BUSINESS PSYCHOLOGY AND
ORGANISATIONAL BEHAVIOUR

To Alison, Geraldine, and Graham

Business Psychology and Organisational Behaviour
A Student's Handbook

Fourth Edition

Eugene McKenna

Psychology Press
Taylor & Francis Group
HOVE AND NEW YORK

This edition first published 2006 by Psychology Press
27 Church Road, Hove, East Sussex, BN3 2FA

http://www.psypress.co.uk

Simultaneously published in the USA and Canada by
Psychology Press
270 Madison Avenue, New York, NY 10016

Psychology Press is part of the Taylor & Francis Group

British Library Cataloguing in Publication Data
A catalogue record for this book is available from the British Library

Library of Congress Cataloging-in-Publication Data
McKenna, Eugene F.
  Business psychology and organisational behaviour : a student's
handbook / Eugene McKenna.—4th ed.
    p. cm.
  Includes bibliographical references and index.
  ISBN 1-84169-391-X (hardcover) — ISBN 1-84169-392-8 (softcover)
  1. Psychology, Industrial.   2. Organizational behavior.   I. Title.

HF5548.8.M384 2006
158.7—dc22

                                        2005014959

ISBN 10: 1-84169-391-X (hbk)   ISBN 13: 978-1-84169-391-0 (hbk)
ISBN 10: 1-84169-392-8 (pbk)   ISBN 13: 978-1-84169-392-7 (pbk)

Cover design by Richard Messing, cover image by Neil Setchfield/Alamy
Typeset in Hong Kong by Graphicraft Limited
Printed and bound in Great Britain by Ashford Colour Press Ltd.

Contents at a glance

Contents

Acknowledgements

This book owes its existence to a number of positive influences originating from many sources, including anonymous reviews. My thanks to the publisher, in particular Lucy Kennedy, Senior Commissioning Editor, and to those mentioned below who either reviewed the third edition of the book, or the draft manuscript of the new edition, and made valuable comments and suggestions that were acted upon:

Professor John Child, Birmingham Business School, University of Birmingham
Dr George Erdos, School of Biology and Psychology, Newcastle University
Dr Susan Miller, Durham Business School, University of Durham
Dr Anni Hollings, Staffordshire Business School, Staffordshire University

Photo credits

Chapter-opening photo credits are as follows: page 2, ©Minnesota Historical Society/Corbis; page 26, ©Jon Feingersh/Corbis; page 66, ©James Leynse/Corbis; page 88, ©Roy McMahon/Corbis; page 132, ©Pawel Libera/Corbis; page 170, ©Rob Lewine/Corbis; page 188, ©Bill Varie/Corbis; page 226, ©Royalty-Free/Corbis; page 264, ©Michael S. Yamashita/Corbis; page 308, ©Tom Fox/Dallas Morning News/Corbis; page 348, ©Randy Faris/Corbis; page 374, © Mike Finn-Kelcey/Reuters/Corbis; page 420; ©Jon Feingersh/Corbis; page 452, ©Susumu Sato/Corbis; page 506, ©Jagadeesh/Reuters/Corbis; page 538, typewriter ©Bettmann/Corbis and personal computer ©Jose Luis Pelaez/Corbis; page 568, ©France Vogt/Corbis; page 606, ©Warren Morgan/Corbis; page 650, ©David Pollack/Corbis.

Preface

A major objective was to produce a text that would introduce the basic concepts and principles clearly with the emphasis on relevance and applications, but at the same time would not over-popularise the subject. Therefore, every effort was made to write the book in a style likely to engage the interest of the student, drawing on numerous real-life examples and research studies relevant to the world of business. The text requires no previous study of psychology or the social sciences. Despite its suitability for use on degree, diploma, professional, and short courses, it can profitably be used by practitioners.

Each chapter has a brief introduction, which maps out the area to be covered, a list of learning outcomes, a summary, a list of review questions, pointers to additional reading, and a bibliography. Particular illustrations of practice and relevant research evidence are contained in numerous "panelled or boxed items" dispersed throughout the book; some of these could be used as mini-cases. When important terms are introduced in the text they are highlighted to indicate their inclusion in the Glossary section at the end of the book. (My particular thanks go to Dr Eamon Fulcher, Lecturer in Psychology, University of Murcia, Spain, for producing this Glossary.) Although each chapter is self-contained, the reader will find within individual chapters numerous cross-references to other topics in the book.

In this new edition of *Business Psychology and Organisational Behaviour* the style of presentation and structuring has been improved and the text has been revised to reflect recent theory and research. Also, additional material appears on important topics, including the following: self-monitoring and sensation-seeking in personality; self-efficacy and social identity in motivation; extra-sensory perception; emotion; knowledge management in learning; investor psychology; trust; virtual teams; upward and lateral leadership; transformational leadership; political skills; virtual organisations and other contemporary organisational issues; culture and diversity; business ethics; corporate governance; innovation; models of change; use of technology in selection; mentoring; career development; e-learning; continuous professional development; bullying at work; cognitive strategies to deal with stress; and workplace counselling.

For lecturers and instructors who adopt the book there is a CD-ROM of learning resources, including a chapter-by-chapter slideshow lecture course, a multiple-choice question test bank, and a set of questions with discussions based on selected themes in each chapter. I am grateful to Dr Serge Rijsdijk, Lecturer in Industrial and Organisational Psychology at Erasmus University, Rotterdam, who has provided invaluable help in creating the multiple-choice test bank and sample discussions, and to Dr Eamon Fulcher who designed and programmed the CD-ROM.

Apart from the new topics referred to above, there have been changes to the structure of chapters. New chapters (5 and 6) have been created as a result of hiving off communication from perception. Psychometric testing, previously discussed in Chapter 2 on Personality, appears in Chapter 3 (Intelligence and Psychological Testing) in the new edition. Career choice has been repositioned from the Personality chapter and is expanded and integrated into the "Careers and career development" section of Chapter 18 (Human Resource Practices: Rewards, Training, and Development) of the new edition. The "learning organisation", previously considered in the human resources chapter on training and development, is now integrated into Chapter 7 (Learning and Memory), while Chapter 14 (Organisational Structure and Design) has been reshaped to accommodate extended coverage of contemporary developments in organisations.

Finally, I hope I have realised my objective in writing this new edition, and hope the reader finds his or her excursion through it a pleasant and rewarding experience.

Eugene McKenna

Part I

Perspectives and Enquiry

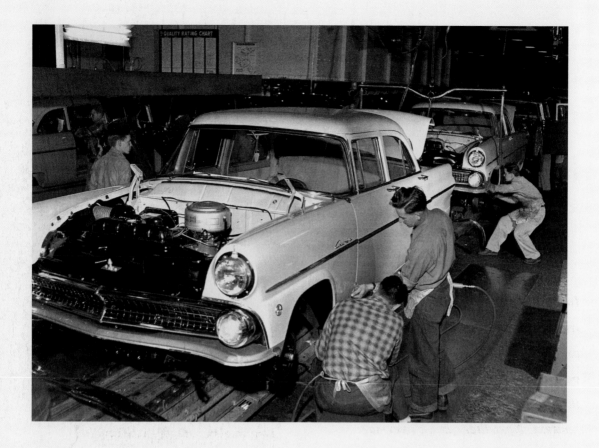

Learning Outcomes

After studying this chapter you should be able to:

- Assess the role played by psychology in the analysis and solution of organisational problems.

- Draw a distinction between the different traditions or schools of thought in psychology and assess their significance.

- Explain what is meant by the multidisciplinary nature of organisational behaviour, and comment on the standing of psychology as a contributory discipline.

- Examine the different approaches used by theorists and practitioners in the study of organisational behaviour over time.

- Assess the changes in the external environment that have brought about fundamental changes to organisational functioning in recent years.

- Identify the role of research in the social sciences, and examine the significance of the scientific method.

- Examine the different techniques available to the researcher when investigating issues or problems in organisations.

Historical Influences and Research Methodology

Initially this chapter is concerned with conveying the nature of the psychological and organisational behaviour perspectives, followed by their development in a historical context. Next there is an overview of contemporary developments in organisation and management. The final section is devoted to an examination of research methodology and the scientific method. A number of issues raised in this chapter are revisited in subsequent chapters.

Contents

INTRODUCTION

This opening chapter sets out initially to explain the nature of both the psychological and organisational behaviour perspectives. Subsequently, as we reflect on the application of concepts from psychology and organisational behaviour, a historical view will be taken. The final section is devoted to research methodology and this reflects the need to be rigorous and systematic in the way evidence relating to behaviour is collected. Therefore, the discussion will unfold as follows: (1) nature of psychological perspective; (2) nature of organisational behaviour; (3) historical perspective; (4) contemporary issues; and (5) research methodology.

NATURE OF PSYCHOLOGICAL PERSPECTIVE

The study of psychology provides valuable knowledge and insights that help us to understand the behaviour of people in business organisations and settings. As a consequence, the manager is equipped with pertinent information about human behaviour when faced with human problems in a business and management context. The contribution that psychology has made to the solution of many human problems encountered in business is significant. It has resulted in (1) better management of human resources; (2) improved methods of personnel selection, appraisal, and training; (3) improved morale and efficiency of operations; (4) a reduction in accident rates; and (5) better working conditions.

Despite these claims to success, it should be stated that psychology is not a panacea for all the human problems associated with business. For example, there are occasions when the outcome of the application of personnel selection techniques is less than perfect. Likewise, a programme to raise the level of morale in a company may, for a variety of reasons, fail to meet the expectations of the management, even though the results provide grounds for optimism.

In the study of human behaviour the psychologist is concerned with a repertoire of behaviour that is both observable (like walking and talking) and unobservable (e.g., feeling and thinking). Animal behaviour has also captured the interest of psychologists.

Different approaches

The development of psychological thought has been influenced by the different traditions associated with the study of behaviour. These traditions are often referred to as "perspectives" or "models of man". The major perspectives can be classified as: (1) the psychoanalytical approach; (2) the behaviourist approach; (3) the phenomenological approach; and (4) the cognitive approach.

Psychoanalytical

The **psychoanalytical approach**, initiated by Freud, ignores or shows little interest in certain areas of contemporary psychology (e.g., attitudes, perception, learning) because of a prime preoccupation with providing help for neurotic patients. This approach, which is discussed in Chapter 2, gave a major impetus to the early development of modern psychology.

In psychoanalysis, the therapist takes note of what the patient has to say, and perceives emotional reactions and signs of resistance to the treatment. In a discussion with the patient the therapist interprets the information emanating from the analysis session. The central thrust of this approach is that people's behaviour can be investigated in a nonexperimental way, that behaviour is determined by some unconscious force, and that behavioural difficulties or abnormalities in adult life spring from childhood.

Behaviourism

Behaviourism is the approach to psychology that is confined to what is objective, observable, and measurable. This approach, which featured prominently in psychology until the 1950s, advocated a scientific means of studying behaviour in carefully controlled conditions. The use of animals in many behaviourist experiments may be influenced partly by the fact that they are less complicated than humans, with a lower propensity to rely on previous experience when faced with a stimulus. Behaviourism, which is discussed in Chapter 7, provided psychology with a number of valuable experimental methods.

However, the preoccupation with behaviour that can be observed and measured objectively has obvious weaknesses. These are primarily associated with the neglect of the processing capacity of the human brain. Factors such as subjective feelings, expectations, plans, and thought processes are ruled out because they do not lend themselves to scientific analysis in the same way that observable behaviour does. In a sense, behaviourism may be viewed as a mechanistic view of people, with the emphasis on the inputs and outputs from the "machine" but with little regard to the functioning of the internal mechanics.

Phenomenology

The **phenomenological approach** amounts to a humanistic reaction to behaviourism. In this approach the emphasis is essentially on people's experience rather than their behaviour. For instance, even though on occasions we all share common experiences, each person perceives the world in his or her own distinctive way. Our unique perceptions—and action strategies based on them—tend to determine what we are and how we react. In the process the individual utilises previous experience, needs, expectations, and attitudes.

Cognitive

The **cognitive perspective**, which focuses on the internal mental states and processes of the individual, has been dominant in psychology since the 1970s and is recognised as a major school of thought. This approach to psychology, which has a fair amount in common with the phenomenological approach, is adopted throughout the book where a cognitive view is acknowledged (such as in perception and human information processing). It seeks to explain features of human behaviour that are not directly observable.

Robins, Gosling, and Craik (1999) conducted research into the trends in the prominence of widely recognised schools in psychology. The following trends were detected:

- Psychoanalytical research has been initially ignored by mainstream scientific psychology over the past several decades.
- Behavioural psychology has declined in prominence and gave way to the ascension of cognitive psychology during the 1970s.
- Cognitive psychology has sustained a steady upward trajectory and continues to be the most prominent school.

NATURE OF ORGANISATIONAL BEHAVIOUR

Many of the concepts examined in this book fall within the boundaries of **organisational behaviour**, a subject that refers to the study of human behaviour in organisations. Apart from the focus on the individual, organisational behaviour is also concerned with the relationship between the individual and the group, and how both interact with the organisation. The organisation is also subjected to analysis, as is the relationship between the organisation and its environment.

The primary goal of organisational behaviour is to describe rather than prescribe—that is it describes relationships between variables (e.g., motivation and job performance), rather than predicting that certain changes will lead to particular outcomes. An example of a prediction is that the redesign of a job (e.g., job enrichment) in a particular way will lead to increased job satisfaction and motivation to work, which in turn will give rise to better performance on the job.

Organisational behaviour, as a social science rather than a natural science, encounters difficulties when identifying, defining, measuring, and predicting relationships between concepts because it deals with phenomena (for instance the human condition) that are more complex than phenomena that constitute the physical world. It adopts a multidisciplinary perspective, but it should be said that

TABLE 1.1

Organisational behaviour disciplines

Discipline	Focus
Psychology	Individual, group, organisational development, occupational psychology techniques
Sociology	Organisational analysis
Anthropology	People's relationship with their environment (e.g., culture)
Political science	Activity connected with the acquisition of power, engaging in political activity, existence of vested interests, conflict generation and resolution, coalition formation
Economics	Economic policy, firm as an economic entity, nature of labour markets, human resource planning
Industrial engineering	Time and motion study and work measurement
Medicine	Occupational stress and employee well-being

psychology as a discipline makes the greatest contribution. The multidisciplinary perspectives are outlined in Table 1.1. The development of organisational behaviour has been associated with the growth of large organisations over the past century, although a preoccupation with issues related to organisation and management has been around for centuries.

The way organisational behaviour is handled by writers of textbooks in this field can differ. According to Buchanan and Huczynski (2004), "organizational behaviour enjoys a controversial relationship with management practice" and some books, such as this one, show a tendency to emphasise the practical application of theory while others adopt a managerial perspective. However, the dividing line between the two perspectives is not clear when viewed across the board.

HISTORICAL PERSPECTIVE

The following are key landmarks in the development of organisational psychology and organisational behaviour: (1) scientific management; (2) classical bureaucracy; (3) principles of organisation; (4) industrial psychology; (5) human relations movement; (6) neo-human relations; (7) systems approach; and (8) contingency approach.

Scientific management

In the earlier part of the 20th century a school of thought, known as scientific management, emerged. This major development—spearheaded by Taylor, Gilbreth, and Gantt—placed emphasis on efficiency and productivity, with the spotlight on the interaction between the person and the job.

The main features of scientific management are as follows:

- Study jobs systematically with a view to improving the way tasks are performed.
- Select the best employees for the various jobs.
- Train the employees in the most efficient methods and the most economical movements to deploy in the jobs.
- Offer incentives (e.g., higher wages) to the most able employees, and use piece rates to encourage greater effort. The piece-rate system of payment offers greater reward for greater effort.
- Use rest pauses to combat fatigue.
- Entrust to supervisors the task of ensuring that employees are using the prescribed methods.
- Subscribe to the notion of job specialisation and mass production.

In scientific management managers are expected to manage (i.e., to plan, organise, and

PANEL 1.1: Scientific management

The principles of scientific management were tested in an experiment in the Bethlehem Steel Company in the USA in the 1920s, where Taylor was a Consulting Engineer in Management. Taylor observed the work of 75 labourers who were each loading 12 tons of pig iron a day on to railway trucks. Having observed the operation, Taylor was convinced that a really efficient worker could handle between 47 and 48 tons a day. Management disagreed, and felt that a more likely output figure would be somewhere in the region of 18 to 25 tons a day under normal circumstances.

To validate his beliefs Taylor conducted an experiment using a Dutchman who was noted to be strong, industrious, and thrifty with his wages, and asked him whether he wished to earn more money. The worker said yes, and Taylor instructed him to do as he was told and he would be paid according to the amount of work done. He was to give no backchat, neither was he to use initiative. When told to walk, he was to walk; when told to put the iron down, he was to do so; when told to rest, he was to rest. After following this routine, the Dutch worker's level of output was 47 tons per day, and for the three years he was under observation he continued to load this amount and was paid a rate 60% higher than his former wage. The other workers were trained in a similar fashion, but only 9 out of a gang of 75 were capable of meeting the target of 47 tons a day; however, everybody's output rose appreciably.

(Brown, 1954)

supervise) and workers are expected to perform the specified operative tasks. In this approach monetary rewards are considered to have a major motivational impact. Although the main exponent of scientific management (Taylor, 1947) believed that his system benefited both employers and employees, it was viewed by the workers as a form of exploitation. Others felt that scientific management contributed to the de-skilling or degradation of work. Needle (2004) refers to the work of Braverman in making the following criticism of Taylorism:

The extensive division of labour means that work becomes fragmented, the machine becomes more important than the worker, and control shifts from the skilled worker firmly into the hands of management, whose position is strengthened by their virtual monopoly of knowledge of the work process.

There is further reference to scientific management in the section on job design in Chapter 4. An illustration of Taylor's approach appears in Panel 1.1.

Classical bureaucracy

The classical theorists, inspired to some extent by the work of the German sociologist, Weber, on the ideal bureaucracy, came forward with a blueprint for organisational design. Here the concern

was with how to organise effectively large numbers of employees into an overall structure. The concept of bureaucracy, propounded by Weber (1947), is as follows:

- A hierarchy of authority, in which the power to act flows from the apex of the organisation to the lowest levels.
- Rights and duties are attached to the various positions within the hierarchy, so that employees know what is expected of them.
- Division of labour, in which activity is categorised by function (e.g., production, finance, etc.), and specialisation take place.
- Rules and procedures, which inform employees about the correct way to process information and run the organisation.
- Documentation, in which information is recorded in written form and committed to the organisation's memory.
- Technical competence, which amounts to recruiting and promoting individuals who possess the requisite qualifications.
- Separation of ownership from control, whereby those who manage the organisation are not those who own it.

There have been criticisms of Weber's concept of bureaucracy along the following lines. It is felt that the bureaucracy (the means) becomes more important than the ends (that which the bureaucracy sets out to achieve); that division of labour breeds rigidity; and that there is alienation because people are expected to perform highly specialised tasks without being able to use much discretion. Also, it is said that classical bureaucracy ignores the significance of the informal organisation, it lacks a human face, and is slow to adapt to change. There is further discussion of bureaucracy in Chapter 14.

Principles of organisation

The **principles of organisation** were expounded by practitioners, such as Fayol (1949) and Urwick (1947), and embrace the following:

*   *Purpose* or *objective* of the organisation.
*   *Hierarchy*, which amounts to the layers of management within the organisation.
*   *Span of control*, which is the number of subordinates reporting to supervisors and managers.
*   *Division of labour* and *specialisation*, whereby the organisation is compartmentalised by function or activity and this allows members to specialise in very specific activities (e.g., buyer, accountant, etc.).
*   *Authority* and *responsibility*, which in the former case means the power to act and in the latter being accountable for the consequences of one's actions as a member of the organisation.
*   *Unity of command and direction*, which signifies that direction and control spring ultimately from one source (e.g., the chief executive).
*   *Communication*, which is the medium through which information flows up and down the organisation and constitutes the lifeblood of the system.
*   *Chain of command*, which is the pathway through which superiors issue instructions and advice and subordinates provide feedback on activities for which they are responsible.
*   *Coordination*, which is a process aimed at ensuring that the different segments of the organisation are pulling together so as to achieve common objectives.
*   *Centralisation* and *decentralisation*, which relate to the level at which major decisions are taken (i.e., at the top or further down the organisation).

*   *Definition*, which relates to important issues such as defining duties, responsibilities, and authority relationships within the organisation.
*   *Balance*, which means getting right the balance between the different parts of the organisation.
*   *Continuity*, which implies that the organisation subscribes to the processes of adjustment and reorganisation on a continuous basis.

The criticism levelled at the principles of organisation is that they tend to play down the importance of the individual's personality in influencing events internally and in the external environment. There is further discussion of the principles of organisation in Chapter 14.

Early industrial psychology in the UK

In the early 1920s **industrial psychology** was established to a greater extent in the UK than in the USA, with notable achievements at both the theoretical and empirical levels (Shimmin & Wallis, 1994). A number of developments are worthy of note. Around 1915 there was an investigation by the Health of Munitions Workers Committee into the poor conditions in munitions factories resulting in low productivity and increased accidents and absenteeism. A recommendation by the Committee led to a reduction in the hours of work and improvements in heating and ventilation, more canteen and washing facilities, and better health and welfare provision.

Following the success of this initiative, the Industrial Fatigue Research Board (later renamed the Industrial Health Research Board) was established to investigate industrial fatigue and other factors, such as boredom, monotony, and physical conditions of work, which were likely to affect the health and efficiency of workers. By the 1930s the Industrial Health Research Board had a wide remit in its investigations, and activity with a physiological and environmental bias characterised much of its work. For example, projects embraced the following themes: posture and physique; vision and lighting; hours of work; time and motion study; work methods; manual dexterity; rest pauses; impact of noise; atmospheric conditions; effects of the menstrual cycle on performance; staff turnover; accidents; and selection and management training.

In 1921 the National Institute of Industrial Psychology (NIIP) was founded "to promote and encourage the practical application of the sciences of psychology and physiology to commerce and industry by any means that may be found practicable" (Shimmin & Wallis, 1994). It conducted a wide range of investigations. The projects undertaken by the NIIP were as diverse as those undertaken by the Industrial Health Research Board, but vocational guidance was a particular speciality. By the 1940s the NIIP was conducting assignments on job analysis, interviewing, psychometric testing, personnel selection, and of course vocational guidance.

By the late 1930s industrial psychology tended to be viewed by workers with suspicion and fear because it was felt to resemble scientific management due to its interest in motion study in order to bring about improved working methods— timing of the performance of workers, using a stopwatch, is necessary in motion study, perhaps conjuring up images of Taylor's approach in his scientific management investigations. But it would be a mistake to attribute Taylorism to the work of the early psychologists.

During the Second World War (1939–1945) there were other initiatives closely connected with the war effort. The Tavistock Clinic—a psychotherapy centre—was involved in the assessment and selection of armed forces personnel, and this type of work enhanced the image of industrial psychology among influential people. According to Shimmin and Wallis (1994), a very important psychological innovation in wartime was the introduction of a new style of officer selection by the War Office Selection Boards in 1942, which firmly laid the foundation for modern-day Assessment Centres.

Another worthy event in the development of industrial psychology was the creation of the Applied Psychology Research Unit at the University of Cambridge. This unit was backed by the Medical Research Council and made good use of its accumulated research findings on human skills and performance when called on to analyse tasks

related to the military. After the outbreak of the Second World War, the unit, drawing on its expertise in human skills and performance, engaged in analysis and measurement of unfamiliar tasks such as gun laying, radar surveillance, and the role of pilots in aircraft. This type of work was invaluable in providing a solid basis for future developments, such as work on skills acquisition and man–machine interactions.

More recent developments

Some commentators do not perceive any real difficulty as far as the standing and application of work or occupational psychology is concerned. For example, this comes across in Arnold's (2005) overview of work psychology. But over the past decade industrial (work) or occupational psychology, despite its popularity, has been at the receiving end of some critical comment. It has been accused of not embracing current developments in mainstream psychology and showing a preoccupation with techniques (e.g., psychometric tests) without sufficient awareness of wider organisational issues. The issues in question (Anderson & Prutton, 1993; Johns, 1993; Offerrmann & Gowing, 1990; Ridgeway, 1998) cover matters such as the following, where the discipline needs to:

- Be appreciative of the strategic issues in business.
- Develop greater sensitivity to critical human resource management considerations and be receptive to a wide range of ideas, including the legal implications of managerial behaviour and what managers feel is expected of them.
- Understand to a greater extent than hitherto the social and political currents within the organisation.
- Be more proficient at speaking the language of business and communicating with a wide range of people.
- Be better able to sell project proposals that have intrinsic appeal to the client.
- Undertake research and consultancy activity in a highly professional way within the ethical guidelines mentioned later.

PANEL 1.2: Hawthorne experiments—Relay Assembly Room

The researchers selected a small group of competent female workers who were engaged in assembling telephone relays. A researcher observed their behaviour and maintained a friendly atmosphere in the group. The workers were fully briefed on the purpose of the experiment, which was stated as to contribute to employee satisfaction and effective work, and were told to work at their normal pace. They were consulted at each phase of the experiment and any changes would only take place in collaboration with them.

Before the start of the experiment the basic rate of production was recorded. Subsequently, output was recorded as and when changes in conditions were introduced. Throughout the series of experiments, which lasted over a period of five years, an observer sat with the girls in the workshop, noting all that went on, keeping them informed about the experiment, asking for advice or information, and listening to their complaints.

The following is a brief summary of the changes introduced, each for a period of 4 to 12 weeks, and the results:

- When normal conditions applied (i.e., a 48-hour week) including Saturdays and no rest pauses, the workers produced 2400 relays a week.
- Piece-work was introduced and output went up.
- Two 5-minute rest pauses, morning and afternoon for a period of 5 weeks, were introduced and output went up once more.
- Rest pauses, up to 10 minutes, were introduced and output went up sharply.
- Six 5-minute rest pauses were introduced, and output fell slightly as the workers complained that their work rhythm was broken by the frequent pauses.
- There was a return to two rest pauses, and a hot meal was provided by the company free of charge after the first rest pause; output increased.
- Work finished at 4.30 pm instead of 5.00 pm, and output increased.
- Work finished at 4.00 pm, and output remained the same.
- Finally, all the improvements in working conditions were taken away, with a reversion to a 48-hour week, no rest pauses, no piece-work, and no free meal. This state of affairs lasted for 12 weeks, and output was the highest ever recorded, at 3000 relays a week.

(Brown, 1954)

- Endeavour to influence legislation on issues of professional interest.
- Publish good ideas and practice through a medium accessed by managers.

Human relations movement

The **human relations movement** arose as a reaction to the earlier approaches (such as scientific management) with their individualistic and over-rational emphasis, and their tendency to explain the behaviour of workers as a response to an environment defined largely in material terms. It was initiated by Elton Mayo, a social scientist from Harvard University, with a series of investigations conducted at the Hawthorne works of the Western Electric Company in Chicago, between 1927 and 1932. Mayo (1949) thought highly of this company and described it as an organisation committed to justice and humanity in its dealings with workers, where morale was of a high order. The first experiment started with an assessment of the influence of illumination on work. For the purpose of this experiment, two groups of workers were chosen. In one group, called the control group, the illumination remained unchanged throughout the experiment, while in the other group, the test group, there was an increase in the intensity of the illumination.

As had been expected, output in the test group showed an improvement, but what was not expected was that output in the control group also went up. This puzzled the investigators, so they went ahead and reduced the level of illumination for the test group; as a result, output went up once more. Obviously, some factor was at work that affected output regardless of whether illumination was increased or reduced. Further experiments became necessary to identify the unknown factor influencing the results. The experiment relating to the happenings in the Relay Assembly Room is briefly stated in Panel 1.2.

Even though the improvements in working conditions in the Relay Assembly Room were taken away, it would appear that the legacy of good human relations practice ensured that productivity would not be adversely affected. Some significant points with reference to the workers' response to their employment situation are as follows:

- The workers collaborated with management in the introduction of the various changes, and good relationships were established with supervisors, with an absence of suspicion between workers and management.
- The workers found the experiment interesting, they approved of what was going on, and welcomed being consulted by management. By being involved in the various deliberations, they experienced an improvement in their status.
- Supervisors were considered to be helpful and interested in the workers' suggestions. This type of supervisory behaviour had the effect of promoting self-respect and the use of initiative on the part of the workers.
- Social activity within the work group developed and manifested itself in a number of ways. For example, natural leaders evolved, people related well to each other, there was a noticeable increase in socialised conversation, and internal discipline became a group rather than a management activity. Also, the need to consider feelings and attitudes was underlined when it was noted that individuals had preferences for seating arrangements (i.e., who to sit next to). The significance of informal organisation was endorsed.
- The motivational effect of social needs and the importance of the social environment was recognised, and a link between satisfaction and productivity was advanced.
- Interviewing and counselling were used to solicit information from the workers and provide support to them. In particular, non-directive interviewing, where interviewees were free to speak about all sorts of things that interested them or troubled them, instead of responding to a direct question, was considered effective. This technique was adopted after using the directive approach initially.
- The notion of the "Hawthorne effect" entered the vocabulary. This signifies that changes in

workers' behaviour could be brought about by the mere fact that they are being observed.

In order to study informal norms more thoroughly, the next experiment focused attention on male workers—wiremen, soldermen, and inspectors—in the Bank Wiring Room, where equipment was wired and soldered before it was checked by the inspector. These workers were not as compliant as the female workers in the Relay Assembly Room. What was noticeable was the solidarity of the men in the face of management action, and this contributed to an informal norm to restrict output, an opposite outcome to that reported earlier. (There is an elaboration of this conclusion in a discussion of group norms in social comparison in Chapter 10.)

Other findings with respect to the bank wiring group were as follows: (1) managers further up the hierarchy were treated with greater respect than the supervisors further down; and (2) the group divided itself into subgroups or cliques and membership of the subgroup had a material influence on the worker's behaviour.

There has been criticism of the human relations movement along the lines that the research methodology used lacked scientific rigour, and there was a lack of concern with broader organisational and environmental issues because of the narrow focus of the research. Also, it was felt that there was a tendency to view the organisation in unitarist terms (i.e., superiors and subordinates share a common outlook, free of disruptive tension and conflict), as opposed to a pluralist view manifested in competing factions with conflict ever present. The latter probably reflects the reality of many organisations. If there was organisational friction, advocates of the human relations approach were likely to suggest basic remedies in the form of involving people, treating them with respect, and improving communication.

Critics are likely to challenge the alleged causal link between employee participation and job satisfaction and between the latter and productivity. They would also take issue with the position of the human relation theorists who maintained that the formal and informal organisation were separate and distinct entities, and that the goals of the

---

PANEL 1.3: Human resource theory

Although people naturally want to receive fair extrinsic rewards (e.g., adequate remuneration) for their effort at work, and they derive benefit from interacting with others in the performance of their duties, other issues are important, such as the following:

- People need to feel that they are making a useful contribution, and that the job offers them the opportunity to be innovative and creative, where they feel a sense of autonomy and receive feedback on their performance. In such circumstances people can be highly motivated.
- Superiors approve of the idea of setting goals or objectives with the assistance of subordinates (i.e., mutual goals) because of a belief that by doing so there will be a greater commitment by subordinates to the achievement of organisational objectives.
- Superiors invite subordinates to join in the various problem-solving activities (i.e., joint problem solving).
- Communication assumes many forms—vertical (up and down) and horizontal—in order to lubricate fully the organisational system.
- People are important resources of the organisation (i.e., human assets) and must be nurtured; hence the importance of training and development.

---

formal and informal organisation were often irreconcilable.

Finally, note an observation by Hollway (1991) on the nature of the human relations movement:

> The Hawthorne studies combined two radical departures from previous industrial psychology. The first involved a shift from the psycho-physiological model of the worker to a socio-emotional one. The second was a change in method from an experimental one whose object was the body (or the interface between the body and the job), to one whose object was attitudes as the intervening variable between situation (working conditions) and response (output).

Neo-human relations

The advent of the **neo-human relations** approach in the early 1950s heralded a more scientific analysis of organisational functioning. It is epitomised in the human resource theory propounded by Miles (1965), and is briefly illustrated in Panel 1.3. There is a recognition that employees have great potential to perform, and they should not be treated as submissive, compliant creatures. Studies covering a variety of perspectives in neo-human relations were conducted by researchers. For example, Argyris examined the relationship between personality and leadership (see Chapter 12); Likert was concerned with groups and management systems

(see Chapters 10 and 12); Lewin focused on group dynamics (see Chapter 10); and Jacques analysed roles and management at the Glacier Metal Company in the UK around the beginning of the 1950s. Drawing on his psychoanalytical work at the Tavistock Institute of Human Relations, Jacques came forward with interesting ideas about the nature of organisations.

Herzberg, influenced to some extent by Maslow, studied work motivation (see Chapter 4). The findings from the studies conducted by Herzberg related to factors giving rise to job satisfaction and motivation. This work aroused much interest in the late 1960s and early 1970s, and had a part to play in the 1972 creation of the Work Research Unit in the UK Department of Employment. It was disbanded in 1992, a period of harsh economic conditions. The objectives of the Work Research Unit were to "promote applicable research, and to encourage the application of organizational principles and working practices that would enhance both industrial efficiency and the quality of working life" (Shimmin & Wallis, 1994). In its heyday this unit was influential in promoting the quality of working life (QWL) principles and practices in British industry. The principles of QWL embrace:

- Adequate and fair remuneration.
- Safe and healthy work environments.
- Work routines that minimise disruption to leisure and the needs of families.

- Jobs that develop human capacities.
- Opportunities for personal growth and security.
- A social environment that promotes personal identity, escape from prejudice, a sense of community, and upward mobility.
- A right to personal privacy and a right to dissent.
- Organisations that are socially responsible.

Systems approach

Before examining this approach, it is appropriate to define a system. A system, consisting of inputs, a transformation process, outputs, and feedback from the environment, is an organised unit consisting of two or more interdependent parts or subsystems, and can be distinguished from its environment by some identifiable boundary. An organisation can be viewed as an open system, as it is continually adapting to and influencing its external environment (e.g., the economy, regulators, suppliers, customers, etc.).

An important contribution to our understanding of the systems approach can be found in the studies conducted by the Tavistock Institute of Human Relations in the late 1940s and early 1950s. A well-known study, using ideas from psychology, psychoanalysis, and open systems in biology, was an investigation of how changes in the application of technology to production influenced social systems (such as work groups) in the coalmining industry. Out of this study came the notion of the organisation as an open system comprising technical and social elements (i.e., a socio-technical system), as well as the idea of organisations as adaptive systems. A major finding was that a change from the old technology to the new technology affected the way groups functioned in the coalmines. This was reflected as a lack of cooperation, tension, and a failure to meet output expectations. There is a discussion of socio-technical systems in Chapter 14 on organisations.

Contingency approach

This approach challenged the view that there are universal answers to organisational questions. Earlier in the chapter the classical theorists of organisation put forward a universal solution to the problem of structuring organisations by advocating the principles of organisation. However, in the contingency approach there is an acceptance of the view that, for example, the structure of the organisation is dependent upon the contingencies of the situation in which each organisation finds itself. Therefore, there is no optimum way to structure the organisation. Instead, one has to look critically at the situation in terms of the tasks to be carried out and the environmental influences when considering the most appropriate structure to achieve organisational objectives.

Examples of major contingency perspectives examined later in this book are the contingency theories of organisation (e.g., Woodward, see Chapter 14) and contingency theories of leadership (e.g., Fiedler, see the "Contingency theories" section in Chapter 12).

CONTEMPORARY ISSUES

In recent years there have been promulgations by management gurus, evidence from researchers, and guidelines from relevant professional bodies on the nature of developing trends in organisation and management. These will be examined in the appropriate parts of this book, in particular the chapters on groups and teams (Chapters 10 and 11), leadership (Chapter 12), and organisation (Chapter 14). In this section the approach adopted is that of an overview.

Organisations cannot be insulated from changes occurring in their external environment. We have witnessed rapid economic growth in countries without a strong industrial tradition (such as in parts of Asia) up until recent times, and slow economic growth in the more mature economies (e.g., Germany), and this has occurred at a time of greater global competition and the easing of restrictions on international trade. As a result, there is a significant increase in competition globally and this has a direct impact on the way companies are structured and managed. For example, employees are expected to be more flexible and to develop a capacity to cope with rapid change.

It is no longer the case that technology used in production and administration is available only to countries with an industrial heritage; in fact, it is more readily available now in many other parts of the world.

Customers are more demanding when it comes to the quality and price of goods and services they purchase, and people generally are more conscious of the effects of industrial waste and pollution on their local environment. There is an ageing population, and that has implications for the nature of the composition of the workforce. Governments across the world are still disposing of state assets through privatisation programmes or partnership schemes with the private sector of the economy, and are exercising restraint in public expenditure. Multinational companies striving for greater critical mass are crossing national boundaries to merge with other companies or to enter into joint ventures with foreign partners. In the European Union the mobility of labour is now a reality, and this calls for sensitivity to other nations' cultures.

Organisations are responding to the challenges posed by the changes highlighted above in a variety of ways, such as:

- Continual reorganisation of divisions, particularly within larger organisations, and selling off businesses that are not performing well.
- Subcontracting noncore services and operations (e.g., security) to other organisations.
- Outsourcing and offshoring key or core activities.
- Developing good relationships with key constituencies (e.g., suppliers, shareholders, customers).
- Streamlining and rationalising processes, eliminating waste, cutting costs, introducing more efficient methods, reducing stock levels, downsizing, and relying where appropriate on techniques such as **business process re-engineering** (i.e., the critical examination of everything the organisation does in order to improve processes).
- Subscribing to continuous improvement of processes, products, and services in order to be more responsive to customers' needs;

adhering to the dictum of "getting it right first time", and using techniques such as **total quality management** (i.e., satisfying consumer needs and promoting worker satisfaction through the continuous improvement of all organisational processes).
- Creating flatter structures in place of the more hierarchical system of organisation referred to earlier, with improved integration of communication and management systems within the organisation, and pushing decision making further down the organisation so that workers are free to make choices about how best to arrange and execute various tasks.
- Creating more teamwork, given the growth of project-based activities within and between functions in the organisation.
- Developing **core competencies**—skills that are crucial for the efficient execution of organisational tasks—and encouraging employees to embrace continuous learning as normal (for managers operating in a global context the development of the mindset and skills necessary to manage in different cultures and to relate to colleagues in other countries is crucial).
- Recognising that differences between people is not something that applies only to individuals in a global setting; it can also apply to differences between people within different countries (this is called **workforce diversity**). There is a recognition that organisations are becoming more heterogeneous in terms of gender, sexual orientation, race, disability, ethnicity, country of origin, and so on—managers should develop skills to deal effectively with the values and lifestyle preferences of those working for them.
- Creating a flexible workforce so that it is more versatile and can easily adapt to the changing conditions (the flexible workforce consists of full-time, part-time, and temporary workers, as well as subcontractors, and it is important that the nonfull-time workers are well integrated into the organisation if the company is to function as a cohesive entity).
- Acknowledging the end of the era of the "secure job" and the traditional path to a career within the organisation.

- Departing from the traditional system of managerial directives or commands and moving to a position of "empowering" workers, and then cultivating self-management as applied to individuals and teams. Managers are expected to sacrifice control to empowered workers who now have to assume more responsibility for the making of decisions; self-managed teams are expected to function without the normal intervention from a manager.
- Promoting the concept of the manager who is more likely to be a facilitator and coordinator, who is fair-minded and employee-centred, and is well equipped with appropriate interpersonal and leadership skills.
- Recognising the ramifications of the drive for continuous improvement, referred to earlier, in terms of frequent changes to the tasks performed by employees. This signals a need for employees to continually update their knowledge and skills (e.g., computer literacy, linguistic skills, and skills as a team player) so that they can operate effectively; also, job descriptions need to be more flexible to cope with the turbulent conditions.

Finally, in a world where people in organisations have to live with the constant pruning of expenditure, a minimum level of resources, job insecurity, more exacting output targets, and highly competitive conditions in the market-place, it is not surprising if the loyalty of the employees to the organisation vanishes and occupational stress becomes a real problem. Also, in these conditions there may be a tendency to bend the rules and engage in behaviour that is not ethical. The issue of ethics is likely to feature more prominently in the future.

RESEARCH METHODOLOGY

Knowledge about human behaviour can be obtained in part through experience, and it is possible to derive some useful insights by this means. However, insight into human behaviour derived from experience has its limitations, simply because

our perceptions of the behaviour of others are not always reliable, partly due to the influence exerted by our attitudes and values. In addition, our observations may be based on a limited and possibly unrepresentative sample that does not provide an adequate basis for generalisation about human behaviour.

By contrast, research provides an approach for obtaining information about many dimensions of behaviour that cannot be acquired through experience alone. When psychologists conduct research into various aspects of behaviour they try to apply the scientific method. Scientific enquiry is based on the assumption that events and phenomena are *caused*. So a major objective of psychological research is to determine what factors cause people to behave in a particular way. However, achieving this objective is extraordinarily difficult because psychologists, unlike physical scientists, have to deal with unpredictable material. Subjects lie, lack self-insight, give socially approved responses, and try to satisfy the needs of the experimenter as they see them.

In reality, a great deal of psychological research at the empirical level is concerned with identifying relationships between events and phenomena, and the question of why people behave in a given manner often remains unanswered. However, identification of relationships can be productive in increasing our knowledge and insight. For instance, a strong relationship between management style and a low level of morale among subordinates might not tell us what particular aspects of management style cause the problems, but it does allow us to focus more clearly on the source of the difficulties.

Research psychologists in the course of their work evaluate claims, impressions, ideas, and theories, and search for real and valid evidence to test and generate ideas about relationships between circumstances and behaviour. As more empirical information about behaviour is accumulated, hypotheses or speculations about certain aspects of behaviour are developed. This can be done in a systematic and controlled way, and the aim is to discover general explanations or theories. In building theories the researcher is engaged in explaining, understanding, and predicting phenomena.

Explaining and understanding are concerned with describing and interpreting what has been observed or discovered. Certain inferences can be drawn from observing a situation (e.g., A causes B or A is associated with B). Also, reliance can be placed on self-reporting by subjects; for example, subjects tell the researcher why they feel dissatisfied with their present job. In this situation the researcher is relying on the meaning people attribute to events in their lives, but we must be wary that the interpretation is not a misrepresentation of reality.

Prediction is concerned with stating that there is a certain probability that, for example, a proposed reorganisation of the company will lead to a particular outcome. Even if the predictive power of social science was impressive, which it is not, predictions could become self-fulfilling prophesies (i.e., the mere act of saying something will happen increases the likelihood that it will), or alternatively the prediction may no longer be relevant because people have taken action to prevent the predicted outcome from materialising. By contrast, the natural scientists' prediction cannot have the effect described previously on the phenomena they study.

As research data accumulate and theories are confirmed, laws and principles are put forward. Although in certain areas of psychology it has been possible to create an impressive collection of empirical evidence that has some theoretical credibility (or a resemblance to the ingredients of a cause-and-effect relationship), much of the research in business psychology and organisational behaviour is at the empirical stage with modest developments in the theoretical sphere.

Characteristics of the scientific method

In order to ensure that the findings of psychological research are as objective, reliable, and quantifiable as possible, the characteristics of the scientific method are adopted. These include: (1) definition and control of the variables used in the research study; (2) data analysis; (3) replication; and (4) hypothesis testing.

Variables used in research are referred to as "independent" and "dependent" variables. The independent variable is the factor that is varied and controlled by the researcher; for example, the level of illumination in a particular task is physically controlled by the experimenter. This could then be related to a dependent variable (which changes as a result of the experiment) and which can be measured, such as counting the number of units of production. In other circumstances the dependent variable could be classified rather than measured. For example, the subject's behaviour (dependent variable) in response to a variation in experimental conditions to stress (independent variable) might be classified as belonging to one of the following categories: (1) remains calm; (2) loses composure; (3) loses self-control. Such classifications should be made in a reliable manner, sometimes by more than one observer.

Apart from control of the independent variable by the experimenter, it is also necessary to control extraneous variables to prevent a contaminating effect. For instance, in assessing the significance of training techniques on employee performance, it would be necessary to ensure that factors other than training methods did not significantly influence the results. Contaminating factors in this case could be educational background, intelligence, age, and experience. In some cases extraneous variables cannot be foreseen, but it must be recognised that they can have a contaminating effect on results, leading to incorrect conclusions.

The requirement to come forward with operational definitions of variables or phenomena that can be subjected to empirical testing is prompted by the desire to bring precision into the meaning of concepts used in research. Ambiguities could otherwise arise. In experimental conditions raw data, often in quantitative form, are collected and summarised, and usually subjected to statistical analysis. Descriptive statistics, as the term implies, are concerned with describing phenomena in statistical terms (e.g., a key characteristic of a sample of managers, such as the average weekly hours spent at work). Inferential statistics are concerned with drawing inferences from the analysis of the data. In measuring the strength of the association between two variables, the question of statistical significance arises. Is the relationship significant or not significant, or is it due to chance?

The psychologist uses inferential statistics to make inferences about general events or populations from observations of samples, and to convey to us some idea of the confidence we should have in those inferences.

Replication arises when an experiment is repeated. We expect to come up with the same result if the study is repeated, otherwise our explanations and descriptions are unreliable. The notion of reliability and validity is discussed in the "Attitude measurement" section in Chapter 9, and in connection with human resource practices in Chapter 17.

A final characteristic of the scientific method is hypothesis testing. The research starts with the formulation of hypotheses, which are predictions or "hunches", preceded by a search of the literature. (An example of a **hypothesis** used in a psychological research project is "Personnel decision situations are more likely to be associated with a consultative or participative style of decision-making behaviour".) Research evidence is then related to the hypotheses, resulting in their acceptance or rejection. Karl Popper is of the view that science proceeds by refuting hypotheses. The researcher then comes up with new observations that challenge new hypotheses.

Techniques and settings

Different branches of psychology use different techniques when applying the scientific method. For instance, in certain branches of social psychology (e.g., attitudes) questionnaires are used. Reinforcement schedules, referred to in Chapter 7, can be used in operant conditioning (part of learning theory). Electrodes that stimulate the brain are the preserve of physiological psychology. The important thing to bear in mind is that the technique used should be appropriate to the research problem in hand. Different settings are used to carry out psychological research, as detailed in the following subsections.

Laboratory experiments

An experiment can be carried out under controlled conditions in a laboratory or work situation where the independent variable is under the control of the experimenter. For example, in Chapter 7 there is an account of the systematic manipulation of the independent variable to demonstrate a causal effect on the dependent variable in the discussion of operant conditioning. In Skinner's experiment on operant conditioning the frequency of the dispensation of food pellets to the pigeon (the independent variable) is varied because the experimenter thinks this will cause changes in behaviour (the dependent variable).

In the laboratory experiment the researcher can control the conditions under which the experiment is conducted and therefore there is a greater likelihood of placing confidence in the conclusions drawn about the relationship between the independent and dependent variables. The findings from laboratory experiments are of limited value in the real world if the situation in the laboratory is too artificial; for example, the subjects are students without work experience and the experiment is concerned with work motivation.

Field experiments

A **field experiment** is designed with a view to applying the laboratory method to a real-life situation and this could be considered a strength. Use is made of experimental and control groups, as was the case with the Hawthorne experiments (discussed earlier) where the field experiment approach was used but with less rigour. Conditions within the experimental group are manipulated or changed, but no such intervention occurs within the control group. For example, the experimental group is subjected to a new system of management and the effects of this change on morale are noted. Later the level of morale within the experimental group is compared with the level of morale in the control group where no such change has taken place. Where experimental and control groups are used it is proper to ensure that the two groups are uniform in a number of critical respects, otherwise variations in outcomes (e.g., morale) could be due to some group characteristic or experience (e.g., expertise, interest, etc.), and not entirely due to the change that was introduced (the new system of management). In practice it is difficult to create groups that are identical in relevant characteristics, such as age, gender, skill, experience, and so forth.

Generally, field experiments are less rigorous than laboratory experiments because outside the laboratory there are many factors that the researcher cannot control but which are likely to affect outcomes. In field experiments one must accept the likelihood of subjects altering their behaviour simply because they realise they are participating in an experiment. This is referred to as the Hawthorne effect, and effort should be made to minimise its impact.

Finally, it may be difficult to gain access to an organisation to conduct this type of research, not to mention the difficulty of putting into practice the basic principles one should adhere to in conducting this type of research.

Field study

The **field study** is conducted in a real-life setting and is principally concerned with survey research methods based on the questionnaire, interview, observation, and the analysis of documents. When various attributes (such as age, qualifications, occupation, and seniority) of a particular population are collected, this is referred to as a "descriptive" survey. When causal relationships or associations (e.g., the relationship between systems of executive reward and motivation) are explored, surveys are "explanatory" in nature. The two types of survey can be interrelated. In the "Attitude measurement" section in Chapter 9 there is a discussion of scales used in attitude surveys. A derivative of this method is the survey feedback technique in organisational development discussed in Chapter 16.

The major advantage of surveys is that comparable data from a number of respondents can be obtained, and patterns in the data can be explored. The major disadvantages are that we may oversimplify behaviour and that, by placing such a heavy reliance on the subjects' verbal reports, the research is exposed to certain weaknesses. These could include shortcomings in the memory of the subject as well as biased viewpoints. In addition, the subject is free to withhold critical information.

Questionnaires. To obtain data all respondents are asked the same questions in the same sequence irrespective of whether the questionnaire or interview is used. Where large numbers of subjects are involved, questionnaires are normally sent to a random sample of the group surveyed (i.e., a section of the total population) in order to reduce costs and time, and they can be completed in a relatively short period of time. Response rates (i.e., the proportion of questionnaires returned) are modest for mailed questionnaires. If the response rate is very low, or the sample chosen is small, the number who responded may not constitute a representative sample.

If a valid and reliable questionnaire is used, it can provide useful information. However, there are commentators who question the suitability of questionnaires for research purposes. There is a view that distortions can creep into the data because vague or ambiguous questions are asked of respondents, and that data obtained following the analysis of responses are superficial.

Questions are also asked about the validity of questionnaires. There are two types of validity— external and internal. **External validity** is concerned with the extent to which the findings of a piece of research can be generalised beyond the specific confines of the setting in which the study took place. Where **internal validity** exists, we are in a position to conclude that the independent variable (e.g., participation in decision making) really does affect the dependent variable (e.g., productivity). If the researcher can control the variables, which would be difficult with survey methods, this will promote internal validity. Normally, there are limitations attached to the external validity of the findings because of the difficulty of applying them in different settings. (Validity is discussed in Chapters 9 and 17.)

There are basically two formats for the questionnaire. One is where the respondent chooses the appropriate response from those listed, and this facilitates the processing of the completed questionnaires using statistical methods and computer processing. A drawback of this format is that respondents are deprived of the opportunity to explain their responses. The other format allows for the presentation of a series of questions, but in this case the respondents reply in their own words. For example, when focusing on rewards there could be a question along the following lines: "What do you think of the performance-related scheme in your organisation?" This format has the advantage of obtaining information not available in the other type of questionnaire. A disadvantage is that respondents take more time to complete the questionnaire, and likewise it is time-consuming for the researcher to analyse and interpret the answers. Of course, it would be possible to design a questionnaire with elements from both formats.

Interviews.   The interview is popular and well established as a means of collecting research data. In the interview, questions are asked of the interviewee, and the answers can be used to supplement the data collected by other means (e.g., the questionnaire). There are two types of interview: one is structured, where a predetermined sequence of questions is asked of the interviewee; the other is unstructured, with no established sequence of questions but the interviewee is given the opportunity to address general themes.

The interview could be a valuable tool for the researcher seeking certain types of information (e.g., the reasons why absenteeism is so high), or when researchers are clarifying their thoughts about the relevance of the selected variables at an exploratory stage in the research process. Although useful information on the interviewee's values, outlook, and experience can be obtained in this way, interviews can be time-consuming and expensive to run with a large number of subjects.

The research interview is a delicate social process. The parties to it are normally strangers and certain social conventions regulate the operation of the process. Both parties (the interviewer and interviewee) have an interest in presenting themselves in a favourable light and have expectations of the other in conditions where the interviewee passes on sensitive and confidential information. Normally the interviewee would expect the interviewer to maintain confidentiality and to be curious, friendly, and objective. The expectations of the interviewer could be that the interviewee is truthful, honest, wishes to cooperate in this form

of social exchange, but, in what might be perceived as an interesting venture, is nevertheless anxious.

Observation.   Memories, thoughts, and feelings (nonobservable data) can be inferred from observing behaviour, though sometimes it may be difficult to infer what causes particular behaviour. For example, what is motivating people to engage in disruptive behaviour or sabotage at work? Sometimes the psychologist uses observation to corroborate the evidence in a self-report. For example, the subject's statements about his or her active involvement in the life of the organisation could be validated by observing the nature and extent of that involvement.

Where the researcher observes the behaviour of workers on the factory floor, with or without their knowledge, as part of a research study, this could be referred to as "naturalistic" observation. In this setting the researcher is collecting information but there is no attempt to influence the respondent. Observation could be unobtrusive, where the observer does not come into contact with people and the latter are unaware that they are being watched (e.g., the use of a surveillance camera to detect unsafe behaviour in a factory).

Observation, as a method of investigation, can be used in a variety of ways. It lends itself to the development of insights that could subsequently lead to hypothesis formation, and it may facilitate the interpretation of data obtained by other techniques. It can be used where subjects (e.g., infants or animals) cannot provide verbal reports. Likewise, it could be suitable where people do not like being interviewed or having to fill in questionnaire forms, or where they might distort the answers.

The psychologist engaged in observation can record the behaviour of individuals and groups as it occurs, although the recording of observations during the actual process of observation can prove difficult. If keeping a record follows the act of observation, the question to ask is how soon after the event does one make the record. Without the benefit of an action playback facility, it is difficult to check the accuracy of one's perceptions. Not all behaviour can be observed, because of the subject's need for privacy in certain circumstances, and it is important to acknowledge the possibility that people may alter their behaviour if they know they are being watched. The observer has to guard against bias stemming from personal prejudice, and must try to maintain objectivity when relationships develop between the observer and other members of the group. In the light of these considerations it is imperative that an observation episode is planned and executed in a systematic and rigorous way. Observation can be structured or unstructured, and it is helpful if there are two or more observers so that they can compare notes and check bias.

Unstructured observation often takes the form of participant observation and is frequently used in exploratory investigations. A participant observer could be knowingly a member of the group he or she is observing. Participant observation can also be carried out in secret (e.g., an experimenter may pose as a convert in a religious sect). A participant observer involved in the life of a group is better placed strategically to understand the complexities and subtleties of behaviour and its meaning than the psychologist who applies standardised questionnaires or creates artificial and restrictive laboratory situations. However, field work is a time-consuming exercise.

In structured observation, the observer knows in advance what behaviour is relevant to the research objectives. A specific plan can be devised to collect and record observations with the opportunity to exercise more precision and control. Although the well-trained observer may produce very reliable results, some of the subtleties detected in unstructured observation may be lost in structured observation.

Analysing documents. The usefulness of the analysis of documents can be seen when critical events in the life of the organisation can be gleaned from the written word. This would have particular significance if it amounted to a confirmation of what was said previously to the researcher in the course of an interview in the order in which it was told. If written information is in quantitative form (like numerical data on absenteeism),

it lends itself to statistical analysis, whereas nonquantitative data (e.g., qualitative information, such as an account of the way a complex contract was negotiated) could be classified by theme or event.

The documents read and analysed by the researcher are called secondary sources and include diaries, letters, reports, minutes of meetings, output statistics, and published work. One must be careful when it comes to the interpretation of this type of data in case the reported events are generalised when in fact they are applicable to a section of the organisation but not to the entire organisation (e.g., productivity gains apply to a function but not to the total organisation). Other secondary sources are industry reports, research reports from external bodies, and so on. In the analysis it should be noted that trends within the industry may not necessarily apply to the organisation surveyed. For example, the organisation may not have suffered to the same extent as the industry at large in terms of a decline in productivity, if this was the case.

Case studies

Case studies probe in some detail the activities or behaviour of individuals or groups within an organisation. The main purpose of this approach is to record in the correct order the way events unfold. If case study activity extends over an appreciable length of time we enter the realm of "longitudinal" studies. This approach can help explain what causes a particular outcome. A case study can be undertaken for different purposes. Where there is a lack of information on a particular topic or event, a case study can be used to create insights for further exploration; but one should recognise it could produce valuable discoveries in its own right. A case study could be particularly useful where the researcher is interested in the impact of a major management technique, such as total quality management. The introduction of this critical event in the life of the organisation is noted and then subsequent developments are recorded.

Action research

Action research can be defined as the application of the scientific method of fact-finding and experimentation to practical problems awaiting solutions. Since this approach to research is problem-centred, it necessitates a close attachment to the organisation and requires delicate negotiation of the role played by the researcher. It requires cooperation and collaboration between the action researcher and members of the organisation. The preferred outcomes of action research are solutions to immediate problems and a contribution to scientific knowledge and theory (French & Bell, 1978). Action researchers are normally outsiders and, unlike change agents who are charged with bringing about specific change, they carry out organisational research.

The research process involves meticulous fact-finding using interviews and the examination of documentation that could result in the identification of problems and their causes. Participative observation could also be used (Meyer, 2001). The information collected will be analysed and synthesised, and action plans to improve the situation will be produced. Next, there is the provision of feedback—that is, sharing with those involved in the change process the nature of the problem and the possible action to be taken—followed by implementation of the necessary action to solve the problem. Overall, this has the effect of giving the recipients of the results of action research the opportunity to analyse solutions better, gain insight, and develop and implement their own solutions to problems.

Using appropriate data at their disposal, action researchers are well placed to evaluate the effects on the organisation of the implementation of action plans. Both researchers and the organisation benefit from the insight and understanding gained of the effects of organisational change (Shani & Pasmore, 1985). A difficulty arises if the organisation does not wish to adopt the researcher's solution to the problem.

Finally, action research has potential in another setting; it has been favourably viewed as a respectable form of qualitative research by academics in the field of management (Eden & Huxham, 1996).

Ethical issues

Those who conduct research in organisations ought to be sensitive to potential **ethical issues**. In this respect the following matters should be considered. A person's right to privacy should be respected. Violation of this principle is evident when subjects are observed without their knowledge, when highly personal questions are asked of them, or, without their knowledge, of their colleagues, or when a participant observer parades himself or herself as, for example, a worker, thereby concealing his or her true identity.

In addition, subjects should be free to decide whether or not to participate in a research study, and should be given the opportunity to obtain detailed information about the study prior to a commitment to take part, or be informed of the nature of the experiment after it has taken place. Also, subjects should be informed of their right to withdraw from the research project at any time. In the experiment on the effects of obedience to authority conducted by Milgram (see Chapter 10), the subjects did not know about the true nature of the experiment. They thought that they were assisting the researcher in gaining an insight into the effects of punishment on learning. In the view of the researcher, it was felt necessary to mislead the subjects, at least at the outset, in order to achieve the goals of the research project. As a general principle, deception should not be condoned and should be avoided in projects that cause distress. It is also necessary to protect subjects from mental and physical harm during the investigation.

Researchers have a moral obligation to maintain the confidentiality of the data. In this respect the anonymity of the respondent is crucial and should be respected, particularly when a statement to this effect is a made by the researchers prior to the collection of the data. A number of these suggestions are contained in a code of practice (British Psychological Society, 2000).

Finally, Francis (1999) feels we should stress the positive aspects of an ethical policy. First, it provides a set of reference points that helps the less experienced psychologist to make sensible social judgements; secondly, it promotes collegiality; thirdly, it provides a neutral forum for the discussion of values in intercultural settings; and, fourthly, it invites us to think of creative solutions to ethical dilemmas. In connection with the latter, it is well to recognise that there is no perfect solution.

FRAMEWORK AND ISSUES

Before moving on to Chapter 2 it seems appropriate to state briefly the framework of the book and the topics covered. The primary emphasis in Part I is to provide an overview and to explain methods of enquiry (Chapter 1); Part II (Chapters 2–9) focuses on the individual; Part III (Chapters 10–13) focuses on the group; Part IV (Chapters 14–16) looks at the organisation broadly conceived; and Part V (Chapters 17–19) examines key management and organisational issues. Among the main issues discussed in the book are:

- historical influences;
- research methodology;
- personality and intelligence;
- motivation and job design;
- perception and communication;
- learning and memory;
- decision making and creativity;
- employee attitudes, job satisfaction, and commitment;
- social interactions of people in groups and teamwork;
- supervision and leadership;
- power, politics, and conflict;
- organisational design, culture and change;
- selection, appraisal, rewards, and training;
- the impact of modern technology; and
- pressure and stress at work.

Explanations of these and other issues dealt with in the book come from the different perspectives identified earlier. As the various chapters draw heavily on empirical or research evidence in psychology, it was appropriate to comment above on the methods used in psychological enquiry.

CHAPTER SUMMARY

- Psychology has a useful part to play in increasing our understanding of human behaviour and of how organisations function.
- The major perspectives in psychology associated with the study of behaviour are the psychoanalytical, behaviourist, and phenomenological approaches.
- Organisational behaviour takes on board a wider range of issues than that normally associated with applied psychology in organisations, though it could be argued that psychology is by far the most influential discipline in the analysis of behaviour in organisations.
- The landmark developments in the evolution of organisational behaviour and organisational psychology include scientific management, human relations, neo-human relations, industrial psychology, classical bureaucracy, principles of organisation, contingency theory, and systems theory.
- Contemporary developments related to modifications to organisation structures and management practices have become pronounced because of the nature and scale of change in recent years.
- Researchers, using the scientific method, gather information on a variety of behavioural issues affecting life in organisations. The scientific method includes definition and control of the variables used, data analysis, replication, and hypothesis testing. The research methods used depend upon the nature of the problem. For example, certain problems lend themselves to scientific investigation in a laboratory or field setting, whereas others are more easily examined using surveys, such as questionnaires or interviews.
- Those who conduct research in organisations ought to be sensitive to potential ethical issues.

QUESTIONS

(1) What is the difference between behaviourism and psychoanalysis?

(2) Identify the disciplines that contribute to organisational behaviour, and assess the significance of psychology as a contributory discipline.

(3) How influential was early industrial psychology in increasing our knowledge of the behaviour of people in organisations?

(4) Discuss major theoretical or empirical developments in the evolution of organisational behaviour.

(5) Examine the major issues affecting contemporary organisations.

(6) Explain the rationale for the different branches of psychology using different techniques when applying the scientific method.

(7) Consider the most appropriate research methodology to use when conducting a study of the motivation of sales representatives.

(8) In what way does adherence to an ethical code influence the approach of the organisational psychologist?

SPOTLIGHT ON RELEVANT READING

Easterby-Smith, M., Thorpe, R., & Lowe, A. (2002). *Management research: An introduction*. London: Sage Publications.

Hollway, W. (1991). *Work psychology and organizational behaviour*. London: Sage Publications.

Howitt, D., & Cramer, D. (2000). *First steps in research and statistics*. London: Routledge.

Robins, R.W., Gosling, S.D., & Craik, K.H. (1999). An empirical analysis of trends in psychology. *American Psychologist*, February, 117–128.

Shimmin, S., & Wallis, D. (1994). *Fifty years of occupational psychology in Britain*. Leicester, UK: The British Psychological Society.

Part II

The Individual

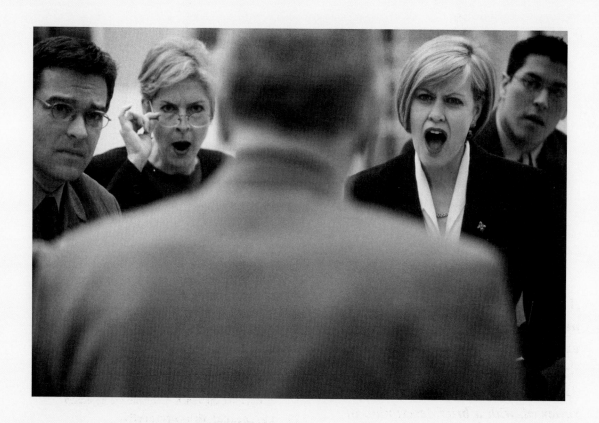

Learning Outcomes

After studying this chapter you should be able to:

- Describe the elements that comprise personality.

- Identify the differences between the idiographic and nomothetic approaches to the study of personality.

- Distinguish between the different perspectives on personality.

Personality

2

A definition of the concept of personality is followed by an examination of research approaches, reflecting complexity in the field. The psychoanalytical perspective is reviewed, with a brief description of projective tests. The latter, which have an indirect relationship with psychoanalysis, are used in consumer motivation research and are complementary to role playing and visualisation. Other perspectives are then discussed, which can be classified as: traits and types; interpersonal; behavioural; and cognitive. All offer valuable insights into the personality factor, and provide a firm conceptual basis for the study of issues connected with culture (Chapter 15), organisational change and development (Chapter 16), and human resource practices (Chapter 17).

Contents

DEFINITION

Repeatedly, we evaluate the people we meet in everyday life. We make subjective assessments of their behaviour. We note their personal appearance and their mannerisms. We listen to what they have to say and watch what they do in different settings. We use this information to make a subjective judgement of the "personality" of the person concerned. This process elicits descriptions of personality traits such as boring, lively, cautious, innovative, rigid, flexible, uninspiring, imaginative, and so on. The definitions that follow capture what is generally meant by personality.

Personality consists of the physical, mental, moral, and social qualities of the individual. These qualities are dynamic and integrated; they can be observed by other people in everyday life. Personality comprises the individual's natural and acquired impulses, habits, interests, sentiments, ideals, opinions, and beliefs as they are projected to the outside world. Personality consists of "those relatively stable and enduring aspects of the individual which distinguish him from other people and at the same time form the basis of our predictions concerning his future behaviour" (Wright, Taylor, Davies, Sluckin, Lee, & Reason, 1970).

Some argue that personality is inherited and determined by genetics. For example, it has been suggested in a 2003 report in *The Lancet* (the medical journal) that schizophrenic behaviour has been linked to genes for the myelin sheaths that surround the nerve cells; it was proposed these might also be a factor in depression. But others maintain that personality is shaped by our environment (e.g., cultural and social forces) and that our feelings and behaviour are learned. (This is a theme considered later in this chapter when the spotlight is on socialisation, and also in Chapter 7 on learning.) Yet others who contribute to the debate acknowledge the influence of both heredity and the environment. (Discussion on heredity and the environment appears in Chapter 3 in connection with intelligence.)

Just as there are many definitions of personality, so there are also many theories of personality.

Nowadays it is easy to justify the study of personality in a business context because of the increasing use of personality testing in employee selection and development. This is a topic that will be discussed in Chapter 3 on psychometrics and as a human resource management issue in Chapter 17. The topics comprising the study of **personality** are presented in the following sections:

*   idiographic and nomothetic approaches;
*   psychoanalytical perspective;
*   role playing or visualisation;
*   trait and type perspectives;
*   interpersonal perspective;
*   behavioural perspective;
*   cognitive perspective; and
*   personality assessment.

IDIOGRAPHIC AND NOMOTHETIC APPROACHES

There are two fundamental approaches to the study of personality—the **idiographic approach** and the **nomothetic approach**.

Idiographic approach

The researcher adopting this approach operates in the belief that the individual is not just a collection of separate traits, but is a well-integrated organism. The individual reacts as a system to various situations, with past experiences and future intentions contributing to present behaviour. Allport (1965) constructed an idiographic portrait of a woman named Jenny, by using the 301 letters she had written over a period of 11 years, and by examining them from a number of different perspectives.

A more recent example is the unique study of Dodge Morgan, the solo circumnavigator, who kept records and completed questionnaires during his 150-day single-handed voyage around the world. A special issue of the *Journal of Personality* was devoted to a report of his experiences (Nasby & Read, 1997). Hampson (1999) goes on to say that "this type of in-depth study of an individual draws on a wealth of idiographic detail to provide a rich description of personality and explanation of life choices. In this case quantitative and qualitative approaches were used to assess Dodge Morgan's personality and to explain why he responded as he did to the various setbacks and adversities along the way."

The emphasis on a very intensive study of individual cases is said to capture the wholeness and the uniqueness of the personality as it functions in the many and diverse situations found in day-to-day life. The approach tries to capture the essence of the total personality, but it is often criticised because it does not lend itself easily to scientific measurement, and because there are difficulties in extrapolating from the particular —the single or few cases—to people in general. This problem could be overcome by studying many more individual cases, but it would prove very costly.

Nomothetic approach

This approach is principally concerned with the collection and analysis of data about groups, and the main objective of the nomothetic approach is the isolation of one or more of the variables of personality. This is done by measuring the variables scientifically under controlled conditions, using a sufficiently large test sample. The approaches adopted by Eysenck and Cattell, personality theorists whose work is considered later, would fit into this category. It is hoped that the relationship between personality traits and behaviour is generalisable and repeatable in other samples of people at other times. This approach is fundamentally opposed to the idiographic approach.

The final comment on the weaknesses of the idiographic and nomothetic approaches to personality will be reserved for a respected academic who has made a close study of personality. Lazarus (1971) makes the point that the idiographic approach is too global and does not possess valued scientific features, such as controlled observation, precision of measurement, or repeatability. Neither does he believe that the nomothetic approach is the correct one, because distortions arise in any

analysis when component parts are studied in isolation and when there is a failure to examine the full range of reactions to the variety of life's circumstances.

PSYCHOANALYTICAL PERSPECTIVE

Freud originated this line of inquiry and his greatest contribution to our understanding of human behaviour was probably his recognition of the power the unconscious has in directing that behaviour (Freud, 1938). This perspective will be discussed with reference to: (1) levels of awareness; (2) structure of personality; (3) defence mechanisms; (4) personality development; and (5) other explanations.

Levels of awareness

Freud classified awareness into three levels: the conscious, the preconscious, and the unconscious.

- *Conscious*. That of which one is aware, is in the *conscious* mind. As I write this section, I am fully aware of what I am doing.
- *Preconscious*. But I am not aware of a great deal of information that, if required, could be brought to the level of awareness. For example, once I had put my mind to it, I could recall the broad details of the way I spent each day of my holiday last year. All such material is said to be *preconscious* in the sense that it is not currently in awareness but, with some effort, can be recalled.
- *Unconscious concerns*. The third level of awareness—the *unconscious* mind—concerns that of which we are totally unaware, and therefore cannot normally be brought into awareness. The material in the unconscious mind comprises drives, desires, urges, some memories, and deep-rooted moral standards. It follows that the individual can be motivated by forces in the unconscious mind of which he or she is unaware, called **unconscious motivation**. For example, one may hear reference to an individual's behaviour as being "entirely out

of character" and difficult to explain, or we recognise a person's behaviour as being due to a strange impulse. These are examples of a lack of insight into forces that are motivating the individual. Psychotherapy or hypnosis could be used to gain a clearer understanding of the unconscious factors that motivate behaviour.

Structure of personality

Freud conceived the structure of personality as comprising three parts, each with different functions: the id, the ego, and the super-ego.

Id

The id is the biological basis of personality. It consists of the inherited characteristics of the individual and can be viewed as a collection of instinctive desires, urges, or needs, all demanding immediate gratification. It is concerned with trying to maintain a balance between the forces within the person that produce conflict and tension. The id finds these conflicts difficult to accept and is therefore keen to reduce them.

The id tends to be irrational and impulsive; it adheres to the pleasure principle. That is, it invites and accepts pleasure and tries to avoid displeasure. It has no values, no sense of right or wrong, no moral standards, and no consideration for other people. The id is cut off from the external world and, because it is frequently kept in check by the ego, it is forced to fantasise in order to relieve tension.

The main force energising the id is the libido. The libido, which is sexual in nature, is also concerned with self-preservation. Sex is interpreted widely by Freud. Pleasurable sensations applied to any bodily function, as well as feelings such as tenderness, friendship, and satisfaction at work, could fall within the definition of sex. After analysing the dreams of battle-shocked soldiers, Freud concluded that, as well as sex, aggression might be an important instinct separate from the libido. This was called the death instinct, and if put into action could, in extreme cases, result in masochism, self-injury, and suicide.

Ego

The new-born child has no ego. Exposed to grim realities—cold, thirst, noise, etc.—which can produce anxiety, and powerless to be rid of these disturbing situations, help is only forthcoming from those close to the child. It is the confluence of forces in the environment acting on the surface of the id that contributes to the formation of a separate mental process called the ego. The internal part of the id will still remain latent as its external part is transformed into the preconscious ego.

The infantile ego is only dimly aware of the external world and tends to be narcissistic—as its needs are met, so it is happy. Objects responsible for the gratification of its needs come from outside. Hunger, for instance, is satisfied by its mother's milk or a substitute. When the infant is free from such discomforts as pressure in the bowels and bladder, irritation of the skin, and extremes of temperature, it falls asleep.

As the child grows up he or she becomes less narcissistic and begins to recognise the omnipotence of the outer world that satisfies his or her needs. There are times when external reality may be perceived as overwhelming and results in fantasies. The ego gradually becomes able to protect the growing child from the internal threats from the id, as well as external threats; in fact, it is the main mental force controlling behaviour in the well-adjusted adult. The ego pursues pleasure; it seeks to avoid unpleasant situations.

Unlike the id, which is intent on the immediate gratification of instinctual urges, the ego is capable of logical reasoning and learning by experience. It clings to the task of self-preservation and postpones or suppresses demands made by the instincts when it feels that meeting those demands would be to the disadvantage of the organism. But there are times when it considers it appropriate to meet these instinctual demands. It is rational in its perspective in the sense that it weighs up situations realistically, taking into consideration such factors as special abilities, aptitudes, temperament, limitations, and the prevailing circumstances.

There are times when the ego is caught off balance, and impulses from the id reach the level of consciousness in disguised forms. The psychotherapist is then offered scope to place interpretations on behaviour such as slips of the tongue, jokes, and so on. In sleep the ego severs contact with the external world permitting the id to express itself. This should not have any adverse repercussions because the ego controls the movement of the organism. Wishes that are warded off when awake now take the stage and reveal themselves in dreams, often in symbolic form. The interpretation of dreams is a well-known approach in psychoanalysis. Anxiety is said to develop when the ego is experiencing difficulty facing the demands of the id.

Super-ego

The super-ego is a new mental process that develops as a result of the weakness of the infantile ego. Eventually it represents the standards and ethical values acquired from parents and society in general. Initially, however, it represents the "voice of the parents" and their moral standards, as perceived by the child. It may be childish and irrational, imposing rigid restrictions that persist into adulthood without much consideration for the changed circumstances. The super-ego is mostly unconscious—thus, if the ego does not live up to its expectations, then conflict develops. When there is conflict, the aggressive forces stored in the super-ego turn against the ego with accusations, creating feelings of depression and guilt.

Depression is said to be self-directed aggression. The manic depressive oscillates between the joy and happiness resulting from the approving super-ego, and the tortures resulting from the feelings of guilt and depression when the super-ego becomes sadistic. At a less severe level, the disapproval of the super-ego is evident when the individual claims to feel bad about something he or she has or has not done, and is troubled by his or her conscience. When somebody feels proud of something they have done, self-congratulation comes into play, no doubt with the approval of the super-ego.

As the individual gets older, the super-ego gradually draws away from the infantile images of the parent; it becomes more impersonal and more related to the objective social and ethical standards to which the individual subscribes. In the course of its development, an individual's super-ego takes over from parent substitutes, such as teachers, admired figures in public life, or high social ideals.

Defence mechanisms

The interaction of the three aspects of personality structure produces constant strife. "Id, the psychic powerhouse, a lawless mob of instinctual urges, demands release; super-ego, the harsh unbending moralist, demands total inhibition of these urges; ego, the rational decision maker, has to try to keep the peace between these two forces and to take into account the demands of external reality" (Mackay, 1973). It is argued that the ego needs reinforcements to function adequately. These are called "ego **defence mechanisms**" and they shed light on our understanding of the behaviour of people. Consisting of at least six major strategies, they are designed to protect the ego from the excessive demands of the id and the super-ego, and to cope with external reality:

- *Repression*. This is the mechanism whereby the ego protects itself from damage or discomfort by denying the existence of a potential threat from within. Distressing feelings and memories are unconsciously removed from the level of awareness. The individual may repress sexual or aggressive desires that would adversely affect the stability of the self. Likewise, the individual may repress painful memories, which, if recalled, would make him or her feel bad. Repression can create problems when the repressed desire or memory becomes so strong that it makes its way into the level of consciousness, perhaps through dreams or some form of anxiety.
- *Suppression*. As a contrast to repression, suppression amounts to the conscious control of desires, fantasies, wishes, or memories. Suppression appears to be a healthier form of defence, for in suppressing a desire a conscious decision is made that, for the time being at least, it will not find expression in its present form.

- *Projection*. This is a mechanism whereby feelings that create acute discomfort are projected onto an object or another person. In this case, the disturbing emotions can be blamed on the other person. The manager who continually interprets other employees' behaviour as conspiratorial or politically inspired might have such tendencies. A student who has a strong desire to cheat in an examination, but somehow cannot go through with it, might become suspicious of other students and unjustifiably accuse them of cheating.
- *Fixation*. This is the mechanism whereby the ego is protected by not proceeding from a particular stage of personality development. So if a child experiences a lot of anxiety about asserting its independence and moving away from being dependent on its parents, the ego refuses to accept the challenge to develop. As far as this characteristic is concerned, it tends to become fixated at an immature level.
- *Regression*. This is the mechanism whereby the ego reverts to an earlier form of behaviour when confronted by a threat. For example, an employee facing a frustrating situation at work may burst into tears or sulk. This form of coping behaviour may well have been successful when dealing with threats of a lower magnitude earlier in life. The child experiencing major difficulties at school may play truant, and as an adult may adopt similar behaviour when confronting significant problems at work.
- *Reaction formation*. This is the mechanism whereby the ego copes with undesirable impulses or desires by developing a pattern of behaviour that is the direct opposite of those impulses or desires. An employee who harbours deep antisocial feelings towards people may develop pleasant mannerisms and good social skills in dealings with colleagues at work as a means of keeping his or her feelings in check. If an occasion arises when this mechanism fails to function properly, colleagues will be shocked by this individual's outburst of hostility.
- *Sublimation*. This arises when an unacceptable impulse is channelled into some socially acceptable action or form of behaviour.

Defence mechanisms are entirely unconscious and the person is unaware of using them. When used successfully, they become a normal feature of coping behaviour whereby the individual can resolve personal conflicts. They also play a crucial part in the development of characteristics of personality. If used unsuccessfully, the ego cannot cope and neurosis or psychosis may result.

Personality development

Freud subscribed to the view that there are three stages of sexual development during infancy. The stages are associated with libidinous satisfaction derived from a preoccupation with different parts of the body. The infant derives pleasure at first from its mouth (sucking its mother's breast or an inferior substitute such as sucking its thumb), followed by pleasure from the anus, and finally pleasure from the genitals. If conflicts are not resolved at any one of these stages, the person may become fixated at that stage, producing a profound effect on character.

Oral stage

The first stage is the **oral stage** and it lasts for a year. During this period in which the infant is highly dependent upon others for its survival, the libido manifests itself through sucking and chewing. Early oral pleasures are perpetuated when the adult indulges in, for example, excessive smoking, eating, kissing, and the chewing of gum. If a person fails to negotiate this stage successfully, and develops an oral fixation, this could lead to adult behaviour such as dependency (as in the original feeding situation), immaturity, optimism or pessimism, sadism, oral aggression (the need to bite), or a suspicious nature.

Anal stage

In the second year of life the anus becomes the focal point for libidinous satisfaction. The infant is intensely interested in the bowel movements and obtains satisfaction from this process. The child establishes that the control of the bowel movements is something with which the parents are obviously concerned. During the **anal stage**, toilet training takes place, and the way this is handled can have significant effects on later development. If the person becomes fixated at this stage, this can affect adult behaviour and is reflected in such characteristics as stinginess, obstinacy, obsessionality, sadism, and orderliness. These characteristics are said to be associated with the early pleasure derived from the excretion and the retention of faeces.

Furnham (2002a) has put forward an interesting view of the after-effects of the anal condition. He speculates that unhealthy responses, such as hoarding mountains of paper in an office, may have their origins in potty training. He acknowledges that hoarding, which is distinguished from storing, is a powerful instinct and many animals do it for survival. But when hoarding becomes pathological it is a real problem. Pathological hoarding has been associated with an obsessive/ compulsive syndrome.

Phallic stage

Around the age of three the child's interest moves towards a preoccupation with the genitals. The main focus is the exploration and manipulation of the genitals, and this is known as the **phallic stage**. The little boy develops feelings of sexual attraction towards his mother and at the same time feelings of jealousy or resentment are directed against his father, whom he looks upon as a rival for the mother's affection. This phenomenon is known as the *Oedipus complex*. In Greek mythology Oedipus Rex, a character from a play by Sophocles, killed his father and married his mother without knowing the identity of either. The Oedipus complex comes to an end in the fourth or fifth year as a result of the boy's fear that his illicit desires might be punished by the father with castration.

The position of the little girl is unclear, although penis envy is attributed to her. This comes about when the little girl recognises the alleged inferior nature of her sexual organ in relation to the masculine one. She develops an envious desire to be like the boy and turns her attention towards her father. Her attachment to her father is crystallised in the

Electra complex. In Greek mythology, Electra connives at the death of her mother, Clytemnestra, who murdered her father, Agamemnon.

The boy resolves the Oedipal conflict by modelling himself on his father and repressing his incestuous urges; the girl, on the other hand, resolves the Electra conflict by the recognition that she might lose the love of her mother if she realised her illicit desires. Unsuccessful resolution of these conflicts for both sexes can lead to major problems in adulthood, particularly problems of sexual identification and **neurotic** tendencies. Those fixated at this stage of development are said to display characteristics such as extreme self-love, excessive ambition, exhibitionism, and bragging. After the phallic stage comes the latency period which lasts until adolescence, during which time sexual impulses are inhibited and satisfying relationships are developed.

Freud has been criticised for the prime emphasis he placed on sexual desires. Lazarus (1971) puts an interesting interpretation on the Oedipus complex. He maintains that the Oedipus complex could be better understood in terms of social relations within the family:

> The boy might come to fear the father not because he literally expects castration, or because of sexual urges toward the mother, but because the father controls power within the family, particularly in the Viennese society of the late-1800s. Also the girl might envy the boy, not literally for his penis, but because in most societies girls are usually considered subordinate to boys.

Psychoanalytical theory sees the origin of personality in the conflicts between the id, ego, and super-ego and in the way in which the conflicts are resolved at each stage of development. Adult behaviour is said to be related to the success, or otherwise, of negotiating the various stages of development.

Other explanations

Some of Freud's followers, notably Jung and Adler, felt that it was unsatisfactory to emphasise persistently the sexual roots of neurosis to the exclusion of other factors. Jung parted company with Freud, to the latter's regret, but shared Freud's views concerning the importance of the unconscious. He maintained that Freud overlooked an aspect of the unconscious, which he called the "collective unconscious". This contains experiences shared by all human beings and is part of our biological inheritance. In effect the contents of the collective unconscious basically reflect the experiences of our species since it originated on our planet. Many psychologists have rejected the idea of the collective unconscious (Baron, 2002).

Another aspect of Jung's theory is the view that we are born with innate tendencies to be primarily concerned with ourselves or with the outside world. Those concerned with themselves are introverts (e.g., cautious, hesitant, unsociable) and those concerned with the outside world are extraverts (e.g., open, confident, gregarious). There is further reference to Jung's concept of the introvert and extravert later in this chapter.

Adler was of the view that human behaviour can be explained in terms of a struggle for power in order to overcome feelings of mental or physical inferiority (Brown, 1961). This contribution was of significant benefit to psychoanalysis because it recognised that nonsexual factors could also lead to conflict, and that neurosis is a disorder of the total personality. In modern developments in the mainstream of psychoanalysis, the ego receives increasing attention, and the influence people have on each other receives a high priority. The quality of the mother–child relationship is a critical interpersonal influence because it is the base of subsequent personal relationships (Peck & Whitlow, 1975).

Some psychoanalysts, who revised Freud's doctrine of instinctual and sexual motives in human behaviour, began to stress the role of social context in the determination of behaviour. As mentioned above, Adler stressed humans striving for superiority in order to compensate for feelings of inferiority (Brown, 1961). According to Fromm (1941), humans have a compelling need to belong, and seek ways of relating to others and escaping from freedom, but in the process conflict and anxiety can be encountered. It would appear that certain advertisements contain messages that can be related to these concepts. The purchaser of a unique car is told he or she will feel superior; only distinctive and discriminating buyers purchase a particular brand of perfume! Likewise, the consumer is told that loneliness will be dispelled once membership of a particular club is obtained.

Horney (1945) felt that the way to appreciate the individual's conflicts was to understand how personality is shaped by the texture of society. In a highly competitive culture the child feels helpless, alone, and insecure because of being dependent on adults. The child develops ways of coping with the basic anxiety generated by these forces. Each way of coping involves a different strategy:

• *Compliance.* This way involves moving towards people—for example, protecting oneself by gestures of affection, dependency, and submission. Compliant people are likely to conform to social norms, to subordinate themselves to the wishes of others, and will tend to avoid conflict. Likewise, they are unlikely to be assertive or to seek power.

• *Aggression.* This way involves moving against people—protecting oneself through aggression, hostility, and attack. Aggressive people want to excel and manipulate others by securing power over them. They need to confirm their self-image because of uncertainty about their talents.

• *Detachment.* This way involves moving away from people—protecting oneself by isolation and withdrawal. Detached people place emotional distance between themselves and others, place a high value on freedom from obligations, their independence, and self-sufficiency, and prefer to use their intellect more than their feelings.

Another application of the psychoanalytical perspective focused on the behaviour of managers in work organisations. Kets de Vries and Miller (1984) identified five neurotic styles among managers:

(1) *Paranoid.* They tend to be suspicious of others, and are exceptionally vigilant for hidden threats.

(2) *Compulsive*. They tend to be perfectionist in what they do and are concerned with the right way of doing things.

(3) *Dramatic*. They frequently draw attention to themselves, and show a desire for activity and excitement.

(4) *Depressive*. They display feelings of guilt, inadequacy, and hopelessness.

(5) *Schizoid*. They show symptoms of withdrawal, lack of involvement, and lack of excitement or enthusiasm.

Where these neuroses are reflected by senior managers, the organisation could be considered sick and action should be taken to treat this condition.

Criticisms of Freud's theory range from its lack of scientific foundation to the difficulty in measuring the many variables systematically. Several of his proposals have not been supported by research findings. In the construction of his theory he relied on a small number of cases. These cases were not chosen to be representative of people generally, and Freud recorded and later analysed the data himself, so the procedures used are open to question. For the reasons already stated, and other reasons, his theory of personality is not currently accepted by most psychologists.

Yet there is a positive side. According to Baron (2002), "his insights—especially his ideas about levels of consciousness and the importance of anxiety in various psychological disorders—have contributed to our understanding of human behaviour and of personality in particular. In these ways Freud has had a lasting impact on personality and on society." There are other views supportive of the impact of Freudian theory. For example, Andrews and Brewin (2000), editors of a special feature on Freud's contribution to personality in *The Psychologist* (the organ of the British Psychological Society), point out that there has been much criticism of his theory and practice over the years, but equally there have been a number of supportive comments from psychologists on his contributions in such areas as the unconscious, dreams, transference, slips of the tongue, and psychodynamic theory.

PROJECTIVE TESTS

An appropriate way to assess personality based on unconscious processes is to use assessment methods that include face-to-face analysis and projective techniques. These methods are expensive and time-consuming to administer and they do not lead to quantifiable results. However, they are used as a framework for motivational research in studies of consumer behaviour. The ideas of Freud were the inspiration behind projective techniques, but the relationship between psychoanalytic theory and projective techniques is merely indirect.

Projective techniques require a person to respond to ambiguous or unstructured situations as a means of exploring unconscious impulses and motives. Subjects are unaware of the purpose of the test; consequently the ego's defences are off guard, and unconscious forces emerge in disguised form. It is the job of the assessor to interpret these responses. Two well-known projective tests—the **Rorschach Test** and the **Thematic Apperception Test**—are examined in the following subsections.

Rorschach Test

The Rorschach Test consists of a series of 10 ink-blots or formless shapes in which one half is the mirror image of the other. An ink-blot, similar to the one used in the test, is shown in Figure 2.1.

FIGURE 2.1

An ink-blot.

PANEL 2.1: What does the Rorschach Test measure?

The Rorschach is a test of perception—more widely used in the US and other parts of Europe than in the UK—which measures how an individual assigns meanings to 10 symmetrical ink-blots. An ink-blot similar to the one used in the test is shown in Figure 2.1. The 10 ink-blots are presented individually to the subject or patient with the question, "What might this be?" Responses are recorded in exactly the words used by the individual. Each response is taken up and probed according to three categories: (1) content (what is it?); (2) location (where on the card do you see it?); and (3) determinants (what makes it look like that?).

The responses are scored and combined in such a way that indices are created to form the basis for hypotheses that lead to interpretation. For example, a shortcoming in a person's interpersonal capability or resource leads to difficulties in handling stress at work. Hypotheses can also be related to evidence or insight from other quarters.

Administration of the test is simple but the scoring is complex. Calculating the indices without a computer-based program could be a time-consuming activity. The final outcome is a profile of personality and psychological functioning. A psychologist who uses the Rorschach Test in his work had this to say about it: "It can extract information that is difficult to obtain using other psychological tests (e.g., self-reporting tests such as personality questionnaires). I have found the Rorschach to be a useful instrument to assist care planning and treatment in complex cases."

(Donnelly, 2003)

The subject is asked to say what the blot resembles. The abnormal personality is likely to perceive gruesome or horrific images in the blots, and this may be indicative of serious conflicts that are still unresolved. The normal personality sees more tranquil images.

There have been criticisms of the reliability of the Rorschach Test (Wood & Lilienfeld, 1999). However, reviewers of the updated version of the test portray it in a favourable light (Weiner, 2001). There is an expanded view of the issue of measurement in Panel 2.1.

Thematic Apperception Test

The Thematic Apperception Test consists of 20 pictures of varying degrees of clarity. An example of a straightforward scene would be a boy reading at a desk. The subject examines each picture and then tells a story about the scene portrayed, including what led up to the scene, the current situation, and what is likely to happen in the future. The responses are analysed and recurrent themes mentioned in the stories are particularly noted. A subject who harbours intense hostility may read hostility in one form or another, such as severe conflict or death, into the stories.

In motivation research in the field of marketing, a similar test to the one described was used (Anastasi, 1979). In a cigar survey a cartoon was used portraying a person coming home from work

who announces to his partner, "I've decided to take up smoking cigars." The respondent is asked to fill in the partner's response. Tests of this type are carried out in the belief that a person may attribute to another person an opinion that he or she holds but is unwilling to express. In order to get around the expression of a direct personal view, a question may be worded in the third person. For example, instead of "What are the health hazards attached to cigarette smoking?", respondents are presented with the following statement: "Some people who smoke cigarettes may suffer from ill-health at some stage in their life." They are then asked, "I wonder if you can guess what adverse effects of cigarette smoking they are referring to?"

Whereas some psychologists find projective tests useful in providing initial clinical insights, others are sceptical of their value in assessing unconscious processes and believe that subjects can quite easily fake the tests (Holmes, 1974). In Chapter 3 there is a discussion of personality testing using a different methodology.

ROLE PLAYING OR VISUALISATION

As well as the use of projective tests in consumer motivation research, role playing or visualisation techniques have been used to create personality descriptions of consumers.

Stereotyping

Over half a century ago a study was conducted in the USA into the consumption of instant coffee, at a time when instant coffee was not widely used (Haire, 1950). Direct questioning of housewives revealed that they did not like its flavour. Subsequently, the housewives were given two shopping lists covering a number of items and asked to describe the personality of the woman who bought the groceries. The main distinguishing feature between the two lists was that one shopping list—"list A"—contained instant coffee and the other—"list B"—included ground coffee.

The results showed that 48% of the women shown list A said the shopper was lazy and did not plan well, but less than 12% of the women shown list B arrived at that conclusion. The shopper was perceived as a spendthrift by 12% of the women shown list A, but none of the women shown list B expressed that view. Again, 16% of the women shown list A said the shopper was not a good wife, but none of the women shown list B expressed that view.

By the addition of a pie-mix to the two shopping lists, and by using two new samples of housewives, the personality descriptions of the shopper using the B list became closer to those of the shopper using the A list. Was it the inclusion of a prepared food item (the pie-mix) that evoked a stereotyped personality description? The original sample was divided into users and nonusers of instant coffee, as the result of a pantry check. Significant differences were found between the two groups of housewives, as illustrated in Table 2.1.

The shopping list study was repeated 18 years later. No significant differences were found between the characteristics attributed by the subjects to the ground coffee versus the instant coffee user. However, a fairly large number of subjects felt that the instant coffee shopper was a busy, active person in contrast to the shopper preferring ground coffee, who was seen as dull, unadventurous, and not very elegant (Webster & Von Pechmann, 1970). A Canadian replication of the original shopping list study concluded with the assertion that the original findings still hold true with a sample of French-Canadians in a middle-class suburb of Montreal (Lane & Watson, 1975).

These studies highlight role playing or visualisation and, although the association between personality stereotypes and consumer behaviour is interesting, it cannot be conclusive. People might find it difficult or impossible to come up with an authentic personality description from a shopping list and, in order not to disappoint the interviewer or to give what is expected, they cooperate. We never know the depth or strength of the personality stereotype (Anastasi, 1979).

In recent years role playing or visualisation has taken a back seat and "brand personality" has come to the fore (see Panel 2.2).

TABLE 2.1

Haire's analysis of shopper profiles (1950)

Descriptions of shoppers	Instant coffee users (%)	Instant coffee nonusers (%)
Shopper is economical	70	18
Shopper is a good housewife (plans well and cares for the family)	29	0
Shopper cannot cook/does not like cooking	16	55
Shopper is lazy	19	39

PANEL 2.2: Brand personality

Apart from a brand's physical and functional attributes, the images and symbolism portrayed by the product are considered very important. But the images and symbolism must have meaning and significance in the minds of consumers. The "Poison" brand of fragrance could evoke a perception of danger, and the "Obsession" brand may be perceived as erotic by some consumers but not by others (Engel, Blackwell, & Miniard, 1995).

The Cooper Research and Marketing Agency in the UK claim to use creative and projective techniques in qualitative and motivational research for clients, by trying to get beneath consumers' conscious rationalisations about a brand, so as to enter their inner world of feelings about the particular personality of the brand being studied. This organisation conducted research in the 1980s into the deeper meaning of the brand of stout known as "Guinness" (Broadbent & Cooper, 1987). The findings indicated that Guinness supplies satisfying, nourishing values, which, at the inner level, relate to fertility and archetypal myths of power and energy. The outward character of Guinness—rich, creamy, black, fascinating to pour and drink—reinforces these images.

Guinness was also perceived at the outer level as bitter, black, and strong, with a social reputation for manliness, mature experience, and wit. This type of thinking led to the creation of a model called the "Guinness Egg" that subsequently resulted in the successful *Pure Genius* advertising campaign. The inner part (the yolk) of the egg was symbolic of the wholesome, natural, mysterious, and poetic characteristics of the brand, and the key symbols used in the advertisement were mist, barley, fire, earth, and sun. The outer part (the shell) was people-centred with manifestations of play, humour, and confident, independent individuals who are in control and proud to be associated with the brand in an appropriate setting (pubs, etc.).

The qualitative researchers emphasise brand personality and product symbolism, as shown by this example. Some might consider their techniques—for example, role playing, psychodrama, and clay modelling—to be controversial, but they certainly generate challenging hypotheses.

TRAIT AND TYPE PERSPECTIVES

Traits

An important means of studying personality is the trait perspective. A trait is an individual characteristic in thought, feeling, and action, either inherited or acquired, and refers to tendencies to act or react in certain ways (Drever, 1964). The possession of a particular trait—for example, anxiety—does not imply that the person will always be anxious; rather, it suggests that the person is disposed to react with anxiety in given situations.

Traits can be placed in particular categories:

- *Motive traits.* These refer to goals that guide the behaviour of the individual; for example, a person may possess a recognisable trait related to achievement.
- *Ability traits.* These refer to the individual's general and specific capability and skill; for example, this category would include cognitive traits such as knowing, perceiving, and reasoning.
- *Temperament traits.* These would include optimism, depression, and various energetic tendencies.

- *Stylistic traits.* These refer to gestures and styles of behaving unrelated to specific tactics to achieve a particular goal.

Traits contain two basic dimensions. One is the manner in which the trait manifests itself at the surface—for example, the display of aggressive behaviour—and the other is where the trait exists below the surface, and the observer has to infer the nature of the quality. Such a quality could be a belief held by the individual or, again, his or her power of self-control. In distinguishing between people, the use of a rich vocabulary of traits can help enormously. Each individual's traits may be considered unique. For example, one person's loyalty, and the way he or she expresses it, will differ from another's loyalty. Likewise the way traits are organised in the individual's total personality can be considered distinctive (Allport, 1961). The trait perspective will be examined with reference to: (1) Allport's trait categories; (2) **Cattell's 16 PF Test**; and (3) the state of trait theory.

Allport's trait categories

Allport puts traits into three categories:

- *Cardinal trait.* These refer to some predominant characteristic; for example, a determined stance taken by a politician on a number of issues.

- *Central trait*. One can have five to ten central traits that distinguish one individual from another; for example, intelligence, a sense of humour, compassion, sensitivity, and honesty.
- *Secondary trait*. These are weak or peripheral and are relatively unimportant in characterising a person or their lifestyle.

Allport emphasises that traits are not independent entities within a person; they are an interdependent set of attributes that come together to produce an effect on behaviour. The following example illustrates this point.

Many traits contribute to the total performance of a person telling a joke or a story at a party. Motive traits (such as entertaining others or showing off) are evident, and stylistic traits (such as being bashful, boring, or delightfully entertaining) are also reflected. In essence, the entertainer's traits combine to form a coherent cluster. This leads to Allport's concept of the self (proprium)— a concept that embraces distinctive and important personal characteristics, such as self-image, self-esteem, rational thinker, or, alternatively, irrational, impetuous, and so on.

Cattell's 16 PF Test

Cattell (1965) is another influential trait theorist. His approach was to reduce systematically the list of personality traits to a small manageable number by using a statistical method called factor analysis. The attraction of this method is that it enables complex data to be quantified and reduced to a more manageable form, though the total research process in which factor analysis is used does contain some intuitive judgement.

Source traits and surface traits. The following example illustrates Cattell's approach. We are concerned with measuring the ability of a group of students in relation to four activities: using calculus; understanding physics; playing football; and skating on ice. We would expect those who do well in mathematics also to do well in physics, but not necessarily to do well in sport. Though we are unlikely to use factor analysis in this situation, if it were used it would reveal two factors, or source

traits, underlying the activities in question— namely, mathematical and scientific ability and ability in sport. The source traits affect the pattern of behaviour that is visible to the observer.

The observable behavioural patterns are called *surface traits*. At work or college a cluster of surface traits—such as possession of a large vocabulary, an understanding of accounting and quantitative methods, and a knowledge of business history—may be observed in the behaviour of the individual. The surface traits could be underpinned by at least three independent source traits—education, intelligence, and a studious temperament. Through various forms of tests, intercorrelations of personality variables, and the use of observational data, Cattell chose 16 personality factors that are said to represent source traits (see Table 2.2).

The source traits are the backbone of the enduring aspects of behaviour, and it is through their interaction that the more readily observed surface traits of an individual are determined. These surface traits happen to coincide with descriptions of personality in everyday use. The factors on the 16 personality factor ("PF") questionnaire used to measure personality are relatively independent, and are not correlated significantly among themselves. So a person's score on any one of these factors should not influence their score on another, though there may be some weak correlations.

After further analysis, Cattell arrived at *second-order factors*, of which anxiety is one. The second-order factors are said to influence behaviour only through the source traits or primary factors. The source traits or primary factors are considered to be more accurate than the second-order factors in describing and predicting behaviour.

Though source traits are said to be enduring aspects of personality, there are circumstances in one's life when predictions of behaviour on the basis of traits alone can be misleading. For example, a person who is suffering from fatigue or who is frightened or under the influence of drugs may indulge in unexpected behaviour.

Cattell recognises that environmental and hereditary factors interact with and influence the source traits to different degrees. The validity of the 16 PF Test has been questioned (Howarth & Browne, 1971), but a more recent version of the

TABLE 2.2

Factors in Cattell's 16 PF Questionnaire (1974)

Low-score description	Factor	High-score description
Reserved, detached, critical	A	Outgoing, warm-hearted
Less intelligent, concrete thinking	B	More intelligent, abstract thinking
Affected by feelings, easily upset	C	Emotionally stable, faces reality
Humble, mild, accommodating	E	Assertive, aggressive, stubborn
Sober, prudent, serious	F	Happy-go-lucky, impulsive, lively
Expedient, disregards rules	G	Conscientious, persevering
Shy, restrained, timid	H	Venturesome, socially bold
Tough-minded, self-reliant	I	Tender-minded, clinging
Trusting, adaptable	L	Suspicious, self-opinionated
Practical, careful	M	Imaginative
Forthright, natural	N	Shrewd, calculating
Self-assured, confident	O	Apprehensive, self-reproaching
Conservative	Q1	Experimenting, liberal
Group-dependent	Q2	Self-sufficient
Undisciplined, self-conflict	Q3	Controlled, socially precise
Relaxed, tranquil	Q4	Tense, frustrated

questionnaire was considered by Cattell to be an improvement on earlier versions (Cattell, 1974). The major criticism of Cattell's theory centres on the proposition that the assumptions governing factor analysis force us to oversimplify personality (Peck & Whitlow, 1975).

State of trait theory

In the 1960s Mischel (1968) came forward with an influential critique of traits. He attacked the idea that people would act in a consistent manner in accordance with the dictates of a trait regardless of the situation. For example, the "shy" person does not always behave in a restrained, timid way in every situation. Trait theory survived Mischel's onslaught, and is alive and well (Buss, 1989; Hampson, 1999).

Deary and Matthews (1993) provided a comprehensive review of advances in personality research, and from their evaluation of this area they make a very strong case for the potency and vitality of trait psychology. They argue that there is broad agreement about personality traits and their biological determinants, and that traits can be called on to explain and predict behaviour. Addressing the Deary and Matthews review, Bentall (1993), a clinical psychologist, raises the

following objections that may be shared by some psychologists:

It is not yet clear whether personality research can contribute to the greater good. Certainly, a greater sensitivity to the ethical and political implications of personality research seems necessary. Personality research as it stands at present is unlikely to be of use to those of us who wish to apply psychology to help solve pressing human problems. It may be that these objections are not fatal. I look forward to a science of personality which is value-free, and which makes specific and useful predictions about how particular individuals will respond in particular circumstances.

Types

When a person shares a pattern of traits with a large group of people, he or she is said to belong to a **personality type**. The following typologies are considered in this section:

(1) the four humours;
(2) Sheldon's typology;
(3) Eysenck's typology;

TABLE 2.3

The four humours

Humours	Temperaments	Behaviour
Yellow bile	Choleric	Active but changeable mood; rapid thinking; highly strung; easily provoked; strong emotions
Black bile	Melancholic	Pessimistic; tendency towards ill-founded fears; resistance to provocation; strong emotions once aroused
High blood pressure	Sanguine	Cheerful; easy going and supremely confident; weak emotions though easily aroused
Excess phlegm	Phlegmatic	Sluggish; supremely calm; slow thinking; resistant to provocation; weak emotions even when aroused

(4) "Big Five" factor theory;
(5) Jung's typology; and
(6) Allport's typology.

The four humours

The best-known typology in ancient Greece was that of Hippocrates in the fifth century BC. He theorised that the body contained four fluids or humours—yellow bile, black bile, high blood pressure, and phlegm. In AD 180, Galen allocated temperaments to the four humours to show how physical conditions in the form of internal abnormalities could affect patterns of behaviour. These relationships are depicted in Table 2.3.

Sheldon's typology

Probably the best-known modern physical typology is that of Sheldon (1954). Working from the photographs of 4000 college students he defined physical types similar to those that appear in Figure 2.2.

FIGURE 2.2

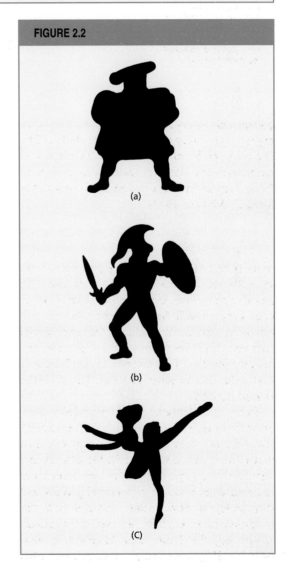

Sheldon's physical typology. (a) *Endomorphic*: Soft round body, stocky but not exactly fat. Large trunk, thick neck, and relatively short legs. Generally relaxed in temperament, loves comfort, sociable and affectionate. (b) *Mesomorphic*: Well rounded with bone and muscle; the Greek God type of body build. The temperament is assertive, noisy, aggressive, and energetic. (c) *Ectomorphic*: A fragile body build, with a temperament that is inhibited in actions, over-restrained, and socially withdrawn, with an inferiority complex.

FIGURE 2.3

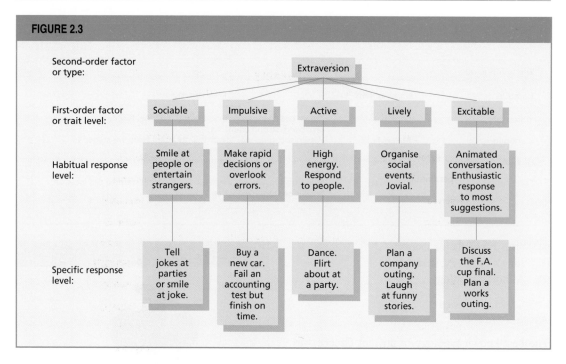

Eysenck's structure of personality as related to extraversion (adapted from Eysenck, 1967).

Eysenck's typology

A prominent type theorist is Eysenck (1953). In his work he stresses the second-order factors or types, as opposed to traits, in the personality of the individual. Take, for example, the personality type known as *extraversion.* It is expressed in the form of a hierarchical organisation in Figure 2.3. Eysenck shares Cattell's view that biological factors are involved in the determination of personality, but, unlike Cattell, much of Eysenck's early work grew out of his interest in abnormal psychology and psychiatry. Eysenck related his own research to the ancient typology referred to in Table 2.3 and found a fairly good relationship with the original theory, as shown in Figure 2.4.

It was in his original study of 700 neurotic soldiers that Eysenck found that factor analysis of 39 items of personal data, including personality ratings, resulted in the establishment of two basic dimensions of personality—extraversion/introversion and neuroticism/stability (Eysenck, 1947).

This structure of personality was substantiated by further research with a large number of subjects. In a later investigation with psychiatric patients, Eysenck established a third dimension of personality, unrelated to extraversion and neuroticism, which he called psychoticism. It should be noted that these dimensions of personality relate to the extreme ends of a continuum, and only very few people would fall into these categories. With regard to extraversion, for example, most people would fall somewhere in between—they would be neither very extraverted nor very introverted.

Extravert. According to Eysenck, the typical extravert is sociable, likes parties, has many friends, needs people to converse with, but does not like reading or studying alone. Extraverts need excitement, take chances, are often adventurous, act on the spur of the moment, and are generally impulsive individuals. They are fond of practical jokes, always have a ready answer, and generally like change. They are carefree, optimistic, and like to laugh and be merry. They prefer to keep moving and remain active, tend to be aggressive, and lose

FIGURE 2.4

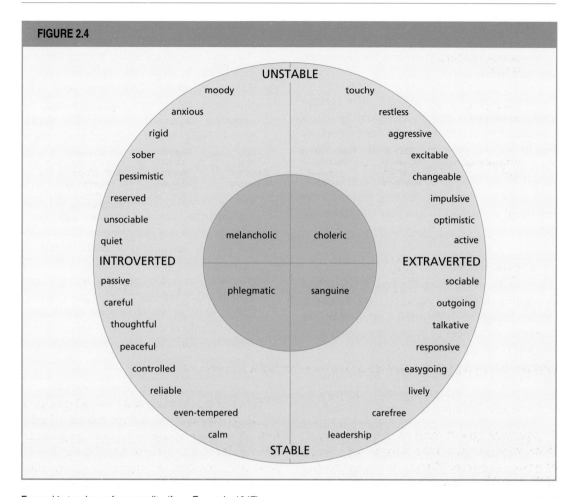

Eysenck's typology of personality (from Eysenck, 1947).

their temper quickly. Altogether their feelings are not kept under tight control and they are not always reliable (Eysenck, 1965).

Introvert. The typical introvert is a quiet, retiring person, introspective, and fond of books rather than people. Introverts are reserved and distant except with intimate friends. They tend to plan ahead, take precautions, and distrust any impulse of the moment. They do not like excitement, take matters of everyday life with proper seriousness, and like a well-ordered approach to life. They keep their feelings under close control, seldom behave in an aggressive way, and do not lose their temper easily. They are reliable, somewhat pessimistic, and place great value on ethical standards (Eysenck, 1965).

Neurotic. The neuroticism dimension is akin to the idea of emotional instability. Individuals who fall into the extreme end of the neuroticism dimension tend to be more prone to worries and anxieties, and more easily upset. They are also likely to complain of headaches, and experience sleeping or eating difficulties. Although they may be more likely to develop neurotic disorders under stressful conditions, in practice the frequency of such events is low and most individuals function adequately in their family, work, and social life. Most of Eysenck's research and theory has been concerned with the extraversion and neuroticism dimensions and, until recently, the psychoticism dimension received less attention.

Psychotic. The psychoticism dimension in its extreme form would be concerned with states such as obsessions, phobias, hysteria, acute depression, and schizophrenia.

Eysenck's concept of personality. His concept embraces the view that an individual *inherits* a particular type of nervous system that predisposes him or her to develop in a particular way. However, the final form personality takes will be determined by the biological basis of personality as well as by the various socialising influences the individual encounters in everyday life (Eysenck, 1967).

"Big Five" factor theory

The **"Big Five" factor theory** dominates current personality research (Bayne, 1994; Furnham, 2002b; Hampson, 1999; McAdams, 1992). The five basic dimensions of personality according to this theory are as follows:

(1) *Extraversion.* Traits associated with extraversion are: being sociable; gregarious; assertive; talkative; and active. It is said that extraverts can be prone to making mistakes and taking risks, and they need lots of stimulation and variety. By contrast, the opposite —introversion—is associated with people who are not necessarily shy or inadequate, but who lack the need for excitement that the extravert exhibits. They are not gregarious and may seem to be ponderous and slow and are likely to emphasise accuracy to the detriment of speed. Unlike the extravert, they think first and speak later and prefer listening to talking, and are more likely to feel happier with written modes of communication than group-centred discussion.

(2) *Agreeableness or likeability.* Traits associated with this factor are: being courteous; flexible; trusting; good natured; sympathetic; kind; co-operative; forgiving; soft-hearted; and tolerant. They are well liked and people who work with them experience them as modest, uncomplicated, with an unselfish concern for the welfare of others. Those who score low in agreeableness may be inconsiderate;

suspicious; unhelpful; argumentative; challenging; with a cynical and sarcastic streak. If they have exceptional ability, they are likely to be tolerated by those with whom they work.

(3) *Conscientiousness.* Traits associated with this factor are: being careful, thorough; responsible; organised; able to plan ahead; hard working; persevering; and achievement orientated. These traits are associated with the work ethic, and people who score highly on conscientiousness are likely to experience impressive accomplishments. But it is said that they can also be rather tight-fisted and intolerant and risk-aversive. Those scoring low on this dimension could be rash or indiscreet and lacking firmness in the way they use time and money, and their personal responsibility towards others is questionable. They could be impulsive and extravagant, and suddenly disengage from a process at a time of convenience to them but not to others.

(4) *Emotional stability.* Traits associated with emotional stability are: being calm; even-tempered; and unruffled. The opposite —*neuroticism (negative affectivity)*—is associated with being anxious; depressed; angry; embarrassed; emotional; thin-skinned; touchy; worried; and insecure. Neurotics are very sensitive, and as a consequence are prone to low self-esteem, guilt, hypochondria, even obsessiveness, and are often better left alone.

(5) *Intellect or openness.* This factor is related to intellect and creativity, and is reflected in openness to experience. It is the most difficult dimension to identify, and those scoring high on it are: intelligent; imaginative; original; optimistic; energetic; curious; broad-minded; cultured; and artistically sensitive. You would expect such individuals to have a wide range of interests, be quite intellectual, and like variety and novelty. They are likely to readily accept change, and are sensitive to the ideas of others. Those scoring low on intellect or openness would find it difficult to handle novel experiences; in fact they could feel uncomfortable and perplexed when facing such circumstances.

They display a certain rigidity and lack of curiosity and this disposition could be wrongly interpreted as a resistance to justifiable change in the workplace.

The "Big Five" factor dimensions and their desirable and undesirable traits are summarised in Table 2.4.

McCrae and Costa (1997) believe that the Big Five structure of personality is a useful general framework but they feel it may be more appropriate if used in cultures that are modern, literate, and industrialised. In an analysis of the Big Five personality dimensions in relation to job performance, Barrick and Mount (1991) concluded that people possessing conscientiousness—e.g., traits such as a strong sense of purpose, obligation, and persistence—generally perform better than those without this set of traits. Another observation was that extraversion (i.e., traits such as being sociable, gregarious, talkative, assertive, and active) was associated with effective performance in occupations connected with management and sales. Obviously, these are jobs where interaction with others constitutes a significant portion of the job.

In another study, Barrick and Mount (1993) explored the extent to which "autonomy" in the job influenced the relationship between personality dimensions and performance in managerial jobs. The opposite ends of the autonomy continuum are as follows. An assembly line job is an example of a job with low autonomy, where the operator is machine-paced in a highly structured job setting with close supervision, and this could be constraining in terms of the expression of personality. On the other hand, an outside sales position, such as a life insurance agent, is an example of a job with high autonomy, where the employee is individually paced, with relatively little job structuring and very little supervision, and this situation could provide more scope for the expression of personality.

The major findings of the study were as follows. Managers with higher scores on conscientiousness (e.g., responsible, persevering, dependable, and achievement-orientated) and extraversion (e.g., sociable, outgoing, and assertive) performed better in jobs with high autonomy when compared with those managers in jobs low in autonomy. Managers with lower scores on agreeableness (e.g., soft-hearted, courteous, forgiving, trusting, and cooperative) performed better in jobs with high autonomy when compared with those managers low in autonomy.

From these results it would appear that the conscientious, extraverted managers perform best in jobs where they enjoy a great deal of discretion in carrying out the various tasks, whereas the agreeable managers perform best in jobs that do not provide much discretion in the way tasks are performed. One possible explanation for the last finding is that highly agreeable managers "may be more likely to comply with rules and be cooperative, and therefore perform better when subjected to a high degree of structure, with little ambiguity, in the pursuit of job objectives"

TABLE 2.4

The "Big Five" personality dimensions and representative traits (from Hampson, 1999): Reproduced by permission of the British Psychological Society

	Traits	
Dimensions	Desirable	Undesirable
Extraversion (1)	Outgoing, sociable, assertive	Introverted, reserved, passive
Agreeableness (2)	Kind, trusting, warm	Hostile, selfish, cold
Conscientiousness (3)	Organised, thorough, tidy	Careless, unreliable, sloppy
Emotional stability (4)	Calm, even-tempered imperturbable	Moody, temperamental, nervous
Intellect or openness (5)	Imaginative, creative, intelligent	Shallow, unsophisticated, imperceptive

TABLE 2.5

Relationship between Eysenck's three-factor system and the "Big Five"

Big Five	Eysenck
Low conscientiousness (undesirable aspect of dimension 3), plus low agreeableness (undesirable aspect of dimension 2)	Psychoticism
Extraversion (1)	Extraversion
Emotional stability (4) (undesirable aspect)	Neuroticism

(Barrick & Mount, 1993). Overall, the results indicate that "autonomy" is an important moderating variable in the relationship between personality and performance.

A major advantage of the Big Five structure of personality, according to Hampson (1999), is that it can assimilate other structures. She cites Goldberg and Rosolack (1994) who demonstrated empirically that Eysenck's three-factor system of extraversion, neuroticism, and psychoticism (previously discussed) can be integrated into the Big Five. The integration is as shown in Table 2.5.

The Big Five model as a predictor of behaviour at work has received impressive endorsement from researchers in recent years, though there are some dissenting voices. Robertson (1998) argues that though the Big Five structure has helped to bring about a remarkable consensus among psychologists, it certainly does not escape criticism; for example, no particular psychological theory accounts for its existence. Schneider and Hough (1995), after reviewing the Big Five debate, are critical of the simplicity of the model and concluded that the time has not yet arrived to view the model as an adequate taxonomy.

Hough (1992) felt the Big Five model needed to be expanded and proposed a nine-factor structure, resulting in subdividing extraversion and conscientiousness and adding two new factors. The new factors are locus of control (the extent to which one feels control over events) and rugged individualism (the extent to which one is decisive, independent, and sentimental). Extraversion was subdivided into affiliation (being sociable) and potency (the extent of impact, influence, and energy displayed by the individual). Conscientiousness was subdivided into dependability (the extent to which an individual is organised, is able to plan, respects authority, and adheres to rules) and achievement (striving for a competent performance).

Cattell (1995), the well-known personality trait theorist whose work is considered above, expresses profound reservations about the five-factor personality theory and finds fault with it on a number of levels, including reliability and statistical testing. However, Hampson (1999) is complimentary about the Big Five structure of personality, but adds that "it remains, for the most part, a description of normal personality and therefore it is not useful in clinical applications as it is in other areas, such as occupational psychology."

In the final analysis, when we look at the relationship between personality and work behaviour we must at all times be vigilant and recognise the potency of crucial variables (e.g., ability and organisational conditions) that can influence outcomes. For example, there are a number of both inborn and learned abilities—such as logical reasoning, linguistic skills, numeracy, manual dexterity, spatial awareness, fund of knowledge and expertise—and personal attributes (e.g., gender, social class, ethnic origin) that can have a significant bearing on the available opportunities for certain kinds of experiences in life, and also influence the manner in which the world treats us.

Let's now move on to a brief examination of other typologies of personality.

Jung's typology

Jung, a prominent psychologist (referred to earlier), whose work preceded that of Eysenck, identifies two broad categories—extravert and introvert. An extravert is outward-looking, responds better to facts, and is more scientific than philosophical. An introvert is subjective, philosophical, a daydreamer, and an artistic type.

Jung entered the domain of traits when he classified personality using primary character-istics. Because a simple introversion–extraversion dichotomy is unlikely to be descriptive enough, due to the tremendous variability among people, Jung introduced four so-called "functions":

(1) *Sensing.* The person is aware of things and processes information through the senses.
(2) *Thinking.* The person understands what a thing is and puts a name to what is sensed.
(3) *Feeling.* The person reacts to things emo-tionally and defines them as acceptable or unacceptable.
(4) *Intuition.* The person has hunches about past or future events in the absence of real information.

This approach concentrates on the information-processing characteristics of the individual (Jung, 1965). These characteristics can be viewed as being located at the ends of the orthogonal axes shown in Figure 2.5.

• A Type 1 person (sensation–thinking) is cold, analytic, lives for the present, is interested primarily in facts, and is extremely practical.
• A Type 2 person (thinking–intuition) is rational, analytic, takes a broad view, and is sociable.

• A Type 3 person (feeling–sensation) is the opposite of Type 2, and is factual, wishes to grasp tangible things, but is emotional.
• A Type 4 person (intuition–feeling) is the opposite of Type 1, and is emotional, sociable, takes a broad view, and is more prone than others to hypothesising.

Myers-Briggs type indicator.   This indicator, or an abridged version of it, is used to identify man-agerial decision styles based on Jung's personal-ity typology (Myers, 1962).

In a study of simulated investment decisions, sensing–feeling executives were more venturesome when undertaking innovative projects than exec-utives falling into the other categories (Henderson & Nutt, 1980). When the focus of attention shifted to the implementation of management science techniques, managers who exhibited sensation–thinking characteristics were said to be more will-ing to construct and accept management science techniques—e.g., linear programming—than were managers who were predominantly endowed with intuition–feeling characteristics. Yet many top-level executives are of the latter type. The manager with intuition–feeling characteristics is said to be more able to implement change and innovation within an organisation if he or she is convinced of the usefulness of the management science techniques (Mitroff et al., 1974).

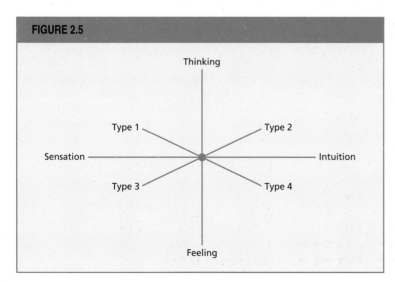

FIGURE 2.5

A graphic representation of Jung's functions of personality.

In a study of personality types in relation to success in business of small retailers, there was no convincing support for any purposeful link between the Jung typology and the performance of small business people, apart from a cautious conclusion that the thinking extravert did best as a small retailer (Rice & Lindecamp, 1989).

Allport's typology

A typology propounded by Allport, Vernon, and Lindzey (1960) has the following characteristics:

* *Theoretical*—pursuit of knowledge.
* *Aesthetic*—striving towards art and natural beauty.
* *Social*—pursuit of humanitarian goals.
* *Political*—pursuit of power.
* *Religious*—spiritual pursuits.
* *Economic*—pursuit of material possessions.

The characteristic that features most prominently in an individual is the determining factor of personality. In a study of managers in diverse cultures and countries, a questionnaire was used bearing some similarities to the typology mentioned here. The results of the study indicate that different values and cultures pose different problems with respect to interaction between people (England & Lee, 1974).

Personality and consumer behaviour

The trait approach to personality has been used extensively in research into consumer behaviour, but the results have been generally disappointing. In the 1970s Proctor & Gamble decided to discontinue the use of personality measures, because the results obtained were not good enough for brand and advertising managers to develop marketing strategies more effectively than they could with alternative approaches. Some would argue that this was not surprising because the standardised personality measures used at that time were more appropriate to clinical settings than to marketing (Engel, Blackwell & Miniard, 1995). They would then go on to say that personality measures designed for the specific purpose of profiling consumers have greater potential to predict the behaviour of consumers with respect to specific products. But, of course, the generalisability of such an exercise is questionable. Notwithstanding what has been said, the trait approach has contributed to the development of psychographics (see Panel 2.3).

Personality types and accidents

As long ago as 1926 researchers were particularly interested in the relationship between personality and accident-proneness, and accident rates (Farmer & Chambers, 1926). Accident-proneness was defined as a personal idiosyncrasy predisposing the individual who possesses it to a relatively high accident rate.

Although aware of the weaknesses of the tests used, the researchers concluded that variations in accident liability are not solely determined by external factors or by chance, but are due in a significant way to measurable individual differences. A relationship was found between accidents and aesthetokinetic coordination; the latter refers to the way the individual uses the hand and arm in response to stimuli recorded and interpreted by the sense organs. Poor integration and nervous instability could lead to accidents. There was a slight indication that the accident-prone are industrially inefficient and more liable to report sick, and consequently react unfavourably to their work environment, but this needed to be confirmed.

In more recent studies the concept of accident-proneness appears to be elusive. It is suggested that the accident-prone personality can be described variously as aggressive, hostile, or overactive, but no permanent or stable personality trait of the accident-prone person can be identified (Haddon, Suchman, & Klein, 1964). It is also suggested that the propensity to accidental injury increases at certain times, such as in conditions of poor vision, fatigue, alcohol use, and where certain hazards or stressors exist in the environment. But these conditions may be of a temporary nature (Hirschfield & Behan, 1963). The young and inexperienced could also be vulnerable to accidents, but likewise this could be a temporary state, just as it could be for a person going through a bad patch of

---

PANEL 2.3: Psychographics

Psychographics incorporates lifestyles or patterns of behaviour adopted by consumers. To gather psychographic data a distinctive technique is used by which consumers are classified by activity, interest, and opinion (AIO). Researchers assemble a large number of items similar to those found in standardised personality and interest inventories. The responses derived from the administration of these inventories are correlated with the buying of products or exposure to the advertising media.

This type of technique measures activities in terms of how people spend their time at work and leisure, their interests expressed as what they consider important in their immediate surroundings, their opinions on social issues, on institutions, and on themselves. Finally, demographic data—such as their age, income, and where they live—may be added. Colonel Sanders' Kentucky Fried Chicken was originally advertised in a folksy, homely, small town way. Then it was established that it was consumed heavily by young housewives with an AIO profile that reflected a more contemporary image. The advertising and packaging of the product were changed to reflect these findings (Wells & Tigert, 1971).

General Foods identified a health-conscious segment of consumers through psychographics. The new market segment for a brand of decaffeinated coffee was active achievers of all ages, as opposed to the previous conception of consumers as elderly people. As a result, the advertisements for the decaffeinated coffee were aimed at consumers interested in adventurous lifestyles (Engel, Blackwell, & Miniard, 1995).

Since the main purpose of psychographic analysis is to understand the lifestyles of core consumers in order to communicate more effectively with their particular market segment, it has assumed importance in a commercial world where change is ever present. The importance of trends in lifestyles is shown by the following examples.

There is growing awareness of the effects of physical fitness and dietary habits on health. People are more conscious of the need to control the intake of such ingredients as salt, sugar, and caffeine, and to reduce or cease the consumption of cigarettes and alcohol. Therefore, it is in the interests of manufacturers to adapt or develop products that appeal to people's desire for a healthier lifestyle. For example, exercise equipment, nutritional and natural food, decaffeinated tea and coffee, and nonalcoholic wines and beers would fall into this category.

The advertising of Alka Seltzer has been influenced by movements to healthier lifestyles—the emphasis is on a product that can relieve the stress symptoms that accompany success, rather than being an antidote for overindulgence (Assael, 1997). Equally, the advertising of established products, such as the condom, reminds people of the value of the product in protecting them against a potent health hazard as opposed to the primary contraception message of earlier years. However, given the steep rise in teenage pregnancies in recent years, the contraceptive message is still important.

In the 1980s the self-centred lifestyle was reflected in the advertisers' emphasis on individualism, pointing to products and services that portrayed a sense of personal achievement.

There is now a system that combines values and lifestyles (VALS). Conceptually, it represents a linkage between the personality angle of psychographics and the activities emphasis of lifestyle research. Although psychographics provides quantitative measures that can be used with large samples (in contrast to the soft or qualitative research associated with the psychoanalytical perspective and consumer motivation research), it should be borne in mind that much psychographic research lacks a solid grounding in personality theory and should be interpreted cautiously.

---

ill-health or stress. Sometimes people are defined as accident-prone if they are not as good as their peers at recognising hazardous situations. It may be more sensible to suggest that it is only at certain times that a person's accident liability increases.

An H.M. Principal Inspector of Factories (Accident Prevention Advisory Unit) in the UK had this to say about accident-proneness (Lindsey, 1980):

Accident-proneness as a concept has little use in practical accident prevention. The concept itself is ill-defined, no stable personality characteristics that can be identified with accident-proneness have been discovered. So therefore, nothing can be done to identify individuals who may be accident-

prone in order to treat them or to remove them from areas of greatest risk. Alternative explanations must be found for persons experiencing multiple accidents. . . . Rather than focusing on accident-proneness we should concentrate on the elimination of risk and provide education to assist employees to cope with unforeseen hazard situations.

Notwithstanding this, a study conducted in South Africa concluded that accident-prone pilots were more neurotic (emotionally unstable) and more extraverted (impulsive) than those who were less accident-prone. Apparently, safe bus drivers in South Africa were stable introverts. In Canada, taxi drivers with a high frequency of accidents were said to have had more disturbed childhoods, to have been more frequently absent without leave while in the forces, and to have displayed more aggression than those who had a low frequency of accidents (Feldman, 1971). Studies conducted among male workers in British industry suggest a highly significant relationship between accidents and extraversion, but no direct relationship between accidents and neuroticism (Craske, 1968).

In recent years, psychologists have been reluctant to stress a fine dividing line between personal factors (e.g., accident-proneness) and environmental factors (e.g., a slippery floor, poor visibility, etc.) when trying to establish the cause of an accident. As a result, the tendency is now to accept the term "accident liability", for by doing so one is acknowledging the involvement of a number of factors, both personal and environmental, in the determination of accident rates (Glendon & McKenna, 1995).

INTERPERSONAL PERSPECTIVE

Psychoanalysis, trait, and type theories attempt to analyse personality in terms of dimensions or insights previously developed by researchers in the field. Interpersonal approaches focus instead on how individuals perceive themselves and their environment, and how a subjective view is matched against objective reality. In effect, individuals try to make sense out of their experience.

The personality theories of Rogers and Kelly are prime examples of the interpersonal approach. Though these theories were developed from the fields of counselling and psychotherapy, they are not concerned with the hidden meanings of an individual's behaviour, as in psychoanalysis. The individual is considered to be in the best position to make statements about himself or herself, and these form the basis for therapy. In this section self-concept and personal construct theory will be discussed.

Self-concept

The important factor in Rogers' theory is the concept of the self (Rogers, 1951). The self in this context comprises the pattern of perception, feelings, attitudes, and values that individuals consider to be unique to themselves. Rogers also refers to the "ideal self", which is the individual as he or she would like to be. In the well-adjusted individual, the difference between the self and the ideal self would not be significant. But where there is a discrepancy between the self and actual experience, imbalance arises and this can result in tension and maladjustment. The consequences of a discrepancy between the self and reality are highlighted in Panel 2.4.

Sometimes when individuals are aware of the state of imbalance, they may change their behaviour to bring it into line with their self-concept, or alternatively modify that self-concept. Rogers also emphasises the importance of different forms of positive gestures in the shaping of the self-concept (Rogers, 1959). These would include approval, sympathy, and love and respect from others, though the conditions to be satisfied before acquiring these benefits could put a lot of pressure

---

PANEL 2.4: Self versus reality

A discrepancy could arise in the following circumstances. Valerie, a female executive, who believes she is sociable and well liked, overhears a conversation in the office in which two colleagues describe her as moody and difficult to relate to. She is shocked as she registers information that is inconsistent with her self-concept. As a consequence, anxiety occurs because of the imbalance experienced. One form of defence could be distortion; that means Valerie changing her perception of reality so that it is consistent with her self-concept. For instance, she may be able to convince herself that the two colleagues' judgement of her is based on an inadequate understanding of her true self, or that they are projecting their own shortcomings on to her. Another form of defence could be repression, which can arise when experiences are clearly perceived as too threatening to the individual's self-concept, and it is used to maintain the integrity of the self.

(Baron, 2002)

on the individual and may elicit defence mechanisms. For example, if the parents value scholastic success, the child is likely to develop a self-concept that emphasises academic achievement. But if the child's performance at school does not match this ideal, an "ego defensive strategy" may have to be used, such as ignoring actual experience. The problem with this is that, as more and more experiences are not allowed to reach the level of awareness, the self can sever contact with reality and the individual becomes increasingly maladjusted. The neurotic individual is placed in a position of heavy reliance on defence mechanisms because of a significant mismatch between actual experience and self-concept.

It is important that the therapist who uses Rogers' ideas is neither directive nor disinterested, but is client-centred. Understanding clients' own views of themselves necessitates an exploration of their total experience. The desired result is constructive change to facilitate greater self-fulfilment of the client. Important conditions for the success of client-centred therapy appear to be the provision of adequate levels of empathy, genuineness, and warmth on the part of the therapist, and an environment suitable for self-exploration by the client of feelings, values, fears, and relationships. This type of approach could be valid in certain counselling situations identified in Chapter 19.

There is some support for the self-concept in studies of consumer behaviour. It appears that consumers prefer brands that relate both to their self-perceptions and to subjective images of brands. In one study the relationship between consumers' self-images and product images in 19 product categories (e.g., club membership, coffee, beer, and wine) was investigated. It was found that the preferences of consumers were positively related either to self-image or to ideal self-image (Landon, 1974). In another study consumers of cars perceived themselves as having characteristics similar to owners of their particular make of car, and saw themselves as possessing a self-concept different from consumers of a competing make (Grubb & Hupp, 1968). The words used to describe the owners of the different makes of car are set out in Table 2.6. These are examples of consumers choosing products that reflect their self-image.

TABLE 2.6

Self-image of car owners

Volkswagen owners	Pontiac GTO owners
Thrifty	Status-conscious
Sensible	Flashy
Creative	Fashionable
Individualistic	Adventurous
Practical	Interested in opposite sex
Conservative	Sporty
Economical	Style-conscious
Quality-conscious	Pleasure-seeking

It is also worth noting that the products we choose can have a material influence on our self-image (Solomon, 1983). Certain products have the symbolic value of a badge and say something about ourselves.

Criticism of Rogers' self-concept theory

A particular criticism of Rogers' theory, with its strong emphasis on personal responsibility or free will, is that it focuses too much on the cognitive dimensions of personality, to the relative neglect of unconscious processes. Also, the use of self-reports can prove unreliable because the client may be unduly influenced by what the therapist expects from the encounter, and may be prone to make socially desirable responses to the therapist. In addition, it can be argued that the client does not have perfect insight into his or her own condition (Peck & Whitlow, 1975).

Personal construct theory

According to Kelly, a psychological theory should be about understanding a person's behaviour with a view to predicting future actions. Humans are seen as scientists who are trying to make sense out of their world. They are continually testing assumptions about various things with reference to experience and evidence. There is no absolute truth or objective reality, but humans can use *constructs* to interpret situations in order to improve their understanding and ability to predict future events.

So a construct is a way of predicting future happenings, and it is only useful if predictions are fairly accurate (Kelly, 1955). If the construct "dishonest" is applied to a person, then a prediction is made about how that person is expected to behave in a position where, for example, he or she handles a lot of money or is in some other way placed in a position of trust.

When using constructs, we are concerned with opposite poles—beautiful/ugly, honest/dishonest, good/bad, warm/cold, intelligent/stupid, and so on. Constructs arise when a person construes two persons or objects as having a characteristic in common, which is different from that associated with a third person or object. Some constructs are more general than others. For example, the construct beautiful/ugly may apply to nearly everything in the world, whereas the construct intelligent/stupid may fit only humans or mammals. Each construct will have its own hierarchy, illustrated in Table 2.7 (Bannister, 1970).

In this example, a person was asked whether he would prefer to see himself as well dressed or badly dressed, and replied that he would like to see himself as well dressed. When asked why, he replied that it was in order to make a good first impression on people. The question "Why?" was repeatedly asked after each reply until the person reached the ceiling of the hierarchy. When asked why he wanted to be happier, he gave no direct response other than saying it was what life was about. Some constructs are classified as superordinate (superior) and are related to a number of subordinate or peripheral constructs. The superordinate constructs that are really stable are considered to be core constructs and give the person a sense of identity and continuity.

If a person can only state one pole of a construct, the other pole is said to be submerged. For example, if a person uses "intelligent" to describe people, the existence of the opposite pole "stupid" is implied, even though it is not used. So if it is asserted that somebody is intelligent, this implies a contrast. To have abstracted the idea of intelligent, a person must be aware of several intelligent people, and at least one stupid person. Thus, at one moment, the person's construct is intelligent versus stupid.

Normally, people revise their constructs in the light of experience. If predictions based on a construct are continually wrong, this could give rise to a revision of the appropriate construct. Constructs, then, may change over time, particularly where they are flexible enough to accommodate new events, although others are relatively inflexible in that they rarely allow new events to be accepted. Constructs that are closely correlated with others are called "tight" constructs, and predictions do not vary; for example, "This is a library, therefore it contains books." When constructs are "loose", it is possible to make a number of predictions in similar circumstances—in the same way that, for example, a track-suit could be used for a variety of sporting activities at a given venue. Generally, constructs should not be too tightly or too loosely organised. Each individual has his or her own personal construct system, and its structure and organisation constitutes that individual's personality.

Important factors in personal construct theory

Anxiety, threat, hostility, and aggression are important factors in Kelly's personal construct theory:

* *Anxiety* is said to arise when the person is aware that perceived events cannot be construed within the construct system. An accountant who cannot decide how to write a management report may experience anxiety. The anxiety

TABLE 2.7

Hierarchy of constructs		
Happier	vs.	Unhappier
↑		↑
Closer personal relationships	vs.	Poorer personal relationships
↑		↑
More accepted by people	vs.	Not so well accepted by people
↑		↑
Makes a good first impression	vs.	Makes a poor first impression
↑		↑
Well dressed	vs.	Badly dressed

arises when the accountant recognises that the challenge with which he or she is presented lies outside the orbit of his or her construct system. The real cause of the anxiety is the realisation that the construct system is inadequate to cope with the situation.

- *Threat* is an awareness of an imminent major change in the person's core construct. An academic construes himself or herself to be an able scholar. However, over the years their research and scholarly achievements are patchy and the number of publications is negligible. Therefore, they have to reappraise their role and find the experience threatening.

- *Hostility* arises when there is a realisation of a mismatch between a construct and its prediction. A senior manager recruits an accountant to provide a management accounting service to the organisation. However, the accountant prefers to operate as a financial accountant. The hostile senior manager does not change his or her view of the accountant, but instead offers inducements and incentives so that the accountant may gravitate towards the provision of a management accounting service.

- *Aggression* is a response that arises when constructs are not working. A sales representative might consider him or herself to be first rate in a large group of companies, but then attends a sales convention organised by head office and encounters other sales representatives with excellent track records. The sales representative finds it difficult to keep up with them, and his or her response is aggression.

It is obvious that Kelly's definitions of anxiety, threat, hostility, and aggression are not quite the same as the conventional definitions of these terms. He has nothing to say about the development of the person, and pays little attention to how the individual comes to construe events. It is as if all that matters is how the individual sees the world at a given moment.

Role construct repertory test

The **role construct repertory test** (rep test) is a method used to arrive at the basic constructs that a person uses, and the interrelationship between

them. The test is based on the premise that a construct can be measured by first noting the similarities and contrasts among events. For example, a person is asked to list a series of people or events that are regarded as important, such as lecturers, friends, relatives, marriage, or the purchase of a house. Once the list is prepared, the person is asked, in the case of people, to give the name of three individuals who can be classified as a lecturer, friend, and relative respectively. The person receives three cards, each card bearing one of the names he or she has given. The person is asked to say in what way two of them are alike but different from the third name. This procedure is repeated with different cards until an adequate number of constructs has been elicited. A simple example of the elicitation of a construct is as follows:

Counsellor: List three people that you most admire.

Client: My friend, my relative, and my tutor.

Counsellor: How are two of these people alike and yet different from the third person?

Client: My friend and my relative are outgoing, but my tutor is introverted.

Repertory grid. A method developed from the rep test is called the repertory grid, and has been used in a variety of settings, including management selection and development activities (discussed in Chapters 17 and 18). This method allows the investigator to use a number of different types of element, such as the title of a job or a name. Constructs may be elicited, or alternatively provided, by the investigator. In the previous example the construct "outgoing" was elicited by the counsellor. In Table 2.8 the constructs provided may be considered critical, in terms of personality characteristics, in an industrial environment. The elements (job titles) are listed as single and paired combinations; the pair share the same constructs (i.e., innovative and optimistic). In this process, more constructs could be elicited until either constructs are repeated or the subjects cannot give any more constructs. Other elements expressed in triad form, in the domain of executive personality

TABLE 2.8

Elements and constructs in a repertory grid

Elements	Constructs
Research scientist ⎫	Innovative
Head of department ⎬ (pair)	Optimistic
Production manager ⎭	Favours status quo,
(single)	pessimistic

characteristics, could be elicited, and this in turn would lead to the elicitation of more constructs.

The final list of elements and constructs will then be used to produce a grid with the elements along the top and the constructs down the side. The subject is then asked to grade each element on each construct using either a 5- or 7-point scale. The grid shown in Figure 2.6 is a simplified representation of constructs and elements after being reduced in number following a consensus process. The grid was the outcome of an elicitation procedure with a group of supervisors attending a short course at an educational establishment (Smith, 1978). To assist with the processing of the grid data, statistical computer software can be used as a prelude to the interpretation of the outcome of the exercise.

BEHAVIOURAL PERSPECTIVE

Though there is no single behavioural position among researchers, there is a significant view that the main source of behaviour can be found in the individual's environment and not within the person. Though genetic inheritance is not discounted, the feeling is that reference to traits, psychoanalysis, and the physiological basis of behaviour is not particularly illuminating. It is maintained that a person's development and behaviour is primarily influenced by what happens to him or her from childhood onwards, and by the learning that takes place. Therefore, the environment is said to exert a powerful influence in terms of behavioural change.

A major exponent of this proposition is Skinner (1974), and his views on conditioning and reinforcement are more fully reported in the discussion of learning in Chapter 7. The following topics will be discussed in this section: (1) reinforcement; (2) imitation; (3) socialisation; and (4) situational variables.

Reinforcement

A behavioural or social learning approach can be illustrated with reference to reinforcement in child training. When the child conforms to certain standards it may receive parental reinforcement in the form of a reward such as an expression of pleasure, a smile, praise, a pat on the head, and so on. The parent has the capacity to shape the child's response. When the child emits an inborn social response, such as a smile, it becomes part of the child's repertoire of responses when it is reinforced.

In the development of language, intermittent reinforcement may also be applied. For example, the mother is positively encouraging the development of language when, periodically, all meaningful language sounds emitted by the child are reinforced. The reinforcer could simply be the expression of delight on the mother's face. However, if the mother does not reinforce or reward the early, crude attempts to pronounce words, this could give rise to a delay in the learning of language. But equally, understanding a child's crude utterances too readily and quickly may encourage late talking. Sometimes it is difficult to establish the reinforcers associated with the child's behaviour. For example, the motives for stealing or lying may be connected with the values of the child's peer group and this is something that falls outside the control of the parents.

Negative and nonreinforcement are also strategies at the disposal of parents:

• *Negative reinforcement* takes the form of punishment and may be appropriately applied in certain circumstances—for example, when a child with insufficient road sense is corrected. Punishment that inflicts pain should be avoided. It may inhibit rather than stamp out

FIGURE 2.6

	Manager	Workers in general	Senior union official	Person W	Top management	Person Y	Government	Person X	Person Z	Junior supervisors	Welfare	Person V	Person U	Staff in general	Managers' staff association
Powerful															
Leaders															
National															
Elected															
Takes management view															
High ranking															
Have control															
Responsible															
Take workers' view															
Employed by organisation															
Impersonal															
Cooperative															
Takes decisions															
Militant															
Communicative															
Good															

5 = definitely yes
4 = yes
3 = uncertain
2 = no
1 = definitely no

A repertory grid (from Smith, 1978). Reproduced by permission of Personnel Publications Ltd.

undesirable behaviour. It may also lead to delinquency, block the flow of communication, and create resentment.

- *Nonreinforcement* can take the form of a threat to withdraw approval, or alternatively actually withdrawing approval, and can be effective when there is a good relationship between the parent and the child. With nonreinforcement, the child's response is likely to become extinct, and further training may be needed in order to reinstate it.

Imitation

Do we always have to experience happenings personally or directly in order to learn? According to Bandura (1969), much learning takes place when we observe what other people do and note the consequences of their behaviour.

The child may imitate the mannerisms of its father, the intonation and favourite phrases of its mother, and the same accent as members of its peer group. Words that are imitated may be used without perfect understanding. Imitation is encouraged where the child observes its role model (e.g., the parent) being rewarded for engaging in a certain work or leisure activity. Likewise, the child finds imitation easy when it is specifically rewarded for copying a role model. Of course, the child could imitate a "deviant" parent but, if the parent is punished for the deviancy, then there may be less likelihood of the child copying the parent.

Socialisation

The child learns the significance of a number of roles in society. There is the realisation that one has to conform to rules, but equally to learn the contradictions inherent in the complex system of rules; in fact, parents may not be able to help in resolving this difficulty. There is the realisation that there are times for competition, and times for cooperation. Bending the rules may be permissible in order to win, but one expects to be penalised if one is caught cheating. One learns to control aggressive and other impulses.

The notion of right and wrong (conscience) is transmitted in a variety of ways and is often developed fortuitously. For example, a child taking money from the father's wallet is stealing, but taking a slice of cake from a plate without permission is bad manners. In the old days it was more acceptable for the young man to "sow his wild oats"; the young girl, however, was expected to preserve her virginity. One finds here a pragmatic acceptance of prostitution but a moral rejection of it. During early socialisation, a number of values are internalised (adopted); these subsequently regulate behaviour without the need for the imposition of control in the form of punishment.

Learning to be male and female is also part of the socialisation process. Boys are often expected to be rough and tough, to play football or rugby, and not to cry. They are often also expected to be assertive and certainly not encouraged to play with dolls. The nonconformist boy is frequently called a sissy. The little boy is more likely to use his fists in an aggressive encounter. The little girl is often expected to play with dolls and be quiet, gentle, and decorous, and to take up a pastime such as ballet. The nonconformist girl is called a tomboy. However, in today's society this stereotyping is being challenged, and roles are changing.

The work of Mead (1935) in primitive societies highlights the effect of child-rearing practices on subsequent adult behaviour. For example, child-rearing practices in the Tchambuli tribe produced males who played stereotyped female roles. The men were domesticated, looked after the children, attended to the household needs, curled their hair, and adorned themselves with flowers. The women were unadorned, had their heads shaven, did the hunting, and generally engaged in masculine pursuits. However, it was the men who were the warriors. Perhaps the male is temperamentally more suited to the performance of aggressive acts, although in the animal world the female can be aggressive when protecting her young.

In recent years the primacy of biological rather than socialisation influences has been emphasised. In a research study published in

The New England Journal of Medicine in January 2004 two researchers at the Johns Hopkins Medical School concluded that the biological forces that make boys feel male and girls female may occur before birth. The researchers studied 14 people who were born with incompletely developed penises that were surgically changed to give them a female identity. These people continued to display male-like behaviour later in life despite attempts to socialise them as girls. They favoured competitive sports and, as children, showed little interest in dolls or other "female" toys. This study throws into doubt the view that gender identity—established in most children by the age of three—is largely based on socialisation. The researchers theorise that hormones active before birth may permanently determine our sense of gender identity (*Financial Times*, 2004c).

In an organisational setting, imitation and socialisation can also be prevalent. This is manifest when the company highlights the behaviour that members (particularly new employees) should emulate. Of course, when a fundamental culture change within the organisation is contemplated, all employees could be involved in the process. A detailed discussion of organisational culture appears in Chapter 15.

A behavioural approach to personality has been criticised because it is said to present an oversimplified view of human behaviour, but particularly because it does not pay sufficient attention to the importance of cognitive processes (Peck & Whitlow, 1975). Another criticism is that inner conflicts and the influence of unconscious thoughts and impulses on behaviour are generally ignored (Baron, 2002).

Situational variables

To complement a behavioural approach, reference is made to the potency of situational variables and how they are selected and evaluated (Mischel, 1973). The same situation or stimulus (e.g., a homeless person on the street asking for money) can elicit a different response in different individuals, even though each individual has a strong caring and compassionate outlook. Also, different situations can elicit similar responses in one individual. The way the person selects information and evaluates it is mediated by values, expectancies, encoding strategies, and the cognitive processing of the individual, which can have a profound effect on his or her response to a particular stimulus. Of course, previous learning of an appropriate nature also has a part to play in this process.

The power of the situation, or the moderating influence of situational factors on the way personality finds expression, can be seen in the way a particular individual reacts to different circumstances. A person is endowed with a particular trait (e.g., is shy) and one would expect him or her to be uncomfortable relating to people. However, this person finds it less of an ordeal addressing a large group in a public lecture than engaging personally with one individual in a small tutorial group. In this case the typical behaviour associated with shyness is not very conspicuous in the public lecture. This type of thinking has been developed in the "cognitive-affective" personality system advanced by Mischel and Shoda (1995). So acknowledging the moderating influence of situational factors allows us to attempt to explain why personality traits alone do not always reliably predict behaviour (Hampson, 1999).

In the following example one accountant has a situational advantage over the other. A balance sheet depicting the financial position of a company is presented to two accountants. One accountant has a particular insight into the quality of the senior management of the company and the state of its market. The other has no such knowledge apart from a superficial understanding of the internal affairs of the company. In these circumstances it is highly likely that the balance sheet will be interpreted differently by each of the two accountants. In other circumstances we would normally be confident that the two accountants would produce an identical response to a particular stimulus. If they encountered a red traffic light while driving in separate cars, for example, one would expect them to stop their cars. Finally, one must acknowledge that situations alone do not determine behaviour.

COGNITIVE PERSPECTIVE

In the opening chapter of this book, there was reference to the cognitive approach to the study of psychology. A cognitive perspective is evident when people's unique perceptions and the action strategies based on them tend to determine who they are and how they react. In the process, they rely on previous experience and future expectations, guided by their attitudes and prominent needs. In this section we will discuss the following relevant concepts: (1) the **internal–external locus of control**; (2) self-efficacy; (3) self-monitoring; (4) sensation-seeking; and (5) field dependency–independency.

Internal–external locus of control

An early behavioural theorist, Rotter (1954), developed the notion of internal–external control of reinforcement. Because of its strong cognitive emphasis, this is considered to be a dimension of personality. Internal–external (I–E) is not a typology. Rather it is a continuum: A person can fall anywhere along that continuum from external at one end to internal at the other. Most people are clustered somewhere in the middle.

Externals and internals

People differ in their attitude to control. Certain people (externals) feel that the outcome of their efforts is controlled by forces and events external to themselves, such as chance, fate, and powerful figures in authority; whereas others (internals) are convinced that control is an internal matter related to their own efforts and talents.

Internals will be confident that they can bring about changes in their own behaviour and environment, whereas externals feel somewhat powerless to bring about change. In an organisational setting internals try to influence work practices and ways of allocating responsibilities and may resist attempts by superiors to closely supervise their work; they may feel more comfortable holding down jobs requiring high initiative but low

levels of compliance. By contrast, externals are more likely to feel comfortable with jobs that are highly structured with greater levels of compliance. With regard to home security, for instance, internals are likely to take certain precautions, such as installing burglar alarms, mortice locks, and bright outside lights, if such action discourages intruders. Externals are much less likely to take such precautions if they believe that a person determined to break into the house will always find a way regardless of deterrents.

Internals and externals view reward or reinforcement differently. Internals are likely to have greater belief that their efforts will lead to rewards, and are likely to respond more favourably to reward systems based on, for example, performance-related pay. If internals receive positive reinforcement after engaging in a particular bout of behaviour, this will increase the likelihood of that behaviour occurring again; negative reinforcement will have the opposite effect. Externals are more likely to believe that positive reinforcement following a particular bout of behaviour was a matter of pure luck, and so there is little point in repeating that behaviour in the future. Faced with a problem, internals expect that defining the situation as one in which personal efforts will make a difference will help them to resolve the problem. On the other hand, externals will operate with the expectation that chance or other uncontrollable factors are critical, and they will behave accordingly.

The importance of expectations

One of the most distinctive assumptions that Rotter made is that human behaviour is determined not just by the rewards that follow it but also by our expectations that the behaviour chosen will, in fact, bring about reinforcement. He believed that an essential human quality is our pervasive tendency to think and to anticipate (Phares & Chaplin, 1998).

The person builds up expectations about the relationship between behaviour and its consequences, and these expectations will be either strengthened or weakened depending upon their similarity to the actual consequences of the

---

PANEL 2.5: Expecting the best and the worst

JC considered it necessary to have an extension built to his house. Following various enquiries he approached a particular building contractor to discuss the costs of such a project. JC will have certain expectations about a satisfactory outcome if the contract is given to this builder. These expectations could be based on his previous experience of doing business with the builder. But if JC had no previous experience of his work, then the expectation that using him would result in satisfactory work could depend on other factors.

He could rely on the recommendation of somebody he knew who had a similar extension constructed by the builder in question, and who was pleased with the outcome. Likewise, he may be able to inspect similar projects undertaken by the builder, with the help of an expert. Of course he could be optimistic about the venture and this could be reflected in a general expectancy that the contract will work out well. If, however, JC is a distrusting person, this will lower his expectancy that doing business with the builder will be a productive exercise. If JC is an external in disposition, the expectancy that commissioning work on the extension will lead to a positive outcome could be dampened.

---

behaviour. In this way the person distinguishes behaviour that brings about predictable results from behaviour that does not. The executive will develop a relatively stable set of expectations regarding the control of his or her behaviour at committee meetings, in terms of results or success either due to his or her own actions, or to some other factor. A further example of expectancy manifesting itself is shown in Panel 2.5.

Externals are likely to be compliant and conforming individuals, prone to persuasion, and ready to accept information from others. Because they expect that they cannot control the consequences of their own behaviour, they are more willing to place reliance on others. Internals seem to have greater confidence in their own competence and they appear to be more independent. They prefer to be in control, and consequently resist any efforts on the part of others to manipulate them.

The most fundamental difference between internals and externals lies in the way they seek knowledge about their environment. The internals, unlike the externals, realise that they are in control of the reinforcement or reward that follows their behaviour, and they put greater effort into obtaining information about their environment (Phares & Chaplin, 1998). Apparently secretarial staff, who were classified as externals, were found to be more reluctant to use word-processing equipment, whereas their nonexternal peers displayed natural curiosity about the potential of the equipment (Arndt, Feltes, & Hanak, 1983).

Reflecting on empirical evidence relating to the personal qualities and characteristics of successful entrepreneurs, Kuratho and Hodgetts (1989) propose that successful entrepreneurs believe that they can achieve success through their own efforts, and are convinced that if they work hard and keep things under control the desired outcome is almost assured. They do not believe that the success or failure of their venture will be governed by fate, luck, or similar forces. These individuals exhibit an internal locus of control orientation. Their view of failure is interesting. They go ahead with a new venture despite setbacks, and freely admit that they learn more from their failures than from their successes.

In trying to increase their understanding of the effects of participation in the budgetary process, academics in the management accounting area might well turn to the concept of locus of control. Brownell (1982) examined the effects of locus of control on the relationship between participation and performance in a budgetary context. Those with an internal locus of control orientation performed best in highly participative situations where they were able to exert much influence. By contrast, those with an external locus of control orientation performed best in conditions of low participation where the potential for exercising influence was that much less. A discussion of the relationship between budgeting and participation appears in Chapter 12.

A questionnaire, referred to as the I–E Scale, has been developed by Rotter (1966) and is used to measure the orientation of internals and externals. The questionnaire consists of 29 items, each of which contains 2 statements. The subject is asked to select the statement that is closest to his or her belief. The following statements bear some similarity to statements on the I–E Scale:

(1) (a) Many people can be described as victims of circumstance.

    (b) What happens to other people is pretty much of their own making.

(2) (a) Much of what happens to me is probably a matter of luck.

    (b) What happens to me is my own doing.

(3) (a) It is foolish to think one can really change another person's basic attitudes.

    (b) When I am right I can convince others.

The concept of the internal–external locus of control has generated a fair amount of research, and the validity of the I–E Scale has been questioned, particularly on the grounds that it is socially desirable to be portrayed as an internal. It is suggested that some people fake the test in order to project a favourable image (Peck & Whitlow, 1975).

Self-efficacy

Self-efficacy is a personality characteristic related to locus of control, but not immediately obvious as such. It is a belief in one's capability to take the appropriate action to produce desired outcomes in a defined task (Gist & Mitchell, 1992). It develops as a result of performing the task a number of times, where one receives positive feedback on achievements, or it can arise from observing colleagues and others being successful in what they do. The greater a person's self-efficacy, the more confidence the person possesses to complete a task successfully, and he or she will try harder to meet challenges in difficult circumstances. People with low self-efficacy are more likely to reduce their effort or terminate an activity. There is further discussion of this concept later, when its role in motivation (Chapter 4) and training (Chapter 18) is examined.

Self-monitoring

The extent to which individuals show consistent behaviour across situations and over time could be an important aspect of personality. Some people adopt the same behaviour in all settings, while others change their behaviour to match each particular situation. Self-monitoring refers to the tendency of individuals to regulate their behaviour on the basis of internal factors (e.g., own attitudes, values, beliefs), or alternatively external factors (e.g., reactions to other people or requirements of a given situation) (Snyder & Gangestad, 1987). Low self-monitors tend to show a high degree of consistency in their behaviour across many situations and are influenced by internal factors. On the other hand, high self-monitors are influenced by external factors and are likely to vary their behaviour to suit the prevailing circumstances (Koestner, Bernieri, & Zuckerman, 1992).

According to Baron (1999), self-monitoring involves more than differences in behaviour. Persons high in self-monitoring are generally better than low self-monitors both at detecting others' emotional reactions and at managing their own nonverbal cues. As a result, they are generally more successful at making a good first impression (Paulhus, Bruce, & Trapnell, 1995). High self-monitors are image conscious and approach new situations by asking themselves, how can I please the people I have to relate to? By contrast, the low self-monitors are likely to ask themselves, how best can I be my true self in the situation I am about to enter. High self-monitors may be seen by others as unreliable, inconsistent, or even manipulative due to their changeable behaviour (Turban & Dougherty, 1994). Both high and low self-monitors in a work setting have been criticised; the former are referred to as chameleons who adjust the way they present themselves to the conditions in which they operate, and the latter are sometimes looked upon unfavourably for inhabiting their own planet and being insensitive to others.

Sensation-seeking

Sensation-seeking is the desire to explore novel and intense experiences, and as far as teenagers are concerned it can predispose them to get involved in high-risk behaviour, such as speeding, experimenting with drugs, and having unprotected sex. Those who are high on sensation-seeking are likely to actively seek adventure and excitement.

Reasons have been put forward by Zuckerman (1990, 1995) to account for the existence of high levels of arousal and a preference for dangerous behaviour. He believes that it has important roots in biological processes and says that high sensation-seekers are people whose nervous systems operate best at high levels of arousal. They seem to have the capacity to ignore irrelevant information and pay more attention to stimuli of an unusual nature; also, it is said that they can cope better with stressful events. A medical doctor writing in *The Times* in the UK made reference to a research finding whereby it was claimed that a dopamine receptor gene, called the novelty gene, explains the personality trait of seeking excitement through the intense pursuit of innovation and change (Stuttaford, 1999). This type of finding is indicative of evidence in support of "nature" in the nurture versus nature debate in personality, which is examined to a greater extent in Chapter 3 on intelligence.

Field dependency–independency

This concept was developed following experiments on perception. A field-dependent person tends to be strongly influenced by the background or surroundings of a particular stimulus. A field-independent person is not so influenced and can differentiate more easily between parts of the stimulus and its surroundings (Witkin, 1965). This concept was extended to embrace cognitive style, and as a consequence entered the domain of personality.

The field-independent person has the capacity to interpret events in a detailed, organised way, and has a clearer view of the constituent parts of the objects or situations encountered. He or she has a clearer view of his or her own beliefs, needs, and characteristics, and of the ways in which they differ from those of other people. To arrive at the cognitive orientation of the personality of the individual using this concept, the person is required to identify a specific item(s) embedded in a more complex figure. For example, there are nine items embedded in Figure 2.7 (e.g., a pumpkin, a clock, a witch's hat, etc.).

FIGURE 2.7

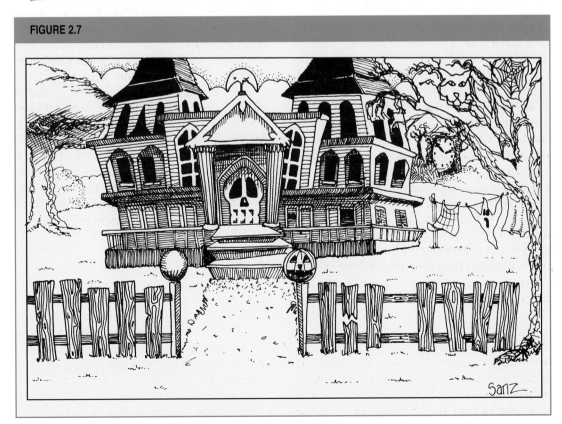

Embedded figures to measure field-independence/field-dependence (based on Pennington, 1986).

People differ in the speed with which they identify the various items embedded in a figure. Field-independent people are fast at locating items because they take an analytical, structured approach to the study of the picture they are viewing. Field-dependent people are slow at locating the items because they are rigidly tuned into the whole picture, and are less able to look at each part of the picture independent of the other parts; generally, they tend to perceive things in a more global fashion.

In one study, subjects had their cognitive style tested prior to being set a task involving the use of a computer program and a set of data to answer a series of questions. It was concluded that cognitive style was related significantly to the number of correct answers. It is interesting to note that field-independent individuals performed particularly well (Egly, 1982).

The field-dependent person tends to be susceptible to social influences and relies less on his or her own judgement. He or she cannot always see how the individual parts fit into the total picture, and finds it difficult to differentiate between them and to relate his or her own beliefs, needs, and characteristics. Likewise, he or she finds it difficult to see a clear distinction between the latter characteristics and those of a similar nature possessed by others.

PERSONALITY ASSESSMENT

It is often recognised that a number of job failures result from personality deficiencies. Being endowed with the necessary intellectual attributes, knowledge, and skills does not guarantee that the individual will be an effective or satisfied worker, or a well-liked colleague. Personality characteristics could be influential in determining success or failure in a job, particularly where substantial interpersonal contacts are involved, as required in selling and managerial or supervisory work. These are areas where the application of personality tests to personnel selection has been explored to a greater extent than elsewhere. Often, the motivation to use the tests is to improve the personnel selection process by cutting down the cost of making errors in selecting people. Methods of personnel selection will be discussed fully in Chapter 17.

Personality tests, which allow a large number of questions about behaviour and preferences to be asked in a comparatively short period of time, along with interest tests, could also be used in vocational guidance and counselling, with the emphasis on placing people in jobs compatible with their personal characteristics. Interest tests measure vocational interests or preferences. The person whose interests are being tested indicates the strength of his or her interests in such matters as various jobs, hobbies, and recreational activities.

Most of the personality tests used are pencil and paper tests with multiple-choice elements. In practice, they are not tests in the sense that correct and incorrect answers are possible to the various questions. They are really questionnaires in which the job applicant or employee seeking advancement in the organisation is requested to state how he or she feels about certain issues, or how he or she would react in certain specified situations.

Psychological testing (or psychometrics), of which personality testing is part, is discussed in Chapter 3.

CHAPTER SUMMARY

- Having defined what we mean by personality, two basic approaches to the study of personality were introduced. These are referred to as the idiographic and nomothetic approaches.

- There followed an analysis of a number of perspectives on personality, starting with the psycho-analytical. This draws heavily on the contribution of Freud and was discussed with reference to levels of awareness; personality structure (id, ego, and super-ego); defence mechanisms (repression, projection, fixation, regression, and reaction formation); and finally personality development. Other explanations are briefly acknowledged.

- Projective tests, designed to assess personality based on unconscious processes, were said to be only indirectly related to psychoanalysis. Two well-known projective tests are the Rorschach Test and the Thematic Apperception Test. These tests, though subject to certain weaknesses, can be used in consumer motivation research. In addition, role playing and visualisation techniques used to create personality descriptions of consumers were explained. The notion of brand personality as an alternative to the latter was mentioned.

- The next major perspective on personality discussed was trait and type theory. Different categories of traits, including Allport's, were described. Cattell was identified as an influential trait theorist. He drew a distinction between source traits and surface traits. His 16 PF Test represents source traits.

- When a person shares a pattern of traits with a large group of people, he or she is said to belong to a personality type. Types, as a perspective on personality, were discussed, initially with reference to the theory of the four humours and Sheldon's physical typology. This was followed by a brief examination of the typologies advanced by two influential psychologists of old, namely Jung and Allport. A derivative of Jung's typology is the Myers-Briggs type indicator. The major part of the discussion was devoted to the important contribution made by another influential psychologist, Eysenck, whose work has some similarities to the "Big Five" factor theory. The latter constitutes a major development in personality theory in recent years.

- There was reference to psychographics and lifestyles as techniques in consumer research designed to compensate for the weaknesses of the trait and type approaches in this area.

- An interpersonal perspective on personality, suitably illustrated, focused on how individuals perceived themselves and their environment, and how a subjective view is matched against objective reality. The notion of the self-concept (Rogers) and personal construct theory (Kelly) were introduced. The important factors in personal construct theory were noted, and examples of the use of the repertory grid (derived from Kelly's theory) were given.

- A behavioural perspective on personality, primarily concerned with reinforcement, imitation, and socialisation recognised that a person's development and behaviour are primarily influenced by happenings from childhood onwards and by the learning that takes place. The weakness of the behavioural approach was accepted, and the relevance of a situational emphasis to complement it was noted.

- A cognitive perspective on personality was acknowledged, consisting of the internal–external locus of control, self-efficacy, self-monitoring, sensation-seeking, and field dependency–independency.

- The concept of personality assessment (testing) was introduced, ahead of its elaboration in Chapter 3 in the section on psychological testing.

QUESTIONS

(1) What is meant by the term "personality"?

(2) Distinguish between the idiographic and nomothetic approaches to the study of personality.

(3) Examine the usefulness of the psychoanalytical perspective.

(4) Identify the differences between projective tests and role playing or visualisation, and comment on the usefulness of these techniques in the field of marketing.

(5) What is meant by the term "brand personality"?

(6) Define a trait, giving examples of different categories of traits.

(7) What significance is attached to trait and type analysis in an employment setting?

(8) Assess the significance of the "Big Five" factor theory.

(9) What is the relationship between personal construct theory and the repertory grid?

(10) Discuss the difference between reinforcement and socialisation in the context of a behavioural perspective on personality.

(11) Define the following terms: (a) compliant strategy; (b) internal–external locus of control; (c) self-efficacy; self-monitoring; sensation-seeking; and (c) field dependency–independency.

SPOTLIGHT ON RELEVANT READING

Hampson, S. (1999). State of the art: Personality. *The Psychologist*, June, 284–288.

Mathews, G., Deary, I.J., & Whiteman, M.C. (2003). *Personality traits* (2nd ed.). Cambridge, UK: Cambridge University Press.

Learning Outcomes

After studying this chapter you should be able to:

* Understand the meaning of intelligence.

* Recognise the different approaches to the construction of models of intelligence.

* Appreciate the significance of emotional intelligence.

* Analyse the ways in which intelligence is measured.

* Identify the influences likely to affect intelligence.

* Draw a distinction between intelligence tests and ability tests.

* Understand the significance of personality tests.

Intelligence and Psychological Testing

There is a link between intelligence and personality, which was discussed in the previous chapter. After defining intelligence, models of intelligence are examined, followed by an explanation of a contemporary development in the form of emotional intelligence. Next, under the heading of mediating influences, the parts played by genetic inheritance, environment, race, age, and culture are briefly explored. Then there is an examination of psychological testing with a focus on the measurement of intelligence using tests that measure general intellectual ability, ability tests (aptitude and achievement tests), which differ in certain respects from intelligence tests, and finally personality tests.

Contents

characteristic

INTRODUCTION

One might well ask whether there is a relationship between intelligence and personality (examined in the previous chapter). According to Phares and Chaplin (1998), intelligence in some ways epitomises the trait approach to personality. Although there is no generally accepted view of intelligence, their definition seems appropriate: intelligence is an ability to adapt to a variety of situations both old and new; an ability to learn, or the capacity for education broadly conceived; and an ability to employ abstract concepts and to use a wide range of symbols and concepts.

Given the importance of intelligence to individual performance, and acknowledging the growing tendency to subject employees to intelligence and related tests, it seems appropriate to explain the nature of intelligence, to identify factors that influence intelligence, to describe the measurement of intelligence using IQ and EQ tests, and to introduce complementary activities such as aptitude and achievement tests used in the employment setting. Also, in the spirit of psychometrics, personality tests are examined alongside other tests belonging to this stable. This chapter covers:

- models of intelligence
- mediating influences (such as heredity, age, gender)
- psychological testing (intelligence tests; aptitude and achievement tests; and personality tests).

MODELS OF INTELLIGENCE

The importance of intelligence is reflected in the controversy over its measurement. (In particular, in the USA there have been repeated attacks on the use of intelligence tests.) In this section we will examine the more traditional models consisting of "g" and "s" factors, primary abilities, the structure of the intellect, and the more recent information-processing models (including emotional intelligence).

Factorial approach

Spearman (1904) proposed that people possess a general factor—called *g*—in different quantities, and a person could be described as generally intelligent or stupid. According to Spearman, the **g factor** contributes significantly to performance on intelligence tests. He also mentioned other factors—called *s* factors—and these are specifically related to particular abilities. For example, an arithmetical test would be aimed at a specific *s* factor. Overall, the tested intelligence of the individual would reflect the *g* plus the various *s* factors. It is interesting to note that when the *g* factor was compared with the *s* factor, *g* was a better predictor of job performance than *s* (Ree, Earles, & Teachout, 1994). A diagrammatical representation of Spearman's model of intelligence appears in Figure 3.1.

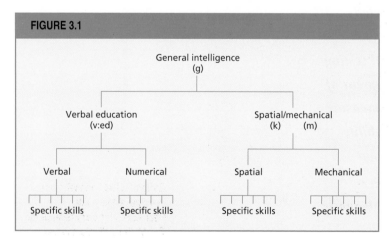

FIGURE 3.1

Spearman's hierarchical model of intelligence.

TABLE 3.1

Thurstone's primary mental abilities (Thurstone & Thurstone, 1963)

Ability	Description
Verbal comprehension	The ability to understand the meaning of words; vocabulary tests represent this factor.
Word fluency	The ability to think of words rapidly, as in solving anagrams or thinking of words that rhyme.
Number	The ability to work with numbers and perform computations.
Space	The ability to visualise space–form relationships, as in recognising the same figure presented in different orientations.
Memory	The ability to recall verbal stimuli, such as word pairs or sentences.
Perceptual speed	The ability to grasp visual details quickly and to see similarities and differences between pictured objects.
Reasoning	The ability to find a general rule on the basis of presented instances, as in determining how a number series is constructed after being presented with only a portion of that series.

Subsequently, Thurstone took exception to the emphasis placed on general intelligence (Thurstone, 1938). He felt that intelligence could be segmented into a number of primary abilities. The seven primary abilities revealed by intelligence tests are listed in Table 3.1. Both Spearman and Thurstone used a statistical technique (factor analysis) to provide a better picture of the types of abilities that determine performance on intelligence tests, and Guilford (1967) proposed a model of intelligence, called the structure of the intellect model. It categorises intelligence on three dimensions:

* operations (what the person does);
* contents (the information on which the operations are performed);
* products (the form in which information is processed).

This model of intelligence is shown in Figure 3.2. In the cube, each cell represents a separate ability —120 in all ($5 \times 4 \times 6 = 120$). A drawback of the

FIGURE 3.2

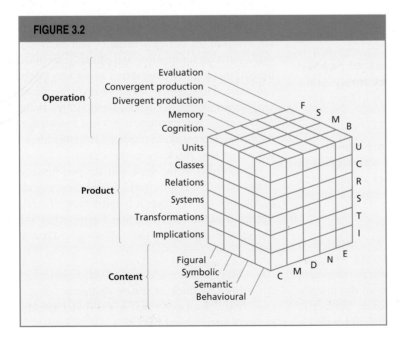

Guilford's (1967) model of the structure of the intellect. Reproduced by permission of the The McGraw-Hill Companies.

Guilford model is that it seems to be a taxonomy or classification rather than an explanation of intellectual activity (Phares & Chaplin, 1998).

Information-processing models

Until the 1960s, research on intelligence was dominated by the factorial approach used by researchers such as Thurstone and Guilford, mentioned earlier. Subsequently, a new approach emerged influenced by the development of cognitive psychology, with its emphasis on information-processing models. The basic proposition in this approach is the attempt to understand intelligence in terms of the cognitive processes that operate when individuals engage in intellectual activities, such as problem solving (Hunt, 1985). In specific terms, the information-processing approach poses a number of questions, such as:

* What mental processes come into play in the various ways intelligence is tested?
* How quickly and accurately are these mental processes operationalised?
* What types of mental representations of information do the mental processes draw on?

Here the emphasis is on attempts to identify the mental processes that underlie intelligent behaviour (Atkinson, Atkinson, Smith, & Hilgard, 1996). The information-processing approach is reflected in Sternberg's (1985) work: he proposed a **triarchic theory of intelligence** involving the individual functioning intellectually in three ways:

* *Componential*. This refers to analytical thinking—recognising, defining, and representing problems—and is associated with success in taking tests. Analytical abilities are applied to relatively familiar problems that are largely academic.
* *Experiential*. This refers to creative thinking, and characterises the person who can dissect experience into various elements and then combine them in an insightful way. Sternberg (2000) provides an illustration of the importance of the experiential approach. Student A was brilliant academically, and did well on

psychometric tests that emphasise memory and analytical skills. She commenced her studies in psychology as one of the top students, but ended the course as one of the bottom students. Why? Though A was brilliant academically, she displayed only minimal creative skills on a course that demanded such skills. (Creative abilities are used to tackle relatively novel problems.) In this case it was not that A was born creatively backward. Rather it seemed more likely that A had previously been over-reinforced or rewarded for her analytical skills to such an extent that there was no incentive to develop or discover whatever creative skills may have been latent in her.
* *Contextual*. This emphasis specifies the real-world contextual functions of intelligence, and those possessing this attribute are likely to be "streetwise", reflected in the behaviour of people who can "play the game" and manipulate the environment. One would expect this person to adapt to existing environments as well as shaping them into new and hopefully better ones. When adapting and shaping fails, they are capable of selecting different environments.

Sternberg's research shows that analytical (componential), creative (experiential), and practical (contextual) abilities are largely independent: "When students' abilities and achievements are assessed for not only memory and analytical skills but also for creative and practical abilities, the students formerly considered as not very bright can succeed in school at higher levels" (Sternberg, Grigorenko, Ferrar, & Clinken-Beard, 1999). In the final analysis what matters is not just knowledge, or the intellectual skills one applies to this knowledge, but how the knowledge is used.

Sternberg is of the view that the performance of the individual is governed by these three aspects of intelligence. He takes a broader view of intelligence than the more traditional approaches and his view encapsulates the following (Atkinson et al., 1996):

(1)   Ability to learn and profit from experience.
(2)   Ability to think or reason abstractly.
(3)   Ability to adapt to the vagaries of a changing and uncertain world.

(4) Ability to motivate oneself to complete speedily tasks one is expected to accomplish.

Another broad view of intelligence is propounded by Gardner (1999). He maintains that there is no such thing as singular intelligence. Rather there are six distinct types of intelligence independent of each other, each operating as a separate system in the brain according to its own rules. The six intelligences are:

(1) linguistic;
(2) logical–mathematical;
(3) spatial;
(4) musical;
(5) bodily–kinaesthetic; and
(6) personal.

The first three types are familiar and are normally measured by intelligence tests. The last three may appear unusual in the context of a discussion of intelligence, but Gardner feels that they should be treated similarly to the first three.

Musical intelligence, involving the ability to perceive pitch and rhythm, has been with us since the dawn of civilisation, and forms the basis for the development of musical competence. Bodily–kinaesthetic intelligence involves the control of one's body motion, and the ability to manipulate and handle objects in a skilful way. For example, the dancer exercises precise control over movement of the body, and the skilled worker or neurosurgeon is able to manipulate objects in a dextrous way.

The last of the six intelligences—personal intelligence—can be divided into two parts: interpersonal and intrapersonal intelligence. The former is the ability to register and understand the needs and intentions of other people and to develop sensitivity to their moods and temperament in order to be able to predict how they will behave in new situations. Intrapersonal intelligence, by contrast, is the ability to develop awareness of one's own feelings and emotions, to discriminate between them, and to use this information as a guide to personal actions. This is the foundation stone for emotional intelligence, discussed later.

It is recognised that some people will develop certain intelligences to a greater extent than others, but all normal people should develop each intelligence to some extent. The intelligences interact with each other, as well as building on one another, but they still operate as semi-autonomous systems. In Western society the first three types of intelligence (linguistic; logical–mathematical; spatial) are given prominence, and of course they are open to measurement by standard intelligence tests. But evidence indicates that the other intelligences (musical; bodily–kinaesthetic; personal) were highly valued at earlier periods of human history, and are valued currently in some non-Western societies (Atkinson et al., 1996). Even in Western cultures, children endowed with unusual nontraditional intelligences, such as bodily–kinaesthetic intelligence, can be groomed to become, for example, a first-rate footballer or a ballet dancer.

Emotional intelligence

Few constructs have captivated the attention of theorists, researchers, and practitioners with such intensity and suddenness as emotional intelligence (Petrides, Furnham, and Frederickson, 2004). The concept of emotional intelligence (EQ, or alternatively EI) was developed by Singer and Salovey (1994) and popularised by Goleman (1998). EI derives its inspiration from the work of Gardner (1999) on multiple intelligence, which was discussed earlier, and has been eagerly embraced by some practitioners in business in recent times. Emotional intelligence is concerned with an individual's emotional and social skills and consists of the following four dimensions:

(1) *Emotional attunement or self-awareness, and people skills*. The person is good at reading his or her own feelings, and has the capacity to empathise with others and take into account other people's feelings.
(2) *Emotional management*. This is reflected in ensuring that the person's emotions (e.g., anger, sadness) do not overwhelm him or her, and that they are appropriate to the situation. It can be seen as an ability to cheer oneself up, or stop a temper tantrum in mid-course by, for example, going out for a walk.

(3) *Self-motivation*. This is connected with the extent to which individuals are good at delaying gratification. A conclusion from the research is that those capable of delaying gratification—i.e., waiting a while to take a reward rather than taking it immediately—were more socially competent and self-reliant than individuals who settled for immediate rewards. Those intent on obtaining immediate rewards had trouble subsequently postponing gratification, tended to be more argumentative, had low self-esteem, and coped badly with stress.

(4) *Self-management skills*. This refers to handling situations without being subsumed or overwhelmed by them.

It is said that those with high EI make personal connections with much ease and are good at defusing explosive situations. Goleman (1998) sees potential in applying EI to organisational settings. He maintains that occupational competencies based on EI play a greater part in first-rate performance than do intellect or technical skill. He suggests that emotional intelligence is crucial in the determination of the effectiveness of leaders; he argues that in challenging jobs associated with people with a high IQ, the possession of an extra dimension in the form of high EI gives leaders a competitive edge. In the final analysis it seems sensible to acknowledge that superior performance is dependent upon both our emotional and our thinking sides.

Dearlove (1999) reports that companies are re-evaluating the leadership qualities they need and are increasingly placing emphasis on the emotional dimension. He quotes the views of the executive development manager at British Telecommunications, who stresses "the importance of understanding relationships. The company is seeking to develop interpersonal sensitivity and a mindset that is about collaboration and understanding what others have to contribute and seeing partnerships as an opportunity to learn." There is a reappraisal of the type of leadership qualities the company requires to meet its ambitions for global expansion through joint ventures and partnerships: "As boundaries get fuzzier and fuzzier, leadership becomes more and more vital. The emphasis is now on relationship management. The critical issue is interpersonal sensitivity. We are moving to a more holistic approach." The issue of leadership qualities and skills is also considered in Chapter 12.

From research into derailed leaders—the rising stars who faded away (see Chapter 12)—at the Center for Creative Leadership in the USA, it was concluded that these executives failed most often because of an interpersonal flaw (e.g., poor working relations, authoritarian) rather than a lack of technical ability (Gibbs, 1995). The Center mounts seminars across the USA for managers who want to "get close" to their emotions, and these sessions are unlike the sensitivity training programmes of old (see Chapter 15).

Woodruffe (2000a) does not seem to be overly impressed by EI as described above. He feels it is another name for competencies, and that the measures of emotional intelligence are not the best method available. This could be better achieved through assessment centre exercises (see Chapter 17) or by multi-rater feedback. According to Petrides et al. (2004), the criticism levelled against the trait EI is that it is indistinguishable from the major personality dimensions.

MEDIATING INFLUENCES: HEREDITY, AGE, GENDER

We realise that people differ in intellectual ability, and many would agree that some aspects of intelligence are inherited. However, opinions differ as to the relative contributions made by our genetic inheritance (heredity) and environment (i.e., what happens to the individual during the course of development).

The environmental conditions likely to determine how an individual's intellectual potential will develop include nutrition, health, quality of stimulation, emotional climate of the home, and appropriate rewards for accomplishments (Bayley, 1970). Inevitably, one feels forced to take a pragmatic position on this issue. For example, heredity and environment interact. Heredity sets the

PANEL 3.1: Nature versus nurture

In 1980 researchers in Dunedin, New Zealand gave 1000 3-year olds a series of psychological tests. Caspi et al. (2003) and his colleagues reassessed these individuals, now aged 26. By and large the children who behaved badly in the original tests were still experiencing problems as adults. For instance, the most irritable and emotionally unstable 3-year olds—classified as under-controlled—tended to be the least adjusted by the age of 26. They were tense, easily upset, antagonistic, and prone to antisocial behaviour. By contrast, the 3-year olds rated as "confident" or "well-adjusted" appeared to be doing well as young adults. This dramatic discovery demonstrated how little the main personality traits had changed. From this one might conclude that crude genetic determinism (nature) may be highly influential.

However, the emerging wisdom is that many bits of genetic material interact in complex ways with a diversified environment to influence intelligence and behaviour. Ridley (2003) maintains that nature and nurture always interact with each other, and that we need to think of our nature as emerging via nurture, rather than predetermined by a genetic blueprint. He cites evidence in support of genes as a dominant force—for example, identical twins separated at birth and brought up in different environments tend to show similar character traits—but equally children's sensitivity to their environment (e.g., upbringing, school, extra-curricular pursuits) appears to vary depending on the precise genetic make-up.

(Prowse, 2003)

scene in terms of specifying the possible limits of achievements for any person in a given situation, but the environment determines how near to these limits of achievement any individual will move in any given situation (Plowin, 2001).

The debate over genetic factors in intelligence raises the possibility of inherited racial differences in intelligence—in particular the question of whether black people are innately less intelligent than white people. Black Americans as a group score 10–15 points lower on standard intelligence tests than white Americans as a group. The controversy focuses not on the difference in IQ but on the interpretation of the difference. Some argue that the two groups differ in inherited ability (Jensen, 1977), whereas others maintain the black–white differences in average IQ can be put down to environmental differences between the two groups (Kamin, 1976). But in an article in *The Psychologist*, Furnham (2000) makes reference to an initiative taken by 50 experts with respect to the influence of the genetic factor. He says that these experts "wrote to the *Wall Street Journal* reacting to a controversial book on intelligence, firmly stating that there are indeed racial differences in the scores. They maintained that intelligence is of great practical and social importance, and that genetics plays a bigger role than does environment in creating IQ differences among individuals." There is further comment on the nature versus nurture debate in Panel 3.1.

If intelligence was simply an innate quality, then IQ would not be expected to alter throughout the life of the person, apart from minor changes due to the measuring instrument used. However, there is strong evidence from a number of sources to suggest that IQ scores fluctuate over time (Anastasi, 1997; Howe, 1998). Also, a person's performance on a test could be influenced by temporary states; for example, the person is affected by illness, is demotivated for some reason, or is going through an emotional upheaval. In addition, intelligence tests tend to measure different things at different ages. For example, test items that require young children to stack blocks and identify parts of the body are quite different from items that are highly verbal, abstract, and mathematical, found in tests for older children and adults.

Botwinick (1984) examines the impact of age on test performance. A decline in performance over time can be attributable to a number of factors. There may be a general deterioration of health, or growing deficiencies of hearing and eyesight. Also, as people grow older they may become more cautious and fearful of making mistakes, and this may undermine their test performance. It is said that giving extra time to older people to do the test, or allowing them more time to familiarise themselves with the test procedures, will often lead to higher scores (Phares & Chaplin, 1998). In the final analysis, it would be wise to distinguish between those with a defective mental capacity because of an age-related infirmity and those who are not disadvantaged in that way.

Furnham (2000) raises the question of gender, stating:

> despite most tests having been devised so as not to show "sex differences", and the received wisdom for many decades being that differences are small, trivial, and not worthy of explanation or research, nevertheless studies relying on self-perception by lay subjects show consistent differences. Males think they are more intelligent than females, and that their male relatives are more intelligent than their female relatives. However, this believed superiority lies primarily in "spatial" and mathematical areas— only a part of fundamental intelligence. For some researchers this remains a shocking finding explained only by sociological processes; for others it represents a reasonable grasp of reality.

Finally, attempts have been made to devise culture-fair tests. These tests attempt to neutralise the effects of forces that distinguish one culture or subculture from another. In essence what is attempted is the removal of factors that reflect cultural background rather than innate ability. These could include language handicap (i.e., lack of total familiarity with the language of the test) or speed of reaction. In the latter case, not all cultures or subcultures subscribe to the view that faster means better. Although sound in theory, culture-fair testing has not worked very well (Phares & Chaplin, 1998). Tests are being reviewed closely, particularly in the USA, if it is felt that they are inappropriately used and act to the disadvantage of a particular racial or ethnic group.

PSYCHOLOGICAL TESTING

Psychological testing is often referred to as **psychometric testing**. The term psychometrics is now used to refer to a broad range of different types of assessments and measurements of intelligence, achievement/aptitude, and personality.

Intelligence tests

Tests are available to measure general intellectual ability. These tests are called "intelligence tests". The first tests resembling contemporary intelligence tests were devised by Binet in France, who had been asked by the French government to create a test that would detect children who were too slow intellectually to benefit from a regular school curriculum. Binet felt that intelligence should be measured by tasks that required reasoning and problem-solving abilities, rather than perceptual–motor skills. The test required the child to execute simple commands, to name familiar objects, to think of rhymes, to explain words, etc. It was both a verbal and a performance test.

Binet joined forces with Simon and published a scale, later revised, in 1905. Binet maintained that a slow or dull child was merely a normal child who was backward in mental growth. Therefore, the slow child would produce a result on the test normally associated with a child younger than him or her. A bright child would perform at a level associated with a child older than him or her. It followed that the bright child's mental age (MA) was higher than his or her real or chronological age (CA); a slow child's MA is below his or her CA.

The selection of items to be included in the test is of crucial importance. Normally one would expect to find both novel and familiar items. The choice of novel items is meant to ensure that the uneducated child is not at a disadvantage. In Figure 3.3, an example of a novel item is given where the child is asked to choose figures that are alike, on the assumption that the designs are unfamiliar to all children.

When familiar items are chosen for the test, there is the assumption that all those for whom the test is designed have had the requisite previous knowledge to cope with the items. The following request and statement provides an example of an allegedly familiar item (Atkinson, Atkinson, Smith, & Hilgard, 1987).

FIGURE 3.3

Novel items used in intelligence tests. The following instructions accompany the test: Mark every card to the right that matches the sample card on the left. You can rotate the sample card but not flip it over. (Cards 2, 3, and 6 are correct in the first line; 1, 3, and 5 are correct in the second line.) (From Thurstone & Thurstone, 1942)

Circle F if the sentence is foolish; circle S if it is sensible.

S   F

Mrs Smith has had no children and I understand the same was true of her mother.

It should be noted that recognition of the fallacy of this statement is valid as a test of intellectual ability for the child who can read and understand all the words in the sentence. The possession of general knowledge and familiarity with the language of the test are necessary to cope with many of the items on intelligence tests. It may be difficult to meet this requirement because of the variability in the educational background and experience of the child. Where the child is tested on novel items, a difficulty may also arise because the discrimination required in a perceptual sense to solve the problem may be found more readily in one culture rather than in another. Nevertheless, the items found in contemporary intelligence tests have endured the rigour of application in the practical world, but it should be noted that the validity of intelligence tests in predicting school performance is applicable only to a particular culture.

Stanford-Binet Intelligence Scale

This was developed in the United States out of the earlier work of Binet, is well known and widely used, and has been revised on a number of occasions. The index of intelligence used is the intelligence quotient (IQ), and this is expressed as a ratio of mental age (MA) to chronological age (CA) as follows:

$$IQ = \frac{MA}{CA} \times 100$$

Using 100 as a multiplier means that when MA = CA, then the IQ will have a value of 100. If MA is less than CA, the IQ will be less than 100; if MA is greater than CA, the IQ will be more than 100.

An IQ between 90 and 110 is considered to be normal, but above 130 it is considered to be very superior. The person with an IQ below 70 is judged to be retarded. As with many differences between individuals, the distribution of IQs in the population approximates the bell-shaped normal distribution curve. Most cases would fall into the mid-value of the curve, with just a few cases at the left and right extreme positions on the curve.

The Stanford-Binet Intelligence Scale was designed to ensure that all items contributed equally to the total IQ score. This means that an individual might perform well on a test inviting the production of geometric forms, but badly on a test of vocabulary. Although the tester might note the strengths and weaknesses, they would cancel each other out in arriving at the IQ score. Under the 1986 revised scale, standard age scores are substituted for IQ scores, and it is now possible to obtain scores for different areas of the test. In accordance with the current view of intelligence as an accumulation of different abilities, a separate score can now be obtained for each of the broad areas of intellectual ability set out in Table 3.2 (Thorndike, Hagen, & Satlet, 1986).

Wechsler intelligence scales

One of the first intelligence tests to test separate abilities, which has been widely used, was

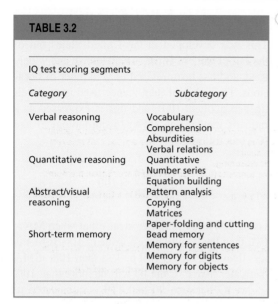

TABLE 3.2

IQ test scoring segments	
Category	*Subcategory*
Verbal reasoning	Vocabulary
	Comprehension
	Absurdities
	Verbal relations
Quantitative reasoning	Quantitative
	Number series
	Equation building
Abstract/visual	Pattern analysis
reasoning	Copying
	Matrices
	Paper-folding and cutting
Short-term memory	Bead memory
	Memory for sentences
	Memory for digits
	Memory for objects

developed by Wechsler in 1939 (cited in Wechsler, 1981). These scales were developed because it was felt that the Stanford-Binet test relied heavily on language ability and did not cater for the needs of adults (Wechsler, 1981).

The Wechsler Adult Intelligence Scale (WAIS) has two sections: (1) a verbal scale; and (2) a performance scale. Each section generates separate scores, as well as an overall IQ score. A similar test with some modifications was also developed for children. The items in the WAIS are shown in Table 3.3. In the performance scale section in Table 3.3 the items specify the manipulation or arrangement of blocks, pictures, or other materials. The stimuli and the responses are nonverbal in this section. The Wechsler scales allow for scores to be recorded for each of the subtests; therefore, the tester has a better view of the intellectual strengths and weaknesses of the individual.

It is claimed that both the Stanford-Binet and Wechsler scales satisfy the conditions for a good test—i.e., they show good reliability and validity. Also, both tests are fairly valid predictors of achievement, particularly at school (Atkinson et al., 1996).

Emotional intelligence questionnaire

A recent trend is to devise measuring instruments for emotional intelligence. For example, ASE—a division of NFER-Nelson—in Windsor, UK, produce an emotional intelligence questionnaire developed by Professor Victor Dulewicz and Dr Malcolm Higgs. In this questionnaire there are 69 items or statements, of which the items listed here are extracts (reproduced by permission of NFER-Nelson). The respondent would indicate the extent of his or her agreement with the statements.

- It is possible to control my own moods.
- In dealing with problems and decisions I take account of the needs of others.
- I find it difficult to maintain performance when faced with disappointment.
- I am effective in building team commitment to goals and objectives.

Another company, Hay McBer, which is part of Hay Management Consultants, has produced a similar instrument—a multi-rater 360-degree feedback instrument, called the Emotional Competence Inventory (ECI). Interested readers are referred to a brief article by Watkin (1999), who highlights what the ECI measures, explains how it was developed, and states how it can be applied to organisations.

Finally, when reflecting on the tests discussed here and the achievement and aptitude tests considered next in this chapter, one should bear in mind the general issues raised later about testing.

Achievement and aptitude tests

These are essentially tests of ability, but differ in certain respects from the intelligence tests discussed earlier. Vernon (1956) drew a distinction between intelligence and achievement as follows:

Intelligence refers to the more general qualities of thinking—comprehension, level of concept development, reasoning, and grasping relations—qualities which appear largely to be acquired in the course of normal

TABLE 3.3

Scale item	Description
Verbal scale	
Information	Questions tap a general range of information; e.g., "How many nickels make a dime?"
Comprehension	Tests practical information and ability to evaluate past experience; e.g., "What is the advantage of keeping money in a bank?"
Arithmetic	Verbal problems testing arithmetic reasoning.
Similarities	Asks in what way certain objects or concepts (e.g., *egg* and *seed*) are similar; measures abstract thinking.
Digit span	A series of digits presented auditorily (e.g., 7-5-6-3-8) is repeated in a forward or backward direction.
Vocabulary	Tests word knowledge.
Performance scale	
Digit symbol	A timed coding task in which numbers must be associated with marks of various shapes; tests speed of learning and writing.
Picture completion	The missing part of an incompletely drawn picture must be discovered and named; tests visual alertness and memory.
Block design	Pictured designs must be copied with blocks; tests ability to perceive and analyse patterns.
Picture arrangement	A series of comic-strip pictures must be arranged in the right sequence to tell a story; tests understanding of social situations.
Object assembly	Puzzle pieces must be assembled to form a complete object; tests ability to deal with part–whole relationships.

development without specific tuition. By contrast, achievement refers more to knowledge and skills which are directly trained.

The use of ability tests to stream children in schools, to admit pupils and students to schools and colleges, and to select people for jobs can arouse passions and much debate. When they were first developed they were approved of as an objective and impartial method of identifying talent in the face of subjective elements in the form of various types of favouritism (e.g., based on class, wealth, politics, and so on). However, they have their critics who label them as narrow and restrictive. In essence this means that they do not measure those characteristics that are the most important in determining how well a person will perform in an educational setting or at work (for example, motivation, social skills, qualities of leadership) and they discriminate against minorities (Atkinson et al., 1996). It should be noted that the factors that make personality tests useful (discussed below) are equally applicable to ability tests.

A distinction is made between achievement and aptitude tests (Atkinson et al., 1996). An achievement test is designed to measure developed skills and tells us what the person can do currently. An aptitude test is designed to forecast what a person can attain with training. However, the distinction between the two types of test is not neat, because the intention is to assess the current standing of those tested, whether the purpose of the test is to assess what has been learned to date, or to predict future performance.

Both types of test include similar kinds of questions. The real differentiating factor seems to be the purpose of the test. For example, on completion of a course in mechanics a test of knowledge of mechanical principles is given to the participants. This amounts to a test of achievement. But similar questions might be incorporated into a battery of tests for those applying for pilot training, because knowledge of mechanical principles has been found to be a good predictor of success in flying. In this case, the test would be considered a test of aptitude.

Although the significant factor differentiating achievement and aptitude tests has been identified here as the purpose rather than the content of the test, nevertheless, the existence of relevant prior knowledge and experience is an important factor to note. An aptitude test assumes little in terms of relevant prior knowledge and experience, whereas an achievement test assumes the person tested has accumulated specific subject matter, the mastery of which is measured by the test.

In practice, the possession of relevant prior knowledge or experience, though not required by the aptitude test, could nevertheless influence the test results. This arises because tests using verbal, numerical, or symbolic material are not totally unfamiliar, and obviously previous education and experience inevitably exert an influence.

Aptitude tests at work

Examples of the types of aptitude test found in the occupational field are examined in this section (Toplis, Dulewicz, & Fletcher, 1987). These tests could be used in the personnel selection process, to be discussed later in Chapter 17.

Verbal ability.   There are a number of tests that measure lower levels of word meaning and comprehension. Some of these tests necessitate an element of reasoning with words. Also, there are verbal tests involving more complex mental operations of reasoning and critical evaluation and these are available for assessing candidates of high ability, such as graduates and managers.

Numerical ability.   There are lower level numerical tests requiring an understanding of, and skill at, arithmetical calculations. In these tests, candidates' existing accomplishments, as well as their aptitude, are being assessed. There are also numerical tests for candidates of high ability, such as graduates and potential managers, which are concerned with higher order numerical reasoning and with critical evaluation of quantitative information.

Spatial ability.   There are tests for lower ability and higher ability candidates requiring mental

proficiency in identifying, visualising, comparing, or manipulating two- or three-dimensional shapes.

Diagrammatical ability.   These tests focus on abstract symbols and diagrams ranging from superficial perceptual tasks to complex abstract logical processes. They do not include verbal or numerical items.

Manual dexterity.   Eye–hand coordination features in tests that fall into this category, and the emphasis is on perception and manipulation involving the fingers and hands. Some tasks require speed with little precision, whereas other tasks place the primary emphasis on precision where speed is considered to be of lesser importance. The abilities involved in manual dexterity tests are relevant to most manual jobs, and are not closely related to the other ability and intelligence tests discussed in this chapter.

Mechanical ability.   These tests are distinct from the manual dexterity tests described in the previous subsection. There is an element of intelligence and reasoning ingrained in them, and they are designed to measure the capacity to succeed and learn in jobs that require mechanical ability.

Scholastic Aptitude Test.   There are certain tests— e.g., the Scholastic Aptitude Test (SAT) in the USA—that measure both aptitude and achievement. SAT is used to test applicants for admission to colleges and it consists of a verbal section that measures vocabulary skills and the ability to understand what is read, and a mathematical section that tests the ability to solve problems requiring arithmetical reasoning, algebra, and geometry. The emphasis is on the ability to apply skills acquired to date in order to solve problems. Questions based on knowledge of particular topics are not included.

Personality tests

Most of the personality tests used are pencil-and-paper tests with multiple-choice elements. In practice, they are not tests in the sense that correct and incorrect answers are possible to the various questions. They are really *questionnaires* in which the job applicant or employee seeking advancement in the organisation is requested to state how he or she feels about certain issues, or how he or she would react in certain specified situations.

Personality questionnaires

The first personality questionnaire used as a placement or selection tool operated as a screening device on soldiers in the First World War. It was used to identify soldiers who it was felt were unable to face the challenge of combat, and it enabled the speedy testing of thousands of candidates. Handling so many people using interviews would be impracticable. The personality questionnaire was called the "Personal Data Sheet".

A personality questionnaire can have "Yes" or "No" answers, although some questionnaires have an intermediate category such as "Don't know" or "Cannot say". A typical item in a personality questionnaire might read, "I feel comfortable with other people":

* Yes
* Don't know
* No

A number of researchers have used the 16 PF questionnaire with managers. The 16 PF instrument comprises 187 questions presented in a forced-choice format. For each question, three possible answers are provided—"Agree", "Uncertain", and "Disagree". The instructions discourage the excessive use of the "Uncertain" response. In this type of process there is always a danger that respondents may distort their true position on various issues by unwittingly giving an inaccurate or a socially acceptable response. However, this danger may be minimised in a supportive climate where questionnaires are completed anonymously.

The Eysenck Personality Inventory (EPI).
This is a device used to measure the dimensions of personality, and lie scale items are included to screen out respondents making socially desirable responses. In evaluating the model of personality

postulated by Eysenck, two clinical psychologists (Peck & Whitlow, 1975) made the following observations: "(a) at present there seems to be little justification for Eysenck's suggestions that psychiatrists, educationalists, or parole boards should base their recommendations for treatment, teaching or probation on measures of extraversion, neuroticism, or psychoticism; and (b) the questionnaires that Eysenck has developed may continue to be useful tools for personality investigators but their practical value in relation to groups or individuals remains to be demonstrated. Despite these reservations, the main body of Eysenck's theory seems certain to prove a fruitful source of ideas for investigation in the field of personality for many years to come."

The EPI has been used as a personality measure in a number of occupational settings. For example, Eysenck (1967) conducted a study of business groups and found that successful business people were stable introverts, but there was some variation across functions. Those working in finance, research and development, and internal consultancy were the most introverted, and those whose activities cut across more than one function were less introverted. In another study, this time in pilot training, Bartram (1995) concluded that applicants for pilot training are much more emotionally stable and more extraverted than the general population.

Kline (1987) analysed a large amount of data from EPI personality questionnaires and endorsed Eysenck's three dimensions—extraversion, neuroticism, and psychoticism. He also identified an additional two dimensions, described as sensation-seeking and obsessionality. A person scoring high on sensation-seeking tends to get involved in activities likely to satisfy his or her need for sensation, such as rally driving or mountain climbing. The person endowed with a significant level of obsessionality displays obsessive behaviour exemplified by an almost unnatural adherence to rules and regulations, often accompanied by a strong preoccupation with tidiness, and sometimes stinginess. Another manifestation of obsessionality is authoritarianism, and should a manager possess this trait there is a likelihood that he or she could adopt an autocratic style of management.

TABLE 3.4

Personality traits on the Thurstone Temperament Schedule

Trait dimension	Characteristics
Active	The person is likely to be in a rush, probably speaking, walking, driving, working, and eating at a fast rate when it is not necessary to do so.
Vigorous	The person usually enjoys physical activity requiring a lot of energy, is active in sport and outdoor occupations, and engages in work requiring the use of hands or tools.
Impulsive	The person is usually happy-go-lucky, likes to take chances, and makes quick decisions.
Dominant	The person has the capacity for taking the initiative and assuming responsibility, and probably takes satisfaction from organising social activities, persuading others, and promoting new ventures.
Stable	The person is likely to remain calm in a crisis, is able to disregard distractions while studying or working, and is not irritated if interrupted when concentrating.
Sociable	The person enjoys the company of others, makes friends easily, and is sympathetic, cooperative, and agreeable in relations with others.
Reflective	The person indulges in meditative thinking, enjoys dealing with theoretical rather than practical problems, and prefers to work alone with material requiring accuracy and fine detail.

Other questionnaire tests. Examples of other tests used to measure personality are the Thurstone Temperament Schedule developed in the USA, and the Saville & Holdsworth Ltd (1984) Occupational Personality Questionnaire (OPQ) developed in the UK. The Thurstone Temperament Schedule attempts to measure personality on seven dimensions. A high score on a particular dimension would reflect the characteristics set out in Table 3.4.

The OPQ was developed from a model of personality which was created initially from a review of existing questionnaires, theories of personality, work-related information, feedback from companies, and repertory grid data generated by employees in companies. It consists of some 11 questionnaires for use in selection, development, counselling, and teambuilding. The OPQ is based on 30 traits listed in Table 3.5.

Jackson and Rothstein (1993) said of the OPQ: "It has not yet been the subject of the peer review process nor the focus of independent research that is necessary for all scientific achievements." Barrett, Kline, Paltiel, and Eysenck (1996) analysed the concept 5.2 questionnaire—one of a series of questionnaires subsumed under the label of OPQ. They concluded from their analysis and the research of others that the OPQ concept 5.2 is overlong and contains a proportion of redundant and quantifiably complex items.

There is little evidence to support the existence of 30 discrete measurement scales, and though it has strengths it could benefit elsewhere from further development. Robertson and Kinder (1993) carried out a major meta-analysis looking at the criterion-related validity of OPQ personality measures and reported supportive findings. The results show that OPQ fares well in relation to other predictors of performance, such as assessment centres, cognitive ability tests, and work samples. These predictors are examined in Chapter 17.

In addition to personality questionnaires, there are other ways of making assessments of personality. In daily life we are constantly making subjective assessments of the personality of others. In a formal sense we use the interview as a method to assess personality. Other ways of assessing personality are described elsewhere in this book; for example, projective tests and the repertory grid were discussed in Chapter 2. And of course there is also graphology (see Panel 3.2).

The remainder of this chapter is devoted to examining psychometric tests from a number of angles:

- standing of psychometric testing;
- advantages of tests;
- disadvantages of tests;
- features of tests; and
- ethical issues.

TABLE 3.5

Traits in Saville and Holdsworth's Ltd's (1984) Occupational Personality Questionnaire

Trait	Characteristics
Relationships with people	
Persuasive	Enjoys selling, changes opinions of others, convincing with arguments, negotiates.
Controlling	Takes charge, directs, manages, organises, supervises others.
Independent	Has strong views on things, difficult to manage, speaks up, argues, dislikes ties.
Outgoing	Fun-loving, humorous, sociable, vibrant, talkative, jovial.
Affiliative	Has many friends, enjoys being in groups, likes companionship, shares things with friends.
Socially confident	Puts people at ease, knows what to say, good with words.
Modest	Reserved about achievements, avoids talking about self, accepts others, avoids trappings of status.
Democratic	Encourages others to contribute, consults, listens, and refers to others.
Caring	Considerate to others, helps those in need, sympathetic, tolerant.
Thinking style	
Practical	Down-to-earth, likes repairing and mending things, better with the concrete.
Data rational	Good with data, operates on facts, enjoys assessing and measuring.
Artistic	Appreciates culture, shows artistic flair, sensitive to visual arts and music.
Behavioural	Analyses thoughts and behaviour, psychologically minded, likes to understand people.
Traditional	Preserves well-proven methods, prefers the orthodox, disciplined, conventional.
Change-oriented	Enjoys doing new things, seeks variety, prefers novelty to routine, accepts changes.
Conceptual	Theoretical, intellectually curious, enjoys the complex and abstract.
Innovative	Generates ideas, shows ingenuity, thinks up solutions.
Forward planning	Prepares well in advance, enjoys target setting, forecasts trends, plans projects.
Detail conscious	Methodical, keeps things neat and tidy, precise, accurate.
Conscientious	Sticks to deadlines, completes jobs, perseveres with routine, likes fixed schedules.
Feelings and emotions	
Relaxed	Calm, relaxed, cool under pressure, free from anxiety, can switch off.
Worrying	Worries when things go wrong, keyed up before important events, anxious to do well.
Tough-minded	Difficult to hurt or upset, can brush off insults, unaffected by unfair remarks.
Emotional control	Restrained in showing emotions, keeps feelings back, avoids outbursts.
Optimistic	Cheerful, happy, keeps spirits up despite setbacks.
Critical	Good at probing the facts, sees the disadvantages, challenges assumptions.
Active	Has energy, moves quickly, enjoys physical exercise, doesn't sit still.
Competitive	Plays to win, determined to beat others, poor loser.
Achieving	Ambitious, sets sights high, career-centred, results-oriented.
Decisive	Quick at conclusions, weighs things up rapidly, may be hasty, takes risks.

PANEL 3.2: Graphology

Parallel to the scientific assessment of personality is the growth in nonscientific methods such as astrology and graphology (handwriting analysis). In the words of two exponents of handwriting analysis, "hand-writing holds the key to one of life's most fascinating and tantalising mysteries—the true personality of another human being" (Greene & Lewis, 1988). Adopting an allegedly "scientific" approach to graphology, called graphonomy, a profile (shown in Figure 3.4) was produced from an inspection of a person's handwriting. The person profiled was a 27-year-old man occupying a managerial position in the buying department of a London department store. Married with one young daughter, he was promoted from the position of sales clerk having spent 10 years with the same firm, wielding considerable authority in his job and carrying significant responsibilities. He was said to be an attractive, outward-going person with many friends.

The results of a study of personnel selection techniques used for managers in the mid-1980s showed that 2.6% of the top 1000 UK companies always used graphology in the assessment of managers (Robertson & Makin, 1986). However, drawing inferences about the personal qualities of the person from an analysis of his or her handwriting is challenged as a reliable form of assessment (Klimoski & Rafael, 1983). (There is further discussion of graphology in the context of selection methods in Chapter 17.)

FIGURE 3.4

| Trait | Score and strength | | | | |
	None	Mild	Moderate	Sub-stantial	Extreme
	0–2	2–3	4–5	6–8	9–10
Independence	0	0	0	0	0
Assertiveness	0	0	0	0	0
Submissiveness	0	0	0	0	0
Perfectionism	0	0	0	0	0
Ambition	0	0	0	0	0
Aggression	0	0	0	0	0
Extraversion	0	0	0	0	0
Worldliness	0	0	0	0	0

A personality profile created by a graphologist (from Greene & Lewis, 1988). Copyright © Souvenir Press Ltd. Reproduced by permission.

Standing of psychometric testing

Over three decades ago Ghiselli (1973) concluded that personality tests have some modest value when used to assist with the personnel selection process. In contrast, a UK study by Blinkhorn and Johnson (1990) casts doubts on the use of personality tests for recruitment and promotion purposes. The researchers looked at the three most widely used and respected tests (including the 16 PF and the OPQ) and concluded that there is little evidence of enduring relationships between personality test scores and measures of successful performance at work.

Jackson and Rothstein (1993), in an analysis of the use of personality tests for personnel selection, take issue with Blinkhorn and Johnson on their conclusions. They maintain that "the criticisms do not accurately or fairly characterise *all* personality measurement in personnel selection research". Despite their reservations, however, Blinkhorn and Johnson do acknowledge that personality testing may be invaluable for counselling purposes, or in other situations where self-perception is as important as the truth.

Later Blinkhorn (1997) expressed profound reservations about the usefulness of psychometric tests when he stated that "test theory has contributed little to our understanding of ability, aptitude and temperament or improved reliable measurement of personal characteristics over the past fifty years". A similar view was expressed by Barrett (1998)—that all the measurement made within occupational psychology is of ambiguous status, and that occupational selection and psychometric testing are unlikely to progress much further in terms of greater understanding and prediction unless they adopt an approach to investigative psychology that is in accord with the principles and axioms of scientific measurement. Duncan (1999), a practitioner, challenges Barrett's view about the ambiguous scientific status of measurement in psychometric testing, and puts forward views defending the scientific basis of psychometrics.

There has also been criticism from a prominent US academic who has conducted research into intelligence, referred to earlier. Sternberg, writing in the *American Psychologist*, states that tests have not kept abreast of developments in psychology; in fact, they are rooted in knowledge that has been around for a long time. Conventional ability tests measure only a narrow range, and results differ with race and sex, which could leave employers open to ethical and legal problems. Sternberg (quoted in Rogers, 1998) refers to the psychometric industry as "an oligopoly of a small number of companies, that have their respective turfs set out for them, and should be subjected to more economic competition and

---

PANEL 3.3: Alternatives to conventional tests

Robert McHenry, Chairman of Oxford Psychologists Press (OPP), a test publisher, and Steve Blinkhorn, Director of Psychometric Research and Development, have serious reservations about conventional tests that show a measure of people's ability to acquire knowledge but do not measure people's ability to apply knowledge. They have joined forces to develop a new concept of testing, which they hope will be superior to conventional tests when it comes to predicting the performance of those tested and reducing the disadvantages alleged to be suffered by ethnic minorities who have taken tests. The new range of tests—called Aptitude for Business Learning Exercises (ABLE)—rests on the notion of teaching people a fictitious concept and subsequently testing them on their ability to apply that concept. An example of providing people with most of the information to do a test and then testing them, rather than testing them on what they already know, would be where candidates are introduced to a fictitious computer operating system and then tested on how well they applied the operating system's rules to solve problems.

Another test in the ABLE series is aimed at establishing whether a person has an aptitude for financial applications; the test is said to be fairer to women who tend to do worse than men in traditional numeracy tests. Here candidates are introduced to spurious financial ratios and shown how to use these ratios to assess the viability of particular projects. The spotlight is on how people learn, how they adapt what they have learned, and how they apply it. These tests are alleged to be fairer than many other psychometric tests, and less disadvantageous to ethnic minorities. Other tests that exist or are being planned deal with a person's motivation to do particular tasks and to assess the ability to think strategically and analyse business decisions (Rogers, 1998). In looking to the future of psychometrics and other approaches to assessment, Maddocks (1998) has recommended the ABLE series of psychometric exercises.

---

more pressure to change. Clients should insist on tests that better reflect what we know today, not 100 years ago." There are signs of activity designed to put forward alternatives to conventional tests (see Panel 3.3).

Advantages of tests

Proponents of personality tests are keen to emphasise their usefulness. It is claimed that, when compared with other selection devices such as interviews and references, personality tests have a number of attractive features:

- Tests provide quantitative data on temperament and ability that make it possible to compare individuals on the same criteria. By contrast, it is possible to find different questions being asked of different interviewees at an interview, and often the language used in references is not the most illuminating in conveying the nature of personal characteristics. Furnham (2005a) would endorse this viewpoint and add the following advantages of personality and ability tests.
- Tests are scientific instruments based on theoretical foundations, and they are reliable, valid, and allow us to distinguish between subjects in terms of good, bad, and indifferent.

- Tests are comprehensive, embracing the basic features of personality and ability that form the foundation of varied behavioural patterns.
- Tests are fair because they prevent corruption, favouritism, and bias being perpetuated because of a candidate's membership of an influential network or club.
- Data generated by tests can be filed and re-examined at a future date to establish how effective this information was in predicting success in the job.

Disadvantages of tests

Having recognised a number of the strengths of personality tests, we are now going to look at some of the weaknesses. The answers provided by respondents to questions on the personality questionnaire could be distorted for a number of reasons, such as the following:

- Subjects may not have sufficient self-awareness to give a response that reflects their true feelings.
- Subjects may not be feeling well and may perform in an unexpected way.
- The questions may be misread for a multitude of reasons (e.g., lack of an adequate educational background).

- Subjects deliberately sabotage the process by giving random, meaningless responses.
- Subjects may deliberately set out to create a false impression. Unlike tests of intelligence and aptitude (discussed above), which are almost impossible to fake—i.e., the candidate comes up with either the right or the wrong answer—tests of personality are open to faking. If a person applying for a job takes a personality test, the motivation to secure the job may lead that person to generate responses that he or she thinks will make them an attractive candidate in the eyes of the employing organisation. There was some evidence in one study to suggest that applicants for the position of salesman faked some of the responses on a personality test (the Cattell 16 PF) because of the high scores they received on two particular dimensions—extraversion and low anxiety. These dimensions are considered to be desirable qualities in a salesman (Poppleton, 1975).

It seems that where a personality test is taken for the purposes of vocational guidance, people are motivated to give relatively truthful answers to the questions because it is in their interest to discover all they can about themselves in order to make sound vocational choices. However, one cannot rule out faking to create a good impression even in these circumstances (Tiffin & McCormick, 1969).

The tester can use forced-choice techniques specifically designed to minimise faking. With a forced-choice item the respondent must choose between answers that appear equally acceptable (or unacceptable), but that differ in validity for a specific criterion. The following is an example of a test item from a personality test (the Gordon Personal Profile) using the forced-choice technique. The respondent is asked to examine a set of descriptions of personal characteristics, and select one description that is most like, and one description that is least like, him or her. The descriptions are: a good mixer socially; lacking in self-confidence; thorough in any work undertaken; tends to be somewhat emotional.

It should be noted, however, that the forced-choice technique reduces but does not eliminate faking, especially by the applicant for a specific job (Anastasi, 1997). Other measures to neutralise faking are disguising the test so that it appears to be something quite different from what it really is, and introducing "lie scales". The latter is a set of questions designed to detect distortion by the person being tested. One approach is to introduce a number of statements depicting ultra-perfect qualities that, bar a few, the normal person could not conceivably possess. If the respondent scores too highly on these items, then the tester can challenge the credibility of all the other responses and disregard the test score. Another approach is to repeat individual test items, sometimes slightly disguised, and then see whether the respondent gives the same answers to both sets of questions.

Serious consideration has been given to the issue of faking by subjects completing personality questionnaires or tests used in personnel selection. In one study the results, which were in line with previous findings, indicated that the questionnaires used were all highly susceptible to faking. Though recognising certain caveats, the researcher found that subjects were able to fake in a selective way by projecting desirable profiles compatible with their perception of the occupation in question (Furnham, 1990).

A number of other shortcomings of tests have been identified by Furnham (2005):

- Tests are invalid—they do not measure that which they say they are measuring and the scores produced do not predict behaviour over time.
- Tests fail to measure certain critical factors, such as the existence of "trustworthiness" and the likelihood of "absenteeism" in organisations.
- Tests are unfair and biased towards particular racial and gender groups. For example, in connection with gender, it is said that males tend to secure more favourable profiles, which act to their advantage when it comes to obtaining jobs.
- Sometimes the necessary skill to interpret the results of the test and produce accurate profiles is absent due to deficiencies on the part

of those charged with this responsibility. This could arise as a result of lack of skill, insight, and experience.

- There is a lack of good "norms" to which the raw scores can be related. Therefore, there is a tendency to use norms more appropriate to a different culture (see the explanation of norms in the next subsection).
- As tests become more established, subjects could acquire them in advance and derive benefit from addressing the questions. In such cases the results may reflect prior preparation rather than the true ability of the candidate.
- Freedom of information legislation might create a situation where those tested could have access to the results and challenge the scores and the interpretation placed on them.

The significance of culture was underlined by Feltham, Lewis, Anderson, and Hughes (1998). They maintain that personality tests make few allowances for cultural differences between countries. By way of example, they refer to a question on a standard test focusing on a need to achieve. Swedes may not respond in the expected way to such a question because they would like to bury any desire to achieve beneath a socially conscious exterior. A project that Feltham et al. were engaged in was to try to get rid of cultural incompatibility in an existing test offered by a consultancy company. Finally, consider also the shortcomings of testing raised in the earlier section on the standing of psychometric testing.

Features of tests

Psychological tests generally possess a number of features (Toplis et al., 1987). With the odd exception they tend to be objective, standardised measures with well-controlled and uniform procedures governing the way the test is conducted and scored. Therefore, the test items, instructions, and time allowed (where a time limit exists), should be the same for every candidate. Also, every candidate should be exposed to the same physical test conditions, such as adequate illumination, appropriate temperature, a distraction-free environment, and adequate space.

Scoring, whether operated manually, or computerised, must be objective to ensure that the tester's or scorer's judgement does not lead to variations in the score. Therefore, the tester has a "key" that contains a value allocated to a given answer. The raw scores derived from values placed on the responses are only significant when they are compared with *norms* for the particular occupational group in question. The norms are the range of scores obtained from a large representative sample of people for whom the test was designed. The sample could, for example, consist of a group of sales representatives in the UK, and the norms relate to the normal or average performance of this group, with degrees of deviation above and below the average. To ensure standardisation and objectivity, a normative score is read from a norms table. Also, this ensures that the subjective interpretation of the data by the tester is removed from the process.

A percentile score is taken from the conversion tables, and this represents the proportion of the reference group (the occupational group with which the individual tested is compared) that has a lower score than the person tested. For example, if a sales representative scored at the 75th percentile on a particular dimension of a test using UK norms, his or her score would be better than 75% of UK sales representatives. Only 25% of UK sales representatives would have a better score.

The manual supporting the test should contain scientific data to show the "quality" of the test and what it is supposed to do. In this context two factors are crucial—reliability and validity. A test is reliable if it gives the same profile on a repeated basis in the same conditions. In other words, the measure must be consistent. A test is valid if it measures what it is supposed to be measuring. A more detailed explanation of these concepts appears in Chapters 9 and 17 in connection with attitude measurement and selection methods.

It should be noted that training those responsible for the administration and interpretation of tests is very important; as is restricted access—for example, preventing candidates getting hold of tests before selection, and therefore reducing the chances of tests being misused.

Ethical issues

Finally, it is worth reflecting on some important ethical considerations in the use of tests for selection purposes (Porteous, 1997):

- Tests should never be used without justification. One should ensure that the test has relevance to the job, and that the individual's score on the test can be compared with at least some aspects of performance on the job.
- Tests should be administered by users with qualifications approved by The British Psychological Society (BPS).
- Tests should not be stored in places with easy general access; instead they should be securely filed.
- The test results of individuals who fail to secure the job on offer should be destroyed or retained without identifying the candidate's name.
- Applicants should receive sympathetic feedback on their test performance, particularly when they were not selected for the job. People are probably more sensitive to not securing the job because they "failed the test" (particularly an intelligence test) than would be the case with an unsuccessful outcome at a selection interview.
- Use should be made of valid and up-to-date tests because the changing requirements of jobs call for a different set of abilities, or because there are changes in the quality of candidates offering themselves for selection.
- Conditions should be created in which all candidates have a reasonable expectation of performing at their best by providing suitable conditions for the administration of the test and by giving a clear statement of what is in store for candidates. Also, give candidates the opportunity to gain practice by tackling sample test questions prior to the actual test. However, one should avoid a situation where coaching for tests is commonplace.

CHAPTER SUMMARY

- After defining intelligence, models of intelligence were introduced.
- The early models, using a factorial approach, dominated the scene until the 1960s. Subsequently, the information-processing model, influenced by developments in cognitive psychology, became influential.
- The tendency now is to take a broader view of intelligence than is found in the more traditional approaches, and one manifestation of this trend is the acknowledgement of the importance of emotional intelligence.
- Also, the part played by heredity and environment in influencing intelligence was recognised as a subject of heated debate, and the effects of age and gender were briefly examined.
- The issue of the measurement of intelligence, using intelligence tests, was noted as being controversial.
- Closely related to intelligence tests are aptitude and achievement tests, which are really tests of ability. A distinction was made between aptitude and achievement tests, and examples of aptitude tests in the occupational field were given.
- Other tests, such as personality tests in wide use were analysed, in particular the EPI and OPQ, and other ways of assessing personality, including graphology, were acknowledged.

QUESTIONS

(1) Discuss the difference between personality and intelligence.

(2) Outline the "models of intelligence", and identify a particular model that appeals to you, giving reasons for your choice.

(3) Assess the significance of emotional intelligence in the contemporary world of work.

(4) Describe the ways in which intelligence is measured, and comment on the controversy over its measurement.

(5) Discuss the relative importance of genetic inheritance and a person's environment as factors influencing intelligence.

(6) Distinguish between achievement and aptitude tests, and comment on their usefulness in a business organisation.

(7) Identify a major personality test and assess its usefulness in an employment setting.

SPOTLIGHT ON RELEVANT READING

Ciarrochi, T., Forgas, J.P., & Mayer, J.D. (2001). *Emotional intelligence in everyday life: A scientific inquiry*. Hove, UK: Psychology Press.

Edenborough, R. (1994). *Using psychometrics: A practical guide to testing and assessment*. London: Kogan Page.

Loewenthal, K.M. (2001). *An introduction to psychological tests and scales* (2nd ed.). Hove, UK: Psychology Press.

Petrides, K.V., Furnham, A., & Frederickson N. (2004). Emotional intelligence. *The Psychologist*, October, 574–577.

Sternberg, R.J. (2000). In search of the zipperump-a-zoo (Broadbent Lecture on Intelligence). *The Psychologist, 13*, 250–255.

Learning Outcomes

After studying this chapter you should be able to:

- Recognise the major aspects of the motivation process.

- Outline the issues considered in the content theories of motivation.

- Explain the differences between content and process theories of motivation.

- Understand the nature of goal-setting and expectancy theories, noting areas of application, and self-efficacy.

- Describe considerations affecting the integration of motivation theories, and appreciate the significance of the concept of social identity.

- Outline ways in which culture influences the application of motivation theories.

- Outline the different approaches to job design.

- Recognise the manner in which job design is used to motivate employees.

Motivation and Job Design

4

A definition of the concept of motivation is followed by an analysis of factors that contribute to a state of arousal, including emotion, in motivated behaviour. After a brief description of frustration, need or content theories of motivation are considered at length, followed by a discussion of cognitive or process theories of motivation. There is commentary on the possible integration of motivation theories, and the growing significance of the social identity perspective. Monotony and boredom at work are examined. The final section takes a broad view of job design and the impact of new technology. This chapter provides a foundation for the later study of job satisfaction (Chapter 9), leadership (Chapter 12), culture (Chapter 15), change and development (Chapter 16), and rewards (Chapter 18).

Contents

DEFINITION

The question of motivation arises when we ask why people behave in a certain way. When people are motivated, they are responding to conditions operating within and outside themselves. Motivation is frequently studied with reference to needs, motives, drives, and goals or incentives. The emphasis on needs and motives highlights the interconnection between motivation and personality.

Needs

Needs can be classified as, for example, physiological, security or safety, social, and ego or esteem needs. It is possible to have a need and do nothing about it, but equally a pressing need can give rise to a specific pattern of behaviour.

Motives

Motives consist of inner states that energise, activate, and direct the behaviour of the individual as he or she strives to attain a goal or acquire an incentive. Motives can serve as a means by which consumers evaluate competing products, such as with the purchase of a car. For example, a car buyer motivated by convenience is attracted to a model with electronic windows, central door locking, and electronic speed control, in preference to a similar car without these facilities.

Drives

The concept of drive is an important feature of many theories of motivation and is linked with theories of learning, such as Hull's theory (see "Classical conditioning" in Chapter 7). An individual is said to be in a state of drive when he or she adopts a pattern of behaviour in order to achieve a particular goal. For example, a hungry person, who is obviously preoccupied with satisfying a physiological need, behaves (i.e., is in a state of drive) in such a way as to indicate that he or she is in search of food or nourishment (i.e., a goal or incentive). When the person obtains sufficient nourishment, the behaviour (the drive) subsides for the time being. The stronger the drive the greater the level of arousal experienced by the individual.

In its original form, drive theory underlined the importance of biological needs and the associated drives. Later it was extended to other types of behaviour not connected with basic drives, such as drives associated with status, achievement, and satisfactory social relationships (Baumeister & Leary, 1995). Drive theory has been around for a long time, but there are some who feel that there are circumstances where it may not be totally applicable. For example, humans have a capacity to pursue actions that increase rather than reduce various drives (Baron, 2002). An illustration of this is when, in order to lose weight, people turn a blind eye to having snacks even when they are hungry.

Arousal and emotion

The thalamus and reticular formation (both areas of the brain) exert influence on the arousal mechanism. The thalamus is the focal point of excitement and depression, pleasure and pain. The function of the reticular formation is to increase or decrease the level of arousal, and, apart from filtering information, it decides what should be passed on to the higher brain and what should be rejected. Obviously a high priority would be given to information that alerts us to a potential danger. An illustration of arousal in the motivation process is provided in Panel 4.1. The emotion of fear features prominently in the illustration—it activated flight. Anger is also an emotion that is considered in the context of motivation, and produces a physiological change in the form of a greater production of noradrenaline, resulting in a "fight" response.

Emotion is a characteristic that is discussed in Chapter 9 in connection with job satisfaction; the justification for considering it here is that the emotion of fear with its inbuilt action tendencies is considered relevant in work motivation (see Panel 4.2.) It also featured in the illustration in Panel 4.1.

PANEL 4.1: Arousal and motivation

A person suddenly realises that what appears to be a harmless cow in a field is actually an angry bull about to charge. There is a high level of motivation to escape, and information is registered in the hypothalamus (an organ with an important central control function), which directs two processes simultaneously. One process is from the reticular formation, which transmits a message electrically through the sympathetic nervous system to the various parts of the body; the other is from the pituitary gland, which, under the control of the hypothalamus, transmits chemically through the adrenal medulla that secretes adrenalin.

The nervous system and chemical processes together prepare the body for effective speedy action by increasing the blood supply to the brain and muscles and decreasing the blood supply to the digestive system; by increasing the heartbeat and rate of breathing; by alerting relevant parts of the brain to ensure that the necessary skill (to run) is properly performed; and, finally, by directing the movement of the body by monitoring the bull's movements, the condition of the ground, where the gate is located, and so on. It is through the coordination of all these processes that the person escapes. After these processes are complete, the level of arousal drops and the person enters a state of relative calm with the help of the parasympathetic nervous system.

PANEL 4.2: Emotion at work

According to Lazarus and Lazarus (1994), every emotion has a unique value judgement supporting it. For example, guilt is caused by violating a moral principle, depression is caused by the conviction that one is no good and/or that life is no good, and fear is caused by a threat to one's well-being. Although one normally associates an emotion with action, as stated above, we do have reason and so have the power to decide whether or not to allow a feeling to express itself in action. For example, we might hate somebody, but we do not physically assault him or her even though we might feel like doing so.

In the context of fear at work, Donkin (2003a) makes an interesting observation: "It seems that fear remains a significant source of motivation—fear of failure, fear of getting fired, of missing a deadline, or losing face. Are these not all powerful emotions that tie people to their regular jobs? How many people are prepared to endure tyrannical bosses, harassment and miserable working conditions simply so that they can hold on to a job?" Donkin asks the questions why so few motivation theories mention fear and why so many managers feel that it is acceptable, even justifiable and desirable, to maintain a climate of fear.

A raised level of arousal implies increased awareness, energy, and speed, and can be effective in the performance of well-learned mental and physical skills. On the other hand, a lower level of arousal is more suited for tasks of a really complex nature. In a work situation we could expect job performance in the former case to increase as arousal increases up to a certain point. In practice it is often difficult to determine in advance the optimal level of arousal for a given job. Beyond the optimum level of arousal performance could suffer if there is a further change in the level of arousal. As a general principle, and as stated above, the more difficult a task the lower the level of arousal, otherwise a reduction in performance will be experienced. This proposal is known as the Yerkes-Dodson law, and it seems to apply in numerous situations. It would be wise to consider this law in the light of individual differences and preferences. For instance, at one extreme there is the person who prefers and seeks high levels of arousal (e.g., sky divers) and at the other end of the scale are people who prefer to be in a low arousal state (Baron, 2002). It is accepted that arousal theory provides useful insights into the dynamics of motivation, but in the light of what was said in the previous sentence one has to recognise some important limitations or constraints. The relevance of arousal theory to marketing practice features in Panel 4.3.

Goals or incentives

Goals or incentives satisfy or reduce the behaviour associated with the drive. For example, the hungry person achieves the goal or acquires the incentive by eating the food, and this could lead to a reduction or elimination of the hunger drive. Various incentive programmes have been designed to motivate people to meet good standards. Tangible rewards, such as jewellery, gifts, and plaques, as opposed to cash, for meeting safety targets, are especially common in the USA.

PANEL 4.3: Arousal in consumer behaviour

In business there are numerous stimuli that influence states of arousal. Colour and print type are examples of stimuli capable of arousing the person who registers them. Colours in an advertisement can capture our attention, portray realism, and may arouse feelings about an object. For example, from common experience, red is associated with danger (fire, blood, etc.), blue with cool rivers and lakes, and orange/yellow with sunlight and comfortable warmth.

Printing typefaces and other graphic elements as stimuli arouse us and also have significant motivational implications. When reading a book, poor legibility of type may decrease speed and accuracy of reading, and increase visual fatigue. In an advertisement poor legibility reduces the motivation to read further, and the ensuing frustration may become associated with the product. Print typefaces, and the layout of printed matter, have to be considered in order to ensure good legibility (Anastasi, 1979). Unfamiliar type and arrangement tends to slow down reading. A passage set completely in capitals rather than capitals and lower case letters, for example, can have an adverse effect on reading speed. At the same time, capitals are suitable for a message that will be read from a distance—for example, on a billboard or motorway signs.

Sometimes companies deliberately change the image and appeal of a product in the hope of influencing the motivational disposition of consumers. The brand image of Marlboro cigarettes was originally elegant and somewhat feminine. The company adopted a strategy to change the product image by conducting an advertising campaign in which ranchers, hunters, and other sturdy outdoor types, often displaying tattoos, were seen smoking Marlboro cigarettes.

Providing incentives for appropriate or acceptable behaviour conjures up images of reinforcement theory, discussed in Chapter 7. This behaviourist theory of learning is relevant in a motivational sense when it maintains that rewarding behaviour with recognition is likely to encourage the repetition of that behaviour. Apart from the tangible rewards mentioned earlier, other forms of recognition are also valid. For example, the person's accomplishments could be recognised by receiving congratulations from a superior soon after the event, either in private or public.

FRUSTRATION

There are occasions when the individual is in a motivated state in order to achieve a particular goal that will satisfy a deficient need—for example, the hungry person is seeking food, or the ambitious employee is seeking a more challenging job. But when an obstacle is placed in the individual's pathway to the achievement of the goal (such as being caught up in a traffic jam preventing a job applicant from attending a selection interview), this can give rise to feelings of frustration and produce either positive or negative reactions.

A positive reaction comes about when the person tries to resolve the difficulty in a constructive manner. For example, in the face of opposition to the implementation of a certain plan of action, a manager might decide to engage in more consultation with those who object to the scheme. It is also conceivable that the frustrating event makes the individual divert his or her energies into the achievement of alternative goals. In the lives of individuals over the centuries, frustrating events could have been responsible for significant personal accomplishments.

However, frustration can generate various forms of destructive behaviour. The individual may engage in physical or verbal aggression, or regress to an earlier form of behaviour when, for example, a display of temper achieved the desired result. There are other circumstances when the individual reacts to frustrating situations in the same way irrespective of the magnitude of the event and, as a result, the reaction may be totally inappropriate in given circumstances (e.g., shouting or making caustic remarks irrespective of the degree of magnitude of the frustrating event). Some individuals show a tendency to give up and withdraw from the situation, whereas others find the atmosphere surrounding the obstacle to the achievement of the goal unsettling and repress the experience to the unconscious mind.

NEED THEORIES

Need theories fall into the category of *content theories* of motivation. They assume that individuals possess a "baggage" of motives awaiting gratification, and there is an attempt to explain motivation in terms of what arouses and energises behaviour. The theoretical perspective of content theorists will be examined in this section.

One particular view of motivation suggests that people strive towards realising their inner potential (self-actualisation) and may suffer some personal disadvantage in doing so. For example, the adolescent may feel it necessary to leave the comfort of the parental home in order to assert his or her independence. Likewise, there are occasions when a person forfeits comfort and security in order to support an unpopular principle or cause. These are examples of a person's desire to satisfy a pressing need. Maslow (1954) identified a hierarchy of needs ranging from the most primitive, which humans share with the lower forms of life, to those associated with the higher forms of life.

Hierarchy of needs

The hierarchy of needs is represented in pyramidal form in Figure 4.1. The foot of the pyramid represents the most basic needs, and the individual strives to move upwards through the hierarchy. Maslow observed that "man is a wanting animal and rarely reaches a state of complete satisfaction except for a short time. As one desire is satisfied, another pops up to take its place." Thus, only if the lower needs are satisfied will the higher needs appear.

Physiological needs. With respect to some physiological needs, there are certain automatic responses to internal imbalances in the human body. A self-correcting mechanism ensures that the level of sugar remains constant in the blood stream (except in diabetics). We are motivated to drink lots of liquid after eating salty foods. When our body temperature becomes too high, we perspire and are motivated to remove a garment or open a window in a room. A feature of physiological needs is that they have to be satisfied regularly. Consumption of products related to these needs is high, and apart from the emphasis in an advertising message on the convenience factor of certain foodstuffs, the nutritional value may also be acknowledged.

Safety needs. Safety needs include physical security, emotional security, job security, a modestly comfortable and predictable routine, and a desire for fair treatment and justice at work. The need for security could motivate the car buyer to emphasise safety features, such as child-proof locks, head restraints, and a collapsible steering wheel when making a choice. The need for security could also be manifest when the individual is convinced that a signalling system is necessary for his or her future security; as a result, he or she is motivated to install a smoke detector in the house. Security needs could be aroused at work when there is uncertainty about continued employment

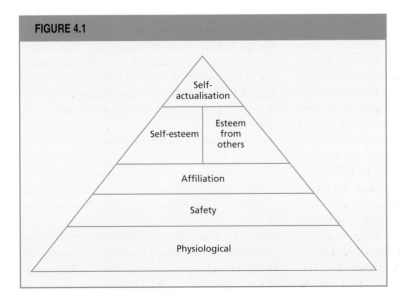

FIGURE 4.1

Maslow's hierarchy of needs (from Maslow, 1954). Copyright 1987, adapted by permission of Pearson Education, Inc., Upper Saddle River, NJ.

with the company. Likewise, the threat of health and safety hazards could arouse safety needs.

Affiliation needs.   Higher than safety needs come affiliation or social needs. These include social contacts, belonging to a group, friendship, and love. Social motivation is also described as dependency (submissive behaviour aimed at an authority figure), dominance, personal relationships (both platonic and sexual), and aggression (Argyle, 1968). It can find expression in many ways. For instance, in order to avoid a feeling of inferiority among others, a consumer may be attracted to the use of a mouthwash to counteract bad breath; and some people may purchase goods that meet with the social approval of others. Similarly, shoppers tend to be more inclined to rely on a friendly sales assistant for information and advice.

Social or affiliation needs act as important motivators of behaviour when the individual has a need to belong to a group at work, which, for example, offers the opportunity to develop meaningful associations with colleagues, to give and receive friendship, understanding, and compassion, and to be accepted by colleagues. There is strong evidence to indicate that social bonding and the need to belong are very influential (Baumeister & Leary, 1995). The consequences of not satisfying security and social needs could be various forms of undesirable behaviour—resistance to change, resistance to budget pressures, antagonism, and an unwillingness to cooperate—intended to defeat the achievement of organisational goals.

Esteem needs.   The next level in the hierarchy deals with esteem needs, divided into self-esteem and esteem from others. Self-esteem includes the need for self-respect and self-confidence, the need to achieve something worthwhile as a result of job performance, the need to be fairly independent at work, the need to acquire technical knowledge about one's job, and to perform one's duties in a competent manner. Esteem from others includes the need for recognition as a result of efficient and effective job performance, the need to be appreciated by colleagues for one's overall contribution at work, and the need to establish a reputation and status in the organisation. The

desire for power would also probably belong to the category of esteem needs.

Argyle (1968) recognises self-image as an essential part of esteem motivation, and there is a tendency to develop attitudes and beliefs towards the self that are consistent and integrated. The person could be motivated to get others to accept and respect the self-image, and perhaps avoid people or alternatively try to change their attitudes if they are not prepared to do so. Furnham (2005a) cites authoritative sources in coming to the conclusion that those endowed with high self-esteem work harder if they are told that things are not going well, tend to be less conformist, and generally are more accomplished. On the other hand those with low self-esteem are more likely to be derailed by a variety of organisational events, including being more upset by negative comments.

Self-actualisation needs.   At the apex of the pyramid are the self-actualisation needs, implying self-fulfilment derived from achievement following the successful accomplishment of, for example, a demanding and challenging assignment at work.

Review of the hierarchy of needs

The sequence of events in climbing the hierarchy of needs is that the gratification of the higher needs follows gratification of the lower needs, and it is often asserted that in Western industrialised society the lower needs are reasonably well satisfied for most people most of the time. As needs that are gratified are no longer determinants of behaviour, it follows that the higher needs assume importance for many people in our culture. This should be borne in mind by those responsible for the design of control systems in organisations.

People seem to have different priorities when it comes to specifying the most important human needs at a particular time. Maslow maintains that if a person has a history of chronic deprivation at a particular need level—e.g., an individual cannot find a job that adequately utilises his or her abilities—this person is likely to be very sensitive to that particular need. On the other hand, where people have previously experienced adequate and consistent gratification of a lower need, they can become relatively unconcerned about subsequent deprivations of that need because their focus has shifted to higher need gratification—as, for example, where an artist's preoccupation with his or her work pushes problems of subsistence to one side. This is similar to the view expressed by Williams and Page (1989) who say that people sometimes seek to satisfy higher order needs even when needs lower in the hierarchy have not been adequately met.

A sample of 1900 managers rated several needs similar to the ones identified by Maslow —security, social, esteem, autonomy, and self-actualisation—in terms of the importance and level of satisfaction associated with each need. It was found that highly satisfied needs were seen as relatively unimportant, and vice versa. There was an exception as far as self-actualisation needs were concerned; they appeared to remain constant, irrespective of how satisfied people felt about them. The self-actualisation needs lost importance only if lower level needs were deprived (Alderfer, 1972). In a study based on the success of managerial trainees over a five-year period in the American Telephone & Telegraph Company, Maslow's concept was also subjected to an empirical test. The successful group (success being measured in terms of fifth-year income) reported the highest satisfaction of achievement, esteem, and self-actualisation needs (Hall & Nougaim, 1968).

Apart from needs that form part of the hierarchy of needs, Maslow acknowledges other needs; for example, a desire for beautiful things could be classified as an aesthetic need. Satisfaction of this need would come from beautiful or attractive surroundings. A person sitting in a room with a picture hung crookedly on the wall may go through the motions of straightening it. Maslow also acknowledges that not all behaviour is motivated, at least in the sense of need gratification—i.e., seeking what is lacking and needed. Though behaviour may not be motivated, it is certainly determined. For example, expressive behaviour could simply be an expression of personality—e.g., a smile on the face may be brought about by an association of ideas or some external stimulus.

The assumptions behind the hierarchy of needs have been criticised as mystical and value-laden, because they flirt so continuously with the evaluation of people in terms of normative judgements of high and low, advanced and primitive, good and bad (Lazarus, 1971). Nevertheless, Maslow's theory has made a significant impact on the development and application of theories of motivation based on "human needs".

In recent years it has still been possible to find evidence supportive of the hierarchy of needs (e.g., Hagerty, 1999). Cary Cooper delved into the "occupational psychology" subconscious and identified Maslow's theory of motivation (along with McGregor's theory X and Y discussed later in this chapter) as the most significant contribution in the field. Both theories are relatively simple and deal with the positive side of human behaviour and motivation (Cooper, 2001a), although referring to theory X as positive is questionable. He goes on to say that "these theories are extremely important because of the changing nature of work, where jobs are now in effect short-term contracts and insecure. As we move towards the Americanised workplace with intrinsic job insecurity, long hours, and a more bottom-line management style, the irony is the American theories of Maslow and McGregor become more important than they were in the last century, particularly for a British workforce."

ERG theory

Alderfer (1972) proposed a hierarchical theory consisting of three need categories:

(1) *Existence (E).* These are needs related to Maslow's physiological needs and certain safety needs.
(2) *Relatedness (R).* These are needs related to Maslow's safety, social and some esteem needs, in particular the need for interpersonal relationships.
(3) *Growth (G).* These are needs related to Maslow's esteem and self-actualisation needs, in particular the need for personal growth and capability to exercise one's creativity.

This matching exercise highlights the fact that there is basically only a general fit between Maslow's and Alderfer's theories. Also, one should recognise that there are no strict demarcation lines between the compartments of ERG needs. An important distinction between the two need theories is that with ERG theory the person will regress to a lower-level need if frustration is encountered. For example, if the individual is unsuccessful at gratifying growth needs, the ERG theory predicts that because of the frustration encountered the person will show an increased desire for relatedness needs. Having satisfied the relatedness needs, the person will strive once again to satisfy growth needs in the hope that this time he or she will encounter a successful outcome. The pattern described could also apply if the person was intent on moving from existence needs to relatedness needs.

Another distinction between ERG theory and Maslow's hierarchy of needs is that, with the former, more than one need could be active at the one time. So instead of progressing up the hierarchy the person may be operating at all levels simultaneously, but obviously to different degrees. Hodgetts (1991) views ERG theory as a workable approach to motivation, with an acknowledgement of a plausible response to frustration when the individual realises it is not possible to progress from one level to the other.

Achievement motivation

A person with a motive to achieve tends to define his or her goals in accordance with some standard of excellence. Six components of the construct—achievement motivation—have been identified by Cassidy and Lynn (1989):

(1) *Work ethic.* This refers to the motivation to achieve based on the belief that performance in itself is good.
(2) *Pursuit of excellence.* A desire to perform to the best of one's ability.
(3) *Status aspirations.* A desire to progress up the status hierarchy and dominate others.
(4) *Mastery.* This refers to competitiveness against set standards, rather than against other people when aspiring to status.

(5) *Competitiveness.* A desire to compete with others and outmanoeuvre them.
(6) *Acquisitiveness.* A desire to acquire money and wealth.

Sagie, Elizur, and Yamauchi (1996) adopted a somewhat different approach to that of Cassidy and Lynn by putting the emphasis on factors associated with tasks only when stipulating conditions for high achievement. For example, it is necessary for tasks to be capable of satisfying the need to achieve, and that these tasks ought to be difficult with uncertain outcomes, but not subjected to excessive risks. In addition, it is the individual (who is expected to be inventive) rather than the group who is responsible for the outcome. This observation is not applicable to all cultures, but it is more valid in the context of the US culture.

McClelland (1967) believes that a society's overall economic performance will be high if the average level of the need to achieve is high in the population (e.g., in the United States). He cites evidence to the effect that in any society the amount of achievement imagery in its children's literature (a reflection of the values society places on achievement) is a fairly good predictor of economic growth in that country for the following 20 years. Apparently, parental expectations and rewards are important conditioning influences on the performances of children high in the need to achieve. The need to achieve (termed "N.Ach") can be modified through a training programme that supports the view that learning is an important agent in motivation. McClelland developed a method for measuring achievement motivation whereby unconscious projections of the individual's dominant needs were analysed. (Projective tests were discussed in connection with personality in Chapter 2.)

Entrepreneurs are said to be high in N.Ach but distinguished scientists are not. Perhaps in the latter case, because of long periods without feedback on progress and working on tasks with low success probabilities, this is understandable. High achievers can flourish if the tasks given to them are challenging but feasible, where they have a sense of control over what they accomplish, and where they are receiving regular feedback on how well they are doing.

High achievers prefer to work on their own where they have control over the outcome of action; they do not like situations where there are no standards to measure their performance by, or where the task is too difficult or too easy. Money is looked upon more as a symbol of achievement rather than an intrinsic motivating factor. The desire for success appears to be the major motivating force; the fear of failure is said to depress N.Ach, causing a person to shy away from achievement-type tasks. Women are said to feel differently about achievement and score lower than men in the tests; the assertion has been made that many women have a fear of success because high achievement is seen as being incompatible with traditional notions of femininity and female roles (Horner, 1970). This situation is likely to be different today!

McClelland has devised programmes to arouse N.Ach in executives by helping the individual to develop self-insight and cultivate the appropriate outlook. Most organisational conditions would appear not to be compatible with the needs of the high achiever, because managers, particularly in large organisations, frequently cannot act alone. However, an association between achievement motivation and budgetary control has been emphasised—"the most sophisticated budgetary system may be of little practical consequence if it fails to elicit the achievement motivations of a significant number of managers and employees" (Hopwood, 1974).

It is recognised that achievement motivation research has been of value in enlarging our understanding of the characteristics of the high achiever, and helpful to managers in trying to develop this need in subordinates (Hodgetts, 1991). A suggested drawback of the research on achievement motivation is the lack of emphasis placed on why people desire to achieve. Instead the emphasis is on identifying, or trying to develop, a desire to achieve (Stahl & Harrell, 1982). This observation could equally apply to a *need for power*, discussed next.

Need for power

A system has been devised for arriving at a need for power profile (termed "N.Pow") in a similar manner to that adopted by McClelland with N.Ach (Veroff, 1953). McClelland (1970), having closely studied the relationship of N.Pow to style of management and performance, concludes that for managers in large organisations, rather than for entrepreneurs, N.Pow is more important for effectiveness than N.Ach.

N.Pow is a motive that involves other people, whereas N.Ach can exclude other people. Because managers in large organisations frequently cannot act alone, they have to depend on influencing others for their success. For this reason McClelland believes that N.Pow is related to success in the exercise of managerial leadership. For example, McClelland and Boyatzis (1982) found an empirical association between success in managerial positions and a moderately high need for power, high self-control, and a low need for affiliation manifest in a warm relationship with others and an ability to empathise with them.

This profile would not be far removed from Miner's (1978) conception of the motivational disposition necessary to manage effectively in large organisations. Miner developed a projective test (similar to the Rorschach ink-blot test described in Chapter 2) of managerial motivation, called the Miner Sentence Completion Scale (MSCS). As the name implies, the test involves completing partial sentences, and is based on the notion that people will project their personalities into their responses. The test is scored in order to give measures of a person's willingness to engage in the following aspects of managerial motivated behaviour:

- positive attitudes towards superiors;
- competitive in the quest for scarce resources;
- assertive, active, with a propensity to take charge of situations;
- directs and controls subordinates, and feels comfortable administering rewards and sanctions;
- highly visible and behaves in such a way as to invite attention, and perhaps criticism; and
- able to perform a wide variety of administrative duties that involve repetitive, detailed work.

Carson and Gillard (1993) concluded from a review of a number of research studies that the higher the managers' motivation to manage, according to the MSCS assessment, the greater the level of success in their jobs. Miner has developed a training course designed to increase managerial motivation by teaching managers and potential managers to behave in a manner consistent with the six managerial behavioural patterns listed.

People might feel uncomfortable about being told that they are high in N.Pow because of the traditional association between seeking power and suppression, exploitation, and tyranny. McClelland (1975a) expresses some observations about those high in N.Pow and suggests two types of group:

(1) At the fantasy level, the first group projects itself in terms of sexual exploitation and the use of physical aggression. They tend to act as impulsive tough guys behaving in accordance with their fantasies.

(2) At the fantasy level, the second group projects itself in a more conventional form, such as winning in a competitive game or election. The members of this group prefer to seek *institutionalised power* with its established environment and rules; they seek posts of responsibility in organisations and have a capacity for creating a good work climate.

Unlike the need for achievement, the need for power is a motive that involves other people in the organisation and is closely linked with management styles (discussed in Chapter 12). One group of managers high in the need for power has been identified by McClelland (1975a) as being competitive, with management potential, in search of responsibility and institutional power. Power is often associated with prestige, status, social eminence, or superiority, and it can affect an individual's self-concept. Sometimes managers who exercise control in organisations are looked up to with respect because they occupy positions of power, although they might feel uncomfortable if they were told they were high in the need for power because of the traditional link between seeking power and its negative associations referred to earlier (e.g., suppression, exploitation, and tyranny). It can be argued as a general proposition that members of an organisation may prefer to exercise influence than to be powerless,

and it is conceivable that managers and workers are much more likely to feel that they have too little, rather than enough or too much, authority in their work.

Certain psychological fulfilment is likely to be derived from the exercise of power, and certain managers get enormous pleasure and satisfaction from influencing the work situation in a way that is compatible with their own interests. There is a discussion of power in Chapter 13. In some respects, the rationale for certain organisational controls may be embedded in the psyche of the manager. But it is all too easy to become preoccupied with the rewards accompanying power and forget its more unpalatable side. Managers in their role of exercising control can suffer frustration and serious tension as a result of a number of organisational demands. Some of these have been identified as extra responsibility, commitment, loyalty, and the burden of taking decisions (Tannenbaum, 1962). (There is a discussion of executive stress in Chapter 19.)

Dual-factor theory

The work of Herzberg (1966) is consistent with Maslow's and McClelland's theories. His dual-factor theory is based on considerable empirical evidence and is built on the principle that people are motivated towards what makes them feel good, and away from what makes them feel bad. His research identifies motivators as factors producing good feelings in the work situation; these are listed in Table 4.1. By contrast he suggests that hygiene factors, also listed in Table 4.1, arouse bad feelings in the work situation.

Hygiene factors are clearly concerned with the work environment rather than the work itself. They differ significantly from motivators in as much as they "can only prevent illness but not bring about good health". In other words, lack of adequate "job hygiene" will cause dissatisfaction, but its presence will not of itself cause satisfaction; it is the motivators that do this. The absence of the motivators will not cause dissatisfaction, assuming the job hygiene factors are adequate, but there will be no positive motivation. It is axiomatic in Herzberg's approach that job satisfaction and job

TABLE 4.1

Dual-factor theory

Motivators	Hygiene factors
Achievement	Company policy and administration
Recognition	Supervision
Work itself	Salary
Responsibility	Interpersonal relations
Advancement	Working conditions
Growth	Status
	Security

dissatisfaction are not opposites. The opposite of job satisfaction is not job dissatisfaction, it is no job satisfaction; the opposite of job dissatisfaction is lack of job dissatisfaction. This is illustrated in Table 4.2.

Empirical endorsement of Herzberg's theory is available. Hodgetts and Luthans (1991) report a number of successful international replications of Herzberg's findings. However, this evidence should be considered in the light of the criticisms voiced later. Adopting Herzberg's approach, a manager should build motivators into the job so as to promote job satisfaction positively; in order to minimise dissatisfaction, hygiene factors should be improved. In the motivation of sales representatives, the motivators and hygiene factors discussed in Panel 4.4 might be considered. There is reference to the motivation of professional/knowledge workers and the motivation of professionals internationally in Panel 4.5.

Earlier it was suggested by Herzberg that motivators are critical factors residing in the job. He prescribes various methods of job enrichment as a way of building motivators into the job. Job

---

PANEL 4.4: Sales motivation

With regard to motivators, sales representatives could be given responsibility for making decisions, such as negotiating prices and terms subject to certain conditions; involved in setting their own sales targets; and given responsibility for planning their own time and journeys. The organisation could ensure that as much relevant information as possible is available to the salesforce, and that feedback of information from the salesforce is acted on and seen to be acted on.

The hygiene factors associated with material reward are likely to receive emphasis. Salary, commission, bonuses, promotions, and competitions are rewards that could be related to the achievement of sales objectives. These objectives could include sales volume, expense control, profitability of sales volume, and new account development. Incentive schemes could be devised for a predetermined period aimed at, for example, the movement of old models from retailers' inventories before the launch of a new product. A system of "prize points" could be used, which would be linked to specific performance targets, allowing each representative to compete against himself or herself. This might be used to raise the level of a representative's performance. As an alternative to money, which may be swallowed up in household expenditure, merchandise incentives (such as holidays abroad) may create greater excitement, with lower tax implications. From the organisation's point of view it is important that extra effort flows from the incentives given, and that the costs of providing the incentives are less than the extra sales revenue (Guirdham, 1972).

Other hygiene factors worthy of mention in the field of sales are an efficient administrative back-up service and good working relationships with colleagues. In a study of the motivation of sales executives in two major companies in the UK, it was concluded that those who held the most favourable attitudes derived satisfaction from the motivators—the job itself, achievement, and scope for development (Smith, 1967). However, if the motivators were in any way restricted, social relationships, security, and other "hygiene" benefits arose as factors promoting satisfaction. Particular hygiene factors (communication and budgetary control systems) aroused dissatisfaction in the more enthusiastic groups.

TABLE 4.2

Herzberg's view of factors contributing to job satisfaction and dissatisfaction

Adequate (Satisfaction)	———— Motivators ————	Inadequate (No satisfaction)
Adequate (No dissatisfaction)	———— Hygiene factors ————	Inadequate (Dissatisfaction)

PANEL 4.5: Motivation of professionals/knowledge workers

Knowledge workers are those who apply their knowledge and expertise to work and produce favourable organisational outcomes. They are likely to come from the ranks of professional and scientific/technical staff. Factors likely to motivate this category of worker are opportunities for personal growth where self-development features prominently, where a high degree of freedom or autonomy in the job exists, where the job offers scope for making a distinctive contribution of value to the organisation, where material (extrinsic) rewards are linked to personal effort, as you might expect to find in individually based performance-related pay schemes (Mullins, 2002). Apart from the latter, motivators appear to feature prominently.

A survey was conducted by Robert Walters (the international recruiter), whereby 3000 professionals drawn from a number of countries (Australia, Belgium, France, Germany, Hong Kong, Ireland, Japan, Luxembourg, New Zealand, Singapore, South Africa, the Netherlands, UK, and USA) were asked what would motivate them to change their jobs. The great majority mentioned better career development and a new challenge, and there was only a slight variation between countries in the responses. The prospect of a better career was the factor that received most endorsement (averaging 40%), though the figure was 53% in Germany and Hong Kong.

Overall money (a hygiene factor) was placed in a position of lesser importance, and the countries where financial rewards were mentioned as a factor were Luxembourg (top of the list) followed by the USA (18%) and Australia (17%). Only 6% of respondents in Belgium cited money as a factor. Company culture and congenial bosses featured modestly in the pecking order. On the basis of this study it would seem desirable for employers to offer professional staff challenges in their jobs and firm career development prospects that could be classified as "motivators".

(Ledger, 2002)

enrichment is an approach to job design (considered in the final section of this chapter) that attempts to make tasks more intrinsically interesting, involving, and rewarding. It comprises both vertical and horizontal loading: Vertical loading entails injecting more important and challenging duties into the job, whereas horizontal loading is akin to job enlargement (increasing the number or diversity of task activities) and job rotation—i.e., moving people back and forth among different tasks. The underlying belief in Herzberg's approach is that increased job satisfaction is an important source of motivation and will lead to better performance because of its association with increased productivity and reduced turnover, absenteeism, and tardiness. There is a discussion of a number of facets of job satisfaction in Chapter 9.

Criticisms of dual-factor theory

There is research evidence that is not entirely compatible with the findings of Herzberg. The following are illustrative of the criticisms made. Dissatisfaction, rather than satisfaction as in the Herzberg model, is associated with performance (March & Simon, 1958). When dissatisfied, the employee will search for alternative courses of action to alleviate this condition. He or she will take into account, and strike a balance between,

the expected value of the reward on offer and his or her own level of aspiration.

Hygiene and motivator factors can both cause satisfaction as well as dissatisfaction (Wernimont, 1966).

There is no recognition in the dual-factor theory of the part played by the expectations people bring with them to the job. For example, when expectations are not met, people can feel dissatisfied (Wernimont, 1966). The issue of expectancy will be considered in the next section.

If there is a mismatch between what people bring to the job (input) and what they receive in return (output), this has significance in terms of satisfaction irrespective of the distinction between motivators and hygiene factors. Here we enter the realm of the concept of equity, which is also examined in the next section.

The mediating influence of culture and category of worker is neglected. For example, an enriched job may have meaning and promote satisfaction for one category of worker but not for another (Hulin & Blood, 1968; Turner & Lawrence, 1965). At Luton in the UK, researchers found that workers sought jobs voluntarily on the car assembly line, and it is interesting to note that these workers had previously given up jobs elsewhere offering interest, status, responsibility, and the opportunity to use their ability and skill (Goldthorpe,

Lockwood, Bechhofer, & Platt, 1970). No doubt they were primarily attracted by monetary or material considerations.

The supremacy of financial reward (accorded the status of a hygiene factor by Herzberg) as a motivating force has been underlined by developments in pay remuneration (Konrad, 2000). In particular, performance-related pay often increases productivity (Bratkovich, 1989), and can result in satisfaction with this system of remuneration (Heneman, Greenberger, & Strasser, 1988). (A discussion of performance-related pay appears in Chapter 18.)

Importance was also attached to pay in an Industrial Society (Wood & Goodhart, 1993) survey, though intrinsic job factors were also important. It was found that good pay, enjoyable work, and a sense of achievement were rated more highly than job security. It was stressed by a spokesperson from the Industrial Society that job security is a concern for everyone, but not an expectation for anyone, because people know they no longer have jobs for life. A good relationship with the boss, good terms and conditions of employment, and status were given a lower priority than job security. One-third of employees were dissatisfied with their work, and only 17% of employees said that they could contribute their full potential at work. The most satisfied employees were public sector workers, and the least satisfied were those in the financial services and engineering sectors of the economy.

The way Herzberg's research was conducted, and the type of questioning used, both have weaknesses (House & Wigdor, 1967). Methodological considerations feature prominently in serious evaluations of the dual-factor theory. Generally, studies that use the same methodology as Herzberg employed—i.e., content analysis of recalled incidents by respondents—are supportive of the theory (Pinder, 1984). Studies that use other methods for measuring satisfaction and dissatisfaction often come forward with results quite different from Herzberg's findings (Hulin & Smith, 1967). Therefore, it should be noted that if a theory is dependent on a particular research method for its substance, as appears to be the case with Herzberg's theory, its validity could be considered questionable.

Theory X and theory Y

While advocating a similar position to that advanced by Herzberg, McGregor (1960) postulates two views of humans—namely, theory X and theory Y.

Theory X is the belief that people are naturally lazy and unwilling to work and must be bribed, frightened, or manipulated if they are to put in any effort at all. This is contrasted with the optimistic perspective of people—theory Y. This view is likely to be held by a manager who believes in providing motivational devices.

A theory Y view states that work is as natural as play; the capacity to assume responsibility for directing one's own efforts is widely, not narrowly, distributed in the population, and, if people are passive, indolent, and irresponsible on the job, it is because of their experiences in organisations and not generally because of some inherent human weakness. McGregor would subscribe to the theory Y view, in the belief that there are more people than is generally believed who are able and willing to make a constructive contribution towards the solution of organisational problems.

COGNITIVE THEORIES

A cognitive perspective in psychology was explained briefly in the opening chapter of this book. The cognitive approach to motivation is primarily concerned with the desire of individuals to produce an effect on their environment and, in the process, to develop certain skills. Early in life, we learn about visual forms, how to grasp and let go of objects, and to coordinate the hands and the eyes. **Constancy**, which is explained in the section on "Perceptual organisation" in Chapter 5, facilitates the stabilisation of our perception, and we develop a cognitive map to guide and structure our behaviour. Individuals in their relationship with the environment like to be active, to explore, to manipulate, to control, to create, and to accomplish things (White, 1960). Likewise, young children like to hold, rattle, and pull toys apart. Monkeys became more skilled with practice at manipulating mechanical devices placed outside their cages (Harlow, 1953).

A cognitive theory of motivation recognises that many aspects of motivation arise when people are fully aware of their motives and actions, and of the risks involved, and make plans guided by their expectations. We find a number of instances where people engage in purposeful behaviour, in which they set a course of action right at the beginning, recognise the obstacles on the way to achieving their plans, and finally overcome the obstacles and feel satisfied with their performance. It appears that the greater the sense of self-control attained, the greater the level of success in carrying out both short- and long-term plans. The most popular cognitive theories are **goal-setting**, **expectancy theory**, and **equity theory**. They are called *process theories*. Unlike content theories, discussed earlier in this chapter, which assume that individuals are endowed with a bundle of motives awaiting gratification and which do not acknowledge individual choice or social influence, process theories focus on how behaviour is initiated, redirected, and terminated. A natural location for **self-efficacy** is under the heading of cognitive approaches to motivation; therefore, self-efficacy will be examined in this section.

Goal-setting

A goal is basically a desirable objective, the achievement of which is uppermost in the mind of a person. Goals can be used for two purposes in organisations:

(1) As motivational devices in the sense that employees work towards meeting these goals.
(2) As a control device when performance is monitored in relation to the goals set for individuals and departments.

Organisational goals might be expressed as, for example, "to reduce overhead costs by 10%" or "to increase sales revenue by 10% over the next year". Subsumed in these organisational goals would be numerous individual goals directed towards achieving the overall goal.

The starting point for a goal-setting theory of motivation is that behaviour is influenced by conscious goals and intentions. The original model of goal-setting was postulated by Locke (1968), who felt that performance was shaped by goal difficulty and goal specificity. Subsequent research has shown a close association between performance and goal difficulty and specificity (Hollenbeck & Klein, 1987).

Goal difficulty. Goal difficulty is the extent to which a goal is challenging and demanding of effort. For a particular athlete a difficult goal could be to secure a place in the national squad for the Olympic Games. This could necessitate a lot of hard work to achieve the goal. For another athlete such a goal would be too difficult to achieve, and it could be considered unattainable. In such a case it is unlikely to have any motivating effect, so the athlete in question puts little effort into training. Therefore, for some people a challenging goal raises the level of performance (Wegge, 2000), while others do not respond positively to difficult goals. Yearta, Maithis, and Briner (1995) take the view that the setting of difficult goals for a particular group (e.g., research scientists) can negatively influence performance at work. Another group of researchers feel that if the difficult or complex goals are set for tasks of an unfamiliar nature, this could have a detrimental effect on performance, but repeated practice at such tasks could reverse the stated effect (Kanfer, Ackerman, Murtha, & Dugdale, 1994). Earley and Lituchy (1991) introduce the concept of self-efficacy (examined below) in the context of goal difficulty and conclude that it is important for goal difficulty to match the individual's perceived self-efficacy. With a raising of the level of performance and the level of self-efficacy, goals and quality standards can be made more demanding or challenging.

Overall, it may be concluded that even though success is not guaranteed when the person faces a difficult goal, most people attach importance in terms of self-actualisation, competency, and extrinsic rewards to the challenge of difficult rather than easy goals (Mento, Lock, & Klein, 1992).

FIGURE 4.2

Expanded model of goal-setting (from Latham & Locke, 1979).

Goal specificity. Goal specificity amounts to a definition of the target to which performance will be directed. An example of a specific goal is to reduce overhead costs by 10%. You will notice the goal is expressed in quantitative terms. In areas where qualitative factors (e.g., state of morale) are considered, specificity is difficult to establish.

Latham and Locke's model. An expanded model of goal-setting, designed to reflect the complexity of the setting of goals in organisations, was proposed by Latham and Locke (1979). This is shown in Figure 4.2. You will notice that goal-directed effort or behaviour in this model is influenced by four goal attributes—difficulty and specificity (as in the original model), plus acceptance and commitment.

Goal acceptance and goal commitment. Goal acceptance is the extent to which a person accepts the goal as legitimate for him or her. Goal commitment is the extent to which the person is interested in attaining the goal, and this is reflected in the extent to which the person will take the necessary steps to attain the goal. According to Latham and Steele (1983), acceptance and commitment

are enhanced by factors such as participation in goal-setting, coming up with realistic and challenging goals, and accepting that goal achievement will lead to rewards that are valued by those involved.

Other researchers view commitment to difficult goals as a natural precondition for effective performance (Hollenbeck & Klein, 1987). Goal commitment can be defined as a willingness not to abandon or lower a goal (Wright, O'Leary-Kelly, Cortina, Klein, & Hollenbeck, 1994), and apparently it is stronger when the goal is made public by communicating it to peers. Those people who believe they can control their fate (i.e., they are of an internal locus of control disposition) and are high achievers, tend to have the strongest goal commitment (Hollenbeck, Williams, & Klein, 1989; Tubbs, 1993). In a meta-analytic review of the research literature, Donovan and Radosevich (1998) endorse commitment as a moderating variable in the relationship between goal-setting and performance, but conclude that it is not as influential as previously suggested.

On the question of a participative style in goal-setting, the case for it is far from clear. However, Arnold, Cooper, and Robertson (1998) maintain that participation in goal-setting in laboratory experiments is an improvement on a style that amounts to simply telling people the goal assigned to them. But participation in goal-setting is less effective than a style that takes the form of assigning goals to people and then offers a rationale or justification for those goals. Wegge (2000) endorses this finding in an exploratory study dealing with groups rather than individuals when he concludes that assigning difficult goals with a "tell/sell" style (see discussion of the leadership continuum in Chapter 12) is in general as effective as setting these goals participatively.

Related to participation in goal-setting is the question of feedback. Good feedback can engender a sense of achievement, accomplishment, and recognition. It highlights present performance in relation to past performance, personal performance in relation to others' performance, and can produce improved and more creative effort (Latham & Locke, 1979). Self-generated feedback—where the employee is able to monitor his or her own progress—has been shown to have greater effect than feedback emanating from official sources within the organisation (Ivancevich & McMahon, 1982).

The next step in the Figure 4.2 model shows how goal-directed effort leads to performance, but the outcome is influenced by two intervening variables—organisational support, and individual abilities and traits. An example of positive organisational support is ensuring that staffing levels and resources generally are of the required magnitude to achieve the goal. Negative organisational support could manifest itself as a failure to repair equipment essential for the execution of the tasks involved in attaining the goal. The abilities, skills, and other personal characteristics required to do the job have also to be considered. A personal characteristic sometimes mentioned in this context is that of *self-efficacy*. This concept was briefly acknowledged as part of a cognitive perspective on personality in Chapter 2 and refers to an individual's belief that he or she is capable of performing a task (Gist, 1987). The greater a person's self-efficacy the more confidence he or she has to succeed in a task. People with low self-efficacy are more likely to reduce their effort or cease an activity, while those high in self-efficacy will try

harder to meet the challenge in difficult circumstances (Gist & Mitchell, 1992). The concept of self-efficacy is given further consideration after the discussion of goal-setting.

The last-but-one step in the model shows that when the person has performed the task, he or she receives various intrinsic and extrinsic rewards.

The final step shows the level of satisfaction being influenced by intrinsic and extrinsic rewards. The relationship between performance, rewards, and satisfaction in Latham and Locke's model bears some similarity to the expectancy model postulated by Porter and Lawler (1968), discussed later in this chapter.

Reflections on goal-setting

Some scholars have expressed views about constraining influences on the effectiveness of goal-setting. Austin and Bobko (1985) maintain that goal-setting theory has not been properly tested in four areas:

(1) Goals that reflect quality, rather than quantity, do not feature prominently.
(2) Goal-setting theory could be compromised in situations where there are conflicting goals, and the person may have to select one at the expense of ignoring the other.
(3) Group goals and performance are neglected in favour of those relating to the individual.
(4) The effectiveness of goal-setting has not been satisfactorily evaluated outside of laboratory conditions.

The last two reservations have been challenged by Pritchard, Jones, Roth, Stuebing, and Ekeberg (1988). They maintain that goal-setting is applicable to groups and is effective outside the laboratory.

The question of goals assigned to people can be a contentious issue. By assigning goals there is an expectation that performance will be directed at the stated goal. But a question to ask is, what constitutes appropriate performance in relation to a particular goal? There is the danger that the organisational conception of appropriate performance may be at odds with notions of acceptable performance as perceived by particular groups (Meyer & Gellatly, 1988).

It is suggested that goal-setting may not be helpful in conditions where novelty surrounds a task, and various strategies are available to tackle the situation. In a novel task—a stock market prediction exercise—subjects who were assigned difficult goals performed worse and changed their strategies more than subjects given a "do your best" goal (Earley, Connolly, & Ekegren, 1989). Perhaps in situations like this too much attention is given to devising strategies to attain goals in difficult conditions, and not enough attention given to task performance!

Evaluation of goal-setting theory

Goal-setting theory has been extensively reported in the research literature on motivation and in the early days was criticised for being a technology rather than a theory, though such criticism is less applicable today (Arnold, 2005). According to Moorhead and Griffin (2004), the critical variables in goal-setting are goal difficulty and specificity when performance is considered. Less importance is attached to acceptance and commitment, and though the theory takes a short-term rather than a long-term view, it is a useful approach to motivation. It has been suggested by Farr, Hoffman, and Ringenbach (1993) that goal-setting as a theory has greater relevance for people who are eager to derive a good learning

experience from the challenge of meeting difficult goals, rather than proving to others their capability to meet exacting standards. Such people are likely to be competent and able performers in the long term.

An avenue through which goal-setting is applied in an organisational context—called management by objectives (MBO)—is discussed under "Development techniques and interventions" in Chapter 16. MBO subscribes to the notion of specific and reasonably demanding goals with a provision for feedback and a participative approach. An attempt to apply goal-setting theory to budgeting within organisations appears in Panel 4.6.

Self-efficacy

Self-efficacy, introduced as an approach to personality in Chapter 2, is a cognitive judgement by the individual and amounts to a belief in one's capability (I feel confident!) to execute required actions and produce outcomes for a defined task. In effect it amounts to a self-assessment of one's capability and has motivational consequences. A strong belief in one's capabilities will sustain the motivation needed for successful performance on both simple and complex tasks. It is said that challenging, complex and autonomous jobs, which could stem from job enrichment, tend to enhance self-efficacy, while boring, tedious jobs tend to do the opposite (Parker, 1998). As individuals gain increasing task-specific knowledge and skill

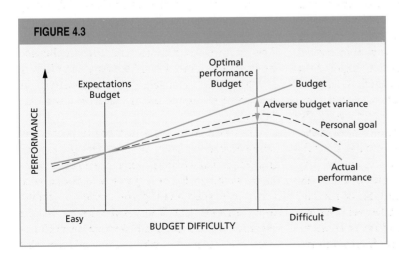

FIGURE 4.3

The effect of budget difficulty on performance (adapted from Otley, 1977).

Budgeting is an example of an important organisational process where goals are set. The application of goal-setting to budgeting will be discussed with reference to *aspiration level, budget standards, budget tightness,* and *bargaining and tactics.*

Aspiration level. In experiments connected with studying the level of aspiration (something within our reach) the setting of goals has received particular attention. We are more likely to be motivated by realistic goals where we recognise the possibility of failure (Atkinson, 1964). Group influence can be an important factor when it comes to fixing the level of aspiration. If one's performance in an activity is better than the average for the group, this may lead to a lowering of the level of aspirations next time round. But equally, if one establishes that one's performance is worse than that of somebody whose standing in the group is low, this could give rise to an upward shift in the level of aspiration (Lewin, 1964). If achievement falls far below the aspiration level, the aspiration level may be subsequently reduced until the disparity is slight (Child & Whiting, 1954). Equilibrium is said to occur when the aspiration level exceeds achievement by a small amount.

Budget standards. Budgets and cost standards are said to motivate employees by acting as goals or incentives, and a fair amount of research evidence focuses on the motivational effects of budget standards or targets of varying degrees of tightness (Hofestede, 1968; Stedry, 1960). Good standards of performance have been associated with high levels of aspiration (Stedry & Kay, 1964). The performance implications of different levels of budget difficulty were analysed using the following procedures.

Goals were set at a normal level (capable of being achieved 50% of the time), and at a difficult level (capable of being achieved 25% of the time). When compared with normal goals, difficult goals gave rise to either good or bad performance. When good performance followed the difficult goal, this goal had become an aspiration level. So where the difficult goal was seen as a challenge (as was the case with high achievers and younger performers), actual performance was better than target. In this situation results were in excess of the aspiration level. Where bad performance followed the difficult goal, the budgetee obviously viewed the achievement of the goal as being impossible, failed to set an aspiration level, and began to show withdrawal symptoms (Stedry & Kay, 1964).

Variation in levels of aspiration appears to be a function of success or failure. It is maintained that success raises the level of aspiration and failure lowers it, and that failure has a more varied effect on level of aspiration than has success. Movements in levels of aspiration are to some extent influenced by changes in a person's confidence in his or her ability to achieve the goal (Child & Whiting, 1954).

Apparently, past budget performance is likely to affect the level at which future budget targets are set. Managers felt it to be in their interest to agree lower rather than higher budget targets, striking a balance between present job security and increasing future income (Lowe & Shaw, 1968). These managers, whose track record may be either impressive or wanting, were quite subtle in the manner in which they tried to influence forecasts in order to win short- or long-term approval or personal benefits.

Budget tightness. Another study tested the effect on performance of varying degrees of tightness in the budget (Hofestede, 1968). As the budget gets tighter, the employee is motivated and aspires to higher levels of aspiration with results lower than the aspiration level. At this stage the budget target is not achieved. Beyond this stage, both levels of aspiration and results fall because the budgetee no longer believes that it is possible to achieve the budget target. This can create negative motivation resulting in a deterioration in performance. Similar findings are reported in a study conducted in the UK (Otley, 1977). As can be seen in Figure 4.3, the budget level that motivates the best performance is unlikely to be achieved most of the time, but a budget that is usually achieved will motivate only at a lower level of performance. In other studies it was concluded that the best performance was achieved in situations where budget targets were clearly understood, and where they were tight but attainable (Kenis, 1977; Merchant, 1981). Department meetings were found to be useful in facilitating the adoption of budget targets as the manager's personal goals. But cultural, organisational, and personality factors all affect an individual manager's reaction to a budget standard (Otley, 1977).

The results of a more recent study confirm the beneficial effect of budget goals in terms of performance. However, it was found that there was another variable to consider apart from budget goals when it comes to variations in performance levels, and that is the completion of interdependent tasks (Hirst & Yetton, 1999).

Bargaining and tactics. We have already seen how success or failure in meeting budget targets gives rise to variations in levels of aspiration, and how past performance in relation to the budget can affect future budget levels. When the budgetees were able to bargain on a budget standard, they presented biased information so as to secure the best personal advantage; this would normally manifest itself in a lower rather than higher budget standard. The budgetees (managers) tried to strike a balance between two objectives—present job security and increasing future income (Lowe & Shaw, 1968).

For example, one manager may disappoint a superior now because of the conservative budget he or she has adopted for the coming budget period, hoping to win the superior's approval when he or she achieves the budget at the end of the budget period. Another manager may feel he or she has little reputation left because of poor past budget performance, but submits an almost unreal forecast (excessively high) so as to win approval now. At the end of the budget period he or she will have to live with the unfavourable consequences of this action. Yet another manager has a high standing with his or her superior because of good past performances, and decides to aim for an easier budget target for the coming budget period, an action that will receive acclaim later when the budget is met. His or her record can quite easily absorb the present disappointment on the part of the superior. Of course there are also circumstances when genuine overestimation or underestimation occurs and this may arise when sales are subject to fluctuation. When sales are rising there is a tendency to underestimate budgeted sales (Lowe & Shaw, 1970). Tactics are discussed in greater detail in Chapter 13.

they acquire self-efficacy (Bandura, 1997), which amounts to the conviction that they can perform tasks at a certain level of skill. People with a high level of confidence in their ability to do a specific job are able to exert more effort, respond more positively to negative feedback, set higher goals, and choose better strategies than people with low confidence.

Searching for good information to solve a problem can be considered in the context of self-efficacy (Wood & Atkins, 2000). Efficacy related to the search could be very core-task or competency specific. For example, a computer expert who has very low efficacy for asking questions in an interpersonal context (e.g., interviews or negotiations) could have a very high efficacy for a computer-based search. Normally, we would expect most managerial work to acquire strong efficacy in varied interpersonal activity.

As well as information search efficacy, we have information-processing efficacy. This is concerned with the individual's belief about his or her capacity to evaluate and process information and integrate relevant information so as to make choices and judgements for effective task performance. Individuals with high processing efficacy are expected to engage in more extensive and deeper processing of information. A real challenge for both the high search efficacy and the high processing efficacy person (e.g., an accomplished stock market day trader or crisis counsellor) arises when he or she is exposed to highly volatile conditions in complex circumstances for a prolonged period of time. In such circumstances the person may doubt his or her capability to handle the uncertainty and the demands of the task. It is said that individuals with stronger beliefs in their capacity to continue coping with high levels of uncertainty and change will respond better to the demands of the task and will be less vulnerable to stress and burnout (Wood & Atkins, 2000).

Because self-efficacy appears to have natural appeal, one might ask whether action can be taken to increase it in various situations. Apparently, self-efficacy can be increased by an uncomplicated procedure. For example, Eden and Aviram (1993) studied such a procedure relating to the self-efficacy of unemployed people, who lost their jobs as a result of "downsizing" and other factors beyond their control and who were trying to find another job. The researchers worked on the premise that it was necessary to increase the self-efficacy of the unemployed participating in the study because the experience of losing a job could result in lower levels of self-efficacy with motivational implications. Those affected could have doubts about their effectiveness as workers and were likely to be despondent about getting another job. To confront the latter the recently unemployed participated in workshops designed to enhance their self-efficacy and this was done through the screening of films in which good job-seeking skills were demonstrated. After viewing the films, participants were offered the opportunity to practise the skills on display and they received feedback and encouragement. The results indicated that the exercise in skills development increased the participants' self-efficacy and the success rate in obtaining new employment was significantly higher than found in a carefully matched control group.

Expectancy theory

A recognisable development within the cognitive theory of motivation was the emergence of expectancy theory. This theory expounds the view that we choose among alternative behaviours—i.e., we anticipate the possible outcome of various actions; we place a weighting or value on each possible outcome, assessing the probability that each outcome will be the result of an alternative action; and, finally, the course of action that maximises our expected value will be chosen. Put another way, people expect to work hard in their jobs only when they believe that by doing so they will better their performance (known as expectancy), that good performance will be recognised and rewarded (known as instrumentality), and that the rewards on offer are the ones they want (known as valence).

Vroom's expectancy model

Vroom (1964) put forward a well-known formulation of expectancy theory, and this is depicted in Figure 4.4. The terms used in the theory are as follows:

- *Valence.* Strength of preference for a particular outcome, which can be positive (desired) or negative (not desired).
- *Outcome.* That which results from action.
- *First-level outcome*: Immediate effect of one's actions—e.g., a "job well done" (this is normally what the organisation is looking for).
- *Second-level outcome.* That which results from the first-level outcome—e.g., a job well done may eventually lead to a promotion.
- *Expectancy.* The probability that a certain piece of behaviour (i.e., certain level of effort in the job) will give rise to a particular first-level outcome (i.e., improved performance).
- *Instrumentality.* Strength of the causal relationship between the first-level outcomes and second-level outcomes (e.g., a strong causal relationship would exist if increased effort had a beneficial effect for the employee, such as a pay increase).

It is possible to quantify valence, expectancy, and instrumentality in Vroom's model. If we multiply each of the first-level outcomes by the expectancy (probability) that an outcome will follow action, and add up the results, we arrive at the strength of motivation to elect for a particular course of action. The preference for a first-level outcome depends on how effective this outcome is in bringing about a second-level outcome that is valued. We can expect the person to choose a pattern of behaviour that has a high motivational force attached to it. Expectancy theory, therefore, postulates that if this process was followed, a person's choice of behaviour would approximate the model's prediction.

Although one can find evidence in support of Vroom's expectancy theory (Van Eerde & Thierry, 1996), there are others who feel the theory is rather idealistic because of the difficulty people are likely to experience when trying to see a connection between performance and rewards. Thompson and McHugh (2002) maintain that on the surface the theory appears to be a simple and powerful tool for predicting behaviour, but it is not free from difficulties connected with measurement. For example, expectancy theory provides a rational-cognitive explanation of individual behaviour. But it may be unrealistic to assume that individuals make rational calculations based on cognitive input in deciding whether or not to act in a particular

Vroom's expectancy model (adapted from Vroom, 1964).

FIGURE 4.5

Porter and Lawler's expectancy model (based on data from Porter & Lawler, 1968).

way (see discussion of the bounded rationality decision model in Chapter 8). Also, the importance of the context in which the individual operates is not given serious consideration. On a more technical level, researchers have experienced some difficulty in replicating the original methodology.

Porter and Lawler's expectancy model

Porter and Lawler (1968) place expectancy theory firmly in an organisational context, with practical ramifications. They also put forward the view that the strength of motivation is dependent upon the person's perceived probability that the motivated behaviour will lead to a desired outcome. Their model is illustrated in Figure 4.5. The factors that affect the amount of effort people put into their work are the value they place on the outcome that they hope will materialise as a result of their efforts and the probability that reward will follow the effort. Porter and Lawler are in agreement with Vroom when they propose that the probability that effort will lead to acceptable performance should be multiplied by the strength of the causal relationship between first-level and second-level

outcomes (instrumentality)—the good performance/reward equation.

But effort is not the only consideration; a person's abilities and traits will also have an effect on performance, as well as the person's perception of his or her organisational role. Based on research evidence, it is concluded that successful managers perceive their roles as requiring the display of inner-directed personality traits, such as forcefulness, imagination, independence, self-confidence, decisiveness, etc. Other things being equal, these managers are expected to perform better than managers who perceive their roles as requiring the display of other-directed traits, such as cooperation, adaptability, caution, agreeableness, tactfulness, etc. (Porter & Lawler, 1968). Managers with other-directed traits are considered less effective as measured by peer ratings, supervisor ratings, and promotions.

The next thing to consider is the relationship between performance and rewards. Rewards are of two types: intrinsic (such as a sense of challenge, achievement, and success) and extrinsic (organisational rewards such as pay, promotion, and fringe benefits). Satisfaction should come about if the receipt of both intrinsic and extrinsic rewards is the consequence of performance; but the level of satisfaction depends on how near the rewards are to what the person perceives as equitable for the services rendered. The closer the fit between actual rewards and perceived equitable rewards, the greater the level of satisfaction experienced.

The feedback loop between satisfaction and reward indicates that rewards associated with higher order needs (intrinsic rewards) assume greater importance as the individual receives more rewards for his or her effort. Apparently the more intrinsic rewards the individual receives the better this is from the point of view of higher future effort. Note that intrinsic rewards are usually more immediate and direct than extrinsic rewards. The emphasis on intrinsic rewards reminds one of Herzberg's motivators; but unlike Herzberg's model in which satisfaction precedes performance, the Porter and Lawler model shows performance leading to satisfaction, with rewards and perceived equity serving as intervening variables. But note the weight given to extrinsic rewards, such as pay, in the Porter and Lawler model.

Reverting to Figure 4.5, the feedback loop between intrinsic/extrinsic rewards and the perceived probability that effort will lead to reward suggests that, if good performance is rewarded, the perceived likelihood that effort leads to reward will grow stronger.

The message conveyed by the work of Porter and Lawler is that not only should jobs be designed or redesigned (job enrichment) so that they pose challenge, variety, and autonomy (i.e., intrinsic qualities), but also extrinsic rewards, such as pay, should be provided and equated with perceived equitable rewards. In addition, there should be a match between the employees' traits and abilities and the requirements of the job. This has already been recognised elsewhere. For example, where workers' abilities and experience correspond closely to those required by their jobs, job satisfaction is said to have a high positive relationship with job performance, whereas in those situations where there is inconsistency the relationship is likely to be progressively lower (Carlson, 1969).

The Porter and Lawler model has not been extensively tested, but the authors have amassed some evidence that is consistent with the model. The message conveyed by this work is as follows: One should endeavour to relate employees' traits and abilities to the job and ensure that employees have accurate role perceptions. This action is likely to contribute to a high level of effort. Also, jobs should be designed so that they pose challenge, variety, and autonomy (intrinsic qualities), but make sure that extrinsic rewards, such as pay, are equated with perceived equitable rewards. Porter and Lawler maintain that some employees with relatively low performance are dissatisfied with the rewards received, and they attribute this condition to the belief that low performers tend subjectively to over-rate their performance relative to that of high performers.

Equity theory

Equity theory as a social comparison theory takes a similar view to expectancy theory on the importance of the underlying cognitive processes governing an individual's decision whether or not to put effort into an activity. But the main thrust of equity theory is that people are motivated to secure what they perceive to be a fair return for their efforts. We are all inclined, consciously or otherwise, to compare each other's inputs (e.g., education, experience, effort, and skill) and outputs (e.g., salary, increases in salary, promotion, and fringe benefits). If we perceive our input as justifying a larger output, or if, on a comparative basis, we believe we are unfairly treated, feelings of inequity can arise (Adams, 1963).

Feelings of inequity amount to a state of discomfort, and apparently this state can also arise when people feel they are overcompensated for their efforts. Feelings of inequity could motivate people to do more or less work depending on the nature of the inequity. The greater the inequity, the stronger the level of motivation. Normally one would expect people to compare themselves with others who are doing similar work or occupying similar positions. It has been suggested that there are six methods at the disposal of people to reduce inequity (Adams, 1965):

(1) Inputs may be modified. For example, if a person believes he or she is not sufficiently rewarded, personal effort (an input) may be reduced. If the person believes he or she is over-rewarded, personal effort may be increased.

(2) Outputs may be modified. For example, the person may demand a better financial package or greater opportunities (an output) in return for the effort that is currently under-rewarded.

(3) Perceptions of self are modified. For example, the person may alter the original perception of inequity by concluding that he or she is contributing less but receiving more than was originally believed to be the case.

(4) Modification of the perceptions of others with whom comparisons are made. For example, the person who experiences inequity may conclude that the other person is working harder than originally appeared to be the case, and therefore deserves the perceived extra outputs.

(5) The person with whom a comparison is made is no longer used. For example, the person may conclude that the other person used as a basis for comparison is no longer suitable and should be replaced by someone else who is considered more appropriate.

(6) Leave the situation. For example, the person believes that the only way to resolve the inequity is to get a transfer to another department, or to leave the organisation.

There is a prominent view in the research literature that equity theory has good predictive powers (Griffeth, Vecchio, & Logan, 1989) and particularly when conditions of underpayment apply (Lord & Hohenfeld, 1979). In another study the importance of social comparison in equity theory was relegated to insignificance. Apparently, there is now a view that some people are more sensitive to perceptions of inequity than others and act accordingly, so it would appear that individual differences have to be considered (Huseman, Hatfield, & Miles, 1987).

In recent years there has been a revision of equity theory using a more explicit cognitive processing perspective along the following lines:

- *Distributive justice.* In the past the focus was on distributive justice—i.e., the perceived fairness of the process of allocating rewards and the amount dispensed to employees (e.g., I am equitably paid when I compare myself with people engaged in similar jobs elsewhere in the organisation). Now we have procedural justice as well.

- *Procedural justice.* This refers to the perceived fairness of the process used to determine the distribution of the rewards (Folger & Konovsky, 1989). For example, in procedural justice there is a perception that the organisation makes available sufficient funds for reward purposes and the reward system is impartial in the sense that it does not favour one group ahead of another.

In a study by McFarlin and Sweeney (1992) it was concluded that both distributive and procedural justice were associated with employee variables, such as satisfaction, commitment, and trust. A message from Robbins (2003) is that managers should be more forthcoming in circulating information about decisions on the allocation of rewards (distributive justice) and raising awareness of what is involved in procedural justice. By doing so they are likely to receive a favourable reaction from employees. A reversal of these conditions could give rise to procedural and distributive injustice. Finally, equity theory has a role to play in the study of motivation, and it would be ill-advised, for example, to ignore it because of one's preoccupation with job design.

As a postscript to the study of both content and process theories above, consider for a moment the relative standing of these two approaches to motivation. According to Thompson and McHugh (2002):

The relative lack of success of process theories in managerial terms is due to the very complexity that makes them less powerful in explanatory terms than content theories. Most management development texts still present content theories in the main because they are simple, easier to demonstrate, and they sound powerful, whereas cognitive/process theories suffer from the very fact that they are multi-factorial and multi-variate, with the implications that there are too many factors which can affect the relations between effort, performance and outcomes; that it is too difficult to place accurate values on variables; that models require assumptions of complex mental calculations, which are hard to reproduce and demonstrate.

The process theories handle the study of motivation in slightly different ways, just as we found with content theories (i.e., need theories) earlier in this chapter. The difference of emphasis is apparent in process theories when expectancy theory and goal-setting theory are examined. For example, with expectancy theory individuals tend to be motivated by projects where the success rate is high. By contrast, goal-setting theory suggests that individuals are motivated by difficult assignments where success is not guaranteed. Of course there are similarities between the process theories. They recognise individual and situational influences that are likely to affect outcomes, and all have an orientation embedded in the future in the sense that they are concerned with how people will behave.

INTEGRATION OF MOTIVATION THEORIES

In the early 1980s it was suggested that more attention needed to be devoted to integrating the various perspectives on motivation (Mitchell, 1982). For example, goal-setting and equity theory could be incorporated into expectancy theory. Also, given the prominence of groups in our lives, there is a need to develop a greater understanding of how group processes affect motivation (see the discussion of social identity theory in the next section and groups generally in Chapter 10). There is scope for developing contingency models of motivation.

Landy and Becker (1987) speculate about the natural arrangement of approaches to motivation. For example, need and equity theories might be best suited to exploring the affective or emotional implications of work, whereas reinforcement models and goal-setting theory could be well suited to understanding specific work behaviour. Expectancy theory would be restricted to the prediction of choices among alternatives. Landy and Becker are adamant in admonishing motivational researchers on the need to identify specific cognitive operations (i.e., cognitive abilities) and explore the role of these operations in various motivational theories. The type of cognitive operations they refer to have been discussed in Chapter 3.

Control theory of motivation

A control theory model of human motivation is put forward by Lord and Hanges (1987), consisting of the following features:

* A standard or goal that the system attempts to achieve.
* A sensor that measures or gathers information important to the system.
* A comparator or a discriminator that compares the sensed information to the standard.
* A decision mechanism by which the system decides what action to take in order to reduce any discrepancy between the sensed information and the standard.
* An effector or response mechanism that enables the system to interact with its environment.

Lord and Hanges believe that control theory provides a viable model for understanding the way specific goals and feedback affect people's behaviour and performance on the job. They believe the model is dynamic, flexible, and that it incorporates responses to changes in standards over time, as well as feedback from the environment. Also, it can be integrated with recent cognitive theory.

Acceptance of this model could lead one to consider the work of another researcher wedded to the control system approach. Klein (1989) has postulated a control theory that provides a general framework within which motivational issues can be addressed. The model, based on integrated control theory, is shown in Figure 4.6.

FIGURE 4.6

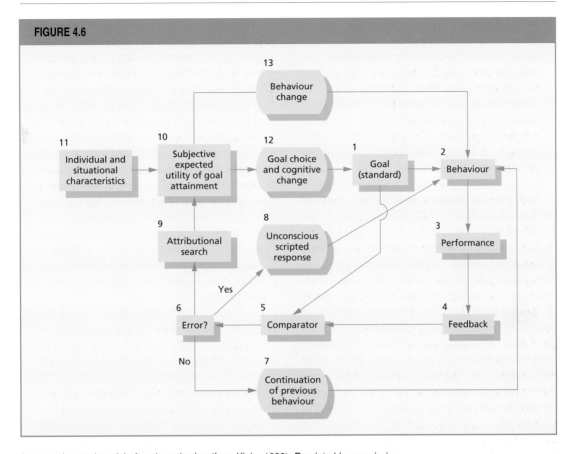

Integrated control model of work motivation (from Klein, 1989). Reprinted by permission.

Control theory operates on the supposition that behaviour is regulated by a system under which an individual's current condition or state is compared with some desired condition or state. If there is a discrepancy between the current and desired conditions, behavioural strategies will be used to reduce that discrepancy. Refer to Figure 4.6 and follow the commentary:

- *Box 1*. A goal or standard is a desired position, which triggers behaviour and performance.
- *Boxes 2 and 3*. The person follows a course of behaviour and performs particular tasks.
- *Boxes 4 and 5*. Feedback on performance is received, and this is compared with the standard, using the comparator.
- *Boxes 6 and 7*. Where no discrepancy or error is detected by the comparator, the person

knows that he or she is on course and that the behaviour to date is acceptable.
- *Boxes 8 and 9*. But if there is an error or discrepancy, two courses of action are open to the person. The first course relates to the familiarity of the situation. Where the situation is familiar, the person engages in an unconscious scripted response. (The idea of a script or cognitive plan that refers to familiar sequences of events and behaviours is discussed in Chapter 7 in connection with memory.) The response in Box 8 brings into existence more behavioural patterns previously learned to confront the error or discrepancy so that it can be reduced. The second course of action arises if the reasons for the discrepancy between actual and desired conditions are not immediately obvious. In Box 9 the person attempts to

attribute a reason for the error or discrepancy. This can give rise to probing questions in an attempt to find acceptable explanations. An attributional view of motivation states that people take action after observing their behaviour through self-perception. **Attribution theory**, which is discussed in the context of perception in Chapter 5, puts forward the view that people become introspective with regard to what caused their behaviour. Was the cause of their behaviour something within themselves or from an external source? The outcome of this questioning will determine their future behaviour.

- *Box 10.* Out of the attributional search come questions such as, is the goal or standard still appealing in the eyes of the person, and what is the expectation of achieving it? Answers to these questions are reflected in the subjective expected utility of goal attainment in Box 10.
- *Box 11.* The individual's personal characteristics, such as needs, interests, and abilities, and situational factors, such as time and resource availability, can influence the value the person places on attaining his or her goal as shown in Box 10.
- *Boxes 12 and 13.* As a result of the impact of personal and situational characteristics on the subjective expected utility of goal attainment, two things can happen. There could be a mental switch and change of goal (Box 12), or a change in behaviour (Box 13), or both. This takes us back to the start of the cycle.

In Klein's model you will notice that it incorporates and integrates numerous psychological perspectives, such as goal-setting, expectancy, feedback, control, attribution, and information-processing. Obviously this model needs refinement, but there is no doubt it has potential as an explanatory mechanism in the field of work motivation. Thompson and McHugh (2002) had complimentary things to say about Klein's integrated control model:

Klein's model is the most powerful development in motivation theory in the last 15 years . . . it integrates cognitive motivation theories, theories of scripted response, theories of causal perception, and attribution and cybernetic theories (information processing and control of action). It is consistent with the theories of social learning, equity, expectancy, and satisfaction theories. It also claims to focus more on individuals' self-regulation in response to external influences than on the effects of those influences, such as providing goals and incentives, as is the case with most motivation theories. Since the model acknowledges the influence of individual and situational factors, such as ability, past experience, social comparison processes, situational constraints and reward structures, this theory offers some hope of reconciling cognitive rational theories with approaches emphasising subjectivity and its construction.

However, the propositions that Klein derives from control theory are still to be tested in any detail. Even so, . . . it does offer considerable insight into the dynamic process of self-regulation in individual action and how automatic and unconscious processes operate simultaneously to initiate and direct behaviour. Although Klein's model represents a more sophisticated and multivariate theory than previous accounts of motivation, any predictions would have to view practical applications as still a long way off.

Others have sought to integrate motivation theories —for example, Locke (1991). Brotherton (1999) also advocates a control and integration view. In integrating diverse factors he shows a preference for facilitation not control in his conceptualisation of motivation. He feels that there is too much of a tendency to feed managers with diets of oversimple and inadequate models of motivation when what is required is more complex approaches of the type we have been discussing above.

SOCIAL IDENTITY PERSPECTIVE

There has been a strong emphasis on individual motivation in the various theoretical positions reviewed in this chapter to date. A trend in recent years is the application of social identity theory to motivation. This approach (which is also acknowledged in the context of inter-group behaviour in Chapter 10 and stereotyping in Chapter 5) takes the view that group-based needs play an important motivational role in which an individual's social identity is crucial. The social identity approach outlines how membership in social groups affects the self-concept. Central to this approach is the proposition that through social identification one sees oneself as at one with the group, or belonging to the group, and individuals define themselves in terms of their group membership and apply the characteristics that are typical of the group to the self. The concept also emphasises that an individual derives part of his self-concept from knowledge obtained through membership of the group, backed up by the value of association with the group, or through the emotional significance of group membership. So experiences derived from group membership are internalised and become part of "who you are" (Van Knippenberg, 2000).

Identification with the group leads to individuals seeing themselves in terms of the characteristics they share with other members of their in-groups. In effect, shared social identity, as opposed to identity based on the individual's idiosyncratic characteristics that differentiate one person from the other (personal identity), makes its presence felt. Identification with the group thus blurs the distinction between the self and the group and turns the group into part of the self (Smith and Henry, 1996). Therefore, the social or collective self is influential in shaping our attitudes, perception, and behaviour. The more one identifies with the group the more one is likely to act in accordance with the group's beliefs, norms, and values. When the latter are internalised and defined as part of the self, people want to follow the rules and live up to those values even if the process is not monitored and rewards or punishment are unlikely. The potency of social identity would be greater if a state such as self-actualisation was a collective rather than an individual experience (Haslam, Powell, and Turner, 2000).

One should not get carried away by the endorsement of social identity above, and heed a word of caution from Van Knippenberg:

even though identification with the group may lead individuals to act in a way typical of the group, this does not always mean that individuals who identify with the group always act in accordance with the social identity based in that group membership. Social identity is only a prominent or striking feature (salient) when it is considered highly functional for the individual. Salience normally enters the equation when a significant event is experienced by the group —e.g., the group merging with another group, inter-group competition or conflict, or the influx of newcomers or outsiders to the group.

With regard to social identity and motivation, Van Knippenberg (2000) is of the view that the motivation to exert effort on behalf of the collective (the group) is affected by social identity, particularly when the latter is *salient*. Where the individual perceives the group to be concerned with good performance, he or she decides to lend a hand. In such circumstances the individual is motivated to voluntarily make a contribution and is not pressurised to do so by the group. Van Knippenberg draws a distinction between task performance and contextual performance. Task performance is job-related (that which one was hired to do). Contextual performance amounts to organisational citizenship types of behaviour—i.e., behaviour that supports the psychological, social, and organisational environment in which task performance takes place, such as helping others, and being willing to act as an able ambassador for the organisation externally. In a sense, contextual performance amounts to voluntary behaviour, and it is optional.

It is said that the relationship between social identity and group performance is most potent when simple tasks are examined. Where tasks are complex it appears that the skill or competency level of the individual would be crucial, but, equally, cooperation and information from the group would be invaluable. There may be a downside in the relationship between social identity and group performance where the group develops lower productivity norms (as was the case with workers in the Bank Wiring Room in the Hawthorne experiments discussed in Chapter 1) because of conflict between management and workers, or where social loafing (see Chapter 10) is tolerated.

PROBLEMS WITH MOTIVATION

Boredom

Monotony and boredom are associated with problems of motivation and, as such, are risk factors in safety at work. Boredom can be caused by a number of factors, and is a particular problem in mass production industries. The following factors may cause boredom:

- *Lack of variety and challenge.* Lack of variety and the absence of challenge due to a short job cycle, which is a result of keeping the number of operations to a minimum, causes boredom. A comment by an assembly line worker in a car plant a number of years ago highlights this problem: "The job gets so sickening, day in day out, plugging in ignition wires. I get through one motor, turn around and there's another staring me in the face. It is sickening" (Strauss & Sayles, 1960). Accidents can occur when employees perform repetitive tasks by instinct rather than thinking about what they are doing.
- *Lack of skill and independence.* Another source of boredom is the lack of opportunity to exercise skill or to act independently. This arises when the work is subdivided and simplified to such an extent that the person feels there is little scope to exercise ingenuity or initiative. As a result, the individual's contribution seems to be negligible. For some people the challenge of the job is important, and when they experience an absence of challenge they feel dissatisfied. But it should be noted that others dislike a demanding job and prefer to day-dream, and this is more likely to be possible in a job that does not offer much of a challenge—in fact in a job that is likely to require only surface attention. However, having pride in one's work and involvement in the efficient execution of one's duties is a good way of keeping alert and thus avoiding mistakes and most accidents.
- *Pace of work.* Another factor contributing to boredom is the inability to control the pace of work, particularly on an assembly line where a machine determines how fast somebody will work. The relentless rhythm of the assembly line makes natural pacing difficult or impossible, although the worker may have some opportunity to vary the pace of work by "bank building". Probably most people want a varied work pace, but some prefer to be machine-paced because they find that there is no need to pay attention to how fast they work, and that in these circumstances there is little interference from the supervisor. Eventually, people accept the rhythm of movement imposed on them.

How does one combat boredom? A number of suggestions appear in Panel 4.7.

PANEL 4.7: Combating boredom

Workers try to alleviate boredom in a number of ways. Some try to make a game out of work by varying the speed of the production line and setting their own subtargets. Some might make frequent visits to the cloakroom or, if the noise is not too loud, engage in conversation. Other outlets can be gambling or horseplay, and the ultimate tactic would be to go absent or leave the organisation altogether. There may also be attempts to change work practices, and active resistance to management initiatives could be mounted.

Management could also take action to alleviate boredom and prevent people from nodding off. Canned music may be used as a means of keeping people at least partially awake. Another method is to startle workers into instant wakefulness by an occasional announcement over the loudspeakers, though this should be done with due care. The taped music could be switched off in mid-bar, followed by a 30-second pause to give the "sleeper" time to wake up, and then an announcement made in a clear-toned, urgent voice that, in a few moments there will be a special announcement.

Items likely to scare people should be avoided, but the announcement ought to be of some interest. An item of low interest would be the dangers of smoking in the toilet, whereas an item of strong interest would be news of a works outing, or the latest score in a major football match. News related to work should be confined to relevant items such as proposed pay increases or a visit by a factory inspector. Controversial subjects should be avoided.

Managerial action in the form of job redesign could be taken to cope with repetitive work (discussed in the section on job design later in the chapter). Technology can also come to the rescue. The appearance on the work scene of the industrial robot and automatic handling systems has had the effect of eliminating repetitive, tedious, and often unpleasant tasks. At Volvo, automatic welding lines replaced manual jigs and manual welding lines, freeing people from hard and tedious work where absenteeism and labour turnover were high. Likewise, the use of paint-spraying robots can eliminate unhealthy and monotonous jobs. The automation of work processes involving asbestos, lead-based products, or intensive dust creation is welcome on health grounds. At the same time, such developments amount to de-skilling of jobs and, in turn, create other problems.

Rest pauses

The effect of a rest pause is particularly beneficial in counteracting repetitive work of a monotonous nature. Heavy muscular work, tasks that require close concentration, and operations involving a continuous standing or sitting posture are also suitable cases for the introduction of rest pauses. The speed of operations at work is another factor to be considered in relation to rest pauses. Work conditions that require a working rate in excess of the natural rhythm of the body are likely to lead to fatigue and, if they cannot be avoided, at least their effects should be alleviated by suitable rest pauses.

Because of complaints about fatigue among operators of VDU equipment, it is suggested that regular rest pauses should be provided for employees who frequently use VDUs. Ideally, continuous work at a VDU should be interrupted by occasional movement or by spells of alternative work. Otherwise it is recommended that mid-morning and mid-afternoon breaks of 10 to 15 minutes are taken, away from the equipment. The maximum continuous work period at a VDU should not exceed 2 hours, and there should be no more than 7 hours viewing in any one day (Anderson, 1980).

Apart from such scheduled rest pauses, the unscheduled rest pause is a feature of repetitive tasks, when the worker decides for himself or herself to take a break. At other times workers experience a lapse of attention (an involuntary rest pause) and this can give rise to mistakes and accidents. It is said that just before a rest pause, inhibition sets in—central nervous fatigue—and this undermines to some extent what has previously been learnt, leading to a lower level of performance. Several minutes after the rest pause, disinhibition and consolidation occur to restore performance to the customary level, which reflects what the employee has learnt about the job to date.

CULTURE AND MOTIVATION

In evaluating motivation theories it is important to consider the significance of culture. There is a view that the influence of US culture is paramount in the development of motivation theories. Adler (2002) maintains that:

> most motivation theories in use today were developed in the US by Americans and about Americans. Of the theories that were not, many have been strongly influenced by American theories. Americans' strong emphasis on individualism has led to expectancy and equity theories of motivation—theories that emphasise rational, independent thought as the primary basis of human behaviour. The emphasis placed on achievement is not surprising given Americans' willingness to accept risk and their high concern for performance. The theories therefore do not offer universal explanations of motivation: rather they reflect the value system of Americans.

Unfortunately, many Americans as well as non-American managers have treated American theories as the best or only way to understand motivation. They are neither. American motivation theories, although too often assumed to reflect universal values, have failed to provide consistently useful explanations for behaviour outside the US. Managers must therefore guard against imposing domestic American management theories in their global business practices.

There is more detailed discussion of culture in Chapter 15. In particular, refer to the work of Hofestede and Trompenaars in the subsection on "Cross-cultural studies".

JOB DESIGN

Job design draws heavily on motivation theory and to a certain extent on organisational theory, discussed in Chapter 14. In this section the primary focus is on:

* job specialisation;
* job rotation;
* job enlargement;
* job enrichment;
* job characteristics model;
* the relationship between job design and new technology;
* social information;
* work schedules; and
* worker flexibility.

Job specialisation

An early feature of job design was **job specialisation**, pioneered by Frederick W. Taylor, the main proponent of scientific management in the 1920s (Taylor, 1947). The following represents the approach he adopted (see also the discussion in Chapter 1):

* Study the way a job is done scientifically.
* Break down a job into its smallest component parts.
* Determine the most efficient way of performing each part of the job, in addition to the design of any tools needed and the layout of the workplace.
* Train workers to undertake the component parts of the job in the way laid down as the best.
* Use money as the primary incentive.

These principles were enshrined in the assembly line production process, with the alleged advantages of proficiency stemming from acute specialisation, less costly and shorter periods of job training, less remuneration because the job is unskilled, and greater managerial control. However, the disadvantages are that the individual's contribution is insignificant and lacks meaning; the individual does not have the opportunity to develop skills to further his or her career; and the work is repetitive and boring with negative side-effects such as dissatisfaction, apathy, and carelessness. Nevertheless, scientific management based on Taylor's principles still appears to be alive (see Panel 4.8).

In the 1950s, Walker and Guest (1952) studied people who worked in a car assembly plant in order to establish how satisfied they were with varied aspects of their jobs. The workers stated that, by and large, they were reasonably satisfied with matters such as pay, working conditions, and the quality of supervision. But they were extremely dissatisfied with the actual work they were doing.

PANEL 4.8: Scientific management—Mark 2

Professor Adler from the University of Southern California studied the work methods at a car factory in California, run by a company jointly owned by General Motors and Toyota. He attributes the company's great success to the widespread application of Taylor's principles of meticulous observation, and continuous refinement of work methods. Workers do their jobs in teams, with a high level of autonomy; for example, the stop-watches and clipboards are in the hands of the workers, not in the hands of supervisors and industrial engineers as in the original version of scientific management.

(*The Economist*, 1993)

It should be noted that job design in the plant was influenced by the principles of scientific management. The workers reported six factors as being responsible for dissatisfaction:

(1) Mechanical pacing by the assembly line, over which workers had no control.
(2) Repetitive work.
(3) Low level of skill required in the job.
(4) Involvement with only a small part of the overall production cycle.
(5) Limited social interaction with colleagues at the place of work.
(6) No control over the methods and tools used in the job.

It was observations from studies such as the one conducted by Walker and Guest that led management to reconsider the advisability of adhering religiously to the precepts of scientific management. It was recognised that the application of the principles of scientific management had implications in terms of efficiency but, if carried too far, acute specialisation would generate a number of adverse side-effects. As a result, there was a determination to devise ways to create less monotonous jobs. In this respect two alternative approaches to job redesign—**job rotation** and **job enlargement**—were developed.

Job rotation

This approach involves moving workers in a systematic way from one job to another in order to provide more interest and satisfaction at work. Supporters of this approach might argue that job rotation is an effective training method because a worker rotated through a number of related jobs ends up with a broader set of job skills. This provides the organisation with greater flexibility. On the other hand, opponents of job rotation maintain that the fundamental problem of routine jobs still exists under this approach. Their view is likely to be that the rotation cycle means that workers experience several routine jobs instead of one. Finally, those who advocate the benefits of job specialisation would argue that job rotation might adversely affect efficiency because one is not taking full advantage of the proficiency that evolves from specialising in one job.

Job enlargement

This approach—often referred to as "horizontal job loading"—entails an expansion of the worker's job to include tasks previously performed by other workers. The rationale for the change is that the increased number of tasks creates greater variety and interest, with a reduction in the monotony and boredom associated with the previous narrowly defined, specialised task. In practice, job enlargement has often failed to live up to expectations. This was particularly the case where the enlarged job was no more than a collection of simple tasks (Campion & McClelland, 1993).

Job enrichment

The disappointing results arising from the adoption of job rotation and job enlargement paved the way in the late 1950s for a more sophisticated approach to job design. This was called **job enrichment** and, as we saw earlier in this chapter, it was underpinned by Herzberg's dual-factor theory of motivation. He advocated *vertical job loading* to promote positive job-related experiences, such as a sense of achievement, responsibility, and recognition. Vertical loading amounts not only to adding more tasks to a job, as you find with horizontal loading, but also to granting the worker more control over the job. Herzberg (1968, 1974) viewed vertical job loading as a vehicle for enriching jobs in the following ways:

- *Accountability.* The person should be held responsible for his or her performance.
- *Achievement.* The person should feel that he or she is doing something worthy of note.
- *Feedback.* The person should receive unambiguous information about his or her performance.
- *Workpace.* The person should be able to set his or her pace at work, where this is practicable.
- *Control over resources.* The person should, where possible, have control over resources used in the job.

PANEL 4.9: Hackman and Oldham's five core job characteristics

(1) *Skill variety.* This focuses on the extent to which a job requires a number of different skills and talents. The job of a personnel specialist would receive a high score on this dimension, as would a nurse working with the elderly in their homes using professional skills of dressing wounds, listening, counselling, being empathetic, and appraising the supports and dangers in the person's home (West, 2000). But the job of an operator on a production assembly line would receive a low score.

(2) *Task identity.* This focuses on the extent to which the job requires the performance of a whole unit, which is identifiable with a visible outcome. The job of a carpenter, who constructs a piece of furniture from raw material, would receive a high score on this dimension, whereas an operator who solders wires on to a piece of equipment would receive a low score.

(3) *Task significance.* This focuses on the extent to which the job makes a significant impact on the lives and work of other people inside and outside the organisation. The job of a surgeon in a hospital would receive a high score on this dimension, whereas the job of a filing clerk would receive a low score.

(4) *Autonomy.* This can be viewed as the degree of freedom, discretion, and independence that a job possesses at both the planning and execution stages. The job of a college or university lecturer would receive a high score on this dimension, whereas the job of an accounts clerk, who is closely supervised, would receive a low score.

(5) *Feedback from the job.* This focuses on the extent to which direct and unambiguous information about the effectiveness of the job holder's performance is available while he or she is engaged in carrying out the job activities. The airline pilot receives information on the progress of the flight from the instrument panel in the cockpit and from ground control. The pilot's job would receive a high score on this dimension, whereas the job of a sales representative, who may have to wait some time to establish the effectiveness of his or her performance, would receive a low score.

FIGURE 4.7

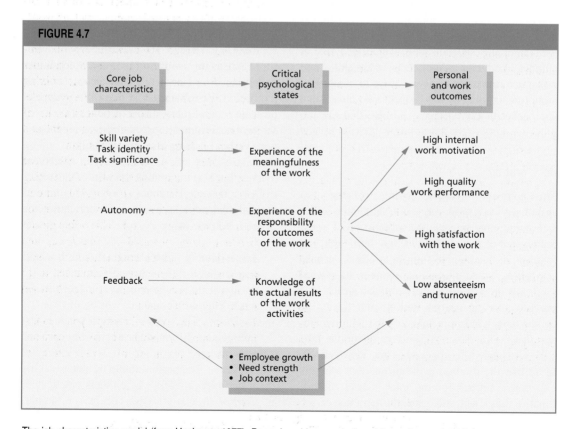

The job characteristics model (from Hackman, 1977). Reproduced by permission of the author and publisher.

There have been mixed results with the application of job enrichment schemes. Early successes were claimed by large organisations, such as AT&T in the USA and ICI in the UK, but equally one has to acknowledge that many job enrichment programmes have failed. Some organisations found them too costly to administer, and others felt that they did not live up to expectations (Griffin, 1982). Criticisms of the theoretical basis of job enrichment—the dual-factor theory—were highlighted earlier in the chapter. Job enrichment has lost the popularity it once had, but some of its ingredients are worth preserving. In the 1970s and early 1980s a new perspective, called the job characteristics approach, occupied a prime position in thinking about job design. It drew on motivational concepts, such as autonomy and feedback, but was enlarged to give serious consideration to differences between individuals in the way they respond to jobs.

The job characteristics model (JCM)

A development of the earlier approach to job enrichment is propounded by Hackman and Oldham (1975). The authors focus on what they call the five core characteristics of a job (see Panel 4.9 and Figure 4.7). The five characteristics are given a numerical value and are then combined into a single index called the motivating potential score (MPS) (see equation below).

The job diagnostic survey, filled out by the job holder, is used to measure the five core characteristics so as to arrive at the MPS calculation. For job enrichment to work, three factors have to be considered: employee growth, need strength, and current job context. For example, the individual with strong needs for personal growth will respond positively to a job that scores highly on the core dimensions (high MPS). But the individual who does not place much value on personal growth or satisfying higher-order needs would find a high MPS situation both uncomfortable and a source

of anxiety. It is also suggested that if an employee is grossly dissatisfied with contextual job factors (pay, job security, or supervision) job enrichment will not be as effective as if the reverse was true. Finally, the MPS is used to assess the extent to which the job is enriched. Where appropriate, the job may be enriched by redesigning it so as to increase its score on the core characteristics.

Hackman, Oldham, Janson, and Purdy (1975) developed a set of guidelines to help managers implement the job characteristics model. The implementing concepts are set out on the left-hand side of Figure 4.8. The motivating potential of jobs can be improved by the application of the following five implementing concepts:

- *Combining tasks.* Enlarge the range of tasks undertaken by an employee so as to increase the variety of the work and the individual's contribution. For example, a receptionist in a suite of offices could undertake tasks additional to his or her main duties, such as word-processing and telephonist duties.
- *Forming natural work units.* Provide employees with a job that incorporates a number of steps from start to finish, rather than offering them a fragmented part of the whole job cycle. This is likely to enhance the significance of the job in the eyes of the job occupant and increase the individual's contribution.
- *Establishing client relationships.* Allow the employee to take responsibility for making personal contacts with people inside and outside the organisation on matters connected with the processing of work. This offers greater freedom, more potential for feedback, and job variety. It can be contrasted with a system whereby the employee is expected to go through a supervisor or other third party when interfacing with clients.
- *Vertical loading.* Give the employee responsibilities normally associated with supervisors, such as the scheduling of work, control of

$$MPS = \frac{\left[\begin{array}{ccc} \text{Skill} & \times \text{Task} & \times \text{Task} \\ \text{variety} & \text{identity} & \text{significance} \end{array}\right]}{3} \times \text{Autonomy} \times \text{Feedback}$$

FIGURE 4.8

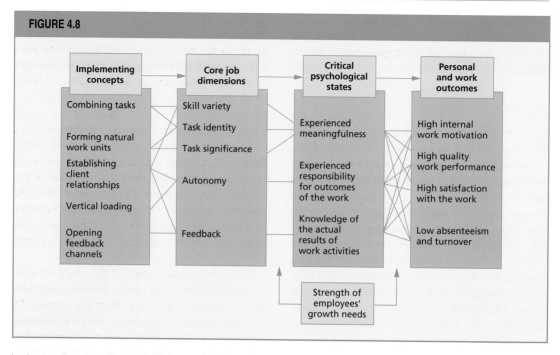

Implementation of the job characteristics model (from Hackman, Oldham, Janson, & Purdy, 1975). Copyright © 1975 by the Regents of the University of California. Reprinted by permission.

quality, determining priorities, recruiting and training, improving work practices, and so on. This offers the employee greater autonomy, with the result that the supervisory role needs adjustment (possibly a delicate situation for the remaining supervisors). Cordery and Wall (1985) argue that supervisors must receive help so as to change from an overseeing or controlling mentality to an enabling outlook.

• *Opening feedback channels.* Give the employee greater opportunities for feedback on performance. This could be achieved through analysis of performance showing how well the employee has done, and perhaps pointing to areas where performance could be improved.

Evaluation of JCM

The JCM has expanded Herzberg's concept of job enrichment and it draws on both needs theory and expectancy theory with its emphasis on

employees seeking to satisfy needs through the job. There is evidence supportive of the model (Kelly, 1992). In a study comparing work motivation in Bulgaria, Hungary, and the Netherlands, Roe, Zinovieva, Dienes and Tenttorn (2000) recognise that there are differences between these countries in the causes of job involvement and commitment, and that the JCM model does not fit equally well in different cultural settings, but they found that two of the critical psychological states in the model—experience of the meaningfulness of the work and experience of responsibility for the outcome of the work—mediated the relationship between job characteristics and motivation. However, weaknesses have been exposed by others. For example, in an evaluation of the model, Moorhead and Griffin (2004) observed that several apparent weaknesses in the model have come to light. First, the job diagnostic survey used to test the model is not always as valid and reliable as it should be. Secondly, the role of individual differences frequently has not been supported by scientific assessment. Thirdly, the implementation guidelines are not specific, and managers are forced to modify at least part of the model to use them. Nevertheless, the theory remains a popular perspective on job redesign.

Groups and job design

So far the focus has been primarily on job design in the context of individual jobs. But there are many situations where jobs have to be designed for groups (for a discussion of groups and teams, see Chapters 10 and 11). There are at least two reasons why one might consider groups in the context of job design. First, it may be more practicable and efficient to use a group to do a job, as with a maintenance crew. Secondly, the organisation may wish to use a group to transform the attitudes and behaviour of members, as with autonomous groups and work teams. This represents job enrichment at the group level and draws sustenance from the job characteristics model.

Autonomous work groups

With autonomous work groups or teams, the groups enjoy a substantial amount of self-determination in the management of their day-to-day work. This is tantamount to group control over the pace of work, the scheduling of work, the arranging of rest pauses, deciding on modes of inspection, selecting new members of the team, and performance appraisal of members. The consequence of this development could be a diminution in importance of the supervisor's role, if not its elimination. Other features of self-managed groups identified by Wall, Kemp, Jackson, and Clegg (1986) are a group of workers who:

- Perform tasks that are interrelated, and who bear responsibility for the end product.
- Possess a variety of skills that enable them to perform all or most of the tasks of the group.
- Are able to evaluate the group's performance, and provide feedback.

A departure from the traditional assembly line system of production in the manufacturing of cars took place in Volvo's plant in Uddevalla in Sweden, where the Volvo 740 model was built using teams (Kapstein, 1989). Each team consisted of seven to ten workers, working in one area, with an output rate of four cars per shift. Members of the team were trained to undertake all assembly jobs; in practice this meant that variety and diversity were built into the system and an average of 3 hours elapsed before a worker repeated the same task. Each team managed itself to a great extent by scheduling work, controlling quality, selecting members, etc. In effect they undertook the duties normally the responsibility of the supervisor. As a result, the teams had no first-line supervisors. However, they appointed a spokesperson, who reported to a plant manager. The latter reported to the chief of the manufacturing unit.

A significant advantage of the way jobs were designed at the Uddevalla plant was the avoidance of the routine and boredom experienced by workers on the conventional car assembly line where the duration of work cycles is no more than 1 or 2 minutes. An absence rate of 20% is associated with Volvo's conventional plants, but this rate dropped to 8% in the case of the Uddevalla plant. Also, the productivity record and quality were said to be better at the Uddevalla plant than at other Volvo plants in Sweden. From what has been said about the nature of jobs at the plant, one could conclude that such jobs score high in motivating potential on the job characteristics model.

Another example of self-managed teams applies to General Motors' joint venture with Toyota in California (referred to earlier in Panel 4.8). The factory workers there are divided into small teams, and each team is charged with defining its own jobs, monitoring the quality of output, and conducting daily quality audits; the latter is an activity previously undertaken by a group of inspectors. The team is also empowered to pull the stop-line cord, which activates a shutdown of the line if a problem is encountered.

Empowerment

In recent years the concept of **empowerment**, previously used by social scientists when dealing with issues concerning the powerlessness of minority groups in the United States, has entered the domain of motivation and job design. It is also used in connection with leadership, power, new organisational forms, and teambuilding (Menon, 2001). Conger and Kanungo (1988b) show a preference for empowerment as a motivational concept associated with "enabling" rather than "delegating". Enabling implies the creation of conditions by management so that people can experience enhanced motivation to achieve desired levels of performance. Apart from providing conditions, such as offering the necessary support and recognition, management is also expected to remove conditions that foster powerlessness.

A valid question to ask is what decisions empowered workers should take. According to Peiperl (1997) the answer is, whatever decisions employees think are appropriate for them to take at a particular time. It is said that without this level of discretion employees cannot be truly empowered. But the latter carries the risk of the manager being less in control and the employee being more exposed. Little empirical work has been done on empowerment. Conger and Kanungo mention some of its negative effects, such as the overconfidence it may create in subordinates, leading to misjudgements on their part. Kanter (1992) contrasted empowerment with the traditional concept of control. She maintained that powerlessness has a corrupting influence in organisations because it forces people to stick to the old rules, and she extolled the virtues of empowering employees to make their own decisions in their dealings with customers in conditions where quality of service is important.

The alleged advantages of the empowered workforce identified by Peiperl (1997) are:

- better customer service;
- flexibility (e.g., being able to respond to changes and opportunities as they arise);
- speed (e.g., swift local action to solve problems);
- formation of important cross-functional links or horizontal connections, which can arise spontaneously without resource implications; and
- certain rewards by way of compensation for the lack of a traditional career path.

However, it would be sensible to be discriminating in the acceptance of empowerment. Wall, Cordery, and Clegg (2002) argue that empowerment as a general recipe for enhancing work performance is flawed if applied universally. But they go on to say that initiatives to empower employees with regard to the execution of their core tasks are likely to be effective if a high level of operational uncertainty exists. Apparently the same outcome would not apply where predictability and less uncertainty exists.

An alternative path to empowerment, called "employee self-management" has been suggested (Shipper & Manz, 1992). The idea behind self-management is that, to a large extent, workers become their own managers. It involves an increasing reliance on workers' creative and intellectual capabilities. Self-management will take root in organisations where formally designated and empowered work teams are established. Apart from the organisational changes that are necessary in order to implement self-management, individuals must master certain basic skills. These are self-leadership skills (learning to lead oneself before attempting to lead others) and skills required to help other people to do the same.

There is further discussion of empowerment with reference to leadership in teams in Chapter 11. In Panel 4.10. there is an example of job enrichment drawing on the concepts of autonomous groups/self-managing teams and empowerment.

Process re-engineering

Process re-engineering is described by Hammer and Champy (1993) as a fundamental rethink and redesign of critical organisational processes, getting rid of processes that are unnecessary or redundant and placing greater reliance on cross-functional teams. It challenges the relevance of traditional bureaucratic structures and control. How does it impact on job redesign? The redesigned jobs are likely to be considerably enriched—e.g., greater variety of skills, including skills in relating to customers and suppliers (where appropriate), more challenge, extra responsibility, and improved pay. However, there is a downside to such a major overhaul of processes and jobs. It is unsettling

Shell UK Exploration and Production embarked on a programme of enriching jobs for offshore oil drilling workers, who are believed to be motivated by money (wages) and the two-week break back on land that alternates with two weeks of 12-hour shifts. Apparently it is difficult to get workers to take responsibility in such circumstances.

An experiment was conducted on two platforms run by the company aimed at improving the involvement of employees and increasing productivity. Tom Brown, the manager of the Dunlin Alpha and Cormorant Alpha platforms, believed that a better strategy to increase productivity was to give people more responsibility for their work. He discounted an alternative strategy which was to reduce manning levels by getting rid of some jobs. He was of the view that the level of worker motivation onshore was better than it was offshore, partly because of the style of management that created an offshore environment where workers were said have "stopped thinking".

Brown set about benchmarking and visited the K-Shoes factory in Kendal in the north of England, which had been running an empowerment programme for two years. He witnessed an enthusiasm among the K-Shoes workforce that he did not see in his own workforce. As a result, he hired the human resource consultancy used by K-Shoes and got them involved in testing out a teambuilding and empowerment programme on the two oil-drilling platforms.

The human resource consultancy introduced upward appraisal for managers: employees filled in questionnaires—focusing on attitudes and practical knowledge—about their bosses, and the managers were then given feedback on their strengths and weaknesses. A certain amount of cynicism greeted this exercise and some people did not feel comfortable with this type of change and gradually moved on. But many wanted to participate in the changes and tried to help each other. After a year, discernible progress was evident. Unlike before, people were now generating ideas to improve production. One example was a pump that never operated to its optimum level because the manufacturer had imposed overcautious limits on the running rate. When this was explained to management by the workers operating the pump, the manufacturer was contacted and confirmed that the pump could run to a higher rate without adverse consequences. In the changed climate there is an emphasis on listening, and comments are seriously considered. The employees with ideas are put in touch with people who can give them an answer. It is important to note that employees on the platforms are close to the tasks and therefore are in a good position to know what they are talking about.

A complicating feature on the two platforms was that only 20% of the production workers were directly employed by Shell, with the rest provided by three separate contractors. A work card system was used because of the contractual arrangements, and this involved a bureaucratic process of approvals and close control of various tasks by supervisors. The system was changed so that responsibility could be given to self-management teams, who were given the freedom to allocate work to team members. As a result, the paperwork and the procedures had to be refined to conform to autonomous groups or self-managing teams. It is claimed that savings of £90 million in production costs, equivalent to about 5% of the oil revenue from the platforms, resulted in the first year of the programme, and this experience led to adoption of similar programmes within the company.

(Donkin, 1997)

for employees during the long period of implementing the process of re-engineering, with the likelihood of them being over-anxious as a consequence of undertaking new jobs and severing contact with familiar routines and colleagues. A critical appraisal of the process of re-engineering organisations is provided by Grey and Mitev (1995), and there is further discussion of this practice in Chapter 14.

New technology and job design

New technology refers to a set of changes produced by the development of microchips, and can be broadly classified as advanced manufacturing technology and office technology. Advanced manufacturing technology includes a wide range of equipment used in the production process,

such as industrial robots for welding and paint-spraying, and computer-numerically controlled machine tools for precision cutting, drilling, or grinding of materials. Office technology places the emphasis on the storage, retrieval, presentation, and manipulation of information, as these are manifested in word-processing equipment and electronic point of sale equipment in stores. The latter uses bar codes on goods, not only to provide the customer with a record of the transaction but also to generate data for use by the organisation in ordering and stock control. Decision support systems, which are discussed in Chapter 8, fall into the category of office technology.

Earlier, the effects of modern technology in displacing labour and eliminating unhealthy and monotonous jobs were briefly considered, and in Chapter 14, the impact of modern technology on the organisation is examined. Here, however, we return to the former theme and continue the analysis of the relationship between technology and jobs. Many years ago in a study of the effects of automation, Blauner (1964) concluded that, instead of increasing feelings of alienation from the task, as was generally the view at that time, automation in the chemical industry actually reduced alienation. In a subsequent attempt to explain Blauner's conclusions, it has been suggested that the subjects in his study were blue-collar workers who performed fragmented manual work. As a result of automation, they became semi-skilled white-collar workers responsible for the monitoring of complete segments of work. Therefore, the consequence of the implementation of the automation process was the creation of enriched jobs; and it was not surprising to discover that alienation assumed a position of minor significance (Crawley & Spurgeon, 1979).

A valid question to ask is whether the same outcome would arise if computers were introduced into traditional white-collar jobs. Apparently, it depends upon the type of white-collar employment that is under consideration. When clerical workers have an involvement with the computer, which amounts to keying data and the retrieval of information, then it is said that the computer system restricts the employees' personal control over their work, with predictable results (Mumford & Banks, 1967). A similar finding was reported in a study of managerial staff in the production function, after a production and scheduling computer system was introduced into three assembly plants of an electronics company. The computer system contributed to changes in the content of the jobs of production planners and resulted in a loss of discretion, culminating in greater control of their work by the organisation. The same applied to all managers who were involved with the computer system; they all felt constrained by policies, plans, and procedures, and were more dependent on the work of others than ever before (Bjorn-Anderson & Pedersen, 1977).

In the two studies cited in the last paragraph there was evidence of alienation springing from white-collar employment (managerial and clerical staff) as a result of the implementation of computer systems. However, other evidence relating to white-collar employment seems to indicate that computer systems produce the opposite effect in particular circumstances. For example, specialists in computing and those in certain managerial positions are at an advantage when they can control the periods of time during which they use the computer. Also, in many cases the computer can enlarge the jobs of users (Kling & Scacchi, 1980). Other evidence showed that the introduction of computers generated more varied, interesting, responsible, and productive work (Oborne, 1994).

In today's world the combined effect of sophisticated computerised systems and reduced staffing levels has led to higher level skills, teamwork, and organic organisational systems. This is exemplified in work practices in flexible manufacturing plants where the power of computer software is evident when the plant is switched from the production of one product to another without changing machinery. With fewer workers in flexible manufacturing plants, it is necessary for them to perform a greater variety of tasks. As a result, there is a greater need for training and the development of higher skills.

Some positive and negative features of computerised information systems have been identified (Strassman, 1982). The *positive features* are:

- Responsibility shifts to the person most suited to carry out the task. For example, the author or journalist keys in information to the computer, and corrects the script or document. This process, together with a freer flow of information between individuals, blurs somewhat the traditional organisational roles. Also, the change in direction of information flows tends to create new social groups with their own particular phraseology.
- The shifts in resources and changing roles lead to enlarged jobs in a qualitative sense—i.e., more varied tasks when in contact with others for secretarial and support staff.
- An increase in communication results from the rapid turnaround of messages due to electronic mail systems.

PANEL 4.11: New technology and job characteristics

New technology has the effect of both enriching jobs and simplifying jobs, and this can occur within the same place of work. In this context the approach of those who introduce the new technology, and the principles underlying the job subjected to design or redesign, are crucial considerations. Therefore, poor planning and implementation of new technology, and poorly designed jobs, are likely to produce a less than satisfactory result.

As a general principle, simplification of jobs is probably more common than enrichment of jobs for workers in manufacturing industry who work on the shop floor.

Where the introduction of new technology results in enriched jobs, some skilled workers may perceive no material change in terms of the quality of the job. Others may perceive a material change in the sense that new skills are now needed, such as abstract thinking, computer literacy, and a broader view of organisational functioning.

Worker resistance to the introduction of new technology in itself is considered to be rare. Nevertheless, the resistance that exists is more likely to be directed at management who may be perceived as using the technology to exploit the workers.

It is not always apparent that management has seriously considered in advance the likely impact of new technology on various job characteristics. Long (1987) attributed failures in the operation of automated systems in the office more to poor planning, poor technical skills of managers, lack of training of users of the system, and uncertainty about the appropriate problems to tackle, than to technical failures.

The *negative features* are:

- The need for increased security measures can seriously disrupt working practices.
- An unhealthy identification with, and a personal attachment to, an electronic workstation may give rise to minor behavioural disturbances.

Arnold et al. (1998) draw a number of general conclusions from the debate on how new technology affects job characteristics (see Panel 4.11).

Wall, Corbett, Jackson, and Martin (1990) identified a number of job characteristics that ought to be considered prior to the introduction of new manufacturing technology. These characteristics, which may have a material influence on the performance of the socio-technical system (i.e., technology and people) and on the level of job satisfaction and dissatisfaction, are as follows.

- *Control.* This refers to control over when tasks are to be done, how they are to be done, and what happens at the boundary of the job.
- *Cognitive demand.* This refers to maintaining acute and constant vigilance over the process of diagnosing and solving problems. Accepting this condition is almost tantamount to acknowledging that advanced manufacturing technology requires sophisticated and flexible operators.

- *Responsibility.* The need to ensure that there is a clear line of responsibility for the technology and the output of the system.
- *Social interaction.* The quantity and quality of interaction between people.

The debate on the impact of technology on jobs and organisational systems is likely to continue for a long time, simply because the rate of change in this field is quite significant. There is now a view that the traditional status of technology as a variable determining a number of aspects of organisational structure, which obviously includes jobs, is in question. What appears to be critical is the impact of decisions to select technological equipment, the capabilities of the equipment, and the way it is used. In addition, the influence of cultural and political forces within the organisation with respect to the use of the technology, and the way key staff control computerised systems, are considerations that have to be borne in mind (Child, 1984a). The effects of technology on jobs that remain within organisations are likely to be two-fold: de-skilling in certain circumstances, and upskilling (increasing demands on skill) in other circumstances. Finally, the way technology affects skill is mediated by the way organisational designers exercise choice in the organisation of work (a view similar to that of Child). So it is difficult to make broad claims about the precise impact of technology on jobs, skills, and dehumanisation of work (Buchanan & Huczynski, 2004).

Further perspectives on job design

Other perspectives on job design include alternative approaches such as social information, work schedules, worker flexibility, and telecommuting.

Social information

Social information in the workplace shapes the individual's perceptions of the job and the way he or she responds to it (Meyer, 1994; Salancik & Pfeffer, 1978). Information on certain facets of work (e.g., management is caring around here) is transmitted to individuals by peers or others and registered as a critical judgement about work. In the example given, the newcomer to the organisation registers the impression that management has a humane streak. Salancik and Pfeffer have constructed a rather complex model, called the social information processing model of job design, which suggests that the needs of individuals, task perceptions, and reactions to work are socially constructed realities. The social information processing model has had a mixed reception from researchers in the field of job design (Thomas & Griffin, 1983); in fact, the way employees perceive their jobs is more complex than the model suggests. It is influenced not only by the social information received about the characteristics of the job, but also by how employees personally register the objective reality with respect to their jobs (Moorhead & Griffin, 2004).

Work schedules

Although not normally associated with job design, work schedules come between the employee and the job. They are aimed at improving the employee's experiences at work in the hope that the individual's attendance, motivation, and commitment will be better. Examples of work schedules are the "compressed working week", whereby the worker works longer hours on, say, Monday to Thursday, so that four days constitute the working week, and "flexitime", whereby the worker is committed to core times at work during the week, but outside those times he or she can choose a flexible work schedule. Flexitime can contribute to individual autonomy because it gives employees more control over their working hours. As a consequence, it has real motivational significance.

An alternative to the traditional work schedule is job sharing, whereby, for example, one employee works in the morning or for half the week, and the other works in the afternoon or for the remainder of the week. Job sharing could be desirable for people who prefer to work part-time, perhaps for family reasons. It can also be beneficial for the organisation because it is able to use the talents of people whose circumstances demand a flexible work schedule. A further example of a work schedule is the permanent part-time worker whose time allocation is expanded or contracted depending on the volume of work. Examples of contemporary work schedules facilitated by telecommuting, referred to later, appear in Panel 4.12.

Legislation has come into force in the UK giving employees with small children the right to ask to work flexibly (Clapperton, 2003). The British Chancellor of the Exchequer, Gordon Brown, made reference to an agenda for extending women's rights in a speech at the 2004 Labour Party Conference. Highlighting how little progress has been made on equal pay, maternity rights, the provision of childcare, and ending discrimination against women at work, he warned that the government had not yet done enough to reduce the gap in pay or to promote flexible working hours (Eaglesham, Turner, and Guthrie, 2004).

Worker flexibility

This approach amounts to a refinement of job rotation, which was discussed earlier. The central tenet of this approach is that it is advantageous to the organisation if employees are trained to perform a number of jobs, and can then be deployed as circumstances dictate. The system of remuneration should reflect this level of worker flexibility. The idea of the flexible worker has a certain appeal. It offers the worker a more varied and exciting range of work experiences than would apply with the normal process of job rotation, and of course the worker receives a financial

In a report published by the Institute of Management (1999), 80% of respondents (managers in 684 large, medium-sized, and small companies across a variety of sectors) said they used flexible work practices. These can include job sharing, reduced hours, home working, teleworking, and flexitime. A manufacturing manager at Hewlett Packard has the option to take time off or work from home, and uses this opportunity to undertake strategic planning or thinking, or to attend to personal matters.

British Telecommunications (BT) has made significant inroads into institutionalising home working in the UK. In 1998 it embarked on its "freedom to work" initiative and conducted an experiment that allowed 600 employees to design their own work patterns. By 2003 the scheme had spread to some 6000 of the company's employees who now work from home, producing a one-off saving of £36 million in office costs for BT and millions of pounds of reduced fuel costs for the rest of society. However, a number of employees who had previously taken up the company's offer of working from home subsequently opted to return to the office.

A manager with responsibility for projects and programmes at BT Syncordia, which designs and manages IT systems, works from home. In his last job he was always on the road and was finding it very difficult to keep abreast of e-mail. He felt that his home in East Anglia would be a better base than the head office in London. Although he still has a fair amount of travelling to do in his job of identifying and implementing current practice, he feels that working from home, with the support of modern technology, helps him to keep on top of the job better. His laptop computer connects with the company's intranet and e-mail via an ISDN line. The mobile phone is also an access point, and meetings are held via a video phone. This manager offers the following advice to somebody who might wish to emulate his example: (a) it helps if you have a room to escape from the family, and work hours have to be respected by them; (b) a heavy reliance on teleconferencing will mean you are not forgotten, but you need to be self-disciplined and your boss must make sure you are kept informed of all material incidents or events; and (c) you have to find ways to avoid feeling guilty because you are not working in the office.

In a recent book on this subject, Vega (2003) emphasises the feelings of loneliness and isolation that can accompany home working, and though it may be a viable and healthy environment for some, it may not be for the majority. She also maintains that people who work off-site may be using their own equipment or "corporate cast-offs", leading to marginalisation, and that the unseen worker suffers not only from creeping technical obsolescence but also is devoid of the opportunity to engage in "personal advertising". The result is said to be diminished status, feelings of loneliness, and personal isolation. The latter would seem to be crucial for a number of people, because they are denied the exchanges with colleagues and others in the office environment even though the frustration of commuting to work is no longer an irritant.

(Clapperton, 2003; Coles, 1999a; Donkin, 2003b)

incentive for becoming proficient at more than one job (Dupuy, 1990).

Telecommuting

This approach to work scheduling seems to be growing in importance and refers to employees working from home. Employees can perform a variety of tasks ranging from processing data to taking orders over the telephone. By offering this arrangement some employers may feel they are able to retain the services of skilled employees who might otherwise be lost to the organisation. Others might feel that there could be a valuable spin-off in terms of efficiency and effectiveness, and the promotion of loyalty from employees working in this way.

This type of work schedule can appeal to employees, who not only get satisfaction from not having to travel to work, but also welcome the freedom it offers in terms of flexible hours, informality of dress, and being able to get on with their work free from numerous office distractions. However, not everybody would welcome such an arrangement. Some employees may feel that they are not privy to important formal and informal discussions about developments at work, and they are denied the opportunity to sense the nature of politics in the main place of work. Others may feel that not being visible in the main office setting could be disadvantageous in terms of career advancement and salary increases. Also, one must not overlook nonwork distractions or difficulties, such as being isolated, interruptions from family and friends, delayed decision making with perhaps an excessive reliance on e-mail, and any lack of self-discipline. (Some other issues are raised in Panel 4.12.)

If people can work from home, they can work from anywhere; therefore, it is not surprising to witness the growth of outsourcing of call centres and other work activities to places like India. When reflecting on home working, one should bear in mind a need for a culture shift, a tolerance of more flexible work practices, and the development of appropriate management skills supportive of this type of initiative. For example, management based on outcomes rather than the physical presence of an employee will be crucial; also, the acquisition of new management skills and the establishment of new, more flexible processes will be critical to the control of the more widely distributed delegation and the management of related work. Because of the dearth of data on the take-up of home working, a 10-year research project, called "Tomorrow's Work", has been set up to look at emerging patterns of work. Microsoft, the Institute of Directors, and the Work Foundation (previously the Industrial Society) are among the organisations involved with the establishment of this project (Clapperton, 2003).

CHAPTER SUMMARY

- The concept of motivation consists of needs, motives, drives, and goals or incentives. Level of arousal, which is related to a drive and emotion, is an important feature of the motivated state. Frustration, which can produce either positive or negative reactions, can obstruct the attainment of the goals of the individual, and as such is an important ingredient in the motivational process.

- Need or content theories of motivation—the hierarchy of needs, ERG theory, achievement and power motivation, dual-factor theory, and theories X and Y—were considered and their shortcomings noted. Illustrations of the motivation of employees, including managers and sales representatives, were given.

- Cognitive or process theories of motivation—goal-setting, self-efficacy, expectancy theory, and equity theory—were discussed, with reference to budgeting in the case of goal-setting. Equity theory was considered relevant in the context of equitable rewards for efforts expended.

- It was recognised that there was a need to integrate the various perspectives on motivation, and therefore an integrated model of work motivation was examined and there was reference to other means to achieve integration. Social identity was considered a concept likely to increase our understanding of motivation at work.

- Problems of employee motivation were highlighted with reference to monotony and boredom, brought about by conditions such as a lack of variety and challenge in the job, lack of opportunity to exercise skill and to act independently, highly repetitive work, and an inability to control the pace of work. All of these can have a demotivating effect. Various measures to mitigate the effects of boredom were suggested. Rest pauses have particular relevance when considering work of a repetitive or monotonous nature.

- Before concluding the discussion of motivation theory it was felt necessary to point out that motivation theories could be culture-bound.

- As a logical extension of the discussion of motivation theories, developments in job design, together with the impact of new technology and work groups on job design, were reviewed. The significance of empowerment, self-management, and business process re-engineering in the context of job design was recognised. Other perspectives on job design, such as social information, work schedules (including telecommuting), and worker flexibility were examined.

QUESTIONS

(1) Illustrate what is meant by needs, motives, drives, arousal, goals or incentives.

(2) In what circumstances is frustration likely to generate destructive behaviour?

(3) Examine the similarities between any two content theories of motivation.

(4) Select any cognitive theory of motivation and explore its application in an organisational setting.

(5) Assess the value of equity theory.

(6) Distinguish between procedural justice and distributive justice in the context of equity theory.

(7) Examine the main features of Klein's integrated control model of work motivation.

(8) What causes boredom among workers in a factory, and what steps can be taken to reduce it?

(9) Why are rest pauses necessary in modern office conditions?

(10) Discuss the suggestion that US culture is paramount in the development of motivation theories.

(11) Examine the range of theories underpinning job design, noting any shortcomings.

(12) Why should one consider autonomous work groups, empowerment, and business process re-engineering when addressing issues connected with job design?

(13) Highlight significant points in the debate about the impact of new technology on job design.

(14) Contrast the dual-factor theory approach to job design with that of the job characteristics model.

(15) Comment on worker flexibility, work schedules, and telecommuting in the context of job design.

(16) Explain what is meant by self-efficacy and social identity in a motivational context.

SPOTLIGHT ON RELEVANT READING

Ambrose, M.L., & Kulik, C.T. (1999). Old friends, new faces. Motivation research in the 1990s. *Journal of Management, 25,* 231–292.

Menon, S.J. (2001). Employee empowerment: An integrative psychological approach. *Applied Psychology: An International Review, 50,* 153–180.

Nicholson, N. (2003). How to motivate your problem people. *Harvard Business Review,* January, 57–65.

Van Knippenberg, D. (2000). Work motivation and performance: A social identity perspective. *Applied Psychology: An International Review, 49,* 357–371.

Wegge, J. (2000). Participation in group goal-setting: Some novel findings and a comprehensive model as a new ending to an old story. *Applied Psychology: An International Review, 49,* 498–516.

Learning Outcomes

After studying this chapter you should be able to:

• Describe the framework that helps to explain the perception process.

• Understand the nature of extra-sensory perception.

• Outline the conventions governing selective perception.

• Identify the factors that make the organisation of perception difficult.

• Explain what is meant by perceptual interpretation, using examples.

• List the considerations to be taken into account when examining misinterpretations in person perception.

Perception

5

The process of perception is an
important activity in the life of
the individual. Our environment,
including the business environment,
is littered with stimuli trying to
attract our attention. The quality of
our perception depends on the way
we organise, process, and interpret
the stimuli or information reaching
our senses. When we interpret a
situation or event, we are then in a
position to respond. To sum up, the
framework for perception can be
described as follows: stimulus–
attention–organisation–
interpretation–response. However,
extra-sensory perception assumes a
different form. But the potential for
misperception has to be recognised.
As an extension of interpretation,
person perception is discussed. The
issues discussed in this chapter
impact on change and development
(Chapter 16) and human resource
practices (Chapter 17).

Contents

STIMULUS

Before any information can be registered it has to be sensed, and this is accomplished through the senses. The eventual response can be an intentional reaction to the stimulus received and processed, but equally it could be a reflex response that is generally outside the control of the person.

When focusing on a stimulus and how it is perceived, there are a number of philosophical views to consider. Although this subject is largely beyond the scope of this text, one such approach may be briefly acknowledged. The phenomenologists (see Chapter 1) are of the view that it is the way we cognitively construe or interpret the stimuli reaching our senses that determines our responses. So what we perceive as reality is a reconstruction of what is in our environment. This reconstruction involves adding information and ignoring parts of the information coming our way; the information added or ignored will depend not only on the experience, education, personality, and training of the perceiver, but also on the purpose for which the information is to be used.

The question is also asked whether perception is innate or learned. It is suggested that normal perception is to some extent learned. In one experimental study, kittens were brought up in the dark except during the period when the experiment was in progress (Held & Hein, 1963). One kitten was strapped into a basket and carried around by an active partner in a rotating arm during the experimental periods (see Figure 5.1). The active kitten had the superior view and developed normal perception, whereas the passive kitten remained effectively blind.

Additional evidence to support the role of learning in perception comes from studies in which humans wore special spectacles that had the effect of turning things upside down and reversed

FIGURE 5.1

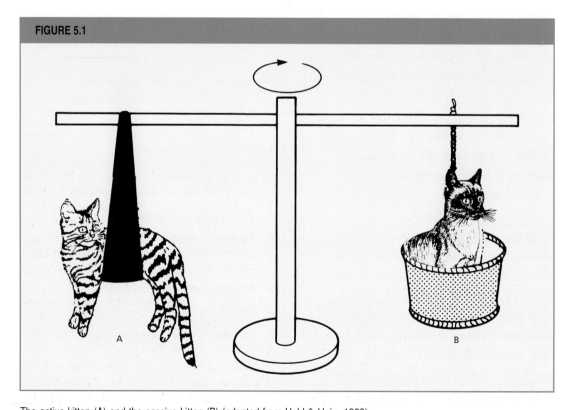

The active kitten (A) and the passive kitten (B) (adapted from Held & Hein, 1963).

FIGURE 5.2

The visual cliff (from Gibson, 1969).

right and left. In other words, their view of the world was inverted. The subjects who participated initially experienced problems with undertaking normal activities, but soon adapted (Kohler, 1962). In another experiment (Gibson, 1969), young animals and human infants were exposed to a visual cliff (see Figure 5.2). This is a patterned area with a steep drop in the middle, which is covered by glass to prevent a fall over the cliff. Both animals and human infants behaved in the same way by avoiding the deep side. The results of this experiment would suggest that perception is either innate or learned at a very early stage in the development of the animal or human.

In the light of the evidence presented above, many psychologists would support the view that perception is influenced by innate factors as well as being the product of experience. Oliver Sacks, a well-established British neurologist working in the USA, reported the case of a 50-year-old man who regained his sight after 45 years of blindness. When this man was tested he could identify visual features (e.g., letters, objects, colours, and motion), which would indicate the influence of nature or innate characteristics. However, the man could not see in the true sense of the word. Since most of his knowledge of the world came to him through the "touch" sense, learning even simple visual relationships required substantial effort (Sacks, 1993). An account of another person in similar circumstances is reported in Panel 5.1.

PANEL 5.1: Role of learning in perception

A Californian—Mike May—lost his sight at the age of 3. He was making a mud pie in the family garden and inadvertently mixed calcium carbide with water. When the mixture exploded he lost his left eye and was blinded in the right eye. At the age of 43 the sight in the blind eye was restored through a pioneering stem cell transplant: stem cells were implanted into his eye to repair scar tissue, and then the surgeons performed a cornea transplant, which restored his sight. This allowed Mike May to see again.

Two years on from the successful operation he was subjected to detailed analysis and it was found that his basic visual capacity was essentially intact and he experienced no deficiencies in simple form tasks, such as distinguishing between a square and a circle. He could also perceive colours and motion as well. But his ability to make sense out of three dimensions was severely impaired. He experienced difficulty identifying common objects, and sometimes could not tell whether an unfamiliar face belonged to a man or woman, or whether the person had a friendly or hostile expression on the face. For example, he could identify the gender of an unfamiliar face only 70% of the time and the expression on the face only 61% of the time. Rather than knowing from experience the stimulus he was perceiving he would make an educated guess, and this facility is improving with the passing of time. Before the operation Mike May was a champion blind skier. After the operation, initially he found the ski slopes terrifying once he was able to see them and would close his eye.

The experience of Mike May indicates that the visual stimuli registered by our eyes tell only part of the story about how we see. The brain must also learn how to process and interpret these signals.

(Henderson, 2003)

THE SENSES

We rely on the senses in order to experience the world around us and to adapt to our environment. Normal stimuli impinging on our senses are taken for granted, and it is when we find ourselves in a situation of sensory isolation that we positively yearn for stimuli from the outside world. When deprived of sensory stimulation, people suffer from disorientation, confusion, and emotional disturbance and are vulnerable to persuasion and pressure. Also in these circumstances, people engage in warding-off depression by dwelling on past experiences.

Humans possess at least 10 sensory channels. Each sense provides a channel through which information received from the world is transmitted to the brain. For each sense receptor at the surface of the body there are nerves that connect it to the brain and certain areas of the central nervous system. These nerves are made up of a bundle of neurones that are responsible for transmitting information by electrical impulses. Because there are different channels through which qualitatively different information flows, each type of information has its own pathway to the brain, but perception, through the different senses, can be integrated.

This is illustrated when we simultaneously hear the lecturer speak, feel the hardness of the chair we are seated on, and feel uncomfortably hot because of the high temperature of the room.

Vision

Vision is perhaps the most important and most often-used sense, and it has been suggested that we obtain three-quarters of our information about the world through sight. The physical stimulation necessary for vision is electromagnetic energy, in the wavelength range between 380 and 780 nanometres (a nanometre is a millionth of a millimetre). All creatures see approximately the same wave band of electromagnetic energy as light, but there are some differences. For example, humans are blind to ultra-violet light, but honeybees and ants can see it. Likewise, humans cannot perceive infrared radiation either by vision or touch because it lies between light and heat, but rattlesnakes are sensitive to it.

The eye

The eye encodes the information it receives as electromagnetic radiation (light) into a form that the human nervous system can use. The retina at the back of the eye transforms the light energy

PANEL 5.2: Dramatic improvement in night vision

In the late 1990s a physicist, Professor Josef Billie, of the University of Heidelberg, Germany, developed a super disposable contact lens that gives wearers the night vision of an owl. It is claimed that it will enable people to see up to five times better than normal in poor light, allowing them to pick up detail as small as facial features from 100 yards. It is anticipated that this development would bring significant improvements in safety during long car journeys at night, and be a distinct advantage to individuals playing sports in poor light and to soldiers on night missions.

The lenses are the outcome of research carried out over a 20-year period, but the commercial potential of this innovation only became a reality in 1998 due to a dramatic decrease in the costs of production. Currently, several leading manufacturers are conducting tests and patents have been applied for.

into electro-chemical energy; this manifests itself as an impulse in the group of nerves running from the eye to the brain (called the optic nerve). The nerve impulses are received by the brain, translated and identified, and the body's reaction to the information is then determined by nerve impulses from the brain to the muscles powering the actions of different parts of the body—legs, arms, hands, and so on.

As well as the wavelength of the light, the intensity of the light determines what we can or cannot see. The human eye is sensitive to light intensities ranging from a low of 5–10 lux to a high of 100,000 lux (a lux is 1 lumen per square metre of surface). Different tasks require different levels of illumination: imagine, for example, the amount of visual detail required to drive a car, with all the complex and changing visual information involved. A driver would, however, tolerate a much lower level of illumination when travelling at 20 mph than at 60 mph, as he or she would have more time in which to resolve dimly seen objects and distances. A recent technological development is very encouraging from the point of view of coping with lower levels of illumination (see Panel 5.2).

When specifying an optimum light level in the workplace (i.e., finding a light level that provides sufficient illumination without causing glare), it is important to consider the nature of the tasks being performed, and also to take account of individual differences. For instance, the performance of people with abnormal vision—e.g., partial sight defect—can be greatly improved by brighter illumination.

The sensory receptors in the eye are divided into two types: rods and cones. The cones perceive different wavelengths of light—i.e., they are sensitive to different colours. The cones are clustered near the centre of the retina. The rods are distributed around the perimeter of the retina, and cannot distinguish between different colours, but are much more sensitive to very low levels of light. Apparently, the primates are the only mammals that can see in colour, but birds and a number of other animals have colour vision. One suggestion is that as most mammals are active at night, they are operating in low light levels; the colour receptors are either not functioning or not present. It has been proposed that mammals do in fact possess all the receptors needed to see colours, but that the process by which the brain recognises the nerve impulses triggered by different colours has not evolved. This type of example highlights the importance of the two sides of visual perception —the physical equipment of the eye and the nervous system, and the psychological processes occurring in the brain to analyse and identify nerve impulses.

The choice of green for use in early VDUs was probably due to the availability of green phosphor. Red is a favoured choice for many displays where light-emitting diodes are used (e.g., in electronic calculators). Red appears to be identified as distinctive more frequently than any other colour of the same brightness, and red numerals are far more legible than green ones.

Colour perception

A number of workplace problems connected with abnormal colour vision have been identified, such as inefficiency, financial loss, personal embarrassment, and danger (Voke, 1982). Mistakes in colour identification with unacceptable consequences that have occurred in the UK include: a day's

TABLE 5.1

Diseases causing colour vision disturbances (from Voke, 1982): Reproduced by permission of Reed Elsevier (UK) Ltd, trading as Lexis Nexis Butterworths

Disease	Colour vision change
Diabetes mellitus	Blue defects
Multiple sclerosis	Red-yellow defects
Pernicious anaemia	Green defect
Addision's disease	Blue-yellow defect
Vitamin A deficiency	Most colours
Congenital jaundice	Blue and green defects
Malnutrition	All colours
Spinal cerebellar ataxia } Friedrich's ataxia	Red-green defect first, then mostly green defect
Brain tumour, trauma, concussion	Red-green or blue-yellow defects
Vascular accidents (stroke)	Various
Cerebral cortex disease	Blue defect
Cortical lesions	Blue defect
Syphilis	Red-green defect, blue defect
Alcoholism and cirrhosis of the liver	Blue defect

production of colour-coded resistors had to be discarded; a crop of unripe tomatoes was picked too early; a buyer experienced difficulty in the selection of cured tobacco leaves; the wrong coloured thread was used in the weaving of a piece of carpet; a red entry was put in the place of a black one in an accountant's records; and a colour-blind electrician received an electric shock from faulty wiring on a piece of equipment. It is therefore important to consider the implications of employing people with defective colour perception.

It is said that 6% of males and 0.5% of females have a deficiency when it comes to discriminating between colours (Oborne, 1995), but very few people are colour-blind. The most common form of deficiency in discriminating between colours is not being able to discriminate between the colours red, green, and blue. The most common type of colour-blind person is the individual who might confuse red with green, or yellow with blue. The relatively rare individual who is really colour-blind (about 0.003% of the population) sees only white, black, and shades of grey. Such a person is described as *monochromat* (Oborne, 1995).

However, it should be noted that certain colours placed on certain backgrounds can be a significant problem for those with normal vision

and may lead to difficulties in focusing on a range of colours simultaneously, causing headaches or fatigue. Mistaking colours can be traced to a genetic factor, and there are a number of diseases associated with colour vision defects. These are shown in Table 5.1.

The human eye experiences difficulty accommodating a variety of colours shown simultaneously on a display, and this can result in fatigue. This is more common when one colour is distanced from another. For example, a wiring operator may have to manipulate a small coloured cable, while also attending to a colour-coded wiring diagram, perhaps several centimetres away from the cable itself. After a time, the operator may find that he or she is confusing the colours of the cables and the colours on the diagram and making errors, actually mistaking one colour for another.

Glare

Light has to be evenly distributed, otherwise glare will result, causing discomfort, visual fatigue, and accidents. Glare is caused by a marked contrast in brightness between two surfaces, which has the effect of concentrating the light in one direction rather than diffusing it (e.g., the effect produced when light descends on shiny metal or glossy paper on a desk).

Glare is something one must consider in relation to lighting and illumination, because it is as troublesome as inadequate lighting. It manifests itself in many different forms. For example, reflections from a VDU screen, from a bright metal trim, from decorations on units, and from the keys and the keyboard can all cause glare. Badly positioned signal lamps can be a source of glare, and glare can also arise because of the positioning and intensity of artificial light.

Glare is apparent when one part of our field of vision is brighter than the level of light to which the eye has adapted. An example of the brighter field of vision is a car headlight at night. Direct glare occurs when the light comes directly from a particular source. On the other hand, reflected glare is caused by very bright reflections from polished or glossy surfaces. When glare interferes with visual performance it is known as *disability glare*; where it causes discomfort, annoyance, irritation, or distraction, it is referred to as *discomfort glare*. It may not be easy to distinguish between the two in practice, but the effects are not in dispute, such as reduced performance through increased arousal and distraction, and the consumption of valuable mental power to avoid the glare. Whatever the source of glare, the visual comfort of the VDU operator is at stake. Steps have to be taken to control glare. One obvious way to control reflected glare from a VDU screen is to do something about the source of glare.

As well as glare, another issue to consider is visual flicker. Instead of our eyes coming into contact with a stimulus in the form of a stable light or illumination, we encounter a light that flickers. Warning lights that flash, or indicator lights, are examples of visual flickering. Excessive flicker from whatever source—e.g., deteriorating fluorescent lights—can have a detrimental effect on both health and working conditions.

Visual displays

These are important in providing the individual with pertinent information. There are several displays in a car that provide the driver with information. The windscreen is a kind of display —sometimes called a real-time display—from which the driver obtains information through vision concerning the speed of the car on the road, and the position of other vehicles. Another display is the instrument panel, which provides information about the internal functioning of the car as well as its relation to other parts of the car–road system. The design of the displays and controls will influence performance. If the driver cannot see the instrument panel, or cannot see through the windscreen, his or her performance will suffer.

Visual displays to show readings can assume different forms. In Figure 5.3 we have the following: (a) a vertical dial; (b) a horizontal dial; (c) a semicircular design; (d) a round design; and (e) an open window design. The smallest percentage of errors in reading the information on display was obtained with the open window design— the dial moves but the pointer remains fixed. The area to scan is the smallest and this could be an important consideration when it comes to accuracy of reading. However, when the direction and rate of movement of the pointer are required, as for example when assessing the speed of a car in motion, the moving pointer is more suitable (Feldman, 1971). Auditory signals may complement visual ones when one is overwhelmed by visual displays. Even in circumstances where visual displays are not overwhelming—e.g., as when reading the speedometer of a car—it might be useful if an auditory signal was emitted whenever the speed exceeded the statutory limit.

Visual perception is an important consideration when a consumer is faced with making a decision, and product advertising and packaging are designed in order to provide visual cues. In packaging, for example, a particular detergent in the past proudly displayed colour stripes with the words "colour safe", obviously appealing to the customer's natural desire to preserve the colour of garments going into the wash. The appearance of the product is critical because it has to compete with other detergents in the same display position in the supermarket. Likewise, expensive cosmetics are found in attractive packaging in order to project a glamorous image.

FIGURE 5.3

Visual display types (adapted from Feldman, 1971).

Hearing

The physical stimulus for hearing is waves of pressure in the air. The sound waves vary in frequency (pitch, measured in Hz), intensity (loudness), and complexity (tonal quality). Sounds that human beings can hear range from low tones of 20 Hz to high ones of 20,000 Hz. At the low end of the sound range we feel vibration more than we hear sound. We hear best in the range 1000–4000 Hz. Many animals, including cats and dogs, can hear high-pitched sounds that we cannot hear, and cats have an upper limit of approximately 150,000 Hz. Frequency and intensity are both important in determining perceived loudness. Tonal quality enables us to distinguish different musical instruments and different voices. But there are other sounds that have little or no tonal quality, and we call them noises—for example, the hissing noise made by blowing air across a microphone. A violin tone, by contrast, has many strong harmonics.

Noise is frequently described as unwanted sound —it can be unpleasant and bothersome, can interfere with the perception of wanted sound, and can be harmful in a physiological sense. Unwanted sound of this type can be referred to as acoustic noise. Too much noise can create an arousal state not compatible with good performance. Noise below 16 Hz is normally described as *infrasound*, and can be produced by any pulsating or throbbing piece of equipment, as we would expect to hear from ventilation systems in offices. Commonly experienced noise levels are shown in Table 5.2.

Continuous noise can have a detrimental effect on both the individual and the group. An example of noise that we invariably find irritating is the constant hum or whine of a cooling fan. The hum from a poor ventilation system, if acute, can be fatiguing and hypnotic. Apart from continuous noise, we also encounter *intermittent noise* in the form of sudden large bangs or impulses coming from any percussion type of machine—e.g., a gun or road hammer. Loud noises are known to cause hearing loss; in the old days boiler-makers and footplate men, for example, suffered impaired hearing because of loud noises (Feldman, 1971). Although people have the capacity to adapt to continuous loud noises, as happens in certain factories

TABLE 5.2

Noise levels related to environmental conditions

Decibels	Type of noise
140	Pain threshold
130	Pneumatic chipper
120	Loud automobile horn
110	
100	Inside underground train
90	
80	Average traffic on street corner
70	Conversational speech
60	Typical business office
50	Living room
40	Library
30	Bedroom at night
20	Broadcasting studio
10	
0	Threshold of hearing

and at parties, distracting noises are tolerated, but soon pose a psychological strain, leading to irritability and annoyance. Distraction, for whatever reason, causes errors.

It hardly needs stating that general architectural design should pay special attention to acoustics in places of work, for any spillover of ambient sound is irritating. Noise can be reduced at source by certain methods of noise absorption, such as placing padding around noisy machinery, using sound-absorbing wall and floor materials, arranging equipment in an appropriate way, and creating screens to reduce the level of reflected sound. Both the Health and Safety Commission in the UK and the European Commission have issued regulations and directives on noise control and

hearing protection. The upper level for exposure to industrial noise in the UK is 90 dB(A).

Finally, we should bear in mind that not all sounds are unpleasant or distracting, and people involved in marketing a product or service recognise the advantages of pleasant sounds. For example, advertisers use jingles—catchy tunes that people can hum or whistle—as a major awareness technique to associate a certain tune with a certain product through repetition. In recent years there has been selective use of popular music from many decades ago in TV advertisements.

Other senses

Smell and taste

The senses of smell and taste are based on the recognition of chemicals by special receptor cells. Smell receptors are located in the roof of the nasal passages and taste receptors are located in the taste buds on the tongue, cheeks, and throat. When chemicals that "smell" or "taste" come into contact with these cells, a nerve impulse is triggered and directed to the brain.

Whole industries have grown up around our perceptions of tastes and smells—many people regularly buy deodorant to suppress "unpleasant" smells, and perfume to make themselves smell attractive. In the late 1960s Proctor & Gamble added a fragrance with no functional benefit to a washing-up liquid. Flavourings are added to many products to disguise unpleasant tastes. Another example of an appeal to our sense of smell to promote sales appears in Panel 5.3.

PANEL 5.3: Smell means business

At Christmas time (mid-1990s), Woolworth's filled 20 of its stores with a seasonal aroma to enhance the festive season and shoppers sensed the mulled wine smell. The festive smell was chosen by a panel of the company's staff, who rejected such alternatives as the aroma of cloves and Christmas pudding, as a measure to increase sales. To create the desired effect, Woolworth's relied on fragrances provided by the British Oxygen Company (BOC) who can also offer odours of freshly baked bread or Christmas trees and sandalwood.

The secret of the technology developed by BOC is that the fragrances are first dissolved in liquid carbon dioxide. The solution can be stored in ordinary gas cylinders and be connected to the air conditioning system using an aroma dispenser. A timer controls the release of the gas, for a few seconds each hour. The system is automatic, unlike the procedure when aerosol cans are used. The fragrance turns directly into a gas to mix evenly with the air, whereas with an aerosol the droplets would drift to the ground.

(Green, 1995)

It is acknowledged that fragrance can enhance alertness and also increase performance on certain cognitive tasks (Baron & Bronfen, 1994). Baron and Kalsher (1996) examined whether the use of pleasant ambient fragrance might be a cost-effective way to combat drowsy driving—a significant cause of injuries and deaths. Participants in the study took part in a simulated driving task, which was performed under varying conditions. The results indicated that performance in the task was significantly enhanced by the presence of a pleasant fragrance, suggesting that the use of fragrance may be an expensive but effective means for maintaining alertness among persons engaged in potentially dangerous activities, such as driving.

Our perception of what is a "good" taste or smell is influenced strongly by social and cultural considerations and, at the same time, we are more disposed to accept a product if it tastes or smells pleasant.

Skin-based senses

Receptors for four different senses are found in the skin: touch; warmth; cold; and pain.

Touch. As for smell and taste, our sense of touch is conditioned by social and cultural factors. We think of smooth baby's skin as "pleasant" and work-roughened or chapped skin as "unpleasant" to touch. These conditioned responses are both used and reinforced by advertising: for example, an advertisement for hand cream, which promises to "leave the skin silky soft", both appeals to our idea of soft skin as being pleasant, and reinforces the idea of soft skin being desirable.

Warmth and cold. Warmth and cold are felt when the receptors in the skin pick up even and continuous temperature changes. The body's temperature is controlled by a complex self-regulating system located in the hypothalamus section of the brain. Under ordinary conditions of rest, the temperature deep in the body is maintained within the normal range of 97–99 °F. Above or below this level problems can arise, such as hyperthermia (heat stroke) when the body temperature reaches

108 °F, and hypothermia (effects of very cold conditions) when the body temperature drops to 95 °F. Naturally, both the extreme temperatures can affect performance.

Pain. The pain receptors appear to be stimulated by tissue destruction. When cells are destroyed, by touching a hot surface for example, a nerve impulse is sent to the brain signalling "pain", which then initiates a series of quick responses, such as snatching the burnt limb away from the hot surface. Interestingly, it has been shown that loss of a limb can often result in the feeling of pain in the limb that is actually no longer there. It is as though we lack the right type of nerve receptors to tell us that a limb is missing, and so the pain signals are used instead. However, one contributor at a conference on phantom limb phenomena maintained that not all phantom sensations are painful (Jarrett, 2005).

Finally, the two remaining senses are kinaesthesis and the vestibular sense.

Kinaesthesis

This is the sense of where one's limbs and body are in space—the way in which you can know where your hand or foot is, even in pitch darkness. The kinaesthesis receptors are located throughout the muscles, tendons, and joints of the body. These sensors inform us of the relative positions and movements of our limbs and of different parts of our body (Matlin & Foley, 1992). A proprioceptive sense (e.g., kinaesthetic), unlike other senses (e.g., vision), does not have a visible organ. But one must not ignore the fact that kinaesthesis underpins a visible sensory organ (e.g., the eyes); the position of the eyes is maintained by muscles that attach the eyes to the socket. The kinaesthetic receptors in these muscles provide information about the degree and direction of the eye's movement.

The worker, relying on kinaesthetic receptors, is kept informed unconsciously of what the body is doing without every part of it having to be monitored. For example, people who do not suffer from a physical disability can climb stairs efficiently because of kinaesthetic feedback emanating from the muscles, tendons, and joints, when in motion. When walking or climbing we do not always have to look down in the direction of our feet in order to know where to place the next step. The kinaesthetic sensory receptors, located in the hand, arm, and shoulder muscles, allow the worker to use the hands efficiently above the head or out of sight.

Receptors located in the muscles convey information about the extent to which a muscle is being stretched, as well as the rate of stretching. Receptors in the tendons provide information about the degree of movement of the joints (i.e., the speed and the direction of movement). Another kinaesthetic receptor is sensitive to deep pressure and to any deformity in the tissue in which it is located. It is now apparent that the kinaesthetic system is made up of a number of sub-systems, all giving the worker information about where the limbs and body generally are positioned in space.

The kinaesthetic system is of critical importance in the field of training and the utilisation of motor skills (e.g., manual dexterity, finger dexterity, wrist and finger movement, and reaction time). Typing is a motor skill, and feedback from the kinaesthetic receptors located in the fingers, arms, shoulder muscles, and joints is valuable information for the typist or keyboard operator, because it allows him or her to be able to sense where the fingers ought to be placed without engaging in a conscious act.

Vestibular

The vestibular system, which maintains our sense of balance and movement, has receptors located in the inner ear and is primarily concerned with maintaining the body's posture and equilibrium. The receptors enable the person to maintain an upright posture, and to control the body's position in space. These receptors also provide information about the speed and direction of the body, the head's rotation, and its position when static—is it upright, upside down, or leaning over?

In conditions of substantial motion found on board a ship in rough seas, certain people can be prone to motion sickness (e.g., nausea, leading to vomiting), though it is possible to adapt to these conditions over time. It is the vestibular system in the ear that triggers the sensation of motion sickness. In another situation, a person suffers from a severe head injury following a road accident or an accident on a construction site; as a result, the balance organs are affected, producing symptoms of dizziness, nausea, disorientation, and so on.

The kinaesthetic and vestibular senses are important parts of our sensory system that are often ignored. Alcohol and drugs can impair the functioning of our sensory system, including our kinaesthetic and vestibular senses. The significance of the final two senses is apparent in a roadside scene where a policeman waves down a suspected drunken driver and asks him to pull over. He requests that the driver stands close to his car, tilts his head back at an angle, and then is asked to touch his nose with each finger tip. Understandably, the driver has great difficulty in doing so!

Overview

The interlocking system of the senses examined here provides a network for registering stimuli both internal and external to an organism. Sense receptors can be overloaded and cease to register stimuli. For example, after a while a person wearing perfume can no longer smell it, whereas others are still immediately aware of it. Senses are also affected by changes in the individual's surroundings, habits, and circumstances. For example, it has been shown that confinement in an isolation chamber promotes an increased tolerance of pain (Feldman, 1971).

The importance of the senses to the world of work is seen when our attention focuses on people's relationship to machines and to the physical work environment. Factors external to the person—the physical stimuli in our environment—and the disposition of the person will be considered shortly.

Extra-sensory perception

Some people accept the existence of extra-sensory perception—that is, perception without a basis in the various sensations in the senses discussed above. Bem and Honorton (1994) refer to it as "Psi"—an unusual process of information or energy transfer that is currently unexplained in terms of known physical or biological mechanisms. Included under the umbrella of Psi are alleged abilities such as telepathy (reading other people's thoughts) and clairvoyance (perceiving distant objects).

Parapsychologists, who examine extra-sensory perception and other paranormal events (or events outside our normal experience or knowledge), suggest that there are several manifestations of this phenomenon, such as the following (Baron, 2002):

- *Precognition.* The ability to foretell future events. Psychics and fortune-tellers make money out of their alleged capability to predict future events.
- *Clairvoyance.* The ability to perceive objects or events that are not registered by our senses, such as knowing which card will be played next in a card game.
- *Telepathy.* A skill used by mind-readers, which involves the direct transmission of thought from one person to another.
- *Psychokinesis.* The ability to change or transform an aspect of the physical world through the process of thought (e.g., bending spoons, moving objects, or making them rise into the air using the mind).

Most psychologists are sceptical about the existence of extra-sensory perception. One reason given for doubting its existence is the repeated failure to replicate instances of this phenomenon (i.e., certain approaches yield results supportive of extra-sensory perception at one moment in time but not at other times) (Milton & Wiseman, 1999). There is also a view that the few experiments supportive of the existence of extra-sensory perception are conducted by those convinced of its existence. While parapsychologists have endeavoured to increase the rigour of their research with improved techniques, most psychologists, such as Hyman (1994), remain to be convinced that something useful will emerge from this research.

ATTENTION (SELECTIVE PERCEPTION)

In everyday life many stimuli vie for the attention of the individual. On commercial television the consumer is bombarded with a large number of messages. Likewise when one enters a chemist shop to buy medicine, one is exposed to many products. The investor interested in the financial health of a company potentially has a welter of information from which to choose. However, we cannot attend to all stimuli, so selectivity must be exercised. Selective perception amounts to picking out those stimuli that are most likely to be important and ignoring the others, with obvious advantages (Matlin & Foley, 1992). But remember it would be detrimental to the perceiver if important information is ignored (Saul & Moore, 1993). Certain conventions govern selective perception, and these are discussed with reference to:

- external physical stimuli;
- absolute and differential thresholds; and
- the disposition of the perceiver.

External physical stimuli

Certain types of external physical stimuli attract our attention, such as size (e.g., large objects); repetition (e.g., events that occur repeatedly); position (e.g., of an advertisement on a newspaper page); colour; moving objects in a stationary setting; novelty; and contrast. All of these stimuli have particular properties that cause us to focus attention on them. These stimuli are discussed in the following sections and then general applications are explored.

Size

In studying the effects of advertising, physical stimuli such as size, repetition, position, and colour have been analysed (Anastasi, 1979). Increasing the size of an advertisement will generally increase its readership—it encounters less competition from other advertisements on a newspaper or magazine page. But obviously there is limited scope for the enlargement of the advertisement. In a large advertisement there is an opportunity to include more illustrations and more text. Advertisements with a large proportion of unfilled background (or "white space") tend to attract attention because of their novelty, stark simplicity, and arresting appearance. With regard to print size, it is suggested that increasing the print size of an advertisement will increase the odds of gaining the consumer's attention (Finn, 1988).

Repetition

Repetition is an important factor aimed at increasing the readership of an advertisement. For those readers who notice the advertisement on more than one occasion, the repeated exposure strengthens the initial impact of the advertisement. Constant repetition is said to produce familiarity, and if a brand is relatively risk-free with some incentive given at the point of sale (e.g., a price discount), shoppers may purchase the product because of accumulated familiarity, even though they have not actively attended to the advertising message.

Position

The position of an advertisement within a magazine or newspaper is crucial. Placing an advertisement near a popular editorial feature gives it an advantage, particularly where the content of the advertisement bears some relationship to the editorial: for example, it is important to place advertisements for books on or near the book review pages. Such a location helps to select an interested audience and attract readers at a time when they are particularly receptive to the appeal of the product. It is claimed that placing advertisements on and inside the front cover, on page 1, and both on and inside the back cover of a magazine creates a significant readership advantage of between 30% and 64% over positions on the inside pages (Starch, 1961, cited in Anastasi, 1979).

With respect to position within a page, it seems that the upper half of a page gets more attention than the lower half, and the left-hand side of the page gets more attention than the right (Berkman & Gilson, 1998). Another study reports greater attention for advertisements located in the front rather than the back part of the magazine, on the right-hand pages rather than the left-hand pages in the open magazine, and on the inside front, inside back, and outside back cover (Finn, 1988). Position is considered important when specific groceries are located in particular parts of a store, and certain items are displayed near cash tills.

Colour

Colour is often used as a device to attract attention and portray realism. In a mass of black and white, a modicum of colour catches the eye. Where colour is still a novelty, as with newspapers, the addition of even a single colour to an advertisement will enhance its attention-getting value. Colour can be used to emphasise the attractive features of a product or to create a suitable atmosphere—high technology products such as cameras are usually produced in black or metallic finishes, although some have been marketed with a less serious, more sporty image, in bright primary colours. Some products, such as cars, come in a variety of colours, but others, such as toothpaste, are in a limited range of colours—it would somehow seem incongruous to use black toothpaste.

Standards (based on psychological research) for the optimum use of colour in coding systems have been adopted by the British Standards Institution after collaboration with industry. There are, for example, colour codes to denote different types of fire extinguisher, for industrial and medical gas cylinders, for the hatched yellow lines at busy crossroads, and for traffic signalling. Colour can be used in the workplace for the enhancement of lighting effects, for creating pleasant surroundings, and for putting across and reinforcing safety messages.

When planning the colour scheme or decor for a room it is important to consider the use to which the room will be put. For repetitive and monotonous activities the overall decor could be made more stimulating by providing small areas of bright colours. A large working area can be divided into smaller identifiable segments by using different colour schemes that complement each other. Where mental concentration is a necessary

TABLE 5.3

The effects of different colours

Colour	Psychological effect	Temperature effect	Distance effect
Violet	Aggressive and tiring	Cold	Very close
Blue	Restful	Cold	Further away
Brown	Exciting	Neutral	Claustrophobic
Green	Very restful	Cold/neutral	Further away
Yellow	Exciting	Very warm	Close
Orange	Exciting	Very warm	Very close
Red	Very stimulating	Warm	Close

feature of office life, the colour scheme should be light and nonintensive.

The effects of colours on the psychological state of the individual should also be considered, because some colours act as a stimulant and others act as a depressant. A dark blue ceiling may appear to be refreshing to begin with, but in time the apparent coldness may become an irritant. Various effects are attributed to different colours and these are shown in Table 5.3 (Hayne, 1981).

Movement

Movement, or the illusion of movement, may also be used to capture attention. People are attracted by neon lighting and by billboards with rotating bars that carry a different message on each surface.

Novelty

People tend to notice distinctive or novel aspects of their environment. That which is novel—e.g., humour, animation, and unusual graphics in an advertisement—stands out and is noticed.

Contrast

Another means of attracting attention is contrast. It is evident in the case of sound on television or in the cinema when there is a difference between the loudness of the programme soundtrack and that of the advertisement soundtrack. It is also manifest in the case of vision when, for example, there is a picture of a product on a completely white background. The contrast between scenes in an advertisement and scenes in the television programme that carries the advertisement should not create undesirable impressions. In selecting programmes for its television advertisements, Kraft Cheese rejects programmes that are excessively violent. The contrast between a programme scene where excessive blood is spilled and a subsequent advertising scene showing a cheese spread in a tranquil setting could hardly be considered appropriate. Panel 5.4 carries an example of a case where the contrast between a TV commercial and a drama gave rise to criticism. Other applications of physical stimuli feature in Panel 5.5.

PANEL 5.4: Undesirable contrasts

In the screening of *The Holocaust* in the United States, the plight of the Jews under the Hitler regime was shown. Viewers complained about the bright and cheerful scenes that appeared in commercials just after the scenes of horror.

There was one particular contrast that was likely to have aroused passions. Lieutenant Dorf was sitting with Adolf Eichmann and other SS officers in their dining room at Auschwitz. Eichmann sniffed the air and remarked that the stench of the chimneys kept him from enjoying his meal. The scene was cut for an air freshener commercial in which a woman called "Snoopy Sniffer" arrived at a housewife's kitchen and informed her that she had house odours.

(Engel, Blackwell, & Miniard, 1995)

A number of the stimuli already identified could be incorporated in the following contexts.

Notices and warnings. Employees must be alerted to dangerous equipment, areas, processes, etc. It is important to attract their attention to the hazards that are present, and to inform and remind them of the safety precautions they should take. This is usually done with notices. Notices and warnings should be varied from time to time in order to attract fresh attention. Warnings are necessary in the following conditions, especially on the factory floor: (a) where a particular hazard cannot be "designed out" of a piece of equipment; (b) where an operator cannot be removed physically from the potentially dangerous point of contact; and (c) where effective guards cannot be installed. Warnings are also needed when no sensory cues are available. An example of such a hazard is radioactivity, to which even limited exposure can have deadly consequences. The radioactive particles produced by certain materials are colourless and odourless, and therefore cannot be detected by our normal sensory receptors. In such cases people need warnings to influence their behaviour (Baron, 1999).

In the UK an employer has a legal duty to inform employees about hazards at work. Employees are more likely to cooperate in keeping rules made for their benefit if they appreciate the risks and the reasons for the precautions.

Warnings may be either dynamic or static. Dynamic warnings consist of warning lights and audible sounds, and static warnings comprise pictures, symbols, and diagrams. Warnings should be universally understood, they should convey why something is a hazard, how it arises from the use or misuse of a piece of equipment or process, and what to do if an injury should occur. Such warnings should also be complete, allow for any literacy or language problems, be conspicuous and capable of attracting attention, and should be updated periodically. "Redundancy" should be built into the information provision process: redundancy in this context is the injection of essentially the same information through two or more sense channels—e.g., vision and hearing.

In the UK there are statutory safety regulations requiring that dangerous substances be supplied and conveyed in containers of sound construction carrying an appropriate warning label. Such labels would include information indicating the general hazards, such as "explosive", "highly inflammable", "toxic", or "corrosive", as well as important health and safety information. The justification for this legislation is that inadequately labelled or badly packed dangerous substances cause accidents and injury.

Illustrations. Illustrations of a product are useful devices to attract attention. For instance, attractive photographs of the product—such as pictures of various appetising foods that can be prepared using the product (e.g., a photograph of a cake along with the recipe for it, displayed on the packaging for flour). Illustrations serve to facilitate comprehension of ideas about the product, to arouse feelings about it, and to help identify the product when the consumer is out shopping. Pictures of people generally rate highly in attention value, but there is evidence suggesting that when human models are used in printed advertisements the appropriateness of the model for the product may influence judgements about product quality (Anastasi, 1979; Kanugo & Pang, 1973). It is essential that the illustrated advertisement does not become an end in itself and detract attention from the product.

Cues. Cues are physical stimuli that act as symbols, giving us an indication of what to expect, and facilitating judgements. The names of supermarkets (e.g., Sainsbury or Tesco), brand names, packaging, and price are cues that convey the quality of the store or product and help us make our decision to buy. Judgements are also made about a company from cues such as the helpfulness of the staff, and the image of the company (e.g., Harrods). Perhaps when we confront a situation where there is an absence of cues about a store, greater reliance is placed on the assessment of the quality of service and product at the time of purchase.

Sometimes reliance on a few cues could lead to stereotyping that might not be justified. This might arise when someone calls at the door selling, for example, insurance. Because of a negative stereotype of a door-to-door salesman, which could be totally unjustified in given circumstances, the customer withdraws from what might otherwise be a fruitful commercial encounter.

A trademark is a reduced cue, serving as a conditioned stimulus for the recall of the product and company name. A trademark may symbolise some advantageous characteristic of the product—e.g., "Long Life" for milk—and often tends to evoke ideas and feelings associated with the product, either through previous advertising or through the customer's own contact with the product. When the trademark is a direct representation of the brand name of the product, as is the case with Kellogg's Corn Flakes, the association between the brand name and trademark is particularly easy to establish and the likelihood of confusion with other products or brands is minimised.

Sometimes a brand name is so strongly identified with a product that it is used as a generic term—e.g., Kleenex to denote any cleansing tissue. In circumstances such as these, there is a danger of associating dissatisfaction with the original brand if the customer is dissatisfied with the purchase of an inferior brand.

Financial data. Published accounting information is a stimulus attended to by the investor, but there are also other sources of information at the disposal of the investor. These can include commentaries and tips in the financial press, government reports on the state of the economy, employers' and trade association reports, stockbrokers' reports, merger reports, the latest inflation and balance of payments figures, and so on.

Clarity. In written official documents and forms, clarity is an important principle. It is very important, for example, for taxation literature to be as clear as possible. The Inland Revenue recognises that good communications with millions of people each year are crucial to the task of assessing and collecting the revenue due from the public efficiently with a minimum of friction. A lot of effort is put into form design and guides to increase the rate of accuracy in the completion of tax returns. In the final analysis the accuracy of tax returns is obviously related to the degree of difficulty experienced in comprehending tax forms and guides. The example of the Inland Revenue is indicative of a determination to strive for clarity in the presentation of a stimulus to the target audience.

PANEL 5.6: Subliminal advertising?

A commercial firm in a New Jersey cinema conducted an experiment. The words "Eat Popcorn" and "Drink Coca-Cola" were flashed alternately on the screen every 5 seconds for 1/3000th of a second during the showing of the regular film. These stimuli were described as subliminal, and the firm claimed that, over the 6-week period this procedure was followed, sales of popcorn in the foyer rose by 57.5% and Coca-Cola by 18.1%.

The report of these results aroused widespread public alarm, and this type of advertising was described as the "super soft sell" and the "invisible sell". The claims made for the experiments could not be evaluated because of the refusal by the commercial firm to reveal the details of the experimental procedure and results.

(Berkman & Gilson, 1998)

Absolute and differential thresholds

Each sense receptor requires some minimum level of energy to excite it before perception is organised. The minimum level is called the **absolute threshold**—a point below which we do not perceive energy. The absolute threshold for light is a flame from a candle seen at a distance of 30 miles on a dark clear night; for sound it is the tick of a watch under quiet conditions at a distance of 20 feet; for taste it is 1 teaspoon of sugar in 2 gallons of water; and for smell it is 1 drop of perfume diffused into the entire volume of a 3-room apartment (Day, 1969). The **differential threshold** is the smallest amount by which two similar stimuli must be different in order to be perceived as different. An example of the differential threshold can be seen in the case of the professional wine taster, who frequently perceives a difference between two bottles of wine that the amateur finds identical.

Thresholds need not only concern the physical stimuli of the real world. For example in accounting, the absolute threshold could be considered as the minimum level of information required by the individual to perceive the overall profitability or financial position of a business. An example of a differential threshold might be a discrepancy in figures detected in the course of a financial audit. To the experienced and competent auditor this discrepancy is serious enough to warrant further investigation, but to the inexperienced auditor the detection of the discrepancy may not signal a need for further action.

It has already been acknowledged that stimuli below the absolute threshold level cannot be perceived. However, on the basis of an experiment conducted in the autumn of 1957 in the USA, it was thought that subliminal perception—perception below the absolute threshold level—existed in and affected buying behaviour (see Panel 5.6). However, it should be noted that in situations like this, factors other than subliminal advertising may influence the results, such as, in the case in Panel 5.6, for example, the presence of a high proportion of teenagers in the audience during the period, changes in the display of the two products and in the sales tactics, and the weather (McConnell, Cutier, & McNeil, 1958).

Subliminal perception is not a mysterious technique for projecting ideas directly into the mind by evading the individual's conscious defences. There is no evidence to suggest that weak stimuli —i.e., stimuli below the absolute threshold level —exert more influence on behaviour than strong stimuli; in fact the reverse is the case. Also, as the stimulus becomes weaker, the probability of misperception becomes higher. With regard to subliminal stimuli, individual threshold differences must be considered—a word flashed across a cinema screen for a short period may have significance for one person because it falls above his or her absolute threshold, but not for another because it falls below the minimum level.

Notwithstanding what has been said, the findings of a study by Zajonc and Markus (1982) would seem to indicate that subliminal stimuli have significance, and that there is a possibility that attitudes are influenced without the individual interpreting stimuli through a conscious cognitive process. Some argue that the subliminal messages of in-store music have a soothing and productive effect on shoppers. But, from another source (Moore, 1982), comes a challenge to the effectiveness of subliminal stimuli. It is claimed that subliminal stimuli are usually so weak that the recipient is not just unaware of the stimuli, but is also oblivious to the fact that he or she is being stimulated. Generally, people are preoccupied with normal stimuli.

Sensory adaptation

Absolute and differential thresholds are known to fluctuate, and this fluctuation is referred to as **sensory adaptation**. Examples are **visual** and **colour adaptation**.

Visual adaptation. When dusk descends the rods take over from the cones in the retina of the eyes. The reverse is true when light reappears. We do not encounter too many difficulties when adapting to different levels of illumination, but the problem of temporary blindness appears with rapid changes in illumination. For example, a change from darkness to light increases the level of illumination falling on the retina of the eyes. In such circumstances the rods are unable to function, and the cones have not had sufficient time to adapt to the new conditions. The natural reaction is to close the eyes, or wear dark or coloured glasses in order to allow the eyes to adapt. The cones react relatively fast—in a couple of minutes—as we move from darkness to light. As we move from light to darkness, the rods react much slower—typically half an hour (Matlin & Foley, 1992). The period of adaptation depends on the previous intensity of illumination. It is for this reason that people who work in a dark environment, as in the photographic industry, wear coloured goggles (e.g., red). They would normally wear the goggles for some time before entering the darkroom. Red is an appropriate colour for the goggles because it has little effect on the visual pigment in the rods (Cushman, 1980).

Colour adaptation. This is manifest in the following illustration. If a person views a bright red stimulus for a few minutes, and then focuses on a yellow stimulus, the yellow appears to be green. Gradually the eye will adapt and return to normality. Such processes have important implications for computer operators spending a long time viewing various colours on a screen.

Adaptation to repeated stimuli

People have the capacity to adapt to stimuli that are repeated, by developing reduced awareness. For example, a worker becomes oblivious to the dangers of operating certain types of machines, and risks having an accident. To account for this phenomenon, one could argue that a stimulus that is repeated contains no new information.

This is akin to a situation whereby people living close to a nuclear power station adapt to the conditions in the absence of an accident. In the process, anxieties subside with the accompanying cognitive reassessment of the probability of an accident. Often, it is the people living furthest away from the nuclear plant who suffer the most anxiety, provoking rumours about the effects of radiation or meltdown. Rumour is the consequence of conditions in which good information is scarce; therefore, it can contain inaccuracies. People living furthest away from the nuclear plant can be compared with those living close to it. The latter have the advantage of being able to see the plant on a daily basis and perhaps learn more about the nature of the hazard. As a consequence, they are better able to adapt to any unconscious fears about the dangers of nuclear power. Any resident living close to the nuclear plant who experiences severe anxiety has the option of moving away, although one recognises that in practice it may not be easy to exercise this option in depressed labour and housing market conditions.

Familiarity with stimuli, where no adverse experience occurs, is a feature of repeated exposure to stimuli. Effectively the person adapts to the situation. However, there are situations when the person fails to adapt to stimuli (e.g., continuous noise) and the result is reduced powers of concentration, leading to poor quality work.

Disposition of the perceiver

Unlike the physical stimuli discussed in previous sections, there are other less quantifiable variables that are unique to the individual. These can be classified as the internal state of the person—e.g., personality, motivation, and previous learning —and affect the way people perceive. The disposition of the individual will be discussed with reference to preparatory set, orientation, intensity of motives, and familiarity of stimuli.

Preparatory set

The preparatory set basically refers to the range of things that, because of our internal state, we are almost programmed to see and register. Items outside the preparatory set are virtually ignored irrespective of what is contained in the stimuli to which we are exposed. The interest we have in certain things influences our attention. Perhaps more women than men are interested in advertisements for children's and babies' clothing, and the position could be reversed when attention focuses on cars and lawn mowers.

Orientation

The particular orientation—the attitude adopted by the perceiver towards a set of physical stimuli, based on interests, background, etc.—is also critical. This is borne out in the results of two classic studies. In the first (Cyert & March, 1963), a group of students was presented with a set of numbers in the form of cost and revenue statements. Both statements were analysed by all the students but there was a 10-week interval between the analysis of the two statements, with one half of the group working first on the revenue statements and the other half beginning with the cost statements. It was found that the context in which the students operated influenced their outlook. When analysing costs they tended to overestimate costs, but they underestimated sales when analysing revenue. Perhaps people are somewhat conservative in outlook when engaged in information-processing connected with money values. By overestimating costs there will be a tendency to minimise losses, whereas by underestimating sales the likelihood of overstating income is reduced.

In the second study a group of managers drawn from a large manufacturing company participated while attending a management course. The managers came from different functional backgrounds (e.g., accounting, marketing, and production) and they were asked to specify the major problem facing a company depicted in a case study that they had read. The majority of managers perceived the major problem as being related to their own area of specialisation (Dearborn & Simon, 1958). However, one should be aware that some of the conclusions in this study have been challenged (Walker, Huber, & Glick, 1995).

Intensity of motives

Perception is selectively affected by personal motives because we pay most attention to stimuli that appeal to fairly intense motives. Thus our perception may be distorted by our motivations. This point is emphasised in the following study. Ten-year-old children were asked to estimate the size of a coin in front of them by varying the size of a spot of light until they thought it was the same shape as a coin from a series, ranging from a penny to half-a-crown. It was found that the estimated size of every coin was larger than its true size. This type of overestimation did not occur with a control group, which tried to estimate the size of cardboard discs that were the same size as the coins. When the experiment was conducted among separate groups from both affluent and poor backgrounds, overestimation was detected in both cases, but was more pronounced among children from the poorer background. Here we observe that perception is accentuated when valued objects are perceived (Bruner & Goodman, 1947).

Where a stimulus is related to a need deficiency, our perception of that stimulus could be acute. The hungry person will display selectivity by tuning into food-related stimuli in his or her environment because of their association with the reduction of a need deficiency (hunger). Selective perception can also help us to cope with a threat. Here our value system assists us by ignoring messages, particularly mildly threatening ones, that tend to question our values, and this can be achieved without conscious awareness.

Studies have also demonstrated how perception acts as a defence in certain circumstances—e.g.,

---

Words were shown to subjects only briefly so that they found it impossible to recognise them. The period of display was then lengthened until recognition occurred. An electronic measure of emotion—the galvanic skin response (GSR)—was used to gauge the electrical resistance of the skin when an emotional reaction was aroused. The words comprised 11 that were neutral and 7 that were taboo (e.g., bitch, whore, rape). Each time a word was flashed the subject gave his or her opinion of what the word was. An emotional reaction (as gauged by the GSR) occurred even in circumstances when taboo words were shown so briefly that recognition was not reported by the subjects.

Taboo words had to be exposed for longer than neutral words before being read because they were apparently more difficult to recognise. When the words were flashed very briefly, and the subjects guessed what the words were, it was found that neutral words were construed in a structurally similar sense. Instead of recognising the word "trade" as such, it was recognised as "trace". However, completely different words were substituted for taboo words.

McGinnies (1949; see Panel 5.7). On the basis of this study one might accept that stimuli of a mildly threatening nature (e.g., a distasteful advertisement) tend to be ignored. Conversely, one may hypothesise that strongly threatening stimuli can capture our attention. So we are protected from the distraction of mildly threatening stimuli, but alerted to the danger of strongly threatening stimuli.

Familiarity of stimuli

Experience of a particular stimulus, such as a particular piece of music, amid a range of stimuli to which we may be indifferent, attracts our attention because of its familiarity. Alternatively, a novel or unfamiliar object amid a range of familiar ones—for instance, a strange face at a social event, or a novel piece of accounting data in a stereotypical accounting report—produces a similar effect. Experience may also predispose us to discount the claims of a product advertiser; we do so on the basis of dissatisfaction experienced as a result of previously using that product. Previous learning creates a tendency to pay attention to familiar patterns, though this might bring about problems when we accept a stimulus that bears a similarity to a familiar stimulus—we see what we expect to see rather than what is!

PERCEPTUAL ORGANISATION

Having focused our attention on relevant stimuli, the next step is to organise the information contained in the stimuli. One of the most notable features of perception is that it is nearly always highly organised. Organised perception is a remarkable achievement when one considers that the information reaching the sense receptors is confusing and disorganised (Eysenck, 1993). However, the organisation of perception could be difficult in circumstances where the stimuli are ambiguous, as we shall see later. The commentary in this section will examine factors involved in making sense of the sensations we experience and transforming them into organised perception. It will cover the following topics:

- ambiguous figures;
- figure/background;
- the Gestalt laws of organisation;
- constancy;
- visual illusions; and
- applications of perceptual organisation.

Ambiguous figures

When we first glance at the lines in Figure 5.4 we may conclude that they epitomise disorganisation. Then we suddenly begin to realise that it is a drawing and could represent either a duck or a rabbit, and then it fluctuates between both images. Likewise, in Figure 5.5 we see either a kneeling woman or a man's face, or perhaps both. With **ambiguous figures** there appears to be a need to create a whole image.

Figure/background

We rarely encounter ambiguity with three-dimensional objects in our normal visual world.

FIGURE 5.4

An ambiguous figure—a duck or a rabbit.

FIGURE 5.5

An ambiguous figure—a kneeling woman or a man's face (adapted from Fisher, 1967).

FIGURE 5.6

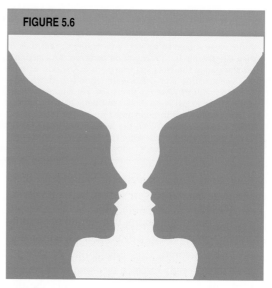

An ambiguous figure—a vase or two profiles.

FIGURE 5.7

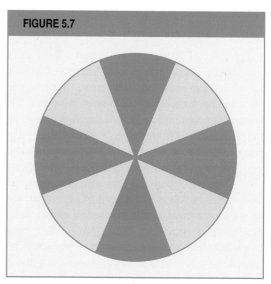

A dark or pale cross.

But with two-dimensional objects we find it difficult to distinguish between background and figure. Figure/background stimuli are presented in Figures 5.6 and 5.7. Two different pictures could be derived from Figure 5.6; at one moment we see a figure of a vase against a dark background, and the next moment we see two profiles against a pale background. In Figure 5.7 we see either a dark cross on a pale background or a pale cross on a dark background. The figure/background relationship is also found in senses other than vision. For example, when we listen to a symphony we perceive the melody or theme as a figure and the chords as background.

These reversible figure/background relationships illustrate the multistability of our perceptual

Multistable figures.

Groupings of vertical lines.

organisation. This is depicted in Figure 5.8 where each image can be "organised" in different ways, generating different three-dimensional or two-dimensional figures. For example, the right-hand image in Figure 5.8 can be seen as a hexagon with lines from the points converging at the centre, or as a cube tipped forward.

Gestalt laws of organisation

A number of rules or laws governing the organisation of perception, sometimes referred to as the Gestalt laws of organisation—area, proximity, similarity, continuation, common fate, and closure—will now be examined.

Area

Where one part of an area depicting an ambiguous figure is smaller in size than the remainder, it is more likely that the smaller area will be seen as a figure and the rest of the total area as background.

Glancing at Figure 5.9A, it is usual to see the small pale areas as the figure of a cross and the large dark area as the background. By contrast, in Figure 5.9B a dark cross set in a pale background is more likely to be seen.

Proximity

In Figure 5.10 we see three pairs of vertical lines instead of six vertical lines. The law of proximity states that items that are close together in space or time tend to be perceived as forming an organised group, or belonging together. When one flicks through the pages of a book, small sections of text with headings stand out from the remainder of the text because of their distance from the previous section.

Similarity

In Figure 5.11(a) most people would see one triangle formed by the dots with the apex at the top, and another triangle formed by rings (i.e.,

Reversible figures.

Examples of perceptual grouping.

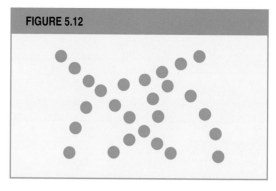

An example of perceptual continuity.

A common fate.

with the apex at the bottom). The triangles are perceived in this way because the dots and rings look different and therefore are organised separately. In a textbook, pictures and diagrams are instantly seen to be similar, and different from the body of the text. In Figure 5.11(b) we do not see a triangle but a hexagon (a six-pointed star) because all the dots are the same. Grouping in accordance with similarity does not always occur. We see Figure 5.11(c) more easily as a six-pointed star than as one set of dots and another set of rings. In this illustration similarity is competing with the principle of symmetry or "good figure"; neither the circles nor the dots form a symmetrical pattern by themselves.

Continuation

There is a tendency to perceive a line that starts in a particular way as continuing in that way. For example, a line that starts off as a curve is seen continuing along a smooth curved course, and, if it changes direction, it is seen to form an angle rather than a curve. Equally, a straight line is seen as continuing on a smooth straight course. Figure 5.12 illustrates the principle of continuation. We see the curved and straight lines as crossing each other and having dots in common, but it requires some effort on our part to perceive a straight line becoming a curved line at one of these intersecting points or junctions.

A numerical illustration of continuation occurs when you are asked to specify a number to follow 4, 8, 12, 16. The most likely answer is 20 because of a tendency to follow a perceived pattern. But in fact any number would be good enough, because you were not asked to maintain the pattern.

Common fate

This arises where elements that are seen as moving together take the shape of an organised group. The soldier in the jungle or wilderness who is perfectly camouflaged against his background is invisible until he moves; when he moves he becomes a figure and remains so while he is in motion. Two of the circles in Figure 5.13 share a common fate because they move in the same direction.

Closure

We compensate for the missing portions of incomplete stimuli so that we perceive a whole rather than a disorganised group. In Figure 5.14, the left-hand drawing is seen as a circle with gaps in it and the centre drawing as a square with gaps in it, rather than as disconnected lines. If these pictures were flashed very rapidly on to a screen, they might be perceived as complete pictures

FIGURE 5.14

Examples of closure.

without gaps. The drawing on the extreme right will also be perceived as a form rather than disconnected lines (e.g., a man on horseback).

All of the principles discussed here also apply to perception using senses other than vision. On the surface the Gestalt laws of perceptual organisation sound plausible, but take note of what two cognitive psychologists have to say about them: though the Gestalt laws of perceptual organisation possess reasonable intuitive appeal, they are merely descriptive statements having little or no explanatory power (Eysenck & Keane, 1995).

Constancy

One way in which people organise their world and make it more understandable is by emphasising stability and constancy. Constancy refers to situations where we see objects as stable despite great changes in the stimuli reaching the sensory organs. An object remains constant despite variations in its size and this allows us to make an adjustment to the reality confronting us. The following are examples of perceptual constancies.

Size

The image on the retina of the eye produced by a nearer object is in fact bigger than that produced by a distant object. However, we make allowances for that fact; e.g., spectators seated high up in the stand are not normally aware of a football player diminishing in size as he moves away from us across the field. We have a remarkable ability to keep the observed size of things constant in spite of large fluctuations in their retinal image.

Shape

The ability to maintain a constant shape in spite of different retinal images is called shape constancy. Like size constancy, it acts to our advantage by keeping our world of perception orderly. Imagine the confusion you would experience in a crowded car park if your car was seen as a different object according to the different retinal images produced from different viewing positions—front, side, back, etc.

Light

Different object surfaces absorb different amounts of light. If a surface absorbs all the light that falls on it, it is seen as black, but if it reflects most of the light it is usually seen as white. We make unconscious inferences about the colour and brightness of familiar materials because we have the advantage of experience of this type of phenomenon. However, with unfamiliar materials, constancy still applies. Apparently, brightness constancy prevails because objects and their surroundings are usually lit by the same illumination source, so changes in lighting conditions occur simultaneously for both the object and its immediate surroundings. As long as the changes in lighting remain constant for both the object and its surroundings, the neural message reaching the brain is unchanged. But brightness constancy breaks down when changes in lighting are not equivalent for both the object and its surroundings (Baron, 2002).

Person

Constancy can also apply to the perception of people. In one study it was demonstrated that there was considerable stability in people's judgements of politicians before and after reading newspaper reports about the politician in question. However, it appears that constancy is strongest when there is no great discrepancy between the position of the politician, in terms of his or her behaviour, before and after the newspaper reports. Even where a marked discrepancy exists, some degree of constancy still remains (Warr & Knapper, 1968).

There is a detailed account of person perception later in this chapter.

Illusions

Under certain conditions constancy does not hold good, and what we see appears to be quite different from what we know to be true. These manifestations are called illusions. Visual illusions are illustrated in Figures 5.15, 5.16, 5.17, and 5.18.

An illusion can be described as a reliable perceptual error; it is stable and not due to a hasty or careless exploration or processing of stimuli on our part. A widely discussed illusion is the Müller-Lyer illusion shown in Figure 5.15. Though the lines A and B in the figure are the same length,

FIGURE 5.15

The Müller-Lyer illusion.

FIGURE 5.16

The Ponzo illusion.

FIGURE 5.17

The moon illusion.

we see A as the shorter line. In Figure 5.16 we see the two rectangles, A and B, as different even though they are the same size.

With regard to Figures 5.15 and 5.16, we can measure the lines A and B and likewise the rectangles A and B and establish that they are equal in length, yet we cannot, even consciously, make the necessary adjustments to *see* them as equal. It has been suggested that the difficulty encountered with many of the two-dimensional illusions is that we misinterpret them as three-dimensional figures, which we expect to obey the laws of perspective (Gregory, 1966). For example, in Figure 5.17 presumably we make some attempt at scaling sizes in accordance with their perceived distance.

The moon illusion is another illustration of this principle. In Figure 5.17 the moon seems to be much larger when it appears on the horizon than when it is high in the sky. But it is the same distance away from us in both cases and the image projected on to the retina is also the same in both cases. Nevertheless, we still see the sizes as different.

The Ames room illusion (Figure 5.18) shows the nearer woman in a room seeming taller than the woman further away, even though both women are about the same size.

FIGURE 5.18

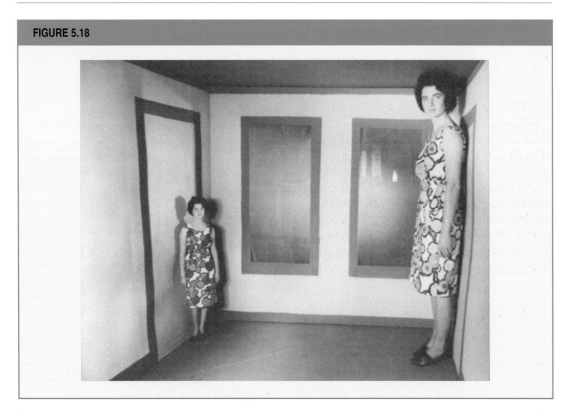

The Ames room.

How do these illusions occur, particularly as we have noted earlier how unconscious inference is introduced in order to maintain constancy? We may attempt to explain the moon illusion on the basis that the moon at the horizon looks further away because of all the information we are given on distance from the intervening terrain. Hence, when we see the moon in this position, we unconsciously "blow up" the image to compensate for this increased distance (Mackay, 1973). In much the same way, we are fooled into believing that the two women in the Ames room in Figure 5.18, who are about the same size, are in a rectangular room and that they are at the same distance from us. But the room is not rectangular; the "short" woman is much further away than the "tall" woman. However, constancy is not maintained, and our judgement of the relative size of the two women is distorted because we have not allowed for distance.

Movement illusions

Illusions of movement that arise from stationary stimuli are not uncommon. For example, an isolated stationary light in an otherwise dark visual field appears to wander after observing it for a while. This is called *autokinesis* and is typically encountered in flying (Hawkins, 1987). The autokinetic effect is a feature of the night flight environment (see Panel 5.8), when a stationary light in a dark visual field appears to move.

Another example of an illusion arising from a moving rather than a stationary stimulus occurs when a person on board a stationary train at a station looks out of the carriage window and sees a train at another platform. In reality the other train is moving, but the illusion is that the person's own train is moving, and this is called the illusion of induced movement. Illusions can also arise from the presentation of stimuli in rapid

---

PANEL 5.8: In-flight movement illusions

There are numerous reported cases of mistaken identity of light, such as the pilot "circling" round the wing-tip light of his or her own aircraft trying to identify it.

Another common illusory problem experienced in visual cruise flights relates to the evaluation of the relative altitude of approaching aircraft and the subsequent assessment of a potential collision risk. At a distance, an aircraft appears initially to be at a higher level, but eventually passes below the level of the observer. Mountain peaks, at a distance, seem to be above the height of the aircraft, but often are actually well below it. Two aircraft separated by only 1000 feet may appear to be approaching each other's altitude, and experience has shown that both pilots may resort unnecessarily to taking evasive action with the possibility of contributing to a mid-air collision.

(Hawkins, 1987)

---

succession. An example of this phenomenon is the apparent slow backward movement of wagon wheels in an old western film.

Applications of perceptual organisation

The principle of the Gestalt psychologists that the "whole is more than the sum of its parts" is seen at work in the illustrations of perceptual organisation discussed here. The principle of organisation is frequently applied in our daily life. When an advertisement for a product is viewed on commercial television, the soundtrack and visual stimuli complement each other and help the consumer to organise the message. Repetition of a message in an advertisement also contributes to perceptual organisation.

For example, a notepad personal computer at an attractive price is advertised in the colour supplement of a Sunday newspaper. This advertisement, which highlights the versatility and usefulness of the computer and associated software, as well as the price, is repeated over a period of time. Eventually, a consumer who has not responded to, or been aware of, initial exposures to the advertisement, sees the advantages of a computer of this size and decides to buy one. Repetition has been instrumental in bringing about the organisation of the consumer's perceptions.

In another case, perceptual organisation with respect to the features of a familiar product affects the consumer's decision when comparing it with competing products. For example, a consumer of Nescafé instant coffee will pick out this brand from among other brands on a shelf in a supermarket, without comparing each brand of coffee feature by feature. He or she has an organised overall perception of the product—cost, taste, etc.

People's ability to organise their perception of individual stimuli into a coherent whole can be affected by particular situations, or blocked by the poor presentation or masking of the stimuli themselves. For example, at an annual general meeting of a public company, private shareholders may feel uncomfortable in a large conference room or hall, and be disconcerted by the need to use microphones to make themselves heard. It is easy for people to mishear or misunderstand the information being discussed or reported, and to form an incorrect impression of what is being discussed or reported. When they try to quiz the senior management they may get to their feet, only to realise that they have not in fact been able to organise their thoughts and questions adequately, and are therefore easily fobbed off with evasions or bland assurances.

The general public can also experience difficulties in organising perception when faced with scientific language. Over two decades ago a report from the Royal Society, the foremost learned scientific association in the UK, warned scientists to stop baffling the public with jargon and learn to communicate with ordinary people as a matter of urgency. The report went on to say that the public should be helped to understand the scientific aspects of such issues as acid rain, nuclear power, and matters connected with in vitro fertilisation or animal experimentation, because of the importance of public opinion in influencing the country's decision-making process. Therefore, the language must be simple, free of jargon, and intelligible to the general lay public (Royal Society, 1985).

PERCEPTUAL INTERPRETATION

Having organised our perception, the next step before an appropriate response can be made is interpretation (Starbuck & Mezias, 1996). Perceptual interpretation occurs when we relate a stimulus (e.g., a physical object or a person) to the individual's cognitive context. The cognitive context consists of various thought processes, ideas, and feelings about experiences and happenings in the world around us, which we have built up based on our own life experiences. It is a primary determinant of perception and response because it embraces such phenomena as our needs, goals, values, education, and training, and accounts for the selectivity in perception that was referred to earlier. As a result, the same objective stimulus or happening could be perceived differently by different people. For example, at the scene of an accident it is not unusual to come across conflicting eyewitness reports.

Consumers see differences between products and it is conceivable that perceived differences between products rest more with the efforts of marketing executives interested in building up a distinctive brand image than in differences in the physical make-up of products. In one study, beer drinkers, who were credited with the ability to perceive differences between certain categories of beer on the basis of such characteristics as bitterness, strength, body, after-taste, foam, aroma, and carbonation, were asked to drink from unlabelled bottles of beer and distinguish differences in taste on a brand basis. None of the drinkers placed their preferred brand ahead of the others. When the same drinkers drank from labelled bottles, there was a marked tendency to express preferences for their favourite brand (Allison & Uhl, 1964). There are a number of complex and interrelated factors that influence brand perception (Berkman & Gilson, 1998), such as: the appeal of the label and packaging; the quality of advertising associated with the product; the consumer's experience of the product and disposition towards it; the product's reliability and the personal satisfaction derived from its use; the specification of attractive features of a product; and the desirable health or environmental factors associated with the product, such as health foods and lead-free petrol.

There are times when stimuli are not accurately interpreted and this can have serious implications. Misperception could arise when the individual's information-processing capacity cannot cope with the stimuli registered, perhaps because of pressure of work, poor procedures, lack of appropriate experience, or lack of training or skill. An important source of error is the inability to analyse and reconcile conflicting evidence due to a less than satisfactory understanding of the work process in which the person is engaged, and failure to attach the proper meaning to information conveyed by instrumentation designed to facilitate effective performance on the job.

In the public inquiry into the circumstances surrounding the collision of two British Rail trains at Colwich Junction, there was evidence to indicate that the driver of the northbound train had difficulty in perceiving the significance of the red lights. The northbound train passed through the red lights before stopping, resulting in the death of the driver of the southbound train and injury to 52 passengers. The driver of the northbound train in his evidence to the inquiry stated: "As a railwayman with 42 years service I saw a double flashing yellow light which means caution, followed by a red signal. I was surprised, as I expected the red signal to change to green, but it stayed at red. I am familiar with the use of flashing lights, but I never had formal training, nor have I seen training videos about the lights." The signalman in his evidence said that he had given clear signals for the northbound train to stop, as the southbound train was coming from the tunnel. A point worth noting in connection with this accident is that the driver of the northbound train was accompanied in the cab by an off-duty trainee driver (*Guardian*, 1986, *Sunday Times*, 1986). Could an animated exchange between them at the critical moment have led to the delayed response to the stimuli in the form of the lights? This report highlights the problem with interpretation in perception and the devastating consequences that follow certain types of misperceptions or perceptual errors. The problem of the interpretation of safety signals is still prevalent, as demonstrated by the more recent Southall and Paddington train disasters in the UK.

The interpretation of stimuli is not confined to human beings. A computerised surveillance system, consisting of a camera linked to a database, which contains the registration numbers of all recently stolen vehicles, has been developed by scientists at the British Home Office (Traini, 1983). The camera scans a stream of traffic and the computer checks the car numbers. When the computer comes across the number of a car reported as stolen, it automatically alerts the nearest police station or patrol. The whole process takes little more than a second. The computer supplies the police with a full description of the vehicle, and even the traffic lane in which it is travelling. The thief who tries to beat the system by using false number plates will not succeed because the computer has access to every valid registration number ever issued. If the camera picks up a number that is not on file, the alarm will be raised automatically. Stealing a car at night is not a way to get round the system because the camera uses infrared light. However, dirty number plates or bad weather can create a problem. The expected recognition rate is 70%.

There is some encouraging news for the blind and partially sighted with the development of the world's first robot guide dog at the Carnegie Mellon University, Pittsburgh, USA (see Panel 5.9).

PERSON PERCEPTION

As an extension of the previous section on perceptual interpretation, we now turn to social interaction, in the context of the interpretations we place on other people's behaviour. Person perception is concerned with the manner in which we perceive the personal characteristics of others, in particular their current mood and their total personality. Various dynamic cues—such as posture, gesture, body movement, facial expression, direction of gaze, tone of voice, rate, amount and fluency of speech, orientation, and distance—are picked up in the course of social interaction and they influence the interpretations placed on other people's behaviour. On occasions person perception occurs without difficulty. However, in an imperfect world there is always scope for misinterpretations to arise.

Misinterpretations

Misinterpretations could become an issue where special factors apply, such as:

* implicit personality;
* logical error;
* the halo effect;
* stereotyping; and
* assumed similarity.

PANEL 5.9: The seeing computer

The robot guide dog will enable its owner to navigate through the home and carry objects. It senses its surroundings with the aid of five different devices as follows: sonar, similar to that used by bats and submarines; laser range finders; infra-red scanners; a camera linked to computer vision technology; and simple collision detectors fitted behind the metal panels of the body. It can respond to simple orders by word or gesture, work out the best route to take, and move about on wheels, avoiding collisions with furniture and with people who happen to cross its path. Powerful artificial intelligence in its central computer allows it to create a map of the home. Its ability to accept that it can make mistakes means it is less accident prone than previous designs.

The robot can use information from its sensors to make decisions, but a unique feature is its ability to cope with uncertainty. For example, it does not believe everything it sees and can accept the possibility that it could be wrong. Eventually, it is hoped that it could climb stairs and survive outside in the less predictable complex world of people and traffic. Robot technology is moving ahead at a fast pace. For example, a machine that moves around a tennis court collecting balls is under commercial development.

(Farrar, 1998)

These should be borne in mind when we discuss the selection interview and staff appraisal in Chapter 17 and, in the next chapter, in connection with communication processes generally.

Implicit personality

Implicit personality theory is part of our "cognitive set"—in essence, it is a set of concepts and assumptions used to describe, compare, and understand people. We carry around in our heads personality characteristics that go together. Therefore, we could arrive at a judgement of what constitutes, for example, the typical school bully. The resultant profile is implicit rather than explicit; therefore, we could experience difficulties if requested to articulate or make explicit the characteristics that constitute the profile.

Implicit personality theories vary with the individual, and the differences are greatest between people of different cultures. In attributing characteristics to people, we can arrive not only at static perceptual judgements (e.g., enduring characteristics such as age, beliefs, ability, manner, and personality traits) but also at dynamic perceptual judgements of characteristics that change, such as specific rather than general actions, moods, emotions, and intentions (Cook, 1971). The use of implicit personality theories for making judgements of interviewees for jobs was found to be an acceptable mode of operation (Rothstein & Jackson, 1984). A number of issues connected with interviews are dealt with in Chapter 17.

Logical error

Implicit personality theory could lead us to form hypotheses or assumptions about what traits go together in a person. Almost intuitively we use this interpretation to form an extensive and consistent view of other people when faced with incomplete information. This is often referred to as the logical error, the assumption being that certain traits are always found together. The following experiment was conducted to test this principle.

Students on a psychology course were given descriptions of a guest speaker before he addressed the class. He was described to one half of the class as "warm" and to the other half as "cold". The lecturer then entered the class and led a discussion for about 20 minutes. When he left the classroom the students were asked to describe him. The students who were told that he was going to be "cold" were more likely to attribute to him traits such as self-centredness, unsociability, humourlessness, and ruthlessness than were the students who were told he was "warm". The students who thought of the lecturer as "warm" were also more likely to interact with him during the discussion (Kelley, 1950). What appears to be happening is that changes in person perception arise from varying even minor cues or stimuli, leading to a totally altered view of the person perceived.

Halo effect

Another tendency, similar to logical error, is called the "**halo effect**". This materialises when we perceive people in terms of the concepts of good and bad; "good" people possess all the good qualities, whereas "bad" people possess all the bad qualities. Somebody given an adverse evaluation at a particular stage of his or her career may find subsequently that, when his or her profile has improved, an evaluation bears the scars of the earlier assessment. Likewise, in an interview situation, if an interviewer perceives in the interviewee a desirable attribute similar to one of his or her own, he or she may make a favourable overall assessment as a result.

The reverse would be true when a deficiency is identified at the outset. This is referred to as the "horns effect". There is evidence to suggest that our perceptions of people are influenced markedly by our initial good/bad evaluations of them. It has been suggested (Osgood, Suci, & Tannenbaum, 1957) that our overall attitudes towards others can to a large extent be determined by our evaluations of them along three dimensions: activity (active versus passive); strength (strong versus weak); and evaluative (good versus bad). The third dimension is considered the most influential.

Stereotyping

Another phenomenon similar to logical error is **stereotyping**. This could be seen as generalised beliefs about the characteristics, attributes, and behaviour that typically belong to certain groups (Hilton & Von Hippel, 1996). For example, we may consider a Scot to be mean or thrifty, or a Jew to be a shrewd businessperson. Therefore we attribute to a member of the race in question the characteristics of the stereotype. Biased perception arises when we rely on the stereotyped image and ignore critical information concerning the individual. It is said that an attachment to stereotypes could lead to an overestimation of the differences between groups (Krueger, 1991). Stereotyping does not necessarily result only in the creation of negative images; it can also be positive. Neither is it a wasteful activity, as one study has shown. Subjects described a student in accordance with a stereotype, as they had no further information on which to work. At a later stage when the subjects became acquainted with the student, they described him for a second time and, on average, it was found that the initial descriptions were the more accurate. A further illustration is highlighted in Panel 5.10. What we should try to do is examine to what extent our impression of others is based on stereotype alone, so that we can make adjustments accordingly.

Do we recall information that is supportive of a stereotype better than information that challenges the stereotype? As a general principle, the answer would appear to be "yes". The main reason why

this is so is that we are naturally reluctant to change a stereotype or belief when faced with evidence challenging it. We may also find the practice of stereotyping useful as a means to protect our identity when faced with threats to our self-esteem or security. But we must accept that there are times when the person is capable of remembering a lot of information that challenges the stereotype, simply because he or she initially went through the motions of examining the challenging evidence in order to test that stereotype (Hilton & Von Hippel, 1996; Stangor & McMillan, 1992).

However, when we are tired or busy there may be a reluctance to address the stereotype; then we are not motivated to explore thoroughly the evidence that challenges the stereotype. Instead we are more likely to remember material supportive of the stereotype (Arnold, Cooper, & Robertson, 1998). When it comes to the actual processing of information, it is suggested that we process information supportive of a stereotype more intensively than information inconsistent with it (Bodenhausen, 1988).

It seems that our desire to stereotype other people springs from our need to create a landscape of our social world in which our identity and the identity of others is expressed in the form of membership of groups. This line of thought is encapsulated in social identity theory (Tajfel & Turner, 1985), which has been applied to group interactions within organisations (Ashforth & Mael, 1989; Hayes, 1992). Social identity theory is also examined in connection with motivation in Chapter 4 and inter-group behaviour in Chapter 10.

PANEL 5.10: Racial stereotyping

In connection with stereotyping, a study was carried out in which students, whose attitudes towards black people were known to researchers, rated a number of pictures according to 25 traits. The pictures depicted 10 Negroid faces and 5 Caucasian faces. The Negroid faces reflected a wide range of Negroid features. Ten of the traits described characteristics of the individual, which could be determined from the features of the Negroid faces. The other 15 were personality traits widely accepted as part of the stereotype of the black person.

Once a student selected a picture as that of a Negroid face there was a tendency to assign to it the personality traits associated with black people as he or she construed them. The student paid no attention whatsoever to the individual differences depicted in the pictures. The results of the study were the same for students with either a less pronounced or more pronounced prejudice. Stereotyping occurred because of a strong tendency to assign traits to an individual on the basis of group membership, despite the fact that individuals vary in the extent to which they exhibit the characteristics of their group.

(Secord, Bevan, & Katz, 1956)

A problem can arise when different groups, originating from various departments, functions, and hierarchical levels, perceive each other in terms of negative stereotypes. This negative stereotyping could be done as part of a strategy to establish a group's own superiority, and justify a reduction in cooperation or collaborative efforts with other groups. This behaviour could be more pronounced when groups have similar standing and where it is felt necessary to emphasise a group's distinctiveness. Where a difference in status between groups is clear-cut, groups of relatively low status may be overly concerned with trying to establish an identity, and they are likely to feel a certain sense of frustration if high-status groups show indifference to them.

Inter-group behaviour of the type just described could hamper understanding and tolerance with negative side-effects. But does it have to be like that? The answer would appear to be "no". Where group members feel that differences in status or affluence between their group and other groups are legitimate, less negative stereotyped views could be found (Arnold et al., 1998). Also, it is possible for a compromise to be reached where group members see themselves and members of other groups as having different but complementary abilities or characteristics (Van Knippenberg, 1984). A necessary first step for developing healthy collective effort is to subscribe to the belief that organisational groups possess complementary strengths. Inter-group conflict is discussed in Chapter 13.

As far as the individual prone to stereotyping is concerned, Devine (1989) has a simple recipe: inhibit the in-built prejudiced disposition and adopt an open-minded thinking process. In practice this is unlikely to be an easy transition.

Assumed similarity

This is the tendency to see others as having characteristics more like our own than is really the case (Feshback & Singer, 1957). We are inclined to project our own emotional or motivational state on to others. In an experiment where subjects were anticipating the receipt of a painful electric shock, it was found that those subjects who reported feeling fear themselves were the subjects who predicted others would be afraid. In other experiments it was shown that those who were asked to predict the behaviour of others usually tended to make predictions more like their own behaviour than the behaviour of the person about whom the prediction was made.

This evidence may be explained as follows. We operate the ego defence mechanism of projection (see Chapter 2) by attributing to others the motives and emotions that we possess but feel uncomfortable about, and, relying on our own experience, we act with the disadvantage of not knowing the internal state of the other person.

Some of the pitfalls in person perception have been identified in this section, and it should be borne in mind that there are a number of situations in business where employees make unrealistic generalisations about the personal characteristics of those with whom they come into contact.

Impression management

Impression management refers to the process by which individuals attempt to control the impression others form of them. Therefore, it would be a mistake to think that the person who is at the receiving end of the perceiver's attention—the target person—is merely passive, while the only person active in the process of person perception is the perceiver. In selection and appraisal interviews, discussed in Chapter 17, the target person is the job applicant and appraisee respectively, who is intent on influencing events to his or her advantage (Silvester, Patterson, and Ferguson, 2003; Stevens & Kristof, 1995; Wayne & Kacmar, 1991), and the perceiver is the interviewer. In reality the target person could be active in trying to create the right impression (impression management) by producing an image of himself or herself for consumption by the perceiver (Schlenker, 1980). The target person could set out to generate a favourable impression through a variety of tactics, some of which are akin to the tactics used in organisational politics referred to in Chapter 13. Rosenfeld, Giacalone, and Riordan (1995) viewed these tactics as:

under enormous pressure to meet a production deadline, at the instigation of a supervisor, and involved short cuts at the expense of safety. In such circumstances, attribution of responsibility to the subordinate for the unsafe act is not as clear-cut as when action is seen as intentional.

Weiner et al.'s scheme

A scheme to classify factors used to attribute causes to the outcome of a behavioural act (i.e., success or failure) was devised by Weiner et al. (1972). Success or failure is attributable to one of four causes: ability, effort, luck, and task difficulty. In Figure 5.20, the four causal factors, together with the dimensions of stability and locus of control, are shown.

The dimension of locus of control, discussed in connection with personality in Chapter 2, can be either internal or external. When the outcome of a particular course of action is under the control of the person, it is referred to as internal. When the outcome is due to circumstances beyond the control of the person (e.g., fate), it is referred to as external. The dimension of "stability" refers to whether the four causal factors are fixed or variable over time.

Illustrations of the operation of this scheme, with numerical reference to the model, are as follows:

(1) An individual performs a task, and the outcome is successful. The perceiver of the individual's performance attributes effort (something that is within the control of the individual—internal—and can vary over time) to successful performance. If the outcome was unsuccessful, lack of effort could be attributed to this eventuality.

(2) An individual performs a task and the outcome is successful. The perceiver of the individual's performance attributes ability (something that is within the control of the individual—internal—and is relatively unchanged over time) to successful performance. However, if an error or mistake occurs, lack of ability is attributed as the cause of the error or mistake. Although ability is fixed in terms of stability, there may be some scope for improvement, and thereby for avoiding errors of this type in the future.

(3) Where an individual exercising reasonable care is struck by falling masonry on a building site, bad luck is the attributed causal factor. Bad luck is perceived as outside the control of the individual and it can vary over time.

(4) An individual may fail to perform well because of the difficulty of the task. This is a causal factor external to the individual, and for the time being it is fixed in terms of stability.

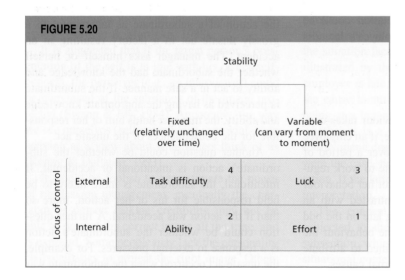

FIGURE 5.20

A scheme for attributing causes to outcomes connected with achievement-type tasks (from Weiner et al., 1972).

It is argued that the way people attribute causes to events can be learned, and distinctive ways of attributing causes emerge (Rotter, 1975). Where people develop in an enabling environment, exercising a fair amount of control over how to influence events in line with their needs, they are likely to attribute more outcomes or events to "internal" considerations. This group can be contrasted with externals—those who believe things happen without their intervention.

An attribution perspective is important because the way an observer perceives an action or behaviour will influence his or her response and provide a foundation for predicting future events. Therefore, it has significance in a motivational sense. Sometimes, scholars approach attribution theory from the perspective of its important motivational properties, and therefore the topic was also acknowledged alongside the theories of motivation examined in Chapter 4. Of course there is a danger in attributing causation to particular actions or behaviour, because we may end up basing our attribution on an oversimplification of reality. As a result, there may be bias in the way we judge others.

As a broad generalisation we tend, as observers of social behaviour, to assume that other people's behaviour is internally controlled (i.e., attributable to their personal characteristics) but for ourselves we exaggerate the extent to which our own behaviour is externally determined—in the final analysis circumstances influenced our behaviour (Nord, 1976). The tendency to take more account of the situation in explaining our own behaviour and less account of the situation in explaining other people's behaviour is sometimes called the "fundamental attribution error". According to Morris and Peng (1994), the fundamental attribution error is to a large extent a Western

idea because non-Western cultures (e.g., Chinese) are more likely to subscribe to external attributions in explaining behaviour.

In appraising the performance of an employee in an organisation (discussed in Chapter 17), effort or ability is often referred to when explaining performance with reference to internal factors. But when performance is explained with reference to external factors, often luck or the difficulty of the job is mentioned. Obviously the attitudes of the appraiser to the person being appraised will have an influence on the final outcome (Fletcher, 1984).

The "ultimate attribution bias" or error is described by Arnold (2005) as "our tendency to attribute good performance by members of our in-group (e.g., our racial group) to internal causes such as ability and effort, but similar performances by members of an out-group (e.g., a different racial group) are attributable to an easy task or help from colleagues." This bias could to some extent explain discrimination (Silvester & Chapman, 1996). In one study (Garland & Price, 1977) the successful performance of female managers was attributed by prejudiced male managers to luck and being an easy task (an external interpretation), but in the eyes of unprejudiced male managers it was attributed to skill and hard work (an internal interpretation). Prejudice is discussed in the context of attitudes in Chapter 9.

Finally, it should be recognised that during the past couple of decades European attribution theorists have been gradually moving away from the individualistic approaches to attribution, as examined here, which is associated with US social psychology. Instead, they have turned their attention to the social purposes of attributions—how people develop shared or collective patterns of attribution (Hayes, 1993).

CHAPTER SUMMARY

- The basic processes in perception are reception of stimulus, attention, organisation, interpretation, and response. Stimuli are picked up by the senses, which consist of vision, hearing, smell, taste, touch, warmth, cold, pain, kinaesthesis, and vestibular. Reference was made to extra-sensory perception.

- Many business practitioners and others recognise the importance of attracting the attention of the perceiver, although this is not always easy. In this context, absolute and differential thresholds are crucial. When they fluctuate this is known as sensory adaptation. The internal state of perceivers is something else to consider when trying to attract their attention.

- Before interpreting the information contained in a stimulus, it has to be organised. The Gestalt laws of organisation govern the organisation of perception. Those involved in business (and others) are naturally concerned with the question of grouping stimuli into an organised whole, but sometimes problems arise. The individual adheres to constancy when organising stimuli, though this can be undermined by illusions. Illusions were discussed with reference to stationary and moving stimuli.

- Perceptual interpretation follows perceptual organisation, and various cognitive aspects of our total personality are activated so that meaning can be ascribed to the information at our disposal. The interpretation of stimuli, such as safety signals and tax forms, can present some difficulties. The perception of a brand is an important consideration for the consumer. The interpretation of stimuli by a computerised surveillance system is a feature of the era of new technology, as is the seeing computer.

- In person perception the following factors feature in a prominent way: implicit personality; logical error; the halo effect; stereotyping; and assumed similarity. Additional factors are the concepts of impression management and attribution.

QUESTIONS

(1) What steps can the business executive take to attract the attention of the target audience?

(2) What significance is attached to the organisation of perception from a business perspective?

(3) Distinguish between absolute and differential thresholds using examples.

(4) What do we mean by sensory adaptation? Assess its significance in any business context.

(5) Discuss the role of subliminal perception in a marketing context.

(6) Why is it necessary to consider the disposition of the perceiver in the process of perception?

(7) What do we mean by the concept of illusions in the field of perception? Illustrate your answer with suitable examples.

(8) Identify the factors likely to give rise to the misinterpretation of information as part of the perceptual process.

(9) What significance do you attach to the brand image of a product in the context of perceptual interpretation?

(10) Examine some adverse repercussions likely to arise from perceptual errors or misperceptions.

(11) What insights derived from interpersonal perception should a sales representative, who is concerned with improving his or her social or communication skills, take into account?

(12) Explain what is meant by: (a) attribution theory; and (b) impression management.

(13) What is the significance of stereotyping in person perception?

(14) Explain what is meant by extra-sensory perception.

SPOTLIGHT ON RELEVANT READING

Baron, R.A. (2002). *Essentials of psychology* (3rd ed.). Needham Heights, MA: Allwyn and Bacon. Chapter 3 (pp. 76–119) on "Sensation and perception".

Sekuler, R., & Blake R. (2002). *Perception* (4th ed.). New York: McGraw-Hill.

Starbuck, W.H., & Mezias, J.M. (1996). Opening Pandora's Box: Studying the accuracy of managers' perceptions. *Journal of Organizational Behaviour, 17*, 99–117.

Learning Outcomes

After studying this chapter you should be able to:

- Comment on the nature of communication.

- Identify the actions involved in the communication process.

- Analyse communication networks.

- Convey what is meant by communications as transactions.

- Identify the barriers to communication.

- Illustrate communication problems.

- Specify ways in which communication can be improved.

- Identify important communication skills.

Communication

6

Communication is the lifeblood of the organization. Perception, as discussed in the previous chapter, plays a central role in communication. In examining the various ways to communicate, emphasis is placed on oral and written communication, nonverbal communication, the influence of new technology, and communication networks. Next there is a focus on interpersonal communication from a psychotherapeutic angle, followed by an examination of the steps involved in the communication process (the communication cycle), and a brief reference to the FIDO principle. Communication barriers and problems are then discussed, plus ways to improve communication. Finally, important communication skills, including active listening and feedback, are introduced. The issues discussed in this chapter have relevance to change and development (Chapter 16) and human resource practices (Chapter 17).

Contents

INTRODUCTION

Perception, examined in the previous chapter, is an important part of the communication process, and at work there are different types of communication. That which is officially inspired is often referred to as formal communication, whereas communication that is unofficial, unplanned, and spontaneous is classified as informal. An example of an informal communication system is the grapevine, discussed later in the chapter. A communication system can transmit information up, down, and sideways within an organisation, and on a one-way or two-way basis. When communication is one-way there is no opportunity to receive a reaction from the receiver of the message. But in two-way communication the receiver of the message can provide a response and is encouraged to do so.

WAYS OF COMMUNICATING

There are many ways to communicate, and in this section oral and written communication, **nonverbal communication**, new technology, and communication networks will be examined.

Oral and written communication

When we use the spoken word, either face-to-face, in a small group, or over the telephone, the sender of a message has the opportunity to observe feedback, answer questions, and provide additional information by way of clarification. It is often faster than other forms of communication and has the advantage of being personal. For example, the human resource or safety practitioner may use the spoken word when he or she feels it necessary to impress upon a factory supervisor the absolute necessity of maintaining permanent machine guards around dangerous machinery where a certain laxity with regard to their use has developed. A disadvantage of the spoken word is the absence of a written record of the dialogue, though conversations can, of course, be taped.

A formal meeting usually consists of both the spoken and the written word. The written component is the agenda, the minutes of the last meeting, and papers distributed previously or on the day. The meeting itself relies substantially on the spoken word. A meeting of the board of directors is an example of a forum to exchange information on the implementation of company policy so as to decide on the appropriate action. In certain meetings, visual aids could be used to emphasise technical issues. Apart from the use of the written word at meetings, a letter, memorandum, or report allows the communicator to organise his or her thoughts carefully, and provides a written record of happenings and transactions for future reference.

Although written communication is an impersonal process, it is generally possible to provide more information to the receiver by this means than through the spoken word. Written communication is somewhat more time-consuming than the spoken word, and it provides little opportunity for the sender to observe feedback and to provide clarification. Written communication amounts to a one-way communication system with a delayed response.

Nonverbal communication

This covers all aspects of communication that are not expressed orally or in writing. It includes body movements, the emphasis and intonations we put on words, facial expressions, and the physical distance between the sender and receiver of a message. Nonverbal body language—e.g., raising an eyebrow for disbelief, shrugging our shoulders for indifference, winking an eye for intimacy, touching our forehead for forgetfulness—conveys meaning and constitutes an important facet of human communication.

Body language, coupled with verbal communication, can often give fuller meaning to the message of the sender, but equally the interaction between the two can create a certain amount of confusion. With the spoken word, a soft, smooth tone creates a different meaning from an intonation that is harsh with a strong emphasis placed on the last word.

Facial expression—e.g., an expressionless or a smiling face—also conveys meaning. On the basis of our perception we may conclude that a person is indifferent, sad, or happy. When coupled with intonations, facial expressions can exhibit fear, arrogance, aggressiveness, shyness, and so on. It has been widely assumed that basic facial expressions are recognised by people worldwide as conveying certain emotions (e.g., regardless of culture, that a smile is an indication of happiness). However, there is research evidence that challenges this view (Russell, 1994). Although facial expression can disclose much about people's emotions, interpretations of such expressions are also affected by the context in which the expressions occur and by various situational cues.

Physical proximity, or distance between people, also conveys meaning. Our liking or disliking for a person may dictate physical proximity. Generally we prefer a shorter distance between ourselves and other people in intimate interpersonal relationships, than in other types of interpersonal relationships. However, this principle could vary depending on cultural influences. It is suggested that in casual interpersonal relationships, Greeks are likely to stand closest to the other person, Scots furthest away, and Americans somewhere in between (Feldman, 1971). So if somebody stands too close or too far away from the other person, after taking into account cultural preferences, unease and difficulties in social encounters could arise.

Other examples of body language interpretation include:

* a handshake denoting a friendly greeting or farewell;
* eye contact indicating a willingness to continue a communication episode;
* sitting on the edge of a chair conveying a nervous disposition;
* sitting back with arms folded indicating an unwillingness to continue with the dialogue; and
* continually looking at your wristwatch at a meeting when you would prefer to disengage mentally and be "elsewhere".

Furnham (1999) recognises that body language is vital to our understanding of each other, and if a person misrepresents a colleague's actions this creates misunderstanding. Body language is an important way to back up verbal communication, but a lot of nonsense is talked about it that is unsupported by the facts. For example, people may move around in their chairs because the chairs are uncomfortable, and not for any other reason. People with their hands in their pockets in low temperatures may just be cold, and not secretive or depressed. People who fold their arms are not necessarily defensive or lacking in confidence, they may be just comfortable doing so.

Nonverbal communication can be a particularly difficult subject to study due to the fact that it can be unintentional, unconscious, and idiosyncratic. When it comes to observation of nonverbal communication, video has a great advantage over live observation. Video observation allows for repeated viewing, which is important in complex sequences of movement. Now there are sophisticated computer programs (THEME) whereby an observer can input information appropriately coded from a digitised video recording directly into a computer, with benefits in terms of analysis, leading to seeing things often hidden from the naked eye (Bull, 2001). There is further comment on the application of modern technology to communication in the next section.

Finally, there is no doubt that nonverbal communication research has considerable practical significance. It can be taught, learned, and improved through what has now become known as communication skills training. This has been used in varied social contexts: for example, employee selection interviews, training of the police, intercultural communication, and therapy with psychiatric patients.

Information and communication technology (ICT)

The application of new technology to the communication of information includes computerised information-processing systems, new forms of telecommunications systems, and a combination of the two. Developments in electronic technology

---

PANEL 6.1: The electronic deluge is getting out of hand

There can be few office workers whose hearts did not lift a little at the news that Phones 4 U, the UK's second biggest mobile phone retailer, has banned its 2500 staff from communicating internally via e-mail. They can still use e-mail to exchange messages with customers and suppliers.

Michael Eisner, chairman of Walt Disney, made the point a few years ago that e-mail has particular pitfalls as a means of communicating with colleagues. It is so easily dispatched that it feels like the spoken word, yet it is as indelible as the written one. An incriminating e-mail will turn up at an inquiry or in a court case, or an angry or unpleasant one will cause long-lasting bitterness among the recipients. Some Wall Street firms that allowed analysts to tell colleagues in lurid detail by e-mail about how little they thought of the stocks they were recommending to investors have paid a hefty price for their actions.

The hegemony of e-mail is too strong to be resisted; we now live in an electronic world, for good or ill. But it is not too late for companies to ponder how internal e-mail could be used more sparingly. E-mails should convey essential information when conversation is impossible; use of the cc: and bcc: should be minimised. Showing off and telling off must be done face-to-face (get people to talk to each other).

(Financial Times, 2003)

---

have brought us faxing, e-mailing, home banking, and video conferencing on powerful PCs, along with mobile phones offering voicemail, text messaging, and PC integration. It is easy to send and receive letters using the computer, and the transmission of data between computers over long distances is a reality. The electronic office has arrived, in the form of a single, integrated system. As a result, numerous categories of employees are plugged into a communication network that uses a combination of computerised data storage, retrieval, and transmission systems aided by telecommunications.

Moorhead and Griffin (2004) give examples of the computer-integrated organisation. For instance, in one company the sales, marketing, finance, distribution, and manufacturing functions exchange operating information continuously and rapidly through computers. A designer sends product specifications directly to those with responsibility for the machines on the factory floor, and accountants can receive online information about sales, purchases, and prices instantaneously. The challenge for the future is the successful integration of the various technologies, and ensuring that social structures and power relationships in organisations are congruent with the new electronic office systems. Also, difficulties, such as information overload, loss of records in the paperless office, and the dehumanising effect of electronic equipment, will have to be faced.

E-mail is becoming increasingly prevalent, though it is often said colleagues seem to be using

e-mails as a poor substitute for face-to-face communication (Cooper, 2002). E-mail is a very flexible way to communicate using computers and telecommunications. It makes possible instant communication, irrespective of the location of those involved, and it facilitates teamwork when all team members receive messages at the same time. However, it may not be the most appropriate medium to vent complicated and emotional issues, and of course there is the question of privacy and confidentiality. The control of this facility is also an issue because there is the potential for its misuse in organisations (e.g., private use). Some employers are using surveillance software to monitor the extent to which employees are engaged in genuine work-related activities, but such action could undermine trust in the organisation. Reservations about the use of e-mail were raised in an editorial in the *Financial Times* in late 2003 and a summary appears in Panel 6.1.

To complement the internet we also have the intranet, consisting of local computer networks inside the company that operate on a similar principle to that of the internet outside the company. The purpose of the intranet is to improve efficiency and effectiveness by allowing employees in different parts of a company to gain access to company information and share information with each other (McCune, 1996).

The real advances in organisational efficiency and effectiveness as a result of modern information technology may come from the ability to

PANEL 6.2: ICT—future trends

For thousands of people, working from home or on the move is already a reality. The prediction of Bernardo Huberman, who works in Hewlett-Packard's laboratories, is that today's techniques relying on mobile phones and laptop computers will in due course appear to be primitive: "You may have handheld devices of some sort, but they will be smaller than today's and much easier to use". The mouse could become redundant, to be replaced by users' movements, such as waving the hand in front of the screen. Also, screens could respond to touch. Already motor vehicles can be driven without human intervention, but this is likely to encounter human resistance. The QWERTY keyboard is likely to survive intact, as keyboarding is a very convenient way of inputting large volumes of textual data, and humans will still have a prominent role in interrogating data.

A permanently switched on communications "cloud"—a vast network connecting millions of different computing devices, from mainframes to tiny sensors—will allow us to speak to or to send messages to anybody around the world without having to log in or log out. We may still be using the internet, but it will not be necessary to fire up web browsers and type in web addresses. Machines will communicate with each other more than they will communicate with people within this global "cloud". For example, sensors fitted around homes and offices will control normal everyday functions, such as turning on and off the lights as people enter and leave rooms. Information sent from one sensor to another could, for security reasons, follow our movements, or track the movements of other things, such as products leaving the factory and going to the consumer. Robots could be voice activated, responding to simple demands.

As a consequence, sharing information will be much easier, and work will be decentralised away from head and branch offices that have taken decades to establish. Most types of work in the next few decades will lend themselves to offshoring (see Chapter 14)—it will become as easy to share information with a colleague on the other side of the world as one in the same room, provided there are no language impediments. Offshore manufacturing—one of the first activities sent abroad—to countries where labour is cheap will continue, coupled with large-scale mechanisation, with greater use of robots.

(Harvey, 2004)

communicate in new and different ways rather than from speeding up existing communication processes. The new technology should help with the dissemination of new ideas and practices, and in the process organisations will become knowledge-based learning organisations.

Certain technological developments (e.g., e-mail) affect the way we relate to each other. E-mail is devoid of the benefits of nonverbal communication found in the face-to-face meeting and the verbal intonations and emotions gleaned from telephone conversations. Video conferencing, which allows people to speak and see each other even though large distances might separate them, may fail to satisfy our affiliation needs in the way that the conventional meeting does. For a glimpse of the way information technology might take shape in the future, see Panel 6.2. (New technology and organisation is discussed in Chapter 14, and new technology and job design in Chapter 4.)

Communication networks

Within the organisation one finds networks of communication that are, in essence, systems of information exchange (small-group communication networks are discussed in Chapter 10). The organisational communication networks that will be discussed here are not the same as the lines of communication found on an organisation chart. The reason for operating outside the formal hierarchical system of communication is that employees find it easier to perform their jobs, or to obtain necessary information, by going directly to employees in other departments. The roles and functions that are crucial for the proper functioning of the communication network and the organisation as a whole are as follows (Pace, 1983):

- *Gatekeeper.* This person occupies a strategic position in the network enabling him or her to control information moving in either direction through a particular communication line. The gatekeeper could be somebody who communicates most frequently with, say, the chief executive, even though he or she could be two levels removed from the latter.
- *Liaison.* This person acts as a bridge between groups by promoting closer relationships between them and ensuring that the necessary level of information to integrate group activities is available.
- *Cosmopolite.* This person acts as a link between the organisation and its external

environment, and has a lot of contact with sources outside the organisation. He or she can be a valuable source of information on outside developments affecting the material well-being of the organisation. The **cosmopolite** could also be an opinion leader within the group.

- *Isolate.* This person tends to work alone, and communicates little with others.
- *Isolated dyad.* Two people who interact with each other, but communicate little with others.

It is beneficial to develop an understanding of these roles in order to assist managers and subordinates to facilitate communication, to capitalise on the strengths and orientations of various individuals, and to foster much needed integration within the organisational system.

A well-known informal organisational communication network is called the "**grapevine**". It amounts to a network of relationships between people that arises in a spontaneous way, and can be used to supplement formal communication channels. The grapevine relies heavily on word of mouth, and opportunity to communicate (e.g., being in the same building) is a prime consideration. A number of factors give rise to the formation of grapevines, such as the following (Davis, 1976):

- There is a lack of information through the formal communication channels.
- A state of insecurity activates people to communicate with each other and build a bulwark against likely threats.
- Conflicts and tensions, often between superiors and subordinates, can give rise to people talking about the issues informally.
- Where there is distrust and dislike between people, the protagonists will try to gain advantage by circulating, informally, negative information about their opponents.
- Where there is a need to spread new information quickly, informal communication channels will often be used.

The grapevine has the capacity to transmit rumour and gossip, as well as authentic information. Some argue that it is generally the carrier of incomplete and inaccurate information that creates negative side-effects (such as dissatisfaction and anxiety), whereas others say that one cannot discount its reliability on all occasions. The proponents of the beneficial features of the grapevine are likely to put forward the following case (Zaremba, 1988):

- The grapevine is an emotional safety valve for the release of frustration in conditions where an individual's anger cannot be realistically directed at an authority figure.
- The grapevine provides groups with a feeling of security and belonging, which in turn fosters satisfaction and group stability.
- The grapevine can raise morale when it transmits positive information about the organisation.
- The grapevine's existence is a constant reminder to managers to be professional in their managerial role, because the informal network can highlight ineptitude and inefficiency.
- The grapevine can act as a feedback mechanism, thereby providing managers with knowledge on how employees generally perceive problems.

COMMUNICATIONS AS TRANSACTIONS

Transactional analysis, made popular by Berne (1964) and Harris (1969), is a theory or concept of personality (in the psychotherapy tradition) that can be used to analyse interpersonal communication. Personality can be viewed as having three major parts or ego states—the **parent**, the **adult**, and the **child**. The ego states appear to resemble the id, ego, and super-ego referred to in Chapter 2. However, transactional analysis is concerned with the changing interactive aspects of the ego states in social intercourse. An objective of transactional analysis training programmes is to help people relate better, ease tension, and accomplish things. A well-balanced person travels from one ego state to another in the light of the situational demands. The three ego states are defined as follows:

is not the best place for the safety practitioner to give serious advice on health and safety matters to a chargehand or supervisor with only lukewarm interest in such advice.

Incomplete feedback

A misinterpretation by the speaker of feedback from the receiver, or no perceptible reaction from the receiver, represent communication barriers. In either case, the sender of the message is denied insight into the position of the receiver with regard to a particular communication.

Rumour

Gaps in the formal communication system can be filled by rumour—and this is normally associated with the grapevine. The grapevine, however, which is part of the informal communication network discussed earlier, often feeds accurate information

into the system. By definition, rumour is false information, and it frequently arises because people are kept in the dark about important matters.

COMMUNICATION PROBLEMS

Perceptual problems are frequently encountered in organisations; these are often referred to as "communication problems" and certain organisational features can accentuate them (see Panel 6.3). Communication within one function of a business, such as the finance department, is likely to be better than between groups drawn from, say, the marketing and finance departments. Likewise, communication between people within a geographical location is usually better than between groups in different locations. In the traditional staff/line relationships (referred to in Chapter 14), sometimes communication between the "staff specialist" on,

---

PANEL 6.3: Impact of organisational features on communication

Division of labour
Division of labour within organisations provides a number of operating advantages. It permits specialisation with the potential for greater efficiency (see Chapter 14), but the introduction of functional specialists breeds the growth of specialised language and terminology. Production managers have their own unique vocabulary, just as accountants have their technical language. These and other factors, such as conventions and outlook on commercial life, make the transmission of information for the purposes of decision making across functional or unit boundaries rather difficult, and may result in distortions and omissions (Litterer, 1973).

Organisational hierarchy
Apart from the division of tasks into specialist functions, an organisation is invariably characterised by an arrangement of tasks in a hierarchical form (as described in Chapter 14). For example, senior managers perform different tasks from those performed by first-line supervisors. The organisational hierarchy may pose problems for the processing and transfer of information. Sometimes, a subordinate modifies information so that it complies with the preferences and prejudices of the superior. This may be done in order to obtain the approval of the superior. There are many occasions when employees of the same status in the organisation provide information and feedback on performance to one another as a normal part of social interaction, but the incidence of feedback is much less between different layers of the organisation. There appears to be a tendency for subordinates to feel uncomfortable when they are engaged in exchanging information with superiors rather than with their peers (Blau & Scott, 1966). They tend to over-interpret and over-react to messages sent by superiors.

In addition to the problem of communication of information between layers of the organisation, there is the problem that results from the tendency of the organisational system itself "to filter information by providing less and less detailed information to the top of the organisation" (Richards & Greenlaw, 1972). As the information makes its way up the organisation, summaries with expressions of opinion, conclusions, and recommendations for action are very prevalent. So it is the inferences drawn from the primary data collected at the lower levels of the organisation, not the detailed data itself, that is transmitted upwards.

Therefore the people further down the organisation who prepare the summaries and draw inferences from the detailed information can exert considerable influence on the decision makers at the higher level. As the top decision maker is unlikely to inspect the raw primary data, he or she should be aware, to an acceptable extent, of the credibility of the major sources of information within the organisation (March & Simon, 1958). However, it is necessary to review this evidence in the light of advances in information technology, which make it possible for senior managers in certain circumstances to gain direct access to information generated further down the hierarchy. A discussion of new technology and organisation appears in Chapter 14.

PANEL 6.4: Communication problems with respect to safety at work

In a survey of the opinions of safety managers together with a cross-section of shop floor workers in 26 factories in the London area it was concluded that there were problems of communication with respect to safety. There was profound ignorance among employees about safety policy, but those who were aware of safety policy obtained details of it from a notice board or from a personal copy of the document. Few employees knew about the Health and Safety at Work Act 1974, except that they were aware of the fact that an individual employee could incur criminal liability. There was surprising ignorance of the operation of safety committees, and there were problems with the reporting of hazards. In fact, many employees were not very conversant with the business conducted in safety committees, though they were aware of the existence of them. Likewise, there were problems with reporting procedures for accidents, and there appeared to be little knowledge of first-aid facilities. Apparently trade unions were a rather more important source of information on the Health and Safety at Work Act than management, though in one company management was a significantly more important source than trade unions.

(Barrett & James, 1981)

---

say, product planning, and the line manager, e.g., the production manager, leaves much to be desired. This problem is often aggravated by a difference of outlook or orientation.

There is always the potential for perceptual problems to arise in the relationship between superiors and subordinates within the hierarchy of organisations. In one study it was found that there were marked differences in perception between superiors and subordinates when it came to assessing the nature of consultation. For example, 70% of the top managers believed they almost always got their subordinates' ideas and opinions in problem-solving sessions on the job, but only 52% of foremen believed this to be so. Similarly, 73% of the foremen believed that they almost always got their subordinates' ideas and opinions in problem-solving sessions on the job, but only 16% of the workers believed this to be so (Likert, 1961). There is further comment on communication problems in organisations in Panel 6.4.

IMPROVING COMMUNICATION

The response of the General Motors Corporation to criticism of the formality of its top-down communication system was to devise a large-scale communication improvement programme. This included public speaking workshops for employees, improving the numerous publications it circulated, providing videotapes of management meetings for employees, and using satellite links between the company's headquarters and the various operational sites to create two-way conversations around the world (Moorhead & Griffin, 2004).

One of the post-merger integration projects devised by Daimler Chrysler to mould the operations of the two companies was to set up a joint private TV station. The initial purpose of this initiative was to give employees a quick visual sense of operations in other parts of the combined company. The station facilitates the transmission of up-to-date information about the group. The output of information from Europe (Stuttgart) is adapted to meet the needs of the US wing of the organisation (Tait, 1999).

In a study of companies with very good internal communication processes at a critical time (such as a period of major restructuring and reorganisation) a number of factors associated with the effectiveness of communications were identified by Young & Post (1993):

- There was a firm commitment to communication by chief executives who were highly visible and skilful at relating to people and allocating sufficient time to them.
- Words were backed by action; there would be a loss of managerial credibility if there was a mismatch between what was said and subsequent action.
- There was a commitment to two-way communication, striking a balance between upward and downward communication, and employees were positively encouraged to communicate upwards.
- There was an emphasis on face-to-face communication—and more so in times of

change and uncertainty—as senior managers established direct contact with employees.

- There was a determined effort by the senior managers to keep the managers further down the hierarchy informed; in fact managers and supervisors at all levels were actively sharing information with their work groups in an attempt to minimise ambiguity and uncertainty.
- There was a noticeable tendency to encourage employees to come forward with bad news (e.g., setbacks, product failures, and customer complaints) as well as good news, and not to penalise the carriers of bad news.
- Because employees vary in the information they need, there was recognition that the message must be relevant and appropriate to the needs of the target audience, and thought was given to the most effective way of getting the message across.
- It is necessary to be constantly aware of the need to be vigilant as far as communications are concerned and let people know relevant facts as quickly as possible, particularly at times of crisis or major change. In appropriate circumstances convey the rationale for the suggested action, and help people understand the relationship between the broader picture (e.g., a crisis in the economy) and the local situation (e.g., the knock-on effect within the company), and, where appropriate, give people the opportunity to draw their own conclusions.

Team briefing

Team briefing, a method used in the UK and pioneered by the Industrial Society (now the Work Foundation), involves face-to-face communication in an organisational group setting. It is a two-way communication process whereby the manager or leader of the group provides up-to-date information to group members, and the latter are given the opportunity to ask questions. The basic rationale for this process is to improve communication and to create a climate for more positive attitudes and employee involvement. This would be particularly appropriate at a time of organisational change when the reasons for the change can be stated and people can be given the opportunity to ask questions.

Team briefing can increase the standing of the supervisor or foreman as a provider of information, and creates a participative forum capable of confronting industrial strife, although (in the absence of good labour relations) it could be viewed by trade unions as a way of undermining their influence (Marchington, 1987). The information transmitted should be relevant to the recipients and cover work-related issues such as corporate objectives, sales volume, and productivity, and how these impact on employees. Team briefing starts at the apex of an organisation, and takes place at a maximum of four levels. The first could be a meeting of senior executives, and the notes from this meeting could be passed down to the next organisational level, with the addition of any information of particular significance at this level. This pattern is repeated until the stage is reached where the line manager or supervisor briefs the shop floor workers.

Because the success of team briefing depends on the skill of the briefer, it is important that he or she is properly trained. Team briefing meetings are likely to be arranged well in advance, at intervals ranging from fortnightly to quarterly according to need. They should be seen as complementing communication systems generally within the organisation.

Storytelling

In recent years Body Shop, the retail chain, has made use of storytelling in an effort to improve communication within organisations. There are now training programmes on how to tell stories, how stories can help participants dream up great visions, and how they can bring soul and spirit to impoverished organisational lives. Body Shop has used stories to make its communication more human.

But how do we define a story? A story is an account of a specific event consisting of a sequence of steps as follows: a beginning, a middle, and an end, with a theme or plot and a sense of audience. We create meaning by ordering experience in a certain sequence within a time frame, and we learn to think about and tell stories early in our lives. Stories can be linked together, and the linking information amounts to separate stories (McLeod, 1997).

In the field of psychotherapy there is a belief that we do not pay sufficient attention to the central role that stories play in our culture and our individual lives when it comes to forming and maintaining our state of health. According to Taylor (1996), the story is more powerful and often more practical than abstract reasoning for imparting many kinds of knowledge. It appeals to us in a total sense by touching our thinking, feeling, and spiritual faculties and acknowledges the view that if we do not know something in an emotional sense we do not know it completely. The story provides us with not only a way of knowing but also a way of remembering, and this is important because, without an ability to recall information from our memory, knowledge is useless.

IMPORTANT COMMUNICATION SKILLS

In any discussion of communications nowadays, the importance of active listening and the provision of feedback is underlined. In addition, the development of skills in listening and in the provision of feedback is advocated (Robbins & Hunsaker, 1996). The skills listed here are important in the context of interpersonal perception. Also, they are critical for the efficient execution of certain human resource practices, such as selection and appraisal interviews, examined in Chapter 17, and organisational development strategies, discussed in Chapter 16.

Active listening

Hearing is not the same thing as listening. Whereas hearing amounts to registering stimuli based on sound, listening entails paying attention to what we hear, interpreting, and remembering the stimuli. Effective listening is an active rather than a passive process, whereby the listener is concentrating intensely on the communication and is keen to understand fully what the speaker is trying to get across. Of course it helps if the speaker is putting across his or her message in a clear and

interesting way. Apart from intense concentration, other requirements for active listening are:

- Empathising with the speaker so that you try to see the subject or issue from his or her point of view, thus increasing the likelihood that the message put across by the speaker is interpreted in the way he or she intended.
- Accepting what is said, and reserving judgement on the content of the message until the speaker has finished; the listener could be distracted from the content of the message if he or she were to concentrate unduly on points of disagreement.
- Taking responsibility for getting the full picture, which means doing whatever is necessary to get the total intended meaning from the information that the speaker puts across; this entails not only absorbing content, but also listening for feelings, and asking questions to facilitate understanding.

It is claimed that effective listeners adopt the following patterns of behaviour (Robbins & Hunsaker, 1996):

(1) *Establish eye contact.* The absence of eye contact could signify lack of interest.
(2) *Show an interest in what has been said.* This may be by a nod of the head or by an appropriate facial expression. Together with eye contact, these responses convey to the speaker that the listener is interested in what has been said.
(3) *Avoid distracting actions or gestures.* Distracting actions or gestures could include excessive glances at a watch and being fidgety. This could convey to the speaker that the listener's thoughts are elsewhere and that disinterest or boredom has gripped the listener.
(4) *Ask questions.* The perceptive listener seeks clarification of what has been said in order to aid understanding. Asking pertinent questions conveys to the speaker that the listener is tuned in to the communication.
(5) *Paraphrase.* This amounts to a restatement by the listener of what the speaker has said,

using his or her own words. Then the listener seeks verification of his or her interpretation of what has been said. Where paraphrasing bears a close relationship to what the speaker said, this could indicate careful listening.

(6) *Avoid interrupting the speaker.* The speaker should be given the opportunity to develop his or her line of thought before an interruption takes place.

(7) *Do not overtalk.* Some people may feel uncomfortable having to sit through a talk without having the opportunity to speak. However, where it is acceptable to ask questions and contribute to the debate, the good listener recognises that it is not possible to talk and listen at the same time, and refrains from overtalking.

(8) *Make smooth transitions between the roles of speaker and listener.* In circumstances where there is one-way communication from speaker to listener (as with a formal lecture), generally conditions are conducive to stretches of uninterrupted listening. But in many situations at work, such as meetings, a person moves from the role of speaker to listener on a regular basis. The effective listener has to be adept at making a smooth transition between speaker and listener, and vice versa.

Feedback skills

Managers are continually faced with providing both positive and negative feedback on various aspects of subordinates' performance. For obvious reasons, the provision of positive feedback is a function a manager could warmly embrace. The same cannot be said of the provision of negative feedback. The average manager could feel uncomfortable in the role of conveyor of bad news: he or she may fear offending the subordinate or does not relish the prospect of coping with a subordinate's defensiveness. It is, therefore, not surprising to find that the provision of negative feedback is frequently avoided or delayed, or when provided it is distorted (Fisher, 1979).

But managers have to face up to their responsibility for the provision of negative feedback,

bearing in mind the potential resistance to it and the circumstances in which it is most likely to be accepted. It is suggested that negative feedback is most likely to be accepted if it is objective—i.e., supported by hard data—and originates from a person with high status and credibility in the organisation (Halperin, Snyder, Shenkel, & Houston, 1976). However, negative feedback that is given by experienced and respected managers of appropriate status can err on the side of subjectivity and still be accepted by subordinates.

The following suggestions have been made with a view to increasing the effectiveness of the feedback process (Robbins, 1991):

specific examples

- *Focus on specific behaviours.* Avoid making vague statements about performance; instead focus on a specific incident, informing the recipient of the reasons for the complimentary or critical remarks.

- *Keep feedback impersonal.* This is particularly important in the case of negative feedback. Criticism should be directed at behaviour related to the aspect of the job the supervisor criticises (e.g., recent unsatisfactory delays in the processing of invoices). Refrain from criticism of a personal nature when commenting on less than satisfactory job performance or other job-related behaviour. The reason for this suggestion is that such action could provoke an emotional response from the recipient of the feedback and deflect attention from the issue of sub-standard performance or other inappropriate job-related behaviour.

- *Keep feedback goal-oriented.* This is done by making sure that the feedback is directed at matters connected with the achievement of the recipient's goals. Using a feedback session in the case of negative feedback to unleash a variety of criticisms, many of which are not directly related to the recipient's inappropriate behaviour currently under review, is a sure way of undermining the credibility and influence of feedback sessions.

- *Short time intervals.* Ensure that the time interval between the relevant behaviour and the provision of feedback related to that behaviour is short. For example, a person is more likely to take suggested action to rectify a personal deficiency shortly after the mistake or malfunctioning occurred rather than after a formal performance appraisal session many months later. Feedback related to a fresh rather than a stale incident is likely to have greater effect. However, one should ensure that rapid feedback is complete and not half-baked because of an urgency to get it to the recipient quickly.

- *Ensure understanding*. This can be fostered by a clear and concise exposition of the feedback and, if necessary, requiring the recipient to paraphrase its content.

- *Ensure control*. Direct the negative feedback towards behaviour over which the recipient has control. Therefore, the recipient must be in a position to do something about the alleged deficiency. If output falls below target because of a failure of a supplier to supply raw materials, the poor output figures can hardly be the direct responsibility of the production manager. Where negative feedback relates to an event that is under the control of the recipient, an enlightened approach would be to offer guidance, where necessary, to improve the situation or solve the problem. This would also take some of the bite out of the criticism.

CHAPTER SUMMARY

- The importance of communication and its link to perception was emphasised.
- There was reference to formal and informal communication; oral and written communication; nonverbal communication; and the role of new technology in the communication process.
- Communication networks were explained with reference to the roles of gatekeeper, liaison, cosmopolite, isolate, isolate dyad, and the grapevine.
- In communication as transactions, transactional analysis—featuring the three ego states of the parent, the adult, and the child—was examined.
- The steps involved in the communication cycle were highlighted.
- A number of the pitfalls that act as barriers and hinder effective communication were considered.
- Perceptual problems frequently encountered in organisations and referred to as "communication problems" were addressed.
- Suggestions were made to improve communication, including team briefing and storytelling.
- Finally, two important communication skills—active listening and the provision of feedback— were examined.

QUESTIONS

(1) Explore the connection between communication and perception.

(2) Identify the modes of communication within organisations.

(3) How important are the following: (a) the grapevine; (b) nonverbal communication; and (c) the role of new technology in communication?

(4) What is meant by communication networks?

(5) What form does communication as transactions take?

(6) Identify the steps in the communication cycle.

(7) Comment on the significance of cultural differences in the context of barriers to communication.

(8) Examine typical communication problems that arise in organisations and suggest ways and means of solving them.

(9) Discuss the importance of storytelling as a method to improve communication.

(10) Define the communication skills applicable to listening and feedback.

SPOTLIGHT ON RELEVANT READING

Bull, P. (2001). State of the art: Non-verbal communication. *The Psychologist*, December, 644–647.

Guirdham, M. (2002). *Interactive behaviour at work*. Harlow, UK: Pearson.

Hargie, O., Saunders, C., & Dixon, D. (1994). *Social skills in interpersonal communication*. London: Routledge.

Nicholson, N. (2001). The new word on gossip. *Psychology Today*, June, 4–45.

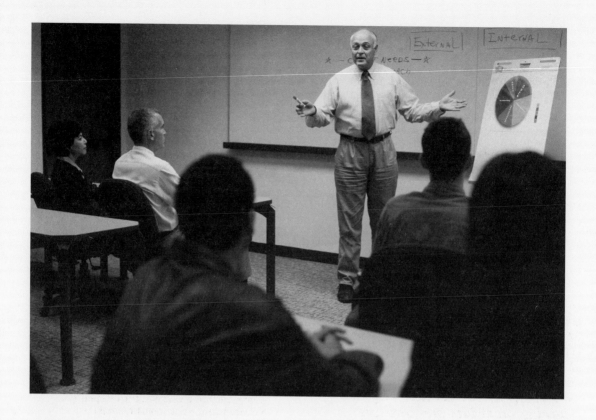

Learning Outcomes

After studying this chapter you should be able to:

* Identify the major approaches to learning.

* Discuss the main difference between operant conditioning and cognitive learning.

* Recognise the commercial applications of classical conditioning.

* Outline the essential features of behavioural modification, and assess its limitations.

* Specify the nature of social learning theory.

* Describe the way memory is categorised, and list the major functions of memory.

* Discuss the important role of recall as a function of memory.

* Explain what is meant by the transfer of learning.

* Assess the significance of knowledge management.

* Recognise the key features of the learning organisation.

Learning and Memory

Although concerned with different functions, learning and memory are related. Generally, learning is concerned with the acquisition of knowledge and skills, whereas memory is concerned with retention and retrieval. The discussion of learning subdivides into classical conditioning, operant conditioning, and cognitive learning. Programmed learning and behaviour modification are discussed as techniques that derive their strength from operant conditioning. Memory is subdivided into short-term, including working memory, and long-term memory. Processes relating to memory functioning are discussed. The transfer of learning (training) is examined, as are knowledge management and the learning organisation. Issues covered help underpin later discussion of information-processing (Chapter 8), attitudes (Chapter 9), culture (Chapter 15), and management development (Chapter 16), and also have relevance to motivation (Chapter 4) and selective perception (Chapter 5).

Contents

LEARNING

Learning covers virtually all behaviour, and is concerned with the acquisition of knowledge, attitudes, and values, emotional responses (such as happiness and fear), and motor skills (such as operating a computer keyboard or riding a bicycle). We can learn incorrect facts or pick up bad habits in the same way that we learn correct facts and acquire good habits. Learning can take place surreptitiously through the process of socialisation in a particular culture.

A generally accepted definition is that learning involves a relatively permanent change in behaviour that occurs as a result of previous practice or experience (Atkinson, Atkinson, Smith, & Hilgard, 1996). This excludes the process of maturation, physical damage or disease, and temporary changes in behaviour resulting from fatigue, drugs, or other causes. Learning cannot be observed directly; we can only observe a person's behaviour and draw the inference from it that learning has taken place. Sometimes a person may have the potential to perform and display what he or she has learned, but unfortunately anxiety intervenes to undermine actual performance. This could occur in an examination, when the anxious student does not perform in accordance with the tutor's expectations.

A distinction has to be made between learning and performance. Performance is evaluated by some quantitative and some qualitative measures of output—e.g., the number of calls a sales representative makes to customers or the quality of action by an executive chairing a committee meeting—but learning acts as a constraint on the outcome. Normally we cannot perform any better than we have learned, though there are occasions when the right motivational disposition and a supportive environment help to raise the level of performance. Increased motivation may improve our performance up to a point but, beyond this, increased motivation may cause a lowering of the level of performance (Spence, Farber, & McFann, 1956).

We shall now turn our attention to a behaviourist approach to the investigation of learning that has been very influential. This draws on the insights derived from classical conditioning and operant conditioning.

CLASSICAL CONDITIONING

Classical conditioning is an association of one event with another that results in a pattern of behaviour. The name of Pavlov is associated with classical conditioning (Pavlov, 1927). He was a physiologist who originally experimented with digestive secretions in dogs, and noticed that the dogs not only produced secretions when they saw food, but also responded to any stimulus that had been regularly associated with the food, such as the sight of the food pan or the sound of the keeper's footsteps. These events prompted Pavlov to investigate the dogs' tendency to salivate in response to a stimulus; this was called a reflex action. Pavlov rang a bell each time he brought food to a dog, and gradually the dog began to associate the ringing of the bell with the presentation of food.

Unconditioned and conditioned stimuli

The unconditioned stimulus (US) is the presentation of the food; the conditioned stimulus (CS) is the ringing of a bell. The act of salivating by the dog is the response. This is often referred to as a conditioned response (CR) when associated with CS, and as an unconditioned response (UR) when associated with US. Before any learning can take place an association must exist between US and UR. Actual learning occurs from the pairing of the bell (CS) and the presentation of a pan of food (US).

Classical conditioning also functions in a human context. If a puff of air is blown into the human eye, a blink automatically occurs. There is an association between the puff of air (US) and the blink (UR). If, however, a new stimulus (e.g., a light) occurs close in time with the US, the new stimulus (CS) brings about the blinking of the eye (CR) (Hall, 1976).

Another example of human conditioning involves a physiological reaction. The small blood vessels close to the body surface constrict in order to try to keep the body warm when it is exposed to the cold; this is known as vasoconstriction. We are unaware of this response when our hands are placed in ice-cold water. After a number of joint presentations of a buzzer and putting a hand in ice-cold water it was established that vasoconstriction (CR) occurs in response to the buzzer (CS) alone (Menzies, 1937).

Extinction and spontaneous recovery

A conditioned stimulus will not last indefinitely unless it is accompanied by an unconditioned stimulus. If the conditioned stimulus is introduced repeatedly without being followed by the unconditioned stimulus, there will be a gradual weakening of the strength of the conditioned response. This is known as "**extinction**", and amounts to a reversal of learning. Pavlov's dog ceased to salivate at the sound of a bell because food did not appear after a number of occasions when the bell was rung.

A conditioned response that has been extinguished may spontaneously recover some of the strength lost in extinction after a period of rest. This is manifest when, after a night's rest, Pavlov's dog increases the number of drops of saliva to the first ringing of a bell the following morning. The degree of spontaneous recovery after extinction will depend on the strength of the association that exists between the conditioned and unconditioned stimuli, and the nature and frequency of the rest periods.

Illustrations of the US/CS associations.   Classical conditioning has become a focus of growing interest as a basic framework for interpreting advertising effects (Allen & Madden, 1985). The marketing executive is interested in creating public awareness of the company's product, and through the medium of advertising attempts to establish a strong association between the conditioned stimulus—the image of the product portrayed in the advertisement—and the unconditioned stimulus (the product itself).

With a limited advertising budget a decision will have to be made as to whether the expenditure should be allocated to one or two major campaigns in a year, or whether it should be spread through smaller but more frequent advertising campaigns throughout the year. For a new product it may be worthwhile to use the budget on an intensive campaign in order to create a strong association for the product, but, for an established brand, the nature of the product and the likely activities of competitors would dictate the desired course of action.

The aim of a marketing strategy could be to associate some feeling of euphoria or satisfaction with the product, so that when consumers enter a store and see the product the associative feeling is aroused. This is reflected in a number of cinema and television advertisements. A scene showing a girl enjoying herself on a tropical beach is followed after a few seconds by a picture of a bottle of a particular brand of alcoholic drink. When the consumer is contemplating the purchase of an alcoholic drink at the off-licence or supermarket, the advertised brand on display can trigger off the image or emotional connotation of the beach and the girl. Similarly, a Hovis bread advertisement depicted the bygone rural conditions of life, followed by people eating brown bread. When this product is seen on the supermarket shelf it is hoped that the consumer will experience a pleasant association between it and the ancient country setting.

In order to entice a consumer to purchase a product, a price discount may be offered. The consumer purchases the product because of the price reduction and continues to do so after the discount has been withdrawn. In this example an association is established between the desirable reduction in price (unconditioned stimulus) and the product brand (conditioned stimulus). If the product in question compares well with the quality and performance of competing brands, the association initially established as a result of the price reduction strategy could continue. In the short term at least, the product may be chosen by the consumer despite the absence of a discount.

Once an action becomes repetitive, such as the continued purchase of the product with the initial price discount, a habit is formed. Many consumers rely on habit so as to alleviate the problem of choice. They tend to buy the same shampoo, coffee, and baked beans that they bought last time, though there has been a trend in recent years for consumers to be price sensitive. A deliberate advertising strategy to foster brand loyalty is reflected in an overt association between the product and the brand. The old slogan incorporating the misspelled name of the product and the name of the brand—"Beanz meanz Heinz"—is a good example of this strategy.

Advertisers exploit associations between social groups and lifestyle, so as to promote products to particular social groups. It is highly unlikely that an advertisement would show a prestige car against the background of a dilapidated small house in a run-down area. A more likely image would be for the car to appear in a context of affluence—near a large house, driven by an attractive, well-dressed woman, and so on. However, if an advertiser wishes to enlarge the market for a particular product, then the product will be shown in a number of different settings, each designed to appeal to a particular social group.

Generalisation

The phenomenon of **generalisation**, related to classical conditioning, occurs when we attribute to a similar stimulus the characteristics of the conditioned stimulus. For example, Pavlov's dog salivated (though to a lesser extent) to the sound of a buzzer. The greater the similarity between the conditioned stimulus (the bell) and the new stimulus (the buzzer) the more pronounced is generalisation. The concept of generalisation can be viewed as the substitution of a new conditioned stimulus for the originally learned conditioned stimulus. It accounts for our ability to react to novel situations where we perceive similarities to familiar situations.

The accountant, when dealing with a new tax problem, may see certain similarities between it and a past problem, and as a consequence is able to draw inferences from the past situation to illuminate the present. This is an act of generalisation on the part of the accountant. It is often assumed when a consumer has a satisfactory experience with a product—e.g., a Sony camcorder—that this will be generalised to other products, such as a compact disc player, made by the company. But generalisation may work to the firm's disadvantage, if an unfavourable experience with a product or service is transferred to a new product or service introduced by the firm. An example would be clients who are dissatisfied with the auditing service they receive from a firm of chartered accountants. Subsequently, the firm creates a first-rate management consultancy service, but the clients concerned, although in need of consultancy advice, feel unable to use the services of this firm.

Generalisation is also evident in the following situation. A child, accompanied by a parent, pays a visit to the dentist. The child will probably respond with a certain degree of anxiety to the odd sensation as the tooth is drilled. But, while in the dentist's chair, the child registers a variety of stimuli—the dentist in a white coat, the "smells" of the surgery, the whine of the drill, and so on. The conditioned response of the child to pain is to be frightened, and this response becomes associated with the other stimuli registered by the child. On the way home the parent and child visit a chemist's shop to buy some medicine, and it would not be surprising if the child was frightened when the chemist appeared in a white coat. Many people experience strong emotional reactions to certain situations because in the past these reactions have been paired with some painful or unpleasant experience.

Anxiety could be produced following a car accident on a particular road. Subsequently when driving down a similar road (CS) the driver experiences anxiety (CR). In fact, an anxiety or fear could spread or be generalisable to other stimuli that bear some relationship to the original stimuli—e.g., riding a bicycle or motorcycle, or using a taxi.

Emotional reactions

An experiment conducted by Watson many years ago shows how emotional reactions may be classically conditioned in humans (Watson & Rayner, 1920). At the beginning of the experiment, an 11-month-old child named Albert was presented with a small white rat and played quite happily with it. Subsequently, there was a change in the procedure whereby an iron bar was struck to make a loud noise behind his ear every time he reached out for the rat. After several pairings of the rat (CS) and the loud noise (US) Albert cried hysterically and tried to crawl away whenever he saw a rat—or any other small, furry object—even when there was no loud noise. He developed a very strong aversive reaction to the rat.

Knowledge about how Albert's phobia occurred has led to the development of several effective procedures for reducing these reactions. In one procedure, called flooding, a person suffering from a specific fear may be forced to confront the fear-eliciting stimulus without an avenue of escape. For example, a therapist may persuade a person who has an irrational fear of heights to walk on to a high bridge and then ensure that the person stays there for some time while under supervision. As no harm arises from this experience, the person may become less fearful of heights (Baron, 2002). In situations where fear-provoking thoughts are too painful to deal with directly, a technique called systematic desensitisation aimed at replacing anxiety with a relaxation response could be used. The client is asked to describe fearful situations, starting with the least fearful ones, then visualises them and relaxes in an alternate fashion. Gradually, the individual learns to relax while imagining situations that are increasingly more threatening.

Discrimination

The opposite of generalisation is called **discrimination**. This refers to the capacity to distinguish between two stimuli so that the appropriate response to the correct stimulus is made. If Pavlov's dog salivates to the ringing of a bell but does not salivate when the telephone rings, we can conclude that it has discriminated between the appropriate and inappropriate conditioned stimuli.

When product differences are easily recognisable—such as the distinctiveness of a Mini Metro or VW Polo—it is relatively easy for consumers to discriminate. In other cases, terms such as "new" and "improved" are used in advertisements as discriminatory cues, though the continuing influx of new products to the market has deadened the

impact of these frequently used words. Stores, such as Harrods, place overwhelming emphasis on the discriminatory cue of quality. Advertisers therefore have to give due care to the strategy of differentiating between the advertised product and competing products. Differentiation is evident when a car manufacturer highlights the positive design features of a particular car when compared with similarly priced competitive models.

However, generalisation that could result in a sales increase not only for the particular brand advertised but also for competing brands may be difficult to prevent in particular circumstances. Take for example an advertisement for Pepsi-Cola, which stresses that those who drink it are cool. There is a danger that this could be generalised to Coca-Cola as well and result in increased sales of that product.

Thorndike (1911), a learning theorist, also gave much thought to the relationship between stimulus and response. He came to the conclusion that problem solving, at least in lower animals, involves a slow, gradual, and at times tortuous trial and error process. He considered learning as a gradual stamping in of correct responses and a gradual stamping out of incorrect responses.

Two basic principles govern trial and error processes: the law of repetition and the law of effect. The law of repetition is self-explanatory. The law of effect states that responses that satisfy the needs of the organism tend to be retained whereas those that fail to satisfy these needs tend to be eliminated. So, if a person gets satisfaction from performing a particular act, that act will tend to be repeated. If you find that Paracetamol is particularly effective over a period of time in removing a headache, this remedy is likely to be repeated.

Another theorist, Hull (1943), recognised the importance of intervening variables in the stimulus–response equation, though Pavlov and Thorndike played down their significance. Intervening variables consist of drive, habit strength, and incentive. A response to a need, such as consumption of a particular product, could reduce the search (drive) for this product, and satisfaction with its consumption could lead to the formation of a habit, though the habit could vary over time. Hull's theory is sometimes described as a theory of conditioned learning, and it incorporates aspects of the work of both Pavlov and Thorndike. However, Hull's real contribution is acknowledging that the internal state of the organism, and particularly motivation, must be considered in explaining learning.

Finally, some of the applications of classical conditioning may raise some ethical issues. In this context, Baddeley (1997) asks the following questions:

Is one prostituting psychology by attempting to use it to induce people to buy things they would not otherwise buy? Or is one simply helping the wheels of commerce to turn, thereby keeping the economy buoyant for everyone's benefit? Even if one has suspicions about advertising, as I suspect one should because of the role it is often allowed to play in politics, then one might still argue that it is important to understand advertising in order to control it. I suspect we shall see a good deal more work in this area in the next few years.

OPERANT CONDITIONING

The basic difference between operant conditioning and classical conditioning is that, in operant conditioning, learners must make some response before their behaviour is reinforced or rewarded.

Reinforcement

The major proponent of the theory of operant conditioning is Skinner, and his work could be considered an elaboration of Thorndike's law of effect. Skinner showed that it was possible to create fairly complex chains of novel behaviour by pinpointing responses and then rewarding them (Baddeley, 1997). In a basic experiment, Skinner (1951) placed a hungry rat in a box in which there was a lever. When the lever was depressed it activated a mechanism to deliver a food pellet. The rat tended to explore the box and, by chance, pressed the lever and a food pellet dropped. It began to press the lever more and more frequently to obtain the food. The food is the reinforcement for the behaviour. This type of experiment was also conducted with pigeons. They pecked a disc in return for food pellets. The animals developed discriminatory behaviour in the sense that the lever was pressed, or the disc pecked, when a light was on but not when it was off. Food is a major form of reinforcement for animals, and this is evident in the training of circus animals to perform interesting manoeuvres in return for rewards.

With humans, factors such as attention, praise, approval, success, and money are major reinforcers. The teacher who pays attention to the troublesome behaviour of a pupil is reinforcing that behaviour. In certain circumstances, such behaviour might profitably be ignored, whereas acceptable behaviour ought to be reinforced by praise or reward. A child may find that asking a parent a question in a civil manner produces hardly any response; however, screaming and shouting in order to attract attention does produce a response, and subsequently the child may adopt this ploy again. Some examples of operant conditioning processes in an organisation are included in Panel 7.1.

For a reinforcer to work it must be perceived by the recipient as being useful and relevant. For

PANEL 7.1: Operant conditioning in organisations

An executive is asked to speak at a board meeting. The stimulus is the request to speak, and the executive responds by giving certain views on matters within his or her area of responsibility. The executive's response may be reinforced by nods and smiles from a prominent director, and the effect of the reinforcement increases the likelihood that the executive will respond with the same or similar views at future meetings.

In another situation, a safety practitioner on an inspection in a factory is impressed by the system of control relating to potential hazards. He or she provides reinforcement by praising those responsible and writing in favourable terms about this experience in the company newsletter.

example, receiving public praise in the classroom may not be regarded as a reinforcement by the young schoolchild who does not want to be seen as the teacher's favourite. The child might work less hard in the future to avoid this embarrassing situation.

Contiguity and contingent

The principles of contiguity and contingent apply to reinforcement. The bigger the gap between behaviour and reinforcement, generally the less the likelihood that the behaviour will be strengthened or diminished. For conditioning to occur there should be only a small delay between behaviour and reinforcement (contiguity). Therefore, when a consumer enters a store to buy a new product, which has been intensively advertised, it is important that it appears on the shelf. Likewise, the commuter on the underground railway who is peckish might prefer to use a vending machine while waiting for the train, rather than satisfy his or her hunger at the end of the journey. Reinforcement should be contingent on the appropriate response; that is, it should be provided only when the desired behaviour occurs, and it should not come too late, otherwise it may be associated with more recent but inappropriate behaviour.

Extinction

If reinforcement is expected but is not forthcoming, the responses associated with it could become extinguished. For example, if the rat in Skinner's box no longer receives food after pressing the lever, it will gradually stop pressing and go back to the previous random exploratory behaviour.

Though reinforcement and reward are associated, reward is not synonymous with reinforcement. For example, a reward could be given without any effect on behaviour. A reinforcer is only a reinforcer if it maintains or increases the probability of responding at a high level.

The learning involved in operant conditioning is sometimes referred to as "instrumental conditioning", because the response of the organism is instrumental in obtaining the reinforcement.

Primary and secondary reinforcement

Reinforcers used in most animal-learning experiments are examples of **primary reinforcers**. Food, drink, and sex fit into this category. A **secondary reinforcer** is one that has derived and developed its reinforcement qualities from being associated with one or more primary reinforcers. Money would fall into this category. When monkeys performed certain actions to secure poker chips that could be exchanged for food (Wolfe, 1936), they responded to the secondary reinforcers (the poker chips). These became reinforcers because the monkeys learned that the chips could secure the food. To be effective, secondary reinforcers must be paired with primary reinforcers.

Positive and negative reinforcement

A number of examples of positive reinforcement have already been given. Skinner's rats and pigeons received positive reinforcement in the form of food. When a person picks up a magazine from a newsstand and derives satisfaction from reading it, then that person experiences positive reinforcement. The same would apply to other fast-moving consumer products; continuous satisfaction from the consumption of the product leads to a learned response and the development of brand loyalty.

Negative reinforcement and avoidance conditioning

With negative reinforcement and punishment, the organism responds to avoid an unpleasant situation. The animal in a maze soon learns not to behave in a certain way in order to avoid receiving an electric shock (a negative reinforcement). An employee may work hard during a period in which the company is going through a difficult time to avoid being made redundant, rather than for the positive reinforcement of success. The motorist with little petrol left in the tank pulls in to a filling station with low standards of service, and unavoidably receives a negative reinforcer in the form of surly, discourteous service. Next time he or she will avoid, if possible, patronising this filling station. In this case, negative reinforcement can lead to avoidance conditioning because cues have been picked up indicating that the same standard of service is likely to prevail in the future. Responses based on avoidance conditioning do not easily disappear, as most organisms are unlikely to try to establish whether or not the original negative reinforcement is still operating.

Other illustrations serve to highlight negative reinforcement and avoidance conditioning. A product is found to be faulty, or it does not live up to the customer's expectations in some way—i.e., it falls short of the manufacturer's claims. In this case, the purchase of the product will be negatively reinforced, and the customer may consciously avoid purchasing it again. This could create problems for the manufacturer because it could be difficult to extinguish a negatively reinforced response. A car manufacturer may experience problems if a product had developed a reputation for rust or faulty parts leading to an above-average breakdown record. It could take a long time to overcome this reputation, even though corrective action was instituted soon after the difficulties were reported.

Punishment

Even though positive reinforcement is said to be more effective than punishment in regulating behaviour, punishment seems to be used in society as much as reward. The link between action or response and reward is visible in positive reinforcement, unlike punishment where it is evident that the action is wrong but the correct response is not specified. However, punishment can play a useful role in stamping out inappropriate behaviour and regulating behaviour, at least in the short term. If a lecturer raises his voice disapprovingly at a student guilty of disruptive tactics in the classroom, the misbehaviour is likely to cease immediately. The sudden cessation of the undesirable behaviour is very reinforcing for the lecturer.

Though punishment has a role to play in changing behaviour, it should be used sparingly. If it is not severe, and there is a clear distinction between good and bad (for example, children playing on the road or with matches could be considered bad behaviour), then problems are unlikely to arise in terms of behavioural abnormalities.

But if punishment is very severe in conditions where it is not easy to distinguish between right and wrong, it may affect negatively both the bad behaviour and other similar good behaviour. For example, administering hard punishment to a child for answering back may not only extinguish this type of response but also it may eliminate intelligent discussions with parents and perhaps others as well, and so it produces unwanted side-effects. Many chronically shy, unassertive individuals report that extremely punitive measures were used against them in childhood, not only when they challenged parental commands but also occasionally when they only tried to voice their opinions on some issue or other. Often, people feel hostile towards punishment because it is viewed as a process that created anxiety in the first instance. Many children have failed to fulfil their scholastic potential because of negative feelings towards teachers and schools that have arisen through earlier traumatic experiences in an educational setting.

To produce the maximum effect, the punishment should come immediately after the undesirable behaviour (Burns & Dobson, 1984). Note the paradox of the heavy drinker, for example, who, despite warnings about cirrhosis, has another drink. If death from cirrhosis was the immediate consequence of having another drink, he or she would decline it. But in reality the immediate pleasure of the alcoholic drink outweighs the distant worry of possible liver failure.

Generally, in order to stop the undesirable behaviour, enough punishment must be meted out early in the process and the recipient must know which aspects of his or her behaviour are looked upon with disapproval. It is always wise to have a positive reinforcement in mind.

There are occasions when organisations have to rely on punishment or discipline, preferably to be used on a progressive basis. This means that each episode of undesirable behaviour—e.g., poor timekeeping, unacceptable work rate, theft, and curt treatment of clients—receives a stronger disciplinary measure than the one that preceded it. For example, the first infringement of the company's rules invites a verbal reprimand, the second is followed by a written reprimand, the third by a suspension, and the fourth by dismissal. It is always wise for managers to provide information on the offence to which the punishment relates and the consequences of repeating the undesirable behaviour.

Vecchio (2003), having reflected on punishment, maintains that the intention to use punishment should be carefully considered in the light of the particular circumstances, and for punishment to be effective the following conditions should be met: "the recipient must recognise that it is not directed at his or her character or self-worth; it should be given as soon as possible after the undesired behaviour; it should be sufficiently severe that it cannot be ignored; it should be used in a consistent way across instances and people; and it should be extremely clear that the reason for the punishment was the specific actions of the transgressor."

Schedules of reinforcement

Examples were given earlier of the nature of reinforcement with respect to animals and humans. Here we examine different ways in which reinforcement is administered. When behaviour is reinforced each time it occurs it is referred to as **continuous reinforcement**. However, reinforcement is not necessary every time a response is made; in fact, intermittent or partial reinforcement may suffice.

Intermittent or partial reinforcement

Reinforcing responses only some of the time can be categorised as fixed ratio, variable ratio, fixed interval, and variable interval.

Fixed ratio. A fixed ratio could be the reinforcement of, say, every fifth response. The fixed ratio schedule keeps the response fairly low after the moment of reinforcement, with a build up to a crescendo just before the next reinforcement, when, for example, Skinner's pigeon would be extremely active pecking the disc in anticipation of obtaining more food pellets.

Variable ratio. A variable ratio could be the reinforcement of, for example, the third, tenth, and then the fifth response. Under the variable ratio schedule, the pigeon produces a very high and steady response rate as it has no idea when reinforcement will come. The variable ratio schedule is the one that is generally not resistant to extinction because the individual or animal never knows when reinforcement will appear again. Although continuous reinforcement is essential in establishing behaviour initially, once behaviour is learned it is best maintained on a partial reinforcement schedule such as the variable ratio basis (Burns & Dobson, 1984). An example of an application of this ratio is set out in Panel 7.2.

It is the irregularity of the reward schedule that makes gambling so difficult to eradicate, because the gambler always feels he or she may be lucky next time. In one experiment (Lewis & Duncan, 1956) people were allowed to gamble using slot machines. The machines were tampered with so that some paid out on every operation of the lever (continuous reinforcement) whereas other machines functioned like normal slot machines and paid out on a periodic basis (partial reinforcement). Then a significant modification took place in the experiment whereby everybody played

---

PANEL 7.2: The variable ratio and absenteeism

The variable ratio schedule in the form of a lottery has been used to reduce absenteeism. The New York Life Insurance Company devised a lottery that rewarded employees for attendance (Halcrow, 1986). Every 3 months the names of central office employees—roughly 4000 of the total of 7500 employees—were placed in a drum. The first 10 names extracted were entitled to a bond worth $200, the next 20 names to a bond valued at $100, and a further 70 names received a day off with pay. At the end of the year another lottery was held for employees with a year of perfect attendance, for which 12 prizes were given—2 employees each received a bond worth $1000, and a further 10 were entitled to 5 days off with pay.

Under this schedule of reinforcement, a good attendance record increased an employee's probability of winning, but a perfect attendance did not guarantee the award of a prize. The use of the lottery as a variable ratio schedule in this case resulted in lower absenteeism rates.

PANEL 7.3: Rat catching and reinforcement

A study by Latham and Dossett (1978) focused on trappers who were paid to catch rats that were eating young trees planted for reforestation purposes. After an initial period on regular hourly pay, half the trappers operated on the basis of hourly pay plus a continuous reinforcement schedule (a specified bonus per rat trapped). The remaining trappers operated on the basis of hourly pay plus a variable ratio schedule (a bonus was paid for an average of every fourth rat trapped). Later these reinforcement schedules were reversed.

Both reinforcement schedules contributed to an improvement in the performance of the trappers, but the continuous reinforcement schedule was at least as effective as the variable ratio schedule. However, when the trappers were split into experienced and inexperienced groups, the variable ratio schedule was superior among the more experienced trappers. But the less experienced group, who were presumably still learning, operated better under a continuous reinforcement schedule.

---

on a machine that was adjusted in such a way that it would never pay out; in other words there would be no reinforcement whatsoever. The subjects who had experienced partial reinforcement were much more resistant to extinction of their responses and they continued to play long after the subjects who experienced continuous reinforcement had stopped.

Fixed interval.   A fixed interval could be the reinforcement of responses, say, every 10 minutes. With the fixed interval schedule there would be a reduction of activity just after the moment of reinforcement.

Variable interval.   A variable interval could be the reinforcement of responses at varying time intervals. The variable interval schedule produces a steady and high response rate.

Applications of partial reinforcement.   The most appropriate partial reinforcement schedule has to be considered in relation to work and business practice. It would be impossible to use the variable ratio schedule as the only method for providing rewards to employees. People expect to obtain their salary on a regular basis (fixed interval), whatever the evidence in support of the variable ratio schedule. However, rewards such as bonuses and praise may materialise on a variable basis. A random partial reinforcement can be used as a basis for sales promotion schemes such as competitions. The consumer may be encouraged to purchase a certain product because it also provides an opportunity to enter a competition and a chance to win a holiday or car. But only a tiny minority of consumers is likely to receive the

stated reinforcement (to win the competition). However, a large number of people may be persuaded to buy the product because of the competition, and then find that the product satisfies their needs. Its purchase has become a learned response.

Continuous reinforcement

As stated earlier, continuous reinforcement amounts to the reinforcement of every response. Some research findings indicate that continuous reinforcement can be as effective as partial reinforcement. In a study of workers planting pine seedlings it was found that a variable ratio schedule based on incentives was no better than a continuous reinforcement schedule; if anything it was less effective (Yukl, Latham, & Elliott, 1976). A further example is included in Panel 7.3. Such findings indicate that one should pay particular attention to differences between individuals when specifying the most appropriate reinforcement schedule. (An alternative theoretical framework for examining the relationship between rewards and performance is the expectancy theory of motivation, discussed in Chapter 2.)

Rules governing reinforcement

Hamner (1983) identified six rules that could be helpful when applying the concept of reinforcement in an organisational context:

(1)   Rewards should vary depending on performance. If everybody received the same reward, irrespective of performance, this would be tantamount to punishing the best performers

and rewarding the poorer ones. It could lead to the best performers reducing their contributions or leaving the organisation.

(2) Managers shape the behaviour of their subordinates by what they fail to do as well as by what they actually do. For instance, a failure to take action on a subordinate's lack of punctuality may be seen as a sign that it is acceptable to come to work late. It follows that managers have to consider the consequences in terms of performance of their lack of action as well as their actions. Therefore, a failure to respond has reinforcing consequences.

(3) Managers should acquaint subordinates with what is expected of them to ensure they receive the appropriate rewards, without restricting their job freedom unduly.

(4) So as to take the necessary corrective action, subordinates should be told when they are doing things wrong. Without feedback of this nature, subordinates do not understand why rewards are not given, or why punishment strategies are being used.

(5) Subordinates should not be punished in front of colleagues. To do so would amount to a double punishment, and could incite an undesirable response. For example, a subordinate in such a situation may experience a badly dented self-image, and may decide to consider ways of settling scores with management.

(6) In order to maintain the necessary level of commitment and motivation, managers should be fair with subordinates, and those doing a good job should receive the appropriate reward.

Concurrent schedule of reinforcement

As a final comment on reinforcement, note that there is a school of thought that says that the principles of reinforcement described above do not do justice to the complexity of human behaviour (Hanisch, 1995). In reality one is faced daily with alternatives and often one must choose one alternative to the exclusion of others. At work it is necessary on a particular day for an executive to choose between, say, preparation for an important meeting, writing an important report, or visiting a client. This example illustrates a concurrent schedule of reinforcement under which a person's behaviour is free to alternate continuously between two or more responses, each having its own schedule of reinforcement. The concurrent schedule of reinforcement has been used to study choice behaviour in both animals and humans (Elsmore & McBride, 1994). We would expect the executive to distribute his or her behaviour between the alternatives specified above in such a way that maximises the reinforcement received for the expenditure of effort.

PROGRAMMED LEARNING

Programmed learning can be discussed with reference to **linear programming** and branching.

Linear programming

Linear programming, which involves presenting very small pieces of information (a frame) at an acceptable level of difficulty to the learner, sometimes using machines, is linked to Skinner's concept of operant conditioning. It is a deliberate attempt to utilise in the classroom the experimental findings of the psychological laboratory, and is a major component of programmed learning.

The learner goes through a sequence of frames and makes a response. For learning to be effective under linear programming, reinforcement should follow immediately after the response; only acceptable behaviour, such as the right answer, is reinforced, and there must be sufficient reinforcements otherwise lack of interest will lead to an extinct response. When the desired response is emitted, being told that the correct answer has been given positively reinforces the learner. Repeating the question negatively reinforces an incorrect response.

Linear programming can be reduced to the following basic principles:

- The subject matter, process, or skill is defined, analysed, and broken down into its elements.

- Material is presented step-by-step in a prearranged sequence, with the steps being so small that the error rate should be close to nil.
- At each step, the learner is given just enough information to ensure he or she makes an active correct response before going on to the next item.
- Learners receive immediate confirmation of the results emanating from their responses, work at their own rate, and check their own progress.

As individuals work at their own pace, some take longer than others to get through the programme. The major disadvantages seem to be that, once written, programmes become inflexible and impersonal. They can also become boring after the initial novelty wears off. The personal intervention of the teacher (particularly the development of personal relationships, which is absent in programmed learning) is often considered to be critical in helping students to maintain their interest and motivation. (Perhaps this would not apply to the teacher with poor teaching skills.)

Skinner (1961) developed teaching machines because he believed that classroom learning was inefficient due to reinforcements being either delayed too long or being absent. This might be an oversimplification, because, although animals like to receive reinforcements without much delay, humans generally favour delayed reinforcement. Humans have the capacity to retain information about reinforcements over a substantial period of time.

Branching

Another technique of programmed instruction is branching. Material presented in branching frames is usually more difficult and mistakes are more frequent. The questions at the end of the frame are designed to determine what, if anything, the learner has misunderstood. This can be achieved by directing the learner to remedial frames that deal with specific misunderstandings, and then directing the learner back into the mainstream of the programme.

Programmed learning is not in widespread use. An enormous number of prepared programmes would be required for large-scale use and presently the take-up rate is at a modest level. However, with substantial growth in the use of computer hardware and software this situation is changing.

BEHAVIOUR MODIFICATION

This is a technique that draws its strength from operant conditioning. It is used to control and change behaviour by reinforcing in a systematic way those actions that are considered important or desirable. A related approach to the control and change of behaviour, which preceded the use of behaviour modification techniques, is that of **shaping**.

Shaping

With shaping, an appropriate reinforcer is selected to suit the occasion, and all positive reinforcements are contingent on the organism moving closer to adopting the desired behaviour. Gradually a chain of behaviour is built up and once the desired behaviour is achieved it will be reinforced continuously at first and subsequently on a variable basis.

For example, a pigeon can be taught to pick up a marble in its beak and deposit it in a box. The pigeon is accustomed to receiving food pellets in a small area, and when the pigeon happens to move near the marble the trainer uses the food reinforcement. As a result, the pigeon will now be more likely to spend time near the marble. The trainer waits until the bird looks in the direction of the marble. The looking increases and the trainer then waits until the bird happens to bend towards the marble before it receives reinforcement. So, in progressive steps, circumstances emerge whereby reinforcement is withheld until the bird performs the complicated movement that is required.

In another experiment, Skinner found that when a hungry pigeon engaged in a particular behaviour at the time it received a reinforcement (i.e., turning round in an anti-clockwise manner when the food came), this behavioural pattern developed into a conditioned response. Between

PANEL 7.4: Shaping and sales representatives

In an encounter between a customer and a sales representative, the customer emits an operant—e.g., a remark that need not be directly related to the topic that is of principal interest to the sales representative. The sales representative moves closer to the customer by a process of reinforcement. This could take the form of a nod, a smile, saying "that's a good point", "how interesting", and so on. Part of the behavioural strategy is to have a large repertoire of reinforcers and to select those most appropriate to a particular situation.

Reinforcement that the customer considers relevant can lead to the emission of another operant. Subsequently the sales representative should be selective in the use of reinforcers—that is, he or she should provide reinforcement when the conversation of the customer shifts a little nearer to the technical matter that interests the sales representative. The sales representative will tend to be effective if he or she is able to provide appropriate reinforcements to satisfy the psychological needs of the customer, on the assumption that the more the customer enjoys the encounter the more he or she will believe the technical case put forward by the sales representative.

the food-giving sessions the pigeon would perform anti-clockwise dances two or three times until the food was presented again. Skinner imputes to the pigeon a certain superstition, in the sense that the bird behaves as if its pattern of behaviour was the cause of the food. As mentioned earlier, shaping is used to control the behaviour of circus animals, and Skinner also trained pigeons to play tennis; they poked a table tennis ball across a table, trying to get it into a trough on their opponent's side (Skinner, 1951, 1961).

Shaping is also common in human learning. Tennis coaches, driving instructors, teachers, and parents all guide their subjects to the desired performance, be it manual, linguistic, social, or emotional behaviour (see Panel 7.4 for an example).

Modelling

An applied learning procedure associated with shaping is **modelling**. The desired behaviour is firmly kept in mind before selecting the appropriate model capable of exemplifying the way to proceed: this could, for example, be an ideal style of supervision. Then a supportive learning situation is created, using role playing. The desirable consequences of adopting the model's behaviour are emphasised, and reinforcement is provided when the model behaviour is achieved. Initially, reinforcement can be continuous, and, subsequently, provided on a variable basis. Modelling procedures can be illustrated with reference to a study (Goldstein & Sorcher, 1974) that was conducted at the General Electric Company (GE) in the USA (see Panel 7.5).

A variant of the GE study was the following exercise in behavioural analysis conducted in a small business (Komaki, Waddell, & Pearce, 1977). Two employees in a grocery store were engaged in stock and sales activities. Their performance, covering a variety of duties, was initially monitored. Subsequently, the clerks were trained

PANEL 7.5: Modelling at GE

The aim of the study was to assist in facilitating the retention of disadvantaged employees. Films were developed to use with both employees and their supervisors. The supervisor films showed and modelled rewards for tact, coolness, patience, thoroughness, and control. The employee films emphasised the courage needed to succeed, the value of working at a job, and success in a job. Other situations depicted were as follows: not quitting; how to teach a task; developing trust; pride in work; reactions to ostracism; the new environment; absenteeism; and lateness. Each film was introduced and summarised by a member of the management team, such as a plant manager in the case of the supervisors, and a famous black athlete in the case of the employees.

As part of the training session, role playing was introduced during breaks in the film show, and instructors and other members of the training group provided continuous social reinforcement when role playing behaviour was similar or identical to the behaviour of the models portrayed. In all, there were five 2-hour sessions for both the supervisors and employees, and the outcome was very favourable from the point of view of the company.

(Goldstein & Sorcher, 1974)

in desired work behaviour, through discussion, modelling, and role playing. Reinforcement took the form of time off with pay, feedback in visual form, and self-recording undertaken by the employees. Following some behaviour modification interventions, performance increased significantly in terms of the employees' presence, assistance given to customers, and the completeness of the stock position.

Role modelling and shaping are relevant to training issues discussed later in Chapter 18 in connection with human resources practices, and to attitudes (Chapter 9), groups (Chapter 10), leadership (Chapter 12), culture (Chapter 15), and organisational change and development (Chapter 16).

Organisational behaviour modification

Two prominent contributors to behaviour modification in an organisational context are Hamner and Luthans. Both adopt a Skinnerian approach, though Luthans goes further than Hamner in his adherence to Skinner's ideas. There is clearly an overlap between the two, but it is useful to present their views separately.

Hamner's approach

Hamner has proposed certain steps or stages that should be followed when introducing a positive reinforcement programme in a company (Hamner, 1977; Hamner & Hamner, 1976). The emphasis is on performance maximisation, maximum positive reinforcement, and minimum negative reinforcement. The attitudes of workers are generally ignored.

(1) Performance should be defined in behavioural terms, and the company should be as objective as possible in devising measures of performance.

(2) Specific and reasonable performance goals should be set for each worker in a form that can be measured; these goals are not meant to be personal goals—they are organisational goals.

(3) The employee should maintain a continuous record of his or her work so that the relationship between the performance goal and actual audited performance is clearly visible. The objective is to highlight behaviour that is associated with positive reinforcements; therefore, the measurement of performance should be frequent rather than infrequent.

(4) The supervisor looks through the employee's own feedback report, as well as examining other indicators of performance such as sales or production records. With reference to the previously set goals and audited performance, the supervisor praises the positive aspects of the employee's performance. This amounts to positive reinforcement and it should strengthen the employee's resolve to achieve performance goals.

The withholding of praise for sub-standard performance in relation to the goals set should give the employee an incentive to improve performance. Working on the assumption that the employee is already aware of his or her deficiencies, there is no reason for the supervisor to be critical. In the final analysis the use of positive reinforcement leads to a greater feeling of self-control, whereas the avoidance of negative reinforcements keeps the individual from feeling controlled or coerced.

Luthans' approach

The approach of Luthans is called the behavioural contingency management model for organisational behaviour modification. It seeks to identify and manage the critical performance-related behaviour of employees in organisations, and consists of a five-step procedure (Luthans & Kreitner, 1975).

(1) The critical behaviour necessary for satisfactory performance should be identified. The causes of good performance or bad performance should be noted, and techniques such as discussion and observation may be used to carry out this procedure.

(2) A measure should be used to determine the strength or frequency of the relevant behaviour, using tally sheets, time sampling, and so on.

PANEL 7.6: Sales representatives and behaviour modification

The importance of understanding what is maintaining a behaviour pattern is illustrated by an example (Robertson & Cooper, 1983) of a sales manager who is concerned about the large number of visits by sales representatives to the home base; the visits are seen to be unproductive chats with colleagues.

The sales manager is acutely aware of the time-wasting involved and is unhappy about the fact that the sales director keeps making comments that large numbers of the salesforce are sitting at the home base doing nothing. It would be logical to establish the apparent rewards for returning to base. The chance to relax and avoid the pressures of being on the road may be one factor to consider. Another, and perhaps more important, may be that the sales representatives have the opportunity for social interaction with their colleagues. It is perhaps the reinforcing effect of the social interaction that is maintaining the undesirable behaviour from the company's point of view.

This analysis could lead to the adoption of a behaviour modification programme as a means of encouraging sales representatives to make fewer visits to the home base. However, the strategy of discouraging them from making frequent visits to the home base as a means to make better use of their time could be defeated if opportunities for relaxation existed elsewhere, or if it was possible to stagger the visits so that only small numbers were at the home base at any one time.

---

(3) A functional analysis of the behaviour is carried out, and this exercise poses a number of questions. What factors caused the behaviour in the first place, and what is sustaining it in terms of reward or avoidance of punishment? It is essential to have a view of the factors that may be maintaining the behaviour in question (see Panel 7.6).

(4) After conducting functional analysis, an intervention process gets under way to modify the appropriate behaviour. Care has to be exercised so that only desired behaviour is reinforced, and it is important to consider the context of the behaviour—e.g., tasks and organisation structure. A wide variety and range of rewards are available, and some do not involve costs, such as friendly greetings and compliments. In Table 7.1 there is a list of possible rewards for use in organisational behaviour modification. This approach represents a major alternative to the expectancy theory of motivation discussed in Chapter 4.

(5) The final step in the procedure is evaluation. The primary aim of evaluation is to establish to what extent intervention has modified the behaviour. One way to achieve that aim is for the intervention process to be removed or reversed, and then the consequences are noted. Various combinations for manipulating the situation can be used in order to assess the impact of the behaviour modification programme.

Illustrations of the practice of behaviour modification appear in Panel 7.7.

Criticisms of organisational behaviour modification

Despite its apparent success, organisational behaviour modification has been the subject of a number of criticisms. The most favourable results emanating from the use of behaviour modification techniques are associated with highly controllable situations, such as a straightforward process in a small business, or variables that are independent and easily isolated (e.g., absenteeism). As research studies move into more complex situations involving subtle interactions between people, and where jobs are interdependent, the success of behaviour modification techniques is open to question.

Furthermore, almost all the research studies have focused on employees in the lower echelons of the organisation, paying less attention to the behaviour of managerial or professional staff. At these lower organisational levels, employees experience greater supervisory control and encounter less complex jobs, and it is said that these conditions facilitate the obtaining of positive results from the use of behaviour modification techniques (Miner, 1980).

The ethical problem of behaviour control and modification has to be considered, and some argue that the systematic manipulation and control of

TABLE 7.1

Organisational behaviour modification rewards (from Luthans & Kreitner, 1975): Adapted by permission of Pearson Education, Inc., Upper Saddle River, NJ

Contrived on-the-job rewards				Natural rewards	
Consumables	Manipulables	Visual and auditory	Tokens	Social	Other
Coffee-break treats	Desk accessories	Office with a	Money	Friendly greetings	Job with more
Free lunches	Wall plaques	window	Stocks	Informal recognition	responsibility
Food baskets	Company car	Piped-in music	Stock options	Formal acknowledgement	Job rotation
Easter hams	Watches	Redecoration of	Passes for films	of achievement	Early time off with pay
Christmas turkeys	Trophies	work environment	Trading stamps	Invitations to coffee/lunch	Extended breaks
Dinners for the family	Commendations	Company literature	Paid-up insurance	Solicitations of suggestions	Extended lunch period
on the company	Rings/tiepins	Private office	policies	Solicitations of advice	Personal time off with pay
Company picnics	Appliances and	Popular speakers or	Dinner and theatre	Compliments on work	Work on personal project
After-work wine and	furniture for the	lecturers	tickets	progress	on company time
cheese parties	home	Book club	Holiday trips	Recognition in house organ	Use of company machinery
Beer parties	Home shop tools	discussions	Coupons	Pat on the back	or facilities for personal
	Garden tools	Feedback about	redeemable at	Smile	projects
	Clothing	performance	local stores	Verbal or nonverbal	Use of company recreation
	Club privileges		Profit-sharing	recognition or praise	facilities
	Special assignments				

PANEL 7.7: Applications of behaviour modification

Apparently, persuading workers to use personal protective equipment, such as earplugs or spectacles, is a significant problem in many manufacturing plants, and there is no doubt that a fair number of accidents at work could be avoided if personal protective equipment was used appropriately. The challenge then is to change the workers' behaviour as a means of avoiding work hazards.

This challenge was taken up in a study within a company, using a behaviour modification programme to alter the habits of workers with regard to wearing ear protectors (Zohar, 1980). Some workers tend to be resistant to wearing ear protectors because they perceive certain costs associated with the practice, such as a very unpleasant adaptation period, a continual concern for cleanliness when using earplugs, and increased sweating around the ear when using ear muffs. Because in this case and in a number of other situations no penalties accrue for not wearing the ear protectors, and the prospect of hearing loss is too distant to be considered significant, the incentive to wear personal protective equipment of this nature is weak. Attempts were made to change the behavioural balance in favour of earplugs by introducing new reinforcers on a less-than-permanent basis. It was considered appropriate to enlist the support of supervisors in the design and execution of the programme. In this way it was felt that there could be mutual superior and subordinate reinforcement, and this could sustain the modified behaviour after the programme had terminated.

In a metal fabrication plant of a company with 2000 employees the management style was production-oriented and authoritarian, and industrial relations were poor as evidenced by the company's history of frequent strikes and high staff turnover. But the company was known for its outstanding safety record, due primarily to top management's involvement in all safety-related issues. Management had tried to increase the use of earplugs by workers before the study was conducted, using group lectures, poster campaigns, and disciplinary action. These efforts seemed to have had limited success.

Control and experimental groups were drawn from two departments involved mainly in lathe-type operations characterised by high-frequency noise levels averaging 90 decibels. Both groups received a standard lecture on hearing conservation, but only the experimental group received immediate feedback as a reinforcer. In order to gauge hearing loss, short audiometric tests were administered at the beginning and end of a work shift, and the audiograms from these tests were shown to the workers immediately after the test. The differences between the beginning of shift and end of shift tests were expressed in terms of temporary hearing loss.

One copy of the audiogram was given to each of the workers, and a second was placed on a special bulletin board in the production area. As well as the data on temporary hearing loss, other information such as a worker's name, age, and number of years in the department also appeared on the bulletin board. Workers were encouraged to try to use earplugs during one of their testing days so that they could observe the effect of noise on temporary hearing loss during that shift. On the other testing day there would be no such condition. The testing procedure was terminated after all the workers had been tested. For a period of 5 months thereafter (the follow-up period) the researchers sampled the behaviour of earplug use. The results indicate that in the experimental group department the use of earplugs had risen appreciably (from 35% to 85%) at the end of the 5-month period. But the control group, who did not participate in the experiment except for listening to the standard lecture on hearing conservation, did not undergo any noticeable change. It took some time for the dramatic rise in earplug use in the experimental group to take place.

The effects of the experimental conditions were complemented by a management prescription requiring the compulsory use of earplugs in the production area. This was an important adjunct to the experiment because, in the changed environment, deviant behaviour (not wearing earplugs) could result in corrective or punitive responses by supervisors. Therefore, this altered the balance in favour of earplug use.

The experiment relied on individual feedback and the expenditure involved was no higher than the costs of a conventional promotion campaign to encourage the use of personal protective equipment. The evidence presented here supports the case for adopting a behaviourist approach to encourage safe work behaviour in these circumstances. Note the reliance placed on feedback in this case. Prompt feedback regarding success or failure is one the most important features of the application of operant principles to practical problems (Baddeley, 1997).

In a study conducted in a large hospital, a behaviour modification programme involving staff from many functions was used (Snyder & Luthans, 1982). Supervisors were given training in behaviour modification, and were encouraged to select problems and behaviours that could be measured, analysed, and adjusted by behaviour modification. Subsequently, intervention strategies were selected and applied. The results of the study indicated that behaviour modification as a process made a very favourable impact on performance in the hospital.

In another study, behaviour modification was used to improve teaching methods in schools for severely handicapped children (Parsons, Schepis, Reid, McCarn, & Green, 1987). The purpose of the programme was to encourage staff to use material and engage in classroom activities that had greater applicability in the real world. The programme was planned and executed by appealing to normal behaviour modification principles, with a successful outcome.

people undermines freedom and is an affront to the dignity of the individual (Robertson & Cooper, 1983). Others assert that operant conditioning principles lack the capacity to explain human action because they are not concerned with the internal functioning of the person (Locke, 1977).

This criticism may have had greater validity in the past, because more recent work on behaviour modification acknowledges that behaviour is better understood as a function of both the situation and the person, and the interaction between the two (Davis & Luthans, 1980).

Reflecting on behaviour modification, Baddeley (1997) concludes that it has both strength and weakness. Its strength is that it will continue to be an important means to help people achieve long-term goals, which individuals currently cannot pursue because of being overwhelmed with short-term distractions and being side-tracked. Giving the person the motivational impetus to overcome these obstacles is where behaviour modification can play an important part. The weakness of behaviour modification is its ineffectiveness if it tries to change the person's habits when this would have the effect of running counter to the realisation of the long-term goals of the individual.

Relevance of social learning theory

Acknowledging the interaction between situational and personal factors, encapsulated in social learning theory, is said to be more productive than the purely situational view contained in operant conditioning. Reference has already been made to a social learning approach in the discussion of personality in Chapter 2. In social learning theory, internal cognitive processes are said to have some effect on behaviour. This could be reflected in a person's expectations about the outcome of a particular piece of behaviour. The individual realises from experience that certain actions will produce valuable benefits, and other actions will result in avoiding future trouble (Bandura, 1977). For example, business people do not have to wait until they experience the shock of a burning warehouse before they are prompted to take out fire insurance cover.

Another aspect of social learning theory is the notion that individuals adopt their own pattern of behaviour by observing and copying or modelling the behaviour of others. On the face of it, the act of modelling one's behaviour on other people's behaviour appears to provide no direct reinforcement. But what if the observer had expectations that certain desirable consequences could flow from adopting the behaviour of the model? The junior executive may copy the behaviour of the successful senior executive (e.g., mannerisms, work rate, management style) in the expectation that such behaviour leads to desired outcomes. Obviously, cognitive activity comes to the fore in this example (the junior executive concludes that the observed behaviour is functional).

The socialisation processes involved in situations like the one described are informal, as opposed to formal processes such as induction programmes for new recruits or the training programmes for established employees. In some quarters there is a belief that the socialisation process should not be left to chance but should be formalised and used in a proactive sense by the organisation if the challenges of today's business world are to be successfully met (Nota, 1988). (As well as the discussion of socialisation in connection with a behavioural perspective on personality in Chapter 2, there is reference in Chapter 15 to organisational socialisation in the context of the development of corporate culture.)

Social learning theorists maintain that although people respond to external reinforcement (e.g., money or praise), people often control and develop patterns of behaviour through the use of self-reinforcement. For example, a positive self-reinforcement could arise when an athlete, having appraised his or her performance in finishing in fifth place in an important race, nevertheless feels extremely satisfied because of the strong competition. Another athlete, having appraised his or her performance, feels intensely dissatisfied with the outcome and rebukes himself or herself. It is now apparent that internal cognitive processes, such as self-reinforcement and expectations as to the outcome of behaviour, should be placed alongside external reinforcement when considering the application of behaviour modification techniques (Arnold, 2005). For further comment on social cognitive theory (Bandura, 1986), refer to the discussion of behavioural role modelling in the "Training processes" section of Chapter 18.

COGNITIVE LEARNING

The main difference between a behaviourist approach to learning and a cognitive approach is that in cognitive learning there is a change in what the learner knows rather than what he or she

PANEL 7.8: Chimpanzees and insight learning

Kohler (1927) placed chimpanzees in an enclosed play area where food was kept out of their reach. Potential tools such as poles and boxes were placed in the enclosure, and the chimpanzees rapidly learned how to use a box to stand on or a pole to move the food in their direction. At times the poles were even used for pole-vaulting.

In this experiment, learning did not appear to develop as a result of trial and error and reinforcement, but came about in sudden flashes of insight. The chimpanzee would roam about the enclosure for some time, and then suddenly would stand on a box, grasp a pole and strike a banana suspended out of normal reach above the enclosure. When the chimpanzees were moved to new situations, the previous learning seemed to be transferred and the problems were solved quickly.

does. The processing of knowledge is therefore important. Cognitive learning consists of two components—insight learning and latent learning.

Insight learning

Much learning involves understanding what is being learned and thinking about it. Even animals behave sometimes as if they had insight into the situation to which they are responding. In a normal experiment in insight learning a problem is presented, followed by a period of time when no apparent progress is made, and finally a solution suddenly emerges. A feature of insight learning is that it can be generalisable to other similar situations (see Panel 7.8).

Latent learning

Latent learning is not manifest at the time learning takes place. The learning goes on in the absence of reward, but when a suitable reward is available the information previously learned can be used. We tend to store knowledge about positive and negative reinforcements acquired through past experience. For example, we may well have registered that a certain type of previous job was a source of satisfaction, whereas another proved unsatisfactory. Likewise, the individual forms many kinds of cognitions about the way the career in which he or she is interested is structured, from the trainee stage right up to the highest position of responsibility.

Cognitions from several different learning experiences may be integrated so that the individual can adapt to new situations and achieve personal goals. Tolman (1948) made an early contribution to the concept of latent learning. He placed a rat in a maze, and the rat developed a cognitive map or mental picture of the maze. The rat learned something about the spatial arrangement of the maze, but this learning was not evident until a reinforcement motivated the animal to behave— i.e., to use an alternative escape route when the original one was blocked. One should add that although the existence of cognitive maps has not been clearly established (Wehner & Menzel, 1990), there is substantial evidence that animals form mental representations of their environment, including memories of positive and negative reinforcements (Capaldi, Birmingham, & Alptekin, 1995).

Skills acquisition

Cognitive learning has relevance in the context of the acquisition of complex skills. Fitts (1962) refers to three phases of skills development, which are conceptually distinct but there could be some overlap:

(1) *Cognitive.* The learner seeks an understanding of the tasks involved, stressing deliberate and conscious action. For example, the learner expresses a wish to ride a bicycle and asks, "What type of bicycle should I choose? On what surface should I practise? What is the best way to ride it?" At this phase the emphasis is on contemplating the action necessary for successful performance.

(2) *Associative.* The association between knowledge and application intensifies. Practice is a key aspect of this phase as the learner goes through the motions of improving

---

PANEL 7.9: Feedback in the learning process

We use information on how we are progressing, and this is called feedback. A lecturer provides a student with extrinsic feedback. This feedback is delayed because it normally arrives some time after the submission of an assignment or piece of homework. Good feedback can assist the person receiving it to improve his or her performance.

Apart from delayed feedback, there is concurrent feedback, which arrives as one is actually engaged in a particular activity, such as the information received from a speedometer and what can be seen through the windscreen of a car while driving. This can result in controlling or modifying our behaviour at that time.

Concurrent feedback is unlikely to be provided by a lecturer on an academic course while the student is preparing an essay, but it is good practice to provide the student with feedback within a reasonable time of the submission of the coursework.

There is another type of feedback, which is called intrinsic feedback. In the discussion of the kinaesthesis and vestibular senses in Chapter 5 (perception) there is an acknowledgement of intrinsic feedback. The kinaesthesis sense provides intrinsic feedback from the muscles, tendons, and joints when the person is in motion and this provides essential information on the relative position of our limbs and different parts of our body.

As to the vestibular sense, which operates through the inner ear, the intrinsic feedback helps maintain the body's posture and equilibrium.

Generally, extrinsic feedback serves two main functions for those receiving it—one is instructional and the other is motivational. The instructional aspect can be seen when a trainer clarifies issues for the trainee or endeavours to impart new knowledge or assist with the acquisition of a new skill. For example, the trainer points out that a particular negotiating tactic is not appropriate and explains that an alternative tactic is likely to produce a better outcome. The motivational aspect is evident when extrinsic feedback serves as a reward. An example of this would be a manager complimenting a co-worker for exceptional performance in a difficult project; this amounts to a rewarding item of news and could enhance feelings of competence and personal control. In another situation the provision of specific feedback on results to individuals faced with challenging goals could be powerful in a motivational sense (Earley, Northcraft, Lee, & Lituchy, 1990). The last observation is also relevant in the context of goal-setting in motivation, discussed in Chapter 4.

Finally, note the following observations by Kreitner, Kinicki, and Buelens (2002): it is wise to ensure that feedback in a work setting is based on accurate and credible information, is appropriately targeted, geared to performance aimed at specific outcomes, and is provided reasonably frequently.

---

performance. For example, much less attention is devoted to the steps involved in riding a bicycle, but practice and the use of feedback lead to an improvement in performance. (There is comment on feedback in skills acquisition in Panel 7.9.)

(3) *Autonomous.* At this phase the performance of the skill becomes increasingly automatic. Now there is much less reliance on attention to detail and invoking memory, and the capacity to withstand distractions (e.g., being asked a question) is progressively enhanced.

Another researcher has postulated ideas similar to Fitts, when he refers to *declarative knowledge*, *procedural knowledge*, and the *tuning stage* (Anderson, 1983, 1987). Again, using the analogy of the cyclist, declarative knowledge is the requisite facts, which are declared, on riding a bicycle. The demands on attention and memory are great during the declarative stage, and when it ends the performer ought to have a good grasp of the guiding principles.

Procedural knowledge is the information utilised during the physical act of cycling. At this stage the guiding principles are solidified as a result of experience (e.g., practice sessions). However, it is possible to encounter a situation where a person has the necessary knowledge on how to ride a bicycle, but is not able to operationalise this knowledge for a variety of reasons such as lack of confidence or opportunity.

Tuning is the final stage where the principles and guidelines underpinning performance are fine-tuned to bring about skilful and automatic performance.

Cognitive learning is closely related to other topics discussed elsewhere in this book. For example, selective perception (Chapter 5) and information-processing (Chapter 8) are important ingredients in the cognitive process. But the heart of cognitive learning is memory.

MEMORY

Memory performs many functions and is involved in nearly every aspect of behaviour. In order to remember new information the individual needs to process or encode the information, store or retain it until it is called for, and be able to retrieve it when required to do so. If any of these processes breaks down for any reason, the result is a failure to remember; in other words, we forget.

Research on learning usually emphasises the acquisition of knowledge and skills, whereas research on memory is largely concerned with retention and retrieval—although, clearly, there is a relationship between these two concepts. The human memory can be supplemented by an external memory. There are many situations where information is available without the need for it to be stored in the individual's memory: brand packaging information, shopping lists, buyers' guides, or advertisements cut out by a consumer are all part of the consumer's external memory.

Research in cognitive psychology shows that the performance of memory is sensitive to the context surrounding the item committed to memory, and is dependent on factors related to the person, the information to be learned, the learning instructions given to the person, and the questions chosen to test memory (Jenkins, 1974). The importance of context is underlined by Horton and Mills (1984) who state that, "if there is a single principle that best describes the current status of the cognitive psychology of human memory, it is that the contextualist thesis is alive and well at both the empirical and theoretical levels." It would appear that those interested in advertising should be aware of the importance of context—defined as consumer processing goals that determine the information committed to memory, and the interfering effects of competitive advertising—when it comes to information contained in advertisements that are committed to memory (Kellar, 1987).

Memory is divided into the following categories: short-term, long-term, and working memory.

Short-term memory

Short-term memory (STM) is said to have limited storage capacity and is capable of holding a small amount of information for a short time. Normally we can remember around seven names, or seven letters in the alphabet, although each of the names may contain many more than seven letters. A feature of STM is the rapid loss of information; therefore, we tend to repeat the information over and over again in order to retain it. An employee is verbally given a customer's telephone number and asked to ring the customer immediately. Without writing the number on a piece of paper, the employee retains the number in his or her STM while dialling it. After making the telephone call he or she is likely to forget the number. Likewise, an accounts clerk holds a list of numbers in his or her STM for a brief period while engaged in mental arithmetic.

Long-term memory

At some stage in the learning process, information is transferred from STM to long-term memory (LTM). When material can be recalled reliably after a day or a week, it is safe to conclude that the information is recalled from LTM. Before the transfer takes place, a fair amount of information can be lost but, unlike STM, the capacity of LTM is substantial and forgetting is slower.

Normally, when we focus on LTM a distinction is made between episodic memory and generic memory (Tulving, 1985). Episodic memory is the memory for particular events or episodes in our life—what happened when and where, as with, for example, a first date! This can be contrasted with generic memory, which is the memory for items of knowledge, such as the size of the population of the UK, or how to prepare a balance sheet from accounting data, or how to construct a particular mathematical equation. A person's generic memory is the accumulation of all his or her acquired knowledge—i.e., the meaning of words, symbols, and facts about the world, etc. One of the most important components of generic memory is semantic memory—that is, the memory that concerns the meaning of words and concepts.

So far the discussion has largely centred on people with normal memories. However, we must recognise that certain injuries to the brain, such as amnesia, and progressive dementia, such as Alzheimer's disease, produce malfunctioning of the memory.

FIGURE 7.1

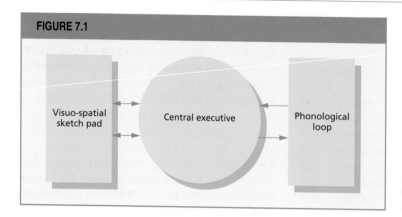

A simple representation of the model of working memory proposed by Baddeley and Hitch (1974). An attentional control system, the central executive, is supported by two sub-systems, one visual and one verbal.

Working memory

There has been a reconsideration of the function of STM (Baddeley, 1999). Rather than looking at STM as a staging post on the journey to LTM, like a temporary left luggage locker serving perception, it should be viewed as an active store (**working memory**), holding information. This information can be manipulated, interpreted, and recombined to develop new knowledge, assist learning, facilitate interaction with the outside environment, and form goals. For example, an employee who previously was made redundant is now working in a factory and is told that the company is proposing to close down its manufacturing operations. The disappointed employee interprets this fresh information together with past experience of an almost identical event (stored in LTM) in the working memory.

A feature of the usable working memory is its limited capacity. Therefore, only some of our immediate past experience is retained, and what is selected is dictated by the nature of the task and the particular circumstances. Another feature is its temporary nature, which is essential for constant updating of information, otherwise there would be the danger of crowding the mind with irrelevant information (Logie, 1999).

Baddeley (1999) proposed a model of the working memory. In the model—shown in Figure 7.1—the central executive is attentive, supervising and coordinating a number of subsidiary slave systems. The slave systems are called the phonological loop

and the visuo-spatial sketch pad. The phonological loop is responsible for the manipulation of speech-based information whereas the visuo-spatial sketch pad takes on board the setting up and manipulation of visual images.

Other major functions of memory, which will be discussed in this chapter, are: encode or process; store or retain; retrieval; and recall.

Encode or process

The storage capacity of STM is, as stated earlier, limited to around seven items or "chunks" of information (Miller, 1956). A chunk may be a single letter or digit or a combination of letters or digits, each combination being a chunk. We can remember a long telephone number (e.g., 35366673) because it can be chunked (35-36-66-73). In essence, a chunk is an organised cognitive structure that can grow in size as information is integrated into it. A brand name could be considered the summary of more detailed information about a product in the eyes of a consumer familiar with that product.

When chunking words, the load on the memory is eased considerably. In order to facilitate memorising, the following words may be chunked to form a sentence:

company	a
The	acquisition
of	reorganisation
necessitates	another

The sentence reads: "The acquisition of another company necessitates a reorganisation."

Schemata

One important type of information in memory that is related to chunks is memory schemata. A schemata is an internal structure, developed through experience, that organises incoming information in relation to previous experience (Mander & Parker, 1976). The experienced stockbroker draws on a well-organised strategy (schemata) in buying or selling shares, and utilises a wide repertoire of dealing strategies, as well as interpreting the mood of the stock market, using his or her knowledge or experience. In addition, the broker may be able to rely on rapid recall from LTM about possible deals. The novice stockbroker would find each item of incoming information difficult to deal with. The information cannot be related quickly and easily to existing stored material because his or her schemata is underdeveloped. This could result in confusion and a lack of ability to process and respond to incoming information at the early stages of learning.

Scripts

A special subcategory of a schemata is a script, which describes a scenario of behaviour applicable to a particular setting, such as a restaurant script, where the sequence includes being seated, looking at the menu, ordering food, paying the bill, and leaving (Gleitman, 1995). A script amounts to expectations about how various types of event will unfold, and its general function is to facilitate cognitive processing. When an incoming stimulus activates a person's script, a rich network of information is tapped that substantially reduces the burden of processing the stimulus. Scripts appear to exert significant influence on both the encoding and retrieval functions and, as a result, script-based information-processing is highly automatic and efficient (Smith & Houston, 1985).

Scripts are said to provide an efficient framework for summarising what has been learned about a task, either derived from experience or observing others, and could be applied to the training of new employees. Because experts should have a greater repertoire of more thoroughly developed scripts for many activities within their task domain, teaching novices the scripts of experts may be an efficient way to train them (Lord & Kernan, 1987).

Rehearsal

As a means of keeping information activated in STM, rehearsal is used. Rehearsal is an activity that recycles the same items of information in STM. For example, a new word encountered in the study of a foreign language is repeated over and over again. Rehearsal is said to occur when items of information are repeated silently or overtly by the individual, and is limited by the capacity of STM to around seven items or chunks circulating in the system. It must not be confused with mere repetition, and it implies an active, conscious interaction with incoming information. Material that is rehearsed is then transferred to LTM.

Coding

It is suggested that there are two basic ways of representing information in memory—i.e., that there are two coding systems (Paivio, 1969). One is verbal, and the other is nonverbal and uses imagery. The latter could arise when one imagines a scene described by a sentence or caption, or a brand name may be associated with some mental image of that brand. On an aerosol can of freshener, a scene depicting a beautiful garden in springtime is obviously designed to create the appropriate imagery. However, it is important from a manufacturer's point of view for the consumer to process the verbal or semantic information in the advertisement. Otherwise, a consumer who processes the imagery only (e.g., a waterfall or a beautiful scene) and fails to relate the claims made in the advertisement to his or her experience of the product, will be badly informed when confronted with product choice in a store. This is an example of the background of the advertisement diverting attention from the message.

It is important to bear in mind that, in processing material, individual differences with respect to priorities, preferences, and prejudices play a significant part.

Store or retain

Various methods are employed to ensure the retention of incoming information. Obviously there is a limit to what can be stored in STM. An eight-digit number (e.g., 13456839) could be broken into manageable chunks (13-45-68-39), making four items, which will facilitate short-term retention. Although LTM can be improved greatly by the individual becoming more proficient at encoding information, there is a distinct limit on the improvement of STM. When it comes to storing and retaining, a high priority is given to information that helps to achieve personal objectives, and information that can be easily stored (Shiffrin & Atkinson, 1969). For example, a consumer plans to compare specified foods in the supermarket on the basis of nutritional content, using only the information printed on the package. All that is required in this particular situation is to commit to memory the brands that the consumer plans to compare in the supermarket. However, if the information on nutritional content appeared in an advertisement or in an article in a health food newsletter, and not on the package, the consumer would have to put more information into his or her memory. Events that are surprising, novel, inconsistent with our expectations, and so on, will often be given priority when it comes to processing and storage—e.g., for a well-established item, a new price or an interesting new feature.

Advertising can facilitate the retention of a message about a product. Frequently new products require the support of an intensive advertising campaign to capture the attention of the consumer. Special promotions such as free gifts or substantial discounts for a set period produce a similar effect. A different strategy is likely to apply to advertising older, more familiar brands. The objective then is to foster long-term awareness and to mount a continuous but less saturated advertising campaign (Myers & Reynolds, 1967).

The remainder of this section on storing and retaining will be devoted to the associative hierarchy, the conceptual hierarchy, conceptual similarity, and the personal system of categorisation.

Hierarchical models

A model for the structure of LTM to facilitate retention is the hierarchical model. This proposes that memory is structured with specific ideas categorised under more general ideas. Thus, the concepts of a canary and an ostrich are categorised under birds, and birds are categorised under animals. At the highest level of the hierarchy (presented as a *conceptual hierarchy* in Figure 7.2), there are a small number of general concepts, and, at the bottom, many specific concepts (Collins & Quillian, 1969). A similar model could be applied to the structure of information about accounting systems. Accounting could be subdivided into financial and management accounting. Financial accounting would include items such as trial balance, profit and loss account, and balance sheet; and management accounting has subdivisions such as direct and indirect costs and various methods of allocating them. The conceptual hierarchy, depicted in Figure 7.2, is a potent tool for facilitating learning. In one experiment, a group that had a brief exposure to 112 words presented in the form of a conceptual hierarchy were far more effective in reporting orally the words they could remember than a random group who did not receive the words in an organised form (Bower, Clark, Lesgold, & Winzenz, 1969).

When a tree of items is associated, but not necessarily as a conceptual hierarchy, it is called an *associative hierarchy*. This is depicted in Figure 7.3. The outcome of experiments on the associative hierarchy is similar to the results achieved with the conceptual hierarchy, but it would appear that the conceptual hierarchy is more organised and meaningful (Bower et al., 1969).

Conceptual similarity

Another way of organising material is the use of a conceptual category. In examining the association between words, one may be able to conclude

FIGURE 7.2

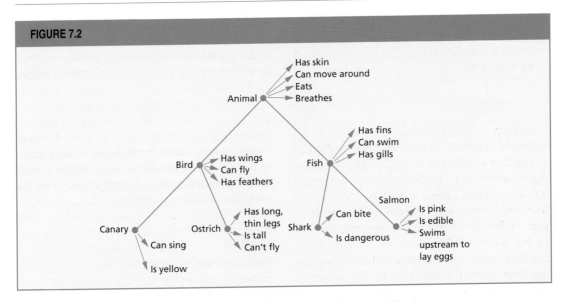

A conceptual hierarchy (from Collins & Quillian, 1969). Reprinted with permission from Elsevier.

FIGURE 7.3

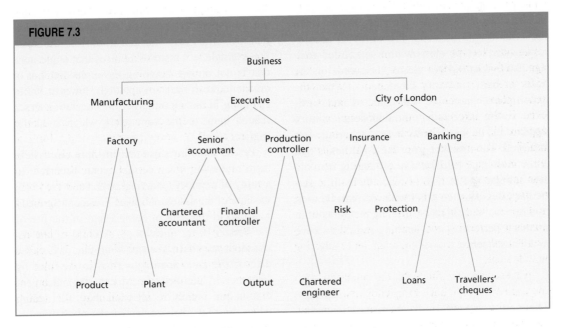

An associative hierarchy.

that certain things are similar conceptually, whereas others are not (Underwood, 1964). Words of both low and high similarity appear in Table 7.2. These were used in a memory experiment in which lists of words, high and low in conceptual

similarity, were spoken by the experimenter. The subjects were told nothing about the differences between the lists shown in Table 7.2. After each list was read, subjects were asked to reproduce as many words as they could, in any order.

TABLE 7.2

Words that are high and low in conceptual similarity (adapted from Underwood, 1964)

Low similarity		High similarity	
Apple	Cruiser	Bob	Foxtrot
Football	Trumpet	Rabbi	Joe
Emerald	Doctor	Cow	Bishop
Trout	Head	Rumba	Dog
Copper	Wide	Bill	Tango
Theft	Blue	Priest	John
Hat	Gasoline	Horse	Minister
Table	Cotton	Waltz	Cat

You will notice that the words listed under high similarity can be grouped under the names of people, animals, clergy, and dances. The scope to cluster words does not exist with the low similarity items. Those who participated in an experiment, but were unaware of the differences between the lists, experienced a high success rate when they unwittingly clustered the words in accordance with the type classification suggested earlier. Those who did not cluster the words on the basis of high similarity fared badly. When the experimental procedure was changed and participants were asked to be on the lookout for word similarities, the best results in remembering were achieved. The message from these studies is that if the individual learns a way of relating items to one another and is able to place them in a particular category, then this framework can be used as a retrieval plan in reconstructing the items from memory. Performance in learning should improve as a consequence.

Personal system of categorisation

There are many occasions when words or meaningful material are presented to us without the assistance of prior categorisation. In such circumstances, it can greatly assist the learner if he or she devises a personal system of categorisation. In Mandler and Pearlstone (1966), words arranged according to a classification system devised by the learner were more readily recalled than words arranged in a predetermined sequence that the learner had to comprehend and follow. The very act of organising the material is in itself an aid to learning, particularly when the learner is involved in developing the system of organisation that is used. This appears to be at variance with the evidence on prior categorisation presented earlier. The principle of one's own system of categorisation can be seen in action in a management training course when, for example, a large group of participants is divided into syndicates to discuss information and present a summary of the syndicate's position.

Retrieval

Retrieval from memory can range from almost immediate access for familiar items to involved, problem-search processes for other items. It is dependent on both the quality of the coding and the organisation of information transferred to memory. Sometimes an item of information cannot be remembered, but then some event occurs that gives the "clue" needed to retrieve the item. For example, a consumer realises that some item that is not on the shopping list is needed, but is unable to recall the item unaided. However, while shopping in the supermarket the consumer sees a related item, or the item itself, which suddenly triggers recall.

People sometimes use real-life episodes to help them remember when certain events occurred. In a study of memory (Warrington & Sanders, 1972) the date of the assassination of President Kennedy was tied to the date of some event in the life of the person being questioned. A child of the respondent may have been born on that day, so the date of the assassination is then worked out by inference. A number of people of the older generation can vividly recall what they were doing when they heard the news of the assassination. Similarly, in the future some people, particularly Americans, may recall what they were doing when they heard the news of the death of the ex-President's son—J.F. Kennedy Jr—who died in tragic circumstances in July 1999.

When recalling what happened at a party, or who was there, a person may engage in imagery retrieval by visualising the room in which the event took place. This may facilitate the recall of the names of those present when the party-goers are known to the person engaged in recall. As regards marketing, an advertiser may use location and imagery to facilitate recall of the identity of the product; for example, the advertisement contains a picture depicting the user of a particular brand of air-freshener relaxing in the woods near a cool, idyllic stream.

Mnemonics

Mnemonics is a method of remembering items by imposing a structure of organisation on the material to be memorised. The example of the advertisement for the brand of air-freshener, referred to in the previous section, could be used as a mnemonic device. This device is known as the *method of loci*, in which people or objects to be remembered are associated with familiar locations. It is a peg system, which provides an organisational framework for learning material as well as offering good retrieval cues. Many of the popular mnemonic devices rely on visual imagery. People tend to learn verbal materials better when they are connected with some visual image. For example, manufacturers incorporate imagery in the brand names of their products—"Thick and Zesty" tomato sauce, and "Easy-Off" oven cleaner.

If a learner wants to remember a particular item in a series (e.g., the third), then a peg system using numbering is useful. A popular system using numbers is as follows: "one is a bun, two is a shoe, three is a tree, four is a door, five is a hive, six is sticks, seven is heaven, eight is a gate, nine is mine, and ten is a hen". This facilitates the development of a mental image of each item. Another mnemonic device is as follows: the sentence "Richard of Virgin is brave" contains the same initials as the colours "red, orange, violet, indigo, blue", and it can be used to remember the colours and the order in which they are listed. The sentence is easier to remember than the list because the sequence is meaningful. Mnemonic devices appear to be suitable when long lists of separate items need to be remembered. By relying on visual imagery, there could be problems when the learner tries to memorise abstract words.

The mnemonic devices have been criticised because they do not foster the development of understanding and reasoning. But this criticism is unfair because really these devices are only appropriate to rote memory tasks. By and large most of the mnemonic techniques are very effective, but the reason why this is so is not known (Eysenck & Keane, 2000).

Recall

The level of arousal (whether calm or active) can affect the ability of the person to recognise and recall. There is a difference between recognition and recall, and this is apparent when we recognise somebody but cannot recall their name. There is reason to believe that recognition and recall improve as a consequence of exposure to repeated messages, though eventually the effects are less pronounced (Bettman, 1984).

A number of difficulties arise with the recall of certain types of information. Material that is meaningful poses less of a problem. For example, the words "college" or "office" are associated with a number of events and experiences. But the same cannot be said of a nonsense syllable (e.g., "nac") (Ebbinghaus, 1885). Nonsense syllables, such as "dax" and "ruf", are fairly unfamiliar to all learners, and we cannot rely on previous experiences to facilitate recall. However, there could be some familiarity with nonsense syllables—dax may be associated with a town in the south-west of France, and ruf sounds phonetically like rough. But not everybody would establish these associations (Burns & Dobson, 1984).

One can never know whether memory genuinely represents what was originally seen, or whether it represents a plausible reconstruction, with perhaps the addition of details that were never present in the first place. There is substantial evidence indicating that human beings have a tremendous capacity for describing what they believe to have happened, but these descriptions may have little relationship to what actually happened (Bartlett, 1932). Often people are unaware that their account of a happening is either invented or inaccurate. It is therefore not surprising to find conflicts of evidence in courts of law when two witnesses provide entirely different accounts of what happened and each swears that his or her account is the correct one.

Bartlett, a British psychologist, conducted classic experiments on the distortion of memory in the early 1930s. Subjects were asked to reproduce stories extracted from folklore of non-Western cultures. The reproductions showed many changes from the original, with some parts omitted, others over-elaborated, and completely new parts added. In fact the subjects had created a new story from their recollections of the original. The reconstructed story was more in line with the cultural expectations of the subjects rather than with the story they had actually heard. For example, certain elements of the plot that had a supernatural flavour were reinterpreted along more familiar lines.

In a variation of the experiment, Bartlett (1932) used serial reproduction, whereby the original story was presented to subject A, who then reproduced it from memory for the benefit of subject B. Adopting the same principle, subject B reproduced the story and told it to subject C, and the identical procedure was adopted for a chain of up to 10 subjects. It should be noted that in this experiment the reproductions of the story, contaminated by memory distortions, were accepted by the next subject, leading to gross distortion of the original story. In order to achieve coherency, the story, though differing considerably from the original, became a story in its own right, revamped with additional material in order to make sense out of it. People's names and other information appeared to get lost. Similarly, the example in Panel 7.10 shows how substantial inaccuracies in recall arise when we amend material to fit our preconceptions.

The findings of Bartlett are relevant in the context of eyewitness testimony. For example, witnesses giving evidence related to a serious work accident in a court of law are sometimes quite confident that their account of what happened is true because it coincides with their expectations of the event. In reality it may not be in line with what actually happened. The event in question—the accident—could have occurred many months ago and the details have become less clear over time. As witnesses try to retrieve information on this past event they may fill in the gaps by making inferences of which they are quite unaware.

A number of studies by Loftus (1975) and her associates have highlighted the problems with eyewitness testimony. For example, the way in which a witness is questioned is an important factor. Asking leading questions of the witness could lead to a reinterpretation of what was originally perceived. A popular current theoretical explanation is that witnesses are confusing information obtained from a source outside the witnessed event (this is called post-event information) with the witnessed event itself (Memon & Wright, 1999).

According to Gleitman (1995), the outcome of Loftus' work is of considerable relevance to the practice of law and the psychology of memory. From a legal perspective it reinforces the importance of the wording of questions, not only in the courtroom but also in prior interrogations in police stations. To those with an academic interest in memory, it shows that remembering is a reconstructive process—i.e., as we are retrieving the past, we are sometimes recreating it. In more recent work, Loftus (2001) focuses on imagination because she found that a number of mental health professionals and police officers were encouraging patients who had no memories of

---

PANEL 7.10: Inaccuracy in recall

In this experiment, two groups were presented with a short passage of prose describing some aspects of the life of a girl. Group A was told that the girl's name was Carol Harris and group B was told that the girl's name was Helen Keller. A week later the groups were asked whether the passage of prose included the statement that the girl was deaf, dumb, and blind. Only 5% of group A said "yes", but 50% of group B said "yes". The information on the girl's disability was not included in the original passage of prose, but apparently Helen Keller was known to a number of people in group B as actually being deaf, dumb, and blind, and they convinced themselves that they were given this information originally.

(Sulin & Dooling, 1974)

abuse to imagine that they had these experiences as children. But witnesses can confuse what they have been asked to imagine what happened with what actually happened!

Forgetting

Forgetting arises when we cannot recall material at a particular time. It may not be due to a loss of information from our memory, but to an inability to retrieve the information because the index system guiding the search is lost or inefficient, or because material has been classified in an inappropriate way so that the normal cues for retrieval are not effective (Tulving, 1968). A number of other explanations are put forward to account for why we forget. As time passes the "memory trace" of what was originally perceived decays. An alternative explanation is that certain processes interfere with the specific information committed to memory, and this undermines our ability to recall that information. There is experimental evidence to suggest that the **interference** explanation is more important than the decay explanation (Waugh & Norman, 1965).

Interference can be expressed in a variety of forms. Some of the important ones are as follows:

- *Retroactive.* The placing of new information in the memory undermines the recall of previously recorded information. For example, a firm of accountants has changed its telephone number. After committing the new number to memory, the client may find it difficult to retrieve the old number.
- *Proactive.* Information that was previously committed to memory undermines the recording of new information. For example, a sales representative who has regularly dealt with the previous manager of a store finds it difficult to remember the name of the new manager.
- *Repression.* The individual subconsciously avoids retrieving information associated with unpleasant events. A patient might forget an appointment arranged with a doctor because of some traumatic experience associated with a previous visit to the doctor's surgery.

- *Emotion.* Anxiety can inhibit the retrieval of information. A student's anxiety about failing an examination may inhibit his or her attempts to retrieve information in the examination room.

The time that information enters memory, be it recent or at an earlier time, is something to consider. The advantage accruing to earlier information is that it is likely to receive more attention. However, it appears that more recently acquired information can be retrieved more easily (the *recency effect*). But imposing a delay of 30 seconds before recall eliminates the recency effect completely, whereas it does not affect significantly the power of recall of information acquired earlier (the *primacy effect*; Glanzer & Cunitz, 1966).

There are some ways of counteracting the effects of forgetting. It has been found that when a period of sleep intervenes between learning and recall, recall is greatly improved (Jenkins & Dallenbach, 1924). Perhaps the absence of the distractions of wakefulness, and the relative inactivity of sleep, may account for this finding. However, if one dreams during sleep (a period when the brain is relatively active), there is some evidence to suggest that more forgetting occurs (Ekstrand, 1972). More recent evidence indicates that sleep has a beneficial effect on long-term memory (Idzikowski, 1984).

Rehearsal is said to prevent forgetting because it keeps replenishing the memory trace. An involved story about an event or happening must of necessity be repeated frequently to facilitate retention and avoid forgetting. A number of the measures discussed earlier in connection with the systematic organisation and arrangement of material prior to transfer to memory assist in combating forgetting.

Effects of ageing

Earlier in the section on long-term memory a distinction was made between semantic and episodic memory. In general the evidence indicates that the contents of semantic memory—that is a person's store of factual knowledge about the world—remain intact (at least in the absence of dementia), but that retrieval is problematic for the majority of elderly people when they are working against a time limit (Maylor, 1996). One can contrast semantic memory with episodic memory (which is a person's store of particular episodes or events that were personally experienced in the past). The elderly person's perception of his or her episodic memory tend to follow Ribot's law, which states that recent memories are forgotten, but remote memories are preserved (Ribot, 1882).

Studies of both semantic and episodic memory can be described as belonging to retrospective memory (recognition or recall of information from the past). This can be contrasted with prospective memory, which can be described as remembering to do something in the future (e.g., taking medication three times a day, or paying the gas bill before the end of the month). It is important to understand the effects of ageing on both retrospective and prospective memory, but many researchers have largely concentrated their efforts on retrospective memory.

Maylor (1996) concludes that memory for both the past and the future generally declines with increasing age, but we cannot take that as universal or inevitable. Thus there is considerable variation so that some aspects of memory are less adversely affected than others, and it is possible to find elderly experts who can perform at least as well as younger experts. Finally, it seems that many older people can learn to compensate for failing memory by adapting their environments to ensure that, for example, important appointments are not forgotten.

Postscript

Finally, it should be noted that the study of human memory has been evolving and changing rapidly in recent years. There has been criticism of laboratory-based research on the grounds of artificiality, and an endorsement of human cognition that recognises the person's interaction with everyday environments. The latter is called the *ecological approach to cognition*, and focuses on how people use knowledge from the past in present discourses. The ecological approach has, however, been vehemently attacked by the laboratory-based researchers. One feature of the ecological approach is discourse analysis, concerned with how people use knowledge of the past in current interactions with others in order to generate shared meanings and to communicate with each other (Conway, 1992).

TRANSFER OF LEARNING (TRAINING)

The basic psychological principle underlying the **transfer of learning** is that of generalisation of stimuli, referred to earlier in connection with operant conditioning. When a stimulus is similar to the original conditioned stimulus it tends to elicit the same response.

Transfer

The transfer of learning (or training) is the process by which the effects of training in one form of an activity are transferred to another form. A claim often made is that the learning of mathematics, or at least the training involved, improves the learner's ability to solve problems requiring logic, whether these are of a mathematical nature or not. The classical curriculum of Latin, Greek, and Rhetoric was considered important in the development of logical reasoning. Many educational programmes are built on the assumption that people have the ability to transfer what they have learned in one situation to another. If transfer was not possible, there would be little justification for formal education; every element of knowledge, skill, and capacity would have to be taught separately.

Lateral transfer

Lateral transfer involves performance at the same level of complexity as the initial learning, but in a different context. If a child has classroom experience of arithmetic calculations with the aid of blocks or beads, this understanding could be transferred laterally at home if the child, having removed two tennis balls from a box of six, realises that four are left.

Sequential transfer

Sequential transfer occurs when we build on a learning foundation. A fact learned today in a subject may have some relationship to a fact or idea learned tomorrow. For example, multiplication draws on an understanding of addition.

Vertical transfer

Vertical transfer occurs when learning at one level, such as comprehending facts about addition and subtraction, facilitates the solution of problems utilising these arithmetic operations. It amounts to a transfer from the simpler components of a task to the more complex ones.

Positive transfer

When training or performance in one task can be transferred to another, positive transfer is said to occur. Positive transfer manifests itself in the following situations: learning Latin may aid the learning of Italian; having learned the skills of ice-skating could mean that learning to roller-skate is that much easier; and mastering the skill of driving a car results in positive transfer to lorry driving.

Negative transfer

Negative transfer is said to occur when previous learning in a particular task hinders learning in another task. This is obvious when a motorist from the UK switches from driving on the left-hand side of the road to the right-hand side while holidaying in France. Errors may arise in a factory when an employee with experience of driving one particular model of fork-lift truck drives another model. The pedals for braking, reversing, and accelerating can differ in sequence from one model to the next. This can be contrasted with the standardisation universally applicable to cars, apart from the difference in the positioning of the steering wheel between cars made in different countries.

The typist of years gone by may have experienced both positive and negative transfer when changing from a manual to an electric typewriter.

Positive transfer occurs when the keys are tapped correctly, but negative transfer occurs when the typist takes action to return the carriage to the beginning of the line. On the manual machine this is done by hitting a lever on the carriage, and on the electric machine by depressing a key. When the typist changes from a manual to an electric machine, performance is initially slowed down by the persistent habit of raising the hand to hit the lever, which now does not exist, at the end of every line.

Personal and organisational influences

It is important to consider personal and organisational influences when considering the transfer of learning. Even though trainees in a training programme may acquire new knowledge and learn new skills, they might still not be able to apply this learning or use those skills when they return to their workplace. As to personal influences, self-efficacy (discussed in Chapters 2 and 4) has been identified as an important variable. Self-efficacy, as a personality variable, is said to be influential when it comes to a trainee's capability to master a particular skill and then reproduce it subsequently in the workplace. People with high levels of self-efficacy are not only more likely to learn new knowledge and develop skills quickly, but they are also more likely to use these skills later in the workplace (Stevens & Gist, 1997).

As to organisational influences, those who have undergone training may not transfer their learning to the workplace because of a fear of appearing foolish in the eyes of established peers who have not experienced this training. There is evidence to suggest that ridicule from peers or colleagues as well as impediments (lack of equipment or facilities) are discouraging factors that prevent the application of new knowledge and skills. However, other factors, such as receiving recognition, support, and rewards, were a source of encouragement in the post-training organisational environment (Tannenbaum & Yukl, 1992).

The message coming across is that the managers of staff who have completed a training programme and are now back at work have a critical role to play in the creation of a positive climate for the transfer of learning. They should provide frequent feedback and reward trainees for using the knowledge and skills they have acquired. They should facilitate the development of a learning culture by wholeheartedly promoting or selling the benefits of training for both the individual and the organisation, and by providing the resources and policies in order to encourage and support training in organisations (Arnold, 2005).

KNOWLEDGE MANAGEMENT

As we learn we acquire knowledge in many areas ranging from work (e.g., a trainee accountant learns how to prepare a profit and loss account) to leisure (e.g., perfecting techniques while actively participating in sport). In business there is a realisation that knowledge management, which consists of the acquisition, stewardship, and use of knowledge, can be a source of competitive advantage in product innovation, improvement of organisational processes, strategic decision making, customer relations, and so on (Earl, 2004).

Knowledge can be viewed as consisting of two types—one tacit and the other explicit. Tacit knowledge is composed of an accumulation of experience in the form of insights and wisdom, which the person may have difficulty in communicating to other people but can easily utilise in the performance of a particular task. By contrast, explicit knowledge lends itself to codification or classification and can easily be expressed; for example, the type of information required to operate a formal organisational procedure. Both types of knowledge are complementary, and it would be an advantage if tacit knowledge could be made available to the organisation (Nonaka, Umemoto, & Sasaki, 1999).

A challenge facing a company is to understand how to share knowledge and to learn from the experience of others. A number of options are open to the company, such as: (a) placing value on knowledge; (b) exploiting the existing knowledge base of the organisation in the best way possible; (c) managing newly created knowledge; (d) collecting and codifying valuable information from a project that

subsequently can be made available to others; and (e) being determined to capitalise on the contribution of knowledge workers. Information technology can be mobilised and is likely to play a prominent role, aided by the development of databases accessed through the internet. On grounds of equity, due recognition should be given to specialists whose expertise is available online, particularly if that expertise is profitably used.

Adherents of knowledge management believe that it ought to be willingly embraced because it places value on people's experience and wisdom, and subscribes to the important idea of making use of knowledge at the disposal of the company. When considering knowledge management, an important and complex issue to address is the question of intellectual property rights. In addition, a crucial consideration is having an organisational culture supportive of this type of development and being partial to frequent communication (Harrison, 2000). In an age when competition is based more on what an organisation knows than what it owns, managers face the challenge of creating cultural environments that foster the development and diffusion of knowledge. If everyone contributes to the repository of knowledge with ideas and suggestions, then everybody has the chance to improve performance by learning from others. Perhaps, however, one is being a bit too idealistic. Panel 7.11 shows that there is some downside to the creation and use of knowledge management.

The concept of knowledge management was embraced in the early 1990s when companies felt it necessary to utilise their underused knowledge and intellectual capital. Reflecting on the use of this concept a decade later, Hansen (2002) makes the point that its implementation has not lived up to expectations. He is of the view that:

knowledge management has become narrowly focused on databases and other electronic means such as online communities and web casts. While these may have some use, they are not far-reaching: in part because they do not alter employees attitudes to sharing and using knowledge. To do so, knowledge management needs to tackle

---

PANEL 7.11: Knowledge management in action

The use of the internet can extend to networks that make it possible to involve stakeholders (e.g., suppliers, customers, or clients) and other organisations. The relationship with a client is illustrated as follows (Cabrera, 2000). A sales executive employed by a telecommunications manufacturer develops a valuable understanding of the client's needs. The sales executive's company has a repository of knowledge on the internet to help sales, production, and research staff share knowledge and discuss ideas about products. The posting of information on the internet could perhaps initiate a discussion with research staff about new trends and it could give sales staff from other divisions of the company hints about how to introduce their products to the clients.

From this illustration, one is likely to conclude that the outcome is advantageous from the company's point of view. But from the point of view of the individual employee it could be a different story. Writing or posting information or a report on the internet may not be a good idea from an individual employee's point of view. It devours time that might otherwise be devoted to more profitable tasks, and sharing information in this way does not generate a commission. Even if the time factor is pushed to one side, sharing knowledge may dilute an individual's competitive position within the organisation. If bonuses and promotions are primarily based on sales figures, helping others might feature low down in the sales executive's priorities. In organisations where knowledge is a source of power it may be naïve to expect people to share ideas just because the company has the technology available to make this happen. Also, one has to consider the position and example set by "free riders" who benefit from the collective effort but do not make a contribution. In such circumstances incentives could be offered to free riders whose record of noninvolvement is conspicuous. Such action could make free riders feel uncomfortable and they take note of the fact that they are not pulling their weight. Generally, it would appear necessary for the organisation to develop interventions that will create cooperative environments where knowledge management systems are likely to succeed. Three conditions have been identified under which cooperation among employees is more likely to take place (Cabrera, 2000):

(1) The less costly in personal terms for people to contribute to the common good, the less likely they will be to withhold their contributions. For example, IBM requires a minimum level of contribution before anyone is considered for promotion. Also, group incentives, such as stock options, may help reduce the perceived cost by creating benefits for everyone from everyone else's performance.

(2) The more clearly people can see the impact of their contributions, the more motivated they are to make the effort. For example, a knowledge exchange system could inform contributors of the number of hits on the internet by readers of their contributions. Or it could allow readers to send back comments on other people's contributions.

(3) Social pressure to foster cooperation is more likely to arise in smaller rather than larger groups. It could be said that as groups become larger individuals may perceive that their contributions do not make a difference. Also, as group size grows appreciably it becomes more difficult to monitor and sanction individual participation and the informal process of social pressure tends to lose its potency. On the other hand, the likelihood of cooperation increases when interactions among participants are solid and frequent, members are easily identifiable, and there is sufficient information available on the actions of each individual.

It is interesting to note the importance of group influences in the comments above. There is specific reference later to knowledge management in the context of affinity groups (see Chapter 11).

---

something more fundamental—the design of a collaborative organization. Helping colleagues across departmental boundaries is commonplace in this type of organization, and HRM systems—e.g., selection, rewards and performance management—ought to be supportive to encourage collaboration.

Hansen advises that one should have a sense of balance when it comes to putting into practice the notion of collaboration. One pitfall that should be noted is that collaboration can be overdone: "before you know it, people participate in meetings without getting anything done, leading to ineffective collaboration that undermines overall performance."

Earl (2004), reflecting on the practice of knowledge management, states that "the promise of knowledge management has yet to be realized. It is not unusual to visit companies claiming knowledge management successes only to find worthy efforts lacking any success. More often, a company has simply relabeled a new IT application as a knowledge management initiative."

As a postscript, in some quarters there seems to be respect for ignorance rather than knowledge. Gray (2003), a senior consultant with the Boston Consulting Group, states that knowledge encourages one to think in well-worn ways, and ignorance allows us to be creative and to question things. Knowledge is everywhere; ignorance is a scarce resource and once it is replaced with knowledge it is hard to get it back. In a review of this article Kellaway (2003a) rightly concludes: "ignorance is not a scarce resource; it is as plentiful as air . . . neither is it precious. It is stupid . . . ignorance gets displaced by knowledge and then comes back effortlessly". Although, there are those who place too much reliance on their knowledge, which in some respects is out of date or obsolete, we should accept that ignorance at work is something that affects our behaviour and is worth noting. In this respect Kellaway makes the point that "the problem with ignorance is that how paranoid we all feel about letting ours show. We strive to look knowledgeable and are terrified that the scale of our ignorance will one day be found out and massive humiliation will follow. The fear is worse than the ignorance itself and leads to pretty sick behaviour. Instead of admitting when we do not know something, we bluff and bluster."

THE LEARNING ORGANISATION

Ideas underpinning the discussion of knowledge management above could be attributable to the concept of the learning organisation. Though we speak of the learning organisation, in actual fact it is the employees who engage in the learning.

It is interesting to reflect for a moment on the idea of a learning organisation, which has captured the imagination of trainers and others in recent years. An idealised view of the learning organisation could be taken, in the form of the biological methaphor (Gherardi, 1997). In this way an organisation could be seen as a body that processes information, reflects on experience, learns, and is endowed with a stock of knowledge, skills, and expertise. An organisation with this capability can adapt by bringing about internal change in response to opportunities in its external environment. In a similar manner it can learn from experience of the operation of the system internally and from the experiences of other organisations, and derive value from the learning experience. As a consequence, the organisation's stock of knowledge and expertise could exceed the repository of individuals' expertise.

Pedlar, Boydell, and Burgoyne (1988) take the view that for an organisation to grow and prosper it has to develop a capacity to respond well to changes in its environment and that the learning organisation can help with the development of that capacity by facilitating the learning of all its employees, and by being alert to the need for continuous transformation. In essence, the aim is to create a culture of continuous learning for all employees. This goes beyond a narrow interpretation of training. Systematic self-analysis of a company's experience, especially its mistakes, is a necessary prerequisite for a company that wants to be a learning organisation. Sharing information about key aspects of the strategic direction of the organisation and important operational issues in connection with the implementation of policy, together with information from stakeholders (e.g., suppliers and customers) is heavily underlined (Pedlar, Boydell, & Burgoyne, 1989).

The managerial qualities of the learning organisation have been described and operationalised (Argyris, 1991; Beard, 1993; Garvin, 1993; Senge, 1990; Senge et al., 1999). These embrace the following:

- Adopt a systems perspective when examining the various strands of interdependent action within the organisation. Systems thinking also encourages employees to keep the big picture in mind, and develop sensitivity to the external environment.
- Be highly focused in effort, be patient, and be introspective and objective when confronting assumptions and ideas underpinning present practices. Double-loop learning, which can amount to adopting a critical perspective whereby things are challenged, would take place here if members use feedback to test the validity of current values and practices. Double-loop learning can be contrasted with single-loop learning. Single-loop learning is learning to correct errors that arise from using a particular set of operating instructions. The first steps in this process are the activities of sensing, scanning, and monitoring the environment, followed by comparing the results obtained with the operating standards (e.g., has

the required quality been met?). The final step entails taking appropriate action to deal with the deviation from the required standard. As stated above, double-loop learning has a critical perspective, which is the process of questioning whether the operating standards are still appropriate; this involves learning to learn. It is said that double-loop learning is critical for the survival of organisations in the volatile business conditions of today. But, according to Doyle (2003), for double-loop learning to occur there must be a climate of openness and trust, where norms and values are subjected to change, where there is a free exchange of information, and where there is shared ownership and commitment to organisational goals.

• Put value on self-development and continuous development, so that expertise is allowed to flourish and problem solving is enhanced. There is a climate characterised by the generation of knowledge and its widespread dissemination, as well as a willingness to modify employee behaviour in response to new knowledge and insights.

• Develop shared views of where the company is now, and a shared vision of the future, reflected in members developing a common purpose and commitment with respect to the primacy of learning in the organisation. Leadership is crucial in promoting a shared vision.

• Promote team learning where members come together and freely share ideas and opinions with each other, in order to improve problem solving. An important principle is putting new knowledge and insights into action. These could be innovations in the way the company is organised and in the management of people, leading hopefully to creativity and flexibility in the contribution of the human resource.

For a learning organisation to function well, it is said that one should pay attention to matters such

as the following (Garvin, 1993): give employees time to reflect on innovative practices; equip them with the necessary skills; break down barriers (either internal or external to the organisation) that frustrate effort; and create learning forums.

Critics argue that the concept of the learning organisation is unrealistic. There could be a clash between insights absorbed from contact with the learning organisation and the experiences obtained from normal training activities (Price, 1997). According to Sloman (1994), the reality experienced by many managers is far removed from what the learning organisation stands for, and its objectives are hardly achievable in a cost-conscious environment. Doyle (2003) maintains:

the greatest obstacle to implementing the principles of the learning organization concerns the transmission and management of knowledge. Much organizational knowledge is tacit or implicit. It is based on unvoiced assumptions, is often rooted in action and is often learned unconsciously through the process of socialization into the organization and through imitation. It is very hard to communicate and transfer to others. As anyone who has been involved in developing an expert system knows, getting human experts to make all their knowledge explicit can be difficult because much of their knowledge does not lend itself to being represented verbally.

Finally, the implementation of the learning organisation could be seen as a threat to the manager's prerogative. Coopey (1996) states that all too frequently the importance of management control and political processes within organisations is ignored, and maintains that because of power differentiation within organisations the potential for both individual and collective effort could be undermined.

CHAPTER SUMMARY

- Learning, which cannot be observed directly, embraces most of our behaviour and can be distinguished from performance. Three major approaches to the study of learning are: classical conditioning, operant conditioning, and cognitive learning.

- Classical conditioning was discussed, with the aid of a number of illustrations derived from business practice, under the following headings: unconditioned and conditioned stimuli; generalisation; emotional reactions; and discrimination.

- Operant conditioning consists primarily of reinforcement. The principles of "contiguity" and "contingent" apply to reinforcement. This concept was discussed with reference to primary and secondary reinforcement, positive and negative reinforcement (including avoidance conditioning), punishment, and schedules of reinforcement. Schedules of reinforcement, appropriately illustrated, were subdivided into intermittent or partial reinforcement, continuous reinforcement, and concurrent reinforcement.

- Programmed learning, which is linked to the concept of operant conditioning, consists of linear programming and branching. Linear programming and branching are techniques of programmed instruction. Behaviour modification, also related to operant conditioning, was discussed in terms of shaping and modelling, and specifically in an organisational context. Certain applications of behaviour modification were introduced. Criticisms of the concept of behaviour modification and the relevance of social learning theory were also discussed.

- Cognitive learning can be categorised as insight learning and latent learning. Phases in skills acquisition were considered in the context of cognitive learning, and the importance of feedback was emphasised. The concept of cognitive learning is closely related to selective perception and information-processing, and draws heavily on memory.

- Memory was classified as short-term, long-term, and working memory, and critical functions of memory were identified as encoding, storing, retrieving, and recalling information. The performance of memory is sensitive to context. Chunking, the use of schemata, scripts, and rehearsal, facilitate the encoding process prior to the transfer of information to long-term memory. Verbal and nonverbal coding systems are used to represent information in our memory. As a means to facilitate the storage of information in long-term memory, devices such as the conceptual hierarchy, the associative hierarchy, conceptual similarity, and a personal system of categorisation can be used.

- Retrieval depends on the quality of the coding system and the organisation of information transferred to memory. In this context, mnemonics and recall were explained. For a variety of reasons, distortions in the recall of information occur. This raises issues about the reliability of eyewitness testimony. Forgetting occurs when we fail to recall information. A number of possibilities were proposed to explain why we forget, and there was a brief reference to ways of counteracting the effects of forgetting. The effects of ageing on memory were examined.

- Transfer of learning (training) was referred to as a process by which the effects of training in one activity are transferred to another. Different types of transfer were described—lateral, sequential, vertical, positive, and negative.

- Knowledge management, and the related concept of the learning organisation, were analysed.

QUESTIONS

(1) Distinguish between learning and performance.

(2) Define the following processes in classical conditioning: (a) generalisation; (b) extinction; (c) conditioned stimulus; and (d) discrimination.

(3) What is the significance of the association between an unconditioned stimulus and a conditioned stimulus in the field of marketing?

(4) Explain the following terms: (a) primary and secondary reinforcement; (b) positive and negative reinforcement; (c) concurrent reinforcement; (d) avoidance conditioning; and (e) contiguity and contingent.

(5) Assess the relative strengths of different schedules of reinforcement in a business context.

(6) Comment on the differences between programmed learning and behaviour modification.

(7) Discuss behaviour modification as a technique used to change work behaviour.

(8) Compare and contrast operant conditioning and cognitive learning.

(9) Outline the different phases of skills development in cognitive learning, and comment on the part played by feedback.

(10) Identify the differences between long-term and working memory, and comment on the effects of ageing on memory.

(11) Using examples from business practice to illustrate your answer, what do you understand by: (a) an associative hierarchy; and (b) mnemonics?

(12) Explain the following terms: (a) chunk; (b) schemata and scripts; (c) rehearsal; (d) interference and decay; (e) primacy and recency effects; (f) episodic and generic memory; and (g) imagination in memory recovery.

(13) Identify the aspect of memory of direct relevance to eyewitness testimony.

(14) What is the connection between learning and training?

(15) Discuss the significance of knowledge management for an organisation exposed to highly competitive market conditions.

(16) Explain what is meant by the learning organisation.

SPOTLIGHT ON RELEVANT READING

Easterby-Smith, M., & Lyles, M. (Eds.) (2003). *The Blackwell handbook of organisational learning and knowledge management.* Oxford: Blackwell Publishing.

James, C.R. (2003). Designing learning organisations. *Organisational Dynamics*, *32*, 46–61.

Warwick, K. (2004). Wired learning: Mind blending. *People Management*, 8 April, 32–33.

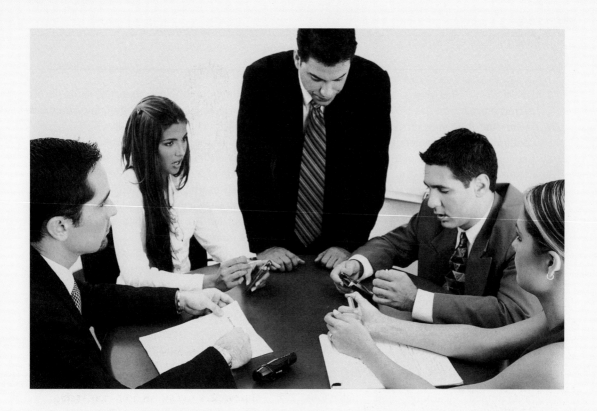

Learning Outcomes

After studying this chapter you should be able to:

* Distinguish between information-processing and decision making.

* Describe the major approaches to information-processing.

* Identify the decision-making models.

* Explain the different types of decisions.

* Recognise the ethical and cultural issues in decision making.

* Define heuristics, subjective rationality, and escalation of commitment, with respect to investor psychology or behavioural finance.

* Explain decision-support systems.

* Assess the significance of individual and organisational influences on information-processing and decision making.

* Explain decision styles.

* Discuss the importance of creativity and innovation.

Information-processing and Individual Decision Making

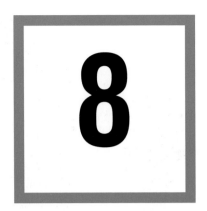

8

Information-processing and decision making are overlapping and related concepts, but there is a tendency among scholars to discuss them separately. This chapter starts with a definition and illustrations of information-processing, followed by an examination of three major approaches to the study of human information-processing. Next is a description of a decision cycle, followed by a discussion of three descriptive decision-making models. A distinction is made between structured and unstructured decision processes. The development of decision-support systems is acknowledged, before closing with an examination of individual and organisational influences on information-processing and decision making. The chapter draws on ideas developed in earlier chapters (e.g., personality, motivation, perception, and memory), and supports discussion in later chapters (e.g., on attitudes, groups, leadership, and organisational culture).

Contents

INFORMATION-PROCESSING

A human **information-processing** perspective is essentially a cognitive view of man. Human beings approach only a few situations in a unique way as information-processors. Instead, information from a person's environment is processed through pre-existing systems of knowledge abstracted from various memory schemata (discussed in Chapter 7) and experiences. These would include beliefs, theories, propositions, and schemes. Effectively, they are structures of knowledge that provide people with an important interpretative function capable of attaching meaning to incoming information as well as augmenting it. These structures also help to resolve certain ambiguities and to draw inferences, sometimes unconsciously, from incoming information, and they create a much broader scene than could be justified by a literal interpretation of the material just received.

The following illustrations refer to the handling of information. Production managers, like most people, have personal goals and aspirations and are motivated to achieve goals. They are fortunate if their personal goals coincide with the goals of the organisation for which they work. In the pursuit of organisational goals, expressed as a specified quantity and quality of output, production managers have to place reliance on information, not always accurate, about such matters as the availability of raw material and manpower,

stock levels, product quality, and the needs of customers. This and other information is used as a basis for making predictions about the business environment that influence the production function and to which it has to adapt.

The processor of information is essentially concerned with identifying and registering cues or stimuli that are perceived to be useful. The intelligent investor will not only pick up cues or information from the published accounts of a company, but will also rely on information from nonaccounting sources, such as stockbrokers, financial analysts, and the financial press (although some of this information may have its origin in the accounting system of a company) (see Panel 8.1).

APPROACHES TO INFORMATION-PROCESSING

There are at least three major approaches to the study of human information-processing. These are the lens model, the cognitive approach, and the process tracing approach, and they will be analysed in that order.

Lens model

The basic principles of this model are that the nature of the task environment exerts a powerful influence on behaviour; that the numerous cues from the environment within the grasp of the

---

PANEL 8.1: Auditors and information-processing

The auditor establishes the appropriate starting point for an audit, and the extent of the assignment, after registering cues from early exploratory work. If the internal control system is perceived to be strong, less extensive tests of a substantive nature are likely to be performed. But if the internal control system is perceived at the outset to be weak, more testing of entries in the accounting records is likely to be undertaken.

The next step is to translate and transform the cues or information into a meaningful pattern in order to facilitate the choice of an appropriate response. Before doing so, however, the information will be evaluated and that which is considered inappropriate will be rejected. Having conducted the audit of the accounting information systems, and having evaluated the data at his or her disposal, an auditor is faced with the task of formulating opinions about the "true and fair" state of the client's financial statements. Before expressing an opinion, professional judgement will be exercised to determine the amount of information to collect, when to collect it, the manner in which it is to be collected, and the implications of the information collected.

The information is rarely, if ever, perfectly reliable or perfectly predictive of the "true and fair" state of the client's financial affairs. Nevertheless, the auditor may be held liable in law should the audited financial statements prove to be unrepresentative of the "true and fair" state when the latter is certified as being the case.

individual are usually imperfect; and that these cues are not very effective at predicting the environment with which the individual has to cope. As a result of the low level of predictability, the individual has to develop a range of processes that act as a response capability in order to achieve the objectives associated with the task (Brunswick, 1955).

The lens model uses linear statistical procedures based on Bayesian decision theory. A primary objective of certain researchers using this approach in the accounting field is to build mathematical models designed to show the relative importance of different sets of information and to measure the accuracy and consistency of judgement. The measurement of consensus and predictability is also attempted.

The lens model is a normative model. A normative model in this context is concerned with how people solve problems, how they predict events, how they make decisions, and so on. To test the model, actual behaviour can be compared with what the model predicts, and if there is a perfect match the model is said to be robust. If there is a mismatch, it is hoped that the discrepancies are reflected in a systematic way. For a company making a major capital investment decision, techniques based on normative principles could be used. Subjective probabilities will also be considered, because certain benefits or costs are expected to accrue following the making of the decision. Subjective probabilities are really different degrees of belief in the truth of a particular proposition. People revise their subjective probabilities as new information is received, so in these circumstances we can expect the company to revise the predictions based on its investment decision.

Research on the lens model identifies the prevalence of conservatism (Snowball, 1980). This means that when people receive new information, they revise their subjective probabilities in the direction indicated by the normative model, even though the revision may be very small. Misperception and bias in the handling of data emanating from a person's task environment explain to some extent the onset of conservatism. When significant revisions are built into a normative model,

it would appear that one is gravitating towards a descriptive model; such a model would describe rather than prescribe the way the individual processes information.

A valid question to ask is whether individuals terminate the search for information at a point before the best or optimal stopping point as specified by the normative model. Sometimes it would appear that individuals have accumulated enough evidence to satisfy their own standards and stop short of the ideal position for the cessation of the search for information. Somebody wishing to buy a DVD player may be advised to consult the *Which?* magazine report on this product. A thorough analysis of the strengths and weaknesses of the various brands covered in the report could be considered a prerequisite to a purchase decision. However, consumers may leaf quickly through the report without studying it closely or completely, and terminate the search for information before the optimal stopping point, feeling that they have enough information to make an acceptable decision.

The usefulness of Bayesian decision theory, which is used in the lens model, has been questioned; criticism is levelled at the static nature of algebraic models for evaluating and combining information, and it is suggested that time would be better spent observing the decision-making process (descriptive theory) (Dillard, 1984).

Cognitive approach

A cognitive approach has already been discussed in connection with the study of personality (Chapter 2) and motivation (Chapter 4). The focal point of attention with this approach in this section is information-seeking behaviour in a complex environment. The assumption is that it is both possible and useful to classify individuals according to how they use information—i.e., their customary style of processing information. (Related concepts—cognitive and decision styles—are discussed later in this chapter.)

Accounting studies based on the cognitive approach attempt to classify users of information by their personal characteristics, employing personality measures and decision style, the objective being to design information systems best suited to the individual style of the decision maker (Libby & Lewis, 1982). However, it is likely to be very difficult to accommodate a tailor-made information system compatible with the personality needs of various individuals in an organisation, though it is recognised that certain information-processing tasks are performed more capably by people with particular cognitive approaches. For example, in examining the problem-solving ability of school-boys, it was found that those who were studying sciences and proposing to continue with their studies to degree level were showing tendencies to be "convergers"—in other words, they tended to be analytical and symbolic in their thinking rather than being imaginative, fluent, and flexible. Those in the arts stream, however, showed a tendency to be "divergers"—i.e., imaginative, fluent, and flexible rather than analytical and symbolic (Hudson, 1966).

A rather crude extension of these different problem-solving orientations to work organisations might suggest that the converger may feel more at ease with tasks that are highly structured, whereas the diverger may find the less structured tasks more suited to his or her mode of operation. The highly structured tasks, exemplified by tight procedures and management techniques, are more prevalent further down the organisational hierarchy than at the top, where the number of relatively unstructured tasks is probably greater. Therefore a convergent outlook would seem to be particularly appropriate at the lower echelons of the organisation. But would a divergent outlook be suited to life at the top of the organisation? The likely answer is yes. Apparently, successful chief executives tend to rely more on "feel" and intuition (divergency-type characteristics) than systematic reasoning—they synthesise rather than analyse, they intuitively know more than they can communicate, and they revel in ambiguity and dislike regularity (Bobbitt, Breinholt, Doktor, & McNaul, 1978).

The cognitive approach is associated with the theories of Schroder, Driver, and Streufert (1967). This work focuses on the reaction of a person's information-processing system to changes in the complexity of the decision environment —particularly changes in the information load. Cognitive complexity has been referred to by Schroder et al. as having three main features: (i) differentiation (numbers of parts); (ii) integration (the degree to which the parts are related); and (iii) order (the clarity with which the layers are arranged in a hierarchy). Cognitive complexity is a function of past experience, and this can be expressed as the amount of information received and the degree of success in negotiating problems in the past.

People facing increasing inputs of information to their processing systems are expected to develop relatively complex cognitive structures. These people tend to rely on more complex sources of information and spend more time searching for and processing information, as if to suggest that they can handle larger amounts of information and are motivated to seek an optimum level of information. A person with an ability to utilise complex conceptual processes (that are integrated in nature), is likely to understand and react favourably to complexity in his or her decision environment. For example, a difficult tax problem is more likely to be resolved by a competent tax specialist than by an accountant with a peripheral interest in taxation. Speed and an ability to cope with a substantial amount of complex data would be a feature of the performance of the tax specialist. Apart from information load, the format for the display of information and the order in which the information is presented are also important considerations.

Process tracing approach

Unlike the other two approaches to human information-processing, this approach goes beyond input–output analysis and attempts to obtain measures of events or processes between the input and output stages (Hayes, 1968). In both the lens model and the cognitive approach, one draws inferences about how the information-processing system works by looking at the relationship between the information received from the task environment and the end result (i.e., the judgement or decision). With process tracing one seeks evidence relating to the actual information-processing activities. The evidence is most commonly sought by asking individuals to describe their thought processes, and this could be done using a technique called protocol analysis. Obviously, memory (discussed in Chapter 7) plays an important part in the process tracing approach.

Protocol analysis

In a study comparing the decision-making processes of experts and novices in the context of a financial analysis task, differences in the style and depth of analysis between the two groups were detected. The research method used in the study was process tracing or **protocol analysis** (Bouwman, 1984). Decision makers were asked to verbalise while engaged in financial analysis, and these verbalisations were recorded on tape. The resulting transcripts, called concurrent or thinking-aloud protocols, provide the data for the protocol analysis. Each subject was given a number of financial cases to process during the financial analysis task. A case contained a general description of the firm and a 3-year set of financial statements, consisting of a balance sheet, income statement, and pages with financial ratios, sales figures, and production data. Each subject was asked to evaluate quickly the financial position of the firm, and to identify the underlying problems, if any.

Protocol analysis starts with splitting up the evidence provided by individuals into phrases, and coding or classifying these phrases with respect to the decision-making activity that they exhibit.

(An example of a decision-making activity would be computing a financial trend or comparing costs and revenue.) Next the decision maker's goals are identified. (An example of a goal would be the objective of the individual to explore indicators of the economic health of the firm, or to discover unusual features of the financial statements.) The next step in protocol analysis is the identification of the decision-making processes in terms of the individual's analysis in relation to the goals he or she has set. The final step is to present a visual representation of the sequence of events leading from the initial examination of the information through to the making of the final decision.

A methodological weakness of protocol analysis stems from the difficulties in eliciting verbal descriptions from subjects. It is the degree of complexity of the task to be performed that exerts an influence on the way the information system functions in the process tracing approach. The task environment, or *problem space* as it is called, determines the extent of the problem. The problem space will then determine the processes used to come up with a solution. This is illustrated in the example in Panel 8.2. The accounting example provided is a simple problem, but the basic processes involved in solving it apply to more complex problems. For instance, if the land in question was leased rather than purchased, the problem would be more complicated. The student would have to establish whether it was a rental lease or a capital lease. He or she would go ahead with the construction of the problem space, combining his or her internal knowledge with the external

---

PANEL 8.2: Problem space and an accounting problem

In an accounting exercise a student is confronted with a statement indicating that "land was purchased for £100,000 cash". The student is asked to make the required bookkeeping entry, and begins by constructing a problem space, which means identifying the type of problem to be solved (Dillard, 1984). In this case it is an accounting problem. The student will then proceed to identify key words in the statement. The word "land" is compared with accounting words stored in long-term memory. When the word is identified, it is categorised by type. For example, a definition of an asset is recalled and is then checked to see if land possesses the characteristics of an asset. If it does, it would be classified as an asset.

Next, the entry in the asset account will be determined by an evaluation of the word "purchased". The information with respect to acquiring an asset would be combined with the student's understanding of the principles of debit and credit. In this case, it would be a debit entry of £100,000 to the land account. The same process would apply to cash, but here it is a credit entry of £100,000 in the cash book. Obviously the manner in which the total process is activated will depend on the skill of the student. What is critical in this example is the interaction of the task environment and the expertise of the information-processor in doing the exercise.

information provided, using a process more difficult than that described in the example.

Finally, when reflecting on this subject it is
easy to concur with Eysenck and Keane's (2000)
view that protocol analysis suffers from the limitation of providing information only about those
processes of which there is conscious awareness.

DECISION MAKING

Before examining decision-making models, a distinction should be made between different types of
decisions made in organisations. Basically, there are
two types—programmed or structured decisions,
and nonprogrammed or unstructured decisions.

A programmed or structured decision is well
defined; the decision maker is aware of the extent
of the decision, and there exists a clear set of
options from which a choice can be made. The
method of evaluating the options has been established and is straightforward. Therefore the decision maker has a well-specified and agreed
decision procedure at his or her disposal (Simon,
1960). This could amount to a decision rule to
tell decision makers which alternative to choose
once they have information about the decision
situation. Then the appropriate decision rule is
used whenever the same situation arises in the
future. The following is an example of a programmed or structured decision (Cooke & Slack,
1984):

A manager has to choose a new packaging
machine from a choice of two models, both
of which are similar to an existing machine
and are known to be reliable. The manager
chooses the machine that offers the most
attractive post-tax discounted return calculated over a 5-year period. This involves
collecting details (such as price and operating costs) of each machine, using a formula
approved by the organisation for capital
expenditure proposals. An order is then
placed for the selected machine and the
goods received section and accounts department are duly notified.

When decisions are unique and not routine,
they can be classified as nonprogrammed or
unstructured. This type of decision is illustrated
later in the discussion of the **implicit favourite
model** and decision making under conditions of
uncertainty. A comparison of programmed and
nonprogrammed decisions appears in Table 8.1.

Turning to our main discussion of decision-
making models, these are of two types: prescriptive and descriptive. Earlier in the analysis of the
lens model, a normative approach was considered
prescriptive in the sense that the model tells us what
ought to be done. The normative or prescriptive
model attempts to impose on the decision maker
the framework reflected in the assumptions of the
model. A descriptive model, on the other hand,
describes the steps involved in making a choice
from among various courses of action open to the

TABLE 8.1

Characteristics of programmed (P) and nonprogrammed (NP) decisions (from Moorhead & Griffin, 1998):
Copyright © 1998 by Houghton Mifflin Company. Used with permission

Characteristics	P	NP
Type of decision	Well structured	Poorly structured
Frequency	Repetitive and routine	New and unusual
Goals	Clear, specific	Vague
Information	Readily available	Not available, unclear channels
Consequences	Minor	Major
Organisational level	Lower levels	Upper levels
Times for solution	Short	Relatively long
Basis for solution	Decision rules, set procedures	Judgement and creativity

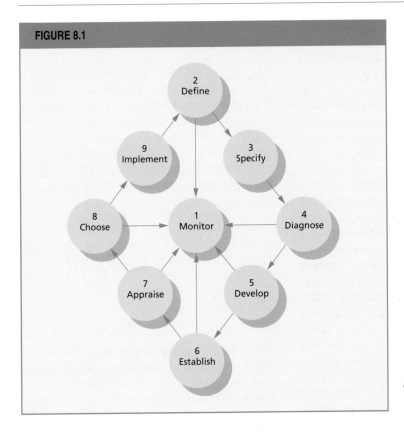

FIGURE 8.1

The decision process (from Archer, 1980).

decision maker (as can be seen in the "Decision cycle" section, next). As we shall discover later, this is not always a rational process.

Decision cycle

A study of over 2000 managers, supervisors, and executives was undertaken in order to determine what steps in the **decision cycle** they used and found helpful. Out of this study came a simple nine-step framework, though the outcome of other studies had a part to play as well (Archer, 1980). This is depicted in Figure 8.1 as a decision process, and it is discussed with reference to a description of a relatively simple decision (Cooke & Slack, 1984).

(1) Monitor. The environment should be monitored constantly to obtain feedback. The decision maker monitors the environment to detect deviations from plans or to pick up signals on the need to take a decision. For example, a company makes specialised quality testing equipment for the food processing industry. The general manager of the company, having monitored the environment, has become aware of the fact that the number of late deliveries of testing equipment to customers is on the increase. Subsequently, this information is reinforced by a complaint from an important customer who has just received a second late delivery.

(2) Define. The problem or situation has to be defined precisely. The information picked up at the monitoring stage could relate to the symptoms of the problem, but not the causes. From initial enquiries it appears plausible that communication difficulties between the production and marketing functions are a contributory factor in the problem of late deliveries. The general manager writes a letter to both the marketing and production managers asking for information on the delivery service to customers and the present utilisation of manufacturing capacity.

(3) Specify. The decision objectives have to be specified, and the likely risks and the constraints should be considered. What the decision makers expect to be achieved is clarified.

(4) Diagnose. The problem or situation is analysed more thoroughly and the causes of the problem are scrutinised. The general manager discusses the problem with the production manager, who states that the reasons for the late deliveries are the unrealistic delivery promises made by sales staff, who are also said to be at fault in not giving manufacturing staff enough notice to plan production when large new orders are received.

Faced with this evidence the marketing manager in conversation with the general manager defends the sales staff. He maintains that prompt delivery is crucial in highly competitive market conditions, and that the company must react quickly to get new business. Inevitably the manufacturing staff cannot expect much notice of new orders. The marketing manager also maintains that the problem is inadequate capacity in the production area due to under-investment in plant over a period of time. Therefore, the production function does not have sufficient flexibility to meet delivery times. The general manager at this stage feels that, due to communication difficulties, neither the production manager nor the marketing manager has critical information at their disposal when making decisions.

(5) Develop. Alternative courses of action or solutions are developed. The options open to the company are discussed at length and the critical options are listed as follows.

(a) Introduce a more sophisticated computerised information system.
(b) All sales staff are required to check with production control before making promises related to delivery.
(c) Put aside an afternoon each week for a meeting when operating managers can discuss matters of prime importance.
(d) All sales staff are required to complete weekly reports on the likelihood of receiving orders from customers in the near future.

It is felt that any combination of these options is feasible.

(6) Establish. At this stage the methods or criteria to be used in the appraisal of the options or alternatives are established. This could be any process that ensures the provision of an adequate amount of information to facilitate realistic promises with respect to deliveries of testing systems to customers, and to improve performance of the delivery service at acceptable cost levels.

(7) Appraise. Alternative solutions or courses of action should be appraised. Each alternative or option is evaluated in terms of the quantity and quality of information it would provide for the production and marketing functions. The costs of implementation of the alternatives would also be appraised. Both costs and benefits would be expressed in quantitative and qualitative terms.

(8) Choose. The best alternative solution or course of action is chosen. In this case a management committee made the decision, and chose two options (rather than one) for implementation. Options 5(a) and 5(d) were either too expensive or were unlikely to produce much useful information. The eventual decision was that 5(b) and 5(c) should be implemented.

(9) Implement. The best alternative solution or course of action is implemented, and the detailed operational plan is discussed at the regular afternoon management meeting. In addition, the marketing manager issues instructions to sales staff to check with a certain person in production control before stating delivery times.

This decision process could revert back to stage 1, when monitoring activity resumes. In this case it was felt that the system had improved, but the general manager was not totally satisfied with the outcome. At a meeting of the management group, the problem was redefined to include some fundamental issues that affected the way the production function was organised, and the decision process started again.

In practice, the process of decision making is unlikely to be as smooth as the model depicted here would suggest. According to Cooke and Slack (1984), "real decision behaviours can exhibit frequent backtracks and jumps forward before an option is finally selected. Thus the decision process may not be smooth but a jerky and hesitant progression involving, at times, one step forwards and two steps backwards."

This descriptive decision process outlined above might well be classified by Behling and Schriesheim (1976) as the econological model of decision making. Other descriptive models of decision making, which they acknowledge, and which will be analysed later, are the "bounded rationality" and "implicit favourite" models.

Econological model

This model describes a logical and orderly way of processing information and arriving at a decision. The resultant decision is considered to be based on rationality (Garvin & Roberto, 2001; Langly, 1989) along the lines of the programmed decision mentioned above. However, there is some evidence to suggest that consumers do not make decisions in the way outlined in the econological model, and a challenge to the model appears in Panel 8.3. In accounting for the shortcomings of the econological or rational model one should accept limitations on the availability of information to decision makers and constraints on their capability to process information. In this connection the following should be noted (Harrison, 1995; Nutt, 1993; Simon, 1957a; Simon & Newell, 1971; Terry, 1968):

- Information available to managers in organisations is usually limited because of the lack of time to collect the ideal quantity of information and the cost of doing so.
- Only a small number of alternative courses of action in the decision situation come to mind because of a lack of data, and sometimes knowledge about a given alternative is not easy to obtain.
- It is often difficult to quantify the chosen alternatives, so that makes comparing them rather difficult.
- Choosing one of the alternative courses of action, so that a decision can be recorded, may not always be possible. For example, two or more alternatives may be equally attractive and the decision maker may have to select a combination of alternatives. Where no single alternative or a combination of alternatives is capable of solving the problem, the decision maker will be forced to obtain more information, or generate more alternatives, or change the decision objectives.
- Because decision makers cannot predict the future, it is unlikely that they will be aware of the consequences (outcomes) of pursuing the alternatives they have subjected to scrutiny.
- There are constraints in the way we seek solutions to problems. Even if the decision maker has full knowledge of all alternatives and outcomes, complete rationality could not be achieved because of the restrictions imposed on the decision process by the capabilities of the human mind as an information-processing

---

PANEL 8.3: Decision making by consumers

In the literature on consumer behaviour a decision model similar to the econological model is adopted (Engel, Blackwell, & Miniard, 1995), but, in a critical analysis of research studies on pre-purchase decision behaviour, it was concluded that for many purchases a decision process never occurs, or if purchase behaviour is preceded by a decision process, this process of choice is likely to be very limited. It typically involves the evaluation of only a few alternatives, it entails little external search for information, few evaluative criteria are used, and the evaluation process is a simple one.

In situations like this it may be more realistic to consider the strong influence of a personal recommendation from a friend or relative, coupled with limited search for and evaluation of information prior to a purchase decision. Other influences on purchase behaviour may be conformity to group norms, imitation, and so on.

(Olshavsky & Granbois, 1979)

system. The system accommodates only one process at a time, it cannot work in a parallel fashion and, as was stated in Chapter 7 with reference to memory, the inputs and outputs stemming from problem-solving activity are initially stored in a small short-term memory or working memory with very limited capacity. Of course, the human information-processing system has access to a substantial long-term memory with fast retrieval but slow storage. All these factors impose restrictions on the way in which the individual's information-processing system will seek solutions to problems.

Given the limiting factors identified earlier, it would appear that decision processes that rely on a consideration of a number of alternatives and outcomes cannot find expression in the way suggested by the econological model. Basically, we suffer deficiencies when comparing alternatives in a simultaneous fashion, rather than a sequential arrangement, and our memory storage system can be a handicap. Likewise, the exercise of placing values on various outcomes of the decision process, and ranking alternatives in order of preference, is constrained by the limitations of our memory. Again we find that being able to select the alternative that will generate the greatest benefit is extraordinarily difficult (Von Neumann & Morgenstern, 1953).

Finally, in the decision-making process it is wise to recognise what course of action would be necessary if the implementation of the preferred alternative encountered severe problems (e.g., a decision to expand the market for a product is no longer valid in the light of the onset of an economic recession). In such circumstances it would be useful if contingency plans existed, and were put into action when the original plans are no longer valid or cannot be operationalised (Ginsberg & Ventrakaman, 1985).

Bounded rationality model

This model is more reality-orientated, and it recognises the constraints acting on the ability of the individual to process information. According to Hardman and Harries (2002), the "idea of bounded rationality in judgement and decision making has proved to be a powerful one, motivating the search for various shortcuts in thinking". Individuals and organisations seek the best solutions when faced with a choice among alternatives, but they usually settle for considerably less than they would like to have (Forester, 1984). The ideal decision would make too great a demand on their data-processing capabilities. Bounded rationality explains decision making in terms of three main processes:

(1) consideration of alternative solutions in a sequential fashion;
(2) use of heuristics to identify the most promising alternatives; and
(3) satisficing.

Sequential consideration of alternatives

When things are going well there is a tendency not to scan the environment in a serious way. But if the external environment poses a threat to the organisation, then a search for solutions to the problems encountered takes place. This is akin to the notion of strategic planning. Fredrickson and Iaquinto (1989) underlined the importance of search for information in particular circumstances. They found that a comprehensive information search and consideration of options contributed to effective strategic decision making in stable external environments (in their study, for example, the environment of the paints industry), but this did not apply in unstable external environments (e.g., the forestry industry).

The search process is said to have three main characteristics (Cyert & March, 1963):

- The search is motivated in the sense that it is activated in response to a current problem.
- It is simple minded in that it begins with the obvious solutions, and only considers other solutions if the simple-minded solutions prove inadequate.
- It is biased because the search for solutions is influenced by the individual's ego, training, experience, hopes, aspirations, and other factors that serve to distort his or her view of the world.

Unlike the treatment of alternatives in the econological model, which requires that all alternatives under consideration be identified before any evaluation takes place, with the bounded rationality model the various alternatives are identified and considered one at a time. Those that prove inadequate in the light of the evaluative criteria are discarded before other alternatives are considered.

Use of heuristics

Making decisions is no easy task, so it is only reasonable to expect people to take short cuts in performing this activity. One group of cognitive shortcuts is known as **heuristics**. Heuristics are rules that guide the search for alternatives into areas where there is a good chance of finding satisfactory solutions. They reduce to manageable proportions the number of possible solutions through which the decision maker must sift (Simon & Newell, 1971). Heuristic models do not attempt to optimise, though they can do so by chance, but they aim to achieve satisfactory sub-optimal solutions. The heuristic approach adopts short cuts in the reasoning process, and it uses rules of thumb, such as the following, in the search for a satisfactory solution (Hinkle & Kuehn, 1967):

- "Buy when prices on the stock exchange move rapidly upwards with a heavy volume of trading."
- "When the stock of goods gets down to four, that is the time to buy more."
- "For accounting purposes, value assets at cost or market value, whichever is the lower."
- In production scheduling, the motto is "first come, first served" or "schedule urgent jobs first" (Weist, 1966).

Heuristic models are generally more complex than these rules of thumb, but equally they can be relatively simple. Tversky and Kahneman (1974) recognise the influence of judgemental strategies in conditions of uncertainty, and analyse three heuristics—representative, availability, and anchoring.

Representative heuristic. This is used when people estimate the probability of an occurrence of an event. It is concerned with the tendency to see the likelihood of an event occurring simply because it resembles similar events. This shortcut approach to decision making can be biased. A person could be asked to state the extent to which an object or event has certain features to permit appropriate categorisation. For example, a selector predicts that a candidate with a qualification from a particular institution is likely to be a success in a particular job because existing employees who attended that institution have turned out to be successful. In the application of this heuristic, consider the situation outlined in Panel 8.4.

PANEL 8.4: Examples of the representative heuristic

Steve is very shy and withdrawn, invariably helpful, but with little interest in people or in the world of reality. A meek and tidy soul he has a need for order and structure, and a passion for detail. Studies find that when asked to guess whether Steve is a librarian or a lawyer, people are much more likely to guess librarian because—with apologies to librarians—Steve sounds more like a librarian. If your answer was "librarian", it is said that you have been influenced overwhelmingly by the representative heuristic. You have concluded that the above profile was a better description of a librarian than a lawyer.

The representative heuristic can be a good rule of thumb, but it can also lead people astray. In the above example, Steve is in fact more likely to be a lawyer. Although he sounds like a librarian, there are fewer librarians than there are lawyers, and the odds are that a given person is more likely to be aware of lawyers. Given this base-rate information, an appropriate answer from a statistical point of view would be that Steve is a "lawyer".

One possible consequence of the representative heuristic in financial markets is that investors may be too quick to detect patterns in data that are in fact random. If a company reports increased earnings several quarters in a row, this heuristic may lead investors to conclude that the company has a high long-term earnings growth rate. After all, past earnings are representative of a high growth rate. However, this conclusion is likely to be premature: investors are forgetting that even though the company looks as if it has a high growth rate, even a mediocre company can produce good quarters of earnings, simply by chance.

Barberis (2001)

Availability heuristic.   This is a tendency to make judgements about the frequency or likelihood of events in terms of how readily examples of them can be retrieved from memory (Vaughn, 1999). Therefore, we tend to consider events more probable if they can easily be imagined than if they cannot. The events falling into this category are those that are particularly vivid, or arouse our emotions, or have occurred recently.

The availability heuristic can be prone to error. For example, those who have been involved in crime may, when asked, overestimate the criminal statistics, unlike those who have not been involved. With the former group, bias creeps into the estimate, and this group is unlikely to consider the influence exerted by their own unique experience on their judgement, or to recall media comments on the statistics, which could present a more authentic view.

The availability heuristic is to view any story through the lens of a superficially similar story. Any comment or story about the prospects of a high-tech firm today could be interpreted with reference to a framework characterised by memories of the dot com bubble.

Reflecting on both the availability heuristic and the representative heuristic, Vecchio (2003) had this to say:

> Both the availability heuristic and the representative heuristic are important tools in drawing inferences. Although they may often lead us to correct inferences, they have the potential to lead us to erroneous judgements as well. It should also be understood that Kahneman and Tversky's notions of availability and representativeness are not, strictly speaking, heuristics in the sense of being explicit and fixed devices or formulas for making decisions. Rather they represent automatic and unconscious processes that are frequently involved in judgement and decision making processes.

Anchoring-and-adjustment heuristic.   A decision can be influenced by what is known as the anchoring-and-adjustment heuristic. This is a mental rule of thumb for reaching decisions by making adjustments in information that is already available to us. So it is concerned with a tendency to pass judgement by starting from an initial position that is likely to influence the final outcome. But bias creeps in when we fail to change our views in the light of new information. We seem to be anchored by our starting point. For example, there is a suggested asking price for the sale of a new house: that is the reference point (anchor) and is a figure from which negotiations between the builder and buyer proceed. In this example, if the asking price is realistic an adjustment in price downwards could be insignificant (Diekmann, Tenbrunsel, Shah, Schroth, & Bazerman, 1996). But if new information (in this case negative) about the neighbourhood in which the house is located comes to life, bias creeps in if we fail to change our view in the light of the new information. In such circumstances the potential house-buyer seems to be anchored by the idea of the realistic asking price.

Anchoring leads investors to make decisions by looking at past share prices, share prices of similar companies, share prices of the sector as a whole, or any other relevant yardstick. It can have the effect of halting a sufficient reassessment of new information (Willman, 2000). The following is an observation from a mathematician who played the stock market (Paulos, 2003):

> People often remember and are anchored to the 52-week high (or low) at which the stock had been selling and continue to base their deliberations on this anchor. I unfortunately did this with WorldCom. Having first bought stock when it was in the forties (US $) I implicitly assumed it would eventually right itself and return there. Later when I bought more of it in the thirties (US $), twenties (US $), and teens (US $), I made the same assumption.

Conservatism might also be a factor in anchoring. When firm opinions are formed, there may be a reluctance to change them even though new information is received to challenge them. For example, Company X, based on its past performance, is seen by investors as having "average"

PANEL 8.5: Investment decisions and satisficing

An example of a computerised behavioural model to simulate an investment decision is provided by Clarkson (1963). The model relied heavily on satisficing criteria in the form of rules of thumb and standard operating procedures. An attempt was made to duplicate the investment decisions of a bank trust officer. Before examining in detail the officer's decision behaviour, numerous bank officials were interviewed. Questions were asked of the officer about how decisions were made with respect to investment portfolios. Transcripts of the responses were studied, the officer was asked to read financial documents and comment upon them, and a model of the trust investment decision process used by the bank officer was constructed.

The following example highlights the predicament of a top decision maker. Kay (2001) comments on the cost of mobile phone licences for British Telecommunications (BT) and asks what could Sir Peter Bonfield (the previous CEO of BT) have in mind when he stated that BT paid too much for its mobile phone licences. The prices paid for those licences were absurd. But BT did not simply have the option of dropping out of the race for third generation services in Europe. BT made a bad decision, but it was still the best the company could have made. We must settle for "satisficing" because our options are constrained not just by the limits of our knowledge but also by the beliefs and actions of others.

---

long-term earnings prospects. Then the company produces much higher earnings than expected. Conservatism predicts that investors will still hang on to their belief that the company is only average, and will not react in a significant way to the good news. The consequence in terms of share price movement is not much change in the share price on the day of the announcement of the results, but there should be a gradual drift upwards in later weeks as investors shed their initial conservatism (Barberis, 2001). This price movement is called "post-earnings announcement drift", and it is said to form the basis of many investment strategies popular with money managers.

Both the anchoring effect and the availability heuristic are exacerbated by other tendencies, such as the confirmation bias. The confirmation bias refers to the way we check a hypothesis by observing instances that confirm it and ignoring those that don't. We are more aware and search diligently for information that might confirm our beliefs (Paulos, 2003). The heuristic techniques discussed above help us to draw inferences from events, but as we have seen not all judgements are likely to be accurate.

Satisficing

In the econological model, the best (or optimal) course of action is chosen after considering all possible alternatives. On the other hand, *satisficing*, as a bounded rationality process, operates on the assumption that decision makers judge alternatives one at a time against certain standards of acceptability, and choose the first alternative that meets the minimal acceptable criteria or the minimum conditions for success. So the decision maker need not evaluate all possible alternatives, but only search until an adequate one is found. Therefore, satisficing means the acceptance of a satisfactory outcome. As a result, the decision maker engages in less information-processing activity than would be the case if an optimal alternative was sought. An example of a decision situation relying on the satisficing process is included in Panel 8.5.

An insight from an expectancy theory of motivation (discussed in Chapter 4) could be applied to the behaviour of the decision maker intent on satisficing. As decision makers explore the various alternative solutions, their aspiration level rises, and next time round they may be a little more adventurous in their search. But as they find it difficult to discover satisfactory solutions, their aspiration level falls and that makes it easier on the next occasion to obtain satisfactory solutions (Simon, 1957b). For a more recent perspective on satisficing, refer to Kaufman (1990).

The bounded rationality model appears to be a more accurate description of the individual's decision-making process than is found in the econological model, but the evidence to support this assertion is not totally conclusive (Behling & Schriesheim, 1976). Much of the supporting evidence comes from computer simulations of the decision-making process, and the decisions studied seem to have a number of characteristics found in programmed or structured decisions.

Intuition. It is now apparent that complexity and uncertainty surround the bounded rationality model, and in such circumstances the decision maker may rely to some extent on intuition. It should not be considered an admission of failure, or a sign of irrationality, if one were to rely on such a nonscientific approach. Robbins (2003) makes reference to intuitive decision making as an unconscious process, created out of distilled experience, that can complement systematic analysis. He then briefly speculates about whether it is an extrasensory power or sixth sense, or a personality trait that a limited number of people have inherited.

According to Behling and Eckel (1991), intuition could enrich decision making in certain situations. In what circumstances are decision makers most likely to use intuition in decision making? One answer might very well mention the following (Agor, 1986):

* The available information relating to the decision situation is rather limited and not very informative.
* There is a lot of uncertainty and few precedents exist to guide us.
* The data in the decision equation do not easily lend themselves to quantitative analysis and what analytical data there are are of limited use.
* The time available to reach a decision is very limited.
* There are many equally attractive options on offer.

Some industrialists or senior executives now use "intuitive consultants" to help them balance the creative and legal sides of their minds and avoid the pitfalls of data paralysis. Here are some comments attributable to these top managers: "intuition offers a short-cut to decision making . . . I take decisions without a logical reason . . . I know when we should follow a certain path." The following is a statement by a self-styled intuitive consultant who teaches a module on intuition at one of the major UK business schools, and who was described as having excellent predictive ability on business matters by the chief executive of a small company providing financial information in the City of London (Overell, 2000):

In recent years I have witnessed a growing interest in the right-brain side of things in business. Clients turn to me to help them understand problems, such as working relationships, financial decisions, or personal matters. All I do is confirm what clients know deep down, and I suppose I provide access to that knowledge. I encourage them to reflect on how they think and how they balance the logical and creative sides of their brains. I also help students meditate, taking them through visualisation and sensory exercises to understand and value their imagination. Some are convinced, others are not.

According to Agor (1986), in cultures where rational analysis is respected, it is conceivable that decision makers will not boast about the power of intuitive decision making. If they use it, they are more than likely to give the credit to analytical approaches when reflecting on the decision made.

Implicit favourite model

Like the bounded rationality model, the implicit favourite model postulates the view that individuals solve complex problems by simplifying the decision process. In this situation the decision maker does not subscribe to the level of objectivity or rationality one might expect. In fact early in the decision process, before seriously exploring all possibilities, a preferred alternative is selected and for the remainder of the time the decision maker places emphasis on confirming that the implicit favourite has been the right choice (Robbins, Millett, Cacioppe, & Waters-Marsh, 2001). The outcome of a research study that looked at the implicit favourite model is reported in Panel 8.6.

In a criticism of the implicit favourite model, it is alleged that it is more a model of decision rationalisation than of decision making. It concentrates on the justification for the choice of the implicit favourite, but it says very little about how the implicit favourite is selected (Behling & Schriesheim, 1976). The model was created as a result of individual decision making in pursuit of

PANEL 8.6: Job search and the implicit favourite

In an analysis of the job-search behaviour of graduate business students it was concluded that decisions were made in a way that could not be explained adequately by either the econological model or the bounded rationality model (Soelberg, 1967). However, in accordance with the predictions of the econological model, the students searched for alternatives in a parallel fashion and evaluated several alternatives at a time. But a departure from the econological model was evident with respect to the lack of weighting attached to the evaluation criteria; also the evaluation criteria were not used in making the final choice. The criteria used in evaluating alternative jobs may, for example, relate to a number of characteristics such as salary level, job interest and challenge, and location. It was also established in this study that the alternatives were not ranked in some order of preference.

An important finding of the study was that the search for information continued after a satisfactory alternative (*the implicit favourite*) was identified—e.g., the choice of a particular type of job that offers interest and challenge with a modest initial salary. What happened next was a lengthy process of investigation soon after the search for alternatives ceased. This took the form of justifying the choice of the implicit favourite by offsetting against it the most attractive of the rejected alternatives—e.g., a job with an attractive initial salary, but rather limited challenge and prospects. Then a rationale was created to show that the implicit favourite was superior to the best of the rejected alternatives.

Once the implicit favourite was chosen, information on the outcome of alternatives was biased in its favour. Also, evaluation elements (e.g., minimum salary and challenge) used in the choice of the most appropriate alternative were adjusted to fit the desired outcome. From an outside, objective assessment of the decision process, it was clear that the implicit favourite was based only on a limited number of dimensions of the decision criteria. A decision was not announced at the time of the choice of implicit favourite; it was not until the most attractive of the rejected alternatives was ruled out in a rather biased analytical way that a decision was declared.

a job, and may not be applicable to organisational decision making where bargaining and political processes could act as significant constraints.

Decision making under conditions of uncertainty

The evidence discussed in the previous subsection relates to a nonprogrammed or unstructured decision, which is described further here.

Nonprogrammed or unstructured decisions

These decisions are not defined clearly either in terms of what the objectives are or who is involved in the decision. In fact the decision situation is blurred, not well understood, and difficult to tackle. The alternative solutions to be considered are not immediately apparent, simply because the situation facing the decision maker has not been seen in its present form before, or under the prevailing circumstances. Because of the novelty of the decision, the decision maker has an unclear view of how to make it; in fact different executives are likely to have different views on both the decision itself and how to tackle it. The following is another example of a nonprogrammed or unstructured decision (Cooke & Slack, 1984):

A manager is keen to make a decision about the nature of the company's product portfolio in the medium term. Reports from sales representatives indicate that the existing product range appears somewhat obsolete in relation to that offered by competitors. The manager has to face a decision either to update the existing range of products or alternatively to offer a new range. This presents a dilemma, more so because the eventual decision will affect a number of areas within the company. The manager proceeds to consult and seek advice from colleagues in other functional areas of the business on the feasibility of his or her own initial ideas about the best way to go ahead. He or she recognises that a new product range will provide a firm foundation for the long-term security of the company, but also realises that any significant expenditure incurred at this stage could threaten the delicate cash-flow position of the company in the short term. It is no easy task to take the right decision in these circumstances.

Apparently, the uncertainty associated with the making of a nonprogrammed or unstructured decision also makes its presence felt at the

---

PANEL 8.7: Implementation of a nonprogrammed decision

A decision was made to transfer staff from one location within a company to another. The chief executive decided that a specified number of staff would be involved in the move, and a senior personnel executive had responsibility to implement the decision. The personnel executive was given wide discretionary powers to use standard operating programmes and to develop new programmes or modify old ones through discussion and analysis. His first line of action was to initiate problem-solving activity by calling a meeting of individuals qualified to contribute to the process of implementing the decision. Out of this meeting came an action programme.

However, as the implementation process neared completion it was evident that matters were not progressing at the level originally anticipated. Because of a reluctance of some staff to move from the old to the new site, quality considerations had to be relaxed and, in certain circumstances, lower-calibre staff were transferred. In addition, the reluctance of certain staff to move created organisational slack at the old site and this was condoned by the workers and union officials alike. The unanticipated consequences flowing from the implementation process, which acted to the disadvantage of the company, were the creation of organisational slack at the old site and the introduction of lower-calibre staff at the new site.

(Dufty & Taylor, 1970)

---

implementation stage. This was highlighted in Dufty and Taylor (1970), a study of the implementation stage of a nonprogrammed decision (see Panel 8.7).

As a final comment on unstructured decisions, it is worth noting that a certain type of unstructured decision—i.e., a strategic decision in an organisation—may be underpinned by a basic structure. From a field study of 25 strategic decision processes, together with a review of the related empirical literature, Mintzberg, Raisinghani, and Theoret (1976) concluded that strategic decision processes, as opposed to tactical decision processes of a routine problem-solving nature, are immensely complex and dynamic, yet they are amenable to conceptual structuring.

To round off this section we shall examine an important decision process that exemplifies uncertainty—the process of negotiation. This is also an example of group decision making, a topic given greater coverage in Chapter 10.

Negotiation

Negotiation is an example of decision making under conditions of uncertainty. It pervades many aspects of organisational life—for example, negotiations are conducted between union representatives and management, between sales executives and clients, and between managers within an organisation on matters connected with the allocation of scarce resources. Before decisions are made, delicate behavioural processes can be detected during the course of negotiations. Morley (1984) has analysed these processes, and the more important ones will now be discussed.

Negotiators take certain courses of action on the basis of their perception of the likely response of the other party in the negotiation process. In this respect the expectations of the other party, including the way the issue or problem under discussion is perceived, is of crucial importance. Negotiators will strive to attain the maximum benefits from the encounter, but equally they are aware of the need to reach an agreement acceptable to all parties. Obviously this will necessitate compromise and modification of positions when circumstances dictate such a course. It is possible to detect different strategies while negotiators are engaged in trying to secure the best possible advantage (Arnold, 2005).

For example, at the outset a negotiator may make high demands and subsequently make concessions. Not to give way on the initial high demands would be a rather high-risk strategy, with the likelihood of not reaching an agreement. Another strategy would be to make low initial demands and subsequently make many concessions, but such a move is likely to produce a quick but lopsided agreement. A final example would be to start with moderate demands and refuse to make any concessions. The moderate demands could please the opposing negotiators at the outset but the refusal to make any concessions could give rise later to their frustration and lack of perceived success from the encounter.

Negotiators have to come to terms with two major forces that impinge on the situation. First, there are the social processes and relationships built up with the opponents at the bargaining table. Negotiators need to maintain good relationships with other negotiators while disagreeing with them, and may resort to light-hearted interventions in their attempt to influence the nature and quality of the relationship and the climate in which the negotiation takes place. Also, where there is more than one negotiator on one side of the table, one would expect them to talk among themselves about how to respond to a proposal from the other side. The display of professionalism of the negotiator is something else to consider because of its association with self-esteem (does the negotiator feel happy with the projected image of problem solver?).

Secondly, negotiators are conscious of the fact that they are acting as representatives of a group that is outside the bargaining process. For example, union representatives are acting on behalf of their trade union, which may have specified the desired result. But in this case there will be situations where the negotiators may have to go back to their masters in the trade union to persuade the latter that the result achieved at the bargaining table is the best deal on offer in the present circumstances, but not as good as the desired result. It has to be acknowledged that negotiations between trade unions and management can be quite complicated because of the influence exerted by external forces (e.g., the impact of employment legislation and the outcome of similar negotiations elsewhere).

The relative strength of the two forces can change as negotiations proceed. At the bargaining table it is possible for friendly relationships to develop between the protagonists. This in turn facilitates the free flow of information, and eventually contributes to a cooperative rather than a competitive spirit, as well as the development of mutual trust and respect. Of course, there is also the potential for conflict, and this could be injected into the proceedings from the outside environment. Another source of conflict stems from inconsistencies in the judgements of negotiators. Deviousness may be attributed to a negotiator because his or her judgement is considered inaccurate or incomplete.

The bargaining process can be complex and clouded with uncertainty. Critical information may not be readily available or, if it is, it may be ambiguous. Alternatively, there may be a lot of information available in numerous documents and the negotiators may find it difficult to grasp their brief. As arguments are presented and manoeuvres worked out, the interests and power base of participants become critical. Uncertainty is often created when a negotiator tries to answer questions on the validity of information presented by the other party. Likewise, negotiators may doubt their ability to defend their position, and are concerned about giving too much away too quickly ("Shall we continue in the hope of negotiating a better deal?"). Negotiators are continuously trying to make sense out of the dialogue and to put it into an ordered perspective.

The influence of culture has to be considered when negotiations are conducted by participants from different countries. An awareness of different cultures is vital to successful negotiations in the international market-place; for example, in some societies one is not encouraged to disagree with people whom one should respect (Wood, 1998). An example of a negotiation episode in the international sphere is one that could be used in connection with the sale of expensive capital goods (e.g., aircraft). According to Wood and Colosi (1997), Westerners, especially north Europeans and Americans, like to get the technical issues resolved first before getting to know the people with whom they are negotiating. On the other hand, those from other cultures emphasise the relationship side first because, before they get steeped in the technicalities of the deal, they want to understand the person with whom they are dealing. In their eyes, if the relationship is strong, any mere technical difficulties can be easily overcome. DuBrin (2002) has proposed a list of suggestions for the American negotiating abroad, as follows:

• Accept that in certain countries there is a preference for a team approach to negotiation.

- Do not overdo the informal approach (e.g., persistence in the use of first names), and recognise the organisational status of your counterparts by adhering to an appropriate degree of formality.
- Recognise that others have a different concept of time. For example, negotiators from China and the Arab world are willing to spend what might seem an excessive amount of time negotiating a deal, including periods devoted to elaborate dining.
- Do not expect full exposure of information from your counterparts, even though you believe that frank disclosure is a valuable negotiating tactic.
- Accept periodic bouts of silence, which seem rather lengthy when viewed from your own cultural perspective. Tolerating spells of silence can be beneficial because it gives the other side the chance to disclose their position.
- Do not be overwhelmed with the desire to clinch a particular deal, and accept a negative outcome gracefully. There is likely to be another opportunity to build on the goodwill developed with your counterparts at the negotiating table.
- Be adaptable by recognising that negotiating tactics have to be modified to work well in cultures other than your own.

Eventually, the outcome of the negotiations will depend upon the accuracy of the negotiators' diagnosis of the delicate interpersonal processes, and the skill with which they make the appropriate moves. Those endowed with a perceptive outlook, who possess a good facility in presenting a case and are shrewd, operate at an advantage. In complex negotiations, particularly of a multilateral nature, a breakthrough in the negotiations may be difficult to achieve. The desired outcome of most negotiation processes is likely to embrace a favourable agreement, the avoidance of a disaster, and improved relationships between the parties concerned.

Other issues

Apart from decision-making models, there are a number of other research issues that can be considered part of the debate on decision making. Hodgetts (1991) recognises three such issues as **simplification**, subjective rationality, and rationalisation. To these could be added escalation of commitment and the influence of culture and ethics.

Simplification

In this case a simplified model of reality is adopted by the decision maker. Familiar situations invite similar responses and a different approach is adopted only if the previous approach did not work out well. Schwenk (1985) maintains that many people make decisions based on their recollections of the facts as opposed to diligently checking their records or other sources of information. However, circumstances could dictate a more refined strategy of data collection. For example, this could arise where the information obtained is incomplete, or a major mistake occurred because of previous reliance on a recollection of facts. There is also a view that people who are attached to a particular belief supporting a piece of behaviour show resistance to new information that challenges that belief. For instance, the heavy drinker could turn a blind eye to new evidence on the dangers of excessive alcohol consumption.

Subjective rationality

People frequently become more conservative as the complexity of the decision situation grows. At the same time, there is the tendency to cease seeking more information, even though such information could be useful and inexpensive to acquire, and heavy reliance is placed on personal judgement (Hodgetts, 1991). Research has shown that individuals often use **subjective rationality** even in circumstances where all the necessary information is available to permit judgements based on objective rationality (Fagley & Miller, 1987).

Fear of failure is evident when people place bets with their own money. People are likely to be risk-takers with small bets, but with larger amounts they are likely to be more cautious, even with favourable odds. Fear of failure (subjective rationality) outweighs the favourable odds (objective rationality) (Schurr, 1987).

People show an aversion to losses greater than the attractiveness of possible gains where the same amount of money is involved. For example, most people would prefer the certainty of winning £750 over a 75% chance of winning £1000; but the same individuals would prefer a 75% chance of losing £1000 over a certain loss of £750. This points to risk-averse decisions when it comes to gains, and risk-seeking decisions when it comes to losses (Kahneman & Tversky, 1984). Therefore, companies facing financial difficulties may take more risks in an attempt to eliminate losses than companies who are doing well and experiencing gains (Fiegenbaum & Thomas, 1988).

In connection with people's reactions to gains and losses, we can now reflect on key ideas from behavioural finance or investor psychology derived from the work of Kahneman and Tversky, cited earlier, and shaped by Shiller (1990). These are related to prospect theory and regret theory.

Prospect theory and regret theory were advanced by Kahneman and Tversky (1979). Prospect theory is concerned with the view that people respond differently to equivalent situations depending upon whether they are presented in the context of a loss or a gain. Typically, people become considerably more distressed at the prospect of losses than they feel happy about equivalent gains (Thaler & Johnson, 1990). We tend to put more weight on the value of a loss, giving it two to three times the importance we give to the positive value of the same size of gain. The aversion to loss means that people are willing to take more risks to avoid losses than to make gains. Odean and Barber (1999) report that investors much preferred to sell off investments that were doing well—the winners in their portfolio. On the other hand, they were very reluctant to cut their losses and sell underperforming investments. This type of behaviour is called the "disposition effect" (Nicol-Maveyraud, 2003). Even when faced with sure gain, most investors are risk-averse, but they become risk-takers when faced with sure loss. In an article in *The Economist* (1994) it was said that, traditionally, financial economists have treated

upside and downside risk as the same, but if we subscribe to prospect theory we are likely to conclude that investors are more concerned with the downside. It was then said the popularity of a crop of mutual funds launched in the mid-1990s, which offer investors protection against sharp falls in financial markets, suggests that people will pay handsomely to avoid a loss.

Regret theory is about people's emotional reaction to having made an error of judgement (Zeelenberg, Beattie, Van Der Plight, & DeVries, 1996); for example, the feelings investors harbour after buying a share that has dropped in value, or not buying a share they once gave serious consideration to that has subsequently increased in value. Investors may avoid selling shares that have decreased in value in order to avoid the regret of having made a bad investment and the embarrassment of reporting the loss. Also, investors may find it easier to follow the crowd and buy a popular share. If that share subsequently goes down in value, the purchase can be rationalised as behaviour shared with numerous others. By contrast, if investors go against the prevailing conventional wisdom, the after-effects could be painful because there is the possibility of feeling regret if decisions do not result in successful investment (Lebaron & Vaitilingam, 1999).

The following observations are in line with some of the above comments: people try to avoid regret; they do not want to appear foolish in admitting mistakes; they go into "denial" and "regret avoidance" and so hold on to "investment losers", and in the process delay having to face up to investment errors. Also, they may be afraid that as soon as they sell poorly performing stock, the price will bounce back up again. On the other hand, they sell shares that are rising in value, so that they are not putting themselves into a position where they suffer regret if the shares subsequently fall in value and they lose out. In fact, selling winners has an obvious feel-good factor even if investors go on to reinvest less profitably (Odean & Barber, 2000; Willman, 2000).

People tend to create rules governing decision making, but in reality such rules are often fallacious. This can be seen when people predict the occurrence of a particular kind of event simply because that event has not occurred recently (Hodgetts, 1991). For example, if a coin is tossed and comes up heads on three occasions, many people are likely to bet that tails will come up next time.

The same information can be presented or "framed" in different ways, so that for one group it has particular appeal in one form, as opposed to another form that appeals to another group. For example, a utility company wishes to encourage customers to settle their accounts on time, and there are at least two avenues open to the company. One is to frame information in the form of a discount if a direct debit to a bank account facility is used, and the other is to put the information in the form of a penalty for late payment. The way the information is presented or framed can have an effect on the decisions made (Tversky & Kahneman, 1981).

In fact the same information can be framed in different ways; in one form it appeals to one group and in a different form it appeals to another. In an article in *The Economist* (1994) on behavioural finance, an example of framing was given. If an investor owns two stocks now worth $20 each, one of which he bought at $10 and the other at $25, he might not sell the latter (even if the price was falling) because he did not want to suffer a loss. However, if he thought about the combined current value of the two shares, he might be happy to sell both as such action would produce a net gain. This helps to explain the popularity of mutual funds, where the investor sees only the combined effect of many deals, despite the fact that the average mutual fund fails to beat the relevant stock market index.

Barberis (2001) mentions framing, which is referred to as "narrow framing". This is an excessive focus on changes in wealth that are narrowly defined. Even when people are saving for their retirement and have a long-term horizon, they often pay too much attention to short-term gains and losses. Moreover, they become obsessive about price changes in a single stock they own, even if it represents only a fraction of their total wealth. According to Barberis (2001): "Narrow framing is dangerous, simply because it can lead people to overestimate the risk they are taking,

especially when they are in loss adverse mode: that is when they are more sensitive to losses than to gains. This is because the more narrowly an investor frames a situation, the more likely he or she is to see losses."

Another undesirable consequence of narrow framing is the "disposition effect", also referred to earlier in connection with prospect theory. This behaviour can be seen "when investors sell stocks: they typically sell stocks that have gone up in value relative to the purchase price, rather than stocks that have gone down. It is not hard to guess at the underlying cause of the disposition effect. If investors pay too much attention to the gains and losses of individual stocks that they own, it is probably difficult to take a loss in a specific stock."

Finally, while recognising its powerful impact, framing can be affected by people's attitudes and can be modified when people are given a more complete picture of the choice to be made. This was found to be the case in a study of health issues with respect to various choices (Rothman & Salovey, 1997).

Rationalisation

There is a view that decision makers not only invoke satisficing (discussed earlier in the chapter), but also that they frequently rationalise. Instead of being concerned with the identification of satisfactory alternatives, the decision maker, who may be in a hurry, rationalises choice by adopting the first feasible option even in circumstances where time was available for further exploration. As stated earlier, some argue that the implicit favourite model has rationalisation built into it, when decision makers rationalise their decision choice by finding some shortcomings with each of the other potential choices.

Escalation of commitment

This arises when there is a tendency to persist in an ineffective course of action, even when evidence suggests that a problem exists and that a particular project is doomed to failure (Bobocei & Meyer, 1994; Hammond, Keeney, & Raiffa,

---

PANEL 8.8: Escalation of commitment by an investor

Imagine an investor who purchased shares in a company— TCM Property Co—for £1.50 per share. Due to a deteriorating overall economic situation and adverse market conditions for the company the share price falls to 50p. At around this time, the company experiences problems with repayment of debt and decides to raise additional equity capital by way of a rights issue of shares (an offer of more shares to existing shareholders, pro rata to their holdings).

The investor subscribes for the allocation of shares to which he or she is entitled at a price marginally below the prevailing market price. The share value falls still further, and the investor acquires additional shares in the expectation that one day the share price will recover when the company's fortunes change for the better. In this case there was no such change because the company went into liquidation.

This is an example of a situation in which people remain committed to a particular course of action despite negative vibrations that all is not well.

1998; Staw, 1981). An example of escalation of commitment with reference to personal investment appears in Panel 8.8.

Staw (1981) has offered explanations for the escalation of commitment. Some projects involve much upfront investment, with little return until the end. These projects require continuous commitment, and those who put up the capital, or provided the funds, must stay the course in order to receive any return on their investment. On other occasions, investors or project managers frequently become so egotistically involved with a project that their identities are immersed in it (Brockner et al., 1986). They support the project as potentially worthwhile despite evidence to the contrary, because failure signals a threat to their self-esteem. There are other occasions when organisational inertia or culture is responsible for allowing a less than satisfactory project to continue. Hantula and Bragger (1999) are of the view that lack of standards of performance and ambiguity surrounding the provision of feedback on performance should also be considered as factors responsible for escalation of commitment.

In the final analysis it is important for the organisation to recognise when it is necessary to stop a project before it results in throwing good money after bad. Obtaining good information based on project reviews is a necessary course of action to prevent the problem of escalation of commitment. Staw and Ross (1988) put forward a solution to the problem by suggesting that one should create an "experimenting organisation" in which every project is reviewed regularly and managers are evaluated on the basis of their contribution to the total organisation rather than to specific projects.

Other strategies to reduce the escalation of commitment have been suggested following a study of a simulated investment decision in a laboratory setting. Simonson and Staw (1992) found that escalation of commitment was reduced if certain conditions were met. Participants were less likely to continue involvement in further investment in an unprofitable project if they were told that their performance was not directly related to their managerial qualities, and that the evaluation of their decision performance would only relate to matters within their control. They were also less likely to invest further when targets were not met, and when minimum targets for a return on a project were suggested as necessary before the project could be considered successful. In another experiment there was less escalation of commitment when the performance of participants was monitored (Kirby & Davis, 1998).

Finally, Baron (2002), citing evidence, puts forward two other reasons why people are less likely to escalate their commitment to a failed course of action. People are likely to refrain from commitment when resources to do so are limited and evidence of failure is really obvious. First, an individual or group can decide in advance that if losses reach a certain level or limit, no further resources will be committed to the project (a private investor could arrange with his or her stockbroker that if losses on dealings in a particular stock reaches a particular level, the stock should be sold). Secondly, escalation is unlikely to occur when people can diffuse their responsibility for making a bad decision (the less we feel responsible for making a bad decision, the less we may be motivated to justify our mistake by committing extra effort, time or money).

Culture and ethics

Increasingly, attention is given to issues related to the impact of culture and ethics on decision making.

Adler (2002) refers to five steps in the decision-making process that ought to be considered in the context of culture, as follows:

(1) *Problem recognition.* Some cultures (e.g., US) emphasise an urgency in solving problems, while others (e.g., Malay, Thai) are inclined to accept situations as they are.

(2) *Information search.* Cultures vary in their data-gathering styles (perceptual styles); e.g., societies that are more fact-oriented would behave differently from societies that are more intuitively inclined.

(3) *Construction of alternatives.* Cultures that are more future-oriented would tend to generate more alternatives than more past-oriented cultures.

(4) *Choice.* The organisational level at which decisions are taken, the speed at which decisions are made, and the degree of risk aversion can be influenced by national cultures.

(5) *Implementation.* The speed with which decisions are implemented, whether or not implementation is done imaginatively, and by whom (e.g., centrally imposed, group-based) can be culturally determined.

Normally we consider certain universal principles when the focus is on ethics. These principles would include honesty, integrity, fairness, justice, respect for people and property, right to privacy, and concern for people's safety. If a particular decision violates one of these principles, it could be considered unethical, even if nobody gets hurt.

Examples of actions in organisations likely to raise ethical issues are untrue information about a product or service, bribes, stealing property belonging to the company, job discrimination, and sexual harassment. But when trying to establish whether behaviour is ethical or unethical, the influence of culture cannot be ignored. For example, bribery is acceptable in certain countries.

When making judgements about what is right or wrong, we would normally review the alleged unethical actions or decisions, as well as focus on their consequences (Trevino & Nelson, 1995).

Many people rely on their own standards of right and wrong to guide their behaviour, and a number would question organisational practices believed to be wrong, but generally it is likely to be beneficial if the organisational environment is supportive of ethical behaviour. One would expect to find an environment supportive of high standards of ethics in decision making where the organisation provides written codes of ethics, where senior managers subscribe to high standards of morality, where recognition and reward are bestowed on those who display high moral standards, where the organisation is not exploiting its staff, and where visible sanctions are applied to those who act unethically (Snell, 1996). Admonishing people about ethics is not enough. According to Vecchio (2003), there should be training aimed at developing ethics. He states that ethical training is intended to aid decision making by clarifying rules and norms, by reducing confusion concerning issues of responsibility, and by providing decision-making frameworks for analysing ethical options. Ethics is raised as an issue elsewhere in the book (e.g., Chapters 1 and 9).

Decision-support systems

A **decision-support system** is a system that provides information to supplement rather than replace managerial decision making. It generally consists of a database that accommodates internally generated data (e.g., costs), but can also include external data (e.g., economic forecasts). The data can be analysed or rearranged using, for example, computer models of varying degrees of sophistication. There are those used in financial analysis where data on cash flow, financial forecasting, and balance sheet projections are available. By contrast, databases in a marketing information system might include sales figures, pricing data, and the costs of marketing a product. These data could be merged with an external marketing database to provide a forecast of sales, as well as effects of different marketing decisions.

The examples given here are related to systems providing decision-oriented data with the aid of a basic computer model. A more sophisticated model would be a system that proposes a decision or a specific recommendation for action. In this situation, the decision-support system has the capacity to provide solutions based on the appropriate software and data input.

Are certain types of decisions more amenable to decision-support systems than others? It appears that decisions on the borderline between structured and unstructured decisions are compatible with the computer models of the decision-support systems. Well-structured decisions can be accommodated by conventional management information systems. But when top management face novel and unpredictable conditions, which require the taking of unstructured decisions, programmed packages may be too restrictive to deal with these circumstances (Oborne, 1994). In decision situations that are highly unstructured, the decision maker will rely heavily on experience, judgement, and even intuition.

With regard to creativity (discussed in the next section), computer-aided creative problem solving could be of great assistance to both individuals and groups. Proctor (1991) provides a useful summary of the different kinds of computerised managerial creativity aids.

INDIVIDUAL AND ORGANISATIONAL INFLUENCES

Individual and organisational factors influence the way in which information is acquired, processed, and used in the making of decisions. The influence exerted by the group on decision making is reserved for discussion in Chapter 10, and some individual considerations in connection with cognitive complexity were discussed earlier in the section of this chapter on the cognitive approach to information-processing. In this section the following influences will be discussed: (a) personality and cognitive style; and (b) creativity and innovation.

Personality and cognitive style

With respect to specific personality factors related to information-processing, it has been suggested that dogmatic and authoritarian personality types display a marked lack of tolerance for ambiguity and uncertainty and consequently are less likely to search for information. They are less capable of dealing with inconsistent information and are unlikely to be flexible in the positions they adopt (Dermer, 1973). (A discussion of personality types appears in Chapter 2.)

Decision makers with machiavellian tendencies could view information as a tool for achieving their personal objectives, possibly resulting in the withholding of information so as to maintain control or to win favours from influential people. The withholding, ignoring, and distorting of information for whatever reason can be detrimental to decision making that rests on the combined or cooperative efforts of a number of employees. Social motives play an important part in interactive episodes or contacts between employees, and as a consequence can affect the quality of decisions where an exchange of information is critical in the decision process.

Decision styles

Whatever decision model is applicable, managers are said to adopt a particular style of decision making as they collect and evaluate information. In Chapter 2, Jung's typology of personality was introduced (Jung, 1923), and this consists of four functions. The orientation associated with each function is as follows:

- *Sensation.* This type likes to solve problems in standard ways.
- *Intuition.* This type likes to solve new problems, relying on hunches, spontaneity, and openness in redefining problems until they are solved.
- *Thinking.* This type tends to be unemotional, carefully considers all options, and uses intellectual processes in decision making.
- *Feeling.* This type tends to be sympathetic and relates well to others, and believes in harmonious and pleasant working relationships.

PANEL 8.9: Decision styles in organisations

---

(1) *Sensation–thinking (ST)*. People who are classified as ST attend to facts and handle them with impersonal analysis. They tend to be practical and matter of fact and develop their abilities in situations of technical clarity. Occupationally, ST is typified by a technician.

(2) *Sensation–feeling (SF)*. People classified as SF attend to facts but they handle them with a warm personal touch. They tend to be sympathetic and friendly, and their abilities can be usefully applied helping people. Occupationally, SF is typified by a teacher.

(3) *Intuition–thinking (IT)*. People who are classified as IT are logical and ingenious, like to explore a number of possibilities, and approach the exercise with impersonal analysis. Their abilities find expression in developments from a theoretical and technical perspective. Occupationally, IT is typified by a planner.

(4) *Intuition–feeling (IF)*. People classified as IF rely on intuitive and nonrational feelings in arriving at a judgement. They tend to explore possibilities with the human touch, are enthusiastic and insightful, and their abilities find easier expression in understanding and communicating. They tend to be sympathetic and friendly, and their abilities can be usefully applied helping people. Occupationally, IF is typified by an artist.

(Taggart & Robey, 1981)

The first two functions—sensation and intuition—are compatible with the collection of information, whereas the last two—thinking and feeling—relate to the evaluation of information in a problem-solving context (Hodgetts, 1991).

The four functions can be expressed as four basic decision styles as follows:

(1) sensation–thinking (ST);
(2) sensation–feeling (SF);
(3) intuition–thinking (IT); and
(4) intuition–feeling (IF).

Taggart and Robey (1981) place these four decision styles in an organisational context (see Panel 8.9).

Mitroff and Kilmann (1976) administered the Myers–Briggs Type I indicator—a personality inventory drawing its substance from Jung's typology—to managers to determine their decision style. In addition, the researchers asked the managers to relate stories about their ideal organisation. They found a strong similarity between the stories of those managers who had the same decision style.

(1) STs depicted their organisation and its infrastructure in a factual way, emphasised the certainty and specific nature of things, and underlined impersonal organisational control.

(2) SFs also concentrated on facts and precision, but did so in a way that highlighted human relationships.

(3) ITs stressed broad global issues, and theorised about organisations in a rather idealistic but impersonal way.

(4) IFs underlined the global nature of things, laced with a concern for personal and humanistic values.

Henderson and Nutt (1980) used the Myers–Briggs Type I indicator to study management decisions. They studied risk-taking and the acceptance of hypothetical capital expenditure proposals. STs were the most reluctant to accept the proposals, perceiving the most risk in making decisions. SFs had a tolerance for greater risk and shared the acceptance of the same proposals. ITs and IFs fell between ST and SF with regard to the acceptance of the proposals.

However, Nutt (1990) would elevate IFs to a position of greater risk-taking when faced with hypothetical risky business ventures, and concluded that top managers' decisions were more influenced by their decision style than were middle managers' decisions. Obviously decision styles have real meaning to people, because Hunt, Krystofiak, Meindl, and Yousry (1989) found that people tend to select advisers with decision styles similar to their own when faced with evaluating hypothetical strategic business decisions.

There have been other attempts to classify decision styles. Arroba (1978) isolates six styles, among them the logical, emotional, and intuitive styles. Generally, the logical style was the style

most often used. Janis and Mann (1982) also identify styles, but their emphasis is on decision
quality, and they underline the way people cope
with the conflict inherent in the decision-making
process. Examples of coping strategies are "defensive avoidance" where the decision maker avoids
the decision by delaying making it or denying
responsibility for it; and "vigilance" where the decision maker conducts a careful search for relevant
information and weighs it up in an impartial way.
The latter is considered to be a good strategy.

Another attempt to arrive at the dominant
decision styles of managers was made by Rowe
and Boulgarides (1992). They came forward with
four styles—directive, analytic, conceptual, and
behavioural—described below. Superimposed on
the four styles is the person's "tolerance for
ambiguity", and it appears on the vertical axis of
the Rowe and Boulgarides' model in Figure 8.2.
Some individuals have a high need to structure
information in ways that minimise ambiguity,
while others have a capacity to handle information in a simultaneous fashion that is more
cognitively taxing. Rowe and Boulgarides' decision styles are as follows:

• Those who are logical and rational with a disinclination to use intuition, and have a low

tolerance for ambiguity; they seek rationality and are said to feel comfortable with a
"directive" style. They do not mind relying on
a minimum amount of information, having
considered only a few alternative courses of
action.

• By contrast, those using an "analytic" style
have a greater tolerance for ambiguity, and they
desire more information and consider more
alternatives than do the users of a directive
style. The analytical decision maker is likely
to be a careful and thoughtful person with good
powers to adapt to changing situations.

• The users of the "conceptual" style go a stage
beyond the individuals with the analytic style,
take a long-term expansive view, and consider
many alternatives; they are also adept at finding
creative solutions to a problem.

• Finally, those using the "behavioural" style
are able to relate well to others; they listen
carefully to other people's suggestions, like to
be accepted, try to avoid situations of conflict,
and are happy to see their subordinates and
colleagues succeeding in life.

Having considered the dominant styles here,
we may be able to allocate a manager to one
particular style, but equally we may find a manager with aspects of all styles in his or her way of
managing. Obviously it would be advantageous
to be knowledgeable or aware of one's decision-
making style in order to be in a better position to
identify one's strengths and weaknesses as a decision maker and plot a course of action that is best
in the circumstances. Also, one should be aware
of "influencers" likely to affect decision styles—
e.g., occupational demands, position in the hierarchy, and national cultures (Dollinger & Danis,
1998).

Left-brain and right-brain dominance

A preoccupation of some psychologists interested
in decision styles is the issue of left-brain and
right-brain hemispheres. Although the brain is
usually viewed as a single structure, in actual fact
it is divided into two halves, joined by the *corpus
callosum*, which is a bundle of connecting fibres.

FIGURE 8.2

Dominant decision styles (from Rowe & Boulgarides,
1992). Copyright © 1992 by the authors and reprinted
by permission.

For most people, the right side of the brain controls the left side of the body, and the left side of the brain controls the right side of the body. Although each hemisphere of the brain has the potential to undertake many functions, there tends to be specialisation.

Where the left brain is dominant, the person is predominantly involved with analytic, logical thinking, especially in verbal and mathematical functions. Where the right brain is dominant, the power to synthesise is evident, but language ability is limited. The right hemisphere is primarily responsible for orientation in space, artistic endeavour, crafts, body image, and recognition of faces. It processes information more diffusely than does the left hemisphere, and it has a capacity to integrate many inputs at the same time (Ornstein, 1977).

There is speculation about the functions of both sides of the brain in the management literature. For example, left-brain dominant people tend to respond best to verbal instructions, whereas right-brain dominant people respond best to visual instructions. According to Lynch (1986), the different orientations in the decision-making process can be summarised in the proposition that, when left-brain dominant people are compared with right-brain dominant people, they tend to be more conformist; prefer structured assignments to open-ended ones; discover things systematically as opposed to by exploration; recall verbal material better than spatial imagery; focus on specific facts, as opposed to main ideas; solve problems in a logical way as opposed to an intuitive way; and work best with ideas that flow in sequence, as opposed to those that show a relationship.

In connection with decision styles, Taggart and Robey (1981) claim a link between the left brain and the sensation–thinking (ST) type, and between the right brain and the intuition–feeling (IF) type. The other types were considered less important in this respect. In today's world, with its numerous complex and difficult problems, it would seem appropriate to admonish managers on the need for flexibility in their information-processing style. Ideally, it would appear to be beneficial for the organisation if the manager could move with ease from one decision style to another in the light of the demands of the situation. The same reasoning could apply to movement within the brain hemispheres where, for example, the logically minded manager could move in the direction of the more imaginative sphere. These are issues that can offer a challenge to management education and development.

According to Hodgetts (1990), this challenge has to some extent been taken up. He relates the experience of the Hawaiian Telephone Company, which introduced tests to identify left-brain dominant and right-brain dominant managers. They were then allocated to a group with thinking styles similar to their own. The left-brain dominant managers were asked to make decisions that required a creative approach, while the right-brain dominant managers were required to make decisions that required a logical and analytical approach. This form of training appeared to be successful.

Other examples of training in this field include encouraging left-brain dominant people to develop their right brain by participating in unstructured activities such as creative day-dreaming, observing colours, listening to sounds in their immediate environment, and cracking jokes in other people's company. Right-brain dominant people are encouraged to develop their left brain by solving mathematical problems and engaging in analytical thinking (Hodgetts, 1990).

Despite what has been said, one should be cautious in accepting the relationship between brain hemispheres and training, as there are some scholars who are extremely sceptical about its substance. A further word of caution is called for when looking at the association between cognitive styles and neurological functioning. Robertson (1985) rightly points out that it is far from clear that cognitive strategy and style can be related to brain functioning in any straightforward way, although some researchers argue strongly that there are links. Levy (1985) maintains that any mental activity is carried out by both sides of the brain simultaneously, and that the two hemispheres work together in harmony. Finally, there are many neuropsychologists who are sceptical about the substance of these findings.

Adaptors versus innovators

Kirton (1984) identified differences in the way people prefer to process information. These differences can be expressed as cognitive or thinking styles, are referred to as adaptors and innovators, and occupy opposite ends of a continuum. Similarities can be found between Kirton's approach and the approaches discussed earlier. The main distinguishing characteristics of the adaptor and innovator are as follows:

- With regard to problem definition, adaptors are more inclined to wait to be handed a problem, whereas innovators seek problems.
- With regard to solving problems, adaptors can be effective in modifying existing systems in conditions of relative stability, whereas innovators derive a challenge from seeking new and possibly unexpected solutions.
- With regard to the implementation of decisions, the adaptors utilise precise, accurate, methodical, and disciplined approaches, unlike the innovators who appear undisciplined with a low tolerance for routine work.
- With regard to personal image within the organisation, adaptors are seen as safe, dependable, and conformist, whereas innovators are seen as mavericks, with lots of self-confidence, and are constantly generating ideas that are not always practical.

It is possible, of course, for the two styles to complement each other but, given the fundamental differences, the potential for a clash of personalities always exists. Kirton attributes the failure to implement innovative ideas in organisations to a clash of styles. Hopefully a way forward can be found to resolve these difficulties by understanding the other person's orientation and accepting it. It is said that adaptors may find some sectors of the economy—for example, public sector organisations—more amenable to their outlook, but it has to be said that these organisations are now becoming increasingly exposed to market forces and the consequent pressures to innovate.

The adaptor and innovator styles could find expression in the culture of departments within organisations, giving rise to inter-group conflict that is referred to in Chapter 13. If, within the organisation, such a state of affairs is frustrating efforts to innovate and change, Kanter (1984) is likely to suggest the need for "integrative thinking" to ensure a team-oriented, cooperative environment in which change is facilitated and innovation flourishes.

Creativity and innovation

Creativity can be seen as the development of new ideas, while innovation, which West (2000) calls "innovation implementation", is the application of those new ideas in practice. Creativity is more a characteristic of individuals, while innovation implementation tends to be accomplished by groups, organisations, or societies.

A number of problems, especially in the area of nonprogrammed decision making, require creative solutions. It stands to reason that organisations that devise creative strategies for dealing with decision making are well placed to gain competitive advantage in a highly competitive business environment. In today's world, many companies are under pressure to improve old systems and products, and organisational growth and survival can be directly related to an ability to innovate (Proctor, 1991). Creativity has a part to play at each stage of the decision-making process. A critical perspective is beneficial in the way a problem is defined, in the generation of alternative solutions, and in the actual implementation of a solution.

Creativity has been defined by Richards (1990) as a universal human process resulting in an escape from assumptions and the discovery of new and meaningful perspectives, or as an escape from mental "stuckness". It seems that creative ideas arise purely by chance, but one has to recognise that generating ideas is not just a chance process: ideas appear to arise by chance only when people are actually looking for ideas. It is recognised that being immersed in one's own subject, and being detached in order to examine it critically, are important factors in gaining creative insights. It is probably safe to conclude that creative ideas do not float into the minds of people who are not curious, or inquiring, or who are not engaged in a hard search for opportunities, possibilities, answers, or inventions (Proctor, 1991).

Creative problem solving stems from creativity. Creative problem solvers allow the imagination to wander, tend to push back constraints that impose limitations on their thinking, make deliberate jumps in thinking, and welcome chance ideas whenever they come along. By contrast, the less creative person (or conformist) proceeds in an orderly way from point to point (DuBrin, 2002). Nowadays, creativity is considered to be a valuable resource for somebody who aspires to a leadership role in an organisation. This view is examined in the discussion of transformational leadership in Chapter 12.

Creative individuals

It is claimed that creative people possess different intellectual and personality characteristics from their less creative counterparts. However, there is one overall distinguishing characteristic, which is flexibility. Creative people are in general more flexible mentally than others, and this allows them to overcome the traditional ways of looking at problems (DuBrin, 2002). Reflect on the characteristics of creative workers that appear in Panel 8.10.

Certain initiatives can be taken to measure individual creativity. A basic approach for measuring the creative potential of employees is for the manager to give them a challenging assignment and then assess both the way they went about completing it and the final outcome. Another approach is the use of standard creativity tests or, alternatively, tests of creativity devised by companies for their own use. A problem may be finding creativity tests that are occupationally specific. Tests of creativity bear a similarity to the cognitive tests discussed in Chapter 3.

Stages in the creative process

One can identify at least five stages in the creative process (Randall, 1955):

(1) *Opportunity or problem recognition.* This is the stage when it crosses the mind of a person that either a problem or an opportunity is waiting to be tackled.

(2) *Immersion.* This is the stage where a person either recalls or obtains information relevant to the problem or opportunity identified in stage 1. The information is unlikely to be evaluated seriously at this stage. What is more likely is to hypothesise about the situation. For example, a manager might say, "I have a faint recollection that the problem or opportunity was tackled in a particular way by a professional acquaintance in another company a few years ago."

PANEL 8.10: Characteristics of creative workers

- *Knowledge.* It is necessary to have a broad background of information, including facts and observations.
- *Intellectual abilities.* These would include intelligence and abstract reasoning. Creative people are expected to be adept at generating alternative solutions to problems in a short period of time, and display a youthful curiosity, not only in their own specialist field but beyond it as well.
- *Personality.* Among the nonintellectual characteristics of creative people are reasonable self-confidence and the ability to handle criticism of their ideas. Although creativity can be fostered by interaction with others, creative people show a tolerance for working in isolation because it puts them into a receptive mood for ideas.

Creative people value their independence, tend to be nonconformist, and do not have strong needs for group approval. They tend to be thrill-seekers, because imaginative solutions to problems give them a thrill (a thrill-seeker has a higher than average need for stimulation, can become easily bored, and as a risk-taker is likely to pursue adventure). Creative people place value on persistence, because they recognise that finding creative solutions to problems involves a lot of concentration and hard work.

In summary, this profile of the creative person fits the popular stereotype of him or her as a maverick, both intellectually and socially.

(Godfrey, 1986; Gover, Ronning, & Reynolds, 1989)

(3) *Incubation*. This is the stage for reflection and consideration, often at an unconscious level. The person is literally sleeping on the problem or opportunity that is beneath the surface. Even when the person is engaged in recreational activity, ideas are maturing and being rearranged.

(4) *Insight*. This is the stage where, as a result of the previous stages, there is a desired outcome reflected as something new. This could be a novel but effective way of tackling the problem or taking advantage of the opportunity. Creative insight should be committed to writing immediately, as it could be easily forgotten.

(5) *Verification*. This is the last stage of the creative process. A person subjects the solution to test by using logic or actual experimentation. It may then have to be verified by the person's superior, or an outside agency, such as a referee or assessor, as when, for example, the insight or solution to a scientific problem is scrutinised prior to publication in an academic journal. Where the issue is connected with an innovative process within a company, resistance could mount at the point of implementation, when it may be branded as an impractical proposal. This could test the perseverance of the creative person.

This progression of stages in the creative process commands a certain appeal. However, creative insight may not evolve in the manner described. The process may be repetitive because the initial outcome of the whole process is considered unsatisfactory, and therefore it requires reconsideration and revision. Also, incubation might very well occur during the verification stage.

Enhancing creativity

Techniques are available to improve creative ability. One such technique is **brainstorming**. It is used to train individuals to be more creative and to tackle complex problems (Osborn, 1957). In a brainstorming session people in a group are encouraged to exchange ideas freely in an atmosphere characterised by little censorship or criticism. The important thing is to be tolerant of all suggested solutions to a problem, however unconventional or unworkable they appear to be. The latter are particularly encouraged because they may act as an impetus to subsequent ideas, which, in turn, could form the basis of a useful solution. Kodak put aside space, called the humour room, for employee relaxation and creative brainstorming (De Salvo, 1999).

With regard to brainstorming, one should point out there is evidence, at variance with Osborn's position, indicating that individuals acting on their own with instructions to produce as many ideas as possible, generated twice the number of ideas per person than did the groups (Lamm & Trommsdorff, 1973). What explanation can be offered for this result? Perhaps individuals in groups are inclined to think that other group members will do their work for them. Also, individuals in groups may be too self-conscious about how others perceive them and their contributions, and show a reluctance to air their views, despite having registered the brainstorming instructions that should have reassured them on this point. An alternative explanation, advanced by Diehl and Stroebe (1987) and known as *production blocking*, states that because only one individual at a time in a group can articulate his or her ideas, other individuals may forget or suppress their own ideas. However, computing technology could have an effect on production blocking. It is suggested that groups linked by computer are capable of creating more ideas than those acting face to face (Hollingshead & McGrath, 1995).

Despite what has been said above about the weakness of brainstorming in a group setting, more recent evidence indicates that being open to the ideas of others, particularly in conditions where group diversity exists, can have a beneficial effect on creativity (Paulus, 2000).

An alternative format of brainstorming is *brain writing* or private brainstorming. This entails individuals arriving at creative ideas by jotting them down. An important requirement of private brainstorming is that a regular time is set aside for generating ideas.

PANEL 8.11: Becoming more creative

- Do not be intimidated by the fact that a large proportion of attempts at being creative are likely to fail.
- Work on your sense of humour; it can promote a lessening of tension and a relaxed disposition, which, in turn, assists creativity. Also, insights can be cultivated by approaching a problem with a sense of humour.
- Get absorbed in and enjoy the work activities in which you are engaged.
- Build up a tolerance for the possibility of failure, and adopt a risk-taking attitude. It is the fear of failure that suppresses creativity.
- Develop self-confidence and courage and persist in your determination to solve your problems.
- Engage in creative hobbies that demand physical and mental effort, on the understanding that creative growth is possible only through constant and active use of mind and body.
- Build up your knowledge base in your specialist area, maintain it in order to foster creative links between one piece of information and another, and search for links between knowledge and practice based on novel outcomes.
- Read widely in fields not directly related to your specialist area, and be aware of links between what you already know and the new information.
- Be alert in your observations, looking out for similarities, differences, and unique features of ideas and things.
- Be open and alert to others ideas, realising that new ideas seldom arrive in finished form. Seize tentative, half-formed ideas and hunches.
- Keep track of your own ideas at all times, and record flashes of insight in a notebook for future reference.
- Identify a specific time of day when you are most likely to be creative, and schedule work sessions accordingly.
- Pose new questions every day, because a questioning and active mind is likely to be creatively active.

(DuBrin, 2002; Randsepp, 1978; Shalley, 1991)

Another technique is De Bono's (1970) imaginative system of *lateral thinking*. This can be contrasted with vertical thinking, which is designed to help people escape from habitual mind patterns. With vertical thinking each step in the cognitive process follows the previous step in an unbroken sequence; it could be considered rational because only relevant information is considered at each step. For example, within an organisation there are many habitual ways of processing and analysing information based on vertical thinking.

But lateral thinking poses a deliberative and provocative challenge to one's preconceptions. It emphasises thinking in sideways mode and invites restructuring conventional ways of looking at a problem. For example, a problem could be looked at from the angle of the solution, and then going backwards to the beginning of the process and looking at it afresh. It is not necessary to be correct at each step in tackling a problem; in fact, one could go down the wrong alleyway, but there could be a weird logic in such a deviation because from this vantage point a better pathway may be visible. One could also use what was once considered irrelevant information as a means to arrive at a new way of examining a problem.

A creativity technique suitable for individual use is *mind mapping*, which is a form of visual thinking (Goman, 1989). Visual aids in various forms are used to enhance creativity. The technique starts with identifying and writing a central theme in the middle of a blank sheet of paper. This is then circled and lines like spokes are drawn whenever new ideas come to mind. The description of the idea will appear on the spoke. If a particular idea spawns another idea, a branch line is drawn with a description of the new idea.

Important principles that people intent on increasing their creativity should bear in mind are set out in Panel 8.11. The principles do not offer a prescription for tackling specific problems, but they can be a useful aid to personal development. To put these principles into action requires self-discipline and a fair amount of control over one's emotions and intellect in order to develop a new set of behaviour patterns and eliminate old ones. From what has been said one may conclude that the path to creativity for the individual seems to be rather an arduous one.

In recent years organisations have adopted a variety of approaches to stimulate creativity and innovation and some of these are highlighted below

(Donkin, 1994c, 1995b; Houlder, 1996; Kehoe, 2001; Sadler, 1993; West, 2000). Important characteristics behind innovations in organisations are said to be persistence and contributions from a number of quarters; sponsorship of creativity where managers are prepared to nurture and protect innovative individuals or teams; and the management of creativity by suitably qualified managers. Siemens, the German telecommunication products company, encourages every member of staff to be more innovative, and to this end has mounted motivation workshops, an innovator's competition, and special training for its staff.

Hasbro, a toy manufacturing company that has among its products Action Man and Sindy, with a third of its sales revenue from new products, makes every effort to ensure that its product designers are in touch with children. It set up a fun laboratory—a crèche with two-way mirrors that accommodates 25 children each day—next to the research and development department.

Merc, the US pharmaceutical company, developed practices to stimulate talent. Among its motivational programmes for scientists is an award scheme to bring them recognition among their peers, and stock options, spread over stages of research and development; the options can only be exercised when the product has been successfully launched on the market.

The 3M company has devised a number of ways of encouraging innovation. For example, it has a rule that technologists are free to devote 15% of their time to any research project that captures their imagination. In addition, they get money to buy equipment or hire extra staff. For an idea to be accepted at 3M it must win the backing of one member of the board. Then an interdisciplinary venture team of researchers, engineers, marketers, and accountants is set up to push the idea further. Otherwise it goes back to the drawing board; but employees are not penalised for failure. The 3M experience is an example of a practical scheme to stimulate, support, and ensure the implementation of innovation. This approach to innovation has resulted in the creation of important products for the company, such as the Post-it Note pad.

Cannon, Du Pont, Philips, and Sony are examples of companies where breakthroughs flourish because they prepare for them. These companies require top management to have a strong vision about where and how to innovate, a strong technological culture, and a clear idea of the needs of the customer. Though one recognises the importance of planning in innovation, there are many times when unplanned spontaneous activity at the lower organisational levels results in innovative developments.

However, innovation cannot be left to chance and it is important to create a tradition of innovation and entrepreneurship. A key to success in innovation management is the dilution of the cultural divide between different functions within the organisation, whereby the production staff do not relate well to the marketing staff, and the latter do not relate well to the R&D staff. One way to cope with this problem is to rotate staff through different functions and use cross-functional teams, as is done in Japanese industry. The ultimate goal is to establish a link between creativity and corporate success, because there are many examples of companies that failed to reap the benefits from innovative ideas—e.g., Apple Computers, which at one time was said to have a technological lead on its rivals, and EMI's ill-fated invention of body scanner technology.

Hewlett-Packard in Silicon Valley provides an example of a company that has not only engaged in technological innovation to match some of the achievements of the companies described above, but has also gone in for developing new approaches to organisational and management systems as a way to foster technological innovation. For example, they avoided hierarchical management structures that might prevent the sharing of innovative ideas, established the principle known as "management by wandering around", introduced the idea of business networking—which contributed to generating clusters of technology companies in Silicon Valley—and adopted progressive employee relations and comfortable working conditions in a business whose growth depended upon the inventiveness of knowledge workers.

A central plank of the 3M company's innovation philosophy is a life-long career. Many companies, including 3M, have suffered from redundancies following rationalisation and cost cutting in recent years. Valid questions to ask are: "How can we be more innovative while paying close attention to costs?" and "How can we encourage people to be innovative at a time when they are overworked, stressed, and experiencing job insecurity?"

West (2000, 2002) specifies conditions appropriate to "innovation implementation" with a team flavour as follows:

- An external threat or challenge is necessary for innovation (e.g., losing market share may be a spur to action).
- Innovation is more likely to occur in work settings where there is a commitment to processes supportive of it. Supportive and challenging organisational environments are likely to sustain high levels of creativity, especially those that encourage risk-taking and idea generation. For example, in a US company that makes cables there was a high commitment to creativity, innovation, and teamwork. In this climate a part-time shop floor worker recommended to the company an inexpensive solution to the problem of wet cables jamming in the high-tech equipment as they moved through the process. This worker suggested positioning upward sweeping brush heads wherever the jam occurred to enable a smooth flow. This was a simple and completely effective solution that saved the company time and money.
- Organisations need to encourage teams by focusing not just on productivity, but also on creativity and innovation as important performance outcomes.
- Imposing stiff challenges for well-integrated diverse groups (in terms of knowledge, skills, and abilities) can be productive.
- People can also be productive where tasks are sufficiently interesting and motivating and people feel safe (where little bickering and undermining of one's position exists and there is not too much competition).
- Reflexivity is something one should consider in the context of innovation; that is, the extent to which team members reflect upon the team's objectives, strategies, and processes, and adapt them as necessary.
- Having a good idea is not good enough. Richard Branson does not succeed by simply being a maverick. He is also able to charm, persuade, and inspire people.
- Conflict has to be given serious consideration. It is a natural outcome of attempts to innovate because it represents a challenge to the status quo, as we find with resistance to change. However, the reverse situation could apply. This arises when innovation is often caused by conflict (e.g., it is the diversity of views that generates friction that leads to the search for better ways of doing things). Managing conflict is an important organisational process discussed in Chapter 13.
- The implementation of ideas for improving workplaces, processes, products, or services can be inhibited where organisational climates are characterised by distrust, lack of communication, personal antipathies, limited individual autonomy, and unclear goals.
- Minority influence in groups, which can be expressed in groups as a consistent and persistent challenge to the majority view, can result in desired change in certain circumstances. Therefore, we should learn to tolerate and encourage dissenting views in organisations in order to develop "seedbeds" for creativity and innovation.

Open versus closed innovation

In a world of "open innovation", businesses use ideas from outside the company. You do not have to generate research in-house to benefit from it. In this type of setting you should buy others' intellectual property whenever it can help to benefit your own business. At the same time you should derive benefit from other companies' use of your company's intellectual property.

Adopting innovation from outside the company can be of great practical significance. For example, a chemical company wanted to find a smaller-scale way of manufacturing a particular compound. Around this time the manufacturing process required nine steps that resulted in poor yields and high costs. By joining forces with an innovation intermediary, the chemical company found an investor (a recently retired chemical engineer in another part of the world) who proposed a two-step process to make the compound. The process worked and it saved the company millions of dollars. The inventor was paid $20,000 for this invaluable solution.

Another, more low-tech example was Proctor and Gamble's response to sluggish revenue growth in 2000; it decided to change its approach to innovation in the consumer goods packaged industry. Its company-wide initiative, called "connect and develop" encouraged business units within the company to reach out to external parties for innovative ideas. The job of Director of External Innovation was created to manage a team of technology scouts. The latter were in search of interesting and promising technologies that were not being developed inside the company. Proctor and Gamble planned to source 50% of its innovation from outside the company, but in 2002 this stood at a mere 10%. The company recognised that within its boundaries there were more than 8600 scientists, but outside there were 1.5 million. Therefore, why try to invent everything internally? The company also planned to sell its own unused ideas to others (Chesbrough, 2003).

Linder, Jarvenpaa, and Davenport (2003) highlight that the Sainsbury supermarket chain is good at using external sources of innovation. The company is interested in identifying ideas that create new market categories, and derives benefit from this information in the sense that it is inspired to sift through external innovation suppliers, and its priority is to apply those ideas in its stores.

The account above of open innovation can be contrasted with "closed innovation", which means that successful innovation requires control from start to finish within the company. Much of the comment on innovation in the main part of the text refers to closed innovation. For example, companies must generate their own ideas, develop them, and translate them into workable forms, because they cannot be sure of the availability, quality or reliability of others' ideas. One would expect organisations in the field of nuclear reactors

and aircraft engines to fall into the category of closed innovation (Chesbrough, 2003).

Intrapreneur

During the last decade, the roles of the **entrepreneur** and the **intrapreneur** have been associated in the literature with creativity. The entrepreneur, who creates and manages a business in an innovative way, must have the creative talent to identify a new product or service. By contrast, an intrapreneur is a company employee who works independently inside the company to develop a new product or service, and adopts an entrepreneurial perspective with the objectives of the organisation firmly in mind (Atkinson, 1986). The intrapreneur, who is a risk-taker (perhaps not to the same extent as the entrepreneur) and operates within a small organisational unit, has the advantage of the company's backing, and the company benefits from his or her creativity. At the same time the company exempts the intrapreneur from many of the restrictions and controls associated with large organisations, and he or she is given special privileges. If the endeavours of the intrapreneur are successful, he or she commands more resources (De Chambeau & Mackenzie, 1986). There has been a trend in recent years to identify employees with intrapreneurial potential, particularly in high-tech companies. The intrapreneur is often referred to as the corporate entrepreneur. Panel 8.12 contains additional information on the intrapreneur, or corporate entrepreneur.

Jennings, Cox, and Cooper (1994) compared the characteristics of the entrepreneur and the intrapreneur. Both entrepreneurs and intrapreneurs exhibit a need to achieve and control, spurred on by early losses or dysfunctional aspects of their background. When compared with the intrapreneur, the entrepreneur is more likely to be a loner, resilient, and a risk-taker—a visionary who challenges the status quo and is innovative in problem solving. He or she will often exhibit an inability to let go, a preference for personalised relationships, an aversion to structure, and a reluctance to accept criticism. By contrast, intrapreneurs tend to be more accomplished in matters of efficiency, acting as team players, with

---

PANEL 8.12: Actions of the corporate entrepreneur

Jennings and Lumpkin (1989) define corporate entrepreneurship as attempts to develop an internal entrepreneurial spirit, philosophy, and structure that will produce a higher than average number of innovations. Corporate entrepreneurs try to tap the resources of creative departments and "venture teams" within the organisation. A venture team is often located out on a limb and is not subjected to the normal rules and regulations of the company. At Convergent Technologies in the USA they used the name "Strike Force" to describe a venture team that is going to develop a new computer. Strike Force, even though it's a small team, nevertheless will be a separate small company within the larger company and it will have the independence to make the best use of its members' ideas, free from the constraints of the normal bureaucracy. Kodak has had 14 venture teams (a company within a company) over a period of 16 years, exploring ideas such as computerised photo imaging, lithium batteries, and technology to project computer images on to a large screen (Daft, 1998).

Another thing corporate entrepreneurs try to do is to tap the creative energy of all employees within the organisation. In this context they try to promote the notion of "idea champions" (Daft, 2004). The latter are like dedicated change agents who are very keen to bring about change, such as innovations, and it is their intention to promote the quality of creative ideas. They will be good at meeting resistance to change head on. In order to encourage ideas champions, the company will offer freedom and slack time to creative people, such as a high-technology company offering one of its creative employees the space and freedom to develop new technologies. There are two types of idea champion—one is a technical or product champion, and the other is a management champion. The technical or product champion is dedicated and prepared to make sacrifices to get his or her ideas for technological innovation accepted and applied. The management champion (a supporter and sponsor of the technical or product champion) believes in the technological innovation put forward and considers it has potential, and has the standing and authority within the company to have it adopted and, importantly, have resources allocated to its exploration.

The two types of idea champions often work together, because collectively they have more strength. An example of the two types of idea champions in action is provided by Black and Decker, where a technical or product idea champion is a full-time product designer who tries to convince others of the merit of his ideas. He invented the Piranha circular saw blade, which is a great seller as a tool accessory, and then he invented the "bullet"—a bit for power drills used in the home. Apparently the bullet was the first major innovation in this product in almost 100 years. His boss acts as a management champion for his ideas (Daft, 1998).

---

an interest in power and wealth. Chell (1999) lends support to some of these observations.

However, there is a substantial view that there is no common set of personality traits predictive of entrepreneurial success. There are lots of different types of entrepreneur. John Mullins, Head of the Entrepreneurship Faculty at the London Business School, is quoted as saying that: "There is no model entrepreneurial character type. There has been an abundance of research over the last 20 years which has found there is little difference between successful entrepreneurs and successful managers." Though some capacity for risk-taking is needed, it has to be accepted that many lucrative businesses have been set up at minimum financial risk (Guthrie, 2003a). As Guthrie (2003b) also notes, "for every ebullient Richard Branson, there is a reflective innovator, such as Jeff Hawkins, founder of Palm Computing. The introverts may get less publicity but enterprise is a valid career choice for anyone with ideas and energy."

CHAPTER SUMMARY

- Information-processing and decision making are related concepts.
- An information-processing perspective, which amounts to a cognitive view of humanity, was discussed with suitable illustrations. Three approaches to the study of human information-processing were identified: the lens model; the cognitive approach; and the process tracing approach.
- Two types of decision models were referred to, but most of the discussion was devoted to an analysis of descriptive rather than prescriptive models. This reflects the interests of behavioural researchers who study applied decision making.
- The steps in a decision cycle were illustrated with respect to a description of a relatively simple decision. Three models of decision making were introduced—the econological model, the bounded rationality model, and the implicit favourite model. Heuristics and satisficing were examined as two important features of the bounded rationality model, and these could be complemented by intuition. There was an analysis of investor psychology or behavioural finance, in which the spotlight was on heuristics.
- Decision making was examined with respect to conditions of uncertainty. Two types of decision were defined as structured and unstructured. The unstructured decision lends itself to conditions of uncertainty, whereas stable or more predictable situations are compatible with a structured decision. The significance of culture and ethics in decision making was discussed.
- Negotiation and bargaining were discussed as examples of decision making under conditions of uncertainty. The impact of culture in negotiations in the international sphere was considered. Issues such as simplification, subjective rationality (e.g., prospect theory and regret theory), rationalisation, and escalation of commitment were also discussed in the context of decision making in conditions of uncertainty. Subjective rationality and escalation of commitment were applied in the context of investor psychology or behavioural finance.
- Decision-support systems were acknowledged as a process that supplements managerial decision making.
- There was an examination of some individual and organisational influences on decision making. The role of personality and cognitive style plus creativity and innovation received due attention.
- Personality and cognitive style were examined from the perspective of the authoritarian personality, machiavellian tendencies, decision styles, left-brain and right-brain processing, and adaptors/innovators.
- Creativity was discussed with respect to characteristics of the creative individual, steps in the creative process, and ways of enhancing it. The nature of open and closed organisational innovation was explored.
- The significance of creativity for the intrapreneur was acknowledged. Differences in the characteristics of entrepreneurs and intrapreneurs were reviewed.

QUESTIONS

(1) Define information-processing with examples drawn from business life.

(2) Describe three approaches to the study of human information-processing. Select one approach and show how it can be applied.

(3) Distinguish between a converger and a diverger in an organisational context.

(4) Identify the steps in the decision cycle. To what extent do decisions in real life follow this process?

(5) Comment on the conditions appropriate to (a) unstructured decisions, and (b) structured decisions.

(6) List the models of decision making reported by Behling and Schriesheim.

(7) Identify the part played by culture and ethics in decision making.

(8) Collective bargaining is a complex negotiation process. Discuss.

(9) Consider the impact of culture on negotiations conducted internationally.

(10) Examine the significance of subjective rationality and escalation of commitment in decision making under conditions of uncertainty, with reference to personal investment.

(11) Discuss the different types of heuristic techniques, using illustrations from investor psychology or behavioural finance.

(12) What do you understand by the notion of decision-support systems?

(13) Comment on the interaction between decision styles and neurological functioning in the way information is processed and decisions are made.

(14) Illustrate decision styles with reference to the model of your choice.

(15) Distinguish an adaptor from an innovator.

(16) Describe the characteristics of the creative person, and discuss ways in which organisations may cultivate creativity among employees.

(17) Describe the way in which innovation is reflected in organisations, and distinguish between open and closed innovation.

(18) List the characteristics of the intrapreneur.

(19) Explain the following terms: (a) intuition; (b) brain writing; and (c) mind mapping.

SPOTLIGHT ON RELEVANT READING

Bragg, A., & Bragg, M. (2005). *Developing new business ideas*. Harlow, UK: Pearson.

Garvin, D., & Roberto, M. (2001). What you don't know about making decisions. *Harvard Business Review*, September, 108–115.

Odean, T., & Barber, B. (2000). Trading is hazardous to your health. The common stock investment performance of individual investors. *Journal of Finance, 5*, 773–806.

Paulus, P.B. (2000). Groups, teams, and creativity: The creative potential of idea-generation groups. *Applied Psychology: An International Review, 49*, 237–262.

Sadler-Smith, E., & Shefy, E. (2004). The intuitive executive (understanding and applying "gut feel" in decision making). *Academy of Management Executive, 18*, 76–91.

West, M. (2000). Creativity and innovation at work. *The Psychologist, 13*, 460–463.

West, M. (2002). Sparkling fountains or stagnant ponds. An integrative model of creativity and innovation implementation in work groups. *Applied Psychology: An International Review, 51*, 355–387.

Learning Outcomes

After studying this chapter you should be able to:

- Recognise the difference between attitudes and values.

- Explain the work ethic and business ethics.

- Identify the important variables in attitude formation.

- List the major functions of attitudes.

- Outline the major concerns with respect to prejudice and discrimination in the workplace.

- Describe ways in which attitudes can be measured and changed.

- Examine the relationship between attitudes and behaviour.

- Distinguish between job satisfaction, organisational commitment, and organisational citizenship.

- Discuss the importance of genetic factors, emotion, and gender in job satisfaction.

Attitudes, Values, Job Satisfaction, and Commitment

9

After a definition of attitudes, a distinction is drawn between values and attitudes. In the context of values the work ethic and business ethics are explored. A brief commentary on attitude formation is followed by a section on the functions of attitudes. Next, the notion of prejudice and discrimination is introduced, and this leads to an analysis of attitude change, attitude measurement and the relationship between attitudes and behaviour. The final part of the chapter is devoted to job satisfaction, emotion, job dissatisfaction, organisational commitment, and organisational citizenship. The chapter has particular relevance in the context of job design (Chapter 4), changes within organisations (Chapters 15 and 16), and human resource practices (Chapters 17 and 18).

Contents

DEFINITION

Attitudes are enduring systems of positive or negative evaluations, emotional feelings, and action tendencies with respect to an individual's social world (Ajzen, 2001; Krech, Crutchfield, & Ballachey, 1962). Attitudes can also be defined as mental states developed through experience, which are always ready to exert an active influence on an individual's response to any conditions and circumstances that the attitudes are directed towards (Allport, 1935). Another definition of an attitude (proposed by Bohner and Wanke, 2002) is as follows: "A summary evaluation of an object of thought. An attitude object can be anything a person discriminates or holds in mind. Attitude objects can be concrete (e.g., pizza) or abstract (e.g., freedom of speech), may be inanimate things (e.g., sports cars), persons (e.g., Slobodan Milosevic, oneself) or groups (e.g., conservative politicians, foreigners)." An attitude to safety could predispose the individual to react in a certain way to hazardous conditions at work. An attitude, which can be positive or negative, acts as a filter. A person tends to select information that is consistent with his or her attitudes and to ignore information that is opposed to them. The expression of an opinion amounts to an interpretation of what has been observed after filtering it through the medium of attitudes.

Three components of an attitude can be identified (see Table 9.1). They are classified as belief (cognitive), feeling (affective), and action (conative), and each component can be either positive or negative (Pennington, Gillen, & Hill, 1999).

The feeling or affective component of an attitude is of prime importance and it can have a significant impact on the other two components. There are occasions when the cognitive, affective, and conative components of an individual's attitudes will be consistent with one another; this is called *intra-attitude consistency*. The person who visits a pub or bar frequently (action tendency), probably believes that the bartender gives a good service (cognitive), and feels that the service and atmosphere are good (affective). However, intra-attitude consistency may not always be achieved, as will be seen later.

The distinctiveness of the attitude components and the interrelationships between them have been subjected to analysis (Kothandapani, 1971). An example of an empirical study in this area is provided by Breckler (1984). Subjects were presented with a live snake, and the next step was to record their reactions by the use of verbal measures of the three attitude components. In addition, the heart rate was measured for the affective components, and there was a measure of coping behaviour (e.g., avoidance of the snake) in the case of the behavioural component.

A subsequent variation of this experiment was not to present a live snake, but to ask subjects to imagine a live snake in their midst. This could invite a different reaction. For example, when you imagine a live snake in your midst, which you believe to be harmless (cognitive component), it is likely that you would not be afraid of it (affective component), and that you would be prepared to handle it (behavioural component). However, a different reaction is likely to occur if you were actually confronted by a snake, however benign.

TABLE 9.1

Components of an attitude

Component	Positive	Negative
Belief (cognitive)	X is safety conscious	X is careless in the way he operates machinery
Feeling (affective)	X can be trusted	X cannot be trusted
Action (conative)	It is easy to relate to X	It is difficult to relate to X

VALUES

There is a difference between attitudes and **values** (but equally, as we shall see, there is an interconnection). Having an attitude implies the existence of an object towards which an attitude is directed. A value is an ideal to which the individual subscribes, it represents basic convictions that a specific mode of conduct is preferable (in a personal or social sense) to any other, and it is relatively stable and enduring (Rokeach & Ball-Rokeach, 1989). Values represent our ethical and moral codes of conduct and are highly influenced by peer group norms and culture. They contain a judgemental element of what is right or wrong, or desirable, and they offer a standard that will guide our conduct and act as a process to evaluate and judge our own behaviour and that of others. The motivational impact of a value is apparent when we strive to attain a particular ideal (Rokeach, 1973). More recently, Maio (2002) had this to say about values: "The significance of values is attributable to the strong social consensus supporting them. As a result, values become empowered by a strong sense of emotional conviction."

A question that is sometimes asked is: What part is played by our genetic inheritance in the determination of values? It is said that the influence of the socialisation process (the environmental factor) accounts for the majority of variation (60%) in work values, leaving 40% identified with genetic factors (Keller, Bouchard, Arvey, Segal, & Davis, 1992). Certain values—e.g., cooperation and achievement—could be developed and reinforced over time and form societal values.

Within a person's value system, there could be a hierarchy of values, with some more important than others. For example, we attach relative importance to concepts such as freedom, equality, honesty, and so on. Values can cloud objectivity and rationality, and when values clash with organisational reality, dissatisfaction can arise. Thus, a prospective employee may possess a value that reflects itself in pay being related to performance, but finds on entering the organisation that seniority is the crucial factor in the determination of pay. Understandably, the person concerned could experience dissatisfaction (discussed later in this chapter).

Values can be classified by type. A typology put forward by Allport, Vernon, and Lindzey (1960) was described in Chapter 2 as consisting of theoretical, aesthetic, social, political, religious, and economic values. Schwartz (1992) placed the values of people into 10 categories, as follows:

(1) benevolence (providing care for others);
(2) hedonism (seeking sensual and emotional fulfilment);
(3) stimulation (sense of excitement);
(4) achievement (success from making use of one's talents);
(5) universalism (attachment to the principles of equality and justice);
(6) power (status and respect from others);
(7) security (feeling safe; internal and external harmony);
(8) tradition (attachment to old ways of doing things);
(9) self-direction (reliance on independent ways of thinking and acting); and
(10) conformity (curtailing impulses and actions likely to violate norms or disadvantage others).

Attitudes and behaviour are the consequence of adhering to a particular value. For example, if an individual places a high value on equality for different races in society, one could expect him or her to have a positive attitude to ethnic minorities and behave accordingly. However, the relationship between attitudes and behaviour is not always predictable, due to the moderating effects of moods and values (George & Jones, 1997). For example, a person is dissatisfied with both their job and work colleagues (i.e., a negative attitude); as a result, one expects him or her not to be forthcoming in helping others (i.e., unhelpful behaviour). But in this case the person possesses a cooperative value and engages in cooperative behaviour, which is the opposite of the expectation.

An attitude can spring from a value. A person who places a high value on honesty may develop a negative attitude towards another person who consistently tells lies. In another context, a person who values justice may develop a positive attitude towards a public figure who is seen to be fostering this cause. But equally the reverse could apply where attitudes change values. For example, an attitude expressed as acute job dissatisfaction could change a person's belief about the importance of work in life generally.

Work ethic

Weber (1958) was of the view that Protestant work ideals and values influenced the growth of capitalism. A person with a firm attachment to the Protestant work ethic sees work as intrinsically good, from which is acquired a certain dignity. He or she is hard working, keen to accomplish things, rational, economical, thrifty, and can expect to receive adequate extrinsic rewards. (By contrast, a Marxist value signifies that work is beneficial because it offers the opportunity to get involved in economic activity while relating to others, but work has been created in a way that is detrimental to the interests of the working classes who need more control over their work.)

One might ask which socialisation processes in childhood are supportive of the Protestant work ethic? According to Porteous (1997), child-rearing practices such as the following could be influential: encouraging independence; encouraging the young to delay gratification of certain needs; encouraging rationality (i.e., most things can be explained, and avoid reliance on luck or psychic powers); and mastery training (i.e., finish assignments successfully, and be proud of a job well done).

When we are focusing on the work ethic, it is easy to turn our attention to the meaning of work. Such questions as the following are relevant. What value and priority are given to work in the light of the many demands on our time? What do we expect to achieve through the medium of work (e.g., psychological growth, material rewards, security)? What commitments do we expect from our employer in specified circumstances (e.g., to facilitate the development of our career), and what commitments can our employer expect from us, particularly those beyond the basic contract of employment (e.g., putting in extra effort when circumstances dictate it)?

Traditionally, the work ethic was strong in countries such as Japan and the USA. In Japan there could be a challenge to the solidity of the work ethic because of the threat to cherished values (e.g., security of tenure, seniority) as a consequence of the ravages of the economic downturn in the last decade. In the USA the central place of work in the life of people has been eroded slightly, except for those who are self-employed (England, 1991), but in countries such as the Irish Republic (the "Celtic tiger") it seems to be on the ascendancy from a low base.

Business ethics

Ethics—beliefs about what is right and wrong, and good and bad—has become a serious issue with some organisations. The principle of **business ethics** is that companies and their employees need a framework to deal with issues, both internal and external to the organisation, that have a moral dimension. Such a framework can have a motivational effect, influence corporate culture, and specify desired behaviour. There is growing interest in business ethics in Europe as a consequence of financial scandals (e.g., the mis-selling of pensions by the insurance industry in the UK; the raiding of the pension fund of the company once controlled by Robert Maxwell) and environmental accidents. Also, there are other examples from recent years, when "infectious greed" (a term used by Alan Greenspan, the US Federal Reserve Chairman) gripped sections of the business community, that are serious grounds for concern.

In court in the north of England in late 2003 were former directors of SSL, the medical group that makes condoms. They were, according to Firn and Tait (2003):

charged with boosting the sales figures by £22m over a 25-month period. The sales figures had been exaggerated by trade loading—selling retailers more products than they needed to make sales figures more attractive than was so in reality. An investigation by accountants/lawyers revealed that unfulfilled orders were at the centre of an elaborate attempt to overstate SSL's profits and sales through the use of fake invoices, which were then washed out of the accounts using inflated exceptional costs.

The main examples of unethical practice in recent years have occurred in the USA (*Time Magazine*, 2002):

Unlike Enron which fooled investors with esoteric and highly creative accounting tricks, WorldCom cooked its books with a scheme which a first year accounting or business student could devise. The company spent more than $3.8 billion on everyday expenses to run its business—just as you might pay your utility bills at home. But instead of reporting those expenses as costs of doing business, WorldCom treated them as money spent to buy assets, such as real estate or equipment. Over a period of 15 months, WorldCom shifted those expenses to its "capital expenditure" category, which allowed it to spread the cost over several years. That made WorldCom's profits (before taxes and other charges) appear $3.8 billion higher than they really were.

A necessary first step in tackling the type of behaviour described above is to acknowledge the importance of the ethical dimension in economic activity. One could say that the collapse of the Enron Corporation in late 2001 has made ethics, the credibility of financial information, and conflicts of interest between companies and their auditors topics of concern for all executives. For some time British companies have been adopting codes of ethics and corporate conduct, and these codes can refer to individual behaviour as well as corporate behaviour (see Panel 9.1), but more is demanded in the light of the prominence given to corporate governance.

Corporate governance

In the USA the Sarbanes-Oxley Act 2002 was passed in the wake of the Enron, World Com and other scandals. The passing of this Act was seen by many responsible business executives as a healthy reaction to the sins of the past. A number of listed companies now pay greater attention to internal control as a consequence of the corporate governance reforms and specific regulations to tackle the abuses of the past. For example, in 2004 the US corporation, General Electric, announced that it was spending $30 million (£16 million) on the internal control requirements resulting from the above Act (Michaels, 2004). Many companies could only afford to incur a fraction of these costs, made up of expenditure on audit, legal, and insurance items, not to mention the costs of senior executives' time.

Some people are now voicing concern about the direction of corporate governance, in particular the proliferation of campaigns against company directors and the burden of reform: Is the administrative cost justified in the light of the benefits? (Roberts, 2004). Corporate governance is also an issue of importance in the UK, but not to the extent it is in the USA.

Bribery

In the context of business ethics, bribing has received much attention. According to Mahoney (1997), a "business bribe might be defined as an inducement aimed at influencing an official to act improperly in the exercise of his or her duties, such as granting a contract unfairly, ignoring safety regulations, relaxing licensing or tax conditions, or otherwise giving preferential treatment for a consideration or material benefit." But one has to acknowledge that there are many bribes aimed at inducing officials to do what they should be doing, whether it be issuing the correct documents in time or discharging the normal duties of their office. This practice could be viewed as extortion rather than bribery, as has happened over the years in Italian society in the normal conduct of business, where the recipients of the inducements were national and local politicians. In Northern Ireland or in the former Soviet Union it might be called protection money. There are further reflections on the use of bribery in Panel 9.2.

There is a view in both Europe and the United States (where codes of ethics have been in existence for a long time) that many of the codes of practice are either ineffective in themselves or they are enforced inadequately (Lorenz & Lorenz, 1989). There appears to be a need for the HR

PANEL 9.1: Corporate halo

About a third of large UK companies, and four-fifths of their US counterparts, now have codes of ethics. Most set guiding principles for the organisation, as well as covering specific areas such as buying policies, safety, and environmental responsibilities. An increasing number of companies, such as British Petroleum, British Telecom, Scottish Power, and Grand Metropolitan are using social and ethical reports. In April 1993 the National Westminster Bank (now part of the Royal Bank of Scotland) produced a document setting out the proper behaviour for its employees in cases where conflicting demands arise, on good banking practice and customer complaints, and on accepting entertainment from outsiders.

There are a number of reasons why organisations produce codes of ethics. Adopting codes of ethics could be motivated by a need to avoid embarrassment in the future. British Airways produced a code of conduct after the bad publicity created by the dirty tricks campaign aimed at its competitor, Virgin Atlantic. Shell's traumas over the way the Ogoni people in Nigeria were treated during the course of oil extraction gave impetus to putting human rights on the agenda and forced the company into making ethical commitments. In other cases, the rationale for producing codes of ethics could be associated with altruistic or philosophical considerations in a world where the image projected by business is less than ideal.

And, of course, there are situations where self-interest has a powerful impact when it comes to embracing ethics. In such circumstances, ethics codes could be used in marketing the company. The cosmetics chain Body Shop received substantial free media publicity as a result of the company's identification with popular social issues, thereby needing to spend less on advertising. Among its strategies was a direct association with organisations such as Friends of the Earth and Greenpeace, and the prominent display of material supporting preferred social causes. Also, Body Shop developed specific programmes, such as trade-not-aid, to implement a policy of sourcing ingredients from the developing world. Companies such as Body Shop that practise "social cause marketing" have come under attack in parts of the media for not living up to their own proclaimed standards. Tesco, the successful supermarket chain in the UK, has concrete social goals expressed in 2004 as a commitment to community-based schemes, such as its computers-for-schools voucher scheme. Tesco has also developed regeneration partnership stores in areas of high unemployment.

In 1992 the Co-operative Bank produced a 12-point code including statements that the bank would no longer lend money to organisations operating in sectors that involved cruelty to animals, trading in arms, and environmental destruction. This code could be viewed, although not necessarily so, as a marketing ploy to attract new business. Between 1992 and 1998 the bank increased its market share by about 3% and it is suggested that placing ethics in such a prominent position produced economic benefits. It is claimed that the Co-operative Bank has an unusually loyal workforce, with over 60% of employees having more than 20 years service.

In 1999 the company secretary of ICI oversaw a review of the firm's code of conduct. Heads of ICI's business units are required by the company's Internal Audit Committee to confirm that they have communicated the ethical code to staff and that any breaches of the code are reported. Staff worried about breaches are encouraged to report to their line manager or the internal auditors. The company secretary believes that ethics can be integrated into ICI's corporate strategy by using high moral standards to attract quality recruits and to win customers, and he sees nothing wrong with using an ethics code for competitive purposes.

In order to help small and medium-sized companies in the UK, the Foreign Office drew up a guide in 1999 to help these companies to act responsibly abroad. The guide highlights best practice on the environment, employment issues (such as child labour), corruption, human rights, and preventing local conflicts over operations such as oil extraction.

The problems connected with the implementation of business ethics have been noted; in particular, the difficulty of sanctioning people who break the codes. Also, there are those who believe that the adoption of ethics codes could blunt the competitiveness of business.

(Donkin, 1998a; Dunfee, 1997; Jack & Dixon, 1993; Maitland, 1999a; Moules, 2004a; O'Reilly, 1998b)

---

function within organisations to be proactive in raising awareness of business ethics, and to encourage consistency between values and behaviour in the age of the green consumer and ethical investor (Pocock, 1989).

ATTITUDE FORMATION

In the formation of attitudes, personality and socialisation are two important variables (personality is discussed in Chapter 2 and socialisation in Chapters 2 and 7). Personality in terms of introversion or extraversion is said to create a disposition favourable or unfavourable to the acceptance of attitudes. Introverts are more susceptible to socialising influences and are more prone to accept the values of society than extraverts, who tend to be undersocialised (Eysenck, 1970). It is said that the authoritarian personality is likely to display attitudes such as deference to superiors, hostility towards inferiors, disinclination to be introspective, with an inclination to project unacceptable

---

In a report by Control Risks Group (1998), London, there are examples of spurious demands for payment from officials of companies. In 1997 the Chinese authorities found that each of MacDonald's 38 outlets in Beijing was subject to 31 miscellaneous fees for purposes as unlikely as river dredging, flower displays on public holidays, and the spiritual well-being of President Jiang Zemin. Only two of the fees charged had any clear legal basis. It is interesting to note that this investigation was initiated by the Chinese authorities because of the fear that corruption was inhibiting foreign investment (Montagnon, 1998).

Sometimes managers are under pressure to deliver results and they succumb to the temptation to pay bribes to secure business or competitive advantage. On occasions agents or middlemen are employed to disguise the offer of inducements. The Control Risks report found that 90% of US company directors believe that their competitors occasionally or regularly use middlemen to get round anti-corruption legislation in competing for contracts in developing countries. But hiding behind agents will not exempt a US company or its executives from prosecution under the Foreign Corrupt Practices Act, which bans US companies from paying bribes.

The US consultant who represented the Kazakhstan government in negotiations with Mobil Corporation (now Exxon-Mobil) for the exploration of an oil field said to be worth $1 billion received a success fee of $51 million. The consultant has been arrested and charged in what seems likely to be the biggest ever violation of the Foreign Corrupt Practices Act. In total the US government have accused him of accepting more than $78 million in fees and commissions from Mobil and other Western oil companies and then illegally transmitting them to senior Kazakh officials. The US prosecutors have filed charges against the executive of Mobil who negotiated the deal. Exxon-Mobil is also the subject of their investigation. If found guilty of violating the Act, the company could be fined tens of millions of dollars, and individual executives could be sentenced to up to five years in prison. Also, in theory the company could be barred from public contracts, and suffer withdrawal of export privileges and suspension of investment protection abroad (Catan & Chaffin, 2003).

Under new legislation in the UK and around the world, companies could pay stiff penalties if they do not carefully scrutinise what their executives are doing to win business abroad. Thirty-five nations have now adopted the Anti-Bribery Convention drawn up by the Organisation for Economic Cooperation and Development (OECD), under which they undertake to make foreign bribery illegal in their countries. The legal change that took effect in the UK in 2002 introduced some of the strictest anti-corruption laws in the world (Sherwood, 2004). It is a criminal offence for any UK citizen or company to bribe foreign officials even if the offence takes place entirely overseas. In late 2004 the UK Serious Fraud Office investigated suspected false accounting in relation to contracts for services between BAE Systems and two companies in connection with defence contracts with the Saudi government. Representatives of the employers' organisation (the CBI) feel that the strict UK legislation puts British companies at a competitive disadvantage. Industry lobbying has resulted in revisions to the bribery rules in December 2004, which are now subject to a judicial review. Corner House, an anti-corruption pressure group, is asking the High Court to set aside the revisions (Eaglesham, 2005).

In developing countries, such as Indonesia, there has been an increase in public disapproval of corruption. It is conceivable that, in the future, companies that manage to do business without offering bribes may be more competitive and more able to attract high-quality staff than those that do offer bribes.

The following rules of thumb for handling gifts and hospitality could be considered (Mahoney, 1997):

- Adhere to company policy, which might require outright refusal.
- Declare anything that is received, or accept it on condition that it is given to charity, in accordance with company policy, and be aware of the need to set a good example for junior colleagues.
- A code of practice may give prominence to the issue of conflict of interests.
- The company policy may stipulate that the value attached to presents that have been given or accepted should not exceed a nominal sum.
- Account should be taken of what is accepted practice or etiquette in a particular market, industry, or region. In certain cultures an exchange of small gifts is a normal and necessary practice when doing business. In other cultures, such as the UK, some expressions of public corporate hospitality have become accepted practice, and have the merit of transparency. However, there are certain misgivings these days about the increasing lavishness of corporate hospitality.

---

impulses on to others. It is also suggested that highly authoritarian individuals are those who have been exposed to harsh and threatening discipline in the home early in life, and they retain an attitude of latent hostility towards their parents (Adorno, Frenkel-Brunswick, Levinson, & Sanford, 1953). A more comprehensive discussion of personality types can be found in Chapter 2.

Membership of a group can be influential in determining the attitudes of individuals. This is illustrated in the Bennington College study of group processes reported in Chapter 10. Socialising influences at work also play a part in the formation of attitudes. It is widely acknowledged that, during training, professional people develop attitudes towards the practice of their chosen vocation that colour their vision and affect their approach to the reality of the work situation. This process of socialisation, by which members of a profession subscribe to the values and beliefs nurtured by the professional group, is termed *professionalisation*. It involves modification of attitudes during the training phase and conformity to group standards, and it embraces acceptance of specific obligations to colleagues, clients, and the public. Thus, entrants to the profession come into contact with various segments of it during training and, apart from acquiring necessary skills, they become acquainted with the typical responses, postures, thought processes, and expectations of the qualified professional.

Some commentators (e.g., Bohner and Wanke, 2002) have specifically raised the part played by genetics and suggest, "there is some evidence, mainly from twin studies, that attitudes may in part be genetically influenced . . . and that the interaction of environmental factors (socialisation) and genetic dispositions may explain part of the variance in attitudes."

FUNCTIONS OF ATTITUDES

Attitudes help individuals to adopt a stable view of the world in which they live. We can only cope with our environment if that environment is reasonably orderly and predictable, so that the individual, the group, or society may know where they stand and what to do (Kelman, 1969). Attitudes facilitate the organisation of diverse thoughts into a coherent pattern. This contributes to the reduction of uncertainty and allows individuals to operate without the discomfort of having to evaluate all stimuli impinging on their senses in order to make the correct response (Pratkanis & Turner, 1994). The mere fact that we impose some order on our social universe makes it easier for others to communicate and relate to us, particularly when they have some insight into our attitudes.

Likewise, an insight into the attitudes of others helps us to understand and interact with them. However, as we saw in Chapter 5 on perception, we still experience difficulties in perceiving and

evaluating people and events in everyday life. It is generally recognised that humans have a need to experience themselves as free agents, and are not just entities reacting to an ordered environment. In fact, there are a number of occasions when we exert influence on our environment.

The major functions of attitudes, which have not been experimentally tested to any great extent, have been identified by Katz (1960) as: instrumental or adjustive; ego defensive; expressive; and acquisition of knowledge. In the words of Pennington, Gillen, and Hill (1999), "the basic idea with this 'functional approach' is that the attitudes help the person to mediate between the demands of the self and the outside world (especially material, social, and informational aspects)".

Instrumental or adjustive function

Individuals strive to maximise rewards and minimise sanctions or penalties in their external environment. They develop favourable attitudes towards objects that satisfy their needs, and unfavourable attitudes towards objects that thwart their needs. In the latter case, a consumer may develop a particular attitude towards a product category and avoid items in that category. For example, a consumer chooses not to use a particular brand of electronic equipment because of a previous bad experience with a similar product from the same manufacturer. By contrast, a successful stay in a hotel may give rise to a favourable attitude that manifests itself in return visits to that or a similar hotel.

Ego defensive function

Individuals develop attitudes designed to protect themselves from exposure to undesirable basic truths or certain realities in their environment. Consumers may attempt to ward off threats to self-esteem by developing positive attitudes towards products, such as grooming aids or an impressive car, that may enhance their self-image. Others may develop favourable attitudes towards mechanisms of defence, such as mouthwashes or deodorants, in order to defend their ego. There are other occasions when the individual projects his or her weaknesses on to others as a means of self-protection and, in the process, develops unfavourable attitudes towards the target group; this could arise in the case of prejudice directed at minority groups.

Ego defensive attitudes may be aroused by internal and external threats, by frustrating experiences, by the build-up of pressures previously repressed, and by suggestions or directives from an authoritarian source. Ego defensive attitudes are difficult to change because of the misdirected nature of the impulses associated with them. For example, an employee encounters a frustrating experience at work, and feels aggressive as a consequence because of the hurt to his or her ego. However, the employee displaces this aggression by directing it at a completely different target such as a member of the family or a pet. Though ego defensive attitudes are difficult to change, it is possible to remove the threats to the attitudes through therapeutic means in a supportive environment, by giving individuals insight into the dysfunctional parts of their defence mechanism.

Expressive function

This attitudinal function contains three main aspects:

(1) It helps to express the individual's central values and self-identity (Pratkanis & Turner, 1994). Consumers express their values in the products they buy, the shops they patronise, and the life-style they exhibit.

(2) The expressive function also helps individuals to define their self-concept, and facilitates the adoption of subculture values considered important (Pratkanis & Turner, 1994). For example, teenagers may dress and behave in a certain way in order to foster their status in an in-group.

(3) The expressive function helps individuals to adopt and internalise the values of a group they have recently joined and, as a consequence, they are better able to relate to the group. An individual who has joined an ecology group may now express values manifest in the purchase and use of a bicycle and the recycling of bottles.

Knowledge function

Individuals need to maintain a stable, organised, and meaningful structure of their world in order to prevent chaos. Attitudes provide the standards or frames of reference by which the individual judges objects or events, and attitudes that provide consistency in our thinking are particularly relevant.

The efficiency of the knowledge function of attitudes is readily observable in consumer behaviour. Attitudes predispose purchasers to prefer a particular make of car, and they do not have to re-examine their values, habits, and lifestyle prior to the decision to buy. However, if existing attitudes are inadequate in resolving a particular issue, then the acquisition of new knowledge could bring about a changed attitude. Consumers are generally information-seekers; they have a need to know and this drives them to gain information that gives meaning to their social world. But sometimes individuals take the easy option and rely on stereotypes to simplify reality.

Of the four major functions of attitudes, the knowledge function is perhaps the weakest in theoretical significance (Reich & Adcock, 1976). However, Pratkanis and Turner (1994) consider the knowledge function important in their socio-cognitive perspective of attitudes. It is also wise to consider the demands of the job environment when looking at the functions of attitudes. Bohner and Wanke (2002) reflect on Katz's functions and make the point that "in contrast to Katz's approach most other conceptualizations, whether contemporary or classic, do not separate the functions of helping to understand and organize the environment and maximizing benefits and minimizing costs".

PREJUDICE

Prejudice is an attitude that predisposes a person to act in an unfavourable or favourable way to another person or group of people (Pennington, Gillen, & Hill, 1999). So it is possible to encounter a continuum of prejudice, ranging from extremely favourable to extremely unfavourable in terms of attitudes, but in practice the word "prejudice" is mainly used with a negative connotation.

The prejudiced person tends to hold a negative view of, for example, racial groups or certain practices. In rural India it was not uncommon to find prejudice against the introduction of new farm machinery or the general acceptance of contraception. The prejudiced person with, for example, a stereotyped view of people of a particular race or creed, may have that view dispelled on meeting somebody who does not fit the stereotype. But equally, the prejudiced person is capable of rationalising the situation in such a way as to conclude that the person he or she met is unique in some respects, and is unlike the stereotype. Therefore, the prejudiced view prevails. For example, an anti-Semite will not be swayed in his or her view of Jews by evidence of their charitable behaviour, nor will those who have a deep prejudice against black people be persuaded by coming in contact with intelligent and industrious people in this racial group. A successful encounter with an estate agent, whereby a person's house was sold in record time to a reliable purchaser, may not dispel that person's prejudice against estate agents—the experience may be viewed as atypical. The prejudiced person can easily slide into behaviour known as discrimination.

Despite legislation in the UK outlawing discrimination in employment, there is a general belief that prejudice based on sex and race leads to discrimination reflected in widespread inequalities at work. Cassell and Walsh (1993) considered the difficulties facing women at work and highlighted some of the barriers that prevent women achieving positions of power in organisations. They concluded that psychology as a discipline needs to understand ways in which gender determines work organisation—particularly the links between gender, power, and organisational culture. O'Brien (1998) takes a rather optimistic view when she reports on the progress US women have made in the corporate world of the previous two decades. Griffith (1998) does not share this view when she states, "while it is encouraging to look on the bright side every now and then, the kind of complacency O'Brien seems to be

recommending may do little to advance the position of women in the workplace". In a recent report by the UK Employers' Forum on Age it was stated that women's promotion prospects suffered from their 20s onwards, even before they have children. Some 37% of men in their 20s held management positions compared with 24% for women. The gap widens as women get older and they never catch up with their male counterparts (Taylor, 2005).

Other forms of discrimination are age discrimination (see Panel 9.3) and discrimination on grounds of disability. In a telephone survey conducted by NOP for the Leonard Cheshire Charity, it was found that disabled people still experience widespread prejudice and discrimination that often make them feel misunderstood and rejected. The charity launched a campaign on the theme of "enabling" disabled people (Brindle, 1998).

Influence of personality, beliefs, and culture

Factors such as personality, beliefs, home background, culture, and conformity can influence prejudice. Earlier, the authoritarian personality was considered important in the context of attitude formation. In a study conducted by Adorno et al. (1953), it was concluded that the most seriously prejudiced people displayed an authoritarian personality. These people put a high premium on status both inside and outside the home, and had a clear view of dominance and submission. They were basically insecure and tended to repress or deny their own personal conflicts; they were conventional in their approach to life with explicit values and rules to guide behaviour; they adhered to socially acceptable behaviour that promoted their interests, and tended to be aggressive towards groups not sharing their views.

A study of anti-Semitism among female university students concluded that those girls who harboured deep prejudice against Jews displayed repressed hatred, jealousy, and suspicion of parental figures (Frenkel-Brunswick & Sanford, 1945). In effect, they projected on to Jews feelings that would normally be directed towards parents and other authority figures in their life.

PANEL 9.3: Ageism in the workplace

Age discrimination is rife throughout the EU. This is evident from the practice of targeting employees over 50 for redundancy and retirement programmes, and advertising vacant positions specifying that applicants must be below a certain age (e.g., 35). Ageism unfairly curtails individual opportunity, and it is likely to become increasingly wasteful in an economic sense because older people who are still capable of making a contribution to society may instead become a burden.

A report produced by the pressure group Eurolink Age blames the restricted opportunities largely on discriminatory attitudes. It is said that too many employers believe that old people are not up to the job or do not possess the right skills, and there is a widespread belief that older people's jobs are more expendable than young people's. Although some people lose their ability and enthusiasm to work in their 50s, it is unfair to lump all older people in that category. If people are fit, productive, and want to work, age should be no barrier. However, where older people are forced out of work, it is often too simplistic to point at discriminatory attitudes. It could be that institutional arrangements give employers artificial incentives to take such attitudes. For example, due to the seniority system, the rewards (e.g., salaries) of older employees are greater than those of younger people, and barriers are created by pensions and retirement arrangements.

The British government's voluntary code of practice on ageism—*Age Diversity in Employment*—was published in 1999. It warns employers against a number of ageist practices, including using terms such as "newly qualified", or "recent graduate" in job advertisements; seeking medical references for older candidates but not for younger ones; barring older staff from promotion on grounds of age, or denying responsibility to younger staff for the same reason. The code also advises employers against making redundancies on the basis of age with either a "last in, first out" policy, which targets young people, or by letting older staff go because of the cost of pension contributions. The absence of sanctions in the code has been criticised as a shortcoming by age and employment organisations, but it is the government's intention to monitor practice through the use of surveys and if necessary consider the need for legislation. The UK government must introduce legislation by 2006 to comply with a European Union Directive outlawing age discrimination in the same way that bias attributable to race and gender is illegal at work. A major reason for delaying the legislation is the concern about how best to deal with workers who want to work beyond the usual retirement age.

The Employers' Forum on Age conducted a survey in 2004 and concluded that it was a myth that age discrimination affected only the 50-plus age group. According to the report, "ageism is even a bigger problem for people in their late teens. Some 25% of school leavers have faced age discrimination compared to 21% of those over 50". Employers are quick to accuse young people of being disloyal and prone to frequent job changes, but "young people are denied interesting and challenging jobs, which is why they move on frequently: it's nothing to do with lack of loyalty."

(Donkin, 1994b; O'Reilly, 1998a; Steiner, 1999; Taylor, 2005)

The authoritarian personality has remained of consistent interest to social psychologists over the past 50 years, and while there are serious flaws with the approach, it may be that the idea of such a personality type appeals to our everyday explanations of behaviour (Pennington, Gillen, & Hill, 1999). A prominent personality theorist, Eysenck (1954), came up with two dimensions of personality, not one, when examining prejudice and discriminatory behaviour in politics—one being tough-minded/tender-minded, and the other radical/conservative. Communists and fascists were found to be at different ends of the radical/conservative scale, but they are both very tough-minded. Liberals were portrayed as rather tender-minded, and neither radical nor conservative. In Eysenck's theory prejudiced attitudes and discriminatory behaviour are more likely to originate from tough-minded people.

It is sometimes said that having differences in beliefs (what we hold true about the world) on important issues is a more powerful determinant of prejudice or discrimination than differences in race or membership of an ethnic group (Rokeach, 1968). This amounts to saying that people who share the same beliefs (belief congruence) could be prejudiced towards those who hold different beliefs. One might challenge the proposition concerning the applicability of belief congruence, because not all people in a group share the same beliefs (Pennington, Gillen, & Hill, 1999). For example, political parties are well known for having different factions within their ranks representing quite different views.

Culture can determine the nature and level of prejudice. In Japan the culture is supportive of flexible working practices, whereas at one time Britain had a reputation for rigid demarcation lines between jobs and skills.

From the results of a survey of South African whites in the apartheid era, three main reasons were inferred to explain prejudice against black people (MacCrone, 1957). One reason was the manner in which the historical strife between black and white had been presented in schools, in textbooks, and at home. The whites were the "goodies" and the blacks were the "baddies", and invariably the blacks were presented as perpetrating atrocities on the whites. Another reason was associated with way of life. Blacks were poorer, had no political rights, and had the least attractive jobs. Finally, the way blacks were treated was considered important. Blacks had to carry identity cards and, if they were imprisoned, they were forced to work—a requirement not imposed on the whites.

Modern racism is likely to be present in our justice system (Pennington, Gillen, & Hill, 1999). In experiments where people acted as mock jurors in making judgements about a case, Gordon (1993) found that jurors set higher bail for a black man accused of committing a violent crime than a white man accused of exactly the same crime.

Influence of the group

Conformity to the dominant norm of a prejudiced group is a critical factor in prejudice. When the individual conforms to a prejudice held by the group, he or she can be seen as favouring the maintenance of this prejudice. Conformity can give legitimacy to extreme behaviour that is based on prejudice. At work this could lead to active discrimination and ill-treatment of minorities. The victims of prejudice are generally held in low esteem by the prejudiced person, and this is considered ample justification for prejudice and discrimination. Sometimes the social status of the prejudiced person is low or declining, and using a scapegoat to compensate for feelings of internal unease is one way of trying to cope with the frustration experienced.

Another concept applicable to the group—social identity theory and self-categorisation—has been considered by Pennington, Gillen, and Hill (1999) in the context of prejudice in an intergroup setting. Here, group membership by itself is seen as a sufficient condition for inter-group discrimination to occur, such as favouring the group to which one belongs and discriminating

against other groups. Social identity theory is discussed in connection with motivation (Chapter 4) and groups (Chapter 10).

Ways of reducing prejudice

A number of suggestions have been made about ways of reducing prejudice. As was mentioned earlier, contact with the victim of prejudice may help to change the attitude of the prejudiced person, but this does not always happen. There are circumstances where the prejudiced person, having worked with the victim of prejudice, concludes that, contrary to expectations, his or her colleague is not, for instance, lazy after all. However, the prejudice may remain firm when generalised to situations outside work (Secord & Beckman, 1974).

Discussion is said to reduce prejudice when the prejudice is of a lower order, but to intensify it when it is of a higher order (Mackay, 1973). When people with opposing prejudices work in an interdependent fashion to achieve a common objective (strive for the achievement of superordinate or common goals), this can have the effect of reducing prejudices on both sides. As described in Chapter 10 on groups, hostility between two groups can be reduced by creating situations that make it necessary for both groups to cooperate in removing obstacles. The notion of cooperative behaviour is endorsed by Gaertner, Rust, Dovidio, Backman, and Anastasio (1993), who advocate getting people to re-categorise themselves so as not to see great differences between different social groups. This could have the positive effect of breaking down the barriers between the in-group and out-groups, and lead to people considering themselves as part of a larger social grouping.

ATTITUDE CHANGE

Many factors are responsible for bringing about a change in attitudes. For instance, marketing executives can attempt to modify those attitudes that strongly influence the purchase of a particular type of product by trying to bring them into line with what the company plans to offer. Take an old British Rail advertisement with the simple message, "Let the train take the strain". It draws attention to the convenience and relaxation of a train journey compared with a similar journey by car.

There are many instances of marketing strategies designed to change attitudes towards a product by attracting attention to the characteristics of the product that have an edge over the competition. For example, a manufacturer may add a supplement to the existing characteristics of a product—a mouthwash ingredient may be added to a toothpaste. In other situations, the emphasis could be placed on an important product attribute. For example, a car manufacturer may attract the consumer's attention to a novel feature in a new model.

Sources of attitude change

Kelman (1958) proposed three sources of attitude change—compliance, identification, and internalisation.

- *Compliance.* Compliance arises when an attitude is adopted for ulterior motives, such as the desire to make a favourable impression on the individual's boss or client. To use an example from the safety field, a worker uses a particular type of personal protective equipment in a factory or building site because he or she wishes to please the supervisor. There could also be another reason, such as the existence of strict rules about wearing it and sanctions, including eventual dismissal, for not using it.
- *Identification.* Identification arises when the individual adopts an attitude in order to establish or maintain a satisfying relationship with others. A student wishing to establish a good working relationship with a lecturer may adopt an attitude reflected in listening attentively at lectures and contributing intelligently at seminars.
- *Internalisation.* Internalisation arises when the new attitude is embraced as part of a cluster of attitudes, because the individual feels comfortable subscribing to that attitude.

Factors contributing to attitude change

A number of specific factors giving rise to a change in attitudes can be identified. These are:

- group membership;
- exposure to the mass media;
- forced contact;
- rewards;
- communication; and
- persuasion.

Group membership

In a study conducted at Bennington College (Newcombe, 1943), there was evidence of a noticeable shift in attitudes as a result of group membership, though there were marked individual differences. It was concluded that the main factor influencing students' decisions to change or not to change their attitudes was their relationship to the family or college. Where students decided to be independent of their family, and affiliated with and derived prestige from the college group, they tended to adopt a radical position on the left of politics. But where they maintained strong family ties, coming from a home where conservative attitudes were more prevalent, there was a tendency to ignore the influence of the college. This was expressed as withdrawal or active resistance. Membership of a group at work, whereby the individual is influenced by some prevailing ideology or practice, can likewise contribute to a change in attitudes.

A "situational view" of attitudes, stressing the power of *social context*, could be considered under the heading of group membership. Social context can influence individuals' attitudes, and this is evident in Salancik and Pfeffer's (1978) social information-processing approach. Socially acceptable attitudes and behaviour could be prescribed through cues and guides in the social information-processing approach. The spotlight could focus on specific attributes of a particular setting (e.g., the office or factory) with an emphasis on the set of attitudes and behaviour of greatest importance (salience) to the individual.

For example, a new recruit joins the accounting department in an organisation, which could be considered a well-established group. In a short space of time, members of the group will communicate with the new recruit on different matters, such as what is expected of a group member in terms of expenditure of effort, what members think of the competency of the boss, the acceptability or otherwise of the salary system, and so on. It would not be unusual to find the new recruit's attitudes and behaviour being at least partly influenced by this experience. In effect, social information emanating from the group influences the new recruit's perception of reality.

Exposure to the mass media

The mass media (press, radio, and television) are often held responsible for a change in attitudes. For instance, campaigns are mounted periodically in the mass media with a strong safety connotation —such as highlighting the risks of driving with excess alcohol in the bloodstream. The aim is to influence attitudes to safety.

On examining the influence of the mass media on attitudes to certain issues, an unexpected conclusion emerged in one study (Katz & Lazarsfield, 1955). Messages presented via newspaper, radio, and television produced insignificant attitude changes initially. However, having repeated the measurements of these attitudes some weeks later, the researchers found significant changes. They put forward the following explanation for the delayed shifts in opinion. Most people, to begin with, are affected in a very small way by what they see and hear in the media, but are then likely to discuss these issues with others whom they know and whose opinions they value and trust. It is only then that attitude change will occur to any marked degree.

Campaigns with a strong safety message may have some influence on attitudes that are not yet formulated or are at odds with those implied by the campaign, but they are more likely to be effective in reinforcing existing attitudes that are consistent or consonant with the message (Glendon & McKenna, 1995).

Forced contact

Closely related to the influence exerted by the group in changing attitudes is the notion of forced contact. For example, placing a worker with negative safety attitudes in a vibrant safety group, whose terms of reference are to promote good safety practice in a company, could result in a change in safety attitudes. But the success of such a venture is likely to depend on the degree of involvement of the recalcitrant worker in the work of the group.

When black and white people were forced to live in integrated housing schemes—i.e., where families were allocated flats and houses irrespective of their race—the three aspects of attitudes (beliefs, feelings, and actions) towards black people by white people improved. A control group observed in segregated housing schemes did not produce a similar effect (Deutsch & Collins, 1951). A related finding was reported during the Second World War, when black troops were integrated into previously all-white US combat divisions. Where black and white soldiers experienced field service together, only 7% of the white soldiers in the mixed units said they disliked this form of integration. But in units that were all-white, 62% of the troops opposed the integration (Stouffer, Suchman, Devinney, Star, & Williams, 1949). It is clear that forced contact in these housing and military situations led to a decrease in racial prejudice.

Rewards

In certain cases, some form of reward may have to be forthcoming before a person changes an attitude. Take, for example, a prejudiced politician with strong views on immigration. Having had a number of refusals from selection committees in constituencies where he would have liked to stand, paradoxically he is eventually adopted by a constituency with a strong immigrant community. In nursing the constituency, his behaviour is at variance with his private beliefs. But if he receives social approval for the way he conducts himself politically, it is conceivable that he will adopt the attitude implicit in his political role. In this case, social approval is the reward that leads to attitude change.

As a means to encourage workers to use personal protective equipment, such as earplugs or earmuffs in noisy factory conditions, changes could be made to both the design and the material to improve the comfort of the wearer (Zohar, 1980). In effect, this is offering the prospect of reward to those prepared to adopt a more positive attitude to safety practice.

Communication

Various facets of the communication process were discussed in Chapter 6. Here a number of specific issues will be considered with respect to communication as a vehicle for changing attitudes.

One-sided or two-sided communication. In a two-sided communication the recipient of the message has a right of reply. The following findings emerged when propaganda was used to change the attitudes of soldiers (Hovland, Lumsdaine, & Sheffield, 1949). A soldier who had received a high school education was more influenced by a two-sided communication, whereas the soldier with a poorer education was more influenced by a one-sided communication. Arguments contained in one-sided communication are effective if the receiver's attitude is in sympathy with the attitude embedded in the message. But an argument contained in a two-sided communication would be more effective if the initial attitude of the receiver was at variance with the attitude embedded in the message. These findings may not be valid in the long term and in conditions where counter-propaganda exists. This principle is illustrated by the following examples.

A productive social encounter in an organisation might arise when *A*, a credible communicator with a deep-seated positive attitude to safety, tries to influence *B* who has a lukewarm attitude to safety. If *A* and *B* held diametrically opposed views on safety, the encounter could be quite different.

A manufacturer of electrical appliances provides information in a one-sided communication when a user's manual is included with the product, although there is scope for two-sided communication when the consumer asks questions of a sales assistant in the store where the appliance was bought. This offers an opportunity to clear up any confusion or difficulties with respect to the operation or use of the product.

In the context of consumer decision making, Chattopadhyay and Alba (1988) maintained that the advantage of one-sided arguments was that the individual receiving the message has more time to think about the issues raised, and this would be of particular importance if the person concerned had limited cognitive ability and was not very familiar with the central issues of the argument.

Reflecting on the question of the relative merits of the two sides of an argument, Tesser and Shaffer (1990) proposed that two-sided communication encourages people to concentrate on receiving the message, at the expense of thinking about its implications in detail, particularly when the issues under review are unfamiliar to the recipient of the message.

Primacy and recency effects. The order in which two opposing arguments are presented is likely to have a bearing on the effectiveness of the communication. Where the first argument put across has the greatest effect, this is referred to as the primacy effect. But where the second argument put across has the greatest effect, this is referred to as the recency effect.

Attachment to the notion of the primacy effect may be implied from the behaviour of a lawyer acting for the prosecution in a court of law. He or she presents the prosecution's case before the lawyer acting for the defence has a say. On the other hand, a politician may feel that the best moment to make a final address before an election is the day after his or her major rival does so; this politician obviously believes in the recency effect.

There is support for the superiority of the primacy effect in certain circumstances (Hovland, Harvey, & Sherif, 1957). A first communication is likely to be more effective if both sides of an argument are presented by the same person, and provided the listeners are unaware that conflicting views are to be presented. If at the end of the presentation the listeners make a public commitment, this is an important factor in endorsing the primacy effect.

Public commitment. This is a powerful strengthener of attitudes (see Panel 9.4). The effect of making a public commitment is to make the

---

PANEL 9.4: Public commitment and the voting age

A group of students were asked to write essays on their attitudes to reducing the legal voting age to 18 years. This came after a session in which they were exposed to an argument favourable to the idea. Half the group members—the public commitment group—were asked to sign their essays and were told that their work would be published in full in the school newspaper the following week. The other group members—the private commitment group—were not asked to sign their essays, and in addition were assured that their views would remain anonymous. Both groups were then presented with an argument that was strongly in favour of retaining the minimum voting age at 21 years, and they were invited to write a short paragraph stating their frank opinions on this matter. The results of this experiment suggest that only 25% of the public commitment group shifted or changed their attitudes, whereas 50% of the private commitment group (whose views remained anonymous) decided to change their attitudes.

(Hovland et al., 1957)

---

person relatively resistant to change in the face of counter-propaganda. But situations like the one illustrated in Panel 9.4 are rather complex because people differ in their interest in particular issues. Likewise, if the issues are difficult to grasp, the intelligence of the person is an important factor. Other factors to consider are the nature of the propaganda to which the individual is exposed, and the nature of the group making the public commitment.

Sequence of presentation.   Is the manner in which the message is put across critical in terms of changing attitudes? To answer this question, a group of researchers conducted two experiments based on the UK court system (Maslow, Yoselson, & London, 1971). A written legal case was presented to subjects and they were asked to reach a decision on whether they considered the accused guilty or innocent. However, before they reached a decision they were asked to study the defence argument put forward by the accused. The defence argument was submitted to two groups, and though the content was identical the presentation was different in each case.

In the first group, the experimenters put forward the arguments in a confident tone of voice—a statement would be prefaced with, "Obviously . . .", "I believe . . .", "I am sure . . .", etc. In the second group, the experimenters presented the arguments with more tentative expressions in the text, for example, "I don't know . . .", "I am not positive . . .", "I am unsure . . .", etc. It was found that when the case for the defence was put forward in a confident verbal manner to the first group, the number

of subjects agreeing with the submission for the defence was significantly higher than was the case in the second group.

In a second experiment, an actor used a tape to submit a plea of "not guilty" and this submission was presented in three alternative forms— that is, in either a confident, or a neutral, or a doubtful manner. So the subjects were exposed to three different modes of presentation. The number of subjects who were sure that the plea was correct was highest when the actor behaved confidently. This was followed by neutral and doubtful modes of presentation in that order.

It hardly needs stating that confidence is an important factor in influencing people in business, and one feels that the able communicator is likely to rely on nonverbal expressions as a means of supplementing the verbal delivery when transmitting confidence to an audience. (Communication skills were examined in Chapter 6.)

Threats and fear.   When dealing with threats and fear, how gruesome should a message be? An advertisement on road safety showing a really horrific illustration of road accident victims may not produce the desired effect, whereas a more temperate reference to road accident victims might be more productive. On this theme, Janis and Feshbach (1963) conducted a study into the effects of different levels of threats to persuade high school students to adopt recommended practices of dental care (see Panel 9.5). The conclusion from the study is that threats should be used with great care, and, although a little fear may be a good thing, a lot of fear may be a bad thing.

PANEL 9.5: Dental care study

An illustrated lecture on dental care was given to three similar groups, but a different level of fear-arousing message was used in each group. In the mild-level threat group, the students were shown decayed teeth cavities, mouth infections, and visits to the dentist. In the moderate-level threat group, there were similar illustrations, but in addition warnings of pain from toothache and dental work were given. In the strong-level threat group, the threats already made clear to the other two groups were reiterated and these were reinforced by warnings of possible intense suffering from secondary diseases, such as blindness, cancer, and major dental surgery. In addition to the three experimental groups, a control group, which received a talk on a different topic, was used. In order to measure the response to the message, the experimenters noted the students' reported changes in teeth-brushing practices and the extent to which they attended a dentist during the following week.

It was found that the mild-level threat produced the greatest change in responsive behaviour (37%), followed by the moderate-level threat (22%), with the strong-level threat producing a small change (8%). The mild-level threat group responded significantly more than the control group. But the strong-level threat group was no different from the control group that did not get a pep talk. These findings indicate that the greater the threat, or the higher the intensity of a fear-arousing message, the lower the intensity of dental protective action.

The three experimental groups were exposed to counter-propaganda (a different message) a week later. The mild-level threat group was more resistant to this message than the other two groups, and the least resistance was felt by the strong-level threat group. This is understandable because the mild-level threat group had already changed their attitudes significantly, whereas the strong-level threat group experienced an insignificant change of attitudes following the initial fear-arousing message.

An explanation put forward to account for the initial reaction of the strong-level threat group suggests that stimuli that appeal to intense fear arouse anxiety in listeners. To try to reduce this anxiety, people become hostile to the speaker and, as a result, are likely to reject the message.

(Janis & Feshbach, 1963)

The common-sense view, unlike the view emanating from the Janis and Feshbach (1963) study, would suggest that a high-level threat is likely to produce a better response in terms of attitude change. Support for this view came from the findings of a study assessing the effect of a talk on the seriousness of tetanus and the need for anti-tetanus injections (Leventhal, Singer, & Jones, 1965). The talk created strong fear arousal leading to a behavioural change in the form of obtaining an inoculation if this was easily available (although such a course of action could be considered medically desirable behaviour requiring little prompting).

It is also suggested that a strong fear appeal in a message is superior to a mild fear appeal in changing attitudes when a threat is posed to an individual's loved ones, when the subject matter of the message is presented by a highly credible source, when the recipient, though vulnerable, has a high degree of self-esteem (Karlins & Abelson, 1970), and when the recipient has the ability to ward off the danger depicted in the message (Rogers & Mewborn, 1976). In a particular situation a speaker with high credibility can arouse high fear in the recipients of the message, but the

logical consequences of total acceptance of the message may not materialise. For example, when subjects were subjected to high fear arousal with respect to the hazards of smoking, they were willing to cut down on smoking but less willing to have a chest X-ray (Leventhal, Watts, & Pagano, 1967).

Sutton (1982), having reviewed a number of studies, concluded that fear arousal in messages produced a consistent improvement in intention to change behaviour, as well as actual changed behaviour, when compared with situations where no fear arousal was applied. Also, he maintained that higher levels of fear led consistently to more change than lower levels. It is important to stress that the effects generated by fear arousal in a message must be placed in their proper context. A valid question to ask here is: Are the suggested remedies to counteract the threat likely to be perceived by the recipient of the message as effective measures, and also does the recipient have confidence in his or her ability to carry out the recommended action (Eiser & Van der Pligt, 1988)? For example, seasoned smokers, faced with persuasive messages to stop smoking or face dire consequences, must believe the advice that giving up smoking is an effective measure in reducing their chances of contracting lung cancer and other diseases, and must have confidence in their ability to successfully forgo cigarettes if they try.

Another question to consider when people are exposed to horrific images is, how relevant the message is to the perceiver's personal predicament. For example, subjects exposed to a communication aimed at generating a high level of fear—where it is stated that improper dental care leads to teeth being extracted, inflamed gums, paralysis, and blindness (see Panel 9.5)—may believe this message, but on reflection are convinced that their own oral hygiene practices are unlikely to result in these devastating consequences, and naturally infer that their teeth have been cared for properly. Therefore, they conclude that there is no need to change existing tooth-brushing behaviour (Fishbein & Ajzen, 1975).

A cardinal principle one must never lose sight of is that people with different attitudes are likely to perceive matters in different ways, and this can be seen clearly in some health campaigns carried out nationally. A fear-arousing message may be construed as a personal attack (and consequently avoided) by the target group whose behaviour the health authority is trying to change. For example, consider the possible reactions of gay men to certain AIDS campaigns in the past.

Attitude dissimilarity or similarity. The similarity or dissimilarity of the attitudes of both the communicator and listener also have to be considered. If the communicator advocates a position that is close to the one held by the listener, the listener will perceive a greater similarity between the two positions than exists in reality; this is referred to as *assimilation*. On the other hand, if the communicator advocates a position that is rather distant from the one held by the listener, the latter perceives it as more distant than it really is; this is referred to as *contrast* (Reich & Adcock, 1976).

Maximum attitude change can be expected when the listener does not hold an extreme attitude on the matter, the issue is not one that appeals to his or her ego, is likely to be considered neutral, and the communicator has high credibility. This might very well describe the conditions in a psychology laboratory, because the typical laboratory setting creates a high credibility source (academic or scientific staff), and the issues dealt with are unimportant when compared to real-life events; therefore, it is no wonder that experimenters usually obtain attitude change (Himmelfarb, 1974). However, this criticism may be unfair if levelled at all studies of attitude change, simply because attitude change as an outcome of field studies has been observed.

Persuasion

Persuasion is an important process in attitude change (Wood, 2000), and persuasive influences were conspicuous in the role of communication as a factor contributing to attitude change, discussed previously. The following issues will be addressed here: nature of persuasion, opinion leaders, credibility of source, and persuasion routes.

Nature of persuasion. An extreme form of persuasion was employed by the Chinese with respect to the re-education (brainwashing) of prisoners of war. Soldiers were coerced into reading aloud pro-communist propaganda over the camp's loudspeaker system. The reason for this was that other prisoners were more likely to accept such ideas from their own colleagues than from the enemy. In one camp, a soldier reared in Brooklyn, New York, delivered the message with a deadpan expression in an exaggerated southern Dixieland drawl as an act of defiance (Mackay, 1973).

Persuasion exemplified in promotional efforts for marketing purposes would appear to be more subtle. A company may wish to change one or more of the attributes of its product or service in order to enhance its corporate image: for example, an airline, primarily a domestic carrier, now wishes to be considered an international carrier. In another situation the consumer is asked to reassess the value of a particular attribute of the product: a pharmaceutical company may stress the absence of an undesirable attribute in its product—e.g., paracetamol, unlike aspirin, is not very harmful to the stomach.

In order to increase the overall attractiveness of a brand, a new attribute of the product is given

---

PANEL 9.6: The power of suggestion

A lecturer, introduced as Dr Hang Schmidt, an internationally renowned research chemist, was presented to a group of students. Dr Schmidt wore a white laboratory coat and spoke with a German accent. The students were asked to report (by putting up their hands) when they smelt a new chemical vapour he was about to release. The lecturer pulled the stopper of a small glass beaker giving the impression that he was releasing the vapour. Then the students sitting in the front of the lecture hall raised their hands, and their reaction spread throughout the hall. Later the students were told that the beaker had not contained any vapour, merely distilled water, and that Dr Schmidt was a lecturer from the Department of German.

   This experiment illustrates the power of suggestion emanating from an apparent expert or credible source. One wonders whether the same effect would be produced if a student dressed in jeans went through the same motions as Dr Schmidt.

(Karlins & Abelson, 1970)

---

particular emphasis in advertisements. Here are a few examples: a birth control element in dog food; the addition of a deodorising feature in socks; the inclusion of a "light to show the way to escape" in smoke detectors; the incorporation of protein in a dishwashing product for "softer hands"; a revolutionary roll-on anti-perspirant that goes on dry; and the "wonder loaf" that is nutritionally superior.

Opinion leaders. An advertiser may wish to influence opinion leaders either individually or in groups. Opinion leaders are people of roughly the same social standing as those who will be subjected to their influence. They tend to be better informed, often more intelligent, and pay more attention to the channels of communication than those subjected to their influence. There could be an opinion leader for different pursuits—e.g., fashion, sport, and politics. As to the recipients of persuasion, it is said that those who succumb too readily to it are anxious (Reich & Adcock, 1976). Their lack of self-confidence, as a result, may make them vulnerable, and their preoccupation with their own thoughts and fears may create a disposition whereby they do not pay enough attention to the persuasive message.

Credibility of source. The credibility of the source of a message has been acknowledged earlier, and it is equally applicable to persuasion. The perceived status (the position or role occupied by the persuader) is also important. Credibility depends on the general trustworthiness, qualifications, dynamism, or energy of the person (Mackay, 1973). What effect has the credibility of the persuader on

whether or not one yields to his or her message? The impact of the credibility of the persuader in a classroom situation is demonstrated in a study (see Panel 9.6) by Karlins and Abelson (1970).

In another experiment, the opinions of students on certain important issues were obtained (Hovland & Weiss, 1951). One week later the students were presented with four newspaper articles dealing with the issues on which they had earlier expressed an opinion. Each article dealt with one of the important issues, and the articles contained a mixture of arguments for and against the topics discussed. The students were unaware of the title of the publication from which the articles were extracted. Subsequently, one group of students was told that an article came from a credible source—for example, from a medical journal in the case of the use of drugs. Another group was told that the article came from a low credibility source—for example, from a mass-circulation newspaper, again in the case of drugs. Once again the attitudes of the students to the issues raised earlier were assessed, and they were compared with the attitudes that prevailed prior to the experiment. A 22% change in attitudes was observed for the group exposed to the high credibility source, as opposed to 8% for the low credibility source.

What is the relevance of the notion of credibility to a commercial organisation? The credibility of a commercial organisation can be enhanced by creating a corporate reputation. This could be achieved by reliable products, good after-sales service, sound warranties and guarantees, using friendly and helpful staff, and acting in a socially responsible manner. Likewise, a supplier could use well-respected stores or speciality shops for an unknown brand, and this could contribute to improved sales.

The high credibility of the source is evident in a consumer magazine such as *Which?* in the UK, because of its established reputation for expertise in providing information on different products. A source with low credibility could be effective if it argues against its own interest (Koeske & Crano, 1968). For example, a tobacco company would have low credibility if it argued that there is no relationship between smoking and lung cancer, but the company could be very persuasive in changing people's attitudes if it argued publicly that smoking definitely leads to lung cancer.

When considering source credibility, what is called the *sleeper effect* should be acknowledged. This develops when, after a lapse of time, a person will be more persuaded by the content of a message and less influenced by the credibility or noncredibility of the source. It is said that credibility is of importance only with respect to attitudes connected with issues in which subjects have a mild interest. But if the subject's ego involvement in an issue is high, the importance of credibility is minimal (Johnson & Scileppi, 1969). Why should this be so? Perhaps there is greater involvement of the self in an issue in this situation and this leads subjects to a position whereby they pay more attention to the content of the message and less to the source. If so, the subject's firm attachment to the attitude relating to the particular issue is the crucial factor, and the credibility of a source that may challenge this state of affairs is likely to be considered unacceptable.

It has sometimes been suggested that "overhearing" and taking notice of a message on an issue in which one has a high personal involvement —instead of being the direct recipient of the message—can produce the intended effect. At least the communicator cannot be accused of attempting to influence directly the eventual recipient who overheard the message. But where the communication is presented directly, the communicator may be suspected of giving desirable information to further his or her own ends (Brock & Becker, 1965; Waister & Festinger, 1962).

It is probably better to think of credibility as applicable to a particular situation, rather than having general applicability, because the credible source may have only a specific expertise to offer. Is it important for the persuader to draw an explicit conclusion at the end of the message? The persuader, on the grounds of effectiveness, does not have to be explicit if the listener is motivated or intelligent enough to draw his or her own conclusion. However, the explicit conclusion is more likely to be effective with the less intelligent listener (McGuire, 1968).

Persuasion routes. These are represented by the so-called "elaboration likelihood model" of persuasion (Petty & Cacioppo, 1985; Petty & Wegener, 1999). According to this model there are two routes to persuasion—the central route and the peripheral route.

The central route to persuasion entails handling the message received with careful thought, and considering the various arguments along with our own ideas in deciding what position to take. We take this route if the issue interests us, where we take notice of the content of the message and the information contained in it, and where the arguments are significant and can withstand serious scrutiny. People who are likely to process persuasive messages through the central route are likely to enjoy thinking, are able to concentrate, feel involved in the issues under review, and consider that they have a personal responsibility for evaluating the message. A critical aspect of the persuasive message for these people is the arrangement of the arguments, and they play down simply remembering the arguments (Cacioppo & Petty, 1989).

The situation is quite different if the message comes by way of the peripheral route to persuasion. Along this route we resort to a more simplistic processing of information, possibly because we do not care much about the issue in question, or because the message is not clearly heard because of background noise or we are otherwise distracted. In such circumstances the content and arguments matter little. What matters more are peripheral cues. Such cues may embrace the speaker's apparent expertise ("experts know their subject"), or likeability ("nice people can be trusted"), or the sheer number or length of the arguments presented, irrespective of how meaty they are ("the more arguments put forward, the greater the likelihood that they are correct"). Also, the reaction of other recipients to the message ("it appears to be well received") is a cue that might be considered (Petty & Wegener, 1999; Wood & Kallgren, 1988).

In recent years a one-process alternative to the above dual-process approach has been proposed (Kruglanski & Thompson, 1999). This is called the *unimodel*, and is an alternative to the central and peripheral routes examined above; the authors deny any useful qualitative distinction between the central and the peripheral routes.

Balance and consistency

A key concept in attitude change is balance and consistency. It is suggested by Festinger (1957) that people try to establish internal harmony, consistency, or congruity among their opinions, attitudes, knowledge, and values. **Consistency theory** was developed in a climate of conformity in the USA when it was believed that people do not like to behave in a manner inconsistent with their attitudes.

Consistency could equally be applied to the structure of a given attitude, whereby the cognitive, affective, and conative components of an attitude are consistent with one another. In a sense, consistency could be internally rewarding and this is tantamount to experiencing internal reinforcement. The concept of consistency can be applied to a cluster of attitudes within the attitudinal frame of the individual, though it is possible to condone minor inconsistencies (Sherif & Sherif, 1967).

Consistency theories

Consistency theories have been divided into three categories, as follows:

- balance theory;
- congruity theory; and
- cognitive dissonance theory.

Balance theory

Balance theory is concerned with both balance and imbalance in attitudes (Heider, 1946). There are times when our intuition tells us that a particular situation is unbalanced or uncomfortable in a cognitive sense. For example, the finance director of a company welcomes the appointment of a new marketing director because he or she believes they share an outlook in common about efficiency and the future direction of the company. However, the finance director suddenly senses that the marketing director has serious reservations about proposed cost-cutting plans. As a result, the finance director expects friction to arise at the next board meeting. This creates imbalance and produces tension, which the finance director attempts to alleviate. In these circumstances the finance director, in order to restore balance, could change his or her attitude to the marketing director from positive to negative, or revise his or her opinion about the matter on which there is likely to be fundamental disagreement, or alter his or her perception of the marketing director's attitude towards the proposed cost-cutting plans.

It should be recognised that people have different thresholds or levels of tolerance for imbalance, and some people may function well in certain states of imbalance and not feel it necessary to reduce the accompanying tension.

Congruity theory

Congruity theory is also concerned with positive and negative attitudes but, in addition, attempts to measure the strength of these attitudes (Osgood & Tannenbaum, 1955). For example, if someone such as a first-class actor for whom we have great respect and who we evaluate as +3 (highly favourable) on an Osgood semantic differential scale (see Table 9.4 later in this chapter), praises a product in a television advertisement (again which we evaluate at +3), then there is no discrepancy. However, if somebody whom we admire greatly (say, +3) makes many complimentary remarks about a product or service for which we have a low regard (say –2), then there is a discrepancy of 5. To reduce the discrepancy, the individual could think less well of the admired figure and view the product or service in a less negative way; this might help to bring the attitudes in question more into line.

Factors to consider when adjustments to attitudes are contemplated are the strength of the attitudes (because generally speaking the stronger the attitude the more difficult it is to change), and the extent to which the person believes in the information disseminated by the admired figure. A consumer could arrive at a conclusion that the admired figure is putting forward favourable views about the product, not because he or she thinks highly of it, but merely because there is a handsome fee for putting across the message.

There are occasions when people actively seek information consistent or consonant with their attitudes. In one study, recent purchasers of new cars were asked to read advertisements for various makes of car including their own (Ehrlich, Guttman, Schonbach, & Mills, 1957). The results showed that they were much more likely to read advertisements for their own car, which they presumably had favourable attitudes towards, than advertisements for cars which they had either seriously considered buying at one stage or cars that had been given little or no consideration. There are other occasions when people strive for consistency by bringing their attitudes into line with newly adopted behaviour. When workers were promoted to the job of foreman they tended to acquire managerial attitudes consistent with their new organisational role. However, when some of them returned to their previous positions as workers they experienced a significant dilution of their recently acquired managerial attitudes (Liberman, 1956).

The consistency between attitudes and behaviour may not apply in every situation. In a study of hotel owners' attitudes towards certain racial groups it was concluded that there were discrepancies between attitudes and behaviour. In their response to items on a questionnaire, some hotel owners resident in the southern part of the USA expressed an intention to discriminate against a Chinese couple, accompanied by a white American, in the provision of accommodation (LaPiere, 1934). But when they came face to face with a well-dressed Chinese couple, travelling with a white American, the travellers were not refused accommodation. Perhaps it is more difficult to discriminate in a face-to-face situation than in private on paper. But equally, it is often easier to be liberal on paper than in face-to-face encounters. In this situation the hotel owner may have had to come to terms with conflicting attitudes, and perhaps the business attitude to making a profit took precedence over the racial attitude or prejudice. Bohner and Wanke (2002) reflect on this finding and make the following observation:

> In the light of contemporary methodological standards, there are a number of flaws in LaPiere's (1934) study: Respondents' attitudes were assessed long after the behaviour in question; it was unclear if the people who responded to the mailing were the same as those who had admitted the Chinese guests; and the "attitude object"— an English speaking (Chinese) couple accompanied by a white American—may not have been identified as members of the Chinese race to begin with.

Cognitive dissonance theory

Cognitive dissonance theory is probably the most important cognitive consistency theory. Cognitive dissonance arises when individuals act in a manner inconsistent with what they feel. If an attitude is not terribly important to the individual, then the behaviour that is inconsistent with it creates relatively little dissonance.

Different situations create different levels of dissonance. For example, a child may experience greater dissonance when having to choose between buying a book and going fishing, than between going to the cinema and going to the theatre. Choice in the face of alternatives then becomes a critical issue. The positive aspects of a rejected alternative and the negative aspects of the chosen alternative are inconsistent or dissonant with the action taken (Festinger, 1957). The easiest way to get rid of this psychological discomfort—i.e., to reduce the dissonance—is to change the attitude to the decision so that it corresponds more closely with the

---

A group of women was asked to rate the desirability of a number of household products. They were told that the manufacturer wanted consumer reactions for which they would receive a reward of one product from a set of two that was available for this purpose. The researcher then manipulated the magnitude of dissonance likely to be experienced. Half the group could choose from two products where there was only a slight difference in the attractiveness of the products (high-dissonance group), which makes the act of choice more difficult. The other half could choose from two products where the difference in the attractiveness of the products was great (low-dissonance group), which makes the act of choice easier.

When both groups made their choice of product they were asked to read four research reports that contained commentaries on the products used in the study. The high-dissonance and low-dissonance groups were divided into subgroups, whereby half the members in each subgroup were given a report on the products that constituted the first choice, and the other half were given reports dealing with products not the subject of choice. Therefore, those provided with reports on products chosen had the opportunity to peruse relevant technical data after they had made their decisions.

The experimental test was repeated when the subjects were asked to rate the desirability of the household products once again. The results showed that the attractiveness of the previously chosen product increased and the attractiveness of the previously rejected product decreased in the high-dissonance group, irrespective of whether or not relevant information about the product was received. In other words, the provision of relevant or irrelevant post-decision information did not have a material effect on individual efforts to reduce the state of dissonance. In the low-dissonance group it was the irrelevant information that increased the attractiveness of the previously chosen product and decreased the attractiveness of the previously rejected product.

Because the results show that dissonance was reduced by the provision of information unrelated to the product choice after a decision was made, the hypothesis cited in the main text (i.e., that the use of supportive information reinforces the chosen alternative and plays down the attractiveness of the rejected alternative) must be rejected. However, the manner in which the research was conducted in this study has been subjected to criticism.

(Brehm, 1966)

---

outward behaviour. One may hypothesise that this may be achieved by deliberately playing down the attractiveness of the rejected alternative and reinforcing the chosen alternative by providing supportive information after the decision was made (Brehm, 1966). This hypothesis has been subjected to favourable empirical testing (see Panel 9.7), although some doubt has been cast on the findings.

The threat of punishment or the promise of reward is relevant in the context of cognitive dissonance (Festinger & Carlsmith, 1959). If individuals are forced to comply, following the use of sanctions or rewards, there will be a tendency for them to change their attitude so that it is brought into line with their behaviour. However, this statement needs qualification in the light of whether or not the force to bring about compliance is strong or weak.

If the pressure used to force compliance is strong, the individual is much less likely to change his or her attitude so as to bring it into line with enforced behaviour. Why should this be so? Because it could be argued that if you were made to change your actions or behaviour by a strong force, you can always say to yourself that if you

had the freedom to express yourself you would do so and would not take the enforced action. In this case, dissonance would be minimal because the individual has little choice in the matter. On the other hand, if the pressure to force compliance is weak—i.e., the force exerted to make you act or behave in opposition to your inner attitude is weak—then dissonance is strong. This might arise, for example, when under the threat of a minor social sanction you behave in a manner contrary to your privately held attitude. To reduce the dissonance would necessitate bringing the attitude into line with the behaviour.

The hypotheses in the previous paragraph were subjected to experimental laboratory tests by Festinger and Carlsmith (1959). Students were asked to carry out boring, repetitive tasks. One group was paid $1 to participate in the test and the other group was paid $20. The first batch of students who performed this task was told to tell the next batch that the tasks were interesting and enjoyable; in fact, the students were asked to tell a lie. The students complied with the experimenter's request, and later the two groups were tested privately on their attitudes towards the original laboratory tasks. The first group, who received the smaller payment, said that the tasks were enjoyable, but the second group, who received $20, said the tasks were boring and uninteresting. Therefore, in accordance with the prediction in the hypotheses, the first group of students had little pressure applied to them and they changed their attitude by acknowledging that the tasks were interesting and enjoyable. This group could hardly justify telling a lie for the money, so dissonance was high. To reduce the dissonance the students had to change an inner attitude by an unconscious means to arrive at the view that the tasks were quite interesting and enjoyable. But the second group of students were subjected to greater pressure to tell a lie, in the form of an incentive of $20, and felt it unnecessary to change their inner attitude to the task; the students were prepared to tolerate dissonance because the rewards for doing so were worthwhile.

In experimental studies like the one described, we cannot always be sure of the exact nature and seriousness of the subject's response and when it is the best time to introduce the rewards. Festinger (1957) identifies some of the possible reactions to a state of dissonance as follows:

- Individuals seek new information that is supportive of their outlook, and will avoid sources of new information that are likely to increase the existing state of dissonance.
- New information likely to increase the existing state of dissonance could be misperceived or misinterpreted.
- The presence of others who agree with a particular attitude that one wants to establish or maintain is sought, and efforts are made to solicit greater social support for one's desired position.
- The individual plays down the importance of the factors contributing to the state of dissonance, and loss of memory intervenes and helps remove key dissonant elements.

Cognitive dissonance theory has been subjected to much criticism on the grounds that attitudes have often been found not to predict behaviour, and that results supporting the theory often turn out to be based on vulnerable experimental evidence. In addition, most people seem able to tolerate great logical inconsistencies, and do not necessarily

avoid information favourable to alternatives not chosen. Neither do most people overexpose themselves to favourable information and, finally, dissonance seems to explain the past rather than predict the future (Tedeschi, Schlenker, & Bonoma, 1973).

A particular criticism of the measures used to gauge cognitive dissonance is the rarity of circumstances in which subjects engage in self-reporting. With regard to our tolerance of inconsistencies, it is argued that people grow used to and expect a certain amount of imbalance in their cognitive make-up and, over time, have managed to adapt to a certain level of incongruity (Driver & Streufert, 1966). Therefore, up to a point, they are not too concerned with means of coping with dissonance reduction.

Cognitive dissonance theory focuses attention on what happens when we act in ways that are inconsistent with our attitudes. The most prominent challenge for dissonance theory came from Bem's (1967) self-perception theory (Bohner & Wanke, 2002). According to this theory, we frequently determine what our attitudes are from observing our own behaviour (*self-perception*). For example, if a person repeatedly takes various safety precautions at work (safe behaviour), that person might conclude that he or she possesses positive safety attitudes through observing his or her own behaviour. It is said that self-perception theory is less applicable when somebody holds a strong attitude related to the observed behaviour, and is more applicable when an attitude or set of beliefs towards the behaviour in question does not exist (Pennington, Gillen, & Hill, 1999).

ATTITUDE MEASUREMENT

How do we measure attitudes? Attitude measurement usually implies measurement of the cognitive component (i.e., the thinking aspect) of an attitude. The most basic way of doing this is to ask a single question, but this is rarely a satisfactory method because it does not take into account the many components of attitudes. Many general attitudes possess a number of facets, and therefore it is preferable to use an attitude scale composed of many questions.

Attitudes cannot be directly observed as such, but can be measured indirectly. We need measures to help us compare the attitudes of individuals or groups, and to be able to register changes in an individual's attitudes over time. The aim is to record numerically what a person thinks about a particular issue (e.g., the new world order, or the political party most suited to governing the country) and it is important that the questions asked have the same meaning for all those who participate in the attitude survey. Among the widely used techniques are the following.

Thurstone scale

This was one of the first systematic approaches to attitude measurement and was developed by Thurstone and Chave (1929). The first step is to write out a large number of statements (perhaps 100 or more), each of which expresses a particular view. These statements should express all possible viewpoints from extremely favourable to extremely unfavourable. An example of statements used for the measurement of employees' attitudes using this method is illustrated in Table 9.2.

Each statement is typed on a separate piece of paper, and a judge is asked to place each statement in anything up to 11 piles. There are nine statements in the example in Table 9.2, so the piles range from statements judged to express the least favourable viewpoint (pile 9) to statements judged to express the most favourable viewpoint (pile 1). Statements judged to express varying degrees of favourableness in between these extremes on a continuum are put into the appropriate pile.

In the construction of the attitude scale the services of as many as 100 judges or assessors are used. The judges are asked not to express their own attitudes, but to be as objective as possible in indicating the extent to which the statement is favourable or unfavourable towards the topic in question. The purpose of allocating statements to piles is to determine the scale value of the various statements. For example, if all judges place a statement in piles towards the favourable end of the continuum of attitudes, we could conclude that the statement expresses a favourable attitude towards the company.

The number of times each statement is placed in each pile is calculated, and a further calculation is made to determine the average location of the statement in order to arrive at a scale value. An imaginary scale value is shown in Table 9.2. The consistency of the judges' assessments for each statement is analysed, and statements placed by all judges in one or a limited number of categories have the greatest degree of reliability. Statements that are placed by the judges over several categories are eliminated. It is sensible to begin with many more statements than are required for the final scale, and to settle for 10 or more

---

TABLE 9.2

An example of a Thurstone scale measuring employee attitudes

Statements	Scale value*
The company values my contribution	9.50
My job is safe as long as I turn out good work	8.25
My boss lets me know what he or she thinks of me	7.20
The company offers rewards commensurate with efforts	6.50
The company needs to improve its training programme	4.80
The company's policy of dealing with people is rather vague	3.00
My job offers little opportunity for the exercise of discretion	2.65
My boss never lets me know what he or she thinks of me	1.50
Many employees stay with the company because they cannot find another job	0.70

* These values would not appear on the scale.

statements that are spread over the entire range of the continuum; these statements would have been consistently evaluated by the judges.

The final material for the attitude scale comprises the selected statements and their scale values. In the administration of an attitude scale, statements appear on printed paper in random order without the scale values that appear in Table 9.2. All employees participating in the attitude survey are requested to tick all statements they agree with: participants remain anonymous. The attitude of each employee is usually calculated as the average or median scale value of the statements ticked. An average of 6.52 would be the outcome of an attitude survey where the second, fourth, and fifth statements shown in Table 9.2 were ticked by an employee. The calculation is as follows:

$$\frac{8.25 + 6.50 + 4.80}{3} = 6.52$$

This employee's average score is at the favourable end of the scale, and therefore it indicates a favourable attitude towards the company (the higher the scale, the more favourable is the attitude in this illustration). On the other hand, an average of 1.73 would emerge if the sixth, eighth, and ninth statements reflected the preferences of the employee. This score would be arrived at as follows:

$$\frac{3.00 + 1.50 + 0.70}{3} = 1.73$$

The average of 1.73 would indicate an unfavourable attitude towards the company.

Likert scale

This method of measuring attitudes is somewhat simpler than the Thurstone method, and is probably the most commonly used attitude scale (Likert, 1932). The individual is asked not only to indicate agreement or disagreement, but also to signify how strongly he or she agrees or disagrees with a number of statements relevant to the attitude being measured. This is normally done on a 5-point scale, though it is possible to use a 7-point scale. The normal practice is to incorporate the various statements in a questionnaire. The following selection of items is extracted from a questionnaire used in a study of union and management attitudes to safety (Price & Lueder, 1980).

(1) Many accidents happen because a worker tries to make things easier or faster at the expense of safety.
(2) Industrial accidents are part of life and must be accepted as such by management and workers.
(3) Many of the present-day occupational illnesses from which people suffer cannot be anticipated or avoided.
(4) The benefits of safety outweigh its costs.
(5) Safety is the most important element of the working environment.

The subject is asked to respond to these statements, indicating the extent of his or her agreement or disagreement and using the scoring method illustrated in Table 9.3. In the example, a value is given to each response category in order to produce a numerical score, and the different scores in each category are added together to arrive at a total score. A high overall score can be viewed as a positive attitude to the issues raised in the questionnaire, whereas a low overall score denotes a negative attitude.

The statements chosen for inclusion in the Likert scale are usually found from experience to be connected with the attitude concerned and

TABLE 9.3	
An example of a Likert (1932) scale	
	Scoring attitude intensity
1	Strongly disagree
2	Disagree
3	Tend to disagree
4	Neither agree nor disagree
5	Tend to agree
6	Agree
7	Strongly agree

would be provided by knowledgeable people. In order to analyse statistically the data on the scale, it is important that a zero point is absent. However, this entails forcing a subject to express an attitude when in fact he or she does not hold one, and this reduces to some extent the validity of the exercise. Because of the way the Likert scale is constructed, most of the scores will fall at the two ends of the scale, and there is less power of discrimination as we move nearer the neutral point.

Osgood's semantic differential

This technique was devised by Osgood and his colleagues as part of a study of the meaning of words; it consists of pairs of adjectives opposite in meaning (Osgood, Suci, & Tannenbaum, 1957). An abbreviated example of pairs of words used by Fiedler (1967) to create a profile of the least preferred co-worker in the contingency model of leadership (referred to in Chapter 12), is shown in Table 9.4.

In the table, a 7-point rating scale is used with zero standing for neutral or "don't know". Numerical values cover a scale from +3 to –3. Alternatively, a scale ranging from 7 to 1 can be used, with 4 as a mid-point. The respondent is asked to give an immediate reaction to each pair of words listed in the table and describe the person he or she prefers the least by placing a cross in one of the seven spaces between each pair of words. The individual's score is his or her total score on all scales of the measure used; the higher the score the more favourable is the respondent's impression of the person assessed.

The semantic differential deals with factors concerned with evaluation (good–bad), with potency (strong–weak), and with activity (active–passive). It could be used in the study of interpersonal perception, and also in measuring attitudes to work where the emphasis is on the emotional reaction of the subject. The semantic differential technique measures attitudes in a rather global way and can be used to advantage among less literate subjects.

Sociometry

Using a natural group, every member of the group is asked to name their preferred partner for a specified activity (Moreno, 1953). They then rank the remainder of the group in order of preference, with reference to questions such as, "Who would you most like to sit next to?" Some knowledge of the "thinking" and "emotional" aspects of an individual's attitude can be obtained by asking, "Why do you want to sit next to X, the most popular person?" The least popular person—Y—can also be identified by this method. This technique, though useful in establishing the popularity of group members, has not been used extensively in the measurement of attitudes.

TABLE 9.4

An example of a semantic differential rating scale

	+3	+2	+1	0	–1	–2	–3	
Pleasant	–	–	–	–	–	–	–	Unpleasant
Friendly	–	–	–	–	–	–	–	Unfriendly
Accepting	–	–	–	–	–	–	–	Rejecting
Helpful	–	–	–	–	–	–	–	Frustrating
Enthusiastic	–	–	–	–	–	–	–	Unenthusiastic
Relaxed	–	–	–	–	–	–	–	Tense
Close	–	–	–	–	–	–	–	Distant
Warm	–	–	–	–	–	–	–	Cold
Cooperative	–	–	–	–	–	–	–	Uncooperative
Supportive	–	–	–	–	–	–	–	Hostile
Interesting	–	–	–	–	–	–	–	Boring
Self-assured	–	–	–	–	–	–	–	Hesitant
Cheerful	–	–	–	–	–	–	–	Gloomy

Reliability and validity

Qualities that are essential to any kind of measure are **reliability** and **validity**. A reliable measure is one that will provide the same reading if that which is measured remains constant. If the same jar of marbles is weighed twice within a day, one expects it to weigh the same on both occasions. This procedure can then be used to test the scales, because the jar's weight can be relied on to remain the same. However, with attitudes one cannot get away with the assumption that they remain the same over time; in fact attitudes may change as a result of being measured. Therefore, the reliability of an attitude measure is more difficult to establish.

A valid measure is one that measures what it claims to measure, though this is sometimes difficult in the social sciences because we normally try to measure something that cannot be observed from the outside (i.e., how somebody thinks and feels about an issue). So the appropriate criterion for establishing validity is often difficult to determine. For a measure to be valid it must first be reliable, though a measure may be reliable but lack validity. A fuller exposition of reliability and validity can be found in the section on selection methods in Chapter 17.

Finally, one of the reasons why work attitudes are measured is to try to establish how satisfied or dissatisfied employees are with their jobs. The concept of job satisfaction is discussed later in the chapter.

ATTITUDES AND BEHAVIOUR

The relationship between attitudes and behaviour is more complicated than one might expect. A positive attitude towards road safety is just one factor among many that influence safe driving (behaviour on the road). Other factors have to be considered, such as driving habits, social conventions, temperament when provoked by another driver, and the attitude of the police to speeding or reckless driving. So it is easy to envisage situations where, because of various constraints, people are prevented from behaving in a manner consistent with their attitudes.

Pratkanis and Turner (1994) put forward suggestions for establishing closer links between attitudes and behaviour. These are: the attitudes held are easily identifiable and retrieved from memory; they are based on a solid foundation of knowledge; they are protective of the self; and the object (e.g., road safety) to which they relate is clearly defined and relevant.

The relationship between an intention to behave and actual behaviour has been the subject of rigorous investigation (Fishbein & Ajzen, 1975). Intentions with regard to behaviour, such as intentions to devise better cost-control measures, are influenced by the accountant's attitude towards controlling expenditure and by various organisational and social influences about the acceptability of this activity. Before proceeding, the accountant is likely to be interested in the reaction of interested parties to his or her ideas and the best way to proceed.

Planned behaviour

In the **theory of reasoned action** there is a recognition that people's actions are best predicted by their intentions (Ajzen & Fishbein, 1980). In turn, intentions are determined by people's attitudes as well as by what they see as expectations of them held by others. The theory of reasoned action, slightly amended by Ajzen and Madden (1986) and called the **theory of planned behaviour** (Ajzen, 1991, 2001) is shown in Figure 9.1. The theory defines an attitude in a particular way. An attitude is expressed as a belief about the consequences of behaviour; it is not concerned about general beliefs or feelings related to the object or subject matter of the attitude. As such it has something in common with expectancy theories of motivation, and, as a result, it is said that this is a good predictor of behaviour.

Along with "attitude" we have to consider "subjective norm" before arriving at "intention". Subjective norm embraces the beliefs of other people whose opinions we value with regard to performing or not performing the behaviour. It would also accommodate a person's desire or lack

FIGURE 9.1

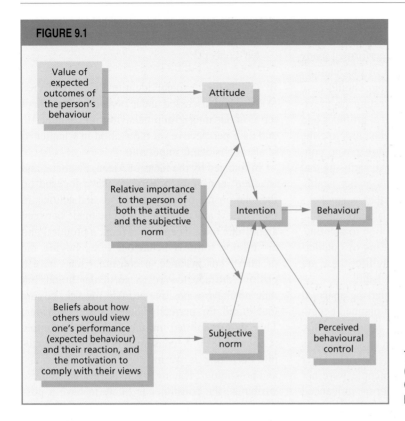

The theory of planned behaviour
(from Ajzen & Madden, 1986).
Copyright © 1986 and reproduced
by permission of Elsevier.

of desire to comply with the opinions of others. Before arriving at a final position on intentions, one should realise that people differ in the relative weighting they attach to "attitude" and "subjective norm".

The theory of reasoned action has been successful in predicting behaviour in a range of areas, such as smoking, alcohol abuse, contraception, and consumer behaviour (Bohner & Wanke, 2002; Sheppard, Hartwick, & Warshaw, 1988), but, as Eiser and Van der Pligt (1988) rightly point out, the theory has not escaped criticism at both theoretical and empirical levels. In the revised version of the theory by Ajzen and Madden (1986), the idea of perceived behavioural control is introduced. This is concerned with the extent to which people believe they can perform the required behaviour in particular situations. As a new variable, perceived behavioural control in Figure 9.1 has the potential to influence behaviour in a direct fashion or indirectly through intentions.

Ajzen (1991) reflects on the theory of planned behaviour, and suggests that the variables called the "relative importance to the person of both the attitude and the subjective norm" in Figure 9.1 should be recognised as situational in nature (that is they vary with circumstances). He then goes on to say that we should closely examine the variables "perceived behavioural control" and "subjective norm" in case there are weaknesses in this part of the model. For example, if individuals mistakenly believe that they are in control of a situation, the delicate link between intention and behaviour can be damaged. Also, it should be recognised that the influence exerted by the "subjective norm" on intentions and behaviour in the model is rather weak because some people are guided by their own conscience rather than the opinion of others.

When Eiser and Van der Pligt (1988) examined the theory of reasoned action—the forerunner of the theory of planned behaviour—they felt it was better suited to a situation where a person is deciding on a course of action for the first time. But often in life the action we consider will be similar if not identical to actions performed many times before. Therefore, a model of the relationship between attitude and behaviour should have the capacity to explain "habit" resting on previous behaviour, which, unlike normal attitudes and beliefs, can be very resistant to change. Note the predicament of the "habitual" smoker who continues to smoke cigarettes despite recognising that this behaviour is damaging to his or her health. However, one has to recognise that a smoker's behaviour can be physically determined—that is, behaviour is activated by an addiction to nicotine, as well as being a functional means of counteracting stressful conditions in daily life; these are powerful forces in sustaining the habit.

Armitage and Conner (2001), having analysed numerous studies of the theory of planned behaviour, were very complimentary about it, while admitting that the variable "subjective norm" was not as influential as the other variables. The latter could mean in this context that people were not prepared to accept that social norms influenced them in a significant way, which is likely to be prevalent in individualistic societies, such as the USA. Bohner and Wanke (2002) take the view that the theory of planned behaviour is superior to the theory of reasoned action in predicting behavioural intentions (and behaviour) when the behaviour under study is difficult to perform, but other studies indicate that this is not true for behaviours that can easily be performed.

Reflecting on the above theoretical advances, Terry, Hogg, and White (1999) state that:

> two decades of research have revealed, across a range of behaviour, general support for the theories of reasoned action and planned behaviour. However, support for the role of the subjective norm in both theories has been relatively weak. Recent research has also examined whether the theory of planned behaviour incorporates all the major predictions of intention and behaviour. One variable that has consistently been found to emerge as an additional distinctive predictor of intentions is self-identity, that is

the extent to which performing the behaviour is an important component of a person's self-concept.

In this context, social identity theory (referred to above and discussed under stereotyping in Chapter 5, under inter-group behaviour in Chapter 10, and as a perspective on motivation in Chapter 4) is also considered important.

Influenced by the ideas of Ajzen, Fishbein, and Madden, consumer researchers have focused on the relationship between intentions and actions. In this context a distinction has to be made between an attitude towards an object (e.g., a product) and an attitude towards behaviour (e.g., buying the product). For instance, a consumer may have a positive attitude towards a particular brand, but may not have a positive attitude towards buying that brand for perfectly understandable reasons. This is exemplified in the following example (Cohen, 1981). A consumer believes that high-pile carpeting is warm, comfortable, luxurious, and prestigious. Having positively evaluated these attributes, the consumer is likely to have a positive attitude towards high-pile carpeting. But is it practicable to buy this type of carpeting if there are pets and young children in the consumer's house? Therefore, a consumer's intention to purchase a product is dependent upon an assessment of how favourable the outcome is likely to be in terms of utility or satisfaction.

Sometimes the attributes of a product gain in importance as a result of external factors, quite independent of any marketing strategy used by a company. For example, when dieticians promulgate the view that products high in fibre content are good for people's health this is likely to influence in a significant way the sale of selected high-fibre foodstuffs.

Alternative viewpoint

An alternative view of the relationship between attitudes and behaviour is put forward by Fazio (1986). He maintains that an attitude influences behaviour by selectively activating various thought processes stored in the person's memory. The consequence of this development is that selective perception of the object to which the attitude relates is created. For example, a lecturer holds a positive attitude towards an object—attending academic conferences. If so, it is likely that he or she will recall positive rather than negative thoughts or associations (evaluative beliefs) with respect to academic conferences. These associations or thoughts will shape the person's selective perception of what academic conferences are like, which in turn will influence a decision to attend one.

From Fazio's perspective, an attitude is dependent upon previous positive or negative experiences, but it influences (rather than being merely influenced by) the evaluative beliefs (e.g., recall of positive thoughts and associations from memory) at the time the person decides on a course of action. This perspective underlines the view that people with different attitudes may see different aspects of an issue as important or salient (Fazio, 2000).

JOB SATISFACTION

When attitudes are discussed in a work context, we often make reference to **job satisfaction** and organisational commitment. The latter will be examined later. Job satisfaction is associated with how well our personal expectations at work are in line with outcomes. For example, if our expectations indicated that hard work generated equitable rewards, and that was the case, job satisfaction could ensue. The opposite situation of shattered personal expectations could lead to job dissatisfaction.

Earlier the question was asked in connection with attitudes generally whether they had a genetic basis. This line of questioning has also entered the discussion of job satisfaction. It is suggested that people's disposition towards life and subsequently towards work, be it positive or negative, is created and sustained by our genetic inheritance (Arvey, McCall, Bouchard, & Taubman, 1994). It is suggested that genetic factors could account for up to 30% of job satisfaction incidents. In many research studies this figure would be arrived at after determining the proportion of total job satisfaction attributable to environmental factors.

But it is questionable whether all the relevant environmental factors are considered; also, there is reason to believe that there are problems with the methodology used in this type of research, and it is difficult to pinpoint the aspects of an individual's disposition that influence job satisfaction (Judge & Hulin, 1993).

Apart from genetic disposition, do gender, age, and education have any influence on job satisfaction? With regard to gender, the evidence is not clear-cut. Lefkowitz (1994) refers to a number of US studies and reports that women's job satisfaction is lower than that for men. However, this finding does not stand when certain variables (e.g., age, education, income, and status) are held constant. In the 1991 British Household Panel Survey, women reported more job satisfaction than men (Clarke, 1996). Some might consider this a surprising result because of the nature of employment for many women—e.g., part-time, insecure, relatively low pay. Perhaps this result is not so surprising after all if one recognises that women can leave jobs more easily than men when they are dissatisfied, and those that remain in employment are more likely to be satisfied.

With regard to age, there is a tendency for job satisfaction to increase with age (Clarke, 1996; Clarke, Oswald, & Warr, 1996). One could speculate on the likely reasons for this result. For example, one could argue that dissatisfied older workers are more likely to leave their jobs through early retirement and redundancy schemes, while the older workers who stay in the organisation might enjoy their jobs. Alternatively, older workers, unlike younger workers, have spent more time in their career and manoeuvred themselves into satisfying jobs; or as workers grow older they may have adjusted their expectations of job satisfaction downwards and therefore it takes less to satisfy them.

On the question of education, particularly higher education, those who were well qualified experienced lower levels of satisfaction due to a failure to meet their expectations (Clarke, 1996). A variety of factors could be responsible for this result, such as work pressure, reservations about the adequacy of remuneration, and less than satisfactory career prospects.

Emotion

The work environment is an arena where experiences such as pleasure, sadness, jealousy, rage, guilt, and love are displayed to the same levels of intensity and frequency as elsewhere in our daily lives (Cassel, 1999). According to Briner (1999a):

> work, like any other domain, both produces and is influenced by emotion. We may, for example, feel envious of a co-worker's success, proud and delighted when we complete a difficult and important task, embarrassed about a barely disguised failure, or angry if a colleague lets us down at a particularly crucial moment. It is, therefore, unfortunate and curious that in conceptualizing and researching how people feel at work, psychologists have almost completely ignored emotion.

Some 30 years ago Locke (1976) captured the affective or emotional aspect of job satisfaction when he defined job satisfaction as "a pleasurable positive emotional state resulting from the appraisal of one's job or job experiences". This is a theme that has surfaced in more recent years (Weiss & Cropanzano, 1996). There is a recognition that we are strongly predisposed to reflect reasonably constant and predictable moods and emotional states, and these determine the satisfaction experienced (George & Jones, 1996). The major mood states are as follows:

- *Positive affectivity.* The person is relatively upbeat and optimistic, seems to be in a good mood, usually has a positive outlook on life, and has an overall sense of well-being.
- *Negative affectivity.* The person is relatively downbeat and pessimistic, usually has a negative view of life, and is normally in a bad mood.

With regard to these mood states, one has to accept short-term variations. For example, the relatively positive affectivity person could be moody (down) after being overlooked for an upgrading, having received a poor performance evaluation, or having been earmarked for compulsory redundancy.

By contrast, the relatively negative affectivity person could be cheerful at times when his or her performance has been favourably evaluated. When the initial impact of the good or bad news wears off, both types described here could revert to their normal states.

Much of the research in the psychology of emotion has focused on negative mood. Clinical psychology, for example, has explored the causes and symptoms of sadness rather than happiness. Few psychological studies have explored the consequences of being really happy (Martin, 2002). In one study of undergraduates conducted by Diener and Seligman (2002), and reported by Martin (2002), it was concluded that:

> Very happy people were found to have a rich social life and to spend less time alone than did moderately happy people. They had stronger romantic and social relationships than did the less happy groups, were more extraverted and agreeable, and were less neurotic. Unhappy people's social relations are worse than the moderately happy people's social relations. The very happy people did not experience more pleasant or good events in their lives than did the other groups, nor was there one factor common to all very happy people. Even the people classified as very happy were not consistently happy; they experienced occasional negative moods. The researchers found it difficult to establish whether happiness caused good social and romantic relations or whether the good relations caused happiness, and also were unable to pinpoint any single factor that produces a high state of happiness.

Wallis (2005) refers to the views of Ruut Veenhoven, Professor of Happiness Studies at Erasmus University, Rotterdam, and Editor of the *Journal of Happiness Studies*. He is quoted as saying that "people are happiest in jobs that afford a certain amount of freedom and scope for decision making and when they have less burdens or responsibilities in life generally (outside the age range 30–50)".

PANEL 9.8: Sequence of work emotions, thoughts, and behaviour

Jane is asked to undertake a difficult project, usually carried out by more experienced colleagues. She feels valued, flattered, and trusted, though she is a little worried by the assignment. While working hard on the project her emotions range from excitement and elation to fear and frustration. But she completes the task and feels proud and relieved. She informs her boss of her proud achievement and shows her the completed work. The reaction of the boss is to point out a trivial error, and she gives no thanks or praise to Valerie. The result is that she feels resentful and angry, and now begins to think that she will never again make a special effort for her boss. She also feels exploited, and is giving serious thought to seeking another job. In the meantime, she does not volunteer to undertake any additional tasks. She starts to feel sad and disappointed, revises her CV, and frequently studies job advertisements.

(Briner, 1999a)

Job satisfaction straddles several related attitudes. For example, people experience fairly strong affective or emotional responses to such things as remuneration, promotion opportunities, relations with superiors and colleagues, and the work itself. In turn, these and related factors could be classified as important causal agents in determining job satisfaction. As we have just seen, Briner (1999a) is a strong advocate of the view that emotion is a fundamental aspect of much of what people do at work. And in the past the tendency was to ignore or play down its relevance (Briner, 1999b). In Panel 9.8 he shows, through a simple illustration, how emotion, thought, and behaviour interact in a reciprocal way.

Causes of job satisfaction

The following are some of the organisational factors one might consider in attempts to establish the causes of job satisfaction (Hodgetts, 1991):

- *Pay and benefits*. The importance of equitable reward is a factor to consider here. One could add fair promotion policies and practices concerning fair pay (Witt & Nye, 1992).
- *Promotion*. The level of satisfaction will depend on the acceptability of the system in operation, be it a system based on merit, or seniority, or whatever combination of the two.
- *Job*. This would embrace (a) skills variety—the extent to which the job allows a worker to use a number of different skills and abilities in executing his or her duties (Glisson & Durick, 1988); (b) interest and challenge derived from the job, in particular moderate challenge

(Katzell, Thompson, & Guzzo, 1992); and (c) lack of role ambiguity—how clearly the individual understands the job (Glisson & Durick, 1988).

- *Leadership*. There has been endorsement of people-centred or participative leadership as a determinant of job satisfaction (Miller & Monge, 1986).
- *Work group*. It would appear that good intra-group working and supportive colleagues have value in not permitting job dissatisfaction to surface, rather than in promoting job satisfaction.
- *Working conditions*. Where working conditions are good, comfortable, and safe, the setting appears to be appropriate for reasonable job satisfaction, though not necessarily high job satisfaction. The situation with respect to job satisfaction would be bleaker if working conditions were poor.

To these factors can be added personality–job fit as a factor influencing job satisfaction. This arises when there is congruence between personality type and the demands of the job. Initially this could be expressed as successful job performance, eventually leading to high job satisfaction (Feldman & Arnold, 1985).

Measuring job satisfaction

The most frequently adopted approach to measuring job satisfaction involves the use of rating scales. These are standard instruments that are designed to provide feedback on specific examples of employee satisfaction and dissatisfaction.

When attitude measurement was discussed earlier in this chapter, reference was made to various rating techniques. A brief restatement of some of the earlier observations is appropriate here.

Rating scales in their simplest form consist of a single "global" rating, whereby an individual is asked to respond to one question—for example: "By and large, how satisfied are you with your job?" The respondent is asked to circle a number between 1 and 5, say, that corresponds with answers ranging from highly satisfied to highly dissatisfied. An alternative rating scale is called the "aggregate score", made up of a number of job facets. This is considered a more refined technique. It identifies key elements in the job and invites employees to express their feelings in numerical form about each element using the method identified earlier in connection with single global rating. The individual scores are added up to create an overall job satisfaction score. The elements could refer to the nature of the job, promotion opportunities, remuneration, supervision, relations with peers, and so on. An example of the type of items appearing in a measure of job satisfaction is contained in Table 9.5

One might well ask which one of the two approaches discussed has the edge as a measure of job satisfaction. A subjective evaluation might lead to a conclusion that the aggregate score approach is superior. However, there is evidence to indicate that single global rating has the edge (Nagy, 2002;

Scarpello & Campbell, 1983). The main advantages and disadvantages of measures of job satisfaction based on rating scales are listed in Panel 9.9.

Other techniques for measuring job satisfaction are **critical incidents** and *interviews*.

Critical incidents

Employees are requested to focus their attention on some situation or incident that is related to job satisfaction. For example, employees are asked to relate what they particularly like or dislike about their jobs. The next step is to have the content of this specific job-related information analysed in order to identify factors that can either cause job satisfaction, or prevent it. With the critical incidents technique, respondents experience greater freedom to express themselves, unlike the situation with rating scales.

However, using the critical incidents approach is time-consuming, with the likelihood of respondent bias. The latter could arise when respondents equate intrinsic job factors (e.g., challenging and stimulating assignments) with liking the job, whereas extrinsic job factors (e.g., style of supervision) are equated with disliking the job. Another way of putting this statement would be to suggest that people tend to like events over which they exercise control, but tend to dislike events or situations that are determined environmentally, and over which they have little, if any, control.

TABLE 9.5

Measure of job satisfaction items from the occupational stress indicator (from Cooper, Sloan, & Williams, 1987): Copyright © 1987 and reproduced by permission of the publishers

How do you feel about your job?	6	5	4	3	2	1
The relationships you have with other people at work						
The actual job itself						
Current career opportunities						
Your level of salary relative to your experience						
The degree to which you feel "motivated" by your job						
The degree to which you feel extended in your job						
The style of supervision that your superiors use						
The amount of participation that you are given in important decision making						

Note: 6 = very much satisfied; 1 = very much dissatisfied.

PANEL 9.9: Measuring job satisfaction with rating scales—advantages and disadvantages

---

Advantages

- They are normally short in length and can be completed rapidly.
- The language used is general, as opposed to being occupationally specific, and therefore it caters for a broad spectrum of employees.
- The responses can be quantified and this facilitates comparisons between groups (e.g., the attitudes of employees in a particular organisation are compared with those in similar organisations) and between periods of time. Normative data are available for certain job satisfaction questionnaires, including the distribution of responses in a representative population.
- The outcome of surveys of job satisfaction could lead to the diagnosis of problems amenable to solutions. At the very least, the survey could provide a forum for eliciting constructive feedback from employees.

Disadvantages

- Not everybody may be honest and straightforward when completing the questionnaire.
- The results may be distorted by the wording of questions and the choice of topics contained in the questionnaire.
- The results may be contaminated by attitudes or dispositions that bear an indirect relationship to job satisfaction. For example, a person may respond negatively to job-related items because of transport problems affecting getting to work on time. Likewise, short-term considerations, such as perceived lack of progress in writing a report with the deadline looming, may provoke anxiety. Matters such as these may create an inaccurate picture of the real state of job satisfaction.
- There may be problems with the validity of the measuring instrument—do the questions really measure job satisfaction?
- There may be problems with the reliability of the measuring instrument—do the questions measure job satisfaction consistently?

Interviews

As a more open-ended approach than critical incidents, interviews offer the interviewee wider scope in terms of response. Also, the interviewer can probe because he or she has the opportunity to ask questions and seek clarification on responses or observations that are unclear. A shortcoming of this technique is that it is time-consuming; also there is the possibility of interview bias, which can arise when the interviewer's preconceptions concerning the issues raised, and misunderstanding of the responses, contaminate the outcome. A fuller discussion of interviews and critical incidents can be found in Chapter 17.

Consequences of job satisfaction

A commonplace view is that if an organisation does not create conditions for the provision of a minimum level of job satisfaction, one can expect certain outcomes or consequences to follow—e.g., deterioration in productivity, employee turnover, absenteeism, and morale. In the light of evidence, however, the relationship between job satisfaction and the outcomes just mentioned may not be as clear-cut as many people think (Hodgetts, 1991). The outcomes that will now be examined are performance, employee turnover, and absenteeism.

Performance

could not afford this negligence

Apparently there is empirical evidence to show that the link between job satisfaction and performance is weak (Iaffaldano & Muchinsky, 1985), a conclusion not shared by Judge, Thoreson, Bono, and Patton (2001). But Ostroff (1992) maintains that when satisfaction and productivity data are collected and analysed at the organisational level, rather than at the individual level, it was found that organisations with more satisfied employees tended to be more effective than organisations with less satisfied employees. One explanation for the weak relationship between job satisfaction and productivity at the individual level of analysis is that the research instruments used may not always capture the many complex interactions and events in the workplace. Research in the UK endorses the role played by job satisfaction in influencing productivity (West, 1998).

Reflecting on the relationship between job satisfaction and performance, at least two moderating variables—namely, job level and machine-paced work—come to mind. Forces such as these could improve the relationship between job satisfaction and performance (Petty, McGee, & Cavender, 1984). With regard to job level or position in the hierarchy, the correlation between job satisfaction and performance are stronger for groups of employees in the supervisory and managerial class. Also, the relationship between job satisfaction and performance is likely to be weaker in the presence of factors outside the control of the worker. For example, an operative on the factory floor may have his or her productivity much more influenced by the speed of the machine or assembly line (something outside the person's control) than by the level of job satisfaction.

Another way of looking at job satisfaction and performance is to reverse the relationship and examine how productivity could influence job satisfaction (Petty et al., 1984). This could be achieved in an indirect way. For example, good job performance could not only lead to feeling good about oneself, but could lead to organisational recognition in the form of improved rewards and opportunities, which, in turn, could raise the level of job satisfaction.

Employee turnover

With regard to the relationship between job satisfaction and employee turnover, Lee and Mowday (1987) conclude that individuals who are satisfied with their jobs are less likely to leave the organisation than those who are dissatisfied. However, it would be wise to acknowledge the potency of moderating or intervening variables in the relationship between job satisfaction and employee turnover. There is a recognition that labour market conditions, expectations about alternative job opportunities, and job tenure within the organisation, all act as intervening variables (Carsten & Spector, 1987; Hulin, Reznowski, & Hachiya, 1985).

In a specific sense, as job tenure increases it is suggested that the employee turnover rate tends to decline, irrespective of the level of job satisfaction (Hodgetts, 1991). This might be explained as follows. There is still commitment to the organisation from long-standing employees who may

not be as satisfied with their jobs as previously but are close to retirement. Also, they are of an age where it may be difficult to get another job of similar status and remuneration package; they cannot see themselves doing any other kind of work; and they are on top of the job to such an extent that its demands put little pressure on them.

The competence of the employee has also been cited as a moderating or intervening variable (Spencer & Steers, 1981). For example, competent performers may stay with the organisation irrespective of the level of job satisfaction because the organisation is intent on retaining their services and bestows certain benefits (e.g., increased pay and promotion opportunities, praise, and other forms of recognition). But the organisation is unlikely to go out of its way to retain the services of poor performers or incompetent employees. In fact, the latter may be encouraged to seek opportunities elsewhere.

A final example of a moderating or intervening variable is the affective disposition (mood) of the employee (Judge, 1993). It is said that those whose mood reflects a more negative outlook and disposition are more likely to remain within the organisation when they experience job dissatisfaction, whereas those with a more positive outlook and disposition are more likely to leave the organisation when dissatisfied with their job.

Absenteeism

There is said to be an inverse relationship between job satisfaction and level of absenteeism—that is, when job satisfaction is low, absenteeism tends to be high (Scott & Taylor, 1985; Steel & Rentsch, 1995). Apparently, high levels of job satisfaction will not guarantee low levels of absenteeism (Clegg, 1983). But yet again one has to accept the influence exerted by intervening variables. The relationships between job satisfaction and absenteeism could be moderated by the importance of the job to employees, the opportunity to use a variety of skills in the job where clear objectives exist, and the existence of good relationships with superiors and peers. These variables could enhance the level of job satisfaction. Even when satisfaction is high, absenteeism could occur when people, feigning illness, take time off

---

PANEL 9.10: Happiness, satisfaction and work

The findings of a report commissioned by the Chartered Institute of Personnel and Development, produced by Guest and Conway (2002) and discussed by Overell (2002a), stated that "life" satisfaction does appear to be related to how work is organised. There are features of work design that have quite a high correlation with happiness. Focusing on the psychological contract (the unwritten agreement that exists between employers and employees; it sets out what management expects from its staff and vice versa), the authors of the report suggest that the traditional psychological contract is no longer applicable. The traditional psychological contract, which involved an exchange of job security for motivation and commitment, is widely held to have been destroyed by globalisation, competitive pressures, the retreat of trade unions, and the need for flexibility.

In its place employers are believed to be shaping a new contract using high-performance practices (such as teamwork, performance management, employee involvement, and communication) to rebuild employee motivation. Employee autonomy (how free the person feels) is said to be a fundamental determinant of well-being. The greater the autonomy over how, where, and at what pace work is done, the greater the life satisfaction, which is described as related to job satisfaction (the two overlap). Professor Andrew Oswald is reported as saying that the employee is likely to be happier if the customer rather than the supervisor controls the pace of work.

Other attributes of the workplace that can add to life satisfaction include a supportive climate, a sense of mutual trust between employer and employee, a dynamic atmosphere, procedural fairness, participation in decision making, and individuals feeling that they are in a strong position in the labour market.

(Overell, 2002a)

---

work to go to some important sporting fixture or attend to some domestic problem, in the realisation that they are not going to lose pay.

Finally, one has to acknowledge the importance of the interaction between job satisfaction and job design (discussed in Chapter 4); this link is also raised in Panel 9.10.

Job dissatisfaction

Before examining the nature of organisational commitment in the next section, one ought to say something about the opposite of job satisfaction, which is job dissatisfaction. The behavioural manifestations of job dissatisfaction could include the following: resigning from the organisation and going elsewhere; being vocal in registering complaints; being reluctant to accept guidance or instructions from supervisors and managers; deliberately not performing part of one's job responsibilities; theft and sabotage; poor overall job performance with a high incidence of errors and wastage.

But a dissatisfied worker could take action to do something positive about his or her predicament by suggesting remedies, getting the boss and union involved, even going as far as displaying loyalty by defending the organisation in the hope that the situation will improve (Withey & Cooper, 1989). In some quarters it is said that dissatisfied workers turn their frustration into

creativity to the benefit of the organisation. In a study of 149 employees of a North American manufacturing company it was found that under certain conditions dissatisfaction can induce creativity (Zhou & George, 2001), but Professor John Hunt, in a newspaper article a few years ago, has stated that he is not convinced by this evidence. He says that creativity is difficult to measure objectively, that creative workers are relatively scarce (perhaps only 15% of the workforce), and that there is not much evidence to suggest that dissatisfied workers are more creative than satisfied ones.

A growing problem, particularly in the USA, is violence by acutely dissatisfied or disgruntled existing or former workers, which has resulted in a number of deaths and injuries each year (O'Leary-Kelly, Griffin, & Glew, 1996). One London computer security company warned companies that they could be subjected to devastating computer hacking attacks from angry employees who face dismissal or redundancy because of cost-cutting programmes (Ayres, 1998).

In a survey of 2500 employed people in the UK, conducted by the Economic and Social Research Council (ESRC), a significant growth in dissatisfaction—notably over long hours and demands such as the intensity of work—was noted. It was said that today's world of work is much less satisfying to employees than the one they experienced 10 years ago. "People are working more intensively, clocking on for more hours and staying in jobs longer. There has been a significant deterioration in employees' commitment to their companies, more so among the better educated and qualified" (Timmins, 2002). This is a view likely to receive some support from Carter (2002), who on the basis of two consultancy reports says that the overall trust staff have in the companies they work for is in decline. What was interesting to note in the ESRC report was that despite the rise in more flexible hours, and team working, the supervision of staff by employers has also increased. Nowadays the conditions just described may not be reflected in increased staff turnover or industrial action, but may be manifested in absenteeism, lower productivity, and inflexibility (Timmins, 2002).

Guest and Conway (2002), in a report commissioned by the Chartered Institute of Personnel and Development, are inclined to take a less pessimistic view of the level of job dissatisfaction and negativity. They maintain that despite some decline in job satisfaction and pressures associated with long hours and a demanding workload, notably among public sector workers, they see no clear and consistent trend towards more negative experience of work, or of its more damaging impact on life as a whole. However, they acknowledge that employee involvement (e.g., participation in decision making) has in fact gone down. Likewise, concern about job security is not growing, but that might be explained by the buoyancy in the UK labour market from the angle of the employee. What is interesting is the finding that job security is not particularly important to a new generation of workers, who are likely to move jobs of their own accord.

ORGANISATIONAL COMMITMENT

Whereas job satisfaction focuses narrowly on the job, commitment to the organisation could be affected by a range of considerations. For example, people may be dissatisfied when they do not receive an expected promotion, or when a salary increase is less than expected. In such circumstances, organisational commitment could be adversely affected.

Commitment, a key ingredient in human resource management, could be defined as the relative strength of an individual's identification with and involvement in an organisation (Mowday, Porter, & Steers, 1982). Involvement could be reflected in the person's willingness to undertake duties beyond the standard requirements of the job. Organisational commitment arises when the employee strongly identifies with the organisation, agrees with its objectives and value systems, and is willing to expend effort on its behalf. But it would be unwise to view commitment as a phenomenon only applicable to a unitarist type of organisation (i.e., a single entity with a united goal). In fact, organisations are made up of a number of factions with different agendas and conflicting objectives, and commitment can be directed to specific aspects of the employee's experience at work—for example, the individual's geographic location, his or her section, department, or subsidiary company, or a trade union (Barling, Wade, & Fullagar, 1990; Becker & Billings, 1993; Coopey & Hartley, 1991; Reichers, 1985).

According to Guest and Conway (2002), employers who adopt appropriate human resource practices and make firm pledges to their workers in the psychological contract could find that commitment as well as satisfaction is higher and staff turnover is lower. But commitment appears to be weaker for employees on temporary contracts and for full-time employees working in an environment characterised by tight management control and ongoing surveillance.

An attempt has been made (see Table 9.6) to identify the component parts of commitment along similar lines to the descriptions of the three components of attitudes (Allen & Meyer, 1990). Using the framework in Table 9.6, one could offer explanations for the causes of organisational commitment. A view applicable to affective commitment might convey the following sentiment: "If the organisation is good to me, I will be loyal and hard working." It appears that intrinsic job factors (e.g., taxing assignments and personal autonomy) rather than extrinsic factors (e.g., working conditions, remuneration, and supervision) are most salient in fostering affective commitment (Dunham, Grube, & Constaneda, 1994; Mottaz, 1988). If, on the other hand, affective

TABLE 9.6

The component parts of commitment

Attitude	Commitment
Affective	*Affective*: A person's emotional attachment to the organisation
Behavioural	*Continuance*: A person's perception of the costs/risks of leaving the organisation
Cognitive	*Normative*: The obligation and responsibility felt by the individual in the organisation

commitment is low, then a desire to leave the organisation could be strong (Meyer, 1997). Of course, actually leaving the organisation is another matter because it all depends on employment opportunities.

A view applicable to continuance commitment unfolds itself as follows. People take stock of their track record, as well as their current worth in the open market. The outcome of this analysis could determine organisational commitment (Myer, Paunonen, Gellatly, Goffin, & Jackson, 1989). A view that might apply to normative commitment suggests that commitment is in some way influenced by the person's nature rather than what happens at work, and that some people are naturally committed, whereas others are not (Bateman & Strasser, 1984).

There are other causal factors to note, such as age and time spent in the organisation, the extent of participation in decision making, and perceived security of employment (Romzek, 1989; Steers, 1977). The participative leadership factor is endorsed by Glisson and Durick (1988), who also stress the importance of the age of the organisation and the educational attainment of employees. An explanation derived from Bem's (1967) self-perception theory, discussed earlier, might suggest that if employees do something that is of obvious benefit to the organisation (e.g., expend exceptional effort), they may reflect on this and then conclude that they must be committed to the organisation.

Instruments are available to measure the various dimensions of organisational commitment examined earlier. One such instrument, developed by Warr, Cook, and Wall (1979), tends to measure affective commitment.

With regard to consequences of organisational commitment, one should note the following. Organisational commitment is said to influence outcomes such as employee turnover and absenteeism (Mowday et al., 1982). As far as work performance is concerned, a distinction could be made between the different components of commitment examined earlier. For example, employees rated "high" on affective commitment tended to be better performers than those rated "low" (Myer et al., 1989). However, this relationship does not stand firm for those rated high on continuance commitment. High, as opposed to low, continuance commitment is partly based on one's poor external job marketability, and a contributory factor for the lack of employment opportunities could be that the person concerned is not very efficient or competent.

The concept of organisational citizenship has been discussed alongside organisational commitment. Organisational citizenship is a term used to describe the behaviour of individuals who make a positive overall contribution to the organisation. For example, such behaviour could be reflected in satisfactory performance at work in the normal course of events, but in addition the good citizen is prepared to work late when required, devotes time to assist new entrants to the organisation, is generally perceived as being helpful, and is committed to the success of the organisation. It is said that there is a stronger relationship between commitment and organisational citizenship than between commitment and job performance (Organ & Ryan, 1995). Finally, commitment is a two-way process, and employees may show a reluctance to commit themselves if they perceive themselves as expendable in the eyes of employers.

CHAPTER SUMMARY

- In defining attitudes, the three components of an attitude (cognitive, affective, and conative) were identified.

- A distinction was made between attitudes and values. With regard to values, a hierarchy of levels was examined as well as their determinants, such as genetic factors. Also, the work ethic and business ethics were examined as important issues in the study of values. It was stated that attitudes, which can be either positive or negative, act as filters in the selection of information.

- Personality and socialisation are important influences in the formation of attitudes. The influence of socialisation at work in the context of attitude formation was mentioned.

- Attitudes perform an important function in helping individuals adopt a stable view of the world in which they live. The functions of attitudes were discussed with reference to Katz's system of classification—i.e., instrumental or adjustive, ego defensive, expressive, and knowledge functions. In this context, a brief reference was made to the demands of the work environment.

- With respect to prejudice, which mainly has a negative connotation when discussing attitudes, the influence exerted by personality, beliefs, group, and culture was noted. The issue of discrimination as an offshoot of prejudice was raised. Suggestions were made about ways of reducing prejudice.

- Attitude change was examined from three angles: sources of attitude change; factors contributing to attitude change; and balance and consistency. Using Kelman's classification system, the sources of attitude change are compliance, identification, and internalisation.

- Factors contributing to attitude change were identified as group membership (where the power of social context reflected in the social information-processing approach was acknowledged), exposure to the mass media, forced contact, rewards, communication, and persuasion. With respect to persuasion, the elaboration likelihood model was examined. The factors contributing to attitude change were illustrated with reference to appropriate examples.

- A key concept in attitude change is balance and consistency. Basically this means that people strive for consistency between the components of an attitude as well as between attitudes and behaviour. Consistency theories were discussed with reference to balance theory, congruity theory, and cognitive dissonance theory. An alternative view to cognitive dissonance, in the form of self-perception theory, was introduced.

- The notion of attitude measurement was acknowledged, and the following techniques were described: the Thurstone scale; the Likert scale; Osgood's semantic differential; and sociometry. The qualities essential to any kind of measure—reliability and validity—were briefly explained.

- The relationship between attitudes and behaviour (drawing on the work of Fishbein and Ajzen) was introduced and illustrated with examples. The updated version of the theory of reasoned action in the form of the theory of planned behaviour was examined. An alternative view of the relationship between attitudes and behaviour, with the emphasis on the role of selective perception, was put forward. Moods and values as moderating factors in the relationship between attitudes and behaviour were examined.

- Job satisfaction and organisational commitment straddle several related attitudes in a narrow and broad sense within organisations, and their nature, cause, measurement, and consequences were analysed. The notion of organisational citizenship was introduced. Gender, emotion (including happiness), age, and education are factors to consider in the context of job satisfaction.

- The behavioural manifestations of job dissatisfaction were noted and there was reference to violence perpetrated by acutely dissatisfied workers.

QUESTIONS

(1) Explain what is meant by the components of an attitude.

(2) Distinguish between attitudes and values, and comment on the genetic basis of values.

(3) Examine the frameworks used to categorise values.

(4) Assess the significance of the work ethic in contemporary society.

(5) Reflect on the relevance of business ethics.

(6) What influences the formation of attitudes?

(7) Outline the functions performed by attitudes.

(8) Explain what is meant by prejudice and discrimination, and discuss the factors that give rise to prejudice.

(9) In what way does compliance differ from internalisation when the focus is on sources of attitude change?

(10) Why is the social information-processing approach referred to as a situational view of attitudes?

(11) Examine the merits and demerits of one-sided and two-sided arguments in the communication of messages designed to change attitudes.

(12) What is "the elaboration likelihood model" of persuasion?

(13) In connection with communication and persuasion, explain the following terms: (a) primacy effect; (b) public commitment; (c) threats and fear; (d) opinion leaders; (e) credibility; and (f) the sleeper effect.

(14) Discuss any one of the consistency theories and explore its application to business practice.

(15) What is the alternative view to cognitive dissonance?

(16) Examine the methods for measuring attitudes.

(17) Explain the theory of planned behaviour.

(18) "The relationship between job satisfaction and outcomes (e.g., performance and absenteeism) may not be as clear-cut as many people think." Discuss.

(19) What are the differences between job satisfaction, organisational commitment, and organisational citizenship?

(20) Identify the component parts of commitment.

(21) Consider the importance of genetic factors and emotion (including happiness) in the study of job satisfaction.

(22) Define job dissatisfaction and reflect on outcomes associated with it.

SPOTLIGHT ON RELEVANT READING

Ajzen, I. (2001). Nature and operation of attitudes. *Annual Review of Psychology*, *24*, 1251–1263.

Bohner, G., & Wanke, M. (2002). *Attitudes and attitude change*. Hove, UK: Psychology Press.

Gavin, J.H. (2004). The virtuous organization: The value of happiness in the workplace. *Organizational Dynamics*, *33*, 379–392.

Guest, D., & Conway, N. (2002). *Pressure at work and the psychological contract*. London: Chartered Institute of Personnel and Development.

Johnson, R. (2004). Diversity—What women want: The glass ceiling is still a firm fixture in most companies, with women finding it difficult to reach board level. *People Management*, 15 January, 26–30.

Wood, W. (2000). Attitude change: Persuasion and social influence. *Annual Review of Psychology*, *51*, 539–570.

Part III

The Group

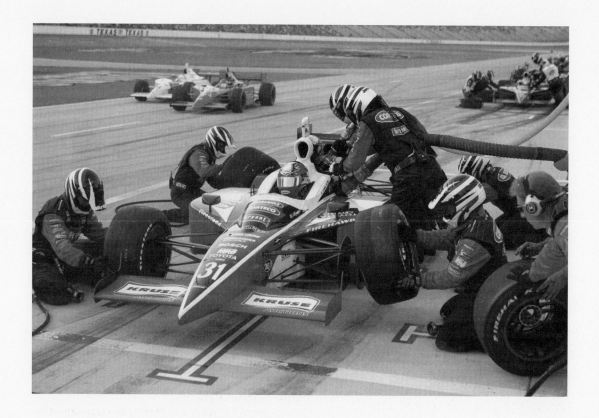

Learning Outcomes

After studying this chapter you should be able to:

- State what we mean by a group.

- List the different types of groups.

- Specify the key characteristics of groups.

- Provide reasons why people join groups.

- Recognise the group processes that exert influence on the attitudes and behaviour of members.

- Distinguish between group norms and groupthink, and discuss the ways in which both influence members.

- Appreciate the significance of social identity in inter-group behaviour.

Groups

10

Following a definition of a group and different types of groups, an analysis is provided of important characteristics of groups, and some reasons are given as to why people join groups. Next, the main focus is on key processes within groups, and this is followed by an examination of inter-group behaviour. This chapter connects with the discussion of autonomous work groups in Chapter 4 and decision making in Chapter 8. It also provides a foundation for later discussion of leadership (Chapter 12), conflict (Chapter 13), and organisational change and development (Chapter 16).

Contents

DEFINITION

How do we go about defining what we mean by a group? In the first instance, we can observe *interpersonal relationships* in a group and note that people communicate verbally and nonverbally. The behaviour of members of the group is influenced by *shared norms*, such as standards of behaviour or expectations. Members strive to achieve a *common objective*, normally under the influence of a leader or chairman. *Interdependency* is apparent when members of the group are dependent on each other for support and help. The more the members of the group interact to finish a job, the greater is the level of interdependency. When members of a group subscribe to common values, beliefs, and objectives, and there is a high level of agreement between them on these matters and how best to achieve the objectives of the group, a state of **cohesiveness** is said to exist. Cohesive groups emphasise the need for close cooperation in order to complete their various tasks in an effective way, and to create conditions in which the personal needs of members are satisfied.

This definition of a group might not include a silent order of nuns who do not interrelate in a dynamic way; also, there are occasions when members of a committee (a group) may not share group norms and, although they work together, one member could achieve his or her goals at the expense of the others. So it is difficult to arrive at an all-embracing definition of a group.

TYPES OF GROUPS

Groups can be referred to as belonging to certain types, and a classification of groups by type follows.

Formal or informal

Groups can be classified as either formal or informal. In a **formal group**, important objectives and roles performed by members are predetermined. For example, the quantity and quality of output, the requirement to adhere to safety standards, and desired behaviour in dealing with charge-hands and colleagues are either implicit or made explicit. In formally constituted groups it is also possible to find informal norms and behaviour.

By contrast, the **informal group** develops in a spontaneous fashion, and the objectives and roles found in this type of group arise from the current interactions of members. Once these objectives and roles are established, members normally subscribe to them because they consider themselves a group member or wish to be considered as such. A friendship or interest group, which consists of individuals who share one or more characteristics and perhaps meet also outside the place of work, could be considered in this context.

Primary or secondary

Groups can also be classified as either primary or secondary. A **primary group** is small in size, face-to-face contact is generally frequent, and relationships tend to be close and often intimate. A family, a playgroup, a sports team, or a tightly knit group of accountants in an organisation could constitute a primary group. A **secondary group** assumes more of an impersonal nature and may be geographically distant. A company, a hospital, or a school could fall into this category. This type of group is not necessarily a psychological group, but membership of it could influence a member's outlook.

Co-acting

A feature of a **co-acting group** is the level of independence experienced by group members. They may undertake either similar or dissimilar tasks within the group, but they do so independently of each other. The interdependency and cohesiveness referred to earlier would not apply to the co-acting group. However, members are likely to relate more to each other at the advanced stages of work processes or assignments where there may be a need for cooperation and coordination.

Counteracting

Counteracting groups have opposing aims and compete for scarce resources. In the process they may engage in a struggle for power and advantage. With regard to what goes on within each individual group, unity of purpose and mode of operation may feature prominently.

Reference

Reference groups may possess a certain attraction and, as a result, individuals may wish to join them, or merely to identify with them in some way. Therefore, a reference group can influence a person's outlook without that person being a member of it.

CHARACTERISTICS OF GROUPS

The following key characteristics of groups will be discussed in this section:

* norms;
* cohesiveness;
* communication and interaction;
* structural factors; and
* group dynamics.

Related topics, such as reference groups and decision making, will be examined later in the chapter in the section on "Group processes".

Norms

Social norms regulate the relationships between individuals in groups; in fact they are guides to behaviour on a number of issues ranging from how tasks are done and level of output to speed of action (Blau, 1995). Norms are collective because they are shared by many members of a group. They are only guides or expectations about what behaviour should be and, as such, allow us to anticipate other people's behaviour in specified circumstances. They are not necessarily followed in all circumstances. However, they can be enforced, and people are either positively rewarded for complying with them or punished for not complying. Norms usually reflect the values of the group (Zaltman & Wallandorf, 1979).

Though norms regulate behaviour in groups, some norms can be viewed more seriously than others simply because of the sanctions associated with contravening them. To depart from a group norm in a street gang could produce significant sanctions, and so members of the gang may break society's laws in order to escape the sanctions. Yablonsky (1967) has shown how an ordinary youth, a member of a violent gang, gets involved in brutal behaviour as a response to group pressure. This illustrates a powerful compulsion to adhere to group norms considered by many people, in this case, to be crude and unacceptable. But for the individual member of the gang, the fear of sanctions far surpasses general moral inhibitions. There are other circumstances depicted in experiments where deviation from a group norm would not activate any significant sanctions apart from the anxiety that would arise as a result of departing from the consensus established by a group. These are examples of internally imposed norms.

Externally imposed norms in, for example, an active military group, are various forms of discipline to which military personnel are required to adhere. Sanctions for the infringement of these norms can be heavy. By contrast, a sports team may typify a situation where norms are externally imposed, but sanctions applicable to deviations from the norms are modest; for instance, a footballer may receive only a caution for indulging in illegal play.

Somebody who chooses to ignore a group norm by, for example, persistently ignoring safety regulations at work can be referred to as a deviant. Pressure can be put on deviants to conform to group norms and this can take the form of verbal abuse, physical assault, silence, blacklisting, and physical exclusion from the group. Sometimes, one or more of these sanctions is levelled at a worker who fails to respond to officially approved strike action—he or she is considered to be a deviant by contravening the norm to withdraw labour in specified circumstances.

Norms are associated with the internal working of the group, but to the outsider it is generally the group's external image that is visible. The outsider recognises private language, technical

FIGURE 10.1

Communication networks (from Leavitt, 1951).

of attention is given to building and maintaining group morale. There is also an emphasis on participative management and encouraging employees to promptly correct any mistakes without stopping the production line. There is an expectation that employees will commit themselves fully, and gladly take up the slack for colleagues absent due to illness.

Some people believe that the overwhelming emphasis on high productivity generates stress, whereas others applaud the job security that success brings in its wake. It is claimed that Japanese management practices in car plants result in greater effort by employees, lower absenteeism, and lower staff turnover (Hodgetts, 1991). The danger of too much cohesion is that it could lead to an insufficient exploration of issues considered by the group. This is a topic that will be elaborated on later when discussing "groupthink".

Communication and interaction

In a study of communication networks, groups of four or five people were engaged in problem-solving tasks in different forms of groupings (Leavitt, 1951). Each person in a group receives a list of symbols (e.g., star, circle, wavy line). Although each list is different, all lists contain one symbol in common. The task is to find out as quickly as possible which is the common symbol. Subjects are only permitted to communicate with one another by written notes. The situations depicted in these studies are not like the small group in which communication is face-to-face and everyone can hear everyone else. They are rather more like situations found in large organisations where a number of people in different parts of the organisation are in touch with one another only

indirectly or, if directly, then frequently through relatively impersonal media such as telephone or e-mail.

The communication networks studied by Leavitt are shown in Figure 10.1. Problems were solved more quickly, there were fewer mistakes, and fewer messages were required in the more centralised network—i.e., the wheel. The person at the centre enjoyed himself much more than the other members of the group, and he was perceived as leader. In the decentralised network—the circle—performance was slower, more erratic, but enjoyable. It is suggested that centralised networks, such as the wheel, lend themselves to the efficient execution of simple tasks, but more complex tasks were found to be more effectively performed by less highly centralised networks, such as the circle or a network in which everybody communicates with everybody else (Shaw, 1964). The complex tasks required more than the mere collation of information in exercises connected with the construction of sentences and solving arithmetic problems. The central person in the wheel could be overwhelmed and overloaded when dealing with incoming messages and manipulating data in the complex tasks; so a centralised network would be inappropriate in these circumstances.

Reflecting on the managerial implications of communication networks, a number of observations can be made. For a work group confronting a variety of tasks and objectives, no single network is likely to be effective. For example, the wheel, with its simplicity and efficiency, can be less than functional in the event of low job satisfaction having an adverse effect on the motivational disposition of group members. If a situation exists where the work group is not adept at sharing information and considering alternatives in decision making, then there is the danger of not being able to handle complex problems requiring high interdependency among group members. Preference for a particular network and the nature of the task have to be considered. For example, a work group that prefers a network in which everybody communicates with everybody else (high interdependency), could experience difficulties in handling simple problems that require little interdependency between members (Hodgetts, 1991).

When people are interacting at work they are essentially engaged in two sets of activities—the accomplishment of tasks and the maintenance of the social fabric of the group. But a balance has to be struck between behaviour related to a task, and behaviour of a socio-emotional nature—i.e., social maintenance of the group. A well-known system embracing the two streams has been developed (Bales, 1950). It is called "interaction process analysis", and the 12 categories used are as follows. Socio-emotional/positive behaviours are:

(1) Shows solidarity, raises others' status, gives help, rewards.
(2) Shows tension release, jokes, laughs, shows satisfaction.
(3) Agrees, shows passive acceptance, understands, concurs, complies.

Tasks/attempted answers are:

(4) Gives suggestion, direction, implying autonomy for others.
(5) Gives opinion, evaluation, analysis, expresses feelings, wish.
(6) Gives orientation, information, repeats, clarifies, confirms.

Tasks/questions are:

(7) Asks for orientation, information, repetition, confirmation.
(8) Asks for opinion, evaluation, analysis, expression of feeling.
(9) Asks for suggestions, direction, possible ways of action.

Socio-emotional/negative behaviours are:

(10) Disagrees, shows passive rejection, formality, withholds help.
(11) Shows tension, asks for help, withdraws out of field.
(12) Shows antagonism, deflates others' status, defends or asserts self.

The 12 categories comprising the interaction process analysis system are claimed to be mutually exclusive. Verbal or nonverbal contributions by members of the group can be classified by a trained observer using this system as an aid in interactive skills training.

Bearing some similarity to the interaction process analysis system is a list of functional and nonfunctional behaviour devised by Benne and Sheats (1948) (see Panel 10.2). They recognise, as Bales does, a balance between task and social factors in the life of a group; they refer to the social dimension as group-building and maintenance. A, B, and C in the lists in Panel 10.2 are considered functional because they serve the interests of the group. By contrast, D is nonfunctional because this behaviour tends to make the group weak or inefficient.

In using a classification, such as D in Benne and Sheats' analysis, people need to guard against the tendency to blame any person (whether themselves or another) who falls into "nonfunctional behaviour". It is more useful to regard such behaviour as a symptom that all is not well with the group's ability to satisfy individual needs through group-centred activity. People need to be alert to the fact that each person is likely to interpret such behaviours differently. What appears to be nonfunctional behaviour may not necessarily be so, for the nature and content of that behaviour as well as group conditions must also be taken into account. For example, there are times when some forms of being aggressive contribute positively to the scene by clearing the air and instilling energy into the group.

Spatial factors

Spatial factors such as geographic proximity can also affect group communication and relationships, and the greater the opportunity to interact with other people the greater the likelihood that such

A: Task roles (functions required in selecting and carrying out a group task)

- *Initiating activity.* Proposing solutions, suggesting new ideas, new definitions of problems, new attack on problems, or new organisation of material.
- *Seeking information.* Asking for clarification of suggestions, requesting additional information or facts.
- *Seeking opinion.* Looking for an expression of feeling about something from the members, seeking clarification of values, suggestions, or ideas.
- *Giving information.* Offering facts or generalisations, relating one's own experience to the group problem to illustrate points.
- *Giving opinion.* Stating an opinion or belief concerning a suggestion or one of several suggestions, particularly concerning its value rather than its factual basis.
- *Elaborating.* Clarifying, giving examples or developing meanings, trying to envisage how a proposal might work if adopted.
- *Coordinating.* Showing relationships among various ideas or suggestions, trying to pull ideas and suggestions together, trying to draw together activities of various subgroups or members.
- *Summarising.* Pulling together related ideas or suggestions, restating suggestions after the group has discussed them.

B: Group-building and maintenance roles (functions required in strengthening and maintaining group life and activities)

- *Encouraging.* Being friendly, warm, responsive to others, praising others and their ideas, agreeing with and accepting contributions of others.
- *Gatekeeping.* Trying to make it possible for another member to make a contribution to the group by saying, "We haven't heard anything from Jim or Jane yet", or suggesting limited talking time for everyone so that all will have a chance to be heard.
- *Standard-setting.* Expressing standards for the group to use in choosing its content or procedures, or in evaluating its decisions, reminding the group to avoid decisions that conflict with group standards.
- *Following.* Going along with decisions of the group, thoughtfully accepting ideas of others, serving as an audience during group discussion.
- *Expressing group feeling.* Summarising what group feeling is sensed to be, describing reactions of the group to ideas or solutions.

C: Both group task and maintenance roles

- *Evaluating.* Submitting group decisions or accomplishments to comparison with group standards, measuring accomplishments against goals.
- *Diagnosing.* Determining sources of difficulties, appropriate steps to take next, analysing the main blocks to progress.
- *Testing for consensus.* Tentatively asking for group opinions in order to find out whether the group is nearing consensus on a decision, sending up trial balloons to test group opinions.
- *Mediating.* Harmonising, conciliating differences in points of view, making compromise solutions.
- *Relieving tension.* Draining off negative feeling by jesting or pouring oil on troubled waters, putting a tense situation in a wider context.

D: Types of nonfunctional behaviour

From time to time, more often perhaps than anyone likes to admit, people behave in nonfunctional ways that do not help, and sometimes actually harm, the group and the work it is trying to do. Some of the more common types of such nonfunctional behaviours are as follows:

- *Being aggressive.* Working for status by criticising or blaming others, showing hostility against the group or some individual, deflating the ego or status of others.
- *Blocking.* Interfering with the progress of the group by going off at a tangent, citing personal experiences unrelated to the problem, arguing too much on a point, rejecting ideas without consideration.
- *Self-confessing.* Using the group as a sounding board, expressing personal, non group-oriented feelings or points of view.
- *Competing.* Vying with others to produce the best idea, talk the most, play the most roles, gain favour with the leader.
- *Seeking sympathy.* Trying to induce other group members to be sympathetic to one's problems or misfortunes, deploring one's own situation, or disparaging one's own ideas to gain support.
- *Special pleading.* Introducing or supporting suggestions related to one's own pet concerns or philosophies, lobbying.
- *Horsing around.* Joking, mimicking, disrupting the work of the group.
- *Seeking recognition.* Attempting to call attention to oneself by loud or excessive talking, extreme ideas, unusual behaviour.
- *Withdrawal.* Being indifferent or passive, resorting to excessive formality, daydreaming, doodling, whispering to others, wandering from the subject.

meetings will give rise to the development of group norms and consensus (Festinger, Schachter, & Back, 1950). It would appear that homogeneity among subjects (in terms of age, intelligence, and social class) is important in this context. Different seating arrangements in groups were associated with different types of group task. Where children were given a competitive task, they chose to sit at right angles at a table, but when they were given a cooperative task they sat side-by-side.

Students participated more in discussions when the seating arrangement was a circular layout of chairs (Sommer, 1967). It is clear that decisions customarily taken by architects and interior designers have a marked effect on group structures and relationships. It is sometimes suggested that the ideal arrangement is the loose oval seating plan adopted by five or so people meeting for informal discussion. A rule of thumb is to increase the distance of people from the hub or centre until they are almost out of the bounds of communication. Then the desks and apparatus required for work can be positioned. Ancillary facilities, such as communal files, rest areas, and soft-drink dispensers should be spread widely so that people are encouraged to stand up and walk around for at least 2 in every 20 minutes. It should be borne in mind that our bodies do not like immobility and our span of attention is limited (Lately, 1982).

Personal space. In interactions with others, we allow people we know well to enter our **personal space**. A stranger entering into this territory could be perceived as a threat. Effectively, he or she violates our personal space by entering a zone not reserved for the invader. The invasion of personal space may cause discomfort, tension, and flight, and could lead to an over-aroused state. A state of over-arousal can be associated with reduced performance. Also, people whose space is invaded could turn away or withdraw, or alternatively ignore the fact that their space has been invaded by creating greater distance between them and the intruder. In public transport, as a train becomes overcrowded, the contraction of space is evident and this could lead to discomfort. To cope with such a situation, people often stare at the floor or into space.

Personal space considerations can be influenced by cultural factors. It is said that the Germans have larger personal space areas, and are less flexible than the Americans. The Latin Americans, the French, and particularly the Arabs require smaller space zones than the Americans (Oborne, 1995).

Landscaped office. One solution to people's need for space is to allow them freedom to arrange the workplace as they wish. The landscaped office does not have boundaries, and offers flexibility in the use of space. In the absence of walls and partitions, the need for personal space and privacy is met by having low moveable screens, and by allowing employees to arrange desks—within limits—as they see fit. The way work groups are scattered would normally reflect the pattern of the process of work. It has been suggested that all staff—managerial, supervisory, and clerical—should participate in the open-plan office in order to foster overall group cohesiveness and increased productivity. Also, the flow of information between the different groups of employees could be facilitated (Brookes & Kaplan, 1972), and there would be an incentive to create a colourful design for the office.

But the concept of the landscaped office has been criticised. It has been said that there would be a pronounced loss of privacy, increased noise, distractions, and interruptions (Nemecek & Grandjean, 1973). In addition, people's absences can be readily seen; the nature of what people are doing is also visible, as are the various interactions in which they are engaged. As a consequence, the question of monitoring and surveillance arises, which can make people feel uneasy. Because of the lack of privacy, people may feel a certain lack of control, even though they may have physical control over the arrangement of the immediate space. There appears to be no strong research evidence to support the claims of the proponents of the landscaped office (Oborne, 1995).

Structural factors

Work groups have a structure that influences the behaviour of members. In this section certain characteristics of groups, often called structural factors, will be examined. These include:

* the nature of the structure and atmosphere;
* roles;
* status;
* composition;
* size; and
* management of the group (leadership).

Structure and atmosphere

The structure and atmosphere of a group have a part to play in facilitating the performance of tasks and the satisfaction of individual needs. The connection between innovation and group structure has been emphasised (Meadows, 1980a, 1980b). Innovation in this sense means the ability to generate and implement new ideas and to cope with change in the application of new technology or work practices, and developing new products. The characteristic of group structure that was related to innovation was the "organic" type. In the organic structure there tends to be less of a bureaucratic outlook on the part of group members, with built-in flexibility manifested in greater awareness of organisational objectives, less reliance on formality with respect to jobs and organisational relationships, and far more consultation and discussion. The research described earlier conveys the message that the management process should be flexible, and that work groups should be handled with a certain sensitivity, particularly when they are involved in problem-solving activities.

Other features of the organic work group are: the group has a high level of autonomy on matters connected with the use of technology and appropriate organisational arrangements; there tends to be flexibility in taking decisions as to when it is appropriate to deploy groups; there exists an appropriate mix of relevant knowledge, abilities, and skills in the group with members having similar values and beliefs, and agreeing on goals to be achieved; people work well together as a team supported by effective communication.

The opposite of the organic group is the mechanistic group, which tends to be bound by rules with established norms for making decisions, and

in which it is difficult to move outside the organisational guidelines. Features of overall organisational structure, including mechanistic and organic systems, are discussed in Chapter 14.

Roles

Members play a particular role in a group, and the way an employee perceives and performs his or her role in a group has a material influence on how the group functions. A role could be defined as a set of expected patterns of behaviour attributable to a person occupying a particular position. Frequently, a role is prescribed by the role occupant's job description. In life we all play a number of roles inside and outside work, and our behaviour can vary with the role we are playing. There are three aspects to roles that should be noted. The first, which has been referred to earlier, is the "expected role". For example, financial accountants are expected to participate in the process of preparing the statutory accounts of the company.

The concept of role expectations can be considered in the context of the "psychological contract". This is an unwritten agreement that exists between employers and their employees, and it sets out what management expects from its staff and vice versa (Robinson, Kraatz, & Rousseau, 1994). In essence this contract defines the behavioural expectations that accompany each role. Management is expected to treat employees fairly, offer a realistic workload, and provide feedback on the employees' performance. Employees are expected to respond by displaying a positive attitude, adhering to what is required of them, and showing loyalty to the organisation.

What is likely to happen if role expectations, as implied by the psychological contract, are not met? If management fails to honour its side of the bargain, the commitment and motivation of staff could suffer, leading to lower productivity, whereas dereliction on the part of employees could give rise to disciplinary action or severance. The psychological contract is a powerful determinant of behaviour in organisations, and therefore it goes without saying that one should not ignore the importance of communicating clearly when transmitting role expectations. There is further comment on the psychological contract in Chapter 9 in connection with job satisfaction and commitment.

The second aspect of roles is the "perceived role", which embraces those activities or behaviours the individual or role occupant believes are necessary to fulfil the expected role. Financial accountants, having realised what is expected of them in the preparation of accounts, engage in various interactions with colleagues that they consider are part of the overall duties. So, from the expected role, a person develops the perceived role.

The third aspect of roles is the "enacted role", which springs from the perceived role. This is the way a person actually behaves. For example, as financial accountants interact with colleagues, they adopt a pattern of behaviour, such as asking questions, discussing issues, uttering words of encouragement, providing information, and so on. Many of the things role occupants say and do during the exchanges will be determined by their understanding of the best way of executing the perceived role.

Role ambiguity. As a person moves from the expected to the perceived role, a big problem is **role ambiguity**. This arises when people are uncertain about their duties, responsibilities, or authority, or all three (Peterson et al., 1995). Role ambiguity can arise because of lack of sufficient guidance in job descriptions or explanations by superiors, and results in confusion, conflict, and lower levels of performance.

Role conflict. This arises when a person performs more than one role, and performance in one role makes performance in the other more difficult (Peterson et al., 1995). For example, successful senior executives may experience role conflict, and attempt to reconcile the expectations placed on them as a spouse, parent, and corporate official. An extreme form of role conflict arises when two or more role expectations contradict each other.

There are at least five types of **role conflict**:

(1) *Intra-role conflict.* This occurs when a person experiences conflicting requirements in the job. For example, in a study of supermarket cashiers it was found that the greatest demands originated from the customers as opposed to managers and co-workers, and that the demands of customers often conflicted with managerial or organisational rules and instructions (Rafaeli, 1989).

(2) *Inter-role conflict.* This occurs when a person experiences conflict between a number of roles to which he or she has been allocated. For example, in the performance appraisal process a manager may experience conflict between the role of evaluator about to make a negative assessment, and the day-to-day role of the supportive manager when faced with a subordinate whose performance is unsatisfactory.

(3) *Intra-sender conflict.* This is seen, for example, when a manager conveys the impression to a subordinate of being very satisfied with his or her performance, and that an upgrading is a mere formality. However, to the great surprise of that subordinate, the upgrading goes to another subordinate. In this case, contradictory messages originating from a single source reach the recipient.

(4) *Person–role conflict.* This emerges when a person's values are incompatible with the behaviour appropriate to the performance of the role. For example, on the issue of ethics in business one study found that 57% of *Harvard Business Review* readers had to confront the dilemma of having to choose between what was profitable for the organisation and what was ethical (Brenner & Molander, 1977).

(5) *Role overload.* This type of conflict arises when a person is inundated with work, and considers it almost impossible to perform the expected role. In such circumstances it is obviously necessary to prioritise the various activities in order to handle them to an acceptable level (Jackson & Schuler, 1985).

Coping with role ambiguity and conflict. A number of avenues are open to those afflicted by problems connected with role ambiguity and role conflict. One approach could be to live with them, but this does not seem to be an acceptable way to

- Directive leadership becomes more acceptable.
- Job satisfaction is lower than in smaller groups.
- Subgroups may spring into existence, and problems could arise when the subgroups do not share the main group's objectives and prefer to pursue rather parochial interests.
- An odd number of members in a group is preferred over groups with an even number because this eliminates the possibility of a tie after votes are cast.

Social loafing.   Members may engage in **social loafing** (i.e., hide "in the crowd") within a group: Why should I contribute conscientiously when I believe others are withholding effort? I'll also withhold effort. And this is more likely to happen in a larger rather than smaller group. In social loafing the average productivity of each member decreases. In other words, the productivity of the group as a whole is not at least equal to the sum of the productivity of each group member because individuals show a tendency to expend less effort when working collectively than when working individually (Comer, 1995).

Explanations for social loafing embrace views such as, if one perceives others in a group not pulling their weight then the perceiver adjusts his or her contribution downwards. In addition, diffusion of responsibility may take root. For example, because a group member realises that his or her contribution to the group effort is incapable of measurement, there is the temptation to ride on the back of the group and coast along at idling speed (Latane, Williams, & Harkins, 1979).

Is the simplicity or complexity of the task influential in terms of social loafing? Robbins (1995) maintains that social loafing can occur even when a task is thought-provoking, where the person is involved in the task, and the activity lends itself to a unique contribution. For example, some workers in self-directed teams in work associated with the generation of ideas in connection with the implementation of proposals look for a free ride. One way of addressing social loafing with a view to reducing it is to ensure that the rewards received by the individual are related to his or her performance (George, 1995), but this could be difficult to achieve in certain areas of practice.

It has been suggested that social loafing is likely to occur in an individualistic culture dominated by self-interest, because it will maximise an individual's personal gain. An example of a society fitting this description is the United States. Social loafing is not expected to appear in collective societies (e.g., China) as it is believed that individuals in such cultures are motivated by group goals rather than self-interest. There is evidence to suggest that the social loafing effect existed among US management trainees but not among their Chinese counterparts. The Chinese seem to perform better in a group situation than working alone (Earley, 1989, 1993). Therefore, it would appear that the social loafing effect is culture specific, being most prevalent in individualistic cultures.

The most obvious way to counteract the effects of social loafing in work situations where cooperation is necessary is to make serious attempts to identify individual contributions and, according to Kreitner et al. (2002), hold group members accountable for identifiable portions of the group's task. Apparently, in circumstances where it is possible to identify personal contributions, and individuals are committed to the group, then we could expect to find forces that could counteract the effects of social loafing, even in individualistic societies (Erez & Somech, 1996).

Finally, many organisations might consider a group of five to seven to be ideal. However, hard evidence about an ideal size for groups is thin on the ground.

Leadership

Leadership is an important structural characteristic of a group. It can be both formal and informal.

Formal leadership is bestowed on the leader or manager of the group by the organisation with the authority to use rewards and sanctions. By contrast, an informal leader derives a mandate from the group members and usually reflects the group's values. In addition, the informal leader can be of practical assistance to members in a number of ways, including acting as spokesperson for the group. Rarely does one find formal and informal leadership residing in one person, comment on the psychological contract in Chapter 9 in connection with job satisfaction and commitment.

The second aspect of roles is the "perceived role", which embraces those activities or behaviours the individual or role occupant believes are necessary to fulfil the expected role. Financial accountants, having realised what is expected of them in the preparation of accounts, engage in various interactions with colleagues that they consider are part of the overall duties. So, from the expected role, a person develops the perceived role.

The third aspect of roles is the "enacted role", which springs from the perceived role. This is the way a person actually behaves. For example, as financial accountants interact with colleagues, they adopt a pattern of behaviour, such as asking questions, discussing issues, uttering words of encouragement, providing information, and so on. Many of the things role occupants say and do during the exchanges will be determined by their understanding of the best way of executing the perceived role.

Role ambiguity. As a person moves from the expected to the perceived role, a big problem is **role ambiguity**. This arises when people are uncertain about their duties, responsibilities, or authority, or all three (Peterson et al., 1995). Role ambiguity can arise because of lack of sufficient guidance in job descriptions or explanations by superiors, and results in confusion, conflict, and lower levels of performance.

Role conflict. This arises when a person performs more than one role, and performance in one role makes performance in the other more difficult (Peterson et al., 1995). For example, successful senior executives may experience role conflict, and attempt to reconcile the expectations placed on them as a spouse, parent, and corporate official. An extreme form of role conflict arises when two or more role expectations contradict each other.

There are at least five types of **role conflict**:

(1) *Intra-role conflict.* This occurs when a person experiences conflicting requirements in the job. For example, in a study of supermarket cashiers it was found that the greatest demands originated from the customers as opposed to managers and co-workers, and that the demands of customers often conflicted with managerial or organisational rules and instructions (Rafaeli, 1989).

(2) *Inter-role conflict.* This occurs when a person experiences conflict between a number of roles to which he or she has been allocated. For example, in the performance appraisal process a manager may experience conflict between the role of evaluator about to make a negative assessment, and the day-to-day role of the supportive manager when faced with a subordinate whose performance is unsatisfactory.

(3) *Intra-sender conflict.* This is seen, for example, when a manager conveys the impression to a subordinate of being very satisfied with his or her performance, and that an upgrading is a mere formality. However, to the great surprise of that subordinate, the upgrading goes to another subordinate. In this case, contradictory messages originating from a single source reach the recipient.

(4) *Person–role conflict.* This emerges when a person's values are incompatible with the behaviour appropriate to the performance of the role. For example, on the issue of ethics in business one study found that 57% of *Harvard Business Review* readers had to confront the dilemma of having to choose between what was profitable for the organisation and what was ethical (Brenner & Molander, 1977).

(5) *Role overload.* This type of conflict arises when a person is inundated with work, and considers it almost impossible to perform the expected role. In such circumstances it is obviously necessary to prioritise the various activities in order to handle them to an acceptable level (Jackson & Schuler, 1985).

Coping with role ambiguity and conflict. A number of avenues are open to those afflicted by problems connected with role ambiguity and role conflict. One approach could be to live with them, but this does not seem to be an acceptable way to proceed. Role problems, as reported in Chapter 19, can be a significant source of stress, and eventually the person could become a victim of stress, leading to resigning from the organisation or withdrawing from certain activities to the detriment of the organisation.

Alternatively, a proactive stance can be taken and, in the event of role ambiguity, the person approaches the superior seeking clarification. In the case of role conflict, a number of approaches may be worth pursuing (Hodgetts, 1991). For example, where conflict due to role overload occurs, prioritise the tasks to be done, and if possible delegate the activities you cannot complete, or arrange for them to be reallocated. Where person–role conflict is experienced, cite the organisation's code of ethics, if there is one and it is supportive of your position, or simply refuse to engage in behaviour that contravenes your system of values. Where inter-role conflict is experienced, recognise that it is necessary to function in a number of areas, and seek the advice and support of others in approaching the unpalatable tasks.

Status

Status is the social ranking given to an individual because of the position he or she occupies in a group. Various factors may contribute to status, such as seniority, title, salary, and power, and any one of these factors could be critical in bestowing status. Naturally, status must exist in the eyes of those who confer it. Because status plays an important role in how people are treated, it assumes importance for many people.

Sometimes status is acquired as a birthright, but generally nowadays people acquire status in an organisational system on the basis of merit. Position in the organisational hierarchy conveys status—for example, the position of the HR director or chief executive. In other situations, groups of employees could be at the same hierarchical level, but the jobs they do are critical determinants of status. For example, a senior accountant and a senior production executive, although attached to different functions, occupy positions at the same level within the organisation. But there may be a general perception within the organisation that accountants enjoy higher status relative to production executives.

There are people in groups whose status is influenced primarily by their personal attributes, but the most powerful combination arises when status rests on both personality and position. Symbols of status, such as titles, are badges of identification that communicate differences in organisational rank, and are said to provide stability and predictability concerning role expectations and the appropriateness of conduct and behaviour. In addition, they provide incentives for people to strive for improved performance and advancement.

Two common problems with status are "status incongruency" and "status discrepancy" (Hodgetts, 1991). Status incongruency arises when there is disagreement among members of the group about an individual's status. For example, a particular executive is perceived to be on the same level in a number of respects with colleagues. However, the particular executive is in receipt of an inferior remuneration package. So there is incongruency between the executive's position and an important status symbol, and this could create some confusion in interpersonal relations.

Status discrepancy happens when people engage in activities considered to be out of keeping with their status. For example, if the chief executive of an industrial company was to lunch with the operatives in the factory canteen, this could be viewed by some as discrepant behaviour in a status sense. It is as if there is an expectation that people should stay within their reference groups—i.e., groups with which they can identify and the values and behaviour of which they have adopted.

Composition

When the composition of a group is considered, there tends to be an emphasis on *homogeneity* and *heterogeneity*. A homogeneous group is said to exist when the profile of members (e.g., age, experience, education, specialism, and cultural origins) is similar in one or more ways that are relevant to the functioning of the group. In the heterogeneous group, the profile of members is dissimilar. However, in a particular work group one could encounter aspects of both homogeneity and heterogeneity. This could arise where there is dissimilarity with regard to some factors (e.g., age or experience), but similarity in respect of a major factor such as a technical specialism (e.g., a research chemist in a drug company). In this example, the tendency would be to describe the group as homogeneous because the major factor is critical in terms of group functioning.

In recent years, "**group demography**" has captured the interest of researchers. This amounts to the degree to which members of a group share a common demographic attribute such as age, sex, race, educational level, or time spent in the organisation. Heterogeneity within a group with respect to age and time spent within the group has been associated with staff turnover (O'Reilly, Caldwell, & Barnett, 1989). That means that groups with members who are of different ages or who possess different levels of experience are likely to show frequent changes in membership due to turnover.

Why should this be so? One explanation is that staff turnover is likely to be greater among those with profoundly dissimilar experience because communication is more difficult, and conflict and power struggles are more likely and more potent when they occur. The increase in conflict makes membership of the group less attractive, leading to the likely departure of members. Also, the losers in a struggle for power are likely to leave or be forced to go (Robbins, 2003). By contrast, a homogeneous group is likely to have less conflict, fewer differences of opinion, freer communication, and more interaction.

Certain variables are said to intervene in the relationship between type of group and effectiveness (Moorhead & Griffin, 2004). A homogeneous group is likely to be more productive in situations where the tasks facing the group are simple and in sequence, cooperation is necessary, and prompt action is required. An example of such a situation would be a minor disaster facing a group of fire fighters from the local fire brigade. A heterogeneous group is more likely to be productive when the task is complex and requires creative effort, and the group draws on a diverse range of skills in its collective effort. A group of advertising executives with mixed backgrounds asked to prepare interesting and novel advertisements projecting the attractiveness of a novel project would fall into this category. A wide range of perspectives could be explored in such a group, with the potential for much discussion and differences of opinion.

Culturally heterogeneous groups—e.g., diversity created by racial or national differences—would also appear to be well placed to offer a variety of perspectives with beneficial consequences. However, members in this type of group may experience difficulties learning to work with each other and solving problems (Watson, Kumar, & Michaelsen, 1993), but difficulties in learning to work with each other could wane over time.

Finally, the composition of a group becomes a critical issue when companies enter into joint ventures with other companies overseas.

Size

The size of the group has some bearing on its performance. Smaller groups give people the opportunity to interact frequently, facilitate the free flow of information, and provide a setting in which it is easier to reach agreement. The larger group has at its disposal more resources, and is more likely to have formalised communication processes and bureaucratic practices. In the larger group the potential influence of any individual is limited, but it is said that groups with more members tend to produce more ideas and seem to be better at problem solving than smaller groups. Beyond a certain point, the rate of increase in the number of ideas diminishes swiftly as the group grows (Shaw, 1981). Also, a stage is reached in the growth of the size of the group when the corresponding increase in the complexity of interactions and communications makes it more difficult for the larger group to coordinate activities, retain cohesiveness, and arrive at a consensus. The larger group may also inhibit participation by some members who despair at the lack of an opportunity to make a meaningful contribution to the deliberations.

Other observations about the consequences of increasing size in groups are:

- Directive leadership becomes more acceptable.
- Job satisfaction is lower than in smaller groups.
- Subgroups may spring into existence, and problems could arise when the subgroups do not share the main group's objectives and prefer to pursue rather parochial interests.
- An odd number of members in a group is preferred over groups with an even number because this eliminates the possibility of a tie after votes are cast.

Social loafing.   Members may engage in **social loafing** (i.e., hide "in the crowd") within a group: Why should I contribute conscientiously when I believe others are withholding effort? I'll also withhold effort. And this is more likely to happen in a larger rather than smaller group. In social loafing the average productivity of each member decreases. In other words, the productivity of the group as a whole is not at least equal to the sum of the productivity of each group member because individuals show a tendency to expend less effort when working collectively than when working individually (Comer, 1995).

Explanations for social loafing embrace views such as, if one perceives others in a group not pulling their weight then the perceiver adjusts his or her contribution downwards. In addition, diffusion of responsibility may take root. For example, because a group member realises that his or her contribution to the group effort is incapable of measurement, there is the temptation to ride on the back of the group and coast along at idling speed (Latane, Williams, & Harkins, 1979).

Is the simplicity or complexity of the task influential in terms of social loafing? Robbins (1995) maintains that social loafing can occur even when a task is thought-provoking, where the person is involved in the task, and the activity lends itself to a unique contribution. For example, some workers in self-directed teams in work associated with the generation of ideas in connection with the implementation of proposals look for a free ride. One way of addressing social loafing with a view to reducing it is to ensure that the rewards received by the individual are related to his or her performance (George, 1995), but this could be difficult to achieve in certain areas of practice.

It has been suggested that social loafing is likely to occur in an individualistic culture dominated by self-interest, because it will maximise an individual's personal gain. An example of a society fitting this description is the United States. Social loafing is not expected to appear in collective societies (e.g., China) as it is believed that individuals in such cultures are motivated by group goals rather than self-interest. There is evidence to suggest that the social loafing effect existed among US management trainees but not among their Chinese counterparts. The Chinese seem to perform better in a group situation than working alone (Earley, 1989, 1993). Therefore, it would appear that the social loafing effect is culture specific, being most prevalent in individualistic cultures.

The most obvious way to counteract the effects of social loafing in work situations where cooperation is necessary is to make serious attempts to identify individual contributions and, according to Kreitner et al. (2002), hold group members accountable for identifiable portions of the group's task. Apparently, in circumstances where it is possible to identify personal contributions, and individuals are committed to the group, then we could expect to find forces that could counteract the effects of social loafing, even in individualistic societies (Erez & Somech, 1996).

Finally, many organisations might consider a group of five to seven to be ideal. However, hard evidence about an ideal size for groups is thin on the ground.

Leadership

Leadership is an important structural characteristic of a group. It can be both formal and informal.

Formal leadership is bestowed on the leader or manager of the group by the organisation with the authority to use rewards and sanctions. By contrast, an informal leader derives a mandate from the group members and usually reflects the group's values. In addition, the informal leader can be of practical assistance to members in a number of ways, including acting as spokesperson for the group. Rarely does one find formal and informal leadership residing in one person, though it is possible. The informal leadership role could be short-lived if the person lacks the ability and skills to exert influence in coping with the changing scene.

In recent years the self-directed group has asserted itself. In self-managed or self-directed groups the leadership rotates naturally to the person best qualified to run specific parts of a task, and supervisory positions become less important and may even be removed. An elaboration of this theme appears in the next chapter, and there is a discussion of leadership in Chapter 12.

Group dynamics

A psychoanalytical view of the dynamics of a group recognises the group's emotional impact on the individual's behaviour because of considerations of conformity, loyalty, and identification with and reaction to the group. According to Freud, libidinal or sexual impulses are inhibited, and identification with the leader takes place, though this could lead to envy and competition between members for the chance to replace the leader (Freud, 1955). A discussion of the psychoanalytical view appears in Chapter 2 on personality.

It is conceivable that when the individual is acting alone, he or she is more reality-oriented and more efficient intellectually than when exposed to the stultifying effect of interaction in a group. From his observational experiments with groups of soldiers undergoing therapy, Bion (1961) refers to the unconscious contributions by members to the group mentality. For example, an atmosphere of hostility in a group does not come out of nowhere; members unconsciously contribute to it even though individually they may deny it. Bion recognises the existence of a mechanism below the surface of the group and made up of three functions, which has the express purpose of resolving group tensions. The three functions are flight or fight, dependency, and pairing:

(1) *Flight or fight.* The group sees its survival as being dependent on either fighting (e.g., use of aggression or physical attacks) or fleeing (e.g., being passive or withdrawing from the scene). Although designed to protect the group and ensure its survival, this could be destructive. The group appears to want to fight somebody in the group, including the leader, or ignore issues by replacing them with anything other than the appropriate issues.

(2) *Dependency.* The group is concerned with procedural matters (e.g., good committee practice) so that it can feel secure. The concern is to ensure that the group continues to exist and function in a predictable way. Equally the group would like to alleviate its insecurity by becoming dependent on a leader or somebody aspiring to that role.

(3) *Pairing.* Two members of the group, one of whom could be the leader, express warmth that could lead to closeness. They enter into discussion, while the remaining members listen and are attentive. The matters under discussion could hinge on a change of leadership or a change in the direction of the group in order to improve its effectiveness.

Anxiety and discomfort can arise as a result of the flight or fight function, complacency and security can stem from dependency, and guilt can follow on from pairing because the group is not making headway in the task of changing the situation. Pressures are generated internally, arising from the dynamics of the group, as well as imposed externally—for example, nursing mentally handicapped patients in understaffed conditions. The psychoanalytical view emphasises the dysfunctional aspects of group dynamics, but it should be noted that the working life of the group is not always dominated by these pressures.

REASONS FOR JOINING GROUPS

People have a need to develop relationships with others, and therefore companionship is one reason why people join groups. Sometimes a job may not be very interesting, but belonging to a work group could provide the interest and diversity that is lacking in the job. When a person enters a new situation or encounters unfamiliar surroundings he or she may feel lost or lonely; it is in circumstances like these that a friendly group can be of immense benefit.

Another reason for joining a group is the need to identify with the group. Belonging to a group where one can share the experiences of one's immediate colleagues can be an important source of job satisfaction and, as a result, loyalty to the group can over-ride loyalty to the organisation. The group may also provide a sympathetic ear when we experience tension or frustration. Likewise, we rely on the group to provide guidance on the correct behaviour to adopt in particular circumstances, or to provide answers to difficult questions. This could apply to an inexperienced recruit in an organisation.

People sometimes join groups in order to obtain power because they wish to control others or want the status that accompanies a leadership role. Some, however, have a desire to be dependent or submissive. Associating with others may not be prompted by a need for dependence; instead it may be a self-protection strategy employed by an individual when, for example, he or she joins a trade union. Finally, groups provide a refuge for those who seek a certain degree of anonymity in a social setting.

GROUP PROCESSES

Group processes are discussed by focusing on the following:

- reference groups;
- social comparison;
- co-action and affiliation;
- social control;
- decision making;
- effective groups; and
- inter-group behaviour.

Reference groups

Groups can exert a powerful influence on the attitudes and behaviour of members. People are not only influenced by groups to which they currently belong, but also by reference groups, which they

refer to in arriving at an opinion or judgement. Reference groups may provide a normative or comparative reference point, or both. They may not always be real groups; it may be a single individual who symbolises a group perspective on life, or it may be a group that never meets— e.g., "well-rounded people".

A *normative* reference group is one from which the individual obtains certain standards. The individual is influenced by the norms, values, and attitudes of the group as well as its total outlook on life. The aspiring entrant to a profession, such as chartered accountancy, may be influenced profoundly by the persona of chartered accountants before being admitted to professional membership. This is referred to as *anticipatory socialisation*.

A *comparative* reference group is used as a focus when the individual compares the predicament and characteristics of members of the reference group with his or her own situation or that of his or her group. Reference groups chosen may be those seen as very similar to the individual's own group or those with which he or she can identify. These groups are important in determining whether the individual feels relatively satisfied or dissatisfied after engaging in the comparative exercise. Both normative and comparative reference groups may be used as positive frames of reference when the groups are admired or envied or, alternatively, as negative frames of reference from which individuals disassociate themselves, or that they reject.

In the study reported in Panel 10.3, Newcombe (1943) concluded that a change in attitude is affected by the way in which an individual relates himself or herself to the total membership group and one or more reference groups within it. A change in attitude could also depend on the strength of the initial attitude prior to exposure to group influences, the perceived discrepancy between the person's attitudes and the attitudes of members of the membership group, and the personality of the individual in the light of perceived pressures from the group. Therefore, a factory operative with regressive safety attitudes who works in a progressive safety environment may not necessarily be influenced by the enlightened attitudes of his or her membership or reference

PANEL 10.3: Reference groups and Bennington College

Newcombe (1943) uses the "reference" concept in his study of women students at an expensive American residential college (Bennington College). In the 1930s most of the girls came from wealthy conservative families and, on arrival at college, held conservative political views. During their 4-year stay at the college they were exposed to the more liberal or radical attitudes of the teaching staff and senior students. A feature of the educational approach at the college at that time was discussion of a wide range of social problems; in part this was prompted by the experience of the Great Depression and President Roosevelt's New Deal. There was also a belief that the girls should be exposed to issues affecting the contemporary world. Over the 4 years a number of the girls experienced a marked shift in their attitudes, from relatively conservative to relatively liberal.

How can this phenomenon be explained? Bennington College was the girls' membership group, but this in itself would not explain the shift towards attitudes held in high regard by the college. The crucial factor appears to be that the college community was taken as either a positive or negative reference group for the political attitudes of the students. The college community was taken as a negative reference group for the girls who remained conservative in outlook; they used the home or family group as a positive reference group. For some girls the college remained a negative reference group for political attitudes, but a positive reference group for social attitudes. But the vast majority of the students did alter their political outlook, taking the college as a positive reference group and possibly the parents and family as a negative reference group.

The girls who remained unaffected by the college's political attitudes may have had well thought out conservative opinions, rather than mere compliance with parental views, prior to joining the college. Alternatively, in the estimation of Newcombe, they were over-dependent on their home and parents, or they had other interests and did not take either the college or home as a reference point for their political attitudes.

group. Likewise, a stubborn and obstinate character may resist group pressures even though acceptance of such pressures could be beneficial to all concerned.

Reverting to the Bennington College study, Newcombe (1967) and his colleagues carried out a follow-up study 25 years later. They found that very few of the women had reverted to the conservative attitudes that they had on entering the college. The women and their husbands, where appropriate, expressed more liberal attitudes than a comparable sample of American women of the same socio-economic grouping. One interpretation of this finding might indicate that the college remained a vital reference group and focus in the lives of the women, and the persistence of their liberal views was assisted by their choice of spouse and friends.

Turning to business applications, reference groups influence consumer behaviour in at least two ways. They set levels of aspiration for individuals by offering cues as to what lifestyle and related purchasing patterns they should strive to achieve. They also define the actual items considered acceptable for displaying this level of aspiration—i.e., the kind of housing, clothing, car, etc. appropriate for a member to retain his or her status in a group. Manufacturers place importance on getting their brand identified with a particular reference group, and advertisers have made effective use of reference groups in marketing a wide range of products.

Social comparison

A reasonable degree of conformity, and hence predictability, is necessary for successful living in a social environment. When we find ourselves in a particular group situation, it is of immense value to have previously given some thought to what others consider the correct response to make in a particular situation—e.g., the best way to behave at an interview. Also, we may consider other people's views before deciding on the most suitable views to express on religious, social, work, and political issues, as well as the use of a particular vocabulary in conversation, or the most suitable clothes to wear at a party. For example, an able quality controller is continually comparing his or her views on quality with those of other experts in the field, as well as relevant line managers who have something useful to say. It is natural for people to compare their own judgements on a particular issue with the judgement of others who are in close proximity to them so that they can check out the validity of these judgements.

Kelman (1958) identifies three processes of social influence that have an impact on the individual—compliance, identification, and internalisation (referred to in the previous chapter as the sources of attitude change):

- *Compliance* arises when individuals conform to the expectations of the group because the group has the power to reward them if they conform to the group's norms or values, and to punish them if they fail to do so.
- *Identification* refers to the process of adopting the characteristics of the group in order to sustain a valued relationship.
- *Internalisation* develops when individuals accept the group's influence because it appeals to their own values and can be instrumental in attaining personal goals.

Group norms in social comparison

As a social comparative influence, norms in work groups can assume a position of importance. A deviation from significant norms may initially invite disapproval that amounts to no more than reminding the culprit that a deviation has taken place. Subsequently, disapproval may assume a stricter and harsher form. Norms, which were discussed earlier in connection with characteristics of groups, can relate to work targets, sharing of resources, and mutual help, and can be affected by events such as changes in work practices, rewards, and employment and economic circumstances.

The Bank Wiring Group, consisting of men engaged in wiring up telephone banks in the celebrated Hawthorne studies (see Chapter 1), developed clear norms about what represented a fair day's work for a fair day's pay. The group set an output level below that which was possible, but that was, none the less, acceptable to management. Sanctions were used to denote disapproval when deviation from norms occurred. If a worker produced at a level far above the output norm, he was described as a "rate buster". Where the level of production was far below the output norm, the worker was described as a "chiseller". A norm unrelated to output was called "squealer", which meant that divulging information on colleagues to superiors was frowned upon. The pressure brought to bear on deviants to conform ranged

from the use of derogatory names, to being ostracised, to "binging" (a hard blow on the upper arm). In addition, the Bank Wiring Group had a standard with respect to what was acceptable behaviour for those in positions of authority. As a consequence, the group applied social pressure on the inspectors and group supervisor to get them to conform to this standard (Roethlisberger & Dickson, 1939).

One of the findings in a study conducted by Lupton (1963) confirmed the Bank Wiring Group finding, but another finding did not. There was a restrictive productivity standard in one factory, Jays, engaged in light engineering, and all employees referred to it as the "fiddle". In the other factory, Wye, which was engaged in the manufacture of waterproof garments, each employee sought to maximise his or her earnings. Various explanations were put forward to account for the differences in group standards or norms. Jays operated in a stable market, had a history of union organisation, a predominantly male labour force with interdependent work, and relatively low labour costs. Wye operated in a small unstable market, had a weak union, a predominantly female labour force with independent tasks, and high labour costs. What appears to be fairly clear is that attempting to maximise earnings in one organisation was tantamount to deviant behaviour, but such behaviour in the other organisation amounted to conformist behaviour.

The Hawthorne and Lupton studies deal with the technical or task-related aspects of group norms. But norms can also be social in nature ("social norms"). This was highlighted in the study of a small group in which the researcher was a participant (Roy, 1960). The group under observation was involved in simple and repetitive work (operating a punch during a long work day). Ritualistic behaviour emerged within the group, which at first was not apparent to the observer, and this became an important part of the group culture. For example, on a frequent basis the long day of boring work was interrupted by events that gave employees the opportunity to interact. The first interruption was "peach time" when one worker provided a pair of peaches for his colleague to eat. Invariably, there were then complaints about the quality of the fruit. "Banana time" followed peach time when the worker who brought in the peaches produced a banana intended to be consumed by himself. Every morning another worker would steal the banana, calling out "banana time", and would eat it while its owner made futile protests. Nevertheless, the latter continued to bring the bananas to work with the intention of consuming them, but never managed to do so. There were other forms of ritualistic behaviour of an interpersonal nature—e.g., "fish time", "cake time", and "window time". Ritualistic behaviour of the type described here can be used to counteract boredom at work, and make the passage through the day a little bit easier.

A classic study dealing with the emergence of group norms in ambiguous or uncertain conditions was conducted by Sherif (1936). Individuals who participated in the experiment were given the job of judging the apparent movements of a stationary pinpoint of light. When the light is viewed in a completely dark room, without any reference points, it appears to move. This is a phenomenon known as the "autokinetic effect". Perception of the magnitude of this movement varies from individual to individual and is influenced by psychological factors residing in the person. When individuals work alone on different occasions, each develops a stable perception of the light. One individual may perceive relatively little movement (e.g., a few centimetres) in a particular direction, whereas another individual may perceive a large movement in a different direction. An individual norm or standard develops and this is repeated consistently from one episode of the experiment to another.

In this study, when individuals work in groups of two or three, announcing their judgements aloud without any collusion between them, each individual is affecting the other's judgement. Gradually, group norms (shared expectations) rather than individual norms or standards are established. The group norm tends to reflect a compromise between the individual norms, whereby extreme estimates of the movement of the light are moderated. Individuals who had previous experience of the autokinetic phenomenon, and had established their own individual norms, gradually gave them

up in response to the behaviour of the group. In fact, the group norms persisted even after the individuals were allowed subsequently to work on their own. A more rapid acceptance of group norms occurred among individuals who had no experience of the experiment before becoming a member of the group. As before, these group norms persisted in the period when individuals later worked alone.

This study illustrates dramatically the powerful effects of group membership on the individual and has some fascinating features. The individual has negligible past experience that can be applied in judging the position of the pinpoint of light. There is the absence of a yardstick, ambiguity is present and, as a consequence, the individual is highly dependent upon others in arriving at judgements. In everyday life this happens with different degrees of ambiguity, but in many situations each of us usually has some past experience (knowledge, facts, beliefs, values, attitudes) that forms a basis for our judgement.

In a laboratory study (Venkatesan, 1966), where subjects were asked to evaluate and choose the best suit from three identical men's suits, it was concluded that individuals who are exposed to a group norm will tend to conform to that norm in a decision-making situation that confronts them when no objective standards are available. However, if the individual's freedom is threatened by being induced to comply with a group norm, then there will be a lesser tendency to conform. The marketing implications of this study would indicate that when objective evaluation is difficult consumers accept information on product quality or style provided by their peer, or reference, groups. Thus peer groups, friends, and acquaintances may be a major source of influence and information that deserves our attention at the stage of buying major products or services. But any attempt to restrict the independent choice of the consumer may be resisted under certain conditions. For example, a neighbour or relative may sell you an idea about a product, but not necessarily the brand to buy or the store to patronise because this advice could very well be ignored (Cohen, 1981).

Even when a situation is clear-cut, where conditions of uncertainty are absent, a group can exert a significant influence on the judgements of the individual. This would be particularly noticeable in situations where one individual is in the minority, and the majority holds a view that is contrary to the view of reality held by the individual. In a well-known study conducted by Asch (1952), groups of eight individuals each had the job of comparing a series of standard lines with several alternatives. They were then required to announce, in the presence of the investigator, which of the alternative lines was the same length as the standard line in each case. Unknown to the one genuine subject in each group, seven individuals colluded with the investigator; each of them was secretly instructed on exactly how to respond. They offered the same incorrect answer before it was the turn of the genuine subject to pass comment. From this experiment emerged the sobering thought that, one-third of the time, the genuine subjects were prepared to deny the information being conveyed by their senses and shifted their judgements, thereby making an error, so as to conform with the group norm or standard.

It is interesting to note that before the group task in the experiment each individual performed on a solo basis with virtually no errors. This suggests that perceiving the similarity or otherwise of the paired lines was not a particularly difficult task and errors can hardly be attributed to an ambiguous stimulus. After the experiments, the researcher confronted each individual who had succumbed to group pressure or influence with the fact that they had yielded to the group in the specified instances. When faced with their mistaken judgements, some individuals admitted that they had realised the seven other members of the group were wrong, but the unanimity in outlook of these members led them to experience severe distress about being deviant, which culminated in yielding to the perceived pressure. Others reported experiencing equal distress, but, sensing the considerable weight of evidence against them, concluded they must have misunderstood the instructions and were wrong. A small proportion of those who succumbed to group influence were amazed at discovering their errors, and reported not being aware of any conflict and could not recall being influenced by other group members.

A number of years later in a replication of the Asch study the researchers found that the subjects—engineering and medical students—were more likely to stand their ground and resist group pressure. However, they felt very uncomfortable doing so (Perrin & Spencer, 1980).

In the Asch experiment we can observe three quite different processes of social influence:

(1) There is the threat of disapproval or rejection because one is a deviant, and it is up to the person to cope with the stress brought about by ignoring the group pressure, or to succumb to group pressure and avoid the stress.

(2) There is the threat arising from doubts about whether the requirements of the task have been correctly interpreted. This could give rise to a search for confirmation or disconfirmation of the accuracy of one's judgement, and, dependent on the outcome of this search, yielding or not yielding to the group.

(3) There is an attempt to neutralise the threat by denial or repression without being aware of this and, as a consequence, accommodating oneself to the wishes of the group.

Apparently the subjects who did not yield to group pressure, and who remained independent, were those who experienced the greatest stress and discomfort. However, this condition was substantially alleviated when the genuine subject was supported by an ally (another genuine subject). Also, a growth in the minority representation—i.e., another genuine subject joining the group—gave rise to a lesser degree of compliance with the group judgement.

Whether the individual yields to the group or resists it is likely to depend on the clarity of the stimulus (i.e., the degree of similarity of the paired lines), whether or not the genuine subject is the only deviant from the group norm, and the personality disposition of the genuine subject. A genuine subject, acting on his or her own, who perceives only a small difference between the standard and alternative lines, and acts invariably in a conformist way, may side with the group judgement.

Group influence may be particularly important in budgeting discretionary costs. These costs would be associated with nonprogrammable and nonroutine tasks and would cover areas such as advertising, research and development, training, and so on. There is no optimal solution as to the amount to spend and there is considerable latitude for the use of judgement in the determination of discretionary costs. The group may exert pressure to achieve uniformity of opinion or consensus, even though this may not be the most appropriate way to act in given circumstances. In accordance with Asch's conclusions, a solitary voice of dissent within the budgeting group may yield to the majority view in circumstances when such a course of action is unwise. But a growth in the minority view may add strength to a position of justifiable resistance. Therefore this may suggest a vote in favour of heterogeneity in group composition so as to increase the likelihood that minority viewpoints will have at least some peer group support, and not face unanimous opposition in the budgeting process. It may also suggest the need for group leaders to develop a group norm embracing the encouragement of responsible disagreement.

The importance of minority influence as an enriching experience has been recognised. Nemeth (1986) states how important it is for minorities to continuously express viewpoints in order to encourage a more penetrating consideration of alternative views, and that the influence of minorities is beneficial whether or not the views they express are right. An independent and confident minority—e.g., responsible nonexecutive directors—is valuable, more so when faced by majorities who encourage convergent, shallow, and narrow thinking.

Wood, Lundgren, Ouellette, Buscene, and Blackstone (1994) are of the view that certain conditions must exist before the minority influence is felt. The minority has a receptive audience (i.e., the majority) and can influence the latter, particularly in situations where the majority do not have to own up to having changed their mind as a result of the intervention by the minority. The minority is more likely to be successful in changing the opinion of the majority when the issues raised by the minority are of peripheral interest (i.e., indirectly related to the message).

Also, it is suggested, on the basis of the perception of group members, that an effective strategy for minorities is to be assertive and consistent in their approach (Van Hiel & Mervielde, 2001). In doing so they are likely to express a number of arguments opposing the view of the majority. Finally, if the minority consists of only one person, who happens to be the leader, this person is likely to have more influence than a one-person minority who is not in a leadership position (Ng & Van Dyne, 2001).

The conformity hypothesis has been discussed in the context of the psychology of the stock market (Eachus, 1988). Because investors are presented with a mass of competing investment opportunities, and are uncertain on how to act, they look around to see what others are doing. For example, when a share price is rising, or the stock market is bullish, it is very difficult for individual investors to resist the pressure to behave as they believe others are behaving. There is more detailed coverage of investor psychology in the section on "Decision making" in Chapter 8.

Finally, a review of conformity studies (Bond and Smith, 1996; Smith and Bond, 1993) identified differences in levels of conformity depending on whether participants were in a collectivist society (e.g., Latin America, Asia) or an individualistic society (North America, Europe) (Collectivism and individualism are concepts also discussed in Chapter 15 on culture.) The conformity studies reviewed by Smith and Bond showed that conformity is higher in collectivist societies, where group harmony is a priority and group influences on the individual are strong, than is the case in individualistic societies. Reflecting on this comparative analysis, Pennington et al. (1999) stress that while this result is interesting and informative it should be viewed with caution on methodological grounds. It should be noted that even a modest amount of blind, unthinking conformity could pose a serious threat to the effectiveness and integrity of work groups and organisations.

Co-action and affiliation

Being in the company of others has a material bearing on the behaviour of the individual. In

---

PANEL 10.4: Affiliation and fear

Groups of college girls in an American university were selected to participate in an experiment in a mythical Department of Neurology. They were greeted on arrival by Dr Gregor Zilstein, the psychologist performing the experiment, who wore a white coat and used a stethoscope. This image was intentional in order to influence the students' behaviour.

The psychologist told the girls that they were about to receive electric shocks that would be either painful (but would do no permanent harm) or not painful, and in either case the electric shock would resemble more of a tickle or a tingle than anything unpleasant. The key question was what the girls would do in this frightening situation. They were told to choose whether to wait with other girls or alone, and to state their preference on a questionnaire. It should be noted that the instructions the girls received, and the presence of the doctor with his apparatus were merely a deception, in order to make the subjects feel afraid. When the girls experienced strong fear, they generally preferred to wait with others, and they preferred to wait alone in conditions of low fear.

(Schachter, 1959)

---

emergency situations it is said that we are more likely to respond quickly if we are on our own than if we are in a co-active situation in the presence of another person (Latane & Darley, 1968). When we are in the presence of others in a group situation, we are inclined to leave it to other members and, if they do not react, perhaps the situation is perceived as not being serious enough. Until we see others acting in a decisive way, there may be a reluctance to act because of the lack of clarity surrounding what is happening. This may occur in an emergency situation when life or property is at risk. If an individual experiences smoke in a room, he or she is likely to respond fairly quickly. However, if a group is confronted with the same stimulus, rapid response may be less likely because of the inclination to discuss the nature of the threat and how to tackle it (Zajonc & Sales, 1966).

In the company of others, be they colleagues or observers, we tend to get aroused and this creates a state of drive that manifests itself in a behavioural response (Latane & Darley, 1968). If the observer of the behaviour is an expert who evaluates the subject's performance, the behavioural response of the subject is likely to be greater; in these circumstances the subject is likely to be apprehensive. A lesser behavioural response is likely when the audience consists of peers who are watching out of interest, and the least behavioural response is noted when subjects act on their own (Henchy & Glass, 1968). Imagine a situation when your own performance as a student or worker is being evaluated by an expert in your field!

Do people prefer the company of others to remaining in isolation? A classic experiment conducted by Schachter (1959), who was concerned with the concept of affiliation, may throw some light on this question (see Panel 10.4). The results suggest that people affiliate with others when suffering from fear. Why should this be? Perhaps they want to compare their situation with others to see if their fears are justified. Apparently people are likely to reduce their anxieties while waiting for a painful experience, but more so when waiting in the company of others, irrespective of whether the people in the group communicate (Wrightsman, 1960).

Sometimes it is argued that knowledge about what might happen in a future fearful event could have a beneficial effect. For example, uncertainty as to the outcome of a visit to a hospital for a medical check-up is obviously a factor that contributes to anxiety. From this one might conclude that increasing a patient's knowledge and understanding of what is going to happen reduces uncertainty, and in turn reduces the level of distress and anxiety.

The latter statement was subjected to testing in a research study consisting of a sample of 40 women undergoing colposcopy (a diagnostic investigation for the detection of cervical cancer). Half the group received a 20-minute verbal and visual presentation of what they were to expect in terms of the medical procedures they would go through and the likely range and intensity of sensations they would experience. The other half received much less information, although the same amount of time was devoted to the talk. Various techniques were used to obtain the views of the women at different stages—i.e., after the information-giving stage (the briefing session), after the medical examination, and after the women returned home (Miller & Magnan, 1983). Surprisingly, the group that received the most information showed increases in anxiety and tension after the briefing session. This level of anxiety and tension decreased somewhat after the medical examination, but still was only marginally below the level that prevailed prior to the briefing session.

How can we explain this result? First, the research took place within a short space of time, with the information-giving (briefing) and the medical examination carried out at one session. This may not have allowed the women sufficient time to integrate and synthesise the information. Secondly, it seems that the information was presented to the women in a one-way communication mode in a formal setting without the women having a chance to ask questions or to check out their understanding (Harvey, 1988), as they would be able to do if a discussion group was used. In exercises of this type, it is suggested that comprehensive information, previously distributed in booklet form well in advance of hospitalisation, together with checking whether the patient has received, understood, and acted on the information presented, is a wise course of action. In such circumstances, one can expect to find a real reduction in anxiety after a briefing session based on the giving of comprehensive information (Wallace, 1986).

Social control

In social control the influence is exercised from above on a vertical basis, rather than on a horizontal basis as in social comparison. Experiments on obedience to authority, such as the famous study by Milgram (1965), have shown that a significant number of people are prepared to inflict pain on others because an authority figure instructs them to do so. Subjects representing a cross-section of the population in an American university town were induced to inflict pain and danger on other people by increasingly large doses of electric shock as a punishment for making mistakes in a learning experiment. Those at the receiving end of the electric shocks—the victims—protested in a dramatic fashion and pleaded for the experiments to cease. This put the subjects into an awkward and difficult position. They had to cope with the demands of the experimenter to continue with the experiment, the pleas of the victims for the experiment to cease, and the demands of their own conscience. A number of people refused to take part in the experiments, and some withdrew after administering a small dose of electric shock. However, others continued to participate and, though troubled by their participation, they accepted the experimenter's logic that it is legitimate to administer an electric shock to a learner who makes mistakes.

When colleagues of the experimenter were present, and they refused to continue with the experiments, this gave subjects encouragement to do likewise in most situations. The effects of group pressure are evident in this situation. The behaviour of the colleagues of the experimenter conveyed to the subjects that first of all disobedience is possible, that no adverse consequences stem from disobedience, and anyway the act of giving a victim an electric shock is improper. The good news is that the electric shocks were not real, though the subjects were not aware of this during the experiment. The cries of the victims' distress came from a tape recorder, which was activated by pressing the "shock" lever. When victims were visible to the subject, through a glass partition, the role of the victim was played by an actor. What was surprising in this series of experiments was the number of people who were prepared to administer electric shocks to somebody who made a mistake in a learning experiment. Another striking aspect of the experiment was that the subjects were in a situation where demands were made on them while they could not compare themselves with somebody in a similar situation. As such, the conditions of the experiment do not correspond with those found in formal organisations.

It is worth noting the operation of social comparison in one phase of the experiments. This occurred when colleagues of the experimenter decided to challenge his authority. From this incident we may conclude that social comparison may play an exceedingly important part in limiting the potency of demands from authority figures.

Milgram's aim was to establish conditions under which a person would blindly carry out the orders of another, even when the task was objectionable and the orders could not be supported by any kind of reasoning. He saw his research as contributing to a reduction of the threat of totalitarian authority systems. His critics felt that he should not have exposed his subjects to the stress they experienced from participating in the experiments, and that studies of such destructive forms of obedience are open to misuse by totalitarian authority figures (Pennington et al., 1999). Nowadays the ethics of research of this nature is a live issue, and many scholars would subscribe to the view that it is important to protect participants in research studies from threatening or traumatic experiences. The question of deception is also important in this context.

Other forms of social control are institutional control and brainwashing. In institutional control the inmate in a prison is frequently stripped of personal props to his or her identity. For example, personal clothing and furniture are not permitted, the mail can be controlled, and frequent association with relatives and friends is not allowed (Goffman, 1961). In brainwashing there is an attempt to undermine people's stability of mind and self-image by not permitting them to relate to friends or identify with their normal group. This is achieved by measures such as segregating members of the group, prohibiting group formation, fomenting mutual distrust, manipulating the news so that only the bad news gets through, and finally exposing the individual to the desired message in a state of social isolation (Schein, 1956).

Individual differences have to be taken into account when considering the degree of difficulty in altering a person's values. It would be more difficult to induce sincere Catholic missionaries to renounce their faith than to persuade army conscripts who are peace-loving civilians at heart to renounce their country's involvement in an unpopular war. Some manipulative measures manage

to secure compliance only, but not identification and internalisation. The value of this type of social control is lost when the individual returns to his or her old environment, but in severe situations the effect of coercive persuasion cannot be reversed.

Decision making

Models of decision making and constraining influences (individual and organisational) were discussed in Chapter 8. Using groups to make decisions has been both strongly endorsed and seriously questioned by behavioural scientists and managers. From early studies of group dynamics the implication appears to be that people are more likely to accept new ideas from their colleagues and leader in the course of discussion than from a leader telling them what to do. It is believed that the individual sees a clearer picture of the situation and, as a consequence, feels involved in the decisions, and finds it easy to bow to the will of the group.

This involvement is considered effective when the focus is on overcoming resistance to change. It is claimed that group discussion makes better use of the available talent or abilities of members. It promotes acceptability of decisions because people have had the opportunity to raise their anxieties or concerns in connection with the problems under discussion. Also, it is considered a democratic way of going about things, although this could be somewhat invalidated if the information put before the group is chosen selectively.

The early studies referred to in the previous paragraph were conducted by Lewin (1958). Groups of housewives were persuaded to buy cheaper, unattractive cuts of meat, which were nutritional, to help economise as part of the war effort. Interesting and attractive lectures were given with supporting leaflets, emphasising the vitamin and mineral value of offal as well as stressing the health and economic aspects of this type of food, with hints about the preparation of dishes. In the method devoted to group discussion a different approach was adopted. The group leader explained the link between diet and the war effort and the discussion focused on the reasons why housewives were not keen to experiment with cheap foods (hearts, kidneys, etc.). It was found that 32% of those who discussed the issues in a group said a week later that they had served at least one of the dishes recommended by their group, but only 3% of the housewives who attended the lectures took the minimum advice of the lecturer. Is the lecture an unsuitable medium in these circumstances? The listener is generally in a passive role, using personal experience to accept or reject the proposals advocated by the lecturer; the listener is generally ignorant of what others are going to decide and there is no "new social norm" to offer guidance.

By contrast, in the discussion group, people are encouraged to exchange views and consider the merits and demerits of buying different cuts of meat. There is an acknowledgement that other people have a valid point of view, and this could lessen resistance to change. The advisability of buying offal is discussed openly, and recipes are introduced when the housewives are mentally prepared for a change. The decision that emerges from the discussion becomes a norm, and when members publicly support the group's decision this can consolidate the individual's intention to buy and, in effect, change her purchasing behaviour. Lewin accepts the power of group decisions in influencing individual behaviour. To him, the exercise of freedom of choice rather than high-pressure salesmanship is critical. In the discussion group a minority position (to buy the cheap meat) developed into a majority position. In fact the previous majority position (not to buy the cheap meat) could now be considered deviant.

One particular facet of this experiment should be noted, which is that the advocated new behaviour (save money and assist the war effort) was obviously an attractive proposition.

In some organisational settings, efforts are made to change the individual's outlook, and group decision making may be used as a vehicle to achieve this objective. In a study adopting similar methods to those used by Lewin, housewives were encouraged to consume greater quantities of fresh and evaporated milk (Radke & Klisurich, 1958). It was found that the group discussion was more effective in changing behaviour than the lecture. The personality of the leader of the discussion group was considered not to be an influential factor. The group was drawn from the same neighbourhood, and unlike the Red Cross Group in Lewin's experiment, members of the neighbourhood group were not members of a club meeting regularly. This might suggest that group decision making can be effective in ad hoc groups.

Lewin is of the view that group discussion could be used as an important method of bringing about social change that is potentially adaptive. However, group discussion as a method could be undermined (as is shown later in the analysis of "groupthink") if the discussion is limited and the group leader manipulates proceedings in a manner that is contrary to the interests of the group. Group decision making is not without its limitations. Assembling a group can consume much time, and reaching a decision may be a more prolonged exercise than if individuals did so on their own. There may be a tendency to conform too readily to social pressures, and domination by a few individuals in a group situation is not uncommon. The latter could be particularly disadvantageous if the members concerned are of below average ability. Responsibility for the final outcome of group deliberations is ambiguous, unlike a situation when a single individual is responsible for a decision and it is clear who is accountable.

In comparing groups with individuals to establish who is best at decision making, it appears that the effectiveness of either will depend on the criteria (e.g., accuracy, speed, creativity, acceptance) used. With regard to accuracy, there is evidence to indicate that groups outperform the average individual in the group (Michaelsen, Watson, & Black, 1989), but the most accomplished individual in the group is likely to outperform the group (Miner, 1984). With regard to speed, the individual is likely to be superior to the group, but the group appears to be superior to the individual on creativity and acceptance of the final decision. However, as stated earlier, groups can fall short of standards of efficiency (e.g., time spent arriving at a decision) normally associated with individual decision making. Group decision making has an affinity with participative leadership discussed in Chapter 12.

Types of decision-making group

Management has to give thought to devising the best format for a group faced with problem solving and decision making. Three formats for decision making are suggested—**interacting, nominal**, and **delphi groups** (Van de Ven & Delbecq, 1974).

Interacting groups. These groups are widely used and involve members interacting in the process of generating ideas about ways of tackling a problem, leading eventually to a group decision using majority voting if necessary. These groups suffer from the deficiencies associated with group functioning discussed elsewhere in this chapter.

Nominal groups. Discussion is restricted during the decision-making process. Members physically present at the meeting state their opinions independently with respect to the problem before the discussion takes place, and remain silent in relation to such opinions during the discussion. This type of forum helps introverted people get involved in group activity. The procedure adopted after presenting the problem to the group is as follows:

- Before discussion takes place, each member writes on paper his or her ideas about the problem under review.
- Then each member in turn presents one idea to the group, using a flipchart or blackboard. There is no discussion at this stage.
- Next, the group discusses the ideas presented, with the emphasis on clarity and evaluation.
- Finally, each member reverts to silence and ranks independently the ideas already presented to the group. The idea with the highest aggregate ranking constitutes the final decision.

A particular advantage of nominal groups is that independent thinking in a group situation is cultivated, unlike the circumstances in interacting groups.

The nominal group technique can be blended with computer technology to create the "electronic meeting" (Dennis & Valacich, 1993). Members of the group, not exceeding 50 in number, sit at a table and each person has access to a computer in which information is keyed in response to issues raised with the group members. Individual comments as well as aggregate votes are projected on to a screen in the room. The electronic meeting has the benefit of speed due to its focus on critical issues only. The identity of the individual whose message is projected on to the screen is not made public, so people can express honest views without the fear of ridicule or reprimand.

Delphi groups. These groups are similar to nominal groups, except for the fact that members do not meet face to face. The following procedure is used:

- Members are told what the problem is and asked to provide a solution. This is done through a structured questionnaire approach.
- The questionnaire is completed independently by each member whose anonymity is maintained.
- The responses of all members are tabulated and each member receives a copy of the set of results covering all responses.
- After having an opportunity to see the range and types of answers, each member is asked again to provide an answer to the original problem. At this stage an individual could change his or her solution.
- The last two steps could be repeated until a consensus position is arrived at.

Delphi groups, like nominal groups, require limited exposure to group influence, but in the case of nominal groups there is a forum for discussion. Delphi groups have a certain appeal when group members are scattered geographically and it would be expensive for them to meet at a central location. However, they consume a lot of time and certainly are not appropriate when a quick decision is necessary. Because of the absence of interaction, obviously there is a total lack of useful insights, which could emanate only from discussion and from people bouncing ideas off each other.

Van de Ven and Delbecq (1974) maintain that the nominal and delphi groups are more effective

TABLE 10.1

Choice dilemma questionnaire: Probabilities of political stability

Tick the lowest probability that, as finance director, you would consider acceptable for the chief executive to decide to build a new plant in the foreign country.

The chances that the foreign country will remain politically stable are:	
1 in 10	☐
3 in 10	☐
5 in 10	☐
7 in 10	☐
9 in 10	☐
Or tick here if you feel that the chief executive should not build, no matter what the probabilities.	☐

than the normal discussion group in problem situations where the pooled judgement of a group of people is necessary. In particular, nominal groups are suitable for situations where people can come together without much difficulty, and for problems needing data that can be produced quickly. By contrast, delphi groups are suitable for situations where the cost and inconvenience of people congregating in one place are high, and for problems that do not require immediate solutions.

Risky shift

Is there a danger that a group is more conservative and cautious than an individual in arriving at decisions and, as a result, may produce poorer decisions? Or, alternatively, are groups prepared to take greater risks? Apparently, some groups are prepared to take greater risks than are individuals, and this is known as the "risky shift" phenomenon (Stoner, 1961, quoted in Brown, 1965). The following is an item from a questionnaire on choice dilemma used for measuring risk-taking (Kogan & Wallach, 1967).

A corporation, dealing in light metals, is prosperous and has considered seriously the possibility of expanding its business by building an additional plant in a new location. It is faced with a dilemma of choice. It can build a new plant in the home country, which is politically stable, and where a moderate return on the initial investment could be achieved, or it could build a plant in a foreign country where there are lower labour costs and easy access to raw materials. The latter

action would mean a much higher return on the initial investment, but there is a history of political instability and revolution in the foreign country. In addition, the leader of a small minority party in the foreign country is committed to nationalising all foreign investments.

As finance director, imagine you are advising the chief executive of the corporation. Several probabilities or odds of continued political stability in the foreign country under consideration are listed in Table 10.1, and you are asked to tick the lowest probability that you would consider acceptable in order for the chief executive to go ahead and build the new plant in that country.

The dilemma is a two-choice situation where the finance director is faced with a choice between a risky but highly desirable course of action, and a cautious but less desirable one. Failure in terms of the risky alternative can be assumed to lead to very unfavourable consequences. For the risky choice there are two possible consequences: (1) the probability of political stability and no nationalisation; or (2) the probability of political instability and nationalisation. In Table 10.1, a 1 in 10 chance represents a risky choice, whereas a 9 in 10 chance represents a cautious one.

When business executives decided on the ranking of investment projects, in a study outside the normal risky shift research studies, they agreed as a group to take more risky decisions than they had chosen as individuals. An appropriate question to ask at this stage is whether people would generally be more willing to take risks in their behaviour when the decisions are real in the world of work?

What aspects of the group's experience account for the risky shift phenomenon? Before a consensus is reached certain aspects of the group discussion are important:

- An upward influence on the level of risk an individual proposes to take emanates from information about the risks other members in the group are prepared to take.
- The emotional interaction arising from the discussion may create a disposition for a shift towards risk to take place.

The act of committing oneself to a group decision is tantamount to lifting the burden off one's shoulders and transferring it to the group and, in the process, the commitment becomes more risky. Because each member feels less personal responsibility for a potential loss, consensus is likely to move towards acceptance of more risk (Wallach & Kogan, 1965).

Cautious shift. It is also suggested that there may be a possibility of a "cautious shift" in group decision making, and this would coexist with a risky shift. For example, certain items under review might be interpreted in a cautious direction after the discussion, whereas other items are biased towards risk. In other circumstances, risk-taking may be ingrained in the culture of the members of the group. In such a case, cultural values could act as a filtering process whereby information generated by the group discussion is interpreted in a particular way. For example, risk-taking business executives from the USA engaged in committee deliberations to justify a decision may select observations arising from the discussion that support their cultural disposition. On the other hand, cautious business executives from Iran may place a different interpretation on the group discussion. In the former case it is likely that persuasive arguments favoured risk, and in the latter case they favoured a conservative view.

Risky or cautious shifts are referred to as **"group polarisation"**. Group polarisation occurs when the attitudes and opinions of the group, in connection with an issue, change during a group discussion (Moscovici & Zavalloni, 1969). The change or shift could be towards a risky or cautious shift. For example, a fund management team may become more cautious about committing funds to a particular investment after a group discussion. Isenberg (1986) stresses the importance of the influence of the group in terms of social comparison (i.e., pronounced identification with the group) and persuasion (i.e., the potency of accurate information supportive of the group) in promoting group polarisation. It is said that the use of a "quantitative decision aid" while deliberating on group issues can help to neutralise to some extent the effects of arguments (based on biased persuasion) on the thought processes of group members (Chen, Gustafson, & Lee, 2002).

Cohesion and loyalty

Sometimes the advantages of group decision making are undermined by powerful psychological pressures resulting from members working closely together and sharing the same set of values. At a time of crisis this puts people under considerable stress. Where a group is cohesive—that is, the group is very important to its members or they have a strong need to stay in it—a high level of conformity can be demanded of members. The conformity is likely to express itself in loyalty to the group, even in circumstances when the policies of the group are malfunctioning. A detailed discussion of cohesiveness appeared earlier in the chapter. There are occasions, for example, when group loyalty makes a mockery of accident prevention (see Panel 10.5).

Groupthink

It has been suggested by a perceptive observer of the functioning of in-groups that as a group becomes excessively close-knit and develops a strong feeling of "we-ness", it becomes vulnerable to a pattern of behaviour known as **groupthink** (Janis, 1972). When consensus-seeking becomes a dominant force, groupthink develops; this is a thinking process that tends to push aside a realistic appraisal of alternative courses of action. It is the outcome of group pressure, impeding the efficient execution of members' mental faculties

In one particular case, the function of factory units was to modify rod-shaped machine tools by cutting or banding them (Chapman, 1982). Before modifying them, one end of each pen-sized tool was dipped in a protective molten plastic substance. After modification some of the tools were sandblasted to make them look better. Almost every one of these actions was undertaken in a grossly unsafe manner.

One Monday the manager told six of his subordinates to make the place presentable because the Factory Inspector was coming round. Three of them were asked to tidy up around the machine and the other three to pick up the boxes of machine tools from the gangway and place them on a long bench. The manager told the group that they could replace the boxes as soon as the visit was over, and gave them a wink, because the bench was required for other things. The Inspector seemed to be viewed as an enemy. The men grumbled about the visit, but the manager said, "Surely we don't want people like Inspectors finding fault with our unit, lads!" This prompted jokes about setting booby traps for the Inspector. When the Inspector left, there was evidence of a lot of anti-safety behaviour. This behaviour would suggest that there appeared to be mindless devotion to the group, particularly in the face of an outside authority figure with powers of sanction.

and interfering with members' ability to test reality and preserve their judgement. [Groupthink amounts to an unintentional erosion of one's critical faculties as a result of adopting group norms.] This is to be distinguished from a similar occurrence as a result of external threats of social punishment. Although groupthink is more likely to affect cohesive in-groups, this is not always the case, and is particularly unlikely to be so where an atmosphere of critical inquiry is a normal feature of the decision-making approach.

The outward signs of groupthink are likely to manifest themselves in a number of ways. Members of groups formed to make decisions show a tendency to be lenient in their judgement of the ideas of their leader or fellow members for fear of being ostracised or disciplined. They go so far as being unnecessarily strict with themselves, placing controls on their own freedom of thought. There is an amiable atmosphere with an absence of aggravation so as to retain the comfortable "we-feeling". As cohesiveness in the group continues to develop, there is a strong urge on the part of each member to avoid "rocking the boat" and this can be instrumental in persuading the individual to accept whatever proposals are promoted by the leader or a majority of the group's members (Neck & Moorhead, 1995).

On the face of it, the scope for deviant thought is considerable in a highly cohesive group; nevertheless, the desire for consensus on all important issues is so prevalent as to discourage the individual from utilising this advantage. When groupthink is forcefully present, deviant thoughts are relegated to insignificance by individuals establishing that their own reservations are not so overwhelming after all and should be set aside, and that the benefit of the doubt with regard to the remaining uncertainties should be given to the group so as to promote consensus. Also, perhaps agreeing is considered more beneficial than the insecurity that is likely to be created should the individual suffer rejection because of persistent deviant thoughts. Groupthink places greatest emphasis on teamwork, with an inherent striving for unanimity within the collective membership. This presents a number of difficulties ranging from over-optimism and lack of vigilance to ineffectiveness and lack of realism in the formulation and implementation of policy.

Janis (1972) proposes the following key characteristics of groupthink:

- illusion of invulnerability;
- belief in the rectitude of the group;
- negative views of competitors;
- sanctity of group consensus;
- illusion of unanimity; and
- erecting a protective shield.

Illusion of invulnerability. Many, if not all, members of the in-group share an illusion of invulnerability. This has some reassuring effect as regards obvious dangers, and is responsible for members becoming over-optimistic and keen to take unjustifiable risks. It also causes them to fail to respond to clear warning signals. Here the group displays an unshaken belief in its endorsed course of action, and in the face of information or views to the contrary its belief remains intact. The group goes as far as discounting warnings or negative feedback by indulging in rationalisations of its action on a collective basis. Inevitably this leads to a reconsideration and renewed commitment to both the underlying assumptions of policy pursued and the policy itself. A further line of action might be reflected in an approach whereby evidence to support the status quo is chosen selectively from any available source or, if necessary, by inventing specious forecasts. Some members of the group or committee may be aware of the misgivings of an outsider about the wisdom of pursuing the policy in question, but display a reluctance to voice concern. Where the group believes it is invulnerable, this can reduce anxiety about taking risks.

The following is an example of a situation where an employee performing a "staff" role encounters the illusion of invulnerability. An accountant acting in an advisory capacity may find that members of a management committee fail to respond to clear warning signals with regard to the financial advisability of pursuing a particular course of action. Because of the illusion of invulnerability, the group discounts the warnings and engages in collective rationalisation in order to maintain its view or belief.

Belief in the rectitude of the group.   There will develop an unquestionable belief in the morality or self-righteousness of the in-group. In this way members can choose to ignore the ethical or moral consequences of the decisions taken. A war cabinet, having placed the minimisation of civilian casualties high on its priority list, may find it easier to prosecute or escalate the war without feelings of guilt. In much the same way a working party or committee within an organisation, having reached a decision to introduce a scheme in connection with performance-related pay, may appeal to the justness and ethical nature of the scheme when fully operational—i.e., it provides able employees with potential benefits. A member whose doubts, following consideration of the scheme, are committed to writing, is likely to suppress them when attending meetings. When an outsider is invited to express his or her observations on the feasibility or otherwise of the scheme, the chairperson is likely to be quick off the mark when the speaker finishes, and to move on to the next item on the agenda if the speaker's observations express misgivings or doubts. At crucial meetings the obvious tactic would be for the chairperson or leader not to call on the doubters to speak. Instead, an attempt would be made to tame the doubters, and in any case not to permit them to go so far as questioning the fundamental assumptions of the proposed action. This would be particularly so if the doubters are members of the in-group.

Negative views of competitors.   There is a tendency to subscribe to negative stereotyped views of the leaders of enemy or competitor groups. Here we find the prevailing attitude of mind supporting the view that these leaders are either too weak or too stupid to meet the challenge of the in-group. In a military campaign this disposition could create an underestimation of the numerical strength of the enemy, or a totally inaccurate assessment of their true intentions. For example, it is reported that because of the rigid attachment of President Johnson's advisers to the domino theory, they ignored the nationalistic yearnings of the North Vietnamese and their wish to ward off the Chinese. Similarly, it was suggested by a social scientist in Britain, who has made a special study of decision making, that the UK government did not pick up certain critical signals prior to the Falklands War (Heller, 1983).

Similarities to the military analogy can be found within organisations among groups competing for scarce resources, and in an external context when policy-making groups make certain assumptions about the quality of the company's competitors.

Sanctity of group consensus.   There appears to be a natural tendency to steer clear of a deviation from what is perceived as group consensus. Members sharing this disposition remain reticent about personal misgivings or doubts and, in addition, are quite capable of convincing themselves of the lack of substance in these doubts. Outside the group situation, in the corridor, such people may, however, feel strongly about the issues in question and convey the antithesis of their true feelings on the matter at the meeting. These individuals may subsequently feel guilty for having kept silent, but it is probable that the circumstances surrounding the group discussion were such as to permit only the raising of matters of minor importance.

Illusion of unanimity.   The illusion of unanimity creates the belief that all members' judgements are unanimous when they subscribe to the majority view. No doubt unanimity is fostered when members are insulated from outside views between meetings, and where the emerging majority view reflects the declared choice of an influential figure (e.g., the chief executive) in the organisation. The presumption of unanimity is upheld when members remain silent. There is an almost unstated assumption that members who respect each other will arrive at a unanimous view. The result of this proneness to validate group consensus is, in the absence of disagreements among members, the sweeping away of critical thinking and testing of reality. This can lead to serious errors of judgement, though it could be argued that the mutual bolstering of self-esteem and morale, which emanates from the process of seeking agreement, enhances the group's capacity to take action.

A range of divergent views about the riskiness of the preferred course of action could be mildly traumatic. The existence of disagreement could give rise to anxieties about the likelihood of making a serious error, and once unanimity is severely dented it is difficult to remain confident about the correctness of the group decision. The onus then falls on members to confront the uncertainties and assess the seriousness of the risks. Therefore, to eradicate this painful state, members are inclined, without realising it, to prevent latent disagreements from coming to the surface, particularly when they are proposing to initiate a risky adventure. However, a nagging doubt may persist if information about difficulties surfaces and is provided by a previous supporter of the group who is of high calibre. There now develops a movement towards emphasising areas of convergence in thinking, at the cost of fully exploring divergencies that might expose unresolved issues. The illusion of unanimity is maintained simply because, generally speaking, the major participants in the group discussion fail to reveal their own reasoning or discuss their assumptions or reservations.

Erecting a protective shield.   Groupthink has the effect of erecting a shield to protect the leader and fellow members from adverse information that might shatter their shared complacency about the morality and effectiveness of past decisions. This situation arises when an influential group member calls a doubter or dissenter to one side and advises him or her on the desirability of backing the leader and the group. Where outside expert opinion is sought, invariably the chairperson will retort by questioning the legitimacy of the assumption underlying it, or ensuring that insufficient time is devoted to discussing it, finally stating why the original decision seems to be a wise one. This type of behaviour manifested itself in the investment decision process referred to earlier, and can also be seen in the following example.

An accountant may be asked to submit a financial appraisal of a project to which the chief executive has a total commitment. Having presented the report, the accountant is horrified to find that the chief executive, instead of assessing the report on its merits, questions the legitimacy of the assumptions underpinning it, and puts aside insufficient time to discuss it. In effect, a shield is erected to protect the group members from what they consider to be adverse information likely to dislodge commitment to the chosen course of action. The accountant then faces a dilemma: having presented an opinion, should he or she accept a committee decision that is quite contrary to it?; would it be better to insist that the report goes on record?; by being too persistent or regularly opposing the group, is there a possibility of increasing isolation and eventual rejection by the group or its leader?

Consequences of groupthink

The consequences that flow from these groupthink symptoms are synonymous with the consequences of poor decision-making practices, and it follows that inadequate solutions to the problems under review are found. Discussion tends to be limited to but a few alternatives, and there is a conspicuous absence of evaluation of many alternatives that should be considered in the decision process. No systematic consideration is given to the question of whether gains, which do not appear obvious in the normal course of events, have been overlooked; neither is any cost assessment placed on the alternatives that have been rejected by the group. Similarly, no serious attempt is made to obtain the views of experts on potential losses or gains. A noticeable trend is for group members to display a positive interest in facts and opinions that support their preferred policy, while ignoring facts and opinions that test it. The decision to launch the ill-fated *Challenger* space shuttle may very well be an example of this frame of mind. Negative information was ignored by the group that made the decision (Moorhead, Ferrence, & Neck, 1991). Finally, there tends to be a failure to establish contingency plans to deal with foreseeable setbacks such as bureaucratic inertia, mishaps, or subtle political manoeuvring by opponents, which could pose a threat to the successful outcome of the course of action chosen.

In the discussion so far the importance of groupthink to processes within organisations has been emphasised. In Panel 10.6, the concept is applied to a particular incident within an organisation concerned with generating commercial nuclear power.

Given the dysfunctional effects created by groupthink, what steps can we take to try to prevent it? There are a number of steps suitable to counteract groupthink:

(1) Encourage individual group members to evaluate what has been said in a critical fashion and place a high priority on an open discussion of doubts and objections where it is perfectly legitimate to disagree or be sceptical. The leader must be prepared to accept criticisms of his or her own judgement, which could have a healthy effect in arresting the rapid slide towards consensus with its adverse effect on critical thinking.

(2) At the beginning of the discussion, as a means of encouraging open inquiry and an objective investigation of a wide range of policy alternatives, the leader should exercise impartiality and avoid stating preferences and expectations with regard to outcomes. Avoid arriving at conclusions on the basis of a consideration of an inadequate number of alternative courses of action. Encourage members to offer suggestions, and be aware at all times that early evaluation of a limited choice of alternatives could have a detrimental effect

---

PANEL 10.6: The Chernobyl disaster

In a psychological analysis of the events leading up to the Chernobyl disaster in 1986—the worst accident in the history of commercial nuclear power generation—Reason (1987) focuses on two perspectives. The first deals with the cognitive difficulties people have in coping with complex systems. The second, which is examined here, is concerned with the "pathologies" of small cohesive groups (groupthink). Reason identified a number of groupthink symptoms as being attributable to the Chernobyl operators, as follows:

- "The actions of the operators were certainly consistent with an illusion of invulnerability. It is likely that they rationalised away any worries (or warnings) they might have had about the hazards of their endeavour."
- Their single-minded pursuit of repeated testing implied "an unswerving belief in the rightness of their actions".
- They clearly underestimated the opposition: in this case, the system's intolerance to being operated within the forbidden reduced-power zone.
- Any adverse outcomes were either seen as unlikely, or possibly not even considered at all.
- Finally, if any one operator experienced doubts, they were probably "self-censored" before they were voiced.

These speculations suggest that the group aspects of the situation were prominent.

(Reason, 1987)

on ideas that are different, novel, or lacking support.

(3) At the stage of the meeting when an evaluation of policy alternatives is required, one member of the group should play the role of devil's advocate, challenging the evidence put forward by those promulgating the majority point of view.

(4) Do not rush into a quick solution of the problem. When you arrive at a first solution or preliminary choice, let it rest for a while, come back to it later and analyse the problem afresh. Where security considerations permit, allow each group member to report back to his or her section or department to establish what people feel about the proposals before a final decision is reached. Expose the problem to outsiders with different special interests from those of group members and ask them to challenge its assumptions and content. The outcome of this exercise would be reported back to the group.

(5) Where appropriate, break up the group into subgroups (each having a chairperson) to examine the feasibility and effectiveness of the proposed policy alternatives. Then the main group should reconvene to settle any differences. Ideally, create more than one group to examine the same question, each group working under a different leader.

(6) Where the group is in competition with another group, it may be advisable to put aside a session to monitor information reaching the group from this source and write alternative models of the rival group's intentions.

The strategy outlined here, though desirable, could be costly in execution and might be considered inappropriate at a time of crisis.

Research on groupthink. Reflecting on the research basis of groupthink, there is a view that, although the arguments for its existence are well stated, the concept has not been subjected to rigorous empirical investigation. Apart from some interviews with participants, there is a heavy reliance on news reports and memoirs, which in some cases might not be totally accurate. Also, much of the research into groupthink has been carried out in laboratories where key organisational conditions do not exist. A challenge to groupthink is made by Whyte (1989), who conceives it as the outcome of risk-seeking in a group faced with impending losses.

Nevertheless, part of the groupthink phenomenon is supported by research, although a number of questions remain unanswered (Choi & Kim, 1999; Montanari & Moorhead, 1989; Park, 2000). It is suggested that an offshoot of groupthink—group cohesiveness—could be functional in generating ideas rather than in repressing them (Aldag & Fuller, 1993), though others are inclined to take the view that cohesiveness makes a group vulnerable to groupthink (Hayes, 1997). It is suggested that an ideal recipe for self-managing groups to use in order to neutralise pressure from groupthink is to adopt a process called "teamthink". This is viewed as a positive thinking approach, ideal for confronting conditions of complexity. Neck & Manz (1994) refer to teamthink as a positive cognitive strategy likely to be found where the focus is less narrow and where there is more open decision making. In this setting the positive beliefs and assumptions of the team help to encourage a fuller exploration of alternatives, thereby helping the team to make better decisions. Schultz-Hardt, Jochims, and Frey (2002) point out the value of appointing somebody to play the role of devil's advocate in order to counteract some of the negative effects of groupthink.

Finally, Esser (1998) concludes in a review of groupthink research that:

> it is too early to pass judgement on groupthink theory. Much more research is needed before we can determine whether the theory is valid, whether modifications of the theory are needed, or whether the theory should be discarded altogether. In the meantime groupthink theory continues to stimulate interest and its research base, though small, is growing. In sum, groupthink research is alive and well, not because it has validated groupthink theory, but because it has stimulated a growing set of testable ideas about group decision making.

Effective groups

Over 40 years ago two academics—Rensis Likert and Douglas McGregor—made interesting observations about the features of effective groups, and one of them (McGregor) had also something to say about the features of ineffective groups. The features of both the effective and the ineffective group are highlighted in Table 10.2 (McGregor, 1960). The profile and performance characteristics of the highly effective group are specified by Likert (1961), and are set out in Table 10.3, and may be viewed as a supplement to the features of effective groups listed in Table 10.2. Many of the characteristics of effective groups listed in Tables 10.2 and 10.3 are ideal types, and, although people may strive to operationalise them, there are formidable behavioural and organisational constraints likely to undermine the process. Nevertheless, they are indicative of good practice with respect to the functioning of groups.

After reviewing the research evidence on making groups effective, Zander (1982) proposed key steps to promote problem solving within the group and to avoid ineffective decision making (see Table 10.4) Over the years a lot of effort has gone into trying to discover the right blend of characteristics in the effective group or team. For example, the spotlight has focused on the leadership and structure of the team (see the commentary on team roles as defined by Belbin and by Margerison and McCann in the next chapter).

Inter-group behaviour

As well as intra-group behaviour, organisations are also concerned with the way groups interact with other groups. This is called inter-group behaviour, and is seen when, for example, organisations use cross-functional teams to tackle difficult technical problems. At a more basic level, it is manifest in normal liaison between different groups in an organisation in order to settle routine matters (e.g., between the marketing and production departments).

Social identity

This concept has been examined earlier in the book in connection with personality (Chapter 2)

TABLE 10.2

McGregor's (1960) characteristics of effective and ineffective groups: Copyright © 1960 by The McGraw-Hill Companies and reproduced with permission

Effective	Ineffective
(a) Informality; relaxed atmosphere; involvement; interest	Formality; tense atmosphere; indifference; boredom
(b) Much discourse; high contributions	Domination by few; contributions often lack relevance
(c) Understanding/acceptance of common aims	Aims ill-defined and misunderstood; conflict between private aims and common aims exists
(d) Listen; consider; put forward ideas	Unfair hearing; irrelevant speeches; members fear ridicule/condemnation
(e) Examine disagreements; dissenters are not over-powered	Disagreements are suppressed or conflict develops; large minority is dissatisfied; disruptive minority imposes its views
(f) Consensus decision making; member feels free to disagree	Lack of consensus; premature decision making; formal voting (simple majority)
(g) Constructive criticism	Personalised destructive criticism
(h) Feelings and attitudes are aired	Feelings remain under the surface
(i) Awareness of decisions/actions; clear assignments	Lack of awareness of decisions; unclear assignments
(j) Leadership role undertaken by most suitable member	Leadership role is jealously guarded
(k) Frequent review of group operations	Not too concerned with deficiencies of the group

TABLE 10.3

Likert's (1961) characteristics of the effective group: Copyright © 1961 by The McGraw-Hill Companies and reproduced with permission

(1) Social interaction skills (e.g., ability to relate to others) required by both the leader and members are well developed.
(2) Relaxed working relationship among members of the group.
(3) Identification with the group and loyalty to all members, including the leader.
(4) High degree of confidence and trust among members, including the leader.
(5) Individual values and needs find expression in the group's values and goals. Because the individual members have helped to shape the group outlook, they feel satisfied with the way in which the group is going.
(6) Acceptance of important group values (e.g., loyalty or safety) by members.
(7) Because individuals wish to achieve something and enhance their personal worth, they channel this motivation to achieve the important goals of the group and at the same time they abide by the major values of the group (e.g., achieve a high level of production without compromising safety standards).
(8) Commitment to the group springs from sharing the group's values and deriving satisfaction from membership. The individual is keen to do his or her best and not let his or her colleagues down.
(9) Supportive atmosphere governs all interactions, problem-solving, and decision-making activities of the group. Suggestions, comments, ideas, information, criticisms, are forthcoming.
(10) Linking functions with other groups: the group endeavours to adopt the values and goals of the groups with which it has a link.
(11) The leader of the group who is carefully chosen adopts a participative management style.
(12) The group is capable of setting attainable goals for members.
(13) Mutual help is forthcoming in order to accomplish the group's goals.
(14) The supportive atmosphere of the group stimulates creativity.
(15) The group has a healthy respect for necessary bureaucratic practices.
(16) A premium is placed on efficient communication processes, and there is little reason to doubt the credibility of the information communicated.
(17) Members tend to exert influence on each other for the common good; this would apply to exerting influence on the leader. The ability of members of the group to influence each other contributes to the flexibility and adaptability of the group.
(18) The attachment to common goals and shared values contributes to the stability of group activities. Members feel secure in using their initiative to make decisions in these circumstances.

TABLE 10.4

Promoting effective group problem solving and decision making (Zander, 1982)

- State the problem clearly, indicating its significance and what is expected of the group when faced with solving it.
- Break a complex problem into separate parts, and make decisions affecting each part.
- Focus discussion on the key issues and, when all avenues are explored, put a stop to analysis, and call for a vote, if necessary, when the time is right.
- Assist members on how to cope with other people's ideas, and then ask them to substantiate the correctness of their own ideas.
- Choose the least objectionable alternative, if no clearly appropriate or appealing solution emerges.
- Before making a final decision, encourage members to consider any adverse repercussions likely to flow from a given solution.
- Be suspicious of unanimous decisions, particularly those arrived at quickly, and avoid them.
- Make sure that those who are charged with the implementation of a group's decision understand exactly what they are expected to do.
- Be on one's guard in order to prevent "groupthink".
- Avoid wide differences in status among members, or alternatively help members recognise these differences and explore ways of reducing their inhibitions with respect to "status" in the group.
- Use brainstorming to generate improved participation within the group, as well as as a device for the enhancement of the quality of ideas.
- Prepare procedures in advance to deal with urgent or crisis decisions.
- Protect the group from the damaging effects of external criticism, but at the same time let the group benefit from critical ideas or observations of a constructive nature that are likely to improve the quality of its deliberations.
- Encourage members to evaluate the skills residing in the group and find ways of improving them.

and motivation (Chapter 4). Tajfel (1970) states that membership of a group is in itself a sufficient condition for the creation of "inter-group discrimination". This is because the social groups to which people belong have a profound impact on the way they see the world. Turner (1981) explains discrimination resulting from group membership as being due to individuals perceiving greater similarities within their own group, and greater differences between their own group and other groups than actually exist in reality. Also, individuals assess and compare themselves using their own group as a yardstick in a quest for "positive social identity" (the source of self-confidence, self-image, and a sense of belonging); but if they do not experience positive self-esteem from membership of their group, they are quite capable of leaving the group, or distancing themselves from it, or trying to change how they perceive the group (Hayes, 1992, 1997).

The social identity approach to teambuilding —the subject of the next chapter—has been considered by Hayes. This involves "developing a strong sense of team (social) identification through establishing clear team boundaries, promoting cohesion through effective communication, and encouraging pride in the team through achievement and through professionalisation". Where members feel proud of their team or section, and see it as having special features, this can have a significant motivational impact (Hayes, 1997).

Social identification is concerned with our need to classify the world into "them" and "us" groups. We see ourselves as belonging to various social groups, which are different to other groups. To belong to different social groups is an important aspect of how we see ourselves. Shared beliefs (social representation) is also an important principle. It is understandable that favouring the in-group (the group to which we belong) could lead to the exercise of bias against out-groups (other groups), who are viewed less favourably than the in-group. If the in-group has high status and importance, there is a danger that its members will have greater potential to exercise bias, though it is conceivable that in-group members could in these circumstances be sympathetic towards

out-groups who are viewed as less fortunate than themselves. Hewstone, Ruibin, and Willis (2002) have suggested a number of approaches to reduce bias harboured by in-groups so that relations between groups can be improved. These include exercises aimed at changing attitudes supporting biases, and influencing behaviour so that in-group members behave in a better way towards out-groups. Other measures could be providing the in-group with more information about the characteristics of the out-group, and the establishment of superordinate goals that could have the effect of uniting groups in pursuit of a common goal. One should acknowledge that inter-group interactions can breed hostile behaviour and may result in open conflict. Inter-group conflict is discussed in Chapter 13.

Reason (1987) recognised inter-group behaviour in his analysis of the Chernobyl disaster. He makes reference to two groups at the plant—the operators and the experimenters—and the relationship between them in trying to explain the catastrophe. Key observations from his analysis include the following points. The operators, probably all Ukrainians, were members of a high-prestige occupational group, and had recently won an award. They probably approached the task with a "can do" attitude with some confidence in their ability to "fly" the reactor. Like other nuclear power plant operators, they would operate the plant using "process feel" rather than a knowledge of reactor physics. Their immediate aim was to complete the test as quickly as possible, get rid of the experimenters, and shut down the plant in time for the start of the Tuesday maintenance programme. But they had forgotten to be afraid of the dangerous beast they were driving. As the Russian report put it: "They had lost any feeling for the hazards involved."

The experimenters, akin to a development group, were electrical engineers from Moscow. Their aim was quite clear: to crack a stubborn technical problem once and for all. Although they would have set the goals for the operators before and during the experiment, they would not, themselves, have known much about the actual operation of a nuclear power station. The Russian report makes it evident that the engineer in charge of this group knew little or nothing about nuclear reactors. Together the two groups made a dangerous mixture. The experimenters were a group of single-minded but non-nuclear engineers directing a group of dedicated but overconfident operators. Each group probably assumed that the other knew what it was doing. And both parties had little or no understanding of the dangers they were courting, or of the system they were abusing.

As stated earlier, when individuals identify strongly with a group, their views of other groups become biased, and harmonious relations may be difficult to achieve (Ashforth & Mael, 1989). The two groups at the Chernobyl plant had some difficulties in relating to each other. In general it is important for groups to relate well when interactions are required for the achievement of organisational objectives.

Performance variables

Inter-group performance can be affected by the following variables (Moorhead & Griffin, 1998, 2004):

• task uncertainty;
• task interdependence;
• time and goal interdependence; and
• resources and location.

Task uncertainty. This arises when groups lack information about courses of action to take or what to do about future events that may affect them, the task, or the organisation. Uncertainties arise from a diverse range of factors relating to technology, markets, the economy, regulatory agencies, etc. Groups may confront these uncertainties on their own, or seek help from another group in an attempt to reduce uncertainties. For example, the personnel or HR department may be able to assist the production department on legal practices with respect to handling staff redundancies.

Task interdependence. This is concerned with the extent to which groups have to depend on each other, necessitating coordination to achieve common objectives. For example, when the output of one group becomes the input for another ("sequential interdependence"), interactions occur and coordination effort is necessary. The research and development department in a pharmaceutical company provides an output that is used as an input to the production department, which, in turn, provides an output that the sales and marketing department handles.

Time and goal interdependence. Goals set at the top of the organisation are expressed further down the hierarchy as subgoals to which various groups subscribe. It is common for deadlines to be attached to the achievement of particular subgoals —e.g., complete a project or task by a certain date—because of the need to harmonise the operations of various groups. Problems arise when groups do not share the same time frames. For example, the research engineer feels that more time is needed before a new product is ready for production—a view not shared by the production department. Those responsible for coordinating the work of diverse groups should be sensitive to the need to resolve such differences so that group interactions flow smoothly.

Resources and location. Groups interact over the availability of organisational resources. There is a greater likelihood of interaction if groups share the same or similar resources, or if one group can affect the availability of resources to another group. Budgetary processes are used to allocate resources between groups. Often one finds heated discussions among groups about rights to floor space and facilities. It is necessary to resolve these matters on an equitable basis.

In connection with location, the closer work groups are to each other the more likely it is that they will interact. Often the relocation of groups on a single floor or in one building is prompted by a deliberate strategy to promote greater interaction. In other situations it may be appropriate to separate groups who are having difficulty relating to each other, in which case the objective is to decrease the frequency of interactions. However, this could create problems if there is a high degree of interdependency between these groups.

CHAPTER SUMMARY

- Having briefly introduced the notion of what is meant by a group, it was suggested that groups can be classified by type—i.e., formal or informal, primary or secondary, co-acting, counteracting, and reference groups.

- The characteristics of groups were identified as norms, cohesiveness, communication networks and interaction episodes, spatial and structural factors (including atmosphere, size, roles, leadership), and group dynamics. Before examining group processes, some reasons for joining groups were briefly stated.

- Group processes were identified as: reference groups; social comparison; co-action and affiliation; social control; decision making; and inter-group behaviour. Reference groups were classified as normative or comparative, positive or negative, and areas of application were noted.

- The significance of social comparison was explained. Group norms as a social comparative influence were illustrated with reference to production targets. The influence exerted by the group in different experimental conditions (e.g., the studies conducted by Sherif and Asch) was acknowledged. Group influence was briefly discussed with respect to budgeting discretionary costs and investor behaviour.

- With regard to co-action and affiliation, relating to others in different conditions (e.g., being evaluated by an expert or being in a state of fear) can have a material bearing on the behaviour of an individual in a group setting.

- Social control is the influence exercised by an authority figure on a vertical basis, rather than on a horizontal basis as in social comparison. Social control was illustrated with particular reference to Milgram's experiments (i.e., obedience to authority). Other forms of social control are institutional control and brainwashing.

- The nature and likely benefits of group decision making were discussed, initially with reference to the experiments conducted by Lewin. The limitations of group decision making were noted. The different types of decision-making groups were examined. The risky shift phenomenon was explained and illustrated using an investment decision as an example. The focus on decision making was concluded with a discussion of groupthink. The key characteristics of groupthink were explained, along with possible steps to counteract it. Reflections on groupthink research were introduced.

- The nature of both the effective and the ineffective group was explained.

- The importance of inter-group behaviour was noted, and social identity was explained. The variables likely to affect inter-group performance—task uncertainty, task interdependence, time and goal interdependence, and resources and location—were identified.

QUESTIONS

(1) Define what is meant by a group, and give examples of different types of group.

(2) What is the difference between an internally imposed norm and an externally imposed norm? Into which category would you place a production target?

(3) Explain the following terms, which are used to describe the characteristics of a group: (a) communication networks; (b) group dynamics; and (c) geographic proximity.

(4) Examine the relationship between cohesiveness and productivity.

(5) Identify the structural factors discussed in the context of the characteristics of the group, and single out the factor(s) that you consider are critical for our understanding of groups.

(6) Give the reasons why you joined your favourite group other than your family.

(7) What is the difference between: (a) a membership group and a reference group; and (b) a normative reference group and a comparative reference group?

(8) Discuss the suggestion that reference groups influence consumer behaviour.

(9) What is the significance of the Hawthorne studies in the context of group norms as a social comparative influence?

(10) Comment on the relevance of the findings of Asch's experiment to a group involved in the budgeting process.

(11) Describe Milgram's work on obedience to authority, and suggest the most appropriate type of organisation where social control is legitimate.

(12) With reference to decision-making groups, explain the following with examples from business practice: (a) group discussion; (b) risky shift and cautious shift; (c) teamthink; and (d) groupthink.

(13) Identify the main characteristics of the effective and ineffective group.

(14) Discuss the factors likely to influence intergroup performance.

SPOTLIGHT ON RELEVANT READING

Bond, R., & Smith, P.B. (1996). Culture and conformity: A meta analysis of studies using Asch's (1952, 1956) line judgement task. *Psychological Bulletin*, January, 111–137.

Brown, R. (2000). *Group processes*. Oxford: Blackwell.

Guest, D., & Conway, N. (2002). *Pressure at work and the psychological contract*. London: Chartered Institute of Personnel and Development.

Park, W. (2000). A comprehensive empirical investigation of the relationship among variables of the groupthink model. *Journal of Organizational Behaviour*, 21, 873–887.

Learning Outcomes

After studying this chapter you should be able to:

- Explain what is meant by a team and recognise different types of teams.

- Outline the developments that have given rise to the popularity of teams.

- Assess the benefits to an organisation from the use of teams.

- Describe models of team or group development.

- Provide examples of contextual factors that might influence teams.

- List the features of a high-performance team.

- Recognise mistakes made in building effective teams and list means of correcting them.

- Explain why there is a need to nurture mature teams.

- Discuss management team development.

- Provide examples of diversity in teams.

- Appreciate the nature of leadership in teams.

Teambuilding

11

Following a definition of teams, types of teams, why they are used, and the likely benefits from their use, there is a discussion of models of team or group development, recognising the importance of contextual factors in group functioning. Next, the notion of the high-performance team is introduced, plus discussion of the problems encountered in teambuilding and ways of addressing these problems. Then there is a focus on the need to enrich or refresh mature teams, and the use of project teams in specified circumstances. The final part of the chapter deals with the different approaches to management team development, diversity or heterogeneity in teams, leadership and empowerment in teams, and the influence exerted by contextual factors.

Contents

DEFINITION

Teams and groups are words that are used interchangeably. Some academics maintain that it is extremely difficult, if not impossible, to distinguish between teams and groups (Guzzo & Dickson, 1996), but others argue that there are differences between the two. For example, a team could be described as a small number of people with complementary skills who are committed to a common purpose, common performance goals, and a common approach for which they hold themselves mutually accountable. A team differs from the work group in its job category, authority, and reward systems (Moorhead & Griffin, 2004).

Developments that have given rise to the use of teams in organisations are trends towards breaking down functional boundaries within organisations and the increasing amount of work based on projects requiring input from people with different expertise and experience. Therefore, when group concepts are applied to certain features of organisational functioning, it is customary to refer to *teams* and *teambuilding*. The appeal of teams in contemporary organisations could spring from the belief that teams typically outperform individuals when the tasks undertaken require multiple skills, judgement, and experience (Mohrman, Cohen, & Mohrman, 1995). There is evidence that productivity and other gains can be achieved as a result of adopting the team-based approach. As a result of moving to teamwork, K-Shoes reported a 19% increase in productivity and significant reductions in rejects in the manufacturing process, and Colgate Palmolive reported a technician turnover rate that was very low—90% of technicians were in post after 5 years (Wellins, Byham, & Dixon, 1994).

The concept of teambuilding originated in the study of organisational development. The latter in its broadest sense (i.e., trying to fulfil the twin objectives of meeting organisational goals and satisfying individual needs) is discussed in Chapter 16. The reliance on teams in organisations has been pronounced since the 1980s. What is noticeable is the shift in research activity from the traditional small group, discussed in the previous chapter, towards task-performing teams embedded in organisations (Ilgen, 1999).

TYPES OF TEAMS

The following different types of teams are discussed in this section:

- work teams;
- management teams;
- top management teams;
- cross-functional teams;
- venture teams;
- quality circles;
- self-managed teams;
- affinity groups; and
- virtual teams.

Work teams

These are relatively permanent and engaged in daily work. There is an example of a work team and the attitude of the unions towards it in Panel 11.1.

Management teams

These teams coordinate the activity of work teams drawn from a number of areas, as well as offering advice and support.

Top management teams

The emphasis on top teams represents an important advance in thinking about executive leadership, since the management of an enterprise is typically a shared activity that extends well beyond the chief executive. The top management team does not have to be a formal arrangement, such as a committee. More often it refers to a relatively small group of the most influential executives at the top of the organisation. Like all resources, an effective senior team requires investment and time to develop (Hambrick, 2000).

Although the idea of top teams is appealing, it may be difficult to put into practice. The top layer

---

PANEL 11.1: Work teams

In the mid-1990s the Royal Mail was using a work system where a postal worker would have responsibility for a particular delivery route. Around this time it was considered more appropriate to create mail delivery teams of roughly nine members, and each member would have responsibility for all routes. It was hoped that the adoption of team working would smooth the confrontation process and emphasise harmony in finding solutions to problems. For example, under the old system a difference of opinion between a foot postman and a postman with a van over the size of packets to be delivered by the van driver would need to be resolved by a manager. But under the new system of team working all team members, including the driver, have a common interest in securing a quick harmonious solution to the problem.

The union—the Communication Workers—complained about the lack of flexibility in the new system. The union maintained that team working seemed to be introducing fixed duties with less job rotation, unsocial hours, and greater demarcation in certain areas, and was at odds with management on this issue. The arbitration service brokered a deal, but this was subsequently rejected by the Council of the union.

Sometimes unions fear that work will be allocated to team members for which they are not adequately rewarded in terms of money or job status, coupled with the reduced opportunities for upgrading, which will have a dampening on pay aspirations. Another concern of unions about team working is the fear that their influence and communication with members will be eroded or undermined. However, it is possible to find some union (MSF) support for team working in the sense that it provides a supportive environment in which the normal preoccupation with authority and status is reduced as members strive to achieve common objectives, though the MSF is also likely to subscribe to the view that team working promotes the individualisation rather than the collectivisation of conflict, as well as the unleashing of competitive rather than cooperative forces within the team.

(Buckley, 1996)

---

of management may find it difficult to function as a team because of a reluctance to modify their approach or sacrifice their individuality or independence, particularly if they have a record of success (Hart, 1996). On the basis of their experience as McKinsey management consultants in the USA, Katzenbach and Smith (1993) concluded that although teams have an advantage over individuals, there are instances where factors such as the time-consuming nature of team working and a culture of individual rather than collective effort, make it difficult for teams to form, particularly at the top management level. Similarly, Kakabadse (1991) found obstacles to the effective functioning of top management teams in companies in the UK and Ireland.

Cross-functional teams

These are drawn from roughly the same hierarchical level, but from different functional areas within an organisation, or even between organisations, and they come together to perform a particular task. They are not easy to manage as they exchange and develop ideas, solve problems, and coordinate complex projects. They take some time to settle down as trust has to be developed

between people coming from diverse backgrounds (Denison, Hart, & Kahn, 1996).

Venture teams

These teams try to tap the resources of creative departments within the organisation. A **venture team** is often located out on a limb and is not subjected to the normal rules and regulations of the company. At Convergent Technologies in the USA they used the name "Strike Force" to describe a venture team set up to develop a new computer. Strike Force, even though a small team, is a separate small company within the larger company and has the independence to make the best use of its members' ideas, free from the constraints of the normal bureaucracy. Kodak has had 14 venture teams over a period of 16 years, exploring ideas such as computerised photo imaging, lithium batteries, and technology to project computer images on to a large screen (Daft, 1998).

At the 3M corporation venture teams are referred to as actions teams. An employee with a promising new idea is given permission to recruit new team members from within the company. These people could become key players in a newly created division if the idea is successful (Daft, 2004).

Quality circles

These teams are concerned with improving quality and effectiveness. The **quality circle** could be considered an extension to the basic philosophy of the participative process. As a group phenomenon, it has relevance to the discussion in Chapter 10. The quality circle advocates participation in the setting of objectives, together with participation in processes leading to a removal of obstacles frustrating the achievement of agreed objectives. The consequences of the implementation of quality circles are said to be enhanced commitment to necessary changes in work practices.

The quality circle became an integral part of the management system in Japan, and the key factor appears to be the involvement of employees at all levels. It is used to improve productivity, product quality, and safety at work, and the benefits claimed following its use are reduced waste, improved communication between management and workers, the creation of a problem-solving environment, increased job involvement, and improved morale.

A quality circle is a small group of employees (4 to 15) who do similar work and report to the same supervisor. The group meets regularly on a voluntary basis to identify and analyse work problems and provide solutions. A large plant could have many quality circles. Employees are encouraged to join a circle, not told to, and they can expect to experience a greater sense of control over their job environment. Members of a circle receive training in the basics of the technical aspects of the job, and in the skills of problem solving and making presentations to management. Interpersonal skills training is an important means of removing the barriers to interactions between people.

The usefulness of the concept of the quality circle must be properly understood, and to this end a publicity campaign could be launched within the company to explain the concept to employees and to request volunteers. The objectives of the circle must be endorsed by management. Some of the main functional considerations concerning quality circles are set out in Panel 11.2.

The following conditions should also be given serious consideration (Collard, 1981). The management should be modest in its expectations initially, and perhaps start with a low-profile pilot scheme. The support and commitment of management, and

---

PANEL 11.2: The workings of quality circles

A quality circle consists of circle members, a circle leader, a facilitator, a steering committee, and circle management. Circle volunteers are those who do the work and are interested in improving the quality of the work environment. The circle leader is a specially trained supervisor or somebody chosen from among the voluntary group. A facilitator, who has to be carefully selected and trained, provides training to circle members, provides a communication channel between different circles, and acts as liaison between the steering committee and management. He or she provides feedback on various activities, exerts influence where appropriate, and deals with conflicting groups.

A steering committee normally comprises first-line supervisors, who have a brief to provide quick responses to requests for funds, and to make sure that the circles get support from technical specialists in the organisation. Circle management provides support, funds, and facilities, and it reviews the solutions recommended by the circle in its management presentations. The presentations are the vehicle through which the group obtains recognition for the work done.

A quality circle meeting, in a quiet room, could last for no more than 1 hour per week. Members of the circle would identify problems that could affect the overall company plan; for example, how to improve productivity by 10% over the next year. The circle would prioritise the order in which problems are to be tackled and, having selected a problem (e.g., how to reduce product defects from 5% to 2%), circle members set realistic goals. Using appropriate analytic methods, a general plan and schedule for the solution of the identified problem are established. Drawing on internal expertise and invited external specialists who act in an advisory capacity, and using external sources of data, the circle discusses several solutions to a problem.

The preferred solution would be tested and implemented after presenting management with a full analysis using appropriate statistical techniques. Where management decide to implement the solution, this should be publicised widely so as to provide circle members with the necessary recognition. Any rejection of a circle recommendation should have the reasons for nonacceptance well stated. The results emanating from circle initiatives should be monitored, and presentations of successful outcomes could go beyond the organisational level in which the circle functions. As an incentive for circle members, in Japan it is not uncommon for directors of a company to be present and participate directly by asking questions at the presentation.

particularly senior management, is crucial. They should demonstrate their support for the programme, in both words and actions, by explaining what is involved, by providing training resources and other assistance, by attending regular presentations made by the circle, and by using the circle for its own purposes. The terms of reference of the quality circle should be clearly stated and communicated.

The safeguards and assurances with respect to the impact the quality circle may have on bonuses, overtime earnings, and job security have to be considered. The union is likely to be sensitive to the question of productivity gains and the way they are to be distributed. The importance of anticipating problems, rather than merely reacting to them, has to be stressed, as well as the need to engage in innovative activities, such as new systems and products. Naturally, circle members would like to see their successes recognised at all levels of the organisation.

In an empirical study of how quality circles work in practice in four US companies, it was concluded that quality circles lend themselves to the solution of basic localised problems of an immediate and solvable nature. They also provide employees with an opportunity to learn how to influence their work situation (Burpeau-Di Gregorio & Dickson, 1983). The Work Research Unit of the Department of Employment in the UK did much in the 1980s to publicise the concept of the quality circle, and was interested in the practical application of the concept (Work Research Unit, 1983). In Japan the enthusiasm for the quality circle is evident, and the concept is adapted to meet particular organisational circumstances. As a result, there are variations in the manner in which the quality circle is implemented (Collard, 1981).

One practice common to all quality circles is that discussions go beyond quality; they include cost, use of equipment, efficiency, errors, and safety. In some cases there is a formal training programme for members; in other cases only leaders receive formal training, and there are also instances where no formal training is provided. In the latter case the skills of supervisors and experts in the group would be used. The circle leader can

be the immediate supervisor of the group; in other cases the leadership role rotates, though it is likely that the majority of leaders come from the ranks of supervisors. Sometimes the norm is to hold meetings in the employees' time without payment, but there are also precedents for meetings to take place in the company's time, with overtime payments for meetings held in the employees' time.

There is evidence to indicate that although quality circles have a short-term favourable effect, their effectiveness over time begins to diminish (Griffin, 1988; Hayes, 1997). Also there have been examples of lukewarm commitments to quality circles by management, as well as trade union opposition. In the latter case it is possible that quality circles were seen as a vehicle to create a more expansive participative culture throughout an organisation that could be construed as a threat. It could become a live issue if there is no agreement between management and the trade union about setting up quality circles. It should be noted that in recent years a number of organisations have discarded their quality circles and replaced them with team-based structures.

A development, not directly related to quality circles but no doubt complementary to them, is called "total quality management". It starts with the vision that concentrated management action can improve the quality of an organisation's services and products at very competitive cost levels, while still satisfying customer needs and increasing market share. Various action strategies are suggested, including securing a high level of involvement and commitment from organisational members (Kanji, 1990). There is a belief that if total quality management (TQM) is handled properly it can deliver gradual but continuous improvements in many aspects of business performance. This is a view likely to be bolstered by the findings of research conducted by the Delta Consulting Group in the United States. Although the study of around 200 large corporations was generally supportive of TQM, problems were identified. Chief executives reported two particular problems with TQM: (a) it took longer than expected to produce results; and (b) some senior managers were not sufficiently skilled in handling it. By contrast, quality officials in the organisations studied emphasised negative views with respect to senior management's knowledge and skill, and identified conflicting values among senior managers, a lack of perceived need for change, and strong resistance to change (Lorenz, 1993a).

Self-managed teams

These teams or groups, with around 10–15 employees, could be considered the successor to the *autonomous work groups* discussed in Chapter 4, and they take on the responsibilities of their former supervisors (Cohen, Ledford, & Spreitzer, 1996). The work of the team consists of planning and scheduling of work, collective control over the pace of work, making operating decisions, and solving problems. A feature of the real self-managed team is the selection of people to join the group, and allowing members to evaluate each other's performance, but the latter, according to Golzen (1993), could be a contentious issue.

Nowadays we tend to extol the virtues of the self-managed team, to the extent that they are considered the ideal recipe to counteract the worst effects of organisational life, such as stress and lack of meaning in work. According to Manz and Sims (1993), by allowing people to manage themselves this type of group provides people with scope to experience more personal fulfilment, gain self-respect and dignity, and feel a greater sense of identification with their work. A valid question to ask is, how does the traditional manager interact with the self-managed team? Sometimes managers do not adapt easily to the role of coach and facilitator required by team-based organisation, particularly if their skills were developed under the traditional hierarchical system of organisation. Some managers feel that they are undermining their job security if they progressively hand over more and more of their traditional "directing" duties to the team.

The degree of freedom enjoyed by a self-managing team is an issue that has to be addressed. One extreme is where the group begins to function without guidance or input from a formal leader. According to Laiken (1994), such a group could become almost anarchic and ineffective, certainly in the short term. In order to achieve the aim of

the leaderless team in the long term, the group will initially need some structure and guidance.

Affinity groups

These teams are composed of professional or knowledge workers who meet regularly to share information, capitalise on opportunities, and solve problems relating to the work team and wider organisation (Van Aken, Monetta, & Scott Sink, 1994). *Knowledge management*, an umbrella term that covers processes and technologies to harness and exploit the know-how and experience of employees, is attracting increasing interest from a number of companies, such as British Telecommunications and British Petroleum (Donkin, 1998c). It is recognised that powerful information technology systems make the sharing of knowledge possible, but without a culture of knowledge sharing in business the necessary cooperation will not exist and therefore the potential of the technology will not be realised. The reluctance to cooperate in the sharing of knowledge could spring from a position where knowledge is regarded as power. There is a more expansive discussion on knowledge management in Chapter 7.

Virtual teams

A virtual team has been defined as a physically dispersed task group that conducts its business through modern information technology (Townsend, DeMarie, & Hendrickson, 1998). Members never meet in a room as a group but they relate to each other, audibly and visually, using computers and telecommunications. For example, information is shared through the internet, electronic mail, and teleconferencing. Through these facilities all members have access to the same information before making a decision, and can move in and out of teams as circumstances dictate.

Although flexibility is an attractive aspect of the virtual team, a negative feature is the lack of face-to-face interaction, which can weaken trust, communication, and accountability. This would appear to be a drawback, particularly in the early stages of the group development process when

---

PANEL 11.3: Features of a virtual team

Jenny Goodbody is Global Change Manger at Process Gas Solutions, a division of the British Oxygen Company, and works in New Jersey, USA. Her team of six people are spread across the world—Australia, Mexico, South Africa, Thailand, the UK, and Venezuela. Once a week they meet through a teleconference, which means Jenny must be wide awake by 6.30 am, while her colleague in Sydney, Australia has got to be in work mode well past 8.30 pm.

As part of an MBA project, Jenny studied nine virtual teams in her company. She found that only one-third of them were successful in meeting their objectives, a finding she says is in line with other research findings on virtual teams.

The following are aspects of good practice with regard to the operation of virtual teams:

- A face-to-face small group meeting right at the start is important, which helps with the nurturing of a key ingredient—the building of trust. The latter develops faster in teams that met face-to-face than in teams that did not. Jenny's team met at the start of their project work. The technical matter discussed hinged on the logic of using a new system and ensuring the change is implemented with the minimum of disruption. (Accenture, the UK consultancy firm, advises companies to set up meetings for global teams at the start of a large project in order to promote creativity and bonding—things that cannot be achieved over the phone: London, 2004b.)
- A distinguishing feature between successful and unsuccessful virtual teams is that the more successful teams make a genuine effort to build trust.
- Team leaders should support the development of trust among team members and should encourage the sharing of social information; for example, information that relates to their country or their family.
- A code of practice setting out how team members are to behave and communicate with each other should be agreed. The code should cover practical things, such as responding to e-mails within a fixed time. The code should also cover issues relating to psychological support, which could include sending encouraging messages to team members as well as acknowledging their efforts.
- Team leaders or coordinators should be skilful in summarising information obtained through interactions (conversations) within the team and made available to all members, but care should be exercised in generating information in case people become overloaded. This could apply to communications through e-mail.
- Ensure that everybody understands each other's role, and keep strong links with the parent organisation.
- Virtual teams should have a sponsor right at the top of the organisation. One of the key tasks of the sponsor is to show interest in the team's progress and be involved in resolving major issues.
- Place strong emphasis on rewarding good performance.

(Maitland, 2004b)

---

face-to-face contact would be beneficial. The challenge is to encourage positive interaction between members of the virtual team without the benefit of face-to-face contact. It is said that for these teams to succeed there should be clarity in the objectives set for them, the existence of the necessary administrative support, appropriate training provided, and last but not least, top management support (Kreitner et al., 2002). According to Child (2005), there is increasing interest in the use of global virtual teams. There is reference to practical features of a virtual team (which is global in nature) in Panel 11.3.

TEAMBUILDING MODELS

It is natural for an organisation to be concerned about the effective operation of the various work groups or teams on both the technical and the interpersonal front. Teambuilding is the process of enhancing the effectiveness of teams, and the term is often used interchangeably with team development (Hogg & McInerney, 1990). The following are the major approaches that will be examined:

- models of group development;
- high-performing teams;
- project teams;
- management team development.

Models of group development

In its development a permanent group is said to pass through four main phases in a set sequence (Tuckman, 1965), with each stage having both dominant task-related and social considerations. A fifth phase applies to a temporary group. The five stages are:

(1) *Forming*. At the level of the task, the primary consideration is to focus on the nature of the job to be done and how best to do it with the available resources. At the social level, members try to establish the most appropriate behaviour to adopt (perhaps cautiously to begin with), and look to the leader or a powerful figure for guidance.

(2) *Storming*. At the level of the task, there appears to be emotional resistance to the demands of the job, particularly when the individual experiences a mismatch between the demands of the job and his or her own interpretation of what the job entails. At the social level, opinions of members seem to be polarised, particularly on key interpersonal issues. There is resistance to the control exercised by the group leader, and members are inclined to stress their own needs and concerns, and attempt to resist group influence.

(3) *Norming*. At the level of the task, there is an open exchange of views and feelings. Co-operation is conspicuous, with a willingness to listen to and accept the views of other members. At the social level, group cohesion develops. New standards (norms) and roles emerge and are accepted by group members. There is an emphasis on harmony, and mutual support is noticeable, as members perceive themselves to be part of a sound group that they wish to preserve. There is a conscious effort to avoid situations typified by conflict.

(4) *Performing*. At the level of the task, solutions to problems are emerging, and constructive attempts are made to complete jobs. The task and social aspects of work are coming together. At the social level, the group has developed a purposeful way of members relating to each other in the performance of tasks and functions, with flexibility being apparent. Interpersonal problems have been resolved, and the energy of the group is channelled into the tasks in hand.

(5) *Adjournment*. This stage amounts to the winding down of a temporary group's activities and it creates mixed emotions in the form of euphoria at completing the tasks and regret at terminating the existence of the group with the loss of comradeship developed over its life.

These five stages are referred to as the **Tuckman model**. The model implies that the group must go through the five stages before it can be effective in terms of performance. But time could be an important factor as far as successful progression within the model is concerned; too little time and issues may not be adequately resolved at a particular stage. Also, issues that are not resolved may go underground only to find expression at a later stage, but the Tuckman model would not accommodate such an eventuality because of its linear nature. However, in practice a number of stages may occur simultaneously, as when a group storms and performs at the same time, or regresses to previous stages. So the model may not progress smoothly in a neat fashion from one stage to the next in the manner predicted.

A slightly different four-stage model has been advanced by Woodcock (1979). The stages of development (in a concise form) are as follows:

(1) This phase suggests that many aspects of life in a team leave much to be desired. There appears to be an unnecessary level of authoritarian management and bureaucratic control. Group objectives are not very clear to members, and predictably there is a low level of involvement in the planning process. The stage is also characterised by poor listening, feelings are not seriously considered, and weaknesses are covered up.

(2) At this stage, suddenly there are indications that the group is prepared to experiment, risky ventures are debated, and wider options are considered. There is now concern for others, more listening, and personal feelings are aired.

(3) In addition to what is happening in stage 2, now there is evidence that the group is more methodical with respect to working practices. Procedures are agreed and ground rules are established.

(4) This stage builds on the foundation laid in stages 2 and 3, by developing new activities from a healthy base. The situation now is characterised by in-built flexibility and appropriate leadership, with the creative use of members' abilities and energy. The group is sensitive to members' needs and cherished principles, and development is a priority.

A more recent model of group development is the **punctuated equilibrium model**. Here there is a flurry of activity at the commencement of deliberations—i.e., changing old practices and introducing new ones—followed by a substantial period of inertia as the group puts into action the plans made at the earlier stage. The last meeting of the group is full of activity aimed at finishing the job. In this model the forming and norming stages associated with the Tucker model are combined. Next, there is a stage characterised by low performance, which is followed by the storming stage and a period of high performance, and finally adjournment (Romanelli & Tushman, 1994).

It is wise to consider the organisational context impinging on group tasks when viewing these models of group development. In a study of airline cockpit crews, consisting of strangers, the group did not need to create plans, calculate the resources needed, resolve conflict, and assign roles to individuals as predicted in the Tuckman model. Instead group members were in a situation where they could refer to the appropriate rules, job descriptions, and other information and resources necessary to perform the task (Ginnet, 1990).

The development of groups and teams, on the lines indicated, cannot be isolated from the prevailing ethos or culture in the organisation. An organisational culture having an impact on team development could be either achievement-oriented or help-oriented. According to Zander (1982), in the achievement-oriented organisation people place value on achieving their own personal ends, with a desire to get ahead and compete with colleagues. They tend to be individualistic and are not too concerned about the needs of the group. The help-oriented organisation has quite a different culture in which people make an effort to help their colleagues grow as people. They ask questions, listen attentively to the answers or observations made, and at all times they are seeking to understand people and situations. There tends to be a determined effort to explain issues in order to assist comprehension of what is entailed.

The culture or atmosphere of the organisation, referred to in the previous paragraph (and discussed in more detail in Chapter 15), cannot be ignored when the operation of teams or groups is considered. In today's organisation, certain groups (for example, the innovative project group, the multidisciplinary research team, the project planning group) are growing in importance, and as a consequence it is necessary for the organisational culture or climate to be supportive of them. An organisation with a supportive culture is likely to have the following features (Thomsett, 1980):

* There is a view that people are an asset to be developed.
* The organisation has a flat rather than a tall shape, and the management style is participative rather than autocratic.
* Innovation is prevalent, with a tendency to take significant risks.
* The control system within the organisation places more stress on internal controls (where the individual or group exercise self-regulation) rather than having an undue reliance on external controls (i.e., controls stemming from close supervision, specialist staff, as well as procedural control).
* The grouping of staff is enlightened, in the sense that people with skills and expertise tend to be brought together in appropriate groups, rather than having people with skills dispersed and located in isolated units.
* The level of commitment is impressive, with a noticeable lack of alienation, and people tend to collaborate rather than compete in a congenial environment.
* People's skills should match the roles they are expected to play, and natural groups should be allowed to form.

Team climate

The central idea behind the notion of a supportive organisational climate is that one is creating an infrastructure in which effective groups can flourish. In recent years the designers of the **Team Climate Inventory** recognised the need to place team functioning in its organisational context (Anderson & West, 1996). This approach examines the relationship between team working and innovation in organisations, stressing factors such as:

(1) A focus on clear and realistic objectives to which the team members are committed (called *vision*).

(2) Interaction between team members in a participative and interpersonally nonthreatening climate (called *participative safety*).

(3) A commitment to high standards of performance, and therefore being prepared to confront weaknesses (called *task orientation*).

(4) Enacted support for innovation, manifest, for example, in cooperative behaviour to develop and apply new ideas (called *support for innovation*). (There is further reference to West's ideas on creativity/innovation in Chapter 8. West (2002) maintains that teams are a useful vehicle for both generating new ideas and implementing them. It is recognised that the diversity of perspectives in teams, together with quality involvement and constructive discussion of issues, is a powerful ally of creativity/innovation. However, there are both positive and negative environmental influences to recognise in this respect.)

The above factors can be assessed with a survey instrument called the Team Climate Inventory (TCI) (Anderson & West, 1994). A shortened version of this inventory was used successfully in a research study in Finland (Kivimaki & Elovainio, 1999).

High-performance teams

In recent times there has been a preoccupation with the characteristics associated with high-performance teams, as follows:

- Abilities and skills. Technical expertise and knowledge about the problems faced, problem-solving and decision-making skills; effective feedback, conflict resolution, and other interpersonal skills (Larson & La Fasto, 1989; Stevens & Campion, 1994).
- Commitment to specific, challenging, and clearly defined goals; goal interdependence —i.e., linking individual goals to group goals (Larson & La Fasto, 1989; O'Leary-Kelly, Martocchio, & Frink, 1994).
- Potency (team spirit in this context); social support (relating positively and helping each other); workload sharing (people are pulling

their weight and free riding is minimised); communication and coordination (Campion, Medsker, & Higgs, 1993).

- Group-based, as opposed to individual, rewards.
- Size. It is suggested that the number should not exceed 12, otherwise create subgroups. Size can provide a cloak of anonymity that diffuses personal responsibility for the consequences of one's actions.
- High mutual trust, where values such as honesty, truthfulness, competence, loyalty, and openness, are present but not easy to sustain (Hosmer, 1995; Schindler & Thomas, 1993).
- Familiarity (in terms of specific knowledge about jobs, colleagues, and the work environment possessed by members). It is said that if familiarity does not extend to the factors mentioned, in particular co-workers, the team could lose momentum during the period of adjustment (Goodman & Leyden, 1991).
- Capacity to tap external sources of repute for information and resources of benefit to the team (Larson & La Fasto, 1989).

What type of team could be considered a high-performance team? One good example is the task-oriented team envisaged by Katzenbach and Smith (1993). This could be used with high-powered executive teams charged with a single complex task such as restructuring a company to meet future challenges. These teams could possess a number of the characteristics of the high-performance teams referred to earlier. When the job is done, the teams disband (Hayes, 1997). The basic principles put forward by Katzenbach and Smith to build an effective team in this context are as follows:

- Create a sense of urgency and direction.
- Choose people on the basis of skill, track record, and potential, and not on the basis of their personality.
- Ensure that the first meeting goes well, and put the accent on action.
- Lay down some explicit ground rules to govern behaviour.
- Focus on critical but urgent matters to address, and set clear objectives.

PANEL 11.4: Characteristics of high-performing teams

(1) Senior managers shape the nature and purpose of the team. The team is then allowed to get on with it and exercises flexibility with respect to planning and attending to operational matters. The team members are empowered. By giving the team clear authority and then taking a back seat, management releases collective energy and creativity.

(2) Successful teams translate the common purpose into specific and measurable performance goals. Specific team goals are related to department or division goals and the focus of attention is on what is required to be done and getting results. This fosters good communication and commitment and if there is conflict it is likely to be constructive and handled well. Feedback on progress towards meeting goals is available and considered important.

(3) The successful team should be of a manageable size (between 2 and 25), but the actual number depends on the demands of the situation. (Earlier there was reference to 12 as the number that should not be exceeded.)

(4) In successful teams there is the right mix of expertise, and the team strives to obtain and utilise complementary skills (e.g., a mix of technical expertise) for the purpose of problem solving and decision making. Interpersonal skills are mobilised to improve the dialogue and interaction and keep the team focused on the matter in hand.

(5) Successful teams develop a common commitment to working relationships. There must be agreement on the scheduling of work, the allocation of tasks, the necessary skill and its development, the ideal approach to decision making, and what is required of team members to justify their continued association with the team. The team deliberates on individuals best suited to the various tasks and how roles are related, and the reporting relationship between the team and others in the organisation. In fact a social contract among members is developed that governs the way they will relate to each other and specifies their obligations in the light of the demands of achieving the common goal.

(6) Members of successful teams hold themselves collectively accountable. It is said that putting the spotlight on individual responsibility is critical to a well-coordinated effort, but effective teams find ways to hold the collective accountable.

(Katzenbach and Smith, 1993)

- Devote a lot of time to interactions between members.
- Provide regular up-to-date information to members, recognise the potency of feedback at all times, and ensure members receive proper recognition and rewards.

Creating an effective team is no easy matter, and the establishment of a team-based organisation could pose a threat to the established management order.

Bolman and Deal (2003) feel that it is important to have a clear and appropriate structure for a team if it is to be successful, and in this respect they highlight the six distinguishing characteristics of high-performing teams devised by Katzenbach and Smith (1993); these (some of which have been briefly referred to above) are set out in Panel 11.4.

Problems with teambuilding

Common mistakes in building effective teams, according to Hackman (1994), are as follows:

(1) Treating a unit as a team but, when it comes to the allocation of tasks, employee selection,

dispensing rewards, performance management, etc., the set of individuals are dealt with on an individual basis.

(2) There is a failure to strike the right balance between the exercise of authority and the use of democratic practices. The right balance would be the avoidance of the extremes. One extreme—complete democracy—is where management specifies neither the means (ways of achieving objectives) nor the ends (objectives of the team). Another is the full-bodied exercise of authority where both the means and the ends are specified by management. Perhaps the best option is to give the team its objectives, and then leave it to the members to decide the most appropriate way to achieve them.

(3) Organisational structures are left unchanged, when ideally they should be dismantled and replaced by an "enabling" structure.

(4) After the teams are formed, they are left unsupported, when in fact they should be provided with adequate material resources, supportive training, relevant organisational information systems, and group-based rewards.

(5) There is an invalid assumption that individuals are eager to work in teams and that they are equipped to do so. In certain individualistic cultures (e.g., the USA) this may not be so. Organisations in such cultures may have traditionally placed value on individual performance; in fact, often a competitive environment that encouraged individual achievement and recognition was nurtured. In such circumstances, training in teamwork is crucial.

Confronting the problems

Hackman offers advice to confront the above mistakes, in the form of a recipe for effective teamwork. The following guidelines embrace much of the advice given:

- Think clearly, and take appropriate action in spelling out the tasks to be performed, the composition of the team, and appropriate group norms (e.g., supportive of helping others).
- Ensure authority is "bounded"—specify the ends, but not the means to the end.
- Issue clear instructions and directions, but keep a sharp eye on motivational implications of such action.
- Recognise the importance of intrinsic motivation (e.g., the excitement and satisfaction from being part of a successful team, coupled with potential for self-development).
- Create a supportive organisational context; for example, selection of team players capable of undertaking their team roles, and rewards (including bonuses) to encourage cooperation and the meeting of team goals. One must not ignore individual performance but it has to be balanced with group-oriented contributions, such as sharing information with one's colleagues, assisting with the training of new colleagues, and helping to resolve team conflicts.
- Provide training and expert coaching in the processes of teamwork. Workshops could be mounted to cover a number of processes such as problem solving, communication, negotiation, conflict management, and coaching skills.

Nurturing mature teams

It can take a long time for a team to become mature, efficient, and effective. It is important for senior management to be fully committed to a team-based organisation. If senior management loses its patience with the team because of the slowness of progress through the cycle of development, the team may be disbanded. The alternative then would be a return to the traditional hierarchical structure with certain drawbacks in terms of the significant commitment of supervisory and managerial time and perhaps losses in efficiency and effectiveness.

Robbins (2003) rightly draws our attention to the need to reinvigorate mature teams because the initial euphoria and enthusiasm wear off and apathy sets in, and the latter could happen at the performing stage of Tuckman's model due to familiarity. The advantages of diversity are diluted by cohesiveness, groupthink may become a problem, and there may be less openness to new ideas and innovation. Therefore, when the initial euphoria has worn off and conflict has surfaced, those responsible for teams should utilise refresher training in areas such as communication, conflict resolution, and team processes in order to restore vitality, trust, and confidence.

PROJECT TEAMS

As is now apparent, a team is a particular type of group. We speak of teams in sport, and in business we have teams that come together at various stages to work on a project. Different specialists could make a contribution to a project at different times. In the early stages of a construction project, the architects, planners, and clients will be actively involved. Later, the surveyors, construction engineers, and builders will have a part to play. The project team changes in composition over time, though some members continue to serve throughout the life of the project and, of course, the contracting agent plays an integrating role, coordinating the various elements. Teams of this nature can be difficult to manage, and to complicate matters they cut across organisational boundaries, as well as permeating inter-departmental barriers.

Project teams, drawing their membership from within the organisation, are essentially multifunctional groups that may only have a temporary existence. They could be formed to solve particular problems and are likely to draw on representatives from different departments, with different backgrounds, values, skills, and affiliations. The problem of integrating members' contributions from diverse specialist areas can be difficult. The appointment of an "integrator" could be crucial in this respect. He or she could oversee the situation, deal with unusual problems that cut right across the group, resolve inter-sectional conflict, and facilitate decision making. In the final analysis, the organisational climate and structure need to be supportive of this approach.

In identifying the problems of introducing change and innovation, Kanter (1984) maintains that there should be "integrative thinking" within organisations in order to cultivate team-oriented, cooperative environments in which change is facilitated and innovation flourishes. In this type of setting Kanter (1999) is likely to advocate the virtues of "soft assets", which are: (i) concepts (ideas and technologies driven by innovation); (ii) competence (skills and abilities to use these concepts, supported by teaching); and (iii) connections (strategic relationships nurtured by collaboration). The soft assets are rooted in human qualities, such as imagination, courage, and sociability, and, according to Kanter, they will increasingly overtake hard assets as factors critical for organisational success.

What has been discussed so far with respect to project teams is the notion of the project team as a group concerned with developments where innovation features prominently. However, in recent years, due to cut backs and rationalisation, teams have been created to plan and execute changes in organisations against a background of anxiety and fear of job losses due to redundancy. What often happens in these circumstances is that these emotional and psychic issues begin to find expression at the level of the group and the organisation, with a regression to primitive thought processes and behaviour and the use of defence mechanisms

(Kanter, 1984). The end result can be irrational behaviour and illogical group decision making.

MANAGEMENT TEAM DEVELOPMENT

A conscious attempt can be made to develop managerial teams already in existence. Before any decision is made to implement a team development programme, several matters have to be considered (Dyer, 1977). For example, one could ask the following questions:

- Why is it necessary?
- Can an appropriate programme be devised?
- Who will be included as part of the team?
- What is the duration of the programme?
- Where should the programme be located?
- Should an external consultant be appointed?

Dyer's approach

A straightforward team development programme has been put forward by Dyer (1984), and it consists of the following steps:

(1) A day should be set aside, away from the place of work and free from interruptions, for teambuilding.
(2) Each individual should provide answers to the following questions before going to a meeting with other members: (i) What prevents you from being as effective as you would like to be in your position? (ii) What prevents staff in your unit from functioning as an effective team? (iii) What do you like about the unit that is worth maintaining? (iv) What suggestions do you have for improving the quality of the working relationships and the functioning of the unit?
(3) At the meeting each person makes a presentation of responses to the questions in step 2, and these are written on a blackboard or a flipchart, under four headings: barriers to individual effectiveness; barriers to team effectiveness; matters people enjoy; and suggestions for improvement.

(4) The group is asked to list, in order of priority, the problems it wants to raise. The list forms the agenda for the meeting.

(5) The group begins addressing the major objective of the session. This would be to remove as many barriers as possible to the smooth functioning of the group. The barrier-removing activity may consist of clarifying the role each member plays, putting right misunderstandings, going in for more sharing of information, changing assignments, or instituting other innovative measures.

These processes are characterised by collecting data to determine the causes of the problem. As a catalyst, a consultant must be sensitive to the group's desire to handle issues through open discussion. There will be a recognition that certain issues can be confronted here and now, other issues perhaps could be dealt with by a task force later, while the remaining issues are not open to change and will have to be left as a constraint that one has to accept. In the quest for solutions to a problem a manager acts as the group leader, while the consultant acts as an observer/facilitator, concentrating his or her attention on the process by which the group arrives at its conclusions along the lines of Schein's "process consultation" (discussed in Chapter 16). The final stage of the process is where action strategies, planned and approved during the teambuilding session, are put into practice. This requires commitment on the part of the manager, with support from the consultant.

Belbin's approach

While Dyer's approach to team development is largely used with existing teams of managers, the approach examined here starts with the proposition that the best way to proceed is to bring together people with a range of skills and expertise to form a balanced and effective team. This concept was advanced by Belbin (1981) and his colleagues, who were concerned with analysing what team member roles were necessary to constitute an effective team. Before members were allocated to a team, they underwent a series of psychometric tests designed to measure the individual's

personality and mental ability. With regard to personality types, the measures used would shed light on dimensions of personality listed here, which are similar to those used by Eysenck (see Chapter 2):

- stable extravert (e.g., social, responsive, talkative, enthusiastic, leader);
- unstable extravert (e.g., restless, aggressive, impulsive, optimistic);
- stable introvert (e.g., passive, thoughtful, reliable, calm); and
- unstable introvert (e.g., moody, anxious, pessimistic, quiet).

Measures of mental ability were also used, and these were designed to detect cleverness, and also creativity, using Cattell's formula for creative disposition. Note that the first step is to classify team members by personality type and mental ability. The next step is for members to be formed into teams and then to engage in an activity testing their skills. Trained observers would frequently record the way members interacted and the nature of their contributions. Categories of behaviour observed were as follows:

- asking;
- informing;
- proposing;
- opposing;
- delegating;
- building; and
- commenting.

Numerical scores would be given to each participating member on each category of behaviour. The scores would reveal who, for example, was doing the most talking, or what type of intervention strategy was used by a particular team member. Performance in the activity testing team members' skills could be related to a certain aspect of personality or ability. For example, was the person who was active in "proposing" one of the cleverest team members, or alternatively was he or she a stable extravert?

Examples of the work-related tests were the executive management exercise (EME) and Teamopoly (based on Monopoly). The EME is a computer-based game that requires users to be involved in producing calculations and analysis in the context of models of business. With Teamopoly the success of teams was measured in financial terms; so a financial yardstick was used to indicate the effectiveness of the teams in attaining their objectives. Also, in this exercise it was possible to detect the reasons for team failures—e.g., a poor team or inefficient use of the team's resources.

Many experiments were conducted by Belbin and his colleagues over a period of 9 years. The following are examples of the tests whereby attempts were made to come up with the right mix of talent in a team on the basis of (1) mental ability and (2) personality:

(1) A high-powered management team was formed consisting of those who scored high on the mental ability tests (i.e., clever people). This group was called the Apollo group, but unexpectedly was placed last among the teams. Apparently, the observers noted that the team did not function very well. In fact, there was fruitless debate, there was a lack of logical consistency in decision making, a number of priority tasks were neglected, members were prone to act independently, and there was an absence of coordinated effort.

(2) A team was formed of particular personality types, using the personality measure referred to earlier. Generally, the extraverts performed better than introverts. In particular, a team of stable extraverts had members who functioned in pairs; they were flexible in the way they operated and communicated well. They used the record sheets of the observers in order to modify or adjust their team's style. But note that when the teams of stable extraverts were engaged in planning activities, they had difficulty in concentrating; as a result, social activities, such as playing snooker, assumed a certain attraction. This led to a situation where they were likely to commit minor errors, and these errors were left uncorrected because of the easygoing manner of members. Apparently, the approach to teambuilding using similar personality types had clear weaknesses.

We can now conclude that management teams categorised solely by either mental ability or personality were less than satisfactory.

Team roles

The next series of experiments focused on teams composed of one particular type of worker. Eight key team roles were identified as follows: company worker; plant; resource investigator; chairperson; shaper; monitor-evaluator; team worker; and completer-finisher. A profile of each team role follows.

Company workers (CW). A CW possessed the following characteristics:

- disciplined;
- tough-minded;
- practical;
- trusting;
- tolerant;
- conservative;
- conscientious;
- exercised self-control;
- firm self-image;
- outward looking.

The experimental CW groups were composed of one team high in mental ability and the other low in mental ability. By and large, the results were negative; these groups failed to get good results and they tended to be inflexible and were lacking in substantive ideas. However, they were strongly committed to achieving the objectives of the team, and generally worked well together towards that end. If the situation in which they operated matched their style, the teams could be reasonably successful, but they did not have the versatility to respond well to new and different situations.

Plants (PLs). For this role, creative individuals who scored high on the mental ability and creative disposition tests were chosen. PLs had the following characteristics:

- individualistic;
- intellectual;

- serious minded;
- knowledgeable;
- unorthodox;
- aloof;
- genius;
- impractical;
- lacking managerial skills;
- loner.

PLs were planted in different teams, and were known as "ideas people". They were skilful at getting their ideas across and having them accepted. But, paradoxically, teams with more than one PL fared no better than those with none.

Resource investigator (RI). An RI tended to be creative, and possessed the following characteristics:

- versatile;
- curious;
- sociable;
- low on anxiety;
- extravert;
- innovative;
- communicative;
- social skills.

Both the RI and PL have creativity in common and could be considered innovative. But the RI was more extravert and more capable in a managerial sense. The RIs looked beyond the boundaries of their group and, as a consequence, injected new ideas from outside into the team's deliberations. Being outgoing, they liked to work closely with people, and were particularly good at utilising resources. I suppose the real strength of the RI was that of collecting incompletely developed ideas from others and making something of them, rather than originating ideas.

Chairperson (CH). Given the importance of the leadership role in a team, the characteristics of the effective CH should be noted:

- calm;
- average intellect;
- self-confident;

- average ability;
- trusting;
- impartial;
- dominant;
- self-disciplined;
- enthusiastic;
- positive thinker;
- reasonably extravert.

Successful team performance was associated with the effective CH profile. Their behaviour at meetings of the group indicated that they were capable of making the best use of resources at their disposal. They showed tolerance when listening to others, but were quite capable of rejecting people's advice when feeling justified in doing so. They had a canny way of intervening at critical points in the discussion, were adept at handling people, and never lost their grip on a situation. They injected a sense of purpose and direction into a meeting and, as a consequence, the discussion was highly focused. They were proficient at making assessments of situations in terms of practical implications.

Reflecting on this personal profile, and noticing that the effective CH is of average ability, a conclusion could be that the ability level is not compatible with his or her impressive track record. It is suggested by Belbin that average mental ability is an advantage, because it facilitates communication with colleagues or team members. Apparently, CHs with below average mental ability had difficulty in following the threads of an argument, were unsure of the number of alternatives open to them in a discussion, and showed signs of indecision. By contrast, CHs well above average mental ability tended to be too erudite in their reasoning at the cost of losing the attention of team members. The intellectual power, underpinned by the status factor (e.g., chairperson's role), had an adverse effect on the quality of communication and had an inhibiting effect on likely opponents within the group; as a result they advocated a cautious stance.

Shaper (SH). Another role, similar to that of the CH, was the shaper. SHs had the following characteristics:

- high achievers;
- highly strung;
- argumentative;
- outgoing;
- impatient;
- dynamic;
- provocative.

SHs were full of nervous energy, and winning was an important goal. They tended to be both a disruptive influence and an arousing force in a group.

Monitor-evaluator (ME). With regard to ME, it was said that in a team with a PL and RI one could find a situation whereby there were a number of conflicting ideas floating about. Therefore, there was a need for a team member who had the ability to evaluate conflicting proposals put forward by the group. Hence the need for an ME with the following characteristics:

- sober;
- clever;
- unemotional;
- uninspiring;
- discreet;
- detached;
- hard-headed;
- low arousal.

MEs were pretty shrewd in their judgements, and had a tendency to think that they were invariably right in their decisions, and anyway their disposition was conducive to taking an impartial view.

Team worker (TW). When one or more team members with real ability and skill cannot work well together or with colleagues, this can undermine the effectiveness of the team. TW is the sort of person who is needed to make the necessary interventions in order to minimise friction and encourage members to divert their energies to constructive ends. TW's characteristics are:

- responsive;
- gregarious;
- sensitive;

- team player;
- somewhat indecisive.

Completer-finisher (CF). Because many teams are reasonably good at instituting initiatives, but poor at sustaining the effort necessary for successful completion, there is a need for somebody like a CF. The characteristics of CFs are as follows:

- perseverance;
- perfectionist;
- conscientious;
- attention to detail;
- anxious.

CFs' role is a real asset to a team. They put enormous effort into the job, with an eye for detail, and show consistent performance. Though CFs appear to be calm and seemingly never frightened or upset, they absorb a fair amount of stress, and though highly controlled they are prone to anxiety.

An assessment of Belbin's approach

When one is reflecting on these eight roles, it is well to remember that there are certain individuals, perhaps a very small minority, who can perform more than one role in a group or team. There are other individuals who lack the necessary competence to perform any of the team roles in a satisfactory way; as a result, they contribute to a team's lack of success. Other factors contributing to a team's lack of success are:

- Where the culture of the situation interferes with the team's ability to confront particular problems and it is not supportive of members acting as specialists.
- Where individuals are not fully aware of what their roles entail, or they are performing a role that accords with their previous experience rather than the role allotted, or the role is changed in an unpredictable way.
- Where there is an unsuitable mix of characters in the team.
- Where the team has no strategy.

In the light of the analysis of Belbin's research work at the theoretical level, it is possible, through careful selection and matching of team members, to arrive at an optimal solution in terms of group effectiveness. That would entail the right mixture of team roles. However, in practice it must be extremely difficult to balance the team role with that of the role in which the manager feels comfortable as a technical expert. Also, for each member to use his or her skill and expertise in a way complementary to existing resources of the group in relation to the job in hand is no mean task. The team can only operate to its best advantage when it has the required set of roles to function as an efficient team. A real constraint is that there is a tendency for teams to be well endowed with shapers and implementers but with an insufficient supply of plants and team workers. In such circumstances plans are formulated and elaborated promptly, but frequently they are insufficiently creative and the discussion amounts to adversarial episodes where some members are discontented (Arnold, Cooper, & Robertson, 1998). Belbin's approach to the design of successful management teams would hardly be appropriate in a very small company not possessing a management team of eight members.

One thing that is certain about the discussion of Belbin's work is that it is a useful piece of research, but to design a successful team with reference to the prescription for the eight roles would be a challenge requiring considerable knowledge and expertise, and it would in itself rank as one of the most creative of tasks! Belbin (1993) referred to six factors connected with team roles behaviour (see Figure 11.1). Note that the titles used to describe two team roles have been changed: company worker is now referred to as *Implementer*, and chairperson has become *Coordinator*.

Dulewicz (1995) tested the inter-method reliability of obtaining Belbin's team roles using data derived from personality measures—the Cattell 16 PF and the OPQ—discussed in Chapter 2. He concluded that there was some evidence supportive of the structure and validity of the team roles identified by Belbin, but he does not support Belbin's Team Role Self-Perception Inventory (BTRSPI). Furnham, Steele, and Pendleton (1993) subjected the psychometric properties of the BTRSPI to empirical test and concluded that there is little psychometric support for the structure of Belbin's inventory. Furnham et al. point out that if Belbin's inventory is to be used for employee selection, it is important that the psychometric

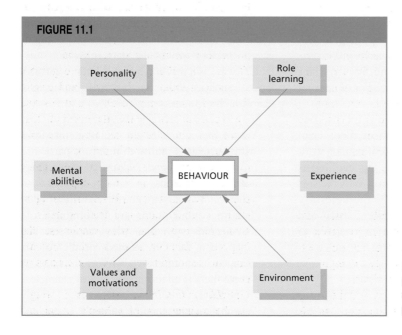

FIGURE 11.1

Factors associated with team roles behaviour (from Belbin, 1993). Copyright © 1993 and reprinted by permission.

properties of the scale are investigated. Barry (1995) reflects on the above criticisms, but on the basis of his consultancy work with top management teams concludes that he has found Belbin's measures extremely useful in the field of management development.

Finally, Arnold (2005) rightly points out that while teams with diverse roles (such as Belbin's team roles) have the potential to be highly effective because of the varied outlooks members possess, they often fail to achieve that potential because of one critical process—integration. It is often difficult to maintain effective integration as teams become diverse in their composition. As we shall see later, diversity is a concept that applies to phenomena other than expertise, such as age, race, gender, and culture.

Team management wheel

Margerison and McCann (1995) go a stage further than Belbin by developing a basic model that links job functions with the roles team members are expected to perform. This model is depicted in Figure 11.2 as the team management wheel, and is based on necessary behaviour (i.e., exploring and controlling) and preferred roles (i.e., advisory and organising). Exploring behaviour includes contacting people, searching for opportunities, and creative pursuits. Controlling behaviour is reflected in adhering to rules regulations, and operating systems with an eye for detail and precision in the performance of tasks. Advisory roles are associated with the provision of support services—e.g., planning, research, and training for main-line activities such as the production and distribution of products and services. Organising roles focus on the main-line activities.

The team roles identified in Figure 11.2 are as follows:

(1) *Reporter-advisers*, who collect and use information in performing a support role.
(2) *Creator-innovators*, who concentrate on generating new ideas, and are likely to emphasise experimentation and new designs.
(3) *Explorer-promoters*, who represent the group or the organisation in establishing outside

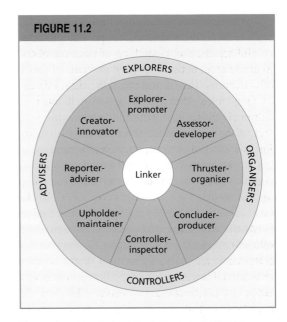

FIGURE 11.2

Team management wheel (from Margerison & McCann, 1995). Copyright © 1995 and reprinted by permission.

contacts so as to publicise new ideas, and attract funds and resources.
(4) *Assessor-developers*, who identify the best way to develop ideas in practice, assessing the viability of proposals with reference to market research and other intelligence data. They may make a prototype, where appropriate, as a means to test their ideas.
(5) *Thruster-organisers*, who show an eagerness to establish exacting objectives, and ensure that the appropriate procedures and systems are in place to facilitate the attainment of those objectives. They show a keenness to remove any obstacles that stand in their way.
(6) *Concluder-producers*, who show consistency and determination in seeing a process or project through to completion, adhering to quality considerations and deadline dates.
(7) *Controller-inspectors*, who emphasise the inspection function to ensure that jobs are done in the correct way, with an emphasis on control.
(8) *Upholder-maintainers*, who place weight on the maintenance of valuable social and

organisational systems and relationships. They try to preserve the best of the old traditions and cultural heritage in an organisational sense, but at the same time they are receptive to the notion of grafting new ideas into the ongoing system without too much disruption.

(9) *Linkers* are those who link people within the team, but they also act as representatives for the team in its contacts with other units and organisations. The emphasis is on coordination and integration—common managerial functions.

Has the team management wheel any weaknesses? According to Barry (1995), citing Furnham et al.'s (1993) criticism of this measure, "there appears to be little or no evidence of the factorial structure of the questionnaire (to confirm the classificatory/taxonomic scheme put forward), nor is there any evidence of the predictive or construct validity of the test. However, it was noted that the instrument does have norms and evidence of internal reliability and concurrent validity." (There is reference to reliability and validity in Chapter 9, plus further explanation of these concepts in Chapter 17.)

Finally, note that Katzenbach and Smith (1993) have suggested an alternative to the "team role" approach. They emphasised the importance of the team having an appropriate blend of skills needed to undertake a particular task. These skills could be categorised as follows:

- technical or functional skills;
- problem-solving and decision-making skills;
- interpersonal skills (e.g., communicating well with others, and promoting social harmony).

It is said the listed skills are more likely to be dynamic and amenable to development over time than are the Belbin's team roles (Hayes, 1997).

DIVERSITY IN TEAMS

Diversity in teams can find expression in different forms. In the previous section both Belbin plus Margerison and McCann emphasised the importance of diversity, when individual strengths and preferred roles are recognised in the allocation of work tasks. But diversity can also be associated with issues such as age, gender, race, and culture. Diversity or heterogeneity brings multiple perspectives to the team discussion because of the varied expertise and orientation, thereby increasing the likelihood that the team will discover creative or unique solutions. Because more time is spent in discussions in this type of forum, the likelihood of choosing a strong course of action is greater. It is suggested that the positive side-effects emanating from diversity decline over time because of the difficulty experienced by diverse groups in working together as a unit. However, unity or cohesiveness could be promoted as members of diverse teams become familiar with each other.

The problem of unifying the diverse team is acknowledged by Jackson, Stone, and Alvarez (1993), and the issue of diverse teams not often realising their potential is recognised by Kandola (1995). The important issue of solid integration is raised by Maznevski (1994). Integration in this sense means having a common outlook, agreeing on mutually acceptable standards, a realistic assessment of any difficulties, showing confidence, nurturing powers of empathy, and communicating well. But since these characteristics or factors are not easy to acquire, it is difficult to achieve integration in diverse teams.

The important issue of cultural diversity has been advanced by Adler (2002). She maintains that in the 1990s the development of global markets created numerous cross-cultural contacts, and that cross-cultural dialogue has become the basis for transacting global business. Today managers do not have to leave their communities in order to work for a foreign-owned company, sell to foreign clients, negotiate with foreign suppliers, and attend meetings with colleagues from abroad. Design teams with members scattered around the world develop revolutionary new products and carry out their deliberations at electronic meetings, relying on e-mail and internet discussions as well as teleconferencing, telephone, and fax.

The potential for impressive levels of productivity in culturally diverse teams is high. These teams can possess insights, perspectives, experience, and breadth of resources, and therefore it is possible to create new and improved ideas. Regrettably, culturally diverse teams rarely achieve their full potential. Kandola (1995) made this point earlier when referring to the potential of diverse teams. It is highly likely that multicultural teams cannot hope to achieve their full potential unless diversity is well managed. The importance of management or leadership in teams is addressed in the next section.

LEADERSHIP IN TEAMS

Leadership, which is discussed at length in Chapter 12, is becoming increasingly important within a team context, and takes on a form different from the traditional role of the first line of supervision or management. Team leadership has a pronounced "facilitating" aspect to it. According to Steckler and Fondas (1995), the team leader's role hinges on two major themes. One is facilitating the functioning of the team, and the other is managing the external boundary of the team.

- *Facilitating team functioning.* Team leaders are troubleshooters; they help the team to analyse and solve problems, and obtain resources from outside the group (e.g., secure help when the team is overburdened with work). They help

with confronting conflict, and can assist with minimising the disruptive consequences of team conflict by asking the right questions, such as: What is the source of the conflict? What issues are at stake and who are the principal characters? What avenues are open to the team to resolve the difficulties? And what are the strengths and weaknesses of the alternatives at our disposal? Team leaders act as coaches when they help team members to improve their work performance by clarifying what is expected of them in the job and offering support. Later, there is reference to good coaching when commenting on effective team leadership.
- *Liaison with external groups and agencies.* These would include management higher up the organisation, other teams within the organisation, customers, suppliers, and others with whom contact is made in order that the team can function. With regard to the external contacts, the leader is acting in a representative role. He or she collects relevant information and shares it with members of the team, explains and clarifies the expectations other people have of the team, and is instrumental in securing the resources required by the team.

Effective team leadership

To be effective as a team leader it is necessary to acquire skills, such as sharing information, trusting others (see Panel 11.5), being patient,

---

PANEL 11.5: Trust and team management

When we see others acting in ways that indicate they trust us we tend to trust them more (a manifestation of the reciprocal nature of trust). On the other hand, we distrust those whose actions appear to break our trust or who distrust us. When we trust a person we have faith in their good intentions, but the act of trusting somebody carries with it the intrinsic risk of betrayal. Our willingness to trust others can be placed at a point on a continuum, at one end is blind trust and at the other end is an unwillingness to trust (Dirks, 1999; Mayer, Davis, & Schoorman, 1995; Williams, 2001).

Good communication, being supported, treated fairly, and respected are key ingredients in the process of building trust. Perhaps the most important principle of all in successful team management, though, is that of respect. Employees' contributions (thoughts, ideas, talents) must be respected, otherwise they will not contribute. Manifestations of respect for employees arise when the organisation provides, for example, adequate training and resources, as well as empowering them. People are quick to establish the difference between real respect and paying lip service to respect, and will react appropriately (Hayes, 1997).

According to Putman (2000), the new workplace, characterised by flatter organisations aided by compensation systems that reward creativity and innovation more than seniority and loyalty, has had a negative impact on trust. He sees it as encouraging fragmentation and individualism, and concludes that the US workplace is not a happier place than it was a generation ago.

knowing when to intervene to help the team, and how best to release control and bestow greater autonomy on the team (Steckler & Fondas, 1995). In addition, leave members in no doubt as to the true nature of the team and what the leader has in mind in terms of targets and processes, so that the leader and team members are on the same wavelength. The use of teamwork metaphors (e.g., family team, team of associates, etc.) to convey meaning could be useful in this type of situation, and this could be influenced by national culture. For instance, in a collectivist society with status differentials (e.g., a South American country) the family team metaphor could apply, while the metaphor for an associates' team (group of individuals loosely related in professional practice) may be used in an individualist society, such as the USA (Gibson & Zellmer-Bruhn, 2002).

Coaching

A particularly useful skill to enhance the team leader's effectiveness is that of coaching. Coaching could be viewed as an informal approach to employee development based on a close relationship between the individual and the other person, usually their immediate boss or team leader, who is experienced in the task (Torrington, Hall, & Taylor, 2005). What actions or behaviour characterise good coaching? It is suggested that one should consider three main skills to be used by a team leader interested in the effectiveness of his or her team (Orth et al., 1987).

(1) Be on the look out for means to exploit the capabilities of team members with a view to improving their performance. Observe their behaviour, be interested, listen carefully to what they have to say, and be sensitive to ways in which performance could be improved.

(2) Create a supportive climate in order to encourage the improvement of performance. This could be achieved by encouraging members to be open and frank in the exchange of ideas and views. Offer guidance and advice when asked, and if members make mistakes treat such incidents as learning experiences rather than as a justification to mete out punishment. Where there are obstacles in the way of improving performance, make every effort to remove them. Always highlight the value of the member's contribution and single out success; where there is a lack of success identify the missing ingredient.

(3) Influence members to change their behaviour by encouraging them to continually improve their performance, always recognising that they themselves must have an important input to the debate on the most appropriate remedial action. If tasks as currently constituted are difficult to handle, make life easier for members by making them more manageable. Finally, as coach, display the desirable qualities (e.g., enthusiasm, commitment, openness, sensitivity, efficiency) you would like members to embrace and internalise.

Empowerment

Allied to the notion of coaching is a concept called *empowerment*, which, when applied, can promote the development of team members. This term became prominent as part of the total quality management movement, although its origins are in issues raised in the era of employee involvement symbolised by participative management (Herrenkohl, Judson, & Heffner, 1999). When properly operationalised it amounts to the leader sharing power and responsibility with team members (Conger & Kanungo, 1988b). A visionary coach is somebody who would appear to have little difficulty handling empowerment, because many of the behavioural characteristics of the coach referred to earlier could usefully be functional in putting empowerment into practice.

Shackleton (1995) makes the following observations about the leader's role in empowerment:

- The leader has genuine respect for the abilities and potential of team members.
- The leader feels secure, otherwise the empowerment of team members could be perceived as a threat to his or her position.
- Mobilise training to tap latent potential of members and build their confidence, using coaching where appropriate.

- Create conditions where team members are keen to assume responsibility rather than being asked to do so.
- Allow sufficient time for empowerment to take root, and praise and encourage people as they work their way through the implementation of this concept.
- Recognise that a side-effect of empowerment is the need for more information.
- Use the reward system to support empowerment.

Observations by Wall et al. (2002) could be added to the above when they identify the conditions to which empowerment is best suited. These are conditions where uncertainty surrounds the job domain, and devolved and prompt decision making is required.

Herrenkohl et al. (1999) believe that employee empowerment is a goal that has proved difficult to achieve. One difficulty is the lack of an agreed operational definition of empowerment.

Randolf (1995) raised a number of issues in an empirical study of companies that adopted empowerment. A first consideration is information sharing, because with a lack of information (e.g., data about the company's market and the intentions of competitors) it is difficult for people to take their responsibility seriously. Another issue is for management to provide more structure as teams move into self-management mode so that they know the extent of their responsibility and can be provided with the necessary skills. A further consideration is that teams must take constructive action to gradually replace the traditional organisational hierarchy and take on board a number of tasks previously the preserve of management (selection, appraisal, budgeting, etc.). Finally, empowered teams should not operate in areas where they lack the requisite expertise (e.g., employment legislation).

It is claimed that empowerment has beneficial effects in terms of productivity and group satisfaction (Keller & Dansereau, 1995). But there are voices of dissent suggesting that not all leadership situations call for shared team leadership based on empowerment, and that the concept of empowerment is problematic (Belasco & Stayer, 1994).

CONTEXTUAL FACTORS

In assessing the appropriateness of teams, and their effectiveness within organisations, it is important that the use to which they are put is realistic in the light of organisational needs and that the efforts of different teams are coordinated (Guzzo & Dickson, 1996). This type of emphasis reflects a concern with the context or environment within which the team operates.

Sundstrom, De Meuse, and Futrell (1990) also call for a broader perspective when focusing on team effectiveness. Apart from team development, with its emphasis on the internal processes of the group, they draw our attention to the need to consider contextual factors and team boundaries. Key contextual factors include: clarity of mission; technology and task design; group autonomy; rewards; performance feedback; training/consultation; the physical environment, and organisational culture. To organisational culture could be added the influence of national culture.

In a major survey of team working in Europe it was concluded that team-based systems are unevenly spread. For example, Sweden with its tradition of participative management and autonomous work groups ranked at the top of the list, followed by The Netherlands, whereas Spain, with its tradition of emphasising status and hierarchy, occupied the bottom position. Germany and the UK were close together mid-way in the table (Benders, Huijgen, & Ulricj, 2001).

When our attention shifts to team boundaries, which was also considered an important variable by Sundstrom et al. above, we are interested in the dividing line between one group and another, what differentiates them, and what are the barriers to the flow of information between groups. If the boundary is too open or indistinct, the team risks becoming overwhelmed and in danger of losing its identity. If it is too closed, the team might become too isolated and lose touch with peers, management, customers, and suppliers. Team boundaries are likely to mediate the impact of organisational context on team development.

In the final analysis, it would appear that team effectiveness is a function of the interaction of team development, organisational context, and group boundaries.

COMMENT

There appear to be mixed views of the usefulness of teamwork (Arnold, 2005). For example, Harley (2001) felt that workers classified as members of a team were no more or no less happy and committed than those not so classified. Proctor and Currie (2002) found that teamwork had advantages as far as the collective allocation of work was concerned, and in encouraging team members to identify with the common goal, but it did not make much of an impact in the sense that performance appraisal continued to be preoccupied with the individual, there was a reluctance on the part of the team to accept responsibility for individual member's work, and there was no noticeable increase in the acquisition of new skills. Griffin, Patterson, and West (2001) found that there was a decrease in the amount of supervisory support experienced by team members, which led to a noticeable reduction in job satisfaction. Paradoxically, it was also found that teamwork resulted in multi-skilling and acquiring extra responsibility (manifestations of job enrichment), which led to an increase in job satisfaction. In this situation, negative influences in job satisfaction could counteract positive ones.

CHAPTER SUMMARY

- The difference between a team and a group was explored, and different types of teams (e.g., management teams, cross-functional teams, venture teams, virtual teams, affinity groups, and quality circles) were identified.
- Organisational and other developments that gave rise to the use of teams, and the consequences associated with deploying teams, were stated.
- Models of team or group development were examined. A well-known model is Tuckman's (forming, storming, norming, performing, and adjournment), and a less well-known but a more recent approach is the punctuated equilibrium model.
- The importance of the organisational context of group tasks, including culture, was stressed.
- The characteristics of high-performance teams were highlighted.
- Common mistakes in building effective teams and ways of dealing with these mistakes were outlined.
- It was recognised that it is important to nurture mature teams.
- The nature and use of project teams was briefly stated.
- Different approaches to management team development were explored, including team development with existing teams of managers, as well as bringing people together with a range of skills and experience to form a balanced and effective team.
- The concept of diversity (of roles, expertise, age, gender, race, and culture) in relation to team effectiveness was discussed.
- Finally, leadership as a facilitating process in teams, in which trust features, was analysed and its relationship to empowerment was examined.

QUESTIONS

(1) In what way does a team differ from a group?

(2) Identify the factors that have given rise to the current interest in teams within organisations.

(3) Comment on the benefits associated with team systems of working.

(4) What is the difference between a work team and a virtual team?

(5) Compare and contrast Tuckman's model of group development with the punctuated equilibrium model.

(6) Assess the significance of contextual factors with respect to teams.

(7) Identify the features of the high-performance team.

(8) Highlight the problems with teambuilding, and suggest means of tackling them.

(9) How does one improve the performance of teams who have a lot of experience of working together?

(10) What is (a) a project team, (b) a venture team, and (c) a global team?

(11) Identify the approaches to management team development, and comment on the approach that has greatest appeal for you.

(12) What is the significance of diversity to the effectiveness of teams?

(13) Examine the role of leadership in modern teams.

(14) Comment on empowerment.

(15) Explain the role of trust in team management.

SPOTLIGHT ON RELEVANT READING

Currall, S.C., & Epstein, M.J. (2003). The fragility of organisational trust: Lessons from the rise and fall of Enron. *Organizational Dynamics*, *32*, 193–206.

Menon, S.J. (2001). Employee empowerment: An integrative psychological approach. *Applied Psychology: An International Review*, *50*, 153–180.

Mueller, F., Proctor, S., & Buchanan D. (2003). Teamworking in its context(s): Antecedents, nature and dimensions. *Human Relations*, *53*, 1387–1424.

Personnel Review (2002). Special issue on Teams. Vol. 31.

Proctor, S., & Currie, G. (2002). How teamworking works in the Inland Revenue: Meaning, operation and impact. *Personnel Review*, *31*, 304–319.

Van der Zee, K.I., Atsma, N., & Brodbeck, P. (2004). The influence of social identity and personality outcomes of cultural identity in teams. *Journal of Cross Cultural Psychology*, *35*, 283–303.

Wall, T.D., Cordery, J.L., & Clegg, C.W. (2002). Empowerment, performance and operational uncertainty: A theoretical integration. *Applied Psychology: An International Review*, *51*, 146–169.

Williams, M. (2001). In whom we trust: Group membership as an affective context for trust development. *Academy of Management Review*, July, 377–396.

Learning Outcomes

After studying this chapter you should be able to:

- Distinguish between leadership and management.

- Identify traits and personal characteristics associated with leadership.

- Recognise the importance of skills and competencies.

- Explain the behavioural styles of leadership.

- Compare macro participation with micro participation.

- Outline the situational theories of leadership.

- Assess the significance of transformational leadership.

- Discuss the part played by gender, culture, trust, upward influence, and derailment in leadership.

Leadership and Management Style

12

*This chapter begins with a
distinction between leadership
and management, followed by a
commentary on traits, personal
qualities, skills, and competencies.
Next there is an examination
of studies in leadership where
behavioural styles feature
prominently. A number of
contingency theories of leadership
are then introduced, followed by an
examination of contemporary trends
in the study of leadership, including
the influence of transformational
leadership. Other important matters,
such as gender, culture, trust, and
upward/lateral influence in the
context of leadership are examined.
The chapter relates in particular
to personality issues (discussed in
Chapter 2), motivation (Chapter 4),
organisational culture (Chapter 15),
and organisational change and
development (Chapter 16).*

Contents

LEADERSHIP VERSUS MANAGEMENT

In this section the similarities and differences between leadership and management will be explored. Some researchers who have studied leadership in organised settings tend to state that people endowed with authority are leaders. Therefore, supervisors and managers within organisations can be called leaders. Many theories of leadership are concerned with managerial influence, and the terms "leadership" and "management" are sometimes used interchangeably. However, some scholars can see differences between management and leadership.

Kotter (1990) felt that leadership and management are two distinctive and complementary systems, each having its own function and its own characteristic activities, but both are necessary for the management of complex organisations. According to Kotter, management is about planning, controlling, and putting appropriate structures and systems in place, whereas leadership has more to do with anticipating change, coping with change, and adopting a visionary stance.

Zaleznik (1986) also perceived a difference between management and leadership. Managers are seen as fairly passive, people-centred operators, intent on keeping the show on the road, whereas leaders seem to be more solitary, proactive, intuitive, empathetic, and are attracted to situations of high risk where the rewards for success are great.

A definition of leadership and management that has a particular appeal is as follows (John Child, personal communication): Leadership is a force that creates a capacity among a group of people to do something that is different or better. This could be reflected in a more creative outcome, or a higher level of performance. In essence, leadership is an agency of change, and could entail inspiring others to do more than they would otherwise have done, or were doing. By contrast, management is a force more preoccupied with planning, coordinating, supervising, and controlling routine activity, which of course can be done in an inspired way. Managerial leadership could be viewed as an integral part of the managerial

role, and its significance grows in importance as we move up the organisational hierarchy.

Watson (1994) provides a useful exposition of the nature of managerial work and how people managed in the difficult circumstances of the 1990s in the UK. He subjected the behaviour of managers in a telecommunications company to detailed analysis. There is reference to the managerial competencies he considered important in Panel 12.1.

The overlap between leadership and management can be seen clearly in the contrast between the two in the work of Mintzberg (1980) and Yukl (Van Fleet & Yukl, 1989) shown in Table 12.1. Mintzberg identifies a diversified range of managerial roles of senior managers, of which the leadership role is an important ingredient. The list of leadership behaviour categories provided by Yukl covers general management activities, but is derived from an exhaustive review of the research literature on leadership. (Aligned entries in Table 12.1 indicate similarities.)

TRAITS, PERSONAL CHARACTERISTICS, AND SKILLS

The traits, motives, and abilities associated with leadership in general, and managerial leadership in particular, will now be examined. (See Chapter 2 for a discussion of the trait approach to personality.) In the early part of the twentieth century the development of psychometric assessment procedures was felt to be very appropriate to the study of leadership. This was a time when there was a belief that abilities and leadership characteristics were inherited, and perhaps finally we could shed some light on the quality of **charisma**.

Traits

In a typical early study, Terman (1904) asked teachers to describe playgroup leaders. They were reported to be active, quick, and skilful in devising and playing games. Nearly 60 years later, Bavelas (1960) saw leadership traits as quickness of decision, the courage to take risks, coolness

---

PANEL 12.1: Management competencies (Watson, 1994, reproduced with the permission of Thomson Learning)

The following scheme of management competencies was devised by Watson (1994), a British social scientist, after studying the behaviour of managers in a manufacturing company in the telecommunications industry for one year. (Note that + indicates good characteristics while – indicates bad characteristics.)

(1) PERSONAL ORIENTATION (CURRENT DISPOSITION)

(a) Achievement and results orientation
+ high but realistic targets (self/others)
+ strive for continuous improvement (processes/results)
+ monitor progress in relation to targets
– muddling through without clear objectives
– content with "adequate" performance
– success is viewed as avoidance of trouble

(b) Initiative
+ initiate actions/want to be in the lead/proactive
+ seek/create opportunities
– react to situations
– respond passively to others' initiatives

(c) Decisiveness and self-confidence
+ faith in judgement to make decisions/take risks
+ periodically accept that mistakes will occur
– lack confidence
– hesitate/postpone until tomorrow the making of decisions
– risk-averse/afraid of making mistakes

(d) Commercial orientation
+ strong sense of enterprise
+ astute and penetrating grasp of market opportunities
+ cost conscious but deeply committed to capital investment
+ interested in "adding value" to whatever is undertaken
– uneconomical in the incurring of expense, or cost control at the expense of future returns
– generally little awareness/interest in finance/markets

(e) Adaptability and capacity to learn
+ flexible in coping with changing situations
+ cool in the face of crisis or adversity
+ learn constantly from experience/observations/external sources
– attachment to traditional ways, regardless of the situation
– panic or withdraw in the face of threats or changes
– feel sufficiently informed already

(2) COGNITIVE STYLE (THE WAY THE PERSON THINKS)

(a) Vision and strategic thinking
+ capability to form a clear and coherent view of a future state from the standpoint of present activities
+ appreciate the significance of current customer-related activities in terms of long-term business success
+ manage the department/function with awareness of its contribution to the overall business
+ recognise the need to adopt a cross-cultural perspective because of the global nature of the business
– adopt a short-term perspective
– see departmental/functional objectives as ends rather than means to overall business performance (inward-looking)
– minimum attention paid to customers
– little awareness or interest in global business

(b) Information search
+ collect/sift information constantly from a variety of sources
+ put an enormous effort into maintaining an "information network" from which is extracted formal/informal intelligence data
– little knowledge/feel for what is happening because of use of limited sources of information (formal)
– overloaded with less than reliable information (managers are bewildered and out of touch)

(c) Use of concepts
+ apply conceptual models/schemes to information received and this helps managers to see trends/patterns, cause/effect relationships, and to establish testable hypotheses
– unable to use conceptual frameworks to make sense of incoming information
– cannot see the "wood for the trees"
– somewhat in the dark as to cause/effect relationships
– little capacity for trying out new ideas

(d) Creativity
+ imaginative and innovative
+ devise new ways of performing established tasks
+ devise new things to do
– too conservative and resistant to new ideas
– feel more comfortable with established practices and take paths created by others

(e) Judgement and decision making
+ critical and objective evaluation of information
+ striking a good balance between available evidence and intuition
+ taking calculated or informed risks
– bias and prejudice creep into managerial judgement
– actions lack a clear logic
– reasoning rests on "cold" raw data without imaginative interpretation, or alternatively it rests on wild guesses/poorly informed hunches/blind self-interest or malice

(3) INTERPERSONAL STYLE (THE WAY A PERSON RELATES TO OTHERS)

(a) Sensitivity and listening
+ sensitive to attitudes/feelings of colleagues and others located inside and outside the organisation
+ treat others and their ideas with respect
+ listen to the ideas/viewpoints of others
+ active elicitation of positive contributions from others
– little respect for colleagues at work
– insensitive to the feelings of others
– preoccupied with own objectives/ideas/feelings with little regard for the views/interests of others

(b) Impact and persuasiveness
+ personal presence/credibility which helps a lot in winning support for the values/strategies held and action proposed
+ persuasive arguments and rewards are used to gain support
+ compliance is gained by force of example
– tend to be ignored
– have little influence on others' ideas/behaviour when given an audience

(c) Planning and organisation
+ formulate plans/objectives and deadline dates with team, backed up with the necessary resources
– teams are in the dark as to what is expected of them; time targets are vague and access to resources is unclear

(d) Presentation and communication
+ information/ideas are communicated clearly
+ the chosen medium is likely to produce maximum understanding
– attempts at oral/written communication result in lack of clarity and confusion
– lack of appreciation for the most appropriate medium
– fail to establish whether the audience understands the message

(e) Leadership, teambuilding, and maintenance
+ team leadership in a positive atmosphere where tasks are allocated efficiently, information is shared, and where team members with up-to-date skills continually improve their performance and meet their targets
+ team leaders in a nonleadership role in a group also contribute positively and constructively
– act in isolation
– wield power by withholding information from subordinates
– insufficient guidance given to subordinates, leading to lack of focus, negativity, conflict, and under-resourcing
– team leaders in a nonleadership role in a group only act to defend or promote a sectional interest

TABLE 12.1

Contrasting leadership and management

Leadership behaviour categories (Van Fleet & Yukl, 1989)	Managerial roles (Mintzberg, 1980)
	(1) Interpersonal roles
	• Symbolic duties as a figurehead
Recognising and rewarding	• Exercising leadership (i.e., creating the necessary culture,
Developing	and providing the motivational stimulus to achieve
Motivating task commitment	organisational tasks)
Interfacing	• External contacts (i.e., obtaining the necessary information
	and resources through contacts outside the department/
	organisation)
	(2) Handling information
Monitoring operations	• Monitoring (i.e., examining actual performance in relation
	to targets using appropriate information)
Informing	• Disseminating—internal (i.e., information that originated
Clarifying roles and objectives	from outside the department/organisation is disseminated
	internally)
	• Transmitting—external (i.e., internally generated
	information is transmitted externally)
	(3) Decision making
	• Strategic change focus (i.e., shaping or reshaping the
	organisation to adapt to external events)
Problem solving and crisis management	• Fire-fighting (i.e., handling disturbances or unforeseen events)
Representing, planning, and organising	• Resource allocating (i.e., making policy decisions about the
	use of resources; negotiating or bargaining with other
	individuals/organisations; budgeting)

under stress, intuition, and even luck. Other traits often mentioned in popular journalism are vision, willpower, cultivating team spirit and loyalty, inspiring followers, integrity, honesty, and sheer physical stamina.

Stogdill (1948) and Mann (1959) conducted independent reviews of the vast literature on personality as a factor in leadership, and concluded that personality had a minor effect in shaping leadership behaviour. Stogdill proposed that a person does not become a leader by virtue of the possession of some combination of personality traits—what is important is that the leader's personality must be compatible with the personal characteristics, activities, and goals of the followers.

By and large, the studies that Stogdill and Mann reviewed were predominantly concerned with the behaviour of children and students in unstructured settings, such as those found outside bureaucratic organisations. But the findings have often been raised with reference to the behaviour of leaders in formal organisational settings, where a different

set of conditions are likely to be important. A point worth stating is that very few of the studies looked at the effectiveness of the leaders studied. Instead, the focus was on people who emerged as leaders—an emphasis to be expected given the nature of the research site (i.e., unstructured settings outside formal organisations).

In a subsequent review, Stogdill (1974) seems to mix personality traits with abilities or skills, though not intentionally, and concludes that the following factors are frequently linked with leadership: activity; dominance; self-confidence; achievement drive; and interpersonal skills. A decade later Lord, DeVader, and Alliger (1986) did a meta-analysis of the relationship between personality and perceptions of leadership and found that leaders had the following six traits to a greater extent than nonleaders: intelligent; extravert; dominant; masculine; conservative; and better adjusted. Kirkpatrick and Locke (1991) suggested that there are six traits that leaders possess when compared with nonleaders: intelligent; desire to lead; energy and ambition; self-confidence; honesty and integrity; knowledge (job-related). Nicholson (2002) emphasised the importance of personality traits in leadership and related the latter to the Big Five theory of personality, discussed in Chapter 2. These are extraversion, conscientiousness, openness, emotionality, and agreeableness.

Some of the above traits were captured by Willie Whitelaw—deputy to Margaret Thatcher, British Prime Minister in the 1980s—when commenting in his memoirs on aspects of Mrs Thatcher's personality. He described her as very energetic and vivacious; dominant; assertive; obstinate; argumentative but listens carefully; not a conciliator; determined to succeed; not a clubable person, and reserved with strangers (Whitelaw, 1989).

When Jack Welch, the former Chief Executive of General Electric, was asked in the late 1990s to indicate the traits he was looking for in the person to replace him he described them as: vision, courage, ability to energise others, an insatiable appetite for accomplishment, ability to make tough decisions and execute them, good judgement, having the self-confidence to hire somebody better than yourself, able to grow businesses and to add new insights into businesses already run (Stewart, 1999). In a profile of Lou Gertsner, who turned round IBM, he was described as gruff, analytical, distant, and intolerant of criticism (London, 2002).

A view has been expressed that a significant character flaw—the opposite to traits listed above—could be functional by making the leader appear human and approachable and by detracting attention from any other flaws he or she may have. For example, Richard Branson of Virgin has a flaw that has been described as inarticulateness, which makes him sound vulnerable when interviewed and encourages viewers to stay on his side, even though deep down we may distrust him as a wealthy, successful person who had a problem with making Virgin Trains run on time (Goffee & Jones, 2000; Kellaway, 2000).

Given the traits proposed by the various authors above, it is easy to conclude that it is difficult to find a set of prominent traits common to effective leaders. Circumstances seem to dictate the relevance of a particular bundle of traits.

Managerial talent

Because of the weakness of the traditional trait approach, the emphasis switched to the identification of managerial talent and ability. In some studies this is undertaken through assessment centres (discussed in Chapter 17), which create simulations of the settings managers are likely to encounter in their work. In other studies managerial performance is measured and related to self-reports by managers of personality and motivation. In the latter studies, unlike the early leadership studies, leadership was viewed as being synonymous with the occupancy of a managerial role. Different criteria of managerial effectiveness arose, ranging from the promotion potential of managers, as perceived by top management, to ratings of competence by the manager's superior.

The requisite managerial qualities reflected a mixture of personality traits, motives, and skills. Bray and Campbell (1974) found that managers most frequently promoted within the American Telephone and Telegraph Company were those who had been assessed early in their careers as scoring high on: oral communication; human relations skills; need for advancement; resistance to stress; and tolerance for uncertainty.

Ghiselli (1971) compared effective and ineffective managers and reported that effective managers scored higher on: intelligence; self-assurance; supervisory ability; need for occupational achievement; decisiveness; and need for self-fulfilment. But they scored low on the need for security.

McClelland (1975b) sees a need for power as a prerequisite to assuming a managerial role. This finding was endorsed by Miner (1978), who, when specifying the motives most strongly linked to those who were most frequently promoted, added the desire to compete with colleagues for limited resources, to be active and assertive, to be visible and influential in handling subordinates, and having a positive attitude towards authority. A summary of this evidence appears in Table 12.2. From this analysis it seems that achievement-orientation, effective communication and interpersonal skills, and the need for power are the characteristics most commonly shared by effective managers. In a snapshot of Sven-Goran Ericksson's

TABLE 12.2

Personal characteristics of effective managers

Ghiselli (1971)	McClelland (1967, 1975b)	Miner (1978)	Bray & Campbell (1974)
Intelligence Self-assurance Supervisory ability		Effective interaction with subordinates	Communication and interpersonal skills
Need for occupational achievement Need for self-fulfilment	Need for achievement		Need for achievement
	Need for power	Need for power Competitive Assertive	
			Resistance to stress Tolerance for uncertainty

(the English football coach's) leadership, it was concluded that Sven is the prototype of the modern managerial leader. He is unflashy and private, aiming for fairness, clarity, and understatement (Birkinshaw & Crainer, 2002).

Goffee and Jones (2002), reflecting on leadership, considered it necessary to stress the importance of traits and personal characteristics in terms of: sheer physical presence, energy, desire for power, strong sense of direction, clear vision, passion (deeply held views and compelling mission); technical skills (superior knowledge), social skills (listening or coaching); and wanting to develop satisfying relationships ("I would like to build strong teams around me").

Skills

Today, the operationalisation of the leadership role would not be complete without an acknowledgement of the deployment of cognitive, affective, and administrative skills—these are skills in diagnosing problems and suggesting sound solutions, as well as having sufficient insight or personal awareness and the necessary interpersonal skills to relate effectively to colleagues in the implementation of decisions (Chell, 1993; Wright & Taylor, 1984).

Hosking and Morley (1988) offer an approach to leadership that is concerned with how leaders process information, understand the leadership environment, and use the knowledge they acquire as an input to a bargaining and negotiating process with others. Construing leadership in this way would inevitably lead to regarding it as a skill. According to Hosking and Morley, a skilful leader is one who can construct and maintain social order, underpinned by systems of power and values. Within this framework, the skilful leader is likely to be very knowledgeable about the environment that governs his or her work, and is adept at interpreting information and making decisions on the basis of an analysis of that information. To develop information about his or her work environment, the leader is expected to build extensive networks of collaborative relationships, which will provide benefits in terms of awareness of matters of perhaps no immediate relevance, but certainly with long-term significance as an information source. Hosking and Morley feel that the excessive emphasis in leadership studies given to superior–subordinate relationships has resulted in a neglect of lateral relationships.

BEHAVIOURAL STYLE

This section is devoted to a discussion of topics and issues that can broadly be classified as the behavioural style approach to leadership. Topics covered are:

- styles of leadership;
- Likert's four styles;
- consideration and initiating structure;
- the leadership grid; and
- participative leadership.

Styles of leadership

The lack of success of the early personality trait approach to leadership, which viewed leadership as a quality anchored in particular individuals to enable them to play roles in society where the exercise of influence is required, gave rise to a new approach. This was known as the behavioural style approach to leadership and was based on the view that leadership processes did not reside solely in the person, but could be cultivated as distinctive patterns of behaviour. The behavioural style approach became popular from the late 1930s onwards, and was promoted by the work of Kurt Lewin (see Panel 12.2).

The studies featured in Panel 12.2 showed that the effectiveness of a leadership style depended on what criterion of effectiveness was used—a criterion of effectiveness could be the morale of the group or productivity. For instance, the morale of the group in the example was better under democratic leadership, but under autocratic leadership a greater number of aeroplane models were constructed by the children (at least while the leader remained present). The choice of subject

matter or topic in these studies was probably influenced by Lewin's experience of totalitarian systems in Nazi Germany. The outcome of the studies had a significant effect on the development of leadership research in the USA after the Second World War.

In other cultural settings, different results were achieved when the earlier studies were replicated (Smith & Peterson, 1988). For example, in Japan the democratic style was more effective when the task was easy, and the autocratic style was more effective when the task was difficult. In India the autocratic style was superior on all criteria. (The impact of culture on organisations is considered in Chapter 15.) A criticism levelled at these studies is that the findings suffer severe limitations if they are applied to the field of industrial leadership.

The ideal autocratic and ideal democratic leadership style have both been considered in an organisational setting (Lowin, 1968). In the autocratic model there is a noticeable absence of credit for suggestions emanating from subordinates and a lack of formal recognition of the efforts of subordinates. The subordinate does not have the opportunity to participate in the decision-making process, and is therefore deprived of feedback that could contribute to a useful learning experience. He or she is prevented from developing an insight into the factors that must be considered in choosing among alternatives in a decision situation.

PANEL 12.2: Early studies of behavioural styles

In order to investigate some aspects of how a group functions under different types of group atmosphere and different types of leadership, experiments were conducted by Kurt Lewin and his colleagues with groups of children (Lippit & White, 1968). The groups were engaged in mask-making, model-making, and similar activities. Different styles of leadership—autocratic, democratic, and *laissez-faire*—were introduced by the (adult) experimenters. For example, the formulation of policy, the techniques and methods to be used, the division of work activities, and the allocation of individuals to work were determined by the autocratic leader without reference to the group, whereas the democratic leader actively involved the children in policy making and generally in the job of dividing and allocating the work. The autocratic leader was very subjective in his criticism and praise and remained aloof from the group except when demonstrating how to do the work.

On the other hand, the democratic leader was objective in his criticism and praise and tried to be a regular group member in spirit without doing much of the actual work. The groups appeared to react very favourably to the imposition of democratic leadership practice. There appeared to be greater group purpose, the individual group members related well to each other, and they displayed less aggression and hostility and more group unity than in the autocratic groups.

The reaction of group members to the *laissez-faire* style was marked with a lower degree of efficiency, organisation, and satisfaction.

TABLE 12.3

Managerial leadership—ideal behavioural styles (adapted from Lowin, 1968)

Autocratic style	*Democratic style*
Direction/obedience	Open communication/positive attitudes
Close supervision	Frequent and constructive dialogue
Control and accountability	Evaluation of suggestions/availability of feedback
Absence of participation and feedback	Consensus, rather than coercion/compromise
Subordinates are poorly informed	Self-direction/self-control
Absence of credit for suggestions	Atmosphere that permits emotional expression
Minimum level of motivation	Conflict is confronted
	Group-based problem solving
	Influence (based on technical expertise)
	Personal/organisational goal congruence

Should the subordinate make a contribution, he or she probably gets no credit for it and, as a result, has little motivation to contribute beyond what is minimally expected.

Under an ideal democratic system, participation by subordinates is more frequent and more constructive. Managers are more prepared to discuss relevant issues with subordinates and to respect their suggestions. When suggestions are received and evaluated, the reaction is transmitted to the subordinate in the form of feedback. This is believed to contribute to a desirable level of motivation and to promote the quality of future suggestions. It is also said to lead to greater involvement and to contribute to high performance standards. A summary of the characteristics of the two styles appears in Table 12.3.

In the light of the above descriptions of leadership, it is useful to describe the styles of two British industrial leaders—Richard Branson of Virgin and the late Robert Maxwell of, what was then, the Mirror Newspaper Group. The style of Robert Maxwell was autocratic. Frequently he would pop in and out of meetings that were in progress simultaneously, so he could see for himself what was happening. He insisted on initialling written authority for the purchase of every new company car and the recruitment of staff to every new position within the company, as far down the line as a secretary. Senior executives had authority to spend up to set limits without reference to him, but they used that right with

great care. Virtually all important negotiations, whether with trade unions, printers, or computer manufacturers, were handled by Maxwell himself. Given the centralisation of control in his hands, there were many delays and inefficiencies, last minute switches in policy, and ill-considered gestures. Paradoxically, his style was reasonably effective most of the time (Bowman, 1990).

By contrast, Richard Branson's style seems to manifest elements of democratic leadership. He is said to have the common touch and mixes easily with people, making them feel as if they are on his level. He believes in modesty, listening to people, and treating them as equals, and displays a sense of humour. He possesses a hands-off leadership style bordering on delegation or empowerment. His managers enjoy the opportunity to run their own show. It is apparent that all managing directors of the companies within the Virgin Group have almost total authority to make their own decisions. Therefore, they experience a high level of autonomy, which has a sound motivational effect. Because of his style he seems to have time and space to enthuse his followers, contributing to a "buzz" that springs from every part of the group (Dearlove, 1998).

Likert's four styles

An expansion of the notion that leadership style consists of two extreme positions—autocratic and democratic—is provided by Likert (1967). He puts forward four styles of leadership to capture the management culture of an organisation:

- *Exploitive authoritative*. The leader uses fear and threats, communication is downwards, superior and subordinates are psychologically distant, and almost all decisions are taken at the apex of the organisation.
- *Benevolent authoritative*. The leader uses rewards to encourage performance, the upward flow of communication is limited to what the boss wants to hear, subservience to superiors is widespread, and although most decisions are taken at the top of the organisation there is some delegation of decision making.
- *Consultative*. The leader uses appropriate rewards, communication may be two-way, although upward communication is cautious and limited—by and large—to what the boss wants to hear; some involvement is sought from employees, and subordinates have a moderate amount of influence in some decisions, but again broad policy decisions are the preserve of top management only.
- *Participative*. The leader discusses economic rewards and makes full use of group participation and involvement in fixing high performance goals and improving work methods and procedures. The emphasis is on a network of accurate information; subordinates and superiors are psychologically close, and group decision making is widely spread throughout the organisation. There is a tendency for a number of individuals to belong to more than one work group in order to promote inter-group links and understanding.

Consideration and initiating structure

Consideration and **initiating structure**, as dimensions of leadership behaviour, were isolated and identified by researchers at the Ohio State University (Fleishman & Harris, 1962). Both factors can be evaluated after an individual completes a questionnaire.

Consideration indicates friendship, mutual trust, respect, and warmth. A leader with a high score

on this dimension is likely to be friendly and approachable, with a good rapport and two-way communication with subordinates, and is willing to help with personal problems, and thereby adopts an employee-oriented (i.e., participative and empowered) approach to leadership.

Initiating structure indicates a concern with defining and organising roles or relationships in an organisation, establishing well-defined forms of organisation, channels of communication, and ways of getting jobs done, and trying out new ideas and practices. A high score on this dimension characterises individuals who play an active role in directing group activities through planning, communicating information, scheduling (including assigning group members to particular tasks), and expecting employees to meet particular standards of performance and meet deadlines.

The job-centred manager (task-oriented) would appear to rank high on initiating structure and low on consideration. The Ohio studies found that the two factors were independent of each other—that is, how a leader scores on one factor has no influence on what he or she scores on the other, although other studies show that the two dimensions are related. This means that a leader can be directive in managing subordinates and at the same time can establish highly supportive relations with them (Weissenberg & Kavanagh, 1972). The outcome of early studies indicated that a leader rated high on both initiating structure and consideration was most likely to be a successful manager. However, some subsequent studies did not endorse this position. An updated analysis of initiating structure and consideration is provided by Schriesheim, Cogliser, and Neider (1995).

It is maintained that behavioural styles that bear a close relationship to consideration and initiating structure are likely to be influenced by cultural norms. For example, in Japan and Hong Kong the operationalisation of the consideration dimension in specific behavioural terms varied from that in the UK and the USA (Smith, Misumi, Tayeb, Peterson, & Bond, 1989). In Panel 12.3 there are observations on the impact of culture in Southeast Asia on attitudes to authority and behavioural style.

PANEL 12.3: Culture and behavioural styles

Acceptance of authority, deference, loyalty, and apparent authoritarianism are prevalent in most South-east Asian cultures. Malay culture, for example, upholds the value of respect for authority and deference towards one's superiors. Similarly, the Thai management style is generally authoritarian with an unequal relationship between the boss and subordinates. The Thai worker is compliant and tends not to challenge his or her superior. In Thailand, benevolent authoritarianism in management invites a response from subordinates in the form of submissiveness, obedience, and loyalty, and these characteristics could be considered more valuable than the subordinate's ability.

Managers from South-east Asia, including Thailand, Malaysia, Indonesia, the Philippines, Hong Kong, and Singapore, are more likely to use a more directive style of decision making than their Western counterparts. They are less likely to share information with subordinates on the setting of objectives and generally do not favour consultation as a style. However, subordinates are more likely to get involved at the implementation stage of the decision process. Generally, the group involved in decision making is likely to be small, and the bias towards centralisation and autocracy is evident.

(Westwood, 1992)

The leadership grid

Another approach to depicting different leadership styles is the "leadership grid" developed by Blake and Mouton (1985), and formerly known as the "managerial grid". In this concept of leadership style, concern for people and production are treated as separate dimensions. Leadership style is not shown as a point on a leadership continuum but rather as a point on a two-dimensional grid. In Figure 12.1, the horizontal dimension of the grid represents the individual's concern for production, and the vertical dimension represents his or her concern for people.

This concept is similar to that of employee-centred and job-centred leadership discussed earlier. In the leadership grid the individual can score anything between the maximum number (9,9) or the minimum number (1,1) on either dimension. The ideal of the leadership grid is to move towards the 9,9 style (team management) where there is an integrative maximum concern for both production and people; this appears to be in the same mould as participative leadership.

Blake and Mouton advocate a phased organisational development programme with the adoption of the 9,9 style in mind. The 9,1 style (task management) focuses wholly on production, and the manager in this category can generally be said to have acute problems in dealing with people, but is exceptionally competent in a technical sense. This style is entirely geared to a high level of productivity, at least in the short term. The superior

makes the decision and the subordinate carries it out without question. Traditionally, shop floor conditions in the motor industry were considered to be a good example of the 9,1 leadership style, and the fact that its past record of industrial relations was punctuated with disputes might be indicative of the shortcomings of task management. It is conceivable that this style of leadership is a major contributor to the polarisation of the superior and subordinate, resulting in the "them" and "us" thinking that is at the root of many industrial disputes.

By contrast, the 1,9 style (country club management) emphasises people to the exclusion of their performance. People are encouraged and supported, but their mistakes are actually overlooked because they are doing their best—the maxim of "togetherness" applies. Direct disagreement or criticism of one another must be avoided and, as a consequence, production problems are not followed up. This style of leadership can evolve easily when competition is limited.

Blake and Mouton have been vehement in their defence of the 9,9 style as a leadership approach for all situations and all seasons, but this claim has been criticised by Bolman and Deal (2003) who go on to say:

The grid approach focuses almost exclusively on issues of task and human resources. It gives little attention to constituents other than direct subordinates and assumes that a leader who integrates concern for task with

FIGURE 12.1

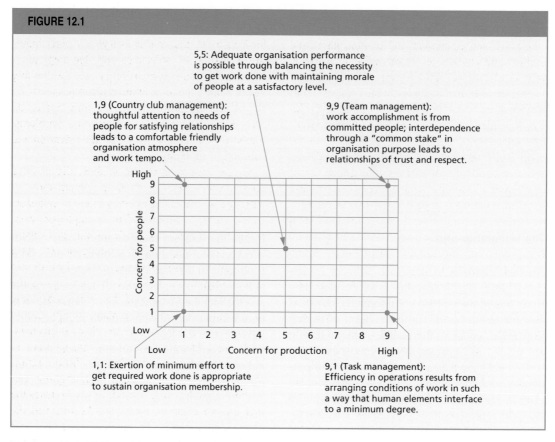

The leadership grid® (from Blake & Mouton, 1985).

concern for people is effective in almost any situation. If structure is unwieldy, political conflict is debilitating or the organization's culture is threadbare, the grid model may have little to say.

Participative leadership

The participative style of leadership has been endorsed in a number of studies. In an early Michigan study of the role of first-line supervisors, it was concluded that the supervisor who often checked up on subordinates, gave them detailed and frequent instructions, and generally limited the employees' freedom to do their work in their own way (i.e., a directive or autocratic style), had a low productivity record. This result was contrasted with the record of high productivity units where there was a high frequency of contact between superior and subordinates, where decision making tended to be pushed down the hierarchy, where superiors were helpful in a constructive way, and generally where good relationships between superiors and subordinates were evident. This profile is congruent with a participative style. In low productivity units, on the other hand, contact between superior and subordinates was low and there existed a high degree of pressure to finish jobs and meet production targets (Likert, 1961).

The following statements seem to encapsulate the essence of participative leadership. The participative style is often conceived largely in terms of a "system of values" governing behaviour, with a commitment to full and free communication, a reliance on consensus rather than on the more customary forms of coercion or compromise to tackle and manage conflict, and an atmosphere that permits and encourages emotional expression as well as a healthy attitude to work (Bennis, 1966).

It is argued that, as the individual moves from the infant end of a personality continuum (basically dependent and submissive, with few and shallow abilities and a short time perspective) to the adult end (endowed with relative independence, autonomy, self-control, many abilities and a few in depth, and a long time perspective), then we have to create conditions to permit self-regulation, self-evaluation, self-adjustment, and participation in the setting of goals. By doing so, it is alleged, we bring about an improvement in productivity and attitudes (Argyris, 1973).

Contrary to general misconceptions, humans have within themselves the capacity to exercise self-direction and self-control in the achievement of objectives to which they are committed. Individuals are likely to assume responsibility rather than to shed it, and if they are lazy, indolent, or passive, it is not due to inherent human weaknesses but attributable to previous organisational experience (McGregor, 1960). There is a recognition that the full potential of human resources is not realised in organisations.

The last point is a theme very much in evidence in a "human resources model" of organisation, not to be confused with human resource management as conceived in the 1980s, and referred to in Chapter 17. The human resources model maintains that there exist in organisations reservoirs of untapped resources and that these resources include not only physical skills and energy but also creative ability and the capacity for responsible, self-directed, self-controlled behaviour. The model also has something to say about the improvement of the quality of decisions and company performance through effective delegation, and that involvement in decisions applies to nonroutine as well as to routine matters. Also, it is felt that providing the opportunity for the exercise of self-direction and self-control should come about in progressive steps in line with growth in the ability and experience of the individual (Miles, 1965).

With regard to the dynamics of participation, Gastil (1994) has proposed some advice. The leader should ensure that everybody participates in the setting of objectives and deciding activities; give people responsibility; set demanding but realistic objectives with explanations, but do so without overpowering people; and, finally, do not suggest solutions to group-based problems, but be vigilant and active in the identification and solution of problems.

In the following classic studies, the positive consequences flowing from the application of participative leadership are very much in evidence. In one factory a group of female employees were given the opportunity to determine their work rate by controlling their own conveyor belt. As a result, quality was maintained and production rose appreciably. It was not until the earnings of the female workers outstripped the earnings of many of the male workers in the plant, chiefly due to the size of productivity bonuses, that various pressures were brought to bear on management to remove the alleged inequality. In these circumstances the plant superintendent arbitrarily revoked, without consultation, the productivity bonuses the women had come to expect and he returned the plant's operations to the previous state. The end result was that things moved again at their "time study" speed, production dropped, and, within a month, all but two of the eight women had left the company (Bavelas & Strauss, 1970).

In another factory, an investigation was undertaken because the company experienced acute resistance by employees to changes in both jobs and methods of work. The consequences of this resistance to change were high rates of staff turnover, many complaints, low efficiency, and restriction of output. It was decided to create both an experimental and a control group, the experimental group participating in the evaluation and redesign of their jobs. The experimental group, unlike the control group, surpassed their previous performance, but only after experiencing an unsatisfactory contribution for a transitional period (during which 62% of employees whose jobs were modified suffered a chronic sub-standard performance or left the job during the retraining stage). An encouraging note to these experiments was

---

PANEL 12.4: Participation in the budgetary process

It is maintained that higher levels of participation in the budgetary process lead to a higher level of motivation to meet budget standards, though this does not extend to the setting of financial standards (Hofstede, 1968).

In one particular study it was found that those who participated in the setting of standards performed better than those who did not, but the outcome from another study suggests that the favourable consequences of participation are limited to the creation of favourable attitudes rather than improving performance (Bass & Leavitt, 1963; Milani, 1975). In a participative process there is an opportunity to obtain feedback on the acceptability of the individual's proposals, and this is said to be a necessary prerequisite for the individual's commitment to the budget (Foran & De Coster, 1974). Likewise, the budget process is likely to be improved by the contribution of the individual's unique and localised knowledge of his or her area of work (Parker, 1979).

In more recent studies the clarity of the budget goal or standard goes hand in hand with participation as factors giving rise to higher levels of motivation to meet budget standards, the actual attainment of budget targets, and an improvement in job satisfaction (Kenis, 1979; Merchant, 1981).

It appears that the personality of the manager involved in the budgetary process is an important variable in the relationship between participation and positive outcomes in terms of satisfaction and performance. According to Bromnell (1981), the relationship is said to be good for those individuals who feel they have a large degree of control over their destiny (internal locus of control), but bad for those who feel their destinies are controlled by luck, chance, or fate (external locus of control). (The concept of locus of control was discussed in Chapter 2.)

---

the impressive performance of control groups when they worked in the same conditions experienced by the experimental groups—i.e., exposed to the participative process (Coch & French, 1948).

Participation in budgeting

The concept of participation has been applied to planning and control processes (e.g., budgetary control) within organisations. At one time this was a fashionable line of enquiry, but less so now. There is a long stream of studies indicating the desirability of participation in the budgetary process (see Panel 12.4 for examples), though one should take note of the qualifying statements.

Sometimes participation in budgeting falls short of ideal practice. In budgetary control the illustration of "pseudo-participation" is embodied in a classic study where there was analysis of the tactics of the controller who encouraged an exchange of opinions but, believing that the line supervisors had little to contribute anyway, was very keen to get their signatures on the new budget signifying their approval (Argyris, 1953). The signatures were then treated as evidence of their approval. However, one should note that if supervisors accept half-heartedly a budget target or budget changes, and are bound by their signatures, it will almost inevitably follow that the initiators of the targets or changes will have to be constantly vigilant, and will have to pressure the

acceptors of the suggested course of action in order to ensure compliance. This is not a favourable situation to be in for somebody who subscribes to the notion of participation as a motivational tool. There is also the possibility of "budget biasing" taking root in a participatory budget system. This amounts to managers inflating costs or reducing revenue at the budget stage (Schiff & Lewin, 1970) so as to make the target more attainable.

In the context of meeting the requirements of the corporate master budget, there is a view that the ability of large groups of lower level personnel to participate in budget planning must be the subject of some doubt for the following reasons (Parker, 1979): they may lack the interest and expertise required for comprehending the range of factors to be balanced in the planning of sales, production, materials, and administration; they may find it difficult to understand the need for identifying limiting factors, and may be unable to coordinate their estimates with those of other draft sub-budgets; and there may be difficulties in comprehending the more sophisticated forecasting and simulation techniques, as well as a lack of full understanding of the broader economic and other environmental factors affecting operations. To finalise a budget with so many people contributing would present many problems for the accountant, and, if planning were to start much earlier in order to accommodate this constraint, estimates may be out of date. For the reader interested in participative budgeting, Shields and Shields (1998) provide a very useful analysis of 47 published studies on this topic.

Criticism of participative leadership

A challenge to the alleged benefits accruing to a participative style comes from a study conducted in four divisions within a company (Morse & Reimer, 1956). In two divisions a participative style was used, decision making was deliberately pushed down the hierarchy, supervisors were trained to use democratic supervisory methods, and there was an appreciable increase in their freedom of action. In the other two divisions greater hierarchical control was introduced by an increase in the closeness of supervision, and there was a noticeable shift upwards in the level at which decisions were made. These conditions prevailed for a year and approximately 500 employees were involved. It was found that both programmes contributed to a significant increase in productivity, surprisingly with a slight advantage accruing to the autocratic system.

Critics of the participative leadership school (Crozier, 1964; Strauss, 1968) harbour a number of reservations:

- There is a tendency to place overwhelming emphasis on personal coordination and control to the detriment of bureaucratic or impersonal control techniques.
- The important role played by bargaining and the use of power in interpersonal relationships is overlooked.
- The democratic or participative style is conceived largely in terms of group harmony and compatibility between personal goals and organisational goals, but the importance of organisation structure is neglected.
- Although generally people would like to exercise some degree of control over their own environment, they may fear the participation process because it threatens their integrity and independence, or they believe they will be controlled to some extent by other participants.
- Should the rewards or benefits that result from cooperating with others prove inadequate, then

withdrawal from the participative process is a likely outcome.
- Participation might lack appeal for those who do not trust each other, who feel intellectually superior to their peers, and who do not have the patience to bother with it and feel it consumes too much valuable time.

More recently Stace and Dunphy (2001) also expressed reservations about participative leadership. They argue that the participative style may be inappropriate in specified circumstances. They feel that if conflicting views were likely to surface in a discussion forum that were difficult to reconcile, then it is highly likely that a participative style would not be suitable because it consumes too much time. Equally, where a strategic change in direction is called for in order to ensure organisational survival, it is likely that a participative style would be inappropriate whereas a more directive style would be functional. For example, the restructuring of the police force in New South Wales, Australia was spearheaded by a newly appointed Police Commissioner charged with stamping out corruption and modernising the force. A firm directive style was considered functional in this context, at least in the initial stages (Stace & Dunphy, 2001).

However, even though senior management could be directive as in the above situation and in leading change (see Chapter 16), middle managers and those beneath them could be more participative in their approach when implementing change. The last point is likely to be endorsed as functional by Wagner (1994) who, in a reconsideration of the research evidence, concluded that overall participation has a small positive effect on the productivity and job satisfaction of group members.

Macro participation

The foregoing discussion dealt with participation at the micro level (primarily at the operational level). Participation at the policy or macro level is discussed briefly here.

In Britain, participation at the macro level has never been a significant practical proposition, though the worker director scheme at the British Steel Corporation in the past was a notable exception. The Bullock Committee report in 1976 was followed by a White Paper on industrial democracy in 1978. The White Paper proposed a structure of joint representation committees composed of all unions at each place of work with a statutory right to discuss company strategy and have access to information. These measures were never enacted. In Sweden, employee directors on the boards of companies have proved a successful venture, and in Germany, the *Mitbestimmung* provides an opportunity for employee representatives to influence policy formulation on supervisory boards.

Global competition and European integration are putting pressure on Germany's law that gives employees equal representation on the supervisory boards of large companies (*Financial Times*, 2004b). The employee representatives on the supervisory boards generally include trade union officials as well as Works Council members (see reference below to the Works Council). The employers' body and the industry federation recently proposed an overhaul of the co-determination or *Mitbestimmung* law, not the law that provides for employee involvement through Works Councils at the operational level. Supporters of the *Mitbestimmung* argue that it has secured social peace in Germany by ensuring that employees are fully aware of the challenges facing their company, but critics point out the distortions it can create; for example, there have been recent examples of supervisory boards failing to exercise control over management of companies (e.g., KarstadtQuelle, the retail group, that nearly collapsed with heavy job losses).

The European Commission's revised 1983 Draft Directive on Procedures for Informing and Consulting Employees (the "Vredeling Directive") recommended giving employee representatives, in organisations employing 1000 or more workers within the EU, substantial general information on the group as a whole and specific information on their own company within the group. Certain business secrets would be withheld. This eventually led to the creation of Works Councils. These are committees made up of representatives from workers and management and can be found in a

number of European countries. These committees operate at the organisational level and meet to discuss a variety of issues including employee relations and business matters and to engage in joint decision making (Holden, 1994).

The Works Council Directive came into existence under the Social Chapter of the Maastricht Treaty in 1991, and the UK used the "opt out" facility to avoid its effect. Therefore, technically UK companies do not have to comply with the provisions of the Directive as far as their UK workers are concerned; however, UK companies with operations in other EU member states would be subject to the Directive for employees working outside the UK. Companies to which the Directive applies are those with at least 1000 employees within the 15 EU member states covered by the Directive, which was implemented in September 1996. They are required to set up European Works Councils (EWCs) with the express purpose of consulting employees and giving them information about their company's performance and prospects.

The alleged advantages of EWCs are that employees will be better able to understand the pressures businesses face and appreciate the need to adapt to change in a competitive world. Also, EWCs could be seen as a means to cultivate the commitment of employees to the achievement of their company's objectives. Some UK companies (e.g., United Biscuits and ICI) have created EWCs in the UK, although they are not required to do so. Drawing on empirical evidence to explore the views of British managers involved in EWCs, Wills (1999) concluded that the British managers in UK-owned firms would appear to have a clear strategy in managing their EWCs, and it appears that EWCs are more likely to be directed by a managerial agenda than a trade union one.

CONTINGENCY THEORIES

By the early 1960s there was recognition that leadership could not be explained satisfactorily in terms of behavioural styles, and there was a general belief that the particular circumstances in which leaders find themselves (situational circumstances) are influential in determining the most appropriate leadership style. Over the years many studies have been conducted trying to establish the critical situational variables (Podsakoff, MacKenzie, Aherne, & Bommer, 1995). In this section the following important contingency or situational perspectives on leadership are considered:

(1) leadership continuum;
(2) influence–power continuum;
(3) Fiedler's model;
(4) a normative model (original and revised);
(5) leader–member exchange (LMX) theory;
(6) path–goal model;
(7) Hersey–Blanchard situational theory;
(8) attribution perspective; and
(9) substitutes for leadership.

Leadership continuum

The first theory to be examined is the revised continuum of leadership behaviour proposed by Tannenbaum and Schmidt (1973). They conceive a continuum (depicted in Figure 12.2) with an autocratic style on the left-hand side, a democratic style on the right-hand side, and varying degrees of influence in between.

The term "nonmanager" is used as a substitute for "subordinate" and this is said to reflect the organisational processes such as industrial democracy and participative management, where subordinates have a greater say in matters that affect them as well as frequently sharing managerial functions. The arrows indicate the continual flow of interdependent influence. The authors of the leadership continuum are inclined to associate a subordinate-centred style with the achievement of the following common objectives shared by managers: to raise the level of employee motivation; to increase the capacity of subordinates to accept change; to improve the quality of decisions; to develop teamwork and morale; and to foster the development of employees.

The theory also considers the situation in which leadership style operates. Situational factors that determine the manager's choice of leadership style are forces in the manager, forces in the subordinate, and forces in the situation.

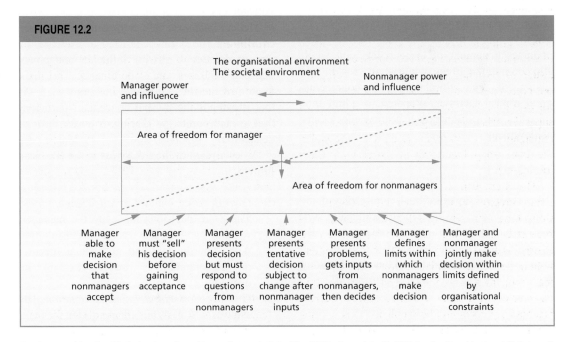

FIGURE 12.2

Continuum of leadership behaviour (from Tannenbaum & Schmidt, 1973). Copyright © 1973 by the President and Fellows of Harvard College and reprinted by permission.

Forces in the manager

A useful starting point is an understanding of the manager's attitudes and predisposition towards an appropriate leadership style. A manager may not subscribe to a participative style because he or she prefers to act alone. Likewise, managers may not wish to involve their subordinates because they lack confidence in them; or if the situation is uncertain, they may feel insecure and prefer to act independently.

Forces in the subordinate

Ideally a manager would expect the following conditions to exist before being prepared to allow the subordinate to participate in decision making. The subordinate has a relatively high need for independence; shows a readiness to assume responsibility for decision making; possesses a relatively high tolerance for ambiguity; is interested in the problem that is considered important; has the necessary knowledge and experience to deal with the problem; understands the goals of the organisation with which he or she can identify; and has developed expectations to share in decision making. In extolling the virtues of the effective followers (subordinates), Kelley (1988) endorses a number of these points and would add commitment to the organisation, trust in their judgement, high ethical standards, courageous, good critical faculties, prepared to admit their mistakes, and a willingness to acknowledge others' achievements.

Forces in the situation

The prevailing organisational culture may determine to some extent the type of leadership style that is best suited to a given organisation. For example, behavioural characteristics of an autocratic nature may be considered functional in some organisations and are therefore reinforced.

Other factors

Other forces in the situation that may somehow restrain the manager's manoeuvrability with respect to leadership style are the size of the working group; the geographical dispersion of subordinates; the secrecy of the issues in question; the level of relevant expertise of the subordinate; and the pressure of time. For example, where the size of the group is large, subordinates are scattered over many company sites, the issues are highly confidential and secret, the subordinate does not have the kind of knowledge that is needed, and the organisation is in a state of crisis, then an autocratic style may be appropriate. The opposite may be true when these situations are reversed.

In the Tannenbaum and Schmidt model there is an interdependent relationship among and between the situational factors and leadership style, because what happens to one variable may have a bearing on another. The model is of some value as a conceptual scheme for identifying different leadership styles and the circumstances that influence them, but it lacks precision in suggesting the appropriate point on the continuum to choose in a given set of circumstances.

The influence–power continuum

Another leadership continuum has been formulated by Heller (1971). He calls it the **influence–power continuum** (IPC) and it is used to evaluate the various degrees of sharing influence and power between superiors and subordinates. The main feature of the IPC—depicted in Figure 12.3—is that it extends the normal concept of participation to incorporate the sharing of power through delegation.

A description of the five styles in the IPC is as follows:

(1) *Own decision without detailed explanation.* These are decisions made by the manager, without previous discussion or consultation with subordinates, and no special meeting or memorandum is used to explain the decisions.

(2) *Own decision with detailed explanation.* The same as in style 1, but afterwards the manager explains the problem and the reasons for the decision in a memorandum or at a special meeting.

FIGURE 12.3

Style 1	Style 2	Style 3	Style 4	Style 5
Own decision *without* explanation	Own decision *with* explanation	Prior consultation	Joint decision making	Delegation

Participation →

Influence →   Power

The influence–power continuum (adapted from Heller, 1971).

(3) *Prior consultation with subordinates.* Before the decision is taken the manager explains the problem to his or her subordinates and asks for their advice and help. The manager then makes the decision. The manager's final choice may, or may not, reflect the subordinates' influence.

(4) *Joint decision making with subordinates.* The manager and his or her subordinates together analyse the problem and come to a decision. The subordinates usually have as much influence over the final choice as the manager. Where there are more than two individuals in the discussion, more often than not the decision of the majority is accepted.

(5) *Delegation of decision to subordinates.* The manager asks the subordinates to make decisions regarding a particular subject. The manager may or may not request the subordinates to report back, and seldom vetoes such decisions.

Heller related the various leadership styles to specific situational circumstances and established certain relationships. The following sample of the findings of a US study is illustrative of a situational perspective.

A large span of control on the part of a senior manager, indicating a large number of immediate subordinates, is associated with time-saving decision styles at the extremes of the continuum— either highly centralised (style 1) or decentralised (style 5).

When senior managers see big differences in skill between themselves and their subordinates, they use centralised or autocratic styles (styles 1 and 2). When they see little difference in skill, they are more willing to share power with their subordinates and use democratic styles (styles 3 and 4). The latter appeals to common sense, in that there is little point in sharing influence with a subordinate who is perceived as not possessing the necessary skill.

Closely related to the last conclusion is the finding that where senior managers have experienced subordinates (measured by age and length of time in the company), they are noticeably more inclined to use delegation (style 5) and to avoid centralised or autocratic styles (styles 1 and 2). General managers and personnel managers used the greatest amount of power sharing, whereas production and finance managers used the least.

Later, Heller's research programme was extended to a number of European countries, providing tests of the original US research. It also introduced some new variables—for example, skills and educational levels, and environmental turbulence and complexity. Taking the US and European studies together, it appears that managers in the UK, Germany, and the USA are inclined to be more autocratic, whereas Swedish and French managers are more democratic (Heller & Wilpert, 1981). The influence of national cultures on management style is discussed in Chapter 15.

The author adopted Heller's leadership continuum to measure the leadership style of chief accountants in the UK. Among the situational factors that influenced their style were the nature of the decisions they faced; the extent of job specialisation in the finance function; the calibre of section heads; the qualities or skills of their subordinates; the number of subordinates reporting to them; and the psychological distance or closeness between chief accountants and their subordinates. Contrary to a general impression at that time, which suggested that accountants are autocratic in orientation, chief accountants placed almost equal emphasis on both autocratic and democratic leadership styles. What was particularly interesting was that they modified their style to suit prevailing situational circumstances (McKenna, 1978).

Fiedler's model

One of the most widely discussed theories of situational leadership is the contingency model of leadership effectiveness, postulated by Fiedler (1967). This theory attempts to predict how style of leadership, leader–member relations, the power vested in the position of leader, and the structure of the job or task harmonise to determine the leader's ability to achieve productive output.

The measure of the style of leadership is the esteem of the leader for his or her least preferred co-worker (LPC). The LPC is the person with whom the leader has found it most difficult to cooperate. To arrive at an LPC score, leaders were asked to rate both their most preferred co-worker (MPC) and their least preferred co-worker (LPC). Leaders who describe their MPCs and LPCs similarly are classified as "high LPC" leaders, whereas those who describe their LPCs much more negatively than their MPCs are classified as "low LPC" leaders. The co-worker evaluated in this way need not be someone the leader is actually working with at the time. According to Fiedler, the LPC score is best interpreted as a dynamic trait that results in different behaviour as the situation changes.

Leaders with high LPC ratings would be psychologically close to their group members; with low LPC ratings they would be psychologically distant. Leaders who describe their least preferred co-workers in a relatively favourable manner (high LPC) tend to be employee-centred in their relationships with group members. They gain satisfaction and self-esteem from successful interpersonal relations. Leaders who describe their least preferred co-workers in a relatively

unfavourable manner (low LPC) tend to be autocratic, task-centred, and less concerned with the human relations aspects of the job. They gain satisfaction and self-esteem from successful task performance. Therefore, the high and low LPC leaders seek to satisfy different needs in the group situation.

The three major variables in the work situation that can impede or facilitate a leader's attempt to influence group members are, as stated earlier, the structure of jobs or tasks; the power in the position of the leader; and leader–member relations.

- *Task structure*. The organisation generally provides support for the leader by structuring jobs with the help of procedures, rules, and regulations. The degree of structure in the job or task can be measured by establishing the extent to which work decisions can be verified, the degree of clarity surrounding the stating of the work goal, the number of methods available for achieving the goal, and the extent to which one can be specific about the solution to the work problem. The leader finds it easier to force compliance in a structured job situation (where the activities to be carried out are specific and clear) than in an unstructured job situation. In the latter, leaders may find it difficult to exercise influence because neither they nor the group members can be dogmatic about what should be done; in fact, the leaders will have to pay attention to inspiring and motivating their followers.
- *Position power*. The power in the position is the authority vested in the leader's position as distinct from any power arising from his or her skill and ability in handling matters occurring within the group. It would include the rewards and punishment at the leader's disposal, the leader's authority to define the group's rules, and his or her appointment being immune from termination by the group. So a leader with strong position power has considerable freedom to reward and punish subordinates.
- *Leader–member relations*. The most important of the three dimensions is leader–member relations. A liked and respected leader, with subordinates who have confidence in him or

her, or one working in a smoothly functioning group, can do things that would be difficult for a leader in different circumstances. Power in the position is the least important of the three dimensions because a well-liked leader can get results without institutional power, and likewise, will not need the power if the task is clearly structured.

Fiedler arrives at a continuum depicting the favourableness of the situation for the leader. This is shown in Figure 12.4. For example, when executive functions in complex organisations were examined, the leader with a low LPC who is autocratic and task-centred (controlling, etc.) was found to be effective in situations both favourable and unfavourable for the exercise of influence. A favourable situation has high task structure, good leader–member relations, and strong power in the position. An unfavourable situation has low task structure, moderately poor leader–member relations, and weak power in the position. But in between these two extreme positions, where the situation is intermediate in favourableness, the employee-centred leader (permissive, etc.) who has a high LPC, was found to be effective. This type

of leadership orientation was associated with policy decision making.

The implications of Fiedler's model for improving organisational effectiveness are either to change the manager's leadership orientation (as reflected in the LPC score) so it is compatible with the situational conditions or, alternatively, to modify the situational conditions in order to bring them into line with the leadership orientation. The latter would appeal to Fiedler because he considers leadership style to be relatively fixed. But if one subscribed to self-monitoring theory, this view could be challenged. For example, high self-monitors (those who are adaptable with a significant ability to adjust their behaviour to situational factors) are likely to adjust their leadership style to changing situations (Anderson, 1990). Fiedler's contingency theory of leadership has been the subject of a significant amount of criticism (Graen, Orris, & Alvares, 1971), but equally there is considerable evidence to support at least substantial parts of the theory (Schriesheim, Tepper, & Tetrault, 1994).

Fiedler has consistently defended his approach, theory, research, and interpretations of the research evidence. There are numerous rejoinders in the

FIGURE 12.4

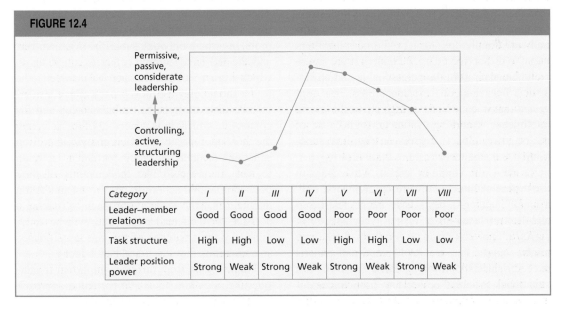

Contingency model of leadership effectiveness (adapted from Fiedler, 1972).

literature on the contingency theory of leadership. Criticisms hinge on the difficulty of measuring task structure, the problem of using the LPC score to differentiate task and human relations-oriented leadership (Schreisheim et al., 1994), and, in particular, the absence in many studies of a leader with an LPC score somewhere between high and low. Fiedler's view, with regard to the latter point, is that middle LPC leaders are not concerned with either task or human relations issues and perform poorly in most leadership situations. But others would dispute this view. Fiedler's model focuses heavily on performance to the neglect of employee satisfaction and, as a consequence, provides an incomplete picture of leadership effectiveness (Gray & Starke, 1984).

Fiedler and an associate have added refinements to his earlier work and they have come forward with a cognitive resource theory that takes into account the intelligence and experience of the leader (Fiedler & Garcia, 1987). Leaders are said to use their intelligence more than their experience in formulating and implementing plans in conditions of low interpersonal stress (a favourable situation or supportive environment), and could get away with adopting directive behaviour. However, they use their experience (i.e., reliance on well-learned patterns of behaviour) more than their intelligence in conditions of high stress (an unfavourable situation or nonsupportive environment), simply because it would be more functional to do so. According to Fielder (1995), stress could emanate from the unreasonable and unsupportive behaviour of the leader's boss. It is suggested that in conditions of high stress the use of intelligence would be dysfunctional because of the negative impact of stress on cognitive functioning (i.e., the leader cannot think clearly when he or she is the victim of stress). With regard to the testing of the cognitive resource theory, only a small number of tests have been undertaken and they produced mixed results (Vecchio, 1990).

As a final comment on Fiedler's work, one might suggest that the intelligence and experience variables should now join LPC and the old situational variables before any pronouncement is made on the contingency model of leadership effectiveness.

A normative model

A "normative" or "prescriptive" model of leadership style has been put forward by Vroom and Yetton (1973). Certain assumptions are made about the consequences of exercising different leadership styles. A significant feature of this model is that it provides a list of considerations a manager may dwell on before selecting a leadership style in different circumstances.

Vroom and Yetton believe descriptions of leadership behaviour, such as employee-orientation and task-orientation, are not strictly operational because they are too imprecise. They maintain that a normative theory of leadership must be sufficiently precise in specifying the behaviour of a leader so that a person may be confident that he or she is acting in accordance with the prescription offered by the theory. To achieve this, they put forward different forms of leadership or decision-making behaviour to cope with both individual and group problems. These are depicted in Table 12.4, and they bear a similarity to the autocratic–democratic continuum shown in Figure 12.2.

In Table 12.4 the approaches or styles classified as "A" are autocratic; "C" are consultative; "G" are group-dominated; and "D" are delegative. There are variations within each letter classification. The right-hand column of the table refers to problems where only one subordinate is involved, and the left-hand column refers to situations in which a group of subordinates is involved. The leader should only use an approach after considering seriously the type of problem faced and the context in which it is placed. Before selecting the most appropriate approach or style in a given situation, leaders must pay particular attention to what they would like the outcome of their deliberations and actions to be. Vroom and Yetton maintain that the leaders' approach to making a decision, or their leadership style, will be determined by the attributes of the various problems and situations they face (see Panel 12.5).

Following on from this, it is important to consider the rules for choosing a particular approach to decision making or leadership style. These are derived by an elimination of the approaches or

TABLE 12.4

Decision methods for group and individual problems (from Vroom & Yetton, 1973): Copyright ©1973 by University of Pittsburgh Press and reproduced with permission

Group problems	*Individual problems*
A1. You solve the problems or make the decision yourself, using information available to you at the time.	A1. You solve the problem or make the decision by yourself, using information available to you at the time.
A2. You obtain the necessary information from your subordinates, then decide the solution to the problem yourself. You may or may not tell your subordinates what the problem is in getting the information from them. The role played by your subordinates in making the decision is clearly one of providing the necessary information to you, rather than generating or evaluating alternative solutions.	A2. You obtain the necessary information from your subordinates, then decide on the solution to the problem yourself. You may or may not tell the subordinate what the problem is in getting the information from him/her. His/her role in making the decision is clearly one of providing the necessary information to you, rather than generating or evaluating alternative solutions.
C1. You share the problem with the relevant subordinates individually, getting their ideas and suggestions without bringing them together as a group. Then you make the decision which may or may not reflect your subordinates' influence.	C1. You share the problem with your subordinate, getting ideas and suggestions. Then you make a decision, which may or may not reflect his/her influence.
C2. You share the problem with your subordinates as a group, obtaining their collective ideas and suggestions. Then you make the decision, which may or may not reflect your subordinates' influence.	G1. You share the problem with your subordinate, and together you analyse the problem and arrive at a mutually agreeable solution.
G2. You share the problem with your subordinates as a group. Together you generate and evaluate alternatives and attempt to reach agreement (consensus) on a solution. Your role is much like that of chairman. You do not try to influence the group to adopt "your" solution, and you are willing to accept and implement any solution that has the support of the entire group.	D1. You delegate the problem to your subordinate, providing any relevant information that you possess, but giving him/her responsibility for solving the problem. You may or may not request the subordinate to tell you what solution he/she has reached.

styles (listed in Table 12.4) that seem to be inappropriate, leaving us with a feasible set of decision-making approaches:

- Where the quality of the decision is important, and the leader does not possess enough information or expertise to solve the problem alone, eliminate the A1 decision-making approach in order to avoid the risk of a low-quality decision.
- Where the quality of the decision is important and the subordinates cannot be trusted to contribute to the solution of the problem with the goals of the organisation firmly in mind, eliminate the G2 approach.
- Where the quality of the decision is important, the leader lacks the necessary information or expertise to solve the problem alone, and the problem is unstructured—i.e., the leader

does not know what information is needed or where it is located because access to it is difficult—then eliminate the approaches A1, A2, and C1. The approach A1 militates against collecting the necessary information, and the approaches A2 and C1 are cumbersome and less effective when a problem-solving orientation is required. In this situation, approaches C2 and G1, which require interaction among subordinates who are knowledgeable with respect to a particular problem, are likely to generate high-quality solutions.

In these three cases, the major preoccupation is to make sure that a high-quality decision is made in circumstances where quality is relevant. In the following four cases, the major preoccupation is to ensure that the decision is acceptable to subordinates when their acceptance of it is important.

PANEL 12.5: Problem attributes and situations faced by leaders

I.   *Decision quality.* The importance of the quality of the decision.

II. *Leadership information/expertise.* The extent to which the leader possesses sufficient information or expertise to make a high-quality decision alone. It is obvious that a leader who makes a decision alone utilises the knowledge and skills he or she possesses. But there are a number of occasions when the leader draws on the resources of the group. Subordinates, as a group, may have the necessary information to generate a high-quality decision. For example, a decision to rationalise the administrative structure of an organisation may require more knowledge and expertise than the leader possesses. In such circumstances one may ask if subordinates can make a valid contribution to the decision process. If not, it may be necessary for the leader to go outside the group for information.

III. *Structured or unstructured problems.* The extent to which the problem is structured or unstructured is significant. Structured problems are those for which the alternative solutions or methods for generating and evaluating solutions are known. An example of a structured problem is deciding when to take legal action for arrears on a customer's account where the amount involved is significant and long overdue. Unstructured problems cannot be dealt with in a clear-cut manner and they appear to be elusive or complex. An example of an unstructured problem is defining the expected life of a new fixed asset for depreciation purposes.

IV. *Subordinate acceptance or commitment.* This is the extent to which acceptance or commitment on the part of subordinates is critical to the effective implementation of the decision. Acceptance of the decision by subordinates is critical when the effective implementation of the decision requires the display of initiative, judgement, or creativity by all concerned. It is recognised that participation by subordinates in the making of a decision is likely to increase the probability of their accepting it.

V.   *Acceptance of autocratic decision.* The likelihood that the leader's autocratic decision will be accepted by subordinates is a further factor. There might be circumstances when subordinates accept a decision imposed autocratically. This may occur when the proposed course of action enshrined in the decision appeals to reason and is intrinsically attractive (e.g., the leader awards his or her subordinates extra holiday entitlement because of their exceptional performance at work).

VI. *Subordinate motivation.* This factor comprises the extent to which subordinates are motivated to achieve the organisational goals as reflected in the problem under review. It is possible to find situations where the personal goals of an employee are in line with those of the organisation. But in other cases the employee's self-interest, as reflected in his or her personal goals, is out of line with organisational goals, expressed as targets and objectives that he or she is expected to achieve. In such circumstances a leadership style, such as G2 in Table 12.4, could pose a potential risk to the quality of the decision because significant control resides in the group.

VII. *Subordinate disagreement.* The final factor is the extent to which subordinates are likely to be in disagreement or conflict over preferred solutions. If there is disagreement, it may be possible to bring about agreement by allowing the group to interact. This could be achieved by using a group-dominated approach to decision making (e.g., C2 or G2 in Table 12.4) where subordinates interact in the process of solving the problem.

(Vroom & Yetton, 1973)

- Where the acceptance of a decision by the subordinate is crucial for its effective implementation, and one is not sure that an autocratic decision-making approach would be acceptable, eliminate the A1 and A2 approaches because neither provides an opportunity for the subordinate to participate in the decision process. By taking this course of action the risk of the subordinate rejecting the decision is minimised.

- Where the acceptance of the decision by the subordinate is critical, and it is uncertain that a decision imposed autocratically will be accepted and subordinates are likely to be in conflict over the most appropriate solution, then eliminate the approaches A1, A2, and C1. The reason for this is that these approaches generally require a one-to-one relationship and involve no significant interaction. These approaches do not provide enough opportunity for those in conflict to resolve their difficulties; as a consequence, some subordinates may lack the necessary commitment to the final decision. The most appropriate approach to adopt in these circumstances is either C2 or G1, which allow those in disagreement to resolve their differences, provided they possess full knowledge of the problem.

- Where the quality of the decision is unimportant, and there is doubt about the acceptability of a decision imposed autocratically, then the approaches that are likely to produce a lesser degree of acceptance by subordinates—A1, A2, C1, and C2—should be eliminated. A participative approach (e.g., G2) would appear to be more suitable in these circumstances.

- Where acceptance of the decision by subordinates is critical, where subordinates can be trusted, and where acceptance is unlikely to be forthcoming if an autocratic approach is imposed, then eliminate the approaches A1, A2, C1, and C2. If these approaches to decision making were used, it would create the risk of a lower level of acceptance of the decision by subordinates. The approach to decision making that would appear functional in these circumstances is G2, which suggests that a high level of influence is exerted by subordinates.

Having now eliminated the inappropriate approaches to decision making, the leader is still left with more than one approach. Vroom and Yetton suggest that decision rules can be used to help with the selection of the most appropriate approach to decision making. To apply this procedure a decision tree can be used. Decision rules are presented pictorially as a decision tree in Figure 12.5. Before examining Figure 12.5, a brief case study is introduced, which is subsequently used to follow the flow of the decision process in the figure.

An office manager is dissatisfied with having to place such heavy reliance on ageing equipment in the office and wishes to explore alternatives. He or she is not very knowledgeable about the purchase and operation of up-to-date substitute equipment. The office manager recognises that the subordinates must feel comfortable and confident using the replacement equipment, otherwise the level of productivity will fall. The office manager's relationship with the subordinates is good and they can identify easily with the company's goals or objectives. However, because of the calibre of the subordinates, and the nature of their work, they would like to have a say in any decision to replace the existing equipment. The

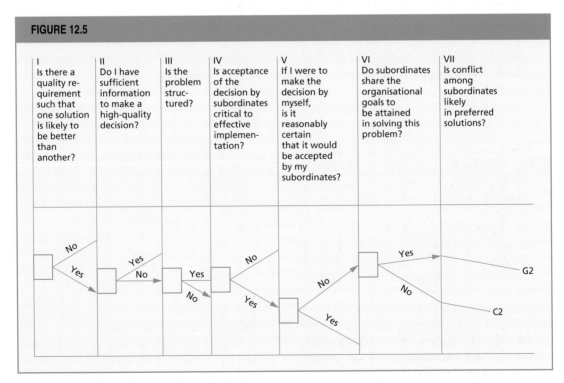

FIGURE 12.5

I	II	III	IV	V	VI	VII
Is there a quality requirement such that one solution is likely to be better than another?	Do I have sufficient information to make a high-quality decision?	Is the problem structured?	Is acceptance of the decision by subordinates critical to effective implementation?	If I were to make the decision by myself, is it reasonably certain that it would be accepted by my subordinates?	Do subordinates share the organisational goals to be attained in solving this problem?	Is conflict among subordinates likely in preferred solutions?

Decision tree for group problems (adapted from the original decision tree of Vroom & Yetton, 1973).

problem facing the office manager and his or her staff is not clear-cut. For example, why is the new equipment necessary at this time and is the expense justified? What about the additional costs, such as maintenance, insurance, and staff training or recruitment?

Which decision-making approach or leadership style for group problems (see Table 12.4) should the office manager use in this situation? (The letters at the end of the decision tree in Figure 12.5 denote leadership style and they correspond to those listed in Table 12.4.) On the horizontal line of Figure 12.5 is a list of questions, posed by the office manager, relevant to the problem. We can go through questions I to VI, using the information provided in the case just described, and arrive at the following answers. (Note that arrows show the flow of the decision process in the decision tree.)

I. Yes, there is a quality requirement (the replacement office equipment must function).
II. No, the leader (office manager) is not very knowledgeable about the replacement equipment.
III. No, the problem is not structured because it is not obvious how to go about the purchase, installation, and operation of the new office equipment.
IV. Yes, the subordinates' involvement in the making of the decision to replace the existing office equipment is crucial for the acceptance of the decision by the subordinates.
V. No, because the acceptance of the decision by the subordinates is critical, and a decision imposed autocratically is unlikely to be accepted.
VI. Yes, the subordinates have the interests of the organisation firmly in mind with regard to the efficiency of the office, and therefore they identify with the goals of the organisation.

In this example, conflict among the subordinates (VII) did not arise. Following the arrows in Figure 12.5, you will notice that the decision-making approach or leadership style associated with this case is G2 (a highly participative style). Given the circumstances reported in the case, it seems to be a sensible outcome. What would be the outcome if the circumstances were slightly different? Suppose the answer to question VI was "No", then the recommended style is C2, in which the leader permits limited participation but takes the final decision alone. The rationale for this may be that, as the subordinates do not share the organisational goals, it is wise for the leader to imprint his or her authority on the decision.

In the Vroom and Yetton prescriptive model, more than one of the five decision-making approaches or leadership styles shown in Table 12.4 may be effective, depending on the answers given to the questions in Figure 12.5. If time is of critical importance, the leader may use an autocratic style, but a participative style could be used when the leader feels it is preferable to spend time developing subordinates. A particular strength of the model is the identification of the factors that influence the effectiveness of the leader. These were referred to earlier as the quality requirement in decisions, the availability of relevant information or expertise, the nature of the problem, the acceptance of the decision by the subordinates, and the commitment and motivation of subordinates.

The theory has a number of attractive features, among them the issue of the involvement of subordinates in decision making. But the research methodology of the model has been criticised. It is suggested that the technique of self-reporting used by managers in devising a decision tree may be open to socially desirable responses (Field, 1979). This could arise when they report that their leadership or decision style is more participative than it really is because they feel it is fashionable to say so. Also, the model may be more applicable to leaders than to subordinates; in fact, subordinates do not always see the relevance of the style dictated by the model. In one study subordinates disliked the managers' autocratic style, even in circumstances where the model indicated this style to be the most appropriate (Field & House, 1990). Another matter to consider is the skill of the leader in putting into practice the chosen decision style (Tjosvold, Wedley, & Field, 1986). For example, the right decision style is selected but it is handled with poor skill, leading to an ineffective outcome.

The Vroom and Yetton model was revised by Vroom and Jago in the late 1980s (Vroom & Jago, 1988, 1995). The attributes of the various problems and situations faced by the leader have now been extended to incorporate the following attributes and questions:

* *Subordinate information.* Do subordinates have sufficient information to make a high-quality decision?
* *Time constraint.* Does a critically severe time constraint limit the ability to involve subordinates?
* *Geographical dispersion (group problems only).* Are the costs involved in bringing together geographically dispersed subordinates prohibitive?
* *Motivation (time).* How important is it to minimise the time it takes to make the decision?
* *Motivation (development).* How important is it to maximise the opportunities for subordinate development?

Another modification to the original model involved the replacement of a yes/no answer to most of the questions (now numbering 12) by a 5-point scale. Vroom and Jago (1988, 1995) point out that the original model assumed that all situations are black and white, "while managers tell us that the most difficult situations they encounter are those that are found in varying shades of grey. Yes and No answers simply do not capture all the meaningful differences that exist among situations." Vroom (2000) has suggested another minor refinement to the original model.

We will now return to the case of the office manager faced with the replacement of equipment and the decision tree based on it in Figure 12.5. In the decision tree of the revised model, but not in the original model, an additional question would be asked of the manager in a time-driven group problem situation. This question, which reads "Do subordinates have sufficient information to make a high-quality decision?" would appear towards the end (right-hand side) of the decision tree. A "Yes" answer to this question, with reference to the case, would indicate the use of a G2 approach (participative) and a "No"

answer would suggest that a C2 approach (consultative) is more appropriate.

The revised model is more complex than the original model and this could discourage its use. It is said to be more sensitive to differences in the various situations. Computer software has been developed that makes it possible for managers to input their answers to the 12 questions. This helps them assess a particular situation quickly so as to arrive at the appropriate leadership style. However, this could be a difficult exercise for the average manager. The revised model has not been subjected to serious empirical examination.

The model put forward by Vroom and his associates recognises that leadership behaviour is flexible and can be adjusted to suit the situation. This view could be contrasted with that of Fiedler, who postulates in his situational model the inflexibility of leadership behaviour, and that we should adjust the situation so that it is compatible with leadership style.

Leader–member exchange (LMX) theory

Like the other leadership perspectives, the LMX theory—also known as the vertical dyad linkage theory—places emphasis on subordinate participation and influence in the decision-making process, but it has distinctive features as well (Dansereau, Grean, & Haga, 1975). It attempts to explain how the nature of the relationship (or linkage) between leader and follower can affect the leadership process.

A distinction is drawn between subordinates who are members of particular subgroups, called *in-groups* and *out-groups*. An in-group consists of workers who the superior believes are competent, trustworthy, and motivated to work hard and accept responsibility. These traits are said not to be possessed by the out-group. As a consequence, the leader feels confident to allocate responsibility for important tasks to members of the in-group, thereby making his or her job that much easier. The leader is grateful to in-group members for making his or her life easier, and reciprocates by offering support, understanding, and a more personal relationship. There is evidence to indicate that in-group members have a higher level of performance and satisfaction than out-group members (Phillips & Bedeian, 1994).

What is the nature of the relationship between the leader and subordinates in the out-group? The leader is inclined not to bestow favours on members of the out-group. They are given tasks requiring less ability and responsibility. Also, out-group members do not benefit from a personal relationship with the leader. In fact the leader's interactions with out-group members is based on his or her formal authority, rather than respect or friendship.

An important implication of the vertical dyad linkage theory is that leadership can be understood better by examining dyads (pairs of relations) made up of leader and member (a vertical relationship) rather than concentrating on what one might call the average leadership style, which, in effect, assumes that all subordinates are treated in the same way (Schriesheim, Castro, Zhou, and Yamarino, 2001). It is unclear how the leader classifies subordinates as belonging to either the in-group or the out-group. However, there is evidence to suggest that leaders consider subordinates to be in-group members where the latter have personal characteristics compatible with those of the leader and are likely to be extravert with a higher level of competence than out-group members (Duchon, Green, & Taber, 1986; Liden, Wayne, & Stilwell, 1993).

The theory predicts that subordinates privileged to be classified as in-group members will enjoy better performance, experience lower staff turnover rates, and enjoy greater satisfaction with their superiors (e.g., Maslyn & Uhl-Bien, 2001). But there have been criticisms of the predictive power of the theory (e.g., in the area of staff turnover), and reservations about the performance measures used. Nevertheless, there is support for this theory of leadership (Graen & Uhl-Bien, 1995; Settoon, Bennett, & Liden, 1996; Vecchio & Gobdel, 1984).

Path–goal model

A **path–goal theory** of leadership, which is somewhat similar to the expectancy theory of motivation discussed in Chapter 4, was developed by House (1971). The main functions of the leader

are, according to this theory, to assist the subordinate to attain his or her goals and to ensure that the subordinate finds the experience satisfying. The theory is concerned with explaining the relationship between the behaviour of the leader and the attitudes and expectations of the subordinate.

The description of leadership behaviour is similar in a number of respects to leadership behaviour discussed in previous sections—particularly initiating structure and consideration—and consists of four dimensions:

(1) *Directive leadership.* The leader lets subordinates know what is expected of them and provides specific guidelines, rules, regulations, standards, and schedules of the work to be done.

(2) *Supportive leadership.* The leader is concerned about the status, needs, and well-being of subordinates, is friendly, and endeavours to make work more pleasant.

(3) *Participative leadership.* The leader goes through consultation processes with subordinates, seeking their suggestions and being considerate towards them in the decision-making process.

(4) *Achievement-oriented leadership.* The leader sets challenging goals for subordinates and shows confidence and trust in the way concern is expressed about their ability to meet exacting performance standards. The leader is also concerned with trying to improve performance.

These four dimensions of leadership behaviour are related to three dispositions of the subordinate, as follows:

• *Satisfaction of the subordinate.* Subordinates will feel satisfied if they perceive the leader's behaviour as being responsible for their present level of satisfaction, or as being instrumental in bringing about future satisfaction.

• *Acceptance of the leader by the subordinate.* Subordinates have no difficulty in accepting the leader.

• *Expectations of the subordinate.* Subordinates expect appropriate effort will lead to effective performance, and that effective performance leads to the acquisition of acceptable rewards. The leader's behaviour produces a motivational effect, and this increases the effort put into the job by subordinates, particularly where subordinates perceive the leader as being supportive and responsible for creating a situation in which they can satisfy their personal needs as a result of effective performance.

The three dispositions of the subordinate can be influenced favourably by the leader, who uses initiating structure to clarify the path to goal achievement, and consideration to make the path easier to travel, in the following ways:

- The leader should arouse, where appropriate, the needs of subordinates for achieving results or outcomes over which subordinates have some control.
- The leader can ensure that subordinates are personally rewarded for attaining their goals.
- The leader can offer coaching and direction to subordinates and therefore make it easier for them to derive a rewarding experience from attaining their goals.
- The leader can help subordinates clarify their expectations about their work experiences.
- The leader can minimise or remove frustrating obstacles in the subordinates' path to the attainment of their goals.
- The leader can increase the opportunities for personal satisfaction that arise from effective performance.

There are two types of situational variables that have to be accommodated in path–goal theory (House & Mitchell, 1974). First, the personal characteristics of subordinates have to be considered. If subordinates feel that their behaviour influences events at work (internal locus of control), they are more likely to be satisfied with a participative leadership style. However, if subordinates believe that their accomplishments are due to luck (external locus of control), they are more likely to be satisfied with a directive leadership style. (The internal and external loci of control were discussed in Chapter 2.) Where subordinates have a high need for affiliation they are likely to be more satisfied with a supportive leadership style, whereas a directive leadership style is more acceptable when a high need for security exists.

Secondly, there are a number of demands or pressures in the job environment that relate directly to both leadership style and the motivational disposition of the subordinate, and they influence the ultimate performance of the subordinate. Where jobs are highly structured and the objectives or goals set for the subordinate are clear (e.g., the processing of an application for a television licence or a road fund licence for a motor vehicle), a supportive and participative style is likely to lead to increased satisfaction. The reason for this is that jobs are already routine and therefore little direction is necessary. By contrast, a more satisfactory arrangement for unstructured jobs would be the use of a directive style, because a directive style helps to clarify an ambiguous task for subordinates (e.g., a clerk in an insurance office finds it hard to handle a difficult claim and the manager explains the best way to proceed).

Apart from job structuring, the complexity of the task is an important situational variable. This is said to interact with the individual's desire to develop his or her knowledge and ability within the job (i.e., a need for personal growth). Not all subordinates share this desire with the same degree of intensity, so it is possible to find two categories of subordinate—one with a strong need and the other with a weak need for personal growth. The subordinate with a strong need for personal growth who performs a complex task (e.g., negotiating the terms of a deal to merge two companies in conditions of uncertainty) is more likely to perform better under a superior exercising a participative and achievement-oriented style. The subordinate with a strong need for personal growth faced with a simple task (e.g., extracting the names of companies on a random basis from a directory of companies) is more likely to perform better when subjected to a supportive style. Where the subordinate has a weak need for personal growth, and faces a complex task, then a directive style is more likely to be effective. But the same subordinate who performs a simple task is more likely to be effective with a supportive

TABLE 12.5

Interaction of leadership style and situational variables in path–goal theory

Situational variables		Effective
Characteristics of subordinate	Features of the job environment	leadership style
Internal locus of control	–	Participative
External locus of control	–	Directive
High need for affiliation	–	Supportive
High need for security	–	Directive
–	Structured jobs	Supportive and participative
–	Unstructured jobs	Directive
Strong need for personal growth	Complex task	Participative and achievement-oriented
Low need for personal growth	Complex task	Directive
Strong need for personal growth	Simple task	Supportive
Low need for personal growth	Simple task	Supportive and directive

and directive leader (Griffin, 1979). These relationships are depicted in Table 12.5.

Path–goal theory deals with specific leadership behaviour and shows how it might influence employee satisfaction and performance. It recognises the importance of situational variables and accepts individual differences. However, studies evaluating the model have generated conflicting results. It is said that the theory (like many others) offers useful insights into employee satisfaction, but has problems predicting employee performance (Gray & Starke, 1984).

Other evidence suggests that the "path–goal" leader, who is able to compensate for weaknesses residing in the subordinate or work situation, is likely to have a beneficial effect on employee satisfaction and performance, provided competent subordinates are not over-supervised (Keller, 1989).

Overall, empirical evidence is supportive, but there is a call for the theory to be refined with the addition of new moderating variables (Evans, 1996; Schriesheim & Neider, 1996; Wofford & Liska, 1993).

House (1996) revisited path–goal theory and suggested that leaders adopt behaviours that complement the abilities and environment of subordinates and that they do so in a way that helps them to overcome and compensate for deficiencies, leading to individual satisfaction and individual and sectional performance. It is felt that this revision

adds a note of clarity to the original model by highlighting the behaviour a leader needs to engage in so as to be effective in assisting subordinates to achieve their goals.

Hersey–Blanchard situational theory

This model adopts consideration (relationship behaviour) and initiating structure (task behaviour) and extends these two dimensions of leadership to form four styles (tell, sell, participation, and delegation). The model places particular emphasis on matching a style of leadership to the maturity or readiness level of subordinates (how willing they are to do a good job, and how able they are to do a job well), and this relationship is said to be crucial in the determination of leadership effectiveness (Hersey, 1984; Hersey & Blanchard, 1982).

Maturity or readiness is considered in the context of a particular task, and consists of two parts—job maturity and psychological maturity. Job maturity relates to technical knowledge and task-relevant skills. Psychological maturity relates to feelings of self-confidence and ability, and people's willingness to take responsibility for directing their own behaviour. A highly mature subordinate would be rated high on both job maturity and psychological maturity, and would be in possession of both technical competence and self-confidence for a particular task. A low-rated subordinate on the two maturity factors for a given task would be considered to lack both ability and confidence. Examples of the relationship between leadership style and maturity are as follows:

• Subordinates who are highly immature would be told what to do (tell). This is a task-oriented and directive style.
• Subordinates who are hovering on the low side of maturity would be persuaded that a particular course of action is the most appropriate (sell). Here there is a tendency to move towards a relationship-oriented style.
• Subordinates who are hovering on the high side of maturity will be treated with a certain amount of consideration and support (relationship-orientation) and allowed to "participate" in decision making.
• Subordinates who are highly mature will be considered capable of exercising self-direction and self-control, and will enjoy a high degree of autonomy. Delegation is the style applicable in this situation.

The Hersey and Blanchard model has intuitive appeal, is simplistic, and is used widely in training programmes, but the theory has not undergone significant evaluation to test its validity. Vecchio (1987) concluded that the predictions of the model were most accurate for subordinates with low maturity, but not very accurate for subordinates with high maturity. Bolman and Deal (2003) maintain that research casts doubt on the validity of the model, and just like the Blake and Mouton model (the leadership grid) referred to earlier, the Hersey and Blanchard model focuses mostly on the relationship between superiors and subordinates and says little about issues of structure, politics, or culture.

Attribution perspective

Unlike a number of leadership theories, this approach focuses on antecedents or causes of the behaviour of leaders and is concerned with how leaders and subordinates perceive each other. In this perspective on leadership we are trying to interpret the behaviour of the leader and attribute causes to it (Green & Mitchell, 1979; Shamir, 1992). Attribution theory is discussed in Chapter 5; in a nutshell, it suggests that we observe the behaviour of others, and then attribute causes to that behaviour.

In the illustration that follows we are trying to seek an explanation for the behaviour of the leader. A leader may react to a subordinate's poor performance in a number of ways. For example, if the leader attributes poor performance to internal factors (e.g., lack of ability or inadequate effort) he or she may issue a reprimand or consider the subordinate as a candidate for training. However, the extent to which the leader likes the subordinate is an important variable in this situation. Dobbins and Russell (1986) maintain that liking or not liking is a variable that could decide the nature of the corrective action (e.g., reprimand or performance counselling) taken by the superior after the subordinate's poor performance.

The leader may adopt a different pattern of behaviour when he or she attributes the subordinate's poor performance to external factors (e.g., poor operating procedures or inadequate allocation of duties), in which case corrective action focuses on the organisation rather than the subordinate. You will note in this illustration that it is what the leader has attributed to the subordinate that determines the leader's response. It is possible that what is attributable to the subordinate is at variance with the subordinate's actual behaviour!

Attribution is a two-way process. Subordinates are also capable of attributing causes to the behaviour of their leaders, and can view the leader as having an effect on their own performance. When subordinates are successful, they tend to rate their leader as successful. When they are not successful, they tend to blame the leader and distance themselves from him or her. Often we find in business that the leader of the group or organisation loses his or her job when there is a lack of success.

Apparently, there is evidence to suggest that men and women differ in their response to poor performers in an attributional context (Dobbins, 1985). An investigation of the differences between male and female leaders' responses to poorly performing subordinates found that corrective actions of female leaders were more affected by likedness and the sex of the subordinate than were the corrective actions of male leaders (Dobbins, 1986). Finally, it appears that little research has been undertaken on the attribution perspective.

Given the importance of perception in leadership, are there any perspectives other than those discussed here that emphasise perception? Meindl and Ehrlich (1987) maintain when we perceive leaders in action there is a tendency to romanticise leadership—that is, we overemphasise its importance and exaggerate the impact it makes in organisational life. This perspective on leadership does not seem to have captured the imagination of many of those interested in the subject.

Substitutes for leadership

Are there situations when leadership is irrelevant? According to some authorities there are occasions when forces in a situation, independent of leadership, offer subordinates sufficient assistance, and they do not have to rely on leaders (Kerr & Jermier, 1978; Podsakoff, MacKenzie, & Bommer, 1996). For example, forces independent of leadership could be the ability, training, and experience of the subordinate, and these could account for effective performance even though the leader of the group is unsatisfactory. In effect, the subordinate requires little supervision. To explain situations in which leadership is considered irrelevant, reference is made to "leadership substitutes" and the "leadership neutraliser".

Leadership substitutes could be the forces referred to earlier (e.g., subordinates' abilities and skills), as well as intrinsically satisfying tasks, explicit formalised goals, rigid rules and procedures, cohesive groups, and knowledgeable officials other than the leader whom the subordinate can consult. For example, where the task is interesting or satisfying, subordinates may be motivated by the work itself and this makes supervision less necessary. Where tasks are simple or repetitive, or feedback on progress is on hand, it is unnecessary for leaders to provide advice or feedback. Likewise, little direction is needed from

the leader when goals or objectives, rules and procedures are clearly stated and accepted. With regard to group cohesiveness, a work group comprising a closely knit team of competent individuals capable of taking initiatives without direction (e.g., a team from the emergency services) create less need for intervention by a leader. (See Panel 12.6 for an account of the leaderless or conductorless orchestra.)

A leadership neutraliser stops a leader from taking action in some way. For example, the leader's position may not be endowed with sufficient power, or the leader does not have adequate organisational rewards to dispense, and there may be physical distance between the leader and subordinates.

The originators of this theory—Kerr and Jermier—seem to be suggesting that effective group performance is dependent on factors other than leadership, and therefore leadership should be recognised as merely another independent variable among many that influence employee satisfaction and performance. Williams et al. (1988) offer support for the theory, though they acknowledge that some problems exist with the construct validity of some of the leadership scales used by Kerr and Jermier. Likewise, Yukl (1994) expresses reservations about certain features of the theory and research but he applauds the value of this work in the way it focuses on approaches to improving group performance. Vecchio (2003) makes a useful point when he states that this theory helps to explain the largely mixed results of studies in leadership, and asserts that studies of leadership that ignore the effect of neutralisers and substitutes may fail to uncover expected relationships.

Comment on situational leadership theory

Having examined a number of reviews of situational leadership theory, Robbins et al. (2001) recognise the intuitive appeal of this area of study, but point out that overall there appears to be very weak support for the validity of situational leadership theory. They also point out that the different situational leadership models and interpretations of variables have led to confusion regarding the results of research studies. They recommend that

PANEL 12.6: The Orpheus process

The Orpheus process refers to a form of internal democracy developed by the successful New York Orpheus Chamber Orchestra, which consistently rehearses and performs without a conductor.

The orchestra consists of 27 highly skilled knowledge workers, who cooperate to solve complex problems. Commitment and involvement by every member of the team is apparent. In the foreword to a book called *Leadership Ensemble* by Seifter (2002), Professor Richard Hackman suggests that the success of the Orpheus Chamber Orchestra points to a new model of leadership in knowledge-based organisations. In such a setting, it would seem that all members share responsibility for leadership, and differences and disagreements can be considered sources of creativity rather than something that should be suppressed in the interest of uniformity and social harmony. How does the Orpheus process work?

A core group (drawn from the instrumental sections) of 6 to 12 musicians is selected to set the artistic tone for each performance. Each instrumental section elects a representative. The core group works intensively on the detailed bar-by-bar decisions that turn sheet music into a symphony or concerto. Within the core group there is a concert master with a lead role in the piece. But this is not a position of authority. The concert master gets the rehearsal going but discussions among the core group are detailed, open, and frank. Rehearsals are then a process of discussion and consensus building, and power and responsibility are put in the hands of the people who are doing the work. Once a basic interpretation has been fully discussed, the full orchestra is assembled and the debate continues. In this setting, decisions made by the core group can be over-ridden if the larger group disagrees with them. It is rare that decisions are put to a formal vote, but it does happen.

The Orpheus process is unlikely to be adopted in a business organisation because of considerations connected with efficiency and cost. It takes the orchestra twice as long to rehearse a piece of music as an orchestra led from the front by a conductor who imposes an interpretation. However, there are obvious strengths in the Orpheus process such as the quality of the personal relationship between team members, which facilitates engagement and the confronting of obstacles.

London (2002)

the diversity of perspectives should be addressed so that a single theoretically sound approach can be pursued.

Bolman and Deal (2003) reflect on the state of situational leadership. They acknowledge that several writers have put forward situational theories of leadership, and go to say that:

> all are limited in their conceptualization of leadership and in the strength of the empirical support. Most fail to distinguish between leadership and management, typically restricting leadership to relationships between superiors and their immediate subordinates, and pay little attention to the exercise of leadership in relationships with all significant stakeholders.

Redefinition of leadership

A redefinition of leadership has taken place and inspirational leadership qualities are back in fashion. This is referred to as **transformational leadership** and will be discussed in the next section. It could be implied that the emphasis given to leadership earlier in this chapter is in the tradition of a transactional model of leadership. This type of leadership arises where the leader enters into various transactions with subordinates, explaining what is required of them in terms of their contributions, and specifies the compensation or rewards they will receive if they fulfil these requirements. It is said that **transactional leadership** is appropriate to stable conditions in the market-place and the environment generally, and to the application of technology in the workplace. Management by exception and a reliance on bureaucratic processes can be functional under these circumstances (Bass, 1990; Yammarino & Dublinsky, 1994). Transactional leadership is exemplified by inward-looking and self-satisfied feelings, and a managerial culture more appropriate to keeping the organisation running smoothly in conditions of equilibrium. But its legacy can be over-control and risk-aversion (Adair, 1990).

CONTEMPORARY TRENDS

Transformational leadership

This type of leadership needs to be fostered at all levels in the organisation when the organisation faces the following conditions: a turbulent environment where products have a short shelf life; greater international competition and deregulation of markets; technology becoming obsolete before it is fully depreciated; and demographic changes are anticipated.

In transformational leadership the emphasis is on people of vision, who are creative, innovative, and capable of getting others to share their dreams while playing down self-interest; and who are able to cooperate with others in reshaping the strategies and tactics of the organisation (e.g., orchestrating a merger, creating a team, or shaping the culture of the organisation) in response to a fast-changing world (Goodwin, Wofford, & Whittington, 2001; Tichy & Devanna, 1986; Yammarino & Dublinsky, 1994). To these qualities could be added the pursuit of high standards, taking calculated risks, challenging and changing the existing company structure, with even the potential for the display (when considered appropriate) of directive tendencies (Bass, 1990).

Reflect for a moment on the following profile of Lord John Browne, Chief Executive of British Petroleum (BP), one of the world's most admired businessmen, then suggest whether or not he is a transformational leader.

Profile of Lord John Browne

Most of the following observations have been made concerning Browne by those who worked with him or knew him well (Buck & Buchan, 2002; Buck, Buchan, Guha, & McNulty, 2002):

- He has a track record of achievement. The exploration and production (E & P) business for BP Worldwide became the most efficient exploration business in the world as a result of his direction.
- He is driven by recognition and power, and relishes the admiration of the outside world for the image he projects and his achievements. But he has a pragmatic view of power. It is better to think you have none than to think you have a lot, and it is limited when it comes to getting things done and making changes. However, it is more effectively used from a position of humility rather than strength.

- He has a high intellectual capability, displays solid professionalism, is endowed with a "can do" attitude (developed in the USA), and has a strong appetite for hard work. He is clever at finding good solutions to difficult or challenging problems, and enjoys doing so, and he has the capacity to implement these solutions with discipline and practicality. All this creates a sense of excitement around him, but if you can't keep up with him and perform you will fall by the wayside.
- He has an obsession for detail and has an ability to grasp complex issues quickly. According to a senior investment banker, he is able to combine the big and small pictures with ease.
- He feels uncomfortable talking about private matters, and can appear remote and aloof.
- He has played a central role in the growth of BP by acquisition since taking over control of the company in 1995—i.e., Amoco in 1998, Atlantic Richfield in 1999, Burmah Castrol in 2000, and Veba in 2001. According to Lord Simon, the previous Chief Executive of BP, "it is doubtful if somebody else had the financial knowledge, commitment, and capacity to do the mergers".
- On mergers, Browne is not convinced that a merger of equals works due to cultural problems; to bring about change it is important to mix cultures by integrating the entities quickly. He feels it is important to avail of the services of a third party (e.g., an HR consultancy) to assist with the selection of the management for the combined company. After the merger deal with Amoco, BP sent 400 top executives to an independent agency for assessment. There were many more redundancies at Amoco, and this reflected the view that the company had its fair share of dead wood. Browne felt that the generous pay-offs to redundant employees (two years' salary) could be justified by efficiency and savings expected in the future. Following the Amoco and Arco deals, the BP style of setting targets and planning were adopted, and more executive positions went to BP staff. Perhaps he displayed a certain ruthlessness in his approach to the merging of cultures,

whereas earlier in this profile a more benign operator came across.

- When it comes to parting company with BP's top 50 employees, Browne does the firing himself: "It is a very, very difficult thing to do and you have to do it in such a way that people's dignity and respect are maintained in this process." Since the company is responsible for changing the individual's circumstances, it has an obligation to help smooth the transition.

- He has been extraordinarily successful in creating value for BP's shareholders and in setting the corporate, political, and environmental agenda.

- As to succession planning, he is committed to it and says, "The most important task of his remaining time with the company (to age 60) is to make sure that there is a strong and deep succession pool". It will be a challenge for him to groom a successor to take over a large and complex corporation.

- It is said by some observers that the company is over-reliant on the abilities of its CEO and BP has become a court with a cult of personality developing around Browne. There is a danger of him not being receptive to advice now that many managers of his own generation, who could challenge his ideas, have left the company and are replaced by a tamer younger generation. Browne is likely to respond by saying that he is receptive to advice from outside experts. But some insiders have the impression that after 7 years as CEO he is impervious to internal advice, or more selective in seeking it.

- One insider reports "a certain resistance" within the company about the heavy reliance on McKinsey & Co (the blue chip management consultants), and there is a feeling that some of McKinsey's ideas come from Browne himself. This sometime happens when senior managers use management consultants to project or promote their ideas. It is not surprising to find that lower-level managers use the same consultancy firm. But Browne rejects these suggestions, and he says that BP uses lots of consultants, not just McKinsey, to provide horsepower and brainpower. He says, "We

rather like consultants who are not agreeable, who are rather outspoken. In the end the company has to make up its own mind and solve its own problems, but in areas where matters are judgemental it is good to be able to test your ideas with people who don't care." He makes an interesting observation when he says he discounts ideas he thinks are stuck in the past, as he maintains that "not all experience of the past is relevant . . . the wise use of experience is to balance the judgement, not to repeat it".

- On delegation he says, you delegate two things —the action required of the person and the limitations on those actions. Wise delegation emphasises only the limitations that are really necessary. Give people space to manoeuvre, otherwise you could stifle creativity and affect motivation by rigidly constraining action.

- He believes fervently in target setting for everyone, and emphasises that targets do not come from the top, but from the bottom up, and they should be given due consideration in discussion. On evaluation of performance in relation to targets set, where the employee's performance is not up to scratch you do not say you are failing; you figure out what is happening and that means looking at root causes rather than outcomes.

- Assessment of performance of units and divisions is an exhaustive and demanding process at BP. Performance gets checked once a month by 33 group vice-presidents, and in summarised form by Browne and his nine executive vice-presidents every month. Browne delves into business units occasionally, a practice that hardly existed in the past.

- He dislikes matrix structures in which managers have to answer to both regional and sector superiors; they are too complex and spawn committees. He also advocates avoiding having people accountable to committees because they do not have passion, or drive, or aspiration.

- He acknowledges the contributions made to the development of the company by his predecessors at BP (Peter Walters, Robert Horton, and David Simon), and believes in building on the leadership acts of predecessors in an established company.

- As to rewards, he accepts that recent scandals in corporate America have shown that incentives linked to share price performance, once considered desirable, can be dangerous. At BP, annual bonuses are related to fundamentals of the company's operations, not its share price. His managers must achieve a certain return on capital and meet targets on health, safety, and the environment. In his own case, an issue was made in the tabloid press of what was considered his excessive compensation, but he maintains that base salary is modest in relation to the amounts that come from variable bonuses, shares, and options related to performance.

- With regard to organisation, BP outsources a relatively large amount of work to oil service companies or computer specialists, when compared with Exxon Mobil and Shell.

- With regard to the use of auditors, he sees nothing wrong with having the same firm of auditors over a very long period of time, but the practice at BP is to change its key Ernest & Young audit partner every 7 years (i.e., rotate people within that auditing firm). The only consultancy taken from Ernest and Young is audit-related in connection with acquisitions and disposals.

- On the wider political front, BP does not try to buy the favour of MPs or political parties. Instead Browne has developed personal ties and regular exchanges of ideas between BP and both the UK and US governments. In the UK Lord Simon, Browne's direct predecessor at BP, probably facilitated this. According to one civil service or government insider, there is a meeting of minds between Prime Minister Blair and Lord Browne, who is a regular visitor to Downing Street. It is said both men admire the other's leadership. Browne received a knighthood and then, two years later, a peerage. It is interesting to note that Browne now has on his staff a friend and ex-colleague of Tony Blair as director of communications.

For the three years to 2002 Browne was voted Britain's most admired businessman by his peers (having transformed BP beyond recognition), but his reputation suffered a blow as BP issued its third production warning in late 2002.

This state of affairs will inevitably lead to much more questioning of the company by market analysts in the future. Analysts are looking for reasons for the failure to achieve production targets. Reference has been made to the breakdown of BP's respected system of internal reporting on the group's corporate culture, which has been criticised for fostering a climate of fear. Browne puts a lot of pressure on managers to achieve exacting targets, and as a result they sometimes commit themselves to targets they cannot achieve. A number of analysts have pointed out that BP's culture might have influenced subordinates not to reveal the full extent of the problems they encountered to higher management levels. Browne challenges the statement that there is a culture of fear within BP (i.e., that people are terrified of giving him bad news). He says: "that is both unfair and untrue. There is a culture of rigour. We are rigorous and grounded in fact and reality. This is a company that tries to understand what is going on and I believe we do. I also believe the culture has not changed in the last 10 years at BP, and I would characterise it as open." Responding to the critics' comments, which also referred to certain weaknesses in the internal communication system of the company, Browne acknowledged that matters could have been dealt with differently in coordinating the flow of internal and external information and hinted that in the company there could be "too much complexity and a little middle-aged spread" following the oil price boom in the early 2000s. He now commits himself to addressing this problem. In future he is likely to put more emphasis on profitability than volume of production, because profits are falling as well. Finally, there remains a strong body of opinion among oil industry experts claiming that Browne is still a superb executive (Buck, 2002; Jones, 2002; Jones & Buck, 2002).

Transformational versus transactional leadership

Transactional and transformational leadership should not be viewed as opposing approaches to getting things done. Transformational leadership is built on top of transactional leadership; it produces levels of effort and performance on the part of subordinates that go beyond that associated with a transactional approach, and is something more than charisma. The pure charismatic leader may want followers to adopt a charismatic view of the world and go no further, but the transformational leader will attempt to cultivate in subordinates the ability and determination not only to challenge established views but to question the leader's opinions as well.

In case we are carried away by the attractiveness of transformational leadership we should pause for a moment and consider the reaction of subordinates. According to Howell and Avolio (1993), subordinates must be ready for the exercise of transformational leadership and see justification for the use of this type of leadership as a means of transforming the organisation.

There are impressive claims for the effectiveness of transformational leadership. For example, Geyer and Speyrer (1997) found a positive relationship between transformational leadership and productivity in Austrian banks.

Characteristics of transformational leadership

The major characteristics of transformational leadership are as follows (Bass, 1990, 1999):

- charisma;
- idealised influence;
- intellectual stimulation; and
- consideration of the emotional needs of each employee.

Bass claims such characteristics are based on the findings of a series of surveys, and on clinical and case evidence. Each of the characteristics will be discussed in turn.

Charisma. House (1977) identified charismatic leadership qualities in an ideal form. Charismatic leaders, through the force of their personalities and interpersonal skills, are capable of articulating an appealing vision linking the present with

the future and are said to have an extraordinary effect on followers or subordinates, without resorting to any formal authority. They have great power and influence, project an attractive set of values and modes of behaviour, and it is not difficult for subordinates to want to identify with them and internalise their values, as well as having a high degree of trust and confidence in them (Pastor, Meindl, & Mayo, 2002).

Charismatic leaders—endowed with determination, energy, self-confidence, and ability—are capable of making self-sacrifices and depart from conventionality in the way they express courage and conviction about their vision; they inspire and excite their subordinates with the idea that together, with extra effort, great things can be accomplished, and they do not necessarily have to offer a carrot in the form of extrinsic rewards (Kirkpatrick & Locke, 1996; Shamir, House, & Arthur, 1993).

Another interpretation of the behavioural dimensions of charismatic leaders, is as follows (Conger & Kanungo, 1988a, 1994):

- They subscribe to an idealised goal that they would like to achieve (i.e., a vision).
- They are able to clarify and state the vision in language that is comprehensible to others, are tuned into followers' needs, and as a result are better placed to motivate people.
- They have a strong personal commitment to their goal and are prepared to take high risks and incur significant costs.
- They are unconventional and act contrary to established norms and are admired if successful.
- They are assertive and possess a lot of confidence in their ability and judgement.
- They act as agents of radical change rather than supporters of the preservation of the status quo.
- They are able to make realistic evaluations of environmental constraints and the resources needed to bring about change.

From the discussion so far some may conclude that the charismatic leader is almost superhuman and a rare specimen of humanity. They may be right! It is sometimes suggested that charismatic leadership is more appropriate when it relates to activities with an ideological flavour, such as religion and politics, and in commerce where dynamic personalities (e.g., Richard Branson at Virgin, Bill Gates at Microsoft) are developing a business. In recent years there has been reflection on the ethics of charismatic leadership, because some charismatic leaders have unduly influenced their followers by acting in an unethical way (Sankowsky, 1995). This could arise where an unbalanced leader of a religious sect leads followers to self-destruction (e.g., the Waco incident and other mass "suicides"). By contrast, one could consider it to be ethical if charismatic leaders use power in a way that benefits mankind (Ciulla, 1995; Howell & Avolio, 1992).

Idealised influence. The leader appeals to the hopes and desires of followers when transmitting to them a sense of joint mission, and inspires them that the vision they share is attainable, and that he or she has confidence in them to contribute to the attainment of that vision.

Intellectual stimulation. The leader is willing and able to show subordinates new ways of looking at old problems, and emphasises that the difficulties they encounter in their work are problems to be solved in a rational way. A climate of intellectual stimulation should be nurtured and cultivated within the organisation.

The "intellectual stimulator" is a powerful ally of his or her subordinates when it comes to problem analysis and solution, and generally in cultivating a climate of intellectual stimulation within the organisation. Browne, the CEO of BP, is said to be well endowed with intellectual curiosity, which no doubt rubs off on those who work with him, as does the attribute of being a competent problem solver. His attachment to nonconformity, expressed as a liking for diversity reflected in different forms, is probably also advantageous (Buck & Buchan, 2002; Buck, Buchan, Guha, & McNulty, 2002).

It could be argued that Jack Welch, the ex-CEO of GE, was an intellectual stimulator in the way he handled and introduced "work-out" and the "boundaryless organisation". The "work-out" initiative was based on the idea that those closest to the work know it best. It amounted to organising and running "town meetings", which enabled employees of the different levels within the company to attend a forum and voice their ideas and opinions concerning operational procedures as well as general ideas that could be of benefit to the company. The boundaryless organisation was a concept developed by Welch to describe his vision of how he wanted GE to be. He was striving to eliminate vertical and horizontal boundaries within GE. For example, by removing vertical boundaries the organisational hierarchy can be flattened, thereby generating wider spans of control, leading to sections and departments being replaced by empowered teams. He also advocated the breakdown of external barriers between the company and its customers and suppliers. One has to accept that the initiatives at GE are difficult to put into successful practice (Daft, 1998; Robbins, 2003).

Consideration. The leader pays close attention to differences in abilities and skills among subordinates, and acts as mentor to those who need to grow and develop. The leader places emphasis on coaching skills, is willing to delegate, and shows a preference for two-way, face-to-face communication. Kotter (1990) places much emphasis on the leader creating conditions in which people satisfy intrinsic needs, such as the needs for achievement, recognition, self-esteem, control over one's destiny, and the ability to live up to one's ideals.

A related concept concerns emotional issues in transformational leadership, and passion is often mentioned as relevant in this context. The ex-CEO of IBM—Lou Gerstner—has spoken of the importance of passion in effective leadership and he believes it goes beyond good cognitive skills and emotional intelligence (e.g., self-awareness, self-control, empathising with others, and being aware of others' impression of us), considered in Chapter 3.

In addition to these four major characteristics of transformational leadership identified by Bass above, we can add:

* vision;
* creativity; and
* the selection and training of talented people.

Vision. It is certainly fashionable nowadays to enunciate the important role of vision in transformational leadership. Vision in this context has been defined as the ability to be sensitive to changes in the organisation's environment, and to be able to perceive a future advantageous position to which the organisation must move if it is to survive (Selznick, 1984). According to Snyder and Graves (1994), a visionary leader has the ability to articulate an attractive, credible, realistic, challenging, attainable vision of the future for the organisation or segment of the organisation, and this vision develops out of the status quo and improves on it. It is important for a vision to get locked into the followers' energies and emotions so that it can activate enthusiasm and commitment. A good vision is a product of a period in time and reflects the strengths of the organisation.

Handy (1989) feels a vision must be reasonably concise, understandable, the leader must be seen to believe it, and that it will remain a dream without the commitment and work of others. It is reasonable to ask how well a vision serves the interest of important constituencies—e.g., customers, shareholders, employees—and how easily it can be translated into a realistic competitive strategy. Bad visions tend to ignore the legitimate needs and rights of a particular constituency (e.g., favouring employees over customers). Or, alternatively, visions are strategically unsound as, for example, when a company that has never been superior to a weak competitor in an industry starts talking about being number one in the not too distant future. That is a pipe dream, not a vision (Kotter, 1990).

The able leader is intent on articulating the organisation's vision in a manner that has meaning to followers, and is keen to involve them in deciding how to achieve it, or the part of it that is relevant to them. The leader is also aware of the significance of providing followers with the necessary technical and psychological support, and believes in recognising and rewarding success. Attending to the courses of action suggested earlier is said to produce real, intrinsic, motivational effects (Kotter, 1990).

Since the 1980s, concepts of corporate strategy and leadership have been brought together to form strategic vision. The role of visionary leadership is an important ingredient in this combination. Westley and Mintzberg (1989) describe various types of visionary leadership. Examples of visionary leaders from the USA are Lee Iacocca, who revitalised the Chrysler Corporation, Jack Welch, who transformed General Electric, Edwin Land, the founder of the Polaroid Corporation and the inventor of the Polaroid camera, and Steve Job at Apple Computer. British examples might be Clive Sinclair, who pioneered the development of the personal computer in the early 1980s, and Richard Branson who put Virgin on the map. As Westley and Mintzberg rightly point out:

> Visionary leadership is not always synonymous with good leadership, and despite their great skills it is a mistake to treat visionary leaders as possessing superhuman qualities. In effect they are products of their times, of their followers, and of their opportunities. As times and contexts change the visionaries of yesterday fade into obscurity, or worse, become the villains of today.

Creativity. Allied to the notion of intellectual stimulation, a dimension of transformational leadership identified by Bass (1990) is the concept of creativity (also discussed in Chapter 8). Adair (1990) sees the creation of new ideas as enriching the organisation's lifeblood in times of fundamental change, and sees an important role for leadership in tapping the fertile minds of young people in the organisation and providing opportunities for their personal development. He extols the virtue of involving layers of management, not traditionally consulted, in the process of strategic decision making. It is only then, he says, that we can expect to secure the necessary commitment for the implementation of strategic decisions. The maxim must be teamwork, with a shared sense of purpose, common objectives, and excellent communication.

In Sadler's (1988) view of creative leadership, there is a recognition that leaders do not have to be innovators themselves, but should be able to recognise the potential for creativity in others and make every effort to develop it. Facilitating the expression of creativity in the organisation is crucial, and a variety of ways of cultivating it are suggested. For example, the company could sponsor artists, invite creative people to exhibit their work in the organisation, encourage individuality, create conditions for people to be exposed to good external sources of ideas, create organic organisational structures, and encourage the formation of networks.

Selection and training.   Given the qualities residing in transformational leaders, it is understandable that attention turns to their selection, training, and development. The new emerging leadership culture is likely to emphasise the value of service and high quality products or services, an entrepreneurial spirit, the removal of unnecessary layers of management, flexible work groupings, and decentralised decision making with people as the key resource (Adair, 1990). Therefore, human resource strategies should focus on selection and training of transformational leaders. Recruiting people with leadership potential is obviously a first step. Thereafter, managing the career patterns of potential leaders is crucial. They must be provided with opportunities to take risks, and to learn from successes and failures. By doing so, they develop a wide range of leadership skills and perspectives, and appreciate early on in their careers both their potential and limitations for producing change.

The value of lateral career moves, unusually broad job assignments, experience in special task force assignments, lengthy general management courses, and the creation of internal and external networks, are considered to be of tremendous importance later in broadening the leader's base as he or she develops (Kotter, 1990). The value of learning by doing is heavily underlined in the development of the experience suggested. Goffee and Jones (2002) emphasise the importance of leaders interacting with as many different types of people as possible, and refer to the current drive to seek new experiences in prisons, charities, or even zoos.

The value of learning by doing is also endorsed by Sadler (1988) who favours a developmental experience for chief executives that uses the leader's own work situation, and the problems encountered therein, as the main vehicle for learning. However, he points out that if people are to learn from experience they will need skilled coaching and counselling, as well as the opportunity to receive feedback. This could best be achieved on a formal action learning programme in management studies, or a similar programme. There is a discussion of action learning and its role in management development in Chapter 18.

Kakabadse (2002) reminds us that to get the best leaders companies should select and groom, as well as coach and counsel, and provide both internal and external training when addressing the needs of future leaders. Some examples of leadership development programmes are set out in Panel 12.7, and there is discussion of selection, training, and development in Chapters 17 and 18.

Tourish and Pinnington (2002) put forward a view that the transformational leader almost resembles the cult leader who is put on a pedestal by followers as a god-like creature who can do

---

PANEL 12.7: Leadership development programmes

Examples of leadership development programmes include Abbott Laboratories. With a turnover of $13 billion, Abbott is a US healthcare manufacturer with 57,000 employees. It brings groups of 35 high-performing, high-potential directors and vice-presidents together for three weeks of leadership development over nine months. Participants examine the leader's role and responsibilities at Abbott, they consider alternative leadership approaches, and they review feedback on their own leadership style and impact.

Du Pont, a US company with $27 billion of turnover and 94,000 employees, has created its own knowledge intensity university, with a set of programmes for training managers on how to identify training strategies, create a culture of urgency, and allocate resources to encourage rapid growth.

(Useem, 2000)

no wrong, and this may promote authoritarianism. This is not a healthy development.

Finally, there are some indications that the transformational leader, particularly at the CEO level, may not be in demand to the same extent as in the recent past. In a profile (Siklos, 2002) of the then CEO-elect (Arun Sarin) of Vodafone there was reference to the new type of CEO:

> . . . he is the latest in a new breed of post-visionary, post-celebrity CEO tailored to today's sober business climate. The high-to-low profile contrast from Christopher Gent to Arun Sarin at Vodafone is not un-like from Jack Welch to Jeffrey Immelt at General Electric, Lou Gerstner to Sam Palmisano at IBM, or Bernard Ebbers to Michael Capellas at WorldCom. For this new breed, internal sales data matters more than stock tickets or framed press clips.

Other important issues

Here we are going to discuss briefly (i) lateral and upward leadership, (ii) gender and leadership, (iii) culture and leadership, (iv) trust and leadership, and (v) derailment of leaders.

Lateral and upward leadership

With regard to lateral leadership (leading out), companies require managers who can lead out (not just down to subordinates) as they increasingly outsource services, use joint ventures, and construct strategic alliances. In other words, the skill of delegating to subordinates is being supplemented by a talent for arranging work (e.g., outsourcing contracts for information services) with partners outside the company. Such lateral leadership is essential for obtaining results when you have no formal organisational authority to guarantee the desired outcome. Lateral leadership could entail in this case the identification of the service to contract out, dealing with the right outside partners to provide the service, and convincing sceptical internal managers that the arrangement will deliver what they want. Lateral leadership requires the following:

- Strategic thinking to understand when and how to collaborate in order to gain competitive advantage.
- Deal-making skills to secure the appropriate arrangements with outside companies and to ensure that they provide a quality service.
- Monitoring the progress of the partnership by overseeing and developing the collaborative contract.
- Change management to spearhead new ways of doing business despite internal resistance.

An unexpected aspect of leadership is upward leadership, or getting results by helping to guide your boss. Rather than undermining authority or seizing power from superiors, upward leadership means stepping in when senior managers need help and support in a way that benefits everyone. It should be noted that it is not always welcomed (Useem, 2001).

In conditions of decentralised authority companies place a premium on a manager's capacity to mobilise support from superiors as well as from subordinates. Effectively one expects managers to lead their own bosses. Where the manager's manager lacks data the subordinate manager should provide the superior with what is needed. Upward leadership depends upon followers who are ready to speak out, solve problems, and compensate for weaknesses at the boss's level, but if it is not done in a subtle way it could be disadvantageous to the person exercising it. When handled delicately, it can be beneficial in career terms to those using upward leadership because it gives them the opportunity to be noticed (Useem, 2000).

Gender and leadership

It is sometimes suggested that women feel more comfortable with the use of a democratic leadership style, which is more in line with contemporary developments such as sensitivity, information-sharing, nurturing, teamwork, flexibility, and mutual trust (qualities associated with transformational leadership). By contrast, men tend to be more directive or autocratic (Bass & Avolio, 1990; Eagly & Johnson, 1990). A number of questions could be asked in connection with these findings. Are women more proficient at handling processes in collaborative decision making? Do women think that the use of a participative leadership style is more likely to lead to greater self-confidence and lead to acceptance from organisational members in a world where men harbour negative attitudes about their competence as managers and where the "glass ceiling" (a barrier to further promotion) is a reality?

More recent evidence suggests that there is no difference in leadership performance between men and women, but men secured an advantage in what might be described as typical masculine pursuits—e.g., military and outdoor pursuits. There was a minor advantage for women in business, education, and government employment (Eagly, Karau, & Makhijani, 1995). At a British Psychological Society Conference in the UK in January 2003, Professor Alimo-Metcalfe proposed that, on the basis of her research, male managers favoured the transactional approach, while women are more likely to take transformational leadership as their guiding light (Muir, 2003).

Culture and leadership

With the advent of global markets, managers may find themselves in the situation of offering leadership to people with diverse backgrounds. Adler (2002) points out that global managers must be sufficiently flexible to adjust their leadership style when crossing national borders and working with people from different cultures. National culture as an important factor in determining leadership style has been well documented (Bhagat, Kedia, Crawford, & Kaplan, 1990; Hofstede, 1991). The impact of national culture is discussed in Chapter 15, and selectively throughout the book.

Hofstede (1980b) asked the question whether US management theories applied abroad, and one of his conclusions was that participative leadership advocated by American theorists was not suitable for all cultures. At the micro level, one can witness the reverse relationship whereby leadership shapes organisational culture. This is evident when a successful entrepreneur shapes the culture of his or her organisation from a position of significant power.

Trust and leadership

In recent years trust has come to the fore as a topic worthy of particular study in organisational behaviour. We have already considered it in connection with teams in the previous chapter. Paul Zak, a neuroscientist at a university in California is reported as saying that the degree to which we are willing to trust others is influenced by factors that operate below conscious control, and may not be amenable to rational or conscious direction as we would like to believe. Zak concluded, on the basis of his research, that it is the level of a particular hormone, oxytocin, in our bodies that strongly predicts how much we are willing to trust others. Oxytocin is strongly released in the body when couples have sex, particularly when reaching an orgasm, leading some neuroscientists to call it the trust and lust hormone (Persaud, 2004).

Another way of looking at trust is to acknowledge that it is rooted in our experience of reliance on another person and it takes time to create the confidence that one can rely on the other person. So we do not trust the other person until they have proved themselves. In any situation where trust enters the frame, risk and vulnerability are inevitable, and there is always the prospect that we could be disappointed or taken advantage of when we freely give important information or promises to another person.

Five key characteristics of trust have been identified as integrity, competence, consistency, loyalty, and openness (Schindler & Thomas, 1993). Integrity refers to honesty and truthfulness, and is probably the most important of the five; it goes to the very core of character. Competence refers to people's technical knowledge and interpersonal skills to deliver what they maintain they are capable of doing. Consistency refers to predictable performance and sound judgement in handling various situations. Loyalty reflects itself when one is confident that a person will not act to one's disadvantage when pursuing a particular line of action; instead the person will act in a loyal way.

In the traitist approach to leadership we looked at personality characteristics, such as honesty and integrity. To these we could add trust, which could be viewed as an important characteristic associated

---

PANEL 12.8: Harvey Pitt—a derailed leader

Harvey Pitt, former Chairman of the US Securities and Exchange Commission (SEC), was an extremely successful senior partner at a prestigious law firm in New York before taking over at the SEC. Many regarded him as the most qualified individual to take up this position. In spite of a very high IQ, renowned expertise, and an impressive track record in the private sector, his public sector career derailed and ended in resignation after only 15 months. Some observers partially attributed this to a style that served him well as a private sector lawyer, but led to a series of errors of judgement as a senior public sector manager.

Fenlon (2002) suggests that the cause of the derailment was not IQ, which was impressive in the case of Harvey Pitt, but was due to the lack of qualities and skills associated with emotional intelligence. These are discussed in Chapter 3 and are said to be powerful predictors of executive success, and the lack of them could cause derailment. Basically they are personal skills, such as self-awareness of strengths and weaknesses, the ability to use self-knowledge constructively and to practise self-control, together with social skills expressed as empathy, and the ability to understand political dynamics, and to influence others constructively.

---

with leadership. After all, it is very difficult to exercise leadership if subordinates do not trust you. On the other hand, trust will exist if subordinates can safely place themselves in the hands of the leader in the belief that he or she will act in their best interests. Unfortunately, the application of techniques such as business process re-engineering and downsizing by management in recent years has had an adverse effect on trust in management.

To build trusting relationships with followers it is suggested that the leader should subscribe to the following principles (Robbins et al., 2001):

- Keep people informed about various aspects of their work and the significance to them of broad corporate activities.
- Be objective and fair in one's dealings with people.
- Build a capacity to share one's feelings with others.
- Tell the truth, since integrity is crucial for trust; be consistent in one's behaviour as mistrust could arise from inconsistency or not knowing what to expect.
- Foster dependability by keeping one's word and promises; maintain confidences because divulging them could be viewed as untrustworthy.
- Project confidence in the way one exercises technical and interpersonal skills.

Derailed leaders

It is not unusual for leaders, who were at one time successful, to go off the rails, given the commercial turbulence and change that has occurred in recent years. For example, some executives are very good at exercising leadership in conditions of growth in markets, but when markets turn sour this could cramp their style. At Novar (previously known as Caradon), the diversified UK manufacturing group now the subject of a takeover bid, it was a drive to improve the quality of management that explained some cases of executive failure (Maitland, 2003). (See Panel 12.8 for a profile of a derailed leader.)

Shackleton (1995), drawing on research evidence from the Center for Creative Leadership, North Carolina, stated that characteristics such as insensitivity, abrasiveness, aloofness, and arrogance were responsible for the downfall of leaders. The most common reason for derailment was insensitivity. This shortcoming was tolerated when the individual operated at a lower level of the organisation, particularly if the person was adept technically. But at higher levels of the organisation, good technical skills do not compensate for an insensitive and abrasive nature.

Other reasons given for derailment were over-managing (e.g., an inability to delegate or empower subordinates), unreliability, an inability to pay sufficient attention to detail, having difficulty building a team, poor relationships with superiors, an inability to think strategically, and being too ambitious at the cost of hurting others. Sometimes being a victim of derailment was a matter of bad luck, such as being a casualty of an economic downturn or declining markets, or the fallout from political strife within the organisation.

Shackleton (1995) also cites evidence from research conducted at the Cranfield School of Management in the UK, dealing with both personality-based and organisational issues that contribute to derailment. Derailed leaders did not seem competent in the exercise of political skills and the way they played the organisational game; they did not seem to be "streetwise". The organisational issues contributing to derailment were moving people too quickly without the necessary experience or proper training, or being too slow to groom people through experience and skills development, or being too harsh with people after making one mistake, or denying people feedback on their performance at the right time. Those with responsibility for management training and development should take to heart the implications of these observations.

CHAPTER SUMMARY

- A number of perspectives can be found in the study of leadership. This chapter opened with a discussion of the difference between leadership and management.
- There followed an examination of the trait approach and the personal characteristics of the leader, recognising the relevance of a mixture of leadership traits, motives, skills, and competencies.
- Leadership or management style can find expression in various forms—behavioural styles—ranging from autocratic to democratic styles. The democratic style is akin to participative leadership, which in one case was applied to the budgeting process. A distinction was made between micro and macro participation.
- A study of leadership would not be complete without an analysis of contingency theories or situational leadership. These theories point to the potency of the leadership environment in determining styles of leadership.
- The major contingency theories examined were the leadership continuum, the influence–power continuum, Fiedler's contingency model of leadership effectiveness, the revised normative model of leadership style, the leader–member exchange (LMX) theory, the path–goal model, Hersey–Blanchard situational theory, the attributional perspective, and leadership substitutes.
- In looking at contemporary trends in leadership, a transactional model was contrasted with a transformational model. Transformational leadership, unlike transactional leadership, seems better suited to conditions of change requiring inspirational or visionary leadership qualities.
- Finally, variables likely to impact on leadership—upward and lateral, gender, culture, trust, and derailment—were acknowledged.

QUESTIONS

(1) Leadership and management complement each other. Discuss.

(2) Distinguish between the early trait approach to leadership and the later emphasis on personal characteristics.

(3) Identify the strengths and weaknesses of participative leadership.

(4) Compare micro participation with macro participation and emphasise the distinctive points of difference.

(5) Identify one contingency theory of leadership that you feel has greatest practical significance, and comment on its features.

(6) Analyse the conditions necessary for transformational leadership to take root.

(7) Briefly explain the following: (a) transactional leadership; (b) the attributional perspective in leadership; (c) leadership substitutes; and (d) leadership derailment.

(8) Reflect on the significance of gender, culture, and trust in leadership.

(9) What do you understand by upward and lateral leadership.

SPOTLIGHT ON RELEVANT READING

Bennis, W.G. (2004). The seven ages of the leader. *Harvard Business Review*, January, 46–53.

Drucker, P.F. (2004). What makes an effective executive? *Harvard Business Review*, June, 58–63.

Fulmer, R.M. (2004). The challenge of ethical leadership. *Organizational Dynamics*, *33*, 307–317.

Goleman, D. (2004). What makes a leader? *Harvard Business Review*, January, 82–91.

Goodwin, V., Wofford, J.C., & Whittington, J.L. (2001). A theoretical and empirical extension to the transformational leadership construct. *Journal of Organizational Behaviour*, *22*, 759–774.

Midgley, D. (2004). The management style of Roman Abramovich (proprietor of Chelsea FC). *Management Today*, November, 76–83.

Vroom, V.H. (2000). Leadership and the decision making process. *Organizational Dynamics*, Spring, 82–93.

Learning Outcomes

After studying this chapter you should be able to:

• Distinguish between power, politics, and conflict.

• Explain micro and macro power.

• Describe the bases or categories of power, and recognise their applications.

• Outline individual and group-based power tactics.

• Appreciate the significance of situational factors in the choice of power tactic.

• Recognise the causes of political behaviour.

• List the political techniques, tactics, or skills, recognising those that are legitimate and those that are devious.

• Identify the ethical dimension in organisational politics.

• Recognise ways of coping with political behaviour, noting the difficulties.

• Discuss the nature of conflict and the different types of conflict.

• Identify the sources of conflict.

• Recognise situations where it would be to the advantage of management to stimulate conflict.

• Assess the styles of conflict management, and the relevance of culture.

• Explain superordinate goals in conflict management.

Power, Politics, and Conflict

This chapter has a group-based perspective. First, definitions of organisational power, politics, and conflict are given, followed by an examination of the bases and types of power. Then the tactics used to gain power and manipulate the bases of power are examined. Following a definition of organisational politics, the causes of political behaviour as well as political tactics (both legitimate and devious) are discussed. The pros and cons of political behaviour are given. Conflict is defined and analysed, and ways of using and managing conflict are discussed. This chapter has particular relevance to Chapter 12 on managerial leadership and Chapters 10 and 11 on groups and teambuilding, respectively.

Contents

DEFINITION

Power refers to a force at the disposal of one person that can influence the behaviour of another. Therefore, X has the capacity to influence the behaviour of Y in such a way that Y performs tasks he or she would not otherwise do. Politics or political behaviour in an organisational context has been defined as activities undertaken by individuals or groups to obtain, enlarge, and use power and other resources to obtain outcomes they desire in situations where there is uncertainty or disagreement (Pfeffer, 1981b). A state of conflict is said to exist when one party frustrates the attempts of another to achieve his or her goals.

POWER

After reflecting on this definition of power, one could conclude that the concepts of power and leadership, discussed in Chapter 12, are closely related. For example, leaders use power to facilitate the achievement of their goals. Both concepts are preoccupied with the ability of an individual to control or influence others and to get someone else to engage in some activity. But there are some differences. For instance, power, unlike leadership, is not the preserve of supervisors and managers, because individuals and groups with different status in the organisation can be involved in the exercise of power (Blackler & Shimmin, 1984).

One important feature of power is that its strength is heavily influenced by dependence. For example, the more Y is dependent on X, the greater is X's power in this particular relationship. In turn, Y's dependence on X is determined by the fact that X controls something that Y values or wants, such as the power to bestow a reward (e.g., a salary increase or promotion). Dependency is enlarged when the resource under the control of a person or group is important, scarce, and cannot be substituted (Mintzberg, 1983a). To create dependency the forces or resources controlled must be seen as important. In a technologically based company the contribution of engineers or scientists may be crucial to the organisation, and consequently others are highly dependent on them.

If a resource is seen as scarce, this contributes to dependency. The possession of specialised knowledge about critical operations of the company by somebody in a modest position in the organisational hierarchy could create the situation where the highest ranked employee is dependent on a person who is lowly ranked. The scarcity factor also raises its head in normal economic conditions when certain occupational groups in short supply are able to exercise power to obtain increased salaries and benefits.

On the question of substitutability, the ability of one person to exercise power over another is dependent on how the latter perceives alternatives to the present job. For example, the greater the number of employment opportunities outside the organisation open to an individual, the less he or she is dependent on the organisation and the less influence is likely to be exerted by his or her boss. By contrast, a higher level of dependence would be expected where the person's external marketability is restricted.

Bases of power

In a classic study, French and Raven (1958) distinguished between five different types of power:

* reward power;
* coercive power;
* referent power;
* legitimate power; and
* expert power.

Reward power

The leader is able to control rewards—e.g., pay and promotion—which subordinates consider to be worth striving for. This type of power can extend beyond material rewards, because many people are motivated by a desire for intrinsic rewards, such as recognition and acceptance. Therefore, reward power also exists when a manager acknowledges and praises good performance by a subordinate. However, if a leader has rewards at his or her disposal to which subordinates attach no value, that leader has no reward power. But if the leader is astute enough to disguise the valueless rewards, he or she may still have reward power.

Coercive power

If subordinates are of the view that the leader is able and willing to use penalties that they dislike —e.g., withdrawal of privileges, allocation of unattractive assignments, denial of promotion opportunities and pay increases, verbal abuse, withdrawal of friendship and emotional support —then the leader has coercive power. In this situation the penalties must be perceived by the subordinates as significant, and there must be a strong probability that they will be used if necessary.

This type of power can still be found in organisations, though it should be noted that certain legislation (e.g., employment protection laws in the UK) offers protection against summary dismissal of disliked employees. The more extreme form of this type of power is physical coercion, but this is less common than it once was.

Finally, the use of coercive power breeds the likelihood of employee hostility and resentment, but there are some who argue that coercive power employed prudently can be useful in ensuring necessary compliance (Hodgetts, 1991).

Referent power

This type of power, similar in concept to charisma, is visible when subordinates think the leader has desirable characteristics that they should imitate. Imitation could mean working the same hours, dressing like the boss, adopting his or her mannerisms, and so on. It could result in an indiscriminate identification with the leader.

Legitimate power

This type of power arises if subordinates believe that the leader is endowed with the right to issue orders that they are obliged to accept. In this case, subordinates tend to look at a title—e.g., director —as conferring on the leader the right to give orders. However, the lines of legitimate power are often blurred in the more organic type of organisations.

Expert power

This type of power emerges when the leader is seen by subordinates as having superior knowledge and expertise that are relevant to the tasks or activities under consideration. The more important the information base underpinning expert power, and the fewer the alternative sources of such information, the greater the power. In practice, this type of power may be confined only to narrow specialist activities and functions, though leadership based on expert power could also be reflected in the other categories of power.

It should be noted that expert power can be found in many parts of an organisation; it transcends positions and jobs, and tends to be less attached to roles with formal authority. For example, a research scientist in an organisation, who is privy to information on scientific breakthroughs of immense value to the enterprise, could be endowed with expert power. The person with expert power has to be able to demonstrate the right type of ability, and he or she must be perceived as somebody with credibility, trustworthiness, and honesty, as well as having access to the required information (French & Raven, 1958).

Other power categories

There are other categories of power, and these are referred to as position power, personal power, and opportunity power.

Position power

This category of power is attached to a post, irrespective of who is performing the job, and is limited to the activities within the boundaries of that power. For example, a directive to a subordinate to commit a crime would fall outside the boundary. Subsumed under position power are legitimate, reward, expert, and some coercive categories of power.

Personal power

Personal power is attached to the person and it subsumes referent and some traces of expert, coercive, and reward power (Moorhead & Griffin, 2004). Those who use personal power can rely on rational persuasion, or appeal to the subordinate's identification with the leader in order to influence events. This type of power inspires much loyalty and commitment, with subordinates acting out of choice rather than necessity. Consequently, they are more likely to accede to requests to adopt a particular line of action. In the final analysis, of course, the subordinate is free to ignore the superior's suggestions.

Opportunity power

This category of power is said to exist when someone can exert power by reason of being in the right place at the right time (Brass, 1984), and by taking advantage of a subordinate position close to a cell of power in the organisation.

Applications of French and Raven's power bases

Using the French and Raven bases of power, Yukl (1994) provides a framework for understanding how power can be employed under different conditions. The bases of power are related to forces residing in the subordinate—namely, those of commitment, compliance, and resistance:

* A committed subordinate will have little difficulty in accepting and identifying with the leader, and may put in the extra effort necessary to complete a project of importance to the leader.
* A compliant subordinate is likely to carry out the leader's wishes provided they do not involve extra effort, but will nevertheless work at a reasonable pace.
* A resistant subordinate is likely to be in conflict with the leader, and may neglect the project as a means of contravening the leader's instructions or guidelines.

When the disposition of the subordinate interacts with the five bases of power, the outcomes listed in Table 13.1 are said to materialise. The following are matters to consider with respect to the use of the bases of power:

* Reward power. The use of reward power has a certain appeal for the leader because it amounts to giving positive reinforcement to subordinates. Rewards should be administered in a fair and equitable way and be related to performance, otherwise the power base of the leader could be eroded. The leader must have the capability to provide the expected rewards, and the rewards must be perceived by subordinates to have value. For example, a promotion without an adequate compensation package may not motivate a subordinate. Rewards should not be offered as bribes or as a means to promote unethical behaviour.
* Coercive power. The use of this type of power could cause resentment and also erode referent power because of the adverse effect it may have on the subordinate's identification with the leader. Therefore, it should be used sparingly. If used in a hostile or manipulative way, resistance is a likely outcome. Where coercive power is used in a helpful, nonpunitive way, whereby the sanctions employed are mild (such as a minor reprimand) and fit the person's failure to respond appropriately, compliant behaviour is all that can be expected from the subordinate. However, a serious misdeed, such as a significant theft or physical violence, would justify an immediate and severe punishment, but the disciplinary procedure should be appropriate and impartial. With regard to sanctions for misdeeds, it is important that rules governing unacceptable behaviour are well communicated. Also, when the rules are broken, a clear picture of what happened and why it happened needs to be created so that the penalty fits the "crime" and to make sure that the wrong person is not penalised.
* Legitimate power. Instructions given by a manager in his or her formal capacity carry a certain amount of influence—and more so in a crisis situation where effective leaders are

TABLE 13.1

Yukl's (1994) adaptation of the French and Raven model (from Hodgetts, 1991)

Type of power used	Outcome as a result of subordinate		
	Commitment	Compliance	Resistance
Reward	If the follower believes that the request is important to the leader, the person will respond appropriately.	If a reward is given in an impersonal way, it is likely that the followers will comply.	If the reward is applied in a manipulative or arrogant way, the followers are likely to resist it.
Coercive	The individual is unlikely to commit himself or herself under the threat of coercion.	If applied in a helpful and nonpunitive way, it is possible that the followers will go along with the directive.	If used in a hostile or manipulative way, the followers are likely to resist.
Legitimate	The follower is likely to go along with the request if it is viewed as appropriate and is politely presented.	If the order is viewed as legitimate, the followers are likely to comply with it.	If the request does not appear to be proper, it is possible that the leader will encounter resistance to it.
Referent	If presented in a subtle and personal way, the follower is likely to go along with the request.	If the request is viewed as important to the leader, it is possible that the followers will comply with it.	If the followers believe that the request will bring harm to the leader, they are likely to resist it.
Expert	If the request is persuasive and the followers share the leader's desire for goal attainment, they are likely to be committed to it.	If the request is persuasive and the followers are apathetic about the goals, it is possible that they will comply with it.	If the leader is arrogant or insulting, the followers are likely to oppose the directive.

viewed as having more legitimate power than they actually possess (Mulder, de Jong, Kippelaar, & Verhage, 1986). Certain behavioural traits are considered desirable in the exercise of legitimate power. For example, politeness in the issue of orders; being courteous when dealing with people, in particular those who are older than the manager; and confidence and calmness when dealing with subordinates who are nervous or anxious about the situation. In some situations subordinates may be unsure of the rationale for courses of action for which they are held responsible, or why in particular it is they that are expected to undertake the task. Therefore, it is important for the leader to explain the order or request given to the subordinate.

• *Referent power.* An important condition with respect to referent power is that subordinates identify with the leader. A common way of achieving this is by selecting subordinates who have similar backgrounds, education, or

training. The reasoning is that people will identify with those who remind them of themselves. However, it would appear that a more delicate means of using referent power is through role modelling, whereby the leader behaves in way that he or she would like subordinates to act. The expectation is that the subordinates will emulate the leader's behaviour.

• *Expert power.* The central thrust of expert power is a leader's projection of an image that he or she possesses the appropriate expertise. This is achieved through subtle remarks about their education, experience, and achievements. For example, a manager, well conversant with the application of information technology in the office situation, states that when he or she "used to work with ICL Fujitsu on computer applications in business, we did it in a particularly innovative way": such a statement is transmitting a clear message with respect to relevant expertise. The maintenance of expert power depends on the continuation of the leader's credibility, and the latter cannot be achieved by pretending to know about things of which one has little or no knowledge. Managers using expert power update their knowledge of issues in their area of responsibility, and are sensitive to the concerns of subordinates. Also, they are keen not to intimidate subordinates by displaying their expertise in an ostentatious manner.

• *Knowledge power.* A base of power that, on the face of it, seems similar to expert power, is knowledge power. However, it is different because it relates to the control of unique information. When that information is required for decision making, it is easy to recognise power based on this source. This type of power is claimed to be effective in terms of satisfaction and performance, and places its holder in a strategic position to exact compliance (Bachman, Bowers, & Marcus, 1968; Robbins, 2003).

A comprehensive review of studies using the French and Raven typology suggests that a majority of them suffer from severe methodological shortcomings, and that much more research is badly needed in this area (Podsakoff & Schriesheim, 1985).

When our interest shifts to an analysis of organisational power, what immediately comes to mind is Etzioni's (1975) three types of organisational power, which are matched with three types of involvement on the part of organisational members (see Table 13.2). The crosses in the table denote the best fit between power and involvement. Any other matching could generate dysfunctional effects. A description of the three types of power and involvement is as follows:

(1) An organisation using *coercive* power attempts to obtain compliance by threats and punishment. This type of organisation may be associated with prisons and similar institutions. The involvement of members that is compatible with this type of power is *alienative*, exemplified by hostile, rejecting, and negative attitudes. These conditions provide a justification for the use of coercive power.

(2) An organisation using *utilitarian* power offers rewards to those who comply with directives, in the belief that it is in their best interests to do so. The involvement of members compatible with this type of power is *calculative*, exemplified by a rational approach aimed at optimising personal gain.

(3) An organisation using *normative* power operates in the belief that members accept directives because of their commitment to the values embedded in the organisation. The use of normative power to influence members is prevalent in professional and religious organisations. The involvement of members compatible with this type of power is *moral*. They are committed to the ethos of the organisation.

Power tactics

People use certain tactics to gain power, as well as tactics to manipulate the bases of power. A rich source of power tactics can be found in Pfeffer's (1992) book on managing with power. He argues that all managers must learn the subtle and demanding craft of "politicking" if they want to succeed, and often even survive. Yukl, Kim, and Falbe (1996) make reference to standardised ways in which powerholders can attempt to get what they want. Power tactics are used by individuals on their own, within groups (intra-group), and between groups (inter-group) in order to influence events. Influence can be used in a positive or negative way (Yukl & Tracey, 1992). When used positively we can expect beneficial outcomes.

TABLE 13.2

Types of organisational power

Types of involvement	Type of power		
	Coercive	Utilitarian	Normative
Alienative	X		
Calculative		X	
Moral			X

Individual and intra-group tactics

In an empirical study of how managerial employees influence others (including superiors, subordinates, and co-workers) and the conditions under which one tactic is more suitable than another, Kipnis, Schmidt, Swaffin-Smith, and Wilkinson (1984) concluded that seven tactics could be identified:

- *Assertiveness*. This would entail setting a deadline date for others to comply with a request, ordering others to do what they were asked to do, emphasising the importance of complying with the request, and repeatedly reminding others of their obligations to perform.
- *Friendliness or ingratiation*. This is designed to make the person favourably disposed to comply with a request. It could amount to flattery by lavishing praise on the person prior to the request, exaggerating the importance of complying with the request, acting in a humble and friendly way when seeking the person's cooperation, and waiting until the person is in a receptive mood before striking.
- *Rationality*. This amounts to using facts and information in a logical way so that the request for action is seen to be detailed and well prepared. The rationale for the request is given, together with a statement of what is required of the person. The originator of the request is portrayed as a competent individual.
- *Sanctions*. This amounts to the use of coercive power, whereby organisational rewards and punishments are activated—e.g., a promise of an increase in salary or a promotion, or, alternatively, ruling out a salary increase or withholding a promotion and threatening to give the person an unsatisfactory performance appraisal.
- *Higher authority*. This consists of efforts to secure support from people further up the organisational hierarchy, and could be exemplified by securing the informal support of superiors and others in higher positions.
- *Bargaining*. This could amount to exchanging favours and benefits through a process of negotiation. Also, the person seeking a favour may remind the other person of benefits the former has bestowed on him or her in the past.
- *Coalition*. This consists of getting help from other parties in the organisation, by building up alliances with subordinates and co-workers. In numbers there is strength, which is evident when employees join trade unions. Coalitions are more likely to be formed where interdependency exists between organisational units, and where broad-based support is necessary for the implementation of decisions.

Kipnis et al. (1984) found that these tactics differed in importance. For example, the most popular tactic was the use of reason, irrespective of whether the influence was going up or down the hierarchy. Table 13.3 shows the tactics, ranging from the most popular to the least popular; but note that (for obvious reasons) the sanctions tactic is excluded from the scale that measures upward influence.

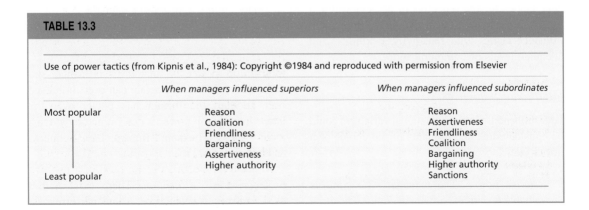

TABLE 13.3

Use of power tactics (from Kipnis et al., 1984): Copyright ©1984 and reproduced with permission from Elsevier

	When managers influenced superiors	*When managers influenced subordinates*
Most popular	Reason	Reason
	Coalition	Assertiveness
	Friendliness	Friendliness
	Bargaining	Coalition
	Assertiveness	Bargaining
	Higher authority	Higher authority
Least popular		Sanctions

Yukl and Falbe (1990) conducted two studies that extended and, to an extent, replicated the research of Kipnis et al. Certain measures of influence tactics were used that did not appear in the earlier research. Also, the research methodology was used in a slightly different way. This research only partly replicated the Kipnis et al. findings for differences in upward, downward, and lateral use of influence tactics. The overall pattern of results suggests that the Kipnis et al. conclusions for influence tactics are considerably overstated. The top four tactics (out of eight) of social influence identified by Yukl and Falbe, in rank order, were consultation (requesting participation in decision making), rational persuasion (called rationality in the Kipnis et al. study), inspiring (arousing enthusiasm by appealing to beliefs), and ingratiation (called friendliness and ingratiation). You will notice that in the later study consultation and inspirational appeals are important additional tactics, and it does not really matter whether one is talking about upward, downward, or lateral influence.

Keys and Case (1990) also discuss the influence tactics most frequently used and those most effective in their impact on superiors, subordinates, and peers. Then they outline five steps necessary to develop and maintain managerial influence: (a) develop a reputation as a knowledgeable person or as an expert; (b) balance the time spent in each critical relationship according to work needs rather than on the basis of habit or social preference; (c) develop a network of resource persons who can be called on for assistance; (d) choose the correct combination of influence tactics for the objective to be achieved and for the target to be influenced; and (e) implement influence tactics with sensitivity, flexibility, and adequate levels of communication.

Situational influences

Four influential factors (situational variables) could be considered as determinants of the choice of a power tactic:

- *Relative power*. The manager who controls valuable resources, or who occupies a position of dominance uses a greater variety of tactics than the manager with less power. However, the former shows an inclination to use assertiveness more often than the latter. Assertiveness and directive strategies generally come into play where there is a refusal or a reluctance to comply with a request. By contrast, the manager with less power is more likely not to persevere with trying to influence others when resistance is experienced.
- *Managers' objectives*. Managers attempt to match tactics to objectives in their dealings with both superiors and subordinates. When the objective is to derive benefits from superiors there tends to be a reliance on friendliness or ingratiation. By contrast, when the objective is to get superiors to accept new ideas, the most likely tactic is to use reason.
- *Managers' expectations of success*. The degree of success in influencing either superiors or subordinates in the past is a strong determinant of the tactic to be used currently. Where managers have been successful in exerting influence, they are likely to use simple requests to obtain compliance. By contrast, where the success rate is low, they are tempted to use the tactics of assertiveness and sanctions.
- *Organisational culture*. This is likely to be an important situational variable. For example, some cultures are supportive of a friendly approach, whereas others may favour reason. Apart from organisational culture, one might also consider ethnic background in the context of influence tactics (Xin & Tsui, 1996). A detailed discussion of the impact of organisational culture appears in Chapter 15.

Inter-group power tactics

Inter-group power is related to influence and dependence. When one group can exert influence over another, the former has power over the latter. Inter-group power is determined by at least three factors (Hickson, Hinings, Lee, Schneck, & Pennings, 1971):

- *Uncertainty absorption*. There exist within organisations specialised groups performing a variety of functions—e.g., industrial relations, pay bargaining, etc. When complex issues arise, the expertise of the appropriate specialist group can be brought to bear on the problems and, in the process, these groups absorb the uncertainty normally associated with such matters. Consequently, the specialist group gains some power over the users of its service.

- *Substitutability.* In the example just given, if the user of the service can obtain a substitute provider (e.g., an external consultant), then the power of the specialist can be reduced or eliminated. However, in practice it might not be possible to substitute external for internal providers in circumstances where an available competent internal facility exists.

- *Integrative importance.* When a group's services—e.g., central computing services—are needed to a significant extent by other groups within the organisation in order that the latter can function effectively, the provider has a lot of inter-group power. The level of power would be less if the group providing the services was needed only to a rather limited extent.

Having endorsed the power tactics mentioned earlier, a group of researchers underline the importance of third-party intervention in the event of the services of another organisation being used to negotiate on behalf of the organisation that is trying to influence events. Advertising is also a tool to consider in the context of the use of power tactics (Butler & Wilson, 1989; Hickson, Butler, Gray, Mallory, & Wilson, 1986).

As we saw earlier, individuals and groups form alliances or coalitions to acquire or enhance a power base. Thompson (1967) identifies some of the cooperative tactics used on occasion by groups in order to expand their power. These are referred to as contracting, co-opting, and coalescing.

- *Contracting*, which does not necessarily culminate in a formal legal agreement, is a tactic arrived at between two or more groups to regulate future action. For example, a management group not wishing to maintain a confrontational stance with a trade union, which is likely to undermine its position, signs an agreement of cooperation with the union.

- *Co-opting* is a process whereby others are admitted to membership of a group, in this case in order to avoid threats to the group's stability or survival. For example, nominees of a bank take their seats on the board of a commercial company after an injection of substantial funds by the bank.

- *Coalescing* comes about when there is a joint venture between one group and another. There is strength in pooling resources for the benefit of the organisation. This would be particularly beneficial when two groups combine their efforts, rather than engaging in wasteful competition.

Reflections on power

Lukes (1974) called for a radical view of power. His explanation of power is similar to radical perspectives on power in organisations, which rely on Weber's and Marx's analysis of class domination based on solid economic foundations, and focuses on power inequalities in society and workers' lack of control of the means of production. Thompson and McHugh (2002) rightly point out that Luke's work has been subject to considerable criticism and that we should recognise that there are great problems with defining power and establishing where it is located.

Over a decade ago a number of organisational theorists interested in power from a radical perspective were attracted by the writings of the French author, Foucault, who provides an insightful analysis of power in a historical setting (Marsden, 1993; O'Neill, 1986). Power in this sense is not something that only originates from a central source. Rather it permeates many corners and crevices of social institutions. At different points in the chain of power there can be resistance to it, and this has the effect of re-creating power with the attendant consequences of changing alliances and tensions.

Thompson and McHugh (2002) provide a useful critical evaluation of the literature on power from the perspective of organisational studies. They distinguish between micro and macro perspectives on power. For example, a micro perspective, such as that taken by French and Raven earlier, would not explain the prior distribution of power, or how some people manage to get access to resources that bestow power, whereas others do not. A macro perspective would recognise that power within organisations has its origins in deeper structures of economic domination in society that give it legitimacy (Clegg, 1977). In this context note the following pertinent observation of Thompson and McHugh (2002):

> A prime example is the concentration of ownership and control in the transnational company. The power to switch resources and relocate operations simply cannot be explained at the level of the single enterprise and its sub-units. Without such a structural framework, we are left with a micro-level analysis capable only of explaining the skills of "politicking" rather than political power. We are also left with a view of managers solely as self-interested manipulators and power-seekers with little understanding of the broader dynamics and constraints that dispose management to use power in the first place.

An alternative route to the origin of power takes us to a position where we need to consider the behaviour of people whose actions are not very conspicuous because of their lack of presence in the scene of action. Power in this sense is attributable to powerful groups outside the immediate scene who prevent various options from being even considered (Bachrach & Baritz, 1962). This is referred to as the "power of nondecision making", and is exemplified by a suppression or removal of options or choices, but the process is not necessarily steeped in resistance by those subjected to the power or who are in open conflict with the wielders of power. Resistance or open conflict might be encountered if unattractive options were imposed on people in a decision-making forum by an authority figure vested with power.

Hardy and Leiba-O'Sullivan (1998) also mention the power of nondecision making in their typology of power, based on a review of the relevant research. The other dimensions of power that they examine are: overt power in the decision-making forum; unobtrusive controls; and power as a network of relations and discourses. They see the power of nondecision making as follows. The decision-making arena is not open to all who have an interest in the outcomes. Power can also be exercised in deciding who should be involved and who to exclude, what items should appear on the agenda, and in forming alliances in order to control the outcome of meetings. On this dimension all power is exercised overtly in making decisions, but much occurs behind the scenes.

Overt power may be derived from the legitimate control of resources, from occupying a particular position in the organisation structure, and from controlling the rewards and sanctions at one's disposal. In this type of situation the location of power is observable, and it can be exercised when the wielder of power feels it necessary to do so to ensure compliance to particular directives.

With unobtrusive controls it is not easy to observe the way rewards are controlled, or alliances formed. Unobtrusive controls operate through cultural norms, generally held assumptions and structures and systems that serve the interests and demands of some players but not others. For example, the operation of power could occur in conditions of political inactivity. Power in this sense operates in unseen ways, and attention should be paid not only to actions and words but also to inactivity and reluctance to speak.

Power can be found in the network of relationships and discourses between people. At this level of analysis power is not regarded as a source of influence that one possesses, or as a force that the wielder can line up so as to achieve his or her objectives in a clear-cut way. This approach to power indicates that we are all subject to the influence of a network of power relations that takes root in every individual perception, action, and interaction. Discourses determine what is seen as important and what is ignored, and they determine how people are perceived, which in turn shapes the way with which people relate to them. Hence certain expectations will be held of managers, and if they do not live up to those expectations they will be regarded as less than satisfactory managers, and this could affect the way subordinates relate to them. Similarly, depending on the circumstance, a particular employee could be viewed quite differently. As a solo performer he or she is seen as competent and committed, but as a team player he or she is seen as semi-detached and uncooperative. The way individuals are perceived and assessed has firm roots in sets of concepts and relationships, often at the unconscious level, which cannot be controlled by any single individual—even those who are apparently powerful.

Hardy and Leiba-O'Sullivan (1998) analyse a case of empowerment—a topic of relevance to motivation (Chapter 4), team leadership (Chapter 11), and organisation (Chapter 14), using the four dimensions of power discussed above:

- In empowerment there is some transfer of overt power in decision making from managers to employees; however, there may be limitations to what an empowered team can decide—for example, their overall budget may be fixed, and hence they have only limited power over the "nondecision-making arena" that sets their own arena of power.
- Unobtrusive controls may operate through peer pressure on attendance, perception, and performance within the team. For example, those who oppose empowerment might be seen as "dinosaurs" and "neanderthals".
- When power is regarded as a network of relations and discourses, attention is drawn to the complexity and ambiguity of empowerment as experienced by individuals. The same event can be seen as empowerment, exploitation, or even as not constituting change. At this level of analysis it is not that one could check the objective facts to see which version is true. Rather, the different people are operating in different "realities" that are real to them. So for some empowerment is experienced as a subtle form of control in which management is extracting greater effort from the workers, while for others it is the chance to exercise greater self-determination. In a sense both are right and both are wrong simultaneously. Greater effort and performance are required and yet there is greater self-determination. But

there are still strong limitations to individual freedom as the organisation will measure output, and the manager and peer group will have expectations that, if flouted, will at least lead to social sanctions such as exclusion from the group. However, the immediate control of supervisory management is removed. The challenge for managers in such situations is to recognise these different levels of reality and enable employees to cope with the ambiguities they entail (Beech & Cairns, 2001; McKenna & Beech, 2002).

POLITICS

The terms politics and power are used interchangeably, but they have distinct (albeit related) meanings (Eisenhardt & Bourgeois, 1988). Politics in organisations has been defined as those activities carried out by people to acquire, enhance, and use power and other resources to obtain preferred outcomes in situations where there are uncertainties or disagreements (Pfeffer, 1981b). Another definition of organisational politics emphasises the fact that it operates outside the narrow confines of formal role behaviour. Political behaviour in organisations is the general means by which people attempt to obtain and use power and it comprises those activities that are not required as part of one's formal role in the organisation, but which nevertheless influence or attempt to influence the distribution of advantages and disadvantages within the organisation according to the agenda set by those engaged in political behaviour (Farrell & Petersen, 1982; Parker, Dipboye, & Jackson, 1995).

A valid question to ask is how prevalent is politics at work? According to Gandz and Murray (1980), it is a common phenomenon in organisations but it is more prevalent at the higher level. They also found that half the managers in their study felt that politics were unfair, bad, unhealthy, and irrational, but recognised that it is necessary to behave politically to progress within the organisation, and that successful executives have to be good politicians. A smaller but still significant proportion of the managers believed that political behaviour influenced decisions in connection with employee selection and the determination of salaries. The results of the study indicate that political behaviour is an undesirable but unavoidable aspect of organisational life.

Causes of political behaviour

A number of elements contribute to political behaviour, ranging from organisational to individual factors.

Organisational factors

Apart from organisational change (discussed in Chapter 16), the following contributory factors could be considered (Fandt & Ferris, 1990; Farrell & Petersen, 1982; Lee, 1993; Miles, 1980).

Ambiguous goals. A certain ambiguity surrounds the meaning of organisational goals; and goals that espouse that the organisation will grow organically (e.g., through acquisitions) in some quantifiable form offer much scope for the adoption of political behaviour to achieve those goals. Behaviour that is politically inspired could rest on strong personal motivation. For example, a top manager in a conglomerate could be arguing strongly for a particular acquisition strategy where it is proposed the company should make a takeover bid for a target company at a very attractive price. Coincidentally, the top manager's family has a substantial stake in the target company!

Organisation structure. Downsizing and team structures do not provide much opportunity to climb the organisational hierarchy, and this creates intense political activity for the limited number of powerful positions that remain. A report in the *Wall Street Journal* concluded that backstabbing had reached an all-time high as workers worried about being laid off attempted to discredit others to protect their own position (Lee, 1993).

Scarce resources. A shortage of resources could come about as a result of cutbacks to improve efficiency, or when there is a significant

reallocation of resources that has the effect of creating difficulties in some areas. When resources are scarce, inevitably some people will lose out in the allocation process (Ferris & Kacmar, 1992). Therefore, it is understandable that certain people engage in political behaviour in an attempt to maintain or increase their share of resources. Managers may present misleading information and lobby key people to obtain a larger budget to expand their departments (Judge & Bretz, 1994). In a sense the existence of scarce resources, which is a common occurrence, offers lots of potential for the use of political behaviour.

Technology and environment. The ways in which technology and the environment affect organisational design are discussed in Chapter 14. The existence of advanced technology and complex environments invariably heralds a need for organisational change. Among the activities incorporated in various responses to change is political manoeuvring to restructure aspects of the organisation in order to preserve or enhance the power base of the politically inspired manager.

Nonprogrammed decisions. The nature of nonprogrammed decisions was discussed in Chapter 8. Situations related to nonprogrammed decision making can be clouded with a poor definition of events and much ambiguity. As a consequence, the scene is set for political manoeuvring.

Low trust. The lower the level of trust, the greater the likelihood of negative political behaviour. For example, a few years ago there was low trust between two influential characters, one Carly Fiorina, the CEO of Hewlett-Packard and the other Walter Hewlett, son of one of the founders of the company. This arose from the acquisition of Compaq Computer, which the CEO considered a strategic move that was opposed by Walter Hewlett. This generated intense political activity on both sides (Daft, 2004). Incidentally, in 2005 Carly Fiorina was fired because of shareholder dissatisfaction with her record of achievement.

Role ambiguity. In conditions of ambiguity surrounding organisational roles, the behaviour prescribed for the role occupant is not clear. There-fore, it is more difficult to establish to what extent the employee is engaged in behaviour demanded by the formal role, as opposed to political behaviour.

Unclear performance evaluation. The art of performance appraisal (discussed in Chapter 17) is far from perfect. There is a strong likelihood of individuals adopting a political stance to further their aims in conditions where there are a lot of subjective criteria in the appraisal process with the result that much emphasis is placed on a single measure of performance, and the lapse of time between the actions measured and the appraisal process is very pronounced.

Organisational culture. The nature of organisa-tional culture is discussed in Chapter 15. It is suggested that the more the culture of the organ-isation emphasises a win–lose outlook to the allocation of rewards, the greater the likelihood that employees will be motivated to engage in political behaviour. The win–lose approach takes total rewards as fixed, so that the gains of any individuals or groups are at the expense of others. Also, the emergence of a culture supportive of participative management or industrial democracy may not be to the liking of managers who were previously attracted by the legitimate power of their positions, which gave them ample oppor-tunity to engage in unilateral decision making. In the new situation it could go against the natural grain to share power with others, but reluctantly these managers use the prescribed committee system and group meetings. However, they do it in a half-hearted way, and seem to be committed to manipulating tactics.

Individual factors

Apart from the organisational factors discussed above, there are individual factors contributing to political behaviour. Normally these relate to the personality or motivational disposition of people. With regard to personality traits, it is said that those who are high in *self-monitoring* (sensitive to what is going on around them and conformist), with an internal locus of control (try to control

the environment and to influence events), and have a high need for power, are likely to be politically active (Biberman, 1985).

At one time there was a tendency to translate basic propositions in Machiavelli's writings into attitude scales to be used to measure the extent to which somebody agrees with his views. (Niccolo Machiavelli put forward a combination of cun-ning and intimidation as a means to the effective control of followers in the fifteenth century.) In one study it was found that employees having views highly compatible with Machiavelli were generally able to control social interactions and were adept at manipulating others (Gemmil & Heisler, 1972). Therefore, one could argue that Machiavellian individuals are better disposed than others to engage in political behaviour. Author-itarian personalities, with a propensity to take high risks, have been shown to engage in fairly reck-less political behaviour (Mayes & Allen, 1977).

With respect to motivation, a high degree of power, autonomy, security, or status can predis-pose an individual to behave politically (Madi-son, Allen, Porter, Renwick, & Mayes, 1980). The adoption of devious political behaviour is said to be influenced by one's investment (in terms of time and effort) in the organisation, by the alternative job opportunities available, and by expectations of using such behaviour successfully (Farrell & Petersen, 1982). So the more a person works con-scientiously in the expectation of securing increas-ing future benefits in the corporation, the more he or she stands to lose if eased out of the job or organisation. Such a person is less likely to use devious political action. By contrast, the individual with greater alternative job opportunities avail-able, because of a favourable job market or stand-ing in his or her occupation or profession, is more likely to risk the use of devious political action. Finally, where there is a low expectation of using devious political action successfully, there is less likelihood it will be used; but that may not apply to those with refined political skills.

Political techniques or tactics

The use of techniques or tactics to promote the political interests of certain organisational members is acknowledged by a number of writers, but there appears to be a dearth of strong empirical evidence on this topic. There has been the suggestion that political skills applicable to managers should become an increasingly important element of management education (Baddeley & James, 1987).

Specific political techniques

In the use of political behaviour, the following techniques are acknowledged (DuBrin, 2002; Mintzberg, 1983a; Pfeffer, 1981b):

* controlling information;
* controlling lines of communication;
* using outside experts;
* controlling the agenda;
* game playing;
* image building;
* building coalitions; and
* controlling decision parameters.

Controlling information. The objective is to control as much information as possible. The more crucial the information, and the fewer the number of people having access to it or part of it, the stronger the influence of the person who is privy to the total picture. For example, a senior manager has at his or her disposal an important report about the company's future. Though it is necessary to confide in some colleagues about certain features of the contents of the report, the senior manager is strategically placed to exert political influence in decision making and related issues.

Controlling lines of communication. Certain people can, as gatekeepers, control the lines of communication as far as access to others is concerned—in particular, access to an important executive. For example, secretaries and personal assistants wield political influence when they regulate access to their boss.

Using outside experts. A manager may achieve his or her objective by using an outside consultant who happens to share his or her views about the matter under review. Although the consultant

may approach the assignment in a professional manner, the recommendations made may be unconsciously biased towards a course of action favoured by the manager. Because the consultant is perceived as somebody occupying a position of neutrality, the recommendations are accepted by others in the organisation and the manager has the satisfaction of having successfully exerted influence to achieve the desired result.

Controlling the agenda. The manager may not feel comfortable with the prospect of having a particular controversial issue thoroughly discussed and acted on at a meeting. The issue could be placed on the agenda as the last item, or alternatively it could be excluded from the agenda, with the manager claiming that it is rather premature to discuss such an important issue that requires further thought. Where the item is placed on the agenda, a tactic open to the manager would be to develop allies by siding with colleagues' views on earlier items in the expectation that they will give him or her their support when the controversial item is discussed.

Alternatively, the manager may rely on a combination of factors. For example, when the controversial item is to be discussed, he or she could rely on what one might refer to as committee fatigue if it was a long meeting, or play on the desire of members to conclude the meeting, and seek support from allies. Other tactics could include exhaustive discussion of prior agenda items, so that the meeting never discusses the controversial item, or only gives it cursory attention. Of course, the issue could be discussed, but the manager may display adeptness in raising new angles to the problem, and concludes that the matter needs further attention before the proposal can be considered firm.

Game playing. Managers operate within the rules of the organisation when playing games. For example, in circumstances where the manager's preferred action is to sit on the fence, he or she could arrange to visit an important customer at a time that coincides with a crucial internal meeting, at which the manager should have declared his or her hand on some policy issue.

People can also play games with the management of information. This could amount to disseminating good or bad news at a time when it is likely to have the greatest impact. For example, with regard to good news, an employee asks satisfied customers to contact his or her manager with favourable comments at a time when the issue of customer satisfaction is high on the company's list of priorities. By taking this line of action, the self-interest of the manipulator of the news is served, but the hopes of others could be dashed. The disseminators of information in this context are unlikely to tell lies or circulate misinformation, because their future credibility would be undermined. But they rely on a carefully considered release of genuine information to serve their needs.

Image building. People may cultivate an outward appearance and style in order to impress influential individuals within the organisation. This is a subtle technique to enhance one's power base in readiness for the exploitation of future opportunities, and could also be used as a supplement to the development of expert power referred to earlier in the chapter. When looking at various aspects of interpersonal perception in Chapter 5, there was an implied reference to image building when discussing impression management. Impression management is a direct and conscious effort by a person to enhance his or her image.

People wish to project a good image for a number of reasons—for example, to secure rewards, attractive assignments, and promotions. Another reason is to acquire more power and hence more control. People interested in impression management could pay a lot of attention to the clothes they wear, the language they use, and the mannerisms and posture adopted, as well as making every effort to be associated with successful projects. However, there is a danger that people who are too strongly motivated by impression management become obsessed by it and resort to dishonest or unethical means to achieve their ends. For example, they take credit for the work of others in an effort to present a better image and to enhance their self-esteem, and in doing so distort or falsify their personal accomplishments (Gardner, 1992).

Building coalitions. An obvious tactic is to befriend people, often in the higher echelons of the organisation, who can help the user of this technique gain access to useful information. Also, being on good terms with the boss's secretary could be considered beneficial by some in developing greater awareness of what is going on. The person using the technique of building coalitions often conveys the impression that by subscribing to his or her aims one would be contributing to the attainment of organisational objectives.

Another tactic could be lobbying by a manager prior to a committee meeting to gain support for certain items on the agenda to which the manager has a deep commitment. Some would consider such an approach acceptable if support for the items concerned would lead to the achievement of organisational goals. Of course, the acceptability of the approach would be questioned if the prime beneficiary of the concerted action was the manager.

The technique of building coalitions is used in the form of reciprocal action. This could arise when X votes for a particular measure sacred to Y, the adoption of which does not materially affect X. In return, Y reciprocates to the mutual advantage of the parties concerned. There are occasions when this behaviour is dysfunctional, but on other occasions it could be functional.

Controlling decision parameters. With this technique managers take a step backward in the organisational process by trying to control the parameters set for making decisions, rather than controlling the decision itself. For example, managers could adopt a stance whereby influence is exerted towards defining or redefining the criteria on which the decision will be based. With respect to a selection decision, the manager could display considerable skill in shaping the criteria—e.g., depicting the ideal candidate for a particular job in terms of age, education, training, experience, etc.—and in doing so creates a profile that happens to resemble that of the favoured internal candidate. In this way the manager has created a situation where the preferred candidate has an excellent chance of getting the job. Therefore, the manager can afford to be less active in the actual selection decision, confident in the belief that the preferred outcome will materialise. Anyway, if he or she were to influence the selection decision directly, there may be accusations of bias because of the way questions were asked or the nature of the discussion.

In addition to these eight techniques, two more deserve mention (Vecchio, 2003). One is to eliminate a political rival by helping that person become more successful and marketable so that he or she is promoted to an attractive post elsewhere in the organisation. The other is to earnestly seek an opening for oneself in the line organisation: this tactic would be particularly appropriate for a staff specialist of old wishing to progress within the hierarchy. Securing a line manager's job is often considered a prerequisite to eventually wielding real power, and the base from which top-level executive appointments are made. However, one must not devalue the role of staff specialists who, of course, can wield power within their own function.

A study of tactics

Finally, of the tactics or techniques discussed in this section, control of information and image building are two of the three most important tactics perceived by a diverse group of managers. The other tactic was attacking or blaming others (Madison et al., 1980). Attacking tactics involved portraying rivals in a poor light in front of the influential members of the organisation. This was often done to create less competition for scarce resources. On the other hand, blaming tactics involved putting the spotlight on somebody else for an unfavourable result or situation in order to deflect attention from oneself.

The fourth tactic in order of importance identified in this study was building support for ideas. This was common among upper-level managers, and it involved getting others to understand one's views prior to a meeting at which a decision is going to be made, then setting out the ideal scenario and inviting others to contribute. Eventually, it is hoped that the others may embrace the views as their own, thereby fostering their commitment to the decision at the meeting.

Political tactics have been described as legitimate—e.g., forming coalitions or bypassing the chain of command—or alternatively as illegitimate or devious, such as sabotage (Farrell & Petersen, 1982). Extreme illegitimate tactics are not widespread because of the likely consequences (e.g., harsh sanctions or dismissals) that may result when the culprits are exposed and successfully charged for wrongdoing.

An alternative view of political tactics as skills is provided by Bolman and Deal (2003). On the basis of a search of the literature, they have come forward with four political skills that they feel the effective manager or leader should possess. These are termed (i) agenda setting, (ii) mapping the political terrain, (iii) networking and building coalitions, and (iv) bargaining and negotiation. You will notice there is a limited overlap (e.g., building coalitions) between this scheme and the one already discussed.

(1) *Agenda setting*. This skill means creating a vision for the organisation after much thought, and making explicit and putting in place the goals and activities required to achieve the mission.

(2) *Mapping the political terrain*. This skill is to some extent aimed at identifying the agendas of other players and trying to anticipate their likely course of action. It is also concerned with identifying influential players who could be of assistance, developing sensitivity to informal pathways of communication, and analysing the strategies most likely to ensure that there is a good chance of achieving what one set out to do.

(3) *Networking and building coalitions*. There is a recognition that it is crucial for the manager to identify people who will be helpful in the process of trying to achieve his or her objectives. Having identified them the next step is to establish their reliability and then to actively seek their cooperation.

(4) *Bargaining and negotiation*. The manager is intent on using this skill to achieve some advantage in his or her dealings with others. In this context there is reference to positional bargaining when it is clear that the manager

has something in mind, which he or she wants to achieve. The manager will then make concessions or concede some ground only if this is absolutely necessary to reach an agreement. The good bargainer will strive to achieve gains for all parties to the negotiation (mutual gains).

Devious tactics

Some devious political tactics are morally difficult to defend (DuBrin, 1978, 2002):

It is quite possible for managers or executives to create enemies because of unpopular or distasteful actions they have taken in denying promotion opportunities, freezing or reducing salaries, displacing people and terminating contracts of employment following, for example, major reorganisations or mergers. One tactic in dealing with this type of problem is to get rid of the individuals who survived but who still bear resentment against the manager's or executive's past unpopular actions and might retaliate at a vulnerable moment.

A tactic referred to as "divide and rule" amounts to a definite ploy to encourage a feud or conflict between subordinates or colleagues by spreading rumours or by promoting competition. The competing individuals may be rivals in the promotion stakes or may be competitors for favours bestowed by the boss. The logic of this approach is that the warring factions will be continually feuding, and therefore unable to mount an attack against the instigator of this tactic. However, the ploy could backfire if the tactics used become too visible.

Where opposing factions are rivals, another tactic is preventing them from attending key meetings or gatherings. The ploy adopted here would be to schedule important meetings or events when the opposition is absent—for example, at another meeting, or on holiday. The instigator of this ploy could then be free to exert much influence in decision making, and perhaps unjustifiably claim credit for the ideas of rivals in their absence.

A tactic, known as backstabbing, occurs when A goes through the motions of being pleasant towards B, while planning B's decline or demise. For example, B's immediate boss is notified by A that B is responding badly to normal work pressures.

Serious blunders

Among tactics considered to be costly political mistakes are the following (Vecchio, 2003):

- *Violating the chain of command.* Where a subordinate approaches the superior of his or her boss, without seeking the latter's permission, in order to act as an informant or complain about his or her predicament, this can be fraught with difficulties.
- *Losing control.* Although behaving aggressively and displaying temper tantrums to achieve one's objectives may be tolerated to a certain extent in competitive sport, such behaviour in the office or factory is unlikely to be condoned. It could earn the person a reputation as being difficult to relate to, and could easily lead to them being typecast as a troublemaker. A sinister twist to events could arise when the person who loses control easily is deliberately provoked in, for example, a public forum, and reacts aggressively. A number of incidents of this nature could adversely affect that person's image and reputation.
- *Saying no to top management.* It may be considered unwise to reject a request from somebody high up in the organisation to undertake a specific assignment. Individuals receiving such a request may feel overburdened with work already and, because they feel that their reputation as an employee is very satisfactory, may conclude that it is acceptable behaviour to decline participation in the assignment. Such a course of action could well be an unwise move. A more acceptable reaction would be to explain the situation with respect to the workload, stating that, if one were to undertake the special assignment, assistance with one's normal duties would be necessary.

- *Challenging cherished beliefs*. Where there are cherished beliefs about the nature of the organisation, it could be unwise (in the presence of influential loyalists) to criticise the myths, folklore, and special feats of the organisation's revered founder. One recognises that people should be free to express their opinions; nevertheless, it may be politically insensitive and unwise to challenge in open debate the truth of beliefs that are widely held within the organisation.
- *Upstaging a supervisor*. A subordinate should refrain from boasting in public about his or her accomplishments or claiming credit for the successful performance of the unit for which the boss is responsible.

Pros and cons of political behaviour

What are the advantages and disadvantages of the use of political tactics? The advantages, according to the findings of a study examining the perceptions of managers on this topic, are career advancement, recognition, status, achievement of goals, effective coordination, and organisational survival. By contrast, the disadvantages are perceived as loss of credibility, demotion, feelings of guilt, divisiveness, and a negative climate (Madison et al., 1980).

Ethics in organisational politics

Since the 1980s there has been a focus on ethics in organisational politics, and naturally questions are asked as to whether people who engage in political activity end up subscribing to unethical practices, such as lying and cheating, to achieve their objectives.

There has been much adverse publicity in recent years about practices such as insider trading in company shares, bribes to acquire large contracts, and raiding pension funds (see the commentary on business ethics in Chapter 9). However, it would be a mistake to view all political activity as unethical. Cavanagh, Moberg, and Velasquez (1981) consider political behaviour to be ethical and appropriate under two conditions— if it respects the rights of all interested parties, and if it is fair and equitable.

Coping with political behaviour

One recognises that it is impossible to eliminate all political behaviour. However, it is possible to take certain action to counteract its worst effects. In an optimistic tone, Moorhead and Griffin (2004), recognising the virtual impossibility of eliminating political activity in organisations, suggest that the manager can limit its dysfunctional effects by resorting to open communication, reduction of uncertainty, and awareness:

- *Open communication* would amount to making known to everybody the basis for the allocation of scarce resources, and curtailing the ability of any individual to control information or lines of communication.
- *Uncertainty* is a phenomenon that inhabits our daily work life and, as was discussed earlier, a number of internal and external factors generate it. Strategies of organisational change and development can create much uncertainty, so it is important for change agents and others to state clearly the way likely future events will unfold, rather than remaining silent on key issues and fuelling speculation and rumour as a consequence.
- *Awareness* of what has been discussed in this chapter about political techniques and tactics, and what gives rise to political behaviour, is a very useful first step to controlling the negative effects of organisational politics.

Vecchio's (2003) recipe, offered to managers to help them combat the dysfunctional aspects of political action, includes setting an example, giving clear job assignments, eliminating coalitions and cliques, and confronting those who play political games.

- Setting an example is evident when the manager acts as a role model by encouraging truthfulness and fair and equitable treatment of others.
- Giving clear job assignments entails the allocation of well-defined and discrete assignments that remove the potential for ambiguity.
- Eliminating coalitions and cliques that are detrimental to work performance could be

achieved by transfers or dismissals, but it may be preferable for individuals to be rotated through different job assignments that could have the effect of enriching their total experience.

- Confronting people who play political games could mean suggesting to the game player that he or she should raise questionable information about an individual in a more appropriate setting, or, if feasible, have it discussed at the next meeting of the group as a matter that requires serious consideration. Adopting this approach conveys to the game player that political games are not condoned.

CONFLICT

Conflict is a phenomenon related to power and politics. In fact, it can be triggered off by political behaviour and can occur between individuals or groups. Conflict is defined as a process that materialises when an individual or group perceives that another individual or group is frustrating, or about to frustrate, the attempts of the former to attain a goal (Thomas, 1992; Wall & Callister, 1995). It can involve incompatible differences between parties that result in interference or opposition, often finding expression in antagonism and the violation of rules and procedures. In its more subtle form it can be reflected in highly controlled forms of interference.

How people perceive conflict depends upon their orientation. This is called the *conflict frame*, the lens through which the parties to a dispute view the conflict situation (Pinkley & Northcraft, 1994). An individual with a relationship orientation would stress the interpersonal aspects of conflict and a person with a task orientation would emphasise the material aspects of a dispute (e.g., money, property). Others play up the feelings dimension (e.g., frustration, anger), as opposed to action or behaviour at the scene of conflict. People with a cooperative perspective would emphasise the importance of all parties to the conflict benefiting, whereas a party with a

"win" orientation is intent on gaining ground even at the expense of the other party.

A somewhat similar exposition of conflict has been put forward by Amason, Hockwarter, Thompson, and Harrison (1995). They classified the conflict found in teams into two types—"C" (*cognitive*) and "A" (*affective*). The cognitive type relates to concrete issues that can be dealt with more at the intellectual level, whereas the affective type relates to subjective matters to be found more in the emotional domain. A recipe for success in teams would be to be more partial towards cognitive conflict than affective conflict because by doing so one is effectively espousing frank disclosures and the articulation of many viewpoints, as opposed to championing disruptive tactics such as directing blame and anger at others.

Conflict can be distinguished from competition: when groups strive for the same goal, harbour little or no antagonism towards each other, and operate according to the rules and procedures, we can expect to find competition.

Conflict has been interpreted differently at different times—i.e., the unitary, pluralist, and interactionist perspectives (see Panel 13.1). The type of conflict supported by current thinking— the interactionist perspective—is described as *functional* or *constructive* conflict, and is said to facilitate the attainment of the group's goals and to improve performance.

Functional conflict is probably best described as low to moderate levels of subtle and controlled opposition, which is likely to lead to an arousal of motivation and could lend itself to activities such as creative or nonprogrammed decision making. Therefore, conflict may be more functional in groups that adopt new and novel approaches to tackle problems—e.g., research, advertising, or organisational change—than in groups performing highly programmed activities found in mass production systems or similar (Jehn, 1995). A similar view is expressed by Perlow (2003) when she argues that reasonable people making difficult decisions in conditions of uncertainty are bound to have differences of opinion that can eventually lead to acceptable conflict. This could create new perspectives and insights, and help promote better decisions.

PANEL 13.1: Differing perspectives on conflict

Unitary perspective

This is the early interpretation of conflict, and it amounted to a definition of a process that was harmful and should be avoided. In early research into groups (i.e., the Hawthorne experiments), conflict was seen as a negative outcome of poor communication, lack of openness and trust between people, and the inability of superiors to respond to the needs and aspirations of subordinates. In conceptualising traditional industrial relations, Fox (1974) made reference to unitarism as follows: Management is viewed as the only source of authority and power and everyone is pulling in the same direction, united by common goals. Conflict and opposition are abnormal and dysfunctional, and trade unions are viewed negatively and are discouraged.

Pluralist perspective

A later school of thought, spanning the period from the early 1950s to the mid-1970s, acknowledged the existence of conflict as a natural phenomenon, and went as far as suggesting that there may be times when it could have beneficial effects on the performance of the group. This outlook claimed that conflict stems from individuals and groups pursuing their own interests. It is the task of management to mediate conflicting claims and bring about an acceptable form of compromise to ensure the functioning of the organisation. Fox (1974), addressing pluralism in an industrial relations context, proposed that organisations are expected to contain groups that have divergent interests and perspectives and each group (the trade unions and the management separately) have power bases from which they can operate. Conflict occurs naturally where there is a clash of interests. Management does not have sole authority, but must compete with other sources of leadership (such as trade union representatives). Although the most common conflict may be between management and the unions, other fundamental differences could arise between managers and others at different levels of the hierarchy and between management in different functions (e.g., finance versus production). Implicit in the pluralist view is that conflict can be resolved when a realistic meeting of minds takes place, which is to the mutual advantage of those involved in the conflict.

Interactionist perspective

This is the current school of thought. This perspective encourages the adoption of a minimum level of conflict—that is, enough conflict to make sure the group is viable, self-critical, and creative. Implicit in this perspective is the belief that too much harmony, peace, tranquillity, and cooperation might create apathy and produce too great a tolerance of the status quo, with a lack of responsiveness to the need for change and innovation.

Functional conflict can be contrasted with *dysfunctional* or *destructive* forms of conflict. Dysfunctional conflict produces uncontrolled opposition and discontent, hampers communication, undermines cohesiveness, elevates in-fighting between members to a position higher than the achievement of group goals, and eventually has an adverse effect on group effectiveness. In its extreme form this type of conflict can gravely disrupt the functioning of the group, and has the potential to threaten the group's survival. It could also lead to workplace violence perpetrated by an alienated employee, or ex-employee still entertaining an unresolved conflict. There is reference to this problem in the discussion of job dissatisfaction in Chapter 9.

In the final analysis one must recognise that the demarcation line between functional and dysfunctional conflict is not clear (Amason, 1996). The issues raised in this section would normally be of interest to commentators who examine the implementation of human resource management policies from an industrial relations perspective.

Types of conflict

Conflict in organisations is manifest at the level both of the individual and of the group.

Individual conflict

Individuals experience frustration when their pathway to achieving personal goals is blocked. Candidates for an internal promotion may feel aggrieved at the way a job description for the vacant post is framed if it appears to hamper their chances of securing the job.

Sometimes employees feel so alienated by organisational conditions that the ensuing conflict expresses itself as sabotage. In the past this could have taken the form of damage to tools or equipment at work, and emanated from general feelings of powerlessness in circumstances where, perhaps, avenues for the expression of dissatisfaction did not exist. Though the underlying causes may remain the same, sabotage takes new forms with changes in technology. Therefore, computing facilities have to be guarded against errors invented by operators, including computer viruses.

Individuals perform a number of roles both at work and at home. There are occasions when the expected behaviour in one work role affects that in another work role, resulting in role conflict. A classic example of this conflict applies to the traditional "person in the middle"—the first-line supervisor—who is expected by management to be part of its team, while the workers feel he or she should represent them and act as their link with management. Another example is that of the individual who is torn between the demands of management for higher productivity and the norms of the group that reflect more modest productivity aspirations.

Role conflicts can also exist where there is a clash between the demands of roles and an individual's values and beliefs—i.e., when the individual is expected to do something that goes against the grain. Another form of role conflict that is experienced by professionals is expressed as the conflict between the need for professional autonomy and the demands of bureaucratic organisation (Child, 1982). (Further discussion of role conflict can be found in connection with groups in Chapter 10 and stress in Chapter 19.)

Group conflict

At the level of the group, particularly in the context of industrial action, reference can be made to collective or organised conflict (Reed, 1989). A group of workers, assisted by a trade union, could engage in certain behaviour (e.g., a go-slow, withdrawal of labour, work-to-rule, or overtime ban) in order to accomplish an objective, such as increased earnings. In industrial action of this nature there could be a high degree of cohesion among those involved with respect to the aims of the action and the best way to fulfil those aims,

but the workers' group could be in conflict with the management group.

While focusing on conflict between groups within the organisation, Hodgetts (1991) classified this type of conflict as **institutionalised** and **emergent conflict**.

Institutionalised conflict. This is evident when, for example, the marketing and production groups vie for advantage during the budgetary process when resources are allocated. In such circumstances, particular groups are preoccupied with their own vested interests and, given that resources are normally scarce, a gain for one group could be a loss for another. This is referred to as lateral conflict and its management is considered a priority in contemporary organisations (Buchanan, & Huczynski, 2004). When lateral conflict is intense and long lasting and people from different functions and departments are suspicious of each other and uncooperative, it is proposed that senior managers should intervene as third parties to assist with the resolution of conflict, or alternatively rely on an intervention by outside consultants (Nugent, 2002). This type of intervention is often referred to as workplace mediation.

The hierarchical arrangement of occupational groups could also inspire institutionalised conflict, because each level of the hierarchy experiences some degree of conflict with the level above it. This is often due to a concern with different sets of priorities. For example, top managers are naturally concerned with the future direction of the organisation, and may place undue demands on lower-level managers who are already burdened with short-term problems connected with the scheduling of work and the meeting of production quotas or other targets.

Emergent conflict. This is seen when two social forces collide. For example, the formal organisation calls for greater productive effort, which the informal organisation resists. The seeds of emergent conflict are sown when the subordinates are convinced that their level of expertise surpasses that of their superiors. It is also evident where staff specialists rely on the influence of senior managers (with whom they may have a special relationship) to impose recommendations for action on subordinate line managers, rather than convincing the latter of the strength of their case.

Sources of conflict

Conflict emanates from a number of sources. Robbins (1974) identifies three specific sources: communication, structure, and personal factors.

Communication

As can be seen from the discussion of the problems of communication in Chapter 6, the potential for misunderstanding is significant. The communication barriers said to be associated with conflict are semantic difficulties, insufficient exchange of information, and noise in channels of communication.

With respect to semantic difficulties, these are said to arise as a result of people's selective perception, inadequate information about others, and differences in training. As regards volume of information, too much as well as too little information is said to provide the foundation for conflict. As numerous people in the communication process filter the information, there is plenty of scope to create incorrect, distorted, or ambiguous messages, all of which can lead to hostility. The channels used to convey information (such as circulars, e-mail, meetings, or the grapevine) have also been considered in the context of the generation of conflict.

Structure

Robbins' (1974) interpretation of structure in this context includes size, specialisation, ambiguity, leadership, rewards, and interdependency. In the light of the evidence, one should add changes to structure and processes (Noer, 1993).

Size and specialisation. These are said to interact; the larger the group and the more specialised its activities, the greater the likelihood of conflict. With specialisation and differentiation within organisations (e.g., marketing, finance, etc.) come

the development of distinctive expertise, and the adoption of a diverse range of goals, sometimes with a parochial outlook. The diversity of goals among groups is a major source of conflict. Members of other functional groupings are likely to be seen as competitors for scarce resources. This can be aggravated by power imbalances between the functional groups, thereby stoking the flames of conflict.

Ambiguity. The greater the ambiguity in defining where responsibility for action lies, the greater the likelihood of inter-group feuding to control resources and organisational domains.

Leadership. Unexpectedly, one may find that too heavy a reliance on participative leadership may stimulate conflict, on the understanding that participation encourages the expression of different points of view.

Rewards. Operating reward systems is fraught with difficulties. If one party secures rewards at the expense of another party, conflict can arise.

Interdependency. An interdependent type of relationship is not uncommon between various groups within organisations. In particular the traditional relationship between line managers and staff specialists is worthy of note. The role of the line manager has often been viewed as that of a generalist concerned with the primary activities (e.g., production) of the organisation. By contrast, the efforts of the staff specialist are directed at supplementing the contribution of the line manager by providing specialised assistance in areas such as accounting, purchasing, marketing, personnel, and research and development.

Over 50 years ago, Dalton (1950) recognised that the staff–line relationship had tremendous potential for conflict. He considered it a delicate relationship whereby the staff specialist must reach a tacit agreement with the line manager in order to foster a workable relationship. But the potential for disagreement and conflict is omnipresent. For example, line managers might resist the innovative proposals of the staff specialists because they feel (a) a lowering of status owing to their

---

PANEL 13.2: Inter-group conflict

A computer was installed in an expanding retail establishment in the 1950s, when mechanised data processing was comparatively new. The organisation became heavily dependent on a group of computer programmers in charge of the installation. This specialist group—graduates who behaved informally and worked outside normal hours—had total control of computer applications (i.e., the group was endowed with expert power). However, the group members did not fit well into the organisation, and they considered the other employees to be staid and bureaucratically minded. The other employees viewed the programmers as immature and full of themselves. Hostile feelings developed between the two groups, resulting in a failure of the programmers to become integrated into the organisation.

Senior managers were unhappy about having to rely on the programmers' skills, and an attempt was made to undermine the programmers' control of technical information. This took the form of a proposal to dismantle the programming function and allocate parts of it to other staff. The programmers responded by projecting their skills as exclusive and withholding information in order to retain the organisation's dependence on them (Pettigrew, 1973).

In a different setting there is a clash between a sales manger and an R&D research scientist. The scientist who differs from the sales manager in personality disposition may feel uncomfortable because the salesman appears to be pressing for immediate answers to technical problems that will take a long time to investigate. This puts a lot of pressure on their relationship (Daft, 2004).

---

inability to formulate such proposals, as well as (b) the fear that the implementation of the proposals would not only cause disruption, but might also expose shady practices and inefficiency in their departments.

Woodward (1965) made specific reference to the ill-feeling that existed between management accountants and line managers residing outside the finance function. Hopper (1978) reported conflict between management accountants and production managers in the budgetary process, due to the failure of the accountants to present information in an easily understandable form relevant to the needs of managers.

It should be noted that there was a significant amount of dissatisfaction with the concept of staff–line, and its applicability has been questioned in conditions of product diversity and increasing complexity in a company's operations (Fisch, 1961). The case in Panel 13.2 highlights the difficulties certain specialist groups may encounter in organisations, as well as differences in outlook held by people from different functions.

Changes to structure and processes. An important source of conflict arises when a fundamental change to structure, systems, and procedures—often resulting in significant loss of staff—leads to negative perceptions of events. In recent years downsizing has been adopted as a strategy to reduce costs and increase efficiency. It is the people left behind that are often in conflict with the organisation, particularly when the policy goes

on for a long time. Then it can develop into conflict between management and the representatives of the workers. Downsizing, in the eyes of the management team who instigated it, may be viewed as "rightsizing", with beneficial consequences in terms of profitability and attractiveness of a listed company to the stock market. To the rank-and-file survivors of downsizing it could be a different matter. In fact it is said that they suffer from guilt, anger, and a sense of loss normally associated with a bereavement as they feel sorry for their colleagues who became the victims of downsizing (Noer, 1993). This theme is considered again in the next chapter.

Personal factors

This heading covers personality characteristics and value systems to which people adhere. It is understandable that individuals who are highly authoritarian and dogmatic, with a leaning towards low esteem, have within themselves the capacity to generate conflict. "Value systems" are a significant variable in the study of social conflict. They determine one's outlook and behaviour, and can be seen as a significant force in prejudice, expressions of views about good and bad practices, and notions of equitable rewards.

There are sometimes conflicts at work based on people disliking each other. There are also instances of conflict based on sexual harassment, where an employee is at the receiving end of unwelcome sexual advances or conduct by a superior or colleague, or has to work in an intimidating or offensive working environment. Most of the time it is women who are the victims of harassment. Sexual harassment could be viewed as a consequence of unequal power in the workplace (Lengnick-Hall, 1995).

Use of conflict

When examining the interactionist perspective on conflict earlier, it was maintained that a certain level of conflict is necessary if a group is to be viable, self-critical, and creative. Certain cues signal the need for managers to stimulate conflict—e.g., when there is an unusually low rate of staff turnover, a shortage of new ideas, strong resistance to change, and the belief that cooperation is more important than personal competence. Conflict stimulation is the formation and constructive use of conflict by management, and its purpose is to create situations where differences of opinion are brought to the surface (Van de Vliert & De Dreu, 1994).

Conflict is constructive when it improves the quality of decisions, stimulates creativity and innovation, encourages interest and curiosity among group members, provides the medium through which problems can be aired and tensions released, and fosters an environment of self-evaluation and change. Conflict is said to improve the quality of decision making when the group is receptive to numerous contributions, particularly those of a unique nature and those advanced by a minority (Priem, Harrison, & Muir, 1995). Conflict, particularly at moderate levels, is also an antidote for groupthink (discussed in Chapter 10). By challenging the status quo it does not allow the group to sit on its laurels and promotes a reassessment of the situation, which is useful during times of change.

Management might profitably stimulate conflict where, for example, it is recognised that competing organisations are improving their product design and production systems and this is likely to lead to the competitor increasing market share. It is therefore concluded that the time is ripe for managers to stimulate innovation and creativity by challenging the status quo. This could entail

taking a fresh view of prevailing attitudes, behavioural patterns, and the existing distribution of power (Van de Vliert, 1985). Creating a conflict situation may provide the impetus for employees to disclose differences of opinion previously kept secret.

In an experimental study, where students played the roles of supervisors and assembly workers, it was concluded that conflict can improve rather than impede decision making. When those with opposing views go through the motions of trying to reach agreement they develop an improved understanding of each other's points of view, focusing on their differences, and arriving at mutually acceptable decisions. The conditions considered best for decision making were called cooperative rather than competitive controversy conditions. Under these conditions feelings of curiosity, trust, and openness were cultivated, and decisions were arrived at that brought together the views of both workers and supervisors (Tjosvold & Deemer, 1980).

Among the measures proposed to produce conflict are the following (Robbins, 1974):

- Appoint managers who are receptive to change.
- Encourage competition by providing incentives (e.g., salary increases, bonuses, and recognition) that are related to performance. However, the competitive situation needs to be properly managed so as to produce creative conflict.
- Restructure the work unit. This would entail rotating staff among jobs and altering lines of communication. Although this is one way to restructure, there is another, and this involves creating new jobs to be occupied by external candidates with values and styles that are the antithesis of the prevailing placid norms.
- Adopt the role of "devil's advocate" in group discussions so that a number of alternatives can be critically appraised and analysed.
- Train people to be more adept at identifying potential problems.

Management of conflict

Because conflict has potentially damaging consequences, it is important that managers are aware of how to manage it. Conflict situations that are disruptive or counter-productive will have to be resolved.

Styles of conflict management

Thomas (1992) identified five major styles of conflict management at the disposal of the manager:

- competition;
- collaboration;
- avoidance;
- accommodation;
- compromise.

As can be seen in Figure 13.1, Thomas places the five styles in a two-dimensional framework comprising assertiveness (the desire to satisfy one's own concerns) and cooperativeness (the desire to satisfy another's concerns).

Competition.   The use of this style in conflict resolution amounts to an attempt to overwhelm an opponent by utilising formal authority, threats, or the use of power. It is a win–lose struggle and is reflected in assertive and uncooperative behaviour.

Collaboration.   This style involves mutual problem solving, whereby all the parties to the conflict come face to face with each other and discuss the issues. For example, the office manager is convinced that the selective application of new technology to work will improve efficiency, but subordinates feel threatened by the changes that are contemplated. This creates a certain amount of conflict among the parties concerned. However, cooperation and the search for a mutually beneficial outcome can emerge when the parties to the conflict are determined to satisfy the genuine reservations of all concerned.

When the collaborative style is used, participants attempt to clarify their differences and consider the full range of alternatives with a view to solving the problem. Collaboration is frequently viewed as a win–win approach because the solution sought by the group is advantageous to all participants. This style is used by marriage counsellors and by social scientists who place emphasis and value on openness, trust, genuineness, and spontaneous behaviour in relationships. The collaborative style is reflected in both assertive and cooperative behaviour.

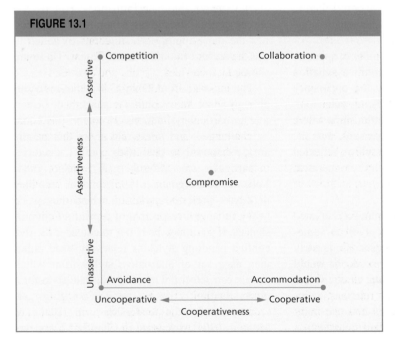

A two-dimensional model of conflict management (from Thomas, 1992).

Avoidance.   One way in which parties to a conflict can deal with the situation is by avoiding the other person in order to prevent an overt demonstration of disagreement. Avoidance takes two forms—withdrawal and suppression. With respect to withdrawal, we may encounter a situation where, for example, the health and safety official finds it difficult to relate to key production executives. The former withdraws from interaction with the latter by sending safety reports up the hierarchical line for downward action. In other cases within a particular department, parties to the conflict could stake out a territory in which each party decides what should be done and does not interfere with the other party. This could be workable if coordination of effort between the parties is not a live issue.

Where withdrawal is not possible or acceptable because of, for example, the necessity for coordinated effort, the parties may suppress their differences by withholding information or not airing their feelings so as not to upset the other party. The adoption of this style has no effect on the cause of the conflict, but by removing the conditions for overt disagreement, a win–lose struggle is avoided. Probably suppression is more widely practised than appears to be the case from casual observation. This style is reflected in unassertive and uncooperative behaviour.

Accommodation.   This style is similar to appeasement, where one party in a conflict situation places his or her interest below the opponent's interest. It amounts to self-sacrificing behaviour, and can be found in personal relationships where one party, for altruistic or other reasons, puts the other party's interest first. This style is reflected in unassertive but at the same time cooperative behaviour.

Compromise.   A compromise situation is created when each party to the conflict gives up something, and there is no winner or loser. If one party concedes ground on a particular issue, one would expect the other to yield something of equivalent value. In the field of industrial relations, compromise is evident in discussions between management and trade unions. In order to arrive at a

settlement to, for example, an industrial dispute, compromise is required. This style is reflected in intermediate amounts of assertiveness and cooperativeness.

Influence of culture

Attempts have been made to assess the influence of culture on conflict handling styles. For example, managers from Jordan and Turkey shared with their US counterparts a preference for a collaborative style, but they differed in their preferences for the remaining four styles depicted in the Thomas model, a version of which was used by the researcher (Kozan, 1989). In another study where a similar model of conflict handling was used, culture also had an effect on styles. For example, Chinese managers in Hong Kong tended to favour harmony and adopt the less assertive styles—e.g., compromise and avoidance—whereas British managers favoured the more assertive styles—e.g., collaboration and competition (Tang & Kirkbridge, 1986).

Situational factors

No particular style of conflict resolution discussed above is applicable in all situations. Following a survey of chief executives, Thomas (1977) specifies the most appropriate situations in which to use the styles of conflict management. These are shown in Table 13.4.

The message from Table 13.4 is that individuals can adapt their conflict management behaviour to particular situations. However, this could be challenged, and one could argue that people are predisposed to deal with conflict situations in particular ways (Sternberg & Soriano, 1984; Volkema & Bergmann, 1995), and in fact they may have preferred styles on which they place heavy reliance irrespective of prevailing circumstances. If so, it may be better to consider the five conflict handling styles as relatively fixed rather than as a set of alternative styles from which people can select the most appropriate style for a given situation.

Surprisingly, the leadership grid (Blake & Mouton, 1964), discussed in Chapter 12, appears

TABLE 13.4

Uses of five styles of conflict handling (from Thomas, 1977): Reproduced with permission

Conflict handling styles	Uses
(1) Competition	When quick decisive action is vital
	On important issues where unpopular actions need implementing
	On issues vital to the organisation's welfare and when you know you're right
	Against people who take advantage of noncompetitive behaviour
(2) Collaboration	To find an integrative solution when both sets of concerns are too important to be compromised
	When your objective is to learn
	To merge insights from people with different perspectives
	To gain commitment by incorporating concerns into a consensus
	To work through feelings that have interfered with a relationship
(3) Avoidance	When an issue is trivial, or more important issues are pressing
	When you perceive no chance of satisfying your concerns
	When potential disruption outweighs the benefits of resolution
	To let people cool down and regain perspective
	When gathering information supersedes immediate decision
	When others can resolve the conflict more effectively
	When issues seem tangential or symptomatic of other issues
(4) Accommodation	When you find you are wrong—to allow a better position to be heard, to learn, and to show your reasonableness
	When issues are more important to others than to yourself—to satisfy others and maintain cooperation
	To build social credits for later issues
	To minimise loss when you are outmatched and losing
	When harmony and stability are especially important
	To allow subordinates to develop by learning from mistakes
(5) Compromise	When goals are important, but not worth the effort or potential disruption of more assertive modes
	When opponents with equal power are committed to mutually exclusive goals
	To achieve temporary settlements to complex issues
	To arrive at expedient solutions under time pressure
	As a backup when collaboration or competition is unsuccessful

to have some value as a way of assessing the conflict management styles referred to earlier (Van de Vliert & Kabanoff, 1990). People are classified into the five conflict management styles on the basis of which of the locations on the two-dimensional grid (i.e., concern for people, concern for production) they occupy.

Superordinate goals

As well as the five styles of conflict management proposed by Thomas (1992), one could consider another strategy. This is known as the setting of common or superordinate goals by feuding groups. It is well established that membership of a particular group could predispose members to view other groups with suspicion and sometimes

hostility. Inter-group discrimination based on social identity is discussed in Chapter 10.

A classic study of inter-group conflict is provided by Sherif (1967). Boys attending summer camps in the USA were allocated to two different groups, and initially were unaware of the other group's existence. The boys participated in the normal activities of a summer camp, and developed norms of behaviour within their groups. An example of the type of conflict situation created by Sherif was informing both groups that the other camp would be using certain equipment, such as canoes, and as a result they would not be able to pursue that activity. This created a win–lose situation, and the two groups harboured strong resentment towards each other. Also, competitive games were used to develop a competitive relationship between the two groups and, when a hostile inter-group relationship emerged, various procedures to resolve the conflict were used. Bringing members of the hostile groups together socially as a means of reducing conflict did not seem to work. Neither did it help when accurate and favourable information about one group was communicated to the other group. Even bringing the leaders of the two groups together to enlist their influence was not productive. In fact social contact of the type described earlier can act as a means of intensifying conflict because favourable information about a disliked group may be ignored or reinterpreted to fit negative stereotyped notions about opponents. (Inter-group discrimination was referred to in Chapter 10.)

Apparently the best strategy for achieving harmony between the groups in conflict is to bring the groups together to work towards the achievement of a common or superordinate goal, and in these circumstances favourable information about a disliked group is seen in a new light. In addition, leaders are in a better position to take bolder steps towards cooperation. Examples of superordinate goals set by Sherif included the breakdown of the camp water supply, which required inter-group cooperation to find the fault, and the breakdown of a lorry used for excursions, which required all members of the groups to pull together on the same rope to get it started. After a series of activities based on different superordinate goals, inter-group conflict was progressively reduced and the two groups began to integrate.

The above principles can also manifest themselves in an organisational setting. An organisation consists of different groups (e.g., the production and marketing functions) and one effect of group membership, in whatever function, is the development of group loyalties. This can result in a parochial view of overall organisational events, with the likelihood that each group actively pursues its own ends to the disadvantage of the organisation as a whole. Conflict can arise when there is competition for scarce resources among the different groups. Budgeting can be used as a process for resolving inter-group conflict, but it may not always be successful in doing so. A significant threat to the survival of the organisation may be instrumental in bringing about more constructive inter-group cooperation and the resolution of conflict.

Although the principle of setting superordinate or common goals as a means to reduce inter-group conflict is appealing, Sherif felt it may not be applicable in all industrial settings because some groups in industry possess much more power than others. There is now greater interest in the significance of power (discussed earlier in this chapter) as a dimension of inter-group relations (Hartley, 1984).

CHAPTER SUMMARY

- Power, politics, and conflict are interrelated. With regard to power, dependency is an important consideration.
- The bases of organisational power identified by French and Raven were discussed, with particular reference to the circumstances in which they can be used. Etzioni's types of organisational power were acknowledged.
- Power tactics used by individuals and groups were discussed, and situational variables that determine the choice of power tactic were examined. There was a section reflecting on power at the macro level.
- Politics in organisations was described, and the causes of political behaviour were noted. The techniques, tactics, or skills to promote the political interests of organisational members were described in some detail, as were examples of devious political tactics and political mistakes.
- The advantages and disadvantages of the use of political tactics were stated. Hints on how to combat the dysfunctional aspects of political action were offered.
- Conflict was examined as a phenomenon related to power and politics; it can occur between individuals or groups. Over time conflict has been interpreted differently—e.g., the unitary, the pluralist, and interactionist perspectives.
- The types of conflict manifest at both individual and group levels in the organisation were discussed, and there was a recognition that conflict emanates from a number of sources.
- There was the suggestion that management might profitably stimulate conflict in specified circumstances, but as conflict has potentially damaging consequences, it is imperative for managers to be able to manage it. Styles of conflict management were outlined, and in this context the use of superordinate or common goals in inter-group activity was emphasised.

QUESTIONS

(1) Distinguish between power, politics, and conflict in organisations.

(2) What is meant by the bases of power?

(3) Reflect on the nature and distribution of power within organisations.

(4) Describe the power tactics at the disposal of individuals within groups, and isolate the ones considered the most important.

(5) Define organisational politics.

(6) What are the organisational factors that contribute to political behaviour?

(7) Distinguish between devious and legitimate political tactics in organisations.

(8) List the advantages and disadvantages of political behaviour in organisations.

(9) What are the skills you would associate with the effective leader or manager?

(10) How does the interactionist perspective on conflict differ from other recognised perspectives?

(11) Define the following terms: (a) conflict frame; (b) cognitive conflict; (c) institutionalised conflict; (d) structured conflict; (e) dysfunctional conflict; (f) opportunity power; (g) alienative involvement; (h) building coalitions; and (i) unobtrusive controls.

(12) Identify the measures proposed to produce conflict in organisations.

(13) Comment on styles of conflict management and the use of superordinate goals.

SPOTLIGHT ON RELEVANT READING

Bragg, M. (1996). *Reinventing influence*. London: Pitman Publishing.

Butcher, D., & Clarke, M. (2002). Organizational politics: The cornerstone for organizational democracy. *Organizational Dynamics, 31*, 35–46.

Clegg, S. (1990b). *Frameworks of power*. London: Sage.

Nugent, P.S. (2002). Managing conflict: Third party interventions for managers. *Academy of Management Executive, 16*, 139–155.

Perlow, L. (2003). *When you say yes but mean no: How silencing conflict wrecks relationships and companies*. New York: Crown Business.

Pfeffer, J. (1992). *Managing with power: Politics and influence in organizations*. Boston, MA: Harvard Business School Press.

Part IV

The Organisation

Learning Outcomes

After studying this chapter you should be able to:

• State what is meant by an organisation, identifying its common characteristics.

• Recognise the significance of using metaphors and typologies in explaining organisations.

• Describe the characteristics of bureaucracy as conceived by Weber, and the principles of organisation put forward by the classical theorists.

• Outline the structural groupings and forms of organisation.

• Assess the significance of the contributions of the contingency theorists in expanding our knowledge of organisations.

• Comment on the importance of strategic choice in the determination of organisation structure.

• Provide an illustration of a socio-technical system.

• Comment on organisation theory from a postmodern perspective.

• Discuss contemporary developments—in particular the network organisation, virtual organisation, and boundaryless organisation, plus outsourcing, downsizing, team-based systems, the flexible firm, and high-performance systems.

• Comment on corporate governance in the context of new organisational forms.

Organisational Structure and Design

14

Following a definition, with common characteristics, and types of organisation, there is an analysis of ideal bureaucracy and its dysfunctional effects. Next is a statement (and criticism) of the classical principles of organisation, and an examination of the various arrangements for organisational groupings, and descriptions of coordinating mechanisms and forms of organisation. A broad view is then taken of the impact of contingency factors (i.e., internal and external environment, and technology) on organisation structure, and there is a recognition of the mediating effect of strategic choice. Following reflections on organisational theory there is an analysis of new organisational forms and reference to corporate governance. The chapter provides the structural framework for the later discussion of organisational culture, change, and development.

Contents

DEFINITION AND COMMON CHARACTERISTICS

An organisation could be described as a collection of individuals who are organised into groups and subgroups and "interact" with each other in an "interdependent" relationship. The individuals work towards "**common goals**", which are not always clear, and the way they relate is determined by the structure of the organisation (Duncan, 1981). Because organisations are complex, this simple definition fails to capture the true reality of this social phenomenon. However, as the chapter unfolds, the nature of organisational complexity will become clearer.

In the above definition some common characteristics of organisation were mentioned. There was reference to subdivision by groups, interaction and interdependency, and the pursuit of common goals. Other characteristics are that people with different abilities, skills, duties, and responsibilities perform specialist tasks (e.g., the job of financial accountant), and this is made possible by the division of labour. As a consequence of the compartmentalisation generated by the division of labour, it is necessary to put in place structures and processes so that it is possible to coordinate a wide range of disparate activities aimed at the achievement of common goals. It should be emphasised that coordination of effort within a function and between functions within an organisation is by no means an easy task. Later in this chapter there is a description of approaches to the coordination of organisational tasks.

Common goals

There is frequent reference to common goals when looking at the characteristics of the organisation. What do we mean by a goal? A goal could be defined as something the organisation is striving to achieve. In its broadest sense it could refer to the overall purpose of the organisation. For example, the overall purpose of an automobile manufacturer would be the production of motor cars and trucks, but equally it could be more specific than that—e.g., to produce a range of motor cars and trucks within a particular time frame.

Essence of organisational goals

Over the years a number of academic writers have attempted to capture the essence of organisational goals. March and Simon (1958) drew a distinction between three types of goals, as follows:

- *Official goals.* These goals are stated in the charter of the organisation, or were established by the founder of the organisation.
- *Operative goals.* These goals reflect the real intentions of the leaders or dominant coalitions within organisations and are concealed from the public. For example, whereas an "official goal" states profit maximisation to ensure maximum short-term returns for shareholders, the real intention of the top decision makers—the operative goal—may be for the organisation to survive and grow by extending its market. Such an action would necessitate a significant retention of profits within the organisation, leading to a lower dividend payment to shareholders (lower returns) in the short term.
- *Operational goals.* These goals could be expressed in quantitative terms. Whereas growth of the organisation may be an operative goal, it becomes an operational goal when it is expressed in percentage terms (e.g., a 7% growth rate). Expressed in this way it makes the task of comparing actual performance with planned performance (goals) that much easier.

Perrow (1970) mentioned five organisational goals, as follows:

- *Societal goals.* These goals refer to the production of goods or provision of services, the maintenance of order, and the maintenance of cultural values in society.
- *Output goals.* These goals are designed to satisfy customer or client needs for goods or services, and this could be viewed as the primary task of the organisation.
- *System goals.* These goals are used to promote the interests of the organisation independent

of its output. For example, these goals could be in the form of an intention to foster organisational efficiency, growth, or to be a leading player in the company's market-place. There is an interaction between systems goals and output goals.

- *Product characteristics goals*. These goals could refer to the production of a distinctive product with style, and they could be derived from either output or systems goals.
- *Derived goals*. These goals apply when top management uses the organisation's power and resources to advance social and cultural causes—e.g., offering more opportunities for employes to develop themselves, helping the community, and supporting the arts.

Simon (1964) viewed goals as a set of constraints limiting scope for action. These are constraints imposed on the organisation and could consist of objectives normally set by management, such as to achieve a particular return on capital, to abide by stated safety standards, and satisfy the needs of customers.

We must be prepared to encounter potential conflict between the goals of individual employees (personal goals) and organisational goals. For example, there are instances when not everybody has the same set of goals or priorities and these do not coincide with organisational goals. At the same time we have to recognise that there are occasions when personal goals and organisational goals are congruent (they fall into line); that is, people satisfy their personal goals—for example, career development—while achieving organisational goals.

From the discussion so far, the nature of goals is not considered problematic. However, if one subscribes to the notion that goals are ideals rarely achievable, then it would be wise to recognise the ambiguous status of goals. Instead of looking at the relationship between organisational goals and related performance, a preferable approach might be to evaluate the overall performance of an organisation against comparable organisations (Mullins, 2002). Another matter to keep in mind when reflecting on organisational goals is the following question: Do organisational goals really exist? Organisations have no goals, only people have goals! It is people as individuals or groups who cooperate or bargain in coalitions and, in the process, set goals. This could arise when a dominant coalition within the organisation comprised of senior management may, after due consultation with appropriate employees, outline a desired course of action that eventually finds expression as organisational goals.

Objectives and policies. Goals form the basis for the objectives and policies of the organisation and it is important that they are clearly stated and communicated to employees. Objectives and policies combined create corporate guidelines for the management and operation of the organisation. Objectives, which should not be too rigidly construed, would ideally set out in explicit and specific terms the goals of the organisation, the aims to be achieved, and the desired end results. They can be expressed in more general terms at top management level, but further down the hierarchy they would be articulated more specifically and would take into account the organisation's prevailing ideology or belief system.

Policy is developed within the framework of objectives and provides a platform for making decisions and taking the various courses of action required to achieve the objectives. Policy is translated into plans, rules, and procedures, and pervades all levels and activities within the organisation. It clarifies the roles and responsibilities of managers and other employees, and provides the guiding principles for decision making across functions (e.g., marketing, production). When the objectives and policy are formulated, and the necessary resources provided, the conditions for strategic planning exist.

Typology

Organisations are a prominent feature of many aspects of life in society, such as the operation of government, business and the church. Various attempts have been made by theorists to classify organisations. Etzioni (1975) created a **typology of organisations** (Table 14.1), which can be associated with particular activities in society. You will

creates competition

TABLE 14.1

Etzioni's typology of organisations

Type	Sector
Coercive (use of force)	e.g. Prison
Utilitarian (use of rewards)	e.g. Retail outlet
Normative (reliance on commitment)	e.g. Church

TABLE 14.2

Type of organisation and prime beneficiary

Type of organisation	Prime beneficiary
Mutual benefit association (e.g. professional body)	Membership
Business concerns (e.g. privatised utility)	Owners (i.e. shareholders)
Commonweal organisations (e.g. Civil Service)	Public at large

notice that the organisations are differentiated in accordance with the primary system of reward used to secure the compliance of members. In Chapter 13 this typology is used to illustrate different types of power based on systems of reward.

Blau and Scott (1966) use a different method to classify organisations. This is done on the basis of the prime beneficiary (the group who benefits!), as shown in Table 14.2.

Metaphors

Another way of describing organisations is to use metaphors. It is suggested that we use metaphors when confronted by the complexity of organisation. A metaphor has been described as a basic structural form of experience through which human beings engage, organise, and understand their world (Morgan, 1983). In describing how an organisation works, the metaphor of the working of the machine is sometimes used. Each cog in the machine performs a highly specialised function, and, provided all cogs operate in the required interdependent way, the machine will perform effectively. The early writers on organisation, introduced later in the chapter, tended to use the machine metaphor. Though it may be helpful to visualise an organisation in this way, an organisation is not a mechanical device like a piece of machinery, and employees should not be treated as cogs or levers amenable to adjustment as the need arises.

Another metaphor could be used to encapsulate some of the properties of an organism, such as an animal or plant. Like an organism, an organisation grows, changes over time, ages, and eventually perishes; but in the final analysis an organisation is not an organism. However, when we use an organism metaphor an emphasis could be placed on the organic features of organisation (e.g., organisational adaptiveness), discussed later in the chapter.

Makin, Cooper, and Cox (1996) point out that we can derive useful insights from the use of metaphors in describing organisations, but then they add a word of caution by suggesting that metaphors should be used in a limited sense because extending a metaphor beyond its useful limits will lead to misunderstanding and ineffectiveness. A metaphor of the sick organisation appears in Panel 14.1. Another metaphor that has had wide currency in recent years is organisational culture, discussed in Chapter 15.

FORMAL AND INFORMAL ORGANISATIONS

Although relationships and contacts operate within the formally established structure, the prevalence of an informal organisation (numerous informal contacts) has to be accepted as a necessary complement to the formal structure. (A related matter was discussed in Chapter 10 when a distinction was drawn between formal and informal groups.) The main difference between a formal and informal organisation is the extent to which they are structured.

Schein (1988) defines a formal organisation as the planned coordination of the activities of a

---

PANEL 14.1: The neurotic organisation

The neurotic organisation can be viewed as consisting of the following characteristics:

(1) *Paranoid*. Suspicious of people and events; heavy emphasis on information-gathering and control to cope with threats and challenges; adopts a reactive approach to the neglect of a consistent strategic outlook; diversifies in order to reduce the risk of reliance on one market.

(2) *Compulsive*. Pays attention to detailed planning, scheduling, and standardised procedures in a hierarchical structure; conducts its business in a thorough way; is conformist; possesses a particular competence that is highly valued and adopted.

(3) *Histrionic*. Hyperactive, impulsive in a reckless way, relishes adventure; there is heavy reliance by decision makers on hunches when making decisions on a wide range of projects; power is centralised and there is a tendency for top management to act unilaterally when pursuing bold ventures.

(4) *Depressive*. There is a noticeable lack of confidence, coupled with an insular, conservative, and inactive stance; there is a heavy reliance on bureaucratic procedures to run the organisation, which is well established serving one mature market.

(5) *Schizoid*. Lacks leadership; chief executive discourages interaction but the leadership vacuum at the top is compensated for by appropriate action one step removed from the chief executive; strategy formulation is heavily influenced by individual goals and internal politics.

(Adapted from Kets De Vries & Miller, 1984)

---

number of people for the achievement of some common explicit goal through the division of labour and function, and through a hierarchy of authority and responsibility. Within the organisation there is a pattern of roles dealing with the authorised activities (e.g., accounting, purchasing, selling) and an organisational blueprint for the coordination of the activities associated with the various roles performed by employees. The organisation exists independent of particular employees and can survive despite excessive staff turnover. The organisational blueprint changes only when roles are redefined by role occupants or senior managers. If such an event was to occur, the organisation itself could change. In the formal organisation a prominent record is the standard organisation chart, which depicts a hierarchy of roles with senior positions at the top and junior positions at the bottom of the organisation.

We speak of informal organisation when members of the formal organisation relate to each other and participate in activities not prescribed by the organisational blueprint. In fact they socialise and establish relationships beyond the requirements of their role, and they aim to satisfy psychological needs (e.g., security, belonging, and a sense of personal identity) in the process. The informal organisation is, by its very nature, a flexible and unstructured phenomenon, where membership and relationships are not preordained and the involvement of members is not always predictable.

An informal organisation can serve a valuable function apart from satisfying the above psychological needs. It opens up an additional communication channel (e.g., the grapevine) and it allows reflection on weaknesses or drawbacks associated with the organisation (e.g., obsolete systems or inability to handle novel or unexpected events). Equally, it could compensate for the tedium experienced in some jobs and may give the individual the opportunity to make a creative contribution to group discussion, which could lead to an increased level of motivation.

Ideally, the informal organisation complements the formal organisation, but one should always bear in mind that informal organisation has the potential to undermine the formal organisation. (It is natural to mention culture when we give some thought to informal organisation, and this issue will be examined in Chapter 15.)

THE NATURE OF BUREAUCRATIC ORGANISATION

Over the years there have been a number of attempts to identify the key features of organisation.

In this section, the following contributions will be examined:

- Weber's ideal bureaucracy;
- principles of organisation;
- structural groupings; and
- Mintzberg's characteristics of organisation.

Weber's ideal bureaucracy

Serious interest in studying the features of formal organisations started with the work of Max Weber many years ago (Gerth & Mills, 1948). It was he who used the much-maligned word "bureaucracy" in his writings. Nowadays the word is viewed as being synonymous with red tape. In the ideal or legal-rational model Weber viewed bureaucratic organisation as technically superior to any other form of organisation and admirably equipped to maintain effective and impartial control. He identified the typical or ideal features of bureaucratic organisation (see Panel 14.2) that were considered to be the most efficient form of organisation. The reason for believing that this model of

organisation has much to commend itself is because the structure (the means) is designed to accomplish organisational objectives (the ends). Also, it is immune from the disruptive tactics of charismatic leaders, or inefficient traditional practices.

Apart from the ideal or legal-rational model, Weber also came forward with other descriptions of bureaucratic organisation—namely charismatic (heavily influenced by a leader) and traditional (where custom and practice predominate). The charismatic leader would possess unusual and exceptional qualities and would have to continually show evidence of his or her fitness to lead the "disciples" in order to be assured of their loyalty. He or she is unlikely to rely on bureaucratic structure as described in the ideal model. (There is reference to a contemporary version of charismatic leadership in Chapter 12.) With regard to traditional practices, there could be situations where power and influence in bureaucratic organisation are derived from traditional rights and duties that have been legitimised in the past (e.g., the monarchy) and status is inherited rather than achieved through

---

PANEL 14.2: Weber's ideal features of bureaucratic organisation

- A hierarchy of offices or positions is clearly stated, with a clear chain of command.
- The functions attached to the positions are known. Tasks should be subdivided and assigned to people with the appropriate level of expertise. Then each person should have the necessary authority and resources to execute his or her duties.
- Officials or employees are appointed on the basis of a contract.
- Selection is based on the possession of an appropriate qualification gained through an examination. Technical competence (rather than personal connections) is the important consideration.
- A salary, and usually pension rights, should be attached to each position, and should vary depending on the position in the hierarchy.
- Officials are only required to honour the impersonal duties of their positions, and are free to tender their resignation. The impersonal bias helps to maintain objectivity in decision making, rather than favouritism or personal prejudice. In order to ensure objectivity in decision making, ownership is divorced from control in that employees, and particularly managers, should not share in the ownership of the organisation.
- It is possible to progress within the bureaucracy through a career structure, and promotion is based on seniority or merit, as judged by superiors.
- Officials must treat their positions as their sole or major occupation, and must not abuse their position by profiting in an illegal sense from the post held.
- Each official is subjected to an organisational system of control and discipline. Standard operating procedures provide greater certainty and help in the coordination of activities.
- Written records are effectively the organisation's memory, and contain not only rules and procedures but also details of past performance that are open to inspection. Written records also provide an information base to facilitate the training of officials.

accomplishments. The customs and traditional methods act as guidelines for actions taken, and the leader is owed a measure of loyalty.

Supporters of Weber's ideal or legal-rational model are likely to maintain that it is functional because it is concerned with efficiency in the creation of structure, with a bias towards objectivity. It is precise and logical in the way it conceives and constructs certain realities of organisational life, but it should only be viewed as an ideal model and not as a working model that lends itself to testing in the real world. The critics are likely to express a number of reservations about its effectiveness. These criticisms can be expressed under the heading of dysfunctional aspects of bureaucracy.

Dysfunctional aspects of bureaucracy

In criticisms of Weber's ideal model of organisation, the central issue is that it neglects the human characteristics (Joseph, 1989; Vecchio, 2003). In particular, the disadvantages, or dysfunctions, of bureaucracy are neglected. These could be expressed as follows:

- *Goal displacement.* Gradually over time the "means" may displace the "ends", when the job itself may become more important than what is supposed to be achieved (Merton, 1957).
- *Conflict.* There appears to be an underestimation of conflict based on ambition because of the assumption that employees would be content with the organisational roles allocated to them. In fact, feelings of alienation or estrangement among employees could arise because of having to execute highly specialised tasks. Related to this is the lack of challenge and novelty that could result in job dissatisfaction and turnover. On this theme of lack of motivators, Argyris (1964) was of the view that compliance with the demands of bureaucracy could stifle initiative and overwhelm the personality of the individual by removing the scope for the exercise of self-direction and self-control.
- *Informal organisation.* The importance of informal work groups as a key source of influence is neglected.

- *Division of labour.* In today's world, extreme division of labour may be out of step with integrated computerised technologies that require teams of highly skilled workers.
- *Relevance.* The model may be more applicable to public sector organisations than to commercial organisations in the private sector.
- *Impersonality.* Taking an impersonal stance, and adhering rigidly to rules, could lead to an inability to cope with special cases, for which the "rule book" does not provide a solution. Also, excessive red tape can result from the emphasis on rules and procedures. Overall, people could feel frustrated with the bureaucratic system's lack of a human face.
- *Adaptation.* Organisations are subjected to pressure from outside to adapt to their environment. In times of rapid change—for example, in markets and in the application of technology—the structure of the organisation could be subjected to profound changes. Managers may resist proposed changes in rules and procedures where they see the price of adaptation as the surrender of authority. Conservatism and inflexibility may prevail to the detriment of innovation.

Quite apart from the stated predicament faced by managers, there could be a lack of flexibility in the response of employees to changed conditions. This could arise when a situation has to be tackled that falls outside the prescribed rules or procedures. This circumstance could be referred to as "**trained incapacity**", because the person is not equipped to cope with the changed conditions and the result is an inappropriate response.

Trained incapacity. A situation sometimes develops where the training provided by the organisation actually interferes with the individual's approach to decision making and problem solving. This arises, in particular, when the decision rules or procedures do not fit the problem or decision under review, but the individual has been trained to operate the rules and procedures, and is not prepared to modify or adjust them to suit the decision or problem in hand. Trained incapacity acts as a process to compartmentalise incoming information and problems into a limited number of categories in a procedure or decision process (Merton, 1957).

This may have an advantage from the employee's point of view because less time is spent on analysing the problem and searching for alternatives, and it provides consistency and predictability in the processing of information. However, it tends to produce rigidity and impairs the capacity of the organisation to react effectively to changed circumstances, when problems cannot be categorised neatly by a predetermined procedure. Trained incapacity is said to portray an approach to decision making whereby the decision makers become so accustomed to making programmed decisions that they even attempt to solve nonprogrammable problems in a programmed way (Kerr, Klimoski, Tolliver, & Van Glinow, 1975).

In defence of Weber's model it should be stated that he put forward a system that focused on the ideal characteristics of a pure bureaucracy, rather than an organisation that already existed.

Principles of organisation

A number of years ago a set of principles of organisation, sometimes called principles of management, were put forward by writers with an applied perspective, such as Fayol (1949) and Urwick (1952). Their motivation to do so was similar to Weber, namely to increase efficiency within organisations. These principles have still some relevance in their original form, but in order to place them in a contemporary setting there will be some additional commentary. The formal structure of an organisation can be depicted with the help of an organisation chart (see Figure 14.1).

Hierarchy

Figure 14.1 illustrates the shape of the organisation, and the different layers of decision making, in the form of a hierarchy. One would expect to find that positions higher up the hierarchy have more power associated with them than positions further down.

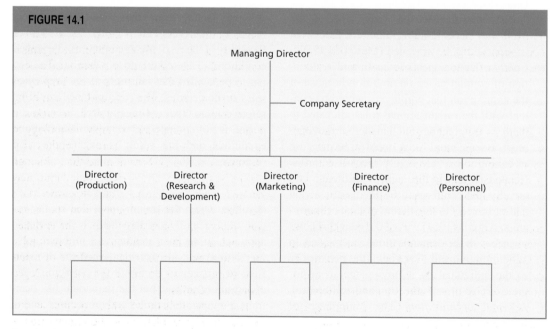

FIGURE 14.1

Functional structure of a manufacturing organisation.

Communication channels

The lines connecting the positions depict the communication channels through which authority is exercised. An organisation chart also shows the relationship between particular jobs or "roles", and the name of the person occupying the role can be inserted.

Chain of command

Organisations can be subdivided on a vertical basis. Figure 14.1 shows the chain of command going downwards from senior management positions to junior positions.

Unity of command

The subordinates receive instructions or guidance from one supervisor, otherwise confusion could arise if there were conflicting orders from more than one boss. Having access to only one official source of assistance and direction could be considered restrictive and may be seen as a negative influence when coupled with the division of labour.

Unity of direction

There should be one manager and one plan for all operations with the same objective. This facilitates unity of action and coordination of effort.

Authority and responsibility

Authority—the right to give orders and the power to exact compliance—is related to bearing responsibility for one's actions. Whenever authority is exercised responsibility comes into play. As a result, authority and responsibility are co-equal. Authority can be delegated within the chain of command but the same cannot be said for responsibility, though this requires clarification. It is accepted that ultimate responsibility cannot be delegated, but there can be delegation of operational responsibility. Authority can be referred to as line authority—i.e., the type of authority that each manager exercises—and it flows through the chain of command. This should not be confused with the authority of the staff specialist (e.g., a person acting in an advisory capacity) whose role it is to help the line manager in executing his or her responsibilities.

The concept of authority had greater validity in an age when superiors were knowledgeable within their section or department. In today's world, over-reliance on authority could be considered dysfunctional if subordinates are well trained and the superior is not fully conversant with everything going on within his or her section. Also, it would be unwise to place reliance on authority to the exclusion of other factors, such as persuasive skills and the power base of the manager.

What is becoming more apparent in the age of delayered organisations (referred to later) is the strengthening of the role of the line manager with the accent on its "enabling" aspects in a climate of teamwork, participative management, and the availability of various specialisms either inside or outside the organisation. Currently, it is customary to refer to authority as part of a larger concept of power. There is a discussion of teamwork in Chapter 11 and power in Chapter 13.

Division of labour and specialisation

As organisations grow in size, it is inevitable that specialisation or division of labour becomes more pronounced. When activities within the organisation are subdivided and tasks are distributed among people, division of labour takes place. Employees specialise in a particular task, and this can bring about increases in efficiency. Also, it makes it easier to train people and to apply technology to tasks, with the potential to increase productivity. However, one should bear in mind that, although certain segments of the working population may be happy with routine jobs and repetitive tasks that flow from division of labour and specialisation, others may have a preference for enriched jobs and can be more productive doing such jobs. In the final analysis the negative effects of repetitive work have to be offset against the alleged economic benefits.

Horizontal division of labour occurs, as can be seen in Figure 14.1, when the organisation is divided into separate departments or units on a functional basis (e.g., production, marketing, finance). With horizontal division of labour comes the opportunity for people to specialise in particular tasks (e.g., cost accounting, production engineering, etc.). But specialisation has some negative side-effects. For example, employees engaged in specialised activities can lose sight of the overall objectives of the organisation. Therefore, their work must be coordinated to ensure that it contributes to the welfare of the organisation.

Centralisation/decentralisation

If the exercise of significant authority and decision making resides in the hands of a relatively small number of people at the top of the organisation, reference is made to centralisation. The opposite phenomenon would be decentralisation, when there is greater autonomy further down the organisation. For example, a significant marketing decision affecting a particular product division could be taken in that division rather than being referred to corporate headquarters. (This could happen within a "product grouping" structure, discussed later.) According to Mintzberg (1983b), factors likely to influence centralisation or decentralisation are spatial differentiation (i.e., geographical grouping, which is also discussed later) and corporate strategy, or managerial preferences (i.e., autocratic or democratic). The advantages of centralisation and decentralisation are briefly stated in Panel 14.3.

Centralisation conjures up images of mechanistic or bureaucratic systems of organisation, and decentralisation is a feature of an organic system of organisation—discussed later—and is influenced by a number of factors, such as corporate strategy, system of management, and various organisational processes. Private sector organisations may lend themselves more easily to decentralisation, but that may not be the case with public sector organisations. Public accountability, regularity of procedures, and uniformity of treatment of issues could have a dampening effect on decentralisation in public sector organisations (Mullins, 2002).

Span of control

Another characteristic of organisation structure is span of control, or span of management. Basically, this means the number of people reporting directly to, for example, a manager or supervisor. The classical management theorists were of the view that narrow spans of control were better than wider ones because they allowed close supervision. Also, it was suggested that spans should vary from three at the upper end of the hierarchy to six at the lower end. However, later empirical work took an opposing view and concluded that wide spans of control tend to create conditions for improved attitudes, better supervision, and more individual responsibility and initiative among employees (Worthy, 1950). The trend in recent

---

PANEL 14.3: Advantages of centralisation and decentralisation

Centralisation
- Stops sub-units becoming too independent.
- Makes it easier to exercise control and coordination.
- Facilitates the implementation of corporate policy.
- Fosters economies of scale and can reduce overhead costs.
- Speeds up the decision-making process.

Decentralisation
- Decisions are taken at the most appropriate level.
- Helps with the improvement of morale and motivation.
- Provides opportunities for the training of managers.
- Permits the positioning of support services close to the relevant operations.

years has been towards wider spans of control. This is compatible with growing empowerment, greater flexibility, speedier decision making, and responding to customer needs (Child & McGrath, 2001). In turn this requires knowledgeable and skilled workers.

The following factors are likely to influence the size of the span of control:

- *Job complexity.* The more complex the job, the greater the justification for a narrower span of control so that the supervisor has the capacity to assist subordinates.
- *Physical proximity of subordinates.* The closer the subordinates are to their boss geographically, the more manageable is a wider span of control.
- *Extent of formalisation* (e.g., existence of job descriptions and well-defined procedures) *and standardisation.* When formalisation is well established, employees have little opportunity to exercise discretion and use initiative in their jobs. These conditions are more likely to prevail at the lower levels of the organisation and in certain functions (e.g., production or finance). The reverse situation (ample opportunity to exercise discretion and use initiative) would apply where formalisation is not well established, often at the higher levels of the organisation. It would appear to be easier to justify a wider span of control when formalisation is well established—that is the jobs of subordinates are governed by well-established rules and procedures (Mintzberg, 1983b).
- *Preferred managerial style.* Some managers might feel comfortable supervising a large number of people (wide span of control), and because of the wide span of control they rely on extensive delegation of authority. By contrast, a wide span of control might cramp the style of other managers with a preference for a narrower span of control.

Mintzberg (1979) also put forward the proposition that the optimum size of the span of control depends on: the extent of coordinating activities within the unit or department; including the level of job specialisation; the extent to which tasks are similar; the type of information required by members of the department; the differences between people's needs for autonomy; and the frequency with which subordinates need to have direct access to the superior. As stated earlier, the size of the span of control has a material influence on the closeness of supervision and the flatness of the structure. For example, when the span of control is narrower it is possible to exercise closer supervision with fewer subordinates reporting to a manager or supervisor. In such circumstances the structure is taller because of the inverse relationship between the size of the span of control and the number of layers in the hierarchy.

Although the debate on the size of the span of control continues (Van Fleet, 1983), today one would expect to find a wider span of control to be associated with the growth in the number of better qualified and experienced staff. Note that the flatter organisational structure (mentioned later), which is created by the wider span of control, is now popular.

Conclusions

It is still possible to find words of praise from authoritative sources of yesteryear for principles of organisation based on hierarchy. Jaques (1990), an influential theorist and researcher, recognised that hierarchy as presently practised has drawbacks, and acknowledged that in business there is a widespread view that managerial hierarchy kills initiative, crushes creativity, and therefore has had its day. He goes on to say:

> Yet 35 years of research have convinced me that managerial hierarchy is the most efficient, the hardiest, and in fact the most natural structure ever devised for large organisations. Properly structured, hierarchy can release energy and creativity, rationalise productivity, and actually improve morale. Moreover, I think most managers know this intuitively and have only lacked a workable structure and a decent intellectual justification for what they have always known could work and work well.

Leavitt (2003) recognises that despite some negative features (e.g., encouragement of distrust, authoritarianism, and fear), bureaucratic structures have a lot going for them as they provide the means of handling complexity, offer structure and predictability, and fulfil our needs for order and security.

Structural groupings

There are a variety of ways to structure organisations. The ones examined here are the functional, process, product, customer, and territorial groupings, together with the matrix system of organisation.

Functional grouping

With **functional grouping** (see Figure 14.1) employees have most contact with those working in the same function, and this helps to foster good communication and cooperation, as well as the sharing of ideas. But a disadvantage is that there is insufficient contact with those in other functions in the organisation. The preoccupation with one's own patch contributes to a narrowing of focus and can hinder the coordination of work activities across functional groups. For example, the finance function fails to provide the marketing function with product costings because it is overstretched preparing end-of-year accounts.

Process grouping

The grouping by process is similar to a functional grouping, but there is one material difference—that the grouping of specific jobs is influenced by a particular work activity. For example, an organisation's manufacturing jobs are divided into well-defined manufacturing processes as follows: drilling, milling, heat treatment, painting, and assembly. Each process would represent a department, reporting directly to the top manager with responsibility for manufacturing (Moorhead & Griffin, 2004). This type of structure promotes specialisation and expertise among employees, with enormous potential for the sharing of information. But then, as in the case of functional groups, it can engender a parochial perspective.

Product grouping

As organisations grow in size the adequacy of a functional structure to serve the needs of the organisation may be called into question. This is said to be particularly the case for multiproduct organisations such as Ford, DuPont, and Coca-Cola, in which a **product grouping** may work well (Hodgetts, 1991). Grouping by product or service materialises when employees who work on a particular product or service belong to the same unit or department, irrespective of their specialism. In the late 1980s, IBM reorganised its business operations into five autonomous units—personal computers, mainframes, medium-sized office systems, communications equipment, and components ("Big blue", 1988). It was hoped that this type of structuring would develop greater communication and technical awareness among employees producing the same product or providing the same service. (One should recognise that IBM experienced a downturn in its market in 1993, though its fortunes changed in subsequent years.)

A major advantage of product groupings is that specialisation and coordination are facilitated by bringing together all activities connected with a particular product or service (Birkinshaw, 2000). Also, each product line can become a semi-autonomous profit centre, making the detection of profitability, or the lack of it, that much easier. A disadvantage is that, as employees align themselves enthusiastically to their own product or service, they lose sight of significant developments and breakthroughs in other product groupings. Also, top management may experience problems connected with overall control if product groupings try to become too autonomous. Another drawback is the demands such a structure makes on managers with general management ability, because they are required to oversee a number of semi-autonomous units. This is obviously a management development issue to be faced by an organisation adopting this type of structure.

Birkinshaw (2000), addressing the global product division, states though it has a disadvantage

---

PANEL 14.4: Product grouping at JCB

JCB, the UK's largest construction equipment company, created product divisions with exclusive responsibility for the future of the main product lines—everything from design and product development to marketing. However, basic manufacturing such as welding are still to take place centrally, while the new product divisions are each to be responsible for painting and final assembly. The stated aim was to create multidisciplinary teams that will sit together and concentrate solely on one product line. The hope is that by identifying more closely with a particular product, the employees at all levels will understand the need for increased profitability, and be encouraged to participate in achieving it.

Certain mechanisms were being put into place to cope with various risks attached to the new structure. For example, one section of the organisation would act as central buyer for parts and components used by the product divisions, in order to take advantage of the company's considerable purchasing power, although decentralised buying could be justified in some circumstances. Other matters needing attention would be how to avoid duplicating contacts with dealers who sell the entire JCB product range.

Benefits of the new structure are said to be that things are moving faster, the incentive to look at new ideas is much greater, and there is much more of a team spirit, with implications for quality improvement. Some grey areas, such as training, remain.

(Baxter, 1993)

---

in that its standardised approach hinders the ability to respond to country-specific differences, nevertheless the global product division is emerging as the most common structure among large global companies. British Petroleum, British Telecommunications, Siemens, Ericson, Sara Lee, 3M, and many other global companies use the basic product division. The US multinational corporation, 3M, went through radical reshaping of the organisation's European operation in the 1990s. In the interests of improved cross-border effectiveness and quicker decision making, 3M pushed most strategic and operational responsibility away from its national subsidiaries (geographical divisions), and centralised it in the form of 19 product divisions called European Business Centres, each with Europe-wide responsibility. As a consequence, the lives of numerous managers in the organisations were transformed, having been given project responsibilities that cut across national boundaries (Lorenz, 1993b). An example of the creation of product groupings in a UK company is featured in Panel 14.4.

Customer grouping

Structures are created to satisfy the needs of particular types of customers under a **customer grouping** arrangement. A department store may have major departments serving different customers (e.g., men's clothing and women's clothing),

and a bank has separate departments for commercial and retail banking. The major advantage of this type of structure is that highly focused attention is paid to the needs of the customer. For example, a buyer in the men's department of a store can concentrate his or her attention on the needs of a particular client group and, overall, possesses a high degree of flexibility when it comes to finding ways and means to improve the relationship with the customer. A disadvantage of this type of structure is that the employee is isolated from his or her counterpart in another customer grouping.

Territorial grouping

When an organisation is geographically dispersed, groupings are created by region within a country or, where appropriate, by world regions. Frequently, sales or marketing groups are divided by geographic region. A significant benefit accruing to this type of structure is that the organisation can cater for the specific needs of a given location (Birkinshaw, 2000). Other benefits are cost reductions and better market coverage (Moorhead & Griffin, 2004), and the provision of a training ground for managers to familiarise themselves with operations in the field (Hodgetts, 1991).

A drawback could be the isolation the work groups in the regions feel when distanced from the nerve centre of the organisation. This could

TABLE 14.3

Matrix organisation

	Marketing	Finance	Production	Personnel
Project A	X	X	X	X
Project B	X	X	X	X
Project C	X	X	X	X

cultivate loyalty to the regional work group of greater magnitude than commitment to the larger organisation. A difficulty for top management is the exercise of overall control in the face of significant devolution of authority to territorial groupings. In a specific reference to territorial groupings by country, Birkinshaw (2000) identifies a disadvantage when he says that coordination across countries suffers, which makes it difficult to achieve economies of scale in development and production.

It appears that territorial grouping or area division is on the decline. In the early 1990s many large companies were organised in this way, such as Nestlé, Shell, and Unilever. Now, these companies have tended to move towards the global product division or some type of hybrid between global product and territorial grouping. In 2001 Unilever, the Anglo-Dutch foods and detergent conglomerate, created two global divisions, one for food and the other for home and personal care. The heads of the two divisions were both given executive authority and profit responsibility for Unilever's operations across 88 countries. The rationale given for this structural change was to accelerate decision making and strengthen the company's ability to harness innovation and awaken the entrepreneurial spirit within the organisation. In addition, the move was designed to put brand management firmly at the centre of Unilever's focus and to speed up its responsiveness to the market (Killgren, 2000; Thornhill, 2000).

Matrix organisation

The matrix structure integrates two different groupings—for example, a project department is superimposed on a functional grouping. This arrangement is shown in Table 14.3. Each function and project has a manager, and each subordinate is a member of each grouping, effectively having two supervisors.

This type of structure used to be popular among US firms in the aerospace and high-technology fields. It has a turbulent history and it emerged in the defence industry as a way of structuring cross-functional teams, and was adopted in the late 1970s by global companies as a way of reconciling the tensions between product divisions and territorial groupings. However, most companies found it unworkable because of the decision-making gridlocks it spawned. The Dow Corporation and Citibank, among others, dropped the matrix organisation in the 1980s (Birkinshaw, 2000), although some organisations, such as Ford, adopted it in the 1990s (see Panel 14.5).

The matrix is a complex system of organisation that requires careful handling for it to be effective. A matrix structure is said to be appropriate when three conditions exist (Daft, 2004; Davis & Lawrence, 1977):

(1) Factors in the organisation's environment require the organisation to give equal weight to responding to external forces and ensuring internal operations are adequate to cope with the demands made on them. This could mean satisfying the customers' requirements, as well as harnessing technological developments in turbulent and highly competitive conditions. Ford and Randolph (1992) provide support for this condition when they state that the matrix system can be highly effective in a complex, rapidly changing

PANEL 14.5: Global matrix

The Ford Motor Company merged its North American and European operations into a single global structure in 1995. A justification for the change was that the old "command and control" culture promoted the power of departmental barons at the expense of innovation, prompt decision making, and cross-functional teamwork. The company created five transatlantic "Vehicle Centres", four located in the United States and one in Europe. Each centre has responsibility for designing, developing, and launching a particular size and type of vehicle for the North American and European markets. In addition, the centres have responsibility for the cash flow and profitability of each product throughout its life. Ford's Asia Pacific and Latin American operations remain separately organised for the time being.

The new structure consists of a matrix organisation, and as a consequence a large number of managers have more than one boss. They report to a manager from the "vehicle centre" to which they are attached, but they also report to a boss in their "functional" department (e.g., manufacturing or marketing).

Within the company there appeared to be a lot of enthusiasm for the new matrix structure. It was suggested that it would promote flexibility, considerable informality, allow for improvisation as situations changed, and would be vital in promoting global teamwork and organisational effectiveness.

Ford hopes to prevent the matrix organisation from being overcome by the problems that have bedevilled this type of structure by proposing to take the following action:

- Take extra precautions to ensure that objectives are agreed precisely between the vehicle centres and the functional parts of the organisation.
- State clearly the roles and responsibilities of individuals in both arms of the matrix.
- Only appoint people to senior executive positions who have proved they are capable of working with colleagues on a collaborative basis.
- Train all those involved in developing cooperative modes of working implicit in operating a matrix system in order to avoid the need for policing mechanisms.
- Adjust the performance appraisal and reward management systems in order to bring these human resource management techniques into line with the new system of organisation.
- Introduce much more intensive and open communication than the organisation has been accustomed to.

Apart from the adoption of matrix organisation, the transformation of the company, called "Ford 2000", included measures such as delayering and business process re-engineering—a topic discussed later.

(Lorenz, 1994a)

environment that calls for flexibility and adaptability.

(2) There are pressures for a high capacity in information-processing. Because of the environmental uncertainty (referred to in the previous condition), and complexity, there is an added need for information-processing. For example, frequent external changes in the organisation's environment and a high level of interdependency between departments require a substantial amount of coordination and information-processing on a vertical and horizontal basis.

(3) There are pressures for shared resources because companies are expected to achieve good results despite limited resources. This could result in the flexible use of people and equipment across projects or product groups. For example, the organisation is not sufficiently large to assign engineers full-time to each project or products, so the engineers are assigned part-time to several projects or products. But this raises the question of recognition of dual authority—to the functional department as well as to the project or product department. Therefore, it is important to have a dual-authority structure in place to achieve a balance of power.

In the matrix system described, the project leader draws on resources from the different functional areas, and members can work on one project for a set period of time, then they return to the "functional" home base, and afterwards are reassigned to another project. The matrix system is said to improve project coordination by assigning project responsibility to a single coordinator rather than having it dispersed among a number of heads of functional departments. Also, communication is said to improve because employees have the

TABLE 14.4

Matrix organisation in a business school

| Subject groups | Programmes | | | |
	Undergraduate programmes	Postgraduate programmes	Post-experience programmes unit	Research & consultancy unit
Accounting/finance				
Economics				
Marketing				
Law				
Organisational behaviour/HRM				
Business policy				
Quantitative methods and computing				
Operations management				

opportunity to talk about the project with colleagues both in the project team and in the functional department. This increases the possibility that solutions to problems arising from the project can come from either group.

However, problems do arise with the implementation of matrix organisation (Daft, 2004; Davis & Lawrence, 1977; Larson & Gobeli, 1987; Lorenz, 1994a):

- The dual system of reporting may give rise to role conflict among subordinates. Also, there could be problems with the operation of the matrix if one side of the dual system of authority dominates.
- Power struggles may come about with regard to who has authority in given circumstances. It could be difficult to achieve full cooperation from the members involved in particular transactions. For example, in the 1960s and 1970s in certain multinational companies management in product and geographic divisions, on which matrix organisation was imposed, debated and fought with each other, and this led to internal conflict, inefficiency, expense, and delay. In many cases it took a lot of effort on the part of powerful coordinators acting as "matrix police" to resolve the disputes.
- In a matrix system there may be the mistaken view that all decision making is vested in the group. As a result, decision-making techniques may be used in inappropriate circumstances.

- Where the design entails many matrices, one on top of the other, establishing who is accountable and who has real authority could be difficult.

A matrix organisation in a business school, at a college or university, might assume a form similar to that set out in Table 14.4. In this structure, a lecturer or professor has a dual commitment, one to the subject group and the other to the programme(s) he or she teaches on. The problems mentioned earlier in connection with the operation of a matrix system of organisation in industry (e.g., multiple superiors) could apply equally in the academic world.

The matrix system we have discussed so far is often described as the balanced matrix, in which one manager has two equally accountable bosses. As seen above, this can be difficult to implement. But a different proposition is suggested, under which, in the case of the global matrix, a manager reports directly to the product division with a dotted-line relationship to the country manager. But this then becomes a more traditional global product division, although the terms "latent matrix" or "unbalanced matrix" are also used (Birkinshaw, 2000).

Conclusions

To conclude the discussion about structural groupings, one can say that a number of organisations experiment with different types of structure, and at any one time a combination of individual groupings discussed in this section may be the most appropriate model. But as Birkinshaw (2000) quite rightly points out, there is no perfect structure; each structure has its own limitations: "Organisation structure, like so many other aspects of business, is hostage to fads and fashions. The matrix has gone in and out of favour a couple of times and companies have moved in pendulum-like fashion between an area division and a global product division."

Before moving on to consider contingency factors, it is interesting to note the views of Mintzberg, a prominent strategy and organisation theorist, who had something to say about organisation structure (see Panel 14.6).

CONTINGENCY FACTORS

Over the years, a great deal of attention has been paid to the study of contingency factors in organisational design. Two major contingency factors are the environment and technology, and it is to these factors that our attention now turns. It will become clear that this approach to organisational analysis has a strong empirical tradition and has spawned many research studies. The major ones are reported in this section.

Environment

Recognition of the importance of the environment is understandable when one considers that a company must be organised in a way that accommodates internal and external factors in its environment if it is to achieve its objectives. Therefore, the design of an organisation should be contingent on forces in its internal and external environment.

Internal environment

An example of the internal environment is the size of the organisation, and the calibre of the people employed. Size of the organisation has been singled out as a crucial contingency variable in organisation design and will be discussed in more detail later. As the number of people in a particular organisational situation increases, the company is likely to resort to more formalised ways of doing things. It becomes necessary to introduce policies, rules, procedures, and other manifestations of "formalisation", because one can no longer expect people to relate informally on a face-to-face basis in the efficient execution of tasks (Child, 1973). With a growth in the size of the organisation there is also the likelihood of an increase in specialised jobs, more standard operating procedures, and paperwork associated with the delegation of authority (Cullen & Anderson, 1986).

PANEL 14.6: Mintzberg on coordinating mechanisms

According to Mintzberg (1979), structure of organisation amounts to the way tasks are divided initially, and then coordinated. He describes five major approaches by which tasks are coordinated:

(1) *Mutual adjustment.* Coordination by mutual adjustment can be seen when employees use informal communication to bring about coordination of each other's efforts. This is perhaps more prevalent in very small organisations.

(2) *Direct supervision.* Coordination by direct supervision arises when the supervisor coordinates the efforts of subordinates. As more employees join the organisation, the coordination process becomes more complex, and direct supervision is necessary. In a small retail shop a few employees can coordinate the work by talking to each other about demand for product lines and the level of stock. But if the retail outlet grows substantially in size, complexity increases, along with the number of full-time and part-time staff. As a result, direct supervision is required.

(3) *Standardisation of employee skills (input).* The set of employee skills required in a particular work situation could be standardised as a result of training. In the hospital service doctors and nurses use skills developed through professional training, and these, together with communication skills, are relied on to coordinate the service to patients. Although mutual adjustment as a coordinating device was mentioned earlier as applicable in less complex situations, it could be used also in complex situations to complement the standardisation of employee skills. For example, the doctors and nurses in the hospital setting may use it when faced with a difficult diagnostic and treatment procedure for patients; they use informal communication to coordinate each other's contributions.

PANEL 14.6: *(Cont'd)*

(4) *Standardisation of work processes.* The work processes refer to the methods used to transform inputs to the organisation into outputs. For example, franchised Kentucky Fried Chicken outlets standardise the preparation of its products, in accordance with a recipe originally devised by Colonel Saunders. Normally, one would expect the standardisation of work processes necessary to achieve the required level of coordination to be conspicuous when the organisation's tasks are fairly routine.

(5) *Standardisation of outputs.* Coordination is achieved when the output (i.e., the product, service, or performance) of the employee meets the required standard or specification. The output could be achieved through the standardised work process described earlier, or alternatively the employee may be given some flexibility with regard to methods used (i.e., departure from the standardised process), provided the outcome meets the specification for the product or service. For example, the shoemaker or repairer has some flexibility in re-heeling a shoe to the required standard.

Standardisation (referred to in points 3, 4, and 5) is usually set by staff specialists (e.g., production engineers or systems analysts) and overseen by line management so that predetermined standards with respect to skills, processes, and outputs can be achieved. In larger organisations, standardisation joins mutual adjustment and direct supervision in order to coordinate the work.

Forms of organisation

Mintzberg maintains that the five approaches to coordination can be combined with dimensions of organisation structure to devise the following five forms of organisation:

*   *Simple structure.* This type of structure could be used by a small recently established organisation (e.g., a supplier of computer equipment) in a dynamic but not complex environment. There is not much specialisation; neither are there many formal policies, rules, and procedures. Also, there appears to be centralisation of authority and decision making, with the owner-manager at the apex of the organisation. He or she uses direct supervision as the primary coordinating mechanism. In order to survive in the market-place the organisation must adapt quickly to its environment.

*   *Machine bureaucracy.* This could apply to a long-established, large organisation in a simple and stable environment. This organisation is characterised by a high level of specialised work activities and well-established formalised ways of executing work. The major coordinating mechanism is the standardisation of work processes. The organisation faces an environment that is simple and stable, and therefore problems of rapid adaptation to changes in the environment do not arise. An example of a machine bureaucracy could be a large insurance company, or a government department.

*   *Professional bureaucracy.* This type of organisation operates in stable but complex environments. The major approach to coordination is the standardisation of skills. Bureaucratic practices are played down, and professional areas of expertise and a community of equals (horizontal specialisation) are given prominence. The relevant professional body acting for the profession has great significance in laying down rules and procedures to govern behaviour. Universities, colleges, hospitals, and professional firms could fall into this category.

*   *Divisional form.* This type of structure could be found in large, well-established companies, with a number of different markets. Apart from the fact that the organisation is divided to serve different markets, it bears a similarity to the machine bureaucracy, and faces a relatively simple and stable environment. Standardisation of output is the major approach to coordination. The way company headquarters exercises control, with decision making split between headquarters and divisions, encourages the adoption of machine bureaucracy in the divisions.

*   *Adhocracy.* This form of structure is applicable to organisations operating in highly technical areas where the environment is complex and dynamic. Experts wield much power, and decision making is dispersed throughout the organisation, with evidence of a strong organic climate. The experts or specialists are not located in their functional specialisms. Instead, they are attached to project groups with a strong market orientation. Coordination is by mutual adjustment, and this is achieved through frequent personal communication processes and various devices to encourage liaisons. The adhocracy, unlike the other structures, is normally established to promote innovation. The organisation could be structured totally as an adhocracy, or alternatively a division could be set up as an adhocracy. Johnson & Johnson, a well-known, large US company, created a new products division over three decades ago to foster innovation, creativity, and risk-taking. This has been a success, with over 200 products introduced in the USA in the past few years (Moorhead & Griffin, 2004).

Mintzberg (1981) stresses the need for the constituent elements of the organisation and its environment to fit together in order to facilitate effective functioning. For example, one combination of fit would be between organisation structure, factors influencing structure (for example, contingency variables—referred to in the next section—such as size, technology, and environment), and the strategy of the organisation. Another example of fit would be an appropriate interplay between the internal constituent elements of organisation structure, such as procedures, specialisation, and decision making.

External environment

An example of the external environment is the range of elements outside the boundaries of the organisation. Within this range are customers, shareholders, competitors, financial markets, human resource markets, government regulatory agencies, supply of physical resources, inland revenue, and cultural influences.

Those who are responsible for the management of organisations ignore environmental forces at their peril. For example, a business organisation that focuses heavily on internal operations to the neglect of registering major shifts in its environment—such as changes in customer tastes, technological innovations, and new regulations—stands to lose out on opportunities. But it would be impracticable for an organisation to explore every minute aspect of its environment. The preferred course of action is for the organisation to monitor carefully those aspects of its environment that are salient, and respond accordingly.

The response could include modification or change to organisation design.

In connection with the external environment, the following concepts will be examined:

* open systems;
* socio-technical systems;
* environmental uncertainty;
* differentiation and integration;
* resource dependency; and
* population ecology.

Open systems.   An integrated view of the organisation's environment has been postulated by Emery and Trist (1965). This is essentially an "open systems" view of organisations where the environment consists of a collection of interrelated parts that relate to the organisation. Four types of environment were identified (shown in Table 14.5):

(1)   *The placid randomised environment* is characterised by organisational goals and problems

---

TABLE 14.5

Classification of the environment by Emery and Trist (1965) (from Moorhead & Griffin, 1989): Copyright © 1989 by Houghton Mifflin Company and used with permission

Type of environment	Characteristics of type of environment	Examples
Placid randomised	Slow change, if any Few interrelationships between environmental components	Few in modern economy Small job workshop or family-operated business in an isolated area
	Few new threats or opportunities Changes are random and unpredictable	
Placid clustered	Slow change Environmental components are interrelated	Container industry Some mass production *manufacturing*
	Change is relatively predictable Some planning is possible	
Disturbed reactive	Moderate change Few large firms dominate Heavy competition Organisations are interrelated within an industry Competitive actions produce reactions	Automobile industry Steel industry Soft drinks industry
Turbulent fields	Very rapid change	Computer hardware and software industry Communications industry
	Change is unpredictable Change may come from technological breakthrough, government regulation, or customer preferences Increasingly prevalent	

that are relatively straightforward and un-
changing. Nowadays it is difficult to find
examples of this simple and almost static
environment. The organisation system coping
with this environment tends to be relatively
small, and has little difficulty in adapting to it.

(2) *The placid clustered environment* does not
change much, but clusters of it interrelate.
The type of organisation that relates to this
environment tends to develop into a big, centralised, and coordinated grouping.

(3) *The disturbed reactive environment* shows
signs of moderate change, with interrelationships between environmental clusters. There
is strong competition between organisations
that are similar in nature. Companies inhabiting this environment possess large-scale
bureaucratic structures.

(4) *The turbulent fields environment* is both complex and dynamic, and features rapid change
springing from parts of the environment
interacting in a rather complex way. Coping
with this type of environment presents difficulties for the organisation; as a consequence,
the organisation may align itself with other
organisations in the same turbulent field.

Socio-technical systems.   An extension of the
open system perspective is the concept of socio-
technical systems. Any complex system consists
of many sub-systems, which, like the overall system, have elements such as those illustrated in
Figure 14.2. A socio-technical systems approach

takes the organisation as an open system accommodating the technical (task) sub-system and the
social sub-system. The technical sub-system receives the inputs and transforms them into outputs.
For example, flour is an input to a bakery, and in
the production process it is transformed into bread.
In a service industry (e.g., a building society)
loan applicants provide personal data about themselves that is used as input. When this information is processed and the application has been
approved, a loan (output) may be forthcoming.

The social sub-system embraces interpersonal
relationships within the organisation, and consists
of personal preferences, mutual trust, insight into
other people's behaviour, antagonisms, and so on.
The task of management is to create socio-
technical systems in which the two sub-systems
reach optimum levels together, and are mutually
supportive. The notion of socio-technical systems
arose from research conducted by Trist and
Bamforth in the early 1950s (see Panel 14.7).

The notable contribution of the socio-
technical approach is the emphasis on jointly
harnessing the technical and social sub-systems
with due regard to the relevant environment. However, Miller and Rice (1967), adopting a similar
analysis, were less confident of the capacity of
organisations to bring about a good fit between
the "task" and "human" sub-systems. The latter
subsystem has a leaning towards retaining routines and practices that could put a dampener on
technological innovation and efforts to bring about
greater profitability.

FIGURE 14.2

Sub-system elements.

PANEL 14.7: Coal mine mechanisation and socio-technical systems

In this research, the process of mechanisation in the coal mines of north-west Durham was observed. The researchers, who were from the Tavistock Institute, noted that the new mining techniques designed to increase productivity failed because they split up well-established work groups, with unfavourable consequences. Therefore, improvements in the technical system occurred, but at the expense of a deteriorating social sub-system.

Traditional methods of retrieving coal by hand involved limited technology, with small teams working their own part of the coal seam. This system created multi-skilled, self-selected, largely autonomous work groups that enjoyed a great deal of independence; in addition, workers obtained a relatively high degree of satisfaction from their work. The work groups did not compete with each other, and relationships were normally harmonious.

With the introduction of mechanical coal cutting (new technology) using the longwall method, workers belonged to shift groups that performed different functions. For example, one shift cut the coal with a mechanical coal cutter; the next shift loaded the coal on to a conveyor; and the third shift propped up the roof and moved the cutter and conveyor in readiness for the next shift. The longwall method was technically efficient, but it produced the following dysfunctional social consequences:

- Self-selected work groups were broken up, destroying some of the loyalty and cohesion required in the performance of dangerous tasks.
- As a result of specialisation by shift, greater coordination from the surface was needed to ensure that one cycle finished before the other started.
- Supervision became closer, and the workers reacted strongly to having to forgo some of their traditional independence.

The researchers argued that a different organisational form could still maximise the technical and economic benefits, and minimise unrest and conflict. This organisational arrangement would still retain the three-shift cycle of the longwall method, but the following conditions would have to be imposed. First, there should be no sharp division of tasks between shifts. Secondly, the miners should be allowed to utilise their multiple skills. Thirdly, there should be a restoration of some of the lost worker autonomy, with less supervision, whereby the work group would be given back responsibility for the allocation of workers to each shift.

(Trist & Bamforth, 1951)

The socio-technical approach is also relevant to job redesign, considered in Chapter 4. For example, the car assembly methods adopted by Volvo were a departure from traditional methods, with a new emphasis on sensitivity to the interface of social and technological systems. Autonomous work groups represent one approach to meeting the human needs and technical demands within organisations, and this is likely to be acceptable to the modern proponents of socio-technical systems. In the final analysis, management can exercise choice when it comes to designing organisations and jobs around the technological system.

There is still interest in the socio-technical systems approach among scholars (Pasmore, 1995), and some argue for an expansion of the approach to capture the dynamic nature of today's organisations, the chaotic environment, and the shift from routine to nonroutine jobs brought about by advances in information technology (Daft, 2004).

Environmental uncertainty. It is claimed that the characteristic of the environment having the most profound effect on organisation structure is uncertainty. Environmental uncertainty is said to emanate from complexity (the number of aspects of the environment—ranging from the economic to the market—that interact directly with the organisation's decision making) and dynamism (the degree to which the environmental aspects change) in the organisation's environment (Duncan, 1972), and it becomes apparent when managers have little information about environmental events and the way they affect the organisation (Daft, 2004).

In a low uncertainty environment there exists insignificant complexity and an almost static rate of change. A company in the cardboard container industry could fall into this category when demand for its product is steady, manufacturing processes are stable, and there is no appreciable change in regulations affecting the industry. At the other extreme there is the high uncertainty

FIGURE 14.3

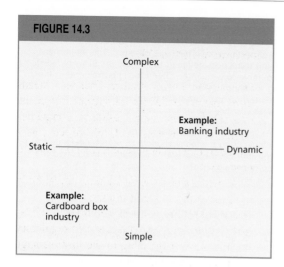

Aspects of the environment in the context of uncertainty (based on data from Duncan, 1972).

environment where there is a state of flux in aspects of the environment impinging on organisational decision making. The banking industry could fall into this category, particularly since deregulation in the financial services markets (Moorhead & Griffin, 2004). A diagrammatical representation of environmental uncertainty, postulated by Duncan, appears in Figure 14.3.

The importance of information-processing in confronting uncertainty in the environment is heavily underlined by Galbraith (1977). He focuses on the acquisition and utilisation of information and suggests various ways in which organisation structure and processes could be altered to handle information. For example, if communication channels within the hierarchy are unable to cope with more complex information, this heralds the need for a more complex information-processing system. Another example would be to set up mechanisms for resolving issues in the event of rules, programmes, and procedures proving inadequate. Other forms of adaptation are to enhance and improve vertical and horizontal information systems, decentralise or divisionalise (e.g., create a product grouping) in appropriate situations, and integrate vertically (acquire another company) in order to tackle environmental uncertainty and overload in information-processing.

Differentiation and integration. The importance of the environment–organisation relationship is underlined in studies examining structural adaptation. A research study conducted by Lawrence and Lorsch (1969) focuses on the volatility of the environment and provides useful insights into the way in which departments within an organisation structure relate to their environment. The study was undertaken involving firms in the plastics, food, and container industries and addressed two critical features of organisation—differentiation and integration.

Differentiation means that within the organisation there are cells or sub-systems, each of which positions itself with respect to its own relevant external environment. For example, a manager near the apex of the structure may be relating to the external environment on matters connected with the impact of interest rates and inflation on the present and future position of the company. Further down the organisation, a manager is linked to the external environment whereby he or she is negotiating with management consultants exploring ways and means of improving production methods and processes. A danger with a highly differentiated organisation is that cells and sub-systems might go their own way to the detriment of the achievement of overall objectives. Hence, there is a need for cooperation and collaboration. It is in situations where there is insufficient cooperation that integration is a valuable process. In a bureaucratic structure integration could be achieved through policies, rules, and procedures governing employee behaviour, but in less bureaucratic structures integration is maintained by mutual cooperation and teamwork on the part of staff.

In the plastics industry the most effective structure adopted by firms seemed to have high levels of both differentiation and integration. For example, functions such as research, production, and sales had the facility to interact effectively with their own particular external environment, but at the same time it was also possible for employees to interact across functions to resolve conflict and achieve integration across the organisation. The research units experienced a lot of pressure to come forward with fresh ideas and product innovations.

Their relevant sub-environment was the most dynamic. By contrast, the production units faced relevant sub-environments that were fairly stable and predictable at the technical and economic levels.

Firms in the container industry operated in the most stable environment, with a low level of differentiation, but surprisingly a high level of integration was considered necessary for effectiveness. The food industry firms were located in between the plastic and container industry firms with regard to the need for differentiation (Lawrence & Lorsch, 1969).

The important point to note about this research is that one has to look beyond the way the organisation as an entity interacts with its environment, important though that may be, and consider how individual functions or units interact with their own external sub-environments. Therefore, contingency factors of organisation design are valid when it comes to issues of structure at all hierarchical levels (Hodgetts, 1991).

Resource dependency. Another matter to consider in viewing the relationship between the organisation and the environment is the importance of resources. In order to survive, organisations must maintain "resource exchanges" with their environments (Yuchtman & Seashore, 1967). Resources can be exchanged in two major ways: by developing links between organisations, and by changing the environment (Daft, 2004). An organisation interested in developing links with other organisations having access to vital resources may develop relationships with these organisations in order to gain a resource advantage. These links may take the form of: joint ventures; mergers and acquisitions; contractual relationships; and co-opting to the board influential business leaders from other organisations as nonexecutive directors. See Panel 14.8 with regard to joint ventures or contractual relationships in the form of strategic alliances.

Instead of making structural adjustments to the organisation in response to changes in the environment, an organisation seeking to exchange resources may try to change its environment so that it is more compatible with the existing structure.

A number of options are open to the organisation that is intent on changing its environment (Moorhead & Griffin, 1992):

- Diversify into other product lines as a means to counteract a decline in revenue from the original business (e.g., tobacco companies buying companies in food, leisure, etc., as a means to reduce their dependence on tobacco products).
- Take part in a trade association or similar body to advance the cause of the industry.
- Get involved in political activities, such as lobbying, to bring about changes in regulatory matters previously acting to the disadvantage of the organisation.
- Engage in activities likely to improve the strategic position of the organisation in its environment, and to lessen the standing of its competitors. It is conceivable that such behaviour could entail illegal activities.

Population ecology. The fit between the organisation and the environment is also dealt with in an approach called the population ecology perspective. Unlike the resource dependency approach, the population ecology perspective is not concerned with managerial interventions in determining the optimal fit between the organisation and its environment. The basic tenet of this perspective is that the survival of the organisation depends on the fit between structural elements and environmental dimensions. This perspective, with its primary focus on the survival of the fittest, is akin to the biological theory of natural selection. When the environment is incapable of supporting all the organisations to which it relates, the companies enjoying the best fit with the environment will survive. Over a period of time it is said that environments select some organisations, or types of organisations, for survival and others for extinction (Aldrich, 1992; Baum, 1996; Hannan & Freeman, 1977).

Organisations need to match their environments to structure using appropriate mechanisms in order to survive. Some organisations are better than others at adapting to their environment. In the early 1990s IBM was so large that adaptation

---

PANEL 14.8: Strategic alliances

In recent years companies have been collaborating on an unprecedented scale. Joint ventures, licensing agreements, collaborative research, technological exchanges, and marketing alliances have become fashionable. The central feature of strategic alliances is that the partner companies remain separate. The impetus for the growing number of strategic alliances is the intensification of competition, faster technological change, and the increasing global nature of markets, which have left companies unable to do everything for themselves. Through cooperation a company can break into new markets, obtain access to new technologies, and obtain economies of scale more quickly than acting on its own and more cheaply than it can buy them in a takeover. But companies also compete in the market-place, and there is also an element of competition in how much they can learn from each other. The airline business is an example of a sector of the economy where strategic alliances have taken root. A number of conditions have been put forward as critical for effective alliances (Douma et al, 2000; Houlder, 1995; Lorenz, 1993c; Skapinker, 2000):

(1) *Each company regards the other as its best partner.* (Problems can arise if the choice of partner is flawed.)

(2) *Mutual need.* Each partner must take what steps it can to ensure that the other continues to need it, and keep in mind how each side is benefiting from the relationship.

(3) *Shared objectives.* There must be clear agreement on what the partners intend to maximise together, and whether they are entering the alliance for the same reasons. It is said that the fastest route to alliance failure is to assume the initial assumptions and objectives will not change over time.

(4) *Shared risk.* Both personal and economic risks must be realistically shared by the partners.

(5) *Trust, social relationships, flexibility, and commitment.* These constitute the heart of a successful alliance, and it takes a lot of time to nurture and develop them. These extend beyond the formal legal contract, and the enthusiasm displayed by the initial deal makers should gradually penetrate various parts of the organisation. Trust is probably the single most important ingredient. Partners need to learn how much they can trust each other.

(6) *Disputes.* There must be recognition that difficult matters must be placed on the table for serious discussion.

(7) *Review and exit strategy.* This is something that ought to be considered at the outset, and there should be a facility for renewing licences after a period of time. For example, if conditions 1 or 2 were to change, it could provide for a parting of the ways without having to resort to court action.

(8) *Implementation.* Ensure that the alliance is well led and properly managed, and that there is sensitivity to the changes that are taking place in the external environment. It goes without saying that progress should be reviewed regularly. Also, consider matters such as cultural incompatibilities. For example, a British company may be rather impatient with the lengthy and involved decision-making process in a Japanese company that is its partner.

Douma et al. (2000) emphasise other points concerning strategic alliances. Alliances, especially in intensive technology industries, can lead to learning races that can quickly erode the very foundation of the alliance. For the alliance to succeed the partners need to agree on the future shape of the industry and the impact this will have on their individual corporate strategies. There should be active liaison and discussion, not just at the early stages but also throughout the life of the alliance. Finally, alliances should be seen as dynamic rather than static, where partners learn from their mistakes and revive and improve the relationship.

---

to a rapidly changing environment became very difficult, but the company managed to survive after a period of major restructuring and refocusing within its markets. Other companies were not so lucky. An example of a company that developed a structure and product that fitted well with the emerging environment is Microsoft under the direction of Bill Gates. Companies like Microsoft fill a new niche in the market-place and attract business from established companies over time.

Hannan and Freeman (1977), the originators of the population ecology perspective, state that many limitations are placed on the ability of organisations to change in order to survive. These limitations spring from a variety of quarters, such as a reluctance to change due to a heavy past investment in plant, equipment, and specialised staff; the track record of the organisation that justifies the current procedures; the mindset and disposition of decision makers; limited information; and the perceived difficulty of changing corporate culture. True organisational transformation is a rare and unlikely event because of the difficulty in surmounting these barriers or limitations. Finally, the analysis used in the population ecology perspective tends to be at a highly abstract level, and the perspective may be of little assistance to the manager because there is little explanation of why some organisations survive and others perish (Bedeian & Zammuto, 1991).

Technology

Scholars interested in the impact of contingency factors on organisational design point to technology—the application of mechanical and mental processes to work—as having a major effect on the way activities are structured. This subsection is devoted to a discussion of the contribution of the technology theorists—Woodward, Burns and Stalker, Thompson, Perrow, and Hall—together with the Aston studies on size and technology. The impact of advanced technology is discussed in the section beginning on page 484.

Woodward's research

To test the applicability of the classical theory of organisation discussed earlier, Woodward (1965) conducted a research study into the relationship between technology and the organisational features of a number of industrial enterprises in Essex, UK. The main theme of her findings is the influence of technology or production systems on shaping organisational characteristics, though the importance of the history of the firm and those who built it up cannot be discounted. The technology identified was manufacturing technology, and firms were classified as follows:

- *Unit and small batch production.* This amounted to one-off items, or a small number of units produced.
- *Large batch and mass production.* More complicated than unit and small batch production, this involved producing standardised parts in very large batches. It is the type of technology used in car assembly plants.
- *Process production.* This was the most complex form of technology studied, where a continuous stream of the same product is manufactured, as in the production of liquids and gases. This classification covers the oldest and simplest production system (unit and small batch) to, at that time, the most up-to-date and sophisticated (process production).

When firms were classified in accordance with the different systems of production technology,

a strong relationship was found between organisation structure and success within each category. In other words, successful firms within a particular production system shared common organisational characteristics. The firms at the extreme ends of the production technology continuum (i.e., unit and small batch and process production), tended to have organic structures, whereas the firms in the middle of the continuum (i.e., large batch and mass production), tended to be mechanistically structured and accorded more closely with the recipe for the organisational form advanced by the classical theorists. Other features of organisation peculiar to firms differentiated by production technology are set out in Panel 14.9. Hodgetts (1991) provides a comparison of some of the organisational characteristics that existed among the successful companies in each of the three production categories (see Table 14.6).

In a later study, Woodward (1970) concentrated her attention on the impact of variations in products, rather than production systems, on organisation design. She tentatively suggested that the nature of management control systems influences organisational structures and behaviour.

It is now over 40 years since the late Joan Woodward developed her classification scheme for production technology. There are those who feel that her classification scheme is still useful for analysing manufacturing organisations, but some critics argue that her production categories are simplistic and fail to capture the true nature of technological complexity (Bedeian & Zammuto, 1991). However, the link between structure and technology is an interesting one. There is now a view that strategy should be added to structure and technology and that these three variables should be aligned, especially when external competitive conditions change. A number of researchers have suggested that the strength of many Japanese firms in many industries can be attributable to a close alignment between strategy, structure, and technology (Schroeder, Congden, & Gopinath, 1995).

Finally, it is interesting to note that in the late 1990s two researchers sought to determine whether Woodward's theory—developed for different technologies—could be of value in an age

PANEL 14.9: Features of firms differentiated by production technology

- Decentralisation was more prominent in process production firms than in large batch and mass production firms.
- Management by committee or group decision making was more common in process production firms, where communication tended to be more in verbal form.
- Communication in large batch and mass production firms tended to be more in written form. Resorting to written communication in large batch and mass productions firms was said to be in some way influenced by the less congenial organisational circumstances associated with this production system.
- The executives working in the large batch and mass production firms displayed greater drive and ambition, but appeared to be subjected to greater stress.
- In the process production firms the quality of industrial relations was very much in evidence, probably due to people feeling less tension and pressure; also, there existed smaller working groups, and a narrower span of control.
- In the large batch and mass production firms the relationships between line managers and staff specialists left much to be desired. Line managers tended to produce memoranda to safeguard themselves in case of comeback on a particular issue by staff specialists. This friction was exemplified in conflicts between accountants (staff specialists) and production managers (line managers). By contrast, there were no significant differences in attitudes or outlook between staff specialists and line managers in process production firms, allegedly because of the high level of interchangeability between line and staff roles. Neither were there problems in unit and small batch production firms, because there was no clear-cut distinction between these two organisational roles—i.e., technical expertise was embraced by the line manager.
- Production control procedures, with some exceptions, were well defined and rigid in large batch and mass production firms, and this had the effect of generating operating instructions, memoranda, and policy directives at a level of magnitude not found in unit and small batch and process production firms. In fact it was difficult to control production and make predictions about outcomes in unit and small batch production firms, and of course the in-built production control mechanisms made the task of control easier in process production firms.

(Woodward, 1965)

TABLE 14.6

Comparison of organisational characteristics among the successful firms in Woodward's (1965) research study (from Hodgetts, 1991)

Organisational characteristics	Unit and small batch production	Large batch and mass production	Process production
Number of employees controlled by first-line supervisors	Small	Large	Small
Relationship between work groups and supervisor	Informal	Formal	Informal
Basic type of workers employed	Skilled	Semi- and unskilled	Skilled
Definition of duties	Often vague	Clear-cut	Often vague
Degree of delegation of authority	High	Low	High
Use of participative management	High	Low	High
Type of organisational structure	Flexible	Rigid	Flexible

characterised by the application of **just-in-time** techniques (Kalagnanam & Lindsay, 1998).

Burns and Stalker's research

Around the same time as Woodward was publishing her findings, another study conducted by Burns and Stalker (1961) investigated 20 industrial companies in England and Scotland to establish how changes in the technological and market environment affected organisation structure and management processes. The companies ranged from a rayon manufacturer operating in a very stable environment to an electronics company operating in a very volatile and unpredictable environment.

TABLE 14.7

Mechanistic and organic structures (adapted from Burns & Stalker, 1961)

Mechanistic system	Organic system
• Organisational tasks are broken down into specialised functions with each employee performing his or her individual jobs without much concern for the overall aims of the organisation.	• Structure has networks based on interests. There appears to be a greater sense of purpose when employees perform their job, with a commitment to the achievement of the goals of the organisation as a whole.
• The duties, rights, obligations, and privileges associated with each job are defined clearly.	• There seems to be less emphasis on defining jobs clearly, and also less of a tendency to stress the status attached to jobs.
• Communication between superiors and subordinates takes place on a vertical basis on matters connected with work. The chain of command is very much in evidence with instructions and directives coming down and feedback going up.	• Employees communicate and relate to each other on a horizontal as well as a vertical basis.
• It is considered legitimate for control and direction to be exercised by senior management, the assumption being that all relevant knowledge is located at the apex of the organisation. The culture of the organisation is typified by an inward-looking perspective, with an emphasis on loyalty and obedience.	• The issuing of directives and instructions by supervisors is of lesser importance than a management process based on consultation and discussion.

Mechanistic and organic structures. The major outcome of the Burns and Stalker study is the categorisation of firms along a continuum, with mechanistic organisation at one end and organic organisation at the other. A mechanistic structure seemed appropriate to a company operating under relatively stable conditions, whereas an organic structure was more relevant to conditions of change, when technology and markets are likely to become unstable and less predictable. Definitions of organic and mechanistic systems are set out in Table 14.7.

In Table 14.8 the different types of companies in the Burns and Stalker study are placed on the mechanistic–organic continuum, with the highly structured bureaucratic organisations on the left, and the organisations with the in-built flexibility on the right (Hodgetts, 1991). The message coming across from this research is that if a company previously operating in a stable environment moves into a turbulent environment, this would necessitate a movement from a mechanistic to an organic form of organisation in order to ensure successful performance.

A prominent feature of the mechanistic system is the precise prescription of the duties involved in various jobs, whereas the lack of a precise prescription and the existence of a significant degree of discretion can be found in the organic system. However, the lack of a precise definition of what a role requires could have dysfunctional effects. Burns and Stalker recognised this when they maintained that managers operating within the organic system were not always sure what they were responsible for because they did not realise the full extent of their authority. Neither did they feel sure of the status of their position within the hierarchy. As a result, they experienced personal anxiety and insecurity. The other extreme—a mechanistic system—is not without its drawbacks. After all, the precise prescription of work roles could be construed as rigid and inflexible which, for some people, could have an alienating effect.

More recent work dealing with this theme broadens the perspective. Apart from structure, the type of job and individual needs are also considered (Porter & Lawler, 1975; Vecchio & Keon,

TABLE 14.8

The position of companies on the Burns and Stalker (1961) mechanistic–organic continuum

Stable ←————————————————— *Type of environment* —————————————————→ Least predictable

Rayon mill	Electrical engineering	Radio and TV manufacturing	Other electronics firms	Electronics development manufacturer
Highly structured	Somewhat flexible structure	Relatively flexible structure	Flexible structure	Very flexible structure
Standing plans	Contingency plans for meeting special eventualities	No organisational charts	No organisational charts	No organisational charts
Carefully defined roles and tasks		No great degree of role definition or job specialisation	De-emphasis on job descriptions	No job descriptions
			Reliance on informal cooperation and teamwork	Emphasis on teamwork and interpersonal interaction to ensure goal attainment

1981). For example, individuals who seek challenge and responsibility at work—i.e., they wish to satisfy higher-level human needs—are more likely to prefer relatively enriched jobs that are capable of stretching them. Such jobs fall more into line with an organic rather than a mechanistic system of organisation.

The book containing the research evidence of Burns and Stalker was reissued in the mid-1990s, 33 years after it was first published. It was praised by a highly respected journalist (now deceased) in the management field for the quality of its ideas, which he said had a profound impact on contemporary theory and practice (Lorenz, 1994b).

Technology and size

Research carried out at the University of Aston, Birmingham (the Aston studies) examined a number of factors likely to influence the structure of organisation in 52 firms. Attention was directed at the transformation of organisational inputs into outputs, and the flow of work (workflow integration). Technology was divided into three categories:

- *Operations technology.* This type of technology refers to techniques used in the process of transforming inputs into outputs.
- *Materials technology.* The focus here is on the specific features of the materials used, such as availability, ease of machining, hardness, and so on.
- *Knowledge technology.* This refers to the soft side of technology, and is concerned with the specific nature, level of sophistication, and complexity of the knowledge required to do the job.

Size, dependence, and specialisation. The importance of technology as an influential factor determining the structure of the organisation was played down, but size, and dependence (i.e., the dependent relationship the organisation has with, for example, a holding company, suppliers, customers, etc.) were mentioned in the research as factors truly influencing structural dimensions. Size was considered earlier in this chapter as an important internal environmental factor. In the Aston studies it was size, rather than technology, that bore the strongest relationship to the following dimensions:

- specialisation (number of specialised roles and activities);
- standardisation of procedures and roles;
- formalisation (the extent to which material appears in written form, such as policies, rules, and procedures); and
- centralisation.

However, technology was related to features of structure within its orbit—i.e., close to the shop floor (Pugh, Hickson, Hinings, & Turner, 1969). A feature of bureaucratic organisation that seemed to influence other bureaucratic tendencies was role specialisation. This means that organisations with many specialists tended to have more standard routines, more documentation, and, as you would expect, a large hierarchy of staff specialists. The same degree of influence was not exerted by centralisation, leaving the researchers to conclude that centralisation cannot be considered an essential feature of bureaucracy (Pugh, Hickson, Hinings, & Turner, 1968). The influence of size in shaping the hierarchy has also been endorsed by Blau and Schoenherr (1971). They found that more specialisation, more formalisation, more layers in the hierarchy, and larger spans of control are associated with increasing size.

Although economies of scale in manufacturing accrue to larger organisations, some large companies seemed to have challenged the notion that bigness is better in production units. The reasons stated ("Small is beautiful", 1984) are: a lower magnitude of investment is required for the smaller plant; a diminishing need to produce a variety of products; a resolve to reduce the number of layers in the hierarchy with fewer lines of communication; and in a number of situations the smaller plant was said to create improved teamwork, to increase productivity, and generate higher profits.

Thompson's research

The classification of technology proposed by Thompson (1967) is long-linked, mediating, and intensive.

- *Long-linked.* This type of technology consists of operations that flow in sequence, with one operation feeding the other. A good example is the assembly line in a car manufacturing plant.
- *Mediating.* This type of technology links different units of the organisation or different types of clients. For example, a building society or bank draws its clientele from investors and borrowers. It resorts to various procedures and controls, within its formal rules, to bring together the two sides of the business. Nowadays, it relies heavily on information technology to assist with this task.
- *Intensive.* This type of technology uses skills and resources in a focused and unique way to accomplish an organisational task. An organisation has its standard procedures, but clients of the organisation must be dealt with individually. For example, in a dental surgery the practitioner deals with the patient in a unique way, using skills and resources with reference to that patient's problem and the way he or she is responding to the course of treatment.

Thompson mentions that organisations design structures to protect their dominant technology. For example, a warehousing facility permits the build-up of manufacturing output and allows the production technology system to operate at a steady state at a time when demand for the product is seasonal or cyclical.

Perrow's research

The classification used by Perrow (1970) is the routine–nonroutine continuum. This categorisation process applies to all organisations, not just to manufacturing companies. Routine technology would be amenable to circumstances where, generally speaking, there exist familiar situations (e.g., a high level of predictability) lending themselves to rational analysis and solution. In these conditions a pronounced degree of formalisation and centralisation can be found, reinforced by low interdependency between work groups, with planning used as a coordinating mechanism. Routine technology could be used, for example, by a company in the manufacture of toothpaste.

Where situations are unfamiliar, and there are no well-established procedures to solve the

TABLE 14.9

Technological systems in relation to flexibility of response

Inflexibility ←————————————————————————————→ Flexibility

Woodward	Large batch/mass production	Unit or small batch products	Process production
Burns & Stalker	Mechanistic		Organic
Thompson	Long-linked	Mediating	Intensive
Perrow	Routine		Nonroutine
Hall	Bureaucratic		Organic

problems (i.e., situations that invite the use of discretion), the technology is nonroutine. This type of technology could be used in the research and development function of a pharmaceutical company. The organisational climate in this setting is likely to be characterised by a flexible system, with much interdependency between work groups and coordination through mutual adjustment. (The latter was explained earlier in the chapter when discussing Mintzberg's work.) There are similarities between Perrow's model and that of Burns and Stalker.

Hall's research

Whereas Woodward's research looked at the influence of technology among organisations (inter-organisational), Hall (1962) was only interested in the impact of technology within organisations (intra-organisational). The research was conducted among five commercial or industrial organisations and five government agencies. He found that departments dealing with situations that do not vary, such as assembly-line work or routine administrative tasks, tended to adopt features of Weber's bureaucratic model (e.g., a hierarchy of authority, division of labour, and procedures for processing work). A more flexible structure was compatible with nonroutine events such as advertising and research. Hall's study substantiates the research of Burns and Stalker, because he established that generally a mechanistic system of organisation (bureaucratic) is more appropriate for routine work, and organic structures more suited for the effective performance of nonroutine work.

A theme running through the empirical work of the technology theorists is the flexibility of the technological system in response to various pressures. The technological systems could be placed on a continuum, ranging from flexibility at one end to inflexibility at the other end. This is shown in Table 14.9.

There may be a tendency to think of the relatively simple technologies (e.g., unit or small batch production systems) as not availing of developments in high technology. But this could be a misleading impression. For in the manufacture of, for example, custom-made products, there are numerous situations where new technology capable of producing a computerised flow of information about the production process goes hand-in-hand with unit or small batch technology (Lengnick-Hall, 1986).

Strategic choice

The importance of contingency factors in organisational design was endorsed empirically in the studies reported above; in other words, decisions to design the organisation were determined by the impact of environment, technology, and size. However, there is an influential view that decision makers at top management level make choices about the strategic direction of the company and, in the process, determine the structure of the organisation. As a consequence, managerial ideology and influence act as intervening variables in the relationship between structure and the major contingency factors of environment, technology, and size (Child, 1972; Montanari, 1978).

FIGURE 14.4

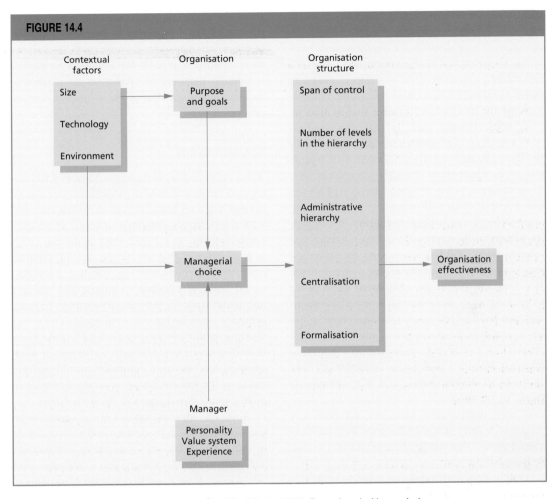

The mediating effect of strategic choice (from Bobbitt & Ford, 1980). Reproduced with permission.

This proposition can be expanded to form a "strategic choice model" of organisational effectiveness, as shown in Figure 14.4. In this model the strategic or managerial choices as far as organisation structure is concerned are influenced by the major contingency factors, both directly and indirectly through the purposes and goals of the organisation, and by certain characteristics of the manager (Bobbitt & Ford, 1980). The effectiveness of the organisation will then rest on the fit between the major contingency factors (contextual factors), strategies influenced by both organisational and managerial considerations, and structural features of organisation. Child (1997)

re-examined the place of the strategic choice perspective in the study of organisations, and considered its contemporary contribution. He maintains that despite the dramatic change in the way theorists have examined organisations over the 25 years since the strategic choice first developed, the concept is still relevant.

Once structure follows strategic considerations, there is always the potential for structure (e.g., centralisation, formalisation of rules and procedures) to reciprocate by influencing strategic decision making (Fredrickson, 1986). The strategy –structure fit was very much in evidence as UK corporations, such as British Airways, prepared themselves for privatisation in the 1980s. A likely course of action by top management in these circumstances is to simplify the organisational hierarchy, eliminate layers of management, dismiss a significant proportion of the workforce, and bring about a cultural shift, such as rewarding management on the basis of merit rather than seniority.

A contemporary view is that organisations with a strategy to promote innovation will opt for flexible systems normally associated with organic structures where there is a strong emphasis on a loose structure, less pronounced division of labour, lower levels of specialisation and formalisation, and a strong focus on decentralisation. The opposite situation—pronounced division of labour and specialisation, with high levels of formalisation and centralisation—characterises a mechanistic structure and might be considered appropriate when a company goes through a period of rationalisation and cost reduction. Of course there could be a situation where organic and mechanistic co-exist. For example, tight controls apply to ongoing activities and looser controls to new ventures or developments, and this scenario is likely to be acceptable to imitators—i.e., those who copy others' good ideas and produce new products or enter new markets once they are convinced there is demand for these products (Galunic & Eisenhardt, 1994).

Finally, the contingency approach to organisation structure has been criticised as being unrealistic because of the expectation that a manager modifies the structure in a rational manner after observing and registering a change in a contingency factor (Moorhead & Griffin, 2004). In practice this would be an exceedingly difficult, if not impossible task. However, Donaldson (1987) provides a defence of contingency theory, and argues that where there is a deficiency in the performance of the organisation due to a failure to respond adequately to changes in one or more contingency factors, one can expect an appropriate organisational response.

Donaldson (1997) continues to defend the contingency perspective, and argues that wide choice is exercised over organisational forms. Organisational structure is seen to be highly determined by the situation (i.e., situational factors). He is cynical about the developing structure–action framework (the belief that free choice is available to actors) in organisation studies. He goes on to say that the more fruitful approach for organisation studies is through pursuing the positivist approach (the traditional empirical approach found in contingency theory).

New technology

When reflecting on the current impact of technology on the structure of organisations, one should acknowledge its broad influence, which contrasts with the narrower emphasis in terms of production technology in the past. Back in the late 1950s it was forecast that computers would promote centralised decision making, because computers would make it possible to collect and transmit information quickly to enable decisions to be made centrally on a better-informed basis. There was also the prediction that considerable economies in staffing levels could be achieved at middle management level because computers would perform many of the information-processing activities of middle managers (Leavitt & Whisler, 1958).

A decade later, the impact of the computer on management was considered in a study conducted in the services industry (insurance companies), and it was argued strongly that computers were likely to increase the centralisation of systems of control in organisations. This applied to clerical functions, and the computer was seen to have a number of capabilities (Whisler, 1970). The computer ties together and integrates areas of decision making and control that were previously relatively independent of one another. Computers monitor, correct, and adjust actions over a much broader area than could be achieved by any human group. And, because of the pyramidal structure of business organisations, the integrative function of computing contributes to the centralisation of control, with a wider span of control for senior managers.

The evidence provided by Whisler, which relates to clerical functions in the service industry, was challenged by evidence from a study of the impact of the computer in a manufacturing industry context (Blau, Falbe, McKinley, & Tracey,

1976). The use of on-site computers was associated with the decentralisation of operational decisions, particularly in granting autonomy to plant managers. But it was pointed out that the physical location of the computer can influence the level of management at which decisions are made; a central location gives rise to centralisation, but where computer systems were distributed throughout the organisation a decentralisation process develops. This accorded with the trend at that time to use more powerful individual microcomputers, which are relatively cheap, and can be easily placed on the executive's desk. The hardware is accompanied by more sophisticated software (e.g., financial modelling) and networking.

Subsequently, the centralisation versus decentralisation debate had been somewhat muted. There was a view at one time that computer applications over a long period were confined to routine accounting and administrative activities, and that there have been no significant changes in the organisational levels at which management decisions were made (Robey, 1977). However, other more recent evidence suggests that we have to be discriminating in the way we view the impact of the computer on the management process and the level at which decisions are made. This could mean that in certain circumstances centralisation is facilitated, but equally in other situations delegation may be assisted.

With new technology in the field of information-processing it is possible to communicate information quickly over a wide area. If that information is based on data input of an accurate and reliable nature, senior managers may not have to rely on middle management and lower-level employees for control information or its interpretation, provided the information can be transmitted from the local area of operations. For example, the scanning of bar-coded or magnetically ticketed items in retailing establishments results in transmitting control data on the itemised sales—i.e., sales registered and outstanding stock—to the store manager and to the central buying department at the company's head office.

Therefore, centralisation is encouraged, particularly when current and comprehensive information is transmitted directly to senior management who, according to Reed (1989), are now in a position to unify and coordinate previously fragmented control systems, thereby justifying a compressed and simplified organisational hierarchy because of the likely removal of layers of middle management. However, in these circumstances one should be aware of the need to use computer programs, if available, to integrate data and draw key analyses from them, otherwise the problem of information overload and complexity for senior managers will pose difficulties. Other influences that account for centralisation are the managerial ethos of the organisation, particularly in those where entrepreneurial or family control is evident, and when production operations are fairly standardised and conditions in the organisation are not complex (Child 1984a; Robey, 1977).

Apart from the centralisation effect, information technology could be used to facilitate more effective delegation. This could be achieved in the following ways:

(1) Units of the organisation could be linked to form a common network, whereby each unit is made more aware of what other units are doing. This promotes awareness of the wider consequences of decisions taken by a particular unit. The local unit is able to inform other units and the central unit of its intentions and obtain rapid feedback. In this way consultation is facilitated, and the local unit is made aware of the intentions of the centre with regard to intervention. The end result could be a reduction in ambiguity and this is likely to encourage local initiatives and discourage intervention from the centre.

(2) The improved analytical facilities offered by information technology—e.g., programs for sensitivity analysis and financial modelling—can enhance the capacity of local units to make sound judgements in the decision-making process. But, as mentioned earlier, the potential of information technology must be married with reliable information or data so that real benefits can be gained. Prior to the onset of the era of information technology, information-processing capacity of a sophisticated nature normally resided at

senior levels of the organisation where specialist staff could be called on to assist senior managers.

Huber (1990) had something to say about both centralisation and decentralisation when he maintained that new information technology will have an equalising effect on power distribution within organisations. People at the lower levels of the organisation will have more information than ever before, and therefore highly centralised structures become less prevalent because people are better able to question decisions. On the other hand, highly decentralised structures will be diluted as senior managers have better access to information that either did not exist previously, or alternatively was not easily accessible.

In what way is information technology likely to have an impact on the role of the manager? Child (1987) maintains that managers and similar employees will be subjected to pressures for simplification and standardisation of their tasks (something that was previously reserved for blue-collar workers), with a possible loss of autonomy. The introduction of computers could lead to a situation where the manager becomes less involved in the collection of information for the purposes of dissemination, simply because other members of the organisation may now have access to information previously denied to them. By reducing managerial tasks that are connected with the monitoring of information, interpersonal contacts between managers and others (an essential feature of the traditional managerial role) may become less important.

This could result in changes in the way people perceive the role of the manager (Eason, 1980). Likewise, it could lead to a diminution of management control when nonmanagerial staff have access to comprehensive and well-structured information (Oborne, 1994). However, there will always be a group of managers somewhere in the organisation, perhaps near the top, whose managerial control will not be undermined by the development of automated information systems; and, of course, there will be others who will experience an increase in their managerial or

supervisory control simply because, with the aid of technology, they are better able to monitor the activities of employees—e.g., the quality of work, costs, and revenue (Kling & Scacchi, 1980).

On this theme, Child (1984b) identified three factors to consider when examining the impact of technological change on occupational groups:

(1) White-collar workers are more likely to control the application of new technology to their own jobs if they occupy a crucial role in decisions about its adoption.

(2) The strength of white-collar groups in the labour market has a material influence on the strength of their position with respect to negotiations about proposals to introduce new technology. In this context, a factor to note is the strength of professional groups to counteract bureaucratic interference with their own concept of what constitutes good professional practice.

(3) Where there is a strong tradition favouring the quality of service based on the personal touch, this could act as a powerful force against attempts to de-skill and automate jobs on grounds of cost. Branch bank managers and officials as a group do not seem to be strategically placed to resist a rationalisation process within the structure of the organisation that could lead to the de-skilling of jobs with the application of modern technology. By contrast, members of the medical profession (e.g., doctors in the hospital service), are better placed organisationally and institutionally to control the advent of technological innovation. This group in the UK has the advantage of having the backing of the influential British Medical Association.

Child and Loveridge (1990) conducted a major study that examined the introduction of information technology (IT) into three areas of service activity—domestic banking, hospital laboratories, and retailing. A particular aspect of the study was the focus on decision-making processes resulting in the choice of IT systems for the organisation, and how these systems would be applied to the work of employees. Among their findings was that employee participation in decisions related to the introduction of new technology had a bearing on the way it was used; the organisational politics surrounding the introduction of IT could lead to a certain resistance to learning to use the new technology in creative ways; and that this resistance was fuelled by the powers enjoyed by different groups within organisations. Scarborough and Corbett (1992) also acknowledge the influence of power.

New manufacturing technology today includes robots, numerically controlled machine tools, and computerised software for product design, engineering analysis, and remote control of machinery. Daft (2004), reflecting on the impact of the new technology—computer integrated manufacturing and advanced information technologies—on organisation, states that for the most part the impact is positive, with shifts towards more organic structures both on the shop floor and in the management hierarchy. These technologies replace routine jobs, give employees more autonomy, produce more challenging jobs, create fewer organisational layers and encourage teamwork, support the trend towards networking (using computer technology to quickly share information and cooperate on projects within and between organisations), and allow the organisation to be more flexible and responsive. Perhaps Daft is rather idealistic when he concludes that the new technologies are enriching jobs to the point where organisations are happier places within which to work.

In connection with networking, one should note that the "intranet", which is the fastest growing form of corporate networking, makes it possible for the "virtual organisation" to take root. In this type of organisation, key activities are performed by headquarters—the nerve cell of the organisation—with other functions outsourced to separate companies or individuals connected electronically to the central office. The speed and ease of electronic communication makes networking a good way to expand operations and keep costs down. More will be said about the virtual organisation later in this chapter.

REFLECTIONS ON ORGANISATION THEORY

The diversity of perspectives on organisational analysis is apparent. However, it would appear that the development of contingency approaches is worth pursuing. One is aware that there are a number of scholars from the sociological tradition who draw our attention to the unsatisfactory state of organisation theory. Reed (1992), in the introductory chapter to an iconoclastic treatise on organisation studies, makes the point that "most of the crucial theoretical questions and substantive issues which define organisational analysis as an identifiable and viable field of study seem to be matters of considerable dispute, not to say deep controversy". Having read the remaining chapters by various contributors, Reed asserts that "diversity, plurality, uncertainty, and fragmentation seem to be the epithets which most easily and readily spring to mind when attempting to provide a general characterisation of the current state of play, in, and future prospects for, organisational analysis".

Postmodern organisation

Clegg (1990a) compares the modernist with the postmodernist organisation. The first is the type of organisation with which we are familiar and that has been analysed in the chapter up to this point. It tends to be rigid, caters for mass markets, and gives pride of place to technological determinism (as we found in contingency theory). There are also highly differentiated functions and jobs (as in classical theory), and a generous sprinkling of job demarcation and de-skilling (Taylorism). Postmodernist organisations are flexible with niche markets, and are the opposite of modernist organisations with respect to differentiation, demarcation, and skill, while actors (key employees) exercise choice as far as the use of technology is concerned (absence of technological determinism).

The postmodernist critique of organisations also recognises that there are multiple and competing views of organisation that are legitimate. It appears everything is open to question and there are always alternative explanations in conditions of diversity. Those advocating this approach have not much time for the modernist view of the existence of a universal objective truth that can be discovered by research methods, often referred to as rational and scientific, which the contingency theorists would like to think they use. The postmodernists recognise that we construct reality as we go along after indulging in self-reflection, aided by the use of language.

In a conversation with a prominent organisation theorist (Professor John Child) in the UK in Devon in August 2001, it was suggested by him that there are two types of postmodernism:

> The first maintains that we have progressed, or should progress, beyond the nineteenth century belief that the world is advancing and converging towards some eventual state of modern civilisation, underpinned by a bureaucracy in the Weberian mould that applies the same rules fairly and honestly to all and guarantees an acceptable order in society. While recognising that bureaucracy and the standardisation it represented had some virtues, adherents of this postmodern perspective argue that the modern approach fails to accommodate the huge variety of local cultural and material needs in society and the sheer speed at which these are evolving.
>
> The second variant of postmodernism goes much further in the direction of seeking to deconstruct the institutions and organisations (and even the language associated with them) that we have taken more or less for granted in the recent past. It regards these as justifying and maintaining an essentially exploitative social order through the ways in which organisations are constituted and the ideology of corporate capitalism that lulls us into taking them for granted. This variant of postmodernism maintains that what each individual says and does is equally valid, and as such it is fundamentally opposed to any form of organisation except for the purely spontaneous and voluntary.

I find the first variant of postmodernism acceptable and constructive in helping us understand so-called new and evolving forms of organisation, as well as the wider cultural and other shifts in society they reflect. It is broadly the approach that Stewart Clegg adopts in his 1990 book on postmodern organisation. I don't find the second variant acceptable, either academically or in terms of the state of society to which it would lead us, for I believe it is likely to lead us to a kind of Hobbesian world in which everyone would be at war with everyone else. I view the first variant as espousing variety and creativity, and arguing for freedom, whereas I fear that the second espouses anarchy and threatens an eventual loss of freedom, which is ironic in view of its aspirations.

NEW ORGANISATIONAL PATTERNS

The concepts examined in this section on contemporary developments in organisations are, in a number of instances, interrelated. They consist of the network organisation, the virtual organisation, the boundaryless organisation, outsourcing, downsizing and delayering, team-based organisation, the flexible firm, just-in-time, and features of organisational design in manufacturing companies (e.g., lean production systems and high-performance systems).

Drucker (1988) maintained that the typical business in 2008:

> will have fewer than half the levels of its counterpart today, and no more than a third the number of managers. The typical future business will be knowledge-based, an organisation composed largely of specialists who direct and discipline their own performance through organised feedback from colleagues, customers, and headquarters. For this reason, it will be what I call an information-based organisation . . . We can perceive, though perhaps only dimly, what this organisation will look like, but the job of building the information-based organisation is the managerial challenge of the future.

Network organisation

According to Miles and Snow (1986), strong competitive pressures (e.g., globalisation, technical change, deregulation, and changing workforce demographics) will eventually create a new organisational form—a unique combination of strategy, structure, and management processes referred to as the dynamic network. Here there would be heavy reliance on self-managed groups and a greater willingness to view organisational boundaries and membership as highly flexible. Taking stock of the situation, Snow, Miles, and Coleman (1992) make the following observations:

> Multi-level hierarchies are giving way to clusters of business units, co-ordinated by market mechanisms rather than by layers of middle management planners and schedulers. These market-guided entities that are flexible with the potential for rapid response are now commonly called "network organisations" . . . Companies could focus on things they do especially well, "outsourcing" a growing collection of goods and services, and getting rid of assets that produce low returns. For example, one company in the network may research and design a product, another may engineer and manufacture it, a third may handle distribution, and so on. Competitive forces are brought to bear on each element of the product or service value chain.

Reflecting on the network organisation, Birkinshaw (2000) makes an interesting point:

> It is a common misconception to talk about the network organization as an alternative to the "organizational groupings" [which were discussed earlier]. In reality the network organization is best seen as an informal overlay that cuts across whatever formal structure is chosen. Volvo Cars is described as a network organization because it has strong project groups that cut across functions, as well as cross-country teams. But it still has a chain of command that lies in product divisions (the car platforms). However, the network organization is a good idea because it gets away from the strict chains of command or "silos" that get in the way of fast and informed decision making.

Strictly speaking, there have always been network organisations to the extent that individual managers related to or communicated with colleagues in other areas. What is new about the contemporary network organisation is the emergence of tools and systems at the disposal of organisations to create such networks. Cross-functional teams, global business teams, dotted line reporting, project groups, and so on are all networking structures. Underlying them are computer systems, and employee transfer and retention policies, all of which are designed to make networking easier.

Network organisations are not only less costly to operate, they are also more agile. By limiting operations to those functions for which the company has or can develop expert skill, and outsourcing functions that can be performed quicker, more effectively, or at lower cost by other companies, the organisation requires less planning and coordination. Also, the organisation can accelerate product and service innovations to keep pace with changes in the market-place. Finally, it is said that the network structure can reinvigorate companies in mature industries that are beginning to stagnate by enabling them to develop new products without substantial investment (Miles & Snow, 1995).

Network organisations are not free from shortcomings. One disadvantage could be little hands-on control. This is evident when operations are not under one roof and there is reliance on outside independent contractors to do the work. Another disadvantage is that companies can experience problems with quality control when many different subcontractors are involved. In addition, some companies have found that subcontractors raise prices dramatically once the company becomes dependent on their products or services (Brown, 1992), and that changes in the number of subcontractors (i.e., additions and deletions) can be disruptive. Equally disruptive is a situation when a subcontractor is going out of business, or there is a question mark over the loyalty of the subcontractor or crucial aspects of the latter's culture are compromised.

Virtual organisation

The **virtual organisation** has been defined as a network organisation with a small core of employees that outsources major business functions (Cascio, 2000). Management outsources all the primary functions of business and the organisational core is a small group of executives, assisted by computer network links, whose major function is to supervise and control activities that are carried out in-house and to coordinate relationships with other organisations that manufacture, distribute, and perform any other activities for the organisation. The coordination and control of external relations can be a time-consuming activity.

The features of the virtual organisation identified by Warner and Witzel (2004) are lack of physical space, reliance on communications technology, mobile work, hybrid forms, boundaryless and inclusive, and flexible and responsive:

- *Lack of physical space.* There are fewer buildings, and those that exist are geographically dispersed.
- *Reliance on communications technology.* Information communications technology (ICT) plays a major enabling role in the virtual organisation and could be considered its lifeblood. There are networks of communication supported by the internet (which enables many employees to share information simultaneously), intranet (private nets within large companies, which are effectively internal communication systems using special software and not available to the public), and extranet (an extended intranet accessible only to selected employees and authorised outsiders). There are also inter-organisational networks that facilitate contact between, for example, a company and its supplier.
- *Mobile work.* It matters less where work is physically located because of the use of communication networks. Therefore, people do not

have to work close to each other. For example, project teams in large multinational companies can draw on members located in different countries, without establishing physical contact.
- *Hybrid forms.* Often a feature of the virtual organisation is cooperation and collaboration between individuals or companies within a loose framework in order to achieve a mutual goal. Such hybrids can have a short- or long-term existence.
- *Boundaryless and inclusive.* Relationships cut across organisational boundaries. The virtual organisation can comprise a company working in close relationship with suppliers and distributors.
- *Flexible and responsive.* A clear feature of the virtual organisation is flexibility and responsiveness. Success is assured if the constituent elements of the virtual organisation are able to relate in a mutually beneficial way, and employees are able to work flexibly.

The potential benefits of the virtual organisation are seen in the way it makes possible the efficient coordination of activities across boundaries of time and space, a reduction in costs, a more flexible combination of activities, and the simplification of management (Child, 2005). But one should be aware of certain limitations. It is often said that a major disadvantage of the virtual organisation is that it reduces management control over important parts of the business. Child (2005) says there are concerns about the limitations of the virtual organisation, especially in terms of its capacity to stimulate learning and innovation, and the vulnerability that may arise from dependence on partners. In connection with the latter, Robbins (2003) makes the following point:

When you farm out your data processing, manufacturing, and other functions you make your capabilities available to your competitors. So virtualization of work diminishes competitive advantages. It leads to rapidly spreading commoditization of everything. Any function that an organization uses to achieve competitive advantage cannot be outsourced.

Boundaryless organisation

Note the reference to the boundaryless concept in the previous section. The term "boundaryless organisation" was actually developed by Jack Welch when he was CEO of GE to describe his vision of how he wanted the company to be. He intended to achieve this by eliminating vertical and horizontal boundaries within GE and also by the breakdown of external barriers between the company and its customers and suppliers. (Robbins, 2003). This he hoped would make GE a "big company/small company hybrid".

The basic ideology behind this boundaryless state is that of trying to eliminate the chain of command, having limitless spans of control, and replacing departments with empowered teams, with a heavy reliance on information computer technology (ICT). Jack Welch found that by removing vertical boundaries, the organisational hierarchy was considerably flattened, which in turn minimised status and rank. This could open the way for greater interaction by employees from different levels of the organisation and promote the practice of participative management and the use of 360-degree performance appraisal.

As for removal of horizontal boundaries, this was achieved by a process of replacing functional departments with cross-functional teams and organising activities around processes. The organisation could use cross-functional teams to work on, for example, new product development. In this type of setting budgets could be allocated to processes, not to functions or departments. Another way management could weaken barriers between functions is to promote lateral transfers, which would involve rotating employees into and out of different functional areas. The rationale for taking this line of action is to transform specialists into generalists.

Among the techniques available to weaken external boundaries are strategic alliances. The latter opens up a pathway to another organisation and offers employees from different organisations the opportunity to come together and work on joint projects. Strategic alliances were considered earlier in the chapter when the concept of "resource dependency" was examined. Another example is the involvement of customers in key organisational processes, such as the selection of staff. There is reference to this type of activity in the discussion of high-performance systems (customer-focused operating units) later in this chapter.

To achieve the boundaryless organisation is likely to be a Herculean challenge. Robbins (2003) quite rightly says that GE has not achieved the boundaryless state, and probably never will, but it has made significant progress towards the ideal form.

Outsourcing

Companies in Europe and the USA have been under a lot of pressure to reduce costs without compromising quality. Outsourcing opens the way to reduce labour costs significantly. It is a term used interchangeably with offshoring, and sometimes with business process outsourcing. Two types of outsourcing are to be found. One is the outsourcing of value chain operations, of which outsourcing the supply chain is the most important. The other is the outsourcing of support activities (research and development, human resource activities, etc.), which supports the value chain, rather than being an integral part of it (Child, 2005).

Companies such as Nike and Reebok in the USA have been successful by concentrating their strengths in designing and marketing the product, and contracting virtually all the manufacturing of their footwear to outside manufacturers or suppliers. Computer companies either purchase their hardware ready made or they buy in all the parts and get involved in the final assembly. In the case of Intel, the design of the processor takes place at two sites in the USA and in Asia. Manufacturing are carried out in the United States (Oregon and New Mexico) and Ireland. Assembly and testing are conducted in Costa Rica, Malaysia, and the Philippines. Intel managers who have the responsibility to coordinate projects across continents argue that a strong corporate culture (referred to in Chapter 15) is more important than ever in this type of organisational arrangement (London, 2004b).

Sainsbury's, the UK supermarket chain, embarked on a massive overhaul of its technology systems and discovered a number of them had not been updated for years and this was having an adverse effect on service to the customer and profitability. Accenture, a UK consultancy firm, took on Sainsbury's 800 IT staff in addition to 200 contractors working on the systems (Voyle, 2003). In recent years British Airways, HSBC, Prudential Insurance and British Telecommunications have switched a number of call centre jobs to India. However, some European countries stand to gain from the outsourcing trend, among them Ireland and countries in eastern Europe because of the closer cultural and linguistic links with other parts of Europe and the more convenient time zones. The Irish Republic has been a major beneficiary of the offshoring trend; it attracted an influx of investment from US and other companies over the past decade. East European countries are trying to follow Ireland's lead.

Unlike the situation in the USA and much of Europe, Japan has not outsourced many of its back-office jobs to organisations in foreign countries. Apart from the language problem, there is the uniqueness of the "customer language" used in Japan (Pilling, 2004). But hundreds of thousands of jobs (in call centres) have moved to remote parts of Japan. Outsourcing in Japan reflects growing competitive pressures and significant changes in the labour market. As companies cut costs, the traditional job-for-life culture is gradually giving way to a more contract-based system. Many companies in Japan like to keep quiet about their outsourcing. According to a spokesperson for IT it, a company that offers outsourcing services for information-related firms, many companies that outsource business are not too keen to disclose the fact that they are outsourcing, and want the end-user of the service to feel they are doing business with the company itself (Pilling, 2004).

Increasingly higher skilled jobs are being outsourced to developing countries, such as India. In May 2003 the mobile phone division of Siemens, the German company, designated Bangalore, India as its global software Research and Development Centre. Other examples are jobs requiring more complex financial skills, such as equity research and analysis or market research

for developing new business. Evalueserve, an outsourcing company located in Delhi, performs research for patent attorneys and consultancy firms in the USA. Novartis, the Swiss pharmaceutical company, employs 40 statisticians in Bombay, who process data on clinical research (Thottam, 2003).

According to Rao (2004), in countries such as India the growth in call centres has created a new breed of employee and a working environment centred round the night shift. Typically, call centre employees in India work at night to service clients in the USA and Europe, and this puts pressure on their working and home lives. In a survey by Dataquest, 40% of call centre employees reported sleep disorders, 19% suffered from eyesight problems, and 34% from digestion problems. Apparently, quite a few companies have encountered problems with their outsourcing arrangements, among them being poor communication, lack of trust, and unrealistic expectations about what could be achieved by outsourcing activities.

Outsourcing has become a sensitive issue politically in both the developed and developing countries. The transfer of business processes (e.g., accounting, human resources) and manufacturing from advanced countries to developing economies has generated popular resentment, particularly in the USA, where some politicians, unions, and lobby groups refer to it as an important cause of unemployment. Similar views have been attributable to commentators in France. In 2004 the French finance minister said people were scared and he wanted France to take the lead in discouraging "offshoring" where possible, and proposed a grant of €1 billion in tax breaks to companies that keep outsourceable manufacturing and service jobs in France, or to relocate them to one of 20 "competitive zones" to be established around the country (Crumley, 2004). A French company, Vivendi Universal, agreed to create two new call centres in France in response to the tax break proposal (Gumbel, 2004).

A report by the United Nations Conference on Trade and Development (UNCTAD) in September 2004 stated that while outsourcing business services is becoming a significant trend, most of it takes place domestically. Only 1% to 2% is done internationally, but it could be described as being at the foothills of a revolution (Gumbel, 2004).

Finally, can we expect any reversal of the offshoring trend? Perhaps we can on a selective basis. A leading Manchester-based manufacturer of control equipment used for measuring water flow, in which it is a world leader, is transferring production jobs from Thailand to the UK (where the wages are five times the level of Thailand) where it will use an automated production line at the company's home base. The chairman of the company is reported as saying that in spite of the disparity in labour costs it will be more effective to do certain kinds of production in Britain, partly because it can be controlled more easily by senior managers (Marsh, 2004).

There are obvious advantages stemming from outsourcing, such as allowing organisations to concentrate on what they do best, where there were previously operational difficulties with the activity or process earmarked for outsourcing, cost savings, and where access to valuable expertise is obtained. However, certain problems arising from outsourcing should be noted. These are loss of crucial skills or competencies, the unreliability of the suppliers, the latter exploiting the client's dependence on them, and lack of sufficient flexibility in outsourcing contracts to handle unusual situations (Child, 2005).

Downsizing and delayering

In the distant past a practice developed to increase the size of advisory or support staff to cope with complexity in the life of large organisations. More recently, large organisations faced with the possibility of becoming victims of corporate predators, or having to rationalise operations because of recessionary forces or to improve profitability, have cut back significantly on numbers of employees, generally in order to create leaner but healthier entities. Particular targets in this pruning exercise have been headquarters or corporate staff, who have become victims of what is called "organisational downsizing", i.e., reducing the size of corporate staff. For example, Mobil and AT&T (both large US corporations) have pruned headquarters and corporate staff drastically, with mixed

results (Moore, 1987). Downsizing has also been associated with an across-the-board reduction in the headcount. Some claim that downsizing will emaciate the organisation in certain key functions, whereas others point to positive outcomes in terms of faster decision making due to the existence of fewer management levels through which decisions pass for approval.

Downsizing and delayering are complementary in the sense that reducing hierarchical levels is a means to achieve downsizing. A flatter structure, obtained by a reduction in the number of layers in the management hierarchy, is justified as a means to simplify management structures, reduce bureaucracy, cut paths of communication, speed up decision making, and push responsibility to lower organisational levels (empowerment). Delayering makes an important impact on managers' lives. The flattening of the management hierarchy also reduces opportunities for promotion, and therefore could impose a restriction on career paths. On reflection, its real impact on career advancement for managers need not be negative, because delayering offers managers still in the organisation the opportunity to assume greater responsibility at an early point in their careers and also to receive favourable rewards for doing so (Child, 2005).

An important distinction is made between reactive downsizing and strategic downsizing. The former refers to situations in which employee reductions are made in response to external events (e.g., severe competition in the market-place) and short-term needs. This could be indiscriminate, across-the-board cuts without regard to a department's strategic value. Strategic downsizing, sometimes called "rightsizing", refers to a carefully thought out process and is designed to support the long-term organisational strategy. It could be associated with transforming the organisation, with the objective of introducing "lean production", business process re-engineering, focus on core competencies, or other aspects of organisational reform (Child, 2005).

To make the downsizing process more palatable, managers can consider voluntary programmes (based on incentives to leave), keeping people informed, allowing those whose services

---

PANEL 14.10: Altruistic action in the aftermath of downsizing

In the face of potential job losses due to downsizing, some companies have adopted a socially responsible stance. The measures they have taken are aimed at keeping people off the unemployment register and facilitating the transfer to new jobs. Companies, such as VW and Hewlett Packard, adopted flexible wage and working conditions in order to minimise the lay-off of employees and reduce costs; for example, laying people off for certain periods without pay, reducing the standard hours and wages, redeployment and retraining, voluntary severance, and confining recruitment, where possible, to internal sources.

In the UK, Pilkington Glass went through a process of massive restructuring in the face of technological and competitive forces that resulted in substantial job losses over a long period of time. The company was altruistic in setting up a trust, which sponsored job creation schemes. These schemes helped to provide advice on financing projects and securing office space, and have assisted nearly 1900 business start-ups and created 15,800 jobs.

In Germany, AEG-Olympia adopted a scheme not too far removed from the Pilkington type of initiative. In 1992 the company terminated production at its typewriter plant in Wilhelmshaven, which employed 2000 workers. The company met the cost of converting the old factory into a Technology Park, and redundant workers who wished to set up business there received two-thirds of their severance pay; the other third was invested in the business. In 1993 the Technology Park opened, initially providing office space for 14 start-up companies, which employed 900 former AEG-Olympia workers, and by 1996 the centre was home to 1500 workers engaged in light industry and services.

(Bilmes & Wetzker, 1996)

---

are dispensed with to leave the organisation with dignity and a suitable package of benefits, including access to an outplacement service. In order to reduce feelings of anger and grief during the transitional stage, off-the-site therapeutic workshops, training sessions and lectures could be made available (Brockner, 1992). The psychological dimension of downsizing is heavily underlined by Kets de Vries and Balazs (1996) when they focus on the cognitive and emotional effects. They examined the patterns of individual reactions, as opposed to the technical and procedural factors associated with narrowly based downsizing strategies. The critical constituents in their analysis are the victims (those who lost their jobs), the survivors (those staying with the company), and the executioners (those responsible for the implementation of downsizing). They offer practical recommendations on how to facilitate the downsizing process. In Panel 14.10 there is an account of socially responsible employers trying to prevent redundancies.

Increasingly the spotlight is on the predicament of the survivors (those who have still got a job). Greenhalgh (2002) has highlighted the following issues attributable to survivors subjected to poorly managed downsizing. A number of studies have shown that survivors of a poorly managed downsizing initiative are likely to feel anxiety and depression. Their work attitudes are also likely

to change and their commitment to the company will have largely disappeared. Their productivity will have taken a serious fall (unless their work lends itself to monitoring) and it is unlikely they will put in extra effort to ensure high quality or customer satisfaction. They are likely to resist change and innovation and could demand militancy from their trade unions. If good labour market opportunities exist, they may be inclined to go elsewhere. This could apply particularly to the better employees, who may be difficult to replace.

Greenhalgh also highlights aspects of a good downsizing programme. It gives people some control over their work lives. They are given choices wherever possible, even if the choice is an unattractive one, such as accepting an unwanted transfer or being asked to leave. For a number of years IBM was a model of industry best practice in providing an understanding of the process, even when market factors forced it into radical downsizing. As a standard operating procedure, IBM managers were briefed on every detail of the downsizing and were entrusted with explaining it to their staff. In addition to direct communication with management through the use of interviews, newsletters were also used to reinforce the message and to address questions asked by employees. Also, a hotline was set up whereby any employee would have a question answered within 24 hours. In addition, senior managers made themselves available whereby employees could have their concerns addressed directly. This was considered effective in discrediting the rumour mill. All the above processes were influential in tackling job insecurity.

Team structure

In Chapter 11 the concept of teamwork was discussed. When management uses teams as a central mechanism to coordinate activities, this is referred to as a team structure or horizontal organisation (Forrester & Drexler, 1999). One way in which delayering, referred to above, can be achieved is by the removal of layers in the hierarchy, making it possible to create teams and in doing so to encourage decentralisation of authority and initiative. In the traditional hierarchical structure authority is vested in the manager, and in the team-based structure authority it is vested in the team or work unit. An important consideration as far as the team structure is concerned is that teams are composed of members who have the necessary information, expertise, and authority to arrive at decisions and execute their responsibilities in an efficient manner.

In the team-based structure there is also a removal or dilution of barriers between departments and functions within the organisation as teams draw their membership from different functions, and this creates a situation whereby more frequent horizontal communication is facilitated. The use of cross-functional teams in an organisational setting can facilitate the coordination of major projects. Finally, a satisfactory outcome would be if the team structure were used to complement bureaucratic structures; that would mean the mechanistic system (formalisation/standardisation) could co-exist with the organic system (flexibility and rapid response).

The flexible firm

Handy (1989) saw organisations as becoming less labour intensive. In his "shamrock" organisation there are three major parts, namely core workers, contractual fringe, and part-time/short-term contract workers. The central core of knowledge-based workers control the main activities of slimmed down organisations. Value is added to the organisation through an input of knowledge and creativity from a core of well-informed employees (knowledge workers) who have ready access to relevant ideas and information. This concept is similar to what Drucker (1988) referred to earlier as the information-based organisation.

The core workers are referred to by Pollert (1988) as a group of employees with permanent employment contracts and job security; they are multi-skilled and able to perform a variety of functions—i.e., functional flexibility—which may cut across traditional occupational boundaries. Therefore, functional flexibility means significantly fewer demarcation lines between jobs. Functional flexibility has also been associated with teamwork. For example, at companies such as Birds Eye Walls, Hardy Spicer, and Cummings Engines, craft workers were moved from their specialist sections and integrated into production teams. Such practices may not be in widespread use in the older plants, though one would expect to find more flexibility in the greenfield sites.

Surrounding the core of knowledge workers would be the outside workers—a contractual fringe—operating on a subcontracting basis and paid a fee rather than a wage. The management of this group (periphery workers) is removed from the organisation that is receiving its services. At Toyota and Matsushita in Japan the research and development staff belong to the contractual fringe (Nakamoto, 1995). A further variation of the contractual fringe is the use of a part-time and flexible labour force. Although this group of temporary or casual workers are less costly for the organisation to employ, because their services will only be used to meet particular demands and released when they are no longer required, they lack job security and this may impact adversely on their motivation and commitment (Feldman, Doerpinghaus, & Turnley, 1994).

When an organisation makes use of the contractual fringe, it could be seen as taking advantage of what Atkinson called numerical flexibility (Pollert, 1988). The results of a research study conducted by Geary (1992) in Ireland indicated that numerical flexibility did not work as well as expected. Eventually, the use of temporary workers was minimised because of the negative side-effects. These shortcomings consisted of the costs of training, the problem of reduced commitment of the permanent workers following the introduction of the scheme, and conflict between the permanent and temporary workers.

Another form of flexibility is called financial flexibility, whereby the organisation adapts its labour costs to its financial circumstances (Pollert, 1988). For example, pay or income could be linked to profits made by the company (e.g., profit-related pay, which is discussed in Chapter 18). Pay could also be related to the performance of specific tasks (e.g., the fees paid to a subcontractor for doing a particular job). Though financial flexibility has a certain appeal, in the eyes of some commentators it suffers a disadvantage in the sense that it would encourage leapfrogging in wage claims and result in bidding up the price of labour, particularly if a national system of pay determination no longer exists.

Whether flexibility is the solution to the problem of organisational restructuring remains to be seen. It can generate conditions of more complexity in a number of areas—for example, in recruitment, preparing contracts, and organising work—and it may not serve the needs of some employers. For instance, Penn, Lilja, and Scattergood (1992) found little evidence of flexibility in eight UK and Finnish papermills, despite conditions of increasing competition and technical change. It was felt that the use of peripheral workers would be less than satisfactory in such a capital-intensive industry where employers rely on full-time workers who are highly skilled and experienced to operate advanced or sophisticated machinery on a continuous basis. There is a mixed picture with regard to flexible working patterns in Europe.

If the adoption of the information-based organisation becomes a reality, coupled with computer-aided production, there is likely to be a significant fall in demand for unskilled and semi-skilled workers and a growth in the number of short-term contract and part-time workers. With this scenario comes the prospect of greater pressure experienced by core workers, and perhaps peripheral workers losing out on training. Further observations on flexibility appear in Panel 14.11.

PANEL 14.11: Working flexibly

In Japan there is an erosion of the social contract that Japanese workers viewed as sacred for half a century. This was exemplified in a job for life in return for unflagging loyalty to the company. Now there is a trend in Japan reflected in a decrease in the number of full-time workers and a substantial increase in the number of part-time and contract workers. Japan has not yet reached the stage where workers can move easily from one job to another. But the labour market has become segmented between relatively highly paid permanent staff and lowly paid temporary and contract workers with few prospects of joining the full-time labour force. Interestingly, the growth of the latter has affected the level of consumer expenditure. The stark reality is that the labour force is much more mobile than it was a decade ago (Pilling, 2004).

Volkswagen (VW), the German carmaker, seems to be adapting to the legislative framework in the EU and acting flexibly. Not only has the company adapted to Germany's rigid labour market, but it has also introduced new working arrangements held as examples of good practice for others to follow. Redundancies have been avoided by high degrees of flexibility. Rather than dismissing workers, they were put on a four-day working week. Another measure is that extra hours worked earlier in one's employment with the company could be banked and cashed in later, allowing workers to work part-time or take early retirement. VW has maintained its reputation for defending the social consensus on which German post-war economic success was built, and for working with the unions through worker's councils on ways to increase productivity. However, investors do not regard VW so benevolently because its recent financial performance has been lack-lustre (Atkins, 2004).

The findings of an Economic and Social Research Council survey do not suggest that the UK has the flexible labour market that it urges other European countries to emulate: "Far from permanent jobs disappearing, 92% of the employed workforce held permanent job contracts in 2000, against 88% in 1992. Contrary to popular belief, people are staying in their jobs longer. Temporary and fixed contract working decreased in the 1990s, and portfolio working remains a minority occupation." The survey also shows a marked divide between skilled and unskilled workers in the use of advanced technology. Among semi-skilled and unskilled manual workers, only 15% use the internet at work.

(Timmins, 2002).

Just-in-time

Production technology is supplemented by production systems based on just-in-time (JIT). JIT was developed by Japanese car firms, and a number of British companies followed their lead. However, one should recognise that not many companies are committed to the concept because they do not understand the practicalities of implementing it (Wickham, 1993). It is essentially a manufacturing and stock system geared to improving the productivity of the plant and a feature of it is that component parts arrive just in time to be used in the manufacturing process. This has the effect of reducing the costs of keeping stocks in a warehouse until they are required. Because of the reduction in buffer stocks, employees are expected to be flexible and to solve problems on the spot, otherwise the next phase of the process would grind to a halt (Tailby & Turnbull, 1987).

The flexibility required of employees is almost tantamount to the possession of multi-skills, so that the worker can move comfortably from one job to another. As a result, there could be the merging of tasks (such as maintenance and inspection) into the overall tasks of a production worker. Obviously, this requires greater knowledge on the part of the workers on issues such as quality control and information on a wide range of jobs, and would have a knock-on effect in terms of payment or reward systems. The advantage of combining skilled and unskilled activities in one person is underlined in a study of a West German car plant (Dankbaar, 1988).

JIT is not just an inventory system with flexible labour utilisation. It requires close managerial involvement in the production process, multipurpose machinery, and reductions in set-up. The system frequently relies on a set of relations between companies and suppliers, reflected in tightly controlled, multiple sources of various inputs through layers of subcontractors (see Panel 14.12). The introduction of JIT appears to have brought about a shift in traditional attitudes to production work, with higher expectations of the skills of operatives. According to Thompson and McHugh (2002), a number of companies use fairly sophisticated selection processes for relatively routine jobs, particularly on green sites. Subsequently, a more exacting system of training is likely to ensue.

The application of JIT in many electronics manufacturing companies has resulted in significant benefits due to the fact that these companies are accustomed to operating with high work-in-process stock levels and long production lead times. The general view is that one should be selective in the application of JIT. For example, it is suggested that JIT is more applicable to manufacturing processes of a repetitive nature than to processes that are nonrepetitive (e.g., production geared to the customers' specification). By contrast, chemical companies with continuous production processes and low stock levels are unlikely to secure the improvements typically associated with JIT (Collins, Schmenner, & Cordon, 1997).

Introducing JIT could necessitate a radical change in the culture of the factory, expressed

---

At Nissan's plant in Sunderland, England, raw materials arrive by the minute. For the Micra's seats, data are read from barcodes on each vehicle as it passes along the assembly line and are transmitted to a mainframe at suppliers Ikeda Hoover, based less than 2 minutes away. Ikeda then builds seats to order, from a range of 180 variations, in 45 minutes. There are similar arrangements with other local suppliers.

Even material from more distant suppliers is collected on a JIT basis. A single haulier collects components four times a day from around the UK, instead of the supplier making its own delivery arrangements. This has cut the road miles needed for the delivery of Micra components by 2.3 million miles a year.

Information technology plays a leading role in running the JIT system at Nissan. Nissan relies to a significant extent on electronic data interchange (EDI)—the paperless communication process whereby orders, invoices, and remittances are sent electronically between computers—to make JIT delivery work.

(Wickham, 1993)

as high dedication and a firm commitment of resources by top management. It could also promote the cause of employee flexibility and multi-skilling. The use of JIT can go beyond the boundaries of the organisation and influence events in another organisation. For example, a company (the supplier) supplies component parts to a car manufacturer (the customer), and the supplier wants to become a "JIT Supplier". In such a case the customer (the car manufacturer) often demands that the supplier has a quality certification so that products do not need to be tested for quality on delivery.

Lean production systems

In the West we have taken particular note of the way Japanese manufacturing companies are organised. Womack, Jones, and Roos (1990) examined Japanese lean production systems and, after drawing comparisons between the Japanese car industry and Western production systems, made reference to the fact that Toyota's manufacturing methods cut development time and defects by 50%. Lean production systems revolve round the following five main principles: teamwork; quality control; customer focus; minimal inventory buffers; and continuous improvement.

In a McKinsey report it was concluded that the weakness of many UK-based manufacturers is not related to low investment or the quality of the workforce, and could be overcome by a big effort to introduce techniques such as "lean manufacturing" and performance management (Marsh, 2001). But there are exceptions, such as the following. British manufacturing practices and management, particularly in certain companies (e.g., Nissan UK, Ford), were altered over the 1980s and 1990s as a result of the influence of the philosophy of lean production systems (Wagstyl, 1996). Output per person has risen significantly, outdated work practices and management have been discarded, there has been a commitment to exacting quality standards and a commitment to continuous improvement, cooperative working relationships between key constituencies (e.g., workers, managers, suppliers)

have been developed, there is a strong emphasis on measurement (e.g., detecting faults and taking remedial action), and a healthier relationship with the trade unions.

In the case of Nissan UK an "evaluation" system was introduced to assess a number of features of the organisation and management of companies supplying Nissan with component parts. The features taken into account include costs, quality, new product development, and quality of management. Understandably, a number of suppliers were not too happy with this type of scrutiny. However, this is an example of the knock-on effect of the adoption of Japanese management and organisation systems in the UK. Although there has been much improvement in the management and organisation of companies who are direct suppliers to Japanese car manufacturers in the UK, it is acknowledged that there is much scope for improvement in companies well down the chain of suppliers in the car component business. One reason for this is that these companies have little contact with Japanese management practices.

High-performance systems

High-performance systems (HPS) borrow concepts from lean production systems but they are distinctive in their own right, and appear to work well in countries (such as the USA) where individualism is strong, lifetime employment is weak, and shareholders are powerful. They were developed in response to an intensification of global competition and pressure from shareholders, and are governed by the following principles, which have been adopted by companies, such as AT&T, DuPont, Ford, Hewlett Packard, IBM, Kodak, and Xerox, when faced with organisational redesign (Useem, 1997):

- customer-focused operating units;
- devolved decision making;
- streamlined management control, including tighter financial control;
- re-engineering of business processes; and
- benchmarking of decisions against their contribution to shareholder value.

Customer-focused operating units

Initially the company obtains a reaction from customers, using techniques such as market surveys and focus groups, and feeds this information directly to managers of operating units. These data would then be treated as input into a range of key decision-making processes, including performance management and employee selection.

In the annual performance appraisal of divisional managers at AT&T, one of the criteria used is customer-value-added (effectiveness in the eyes of major customers). South West Airlines sought the help of a particular category of customer (frequent fliers) in some of its recruitment and selection events. The rationale for the customer focus is that the organisation is more likely to be responsive to changing market trends if management has routine contact with customers. In such a process the customers' interests and concerns are given serious consideration in important decision-making processes within the organisation. Feedback from customers could also be used in the determination of rewards for employees who have been particularly creative and effective in satisfying customers' needs.

Devolved decision making

Authority is pushed down the hierarchy giving operating units greater power. The way this is achieved is to replace the functional grouping approach to organisation (e.g., production, marketing, etc.), referred to earlier in the chapter, with strategic business units (SBUs) consisting of broad product categories within which are housed functional specialisms. (Some would argue that this is similar to product grouping, which was also examined earlier.) An SBU could be subdivided into micro enterprises (the smallest operating units). SBUs are customer-oriented with responsibility for formulating strategy, and are held responsible for results. The number of SBUs within an organisation varies greatly from one company to another. For example, Du Pont has grouped some 60 profit centres into 14 SBUs.

The relationship between the SBU and the headquarters of the organisation can vary, with some companies retaining more centralised functions than others. However, the SBUs all share one thing in common—responsibility for profit or loss. So you can imagine that the management controlling an SBU feel that they are running a quasi-independent business with the power to act, and this has obvious motivational implications. The management of the SBU would also be active in cross-boundary management, relating to and influencing those outside the unit. The top managers of SBUs and micro-enterprises are expected to be generalists, charged with meeting the objectives of their divisions or units.

Streamlined management control/tighter financial control

Rationalisation results in the number of staff at headquarters and the number of layers of management being reduced, leading to wider spans of control and flatter structures. Operating units receive fewer policy directives from headquarters but, on the other hand, they receive tougher financial directives. The corporate staff at IBM's HQ was reduced from 5100 to 3900 in its 1993–1995 restructuring exercise, and the headquarters were subsequently put up for sale.

Re-engineering of business processes

Business process re-engineering (BPR) is "the fundamental rethinking and radical redesign of business processes to achieve dramatic improvements in critical, contemporary measures of performance, such as cost, quality, service and speed" (Hammer & Champy, 1993). In re-engineering, the project team, including senior and experienced managers, questions all aspects of the business, taking nothing for granted. The following are the main characteristics of BPR (Cordon, 1997):

- Redesign processes that cut across functions and departments. This is an area where there is great scope for improvement.
- Redesign processes by minimising the lead time for the total process. For example, reduce the time from delivery of the goods to the collection of payment from the customer.

- Where appropriate, push decision making down to the lowest levels of the organisation where relevant information and knowledge reside, making it possible to empower workers. A spin-off of such action could be the elimination of hierarchical levels, resulting in a lean and flat organisation, as was mentioned earlier.
- Use information technology as an enabling mechanism to speed up processes and cut down on paperwork. It is said that quite a few projects failed because they came to be seen as IT projects rather than BPR projects utilising IT.
- So as to increase the likelihood that the proposed radical changes to the inter-functional processes are accepted by the rest of the organisation, top management should be responsible for introducing BPR and for its implementation.

Dramatic improvements in productivity have been achieved in a relatively short period of time. For example, accounts payable at the Ford Motor Company were reduced by 75% (from 500 to 125)

aided by the installation of powerful data retrieval systems and the elimination of most paperwork from the process of ordering and receiving products from suppliers (Useem, 1997).

Finally, there are many reports of savings of 50% of cost and time when BPR is well conceived and properly implemented, but there is also evidence to suggest that it fails to produce the anticipated benefits. According to Case (1999), the popularity of BPR among Western management seems generally to be on the decline. Case is very critical of BPR and goes on to say "that there will be future BPR embodying technological principles and motives of similarly exploitative intent, and that management studies scholars should discredit such instrumental devices". Consultants who were eager to operationalise this concept now appear to prefer to peddle knowledge management. Mumford and Hendricks (1996) provide an overview of the rise and fall of BPR and make reference to US management's growing disillusionment with the idea. There is further reflection on BPR in Panel 14.13.

PANEL 14.13: Process re-engineering

This employs some of the same tools and techniques as TQM, and attempts to create a more dramatic impact on business processes over shorter periods of time.

The twin cores of process re-engineering are the radical redesign of business processes and their operation by cross-functional teams. Process re-engineering poses a direct challenge to the division of labour and the need for hierarchical control. In many organisations, orders and projects pass up, down, and across a succession of separate vertically structured "functional" departments, often waiting hours or days for the next task to be carried out. In a process re-engineered organisation, tasks that were previously separate are replaced by a seamless process, and functional boundaries are either bridged or removed entirely, with a "process owner" often overseeing everyone involved. Narrow job descriptions are abandoned, and multi-skilling is warmly embraced, supplemented by a small pool of specialist staff to be called on as necessary (Hammer & Champy, 1993).

The concept of process re-engineering has been applied at Bell Atlantic and AT&T. There has been an abandonment of the numerous, traditionally fragmented, start–stop work tasks, routines, and procedures, which have been replaced by a handful of unitary processes designed from scratch to operate smoothly, from first contact with the customer through to order completion (Lorenz, 1993d).

In 1989 the condition of the manufacturing facility at HarperCollins Publishers in Glasgow was described as "enormously serious", if not terminal. The cosy days of long print runs were gone. In the new cut-throat market-place, customers demanded smaller orders more frequently, and the inflexible plant could not respond. According to the business development director, the option of doing nothing expired. A strategy was formulated on the following lines—develop people, simplify processes, and then automate. The implementation of the strategy resulted in a reduction in paperback book production lead times from 5 weeks to 10 days, and hardback lead times from 8 weeks to 4 weeks. Also, 33% was taken off the cost base. According to the chief executive, "top-level commitment was important, but equally people and their commitment was crucial. If companies embark on this journey without their employees understanding what is happening, or why, they are lost. With re-engineering, everything people have banked on is no longer there. If they do not know why, they get insecure—you have to communicate. Once they are committed, they generate ideas, and drive change forward" (Rees, 1993).

One has to bear in mind that changes in processes have implications for cultural change, examined in Chapter 15, particularly when the old command and control mentality of managers and employees is replaced with new sets of behaviour, such as empowerment, teamwork, feedback, and customer responsiveness. Also, there is the danger that radical culture change could undermine the effectiveness of process re-engineering.

Benchmarking of decisions against their contribution to shareholder value

We normally speak of benchmarking when a company makes a very serious attempt to compare its practices with the best in the industry. The reason for doing so is to aspire to and adopt higher levels of professionalism and performance. To carry it out effectively requires an open mind, an objective approach, and a willingness to learn from others.

Benchmarking as used in this section is an activity concerned with seeing a connection between organisational actions or decisions and shareholder value. In this context a question might be asked, such as: How effective is management at producing wealth for shareholders? The link between management action and shareholder value is seen increasingly in the connection between share option schemes and company performance.

Quick response production

High-performance systems (HPS) are suitable in conditions where mass production systems operate, that is where work is broken down into very small tasks with dedicated workers and machines. In such a system, if the product undergoing manufacture is going to be changed the production line has to be shut down for substantial re-tooling (i.e., changing machine tools and the way tasks are organised). By contrast, "quick response production" (QRP) in which Japanese companies are adept and have the edge is "customised production". In this system the output is directed at meeting the specific orders of customers rather than producing for stock. Production systems of this type change frequently in response to alterations in the design of products and changes in the quantities produced (production runs). Where production runs are short, mass production systems would be too expensive as well as being too slow to change.

Features of QRP systems, when contrasted with normal mass production systems, are as follows:

- Manufacturers are better able to respond to the need for changes to products, following changes in consumer tastes, because products can be varied or changed without substantial re-tooling.
- There is a need for smaller teams of workers with higher skills and flexible tools. Because workers perform a wider range of tasks, there is a need for more varied skills.
- Greater autonomy is experienced by employees because the workflow is not as tightly controlled as it would be on the assembly line in mass production systems.

HPS has taken root in manufacturing industry, and is influenced by the development of lean production systems in Japan, but it appears to be absent from other sectors of the economy (e.g., the financial services industry), where operations with regard to processing work (standardisation, repetition) resemble the assembly line. In Panel 14.14 a number of issues are raised in connection with HPS.

Corporate governance and new organisational forms

It is suggested that corporate governance (a topical issue discussed in Chapter 9) and organisational forms are complementary (Child & Rodrigues, 2003). Corporate governance is concerned with the ways in which agents of the company (e.g., directors) can be held to account for the attainment of organisational goals, while the drive to develop new forms of organisation comes from pressures to achieve goals more effectively given the changes in the current business world. New organisational forms generally involve, as we have seen, a decentralised structure with a flat and flexible hierarchy, and partnerships between companies.

Child and Rodrigues call for a change in corporate governance to reflect the changes in organisational forms that are under way, because in traditional forms of corporate governance control was achieved by a combination of rigid hierarchy and bureaucracy. They argue that new organisational forms can be reconciled with the current requirements for corporate governance

---

PANEL 14.14: Reflections on HPS

The following are some of the issues that arise from the adoption of the principles of HPS in a climate characterised by strong global competition, foreign investment, and cross-national joint ventures.

- Less overall division of organisations by traditional functions (e.g., marketing, finance, etc.) and more structures in the form of self-contained divisions (e.g., SBUs) are likely.
- Flatter organisational hierarchies and broader spans of control are likely to be commonplace. As a result, more decentralisation of authority to individuals and groups will occur, but there are likely to be restrictions on employee authority due to technological constraints (e.g., the nature of production technology). Authority is likely to be exercised in a less authoritative way, accompanied by more participation in group decision making (within and between teams) by knowledgeable and skilled workers. With the growth of empowerment, autonomous groups will increasingly undertake tasks previously undertaken by managers.
- Conditions in the internal labour market (e.g., good rates of pay, security, job prospects) are likely to become less attractive, and a more common sight will be insecure and temporary workers. More will be demanded in effort and pace from workers, and as a consequence there will probably be extra vulnerability to occupational stress.
- The skill base of the workers, in particular the possession of complementary skills, is likely to be of prime importance. Within teams there will be scope to acquire and use a broader range of skills, due to the variety of activities and job rotation, and this could be beneficial in terms of job satisfaction and low levels of turnover and absenteeism. Upskilling (enriched and more demanding jobs) and de-skilling (jobs with limited discretion and initiative), though opposite, are likely to co-exist.
- Benchmarking (picking up good ideas with respect to practice from relevant sources), and having the capacity to apply this knowledge, is going to be critical when it comes to good performance in the workplace.
- Accountability for results will be given much prominence, and the interests of shareholders are unlikely to be ignored because, in the case of public companies, powerful institutional investors will demand more accountability from top management on corporate performance.
- Organisations are likely to adopt humanistic values and this will be advantageous in human resource terms.

Finally, it is recognised that though some of these issues will tend to promote commitment from employees, there will be instances where employee commitment is not forthcoming because of the position taken by management (e.g., redundancies). As a consequence, management will have a more difficult task when taking measures to ensure acceptable performance.

(Adapted from Cappelli & Rogovsky, 1997; Useem, 1997)

---

through a number of complementary developments, such as co-opting employees and junior partners into the ownership and governance of the enterprise, more inclusive forms of control, mutual monitoring, and promotion of trust.

Co-opting employees into the ownership and governance of the enterprise is reflected primarily in employee share ownership schemes (ESOPS), but also gain sharing schemes. The idea is that ownership provides clear rights to participation in governance. In particular, the informed views of minority joint venture and other alliance partners are currently often ignored to the detriment of the partnership.

As to inclusive forms of control, the idea is to move the control process from being top-down, hierarchy-based to a more collective form. Examples would be 360-degree appraisal and mutual monitoring. Mutual monitoring is a system in which all members of an organisation are encouraged to report any misdemeanours and are protected in so doing (i.e., "whistle-blowing"). It is consistent with more inclusive forms of control. All parties are involved in the promotion of trust, which can be supported by a clear understanding of mutual obligations—the "psychological contract". The primary onus, though, falls on management, which has often taken actions that breach trust.

CHAPTER SUMMARY

- After defining what is meant by an organisation, there was specific reference to goals, objectives, policies, typologies, and metaphors. A distinction was made between formal and informal organisation.

- Then there was a discussion of Weber's ideal bureaucracy, which offered prescriptions with respect to positions, tasks, contracts, rewards, career structure, control, records, impartiality, and ownership and control. The dysfunctional aspects of bureaucracy were discussed with reference to goal displacement, conflict, informal organisation, division of labour, relevance, impersonality, and adaptation.

- Principles of organisation were identified as embracing hierarchy, communication, specialisation, chain of command, centralisation, and span of control. These principles have been derived from the classical principles of organisation. Although some of these principles have value as basic concepts, they have been subjected to criticism.

- Structural groupings were defined as functional grouping, process grouping, product grouping, customer grouping, territorial grouping, and matrix organisation. There were reflections on the future of the hierarchy.

- Mintzberg's coordinating mechanisms within organisations were defined as mutual adjustment, direct supervision, standardisation of employee skills (input), standardisation of work processes, and standardisation of outputs. When these coordinating mechanisms are combined with dimensions of structure, we are in a position to specify different forms of organisation as follows: simple structure; machine bureaucracy; professional bureaucracy; divisional form; and adhocracy.

- Contingency factors of organisation were identified as the internal environment (including size), the external environment (comprising various external agencies), and technology. Size was discussed initially with reference to the internal environment, and later as a determinant of structure. The external environment was analysed with reference to types of environment, environmental uncertainty, differentiation and integration, resource dependency, and population ecology. The organisation as an open system, and as a socio-technical system, featured early in the discussion of contingency factors.

- A variety of theoretical perspectives (e.g., Woodward; Burns & Stalker; Thompson; and Perrow) formed a basis for examining the impact of technology on organisation. Size and technology as determinants of organisation (i.e., the Aston School) were also discussed.

- The impact of new technology was also discussed, and the role of strategic choice was mentioned. There were criticisms of the contingency approach.

- Postmodernism was discussed when reflecting on organisation theory.

- The final section was devoted to an examination of new organisational patterns, such as network organisation, virtual organisation, boundaryless organisation, outsourcing, downsizing and delayering, team structure, the flexible firm, just-in-time, lean production systems, high-performance systems. The significance of corporate governance in new organisational patterns was acknowledged.

QUESTIONS

(1) Distinguish between a formal and an informal organisation.

(2) List the common characteristics of an organisation.

(3) Examine the principles of organisation in the light of criticisms.

(4) What do we mean by the dysfunctional aspects of bureaucracy?

(5) Compare and contrast the "functional grouping" with that of matrix organisation.

(6) What is the outcome of combining Mintzberg's five coordinating mechanisms with dimensions of structure?

(7) Examine the role of the external environment as a contingency factor.

(8) Explain the following terms: (a) metaphor; (b) typology; (c) prime beneficiary; (d) disturbed reactive environment; (e) differentiation; (f) resource dependency; (g) population ecology; and (h) just-in-time.

(9) Assess ways in which technology, both old and new, influences organisation.

(10) Examine the role of size as a determinant of organisation structure.

(11) Explain the following terms: (a) formalisation; (b) mediating technology; (c) organic system of organisation; (d) strategic choice; (e) downsizing/delayering (f) information-based organisation; (g) the virtual organisation; (h) lean production systems; (i) corporate governance and organisation.

(12) Comment on an open system of organisation, with reference to socio-technical systems.

(13) Explain what is meant by postmodernism in connection with organisational theory.

(14) Examine the nature and significance of both the flexible firm and network organisations.

(15) Comment on the features of high-performance systems.

SPOTLIGHT ON RELEVANT READING

Child, J. (2005). *Organisations: Contemporary principles and practice*. Oxford: Blackwell.

Leavitt, H.J. (2003). Why hierarchies thrive. *Harvard Business Review*, March, 96–102.

Morgan, R.E. (2003). Outsourcing: Towards the shamrock organisation. *Journal of General Management, 29*, 35–52.

Warner, M., & Witzel, M. (2004). *Managing in virtual organisations*. London: Thomson.

Learning Outcomes

After studying this chapter you should be able to:

- Appreciate the difference between culture and climate within an organisation.

- Recognise the various manifestations of organisational culture.

- Specify the different approaches to analysing organisational culture.

- Describe the ways in which companies go about changing and developing culture.

- Discuss the advantages accruing to the organisation from having developed the appropriate culture.

- Assess the significance of cross-cultural studies and cultural diversity.

- Appreciate the significance of contemporary issues and the current status of culture.

Organisational Culture

15

The chapter opens with definitions, types, and major aspects of corporate culture. There is a difference between culture and climate. Next, ways of analysing organisational culture are discussed, followed by an examination of approaches (including organisational socialisation) used in changing and developing organisational culture. The benefits derived from culture are then specified and, finally, national cultures and their impact on organisational characteristics are introduced. This chapter draws widely on ideas developed in other chapters. For example, attitudes and commitment (Chapter 9), group norms (Chapter 10), socialisation (Chapters 2 and 7), management style (Chapter 12), creativity (Chapter 8), organisational forms, change, and development (Chapters 14 and 16), and human resource practices (Chapters 17 and 18).

Contents

DEFINITION

Culture has been the subject of investigation in social anthropology, where researchers have sought to understand the shared meanings and values held by groups in society that give significance to their actions. Anthropologists try to get to the root of the values, symbols, and stories that people in a society use to bring order and meaning to their lives. Goffee (1997) defines culture as historically created guides for living and collective mental programming, and these are derived from deep assumptions that are not directly accessible but may be reflected in the values, attitudes, and behaviour of individuals and groups. The assumptions are learned, not innate, they have a pattern, are shared, and passed down through the generations.

At the organisational level we speak of **corporate culture**, which amounts to a consideration of organisational values and norms, with the focus on assumptions and beliefs. Organisational or corporate culture is still an important issue, but does not grab the headlines in the same way that it did about two decades ago, when it was the subject of intensive study. According to Pettigrew (1979), organisational culture consists of the behaviour, actions, and values that people in an enterprise are expected to follow. Alternatively, a definition by Moorhead and Griffin (2004) states that organisational culture is a set of values, often taken for granted, that helps people in an organisation understand which actions are considered acceptable and which are considered unacceptable. Often these values are communicated through stories and other symbolic means.

Schein (1990), in an analysis of organisational culture from an organisational psychological perspective, comes forward with the following definition of organisational culture:

A pattern of basic assumptions, invented, discovered, or developed by a given group as it learns to cope with its problems of external adaptation and integral integration, that has worked well enough to be considered valid and, therefore, is to be taught to new members as the correct way to perceive, think, and feel in relation to those problems.

You will notice the words "integration" and "adaptation" in Schein's definition. Integration means that members develop a collective identity and are capable of working well together. It is concerned with day-to-day working relationships and determines how people communicate within the organisation, as well as establishing what behaviour is acceptable or not acceptable and how power and status are allocated.

Adaptation is a force that helps the organisation to adapt to its external environment. It facilitates the meeting of organisational goals and dealing with outside influences. This aspect of culture helps guide the daily activities of employees to meet certain goals, and can help the organisation to respond promptly to customers' needs and the actions of competitors. In research conducted by Kotter and Heskett (1992) it was maintained that superior financial performance in most market conditions is significantly dependent on having a culture that helps the company anticipate and adapt to changes in its environment. A primary conclusion from the study is that there will only be appropriate adaptation by the company to its environment if all members care deeply about the company's competitive performance, and if the needs of key constituencies—customers, shareholders, and employees—are given serious attention. The company must anticipate and respond appropriately to changes in the preferences and priorities in any of these constituencies.

It is important to note that the values that make up an organisation's culture (e.g., never lose sight of the customer) are often taken for granted. In other words, they are basic assumptions made by employees, do not necessarily appear in a document, and are not necessarily transmitted in a training programme, although they can be expressed in written form. Organisational culture probably exerts the greatest influence on individual behaviour and actions when it is taken for granted. One of the major reasons why organisational culture is such a powerful influence on employees within an organisation is because it is not explicit; instead, it is an implicit part of the employees' values and beliefs.

ASPECTS OF ORGANISATIONAL CULTURE

The culture of the organisation is perceived by Trice and Beyer (1984) as consisting of four major aspects:

- rites and ceremonies;
- stories;
- symbols; and
- language.

Rites and ceremonies

Rites and ceremonies help employees identify with the organisation and its successes and provide vivid accounts of what a company values. They can be considered special occasions that reinforce special values, that create a bond between people to foster common understanding, and honour heroes who stand for important beliefs or achievements. The following are examples of the different types of rites.

- *Rites of passage* (e.g., induction courses) facilitate the entry of employees into new social roles or jobs, and can increase the status of employees.
- *Rites of enhancement* foster stronger social identities and increase the status of employees. For example, there could be a ceremonial launching of a new product at which employees are present, or an address by the chief executive at the "Salesperson of the Year" event. At events of this nature, often held at a large hotel or conference centre, successful sales representatives receive various gifts for meeting sales targets. Offering public recognition for outstanding performance can have a motivating effect. Other rituals take place when employees take advantage of the opportunity to socialise and relax with each other at informal company social events.

- *Rites of renewal* (e.g., management training and development) are reflected in various training and development activities.
- *Rites of integration* are activities that create common bonds and good feelings among employees and can have the effect of increasing commitment to the organisation.

Stories

This is a form of communication that focuses primarily on vignettes and anecdotes about the dedication and commitment of corporate heroes and managers, or the devotion of ordinary employees. The stories are told to new employees to inform them about the organisation. There are true stories founded on events showing employees displaying heroism or, for example, adhering to high quality standards. Also, the great achievements of the leadership at the inception of the company could be highlighted, as could accounts of great career achievements, ways of getting round the rules and regulations, what one learnt from past mistakes, how the organisation coped with a major crisis, and how a restructuring of the organisation was carried out (Boye, 1991). Stories like these help with explanation and legitimacy by placing the present in some relevant historical context.

But there can also be myths, lacking foundation in fact, where older employees recall past happenings. These could be supplemented by legends—accounts of actual events fleshed out with fictional details—as well as by folk tales, which amount to fictional stories with a message. Stories keep alive the primary values of the organisation and provide employees with a shared understanding. To foster recognition there are symbols and slogans and logos or emblems (e.g., the Mercedes symbol), and these represent an important identification sign.

Symbols

A symbol is something that represents something else. For example, rites, ceremonies, and slogans are all symbols; they symbolise the deeper values of the organisation. But physical artefacts are also symbols. They convey something distinctive about the organisation, and range from the physical layout and decor of offices to the nature of office furniture. Open-plan offices with common areas may indicate a certain degree of informality and may convey something about the social and psychological climate of the organisation (e.g., less emphasis on status; flexibility; etc.). Material symbols, such as size of office and quality of its furnishings, access to a company apartment in a prime location, and use of a chauffeur-driven car, convey to employees certain aspects of status and importance, as well as management culture.

Language

Organisations develop distinctive terms (specific sayings, slogans, or metaphors) to describe people, buildings, and events, and the acronyms and jargon used could be alien to the new entrant. The development of a common language can have a unifying effect within the organisation. Examples of terms used to describe particular groups include the Walt Disney organisation referring to the workforce at its theme parks as the cast, the customers as guests, and when staff work with the public they are on the stage. McDonald's refers to its workers as crew members.

TYPES OF CULTURE

In this section the opening subsection explores the difference between culture and climate, following which a distinction is made between dominant and sub-cultures and between strong and weak cultures.

Culture versus climate

Organisational culture is based on the history and traditions of the organisation with the emphasis on values and norms underpinning employee behaviour, whereas organisational climate is concerned with the current atmosphere within an organisation. Some argue that both culture and climate are concerned with the social context

of organisations and affect the behaviour of employees (Denison, 1996), but it is possible to acknowledge differences between the two concepts.

Climate looks at the current connections between individuals, groups, and performance and it lends itself more easily to change by management in their attempt to influence the behaviour of their subordinates. It is a feature of the organisation experienced by employees on a daily basis. Most descriptions of organisational climate ignore values and norms. Climate is not as subtle or enduring as culture and is probably more akin to morale. According to Furnham (2005a), the internal climate of the organisation incorporates the nature of the organisation's communication networks, rewards system, leadership styles, and other factors, and though it may be seen as part of corporate culture the differences between culture and climate are not very clear.

Organisational culture refers to the historical context within which events occur, and recognises the impact of the historical context, but it is more difficult to change in the short term because of its longevity.

Dominant and sub-cultures

Many big companies have a dominant culture and numerous cells of sub-cultures, which are attached to different roles, functions, and levels (Hampden-Turner, 1990; Sackmann, 1992). Therefore, if we accept the existence of numerous sub-cultures, a natural conclusion is that very few beliefs, attitudes, or values are shared by all organisational members. A dominant culture, normally referred to as the organisation's culture, reflects core values that are shared by the majority of the employees. In effect this is the distinctive personality of the organisation.

By contrast, sub-cultures are found in departments, divisions, and geographical areas, and reflect the common problems or experiences of employees who reside in these areas, and could be considered functional (Tushman & O'Reilly, 1996). A sub-culture could consist of the core values of the dominant culture as well as the values unique to the department or area to which it

---

PANEL 15.1: The sub-culture of the dealing room

Many dealing rooms in merchant banks and stockbroking firms are dominated by one simple system of values: win or be damned. If dealers make large profits for the organisation, the rewards (both material and psychological) are very significant. Not only is the personal remuneration substantial, but also the dealer's status in the firm and the market generally is considerably enhanced. However, if the dealers' performance is poor in terms of profits generated or losses sustained, the reverse situation applies. They could feel humiliated or isolated and risk losing their job with detrimental personal consequences. Always in the background is greed or fear, in particular, fear: fear of losing the job, and fear of public humiliation. It is fear that prevents dealers from cutting their losses as well as forcing them to get out of profitable positions early.

Dealers live in a unique "sub-culture", one that encourages overconfidence and insulates them from the outside world. On the trading floor boldness is looked upon as the most important virtue, and the traders' faith in themselves is boosted by their substantial remuneration package. A moment's hesitation or uncertainty could undermine a transaction. Dealers tend to behave as if omnipotent, they brag about the size of their deals, and hero status is bestowed on anyone making large sums of money. Because of the high rewards, they are encouraged to take unwise risks.

There is a loss of perspective on outside events, with a tendency for dealers to shield themselves from too much information that could metaphorically lead to paralysis. There is the illusion that the computer screen gives them a window on the outside world, even though it is no more than a series of rapidly changing numbers. Erratic behaviour is condoned if not encouraged, and shouting matches are part of the scene on the trading floor. The dealers display emotional volatility, and this is accepted as long as they are generating good profits. A dangerous cocktail is the mixture of emotional volatility, overconfidence, and access to large amounts of capital.

In the mid-1990s, following the disastrous deals entered into by Nick Leeson at Baring Securities, Singapore, which had a fatal effect on the financial viability of the parent company, there has been much debate on the need to tighten operating procedures and to counteract the culture of individualism, competition, and insecurity symbolised by incidents of this nature.

In 2004 in a British court of law the spotlight was on the trading room culture when a senior trader employed in London's financial district was claiming damages because of bullying at work. In this case questions were asked about the extent to which foul language and bullying were part of the dealing room culture. (There is further comment on this case in the section on bullying in Chapter 19 on stress.)

(Griffith, 1995; Tait, 2005; Weaving, 1995)

---

relates. Also, a sub-culture could manifest itself as a management culture or a staff culture. There could be differences and clashes between one sub-culture and another, especially in organisations without a strong overall culture, and between sub-cultures and the dominant culture. For example, the sub-culture in the dealing room of a merchant bank could be different from the sub-culture in the department concerned with the clients' investment portfolios (see Panel 15.1).

Finally, consider the following statement about sub-cultures (Furnham & Gunter, 1993):

> Sub-cultures can assume varying degrees of significance within the organisation, and can be beneficial if they adopt a common sense of purpose, but problems arise where they have different priorities and agendas. Then sub-cultures can clash with each other or with the overall corporate culture, impeding organisational functioning and performance.

Strong versus weak cultures

Often a distinction is drawn between strong and weak cultures (Gordon & Di Tomaso, 1992). As you would expect, a strong culture will have a significant influence on the behaviour of employees, primarily because of the intensity with which people are attached to and share the core values of the organisation. This is so because there is widespread agreement among members about what the organisation stands for. The result is the creation of an internal atmosphere of high behavioural control, as opposed to bureaucratic control; that is, the stronger the culture of an organisation, the less management need to be concerned with developing formal rules and regulations to guide employee behaviour.

The argument put forward is that strong cultures make the greater impact on the behaviour of employees; it is said that there is likely to be greater cohesiveness, loyalty, and organisational commitment—qualities that are likely to encourage people to stay rather than leave the organisation. Why should that be so? In a strong culture the core values of the organisation are widely shared and eagerly embraced by a large number of employees, who are deeply committed to them. It is said that organisations with a strong culture perform better than those without such a culture (O'Reilly & Chatman, 1996). In recent years, as organisations have created flatter structures, introduced team systems of working, released bureaucratic control, and empowered employees, some would argue that the shared meaning generated by a strong culture ensures that everyone is moving in the same direction.

From a perspective of "diversity" a strong culture could be considered a liability because it would not accommodate the diverse behaviours and strengths that people of different backgrounds can bring to the organisation. There could be a bias or insensitivity to people perceived as different on racial, ethnic, gender, or other grounds, and this could be reflected in judgements made when recruiting and selecting new employees (Cox, 1993). Even though there might be a view that diversity could have an enriching effect, at the same time there is often a wish to recruit new staff who will experience little difficulty in embracing the organisation's core cultural values.

We should not ignore the potentially dysfunctional aspects of a strong culture. This is evident when strong cultures, which worked well in the past, may have become barriers to change when the old ways are no longer valid.

Finally, if there is little agreement among members about the organisation's core values, the culture is said to be weak.

ANALYSING CULTURE

These are a number of approaches to analysing the values embedded in organisational culture. Examined here are those of: (i) Harrison, (ii) Ouchi, (iii) Peters and Waterman, and (iv) Deal and Kennedy, plus two other more recent approaches of (v) O'Reilly, and (vi) Xenikou and Furnham. Taken together these analyses provide useful insights into strands of organisational culture.

Harrison's four types

Harrison (1972) identified four types of culture found in organisations as power culture, role culture, support culture, and achievement culture:

(1) *Power culture* is found where senior managers exert considerable influence and power within the organisation, and the managers are likely to manage in an autocratic way.
(2) *Role culture* relates to situations where positions within bureaucratic organisations are the focal point of attention. The demands of bureaucracy (in terms of, for example, compliance with rules) are prominent.
(3) *Support culture* applies where the organisation possesses values and mechanisms to integrate people within a community. The culture promotes a sense of community.
(4) *Achievement culture* values success and personal growth. The climate encourages people to exercise initiative in conditions of high levels of autonomy.

Handy (1985) has been influenced by this typology, and proposes four types of culture related to the structure of organisation. These are power and role cultures (as in Harrison's definition), task cultures (e.g., successful completion of tasks by teams managing projects), and person cultures (where the organisational setting is supportive of the individual in his or her pursuit of technical or creative accomplishments).

Ouchi's approach

Ouchi (1981) analysed the organisational cultures of three groups of companies, described as: typical American; typical Japanese; and type Z American. A list of seven points was developed to facilitate the comparison of the three types of companies:

(1) commitment to employees;
(2) evaluation;
(3) careers;
(4) control;
(5) decision making;
(6) responsibility; and
(7) concern for people.

From the analysis it emerged that the cultures of the typical Japanese companies and type Z American companies are quite different from the cultures of typical American companies. These differences reflect the success of the former as opposed to the latter.

Commitment to employees

The typical Japanese and type Z American company subscribe to the cultural value of endeavouring to offer long-term employment, and would lay off employees only as a last resort. This commitment would seem to have greater currency in Japan. In the USA an employee could be dismissed for unsatisfactory performance in a type Z company. By contrast, the typical American company would have a cultural expectation of short-term employment, whereby workers would be laid off when there is an adverse change in the company's fortunes.

In Japan today, the recent deep economic recession has posed a serious challenge to the system of lifetime employment. Many people have lost their jobs for the first time. Such happenings cause deep psychological distress because of people's close identification with the company, and because unemployment is considered such an embarrassment. In some cases, people joined the ranks of the *shanai shitsugyo*, or in-house unemployed, where their salary is paid but they have nothing to do (Pollack, 1993). According to the chairperson of Mitsubishi, a leading metals and ceramics supplier in Japan, the tradition of lifetime employment will change, but it will take a generation—so expect no revolutions (Dawkins, 1993). But when we take a snapshot of the scene in 2005 we can see that changes are taking place at an impressive rate, and flexible working is becoming part of the occupational landscape.

Evaluation

Promotion is slow in the typical Japanese company and type Z American company because evaluation of an employee's performance, using both quantitative and qualitative measures, takes place over an appreciable length of time. By contrast, in the typical American company the emphasis would be on a rapid process of evaluation, based primarily on quantitative measures, where short-term thinking is encouraged.

Careers

In the typical Japanese company, having a career steeped in experience of a number of different business functions is valued, although the career path in the type Z American company would not be as broad. The adoption of the values of specialisation—reflected in experience of only one or two business functions—leads to a narrow career path in the typical American company.

Control

Control is a normal feature of life within an organisation, and without it the coordination of activities would be almost impossible. Most of the typical Japanese companies and type Z American companies use organisational culture as a powerful control mechanism, from which can come guidance on how best to act. Stories convey what superiors expect subordinates to do. By contrast, in the typical American company guidance is more likely to emanate from formal bureaucratic processes (e.g., explicit directions in job descriptions and procedures) and not from implicit cultural values. If stories exist, they are likely to highlight the benefits of sticking to the written guidelines.

Decision making

The vehicle for decision making in the typical Japanese company and the type Z American company is the "group", based on sharing information and an attachment to consensus. By contrast, in the typical American company individual decision making occupies a prominent position, and a consultative process is not a prerequisite for the taking of decisions.

Responsibility

On the question of responsibility for decisions, there is a divergence in the practices of Japanese companies on the one hand and the two types of

American companies on the other. In Japan, strong cultural values are supportive of the group bearing responsibility (collective responsibility), whereas in both the type Z and typical American companies there would be an attachment to the notion that a single person, rather than the group as a whole, ultimately bears responsibility for decisions made by the group.

You will notice that in the Japanese company, group decision making and collective responsibility go hand in hand, as does individual decision making and individual responsibility in the typical American company. However, the type Z American company is different in this respect, with group decision making coinciding with individual responsibility. This might be explained by attributing to certain American managers a skill in securing positive responses from the group in the decision-making process, but resorting to individual responsibility, because, by so doing, they reflect strong cultural norms of individuality and individual responsibility prominent in American society.

Concern for people

In the typical Japanese company and the type Z American company, the concern for people extends beyond the boundaries of the organisation, embracing their home-life and focusing on their outlook. In the typical American company there is a narrower concern for the worker, and the concern that exists is primarily geared to the workplace.

Ouchi maintains that the cultures of the typical Japanese company and the type Z American company assist them in producing better performances than the typical American company. It is interesting to note that successful Japanese car manufacturers located in the UK imported the management style and culture that have proved so successful in Japan. They did not skimp on well-directed investment in employees and in operations over long periods of time. As a result, generally speaking, they experienced sound improvements in long-term performance.

At this stage an interesting question to ask is: Does this scenario, which applies to the organisa-

tion culture of the typical Japanese company, prevail in all sectors of the Japanese economy? It would appear that the answer is no if one lent credence to the profile of Japanese banks, particularly when factors such as quality and efficiency are noted (see Panel 15.2).

Peters and Waterman's approach

In their popular book, *In Search of Excellence*, the authors emphasised the relationship between organisational culture and performance (Peters & Waterman, 1982). From a sample of highly successful American companies at that time (e.g., IBM, Boeing, Walt Disney, and McDonald's) they tried to identify management practices associated with success, eventually analysing cultural factors leading to successful management practices. The eight cultural factors—attributes of excellence—were as follows:

(1) *Bias for action.* Managers are expected to make decisions (even though all the necessary information may not be available) in conditions where delaying making a decision is tantamount to never making a decision. Delays would open the way for competitors to seize the opportunity.

(2) *Closeness to the customer.* The customer is a source of information about existing products, a source of ideas about new products in the future, and ultimately the rock on which the current and future financial performance of the company rests. Therefore, it is important to identify and meet customers' needs, and to take the necessary action to retain customers' loyalty.

(3) *Autonomy and entrepreneurship.* To foster an innovative climate the organisation is divided into more manageable smaller business units. Then, independent, creative, and also risk-taking activity is encouraged.

(4) *Productivity through people.* Ingrained in the organisational culture is the belief that treating people with dignity and respect is essential. Also, the organisation provides opportunities for people to realise their potential.

PANEL 15.2: Profile of Japanese banks

Japanese banks have a worldwide reputation for incompetence and financial weakness. In the 1990s they struggled with the massive burden of bad loans advanced in a period of acute speculation in the 1980s. Some observers maintain that the Japanese are first class at making widgets but lack the sophistication, innovative spirit, and general all round genius that are essential to success in international finance. Why should this be so? It could be said that the management systems that led directly to success in manufacturing (i.e., long-term view when making investment decisions; building consensus within the organisation) are causes of failure in financial markets.

Striving for consensus is not the best approach to adopt in conditions where trading decisions have to be made in seconds. Equally, adopting an organisational practice (e.g., job rotation every two or three years) might give executives in an electronics company a well-rounded view of the business, but it is not ideal for staff dealing in increasingly complex financial instruments. Perhaps these matters may not have played a key role in the problems experienced! Maybe the large number of bad debts arose because at the time the loans were issued the lenders did not anticipate the extent of the future economic downturn (i.e., poor judgement). Another likely explanation for the cause of the problem is that the regulatory framework put in place by government officials stifled creativity and flexibility, and promoted complacency and over-reliance on the authorities for protection. This left the banks weaker in the deregulated markets of the 1980s.

However, it is said that the most likely explanation for the malaise and poor performance was that the post-war Japanese banks were providing scarce capital to manufacturing industry at cheap rates with too little regard for their own performance. The shareholders of the banks were happy with this situation because many of them were manufacturers benefiting from the cheap loans. As the manufacturers matured in the 1980s, relying less on the banks for funding, the banks were forced to look elsewhere for customers. That led them to make the disastrous lending decisions that have now left their international reputation in tatters, and no match for their overseas competitors (Baker, 1996). Recent developments in Japan, such as the proposed merger of two of its biggest banks based on sound business logic, may indicate a revival in the Japanese banking sector (*Financial Times*, 2004a).

(5) *Hands-on management.* It is important for senior managers to maintain close contact with business operations. Managers should leave their offices and wander around the plant and other parts of the workplace.

(6) *Stick to the knitting.* There is reluctance on the part of management to enter business fields outside their area of expertise. The practice of operating businesses in unrelated industries is frowned on, and runs counter to a strong cultural norm.

(7) *Simple form, lean staff.* This type of structure is reflected in fewer management levels and relatively small groups of corporate staff. The main emphasis is on the performance of employees, not the size of the establishment.

(8) *Simultaneous loose–tight organisation.* On the one hand the adoption of the company's cultural values tends to create tightly organised organisations, wedded by common cultural bonds. On the other hand, the company is loosely organised, with lower administrative overhead costs, fewer rules and regulations, and a leaner establishment. The loose structure is said to be functional because it is supported by the common values accepted by employees in the organisation.

Because of the popularity of this work in the 1980s it was perhaps inevitable that it would invite criticism (see Panel 15.3). The message now projected by serious researchers on corporate culture is that cultures appropriate to today's business environment may be unsuitable, or even lethal, in tomorrow's. As stated in Panel 15.3, many of the companies praised by Peters and Waterman encountered difficulties soon afterwards.

Deal and Kennedy's approach

The research of Deal and Kennedy provides another way of comparing and contrasting organisational cultures. Two important factors shape the organisational culture; the first is the extent of the risk connected with the activities of the company, and the second is the speed of feedback on the outcome of employees' decisions (Deal & Kennedy, 1982). These factors are portrayed in Table 15.1, with risk on the vertical axis and feedback on the horizontal axis. The Deal and Kennedy approach consists of four cultural profiles— tough-guy macho; work hard, play hard; **bet your company**; and process—which appear in Table 15.1. In the discussion that follows, an attempt is made (based on Deshpande & Parasuraman, 1986)

PANEL 15.3: Criticism of Peters and Waterman's approach

The research of Peters and Waterman has been subjected to criticism, with the lack of rigour in research methodology a prominent theme among critics. According to one critic, the samples of companies chosen were treated in a free and easy and uncontrolled manner (Silver, 1987). Some were deleted from the original list, and evidence from companies not included in the sample was used.

It is asserted that the tenuous link between cultures, excellence, and performance ended up as highly fragile. Included in the sample were companies with far from excellent performance, and a significant number of them subsequently encountered difficulties (Thompson & McHugh, 2002). A taste of the reality of the "people orientation" of one of the companies (McDonald's) is given by a critic. Behind the hoop-la and razzle-dazzle of competitive games and prizes lies the dull monotony of "speed-up" and de-skilled work based on the principle of the founder of scientific management (Taylor) at McFactory. The fuel of McFactory is cheap labour, teenage workers, part-time employment, minimum wage, and nonunion workers (Silver, 1987).

Recognising the validity of the criticisms of the methodology used in Peters and Waterman's research, it is only fair to stress that this work had significance in promoting an attitude change in favour of the husbandry of human resources in organisations.

TABLE 15.1

Deal and Kennedy's (1982) organisational culture profiles and examples of companies in each category: Copyright © 1982 and reproduced with permission

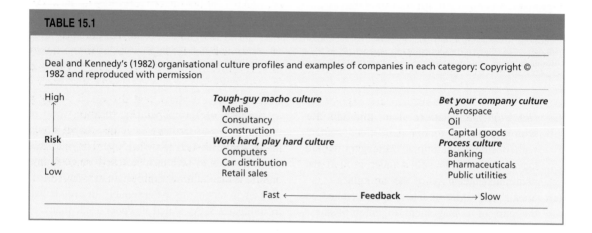

to relate culture typology to strategic issues connected with marketing and the product life cycle.

Tough-guy macho (high risk/fast feedback)

The heroes in this culture are tough, individualistic, superstitious, and risk-takers. They keep up with fashion, and embrace trendy lifestyles. They prefer sport that lends itself to solo performance (e.g., squash), and enjoy competitive verbal interactions. They turn a blind eye to cooperative assignments, stress the short-term nature of situations, and rarely learn from their mistakes. The entrepreneurial type in a company run by the owner typifies this culture. Organisations associated with this culture can be found in construction, cosmetics, television, radio, venture capital, and management consultancy. The **tough-guy** **macho** culture is said to be associated with a situation involving the launch of a new product that does not yield much in the way of profits (Deshpande & Parasuraman, 1986).

Work hard, play hard (low risk/fast feedback)

The heroes in this culture are super salespeople, friendly, not superstitious, fairly conventional in dress, prefer team sport, and socialise in the company of others, and they have a high work rate with quick solutions to problems. They have a short-term perspective and are likely to be associated with companies in the following areas: computers, car distributors, estate agencies, mass-produced goods, and door-to-door selling. Deshpande and Parasuraman (1986) suggest that a **work hard, play hard** culture relates to the situation when the product becomes a cash cow (as defined by the Boston Consulting Group), and the market share is large but not really growing.

Bet your company (high risk/slow feedback)

The heroes of this culture are technically competent with respect for authority. They show a tendency to double-check their decisions, are extremely slow, have a tolerance for ambiguity, and a capacity to make breakthroughs in a scientific sense. Their dress and lifestyle are fairly conventional and are compatible with their rank in the organisation. They like sport where one is not sure until the end what the outcome of the contest is going to be (e.g., golf), and they act as role models and mentors for younger members of the organisation. The organisations they are attached to (e.g., in oil, defence and aerospace, mining, and capital goods manufacture) are exposed to short-term changes in the economy and can face cash flow problems. A bet your company culture is more suited to a situation of increasing market share and when the launched product becomes what the Boston Consulting Group call a "star" (Deshpande & Parasuraman, 1986).

Process (low risk/slow feedback)

The heroes in this culture are rather cautious and protective of their position, which requires the display of an eye for detail, order, and punctuality within the context of well-defined procedures. They put a lot of time into their work, but realise that initiative is not at a premium, whereas red tape is high on the agenda, as is a penchant for discussing memoranda. Their modest lifestyle reflects their rank, and they generally engage in low-key sporting activities (e.g., jogging). The organisations they are attached to are located in banking, insurance, public utilities, governmental agencies, and pharmaceuticals. Deshpande and Parasuraman (1986) associate a **process culture** with a small market share in a growing market, and when the product flops.

Hodgetts (1991) used the Deal and Kennedy framework to categorise the culture of AT&T in the late 1980s. The company, prior to the break-up of the telephone industry in the USA, held a virtual monopoly in the telephone business, and was technology-driven, placing a lot of emphasis on research and development. Among its achievements were touch-dial and portable telephones. After the break-up, competition became severe; the company's culture could now be more accurately described as work hard, play hard, with a very heavy customer-driven momentum.

The cultural profiles shown in Table 15.1 could also be applied to particular functions within business. For example, a research chemist might be classified as the bet your company type and an accountant in a pharmaceutical company as a process type. When companies or individuals move from one type of culture to another, the problems of adjustment should be uppermost in the minds of management. For example, an executive used to functioning in a process culture could experience real culture shock and distress if abruptly moved to a work hard, play hard culture.

The evidence presented so far supports two major conclusions. First, that organisational cultures vary between companies and, second, that organisational cultures influence performance.

Other approaches

Seven primary characteristics of organisational culture have been proposed by O'Reilly, Chatman, and Caldwell (1991) and Chatman and Jehn (1994):

(1) *Innovation and risk-taking* (the extent to which employees are encouraged to take risks and be innovative).
(2) *Attention to detail* (the extent to which employees are expected to display precision, analysis, and attention to detail).
(3) *Outcome orientation* (the extent to which management take into account the outcome of decisions on employees).
(4) *People orientation* (the degree to which management decisions take into account the impact on people of output and productivity).
(5) *Team orientation* (the degree to which work activities are organised around teams rather than individuals).

(6) *Aggressiveness* (the degree to which people are aggressive and competitive rather than easy going).

(7) *Stability* (the degree to which organisational activities emphasise maintaining the status quo in contrast to growth).

Xenikou and Furnham (1996) also put the spotlight on the characteristics of organisational culture when they came forward with the following measures:

*   *Humanistic–helpful.* Members are expected to be supportive, constructive, and open to influence in their interactions with others.
*   *Affiliative.* Members are expected to be friendly, open, and sensitive to others.
*   *Approval.* Members feel that they should agree with others and gain their approval, and be liked by others.
*   *Conventional.* Members are expected to conform, follow the rules, and make a good impression.
*   *Dependent.* Members respond to centralised decision making by doing what is expected of them and pleasing authority figures.
*   *Avoidance.* The organisation fails to reward success, but is quick off the mark when it comes to punishing members for their mistakes. As a result, members try to avoid taking the blame for mistakes.
*   *Power.* Members believe they will be rewarded for controlling subordinates and being responsive to the demands of superiors, and for being seen to be in charge.
*   *Oppositional.* Members gain status and influence for being negative and confrontational.
*   *Competitive.* Members are rewarded for working against their peers and for outperforming others.
*   *Competence/perfectionistic.* Members are expected to work hard doing the right things, avoid mistakes, keep their eye on the ball, and work long hours.
*   *Achievement.* Members set challenging and realistic goals and pursue them with enthusiasm.
*   *Self-actualisation.* Members are encouraged to gain enjoyment from their work, take on new and interesting assignments, and develop themselves.

CHANGING AND DEVELOPING CULTURE

A variety of reasons and circumstances give rise to cultural change and development. For example, a serious crisis (e.g., a financial disaster or the collapse of the market for the company's product) hits the organisation and the shock challenges the status quo and questions the relevance of the existing culture; or, there has been a change in the top management of the company, with values at variance with the existing culture, or, the existing system and the values underpinning it are unsuitable. For particular circumstances that gave rise to the need for cultural change in a bank, see Panel 15.4.

In 1998 Shell, the multinational energy corporation, set about transforming its culture with an ambitious programme to remove traditional organisational barriers, such as slow decision making, bureaucratic inertia, and technical and business arrogance that threatened to stifle innovation. The aim was to instil a renewed sense of freedom within the company, while retaining the "cultural and behavioural glue" that had made it a successful international company. An important aspect of the transformation was to create business units that reflected the demands of current markets and customers, and that meant replacing the old hierarchical management model with a system that combines unconventional thinking with flexible and rapid organisational responses. Other aspects of the transformation were the introduction of ambitious performance targets and a drive to achieve greater diversity in the senior management, including a commitment to raise the number of top women managers from 4% to 20% within a few years (Corzine, 1998).

There are a number of ways to change and develop organisational culture. To begin with, the norms and desired behaviour must be made

Citigroup, the world's largest financial services group, has been hit repeatedly by scandals that have cost it billions of dollars in fines and compensation, and in the process damaged its reputation. A major factor responsible for this unsatisfactory situation is the pursuit of short-term profit at the expense of long-term reputation. This is a result of the way the company was formed—a series of mergers and acquisitions during the 1990s that brought together diverse businesses, such as investment banking, credit cards, retail banking, and lending to poor people. During this period the emphasis was on cutting the costs of support activities, such as reducing the cost of back office activities, and setting tough profit targets for the operating subsidiaries that enjoyed considerable autonomy. In this cultural setting, executives and managers who "cut corners" to meet quarterly targets could earn large performance bonuses. Therefore it is not surprising that serious irregularities or lapses occurred.

In 2005 the CEO, Chuck Prince, made it clear he was unhappy about this state of affairs, and announced plans to change the culture of Citigroup. He said he was eager to build a corporate culture that strikes a good balance between short-term operating profit and the long-term reputation of the company. The measures proposed range from basic steps, such as reviewing the company's value aspirations and setting up an ethics hotline to report unacceptable practices, to more substantial ones, such as the introduction of a common performance appraisal system for senior managers. This could be described as a primary mechanism (adopting the terminology used by Schein later) and resulted in replacing 50 performance appraisal systems the company collected from its growth by acquisition. Another primary mechanism—performance-related pay—is to be linked to the profits of the individual businesses as well as to the company's overall performance.

An obstacle in trying to promote a cohesive culture is the difficulty of moving key staff between divisions in order to promote the values now considered important. In this respect it is said that it is difficult for senior executives with no experience of a particular business to control them. Another difficulty encountered in financial services conglomerates arises from conflicts of interest; for example, one arm of the organisation is advising companies on the issue of shares or other securities and another arm is trying to sell those shares or securities to investors. Chunk Prince faces a challenging task in his endeavour to change the culture of Citigroup.

(*Financial Times*, 2005).

explicit, and then reinforced by top management. O'Reilly (1989) has recognised four approaches to the development of organisational culture:

- participation;
- information from others;
- symbolic action; and
- comprehensive reward systems.

Participation

The concept of participation has already been discussed in Chapter 12. It is essentially a process to facilitate the involvement of people in activities considered important by the organisation, and then to offer them recognition for their contributions. It is hoped that voluntary participation through appropriate mechanisms (e.g., quality circles, suggestion schemes, and advisory forums) will activate responsibility for people's actions and develop commitment to the ideals and policies of the organisation. In this way participation helps to develop and reinforce culture.

Information from others

A group situation is a powerful setting for the reinforcement of cultural values by colleagues or co-workers, as is apparent when looking at the influence exerted by work groups, discussed in Chapter 10. Where cultural values (e.g., ways of handling customers' complaints) have permeated the fabric of the group, one could expect older workers to provide hints and guidance to new employees on appropriate action and behaviour. If the culture is strong, this could give rise to uniformity of action with respect to certain practices in the organisation.

Symbolic action

One form of symbolic action is a certain type of management behaviour considered important in the organisation. For example, if the chief executive of a supermarket chain were to make periodic visits to the company's stores to talk to staff about business and nonbusiness related issues, this could reinforce the importance of this type of managerial style and behaviour.

As stated earlier, a common type of symbolic action is story-telling. For example, the experienced manager tells the new employee about a new recruit in the old days—now a senior manager—who went beyond the call of duty to rescue an awkward situation arising from the breakdown of the production system. The moral in the story is that those who put extra effort into the job will be rewarded with promotion. Story-telling is created as an exercise to reinforce attitudes and beliefs, the adoption of which is critical for corporate success. It is a process that helps to develop and sustain the culture of the company, and was also mentioned with regard to communication in Chapter 6.

Research in social psychology indicates that people use stories or information about a single event more than they use multiple perspectives in arriving at judgements (Borgida & Nisbett, 1977). For example, it is conceivable that a neighbour's bad experience with a particular make of car could influence your decision not to purchase that brand, despite favourable statistical evidence about the reliability of the product.

Another type of symbolic action is the mounting of ceremonies to reinforce organisational culture. Examples of these were given earlier when reference was made to recognising the performance of outstanding sales representatives. The rewards given at these ceremonies are meant not only to recognise past performance but also to encourage particular groups of employees to continue working even harder.

Comprehensive reward systems

There is a discussion of monetary and non-monetary reward systems in Chapters 4 and 18. Most organisations recognise and reinforce approved behaviour and, consequently, individual employees in such organisations feel a sense of satisfaction and accomplishment. Performance-related pay, for example, is often seen as a key factor in shaping employees' attitudes, and the end result is to create a performance-conscious culture (Fowler, 1988; Hendry, Pettigrew, & Sparrow, 1988). In Japan today the appeal of performance-related pay has put the spotlight on the issue of seniority versus merit (see Panel 15.5).

Although it is acceptable to reward good performance, it would be unwise to punish those who fail to reach the desired standards because of a depressing effect this could have on others, perhaps eventually leading to a risk-averse outlook (Hodgetts, 1991).

PANEL 15.5: Seniority versus merit in Japan

The Japanese system of paying employees according to seniority worked well for companies while the economy was growing. It fostered corporate loyalty and allowed companies to repay that loyalty in the form of increasing salaries. Seniority was also a method of assessing an employee's contribution to the company, and it complemented the Japanese belief in the value of experience and in the wisdom of old age. But it created a comfortable environment in which mediocre performance was condoned. As the employee's basic salary increased each additional year worked with the company, there was little incentive to improve job performance.

The maturing of the Japanese economy, and the ageing population, have undermined the seniority-based pay system in recent years. It was reported that Nissan considered abolishing seniority-based pay for nearly 3000 managers and putting them on a performance-related pay scheme. The news that one of Japan's most prominent industrial groups was planning to get rid of the cherished tradition of seniority conveyed to Japan's hard-working "salary man" that the secure life of ever-rising incomes could no longer be taken for granted.

A growing number of Japanese companies are experimenting with schemes that allow salaries to better reflect an employee's performance. Fujitsu tried to do this with the bonuses its managers receive twice a year. Honda uses a salary system that links pay to the previous year's performance. One lingering fear, even among companies that have embraced performance-related pay, is that greater emphasis on individual performance could destroy the group harmony that has served Japanese companies so well in the past. However, the changing economic environment is dictating the need to consider merit in systems of pay.

(Nakamoto, 1993, 2001)

Organisational socialisation

Closely related to the above approaches to the development of organisational culture—particularly information from others and symbolic action—is organisational socialisation. The concept of socialisation was discussed in the context of a behavioural perspective on personality in Chapter 2, and in connection with learning in Chapter 7. It is the process by which children learn, for example, to adopt various behavioural patterns, and to recognise what is both acceptable and unacceptable behaviour according to the norms of the society in which they live.

In a similar way to that in which people are socialised into society, they are also socialised into organisations. They perceive over a period of time notions of acceptable and unacceptable behaviour, modes of interaction with others, and ways of expressing their feelings, and this helps them to adapt to the organisation (Chao, O'Leary-Kelly, Wolf, Klein, & Gardner, 1994). In the context of culture, organisational socialisation has been described as the process through which employees learn about a company's culture, subsequently passing their knowledge and understanding on to others (Moorhead & Griffin, 2004). It is recognised that the important factor in organisational socialisation is the behaviour of experienced people as perceived by newcomers to the organisation (Barney, 1986). This behaviour would include story-telling, and the contents of the stories could be used subsequently by new employees to guide their actions.

The example set by leaders or top managers acting normally or in their role as coach, has been identified by Schein (1985) as "primary mechanisms" for changing culture. In a similar vein, Trice and Beyer (1991) underlined the importance of what top management say and how they behave in influencing the culture of the organisation. Top managers create norms that filter through the organisation and cover such activities as the desirability or otherwise of risk-taking, the extent of employee autonomy, the behaviour most likely to secure pay increases and promotions, the extent of employee autonomy, and the most appropriate dress to wear. At Southwest Airlines

in the USA, Herb Kelleher, the Chief Executive who founded the company, exerted a powerful influence in shaping the corporate culture. The core values of this culture included humour and altruism (Quick, 1992).

Informality seems to be the hallmark of the management style of Ingvar Kemprad, the Chief Executive of IKEA (the large Scandinavian home furnishing chain). The way he treats his staff and customers reflects his philosophy of life. He is endowed with a genuine warmth and interest in people, which is no doubt one of the most important reasons for his success. Due to his influence the company has a culture in which informality and simplicity are a striking feature. This is also reflected in the neat but casual dress of the employees—jeans and sweaters—and the relaxed office atmosphere where practically everyone sits in an open-plan office (Kreitner et al., 2002).

Schein (1985) also recognised the importance of the criteria used in certain human resource practices (e.g., selection, appraisal, rewards, promotions, and terminations) as important primary mechanisms in cultural change. For example, the criteria applicable here would relate to what selectors consider important characteristics in hiring staff, the most appropriate behaviour to secure career advancement and rewards, and what to avoid in order to reduce the likelihood of being made redundant.

The importance of human resources practices in transmitting culture has also been emphasised by Harrison and Carroll (1991). In the selection process one can envisage selectors making a serious effort to recruit people who have values consistent with the cultural values of the organisation, or who at the very least possess a fairly good proportion of those values, so that at the end of the day there is a good fit between the person and the organisation (Kristof, 1996). According to Chatman (1992), recruiting individuals whose values do not align with the cultural values of the organisation is likely to lead to a situation where employees lack motivation and commitment and experience dissatisfaction with their jobs. Sheridan (1992) suggests that such individuals are more likely to experience higher turnover rates.

Also, one must not ignore the part played in the socialisation process by formal training, as well as by pamphlets and statements prepared by the company on the culture of the organisation. But equally one should recognise that in some organisations the rhetoric used in pamphlets and training programmes bears little resemblance to the reality of the actual culture as reflected in people's behaviour. For example, a pronounced "people-centred" culture could be enshrined in the publicity literature, but the actual behaviour of managers may be the antithesis of these sentiments.

Finally, one can view organisational socialisation as consisting of three major phases. The first phase is the pre-entry stage where, for example, a trainee lawyer absorbs certain facets of the legal process from undertaking professional studies prior to joining a legal practice. The second phase is reflected in the way the entrant confronts organisational reality armed with the assumptions and values developed during the pre-entry stage. The third phase is manifest in the way the individual comes to terms with work norms, internalises them, and adapts to the organisation.

Having developed a culture appropriate to the company, the organisation cannot sit back and let things happen. The culture must be maintained by reinforcing beliefs, and making sure the cultural values are supported and sustained over time. Basically, this entails a first-rate process of communication of the beliefs and values to all employees, fostering commitment to the culture, and then rewarding people for their commitment (O'Reilly, 1989).

PANEL 15.6: Facilitators of cultural change and development in UK organisations

---

* In order to create a climate for change it is helpful to have a receptive external environment, together with managerial skills to take advantage of that environment.

* It is important to have a very clear and consistent drive for change from the apex of the organisation. This could emanate from the leadership displayed by senior or top managers brought into the organisation from outside, or from internal managers who have been pressing for change from a powerful internal position for some time. Pettigrew (1985) describes how Sir John Harvey-Jones and others at ICI had the licence and ability to think the unthinkable and to say the unsayable. In effect, they were a counter-culture force that changed culture and fostered corporate success, using a more open management style with pronounced decentralisation, together with simplification of the management structure. In addition, there was much emphasis on management and organisational development.

* Somewhat paradoxically, the agents of change at the top of the organisation have inarticulate and imprecise visions.

* Inconsistent action or behaviour is used by key figures in the new administration as a means to raise the level of tension within the organisation so as to promote change.

* "Deviants" and "heretics", both internal and external to the organisation, are allowed to say the unsayable and think the unthinkable. Either internal or external consultants could be used in this context.

* As a means of releasing energy, people are moved about within the organisation and their jobs are changed.

* New forums are created where problems are aired and shared, and where energy is directed at the need for change.

* The nature of the management process at the apex of the organisation is changed. For example, there could be a move from management as a divisive force to it being more coherent and cohesive.

* When the desired cultural change is achieved, structural arrangements should be changed to complement the event. Then the changed culture and structural arrangements could be fortified by the use of the organisation's reward system.

* The key role models who, through their behaviour, project crucial aspects of the new culture, should be identified. These are the people who raise the level of awareness about the cultural change, and reinforce it continuously.

* The message that encapsulates cultural change is transmitted deep into the organisation with the help of training and development strategies. If necessary, the organisational communication processes should be revamped to transmit the message.

* The agents of change should persist with their strategy, but equally they have to be patient because breaking down the core beliefs of the old culture is quite a complex process. Sensing and articulating the new issues and convincing others that they are worthy of serious attention is no easy task, and this stage could be studded by very inarticulate and imprecise visions of the future.

(Pettigrew, 1990)

Before concluding this section, we should note briefly the outcome of research into cultural change and development at ICI, Jaguar, and other companies in the UK and examples of techniques used in culture change at RWE in Germany and Kerry Foods. In this context, a variety of factors could be viewed as important facilitators (see Panels 15.6 and 15.7).

SOME CONTEMPORARY ISSUES

In this section the link between culture and contemporary issues, such as ethics, customer responsiveness, spirituality, and the learning organisation, will be briefly examined.

Ethics

Ethics is the code of moral principles and values that govern the behaviour of people with respect to what is right and wrong, and it can go beyond behaviour governed by the legal system. (There is a discussion of ethical issues in Chapter 9.) In recent years serious corporate accounting scandals, charges of insider trading, and company executives making personal use of company funds have served to focus attention on issues related to corporate ethics. Organisations should be active in promoting an ethical culture. The following measures might be considered relevant (Robbins, 2003; Smith, Grojean, & Ehrhart, 2001):

- Management, particularly top management, should lead by example and act as a responsible role model on ethical issues.
- Strive for the minimisation of ethical ambiguities by producing and circulating an organisational code of ethics. This document should state the organisation's primary values and ethical rules that employees are expected to follow.
- Be visible when it comes to rewarding ethical acts and disapproving and punishing unethical ones.
- Put in place procedures to enable employees to discuss ethical dilemmas and report unethical behaviour without fear of reprimand. An individual, such as an ethical counsellor, could oversee this process.

PANEL 15.7: Changing culture at RWE and Kerry Foods

RWE

RWE, the Essen-based power and water corporation (utility), is adapting to the forces of globalisation. Less than a decade ago the 100-year-old former Rheinisch-Westfalische Elektrizitatswerk was a stuffy industrial organisation of considerable size with interests as diverse as printing press manufacturing, and telecommunications, with a shareholder base dominated by Rhineland municipalities with multiple voting rights.

In 1998, after much discussion and negotiations, RWE abolished the municipalities' multiple voting rights and over the next few years became a global player, growing by expensive international acquisitions at a fast pace. Among the companies acquired were Thames Water in the UK and American Water Works. In a short space of time, 50% of income was generated abroad and 50% of employees were working outside Germany. It became Europe's third biggest listed utility, after German rival Eon and Italy's Enel. But the company grew too fast and debts soared. What was the company's response to this serious situation? In 2002 the late Friedel Neuber, former head of the state-owned West LB Bank and then chairman of RWE's supervisory board, appointed a Dutchman, Harry Roels, as CEO. It was a rare example of a foreigner taking a top job at a big German group. Roels, aged 56, a chemistry graduate, had spent 30 years working for Royal Dutch/Shell.

Roels stated that "culture change" was one of his priorities at RWE, and he expected it would go on for five years. He also said that to be "a truly international company you need a culture and leaders that are as international as its assets, and that is what we are working on". The following are some of the changes introduced, as well as his views on critical issues:

- A programme of disposals has been undertaken, particularly noncore businesses (e.g., the printing machinery manufacturer), leaving RWE focused on gas, electricity, and water. A key consideration when Roels became CEO was to reduce the company's debt, which was in excess of €23 billion. Debt has now fallen to below €15 billion. The policy now is for the company to engage in organic growth, instead of growing by major acquisitions. However, Roels does not rule out smaller or medium-sized acquisitions to round off the product portfolio, particularly in the

---

PANEL 15.7: (Cont'd)

---

gas and electricity industries, rather than in the water industry, where links between water companies and municipalities make consolidation unlikely.

- Roels created a "group business committee" consisting of 12 executives from across the group (RWE), as opposed to the five-strong legally required *Vorstand* (management board). He found that the *Vorstand* had weaknesses in taking a balanced view of business issues across the group. By contrast, the group business committee became much more effective as a forum in which individual executives had to raise issues and defend their ideas. (Something similar to the group business committee was set up by Josef Ackermann, the Swiss-born CEO, at Deutsche Bank.) The creation of the group business committee has significance beyond mere organisational change. Previously RWE operated like a classic German conglomerate, whereby different parts of the group acted independently or competed with each other. It is said that Roels has driven another nail in the coffin of the traditional German conglomerate. He is very keen to emphasise the importance of the group, and that means "not putting the division first, but putting the group first".

- Non-German ways of working have been introduced. Certain formalities in addressing people (e.g., Herr Doctor) have been discouraged, and all members of the board of directors have agreed to call each other by their first names. Harry Roels is always addressed as Harry by his subordinates.

- There are other little symbolic things one should note. Roels feels that senior executives should eat with other employees in the canteen. Also, he has abolished the practice of somebody standing by the door and opening it for him the moment he arrives at the company's headquarters by car.

- Roels speaks English fluently. He has arranged things so that there are international groups of people meeting together and communicating partly in German and partly in English, leaving people to use the language with which they feel most comfortable.

- Roels sees limits to culture change. Something he shares with a number of German chief executives, including Jurgen Schrempp (CEO of DaimlerChrysler) is that he is not in favour of reforming Germany's *Mitbestimmung* or co-determination laws, by which half the supervisory board is made up of employee representatives. He says RWE has had a long and basically positive experience with *Mitbestimmung*, and he values the involvement of employees. He goes on to say, "at the end of the day change can best be executed in a climate of trust and cooperation or consensus rather than in a conflict-ridden environment". (Incidentally, Germany's main employer organisations think *Mitbestimmung* is an anachronistic system that makes German companies uncompetitive.)

(Atkins and Milne, 2004)

Kerry Foods

Kerry Foods (the Irish food products giant) was growing rapidly as a result of acquisitions. This brought in its wake problems arising from the harmonisation of working practices and changing the nature of jobs in the UK (e.g., the job of a van driver delivering food products to retail outlets was changed from merely a delivery role to that of a sales position). There was a desperate need to cultivate a single-team ethos within the enlarged organisation because of what was happening in the depots where the drivers congregated and collected the food products for delivery. For example, there was widespread distrust of head office, some depots were performing much worse than others, some drivers would not complete their rounds, absence rates and staff turnover were high, and there were numerous complaints from customers.

It was not surprising in these circumstances for the personnel and training manager of the company to conclude that there was something desperately wrong with the company's culture. She decided to conduct a culture "health check", drawing on the services of the Department of Economic Psychology, University of Essex, which had developed a cultural audit tool called the Nine Key Factors Survey. Based on nine measures of work culture, a survey was undertaken whereby staff were asked to assess their employer on factors such as fairness, respect, trust, acceptance, team spirit and development. Each factor would receive a rating out of five, and there was also an overall score. The results highlighted problems that needed further investigation.

Out of this investigation came the realisation that, for example, employees were less than enthusiastic about the numerous initiatives that originated from the UK head office in Andover, Hampshire, such as expanding the van delivery role to incorporate sales activity, the advent of Saturday working, and the introduction of hand-held computers for stock control. In addition, fundamental supervisory and managerial problems were identified in the depots, such as a too relaxed management style or one that encouraged dissent among subordinates. Various training programmes (e.g., induction, leadership, coaching, teambuilding), face-to-face meetings, and incentives were introduced to tackle these problems. Some problems were difficult to solve, including trying to create team spirit and loyalty to a remote head office from lone salespeople (van drivers) operating from 27 different depots, but reasonable success has been achieved.

There is now evidence to indicate that employees are beginning to trust the management more than in the past and the business is more successful. Finally, note a concluding comment from the personnel and training manager: "It has to be accepted that the organisation is a depot-based business, and that it would be futile to impose an inflexible culture on the many depots across the country. One has to recognise that the culture in some depots will be different from others."

(Littlefield, 1999)

Customer responsiveness

In recent years there has been emphasis on customer-responsive cultures. In this type of culture one could expect to find a number of measures to promote the interests of the customer, such as the following (Bettencourt, Gwinner, and Meuter, 2001; Robbins, 2003):

• Recruit and select people who possess personality attributes and attitudes in line with a high service orientation. These could include an outgoing and friendly disposition coupled with a desire to provide high standards of service.
• Key managers within the organisation should show their commitment to customer care by words and deeds.
• Employees who provide a good level of service to customers are well rewarded; in effect the organisation makes pay and promotions dependent upon impressive service to the customer.
• Flexibility and autonomy should be injected into the jobs of those charged with meeting the customer's requirements. This would be consistent with the concept of empowerment.

Spirituality

Spirituality in the workplace is not concerned with organised religious practices. However, it is concerned with the inner life of the person, and looks at ways in which that inner life can enrich and be enriched by meaningful work in an organisational setting. Those who subscribe to spirituality in this sense would like to see the development of an organisational culture that recognises that people have a spiritual side to their make-up, are eager to seek meaning, purpose and fulfilment in the work they do, and to strive for satisfaction from connecting with other people and feeling they are part of a community (Ashmos & Duchon, 2000; McCormick, 1994). A number of reasons are given for the preoccupation with workplace spirituality. These include a desire to obtain something of significance from life in a world where, increasingly, organised religion has lesser meaning for

many people, where existing work may lack meaning, where there is a need to counter-balance occupational and life's pressures, and a desire to bring personal values and beliefs more into line with work-based values.

If one were to profile the culture of the spiritual organisation it is likely that the following features would be heavily underlined (Robbins, 2003). There would be a climate of openness where people feel free to air their feelings and emotions without the realisation that they will be disadvantaged; where mutual trust and honesty exist; where people are highly valued and their growth and development are a key issue; and where empowerment is a striking feature of the organisational landscape. Some would not condone this type of emphasis when it comes to shaping the culture of the organisation and are likely to point out that spirituality and profitability are not natural bedfellows. However, there is evidence to indicate that there is a positive relationship between the two.

Learning organisation

In Chapter 7 the concept of the learning organisation was examined, and it was stated that the learning organisation could help with the development of the company's capacity to respond well to changes in its environment by facilitating the learning of all its employees, and by being alert to the need for continuous transformation. In essence, the aim is to create a culture of continuous learning for all employees.

Following a review of the relevant literature, Daft (2004) maintains that one of the potent characteristics of the learning organisation is a strong organisational culture that incorporates the following values. Employees are aware of the whole system and how the constituent parts fit together. The emphasis on the whole minimises the significance of boundaries, and despite the existence of sub-cultures, there is a strong commitment to the dominant culture. Also, equality and trust are primary values and it is apparent that the culture of the learning organisation creates a pronounced sense of community and caring for one another. The emphasis on treating everyone with care and respect generates an atmosphere of trust where people feel secure. This allows experimentation in a climate where people do not feel too inhibited about making mistakes, and learning is an ongoing process. Finally, the culture within the learning organisation encourages risk-taking and a commitment to change and improving systems and processes. A basic value of the learning organisation is to question the status quo. For those who are innovative with respect to products and processes there is due recognition for their contributions via the dispensing of appropriate rewards. Some might view the values of the learning organisation outlined here as rather idealistic; however, as a set of principles they are worth considering.

BENEFITS OF CULTURE

A number of benefits accrue to organisations from the development of an appropriate organisational culture. Hodgetts (1991) identifies the more important as:

- effective control;
- normative order;
- promotion of innovation;
- strategy formulation and implementation; and
- strong commitment from employees.

Effective control

A strong culture is reflected in shared beliefs and expectations that exact compliance. As such, organisational culture acts as a control mechanism in regulating behaviour (O'Reilly & Chatman, 1996). As culture seeps through the organisation, people register what they should do (e.g., perform efficiently and effectively and keep a firm grip on the quality of the product or service) and what they should not do (e.g., engage in poor teamwork or be disrespectful to customers). When employees do not act in accordance with the beliefs and values of the culture, managers and colleagues are likely to intervene and initiate corrective action.

An example of measures taken to exert control in a cultural context involved the founders of a consultancy firm who established an open and charismatic managerial style capable of generating strong emotional ties among the consultants employed. The work undertaken by the consultants tended to be variable and flexible, and not amenable to conventional mechanisms of control. Obviously, this presented a problem for the management, more so because the work was carried out at the workplace of the client, with the potential for weakening the consultant's sense of identity with the firm. A corrective measure used in this situation was to develop a large number of social and leisure activities, underlining the value of fun, body contact, and support from colleagues. In addition, presentations were made about the firm's performance in order to promote favourable perceptions. The outcome of these processes was the building of social and emotional ties, and the adoption by the firm of a community culture (Alvesson, 1988).

Normative order

The use of norms to guide behaviour (discussed in Chapter 10) is intimately connected with effective control. Norms reflect the culture, and in strong cultures they attract wide support and promote consensus. In weak cultures the consensus may still be there, but the support is weak. The problem with strong cultures that underpin strategies and behaviour is the great difficulty in changing them when business conditions dictate different directions with respect to markets and behaviour. This was a challenge faced by Louis Gerstner when he took over at IBM in 1993. His aim was to reverse the company's conservative, risk-averse culture, and by the late 1990s he seemed to have achieved some notable successes. One particular course of action he took was to relax dress standards to create a more relaxed and less rigid atmosphere at IBM.

When strong cultures support the right strategy for a company and norms are supportive of change, the marriage of culture and strategy is a powerful mix in terms of company performance (Kotter & Heskett, 1992). But strong cultures that are the reverse of efficiency and effectiveness (such as, "quality is an expensive luxury") could be counter-productive (Miller, 1994).

Promotion of innovation

Innovation is an emerging issue in the domain of organisational culture. Innovation can be viewed as an activity connected with the generation of new processes, products, or services. An example of an attempt to be innovative in research and development was a joint venture set up by Siemens, IBM, and Toshiba. The culture of an organisation can encourage creative thinking by the development of norms that support the promotion of innovation.

O'Reilly (1989), having investigated norms supporting innovation across a wide range of industries, found a high degree of commonality between them in terms of their importance to managers, and that certain norms (listed in Table 15.2) were found to be useful in supporting and facilitating the process of innovation. Apart from the encouragement of creative thinking, subscribing to the norms supportive of innovation was helpful to staff when faced with conflicts that emerge when ideas are proposed and implemented.

TABLE 15.2

Norms that promote innovation (O'Reilly, 1989): Reproduced with permission

Norms to promote creativity	*Norms to promote implementation*

(1) Risk-taking
• Freedom to try things and fail
• Acceptance of mistakes
• Allow discussion of "dumb" ideas
• No punishments for failure
• Challenge the status quo
• Forget the past
• Willingness not to focus on the short term
• Expectation that innovation is part of job
• Positive attitudes about change
• Drive to improve
 	
(2) Rewards for change
• Respect for new ideas
• Build into the structure:
  • budgets • opportunities • time
  • tools • resources • promotions
• Top management attention and support
• Celebration of accomplishments
• Suggestions are implemented
• Encouragement
(3) Openness
• Open communication and share information
• Listen better
• Open access
• Bright people, strong egos
• Scanning, broad thinking
• Force exposure outside the company
• Move people around
• Encourage lateral thinking
• Adopt the customer's perspective
• Accept criticism
• Don't be too sensitive
• Continuous training
• Intellectual honesty
• Expect and accept conflict
• Willingness to consult others
	(1) Common goals
	• Sense of pride in the organisation
	• Teamwork
	• Willingness to share the credit
	• Flexibility in jobs, budgets, functional areas
	• Sense of ownership
	• Eliminate mixed messages
	• Manage interdependencies
	• Shared visions and a common direction
	• Build consensus
	• Mutual respect and trust
	• Concern for the whole organisation
	(2) Autonomy
	• Decision-making responsibility at lower levels
	• Decentralised procedures
	• Freedom to act
	• Expectation of action
	• Belief that you can have an impact
	• Delegation
	• Quick, flexible decision making
	• Minimise the bureaucracy
	(3) Belief in action
	• Don't be obsessed with precision
	• Emphasis on results
	• Meet your commitments
	• Anxiety about timeliness
	• Value getting things done
	• Hard work is expected and appreciated
	• Empower people
	• Emphasis on quality
	• Eagerness to get things done
	• Cut through the bureaucracy

Strategy formulation and implementation

There are occasions when organisational culture informs the adoption of a particular strategy for the company. For example, an important feature in the financial and market success of the US corporation, Motorola, is its strong commitment to substantial investment in research and development, and to the commercial exploitation of the ensuing inventions. The culture of the company has been created around significant research and development, high quality, and active enthusiasm for customer service (Thierren, 1989). What is interesting to note is that this culture has bolstered the strategy of the company, providing the impetus for the development of new products—e.g., lightweight cellular telephones and wrist-watch pagers, which were hailed as major technological breakthroughs.

In the mid-1990s corporate creativity associated with "reinventing strategy" became an issue. Hamel (in an address to the 1993 annual conference of the Strategic Management Society) maintained that companies are pressurised by investors to improve the efficiency of their current operations and resources, but are not sufficiently stimulated to create new markets, products, or even industries. Downsizing seems to rule, with an epidemic of corporate anorexia (Lorenz, 1993e). Observations attributable to Hamel on reinventing strategy appear in Panel 15.8.

Employee commitment

The interaction of people and culture has reinforcing qualities, frequently resulting in committed employees. As employees develop their skills on the job, including interactive skills, there is a favourable impact on the level of morale, which, in turn, enhances commitment to the organisation. The commitment is said to go through three phases, as identified in the three sources of attitude change introduced in Chapter 9—i.e., compliance, identification, and internalisation.

With regard to compliance, people conform in order to obtain some material benefit. When they reach the identification stage, the demands of culture are accepted in order to maintain good relationships with colleagues. In the final phase—internalisation—people find that the adoption of the cultural values of the organisation produces intrinsic satisfaction because these values are in line with their own personal values. In many ways this is an ideal state as far as the acceptance of organisational values is concerned (because of the identification with the company), and, if widespread, is indicative of a strong culture.

The benefits of culture could be short-lived when unwelcome mergers or hostile takeover bids undermine the stability of corporate culture. It may not be easy to sustain loyalty and identification with the company when possible threats to job security or the removal of benefits are perceived.

PANEL 15.8: Reinventing strategy

Restructuring (downsizing and delayering) was necessary because it made companies smaller, and so was business process engineering because it made them better. But without the reinvention of strategy they would not become different and better. The only way a company can get ahead is to foresee the next round of competitive advantage and evolution in its industry and to create it. The biggest rewards will ultimately go to companies that transform their industries, change the rules of the game, redraw industry boundaries, and establish fundamentally new competitive parameters. The primary goal must be to become the architect of an industry's transformation.
   Note the barriers to reinventing strategy:

* There are too many senior people in the organisation from the same industry, discipline, or cultural background who are blind to new opportunities.
* There are powerful figures in organisations with out-of-date knowledge.
* There are obvious difficulties because the industry is still emerging and its boundaries are ill-defined. In which case it would probably be better to concentrate on and exploit the organisation's core competencies.

(Lorenz, 1993a)

PANEL 15.9: Difficulties in merging cultures

DaimlerChrysler

Fusing the Daimler (German car manufacturer) and Chrysler (US car manufacturer) operations in the late 1990s was seen as difficult because of the determination of Germany's powerful unions to resist the Americanisation of working practices. Frequently these unions warned against the Americanisation of German companies because they believed it represented cheap labour, poor job security, and less union power.

On the other hand, American managers found it difficult to accept the German consensus approach to management. This was reflected in joint decision making at factory floor level (and no member of a works council could be sacked). Also, the generous social benefits in Germany were foreign to Chrysler's workers in Detroit, while certain management concepts or practices applied in the USA were new to German executives. These included stock option plans for senior executives, performance-related pay, "lean management", and the working lunch.

Chrysler has gone through tumultuous times since the 1998 merger with Daimler-Benz. DaimlerChrysler took serious action to combine what it saw as the best of its European and North American cultures shortly after the merger took place. Several groups of senior executives from each side of the Atlantic were brought together at IMD, the Swiss Business School. The US and German executive groups were each asked to list the other group's positive and negative attributes. Each also had an opportunity to defend itself in the face of comment from the other group. In early 2005 it appears the hard work that has gone into making the corporate marriage work is paying off. The company is receiving praise for its eye-catching new models, and is gaining market share and some improvements in profitability.

(Burt, 1999; Simon, 2005; Woodhead, 1998)

Kmart and Sears

We will have to wait some time to establish whether or not another corporate marriage in the making, which does not straddle country boundaries, becomes a successful reality. Recently it was proposed that two US companies—Kmart and Sears—would merge. Eddie Lambert, the Chairman of Kmart made the point that the two "cultures" should merge. He went on to say that one cannot expect this to happen overnight, and expressed a preference for a culture that was customer-focused and store-focused, but acknowledged that getting the right blend might not be easy.

Sears, founded in 1886, is one of the USA's most established shopping institutions. Although it discounts its products, it is not a pure discounter like Kmart, which celebrated its centenary in 1999. In Sears stores there is a high level of product knowledge and customer service among staff, and this is most noticeable when they are selling home appliances. In fact, this is the type of culture the Chairman of Kmart would like to see in the company that will evolve from the merger. Service to the customer does not currently feature prominently at Kmart, where convenience and price receive prime emphasis, and product knowledge is of lesser importance.

In the negotiations between Sears and Kmart, concrete steps have been take to ensure that a smooth integration of the separate entities will take place. This is likely to be facilitated by the fact that in recent years there are signs of the cultures of the two companies becoming closer. According to a senior US consultant (Booz, Allen, and Hamilton), Kmart has been trying to sell more branded products, while Sears has been adding more soft goods to its stores. A senior analyst at Deutsche Bank says: "I am not exactly sure what Kmart's culture is; it's very clear what Sears' culture is. But they could both benefit from each other's management styles."

(Politi & Foster, 2004)

In other circumstances, the expected benefits of a merger of companies or a joint venture fail to materialise. For example, harmonisation of outlook does not occur because employees accustomed to performing their duties in a particular way are unable to subscribe to a different set of values brought about by the change in strategic direction of the enlarged enterprise (see Panel 15.9). On this theme Cartwright and Cooper (1993) draw our attention to their conclusion that the failure of a number of company mergers to realise their economic potential could be primarily attributable to conflicting organisational cultures.

As a final comment on commitment, Peters (1992) advises employers to look for passion and commitment towards the work itself rather than loyalty to the company. However, this could be problematic for those who have very mundane jobs.

INTERNATIONAL COMPARISONS

Earlier (in reporting Ouchi's work) there was reference to comparisons between US and Japanese companies. In this section there will be an examination of cultural differences at the societal level likely to impinge on the way organisations operate. Those whose work takes them across cultural and national boundaries face different legal and political systems, as well as different primary values and practices that characterise particular countries.

Increasingly, managers in organisations are thinking internationally, and this is prompted by the enlargement of the European Union, developments within the former Soviet bloc, the growing importance of the Pacific Rim countries (e.g., China, Japan, South Korea, Taiwan, Hong Kong, and Singapore) and developments in other countries, such as India. The means at the disposal of managers to assist them in understanding and coping with cultural barriers that exist between countries are, basically, training programmes and direct experience of interacting and doing business with international clients and customers.

Cross-cultural studies

Hofstede

Hofstede (1980a), a Dutch organisational sociologist, developed a 32-item scale to measure work-goal or work-related values, and administered it to equivalent and stratified samples of IBM staff in 40 nations when he was a research director at the company. He obtained average scores on the items for samples of each nation, calculated a correlation matrix among the average values for each nation on the 32 items, subjected the results to factor analysis, and obtained four factors (see below). He then mapped the 40 countries empirically by locating their factor scores along the four dimensions (Hwang, 2005). Similarities and differences between national cultures were found. The research data were analysed in such a way as to eliminate any differences that might be due to varying practices and policies in different companies. As a result, any variations found between countries were attributed to national culture. The four dimensions (listed here and in Table 15.3) showing differences between national cultures that were discovered (and a culture could be rated high or low on these dimensions) were:

- power distance;
- uncertainty avoidance;
- individualism–collectivism; and
- masculinity–femininity.

Power distance. This dimension evaluates the extent to which a culture encourages superiors to exercise power. A culture ranked high in power distance encouraged the expectation that superiors wielded much power, with the recognition of a power imbalance between superiors and subordinates. Although subordinates showed a preference for a directive management style, this culture exemplified low trust between superiors and subordinates. Also, subordinates tended to be passive, organisation structure tended to be tall, and decision making centralised. Examples of countries falling into this category are Panama, Korea, Hong Kong, and Singapore.

In the light of this cultural orientation, consider the following incident involving Asian airline employees. After analysing the circumstances of the crash of a passenger jet in Guam in August 1997, in which 228 people lost their lives, the American investigators believed that cultural deference to authority among the Korean crew was one of two major factors contributing to the tragedy; the other was the crew's unquestioning belief in the autopilot (Rhodes, 1998).

In a culture ranked low in power distance there was a closer relationship between superiors and subordinates, with greater mutual trust, and a firm expectation by subordinates to be involved in decision making. Apart from the tendency towards decentralisation, organisation structures would tend to be flatter. The UK, USA, The Netherlands, Australia, and Canada would fall into this category.

Uncertainty avoidance. This dimension is concerned with the extent to which a culture encourages or discourages risk-taking. In certain cultures—e.g., Japan, Iran, and Turkey—there tended to be strict laws with stiff penalties for deviants. Need for security was high, and those with expert knowledge were respected. Managers tended to be low risk-takers. Cultures rated high on uncertainty avoidance adopted particular strategies to counteract the high levels of anxiety and stress stemming from uncertain situations. These strategies included working hard, not changing jobs, and being unsympathetic to those not obeying the rules.

TABLE 15.3

Four dimensions on which national cultures vary (adapted from Hofstede, 1983)

Dimension	Low	High
Power distance dimension (POW)	(Australia, Israel, Denmark, Sweden) • Less centralisation • Flatter organisation pyramids • Smaller wage differentials • Structure in which manual and clerical work are equal jobs	(Philippines, Mexico, Venezuela, India, Brazil) • Greater centralisation • Tall organisation pyramids • More supervisory personnel • Structure in which white-collar jobs are valued more than blue-collar jobs
Masculinity–femininity dimension (MAS)	(Sweden, Denmark, Thailand, Finland, Yugoslavia) • Sex roles are minimised • Organisations do not interfere with people's private lives • More women in more qualified jobs • Soft, yielding, intuitive skills are rewarded • Social rewards are valued	(Japan, Australia, Venezuela, Italy, Mexico) • Sex roles are clearly differentiated • Organisations may interfere to protect their interests • Fewer women are in qualified jobs • Aggression, competition, and justice are rewarded • Work is valued as a central life interest
Individualism–collectivism dimension (IND)	(Venezuela, Columbia, Taiwan, Mexico, Greece) • Organisation as "family" • Organisation defends employee interests • Practices are based on loyalty, a sense of duty, and group participation	(United States, Australia, Great Britain, Canada, The Netherlands) • Organisation is more impersonal • Employees defend their own self-interests • Practices encourage individual initiative
Uncertainty avoidance dimension (UNC)	(Denmark, Sweden, Great Britain, United States, India) • Less structuring of activities • Fewer written rules • More generalists • Variability • Greater willingness to take risks • Less ritualistic behaviour	(Greece, Portugal, Japan, Peru, France) • More structuring activities • More written rules • More specialists • Standardisation • Less willingness to take risks • More realistic behaviour

In the opposite situation, where cultures are rated low on uncertainty avoidance—e.g., Hong Kong and Taiwan—people tended to experience less stress from ambiguous situations, and attached less importance to adhering to the rules. Generally, people had strong feelings of personal competence and managers seemed more prepared to take risks.

Individualism–collectivism. This dimension evaluates the extent to which a culture possesses individualistic features rather than group or societal features. The individualistic orientation, prevalent in the UK, Canada, and the USA, puts the spotlight on such characteristics as achievement and the use of personal initiative, with more inward concerns based on the self and the family.

By contrast, in a collectivist culture—e.g., Singapore, Philippines, and Mexico—the individual receives help and support from the extended family and tribal group, and is expected to reciprocate with loyalty. The emphasis could be on belonging, having a sense of duty, and a strong belief in the power of group decision making.

Masculinity–femininity. This dimension portrays the type of accomplishments valued by the culture. In societies where masculinity prevailed—e.g., the UK, Germany, Japan, South Africa, and Italy—emphasis was placed on money, material possessions, and ambition, with clear lines drawn between male and female roles. A lot of emphasis could be placed on challenge and advancement, and people are encouraged to be individual decision makers.

By contrast, where femininity prevailed—e.g., The Netherlands and Scandinavia—emphasis was placed on cooperation, friendly atmosphere, job security, caring, quality of life, and the environment, with blurred lines drawn between sex roles, and greater sexual equality. Group decision making is encouraged, and managers find it easy to subscribe to the value of giving autonomy to subordinates.

More recent work undertaken by Hofstede has added a fifth dimension to his model, called "long-term orientation"—i.e., personal thrift, perseverance, and adoption of traditions to the modern world. He also changed the masculinity/femininity dimension because of its sexist overtones. The long-term orientation dimension appears to be a particularly distinctive feature of East Asian cultures (Goffee, 1997; Hofstede, 1993). Hofstede located 40 cultures on a global cultural map, with each of these dimensions representing a continuum along which each culture is placed.

There have been criticisms of Hofstede's original work. For example, Tyson and Jackson (1992) maintained that:

> Hofstede's work deals in generalisations. There may indeed be national characteristics, but it is likely that there are major variations within societies. The notion that all managers have the same vision of power distance or uncertainty avoidance in the US or UK, for example, is absurd. The diversity at the organisational level means we must only use this research with caution, and not seek to perpetuate stereotypes.

Similarly, Furnham and Gunter (1993) stated that "there appears to be very little evidence demonstrating the veracity, as opposed to the simplificatory appeal, of the different systems. They offer little in the way of process (e.g., their origin, maintenance, and impact); instead they are descriptive."

Though Hofstede's research and findings may have weaknesses, it would be unwise to relegate to an insignificant position the need to understand values underpinning culture, and the impact of culture on organisations. Other researchers have adopted Hofstede's approach to cultural clustering (i.e., the grouping of similar cultures). For example, Ronen and Shenkar (1985) concluded that most countries could be classified using eight basic cultural clusters—Nordic, Germanic, Anglo, Latin, European, Far Eastern, Arab, and Near Eastern.

Trompenaars

A more recent cross-cultural model is provided by Trompenaars (1993). He has been influenced by the work of Kluckhohn and Strodtbeck (1961) on value orientations and Hampden-Turner's (1983) dilemma theory. His research revealed seven dimensions of culture, five of which will receive most attention here because of their relevance to business organisations.

Universalism versus particularism. Universalism means essentially that what is good and true can be discovered, defined, and applied everywhere. Particularism means that unique circumstances and relationships are more important considerations in determining what is right and good than reference to abstract rules. Examples of countries at the universalism position are the USA, Austria, and Germany, whereas Indonesia and Venezuela would fall into the particularism category.

Individualism versus collectivism. This is a dimension of culture already acknowledged by Hofstede and others. Individualism is prevalent when individuals, for example, achieve things on their own and assume personal responsibility, whereas in a collectivist setting individuals function through groups, assuming joint responsibility for outcomes. Examples of countries at the individualism end of the continuum are the USA, the UK, and the Czech Republic, whereas Japan, Singapore, and Thailand fall into the collectivist category.

Neutral versus affective. Neutral means that emotions should be held in check. There is a tendency in neutral cultures to view the expression of anger or delight in the workplace as unprofessional. Those of a neutral disposition do not readily express what they think or feel, they are uncomfortable with physical contact outside their private circle, and feel embarrassed or awkward at public displays of emotion.

Affective means that it is natural to openly express emotions. Those of an affective disposition display immediate actions either verbally or nonverbally with an expressive face, raised voice, and body gestures; they are at ease with physical contact. Examples of countries classified as neutral are Japan, the UK, and Singapore, whereas Brazil, Chile, Mexico, and The Netherlands fall into the affective category.

Specific relationship versus diffuse relationship. Specific relationship means that there is a preference for people to keep their public and private lives separate, guarding the latter very closely. There is a tendency to display mostly a public face. People appear to be abrasive, open, and they get to the point quickly, but equally they have the capacity to vary their approach to fit the circumstances.

Diffuse relationship means that the private face is far more prominent than the public face, and in normal relationships it is possible to detect more of the inner-self of the person. Work and private life are closely linked, and there is a certain consistency in the person's approach. The person appears rather introverted, closed, and indirect in utterances, often evading issues and "beating around the bush". Examples of countries classified as specific relationship are the UK and the USA, whereas Spain, Chile, and Venezuela fall into the category of the diffuse relationship.

Achievement versus ascription. Achievement means subscribing to values embedded in the Protestant ethic. People work hard to improve themselves, they emphasise accomplishment, are ambitious, and try to do even better than previously.

Ascription means that status is attributable to respected and admired figures (e.g., elders, highly qualified), with a tendency to show respect for those who have acquired status, and this is quite independent of task or function. Examples of countries associated with achievement are the USA, Germany, Sweden, and Switzerland, whereas

Indonesia, Venezuela, and Chile fall into the ascription category.

The other two dimensions of culture are the way time is viewed and attitudes to the environment. For example, the UK has a greater sense of the past than the USA. With regard to attitudes to the environment, some societies feel that their destiny is in their hands and they have greater control over their environment than others who do not have this outlook.

Cultural diversity: Teams and leadership

In this section cultural diversity will be viewed from the angle of multi-cultural teams and how managerial leadership is influenced by national culture. In the last decade the development of global markets has created numerous cross-cultural contacts, and the ensuing dialogue has formed the basis for transacting global business (Adler, 2002). This has implications for the development of culturally diverse teams, where people from different cultures relate to each other, aided by the power of new technology when it comes to communication systems. The output of culturally diverse teams can be impressive if diversity is well managed. It is said that the potential of diverse teams is not fully realised unless one pays particular attention to the way those teams are managed (Kandola, 1995).

To operate successfully across cultures it is important to be able to recognise cultural differences and be adaptable (Marx, 1999), as well as viewing the organisation as international in orientation. To satisfy the latter it would seem necessary to be aware of political currents likely to affect international trade, to have a management and organisation system tuned into the demands of world markets, and management development activities that nurture an appropriate international outlook (see Panel 15.10). On the theme of management development, one may well ask what type of managerial leadership is appropriate in particular cultures. As a broad principle one can acknowledge that culture influences leadership style (Koopman et al., 1999). More specific associations will now be examined.

PANEL 15.10: Coping with cultural shock

Most managers can be effective abroad if they work hard on the "adaptability" factor. Understanding how people in other cultures think is not enough. International managers must deal with people's emotions and develop their social skills in order to be successful. Adaptability is a process that starts with excitement and curiosity—the honeymoon phase—and moves back and forth between feelings of anxiety and well-being before arriving at full cultural adjustment. The ideal is to reach a compromise between preserving one's own identity and being open to alternative ways of doing business.

It is important to recognise cultural differences in the way people from different countries behave and do business. For example, in Germany long working hours are a sign that someone is not clever enough to finish tasks within normal hours, and humour is not welcome in business. In France lunches of 2 to 3 hours are normal, but it is acceptable to discuss business over the dessert. The Chinese are extremely flexible and are able to juggle demands on their time. In Japan people stand up when a superior enters the room. British managers are exceptionally good at dealing with ambiguity, they can be very flexible, and are very good at dealing with adversity. In the USA salaries help to define social status, and there is no social taboo about asking people how much they earn. Also, in the United States the business pressure is severe, and Americans feel that the US business culture is the right one, because of less exposure to other cultures in their youth.

One should be sensitive to potential areas of friction. For example, managers from the USA and the UK may find it hard to adapt to the political and hierarchical business structures in France. The Germans, accustomed to structure and predictability, may be put off by the fluid, agendaless approach adopted in Brazil. In both Germany and Japan, emphasis is placed on long-term relationships and quality. Type "A" personalities, discussed in Chapter 19, may not function well in certain regions. These dedicated high achievers may function well in individualistic societies, such as the USA and the UK, but in Asian countries (consensus-driven cultures) their impatience and intolerance can be a liability.

Finally, the ideal qualities of the international manager are said to be: curiosity, flexibility, communication skills, assertiveness, team working, stress resistance, and self-reliance.

(Maitland, 1999b; Marx, 1999)

In some cultures leaders are respected when they take strong decisive action, whereas in other cultures consultative and participative decision-making approaches are more valued. According to Den Hartog et al. (1999), in a culture where authoritarian leadership is valued it would be pointless acting in a way more characteristic of a participative or democratic leader. But in a culture that endorses a more nurturing and humanistic leadership style, being sensitive and considerate as a leader could be functional. Using Hofstede's framework, examined in the previous section, masculine cultures are probably more tolerant of strong directive leaders than feminine cultures. In the latter case it is more likely that there is a preference for more consultative, considerate leaders. Also, in "high" power distance cultures, as defined by Hofstede, authoritarian leadership styles may be more acceptable. In this type of setting, dominance and overt wielding of power may be considered appropriate. By contrast, in more egalitarian societies and cultures leaders may be more prone to emphasising less social distance between themselves and their followers, thereby striving for equality with others (Den Hartog et al., 1999).

House (1995) reflected on the North American cultural influence on theoretical developments in managerial leadership, and concluded that the following orientation is apparent. There is an emphasis on individualistic rather than collectivist approaches; rationality takes pride of place over ascetics, spiritual values, or superstition; reward systems assume more of an individual rather than group character; people are more self-centred than altruistic in their motivation; the responsibilities of followers rather than their rights receive emphasis; and the primacy of work in people's lives and the sanctity of democratic values are conspicuous.

Convergence or divergence?

In comparative studies of different countries, a combination of culture and other factors (e.g., laws, state institutions, and mechanisms of economic control) influence various organisational processes. For example, in Chapter 12, when discussing macro participation, we witnessed differences between the UK and Germany. Likewise in Chapter 13, we noticed the influence of culture when looking at styles of handling conflict in different national settings, and, in Chapter 17, cultural differences are highlighted with regard to the use of management selection methods. Therefore, distinctive national circumstances should be considered when examining the application of concepts from organisational behaviour—e.g., leadership and motivation—to the organisational world.

An alternative view is that instead of the divergence acknowledged here, we could expect a form of convergence to arise where similarities between organisations in different countries will be more significant than differences, particularly for the multinational company. The latter allows staff from different countries to rub shoulders, and the combination of similar experiences and exposure to common organisational socialisation processes facilitates the transmission of ideas and the absorption of common values. Certain organisational cultures (e.g., the old IBM culture) can be so potent as to hold in check national culture as determinants of behaviour. However, generally one has to acknowledge a fair amount of diversity between countries.

COMMENT

According to some commentators, "the concept of culture has lost much of its value as a tool for analysing and interpreting the behaviour of people within organisations, and has reached the decline stage in its life-cycle. It may never be exterminated, but is unlikely to be as hot a topic in the 1990s as it was in the 1980s" (Oglonna, 1992). Hayes (1996) maintains that theoretical advances in organisational culture have not addressed questions such as how shared beliefs and collective understandings develop within the organisation in the first place and how they become transmitted and negotiated between individuals. Her preference is for the work group to become the unit of analysis (refer to social identity theory, discussed under inter-group behaviour in Chapter 10).

Furnham and Gunter (1993) conclude that "the corporate culture concept issue debate is here with us for some time to come. While it will no doubt lose its popular appeal as it gets replaced by yet another popular 'solution' to all management problems, it has uncovered enough of a hornet's nest among academics from different disciplines and epistemological perspectives to provide arguments and research for many years to come." Finally, Wood (1997) argues that culture on its own is not enough and we should recognise the potency of ideology (a systematic set of beliefs and values) and personality. Ideology and personality cut across national culture and provide a platform on which individuals from different cultures share a position.

CHAPTER SUMMARY

- Culture is a complex phenomenon and not easy to define. One definition of corporate or organisational culture suggests that it "consists of the expected behaviour, actions, and values that people in an enterprise are expected to follow". It is reflected in rites and ceremonies, stories, symbols, and language. A distinction was made between culture and climate. Culture was viewed as strong or weak and, in addition to dominant cultures, sub-cultures were acknowledged.

- Researchers and practitioners have come forward with different approaches to capture the values embedded in organisational culture. For example, the approach of Harrison related culture to organisation. Ouchi's approach consists of a list of seven points used in comparing three types of companies—the typical American, the typical Japanese, and the type Z American. The cultures of the typical Japanese companies and type Z American companies were different from the cultures of typical American companies.

- Another approach is that of Peters and Waterman, who identified management practices associated with success. They pinpointed cultural factors—attributes of excellence—that led to successful management practices. This work has had a good reception, primarily among practitioners, but the research has been criticised by academics.

- Deal and Kennedy's approach compares and contrasts organisational cultures using four cultural profiles. These profiles are considered in the context of risk and feedback, and are applicable at both the organisational and departmental levels. Two other less well-known approaches were introduced.

- There are a number of ways to change and develop organisational cultures, such as participation, information from others, symbolic action, comprehensive reward systems, and organisational socialisation. The development of culture at ICI, Kerry Gold, RWE, and other companies was mentioned.

- Contemporary issues—ethics, customer responsiveness, spirituality, and the learning organisation —and their impact on culture were discussed, shortly after raising issues about cultural change and development.

- Certain benefits, such as effective control, normative order, promotion of innovation, strategy formulation and implementation, and strong commitment from employees are said to accrue to the organisation from the development of an appropriate organisational culture.

- A section on international comparisons was devoted to how national cultures influence organisation structure and processes. Hofstede is a major contributor to this debate. He differentiated between national cultures on the basis of power distance, uncertainty avoidance, individualism–collectivism, and masculinity–femininity. Trompenaars has also made a contribution in this area, and his cross-cultural model was explained.

- Cultural diversity with respect to teams and leadership was mentioned. The issue of convergence in the application of behavioural theories across cultures was addressed.

- Finally, the current status of culture was briefly noted, and a suggestion was made that it would be wise to consider the influence of personality and ideology alongside culture.

QUESTIONS

(1) What is meant by corporate or organisational culture and how does it differ from organisational climate?

(2) Distinguish between dominant cultures and sub-cultures, and between strong and weak cultures.

(3) Identify ways in which culture manifests itself within organisations.

(4) Examine the frameworks for analysing organisational culture, and state which one you feel is the more credible.

(5) How do companies go about developing and managing culture?

(6) Examine the benefits of culture and comment on the role of symbolic action.

(7) Comment on the outcome of research into cultural change and development in the UK.

(8) What do we mean by organisational socialisation?

(9) Analyse the outcome of the cross-cultural studies conducted by Hofstede and Trompenaars.

(10) What is meant by cultural diversity in an organisational setting?

(11) Why should a company consider ethics, customer responsiveness, spirituality, and the learning organisation when reflecting on the appropriate culture to adopt for the organisation?

(12) Reflect on the criticisms of organisational culture.

SPOTLIGHT ON RELEVANT READING

Detert, J.R., Schroeder, R.G., & Mauriel, J.J. (2000). A framework for linking culture and improvement initiatives in organisations. *Academy of Management Review, 25*, 850–863.

Hatch, M.J. (1993). The dynamics of organisational culture. *Academy of Management Review, 18*, 657–693.

Hwang, K.K. (2005). The third wave of cultural psychology. The indigenous movement. *The Psychologist*, February, 80–83.

Schein, E.H. (1990). Organisational culture. *American Psychologist*, February, 109–119.

Smith, P.B. (2004). Nations, cultures, and individuals. *Journal of Cross Cultural Psychology, 35*, 6–12.

Learning Outcomes

After studying this chapter you should be able to:

- Describe organisational change, using an appropriate model.

- Assess the models or approaches used in planned organisational change.

- List the reasons why there is resistance to organisational change.

- Outline the approaches used to counteract resistance to change.

- Understand the issues to consider when implementing change.

- Analyse the structural and behavioural techniques or interventions at the disposal of those concerned with organisational development.

- Recognise the issues raised in connection with an evaluation of individual and group interventions in organisational development, and describe an alternative viewpoint.

Organisational Change and Development

16

After a description of the nature of change, models of change and ways of planning organisational change are described. The emphasis then switches to ways of implementing change, including an analysis of sources of resistance to change and approaches to controlling such resistance. The final part of the chapter concentrates on organisational development through structural and behavioural science-based techniques, followed by an overall evaluation of organisational development. This chapter's principal links to material discussed elsewhere in the book are teambuilding (Chapter 11); power, politics, and conflict (Chapter 13); culture (Chapter 15); training (Chapter 18); attitude change (Chapter 9); managerial leadership (Chapter 12); personality (Chapter 2); motivation and job design (Chapter 4); and organisation design (Chapter 14).

Contents

ORGANISATIONAL CHANGE

Change is omnipresent in society, and is reflected in many forms. It is not a recent phenomenon; in fact it has always been with us, but now it is more intense and occurs more frequently and more rapidly than in the past. We find changes in values and tastes in society generally having an impact on markets, and ultimately they affect the way companies are organised and managed.

Likewise, there are changes within organisations brought about by the application of new technology to work processes and products, alterations to structure, jobs, physical setting (space and layout), and modification to employee attitudes, expectations, and skills (Robertson, Roberts, & Porras, 1993). If these changes were carried out successfully they could lead to competitive advantage for a company in the market-place. Recently in certain countries we have witnessed changes in practices within organisations, such as the creation of back-up systems and greater employee security in response to international terrorism. These are examples of organisations responding to events in their environment. Organisations can also influence their environment by internally generated changes, such as innovations that command wide acceptance in the external world. IBM, which is now an economically healthy corporation, was in need of fundamental change in order to survive when Lou Gerstner took over as CEO in 1993 (see Panel 16.1).

Models of change

An explanation of the life cycle of a business organisation is offered by Woodward and Bucholtz (1987) in their **growth curve model of change.**

PANEL 16.1: Change—IBM's historic turnaround

After leading the market for years, IBM entered the 1990s on the brink of disaster, as competitors intensified the pressure on the company. Between 1991 and 1993 IBM reported losses of $16 billion. In 1993 alone it lost $8.1 billion on sales of $62.7 billion, and this was the year that Lou Gerstner was appointed CEO of IBM, the first outsider to become chairman and chief executive of the company. Though he was well conversant with marketing and had a sound appreciation of the needs of customers of computing equipment, he had little of the technological background that people at IBM were able to identify with, and many commentators were sceptical of his chances of success in his new role.

Gerstner recognised the value of the IBM brand and its potential impact on the market and the marketing process, and made customer contact a priority for the company. He enthusiastically solicited the views of customers and encouraged a greater customer focus. He soon established that the culture of the company was insular and stifled experimentation. There was an IBM way to do everything, and although IBM people knew how computers worked, they placed less emphasis on what computers could do for the customer.

As part of his efforts to change the culture of the company he believed that greater flexibility and market responsiveness were needed, and decided to move employees out of the firm's corporate office buildings in New York and Chicago, which had come to symbolise insularity, bureaucracy, and lack of cost control within the company. He is reported to have said that the two IBM skyscrapers in New York and Chicago were more appropriate for lawyers or investment bankers than an industrial giant like IBM. He also changed IBM's focus from selling computer hardware products to selling more complete offerings, designed to meet customers' business needs, by bundling hardware with software and service. This necessitated a high degree of collaboration between the company and its customers in defining the latter's needs.

To achieve the restructuring that was necessary the company was forced to shed a large number of staff, even though such action was alien to its policy of lifetime employment. Generous voluntary redundancy schemes were introduced and various forms of assistance (e.g., counselling and time off to get another job) helped ease the exit of employees. The company did not want to lose key staff, and made a determined effort to identify the people it wanted to retain, and then encouraged them to stay. It used communication processes wisely to keep people informed why the reorganisation was necessary and what was required to achieve it. There is no doubt that the high trust created over the years in IBM was a significant factor in helping to bring about the major reorganisation that resulted in laying off substantial numbers of staff.

Though no longer with the company, Lou Gerstner relied significantly on transformational leadership to bring about change, and the measures he instituted while at the helm ensured that IBM is still a key player in its industry in 2005.

(Kumar, 2002)

In this model the organisation passes through three phases in the sequence formative, normative, and integrative.

(1) *Formative phase*. In this phase there is a lack of structure coupled with entrepreneurial endeavour, with a bias towards risk-taking, and there is a reliance on trial and error where mistakes are viewed as learning opportunities in a climate of innovation. The organisation is intent on making a predictable impact on its market.

(2) *Normative phase*. The emphasis now switches to underlining the importance of stability and ensuring the existing structure organised along bureaucratic lines is able to cope with the demands on it. There is less sympathy for those who make mistakes and this adversely affects people's willingness to take risks. Involvement in innovation is more likely to be confined to a formal research and development unit rather than being widely dispersed. Though the organisation is content to maintain the current position, a turbulent environment is responsible for moving the company to the next phase.

(3) *Integrative phase*. In this phase there is much ambiguity and uncertainty because of the impact of the environment and the resultant organisational change. Senior management is forced to re-examine the organisation's mission and policies and institute a number of changes, hopefully relying on visionary leadership and refined interpersonal skills. Obviously there will be resistance to change, particularly from those who find it a painful experience. During the integrative phase there is tension created by the effects arising out of the collision of the forces for and against change. This phenomenon is recognised in Lewin's force field theory, which is discussed in the next section.

Another approach to understanding how change unfolds can be seen in the following sequence of actions (Stace, 1996; Stace and Dunphy, 2001):

(1) *Fine tuning*. Set out to improve objectives and practices at divisional or department level.

(2) *Incremental adjustment*. There is no radical change at this stage, but noticeable modifications to strategy, structure, and processes take place.

(3) *Modular transformation*. There is a major restructuring of departments or divisions, where the focus is on parts rather than the whole organisation.

(4) *Corporate transformation*. This is akin to strategic change in organisations. Radical shifts in policy come about accompanied by significant changes to mission statements, key cultural values, power distribution, structures, and processes.

When reflecting on models of change we should note the views of Dawson (2003). In a processual/contextual perspective on change he maintains that there are no universal prescriptions on how best to manage change. Major change is both a complicated and a political process that takes time to plan and implement. It is important that change strategies are sensitive to the human resource considerations and the context in which they will take root. It must be recognised that it is a phenomenon that is perceived differently by the various actors within the organisation and that communication is an essential ingredient in the change process. Involvement in the change process is a learning experience whether or not it is successful. Training is a natural complement to change, but all too often training is inadequate to underpin change.

Planning change

It is not good enough for an organisation to respond to change; it must try to anticipate it as well. This would necessitate the planning of organisational change as part of the organisation's strategy, as we saw in the case of IBM earlier in the chapter. Planned change is based on the understanding that agreement can be reached between all the parties involved in the change process and that they are interested and committed to the project. This might be an oversimplification, as will be seen later, because there is almost a recognition of the non-existence of conflict and politics.

The following are approaches that facilitate a movement from a current position to a future desired state:

- process model;
- continuous change process model; and
- emergent approach.

Process model

Lewin (1951) has described a three-step change process as involving unfreezing, changing, and refreezing. Despite its longevity, it is still possible to find important supporters of this approach to planning change (Hendry, 1996).

- *Unfreeze or unlock from existing behaviour or practice.* This is the stage where employees recognise the need for change. A key consideration in the unfreezing process is informing people about the absolute importance of change and how it will affect their jobs. It is important for people to see that the current organisational activities to which they may be attached are not good enough, and that the proposed change is called for (e.g., restructuring the organisation, or the introduction of a new procedure) in order to transform the situation.
- *Change or move to a new level.* This is the actual movement from the old situation to the new situation, and involves a process that alters existing relationships or activities.
- *Refreeze behaviour at this new level.* This amounts to making the changed behaviour of people relatively solid and not easily reversed. Without refreezing, the old ways of doing things may dislodge the newly acquired behaviours (such as revised management practices reflected in a different way of relating to subordinates). With regard to newly learned skills, it is obviously important that these are repeated in training sessions and that the organisational environment is conducive to the practice of these skills. In addition, rewards for trying to change the status quo are matters to consider. The application of learning theory, particularly reinforcement (examined

in Chapter 7), is relevant during the refreezing stage, and so is group decision making (considered in Chapter 10) when people are faced with accepting change. Some might argue that refreezing may not be the right thing to do in certain conditions. For example, it is suggested that refreezing is not particularly appropriate for organisations operating in turbulent environments (Dawson, 2003; Kanter et al., 1992). It would be unwise to freeze or set in concrete new ways of doing things, since contemporary organisations need to be flexible and adaptable. However, advocates of refreezing would argue that this process is necessary to avoid reverting back to the previous conditions, which are likely to have been unsatisfactory.

Continuous change process model

An alternative model is the **continuous change process model**, which incorporates facets of the Lewin model. It is considered more realistic because it examines organisational change from the perspective of top management and recognises that change is continuous (see Figure 16.1) (Moorhead & Griffin, 2004). Top management will be active in specifying the likely outcome of the changes proposed, having in the first instance indicated that certain changes are necessary. Also, alternatives for bringing about change are discussed and evaluated, and the most acceptable alternative is adopted. In the continuous change process model note the role of a change agent.

Change agent.   He or she is the person charged with managing the efforts aimed at change. The change agent could assist management with choosing the most acceptable way to proceed. A change agent could be an internal or external consultant. As an internal consultant, he or she could operate with the advantage of having a deep insight into many aspects of organisational functioning, but of course there is the danger of a lack of objectivity because of proximity to the situation. By contrast, an external consultant may be viewed by organisational members as more impartial and detached, and, as a consequence, more acceptable.

FIGURE 16.1

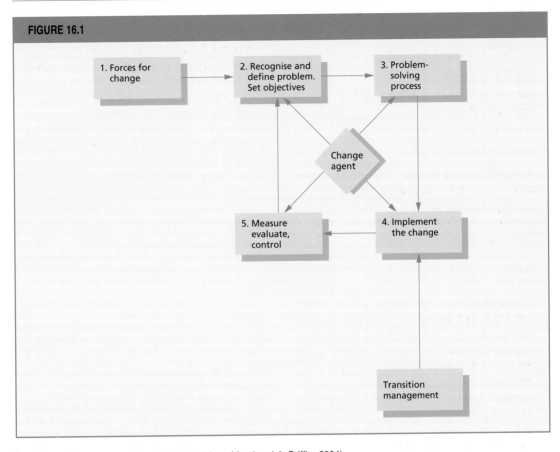

Continuous change process model (adapted from Moorhead & Griffin, 2004).

The arrival of the change agent may be greeted with satisfaction because his or her work offers an opportunity to change the organisation for the better in the eyes of employees dissatisfied with the status quo. The processes of unfreezing, changing, and refreezing are used by the change agent during the implementation stage (step 4 in Figure 16.1). In step 5, the change agent and top management evaluate the extent to which the change is producing the desired outcome. The actual outcome is measured against the objectives set for change earlier in the model, and deviations are handled appropriately. The change agent will naturally be involved in all phases of the change process and, if capable, should be of immense help to the various parties by injecting into the discussion new ideas and opinions that challenge existing practices. This could be painful for

some, but is likely to be beneficial in facilitating the change process. In Panel 16.2 there is a profile of the change agent.

There are many occasions when change is a major and complex task, taking a considerable amount of time to implement fully. In such circumstances it has to be managed carefully. The process of planning, organising, and implementing change in a systematic way from the inception of the change to the future desired state is called transition management (as shown in Figure 16.1). One must realise that once the change process begins, the organisation is in a transitional phase, probably somewhere between the old status quo and the planned future state, but normal business has still to continue (Ackerman, 1982). It is necessary for managers within the organisation to become transition managers and

---

PANEL 16.2: Profile of a change agent

Generally, change agents must have the backing and support of top management and it is suggested (Beer, 1980) that they should possess a number of attributes, including status, credibility, and expertise in the eyes of those who relate to them. Also of importance is the trust people have in change agents because of the sensitive way in which they must handle information. Kanter (1989) would endorse a substantial part of this profile, and would include satisfaction in personal accomplishments, self-confidence, independence, ability to foster cooperation, ability to engage in dialogue with people across business functions, and respect for the proposals of change. To the qualities and skills mentioned could be added self-management skills, general consultancy skills, and a good grasp of OD intervention techniques (Cummings and Worley, 2001).

Egan (1994) stresses the importance of the change agent being skilled and effective in the use of political strategies. To be adept at the use of political strategies in the implementation of organisational change a change agent has to develop sensitivity to how organisational politics manifests itself; be familiar with communication processes and the informal aspects of organisation and use them to his or her advantage; make a serious effort to understand key players and relate to powerful figures; seek reciprocation from those who were supported or helped in the past; know when to be conspicuous and when to work out of sight; create a sense of occasion when the situation demands it; and generally be competent in negotiations.

Buchanan and Badham (1999) endorse the importance of the political dimension when they maintain that political behaviour is an accepted and pervasive aspect of the change agent's role. They maintain that the change agent seems to use skills or tactics beyond the range normally associated with the accepted political or power tactics used in organisations.

---

liaise effectively with the change agent. If necessary, a transition management may be required to exercise overall control of the business during the transitional stage. Also, it is suggested that the natural constituency of the organisation—i.e., employees, suppliers, and customers—should be kept fully informed of the changes. This is an important aspect of transition management (Tichy & Ulrich, 1984).

Emergent approach

In the continuous change process model discussed previously, note that top management are influential in setting the agenda for change. By contrast, the emergent approach views initiating and implementing change as driven from the bottom up rather than the top down. This is functional because the rapid pace of change in a dynamic and uncertain business environment make it impossible for a small clique of top managers to decide on the most appropriate response (Wilson, 1992). In a study of organisational change in six large US corporations, Beer, Eisenstat, and Spector (1990) found that the most effective senior managers recognised their limited power to prescribe corporate renewal from the top. Instead, they defined their role as creating a climate for change by specifying the direction in which the company

should move, without insisting on specific solutions during the early phases of the company-wide change process.

It would appear unrealistic to expect a chief executive to appreciate the necessary level of detail required to effect change in areas of the organisation far removed from the centre. Eventually, top management will be active in aligning structure and systems with changes at the periphery of the organisation in order to achieve enduring organisational change. Beer and his colleagues do not rule out the instigation of change from the top, but they are keen to point out that many senior executives—who developed in an era when top-down hierarchical influence was the primary means for organising and managing—must learn from the younger unit managers closer to the scene of action. According to Child (2005), the emergent approach modifies rather than diminishes the role of senior management in organisational change.

In the emergent approach change is an open-ended and continuous process of adapting to changing circumstances, and is seen as a process of learning and not just a method of changing organisational structures and practices (Dawson, 2003). A rather fluid situation in an imperfect world is likely to characterise the emergent approach. In this setting there is a recognition of power relationships and pressure from vested interests (Burnes, 1996), the forming and disbanding of coalitions, coming to terms with imperfect knowledge, and short spans of attention. As a result, pragmatism prevails in trying to balance the needs of the organisation and the varied interests of its members. Bolman and Deal (2003) admonish us to be on the look out for conflict as well. Some individuals support the change but others are steadfast in their opposition to it. Too often conflict exists in a suppressed state, but it has the potential to surface and can be destructive.

It appears that the advocates of emergent change tend to adopt a contingency or situational perspective (Dunphy & Stace, 1993) when it is maintained that there is no simple prescription for managing movement from the status quo to a future desired state due to the constraints of time and contextual variables. The most we can expect is to recognise the complexity of the issues and identify the range of available options. In this context the focal point of attention is likely to include structure, culture, and the learning organisation. These are concepts explored elsewhere in this book, and will be briefly referred to in the section on organisational development techniques later.

Finally, it could be argued that the continuous change process model considered in the previous section might be more suited to relatively stable and predictable situations where change can be driven from the top down, whereas the emergent change approach is more functional when an organisation faces a dynamic and uncertain environment of the type frequently encountered in the contemporary world. Like most, if not all approaches, the emergent approach is not free of shortcomings.

IMPLEMENTING CHANGE

Earlier in relation to the continuous change process model, and in the account of Lou Gerstner's stewardship of IBM, we saw that top leaders are influential in articulating the company's vision and setting the agenda for major change. But one must recognise that managers and employees throughout the organisation are involved in the process of change. In Kotter's model of a change process there are eight stages that can be used to successfully implement change (Kotter & Cohen, 2002). These stages, listed below, could be viewed as a change process moving through time, though not necessarily moving in a linear sequence. In reality, stages can overlap and change agents need to go back to earlier steps. It will be apparent after registering the steps in the model that major strategic change is on the agenda.

(1) *Establish a sense of urgency.* Make it clear that change is really necessary for the organisation to survive and prosper. Obviously an organisational crisis is a powerful stimulus to convey the need for change, but a crisis alone is not sufficient justification to signal the need. There are many situations when it is necessary for the company to implement change in order to maintain competitive advantage. This stage helps with the unfreezing aspect of the Lewin model discussed earlier.

(2) *Establish a coalition.* Those who wish to institute change must recognise the need to put together a strong enough team to direct the process, otherwise the change initiative is unlikely to get off the ground. Hence the need to build a coalition of people throughout the organisation who have enough power and influence to lead the change process. Shared commitment and top management support are essential. It is important that the coalition should include lower-level supervisors and middle managers. For more modest changes the support of influential managers in the departments affected by change is crucial.

(3) *Create a vision and strategy for change.* The guiding coalition should develop a shared vision that can easily be communicated to those affected by the change. When formulating and articulating a compelling and uplifting vision that will guide the change process it is suggested that: (i) you convey a picture of what the future will look like; (ii) it appeals to the long-term interests of employees, customers, stockholders and others

who have a stake in the company; (iii) it comprises realistic, attainable goals; (iv) it is clear enough to provide guidance in decision making; (v) it is general enough to allow individual initiatives and alternative responses in the light of changing conditions; and (vi) it is easy to communicate and can successfully be explained in five minutes (Hayes, 2002).

(4) *Communicate the vision and strategy through a combination of words, deeds, and symbols.* All those affected by the change should be communicated with repeatedly. Those affected by change—employees and other stakeholders —observe those responsible for change for manifestations of their commitment, so communicating by example is crucial.

(5) *Remove obstacles that impede the accomplishment of the new vision, and empower people to move ahead.* Obstacles (such as reward systems that pay insufficient attention to performance, restrictive regulations, and inflexible organisational structures) that prevent people from acting to realise the vision should be identified and removed. Other obstacles may be less tangible, such as values and beliefs that impede experimentation and moving forward. Empowering people to act amounts to creating conditions where people can experience enhanced motivation to achieve desired levels of performance. (This concept is discussed in Chapter 4.) You would expect empowered people to believe in themselves and are confident that they have the support of others to make things happen.

(6) *Produce visible signs of progress in the form of short-term victories.* It is recognised that achieving major change can take time. Given this reality, there is a danger that the effort put into bringing about change may subside or slow down as people lose the initial sense of urgency and their attention moves elsewhere, particularly to important operational issues. One way to guard against this is to seek short-term or early wins (where progress is visible). This is of value because people involved in making things happen receive recognition for their good work.

(7) *Stick to the change process and refuse to give up when conditions get tough, and don't declare victories or achievements too soon.* Though early wins are advocated to maintain the motivational impetus and to promote continued effort implementing change, we are cautioned against declaring victories or wins too soon as this could damage the momentum.

(8) *Nurture and shape a new culture to support the improvements and innovations that are taking root.* Those instituting the change are keen to ensure that changes are consolidated. This will be made easy if they are able to show that the change has brought about beneficial alterations or modifications to attitudes, behaviour, and organisational processes, which in turn have resulted in improved performance. There should be constant reminders of the benefits of the changes introduced until they form part of the accepted culture of the organisation.

Bolman and Deal (2003) have taken Kotter's model and combined it with four ways in which they view organisations—i.e., the structure, symbolic (culture), human resource, and political frames—and claim this approach provides a powerful vehicle for successfully managing change.

For example, consider the first stage (developing a sense of urgency) of the Kotter model and apply the Bolman and Deal "frames" to it:

Strategies from the human resource, political, and symbolic strategies all contribute. Symbolically leaders can construct a persuasive story by painting a picture of the current challenge or crisis and why failure to act would be catastrophic. Human resource techniques of participation and open meetings would help to get the story out and gauge audience reaction. Behind the scenes leaders could meet with key players, assess their interests and negotiate or use power as necessary to get people on board.

As another example, Kotter's fifth stage calls for removing obstacles and empowering people to move forward. Structurally, this is a matter of identifying rules, roles, procedures, and patterns blocking progress and then working to realign them. Symbolically, a few public hangings (for example, firing, demoting, or exiling prominent opponents) could reinforce the message. Meanwhile, the human resource frame counsels training and provides support and resources to enable people to master new behaviours.

Note the emphasis on training in the last sentence, a topic that is discussed in Chapter 18. Many change initiatives fail because managers do not spend sufficient time and money developing the necessary new knowledge and skills. Companies such as GE, the large US corporation, recognise the value of training for managing change. In such cases middle managers are required to attend courses with the aim of helping them to become better at leading and managing change. Obviously the companies concerned are not content to place total reliance on the manager's experience; instead they support and accelerate the manager's learning.

But apart from the lack of formal training, there are other contributory factors responsible for the unsuccessful implementation of change, such as insufficient time and energy devoted to managing the change process and marketing the change to employees (Manzoni, 2001). From studies of both successful and unsuccessful change efforts in organisations around the world, Kotter and Cohen (2002) concluded that too many change initiatives fail because they rely too much on data gathering, analysis, report writing, and presentations, instead of a more creative approach aimed at grabbing the feelings that motivate useful action. Therefore, the efforts of change agents are not as effective as they might be because they rely entirely on reason and structure and neglect human, political, and symbolic (culture) elements (Bolman & Deal, 2003).

Resistance to change

Change creates uncertainty as to what the future holds, and as a consequence can lead to personal insecurity. Therefore, it is not surprising to encounter resistance to change within organisations.

An organisational change, such as a move to a better office, can be warmly accepted, simply because it is seen to have obvious advantages. But not all changes fit into this category. Where changes create ambiguity and uncertainty, then resistance to change is likely to emerge. In essence, the resistance is not to change as such —rather it is to the personal loss (or possibility of personal loss) that people believe will accompany the change (Burke, 1982).

There are occasions when employees (both superiors and subordinates) fear the introduction of new technology to their work because of a feeling that they may be unable to cope with the job in the changed circumstances. Also, certain employees, particularly the older ones, fear that they may lose the personal investment (in terms of skill and experience) in the current system. For example, print workers in the UK newspaper industry vehemently resisted proposals to computerise their work in the early 1980s because of the perceived ramifications of the proposed change in terms of job loss, status, benefits, and conditions generally.

Sources of resistance to change

Katz and Kahn (1978) identified six sources of resistance to change operating at the level of the organisation. Most of these sources are people-centred and are connected with people being fearful of loss in one form or another—e.g., loss of power, or resources, or the loss of the security of a predictable routine. The six sources, which do not necessarily reside in all situations of organisational change, are detailed in Panel 16.3.

Moving away from the organisational level, a number of specific individual factors have been identified as sources of resistance to change (Bedeian & Zammuto, 1991; Nadler, 1983; Zaltman & Duncan, 1977):

• *Habit*. A change to well-established procedures and practices could create discomfort and resistance on the part of a person who is very familiar with the current system. Inevitably this person is expected to make an extra effort (without necessarily receiving extra

---

PANEL 16.3: Sources of resistance to change at the level of the organisation

- *Over-determination.* The structure of the organisation is designed to maintain stability by resorting to an elaborate process regulating such activities as recruitment, selection, training, rewards, and performance appraisal. The organisational system is over-determined in the sense that lesser control or safeguards could achieve the same outcome. As a result, the elaborate structure could become an impediment to change.
- *Narrow focus of change.* On many occasions efforts to introduce change in organisations take a rather narrow focus, instead of considering the likely knock-on effects arising from the existence of normal interdependencies between tasks, structure, and people found in organisations.
- *Group inertia.* The norms of the group constrain attempts by individuals to change their behaviour. In fact the group is obstructive. This could arise when the group refuses to engage in complementary behaviour in order to reinforce the position of the individual.
- *Threatened expertise.* A change to a job may result in an alteration to, for example, the skills requirement of that job. Such an eventuality may pose a threat to people's expertise developed over many years, with the inevitable consequence of resistance to change.
- *Threatened power.* A reorganisation may lead to changing the existing pattern of decision making. For individuals who benefited in the past from exercising the power to make decisions, but now stand to lose a significant part of their power base, the reorganisation may trigger resistance to change.
- *Resource allocation.* Individuals could be quite content with the way resources are currently allocated to them. A change that heralds less than satisfactory arrangements for individuals previously satisfied with the status quo is likely to be resisted.

(Katz & Kahn, 1978)

---

remuneration) to learn the new mode of operation. It is therefore understandable that this situation could give rise to resistance to the proposed change.

- *Security.* Doing things in a familiar way brings comfort and security, and people are likely to resist change if they perceive their security to be threatened.
- *Economic considerations.* People may fear that change could threaten the very existence of their jobs as presently constituted, and eventually lead to the loss of a salary or wage. As a result, they resist change.
- *Fear of the unknown.* Some people fear anything unfamiliar. Any disruption of familiar patterns within the organisation, such as changes in reporting relationships, may create fear. This might arise with people thinking that their flow of work will not be as smooth and as fast as previously because they believe it will take time to get to grips with the changed arrangements.
- *Lack of awareness.* Due to selectivity in perception, a person may overlook a critical factor in a change process. It could be that the factor ignored—e.g., requiring a double signature on travel expense claims—is something

the person is opposed to, and somehow it is conveniently overlooked. As a result, there is no change in the person's behaviour (at least initially) as far as the changed practice is concerned.

- *Social considerations.* The motivation to resist change may spring from a group. If a change to rules and regulations was unilaterally imposed by management, but resisted by a work group, a member of that group may oppose the change simply because acceptance of the change could amount to disapproval and perhaps be subjected to the application of sanctions operated by the group. (Group inertia was mentioned earlier as a source of resistance to change at the organisational level.)

An alternative perspective on the main sources of resistance to change, with some similarity to issues discussed above, is as follows (Bedeian & Zammuto, 1991):

- *Parochial self-interest.* People are anxious to maintain the status quo because of the benefits associated with it. Change could pose a threat to present advantages in terms of power, status, and security, and could undermine valued relationships developed over time, lead to unwanted geographic moves, and deny opportunities for social intercourse. Also, people may have invested heavily in knowledge and skills related to current jobs and systems, and see change as a threat to this investment. For these reasons people resist change.

- *Misunderstandings and lack of trust.* If people do not understand what the change entails, why it is necessary, and what it is likely to lead to, then resistance can be expected. Where there is a climate of mistrust between managers and subordinates, management may be reluctant to disseminate information about proposed changes. Where information is given it may be incomplete or distorted. If this is the case, then one can expect to find conditions conducive to the creation of uncertainty and the spreading of rumours. Such a situation creates a climate in which people feel threatened. As a consequence, they become defensive and erect barriers to further flows of information about the proposed changes.
- *Contradictory assessments.* Not everybody shares the same view of the impact change is going to have. People will see different advantages and disadvantages to change. This situation is more prevalent when information about change is inadequate, and where certain key people are not well briefed. However, it is alleged that certain beneficial happenings spring from what appears to be an unsatisfactory situation—namely the airing of constructive criticisms, hopefully leading to an improvement in the proposals for change.
- *Low tolerance of change.* People tend to have different abilities and skills to handle the ambiguity and uncertainty heralded by change. If the proposed changes require people to think and behave in a manner that they are not accustomed to, then one can expect a challenge to the concept the individuals have of themselves. If people have low tolerance for the ambiguity and uncertainty associated with change, this could be expressed in fundamental reservations about their competency to cope. Their apprehension and anxiety could motivate them to oppose or resist changes,

which, at the cognitive level, they acknowledge as beneficial.

A specific reference to the role of personality in the context of the tolerance of change is acknowledged in the last point. Leonard (1984) makes reference to the personality equation when looking at the individual's resistance to control systems within organisations and this has obvious relevance to the observations of Bedeian and Zammutu. This places personality, discussed in Chapter 2, in a firm interface position with sources of resistance to change. It is understandable that news of a major change to the person's job or place of work will arouse deep psychological feelings related to self-esteem and achievement, and produce a knock-on effect in terms of motivation and performance. This raises the question, how does the individual cope with news of significant change affecting his or her little universe? A "cycle of coping", which covers five steps and traces the individual's reaction to change, has been proposed (Carnal, 1990). The statements in the cycle of coping (see Panel 16.4) might be viewed as generalisations; however, reflecting on them when considering reactions to change could be useful.

Apart from personality, one should not ignore the role of politics. Because change affects the status quo, it is not too difficult to envisage a situation where it generates political activity (Pfeffer, 1992), which is the subject of analysis in Chapter 13. Power struggles will influence to a great extent the amount of change and the speed of change. It is understandable to find that those well advanced in their careers are likely to resist change, and if they are in key positions they may not be the most suited to take a leading role in heralding change. In fact it is not unusual to call on new blood from outside when a fundamental change to an organisation is anticipated (Ocasio, 1994).

Controlling resistance to change

Encountering resistance to change should be used as an opportunity to re-examine the proposal for change. Resistance can be constructive if it forces

---

PANEL 16.4: Personality and change—cycle of coping

- *Step 1* is "denial" as the individual is confronted with the proposal for change. A typical reaction is that change is unnecessary, and there could be an enhancement of the person's self-esteem because of an attachment to the present way of doing things. Where a group is involved, the threat posed by the proposal for change could lead to a reinforcement of the ties between members, and performance remains stable.
- *Step 2* is "defence" and at this stage the realities of the decision to institute change become apparent as early deliberations lead to the formulation of concrete plans and programmes. Faced with this outcome people become defensive in order to defend both their jobs and the way they have executed their duties and responsibilities. This stage produces an adverse effect, which manifests itself as a lowering of self-esteem, motivation, and performance.
- *Step 3* is "discarding" and, unlike the previous stages, which emphasised the past, this stage puts the spotlight on the future. There is a change in perceptions as people realise that change is necessary and inevitable. Although performance is still on the decline, there are signs that self-esteem is improving as people get to grips with the new situation.
- *Step 4* is "adaptation", where people are beginning to come to terms with the new techniques and processes. Naturally it will be necessary to modify and refine the new system and if people are involved in this exercise they are likely to experience an increase in their self-esteem. However, performance still lags behind the growing level of motivation, particularly in situations where it was necessary to have an understanding of new methods and techniques.
- *Step 5* is "internalisation", where people finally make sense of what has happened, and the newly adopted behaviour is now becoming part of people's repertoire of behaviour. One could now expect an improvement in self-esteem and motivation and this, coupled with the better use of people's abilities, could give rise to raised levels of performance.

---

managers to interact more frequently with subordinates, to review the decision to introduce change, and perhaps to explore alternative ways to meet the desired objective. It is possible that the alternative means to the desired end may be an improvement on those originally proposed, and equally could involve less resistance. Also, the action taken by management to review the proposed change that is the cause of resistance may be perceived by employees as a desirable symbolic gesture, conveying the impression that management cares about them and has respect for their viewpoint (Pfeffer, 1981a).

Six approaches have been put forward as ways of controlling resistance to change (Kotter & Schlesinger, 1979):

(1) education and communication;
(2) participation;
(3) facilitation and support;
(4) negotiation and agreement;
(5) manipulation and co-optation;
(6) coercion.

Education and communication

The reason for resorting to education and communication is to convey to employees the logic of

the change, for by doing so it is assumed that resistance can be reduced. Education and communication can take place through the use of memoranda, reports, one-to-one discussions, and group presentations.

An important consideration for the use of communication and education as an approach is the belief that the source of resistance lies in misinformation or poor communication (see Panel 16.5). Therefore, it is assumed that misunderstandings will disappear and resistance becomes less of a problem if the full facts are placed at the disposal of employees. However, in a climate of mistrust an approach of this nature may not result in bringing about change successfully. Also, it could be a time-consuming exercise.

Participation

This approach, discussed in Chapter 12, is adopted in the belief that if people capable of making a valid contribution are involved in the decision process leading up to the sanctioning of change, they are unlikely to resist the outcome of a decision to which they have contributed. This type of involvement gives people the opportunity to utilise their knowledge and skills and allays their fears about the impact of change on them. Also,

---

PANEL 16.5: Poor communication in workplace change

According to John, who recently resigned as an employee in the finance department of a European airline, a major reorganisation of the company resulting in substantial redundancies was badly handled. The reorganisation and resultant redundancies were announced in an unplanned way and generally poorly communicated, and the workload was redistributed without any consultation, let alone assistance or incentives. Before the reorganisation and proposed redundancies, employees felt they were already overworked and when they were allocated duties far in excess of those listed in their job descriptions they resigned in large numbers.

The above observation comes from a study based on a survey of UK employees at different organisational levels, commissioned by OPP, a business psychology consultancy. According to a change consultant at OPP, employees are not asking for less change. However, they are demanding more involvement and clearer explanations of the reasons for the change, the expected benefits of change, and honesty about how things are going. The results indicate that senior managers emphasise the need to communicate clearly the objectives and potential benefits of reorganisation, but employees further down the line feel that senior managers fail to do so. A majority of these employees say that change tends to be imposed rather than discussed, and say that senior managers are the only ones consulted.

(Maitland, 2004a)

---

it is likely that they are going to be committed to the change. However, the potential for compromise on decisions relating to change in a participative forum is always present. This could be considered a drawback of the participative approach, and so could the time consumed in this process.

Facilitation and support

Various supportive mechanisms to reduce resistance, such as counselling and training, could be used. These could eventually facilitate the process of adapting to change, particularly in conditions where fear and anxiety are high among employees. Again, this approach can be time-consuming and expensive. Earlier the importance of training was emphasised. In the final analysis people need time and help to disengage from the current state and think constructively about the future. This can be particularly helpful when they feel a sense of loss connected with the letting go of something they value.

Negotiation and agreement

A negotiation process could be used in cases where it is believed that resistance to change is coming from a powerful group. This group may stand to lose a substantial advantage as a consequence of the change. As a result, management negotiates with those resisting change to pave the way for the satisfactory implementation of the proposed

change. Inevitably, the resistors will exact something of value in exchange for their cooperation. The problem with this approach is that others who accepted the change willingly may now see the possibility of improving their position through negotiation. The resultant effect could be to increase the cost of implementing change and increasing the time required to negotiate the change with all interested parties.

Manipulation and co-optation

These two approaches may be used if, for some reason, it is not possible to employ the methods already discussed. Manipulation is a covert measure to influence events, where situations are depicted in a favourable light to the point of distortion, and perhaps critical information is withheld, in order to force people to accept change. For example, there may be a threat by management (which happens to be untrue) to axe a section unless employees climb down in their opposition to some fundamental proposals for rationalisation of that section.

By contrast, co-optation is a mixture of manipulation and participation. Prominent figures, perhaps the leaders in the group resisting the change, are involved strategically in the decision to promote change. Their advice is sought not as a means to enrich the decision but as a way of implicating them in the process so that eventually their approval is forthcoming. An extreme example of such an eventuality is where a recalcitrant shop steward of the old school is co-opted on to a committee contemplating a change that is resisted in his or her part of the organisation.

Both manipulation and co-optation do not require a heavy investment in time, and it is possible that the tactics involved are initially effective in neutralising the influence of opponents. But equally one has to acknowledge that the tactics could become ineffective if the recipients of undue influence feel they are being exploited or deceived. The end result would be a total undermining of the credibility of those engineering change.

Coercion

Obviously this would be a measure of last resort for some managers. Coercive tactics may be employed when managers instituting change dispense or withhold valued outcomes in order to motivate people to change. For example, management is prepared to take action, such as a threat to close down a plant or make people redundant, if resistance to proposed changes in work practices continues. It is conceivable that this is an expeditious approach to dilute resistance to change. Nevertheless, the consequences of using such tactics could be disadvantageous in terms of morale and commitment in the future. Also, compliance may only be secured as long as the manager instituting change continues to monitor the situation and maintains the threat of withholding valued outcomes.

Hayes (2002) suggests that:

> in spite of the risks of long-term resentment and the possibility of retaliation often associated with coercive change strategies, there may be occasions when their use is appropriate. These may include situations where those at the receiving end of coercive strategies do not perceive the proposed change as important and are not convinced of the need for change, and where speed in bringing about change is essential.

A summary of the main points relating to these situations, where the different approaches

to controlling resistance to change are used, together with the advantages and disadvantages of each approach, appears in Table 16.1.

Note that the above six approaches of controlling resistance to change are to some extent complementary to Kotter's eight-stage model of the change process examined earlier. Therefore, it could be productive if after reading this section you revisit the Kotter model and reflect on action associated with the implementation of change.

ORGANISATIONAL DEVELOPMENT

Organisational development (OD) has been defined as "the process of planned change and improvement of organisations through the application of knowledge of the behavioural sciences" (Moorhead & Griffin, 2004). To supplement this definition one can use other definitions to reflect the broad coverage of the process. Organisational development has been described as an involved network of events that increases the ability of members of the organisation to solve problems in a creative fashion, to assist the organisation in adapting to the external environment, and to manage organisational culture. It embraces a broad range of interventionist processes from changes in organisational structure and systems to psychotherapeutic counselling sessions with individuals and groups in response to changes in the external environment. According to Beer and Walton (1987), the interventions seek to improve the effectiveness of the organisation and contribute to employee well-being.

In the past OD focused primarily on interpersonal relationships and group processes (such as T-groups, process consultation, teambuilding, and third-party intervention, which are discussed in the next section) and underplayed organisational efficiency and effectiveness (Cummings & Worley, 2001). Since the 1980s, OD has broadened its perspective and has become linked more closely with strategic planning in organisations, and is concerned with aligning strategy with culture and the external environment. Other interventions mentioned by Cummings and Worley (2001) are

TABLE 16.1

Approaches for controlling resistance to change (from Kotter & Schlesinger, 1979): Copyright © 1979 by the President and Fellows of Harvard College and reproduced with permission

Approach	Commonly used in these situations	Advantages	Drawbacks
Education and communication	Where there is a lack of information or inaccurate information and analysis	Once persuaded, people will often help with the implementation of the change	Can be very time-consuming if lots of people are involved
Participation and involvement	Where the initiators do not have all the information they need to design the change, and where others have considerable power to resist	People who participate will be committed to implementing change, and any relevant information they have will be integrated into the change plan	Can be very time-consuming if participators design an inappropriate change
Facilitation and support	Where people are resisting because of adjustment problems	No other approach works as well with adjustment problems	Can be time-consuming, expensive, and still fail
Negotiation and agreement	Where someone or some group will clearly lose out in a change, and where that group has considerable power to resist	Sometimes it is a relatively easy way to avoid major resistance	Can be too expensive in many cases if it alerts others to negotiate for compliance
Manipulation and co-optation	Where other tactics will not work, or are too expensive	It can be a relatively quick and inexpensive solution to resistance problems	Can lead to future problems if people feel manipulated
Explicit and implicit coercion	Where speed is essential, and the change initiators possess considerable power	It is speedy, and can overcome any kind of resistance	Can be risky if it leaves people mad at the initiators

changes to the structure of the organisation, such as adjusting socio-technical systems, business process re-engineering, delayering and the creation of the network organisation discussed in Chapter 14, and aspects of human resource management, such as performance management, employee development, reward management (discussed in Chapters 17 and 18), and stress management (Chapter 19).

DEVELOPMENT TECHNIQUES AND INTERVENTIONS

Organisational development can be focused at different levels. For example, techniques could be used (individually or collectively) for any or all of the following purposes:

• to alter the organisation and culture, and utilise the learning organisation;

• to redesign tasks within the organisation;
• to change the outlook of individuals and groups.

Structure, culture, and learning organisation

Beer et al. (1990) believe that an effective way of bringing about change is to restructure organisations in order to place people firmly in a new organisational context, requiring them to take on board new duties and responsibilities. This could have the effect of putting pressure on them to change their attitudes and behaviour in appropriate circumstances.

A structural change could entail a move from a functional group to a matrix organisation. It could also involve the removal of layers of management, with wider spans of control, to create a flatter and less bureaucratic organisation. Likewise, authority and reporting relationships could be changed, as could the size of units or departments. Many of these changes could have a knock-on effect. For example, the decentralisation of authority could give rise to greater individual autonomy at the lower levels of the organisation, and accelerate the decision-making process. The role of technology in structural change is acknowledged later. Changing structures in order to promote innovation, a topic discussed in Chapters 8 and 15, is considered worth pursuing (Damanpour, 1991). There is an elaboration of the organisational issues discussed here in Chapter 14.

Various techniques and processes (e.g., new technology, total quality management, business process re-engineering), which are discussed elsewhere in this book, have been used to bring about profound changes in order to improve the organisation's performance and competitiveness. New technology has had a significant effect on the design of information systems and organisation. Information technology has contributed much to the delayering that has taken place in organisations in recent years. It was possible to remove layers of management that acted as filters for information flowing up and down the hierarchy. Instead, those seeking information were able to access files and databases using computers. Information technology has had a favourable impact in terms of the democratisation of organisations, because of greater access to information; it has improved decision making because of the quantity and quality of data available; and has assisted with the globalisation of business because of more reliance on networks and less reliance on the telephone (Thach & Woodman, 1994).

Total quality management (TQM), which first made an impact in the mid-1980s, is an organisation-wide attempt to improve quality through changes in structure, systems, practices, and employee attitudes. Business process re-engineering (BPR) sets out to obtain significant improvements in organisational performance by endeavouring to enhance the efficiency and effectiveness of key business processes. However, the success of TQM and BPR is not impressive. Zairi, Letza, and Oakland (1994) maintain that there is a high failure rate in the application of TQM in Europe, and Wastell, White, and Kawalek (1994) suggest that BPR has achieved less than expected.

Changing the corporate culture (see Chapter 15) became an important strategy to transform the organisation in the early 1980s, and although not a burning issue at the present time it is nevertheless important. Obviously it is wise to have an understanding of culture before undertaking change (Clarke, 1994), because adherence to certain cultural values and traditions can slow down or undermine change. The importance of cultural change in the context of placing value on diversity has been advocated (Allen & Montgomery, 2001). However, there are voices that are not convinced of the desirability of changing culture to create advantages for the organisation (Wilson, 1992).

Nowadays the "learning organisation" is likely to be considered a useful means of promoting receptiveness to change. It is claimed that a learning organisation is proficient at generating, obtaining, and disseminating knowledge and at modifying behaviour to reflect new knowledge and insights (Garvin, 1993). There is a discussion of the learning organisation in Chapter 7. What changes are needed to transform the normal organisation into a learning organisation? It would seem necessary to have a corporate strategy in which there is a commitment to change, innovation, and continuous improvement, as well as adopting the features of the contemporary organisation (discussed in Chapter 14) and the reshaping of culture to encourage risk-taking and functional rather than dysfunctional conflict (Robbins, 2003).

Task redesign

The redesign of tasks was considered in Chapter 4. Here it is examined as a factor in OD. When changes to a job are contemplated it is critical to evaluate the organisational structure, especially the work rules and authority for decision making within the department (Moorhead, 1981), quite apart from specific changes to the jobs concerned. The process adopted is what one would expect when faced with any major change. For example, there is initially a recognition of the need for change, followed by selecting the appropriate intervention (e.g., job redesign to give employees more freedom in the choice of work methods or the scheduling of work), and an evaluation of the change, bearing in mind a variety of influences (e.g., technology, leadership, group dynamics, costs, implementation) connected with the context of the proposed change (Griffin, 1982). (The relationship between technology and task design was discussed in Chapter 4.)

Individual and group emphasis

The OD intervention strategies falling into this category are aimed at changing the attitudes and behaviour of members of the organisation by resorting to processes of communication, decision making, and problem solving. Human growth, participative and collaborative processes also feature prominently (Pasmore & Fagans, 1992). Among the well-known people-centred change techniques are:

* sensitivity training;
* survey feedback;
* process consultation;
* teambuilding;
* grid development;
* management by objectives; and
* conflict management.

Sensitivity training

By the mid-1960s sensitivity training, often referred to as T-groups, had become an accepted management fad very much in tune with the optimistic spirit of the times. The US National Training Laboratory and the Tavistock Clinic in London became centres of management research espousing this approach. It is a method used for changing behaviour through interaction of an unstructured nature in a group setting. The group can consist of 10–15 members supported by a professional trainer, and is referred to as a T-group (training group) or encounter group. Groups can remain in existence for up to 2 weeks in a secluded location, though they could function in a company or college setting. A feature of the atmosphere within the group is the openness with which people discuss their ideas, attitudes, and outlook, and the way they interact with others. The professional trainer plays the role of a facilitator rather than a leader, and group members

learn from participating and observing rather than from being told what is correct or incorrect.

The main purpose of the T-group is to give members the opportunity to enhance awareness of their own behaviour and the behaviour of others, as well as to increase sensitivity concerning how others perceive them (Campbell & Dunnette, 1968). Proponents of this technique would expect certain desirable consequences to flow from the exposure of participants to the group processes. These would include a greater capacity to empathise with others, to be a better listener, to be more tolerant of other people's ideas, to be more open, and to be better able to resolve interpersonal conflict.

Evidence has been cited that T-groups can generate negative psychological effects for a significant minority of participants (Lieberman, Yalom, & Miles, 1973). The process of exposing their personality incurs costs in terms of traumatic experiences for certain people. In general, it is maintained that sensitivity training changes the behaviour of those who participate in it, but there is considerable debate about whether the changed behaviour is incorporated into the normal work behaviour of the person on his or her return to the job.

In some ways it is not surprising that the T-group never made the impact its supporters expected. It could be argued that the values exemplified in a strong belief in the importance of openness and trust for effective cooperative effort, which was prevalent in the 1960s, were in conflict with the norms of most organisations. Makin, Cooper, and Cox (1989) point out that sensitivity training was never widely accepted, and has now fallen into disuse mainly because of the differences between the values of T-groups and those of most organisations. Because of this clash of values, there was a poor transfer of learning from the training situation to the real organisational world with its intricate political processes, where factionalism and infighting were part of the scene (London, 2004a).

Survey feedback

This technique is designed to collect data that are subsequently analysed, summarised, and returned to those who took part in the survey. The outcome of this exercise is used in identifying problems connected with change, and to provide an informed input to the solutions proposed. The use of survey feedback techniques in organisational development is different from their use in normal attitude surveys. As part of an OD process, data from the survey are distributed to groups of employees at all levels of the organisation and used by them in their natural groupings to assist in the identification and solution of problems. Data would not be handled in this way with a normal attitude survey where senior management would receive the findings and then decide on the most appropriate course of action to take.

The change agent interviews selected employees from various organisational levels to determine the important issues to be examined during the data-collection stage of survey feedback. It would be invaluable if a questionnaire were designed specifically for data collection. Of course it would not be necessary to prepare a questionnaire if it is proposed to use a standardised instrument (i.e., a questionnaire already prepared externally) of a reliable nature. The latter may offer the facility to use comparative data from other organisations. To ensure the anonymous nature of individual responses, the questionnaire results are analysed and summarised by unit or department (Franklin, 1978). A summary of the results for use in the group feedback sessions is prepared by the change agent.

The feedback meetings are best handled when run by a "family group", which could be the manager and subordinates in a particular unit. Family groups are held down to small numbers in order to promote interaction and discussion among members. Meetings are run by the managers rather than by the change agent in order to emphasise that ownership of the exercise resides in those involved in day-to-day activities. It is important to ensure that the role of the change agent is confined to that of an expert and a resource at the disposal of the group. In essence the change agent assists the manager in preparing for the meeting by reviewing the data, devising ways of identifying and solving problems, and stimulating discussion at the meetings.

The actual feedback that the groups receive is principally a series of profiles on such matters as the effectiveness of communication, the level of job satisfaction, the nature of decision making, and the quality of managerial leadership. During the actual feedback sessions the group members discuss the profiles and the problems that the data bring to light. The next step is for the group, with the assistance of the change agent, to concentrate on the lessons to be learned from the information presented at the feedback session, and to devise action plans aimed at bringing about the organisational improvements. Several sessions may be required to consider the plans and the best way to implement them. Also, follow-up action is crucial to establish to what extent the processes concerned have improved.

The survey feedback technique is a popular organisational change and development intervention. In comparing socio-technical systems, job redesign, and survey feedback interventions, Pasmore (1978) suggested that the survey feedback approach was of value: not only did it help management to understand feelings of employees about an issue, but it also formed the basis for building trust between the management and workforce. However, the effectiveness of feedback meetings could be undermined if the findings are perceived as threatening. In such circumstances it is suggested that a group of managerial colleagues be created to review and discuss the findings before the meetings are arranged with subordinates in the family groups (Alderfer & Ferriss, 1972).

Process consultation

There is some similarity between this technique and sensitivity training, in that it is concerned with improving organisational effectiveness through involving people in the resolution of interpersonal problems. However, it is more task-oriented than sensitivity training. An important feature of process consultation is using an outside consultant to help the client, usually a manager, to perceive, understand, and take action with respect to processes within his or her sphere of influence (Schein, 1969). These processes could include communication patterns, interpersonal relationships, the flow of work, roles, group norms, group problem solving and decision making, leadership styles, exercise of authority and power, and inter-group activities.

There are three stages in process consultation, described in the following subsections.

Stage 1. This is the initial contact with the client organisation. At this stage an assessment is made of whether or not the consultancy is likely to be successful. The assessment is based on the initial impressions of the client's intentions and suitability to embark on a project of this nature.

Stage 2. This consists of setting up an exploratory meeting between the contact person (the client), the consultant, and a group of employees who are likely to have status and influence, but at the same time can appreciate the true nature of process consultation and have the ability to identify problems. At this particular juncture it would be advisable to include people who are not basically hostile to the process. The consultant will seek to establish the nature of the problem, and whether he or she is sufficiently interested in it and can be of assistance. If the consultant accepts the assignment, future plans can be devised.

There are two aspects to the contract that exists between the consultant and the client—one relates to the provision of a consultancy service, including the fee, and the other is called the psychological contract that deals with the expectations the consultant and client have of each other. For example, the client's expectation of the consultant could include the acceptance of expert opinion on how people problems should be managed as well as an evaluation of staff. The consultant's expectation of his or her own role and that of the client could include a personal expectation to put effort into the diagnosis and exploration of issues, to be supported by the organisation in collecting data, and to receive the commitment of staff to the project.

At preliminary meetings there is clarification of what is necessary in order to engage in process consultation. For example, there is a need for trust; the total organisation is to be seen as the client; the consultant must not be viewed simply as the "expert"; and any misunderstandings should be cleared up. Also, it must be emphasised that the role of the consultant is that of a listener who may appear relatively inactive and certainly does not want to get involved in discussions of the content of subject matter addressed by the group. However, he or she may be asked by the group to comment on interpersonal processes, in which case feedback is given, as well as encouragement to come up with solutions to group problems.

Stage 3. This involves the establishment of systems of working. A good starting point would be the apex of the organisation, where the greatest impact and influence for change can be achieved. The focal point for observation must be interpersonal and group processes aimed specifically at staff working on real jobs. Consultants should think clearly of the likely implications of what they say, because every question they ask is seen as an intervention. When the consultant is engaged in information gathering it is felt that the interview is preferable to the survey questionnaire in data collection, because the questionnaire would tend to distance the consultant from the client due to its impersonality. It is important for the consultant's questions to be relevant and not obscure. Good questioning could provide the client with an enlarged perspective of behavioural processes within the organisation.

It is now apparent that the consultant adopts two approaches—one is the gathering of information and the other is an intervention—although the two can be closely related. Schein (1969, 1987) has classified interventions as follows:

- *Agenda setting.* Here the group may put the spotlight on issues connected with "process" or rearrange the agenda for action.
- *Feedback.* When feedback is given to individuals or groups it should be done in a sensitive way, bearing in mind people's feelings.
- *Coaching or counselling.* For instance, from the feedback process it materialises that a manager registers an inappropriate piece of behaviour, and he or she wants advice on ways of changing it.

• *Structural suggestions*. This could mean creating awareness of the advantages and disadvantages of various structural attributes of the organisation. Because the consultant's role is connected with enabling clients to solve their own problems and not to solve problems for them, suggesting how work should be structured and executed is a rare occurrence. He or she is not really in a position to undertake such a role in normal circumstances.

The final stages are taken up with trying to obtain appropriate measures to evaluate the effectiveness of process consultation, and for the consultant to disengage from the exercise. A gradual rather than abrupt disengagement is advisable.

Schein makes the point that process consultation is fundamentally different from other types of consultancy, such as the purchase model and the doctor–patient model. The purchase model is applicable when the organisation identifies its problems without outside help and then appoints a consultant to solve them. In the doctor–patient model, the consultant conducts a diagnostic examination of the organisation and suggests remedies. With the purchase model the difficulty could be that the organisation has defined its problems incorrectly, or the consultant chosen may not be the most suitable. With the doctor–patient model, the difficulty could be that the diagnosis is resisted, or the remedies are not implemented. In the case of process consultation, it should be reiterated that the consultant's role is not to suggest solutions to problems, but to help management understand organisational problems as clearly as possible, so that appropriate solutions are likely to be found.

In an assessment of a number of interventions based on process consultation, the majority of them were considered positive (Golembiewski, Proehl, & Sink, 1982). However, a major limitation of the process consultation technique would be a skill deficiency on the part of the consultant.

Teambuilding

In circumstances where interaction between members of a group is crucial for effective performance, developing or building teams may be useful. A detailed discussion of teambuilding appeared in Chapter 11, and it is useful to refer back to the issues raised there. The main purpose of teambuilding is to assist people with related or interdependent jobs to examine ways in which their team works together, at the same time identifying strengths and weaknesses, and developing plans to improve team functioning. In essence, teambuilding is a task-oriented activity with an emphasis on interpersonal interaction. Processes taken into account in teambuilding are setting goals, developing interpersonal relations, role analysis to clarify team members' jobs, and an overall analysis of the team process. There is also an endeavour to use substantial contact among members to foster trust and openness, and there is a pronounced emphasis on changes that will lead to improvements in specific aspects of team performance.

Teambuilding starts with a diagnostic meeting at which members of the team, in the company of the change agent, discuss in an open, unstructured way the current position on the functioning of the team. Each member is given ample opportunity to state the goals and priorities of the team together with its strengths and weaknesses, and what action is necessary to improve its effectiveness. The viewpoints expressed serve as a basis for discussion, which can lead to an agreed position within the team on desirable changes. At subsequent meetings, plans can be developed to implement the changes. Finally, the effectiveness of teambuilding has received some empirical endorsement (Golembiewski et al., 1982; Macy & Igumi, 1993), but one can also find evidence showing that the effects are not substantial (Buller & Bell, 1986).

Inter-group development. Teambuilding on an inter-group basis can be referred to as inter-group development. It has become an issue in OD because of the damaging effects inter-group conflict (discussed in Chapter 10) can create. Inter-group development sets out to change the attitudes, stereotypes, and perceptions that groups have of each other in order to foster cooperation and communication between them. The intervention is either initiated by a consultant using groups from the same department or, alternatively, groups from different departments, whose cooperation is necessary for successful organisational performance, can be used. The steps involved are as follows (Hodgetts, 1991; Liebowitz & De Meuse, 1982):

- The inter-group intervention starts with the leaders (or all members) of the two groups meeting together when it is established that the relationships between them can be improved.
- Working in separate rooms the two groups prepare two lists—one contains the groups' perceptions, attitudes, and feelings about the other group, and the other consists of what the group thinks the other group is saying about them.
- The two groups meet to share the information that they have listed, with each group stating how the other is perceived. At this stage the consultant invites questions on clarification of meaning, but not discussion of the listed items.
- The two groups return to their rooms to discuss the insights they have formed concerning themselves and the other group. It is conceivable that a fair amount of friction or differences of opinion between the two groups is based on faulty perceptions and communication difficulties. If this is recognised, the gulf between the two groups may be less than originally thought.
- The two groups resume their meeting, and again compare their lists. They cooperate in preparing an overall list of issues or difficulties that still need to be resolved. Items are listed on the basis of priority and action strategies are created, specifying what has to be done, when, and by whom. At this stage the intervention by the consultant ceases.
- In some situations there could be a review to establish whether the action plans have been implemented in order to see if the purpose of the exercise has been achieved.

In reviews of the effectiveness of intervention based on inter-group development it is suggested that, although attitudes can improve among members, the positive effects in terms of behavioural change and organisational performance are more elusive (Friedlander & Brown, 1974).

Grid development

This is based on the leadership grid (formerly called the managerial grid) postulated by Blake and Mouton (1985), which was discussed in Chapter 12. The grid accommodates a "concern for production" and a "concern for people", as a means of analysing and improving the individual leadership styles of managers. The programme based on the grid is formulated with the express purpose of helping managers to identify their current as well as their ideal leadership style, and then to take action to move towards the latter. The six phases in the programme are set out in Panel 16.6.

Although Blake and Mouton cite evidence to support their approach to organisational development, there have been criticisms of the methodology used. Also, there is recognition that although people may show changes in attitudes towards styles of management, changes in actual behaviour have been more difficult to prove (Gray & Starke, 1984). The most fundamental criticism relates to leadership style in the form of a 9,9 team manager (high on production, high on people). Blake and Mouton make the assertion that this type of manager will always be the most effective regardless of the situation, but evidence from situational leadership would challenge that assertion (Bernardin & Alvares, 1976).

Management by objectives

Management by objectives (MBO) can be used as an organisation-wide OD intervention, but unlike the leadership grid it has assumed a variety of forms over the years. The key elements of MBO are identifying the goals of the organisation, setting specific goals for employees (the achievement of which will bring about the attainment of organisational goals), and evaluating the progress of employees in trying to attain their individual goals and providing performance feedback (Rodgers & Hunter, 1991). The following are features common to most MBO programmes (Szilagi & Wallace, 1983):

PANEL 16.6: Leadership grid technique for inter-group development

(1)   Managers attend a seminar, which is held outside the organisation and goes on for roughly a week. They concentrate on reading relevant material, diagnosing their leadership styles, engaging in problem-solving exercises, developing skills to take action in teams, offering critiques, and enhancing communication processes.

(2)   Teamwork is improved by giving managers and their subordinates the opportunity to apply the knowledge and skills acquired in the first phase of the programme to their specific situation. There is also a determination to locate and understand the impediments to group effectiveness, to identify members' preferences for the way to operate, to foster a climate where the work of individuals is examined in a critical but constructive manner, leading to the creation of a timetable and set of objectives for improving the performance of the group.

(3)   The emphasis now swings from a preoccupation with events within a work group (intra-group) to attempts to develop closer integration between work groups (inter-group). Each group specifies what it considers to be ideal inter-group relationships, and shares these views with other groups. Representatives from groups that interact are asked to set in motion discussions about developing and implementing these ideal types of relationships.

(4)   This phase could last for 1 year and concentrates on the development of an ideal strategic plan for the organisation. The formulation of the strategic plan is put in the hands of the top management group. In this exercise there is a commitment to excellence, and the planning process is studded with much discussion and evaluation of ideas and suggestions. Attention is also given to matters connected with implementation.

(5)   This phase can consume a considerable amount of time (frequently 2 to 3 years) as the organisation tries to bridge the gap between the status quo and the future desired state for the organisation. Planning teams, supplemented by top management, will be busy establishing what has to be done in order to move in the desired direction.

(6)   The final phase places the emphasis on stabilisation. This means that every effort is made to ensure that changes made following earlier phases are not undermined by a reversion to old behaviours. The new methods and practices that have been introduced are reinforced, and when progress is reviewed any deviations are earmarked for future corrective action.

(Blake & Mouton, 1985)

- *Diagnosis*. This will lead to developing an understanding of the needs of employees and aspects of their relevant environment at work.
- *Planning*. This entails various activities connected with learning to handle the MBO approach, getting management's commitment to it, and considering the overall goals and strategies of the organisation.
- *Defining the employee's job*. The nature of the job and the duties and responsibilities must be defined before individual goals can be set.
- *Goal-setting*. The goals for a specified period of time, usually a year, are set by the subordinate. Attention is given to identifying goals, setting priorities, target dates, and the modes of measurement to be used.
- *Superior's review*. The superior reviews the subordinate's initial goals, provides feedback, and offers suggestions for improvement. Then the subordinate and superior arrive at an agreed set of goals for the subordinate for the specified period.
- *Interim review*. Periodically throughout the specified period the subordinate and superior

meet to discuss the progress made, as well as to adjust the agreed goals to reflect new information or changing environmental circumstances.

- *Final review*. At the end of the period for which the goals are set, the subordinate and superior meet to review the results. The emphasis is on analysis, discussion, feedback, and input to the next MBO cycle. The cycle repeats itself for the next period.

The effectiveness of MBO, in terms of better communication, improved planning, and positive attitudes towards systems of evaluation has been endorsed (Carroll & Tosi, 1970). However, there has been criticism, such as that MBO programmes generated too much paperwork, overemphasised production, and failed to involve all levels of management (Gray & Starke, 1984). According to Rodgers, Hunter, and Rogers (1993), MBO programmes fail because they do not live up to the expectations of management. In an exhaustive study of the effectiveness of MBO programmes, it was concluded that positive results were lost after a lapse of about 2 years (Kondrasuk, 1981).

Conflict management

A consequence of engaging in initiatives to bring about organisational change and development is the creation of conflict. To handle conflict of an interpersonal nature one could make use of expert intervention by a third party, who may be internal or external to the organisation. If one were to invoke an intervention based on Walton's (1969) interpersonal peacemaking, it would involve the adoption of a well-managed confrontation. For the confrontation to be successful the following conditions have to be met:

- both parties must have an interest in resolving the conflict;
- a relationship manifest in equality of power should exist between the two parties;
- the time chosen for the parties to confront each other should be just right;
- each party should have adequate time to air his or her views and to resolve differences of opinion before moving on to explore common ground;
- the social conditions should be characterised by a climate of openness, and mutual understanding should be fostered by effective communication; and
- the stress and tension in the encounter should be controlled and maintained at a moderate level.

Normally one would expect the third party or consultant to carry out preliminary meetings (interviews with the two parties on neutral ground). Questions such as how formal the first meetings should be, how long the meetings should last, and whether people other than the two parties should be invited, will have to be addressed. In the actual confrontation meeting, the role of the third party or consultant demands considerable skill in managing the process and guiding the confrontation towards an encouraging outcome. The consultant should set the agenda for the dialogue, prescribing what should be discussed at different stages of the confrontation. He or she should:

- ensure that the two parties have equal time to air their views;

- encourage the parties to give due weight to a diagnosis of the problems confronting them;
- summarise and restate the issues in question;
- deal delicately with interactions that are potentially damaging in the context of the continuation of the dialogue;
- provide feedback and comment on the proceedings as they occur; and
- settle the agenda for further meetings.

This type of interpersonal peacemaking intervention could be difficult to operationalise because of the exacting conditions necessary for its use and the qualities required of the consultant. However, Walton's model appears intuitively plausible, and is supported by his own anecdotal case histories. He believes it worked for him.

OVERALL EVALUATION OF ORGANISATIONAL DEVELOPMENT

In the earlier discussion of OD interventions, particularly those that focus on "changing the outlook of the individual and group", assessments were made after an examination of each intervention. Now it is time to reflect generally on their effectiveness.

The OD interventions focusing on the individual and group are by and large based on humanistic and democratic values, such as respect for people, trust and support, participation, open confrontation of issues, participation, and power equalisation (Burke, 2000). Factors such as political systems, organisational conflict, and so on do not feature prominently in the change agent's agenda, though one has to admit that OD has, in recent years, broadened its perspective. Apart from humanistic considerations, matters connected with job redesign and organisational structure are now taken on board, as well as strategic factors related to the overall direction of the organisation.

There are some issues that need to be emphasised when it comes to the implementation of behaviourally oriented OD interventions. First, there are the political forces prevalent during times of change (Shein, 1985). It would be unwise to ignore the political dimension and the impact that change interventions can have on the balance of power within the organisation. (Power and politics are discussed in Chapter 13.)

Secondly, there are individuals who feel uncomfortable engaging in a process that demands a frank disclosure of their feelings and attitudes, even if participation is voluntary. Such a process could be seen as invading a person's privacy and reducing personal freedom. There is also the fear that, though the climate surrounding the intervention is benevolent and supportive, sensitive information may be used vindictively at some later stage against the person who has divulged his or her fears or concerns.

Thirdly, the values ingrained in OD interventions are likely to be out of step with organisational cultures that are characterised as strong on bureaucratic control, risk-averse, intolerant of conflict, and insignificant in supportive management. Of course, OD values could also be incompatible with particular national cultures, in which case negative outcomes can be expected. Therefore, the greater the match between OD values and a country's cultural dimensions, the greater the likelihood that OD intervention will succeed (Jaeger, 1986). (There is a discussion of culture in Chapter 15.)

Despite the acceptability of OD as a useful organisational tool, there has been little systematic evaluation of its effects. Where research studies on the effectiveness of OD have been undertaken, it is suggested that one should turn one's attention in the first instance to the methodology used. Terpstra (1981) argues that the more rigorous the evaluation research relating to whether or not particular interventions had the desired effect, the more difficult it is to find evidence supportive of OD. That means that with well-designed research, using a random selection of subjects, control groups, and sophisticated analysis, one is less likely to find evidence of the effectiveness of OD. Terpstra makes the point that because the results of less rigorous research are often ambiguous, there is an unconscious bias on the part of researchers evaluating the effectiveness of OD to interpret the results as supportive, and that high expectations on the part of top management and

pressure from the latter might also contribute to this bias. On the theme of expectations, Evden (1986) asserts that where gains stem from OD interventions, they can be attributable to managers being convinced by consultants that an intervention would succeed. This is communicated down the organisation through supervisors to workers, and any productivity improvements are due more to raised expectations about the effectiveness of OD than to the intervention chosen.

Worren, Ruddle, and Moore (1999) rightly pointed out that during the 1990s an increasing dissatisfaction with the traditional OD came to the surface. Change management is now considered the preferred way to proceed. It could be considered broader than OD in that it includes a wide range of intervention strategies that may enhance human performance directly or indirectly, including process consultation, work structuring, strategic HRM, and the design or development of information technology solutions (e.g., user interface design). OD practitioners, with their people-centred approach, now acknowledge that they forgot about markets, strategies, and computers. In the field of planned organisational change one of the few things we know with certainty is that change programmes are rarely successful if they are directed at only one component in isolation from the others.

As a final comment on OD, note the verdict of Bradford and Burke (2004): answering the question, "Does OD have a future?", the authors come forward with the following answer:

We believe OD has much to offer in its emphasis on releasing the human potential within the organization. It has developed many valuable approaches. It has stressed the importance of values at a time when too much behaviour is valueless. It would be a shame to have this lost. But for the field to grow and develop, it must do more in defining what it is and what it is not. It must also be more demanding of what is required to be a competent professional. Doing that will not be easy and we do not offer easy answers.

Appreciative inquiry

In recent years there has emerged a school of thought—appreciative inquiry—that takes a position opposite to the traditional people-centred OD approach of identifying a problem and then finding a solution to it. In the appreciative inquiry approach, instead of being on the look out for problems, the practitioner sets out to identify the unique qualities and special strengths of the organisation. Once this is done, effort is directed at improving these features so as to enhance performance and organisational success (Copperrider & Whitney, 2000).

In appreciative inquiry the spotlight is on isolating what is good about the organisation and making it better, rather than laying blame, with the resultant defensiveness, for various problems that may have surfaced. Appreciative inquiry can assist in promoting change by building on the organisation's strengths. It consists of four steps (within the confines of a group with a change agent in attendance) and lasts for a few days:

- *Stage 1 (discovery)*. Group members are given the opportunity to express points of view about the qualities and strengths of the organisation.
- *Stage 2 (dreaming)*. The information obtained at the discovery stage is used to speculate about a possible future scenario for the organisation. For example, the group could imagine a situation at some point in the future and state in what way it is likely to be different from the situation right now.
- *Stage 3 (design)*. Group members will give serious consideration to the outcome of stage 2 and try to reach some form of consensus or common ground on the future shape and purpose of the organisation, isolating its unique qualities and strengths.
- *Stage 4 (describe the organisation's destiny)*. Building on stage 3, the emphasis will be on how the organisation can move forward to the desired or preferred state. At this stage the approach is essentially preparing action plans and implementation strategies.

CHAPTER SUMMARY

- Having defined what we mean by change, models of change and a processual/contextual perspective were introduced.

- The need to plan organisational change was stressed, and the process model, the continuous change process model, and the emergent approach were suggested as approaches. In this respect the role of the change agent is important.

- Ways of implementing change were discussed, with a focus on Kotter's model of a change process, plus, in this context, brief reference to the Bolman and Deal frames.

- Then there was a discussion of resistance to change. The sources of resistance to change at the organisational level were listed as over-determination, narrow focus of change, group inertia, threatened expertise, threatened power, and resource allocation. At the individual level they were identified as habit, security, economic considerations, fear of the unknown, lack of awareness, and social considerations.

- An alternative explanation of sources of change suggested that key considerations are parochial self-interest, misunderstanding/lack of trust, contradictory assessments, and low tolerance of change. A cycle of coping with change was examined.

- Approaches to controlling resistance to change were identified as education and communication, participation, facilitation and support, negotiation and agreement, manipulation and co-optation, and coercion.

- Organisational development (OD) was identified as the process of planned change and improvement of organisations through the application of knowledge derived from the behavioural sciences.

- General strategies to bring about organisational development were specified, and various techniques and interventions were stated. These interventions operate at different levels—i.e., organisation structure, culture, learning organisation, task redesign, and the individual/group. For example, at the organisational level techniques such as TQM and BPR, supported by modern technology, have been used as interventions.

- With respect to interventions at the individual/group level, a number of people-centred techniques were discussed. These are sensitivity training, survey feedback, process consultation, teambuilding, leadership grid, management by objectives, and conflict management.

- The final section reflected on the effectiveness of OD interventions, and there was reference to an alternative viewpoint in the form of appreciative inquiry.

QUESTIONS

(1) Define organisational change.

(2) Identify the features of your preferred model of change.

(3) What is the difference between the process model and the continuous change process model in the context of planning organisational change?

(4) Discuss the justification for the emergent approach when planning organisational change.

(5) What significance do you attach to Dawson's processual/contextual perspective?

(6) How useful is Kotter's model of a change process in developing our understanding of the implementation of change?

(7) Describe the approach adopted by Katz and Kahn to the sources of resistance to change, and state how it differs from that suggested by Bedeian.

(8) How would you go about controlling resistance to change?

(9) Identify the distinctive features of appreciative inquiry.

(10) "It is not good enough for an organisation to respond to change; it must try to anticipate it as well." Discuss.

(11) Define the following terms: (a) action research; (b) group inertia; (c) co-optation; (d) change agent; and (e) cycle of coping.

(12) Define organisational development.

(13) What do we mean by people-centred change techniques in organisational development?

(14) How important are organisation-based interventions in organisational development?

(15) Comment on issues related to an evaluation of organisational development.

SPOTLIGHT ON RELEVANT READING

Bradford, D.L., & Burke, W.W. (2004) (Guest Editors). Is Organisational Development in crisis? Special issue of the *Journal of Applied Behavioural Science*, 49, (December).

Burnes, B. (2004). Kurt Lewin and the planned approach to change. A reappraisal. *Journal of Management Studies*, 41, 977–1002.

Dawson, P. (2003). *Understanding organisational change: The contemporary experience of people at work*. London: Sage.

Hayes, J. (2002). *The theory and practice of change management*. Basingstoke, Hants: Palgrave.

Kotter, J.P., & Cohen, D.S. (2002). *The heart of change. Real life stories of how people change their organisations*. Boston, MA: Harvard Business School Press.

Wright, G., van der Heijden, K., Bradfield, R., & Cairns, G. (2004). The psychology of why organisations can be slow to adapt and change. *Journal of General Management*, 29, 21–36.

Part V

Management and Organisational Issues

Learning Outcomes

After studying this chapter you should be able to:

- Recognise the features of HRM and identify factors responsible for its development.

- Assess the significance of job analysis as an activity associated with recruitment and selection.

- List the methods used in employee selection and discuss their usefulness.

- Outline the issues involved in "fairness" in employee selection.

- Discuss the reasons why an employee's performance is evaluated.

- Outline the criteria and techniques used in performance appraisal.

- Explain what is meant by administering the appraisal system.

- Recognise the role of the feedback interview in the use of appraisal information.

- Describe the problems with appraisal and state how they might be overcome.

- Specify the conditions associated with an effective appraisal system.

Human Resource Practices: Selection and Appraisal

After a brief review of human resource management, this chapter examines human resource practices with respect to personnel selection and performance appraisal. The section on selection puts the spotlight on job analysis, description, and specification, followed by selection methods and their fairness, validity, reliability, and utility. The performance appraisal section analyses the goals of performance appraisal and the evaluative criteria and techniques used, plus issues surrounding administering the process, using appraisal information, and dealing with problems. Conditions for a successful scheme are outlined. The balanced scorecard is introduced. This chapter complements Chapter 18. Issues related to personality and intelligence testing (Chapters 2 and 3) and interpersonal perception (Chapter 5) are particularly relevant to this chapter.

Contents

HUMAN RESOURCE MANAGEMENT

Nowadays, human resource practices operate within a framework provided by **human resource management**, and a brief explanation of this process is appropriate before we move on.

A major theme running through human resource management (HRM) is the acknowledgement that employees are valued assets of the organisation, that there should be an active interplay between a strategy for the human resource and the main strategy for the business, that corporate culture should be managed so as to make it compatible with the requirements of corporate strategy, and that seeking the commitment of employees to the organisation has far greater value than mere forced compliance. To elicit commitment, reference is often made to mutuality. This represents HRM policies that promote mutual goals, mutual influence, mutual rewards, and mutual responsibility. In a climate of mutuality the cause of commitment is advanced, with alleged benefits in terms of productivity and employee development, although it is recognised that mutuality is a fragile phenomenon (Armstrong, 1992).

Another feature of HRM that is often mentioned is the existence of the "common interests" of management and employees in the profitability of the enterprise. This is said to lead to the tapping of a substantial reservoir of initiative within the workforce. There is also a concern within HRM for the organisation to respond appropriately to forces in the company's environment by becoming flexible, adaptive, and competitive. For example, an organisation could respond to environmental forces by increased decentralisation in order to facilitate a better reaction to market forces. In line with delegation, there could be greater employee autonomy and accountability for the efficient use of resources. Flexibility may be injected into the roles employees play in teams (e.g., autonomous groups; self-managing teams), and is manifest in a wider range of skills (multi-skilling).

HRM, as a strategic approach to acquire, develop, manage, and motivate people, became popular in the 1980s, and in some cases it absorbed and extended the personnel management function in business. It draws on a number of the behavioural ideas discussed in this book, but at the same time it adopts a hard-nosed business orientation (McKenna & Beech, 2002). According to Guest (1994), one can identify some contributory factors to the development of HRM, as follows:

- The competitive advantage of Japanese systems of management, which was attributed to the effective use of human resources.
- The study of Japanese systems of management by US academics on the theme of making good use of human talent, and developing cultures of mutual trust and commitment.
- The growth of the service sector of the economy, which put the spotlight on the effective management of employees.
- Dissatisfaction with the capability of traditional personnel management to meet new challenges.
- The prior existence of complementary US behavioural solutions (e.g., job redesign, participative management, quality of working life, employee relations) to organisational problems.
- The impact of the excellence principles (i.e., Peters & Waterman) which stressed the soft issues—staff, systems, style, skills, and shared values—as opposed to the hard issues in the form of strategy and structure.
- The growing importance of corporate culture and its role as a powerful and efficient control system in the management of organisations.
- The significance of the contributions of academics in the field of corporate strategy, with respect to market and customer orientation and cost.

Guest states that, because HRM is a concept which originated in the USA, we should recognise a number of factors likely to affect its implementation when applying it in Europe. In this context there are issues such as cultural diversity and complexity, pluralism as opposed to unitarism, collectivism instead of individualism, the legal process on matters affecting labour, and social responsibility and partnership.

In a survey undertaken by Watson Wyatt's Human Capital in the UK it was stated that some human resource strategies in companies were correlated with increases in shareholder value; for example, good reward management systems and recruitment and selection practices. However, there were shortcomings when training and development was considered, as well as the utilisation of the skills of temporary employees (Donkin, 2002).

The human resource or personnel management practices of primary interest to the occupational/organisational psychologist and the personnel/HR practitioner are personnel selection, performance management, reward systems, and training and development. Measurement is common to selection and performance appraisal, and therefore these two topics will be discussed in this chapter, while rewards, training, and development are covered in the next chapter.

PERSONNEL SELECTION

Selection is the final stage of the overall recruitment process and it is concerned with choosing from a sample of job applicants the individuals best suited to the jobs available. An earlier stage is the activity of recruitment, which is concerned with attracting a pool of candidates (using advertisements, agencies, etc.) for the vacant position, as well as producing a shortlist of candidates whose background and potential are in accordance with the profile contained in the job specification, referred to later. Selection is normally used to decide who shall enter the organisation, and it can be contrasted with the placement process, which involves matching people already in the organisation to the available jobs. The principles associated with selection could equally apply to placement. Before the recruitment and selection techniques are used, it is necessary to analyse the appropriate jobs.

Job analysis

Job analysis is designed to produce systematic information about jobs, including the nature of the work performed, the equipment used, the working conditions, and the position of the job within the organisation (Arnold, 2005).

Techniques and procedures

The techniques and procedures used in job analysis are wide ranging (Spector, Brannick, & Coovert, 1989), but the sources of job analysis data can be categorised as follows:

* written material;
* job holder's reports;
* colleagues' reports; and
* direct observation.

Written material. For jobs already in existence, there are likely to be written job descriptions within the organisation. A job description is a written statement of what a job holder does, how it is done, and why it is done. If this is comprehensive and up to date, it can provide the analyst with useful information. A job description can be supplemented by other written material, such as organisation charts and training manuals.

Job holder's reports. The job holder is asked by the interviewer to state the main tasks applicable to the job and the manner in which they are executed. Although the interviewer is expected to be thorough in his or her questioning, all relevant questions may not be asked. This could be a problem made worse by subjective and biased reports by the job holder. To counteract these difficulties, it may be helpful if workers complete diaries or activity records. Though time-consuming, this approach avoids the problem of placing total reliance on the worker's memory in an interview situation.

Another technique deals with critical incidents (Flanagan, 1954). Here, the job holder is asked to recall specific incidents related to either very good or very poor job performance. Doyle (2003) invokes attribution theory when examining a problem with the critical incidents approach. When you ask people to specify critical incidents that are associated with poor performance, they tend to attribute the poor performance to the limitations of others and to events beyond their control. So the tendency to attribute poor performance to external causes or events and good performance to the employees' own abilities is referred to as the cardinal attribution error.

There are other approaches to job analysis relying on the perceptions of the job holder obtained by structured questionnaires. These can be very comprehensive, covering areas such as information input to the job, orientation of the job (extent to which the job is directed towards data, people, or things), traits and skills required to do the job (reasoning, decision making, relating to others), and the output of the work process (Arnold, 2005).

Colleagues' reports.   As a means to provide comparative data, one could rely on the perceptions held by superiors, peers, and (where appropriate) subordinates of the job holder's activities.

Direct observation.   This amounts to direct observation of the way a particular job is done. Of course it is possible that the observer fails to detect some interesting features of the job, thereby undermining the credibility of the exercise, and the job holder may behave unnaturally because of being observed. However, direct observation offers potential in generating useful insights, more so perhaps if the analyst is a participant observer, engaged totally or partially in the job.

Criticism: some commentators accept the demise of traditional job analysis. If jobs have a short life span, job analysis is somewhat impractical. Also, bearing in mind technology impacting on and changing jobs on a frequent basis, it is becoming exceedingly difficult to predict the type of person the organisation will need in the future, but that does not rule out the need to base HR decisions on good information that also takes into account the needs of business (Doyle, 2003; Furnham, 2001b).

Post-job analysis

Having analysed the job, the data can be used for a number of different purposes, such as a job description and job specification. These are useful documents to have when reflecting on vacant positions and preparing job advertisements.

A job description contains an outline of the job, the tasks involved, the responsibilities and the conditions. The "flexible" job description is becoming popular. This will normally outline the nature of the tasks, and mention the job holder's competencies and skills, but it will not specify which team or group the job holder belongs to, nor will it state the precise nature of their responsibilities. The reason for the open-ended nature of the job responsibilities is to provide flexibility in the event of changes in the emphasis or direction taken by the organisation.

A job specification can be produced, stating the minimum acceptable qualifications in terms of knowledge, skills, abilities, attitudes and interests that an employee must possess to perform a given job successfully. A traditional approach to assist with the preparation of a job specification was Rodger's (1952) seven-point plan. The variables in this plan were:

* physique (health, appearance);
* attainments (education, qualifications, experience);
* general intelligence (intellectual capability);
* special aptitudes (facility with hands, numbers, communication skills);
* interests (cultural, sport, etc.);
* disposition (likeable, reliable, persuasive); and
* special circumstances (prepared to work shifts, excessive travel, etc.).

Nowadays, there is a tendency to highlight critical competencies associated with successful job performance. A competency would refer to an underlying individual characteristic, such as an ability to communicate, to solve problems, to delegate effectively, and to act as a good team player. Another trend is making explicit "key results areas" at the time the job specification is prepared. Here, obtaining results receives serious attention and so the emphasis is on outputs (e.g., quantity, quality, cost) and not on inputs (e.g., skills).

It should now be apparent that the job description and job specification are critical documents at the disposal of selectors.

Selection methods

Those concerned with selecting applicants for jobs have at their disposal a number of selection methods, such as the following:

- selection interview;
- psychometric tests;
- work sample tests;
- assessment centres;
- biographical information; and
- other methods.

Not all the selection methods listed are equally useful. By far the most widely used method is the selection interview.

The selection interview

One has to recognise national or cultural considerations with regard to the use of the selection interview. It is said that German companies make less use of interviews than do companies in other European countries (Shackleton & Newell, 1994). The selection interview entails interaction between people, and has been referred to as a "conversation with a purpose". Achieving the purpose of the interview involves complex transactions of obtaining and giving information. Both the interviewer and interviewee bring hopes, fears, expectations, misconceptions, and many other cognitions to the interview process. By using appropriate behavioural strategies, the interviewer and interviewee hope to realise their objectives, and roles are adopted to further the aim of a successful outcome. If the parties to the interview process act skilfully, this should improve the quality of the interactive episode (Wicks, 1984). Skilful performance in this context is a function of skills connected with self-awareness, awareness of social interaction processes, and self-presentation based on an appropriate foundation of knowledge or information.

However, a satisfactory outcome to the interview process also requires adequate preparation for the actual event. The interviewer should be well briefed, rehearse the interview, and anticipate the actions required. In a job interview it is important to put across information about the organisation and an adequate description of the advertised job. It is suggested that research on interviewing, as a device to select people for jobs, is fragmented and produces findings of little value to selectors (Harris, 1989; Lewis, 1984). However, on the basis of a comprehensive review of evidence about selection interviews (Arvey & Campion, 1982), it was concluded that the following features were present:

- The selection interview offers some insight into a person's sociability and verbal fluency from a sample of his or her total behaviour.
- Though the selection interview may not be a valid process, it is easy to arrange and interviewers have faith and confidence in their judgement in interview situations.
- Though the selection interview may not be a valid process, it presents an opportunity to sell the job to the candidates being interviewed. It is difficult to identify an equally efficient alternative.

There is evidence that is supportive of the suitability of the interview in assessing a job applicant's intelligence, level of conscientiousness, level of motivation, and interpersonal skills (Cascio, 1991; Huffcut, Conway, Roth, & Stone, 2001). It is suggested that these attributes are related to performance in management positions. Therefore, it is not surprising that applicants for senior management positions attend numerous interviews with headhunters, board members, and other executives before a final selection decision is made. Likewise, interviews are used frequently when deciding on the composition of teams.

In the interview situation the interviewers could be looking for attributes beyond the specific job-related skills. For example, there could be a focus on "the applicant–organisation fit", in the sense that selectors are looking at the personality characteristics of the candidates, their personal values and attitudes, and their flexibility and commitment to see if they can fit into the organisation's culture (Barclay, 1999; Dipboye, 1994). The applicant–organisation fit approach could be very relevant when conditions within organisations are in a state of flux, and significant change affecting jobs is on the horizon (Torrington, Hall, & Taylor, 2005). According to Chatman and Cha (2002), General Electric described its desirable candidates as:

> those who stimulate and relish change and are not frightened or paralysed by it, seeing change as an opportunity, not a threat, and have a passion for excellence, and hating bureaucracy and all the nonsense that comes with it . . . Cisco Systems developed culturally consistent selection criteria that targeted candidates who were frugal, enthusiastic about the future of the internet, smart and not concerned with status . . . Also, the company targeted "passive applicants"—people who were satisfied in their current jobs, and not job hunting, but who might be lured to Cisco; and it developed a fast easy-to-use website for them to learn about Cisco.

Despite the claims to success, the interview process has been subjected to some fundamental criticisms. Many of these criticisms are levelled at the interviewer. In panel interviews a proper role for each interviewer is sometimes not adequately specified. Poor interviewing skills of individual panel members compound this. Generally, there are too many occasions when interviewers spend time on irrelevant matters, missing the opportunity to explore a significant point in detail. Also, the public relations aspect of interviewing is ignored (Wicks, 1984). Other criticisms hinge on the following observations (Phillips & Dipboye, 1989; Pulakos, Schmitt, Whitney, & Smith, 1996):

(1) Interviewers make perceptual judgements that are often inaccurate.

(2) Interviewers are poor at reaching agreement when rating interviewees.

(3) Different interviewers see different things in the same interviewee, and thus arrive at different conclusions.

(4) Interviewers arrive at early impressions that quickly become entrenched in their perceptual judgement. Negative impressions arising from negative information received early in the interview can become more heavily weighted than the same information given later.

(5) Many decisions are arrived at by interviewers early in the interview and change very little after the first 5 minutes of the interview. So the absence of unfavourable characteristics early on in the interview could act to the advantage of the interviewee.

(6) Prior knowledge about an applicant has the effect of biasing the interviewer's evaluation.

(7) Interviewers tend to favour applicants who share their attitudes.

(8) The order in which applicants are interviewed influences evaluations.

(9) Negative information is given an unduly high weighting.

(10) An applicant's ability to do well in an interview is irrelevant in most jobs.

Structured versus unstructured interview. In recent years the superiority of the structured interview over the unstructured interview has been endorsed, but nevertheless it is said that the selection interview is frequently conducted in an unstructured way (Van der Zee, Bakker, & Bakker, 2002). The unstructured interview is said to have shortcomings, among them their casual nature, random questions, and that they are short in duration (Campion, Palmer, & Campion, 1997). With regard to the structured interview, there are advantages in standardising questions, recording information, and rating applicants. The benefits in requiring interviewers to ask only job-related questions are stressed as a means to reduce the incidence of irrelevant information, prejudice, and bias in selection decision making (Conway, Jako, & Goodman, 1995; Huffcut & Arthur, 1994; Posthuma, Moregeson, & Campion, 2002). According to Boyle (1997), structured interviews, conducted by trained interviewers using systematic assessment procedures to target key skills and attributes identified by job analysis, are now recognised as comparable to the best selection methods. But interviewers who favour a more discursive style of interviewing complain that the format for the structured interview is too constraining. Further, there have been accusations that highly structured interviews are, in reality, veiled verbal reasoning tests.

The structured job-related interview is akin to the *situational interview* proposed by Latham and Saari (1984). The approach to situational interviewing starts with a comprehensive analysis of the job. Key situations within a job are produced, with the support of job experts. Then benchmarks are devised for interviewers to use when scoring the responses of the interviewees. The interviewers should be well trained and experienced. The interview questions are based on, for example, a mini case study related to incidents and circumstances associated with the job in question (Robertson, Gratton, & Rout, 1990).

Psychometric tests

Psychometric tests used in personnel selection can be divided into two categories. These are personality tests (e.g., the 16 PF or OPQ) and cognitive tests (e.g., general intelligence, numerical ability), which were discussed in Chapter 3. As you will see from the commentary in Chapter 3, among the tests examined are tests of aptitude—i.e., those measuring general mental ability or general intelligence, and those measuring specific abilities or aptitudes—and attainment tests, which measure the skills an individual has already acquired. The usefulness of personality tests as predictors of performance in a job has been questioned (see below and Chapter 3), but there have been suggestions that profiling personality for the purpose of making judgements about performance at work has some value (Day & Silverman, 1989). By contrast, cognitive ability testing across different occupational groups seems to have greater success. (At this stage it would be useful to refer to the discussion of testing in Chapter 3, before reading the remainder of this section.)

With the growing significance of ethical problems in organisations—including an increase in theft and fraud, drug and alcohol problems, cases of bullying and violence, etc.—a psychometric test (pencil and paper test in the form of a standardised integrity questionnaire) to measure integrity is making its presence felt at the point of selection, in order to screen out high-risk applicants (Furnham, 2005b; Ones, Viswesvaran, & Schmidt, 1993). The reason for this development is that employers in the USA, and to some extent in the UK, are becoming more concerned about the integrity of their employees (see Panel 17.1 and the comment on polygraphy later in this chapter).

PANEL 17.1: Integrity at work

In the top eight qualities ranked by employers in the 1989 Michigan Employability Survey are listed integrity, trustworthiness, and conscientiousness (Baldry & Fletcher, 1997). Integrity or honesty should not be viewed as fixed in concrete in our personality. There are many situational variables (e.g., management ethos) that interact with our predispositions to determine the degree of honesty exhibited.

The term integrity as applied within the workplace covers many aspects of employee behaviour. There is behaviour that breaks the civil law (theft, fraud, and embezzlement); behaviour that breaks the organisation's rules (in matters such as absenteeism, malingering, and tardiness); and behaviour that contravenes the norms of behaviour that are established within a work unit (e.g., not pulling your weight).

When integrity tests were first introduced in pencil and paper format in the selection process they were generally regarded as direct alternatives to the polygraph (the lie detector). Questions are asked about specific behaviours in hypothetical situations; in addition, respondents are asked if they committed certain acts of deviance in the past. The assumption is, with regard to overt test items, that past behaviour is indicative of future behaviour. The covert test items assess specific personality traits of respondents.

On the basis of research carried out in the USA, the use of integrity tests is fraught with difficulties. It has been suggested that overt test items are too intrusive and as a result do not appeal to respondents. By contrast, the use of covert test items could create a situation where selection decisions are being made on the basis of personal characteristics that are irrelevant to the individual's level of integrity (Rosse, Miller, & Ringer, 1996). In the light of the research evidence it is apparent that psychometric measures applied to integrity testing should be used with extreme caution. The decision to reject a candidate because they pose a high risk of engaging in deviant or dishonest behaviour is a conclusion that should be arrived at on the basis of more than just their score on one integrity test. Of course, we have to recognise that there are other more traditional techniques with the potential to assess integrity, such as references, interviews, and simulation exercises (Baldry & Fletcher, 1997; Fletcher, 1995). The evidence of the predictive power of these tests is impressive according to some authorities (Schmidt & Hunter, 1998).

The use of psychometric tests in selection, and in employee development (see Chapter 18), is perfectly acceptable to many. However, what is disturbing to some is the practice of using such tests to determine which long-serving employees to discard. Dixon (1994) reported on a situation where this occurred. At the finance section of the London Borough of Southwark, constituting about 120 employees, a long and complex test was administered. This was believed to be a personality test and staff were assured that there were no correct answers to any question. After the results were analysed, 19 staff were told to stop working immediately and were escorted from the office. A further 10 staff were told they were considered unsuitable for employment.

Some psychologists admonish us to be cautious in our acceptance of personality tests as a selection device. According to Doyle (2003):

> I would say that personality measures should be used with great caution in selection. They can provide useful additional information, but it requires very careful interpretation of individual scores and sensitive feedback . . . The conclusion drawn from the results of personality inventories must always be regarded as tentative . . . The real value of personality inventories may be more in career guidance/management and personal development, than in selection . . . They can also be very useful in teambuilding.

Finally, in reflecting on the future of psychometric assessment, Fletcher (1997) makes the following observation. The use of psychometric tests in organisations is facing the greatest challenge it has come up against in many years—perhaps ever. The main challenge comes from the nature of the changes in organisations themselves—downsizing, delayering, and so on. He calls for ethical and fair practice in assessment. He goes on to say that the current balance of power is heavily slanted in favour of the selectors. Selection should become a joint venture between the selector and the candidate. Then we could expect candidates to be honest and more cooperative.

Work sample tests

These tests require the applicant to perform a task or set of tasks that are considered, following job analysis, to have direct relevance to the job in question. Thus the applicant is requested to demonstrate his or her ability by performing part of the job. The activities involved can be wide ranging (Robertson & Kandola, 1982). In the selection of a skilled factory worker the candidate would be asked to perform a variety of typical tasks on a specially built simulated line in a car plant. Another example would be where the applicant may be asked to type a letter, or operate a machine, or take decisions similar to those taken in the job in question. This is done through the use of in-tray exercises where the applicant is presented with a collection of letters, memos, etc., and is asked to deal with them. A more abstract version of the last approach would be to present applicants with a series of hypothetical situations and then ask them how they would respond. This is sometimes referred to as situational interviewing.

Other approaches are the testing of the applicant's knowledge of areas considered to be directly relevant to performance on the job, and group discussion or decision making. The latter is evident when two or more applicants come together to discuss a particular topic, and their performance in the discussion is evaluated. This approach is suitable for testing applicants for a job where an individual's performance in a group situation is crucial for job success.

When work sample tests are administered to experienced applicants, the psychomotor tests (e.g., typing) and the in-tray tests seem to command a superior position. Work sample tests can also be administered to applicants who are not trained in the relevant job. In fact the main purpose of these tests, which can overlap with tests of cognitive ability, is to assess whether or not an applicant is suitable for training. Trainability tests have been developed for many occupational groups with reasonable results (Robertson & Downs, 1989).

Assessment centres

Assessment centres make use of many different methods, including interviews, psychological tests, in-tray exercises, written tasks, and group discussions, and can be considered a systematic, effective, and reliable approach. They can last for a few days or a week, or alternatively they can be as short as a day. In assessment centres candidates are observed carrying out a variety of assignments, either as individuals or as part of a group (Woodruffe, 2000b). A feature of the assessment centre is that a competency or skill is assessed from at least two angles. For example, the ability to exercise leadership could be assessed by the use of a group exercise, arranged as a meeting, and by the use of a personality test. Similarly, the candidates' numerical strengths could be assessed using a test of numerical reasoning and by a business statistics exercise. Simulation exercises could also form part of an assessment centre. These consist of role playing and in-tray exercises. Another exercise involving competing groups could be a business game, which simulates the decision-making process in the context of making the best use of resources at the disposal of a company.

When assessment centres are used to evaluate people who already work in the organisation, as described later in this chapter in connection with performance appraisal, they are often called *development centres*. In the latter context the information derived from the assessment centre is used to facilitate decision making in connection with promotions and career development.

Assessment centres, first used in selection on a small scale, now appear to be an increasingly popular method of personnel selection. Applicants for a job are usually assessed by trained assessors who normally hold fairly responsible positions in the organisation. These assessors observe applicants' performance on the various exercises and arrive at a consensus of opinion about the suitability of each applicant.

There is no doubt that assessment centres are viewed favourably as a selection method. The belief is that a combination of selection methods found in an assessment centre can significantly improve the probability of selecting appropriate applicants, and in particular candidates for managerial positions (Jansen & Stoop, 2001; Thornton, 1992). Proponents of assessment centres would argue that the data obtained from applicants are comprehensive and comparable, and the methods used give applicants the opportunity to demonstrate capabilities unlikely to find expression in an interview alone. In addition, the total experience of the assessment centre is said to be invaluable for the applicant, while for the assessor it is an opportunity to develop skills in the objective assessment of people and in presenting personnel data in a professional way.

Among the issues addressed by critics of assessment centres are that there is a need for substantial investment in resources to create and operate these centres, including the need to select and train suitable people as assessors. Also, the lack of commitment from top management (if that proves to be the case) may have a dampening effect on both assessors and applicants; and putting the spotlight on behaviour that can be observed and measured has its shortcomings when less visible and less easily assessed skills are ignored.

The increase in the use of assessment centres over the years has been impressive and they are increasingly applied to groups other than managers in both selection and career development.

As a postscript, it is worth reflecting for a moment on the evolution of assessment centres as identified by Goodge (1997), who refers to three generations of assessment centres. He states that for external recruitment the most cost-effective option is the first generation of the assessment centre, which was used solely for assessment purposes, initially in military selection at the time of the First World War.

The second generation of the assessment centre began to emphasise development, and innovations took place in the early 1990s. Off-the-shelf exercises and psychological tests were replaced with real-life business problems. Contemporary business issues, often presented live by senior managers, took the place of stale in-tray exercises, group discussions, and personality questionnaires. This aspect captures the original character of assessment centres as practical auditions for management. The centre empowers individuals by allowing participants to collect information and think through the assessments. Exercises become open and honest discussions about performance. The assessors become coaches and advisers, spending much more of their time helping individuals draw conclusions and thinking through the implications. After the completion of the exercises it is those being assessed and not the assessors who write the reports, with assistance from the assessors. Empowering participants improves their motivation and acceptance of the process, without the assessment losing its rigour.

The third-generation assessment centres form part of a larger, performance-enhancing process. Providing a detailed view of the person is the foundation of a good personal development plan. Half the time devoted to the centre's activities is spent on career and development plans, featuring joint decision making between the superior and subordinate. Personal mentors could also be involved in this process to facilitate overall personal development. Development of competencies is also an issue.

Finally, it is acknowledged that assessment centres are good at predicting the potential of people (Cook, 1998). Given that the results of assessment centres are available to those who determine the progression of employees within an organisation, it is possible that those who obtain good results are subsequently given stiff targets and more challenging tasks, which builds confidence and key skills, eventually leading to promotions!

Biographical information

This method is used to relate the characteristics of job applicants to the characteristics of successful job holders, and is most likely to be used by organisations faced with a large number of vacancies for which they receive a very large number of applications.

Applicants for a job within an organisation are likely to complete an application form and other documents in which they are expected to provide certain biographical information about matters such as age, previous employment, education, training, and personal history. When such information is used in a systematic way, this method of personnel selection is often referred to as the biodata approach. Its fundamental characteristic is the identification (with an appropriately large sample of candidates) of correlations between items of biographical information and outcome measures on the job, such as performance or absenteeism. Items of biographical information shown to have a significant relationship with work outcome factors (e.g., performance) are accommodated in a questionnaire, which may be administered to applicants.

The more important questionnaire items used in predicting success in the job are given the higher points weighting. For example, for the job of senior economist in a bank, graduate status and a specified number of years' experience doing similar work could command a higher points allocation than a period of employment as a professional footballer. The weighted items are added together to produce a total score, which is then used to accept or reject applicants. Prior to the preparation of the questionnaire it is advisable to use more than one sample in compiling the data and to keep the relationship between the biodata items and work outcomes under statistical review over time.

Studies have demonstrated the usefulness of biodata in selection (Asher, 1972; Brown & Campion, 1994). However, it is said that a number of problems arising from the use of biodata come about as a result of not being sufficiently critical in considering why there is a relationship between an item of biographical information (e.g., membership of clubs) and a particular beneficial outcome at work (e.g., capability as a team player). To confront problems of this nature it is suggested that one should engage in theoretical rationalisation of the nature of the relationship, and only retain biodata items that can be seen to be rationally connected to the appropriate work outcomes (Owens & Schoenfeldt, 1979). Though the rational approach has appeal, it appears that a combination of approaches (e.g., rational, empirical) might produce the best set of results (Stokes & Reddy, 1992). A drawback of the biodata approach is the time involved in its use and the size of the sample needed (Torrington et al., 2005).

Other methods

There are a number of other methods used in personnel selection, including references, peer assessment, self-assessment, telephone screening, graphology, polygraphy and the internet.

References. Along with interviews, references are widely used as a selection method. The results of a survey of the techniques used for managerial selection revealed that although large organisations are increasingly using assessment centre type exercises and biodata, most organisations still select managers on the basis of interviews and references (Robertson & Makin, 1986; Shackleton & Newell, 1994). Normally, employing organisations take up references only when a job offer is imminent, but there are occasions when references are used as a screening device prior to the preparation of the final shortlist of candidates. Generally, the available research evidence does not support the popularity of references as a means of obtaining a third party's opinion of an applicant's credentials and achievements. It is said that bias is almost built into this method because the candidate is likely to nominate a referee who is capable of conveying favourable information and impressions, and a positive recommendation. Practical suggestions to optimise the usefulness of references as a selection method are available (Dobson, 1989).

Nowadays employers have to be aware that employees may challenge and possibly resort to litigation if they were to receive an unsatisfactory reference, even if it amounted to an honest assessment. (For further comment on the legal implications of providing references see Panel 17.2.) Some commentators advocate taking references over the telephone, but this gives employers less time to marshal their thoughts and use words carefully, unless of course they had advance notice and adequate time to consider the views to be expressed. Another problem is that some candidates are opposed to the idea of their present employer being approached to provide a reference when they have not yet been offered the job. But there are others who would welcome their employer knowing that they have applied for another job and that they are being seriously considered for it, although not yet offered it, particularly if the job in question is of higher status than their current job. Doyle (2003) makes an interesting point with regard to the substance of references. She asks is it realistic to assume that insight into the past behaviour of a candidate, found in a reference, is useful in predicting future behaviour, particularly if the job applied for and its setting are so different from the present or previous job?

Peer assessment. When colleagues or peers are favourably placed to make an assessment of a candidate, peer assessment can be productive. It is probably more suited to particular work environments, such as a college or university, than to others, and for certain purposes, such as career counselling, rather than selection (Roadman, 1964). Support for peer assessment has come from a study of nonunionised, hourly paid employees working in a food-processing plant. This group were on relatively short tenure, had good experiences with previous peer assessment exercises, and did not hold the view that peer assessment contains a friendship bias (McEvoy & Buller, 1987).

Self-assessment. This could start with giving candidates a realistic view of the job, and this information could be sent to prospective candidates at the time an application form is sent out. The information provides candidates with a realistic job preview, and in doing so they are better placed to evaluate their suitability for the job on offer. This method is rarely used in selection. It is said to suffer from leniency errors (Fox & Dinur, 1988) among other shortcomings.

Telephone screening. This method, which could be part of a wider selection process, could be used instead of an application form and has the advantage of a prompt response. It is important that this method is operationalised in such a way that standardised information is asked of each candidate. What is not straightforward is deciding on the spot the person's suitability in the light of the set standards.

B&Q, the UK DIY retailer, uses telephone screening (Overell, 2002b). To begin with, a human being at a call centre will note personal details and preferred hours that the applicant hopes to

---

PANEL 17.2: Giving references can be a hazardous business

Comments in a reference that prove to be ill-judged or inaccurate can result in legal action. An employer should not defame an employee who is hoping to leave the organisation. There are exclusions in the UK Data Protection Act that may prevent employees seeing what they believe are erroneous references; however, these exclusions will not prevent the references being disclosed in general litigation.

References should avoid making any comment that could be discriminatory. Recent UK case law has extended both the Race Relations Act and the Sex Discrimination Act to cover the issue of references. Statements such as, "A left our employment and subsequently brought a claim against us for sex and racial discrimination" will create liability for the employer because such statements could be seen as victimising the employee for taking action.

Prospective employers should be cautious about acting on information received from former employers. A prospective employer who decides not to appoint someone, knowing that she/he has claimed against a previous employer, is also guilty of discrimination. This situation is similar to where an employee has a disability and this is mentioned in a reference, or where there is mention of a poor attendance record without adequate explanation.

An employer should not forget obligations to other employers. If an employer writes a misleading reference where the qualities or skills of the employee are overstated, and the new employer suffers loss, the provider of the reference may be liable to the new employer. For example, an employee, suspected of dishonesty but whose guilt is not proven, enters into an arrangement with the employer to leave the company on grounds of redundancy and receives a good reference containing a statement indicating that he or she was a trustworthy employee. The employee obtains a job with a new employer and subsequently is caught stealing in the new job. Then the new employer reviews the reference and seeks the assistance of a lawyer.

Generally, employers are under no obligation to provide a reference, and would be better off not providing one if the reference cannot be balanced and fair. Increasingly, employers are adopting strict policies on giving references. Some issue references with a minimum amount of information, sometimes with a statement that further information may be given over the telephone. At least in the latter case it is more difficult to prove what is said. Perhaps in the future references may only be provided where a good employee has decided to leave for reasons unconnected with the employer's behaviour or business.

(Bradley, 2004)

---

work, but the interview is conducted by machine. The aim of the automated system is to assess an applicant's values, outlook, conscientiousness, aspirations, integrity, and cleanliness. By pressing numbers on the phone, candidates respond to questions designed to assess their personalities in order to establish whether they fit the culture the company wants to create in its stores. After conducting the interview, the system generates a score and creates a letter that informs candidates whether they are suitable for work at B&Q. Those who make the grade are put on to a database and managers at one of the numerous stores can choose from the shortlist. Names, dates of birth, and other indicators of ethnicity and gender are removed to try to eliminate discrimination. It is only at this stage that previous skills and experience are scrutinised. The final selection is carried out by traditional face-to-face interview.

Graphology.   An alternative label for this method is handwriting analysis, and it is based on the assumption that applicants reveal their personality characteristics through their handwriting. A

description of this method appears in Chapter 2. Handwriting analysis is a frequently used selection method in France.

In a study comparing the methods used to select managers in 73 British and 52 French organisations, more than 77% of French firms used handwriting analysis to select managers, as opposed to 2.6% of British firms (Shackleton & Newell, 1991). Among the French firms it is interesting to note that the greater use of this method is found outside the larger organisations. The question is asked whether the larger organisations are perhaps better informed about the lack of scientific respectability of this method (see Panel 17.3). The interested reader should refer to Salgado, Viswesvaran, and Ones (2001) for a commentary on the evidence relating to graphology.

Polygraphy.   The lie detector test or polygraph might be considered by some to be particularly appropriate for selecting people for jobs involving the handling of cash. The polygraph is used to measure emotional stress shown by variations in blood pressure, pulse rate, perspiration, palm

---

Graphology was used by a UK investment bank, which required job applicants to submit handwriting samples for analysis. The handwriting test came towards the end of a long selection process, and although the results of the test were taken seriously, an applicant would not be rejected on the outcome of this test alone. Similarly, Rhône-Poulenc, the French chemicals company, used handwriting analysis to sift application forms at one time. Now it only uses it where there is doubt about a candidate's suitability, and even then the candidate would be called for a second interview. A decision is never made on the sole basis of a graphologist's comments. The handwriting analysis is one of a number of techniques designed to create an overall picture of a candidate (McGookin, 1993).

A report published by the British Psychological Society, *Graphology in Personnel Assessment* (1993), concludes that graphology is not a viable means of assessing a person's character or abilities. There is no scientific evidence to support the claims of graphologists, and there is no relationship at all between what graphology predicts and subsequent performance in the workplace. This is a view endorsed by research evidence provided by Tapsell and Cox (1997). They maintain that there is no evidence to support the use of graphology in personnel assessment.

There is a new generation of lie detectors, which are said to pick out lies by measuring stress levels in the voice. This equipment is called the "voice risk analyser" and it was developed in Israel for use by secret service agents. It differs from traditional lie detectors that measure sweat. The machine assesses a caller's response to straightforward questions, such as their name and address, which it uses to analyse the person's normal voice pattern. It then detects whether this pattern alters when the person is asked a more direct question on a subject such as whether an insurance claim is genuine. The makers say the machine is able to screen out those who are nervous or stressed from those that are lying. Insurance claims by those judged to be lying are then subjected to more rigorous investigations. Insurance companies have found that suspect claims have been dropped as soon as the company expressed concern. Several UK insurance companies are using lie detectors and in 2004 recorded a 20% fall in fraudulent claims. The voice risk analyser machine is being used by at least five insurance companies, including Axa, Halifax, and Highway Insurance. Other companies, including banks assessing loan applications, recruitment companies, and even dating agencies, are said to be planning to use the new equipment.

It is reported that a number of government departments in the UK are either assessing the effectiveness of the voice analysis equipment used in the private sector or are studying plans to introduce the new technology to help government employees in the identification of members of the public who are not telling the truth over the telephone in areas such as tax, social security benefits, and immigration. Several government departments are in negotiations with Capita, the IT firm that has purchased the rights to distribute the detectors within the public sector.

It should be pointed out that the introduction of the new technology, which is prohibited in several countries, is also likely to be opposed by campaigners concerned with privacy. In an investigation by the US Air Force research laboratory it was concluded that the voice-based lie detectors "do recognize stress through voice analysis; however, although these systems state they detect deception, it was not proven."

(Winnett, 2005)

---

sweating, and respiration as applicants answer questions. In recent years brain activity has also been measured, and the bodily and brain activity can be displayed via ink writing pens on to charts or via a computer VDU (British Psychological Society, 2004b). More recently, as described in Panel 17.4, the voice is considered. The reasoning behind the polygraph is that telling a lie is stressful, and the stress will be reflected in physiological reactions. But it should be kept firmly in mind that the polygraph measures emotional stress and is not a measure of lying. Many causes of emotional stress not related to lying may cause a person to fail a lie detector test. Also, many people can lie without being detected by a polygraph (Hall & Goodale, 1986).

In a penetrating critique of the typical lie detection technique, Lykken (1974) concluded that empirical reports of high success rates are open to serious question, and a theoretical analysis of the customary procedures indicates that the expected probability of valid judgement is very low. There is no doubt that this method has severe limitations as a selection device. At one time the polygraph was widely used in an employment context in the USA, but in 1988 the US Employee Polygraph Protection Act was passed. This legislation prevented the use of the polygraph for pre-employment screening except by some government agencies and certain strategic industries, such as nuclear power. In the UK a working party consisting of prominent psychologists was set up by the British Psychological Society and reported that the use of the polygraph in employment and security screening is not justified by the available research evidence, and that the use of the polygraph in attempts to detect deception raises issues concerning human rights and professional codes of practice (British Psychological Society, 2004b). For further comment on the evidence relating to polygraphy, refer to Salgado et al. (2001), and for comment on proposals for its use outside selection see Panel 17.4.

Internet. The internet has a lot of potential as a recruitment and selection device, and has grown in importance in recent years. It could consist of the employer's own website, and jobs could be advertised alongside the organisation's products and services. Alternatively, the job could be advertised by an employment agency on the internet, and when the responses are processed the agency sends off a shortlist of suitable CVs to the employer. Although it is cost-effective, a shortcoming is the enormous amount of applications that could be generated.

A number of issues have been raised (Torrington et al., 2005). Sometimes a candidate is asked to apply online by completing an application form or taking a psychometric test, but there is no guarantee that the candidate has in fact completed the test, or that it has been completed within a standard, pre-determined time limit. Some candidates might be harbouring fears about confidentiality and security when putting their personal details online. Sometimes there are concerns about the tactics of agencies (e.g., copying CVs from competitors' sites) in building up a stock of good CVs in order to impress client organisations.

Fairness

Ideally, any selection method must be judged by the standard of fairness, which is the tendency to treat all applicants alike and to provide them with an equal opportunity to gain employment. In reality many organisations, whether intentionally or not, have a history of systematically eliminating a portion of applicants from the selection process on the basis of such personal characteristics as race, colour, sex, disability, and even body weight. The bias against overweight job applicants has been empirically endorsed by Pignitore, Dugoni, Tindale, and Spring (1994). Body shape in the form of obesity could affect people's self-concept and this might affect the way they present themselves in forums such as the selection interview. In the case of people with a severe sensory disability (poor eyesight), Reid (1997) concluded that there was an inadequate number of tests for assessing the intellectual functioning of visually impaired adults. It is possible that the lack of fairness in selection might be due to the weaknesses of the methods used, thereby providing selectors with the opportunity to introduce their prejudices and biases. As a result, some people may be treated unfairly.

However, there is reason to believe that personnel methods and practices may often operate in a way that is systematically unfair to particular groups, such as women or ethnic minorities. For example, there is a view that some racial and ethnic minorities do not perform as well as other applicants in many tests of intelligence and aptitude, and therefore are not selected at the same rate. The difference in selection rate is usually referred to as "adverse impact" (Kellett, Fletcher, Callen, & Geary, 1994; Robertson & Cooper, 1983), but equally it should be recognised that a good test is not unfair or biased just because members of different subgroups in society obtain different scores. There is further comment (see Panel 17.5) on adverse impact, which is a problem that arises more frequently in connection with the use of cognitive ability testing (Robertson & Smith, 2001).

Considerations such as the above have given rise to legislation and other practices to offer protection to certain types of applicants. Even though legislation is on the statute book—e.g., the UK Race Relations Act 1976—unfair discrimination still exists. Brown and Gay (1985) found that a disproportionate number of black applicants in

PANEL 17.5: Adverse impact—the case of the Paddington guards

Eight guards at London's Paddington Station, with the support of the Commission for Racial Equality (CRE), took British Rail to court over alleged racial discrimination after they failed the train driver assessment process. The assessment process included published psychometric aptitude tests, a personality questionnaire, an interview, and tests of vigilance and attention taken from a European railway administration test.

Following a review of the test performances of white and ethnic minority applicants, it became clear that the aptitude tests, particularly the test of verbal comprehension, were a source of "adverse impact". The CRE had already identified a similar problem with the published aptitude tests, which were used as part of an assessment process by London Underground for management appointments. Like London Underground, British Rail reached an out of court settlement before the tribunal, as part of which the British Rail Board agreed to review the assessment process and implement an improved one (Kellett et al., 1994). One course of action was to run workshops on test taking, where the guards from ethnic minorities were not used to a test-taking culture. They were given instruction on helpful hints on taking tests, and they were given material on which to practise.

(Torrington et al., 2002)

the UK were not invited to attend various job interviews, even though they had similar qualifications to white applicants. Fletcher (1994) considers the question of equal opportunities and fair testing to be an issue of growing importance, but he also considers as essential the acknowledgement of an ethical framework for assessment practice. Over a decade ago Kellett et al. (1994) rightly called for closer collaborative relationships between interested parties, including employers, test publishers, professional bodies such as the British Psychological Society and the Institute of Personnel and Development, statutory bodies such as the Commission for Racial Equality and the Equal Opportunities Commission, and the academic world, if standards of professional test practice are to be developed and modified.

Validity

The critical phase of the selection process arises when a decision is made to hire or reject a candidate. In arriving at the decision, various strands of evidence relating to the present or past performance of candidates—e.g., references, psychometric test scores, interview performance—are considered. This evidence, which is used to decide on the suitability of candidates for the job in question, is referred to as a predictor. Prediction here means predicting future job-related behaviour (such as the quantity and quality of the employee's contribution) on the basis of current or past performance with the help of selection methods.

Criterion-related validity

Before we can test the validity of selection methods—i.e., whether high or low scores on the selection methods are associated with good or bad performance in the job—information has to be collected on the job-related performance of the person who was selected for the job. This type of performance, which can be gauged by measures such as output data, supervisor's ratings, etc., is referred to as the criterion. Output data are referred to as objective criteria, whereas supervisors' ratings are referred to as subjective criteria. Cook (1994) mentions that there are relatively few types of work in which performance can be measured adequately by objective criteria alone. Therefore, in at least 60% of cases and possibly more than 75%, one has to settle for more subjective criteria, and the problem here is that it is subject to a range of biases. A similar view is expressed by Torrington et al. (2005) when the authors state that "current performance is often assessed in an intuitive, subjective way, and while this may sometimes be useful it is no substitute for objective assessment".

Criterion-related validity refers to the strength of the relationship between the predictor and the criterion, usually referred to as a validity coefficient. A perfect correlation between the two variables is represented by 1.0, whereas zero denotes no correlation. When criterion-related validity is high, applicants who have high predictor scores also have high criterion scores, and applicants who have low predictor scores also have low criterion scores. Where the predictor–criterion relationship is perfect (a validity coefficient of 1.0), we should be able to predict a criterion score from a predictor score. In reality this idealised state is not achievable. It is very unusual to obtain validity coefficients much in excess of +0.5 (Robertson & Smith, 1989), but it should be noted that validity coefficients significantly less than +1.0 still offer a foundation for improved personnel selection.

It is now apparent that criterion-related validity requires at least two measures for each applicant: a selection test score and a job performance score. There are two different ways to obtain these scores: predictive validity analysis and concurrent validity analysis.

Predictive validity analysis. Predictive validity is measured by relating test scores to measures of future performance, such as production rate, appraisal scores, or whatever criteria are deemed important to the organisation. The selection method—e.g., a psychometric test—is administered to job applicants, but decisions to recruit are made without reference to the test scores. In other words, the organisation will rely on whatever selection methods are currently in use while the criterion-related validity of the new selection method is being studied. After a number of months the job performance of those employed is measured and is correlated with the test scores to establish validity. If valid, the selection method will be used as an assessment device. As this type of validation process permits the selection of some candidates who will fail to perform adequately, it is suitable only for organisations that select numerous applicants, and that are seeking strong evidence that their selection methods are valid.

An advantage of the predictive validity analysis approach is that data are examined under conditions that are very similar to those under which the selection test will actually be used. For instance, the selection test scores are obtained from actual job applicants who have indicated a real interest in gaining employment. The scores of the successful candidates are then examined at a later time to determine how well they predict performances on the job.

However, predictive validity analysis has two major drawbacks. First, there cannot be many employers who are prepared to administer a selection test to job applicants and then ignore the applicants' scores when making selection decisions. Secondly, the predictive validity analysis approach takes time. The successful applicants must be given enough time to learn their jobs and demonstrate their abilities. Because of these drawbacks, many employers and psychologists rely on the concurrent validity analysis approach.

Concurrent validity analysis. The selection method (e.g., psychometric test) is administered to a group of current employees, rather than job applicants, and their test scores are correlated simultaneously with data on the measurement of job performance obtained from their personnel files or from their supervisors. In other words, the two exercises are carried out concurrently. This is a much more practical procedure, but it does not necessarily yield a good estimate of predictive validity.

With concurrent validity analysis there is no lengthy time interval between taking the test and gauging subsequent job performance because job holders complete the selection test that the organisation is experimenting with at the same time they have measures of their job performance taken or extracted from their personnel files. Another reason why concurrent validity is acceptable to employers is that they do not have to ignore anybody's test score.

A drawback of the concurrent validity analysis approach is that people who score on the selection test that is being tried out, and whose job performance is concurrently evaluated, may not be very representative of the population from which actual job applicants will emerge (Saal & Knight, 1995).

An important consideration with respect to validity studies, regardless of whether the approach is predictive or concurrent analysis, is that the initial validity study dealing with a fair number of predictors should always be followed by a cross-validation study on a second sample of people in order to cross-check the results obtained (Arnold, 2005).

With respect to selection, criterion-related validity is the most important type of validity, but face, content, and construct validity are also significant.

Face validity

A selection method or test that portrays face validity gives the appearance of measuring whatever is intended to be measured. For example, a typing test looks as if it measures typing skills.

Content validity

Like face validity, content validity is usually a judgemental rather than a statistical procedure. A predictor displays content validity when it incorporates a representative sample of the behaviour in the job being measured. For example, a content validity test of a car mechanic's ability would be expected to cover the key activities undertaken by a competent mechanic. A feature of this approach is that the skills can be observed and understood without appealing to abstract and unobservable traits or constructs.

Construct validity

This type of validity is appropriate when it is the intention to assess the abstract traits or psychological constructs that are felt to underlie more concrete, observable forms of behaviour. For example, intelligence, job satisfaction, and motivation are examples of constructs that help explain a wide variety of job-related behaviours. Construct validity involves drawing hypotheses about the likely connection between the concept of interest (e.g., intelligence) and other events. For instance, in order to demonstrate the construct validity of a measure of intelligence, one might hypothesise that high scorers on this variable would do better than low scorers in a particular type of task. The next step would be to find evidence to support or reject the hypothesis. An important factor in understanding what a psychological test measures is the exploration of the construct validity of that test.

Reliability

An important feature of any measuring instrument, be it a predictor or criterion, is reliability—i.e., the consistency with which it produces results (Robertson, 1994). An example of an unreliable measure is when a candidate produces different scores when he or she takes a test on two different occasions. For example, a person takes an ability test and gets a low score on one occasion, but some time later he or she gets a high score on the same test. This might be due to the existence of special circumstances (e.g., the person was unwell or misread the instructions on the first occasion). However, if the performance of a number of people varies significantly from one testing occasion to another, then there is a question mark over the reliability of the test.

In the final analysis, a measuring instrument used in personnel selection—i.e., a predictor or criterion—must be both valid and reliable. But this may not always be the case. According to Brotherton (1980) the issues and technicalities involved in validation are often not understood, except where occupational psychologists are associated with the shaping, review, and evaluation of selection procedures.

Utility

The use of personnel selection methods can be expensive, and having predictors with good predictive validity is no guarantee that selection tests will be cost-effective in use. When more jobs are available than applicants to fill them, the use of any selection test is likely to be of little benefit. In such circumstances the "selection ratio" is greater than 1.0. Nevertheless, it would be wise to use selection methods in conditions where a selection ratio is in excess of 1.0, and if necessary leave jobs unfilled rather than offer employment to unsuitable candidates. When the selection ratio is less than 1.0 (i.e., there are more applicants than jobs) obvious advantages can be gained from the use of selection methods.

Finally, the cost of personnel selection should be offset against the benefits, and it should be borne in mind that bad selection can have a damaging effect on the organisation over a long period as sub-standard job holders who were poorly selected continue to serve the organisation.

PERFORMANCE MANAGEMENT / APPRAISAL

It is a common event in many spheres of work for the performance of subordinates to be evaluated by superiors and others as a means of developing human resources, with productivity firmly in mind. The normal practice is for the results of the appraisal process to be shared with the subordinate in a positive way so that the individual concerned is given the support to put right deficiencies or maintain good practice. Nowadays performance appraisal is often referred to as performance management when placed in an HRM context.

In performance management there is an emphasis on mutual objective setting and ongoing performance support and review in the context of a sympathetic organisational culture, but according to Torrington et al. (2005) the term "performance management" remains beyond precise definition. Performance management needs to be line manager-driven rather than HR-driven, and for this to happen appropriate action has to be taken. Putting line managers side by side with HR managers in a working party to develop the system is important because the influence of the line manager is crucial. According to Doyle (2003), performance management is best thought of as a philosophy (like that of a learning organisation), rather than a particular set of policies and practices. Williams (1998) feels performance management is all about employees sharing what the organisation's goals are, and helping people to understand their contribution to those goals. In this way the performance of people and organisations is managed. The building blocks of performance management are the creation of a mission statement and business plan, which is clearly communicated throughout the organisation, with ample opportunities for everyone to contribute to its formation. Then one has to clarify how the individual's performance is going to fit

into the whole, subsequently defining, measuring, and rewarding individual performance (Doyle, 2003).

Goals of performance appraisal

Apart from the justification for using performance appraisal, mentioned earlier, there are other reasons why performance of employees is evaluated. These could be grouped into two broad categories. One amounts to an appraisal with a judgemental bias and the other has a developmental bias (Fletcher, 2000; Harris, Smith, & Champagne, 1995).

Judgemental

The focus is on past performance, and the available data are used as a basis for the following purposes:

- To assist with decisions about levels of compensation or reward. This would apply, in particular, to circumstances where a system of performance-related pay is in use.
- To assist superiors to evaluate the suitability of the subordinate for training and development. This could include the identification of employees with high potential, and the spotting of obstacles or barriers to performance. Generally, the emphasis here is on identifying skills and competencies that are currently inadequate but for which remedial programmes exist.
- To assist managers to make informed decisions about matters such as promotions, demotions, transfers, and dismissals.
- To validate the effectiveness of past employee selection decisions, and the adequacy of previous training.

Developmental

The focus is on the future, and the available data are used for the following purposes:

- To create a dialogue between the superior and subordinate on performance-related matters in order to clarify misunderstandings, provide relevant information, and establish agreement on expectations on both sides.

- To provide a supportive setting in which superiors meet with subordinates and provide them with feedback on their strengths and weaknesses.
- To be proactive in the identification of training and development opportunities, and to remove barriers that are likely to have an adverse effect on performance.

Doyle (2003) believes:

if a development appraisal is done well and it is linked to personal development plans that are aligned to business objectives, the interview based on it can offer a great deal . . . Development reviews can raise difficult issues in a constructive context, can clear the air of misunderstandings, resentments and frustrations, can raise the performance of weaker staff and encourage the best, improve superior–staff relationships, motivate the demoralized, and help everyone to work towards common goals . . . Development reviews can give people the chance to discuss what they really want to do in the future to further their goals/aspirations.

It is considered good practice not to combine the judgemental and development aspects of appraisal. Should they be combined in one session, people may not be frank and truthful about their strengths and weaknesses if they felt this could be detrimental to their career advancement or level of pay. Equally an appraiser cannot easily play a counselling role, normally associated with a developmental appraisal, when adopting a critical stance while operating in an evaluative or judgemental mode.

Criteria for performance appraisal

The importance of specifying the criterion or criteria to be used in performance evaluation must not be understated. Criteria used could embrace task outcomes, behaviours, and traits.

Task outcomes

This could be the actual quantity of goods produced or, for instance, the number of invoices processed by a sales clerk over a certain time period.

Behaviours

Performance, though complex and multifaceted at times, can be expressed as the actual behaviours expected of an employee at work. A starting point is job analysis, which amounts to a precise statement of the activities that constitute a job. An observer collects all available information on a particular job and normally interviews the current job holder and the immediate supervisor. From this exercise a job description will be prepared, which consists of a list of descriptive statements defining the responsibilities of the job holder.

Sometimes it is not possible to identify task outcomes that can be directly related to the efforts of the individual. For example, it may be difficult to identify individual performance when the person is a member of a group with highly interdependent activities. In such circumstances it is possible to evaluate group performance. Also, employees who act as advisers or internal consultants may fall into the category of individuals whose specific task outcome it is difficult to identify. To overcome these difficulties, the organisation may specify behaviours that would form the basis for evaluation. These behaviours could include the speed with which tasks are accomplished, and the style of behaviour used (e.g., management style) during interactions with other people.

Traits

This is beyond doubt the poorest set of criteria, but one still finds heavy reliance placed on it in organisations. Traits refer to projections of the personality, discussed in Chapter 2, and labels such as "displays confidence", "is cooperative and friendly", "is bright", and "has the right attitude", are not necessarily related in a positive sense to performance on the job. However, management in organisations seems to have an attachment to traits as criteria for assessing an employee's performance.

Performance appraisal techniques

When the emphasis shifts from the criteria (the things we evaluate) to techniques (how the appraisal is done) we enter the domain of methods used to evaluate performance. The major performance appraisal techniques used in the evaluation of individual performance, or the evaluation of individual performance when compared with other people's performance, are as follows:

(1)   Individual evaluation
   • graphic rating scales;
   • essays;
   • behaviourally anchored rating scales; and
   • behavioural observation scales.

(2)   Comparative evaluation
   • ranking;
   • paired comparison; and
   • forced distribution.

(3)   Multi-rater comparative evaluation
   • objective judgement quotient (OJQ) and 360-degree feedback; and
   • assessment centres.

Individual evaluation

Graphic rating scales.   This is a basic method of rating the performance of the individual. Where a global measure is used, the rater places a tick on the point of the scale that appears to be a good reflection of the level of performance of the employee. This is illustrated in Table 17.1. Where multiple measures of performance are used, the rater marks the point on each scale that is indicative of the performance of the employee (see Table 17.2).

TABLE 17.1

Global measure of performance on a graphic rating scale

Name of employee	Poor	Below average	Rating Average	Above average	Excellent
John Smith					

TABLE 17.2

Multiple measures of performance on a graphic rating scale

Name of employee			Rating		
John Smith	Poor	Below average	Average	Above average	Excellent
(1) Quantity					
(2) Quality					
(3) Expertise					
(4) Initiative					
(5) Cooperative					
(6) Commitment					

Graphic rating scales are easy to develop and administer, and lend themselves to quantitative analysis and comparison between employees, although they do not provide the richness of data produced by some of the other techniques. They have, however, been in existence for a long time and are popular in some quarters.

Essays.   The rater writes a narrative describing an employee's strengths, weaknesses, potential, performance to date, and suggestions for improvement. This record could be based on the memory of the rater or drawn from his or her diary entries, and could provide much more insightful information on an employee's performance than can be derived from a graphic rating scale. However, one has to bear in mind that a rater's memory may not be the most reliable, and diary entries may fall short of what could be considered a good record. In such circumstances the essay method of rating is less than satisfactory.

Other matters to consider in connection with essays are that comparisons between employees whose performance is evaluated are not possible because of an absence of comparable points in narratives on various individuals. Also present is the danger of describing personality traits, rather than describing incidents of good or poor performance, particularly when an inadequately trained evaluator uses the method.

Finally, essays are not as easy to develop or use as approaches relying on numerical analysis, with or without computer application.

Behaviourally anchored rating scales.   These scales integrate graphic rating scales with descriptions of workers' behaviour that characterise or "anchor" various points on the scales. A sample group of raters could be asked independently to suggest examples of behaviour for each point on the scale in order to collect a variety of behavioural examples. Under this method, the framework used to evaluate performance consists of a number of scales, with each scale representing an important aspect of job behaviour (Smith & Kendall, 1963).

An example of rating factors in behaviourally anchored rating scales appears in Figure 17.1. The rater places the individual on an anchor along the continuum of each scale. The behaviourally anchored rating scales are developed by people, called experts, who are familiar with the jobs under review. They verify that the statements are clearly written and accurately describe actual behaviour of job occupants (i.e., critical incidents). Then the scales are developed whereby the statements of job behaviour are positioned on the scale and given a numerical value.

Although it is claimed to be a reliable measure, it has potential disadvantages. These relate to the expense of developing and maintaining the system, because scales may need updating as jobs change with the progressive application of new technology. Also, the raters experience difficulties when the anchors do not coincide with the actual behaviours observed.

Behavioural observation scales.   Yet another attempt to develop performance rating scales linked to actual behaviour was made by Latham and Wexley (1981). They used behavioural observation scales that were developed from a critical incident technique, similar to that used to compile the behaviourally anchored rating scales, in which job occupants and supervisors generate performance behaviours inherent in the job. The evaluator is required to indicate the *frequency* with which an employee displays a specific behaviour. This differs from behaviourally anchored rating scales where the evaluator is asked to define superior versus inferior performance, and the employee is assessed on having displayed a particular behaviour during a specific rating period.

Behavioural observation scales are favourably viewed as an instrument that is easy to use, and is versatile in the range of applications—e.g., setting goals, provision of feedback, and identifying training needs (Latham, Skarlicki, & Siegel, 1993).

Comparative evaluation

When one person's performance is evaluated against another or others' performance, we enter the realm of multi-person comparisons. Comparative evaluation is a relative rather than an absolute appraisal device.

FIGURE 17.1

1. Job capability

☐ Not observed	☐ Has gaps in fundamental knowledge and skills of job.	☐ Has satisfactory knowledge and skill for the routine phases of job.	☐ Has excellent knowledge and is well skilled on all phases of job.	☐ Has exceptional understanding and skill on all phases of job.	☐ Has far-reaching grasp of entire broad job area. Authority in the field.

2. Planning ability

☐ Not observed	☐ Relies on others to bring problems to attention. Often fails to see ahead.	☐ Plans ahead just enough to get by in present job.	☐ Is a careful effective planner. Anticipates and takes action to solve problems.	☐ Capable of planning beyond requirements of the present job. Sees the big picture.	☐ Capable of top-level planning. A high-calibre thinker and planner.

3. Executive management

☐ Not observed	☐ Is a poor organiser. Does not really make effective use of material or personnel.	☐ Maintains ordinary efficiency of operation. Control could be improved.	☐ Gives economy of operation careful attention. Makes wise use of personnel and materials.	☐ Maintains effective economy. Carefully weighs cost against expected results.	☐ Highly skilled in balancing cost against results to obtain optimum effectiveness.

4. Leadership

☐ Not observed	☐ Often weak in command situations. At times unable to exert control.	☐ Normally develops fairly adequate control and teamwork.	☐ Consistently a good leader. Commands respect of subordinates.	☐ Exceptional skill in directing others to great effort.	☐ Leadership qualities reflect potential to highest level.

A behaviourally anchored rating scale (from McBriarty, 1988). Copyright © 1988 by IPMA-HR, and used with permission.

Ranking. This involves taking all employees doing a particular type of job and then, using a global criterion, ranking them by performance after reflecting on the various individual contributions. This method compensates for the weakness of the individual methods discussed earlier by stressing the relative performance of employees. Invariably it is easier to rank the top and bottom performers before consideration of those in the middle. Ranking based on a global criterion of performance has its shortcomings because of the tendency to reduce a very complex set of behaviours to a single value. Also it is difficult to use ranking with a large number of employees, and rankings do not disclose degrees of difference in the levels of performance. When critical decisions are made—e.g., transfers, terminating employment, promotions—it is inevitable that rankings would have to be supplemented by additional information on employees.

Paired comparison. This is a variation of the ranking method, and requires the evaluator to appraise each employee in conjunction with all other employees in the set before making a judgement. The evaluator usually compares two people at a time on one global performance criterion. The better and weaker performer in each pair is identified, and eventually a list is prepared where people are placed in rank order based on the number of good scores achieved. Because ranking is by pairs the evaluator is not overwhelmed and confused by having to cope with too many employees at one time, but, with increases in the size of the pool of individuals to be appraised, this method shows potential weaknesses associated with handling more and more comparisons.

Forced distribution. With this method the evaluator is required to place employees into particular categories according to their performance. For

example, one system would be to create three categories with an equal distribution of people, as shown in Table 17.3. Alternatively, there could be a larger number of categories with variable distributions, as in Table 17.4.

In the case illustrated in Table 17.4, the evaluator must assign specified percentages of employees to each of the five categories. You will notice that an imposed normal distribution applies in the illustration, which suggests that 40% of performance falls into the average category. This could create difficulties if, for example, employees in a particular department were predominantly either superior or inferior performers, in which case a skewed distribution would be more appropriate. By placing all employees into a few groups, the forced distribution method produces less information than the straight ranking method.

Multi-rater comparative evaluation

Objective judgement quotient. The objective judgement quotient (OJQ) method (Edwards, 1983) operates on the principle of using more than one rater, with different evaluation methods.

TABLE 17.3

Distribution among categories—equal

	Categories		
	Below average	Average	Above average
Distribution	33⅓%	33⅓%	33⅓%

TABLE 17.4

Distribution among categories—variable

	Categories				
	Unacceptable	Poor	Average	Above average	Excellent
Distribution	10%	20%	40%	20%	10%

The performance of individuals is compared with that of others using a number of raters, including the supervisor. The outcome of this exercise is the creation of a "performance profile" showing the position of each appraisee on the performance criteria in comparison with all other employees who have been appraised.

Another example of the multi-rater technique is the 360-degree feedback system, discussed later.

Assessment centres.   An assessment centre is also an example of a technique involving multiple raters where comparative evaluation can be used. When used as a *development centre* it is a method of appraising managerial ability with the future firmly in focus, under which the appraisal of managerial abilities and skills takes place over a few days. The overall appraisal normally consists of interviews, psychometric testing, simulations (such as an in-basket exercise whereby the participant copes with a collection of correspondence from a manager's incoming mail), peer appraisals, and appraisal by experts in attendance. The aim of an assessment centre is to appraise current ability as a basis for making judgements about the suitability of the participant for promotion to a more senior position. There is reference to assessment centres in the context of training and development in Chapter 18 and a more detailed discussion of assessment centres featured earlier in this chapter.

Administering the appraisal system

Formal performance evaluation is normally conducted on an annual basis, but employees receive informal feedback on their performance from superiors on a frequent basis. The formal review does not have to take place at the same time of the year for all employees, but it normally does, and precedes the annual process for the determination of rewards. Where the performance review in the organisation takes place on the anniversary of the employee joining the company, evaluations can be dispersed throughout the year, and this could help supervisors by spreading the burden of conducting appraisals over a longer period.

For employees serving a probationary period, the end of that period normally signals the need to conduct an appraisal, even if the time does not coincide with the organisation's annual review or alternative arrangements. After the evaluation of the employee at the end of the probationary period, a decision will be made as to whether or not the person's employment will continue.

Whether an organisation should stick rigidly to annual or semi-annual performance reviews is open to question. A number of influences could be considered. For example, it may be more important to conduct an appraisal when a distinct unit of work or assignment has been completed, or when the organisation needs information on employees' performance on completion of a particular project. A number of ways of evaluating performance outside the traditional annual process have been suggested (see Fedor & Buckley, 1988). For example, the Advisory Conciliation and Arbitration Service (ACAS) in the UK favours appraisal as an ongoing process (not an annual review), which amounts to something similar to a kind of continuous coaching arrangement (Overell, 2003).

Apart from the frequency of performance appraisal in a formal sense, another matter to consider in connection with the administration of the system is who is charged with carrying out the appraisals? The simple answer is that there can be more people involved than the obvious person, i.e., the supervisor. Those charged with carrying out appraisals can be listed as:

- supervisor;
- self;
- peers;
- subordinates (upward appraisal); and
- 360-degree (multi-rater) system.

Supervisor

The immediate supervisor is often considered to be the most logical choice of candidate for the role of evaluator of a subordinate's performance. Naturally it is felt that the immediate supervisor is well placed to observe the subordinate's behaviour and to judge his or her relative contribution to the effectiveness of the department. The supervisor could note the extent to which the subordinate has met the objectives set for him or her for the period under review, with or without the involvement of the appraisee in the setting of the objectives. Naturally the appraiser will be sensitive to issues affecting performance that lie outside the control of the appraisee. Alternatively, the subordinate's performance could be appraised against each task specified in the job description, or key accountability. Performance could also be appraised against job competencies, in which case, for example, an overall competency profile could be identified for a particular job and this could be used in performance appraisal.

Despite what has been said above, it is sometimes conceded that supervisors are not sufficiently close to their subordinates to enable them to pass judgement that is likely to be useful. The reasons given include the fact that supervisors may be geographically distant from certain types of subordinate (e.g., sales representatives in the field), preventing them from observing their behaviour. Also, supervisors are generally too absorbed in roles other than monitoring the performance of subordinates—such as representing their section or department, or handling budgets and report writing (Vecchio, 1995).

Self

This approach to performance evaluation may be suitable when appraising and comparing an individual's performance on certain dimensions, such as the quality of performance, interpersonal skills, and leadership. It is claimed that employees have the capacity to evaluate themselves in an unbiased manner (Mabe & West, 1982). Self-appraisal is particularly appropriate in the context of employee development or management development, but there is a danger that sometimes self-ratings may amount to a distortion of reality and be out of line with supervisor ratings (Bretz, Milkovich, & Read, 1992). Fletcher (1993) maintained that people are capable of rating themselves, but the question is, are they willing to do so? He goes on to say that one of the best ways for individuals to assess themselves is to rate different

aspects of their performance relative to other aspects of their performance, rather than relative to the performance of colleagues or others. In that way individuals can be more discriminating.

One way of improving the effectiveness of self-ratings is to combine them with supervisor ratings (Teel, 1978). Here the supervisor and subordinate complete the evaluation separately, using identical forms, and subsequently meet to compare the responses. In a supportive environment this approach has value in allowing both parties to exchange perceptions of the subordinate's behaviour and performance at work.

Self-ratings could be used where participative management processes exist, such as management by objectives (examined in Chapter 16). As stated earlier, self-ratings are particularly useful in training and development situations where subordinates obtain insight into the progress they have made to date. However, Vecchio (1995) suggests that self-ratings rarely have much influence on decisions about promotions, salary increases, transfers, etc.

Peers

Appraisals conducted by peers or co-workers are a rare event, but as a mode of evaluation this type of appraisal has some strengths. Peers are in a good position to observe a colleague's performance in a variety of situations over long periods of time. According to Korman (1968), one outcome of being in contact with co-workers for an appreciable length of time is the creation of more accurate assessments and predictions of each other's performance. Although peer ratings are likely to be more reliable than self-ratings, they are vulnerable to a number of potential biases. For example, one major limitation is that people are likely to rate their friends more favourably (De Nisi & Mitchell, 1978). Also, better performers may receive tougher evaluations at the hands of less able performers intent on protecting their own image.

Subordinates (upward appraisal)

Subordinates of supervisors or managers could be asked to evaluate their boss's performance. This exercise, which is not in widespread use, should be subject to anonymity, though the latter may be difficult to preserve where a group is small. The appraisal is likely to generate a number of impressions of the boss's performance, which could signal a weakness. Many subordinates may feel unhappy about participating in this type of appraisal because they feel that it is not their responsibility to evaluate their superior, or that they are not well placed to undertake an upward appraisal, or that they may fear reprisal.

It would be unwise to completely ignore subordinates' appraisal of their superiors, because the process could be valuable in providing feedback for the recipient to consider when reflecting on personal performance. In the field of training, and some branches of education, trainees or students are asked to complete evaluation forms at the end of a course. The data, when analysed, could be used to isolate deficiencies that should be addressed, or to form a basis for providing extra material rewards or career advancement when the overall evaluation is consistently very favourable.

Although subordinate appraisals have been conducted successfully in the past in certain well-known companies (e.g., IBM and Pepsico), nevertheless the resistance of superiors is probably the greatest barrier to implementation of the process. Some managers feel that their power will be usurped. Others object emotionally, if not intellectually, to the idea of a subordinate evaluating their performance. Often they are also concerned that an overemphasis will be placed upon being popular as opposed to being respected (Nevels, 1989). Likewise, it appears that managers would not be too happy if their rewards were determined by appraisals carried out by subordinates (Ash, 1994).

According to Fletcher (1993), upward appraisal is only likely to be used on the odd occasion as an additional activity, rather than as an integral part of the appraisal process. It is probably less acceptable than the more conventional approaches (Torrington et al., 2002). Furnham (1993b) argued that enthusiasm for subordinate appraisals (the bottom-up system) has to some extent "gone off the boil", but he feels that if the system is working well it is both efficient and equitable. However,

the conditions for a successful system should be noted, namely: trust in staff to be honest, fair, and constructive; there must be real commitment to the notion that communication is a two-way process; and, finally, the ratings of subordinates must be taken seriously and acted on.

360-degree feedback (multi-rater system)

A multi-rater system embraces the ratings of several people who are familiar with the employee's performance (Conway, 1996). A number of these people could be outside the immediate work environment of the person to be appraised. They could be clients or customers who are asked to give their considered judgement of the person concerned, and managers or supervisors from other sections and departments who are one hierarchical step above the person to be appraised. Other people likely to be involved as appraisers are consultants who would normally be commissioned to undertake appraisal of the performance of the more senior managers. They would tap a variety of sources (e.g., superiors, peers, clients) before making a judgement. The confidential nature of the exercise must be accepted by the raters, and it is important that they feel confident about being open and honest in their judgement.

The multi-rater system described above has been formalised in the 360-degree feedback system (Antonioni, 1996). This system of performance evaluation is very useful because it offers a wider range of performance-related feedback than is offered by the traditional evaluation methods. It goes beyond a narrow focus on quantitative issues (e.g., percentage increase in sales or productivity) and incorporates qualitative issues, such as diplomatic or political skills, quality of interpersonal relations, and leadership inspirational qualities.

Sederburg and Rogelberg (1999) view the 360-degree feedback system as a "potentially powerful intervention that can positively make an impact on individual and organisational effectiveness if educated and careful methodological decisions are made and implemented". According to Warr and Ainsworth (1999) the corporate culture must be supportive of this type of appraisal for it to be

TABLE 17.5

Advantages and disadvantages of using different appraisers (adapted from Vecchio, 1995)

Source of appraisal	Advantages	Disadvantages
Immediate supervisor	Makes decisions on rewards Has perspectives on all subordinates	Personal bias possible Supervisor may be removed from subordinates
Self	Unique perspective A useful basis for comparison Useful for self-insight	Likely to be too lenient
Peers	Greater exposure to appraisee More accurate assessment	Competitive atmosphere confounds usage
Subordinates	Can give diagnostic-type feedback	Can subvert the leader's authority
Superiors of other units	Can be less subjective	Too removed from the individual
Customers or clients	Gives input from immediate client group	Only sees limited facet of appraisee
Consultants	Complete, thorough appraisal	Too expensive for use with all employees

effective. They also make the point that, since this system draws more on subjective than objective evidence, it is important that judges and facilitators understand the factors that can affect the information that is created and applied.

The 360-degree feedback process is usually operationalised through a carefully constructed questionnaire, although the information could also be collected on disc or by electronic mail. The contributors to the rating exercise are asked to score on a given scale the extent to which the individual displays stated behavioural competencies and associated behaviour. The information collected is then grouped and printed in a feedback report, which is interpreted by an internal or external facilitator and then discussed with the appraisee in a feedback session (Brett & Atwater, 2001). The outcome would be a commitment by the appraisee to action plans for improved performance where weaknesses were identified (Clifford & Bennett, 1997). So the logic of the whole exercise is that individuals can use this information to change their behaviours, improve performance, and set and meet development goals and action plans (Torrington, Hall, & Taylor, 2005).

However, there are potential problems. Given the numerous sources of appraisal data in the 360-degree feedback system, there is a greater opportunity for observations to be made that could be hurtful or threatening (Hoffman, 1995). In a survey of 800 UK organisations, the Industrial Society (now the Work Foundation) identified the main obstacle to implementing the 360-degree feedback system to be that people felt threatened by it (Clifford & Bennett, 1997). On a different note, Fletcher (1998) expressed reservations about some of the questions that appear in the 360-degree appraisal systems when he points out, on the basis of his research, that they did not measure the behaviour they were designed to assess. He admonishes companies to be vigilant and evaluate the worth of these systems before using them. Finally, in a survey conducted by Watson Wyatt's Human Capital, doubts have been cast on the effectiveness of 360-degree appraisals (Donkin, 2002).

A listing of the advantages and disadvantages of the different agencies for conducting performance appraisals appears in Table 17.5.

Use of appraisal information

The information produced by the performance appraisal system can convey, for example, that an employee should be considered for extra rewards, or is ready for promotion, or is in need of additional training, or is so seriously deficient in the necessary skills to do the job that he or she should be replaced. Also, the appraisal information can be used to prepare forecasts of staffing needs and inform decision making in areas such as succession planning, recruitment, training, and management development. The outcomes described can be of benefit to both the employee and the organisation if the appraisal system works well. An important process for providing information to those whose performance is appraised is the feedback interview.

Feedback interview

The feedback of information to those appraised is said to have a beneficial effect on performance (Erez, 1977). Employees normally like to know how well they are doing, and a mechanism for providing such information is the feedback interview. The purpose of this interview is normally to provide a supportive climate in which positive suggestions to improve performance would be discussed. Ideally this type of interview should have a number of the characteristics of a counselling session. It should be borne in mind that the impression the subordinate receives about his or her appraisal has a material effect on both self-esteem and future motivational disposition.

In practice, there is evidence to indicate that one outcome of the interaction of superior and subordinate in sharing appraisal information in the feedback interview is emotional tension and defensiveness (Vecchio, 1995). For example, superiors could feel very uncomfortable when relaying to subordinates the message that their performance has been below expectations. This situation could be made worse if the superior accumulates negative performance-related information over time and unloads it during the feedback interview (Meyer, 1991); also, the vindictiveness of some managers (appraisers) has been recognised (Overell, 2003). For these and other reasons, superiors may be tempted to cancel or delay the reviews, or avoid raising issues likely to be contentious. Of course reporting good news should present little difficulty for the supervisor in the normal course of events, though it is possible to find situations where good news is not perceived as good enough by those receiving the feedback. Heneman (1974) maintains that because subordinates generally view their performance

as better than it really is, they are likely to feel discomfort when they disagree with the superior's assessments.

The sincerity, credibility, and power of the appraiser, and the fairness of the appraisal process, are said to be important variables in the feedback interview (Ilgen, Fisher, & Taylor, 1979; Nathan, Mohrman, & Milliman, 1991). According to Ilgen et al., the appraiser must be perceived as credible before an appraisee is prepared to accept and respect the feedback. Acceptance of the feedback will be reinforced when the appraiser is viewed as not only credible but also able to wield power (in terms of authority to dispense rewards and sanctions). Where the appraiser is seen as lacking in credibility or power, the appraisee is likely to seek feedback from other sources—e.g., peers, self, or subordinates—and where there is a divergence between the views of these sources and the formal evaluator, the judgements of the alternative sources may be accepted as a means of shielding self-esteem.

According to Burke, Weitzel, and Weir (1978), to enhance the effectiveness of the process a number of steps should be considered with respect to the feedback interview (see Panel 17.6).

Problems with appraisal

The quality of measurement systems is very important in performance appraisal. The measurement method produces the information used in a variety of decisions connected with promotions, transfers, training, salary increases, and so on. As was seen earlier, the focus of the approaches to measurement varies. In some cases the emphasis is on outcomes, whereas in other cases it is on behaviours and personality traits. Unfortunately events do not always work out well, and problems surface (see Panel 17.7).

In a good performance appraisal system the measurement methods must be valid, reliable, and free of bias, producing ratings that are not too lenient, or severe, or bunched in the middle (central tendency), and that are free of halo and timing errors. But there are situations where imperfections creep into the performance appraisal process, and these will now be discussed.

PANEL 17.6: Effective feedback interviews

- The appraiser should prepare carefully for the interview, and this involves collecting and reviewing available records on the appraisee's performance, such as quantity and quality of output, attendance record, commitment, etc. An outline of the points to be dealt with at the interview should be prepared in advance in order to sharpen the focus of the interview.

- In the notice of the interview, the appraisee should be told of its primary purpose—e.g., personal development or pay linked to performance—so as to be in a state of readiness.

- At the beginning of the interview the appraisee could be given the opportunity to comment on his or her performance. This could create a participative tone to the interaction right from the start, with alleged beneficial side-effects.

- In providing crucial feedback data to the appraisee, the focus should be on issues rather than aspects of personality. An example of a comment hinging on personality traits is "You don't come across as somebody who has a need to achieve". Where personal characteristics—e.g., the way a person speaks or dresses—are relevant to the position occupied by the appraisee, it would appear to be acceptable to have these matters discussed at the interview. Otherwise it is sensible not to make an issue of the distinctive ways in which individuals express their personality.

- Where it is necessary to voice criticism, the appraiser should do it without adopting a hostile stance. Also, it should be clearly articulated why past behaviour is unacceptable. If it was a matter of poor performance, or shoddy work, the consequences for people inside and outside the organisation could be emphasised.

- Having made the criticism, the appraiser should listen attentively to explanations proffered by the appraisee and, after a discussion, the two parties should formulate an approach to resolving the difficulties with an intention to monitor the implementation of the solution. As people generally have a low tolerance for criticism, in circumstances where numerous criticisms could have been levelled at the appraisee it would appear wise to limit the criticism to a couple of problems.

- The identification of good performance is as necessary as suggestions for the improvement of poor performance. There is a belief that early in the interview the appraiser should emphasise the positive aspects of the appraisee's performance, then move on to the negative aspects, finally terminating the dialogue with more positive comments. This is known as the sandwich approach to the provision of feedback. It is claimed that by stressing favourable aspects of performance early in the interview the appraisee is likely to be less defensive. Equally, closing the interview with similar comments help to maintain good working relationships. However, there are those who feel that the sandwich approach may emasculate the critical evaluation aspect of the process.

- Towards the end of the interview it is useful to summarise the action required of the appraisee in order to improve performance. In addition, the appraiser could offer assistance in removing obstacles to achievement, and by doing so could be perceived less as a judge and more as a coach or counsellor by the appraisee.

- The provision of feedback is not something that should only take place in the formal appraisal session. Frequent feedback on an informal basis about a person's positive and negative performance shows that the supervisor is interested in his or her work, and provides a solid base for the formal feedback interview.

(Burke et al., 1978)

PANEL 17.7: Failures in appraisal

Longenecker (1997) conducted a survey and found that the most common reasons for the failure of an appraisal system for managerial staff were: (a) unclear performance criteria, or an ineffective rating instrument; (b) a poor working relationship with the boss; and (c) the appraiser lacking sufficient information on the appraisee's actual performance. Other reasons given were lack of ongoing feedback, and lack of focus on the improvement of performance through management development schemes.

Lesser concerns that were expressed were inadequate skills of appraisal and the performance review process lacking adequate structure or content. A particular concern, ventilated by Torrington et al. (2002) is the importance of the "ownership" of the appraisal scheme. If it is designed and imposed by the HR department, that would leave little ownership of the system by line managers. Also, if the paperwork has to be returned to the HR department, the system may be viewed as a form-filling exercise for somebody else's benefit with no practical value as far as performance on the job is concerned.

Doyle (2003) also recognises unskilled behaviour on the part of the interviewer conducting the appraisal, and goes on to point out that often there are difficulties experienced by appraisers (managers) when relaying negative feedback to the appraisees. Also, many employees will react with defensiveness, anxiety, and depression when negative feedback is poorly given.

Validity

The validity of a performance appraisal method rests on the extent to which it reflects the actual performance of the employee. The validity of a measure would be called into question in a situation where, for example, it is acknowledged that in a particular group Valerie is the best performer, but formal indicators of performance evaluation show her as average. There are different types of validity:

(1) *Content validity*. This is the extent to which the measuring device adequately addresses all the important features of performance in a job. If the measurement method does not assess the full content of job performance, one can question its validity. For example, a test of a trainee driver's ability to drive a car would not have content validity if it did not have a hill start and an emergency stop.

(2) *Convergent validity*. This depends upon the extent to which different measures of performance agree in their assessment of the same performance. If Valerie's performance was rated as high by one measure, and as low by another, obviously the ratings of the same performance do not agree. Therefore, one questions convergent validity in this situation.

(3) *Discriminant validity*. This rests on the extent to which ratings on a subset of performance (e.g., quantity of output) are in agreement with, and differ from, agreed ratings on another subset of performance (e.g., quality of output). This could be seen when two raters agree and rate Valerie high on quality of output but low on quantity of output.

Reliability

The reliability of a measuring instrument rests on the extent to which the results obtained are consistent. Where the same performance is measured on a number of occasions (using the same methods) and the results are very similar, the measuring instrument can be considered reliable. But if the results are very different, one could question the reliability of the method of measurement. Another matter to consider in connection with reliability is *inter-rater reliability*. If an employee's performance is evaluated by more than one evaluator, and the ratings are consistent, inter-rater reliability is high. On the other hand, if the ratings differ, one can question the reliability of the measure. (The topic of reliability and validity was dealt with earlier in the chapter in connection with the employee selection process.)

Bias

As well as validity and reliability, bias is another issue to consider. It can undermine impartial judgement in assessments of performance. Bias is not only reflected in assessments made with reference to specific criteria, but also stems from applying different criteria to different appraisees. The information acquired from a biased assessment is less meaningful, undermines the purpose of the appraisal process, and contributes to career dissatisfaction among employees (Greenhaus, Parasuraman, & Wormley, 1990).

In the UK, and other countries as well, steps are taken to tackle discrimination in employment. Legislation has been introduced to safeguard groups of employees (e.g., women and minorities) who are very likely to be victimised by bias in employment practices, such as performance appraisal. There still appears to be a lot of scope for improvements in confronting discriminatory practices. In 2001 in the British Civil Service it was found that the performance appraisal system discriminated against ethnic minority and disabled workers. White employees received better average performance marks than ethnic minority employees across all age groups, while nondisabled workers received better scores than disabled colleagues. As a means to cope with such problems, the Civil Service Management Board set up an independent assessor system, allowing disgruntled employees a right of appeal (Overell, 2003). (There is reference to discriminatory practices in Chapter 9.)

Leniency, severity, and central tendency

Leniency, severity, and central tendency materialise when evaluators show a tendency to rate performance at a consistently high level amounting to overstatement (leniency), or a low level amounting to understatement (severity), or at about the mid-point, restricting the range (central tendency). In each situation the rater is incapable of distinguishing between different levels of performance. This is akin to the notion of low differentiation identified by Pizam (1975). Low differentiators tend to ignore or suppress differences and use a limited range on the rating scale. This is unlikely to be the case with high differentiators, such as the cognitively complex person. The latter has a capacity to grapple with a number of issues at the same time, and in the case of leniency tends to be less lenient (Schneier, 1977).

The purpose of the appraisal is said to be a factor affecting leniency, particularly in self-rating exercises. Employees who rated themselves tended to exercise leniency when the results were used for the dispensing of rewards or sanctions. But when they knew that others would check their ratings, more accurate ratings were evident (Farh & Werbel, 1986).

Halo error

This was discussed in relation to the halo effect in interpersonal perception in Chapter 5. Basically it is the tendency of the evaluator to allow an assessment of an individual on one trait to influence his or her evaluation of that person across the board (Balzer & Sulsky, 1992). For example, an appraisee may come across as articulate, for which a favourable assessment is given, and this favourable impression is then generalised to other individual characteristics, without regard to actual performance. It is said that the cognitively complex person is less likely to commit halo errors (Schneier, 1977).

Similarity error

This arises when evaluators place special emphasis on the qualities of the person appraised that resemble those seen in themselves (Judge & Ferris, 1993). For example, where an evaluator perceives himself or herself as assertive and sees this quality in others during the appraisal process, then those candidates who are perceived as assertive benefit, whereas those without this characteristic are penalised.

Timing errors

The moment in time when appraisals take place can be critical. It is said that evaluations made after the performance has taken place are more accurate (Heneman & Wexley, 1983). Rating errors can occur when there is an appreciable amount of time between performance and the rating exercise. But the evaluator can reduce rating errors due to the lapse of time by relying on numerous observations of performance over time, and by recording observations soon after the appearance of the relevant bouts of behaviour.

Another type of error—recency error—comes about when the evaluator recalls only the most recent behaviours of the person appraised. This could be problematic because most employees are vigilant and likely to perform well in the period close to the performance review. Should the evaluator place heavy reliance on this bout of behaviour, bias in the appraisal could materialise.

Other factors

Two further factors likely to distort the performance evaluation process are the single criterion and using an appraisal process to justify a prior judgement on the performance of the employee (Robbins, 1998).

The use of the single criterion is evident when a single dimension of performance—e.g., the receptionist skills of a secretary—gains prominence in the evaluation process, whereas other dimensions—e.g., keyboard skills—are excluded. In such circumstances the secretary would be expected to pay most attention to the single dimension of performance to the neglect of the other job-related dimensions.

In the case of formal evaluation following the prior judgement of the employee's performance, the appraisal decision is made before the objective information to support the decision is sought (Woehr & Feldman, 1993). This may appear irrational, but in practice there could be other nonperformance criteria—e.g., seniority—based on preferences or values in operation that are not part of the formal appraisal process.

Tackling appraisal problems

A number of remedies might be considered to address some of the problems connected with performance appraisal, as follows:

- Multiple job criteria should be identified and evaluated. That means that all those aspects of the job that are related to successful performance should be stated and assessed.
- The importance of personality traits alone as predictors of performance should be de-emphasised. A distorted picture could be presented if there was a tendency to isolate personality traits—e.g., extravert, reliable—as the only factors responsible for performance. You should note that people could possess desirable personality traits but these characteristics may not be directly responsible for good performance.
- Multiple evaluators should be used as a means to increase the accuracy of appraisal information. In international ice-skating competitions multiple evaluators are used to rate the performance of the skaters. Also, in 360-degree appraisals, discussed earlier, use is made of multiple evaluations.
- There should be a move to evaluate selectively, whereby evaluators assess only in areas in which they are qualified to pass judgement (Borman, 1974). For example, one evaluator may concentrate on knowledge of the job and another on competence in doing the job.
- Mount a training programme for evaluators. For example, there could be the opportunity to be briefed about the nature of rater errors and to become familiar with appraisal techniques (Smith, 1986). According to Bernardin (1978), a training programme where managers are able to practise the art of observing and rating behaviour could help with eliminating or minimising halo and leniency errors. As a general principle, it would be sensible not to treat the training of evaluators as a

one-off event; instead it ought to be mounted periodically. Apparently employees usually consider appraisals of performance fair if raters receive the appropriate training and use some form of diary to record actual events (Greenberg, 1986).

- The principle of "due process" in performance appraisal as enunciated by Taylor, Tracy, Renard, Harrison, and Carrol (1995) ought to be considered. This means that employees are likely to respond positively to the appraisal system when the following conditions apply: employees will have confidence in the system if they know what is expected of them in terms of performance, where any unwelcome deviations from standard are articulated in a fair way and the individuals concerned have a right to reply, and where the final evaluation decision rests on evidence with an absence of bias.
- Involve employees in the setting of realistic and well-defined performance targets, provide them with feedback based on accurate information, and allow time for discussing the feedback (Roberts, 1994).

From the viewpoint of a large US company, Lawler, Mohrman, and Resnick (1984) maintain that performance appraisal in an organisation is only as good as its overall human resources climate, strategy, and policies, and especially the processes of fitting it to these. It is unrealistic to expect to have an effective performance appraisal system where jobs are poorly designed, the culture is negative, and subordinates are asked to be passive and do what they are told. At its best, it's two people sharing their perceptions of each other, their relationships, their work, and their organisation—sharing that results in better performance, better feelings, and a more effective organisation. At its worst, it is one person in the name of the organisation trying to force his or her will on another, resulting in miscommunication, misperception, disappointment, and alienation. The best is achievable, but only with considerable effort, careful design, constant attention to process, and support by top management.

Perspectives originating in the UK would tend to suggest that the following conditions are

---

PANEL 17.8: Performance appraisal in practice

Shaun Tyson, Professor of Human Resource Management at the Cranfield School of Management, UK is quoted as saying that "appraisal requires interview and counselling skills of a high order, which many managers don't possess. They don't prepare, don't have time, don't have skills to conduct interviews and, where the relationship with the person being appraised is not good, might make it even worse. People go into the appraisal highly motivated and come out highly demotivated." The comment by Tyson has been endorsed by Overell (2003) who cites evidence that a lot of managers don't have the interpersonal skills to give negative comments in a constructive way—there is a very British fear of criticism.

Ian Parkes, Director of Organisation Development at Amersham Pharmacia and Biotech, UK, who used a 360-degree feedback system for 3 years, says that:

> generally appraisal causes confusion because it tries to do too many things. It tries to set objectives and set performance against them, give personal development planning and obtain information for salary planning. The part that loses out the most is development . . . We use the 360-degree feedback as an optional extra to help our leaders and managers increase their self-awareness and improve their performance. But it must be done with care. They are given help to understand the feedback and translate it into development plans.

Lorraine Trainer, Head of Human Resources at Coutts Banking (part of RBS), UK, says that 360-degree feedback, which is being used increasingly, is valuable but not enough: "It is naive to rely on appraisals for staff development. The problem we encounter is that people fill in forms that are then filed and then forgotten. Most organisations would recognise that fact."

(Coles, 1999b; Overell, 2003)

---

compatible with a successful performance appraisal or management system (Fletcher & Williams, 1992; Income Data Services, 1992):

- A proactive rather than a reactive strategy for performance management.
- A climate within which people feel secure.
- Line managers are involved to an acceptable extent in deliberations and action connected with the system.
- The financial considerations (e.g., bottom-line results) and the bureaucratic infrastructure supporting the system are not overstated.
- The introduction of the system is not justified entirely by the need to operationalise a performance-related pay scheme.

For other views on the performance appraisal process see Panel 17.8.

Team appraisal. An important point to note is that, given the growing popularity of team systems of working, acknowledged earlier in the book, serious attention will have to be given to evaluating teams rather than individuals. The difficulty likely to be encountered with the assessment of teams is finding appropriate performance measures and relating team performance to goal achievement. Robbins (2003) suggests a number of actions along the following lines: relate the team results to the organisation's goals; assess the effectiveness of the team in meeting customers' requirements, with the accent on delivery and quality; consider the part played by individual team members in supporting team processes and accomplishments; and ensure that both individuals and the team define their objectives, for by doing so it helps clarify individual roles and promotes team cohesiveness.

Balanced scorecard. Nowadays there is a preoccupation with demonstrating the contribution of strategic HRM to organisational performance. One method for doing this is the balanced scorecard (Kaplan & Norton, 1996). A stakeholders' perspective is adopted, operating on the assumption that for an organisation to be successful it must satisfy the requirements of key stakeholders —namely investors, customers, and employees. Investors are interested in financial performance (economic added value), while customers are interested in products or services that are measured by customer value added. But for employees (the human resource) the organisation can use attitude surveys, skill audits, and performance appraisal data to measure factors such as the quality of the place of work, and opportunities for professional development and growth. These data throw light on what people do, what they know, and the role played by HRM and other systems in helping to identify targets and measure performance in relation to those targets (Beardwell, Holden, & Claydon, 2004).

CHAPTER SUMMARY

- Human resource management provides a framework within which human resource practices operate. The main features of human resource management were outlined and some contributory factors to its development were stated.
- Human resource practices examined in this chapter were personnel selection and performance appraisal.
- Job analysis was noted as the first step in the selection process. Sources of job analysis data were given as written material, job holders' reports, colleagues' reports, and direct observation. A natural outcome of job analysis, when recruitment is contemplated, is the preparation of a job description or flexible job description, and a job specification or required competencies. Sources of recruitment were briefly acknowledged.
- Selectors have a number of methods at their disposal. These include the structured and unstructured selection interview, psychometric tests (including integrity tests), work sample tests, assessment centres, biographical information, and other methods such as references, peer assessment, self-assessment, telephone screening, the internet, graphology, and polygraphy. The evolution of assessment centres and a challenge to psychometric tests were briefly mentioned. The notion of fairness was introduced.
- Validity and reliability were raised as important issues. Validity includes criterion-related validity, face validity, content validity, and construct validity. The utility of the selection process was noted.
- The goals of performance appraisal were stated, and the judgemental and developmental nature of performance evaluation was explained. The criteria used in performance appraisal or evaluation embrace task outcomes, behaviours, and traits. The major appraisal techniques discussed were graphic rating scales, essays, behaviourally anchored rating scales, behavioural observation scales, ranking, paired comparison, forced distribution, OJQ, and assessment centres.
- In the administration of an appraisal system, questions addressed were the frequency of appraisal, and who is charged with carrying it out—i.e., the supervisor, self-appraisal, peers, subordinates, and others such as clients or customers, or consultants. In the latter context the 360-degree system was examined, and the importance of training was emphasised. Appraisal information can be used for a variety of purposes, and the nature and effectiveness of the feedback interview were considered.
- The measurement methods in appraisal were discussed with reference to validity (convergent and discriminant), reliability, bias (leniency, severity, and central tendency), halo error, similarity error, timing errors, and other considerations.
- Ways to tackle the problems of appraisal were suggested, and conditions compatible with a successful performance appraisal system were listed.
- The need to evaluate teams was briefly acknowledged.
- The balanced scorecard approach was introduced as a measure to provide an integrated framework for balancing the interests of various stakeholders.

QUESTIONS

(1) What is the difference between recruitment and selection?

(2) Describe the sources of job analysis data.

(3) Distinguish between a job description and a job specification.

(4) Discuss the usefulness of psychometric testing.

(5) Why is there a need for integrity tests?

(6) What is meant by an assessment centre?

(7) Explain an unstructured selection interview.

(8) What considerations should be taken into account in writing references on employees?

(9) Assess the significance of telephone screening and use of the internet in employee selection.

(10) What is understood by the "applicant–organisation fit" approach to the selection interview?

(11) Comment on graphology as a selection method.

(12) Discuss the issue of fairness and an ethical approach in employee selection.

(13) Explain the terms criterion and predictor with respect to the validity of selection methods.

(14) Specify the goals of performance appraisal, and state how a developmental evaluation differs from a judgemental one.

(15) What do we mean by criteria in the context of performance appraisal?

(16) Having reviewed the major appraisal techniques, rank them in order of importance from your point of view.

(17) Comment on (a) self-appraisal, (b) appraisal of superiors by subordinates, and (c) the 360-degree system.

(18) Define the following terms: (a) convergent validity; (b) central tendency; (c) construct validity; (d) feedback interview; and (e) adverse impact.

(19) How does one go about tackling the problems of appraisal?

(20) Identify the conditions necessary for a successful performance appraisal system.

(21) Explain what is meant by team appraisal.

(22) What is the balanced score card?

SPOTLIGHT ON RELEVANT READING

HRM (general)

Guest, D. (2001). Human resource management: When research confronts theory. *International Journal of Human Resource Management, 12,* 1092–1106.

Guest, D., & King, Z. (2004). Power, innovation, and problem solving: The personnel manager's three steps to heaven. *Journal of Management Studies, 41,* 401–423.

Watson, T.J. (2004). HRM and critical social science analysis. *Journal of Management Studies, 41,* 447–467.

Selection

Jansen, P.G.W., & Stoop, B.A.M. (2001). The dynamics of assessment center validity: Results of a 7-year study. *Journal of Applied Psychology,* August, 741–753.

Robertson, I.T., & Smith, M. (2001). Personnel selection. *Journal of Occupational and Organisational Psychology, 74,* 441–472.

Roe, R.A., & Van den Berg, P.T. (2003). Selection in Europe: Context, developments, and research agenda. *European Journal of Work and Organisational Psychology, 12,* 257–287.

Woodruffe, C. (2000b). *Development and assessment centres: Identifying and assessing competence.* London: Chartered Institute of Personnel and Development.

Appraisal

Brett, J.F., & Atwater, L.E. (2001). 360-degree feedback: Accuracy, reactions, and perceptions of usefulness. *Journal of Applied Psychology,* October, 930–942.

Fletcher, C. (2001). Performance appraisal and management. The developing research agenda. *Journal of Occupational and Organisational Psychology, 74,* 473–487.

Goodge, P. (2005). How to link 360-degree feedback and appraisal. *People Management,* 27 January, 46–47.

Latham, G.P., Almost J., Mann, S., & Moore, C. (2005). New developments in performance management. *Organisational Dynamics, 34,* 77–87.

Learning Outcomes

After studying this chapter you should be able to:

- Recognise the difference between extrinsic and intrinsic rewards.
- Outline ways in which rewards are determined.
- Specify the likely make up of a compensation package for senior managers in a large company.
- Describe the factors likely to influence the acquisition of skills.
- Provide illustrations of the way government has encouraged training over the years.
- Discuss ways in which training needs are assessed.
- Examine the justification for setting training objectives.
- Identify the training methods used in on-the-job and off-the-job training.
- Outline the part played by e-learning in contemporary training.
- Provide an illustration of continuous professional development.
- Give examples of trainee-centred training processes.
- List important features of management development.
- Discuss the role of career planning in contemporary organisations.
- Examine the influences likely to affect career choice.
- Recognise the approaches to the evaluation of training.

Human Resource Practices: Rewards, Training, and Development

The chapter opens with a definition of rewards, followed by a discussion of the purpose and philosophy of reward systems. Methods used in the determination of rewards are reviewed, along with compensation packages. The training and development section starts with an examination of factors likely to influence the acquisition of skills, and this leads to a justification for training and development within organisations. Next there is an analysis of the training process, management development, and career choice and planning.

The need to evaluate training is emphasised. Issues discussed in this chapter have particular relevance to Part IV of this book, plus to Chapter 4 on motivation and Chapter 7 on learning.

Contents

REWARDS

Reward systems in organisations are at the disposal of managers in order to attract, retain, and motivate people in the desired direction. Therefore, motivation theory, discussed in Chapter 4, is relevant to rewards, as is the concept of reinforcement as part of learning theory, discussed in Chapter 7. The reward system comprises the various organisational activities aimed at the allocation of compensation and benefits to employees in return for the effort and contributions they make to the achievement of organisational objectives. It interacts with the performance appraisal process when judgements are made about the adequacy of employee performance and how it should be rewarded.

Rewards can be divided into intrinsic and extrinsic components. Extrinsic rewards—e.g., money and other material benefits—originate from sources that are outside, or external to the individual. By contrast, intrinsic rewards may be described as feelings of achievement, responsibility, or personal growth (which were discussed in connection with motivation theory in Chapter 4). The visibility of extrinsic rewards is pronounced when managers use compensation packages in influencing subordinates to improve performance. Though less visible, intrinsic rewards come to the fore when the redesign of jobs leads to a situation whereby opportunities are created for the enjoyment of intrinsic rewards.

Purpose and philosophy

The purpose of the reward system is to attract, retain, and motivate qualified employees. An overall philosophy governing compensation or reward systems is as follows (Moorhead & Griffin, 2004):

• fair and equitable rewards;
• a recognition of the importance of each employee's contribution to the organisation, although in practice it is difficult to measure these contributions in an objective way; and

• the compensation package on offer must be competitive in the external employment market in order to attract and retain competent staff (Boyd & Salamin, 2001).

Although these statements can be taken as a guiding philosophy, an organisation must develop a philosophy of compensation based on its own needs and the conditions prevailing in the organisation. With an eye on more operational issues, a well-developed philosophical statement is likely to include the purpose of the system, offer a framework for making compensation decisions, and endeavour to accommodate relevant variables, such as labour market conditions, general economic conditions, changing technology, and equal opportunities. (There is comment on the importance of equal opportunities—pay parity in a gender context—in Panel 18.1). Apart from accommodating the relevant variables mentioned above, there should be some indication of the type of behaviour or performance—e.g., effective contributions, attendance, loyalty, and conformity—to be encouraged by the reward system. Rewards convey meanings, and, apart from their objective significance in terms of size or relative importance, they also possess symbolic value.

Determination of rewards

Traditionally, many extrinsic reward systems have been determined by collective bargaining whereby management and employee representatives (usually trade union officials) negotiate wage rates for large groups of employees. This approach to wage determination often relied on a technique known as job evaluation, which was used to determine the relationship between jobs and to establish a systematic structure of wage rates for those jobs. It is concerned with internal relativities. This means that individuals undertaking the same type of work would receive equal rewards. Job evaluation is only concerned with the assessment of the job, not the performance of the job occupant, and it should only take place after a reliable job description has been prepared. Job evaluation measures differences between jobs, which are then placed in appropriate groups in rank order.

PANEL 18.1: Equal opportunities and rewards

Back in the mid-1990s pay parity between male and female workers was raised as an issue when the Equal Opportunities Commission (EOC) said that the UK government was failing to implement European Community law on equal pay. Ministers in the Conservative government at that time denied that Britain was dragging its feet over implementing equal pay legislation, and pointed out that the equal pay issue should be placed in a wider perspective. For example, they said that the UK's flexible deregulated labour market helped to create the biggest female job market in Europe, and women in the UK were less likely to be unemployed in a recession than men. Also, the costs of pay parity should be considered in the context of job creation.

The equal pay concept was widened by a 1975 European Community Directive, which stated that it was no longer the aim to ensure that men and women received the same pay for doing the same or similar jobs; there was also to be equal pay for work of equal value. To operationalise the latter could be difficult. This was not helped by the UK law on equal pay, the wording of which was considered imprecise. A number of "equal value" claims, where women felt disadvantaged, were heard before Industrial Tribunals (Goodhart, 1994; Taylor, 1993).

Recent research commissioned by the EOC in the UK showed that a woman graduate aged 22 to 24 is likely to earn 15% less than a man with the same degree in the same subject (Eaglesham, Turner, & Guthrie, 2004). The inequality of pay between men and women is compounded by motherhood, particularly for women in lower-skilled jobs. According to the EOC, more than one-third of the pay gap stems from the problems women face juggling childcare and paid work. The EOC also mentions other causes for the pay gap between men and women as (i) discrimination, (ii) occupational segregation (meaning, for example, that more women are employed as low-paid care assistants than as higher earning plumbers), and (iii) the unequal impact of responsibility for other people—e.g., elderly relatives (Brisco, 2004).

The older the age group studied, the wider the gender pay gap becomes. This is partly because older women are more likely to have spent time out of the labour market caring for children or elderly dependants. There is also a generational factor. While the gender pay gap with respect to educational qualifications has closed in recent years, the difference is still significant between men and women over 40 years old.

The British Prime Minister—Tony Blair—is reported as being committed to equal pay for men and women, as part of "a fair deal for all at work". Measures taken in an attempt to honour this commitment are in the policy pipeline. A Commission on Women and Work—the Prosser Commission—is due to report to the Prime Minister in 2005. It has been given the brief to consider measures to tackle the pay gap between the sexes, including a statutory requirement for employers to carry out regular pay audits (Eaglesham et al., 2004).

Schemes of job evaluation can be classified as quantitative or nonquantitative.

Quantitative approach

The quantitative approach consists of (a) factor comparison and (b) points rating.

Factor comparison. A first step is to identify landmark jobs within the organisation. These are well-known jobs that are currently compensated at an appropriate rate. The landmark jobs are analysed with a view to establishing the extent to which they draw on certain job factors, such as mental requirements, physical requirements, responsibility, and so on. The overall pay applicable to the landmark jobs is apportioned to each factor depending on the importance of the factor to each job. For example, if mental requirements (e.g., knowledge, skill, complexity) has a job factor weighting of 70%, then 70% of the pay attached to the landmark job will be allotted to mental requirements. The next phase of the evaluation process is to engage in a comparative exercise whereby the other jobs (nonlandmark jobs) are examined to establish how they relate to the chosen job factors. These jobs are placed on a job comparison scale that makes use of the landmark jobs, and the pay rates attached to them, as anchors.

Points rating. This procedure, once widely used, requires an analysis of factors common to all jobs. The factors it uses include skill, responsibility, complexity, and decision making. Each factor is given a score from a range of points (minimum to maximum) and this depends on how demanding it is. The weighting a factor receives is determined by the number of points allocated to it and results in its relative importance in the hierarchy of jobs. It requires a lot of preparation and effort to operationalise this procedure.

Nonquantitative approach

The nonquantitative approach consists of (a) ranking and (b) job classification.

Ranking. This procedure involves comparing jobs on the basis of, for example, knowledge/skill, discretionary features of decision making, and task complexity, and then arranging the jobs in order of importance or value, together with the appropriate level of pay.

Job classification. Jobs are placed into a number of grades, bearing in mind differences within jobs on the basis of knowledge/skill, responsibility, training, type of decision making, and so on. The job classification procedure, with a predetermined number of grades and with a pay structure to match, is relatively straightforward and inexpensive.

Another approach

A more recent development is the single factor approach called "competence and skill analysis". To operationalise this approach would require in the first instance an analysis of the competencies or skill requirements of a job, and then establishing whether the individual's competencies are relevant to the needs of the organisation. This approach has particular value in situations where the application of skills has a material bearing on outcomes, as in the case of scientific and professional staff, and could be suited to modern conditions of flatter organisational structures where there is an emphasis on flexibility, multi-skilling, and teamwork.

Advantages and disadvantages of job evaluation

As you would expect, there are both advantages and disadvantages of traditional job evaluation (Armstrong, 2003). As to the advantages, it is said to be an objective, logical, and fair (free of managerial influence) approach to the determination of a pay structure. It is said that job evaluation is often viewed favourably by industrial tribunals as a visible mechanism for underpinning a reward system.

As to disadvantages, problems could arise if it is found that the evaluators are not objective in carrying out the process. Also, it could be costly to install and maintain the system after it is implemented. In connection with maintenance of the system, extra expenditure could be incurred if job upgradings arise as a result of the evaluation process, but savings on downgradings may not follow where protected grade status exists for current employees.

The rigidity of job evaluation systems and the underlying attitudes have been subjected to criticisms (Wickens, 1987). It is felt they result in a level of bureaucracy that runs counter to the notion of flexibility and adaptability ingrained in HRM thinking. Job evaluation operates on the assumption that there is a collection of tasks performed by a job occupant working in a stable reporting relationship in a traditional bureaucratic organisation. But as new organisational forms emerge, such as delayering and flattening of structures, employees will be required to be more flexible and versatile in the work domain. This rules out a "demarcation of jobs" mentality and introduces a recognition of the need for flexible job descriptions and acceptance of frequent changes to job boundaries.

Another disadvantage of traditional job evaluation systems is that these systems dispense a uniform rate of pay to workers at a particular grading irrespective of their performance. While it may seem equitable to offer the same reward to different individuals doing the same job on a particular grade, one has to recognise the possibility of variations in their performance.

Finally, Murlis and Fitt (1991), both of Hay Management Consultants, provide a spirited defence of job evaluation. Though they recognise that job evaluation is not a wholly scientific process, its true value can be seen as a means of "improving objectivity in the management of vertical and lateral job relativities" with respect to pay. They conclude that the need for defensible pay decisions, based on well-implemented job evaluation schemes, will not go away.

External influences

The internal relativities emphasis outlined above is becoming less important when grappling with the determination of rewards. It appears that external market and environmental conditions are now of greater importance. Over the past 25 years the power of trade unions has been weakened by legislation in the UK. For example, the system of the "closed shop" where everybody doing a particular job that is covered by a trade union agreement is required to join the union, is now illegal. A large number of employers have taken steps to move away from collective bargaining systems to more individual-based systems (e.g., performance-related pay, which is discussed later).

External competitiveness, rather than internal equity (which is associated with job evaluation schemes), is a major consideration when it comes to the determination of rewards. This can be seen when companies adopt market-driven reward systems where the rate for the job reflects the rate required to attract recruits rather than the rate determined by an internal grading structure based on job evaluation.

Companies can draw on a number of sources of information on the levels of pay and employment conditions offered by competing organisations in the labour market. These include official national statistics on incomes and economic data, income data services from private agencies, company surveys where personnel or HR specialists seek information on compensation packages from their counterparts in other organisations, data from a network of organisations committed to the exchange of information on a frequent basis, and data collected from external job advertisements and from external candidates applying for vacant positions within the organisation. It is important to compare like with like and not to rely on a mere job title. Before getting involved in comparative analysis it is important to be guided by a reliable job description.

Types of reward

Both direct and indirect compensation packages could incorporate a diverse range of rewards. A direct compensation package might include the following rewards:

- time rates;
- payment by results;

- bonus and profit sharing;
- gain sharing;
- stock option plans and long-term compensation;
- stock ownership plans;
- performance-related pay;
- skill-based pay; and
- flexible benefit system.

Time rates

A payment system based on **time rates** relates to the number of hours worked, and is common in collective bargaining. Time rates can be classified as an hourly rate, a weekly wage, or a monthly salary. Normally, part-time workers receive an hourly rate. As we saw earlier, the result of job evaluation is putting grades to jobs, and each grade has a particular level of pay attached to it. Often within a grade there is an incremental scale, which employees move along on the basis of one point each year until the maximum of the scale is reached. However, within the incremental scale there is normally a bar that has to be successfully negotiated before progression can continue. Other considerations are the amount of overlap between each grade, and movement from one grade to another. The time rates system rewards experience rather than performance. For example, the employee receives an incremental award, normally on an annual basis, for serving time in the job.

A stated advantage of the time rates system is that it is open to inspection and is equitable in the sense that employees doing the same job will be on the same grade, though there could be differences in income because of employees being on different points on the incremental scale. Other advantages are that the system is relatively easy to administer, it does not emphasise quantity of output to the detriment of quality, and it encourages the retention of staff by creating stability when people realise that gradual increases in rewards materialise as a result of progression within grades.

Although advantages accrue to piece rates because of the likelihood of productivity gains due to growing employee competence with the passing of time, in practice there is little motivation for a member of staff to increase their productivity. For example, a worker who receives £400 a week under a time rate system increases his or her productivity by 50%. This outcome is of economic advantage to the organisation but there is no monetary return to the employee. This raises the question of why an individual should raise performance if good and bad performers on a particular grade receive the same pay. Also, our notion of progression up a hierarchy of grades by way of career development will have to be revised in the light of delayering and flatter organisational structures.

The spotlight was put on time rates in the UK in 1999 with the establishment of the national minimum wage, when the government set the adult rate at £3.60 an hour. Recently the government announced that from October 2005 the rate is to be increased to £5.05 an hour. This rate applies to most workers in the UK, including home workers, commission workers, part-time workers, casual workers, and piece-rate workers. Initially the Inland Revenue and the Contributions Agency were charged with ensuring that the minimum wage was paid to employees, and the Low Pay Commission monitors how the system operates in practice. Refusing to pay the national minimum wage is a criminal offence, which can result in a substantial fine, and dismissing a worker because he or she is eligible for the national minimum wage will count as unfair dismissal.

According to Income Data Services, increasing numbers of employers are setting pay rates for the lower paid above the official minimum wage in order to maintain a competitive advantage in hiring staff. Established UK retailers, such as Tesco, Marks & Spencer, and Dollond and Aitchison, pay rates well above the national minimum wage (Turner, 2004a), but recently the body representing employers in the UK—the Confederation of British Industry (CBI)—has asked the Low Pay Commission to consider freezing the level of the minimum wage in October 2005 and not raising the adult rate above £5 until 2006. The CBI's position is in sharp contrast to that of the Trades Union Congress, which suggests that the 2005 rise should be a higher percentage increase than the increase in 2004 (Moules, 2004a).

The importance of pay as a reward is highlighted in Panel 18.2

Payment by results

One way to address the criticisms of the time rate system is to introduce a **payment by results** system (PBR). This system links pay to the quantity of the individual's output. A forerunner of PBR is the piece-work system where pay is linked to the number of units of work produced, and this was common in manufacturing industry. For example, if the piece rate is £1 per unit and a worker produces 200 units of output the income received is £200. Any figure above or below 200 units would lead to more than or less than £200. Another example of a PBR scheme is the commission received by sales representatives, which depends on sales volume.

The justification for PBR schemes would embrace the following. The employee is motivated to put in extra effort because by doing so he or she will receive additional income. Although there is an absence of overall equity in the sense that not everybody doing the same job will receive the same level of income, there is a sense of fairness in that the level of reward is related to the level of production. Also, there are likely to be cost advantages as wages are directly linked to production, and as a consequence less supervision is required.

It is possible that PBR schemes associated with the individual will stimulate the quantity of output, but management must be on its guard in case increased output is at the expense of quality. An example of the adverse impact on quality is the dramatic increase in the scrap rate following an increase in a PBR worker's output in a factory. Therefore, if there is a PBR scheme in operation, there are obvious advantages in having quality control mechanisms in place. Other difficulties that might arise are that certain jobs may not lend themselves to the measurement of output, safety standards may be compromised because of the drive to increase production, and problems could arise if the PBR scheme is viewed by workers as a device to obtain greater effort from them without commensurate reward.

Because of the importance of pay in compensation packages, it warrants further attention. For many people pay is the most important organisational reward, and its importance is reflected in the attention the salaries of senior executives received during the boom conditions of recent years. It indicates comparative worth, and adjustments to pay can be viewed as a source of satisfaction or dissatisfaction.

On the question of openness, most pay systems rest somewhere between complete secrecy and complete openness. An open system may clarify the relationship between pay and performance, but of course it is important for managers (because of the motivational implications) to defend the system to those who are paid less. In a secret system, employees tend to overestimate co-workers' pay, and this can cause motivational problems (Garvey, 2002; Lawler, 1981).

The applicability of participation has been raised in connection with pay systems. A group of appropriate people, including human resource experts and employees, might discuss and vote on the pay of other employees; a manager's pay might be determined by a group of peers; and employees might set their own pay based on their perceptions of their performance (Lawler, 1981). Allowing individuals and work groups to set their own wages or salaries may not be appropriate for all organisations, but it might be successful in organisations characterised by a climate of trust, joint problem solving, and a participative leadership style. When conditions get tough, pay is likely to be centrally determined by those who hold the purse strings.

It is said that pay is used frequently as an organisational reward because it possesses certain optimal characteristics, such as the following (Lawler, 1981):

- *Importance*. A good reward should be valued by its recipients. There is no doubt that pay is important to most people.
- *Flexibility*. The size of a reward should be flexible. For example, it is easy to adjust the size of an increase in salary, but taking a proportionate part of a reward would not apply to, for example, promotions.
- *Frequency*. Pay can be used as a reward relatively frequently without losing its worth, but some rewards, such as verbal praise, can lose their value if used repeatedly.
- *Visibility*. The relationship between a reward and performance must be obvious to ensure that a reward is effective. Because of the visibility of pay, employees can easily see the relationship between pay and their own performance.

There is a general perception that performance and pay are closely related. However, in one survey this view was challenged when it was found that only 22% of US workers had faith in the link between hard work and the payment received (Lawler, 1984). But one has to acknowledge that hard work may not always lead to accomplishments of a high order, and anyway reality is studded with forces likely to undermine the employee's best intentions. These include uncooperative colleagues, unanticipated interruptions, and faulty equipment.

Finally, it is important that if success is to be achieved, the following should be noted: that PBR schemes are well conceived; that it is possible to undertake work measurement and output measurement; that good prior employee consultation and communication take place; and that there is a healthy rapport between management and workers (Cannel & Long, 1991).

Bonus and profit sharing

A bonus could be based on the performance of a unit or organisation, and profit sharing could amount to a distribution of a proportion of profits at a predetermined rate to all employees. The original idea of profit sharing was that costs could be made variable by linking pay to profits. With profit-related pay employees reap the rewards in good times and share the pain in bad times. It is

possible to design systems so that employees are safeguarded when profits fall. Companies can use profit-related pay as a bonus paid in addition to existing salary, or by getting employees to swap part of their salary for profit-related pay. The tendency is for these schemes to cover all or most employees as opposed to only senior grades as in the past.

Profit-related pay may not be suitable for all companies. The companies that have little to gain from such schemes are those with very low-paid workers, who pay little tax, or where profits are so volatile that they are impossible to predict. Some companies steer clear of profit-related pay because they prefer incentive schemes based on individual rather than group performance.

Finally, it is interesting to note a conclusion from a study conducted by the Economic and Social Research Council in the UK: annual bonuses paid to chief executives lack disclosure and are poorly linked to company performance (Tucker, 2004).

Gain sharing

This scheme could amount to passing on to employees income or benefits as a result of reductions in costs, or arising from ideas related to improvements. It is viewed as a variable pay scheme in the category of a group incentive plan and has received a fair amount of attention, particularly in large manufacturing plants in the USA where unions are strong (Gomez-Mejia, Welbourne, & Wiseman, 2000). The amount of money allocated to this incentive scheme is unpredictable and is determined by improvements in the productivity of the group or section from one period of time to another. By focusing on productivity gains rather than profits, the incentive plan recognises worker contributions which are less influenced by external factors, and therefore the gains can be passed on to employees irrespective of the profitability of the organisation.

Stock option plans and long-term compensation

A stock (or share) option plan could amount to setting aside a block of shares in the company for employees to purchase at a reduced rate, in the belief that employee shareholding at preferential rates leads to extra commitment and more effort, which in turn can be reflected in an increase in the value of the shares. Over the last few years disquiet has been expressed about stock option plans. In an editorial in the *Financial Times* as long ago as August 1999, there was a general criticism of share option schemes as constituted at that time:

> It was suggested that options are a potential claim on the company's future profits and so reduce the payouts available to the other shareholders. Unless they are associated with genuine superior performance, the effect must be to dilute the value of the company's shares. If shareholders could see

how much option schemes were costing them, they would no doubt insist on tighter performance criteria for triggering options. These have become notoriously lax. In many cases executives get big rewards if their companies do no more than keep pace with the average growth of the economy.

Long-term compensation refers to management receiving substantial additional income from share price performance, return on capital, earnings per share, or a combination of these. This method of compensation could be a source of controversy because of the large sums involved and the basis of the payments. More recent observations on stock options and long-term compensation appear in Panel 18.3.

Stock ownership plans

In addition to stock option plans, there are **stock ownership plans** where employees own some stock in their companies. Stock ownership plans are said to promote employee satisfaction (Buchko, 1993), provided employees have the opportunity to experience psychologically a sense of ownership of the company. To satisfy this condition it is claimed that employees have to be regularly briefed on the health of the business and are able to exercise influence through a participative decision process (Pierce & Furo, 1990).

Performance-related pay

This phenomenon is concerned with the explicit link between financial reward and individual, group, or company performance (Johnson, 1998). It goes beyond a narrow definition of pay (e.g., time rates) and subscribes to a broad interpretation of financial rewards ranging from pay incentives and bonuses to profit sharing and equity share schemes. Unlike the payment by results schemes considered earlier, **performance-related pay** (PRP) considers not only results or output but also the actual behaviour of the employee in the job. Examples of rewards linked to performance are a lump sum, or a bonus as a percentage of basic salary, or accelerated movement up a pay scale.

PANEL 18.3: Share options and long-term incentives

In the 1990s the use of share options by directors of large companies, particularly the privatised companies in the UK, was a contentious issue. But there was often a reluctance on the part of institutional investors to criticise even the most staggering rewards of company directors if they experienced a dramatic increase in their investments. These rewards were felt to be inadequately related to management performance and sent a poor signal to employees who were not included in the scheme. It is acknowledged that not enough was done to ensure that the benefits of success were widely shared throughout the workforce. If we require creative contributions from all employees in contemporary organisations, why can't we share benefits, rather than bonuses or stock option benefits going to the few.

In the late 1990s Safeway—now part of Morrison's, the supermarket chain—was intent on providing share option schemes for the many. The company granted share options to all permanent employees based on the number of hours they worked. The share options were normally to be exercisable between 3 and 6½ years from the date they were granted, and of course employees benefited as the share price rose. An innovative feature of this scheme was that the size of the share options granted each year depended on the customer care performance of the store each employee had worked in over the previous 12 months.

Generally, there is a growing feeling that share option schemes should be reserved for exceptional performance and not for meeting the requirements of a normal job.

Following the Greenbury Report in 1995, long-term incentive plans (L Tips) have been viewed as an alternative to share option schemes for senior executives. They can profit from the sale of shares granted as share options 3 years later if targets (e.g., earnings per share measured against a comparator group of companies) are met.

In 1997 the chairman of Unilever expressed doubts about the usefulness of L Tips if the stock market turned bearish (i.e. share values fall). Some US companies adjust the terms of their stock option schemes (i.e., the price at which the option is exercised is reduced), particularly when the stock option is the main form of remuneration and where share prices proved more volatile than the market at large (e.g., Apple Computer).

Unilever put forward a revised share option scheme, where company performance will be based on the real growth of the business and the value created above the rate of inflation, rather than merely relying on performance relative to other companies forming the comparator group.

The results of a 2004 survey on executive directors' pay, undertaken by Deloitte and Touche in the UK, indicate that a number of companies are cutting back on share option schemes as changes in accounting rules, pressure from shareholders, and weak equity markets have combined to make this system of remuneration less attractive. The survey also shows that only 20% of pay schemes introduced in the past year were share option plans, compared with 60% in the same survey 3 years ago. Overall, 83% of FTSE 100 companies had share option plans in place, down 10% from a year earlier.

Companies tend to be moving towards other forms of incentive pay, including deferred bonuses or performance share plans where stocks are awarded to directors or senior executives only if certain benchmarks are met, rather than granting share options the worth of which is entirely dependent on the movement in the share price. The new international accounting standard on share options, which came into force in January 2005, will force companies to account for the grant of share options in the profit and loss account. This is a stimulus for a lot of companies to look at their share option schemes with a view to establishing whether they are getting value for money. The rethink of share option schemes has also been influenced by the reaction of shareholders, who view them as an expensive and inefficient way to reward executive performance that may not be related in a significant way to share price movement. Also the weakness of the market for equities in the past few years has reduced the value of previously granted share options, and this could be another justification for dispensing with their use.

(Beattie, 2004; Donkin, 1998b; Fitzgerald, 1997; Hampson, 1998; Waters, 1998)

The key fact for managers to remember is simply that if they expect rewards to motivate performance, employees must see a clear direct link between their own job-related behaviour and the attainment of those rewards (Deckop, Mangel, & Cirka, 1999).

However, some disquiet has been expressed by shareholders who have witnessed over-generous compensation packages for senior executives who have presided over operations where success is conspicuously absent. They would almost certainly concur with the following sentiments (*Financial Times*, 1993):

One of the yardsticks against which top people's remuneration packages should be judged is whether the directors feel the pinch when the company underperforms. Yet a study this week from Income Data Services confirms once again that the balance between risk and reward in the typical executive contract is all too often weighted in favour of the director against the company and its shareholders.

The single most important objective of performance-related pay is to improve performance by retargeting the remuneration system so that it is more sensitive and responsive to a company's and an employee's needs. The achievement of this objective would necessitate the nurturing of a performance-oriented culture that stresses pay for results, not effort, and rewarding the right people (whereby the high rewards go to those who merit them). Due consideration has to be given to group performance where teamwork is necessary, as well as to individual performance. It is obvious that the setting of performance standards and the quality of the appraisal process are critical for the success of performance-related pay systems.

There is some evidence to suggest that individually based bonus schemes, relying on objective measures of performance, promote business success, efficiency, and gratification of some individual needs (Brading & Wright, 1990; Lawler, 1977). But we are advised by Lawler (1977) to dwell on some of the negative effects generated by such schemes. These are likely to include the danger of individuals with superior performance being ostracised, and performance reports being falsified. Halligan (1997), on the basis of empirical evidence, attacks individual-based performance-related pay schemes. These schemes seemed to have encouraged Inland Revenue staff only to look after themselves, which can be counter-productive. It was felt that these schemes generated much resentment as staff faced conflict between the quantity and quality of their work. Some 60% of respondents felt that individual performance targets were imposed by managers, rather than being the outcome of discussion. Other evidence seems to underline the importance of good administration of performance-related pay schemes, and ensuring rewards are competitive (i.e., external comparability in the determination of rewards).

Exponents of group and organisation-wide performance-related pay schemes refer to the greater sense of cooperation rather than competition among employees that such schemes create —e.g., sharing information with other team members, training new colleagues, helping resolve group conflict, and encouraging the development of skills of use to the group. Halligan (1997) felt that group-based schemes rather than individual-based schemes may have greater effect.

Lawler (1977) is emphatic in stressing that there is no single best pay incentive plan, that each situation must be examined in terms of its unique characteristics, and that it is possible to have multiple or overlapping plans. In a later publication, Lawler (1984) seems to favour profit sharing, share ownership, and gain sharing as rewards that have good motivational implications for both managerial and nonmanagerial staff.

The following are characteristics associated with a successful performance-related pay scheme (Brading & Wright, 1990):

* Business objectives have to be translated into meaningful performance criteria for individuals and groups, and it must be possible to be able to appraise performance in an objective way.
* Individual performance plans, or specific targets related to group or company performance, must be clearly stated and communicated at the outset. This can prove difficult where qualitative contributions are assessed.
* Jobs must be defined in ways that convey clear meaning to individuals and the company.
* For the scheme to be taken seriously and produce the desired motivational impact, significant rewards must be on offer.
* There must be sufficient differentials between levels of performance rating, otherwise high performers are inadequately rewarded and average performers are insufficiently motivated to improve.

Finally, training is required to ensure that the total process of setting performance standards, appraising performance, and allocating rewards is handled properly. The evidence supporting the pay–performance equation is not conclusive. In a meta-analysis of a large number of studies it was concluded that there was a small positive correlation between financial rewards and quantity of output, but this did not extend to the quality of output where no impact was detected (Jenkins, Gupta, Mitra, & Shaw, 1998).

Additional observations on performance-related pay (PRP) appear in Panel 18.4 where the appeal

---

PANEL 18.4: Appeal of performance-related pay (PRP)

The following could account for the appeal of PRP schemes:

* PRP emits a powerful signal for a broad change of business culture.
* It symbolises moves towards individualising employer/employee relations.
* The scope to reward people through promotions becomes more difficult as organisations become flatter (after removing layers of management). Therefore, PRP and a widening of pay scales, is one solution to their problem.
* A number of companies make savings in salaries when automatic increments on pay scales are abolished following the introduction of PRP.
* People making a substantial contribution in their job get a better deal than poor performers.
* People making an excellent contribution at a particular level do not have to be promoted to a level where they may not be equally effective in order to secure greater financial benefits.
* PRP, unlike a piece-rate system, takes into account factors that are not easily quantifiable, such as commitment and initiative.
* There is less opportunity for workers to get together to relate their output to pay, in the way they were able to do with piece-work schemes—the latter was the basis of the strength of shop stewards in industries such as vehicle manufacturing.
* The appeal of PRP is that it is determined by subjective managerial judgement following employee appraisal rather than by market forces, and often there is a ceiling on the budget allocated to PRP. In some companies PRP is not set at the same time as the appraisal of performance to enable a discussion of strengths and weaknesses to take place when pay is not directly an issue. Even though PRP is influenced by the annual appraisal, it is not determined by it.

(Goodhart, 1993; Wood, 1993)

PANEL 18.5: Movement towards performance-based pay in Japan

Traditionally Japanese companies guaranteed employees a monthly salary as well as a twice-yearly bonus, equivalent to about 5 months of annual pay. In recent years Japan suffered badly from its worst economic recession in post-war history. In this climate some companies have moved towards performance-based pay. This trend signals ending pay based on age and experience, and the beginning of a meritocratic system. A first move seems to be cutting the bonuses, and then supplementing the reduced bonus with an additional amount determined by performance. In 1995 Fujitsu went down the meritocracy path by paying employees according to performance. Employees were evaluated against pre-established goals, and the evaluation determined the bonus to pay.

It appears that there is a modest movement towards remunerating top executives on the basis of performance through the use of share option schemes. But executives in Japan do not enjoy the generous rewards of their Western counterparts. In Japan one encounters a more egalitarian spirit, manifest in the sharing of corporate profits equally. For example, the percentage increase in the income of the chief executive in Japan is likely to be in line with the rise in the income of the ordinary worker. The introduction of stock options may signal changes in attitudes, but developments in performance-based rewards are likely to be gradual and hesitant.

(Nakamoto, 1998; Nusbaum, 1999)

---

of PRP is given prominence, and there is specific reference to the Japanese experience in Panel 18.5. As a postscript to the discussion, consider the following provocative views that challenge the value of incentives (Kohn, 1993, 1998). Kohn maintains that the rationale for performance-related pay rests on a mistaken view of what motivates people:

* Pay occupies a dubious position as a motivator, and generally there is too much emphasis on financial rewards.

* Financial rewards secure at best only short-term compliance.
* Financial rewards do not change attitudes that underlie behaviour or commitment to any task, they merely alter them temporarily.
* The link between top managers' pay and company performance is not proven, and this still applies when qualitative as opposed to quantitative measures of performance are used.
* The more complicated the task in cognitive terms the more ineffective are financial rewards as a motivating force.

- Incentive schemes undermine cooperation between employees, and encourage subordinates to engage in obsequious behaviour. They can also undermine intrinsic motivation.
- Reliance on the use of financial rewards to solve a problem masks reality. Money is thrown at a problem as opposed to striving for people-centred solutions, such as trusting people, and offering them autonomy and support.
- Incentive schemes discourage people from using their imagination and cause them to display less enthusiasm about their work. They also minimise challenge, encouraging employees to refrain from taking risks; hence, the first casualty of financial reward is creativity.
- The dispensing of financial rewards encourages a narrow focus that highlights the relationship between the rewards and job performance, and this can lead to the falsification of records to secure rewards.
- Even when incentive schemes are group-based rather than individual-based, active employee involvement in the organisation is thin on the ground.
- When incentive schemes are well established there is an inclination for managers and supervisors to exercise relatively less leadership.

Kohn's preferred strategy is for companies to enhance the quality of job content for employees, allow them to share in decision making, and to create a climate of support. Though this appears to be a firm endorsement of the value of intrinsic motivation, he believes that extrinsic motivation also has a part to play, in the sense that monetary rewards should be provided at an adequate level. (Refer to Chapter 4 to refresh your knowledge of motivation theory.)

Skill-based pay

Skill-based or competency-based pay is determined by the range of the expertise of the employee (e.g., the number of skills acquired or the number of tasks that can be undertaken!) (Murray & Gerhart, 1998). It allows employees to improve

their earnings without having had a promotion. For example, if employees working on the factory floor extend the range of their skills to incorporate, say, maintenance duties, quality inspection, and perhaps the exercise of some supervisory skills, they could obtain additional income. Therefore, it encourages employees to acquire a broader range of skills, which enhances their flexibility in an era of new organisational forms where there is a need for more generalists and fewer specialists. By broadening their job perspective people can dilute a mindset of insularity and gain a better understanding of other employees' jobs; this creates conditions supportive of communication across the organisation. Skill-based payment schemes have been considered beneficial in terms of job satisfaction and performance (Lawler, Ledford, & Chang, 1993).

As regards downsides, in skill-based pay we are paying for the acquisition of skills, and a problem could arise if the acquired skills become obsolete or are no longer required. Robbins (2003) makes an additional observation: maybe employees could be overwhelmed by the experience of continual learning/growth and pay increases.

Skill-based pay has significance in the context of learning and motivation theory. It acts as a reinforcer in the encouragement of continuous learning, broadening one's perspective as a generalist and relating to others. By enlarging the skill base of the employee the person could experience challenge and achievement, a state compatible with content theories of motivation (e.g., motivators) where psychological growth features prominently. On another motivational front, skills could be considered an important input in the context of equity theory.

Flexible benefit system

A cafeteria or flexible benefit system places the spotlight on giving choice to employees when faced with a number of benefit options. As such this system has relevance in the context of the expectancy theory of motivation because it allows employees to select a reward system that fits their individual needs. Employees can consider their needs and their particular circumstances before

---

PANEL 18.6: Flexible work options

At Price Waterhouse (now PriceWaterhouseCoopers), a large international firm of chartered accountants and management consultants with offices in the UK, a flexible benefits scheme allowed employees to give up part of their salary in exchange for extra holiday. The scheme, together with a collection of family-friendly policies, was responsible for the firm getting a best practice award in 1998. The award came from Opportunity 2000, the business-led campaign to increase women's participation in the workforce.

The flexible benefits system was introduced in 1997 because the firm recognised in the mid-1990s that it was losing too many women. But the system was designed to appeal to all staff. By way of example, a manager in the firm opted for the following: 5 days of extra holiday to move house, a company car, extra death and long-term sickness benefits, and supermarket vouchers to cut the cost of her shopping. However, she did not opt for a pension because of the attractive pension benefits enjoyed by her husband. She also benefited from the firm's flexible working arrangements, which allow her to spend school holidays with her three children. In another case one of the benefits taken by an employee was childcare vouchers, used to meet the cost of a day nursery.

Before the scheme was introduced in the UK there was widespread consultation with employees. It should be recognised that schemes like this one are complex and take time to become established because of cultural constraints.

(Maitland, 1998)

---

selecting the appropriate benefit package from a menu of benefit options. The flexible benefit system is a departure from the traditional model of a single system of remuneration for everybody (Meyer, 2000). The major rationale for the flexible system is that the traditional programmes do not meet the needs of today's more diverse workforce —e.g., single people, double income families, etc. (Barber, Dunham, & Formisano, 1992). A flexible system in the UK could consist of pay, company car, additional holiday entitlement, private health insurance, membership of social clubs, modification to working hours, mortgage loan subsidies, and other benefits. An illustration appears in Panel 18.6. Though flexible benefit systems can be complex and costly to run, they have value in recruiting and retaining staff.

A large number of the incentive schemes discussed in this section are normally designed to provide extra income for certain types of performance. Apart from the direct incentives already referred to, there are other benefits—on-the-job and off-the-job benefits—which are found in indirect compensation systems. On-the-job benefits could refer to payment for time associated with lunch breaks, rest periods, and tea breaks, whereas off-the-job benefits refer to vacations, sick leave, holidays, and so on. Other indirect benefits include contributions to life and health insurance cover, and occupational pension schemes. In addition, there could be special privileges—e.g., use of the

company's accommodation or transport—or rewards for certain types of accomplishment.

TRAINING AND DEVELOPMENT

Learning and training

In Chapter 7 training was described as the transfer of learning. (You may wish to refer to the brief introduction to training in Chapter 7 before continuing reading this chapter.) Employee training can be defined as the systematic acquisition of skills, rules, concepts, or attitudes that result in improved performance on the job (Goldstein, 1986). Employee training may be very specific, as in the case of showing a trainee driver how to perform a gear change, or it may be less concrete as in training a manager to adopt a particular leadership style.

Skill acquisition

A number of factors are said to influence the acquisition of skills to perform effectively. Most of these factors were proposed following simulated training sessions, rather than real-life training situations. However, they command a certain degree of acceptance. The issues considered here are knowledge of results or feedback, part or whole methods, and massed or distributed practice.

Knowledge of results or feedback

Feedback comes from two sources—one from the external environment and one from the internal environment. The external environment could be the display section of a machine in front of an operator. The internal environment could be the operator's own muscles and nervous system. Both these sources provide continuous feedback so that, in effect, the operator is always receiving knowledge of results.

In driving a car the learner has a feel for the car while operating the clutch and accelerator pedals simultaneously (feedback from the internal environment), and receives feedback from the external environment when reading the dials on the dashboard. The driving instructor will provide augmented feedback in the form of verbal knowledge of results by telling the learner that he or she is engaged in movements that are either right or wrong. The instructor could also offer explanations to assist the learner.

Knowledge of results, preferably with appropriate comments, is important to the student on a course where continuous assessment is used, and to the business executive who wants to know how well operations are progressing, so that remedial action can be taken if necessary and objectives modified accordingly. Feedback should be precise and the trainee should be given adequate time to assimilate it (Rogers, 1974). Feedback should be appropriate to the stage of learning that the learner has reached, and it should concentrate on those aspects of the task that are critical for good performance. A trainee can become very dependent on feedback, and removing it could cause a deterioration in performance. This would be particularly so if its removal took place early on in learning. (The concept of feedback is also considered in the context of cognitive learning in Chapter 7.)

Part or whole methods

Using the part method the task is broken down into sections, and this method is suitable where learning does not suffer from compartmentalising a body of knowledge. So, if the task lends itself to chunking, and where some elements of the task are more difficult than others and require more time to be devoted to practising them, this can be a useful method.

Typing is an example of an activity best learned by this method, where each letter is practised on the keyboard before attempting whole words. Likewise with swimming, where the components of breathing, arm stroke, and kicking are practised separately at first. Though the part method may appear appropriate for the actor learning the lines of a long play, and it may have beneficial motivational effects in the sense that the learner can reach the learning objective more quickly, it has disadvantages. For example, in linking the parts to form the whole the learner might get the sequence mixed up.

When the whole method is used, the total task is practised until mastered. Tasks that are best learned by this method include those where integration and rhythm are the critical features of the skill. For example, some tasks, like learning to drive a car, would lose their meaning if broken into chunks. In addition, the whole method is preferable when the total task is small enough to avoid resorting to numerous rests and when the learner is quick to learn and is intelligent.

A compromise between the part and whole methods is the *progressive (cumulative) part method*, which has been used for training older workers (Belbin, 1964). The task is broken into its constituent elements; the first element is practised until mastered, when the trainee proceeds to the second element and practises it in combination with the first. When this combination is mastered the third element is added, and so on until the whole task has been learned. Older trainees often suffer from an impairment of short-term memory and, if the task is learned by the part method, the first element can be forgotten by the time the last element is learned. However, the whole method is also unsuitable because it tends to overload older trainees. The progressive (cumulative) part method attempts to prevent overload and minimises the likelihood of forgetting the earlier elements of a task by a constant process of rehearsal.

FIGURE 18.1

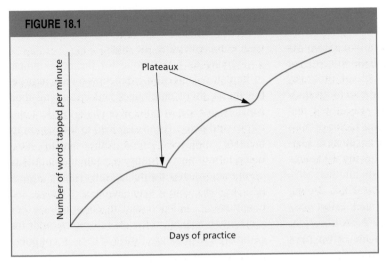

A learning curve (adapted from Bryan & Harter, 1899).

Massed or distributed practice

Should the elements of learning a task be massed together, or should they be spaced or distributed over a period of time? When the student is cramming in preparation for an examination, he or she is engaged in massed practice. In such circumstances some students could be highly motivated with less time to forget the study material. For some people, massed practice can result in boredom and fatigue and impair performance. However, this condition could be alleviated by the introduction of suitable rest pauses. (The role of rest pauses in motivated behaviour was discussed in Chapter 4.) Massed practice would appear to be particularly suited to a problem-solving exercise where it is important to persevere with the task until a solution is found.

Distributed or paced practice seems to be more beneficial for motor skill learning (e.g., typing) than for verbal or more complex learning. But as the material to be learned increases in quantity and difficulty, then paced practice has a useful function (Bass & Vaughan, 1966). In a verbal learning experiment, paced practice was found to be superior to massed practice (Hovland, 1938). Two groups of subjects learned a list of 12 nonsense syllables. One group, which adopted massed practice, had a 6-second rest between each run through the list. The other group, which adopted paced practice, had a 2-minute rest. The two groups were then given scores for the number of syllables that were reported correctly. The spaced practice group was superior to the massed practice group. It would be unwise, however, to generalise this result to all instances of verbal learning.

Learning curves

The trainer must realise that learning takes place in a piecemeal fashion along increasingly difficult paths, and this can be depicted in the form of a learning curve (shown in Figure 18.1). During the course of training, the learning curve sometimes shows a levelling off, after which it rises again. The point on the curve where little or no learning seems to be occurring was termed a plateau in a classic study of trainee telegraphists (Bryan & Harter, 1899).

One suggestion to account for the shape of the curve is that the first plateau denotes the point at which the trainees mastered the motion of tapping individual letters but had not yet progressed to tapping whole words. The second plateau denotes the point at which the trainees mastered whole words but not phrases. These plateaux were supposed to represent a period in the learning process when the skill concerned was in the process of reorganisation. This has been challenged in the light of subsequent studies in this field (e.g., Keller, 1959). It should be noted that the plateaux do not appear during the learning of all skills, but where they can be identified the trainer should take particular care in explaining to the trainees the reasons for their lack of progress, otherwise the trainees may become demotivated.

In a study of taxi drivers it was noted that driving performance improved by a factor of 50% in 7 weeks, but then it remained constant (a plateau) for 12 weeks. Over the following 10 weeks additional training brought about another 50% improvement in performance (Chisseli & Brown, 1955). When learning to drive, much effort goes into the development of hand–foot coordination. As driving proficiency increases the driver pays more attention to monitoring road conditions, predicting the reactions of other drivers, and so on.

TRAINING PROCESSES

Organisations need individuals with relevant abilities, skills, and experience in order to function well. The organisation could resort to recruitment from outside the organisation to secure the services of people with these qualities, or draw on the services of outside consultants or subcontractors. Alternatively, it could place heavy reliance on nurturing existing employees through an adequate system of training and development.

Training and development are terms that are sometimes used interchangeably. In the past, training was associated with improving the knowledge and skill of nonmanagerial employees in their present jobs, whereas development was normally reserved for managers when the organisation was looking ahead. In contemporary society such a distinction is difficult to defend because, in the age of HRM, the development of all employees is of prime importance. We have to think about development when pervasive issues such as multi-skilling, flexibility, and commitment have to be faced for all organisation members, and training for managers is a live issue when attention focuses on the current operational skills or competencies, quite apart from the qualities (e.g., personal development) associated with management

development. It now seems more appropriate to think of training and development as interactive—each complementing the other.

Training as a technique for the development of human resources is preoccupied with improving the skills of employees and enhancing their capacity to cope with the ever-changing demands of the workplace. It can also lead to the empowerment of employees. Among other benefits attributed to training are improvements in the quality of operations and output, greater safety awareness, higher levels of satisfaction, motivation, and commitment, and potential to communicate key issues with respect to the overall direction of the company (Armstrong, 2003). There is comment on various training activities undertaken by companies in Panel 18.7.

National developments

A brief historical view of training initiatives in the UK precedes putting the spotlight on the current responsible body—the Learning and Skills Council.

In the 1960s training in the UK received official endorsement with the establishment of the Industrial Training Boards. The emphasis was on off-the-job training, when it was felt necessary to specify the knowledge, skill, and attitudes required by the employee to do the job (i.e., training needs) before suggesting the ways and means of satisfying the stated needs. In order to establish whether or not the training was effective, the training outcome would be evaluated using appropriate measures. Nowadays, we would be inclined to be more rigorous in planning the training programme and specifying the training objectives or outcomes (i.e., what the trainee should be capable of doing after the training course ends).

Over the years there have been criticisms of the poor training record of the UK. The Conservative government in the 1990s felt a new initiative in the field of training ought to be introduced, because it considered the previous training initiatives (e.g., the Training Boards mentioned earlier) did not succeed due to their centralised and bureaucratic nature. Instead, the preference in the early 1990s was for was a decentralised

PANEL 18.7: Training initiatives

British Telecommunications (BT) has accepted the importance of training to support the achievement of business objectives. One of the biggest business units within BT is supplying services to corporate customers with multiple sites, and this has become a £1 billion enterprise, employing 20,000 people. But BT is eager to extract more milk from this cash cow, and is working hard to win more contracts and squeeze more revenue out of existing deals. BT felt it was losing out on the opportunity to develop further business from its existing clients. In partnership with a sales training and development consultancy, it launched a "business managers' academy", a series of workshops and programmes designed to develop the skills of its executives in building relationships with customers. The company wanted something more sophisticated than selling equipment out of a box. The introduction of new technologies, such as broadband, wideband and mobile, enabled salespeople to offer more complex solutions, and this could lead to the client outsourcing all its telecommunications to BT. The BT academy offers a range of opportunities for managers to develop their skills, with a focus on customers (Eglin, 2005).

Various training areas have been identified as important (Witzel, 2004): with war and terrorism affecting a number of regions of the world, security training remains a priority. Another area of importance is corporate governance. This is supported by recent legislation, including full implementation of the Sarbanes-Oxley Act (USA) and the European Information and Consultation Directive, and relevant employees need to be trained to be aware of the consequences.

Following a number of scandals that damaged the reputation of Citigroup, the world's largest financial services company, thousands of employees throughout the globe recently attended presentations and watched a film on the history of Citigroup. The film emphasises that the group's reputation rests on the integrity of past employees and that it is up to current employees to enhance not damage that reputation. This training initiative is related to culture change, and is supported by a number of other actions such as changes to the performance-related pay system, strengthening of internal controls, and the establishment of an "ethics hotline" for staff to give anonymous feedback on managers (Wighton, 2005).

system, with the participation of industry and commerce. Training and Enterprise Councils (TECs) and their Scottish equivalent, Local Enterprise Councils (LECs), were established as the focal point of local training initiatives.

TECs were allocated government funds, which they controlled, but they also had access to private funds. The majority of the membership of a TEC was drawn from industry and commerce, and the rest originated from the spheres of education and training, trade unions, and voluntary organisations. A TEC surveyed the local scene and took note of indicators of economic growth and skill shortages, and then prepared a training plan for submission to the Department of Education and Employment. Funds for the various training initiatives were allocated to the TEC on the basis of the plan it submitted and its track record, but much of the actual training was carried out by independent providers.

A further government initiative was the establishment of a national framework for training —National Vocational Qualifications (NVQs)— which brought into line "training" and "skills used in jobs". NVQs set various standards of performance or *competence* at work depending on the type of job. The Training Agency defined competence as the ability to perform the activities within an occupation or function to the standards expected in employment. A specific "competency" would refer to a characteristic such as an ability to communicate, to solve problems, to delegate effectively, and to act as a good team player. Training was geared towards meeting the requisite standards and was by an accredited tester who was normally a manager or supervisor qualified to act in this way. Qualifications were issued to those who were successful. NVQs gave employees the opportunity to continue developing their skills and competencies along a pathway ranging from a basic level to a higher level associated with a significant management position.

Doubts have been expressed about the extent to which the competency approach captures the required range of skills and their transferability to the work situation (McKenna & Beech, 2002). It has been recognised that although NVQs have important strengths in terms of significant employer support and the development of skills and competencies relevant to work, one major weakness is the lack of attention to the general skills of numeracy and literacy. There is no requirement for general literacy and numeracy skills to be developed and assessed to gain an NVQ award

(Steedman, 1998). According to Steedman, there should be a move towards including within the NVQ framework the literacy and numeracy skills currently outside it, and this could have the effect of motivating many adults presently low in numeracy and literacy to improve their situation.

Another initiative, administered through the TECs, was the "Investors in People" scheme (IIP). Those responsible for this scheme advised companies on how to develop their training to nationally recognised standards, and the main concern seemed to be to ensure that the proposed training supported the implementation of the corporate plan. A company had to show evidence of conducting systematic planning and review of its training programme in order to be recognised by IIP. Recognition followed after a satisfactory visit from TEC officials who evaluated the progress made by the company. At one time the employers' association (the CBI) criticised the procedures used by IIP as being too bureaucratic and the costs of the assessment process too high (Hilton, 1992), but in a report based on a 3-year government-funded study and produced by the Institute for Employment Studies, University of Sussex, it was concluded that IIP was having a positive impact in the workplace (Bolger, 1996). At that time employers saw a number of benefits springing from their involvement with IIP, as follows: a more systematic and focused approach to training based on business needs; improved employee communications; a better understanding of business among employees; and higher levels of motivation and skill among their workforce.

Finally, in recent years the British government abolished TECs and replaced them with a national learning and skills body, which gives local councils the role of coordinating and funding all work-related further education and training. The Learning and Skills Council (LSC) in the United Kingdom, with a strong business representation, replaces the TECs and the Further Education Funding Council and is set to carry out a major reform of post-16 skills and education. The LSC consists of 47 local councils or subsidiaries, which will enjoy considerable freedom to reflect local needs; but the national council—which will assume real strategic power—will oversee the work of further education and sixth form colleges, and work-based training and education.

The LSC has an ambitious plan to spend a substantial amount of money on training and teaching adults, especially those with poor basic skills needed by industry and those coming from disadvantaged areas. A priority is to tackle Britain's chronic record in adult illiteracy and innumeracy. Those with poor reading, numeracy, and writing skills will be introduced to learning via internet access points in the workplace, libraries and other public areas. It is hoped that the LSC will act as a regulator for industrial spending on training, helping to direct and increase the £20 billion plus spent privately by companies and other employers, and provide quality assurance so that companies can choose effective training schemes. Under this system multinational companies will not have to negotiate with numerous local councils or subsidiaries; instead they can go directly to the national council. This arrangement is likely to be an improvement on the old system.

Another important activity to be undertaken by LSC will be to gather high-quality intelligence data in the market-place to enable it to track skills gaps in industry (Kelly, 2000; Pike, 1999). The debate continues, and in recent times the government has outlined proposals for more and better vocational and occupational courses, and arrangements with employers to improve skills levels, with a promise of selective support for employers (Bream, 2003).

Needs assessment

The first step in the training process is to conduct a systematic assessment of training needs (to be followed by training objectives and training methods in that order). The assessment of needs can be considered at three levels of analysis (Wexley, 1984):

(1) organisation analysis;
(2) task analysis; and
(3) person analysis.

A fourth level—demographic analysis—can also be added (Latham, 1988).

Organisation analysis

In examining the aims and objectives of the organisation, particularly their implementation, it may be possible to identify barriers to their achievement as well as avenues to explore. These could include the following:

- There is poor production planning and control, unacceptable errors and waste, and poor management and work distribution.
- There is a need to upgrade skills in the light of technological advances.
- There is a belief that training has a part to play in building up the capability of the organisation to meet various challenges, such as increased local and global competition.
- Specific developments herald a need for training because of reorganisations, changes in the status of companies due to mergers, alliances, disposals of parts of the organisation, occupational obsolescence, and the emergence of new occupations due to changes in the structure of the economy and the shift from manufacturing to service industry (Bernardin & Russell, 1993).

If we feel the barriers to the achievement of organisational aims and objectives can be removed by training rather than by some other activity, then we are, in effect, taking the first step in an assessment of training needs at the organisational level.

Research in the area of organisational analysis seems to be concerned with two strands of analysis. First, there is the recognition that training should be linked to corporate strategy, and, secondly, it is suggested that organisations have an ethical responsibility to minimise the technical obsolescence of their employees (Latham, 1988). With regard to the first strand of analysis, Brown and Read (1984) make the point—which had greater relevance in the past—that the difference in productivity between UK and Japanese companies could be narrowed significantly by taking a strategic view of training policies. This would entail harmonising business and training plans. Hussey (1985) sympathised with this viewpoint when he argued that **training objectives**, particularly for management development, should be reviewed by top management when a major change in corporate direction is anticipated. Also, he believes that training should not be pursued for the improvement of the individual with the expectation that it will benefit the organisation. On the contrary, training should be undertaken for the benefit of the organisation in the realisation that this will eventually act to the advantage of the individual.

The second strand of analysis epitomises an approach to training whereby the organisation is committed to such activities as retraining workers to create a more flexible and adaptable workforce, with the added advantage of fostering corporate loyalty, training in job-search skills, and basic adult education.

Task analysis

This approach focuses on (a) the objectives and (b) the outcomes of tasks performed by employees. Tasks are broken down into their constituent elements or operations. For example, the assembly of an MFI kitchen or piece of furniture, consisting of certain main operations and a number of further operations that, in turn, are suitable for subdivision, is an example of the process involved in order to create a particular product. The latter is the outcome of the task.

The first step in task or job analysis is to make sure that existing jobs produce outcomes that are consistent with the overall goals of the organisation. Where there is a significant discrepancy, it may be necessary to redesign existing jobs or to design new jobs, to rectify the situation.

Given a suitable match between the goals of the organisation and the outcomes of tasks, the second step is concerned with identifying actual behaviours required of job holders if the required outcomes are to materialise. We have now arrived at a stage in the needs assessment process that has direct relevance to training. For example, if deficiencies in actual job behaviours are identified, this can signal the need for training. Techniques of job analysis are discussed in connection with personnel selection in Chapter 17.

Moving on from task analysis to the design of specific training programmes is one of the most challenging aspects of employee training (Goldstein, 1980). In this context it is wise to specify the knowledge, skills, and attitudes (KSAs) that employees must possess in order to perform successfully the necessary job-related behaviours identified through task analysis:

- *Knowledge* refers to evidence of having absorbed and understood items of information needed to perform adequately in the job. It can be obtained from formal education and training as well as from on-the-job experience.
- *Skills* are manifest when a person operates a machine, solves a difficult problem, and relates effectively in an interpersonal way to people, and these skills are nurtured over time.
- *Attitudes*, in this context, refer to the emotional or affective feelings and perspectives held by a person. An attitude may affect whether or not a skill is exercised in the manner prescribed. For example, a driver is capable of driving a car on the motorway—which is a skill—and is aware of the fact that the speed limit is 70 mph, but travels at 100 mph on stretches of the motorway because he or she seems to harbour unsafe attitudes.

KSAs are normally identified with the help of job experts (e.g., occupational psychologists, management consultants in this field, and managers). Training programmes can then be designed to facilitate the learning of these KSAs. There has been criticism of the KSAs. According to Arnold (2005), the use of KSAs is rather confusing. The simplistic distinction between knowledge, skills, and attitudes, though useful as an explanatory device for identifying different types of learning, is inadequate in a number of ways, particularly in drawing a fine distinction between knowledge and skill. In practice the overlap between the two can be very pronounced. He suggests that the different types of learning (called capabilities) developed by Gagne (1977), listed below, are considered more comprehensive than the list of items found in the KSAs. These capabilities are:

(1) basic learning, as found in the formation of simple associations between stimuli and responses in classical conditioning;

(2) intellectual skills, at different levels, starting with being able to distinguish between cues, then classifying objects and defining concepts, and finally seeing new relationships from existing ones;

(3) cognitive strategy, as evidenced in such activities as learning to learn;

(4) verbal information, as reflected in an ability to state specific information;

(5) perceptual motor skills, as seen in driving a car; and

(6) attitude.

Based on a study aimed at establishing the most relevant and difficult areas related to retraining, Downs (1995) maintains that the jobs of the future will require less memorising of facts and procedures, few physical skills, and far more conceptual ability. A similar stand is taken by Ford and Kraiger (1995), who argue for a more sophisticated approach to training because of the existence of more mentally taxing tasks within highly complex jobs. Such findings are relevant when considering training needs.

Person analysis

This level of the needs assessment process puts the spotlight on those who need training, as well as the type of training required. There are different ways of collecting data during this phase. Performance appraisal information could be available for those already holding down jobs. For those who are about to join the organisation, information derived from the use of selection methods could be used. Alternatively, the opinions of key individuals in the organisation could be sought, using questionnaires or interviews. Whatever method is used, it is no easy matter trying to establish who is in need of training (Latham, 1988). In fact, because of the spread of change in technology, all jobs appear to be in a state of flux; therefore, person analysis will have to focus on potential, rather than current knowledge and skill, as well as motivation (Furnham, 2001b).

Demographic analysis

The fourth level of analysis in the needs assessment process, called demographic analysis, takes a macro view in the sense that it considers the needs of populations of individuals (e.g., women, people over 50, etc.) from a policy perspective rather than from the standpoint of the individual employee within the organisation (Latham, 1988). Demographic studies have been conducted to identify the training needs of populations of workers by, for instance, age, sex, and position within the organisational hierarchy.

For example, Berryman-Fink (1985) examined the views of male and female managers on the communication and training needs of women in management. Both male and female managers identified four communication skills for which female managers needed training—assertiveness, confidence building, public speaking, and dealing with men. By contrast, male managers needed training in listening, verbal skills, nonverbal communication, empathy, and sensitivity.

Training diversity.   Having acknowledged diversity due to gender, one should point out that a rapidly expanding area of training in recent years is diversity training (Rynes & Rosen, 1994). This consists of awareness training and skill-building training. Awareness training is concerned with understanding the need for and meaning of the importance of diversity in the organisation, whereas skill-building training is aimed at getting people to recognise cultural differences in the workplace. An essential feature of diversity training is raising the level of awareness with respect to individual differences and cross-cultural issues, as well as scrutinising and challenging stereotypes. Thayer (1997) reflected on the popularity of diversity training in the USA and concluded that programmes appear to be introduced without a proper person analysis to determine people's attitudes. He feels there is a real need to establish the type of training initiatives that are effective.

Training objectives

Before formulating objectives for training, it is necessary to have conducted an assessment of training needs. This could have taken the form of, for example, task analysis, reported earlier, where a detailed view of the operation of a task is obtained. Such analysis is necessary in order to be in a position to state clearly the "outcomes" from the training programme. These outcomes will eventually manifest themselves in training objectives, which will state what the employee will be able to do at the end of the training session, and are often referred to as *behavioural objectives*. In addition, one would expect some reference to standards of performance and the conditions under which the behaviour takes place. For example, on completion of the training the trainee will be able to operate a word-processing program on a computer to a specified degree of accuracy.

In some training sessions a list of behavioural objectives does not materialise in the manner just described. Instead, competence at the end of a training session is assessed by the use of various tests or job simulation exercises. Whatever system is used (setting behavioural objectives or some other method), it is important to specify the preferred outcomes from the training programme at the outset, so that trainees are offered programmes to help them achieve the desired standard.

There are particular training situations that do not lend themselves to the setting of specific and precise objectives. In this case—for example, experiential learning exercises discussed later in this chapter—it is acceptable for objectives to be relatively general. The reason is that the learning taking place has unique significance for the individual, and each person derives different benefits from the experience.

Training methods

From what has been said it is now apparent that the training methods used should have been chosen or developed following the statement of training objectives, and not the reverse. A variety of techniques, methods, and procedures are available. These include lectures, films, videotapes, computer-assisted instruction, case studies, conferences, simulation, behaviour modelling, coaching, and mentoring.

There are a number of questions one can ask about the various techniques. Does the technique emphasise content (information), process (behaviours), or both? Where does the training occur—on-site or off-site? Does the training emphasise psychomotor skills, cognitive skills, social skills, or a combination of all three? In the final analysis, what we must try to achieve is to ensure that the technique or techniques chosen are appropriate in the light of the identified training needs.

One-way communication

Lectures in their purest form, together with videotapes and films, are examples of a one-way flow of information from the trainer to the trainees. Unless the lecturer or trainer is prepared to respond to questions and provide feedback, the lecture method requires the recipients of information to be passive, with no opportunity to assess how well or how badly they are absorbing the message that is put across. Often the motivation of the audience is taken for granted, and their individual needs and abilities are ignored, with little or no reward given. Sometimes lectures are considered quite boring and difficult to comprehend.

In defence of one-way communication through the methods described, it could be argued that these methods are efficient in the use of time and money, and are suitable for communicating substantial amounts of information to large numbers of trainees in the minimum amount of time.

Computer-assisted instruction

This is similar to programmed learning discussed in Chapter 7. Computer-assisted instruction adopts the principles of programmed instruction and adds the power and flexibility we associate with rapidly expanding computer technology. The phenomenal growth in the use of computers makes this method of training more accessible in the home and the office. The trainee can interact with the computer in the form of a dialogue.

Computer-assisted instruction utilises two important learning principles—motivation and feedback. The motivation of trainees is normally high because of their interest in the process, and they are allowed to progress through the material at their own pace with the benefit of immediate feedback. However, transfer of learning is not always assured, except where, for example, the computer is used to enhance the realism of simulator training. It is said that in order to impart a given amount of material, computer-assisted instruction places lower demands on the time of the trainer and trainee during the actual training session than do other methods, such as the lecture. However, there are no meaningful differences in the achievement scores between those trained under conventional training methods as opposed to computer-assisted instruction (Goldstein, 1986; Wexley, 1984). It should be noted that the preparation of packages used in computer-assisted instruction can be time-consuming as well as expensive.

Conferences

A conference could be described as a carefully planned meeting with a specific purpose. The proceedings rely heavily on verbal communication between trainees, and this can help them understand concepts and influence attitudes.

Case studies

This method relies on presenting a written report describing an organisational problem to trainees. On an individual basis, the trainee analyses the problem, makes certain assumptions about a number of events, and puts forward a set of solutions. Subsequently, trainees meet as a group and, with the assistance of the trainer, present and discuss their solutions and identify underlying principles.

A consistent criticism of lectures, conferences, and case studies rests on the issue of transfer of learning. Information obtained from a conference or lecture may have limited effect if the trainee returns to an organisational setting that does not support the application of such information. With regard to case studies, the outcome of these exercises may involve embracing principles that cannot easily be applied in the trainee's real-time organisational situation (Saal & Knight, 1995).

Simulations

When we provide approximations of real-life situations and events, we are essentially using simulations in training. The purpose of simulation is to reproduce an actual work situation under the control of a trainer, whereby the latter is able to provide trainees with useful and rapid feedback, and influence their motivational disposition. Training simulations can be used not only when trainees are working with materials and machines, but also when engaged in interpersonal processes. Simulations are generally far less expensive to run than training people in real-life situations, and the more realistic a simulation the greater the expected transfer of learning.

A good example of a machine simulator is the flight simulator used for training pilots. The trainee pilot can learn the appropriate response to all types of routine and hazardous conditions under controlled circumstances without the risk of injury or damage to the equipment. Advances in computer technology have created more complex and sophisticated flight simulators, but we are still rather ignorant about how seriously the trainee pilot reacts to these cleverly devised reproductions of reality with their impressive audio-visual effects. After all, the trainee pilot knows that when he or she "crashes" into a highly populated neighbourhood there is still a tomorrow! In factories, trainees use simulators that are less complex than flight simulators. This is called *vestibule training*, and the trainees learn how to operate a piece of machinery away from the disrupting influences of the factory floor.

Role playing is a good illustration of an interpersonal simulation. Trainees go through the motions of playing a role related to work behaviour. If the trainees take the process seriously by eagerly embracing their assigned roles, role playing can be an effective method. It is suggested that if there is an acceptable level of motivation, and the role-playing situation is a good representation of reality, then there is some chance of the transfer of learning back to the role players' actual jobs (Saal & Knight, 1995).

There are variations in the way role playing is conducted. Reverse role playing is practised when a person takes on a role that is some other person's role. For example, A (a social security clerk) takes on the role of B (a claimant) in order to appreciate the client's perspective. There is also multiple role playing where a number of trainees are divided into teams. Each trainee acts out a situation, and subsequently compares and discusses the results with the other trainees.

Other types of interpersonal simulations include business games, as well as the case studies referred to earlier. With business games, trainees are required to make decisions in conditions that approximate circumstances found in the normal business environment. Business games can be operated using sophisticated computer packages, such as real-time organisational simulation in which participants manage a fictitious company. This could be used as a diagnostic tool for identifying management training and development needs in an assessment centre, and for assessing team interaction as part of teambuilding programmes (Wexley, 1984). Teambuilding is discussed in Chapter 11, and management development later in this chapter.

Behavioural role modelling

This method, similar in some respects to the applied learning procedure referred to earlier, has captured the attention of practitioners and researchers and has grown in popularity. It is based on Bandura's social learning theory, more recently called *social cognitive theory* (Bandura, 1977, 1986). Apart from learning from one's direct experience, people may learn from observing the behaviour of others. This is referred to as vicarious (second-hand) learning. So trainees may learn new ways of behaving from observing the behaviour of role models. Vicarious learning is one of the major ways in which social cognitive theory differs from operant conditioning referred to in Chapter 7. Originally, behaviour modelling was used in clinical psychology, treating people with phobias, but increasingly it has been applied to industry.

Mann and Decker (1984) summarise the components of behaviour modelling as follows:

- *Modelling*. The trainee observes another person engaging in desired behaviour for which he or she receives a reward. The trainee receives vicarious reinforcement by observing the role model receive the reward.
- *Retention processes*. The trainee encodes the observations for recall later.
- *Rehearsal*. The trainee goes through the motions where the actual observed behaviour is rehearsed or practised.
- *Social reinforcement*. The trainer and the other trainees reward the trainee for imitating the previously observed role model.
- *Transfer of training*. The trainee tries out the newly learned behaviours in his or her job and reports successes or failures back to the training group.

Behavioural role modelling is concerned with the trainee's motivation, provision of feedback, and the transfer of learning. By emphasising the importance of observation and vicarious reinforcement to learning, in addition to actual practice and direct reinforcement, it takes us a stage further than the traditional behaviour modification techniques discussed in Chapter 7. Closed-circuit television could be used to present role model behaviour that trainees should attempt to imitate. There is encouraging endorsement of this training method in the literature. For example, it was successfully used in a project designed to improve interpersonal relations among black employees and their predominantly white supervisors in a South African pharmaceutical company (Sorcher & Spence, 1982).

On-the-job training

Among on-the-job training methods are induction courses, coaching, and mentoring.

Induction. Induction courses are normally held during the first week of employment. New employees are usually informed about company policies, procedures, corporate culture, the nature of their role, where their job fits in the scheme of things, and are introduced to their colleagues. This is considered preferable, particularly on grounds

of anxiety reduction, to throwing people in at the deep end and expecting them to make sense of their environment and learn the correct procedures the hard way. It is suggested that the Western approach to induction contrasts sharply with the approach used by Japanese companies, where employees receive intensive and prolonged induction training (Price, 1997).

Coaching. Coaching is typically a short-term phenomenon that starts with a learning goal and is concerned primarily with performance and the development of definable skills (Clutterbuck, 2001a). It entails occasionally giving employees feedback and advice about aspects of their job performance, and is normally provided by the immediate supervisor or close colleagues in addition to their normal responsibilities. But sometimes managers coach people from outside their own teams. Unlike teaching, which involves telling people how to do something, coaching is all about showing people how to apply knowledge they have already, and can be particularly useful in generating ideas and getting people involved in the management of the change process. Coaches set challenging tasks, clearly outline expectations, monitor progress, offer advice, carry out frequent appraisals, encourage and prepare subordinates for promotion, and allow them to deputise (Conway, 1994).

Coaching is essentially a way of enhancing the soft skills (e.g., self-awareness, flexibility, interpersonal understanding, conceptual thinking) of senior staff to complement the more technical skills they develop through other forms of training (O'Reilly, 1998d). The prevailing view appears to be that there is a need for effective coaches, who are nonthreatening, proactive, and able to grasp issues and challenges before they escalate into problems, and that ownership of coaching as a tool in the management of change should reside initially at the top of the organisation and percolate downwards.

Mentoring. Mentoring is usually a longer-term phenomenon and is more concerned with helping the employee or executive to determine what goals to pursue and why. It seeks to build wisdom—the ability to apply knowledge, skills, and experience in new situations and to new problems (Clutterbuck, 2001a).

Mentoring normally arises when senior organisational members take responsibility for the development and progression of selected individuals. The practice of mentoring could be viewed as a relationship between two people; one is senior and acts as an adviser to a younger executive, preferably in a different section. The role of mentor has at least three functions: to give advice on career options; to provide social support; and to help mentorees be more effective in their current roles (Hunt, 2001). According to Clutterbuck (1986), mentoring is often seen as similar to coaching, counselling, sponsorship, and apprenticeship, but he concedes that it is something more distinctive. But apparently there is no reason why mentors cannot use a variety of roles—e.g., sponsor, teacher, devil's advocate, and coach—when doing their job (Farren et al., 1984).

Mentoring is a growing activity, with perhaps 50% of medium to large-sized organisations either operating organised schemes or actively encouraging the creation of informal mentor–protégé pairings (Arnold, 2005).

We would expect a mentor to be somebody who possesses the following characteristics (Brown, 1990; Clutterbuck, 1986, 2001b; Conway, 1994; Hunt, 2001; Hunt & Michael, 1983):

(1) The mentor is a person who does not have the normal superior–subordinate relationship with the mentoree (the protégé). The relationship is more open-ended with less immediate attention to attaining goals than other organisational relationships, but it is a protected relationship in which learning, experimentation, and risk-taking can occur and potential skills are developed with outcomes expressed as competencies.

(2) The mentor possesses self-awareness, and this is important when it comes to developing and using rapport and in recognising the boundaries of his or her capability to help.

(3) The mentor is a good listener, is well able to empathise with the protégé, is able to relate well to people and establish rapport with the protégé, which is often based on shared interests, and is willing to use his or her power to influence events. The mentor should avoid encouraging an over-dependent relationship.

(4) The mentor is knowledgeable, has high status, a strong power base in the organisation, and has the ability to place issues in a broader context. He or she also has a capacity for conceptual modelling (i.e., has a broad portfolio of models to help the executive analyse and understand interactions, as well as being able to evolve new models as part of the dialogue).

(5) The mentor is involved and willing to share his or her expertise with the protégé and promotes the latter's self-development, and does not feel threatened by the protégé's potential for equalling or surpassing him or her in status. In fact the mentor has a genuine interest and pleasure in the achievements of the mentoree.

(6) The mentor is willing to challenge, where appropriate, the ideas and judgements of the protégé in order to force a re-examination of the issues, and in the process is providing good feedback. Constructive criticism is just as important as encouragement.

Although positive benefits (e.g., improved income, accelerated promotions, and satisfaction with career progression later in life) have been associated with mentoring received early in a career (Dreher & Ash, 1990), the way mentoring is operationalised can be problematic. Bell (1998) makes the assertion that most attempts at mentoring are so clumsy that they end up as torture sessions for the protégé. Some mentors fail to provide a good service for the following reasons: they are too patronising; are inclined to lavish too much praise; are too interventionist; are too much of the comedian where more laughter than learning is evident; and they are lacking in the appropriate interpersonal skills.

According to Bell, the role of the mentor is changing. As companies become more decentralised, mentoring may have to be conducted long distance. Also, the hierarchical nature of mentoring is changing, so that the ideal mentor is not necessarily a senior executive. An example of a successful learning relationship is cited, whereby the general manager of a Marriott hotel, who had an abrasive style, sought the help of a front desk clerk at the hotel entrance to help her improve her presentation to customers. It is possible for some mentoring relationships to last only for a few sessions but others can continue and flourish over a decade. Arnold (2005) reflects on mentoring, and makes the following observation:

> It is likely that some mentoring schemes work better than others. It is probably important that mentors and protégés want the relationship, and they may well need training and orientation in order to make the most of it. The goals of the mentoring scheme should be clear and specific. The mentor's work performance should be assessed and rewarded partly on the basis of how effectively he or she is carrying out the mentoring role. The culture of the organization should be one that values personal and professional development. Even then there is a danger that mentors will hand on outdated knowledge and skills to protégés, especially in times of rapid change.

There is some overlap between mentoring and coaching. The most effective coaches share with mentors the capability to help the learner develop the skills of listening to and observing themselves, which leads to much faster acquisition of skills and modification of behaviour. Coaches also share with mentors the role of critical friend— confronting executives with truths no else feels able to confront them with. Whereas the coach is more likely to approach these issues using direct feedback, the mentor will tend to approach them through questioning processes that force the executive to recognise problems for themselves (Clutterbuck, 2001b). A related technique is counselling, which is directed at helping the individual overcome specific psychological barriers to performance or helping them deal with dysfunctional behaviour. (There is further discussion of counselling in connection with stress reduction in Chapter 19.)

Coaching and mentoring are approaches that could be usefully applied in management development, but there are some signs that coaching as a preferred way of developing people is superseding mentoring. It may well be that the terms coaching and mentoring are interchangeable, but it may also suggest a shift to a more performance-focused approach where the emphasis is more on improving quality of work now (the coaching emphasis) than on long-term career or general psychological well-being, as in mentoring (Arnold, 2005).

Many of the approaches to training, mentioned above, place a lot of control in the hands of trainers. They set objectives, specify the contents of training programmes in terms of realistic tasks and skills, and, finally, ensure that the success rate in achieving objectives is sufficiently high. This overall approach has been referred to as the traditional approach to learning (Blackler & Shimmin, 1984). It is considered valid in the realms of operative, supervisory, and management training when knowledge and experience of a technical process are required. For example, the technical aspects of procedures governing machine operation and maintenance, budgetary control, and production planning and control would lend themselves to the traditional approach.

One alternative approach incorporates the belief that learning is an active process best undertaken when individuals participate in and take responsibility for their own learning. This offers the trainee the opportunity to have a say in what the learning programme should accomplish, to exercise greater self-direction and control, and to remove the barriers to the attainment of learning objectives. The eventual outcome is said to increase sensitivity and lead to a continuing growth in self-awareness (Blackler & Shimmin, 1984).

Management development

Out of the self-control and self-awareness perspective has come management development with a firm humanistic flavour. The emphasis is on improving the sensitivity and self-awareness of the individual as a person and as somebody who interacts with others to bring about changes for the better in organisations. Stemming from this approach is sensitivity training (or T-groups), discussed as an organisational development intervention strategy in Chapter 16. Approaches to the training and development of managers at the present time are much broader than sensitivity training and related techniques. The alternative approaches—e.g., action learning, competencies, assessment centres, outdoor exercises—will be examined later.

Programmes aimed at developing managers are similar in some ways to general training programmes because they attempt to improve certain abilities, skills, and perspectives. Management development was defined by a UK governmental agency (the then Training Services Agency) nearly two decades ago as "an attempt to improve managerial effectiveness through a planned and deliberate learning process". This definition could still be considered valid. The main objective of management development is to ensure that executives are developed to meet the organisation's short and long-term requirements for specialist managers and general managers (Mumford, 1987).

In the 1980s there was a plethora of reports pointing out the inadequacy of provision in management education and training in the UK (see Sisson & Storey, 1988, and the reports cited there). Invariably, an expansion in the provision of programmes was advocated, with a stricture that they should be geared more towards the needs of organisations for managerial talent at all levels. However, differences between cultures on the best way to develop managers have to be recognised. For example, Germany and Japan have no real tradition of mounting MBA programmes to provide a focused educational experience for managers, though these programmes are well established in the USA and the UK. However, the situation is changing in Germany with the creation of private universities offering a growing number of MBA courses. In fact the German authorities have changed the university framework law to offer master's degrees in addition to the traditional German degrees (Harnischfeger, 1999).

Most developed countries would take seriously the training and development of managers in their own distinctive way, but the special needs of managers expected to manage across cultures have to be recognised. These managers should be able to manage cultural diversity while recognising and respecting their own cultural origins (Goffee, 1997).

Management competencies

There has been a shift towards competency-based education, with its heavy reliance on skills development, and an emphasis on the importance of a partnership between educational and training establishments and the organisations in which managers or potential managers work. As stated earlier in this chapter, competency is defined as the successful application of skills, knowledge, and ability to the standards required in employment. This approach has been used successfully and has evolved rapidly in the UK in the last 20 years due to its use in the national standards programme and NVQ movement (Shevels, 1998; Woodruffe, 1993). The emphasis on **management competencies** in management education and training stresses the nature of a manager's experience and the notion that experience is a great teacher. You will notice that learning from experience is enshrined in action learning, which we will examine in the next section. However, there are differences between the two approaches. One major difference is that the tutor or facilitator in action learning as we will see adopts a noninterventionist role to a far greater extent than does his or her counterpart in competency-based management education.

The emphasis on competence—the ability to put skills and knowledge into practice—stresses outputs from the management development process. This approach stands in marked contrast to the traditional academic model of studying a body of knowledge and then being tested by a formal examination, primarily on retention of information rather than understanding and application, and a written assignment. Those who subscribe to the traditional academic model would argue that it fosters understanding and perhaps limited application initially, but believe that managers need theories and concepts to assist them in interpreting their experience, otherwise they are unlikely to move outside the boundaries of their own experience with the real danger of becoming incompetent or even obsolete (Berry, 1991). Finally, perhaps we can look forward to a future in which the academic model and the experiential model can coexist and complement each other for the betterment of the provision of management education and training.

Action learning

The concept of **action learning** is not new, but increasingly in recent years there has been noticeable interest in applying pure or adapted ideas of action learning to management training and development. Revans (1971) argues that traditional learning is concerned with providing knowledge to answer questions, the solutions to which are known in advance by the instructors. Action learning takes a different approach whereby students are asked to consider problems for which there are no obvious solutions, but which can be tackled by reinterpreting experience. Revans would view action learning as an activity whereby the student goes through a process of recognising that the relevant knowledge does not provide a solution to the problem under review; therefore, it is necessary to rely on experience to engage in "questioning insights".

The following is what one manager, who was a student on a formal action learning programme, had to say about his overall experience (Caie, 1988):

> There was a lot of learning from each other in sets (groups), either in a formal setting or at a distance. Often this learning involved insights into the person's character and how individuals performed in groups, rather than simply factual knowledge about members' businesses and experiences. Using real work situations as a learning environment for the project work proved invaluable and members learned a tremendous amount from the experiences of others.

There are two outcomes of action learning —one is the solving of problems right up to the implementation stage, and the other is learning while doing so. The latter involves developing a greater understanding of the learning process and of one's preferred approaches to learning. In addition, it could give rise to a reformulation of preferred approaches to learning with the potential to transfer them to the work situation. Concerning learning to learn, there is a recognition in Kolb's (1974) work that people learn in different ways. Practitioners in action learning have adapted these ideas (Caie, 1988). For example, a person may prefer to learn through new experiences (the *pragmatist*), by observation and reflection (the *reflector*), by conceptualisation (the *theorist*), and finally by experimentation (the *activist*). In practice it is unlikely that people adopt absolute positions on learning style, but they are more likely to have a leaning towards one style rather than another.

Once people have understood their own learning styles, derived from a questionnaire, there is the opportunity in formal action learning programmes to become more balanced or broad-based learners by practising the learning styles that are less familiar to them. Alternatively, a conscious decision could be made to develop their strengths, and that could mean developing their particular orientation in learning style. A systematic relationship has been established between learning style and personality. Individuals with different personalities were found to have different cognitive styles, and to resort to different decision-making strategies. Those with different cognitive styles approached learning in different ways (Furnham, 1992).

Assessment centres

Increasingly companies are using assessment centres (described in Chapter 17), particularly in connection with two of the issues referred to earlier—selection and identification of development needs. It is suggested that assessment centres, or development centres when used in this context, are an efficient way of helping individuals get a clearer and better picture of their strengths and weaknesses, and of specifying the action required to facilitate their future development (Griffiths & Bell, 1985). The specified action entails a variety of planned educational and training programmes as well as experiences on the job.

Indoor/outdoor exercises

Apart from programmes that emphasise the dissemination of relevant knowledge in areas such as strategic planning, marketing, finance, operations management, and human resource management, participants can get involved in indoor exercises such as leading a discussion in a group, or acting as a leader in a complex task such as a difficult project. Alternatively, there are outdoor tasks that normally consist of some degree of physical deprivation (e.g., getting cold and wet). Exercises of this nature are designed to simulate real-life situations because they involve an element of stress, the need to inspire teamwork, problem solving, resolution of conflict, the exercise of interpersonal skills, and the maintenance of morale.

When one reflects on the indoor exercises it is easy to conclude that the problems encountered lack realism, and that they are unlikely to generate stress in the way that real-life situations do. On the other hand, the outdoor exercises are for real, in the sense that bad decisions could result in groups losing their way, experiencing acute discomfort, or even real danger. Although risks to the person are closely controlled, they are still present to a sufficient extent to generate stress and danger. In the mid-1990s a British Rail executive died while potholing on an outdoor training exercise. In 1998 there was an unfortunate incident during another exercise when a group of trainees from Eagle Star Life on a motivational course in Cheltenham, Gloucestershire, were encouraged to shed their inhibitions along with their shoes and walk barefoot over a bed of hot coals. They were treated for serious burns, and two were detained overnight in hospital.

Sadler (1988) acknowledges the weaknesses of the outdoor exercises. The circumstances relating to canoeing, abseiling, and mountaineering are radically different from those relating to organisational problems connected with mergers, technological change, and international competition. The stress experienced by the more athletic members of the management training group is much less than for those who are not that way inclined. In particular, those who are experienced and skilled in the types of outdoor activities undertaken enjoy a significant advantage. The outward-bound type of activity is obviously more appropriate for younger managers in junior positions than those already in senior positions.

In an assessment of the value of rigorous outdoor training courses for the development of executives, Furnham (1993a) has this to say:

> Outdoor training is neither a panacea, nor a total waste of time. Where there is a match between what a company wants and what a course can offer there is the likelihood of course participants enjoying an enriching and invaluable experience. A bad course with no planned outcomes may result in increased employee cynicism, on top of colds, scratches, and occasionally very bruised egos. Outdoor training courses should not be dismissed as nonsense nor embraced as the only solution. Chosen judiciously, and run well, outdoor training can provide a unique learning experience.

In the spirit of the last statement it is worth noting the attitude of trainers to outdoor training in the late 1990s. According to O'Reilly (1998c), trainers are keen to bury the macho image of training in the great outdoors, and are placing emphasis on developing minds and building teams rather than testing endurance. Ashworth (1999) reported that Marks & Spencer, Sainsbury, and Allied Domecq were among UK companies who are beginning to see the advantages of a more creative approach to teambuilding—one that is less threatening and more enjoyable. It appears that reliance on communication workshops using body language only and the live arts rather than ropes and freezing mud are proving to be the new source of inspiration when it comes to bringing out the best in employees.

Lively Arts, London, got course participants to stage their own performances with the help of stage performers and technical staff drawn from the opera, theatre, circus, and film. Supporters of this approach believe that the arts have a role to play in releasing creativity. Cranfield University School of Management ran a management training course around Shakespeare's plays both at its campus and at the Globe Theatre, London. The course's creator (the son of the late Lawrence Olivier) said that the play *Henry V* drives home the point that a successful leader must be an actor. Like Henry, who embodies inspirational leadership, he must know when not to show fear and when to display enough to appear human to his followers (McKee, 1999).

Recently, the Roffey Park Management College was offering a one-day course on the "The Art of Leadership with Shakespeare's *The Tempest*". In the publicity brochure there is reference to this workshop led by Olivier Mythodrama in the following terms: "*The Tempest* play is steeped in magical mystery, revealing the vital ingredients of the successful change initiative, and this unique form of experiential learning combines theatre practice, psychology, mythology, and organisational development to develop authentic leaders" (Roffey Park Newsletter, 2004). It is claimed that by "acting out" their desired leadership behaviours, and the leadership role they find most challenging, the participants can overcome their leadership "blind spots" and enhance their expertise. This process creates an embodied memory of their learning, which they then apply in their everyday challenges in the workplace (Roffey Park Newsletter, 2005). It remains to be seen if this form of management development is successful.

Sadler (1988) suggests other ways in which managers can be developed by being exposed to real-life situations that generate an element of stress, but do not expose participants to physical dangers and discomfort associated with the traditional outward-bound exercises, as follows:

- Plan and provide a day's outing for mentally handicapped children.
- Plan and execute a presentation to senior pupils in a secondary school to persuade them of the desirability of pursuing a career in industry.
- Plan and conduct a survey of the attitudes of young people in ethnic minorities towards job opportunities and discrimination in employment practices.

There appears to be constant experimentation on the best way to achieve teambuilding, creativity, and other goals of outdoor training events. Strategic planning, exchanges of best practices between different departments, and creative thinking, can be generated through carefully structured "away days". For example, away days are gaining popularity in the public sector (White, 2002). Surrey County Council uses them to improve staff performance and the way its services are delivered. The Head of Service Development and Staff Relations is reported as saying that every away day is carefully planned to achieve a range of aims as well as monitoring progress in the attainment of those aims, so that the organisation is in a position to judge effectiveness and value for money. Locations are carefully chosen to offer the facilities required with the accent on affordability and reasonable distance from the office. For instance, rooms were hired in a building in a small island on the River Thames, close to the headquarters of the Council in Kingston-upon-Thames. It was only 10 minutes away from the office, but it provided a complete change of scene and was ideal for creative strategic thinking. Issues explored at these sessions ranged from exchanging information on best practices between departments to managing change. One technique is to "road test" proposed changes by having staff play the part of people with typical organisational problems and then ask them to examine how new processes or structures might address those problems.

E-learning

E-learning refers to information and knowledge delivered through the medium of information and communication technology (ICT), and is typically associated with the internet. Learners can operate online to carry out programmed exercises, read material, and gain information of particular use in the performance of the various tasks in their jobs. Technology-based learning is said to have a number of advantages. First, it means that learners can access knowledge at any time convenient to them. Secondly, information can be transmitted to employees at high speed, and regular updates to material are possible. Thirdly, organisations whose workforce is geographically dispersed can enable all employees (or particular groups) to have the same information (Masie, 1999).

Glenmorangie, the Scotch whisky distiller, uses e-learning packages on a range of courses over the company's intranet to its far-flung outposts. This is a tremendous advantage for the distillery employees, who would otherwise face a 3-hour drive to get to the training room at the company's headquarters. Those working in the Isle of Islay would need to catch a flight. Glenmorangie has halved its training budget since adopting the technology 2 years ago (Moules, 2004c).

However, one should be aware that e-learning might not be suitable for all learning styles and tasks. In many e-learning packages there is no opportunity for hands-on learning (learning by doing) and there is an absence of feedback from other participants, and lack of the discussion one would expect to find in traditional training situations. However, there are some practices where e-learning is supported by contact with other trainees. This could take the form of access to other participants who have had similar experiences and who are able to share their learning and receive feedback.

Continuous development

It is almost commonplace nowadays to hear the view that training should be a continuing process with the accent on self-development, as mentioned earlier. This is prompted by the suggestion that employees cannot, in a rapidly changing world, rely on the knowledge and skills acquired in gaining their initial qualifications. Nearly two decades ago the Institute of Personnel Management (now the IPD) produced a code of practice relating to personal development and the demands posed by jobs. A starting point is the assessment of the organisation's present and future training needs; this is done by extracting from the corporate plan the pool of employee knowledge and skills required to implement that plan. Predictably the importance of learning from confronting and solving problems at work is underlined.

The role of top management in cultivating a climate of continuous development is given special mention in the code of practice. Top management is admonished to place high on the corporate agenda the frequent formal review of training activities aimed at the development of employee competencies. In the final analysis it should be recognised that it is wise to promote the view that one should make learning a habit and to accept the idea that work problems offer opportunities for learning. Ideally it is hoped that well-conceived continuous development aimed at helping the individual also helps the organisation to achieve its objectives.

Continuous professional development (CPD) has become compulsory in most core accountancy disciplines. Also, lawyers (solicitors and barristers) need to show evidence of the minimum number of hours devoted to continuous professional development in order to retain their practising certificates (Plimmer, 2004). According to the British Psychological Society (BPS), mandatory continuous professional development will in the near future apply to all chartered psychologists who hold a practising certificate (British Psychological Society, 2004a). It requires individuals to be able to show that they are engaging in the CPD process. The CPD records should be submitted to the BPS in the form of a summary log, which includes details of the CPD process undertaken in the previous year, as follows:

- The professional development needs identified for that year.
- The professional activities undertaken.
- An overview of the individual psychologist's review and reflection of the learning outcomes and how this relates to their own professional practice.
- Any further development needs identified as a result of the review and reflection.

It is apparent that professional bodies are paying more attention to CPD. These bodies are naturally concerned with maintaining professional standards, staving off government interference, and retaining their grip on self-regulation of the profession. However, much of the burden has fallen on the shoulders of members who have been forced to foot the bill for training and development themselves.

The UK Financial Services Authority takes a tougher line, presumably influenced by the mis-selling of financial products in the past. It now requires employers to be responsible for keeping their staff's competencies up-to-date, with companies who fail to do so being liable to severe fines (Plimmer, 2004).

Careers and career development

In this section the major themes to be addressed are career choice and career planning. The latter is important in the context of employee development.

Career choice

Holland (1997) developed a theory of career choice rooted in personality. It is maintained that people in each personality type (listed in Table 18.1) gravitate towards a small set of jobs. The reason they do so is because they are seeking work compatible with their likes and dislikes. There is research evidence to suggest that when

people choose a career that matches their personality they are more likely to be satisfied with their choice and less likely to change professions (Feldman & Arnold, 1985). Arnold (2005) acknowledges that research has not always supported Holland's model; nevertheless, the model is very valuable because it provides a structure for understanding and assessing individuals and occupations. In a review of the relevant literature, Furnham (2001b) states that Holland's ideas have provided an excellent springboard for researchers in this area to develop and refine their own ideas and tackle the difficult problems of measuring the fit between the person and the organisation (P–O fit) and understanding its consequences. But at the same time he advises us not to be afraid to criticise this theory or offer a different, perhaps more promising approach.

Schein (1996) introduced the concept of career anchors, which could be viewed as having relevance to personality, particularly to our self-concept. Career anchors consist of a combination

---

TABLE 18.1

Personality types and career choice (adapted from Holland, 1997): Copyright © 1997 by Psychological Assessment Resources Inc. and used with permission

Personality	*Occupational type*
Realistic—Tends to like, and has proficiency in, activities requiring physical strength and coordination	Farming, carpentry, architecture
Investigative—Tends to get involved in observing, organising, and understanding data, and generally enjoys and is adept at abstract thought. But dislikes social activities and situations where persuasive powers are expected to be used	Mathematics, engineering, dentistry
Social—Enjoys the company of others more than being engaged in intellectual or physical activity. Tends to be warm and caring and enjoys the process of informing, training, and enlightening others	Religion, social work, diplomatic service, teaching
Conventional—Likes rules, regulations, structure, and order and is prepared to subordinate personal needs to situations where personal or organisational power and status exists. Is usually well organised but generally is not very imaginative	Accounting, finance, military, clerical work
Enterprising—Enjoys activity rather than observation and reflection. Likes to use verbal communication skills to persuade others and gain power and status	Publishing, industrial relations, sales management
Artistic—Dislikes ordered and repetitive situations. Likes to express feelings and ideas, and be expressive and imaginative. Enjoys drama, music, and art	Advertising, interior design, drama, art

of abilities, needs, motives, and values, and become visible in the early stages of a career as a result of people reflecting on their experiences to date. But one has to recognise that if forced to choose only one anchor, this could be a difficult decision. The chosen anchor is the real career anchor and can be associated with effective career management. It could be said that people will be most satisfied when they choose an occupation and organisation that are in line with their preferred career anchor. The list of alternative anchors to which people may subscribe is as follows:

- Managerial competence (there is a preference to manage other people, and issues such as leadership, taking responsibility with a desire to get on, assume importance).
- Technical/functional competence (there is a strong desire to cultivate specialist knowledge and skills in one's area of expertise, and people tend to identify with their work).
- Security (there is a striving for reliability and predictability in one's employment, and this could be reflected in an attachment to the notion of a job with security of tenure).
- Autonomy and independence (there is a need to be free of too many restrictions, whether they are rules and regulations with regard to the content and context of jobs, or how to behave).
- Entrepreneurial creativity (there is an urge to be creative in a number of ways, ranging from product innovation to running one's own show).
- Pure challenge (there is nothing more appealing than winning against the odds, faced with stiff competition).
- Service dedication (there is nothing better than work that fits well with one's values and beliefs, particularly in organisations with cultures that reflect those values).
- Lifestyle integration (there is a strong desire to strike a good balance between work, home, and leisure activities).

After reflecting on the above framework, the following observations could be made:

- People with a security anchor may tolerate a job lacking in stimulation and challenge in a stable environment but that is high on security with a reasonable salary. However, secure jobs are not as plentiful today as they were in the past.
- Those with a service dedication anchor might find a job in education or in the hospital service appealing.
- Those with an autonomy and independence anchor, such as an academic or research scientist, would prefer an environment where they are not closely supervised and are free of unnecessary restrictions.
- Those with an entrepreneurial creativity anchor may find self-employment in a dynamic and creative environment an attractive proposition.
- Those with a lifestyle integration anchor, would prefer a situation where it is possible to experience a good balance between work and nonwork life, and would not take kindly to a situation where there has been a substantial increase in workload due to a significant cutback of employees within the organisation.
- Those with a pure challenge anchor might find the job of a foreign exchange dealer attractive. Before the demise of the career of Nick Leeson of Barings Bank in Singapore, the job appeared to offer lots of challenge in conditions of uncertainty.
- Those who enter a graduate trainee programme under a scheme to produce general managers within the organisation may be attracted by the prospect of becoming a manager with potential for further progression along the managerial route.

According to Schein (2001), discovering career anchors is not difficult. It is based on a thorough analysis of one's educational and job history, always focusing on why various decisions were made. This is done best in an interview situation.

In reality, when it comes to the actual process of career choice the situation could be clouded with ambiguity. For example, individuals may lack self-awareness and be unable to assess accurately their likes and dislikes, or their strengths and weaknesses; or they may have insufficient knowledge or insight into occupations even after tapping relevant sources of information; or they may lack a rational or intuitive decision capability when faced with evaluating the various career options. Career choices are remade over time and many significant developments can occur between the initial choice and subsequent modifications to choices (Arnold, 2005).

Given the increasing frequency of job changes in today's world, naturally attention is increasingly given to how individuals and organisations can manage transitions from one job to another. Nicholson (1990) put forward a model called the transition cycle. It highlights the dynamics surrounding a job change beginning with the step where the individual prepares for a new job, then coming to terms with and adjusting to the demands and conditions of the job, and finally consolidating and stabilising one's position. For many this could become an experience that repeats itself all too frequently.

Career planning

When attention focuses on career prospects we are entering the domain of career planning. In a management development context, it could be viewed as a managed process of dialogue between each manager and the organisation about career prospects, aspirations, skills, and development needs (Burgoyne & Germain, 1984). This process could be related to a cycle of events, usually on an annual basis, consisting of performance reviews for each person, together with an exploration of career potential and a clarification of learning needs.

The events described previously would be linked to organisational planning, and the two together would be phased to inform the formation of corporate policy, as well as its implementation. In this way individual managerial careers are reviewed in the light of changing corporate directions, and corporate directions are considered in the light of available information on the skills, aspirations, potential, and the agreed future vision of the management team in the organisation.

The purpose of career planning is to ensure there is an enhancement of individual and organisational performance, and it is said that career planning in organisations can help companies identify qualified personnel and future managers, improve job satisfaction and other attitudes, increase the involvement of key employees, and improve the vital match between individual and organisational wants and needs (Granrose & Portwood, 1987).

A word of caution comes from Williams (1984) who feels we should broaden our view of the notion of career planning. He maintains that careers are not the exclusive property of managers and professionals—they should be applicable generally to, for example, clerical staff and part-time employees. Also, he states that the upward and onward view of a career does not always fall into line with current conditions whereby organisations that survive are leaner and fitter with fewer promotion opportunities (see Panel 18.8).

The continuance of these conditions would necessitate a shift away from a career with in-built advancement to an increased emphasis on career development at the same organisational level, or within the present job. With fewer promotions available, lateral moves—for instance, job rotation—provide opportunities for continual career development. Also, temporary secondments or exchanges with other organisations might be considered, provided the eventual re-entry of the employee is carefully planned. However, employees with the most marketable skills, faced with limited advancement opportunities within their own organisation, will probably explore external openings despite a highly competitive labour market.

Career planning categories

The following are some of the ways of categorising career planning (Morgan, Hall, & Martier, 1979; Moorhead and Griffin, 2004):

• career pathing;
• career counselling;
• human resource planning;
• career information systems; and
• special programmes.

PANEL 18.8: Career plateau

As organisations engage in restructuring with the inevitable consequence of fewer layers, the effect on the number of promotions will be pronounced. With a decreasing number of rungs on the career ladder, a career structure plateau will be a fact of life for many people. The results of a study conducted by a research group at Sundridge Park Management Centre suggest that managers are adapting to the changing circumstances because they believe that there are career development alternatives to "promotion" as an organisational reward. The research focused on 1646 managers from eight organisations in the UK finance sector, and many of these organisations had been restructured in the last 5 years.

Respondents (managers) were asked how likely they were to accept a variety of career alternatives if faced with them now. Four career types emerged, although they are not completely mutually exclusive:

(1) *Career flexers*. These managers are likely to accept a wide variety of jobs, and although they may not strive for upward hierarchical moves they would like their jobs to have attractive features. They tend to be younger and more ambitious than the average manager, and tend to have spent less time in their present or immediately previous job.

(2) *Ambitious careerists*. These managers are especially eager to be promoted and groomed for higher level positions. They have a particularly firm belief that promotion will come their way; this belief is more potent the younger they are, and the less time they have spent in their present and previous jobs. They are particularly hostile to any downward move, and they are confident that they will not be made redundant.

(3) *Career disengagers*. These managers are interested in retirement, redundancy, and part-time working. What they would like to do is stop working full-time, either immediately or gradually. The longer they are in the job the more bored they feel, and generally they could belong to any age group. But there is some evidence to indicate that this age group consists of older people who are no longer ambitious, and who hold an expectation of being made redundant or of being offered early retirement.

(4) *Career lifers*. These managers would like to be told that they can remain in their present job until they retire, and would welcome a loyalty bonus. They tend to be older, and are convinced that promotions are a thing of the past.

The research shows that there is considerable variety in the career aspirations of managers in mid- or late career. The challenge facing organisations is to cope adequately with these different career needs. If the challenge is accepted, a natural course of action would be to recast the traditional career structure, and remove the stigma attached to the plateau, because managers nowadays are reaching the plateau much earlier—between the ages of 30 and 40—as opposed to between 45 and 50 in the mid-1980s.

Finally, one has to consider the importance of "job mobility" as a predictor of beliefs, feelings, and career types, the extent to which organisations differ with respect to job mobility practices, and the differences between the genders.

(Herriot & Pemberton, 1995)

Career pathing. Ideally career paths extend over an appreciable period of time (i.e., a 5- or 10-year period), and are updated periodically, with a series of experiences that lead to a particular destination—e.g., a higher level position within the organisation. Some career paths may include assignments overseas to help the individual gain an understanding of the international operations of the organisation. However, overseas assignments should be carefully considered, ensuring the suitability of applicants for such assignments.

Di Prete (1987) suggests that most organisations are unlikely to adhere too rigidly to specific career paths; instead they are likely to provide opportunities for both lateral and vertical movement to enable individuals to develop their skills and breadth of experience. Arnold (2005) maintains: "career path information is said to be provided in about one-third of organisations, which is perhaps surprising given frequent and major structural changes and the disappearance of career paths in many organisations".

A live issue in recent years has been the development of career structures for technical staff, such as engineers and scientists (see Panel 18.9).

Career counselling. Counselling is a process aimed at helping people to explore a problem and alternative ways of dealing with it so that something can be done about it. The over-riding goal is to help the clients of the counsellor to help themselves and take responsibility for their own lives. It is based on the belief that within individuals there is a capacity to grow in maturity and take on responsibility if the conditions are right. You would expect the counsellor to be sympathetic,

---

PANEL 18.9: Career structures for technical staff

There is a growing recognition in some European high-technology companies that scientists and engineers are a prime resource and that the management structure should be altered so that employees can be rewarded for the quality of their research, rather than how many staff they control, or their skill at managing a budget. According to the Technical Director of ICL (UK), part of Fujitsu of Japan, there were instances of quite good technical staff trying to turn themselves into managers so that they could advance their careers, even though the main benefit they brought to the company was their technical contribution.

In 1990, after 10 years of informal arrangements, ICL introduced its technical career structure to show junior staff how they can develop their technical skills. As one recent entrant at a reasonably senior level at ICL said: "I could see there were people very high up in the company who were doing purely research, free of line management responsibilities but with a good salary." However, the Technical Director expects a "strategic" contribution from the senior engineer, such as taking responsibility for the design on which their team is working, or demonstrating ability to work with, for example, the marketing department.

Titular rewards are given to engineers who reach the top. To date 10 employees are ICL Fellows, and 25 have received the title of Distinguished Engineers, with more to follow. Distinguished Engineers are expected to meet regularly to discuss developments and exchange ideas. According to the Chief Engineer at ICL, the technical career scheme has been successful in acknowledging the value of the technical staff, and retaining skilled staff.

Another company, British Telecom, unveiled its professional career-path scheme. The aim of the scheme is to support the career development needs of technical and specialist staff. According to the Management Development Manager, the scheme should prove useful in maintaining the specialist's enthusiasm and innovative thinking within the growing demands posed by "flatter" organisations, in which sideways rather than upwards moves become commonplace.

(Bradshaw, 1993)

---

genuine, nonjudgemental, and able to create an atmosphere of trust and acceptance in the quest to understand empathetically the client's behaviour and the reasons for it. Other skills used by the counsellor are active listening, clarifying issues, reflecting on what comes across in the disclosures, summarising the position put forward by the client, and offering guidance.

The emphasis with respect to the career counselling approach is to enable the employee to recognise and understand the opportunities and constraints in career development (Natham & Hill, 1992). The following issues could be raised with employees during an effective career counselling programme (Van Maanen & Schein, 1977):

- Career goals, aspirations, and expectations of employees for 5 years or longer.
- Opportunities that exist within the organisation, and the extent to which the employees' aspirations are realistic and coincide with the available opportunities.
- Identification of what would have to be done by employees in the way of additional self-development in order to benefit from the new opportunities.

- Identification of new job assignments that are necessary in order to prepare employees for further career growth.

According to Arnold (2005), personal development activities, such as career counselling, probably feature in not more than a quarter of organisations. (There is further reference to counselling in Chapter 19.)

Finally, reflecting on the concept of career counselling, Furnham (2001a) maintains that "it seems to be outdated precisely because we are being constantly told that there is no such thing as a career any longer. We will all have, if lucky, multiple careers—we will be personal portfolio managers—and therefore what advice we need will be quite different."

Human resource planning. This involves forecasting an organisation's human resource needs, creating charts that show planned succession, and producing a record of the skills and abilities needed by individuals in order to progress within the organisation. The complex aspect of human resource planning is implementing the plans based on the assessment of individual and organisational needs.

Career information systems. There are many ways in which the organisation can provide career information to help employees make their own choices about available opportunities. Vacancies can be advertised internally on notice boards, or through an internal newsletter or job vacancy bulletin. Career information can be conveyed by senior managers to staff using leaflets, videotapes, talks, and discussions. This type of activity could be beneficial for the organisation and increase the motivation of employees.

Special programmes. There are a variety of ways of facilitating disengagement from the organisation or progression within it. Pre-retirement programmes, for example, could assist with adjusting to a different lifestyle after leaving the organisation. Likewise, outplacement programmes are designed to help people who are leaving the organisation, either voluntarily or involuntarily. They help people preserve their dignity and self-worth when they are made redundant or dismissed, and can reduce negative feelings about the organisation.

There are programmes to help people change career direction from technical posts to managerial ones, and programmes developed for minorities and women to help solve their special problems (Bowen & Hisrich, 1986).

Career management. This is the process by which career planning is implemented. To create the right climate the support of top management is necessary. In addition, all human resource activity throughout the organisation must be coordinated, all employees should be involved, and realistic feedback should be provided (Moorhead & Griffin, 2004). The importance of the role of the supervisor in the process is heavily endorsed (Leibowitz & Schlossberg, 1981). The supervisor's role would embrace the following:

• communicating information about careers;
• counselling subordinates to help them identify their skills and the options open to them;
• evaluating subordinates' strengths and weaknesses;
• offering subordinates coaching, or teaching skills and behaviour;

• advising subordinates on the realities of organisational life;
• serving as a mentor or role model for subordinates; and
• attracting subordinates' attention to opportunities.

Outcome of career planning

A number of beneficial outcomes have been attributed to career planning (Leibowitz & Schlossberg, 1981; Williams, 1984).

• Employees develop more realistic expectations of what is expected of them at work, and what sort of a future they are likely to have in the organisation.
• Increased awareness of available opportunities and of organisational constraints.
• Supervisory roles in career counselling are clarified, and there are better quality discussions between superior and subordinate.
• Greater sense of personal responsibility for career planning and development.
• Clearer understanding of values, interests, abilities, and personal characteristics.
• Better ability to resolve job–career–family concerns.
• More effective use of personnel systems within the organisation.

The overall benefits are reflected as a strengthening of commitment to careers when individuals develop plans to take responsibility for their careers. Ultimately it is claimed that the organisation is well placed to make better use of employees' talents, employee turnover is reduced, and there is an increase in the performance of individuals and the organisation.

Certain dysfunctional consequences can occur if the career planning system raises people's expectations unrealistically (Moorhead & Griffin, 2004). These are an increase in anxiety, supervisors spending too much time counselling their subordinates, and human resource systems becoming overloaded. The end result could be frustration, disappointment, and reduced commitment, with the under-utilisation of talent, an increase in employee turnover, and a deterioration in both individual and organisational performance.

Nicholson and Arnold (1989) identified four defects in career development systems in organisations that are likely to undermine their effectiveness:

(1) Career moves are determined by rules and procedures that are unresponsive to changing conditions and do not accommodate exceptions.
(2) Career opportunities are created by managers intent on advancing their own interests to the detriment of the organisation or the individual whose career is under review.
(3) People are in the dark as to where they are going because possible career pathways and ways of using them are not stated.
(4) Unnecessary restrictions are placed on certain career moves, particularly sideways transfers between functions.

Herriot (1992) has come forward with some interesting ideas about careers in organisations. He maintains that the idea of "career" is still important, despite the fact that the notion of a career for life in an organisation is fast disappearing. He maintains that only those organisations that "negotiate" careers will retain the people they need to face the future with confidence.

In a later publication, Herriot and Pemberton (1996) propose a model that captures the complexity of careers in the turbulent conditions of contemporary organisations. These conditions caused by restructuring in response to competitive forces have contributed to making the careers experienced by numerous people less predictable than they once were, and therefore a sense of injustice and broken promises are quite common among employees in organisations. The model of the organisational career highlights perceptions of the psychological contract that exists between the employer and the employee, and in this sense equity is crucial.

The psychological contract represents the informal written understandings between employers and employees, and in this setting it relates to careers. In the past it was viewed as a long-term

relationship, but now, in the cost-cutting, leaner organisations, it is more like a short-term economic exchange (i.e., the employer offers a job and increased pay for higher performance in return for increased effort by overworked and stressed employees). According to Herriot and Pemberton (1995), many employers do not stick to their side of the bargain, and this is a source of great disappointment and resentment to employees. Where there is violation of the psychological contract by the employer, the employees have options open to them—leave, or stay and keep out of harm's way, or stay and retaliate.

Evaluation of training and development

Essentially we are concerned with trying to establish the reliability (consistency) and validity (effectiveness in meeting objectives) of training programmes. This necessitates establishing a relationship between the training methods used and some measure (or criterion) of performance, and can only be done by examining the trainees' capabilities after training. If trainees meet the training objectives when they are assessed at the end of the programme, this shows internal or training validity. But if, after completing the training programme, it can be shown that the trainees' performance at work is up to the desired standard, then external or performance validity is achieved (Goldstein, 1978).

When evaluating a training programme it is desirable to go beyond a narrow concern with validation. One would obviously be interested in the trainees' general reactions to the programme—and make use of this information. The views of trainees should be carefully handled. It is known for trainees to be thoroughly satisfied with a programme merely because the instructor or trainer did a good job entertaining them. In other circumstances, the trainees come forward with a less than satisfactory evaluation because the instructor or trainer worked them very hard, or was unpopular for some reason. Feedback of this type may fail to inform us whether or not training was effective in achieving its objectives.

Naturally, a major preoccupation is likely to be the extent to which there is a transfer of learning

PANEL 18.10: Effectiveness of training

Training must be fit for its purpose. The aim should be to make the business stronger, healthier, and more creative. That means that training programmes must suit the needs of business; if they don't, then they are wasted effort. There is evidence suggesting that many employees do not understand the purpose of training programmes on which they are sent, or see no value in them. In a survey undertaken by Cambridge University it was concluded that UK companies are wasting up to 20% of their training budget because employees fail to attend programmes on which they are enrolled. This could be compounded by a situation where trainees attend the training programme but derive little benefit from it. Perhaps this could be of a greater order of magnitude. But it would be unwise to lay all the blame on the shoulders of the trainees. The world of work is full of trainers and training programmes that do not deliver value for money, and all too often human resource managers fail to exercise sufficient care in their choice of training provider.

(Witzel, 2004)

from the training programme to the place of work. For example, a trainee may pass the competency test at the end of the training programme but fail to transfer the learning to the job because of some inhibition, or due to a firm attachment to the old work methods. For reservations about the effectiveness of training programmes, see Panel 18.10.

Kirkpatrick (1967) provided a framework for collecting information for the purposes of evaluating training. It consists of four levels, as follows:

(1) *Reaction* (e.g., responses on the difficulty, depth, and length of the training).

(2) *Learning* (e.g., knowledge acquired as a result of the training, following the use of an appropriate method of assessment soon after the end of the training session, or alternatively much later). The learning stage could entail providing tests on a pre- and post-training basis to establish the extent to which the trainee has achieved the learning outcomes of the training session.

(3) *Behaviour* (e.g., if skills are developed following training, the extent to which the trainee uses those skills to an appropriate standard). The behavioural stage is connected with the transfer of learning, discussed in Chapter 7, and deals with the extent to which trainees demonstrate the skills acquired during training when they return to the workplace. One should be realistic about the time factor, because new skills may be competing with old ones and take some time to be fully operational. The evidence collected at this stage is

the unbiased view of the trainee's manager on the improvements detected, aided by indicators of performance, such as number of customer complaints, number of mistakes, etc.

(4) *Results* (e.g., the extent to which the training has produced the requisite results in the workplace). The extent to which the training produced an impact on organisational effectiveness can be difficult to establish, as is mentioned below. It is said that a relatively small percentage of companies evaluate post-training behaviour (Patrick, 1992). Perhaps if there is a reluctance to measure its impact, there is an implicit belief in the effectiveness of training, particularly if adequate resources are devoted to it and it is recommended by authoritative personnel in the organisation.

The normal expectation is that the above framework would unfold in the manner indicated. However, this has been challenged. For example, it does not automatically follow that "learning" would definitely lead to "results", simply because a situation could arise where the trainee learns the appropriate knowledge but subsequently is not able to use it in the job as a result of lack of encouragement and support from the boss or colleagues (Alliger, Tannenbaum, Bennett, Traver, & Shotland, 1997).

Another approach to the evaluation of training was proposed by Hamblin (1974). He would envisage the transfer of learning being evaluated by the trainee's manager or training specialist to establish whether or not behaviour has changed as a result of the training. The following include some of the techniques used for this purpose:

- *Activity sampling* and *observer diaries*. The trainees are observed to see to what extent they are putting into practice the knowledge, skills, and attitudes acquired through training.
- *Critical incidents*. Key incidents at work are analysed to establish to what extent new patterns of behaviour are present.
- *Self-recording*. The trainees record how they perform certain activities.

The organisation will be looking for evidence of how the changed job behaviour influences other employees and the way the company functions. This would mean measuring changes in overall organisational functioning with respect to output, costs, and productivity, but such an exercise would be difficult to undertake.

When trying to relate training outcomes to organisational effectiveness—the issue raised in connection with "Results" in the Kirkpatrick framework above—we run up against the problem of establishing whether the training variable, or a combination of other variables, was responsible for organisational success. For example, consider the case where the training of sales representatives in an insurance company coincided with renewed public interest in life policies, and an upturn in the economy leading to increased earnings from the sale of policies. The extent to which training of sales representatives was responsible for increased sales revenue may be difficult to establish. Such difficulties are often referred to as threats to validity. As a means to control the many threats to the validity of the evaluation of training, experimental designs can be used, although the typical conditions that prevail in real organisations may make this investigation impossible.

Probably it is true to say that there is a scarcity of good training evaluation studies, and that as a general principle one may state that it is easier to find reports of successful validation of training in perceptual motor skills, which are more amenable to straightforward testing of what has or has not been learned, than in supervisory and management training. In the latter case, complex learning is at stake, involving the use of concepts and the transfer of learning to different situations. As a consequence, it is more difficult to demonstrate the effectiveness of supervisory and management training.

A final matter to consider is training people to improve their assessment skills, particularly in task analysis. This is referred to as "rater learning". According to Latham (1988), research in this area has focused almost exclusively on performance appraisal rather than training needs analysis.

CHAPTER SUMMARY

- Rewards were viewed in both intrinsic and extrinsic terms.
- After stating the purpose and philosophy of reward systems, attention turned to the determination of rewards through job evaluation schemes based on the quantitative and nonquantitative approaches. Another approach is based on competence and skill analysis. The advantages and disadvantages of job evaluation were stated, and the importance of external influence in the determination of rewards was strongly emphasised.
- Examples of compensation packages were given—i.e., time rates (including the minimum wage), payment by results, bonus and profit sharing, gain sharing, stock option plans and long-term compensation, stock ownership, and performance-related pay.
- Factors likely to influence the acquisition of skills were acknowledged as knowledge of results or feedback, part or whole, and massed or distributed practice. The relevance of learning curves was emphasised.
- The employee training process was discussed at length, starting with the importance of training and development to the competitiveness of the organisation and then moving on to an account of various national initiatives.
- The discussion continued with a focus on the assessment of training needs with analysis at the organisation, task, person, and demographic levels.
- The emphasis then switched to an explanation of training objectives and a listing of training methods. The latter include lectures, computer-assisted learning, case studies, simulations, conferences, behaviour modelling, coaching, and mentoring.
- A distinction was made between on-the-job and off-the-job training, and trainer-centred and trainee-centred methods. A manifestation of the latter is action learning.
- E-learning was introduced and its growing importance emphasised.
- Approaches to management development covered were action learning, management competencies, assessment centres, indoor and outdoor exercises, and formal educational programmes (e.g., MBA).
- Career choice and career planning were examined and outcomes of career planning were acknowledged. The complexity of careers in contemporary organisations was emphasised, along with the defects of career development systems. In the context of careers, the psychological contract was mentioned.
- The need to evaluate systems of training and development was emphasised.

QUESTIONS

(1) Define extrinsic rewards, and specify the purpose and philosophy of reward systems.

(2) What are the differences between the quantitative and nonquantitative approaches to job evaluation.

(3) In what way does the type of reward system known as payment by results differ from performance-related pay?

(4) Define the following: (a) part or whole method; (b) massed or distributed practice; (c) action learning; (d) competencies, and (e) e-learning.

(5) Why is it important to carry out an assessment of training needs before setting training objectives?

(6) Review the training methods at the disposal of the trainer, and indicate the method(s) you consider appropriate in the training of: (a) airline pilots; and (b) sales representatives.

(7) List the activities that comprise a well-developed management development programme.

(8) Consider the factors that one ought to take into account when examining career choice.

(9) Comment on the suggestion that planning a career is as important today as it has ever been.

(10) Comment on why it is necessary to evaluate training, and mention the important issues involved in such an exercise.

SPOTLIGHT ON RELEVANT READING

Rewards

Arkin, A., & Downard, B. (2005). Reward—eyes on the prize: The process of developing the best packages to attract and retain staff is becoming more complex. *People Management*, 10 February, 29–35.

Armstrong, M. (2002). *Employee reward*. London: CIPD.

Freeman, C. (2004). Viewpoint—Women play salary catch-up: Despite equal opportunities legislation, male workers are still being paid a lot more than their female counterparts. *People Management*, 25 March, 27.

Training and development

Merrick, N. (2004). Modern romance: Employers are about to be urged to take another look at modern apprenticeships, but are they less cumbersome and bureaucratic now. *People Management*, 25 March, 16–17.

Reynolds, J. (2002). Method and madness: The real value of e-learning. *People Management*, 4 April, 42–43.

Reynolds J., & Slowman, M. (2004). In the driving seat: Traditional training has its place, but is teaching people what the organisation wants them to know the best way to unlock their potential. *People Management*, 12 February, 40–42.

Schein, E.H. (2001). The anchors that dictate our careers. *FT Mastering Management Series*, Part 13, 8 January, 2–4.

Stewart, J., & Tansley, C. (2002). Training in the knowledge economy. London: CIPD.

Learning Outcomes

After studying this chapter you should be able to:

• Define stress and describe its physiological manifestations.

• Recognise the nature of burnout and PTSD.

• Outline the different facets of organisational life associated with stress.

• Discuss the remedies that are available to counteract the stressful state.

• Examine the preventative health management programmes designed to create healthier organisations.

Health and Work: Stress

Contents

This chapter begins with a definition and manifestations of stress, which include burnout and post-traumatic stress disorder. Next there is an examination of stressors attributable to the self, the organisation, and outside influences. Remedies for the alleviation or elimination of stress are then examined, and there is a commentary on health promotion and related programmes. This chapter has particular relevance to personality (Chapter 2), role analysis (Chapter 10), and new technology and job design (Chapter 4).

DEFINITION

Before looking at various facets of organisational life that can generate stress, it is appropriate to be more precise in specifying what is meant by a stressful condition. To use an analogy from physics, **stress** arises because of the impact of an environmental force on a physical object; the object undergoes strain and this reaction may result in temporary distortion, but equally it could lead to permanent distortion.

In human terms any situation that is seen as burdensome, threatening, ambiguous, or boring is likely to induce stress. This is the type of situation that would normally strike the individual as deserving immediate attention or concern and is viewed as unfortunate and annoying. There tends to be the feeling that the situation should not exist, but because of it the person feels disappointed or annoyed and eventually is prone to anxiety, depression, anger, hostility, inadequacy, and low frustration tolerance. This could be considered dysfunctional stress, or distress.

In other circumstances, pressure arises when the individual is expected to perform in a particular manner and finds it a source of discomfort and anxiety, but at the same time finds the experience a source of excitement, challenge, and personal growth. It could be said that when under some pressure—mild levels of stimulation—we function better because we are more aware, more attentive, clearer in our thinking, and physically alert. This could be considered functional stress or "being in the stress comfort zone". Some see this as a healthy form of stress. For example, the pressure of accountability for one's own work or the meeting of a deadline could produce a positive effect leading to a feeling of pride and accomplishment. Of course excessive pressure can be detrimental, contributing to poor performance.

It is suggested that there are no objective criteria good enough to describe a situation as stressful (Briner, 1999a, 1999b; Briner & Reynolds, 1993); only the person experiencing the internal or external threat can do this (Lazarus, 1966). (Although not a representative view, Briner, 1999a,

1999b has reservations about the relevance of stress and its management. He would prefer us to focus on our feelings and emotions at work, rather than dabbling in what he sees as the problematic concept of stress.) However, the potential for stress exists when an environmental pressure is of such a magnitude as to threaten the individual's ability to cope with it in conditions where successful coping is a rewarding experience (McGrath, 1976). In practice this means that one could find an individual flourishing in a setting which, for another, creates suffering and stress-related illness.

In everyday life we rarely encounter severe stressful situations, such as prolonged lack of sleep or physical torture. Instead, weaker but important generators of stress such as the death of a spouse, divorce, impairment of one's faculties, loss of a job, rejection by a colleague, unrequited love, or failure in examinations, all play a crucial part. But people respond differently to stressors. For example, on retirement one group of executives may feel severely depressed, another group may feel moderately sad and frustrated, and a third group may feel content and happy. For others, travelling in a train is less likely to be stressful than travelling by car or by aeroplane. Many of us would find it less stressful to work in difficult or dangerous conditions with people we trust than in similar conditions where we distrust others or lack confidence in ourselves.

Physiological reactions

When a person perceives a situation as frightening or threatening, as could happen in a job that involves risk or danger, a pattern of physical changes in the body is activated resulting in the "flight or fight" response. These changes are regulated by the autonomic nervous system, which consists of many nerves that connect the brain and spinal cord to the various organs of the body. The autonomic nervous system is divided into two parts—the sympathetic and parasympathetic systems.

The sympathetic system—which is dominant for a very stressed person—increases the heart rate and blood pressure and directs blood to the peripheral muscles. It tends to be active when we are preparing for action. It discharges the hormones known as adrenaline and noradrenaline from the adrenal glands. These hormones affect many organs when they enter the blood stream. The liver is activated to dispense glucose, the heart beats faster, and increased arousal is triggered by the flow of adrenaline to the brain. If the person experiences only mild stress, the flow of adrenaline to the brain can produce excitement and pleasure as well as improved performance.

What we should be concerned with, of course, is the frequency of the temporary physical changes in the body (as just described) in the face of acute stress, because the end result could be the onset of permanent physical changes causing illness. The critical factor to note with regard to acute stress is that frequently the fight or flight action mentioned earlier is inappropriate or not possible, and problems arise from the continuous pressures on our system from which there is no escape. Our bodies continue to react, with the result that the build-up of tension develops. If the threatening stimuli continue, we are faced with exhaustion and eventually reach the stage of collapsing under the strain (psychological breakdown).

The opposite to the sympathetic system is the parasympathetic nervous system. It decreases the heart rate and blood pressure, and diverts blood to the gut; it tends to function when we are calm and relaxed.

A specialist in occupational medicine (Murray-Bruce, 1983, 1990) described the body's reaction to stress in the following terms:

> The heart and breathing rates increase, blood pressure goes up, sweating increases, muscles get tense, the eyes widen, and there is heightened alertness. Tense muscles cause headaches, backaches, shoulder and back pains. Clenched hands, clenched jaws, and hunched shoulders are tell-tale signs of stress, along with frowning and fidgeting, finger tremor, and the mopping of a sweaty brow. An anxious person has "butterflies" or churning in the stomach, a dry mouth, weak legs, nausea, a thumping heart, breathlessness and a feeling of light-headedness.

Course participants at a management college reported on symptoms of stress that they had previously experienced. These included dim or fuzzy vision, some chest pains, unusual heart beats, occasional sleep difficulties, frequent episodes of irritability, tiredness, or depression (this was by far the most frequent), and periods in which their work performance was impaired for a few days (Melhuish, 1977).

The following is what a 37-year-old teacher and head of department at a large comprehensive school in the UK, and also a mother of two children, was reported as having said about her plight:

> I am exhausted all the time; I do not sleep very well and when I wake up at night I panic about work; I am losing weight; eczema flares up when the pressure increases; frequently I feel guilty because I do not see enough of my children; I overreact when little things go wrong; recently I could not stop crying at weekends; and my marriage would have collapsed by now if I had not such an understanding husband. I cannot go to senior management because it would sound like I cannot cope, and with a new head in the school I feel under even more pressure to perform. I realise that for the sake of my health and marriage, something will have to change.

In this case the acute pressure or distress stems from trying to cope with a demanding job coupled with work in the home. As we shall see later, the effects of stress can be fatal.

Cost of stress

We are becoming increasingly aware of the true costs of stress at work. According to the Confederation of British Industry (CBI), stress at work was a big factor in the absences of employees from their place of work (CBI, 2001). In 2000 the absence figure was nearly 8 days per employee at a likely cost of about £11 billion, which was lower than it was a decade earlier. To these costs could be added rising medical costs and the cost of a reduction in the quality of work.

On the emotional side, one has to recognise the existence of negative feelings. By impairing the psychological and physical well-being of an employee, stress also affects the employee's family. At the level of society, the effects of stress are reflected in an increase in welfare costs, an increase in socially disruptive behaviour (such as alcoholism and drug abuse), and less involvement in the community. In addition, employers are meeting increasing costs as a result of compensation claims from employees who suffered stress-related illnesses as a result of their experiences at work (Earnshaw & Cooper, 2001). (There is reference to UK cases in the section on role overload later.)

Burnout

Burnout, though not the same as stress, is a related concept. It has been defined as consisting of the development of negativity in a person's response to others, a lowering of one's estimation of personal achievements, and total exhaustion on all fronts (Lee & Ashforth, 1990). Those suffering from burnout lack energy, are fatigued, feel nothing they do is rewarded or encouraged, lack adequate control of their work life, feel helpless, and harbour pessimistic views about life generally (Demir, Ulusoy, & Ulusoy, 2003).

Factors causing burnout are many and varied, including stressors in organisations (which will be discussed later), and unrealistic expectations or ambitions. The consequences of burnout bear some similarity to the consequences of stress (e.g., absences from work, low commitment, and problems relating to colleagues and others). Those affected by burnout are often competent and able executives and, in particular, they can be found in the helping professions, such as counselling, teaching, childcare, nursing, and policing (Cook, 1988). In connection with the police, it is said that burnout is caused by factors such as anxiety from life-threatening situations while carrying out their duties, competitive strivings within the police force in the context of career advancement, the impact of bureaucracy, frustrations about the way the criminal justice system is administered, and insufficient social contacts (Goodman, 1990).

Finally, some argue that burnout could be viewed as a coping mechanism, because it forces the person to disengage from perhaps a pressured existence.

Post-traumatic stress disorder (PTSD)

PTSD occurs in people who have encountered a trauma in which they experienced, witnessed, or were confronted with an event involving actual or threatened death, serious physical injury, or a threat to one's physical integrity. Examples include military combat, physical assault, rape, industrial accidents, and fires in the home and at work (Andreasen & Black, 2001).

The concept of psychological trauma was accepted by the judiciary in the UK over 15 years ago when two booking clerks and a fireman were awarded damages of £65,000 and £34,000 respectively for trauma following the King's Cross London Underground fire disaster, which claimed 31 lives (Frost, 1990). This type of trauma is related to accidents at the workplace, fire, crashes, or similar disasters. By contrast, cumulative trauma could arise from, for example, prolonged exposure to organisational stress. This will be discussed later. PTSD is likely to manifest itself among survivors in the tsunami-hit parts of Asia as a result of the disaster that hit that region in late December 2004. In Thailand, for example, teachers, monks, and other community leaders are being trained in how to recognise and deal with signs of psychological trauma and distress, especially among children (Kazmin, 2005).

PTSD is recognised as a mental health problem (Thompson, 1997). Physicians and psychologists frequently consider PTSD in connection with veterans of Vietnam, the Falklands, or other wars (Hunt, 1997; Orner, 1997). These veterans suffer the classic symptoms of PTSD. They cannot stop thinking about, dreaming about, or having nightmares about traumatic wartime experiences. They might react to any sudden loud noise, such as a car backfiring, by trying to gun down the enemy—they have a flashback and relive the war experience. They also display an inability to maintain previously close relationships, and often suffer from drug and alcohol abuse. People who suffer

---

Mr Jones, a 55-year-old married man, had a perfect work record as a labourer until he suffered a severe crush injury to his legs while he was at work. After more than a year of a series of orthopaedic operations and a painful rehabilitation, he returned to work.

About 6 months later he began to experience recurrent episodes of apprehension, light-headedness, dizziness, and nausea. Eventually, during one of these episodes, he was rushed to a nearby hospital emergency room. He was subsequently classified as disabled because of the repeated episodes, although no abnormalities were identified during medical evaluations.

He was then referred to the occupational medicine clinic. Prior to the clinic's evaluation of his condition, the possibility of PTSD was not considered because there was no recognised connection between his occupational trauma and the subsequent delayed appearance of his symptoms. In the clinic he reported that his recurrent episodes were triggered by reminders of the accident. He first experienced the episodes at work when the man responsible for his accident returned to the work site. The symptoms would also appear whenever he walked past the plant. He was plagued by nightmares about the accident, and, even while awake, he would suddenly see the load of steel that had crushed his legs rolling towards him. He desperately attempted to avoid any reminders of his workplace, and had to make sure that he never walked by the plant. He became severely depressed.

(Schottenfeld & Cullen, 1986)

---

from this disorder often try to blank out the experience. When this fails, they display symptoms including sleeplessness, anger, and extreme jumpiness. According to Dr Curran, a Consultant Psychiatrist at the Mater Infirmary, Belfast, and a specialist in PTSD, these symptoms can often be emotionally crippling (Frost, 1990).

Though not generally recognised, the PTSD syndrome could also apply to occupational injuries. From the caseloads of medical practitioners in an occupational medicine clinic, it has been recognised that some patients with medically unexplained symptoms were suffering from PTSD (Earnshaw & Cooper, 2001; Schottenfeld & Cullen, 1986). A typical PTSD case in an occupational setting is described in Panel 19.1.

A combination of drug therapy and psychotherapy are used in the clinical management of patients with PTSD. Re-experiencing the trauma is often blocked by some tricyclic antidepressant medications, and depressive symptoms may be ameliorated by antidepressant medications. This would be complemented by psychotherapy where the patient is helped to explore the psychological and emotional reactions experienced (Schottenfeld & Cullen, 1986).

Britain's first in-patient facility for PTSD sufferers was set up at Ticehurst Hospital, Kent. The director, a former air force psychiatrist, hoped that by addressing the problems of PTSD, people can avoid long-term problems such as chronic heart disease, abnormal blood pressure, and diabetes, which research has shown are connected with stressful incidents (Rogers, 1993). Another treatment centre—The Traumatic Stress Clinic, London—was opened in the mid-1990s.

A more recent but related condition is acute stress disorder. It occurs in some individuals after a traumatic experience, and could precede PTSD. Symptoms could include emotional numbing, such as feeling detached from others, a feeling of unreality, and amnesia. Although amnesia is not in itself a defence in a court of law, the underlying cause (post-traumatic state) might be so judged (Andreasen & Black, 2001).

Apart from the suggested remedies (medication and psychotherapy) outlined above, counselling (considered later) is also offered to survivors of serious incidents, such as a major disaster. There is reason to believe that this intervention may not be as effective as is generally believed. Doyle (2003) cites research evidence provided by Rick and Briner (2000) who concluded that sometimes the counselling can do more harm than good because it can make the victim relive the experience and compound the original trauma. Also, a limitation was that the counselling varied in quality. However, the victims appreciated the altruism of those who funded the counselling service (e.g., employers, government, etc.).

TABLE 19.1

Factors causing stress to the individual at work

Stressors

From within the organisation	*From within the individual, plus outside influences*
• Role overload/underload • Role ambiguity • Role conflict • Redundancy and early retirement • Responsibility for people • Machine-paced and repetitive work • Decision latitude and job control • Shift work • New technology: VDU work	• Personality • Work relationships • Career development • Family considerations

---

STRESSORS

Among the typical stressful conditions facing people at work are the following (Cox, 1994; Kay, 1974; Kearns, 1973; Sofer, 1970): too much or too little work; time pressures and deadlines to meet; having to make too many decisions; endeavouring to cope with changes that affect the job; concern about the costs in monetary and career terms of making mistakes; excessive and inconvenient working hours; highly repetitive work and lack of job variety; the necessity to work fast; erosion of salary differentials; job insecurity and the prospect of redundancy or being forced into premature retirement; disparity between real authority and authority vested in the job; the feeling of being trapped in a job without much chance of getting a similar or better job elsewhere; a perceived mismatch between performance on the job and the financial benefits secured; reservations about the value of the job in contributing to the output or welfare of the organisation; poor relationship with management and lack of management support; conflicting demands of work and home.

In practice, one may find certain organisationally devised ways of alleviating pressure at work:

For example, deadlines could be set at an unrealistically early date to permit a margin of error so that mistakes or shortcomings could be rectified before it is too late; decisions could be made in groups so as to share the burden of responsibility for a decision; and duties could be reallocated in a department when an individual is very busy and is forced to shelve certain duties. However, there may be occasions when these devices are not directly at the disposal of the manager.

It is now time to examine in some detail the factors that have potential to cause stress at work. These factors are divided into two major categories as: factors within the organisation and factors within the individual, plus outside influences. An expanded version of these factors is included in Table 19.1.

Stress from within the organisation

The discussion of stress within the organisation will begin with an analysis of roles, a topic examined earlier in Chapter 10.

Role overload

A relationship exists between too heavy a workload—i.e., taking and making more telephone calls, more office visits to and from other people, and more meetings for a given unit of work—and heavy cigarette smoking; the latter is an important risk factor as far as coronary heart disease is concerned (French & Caplan, 1970). Too much work can also give rise to a number of symptoms of stress, such as escapist drinking, absenteeism from work, low motivation to work, lower estimation of oneself, and unwillingness to suggest improvements to work procedures and practices (Margolis, Kroes, & Quinn, 1974). Working at more than two jobs that required an excessive number of work hours (60 plus per week) was found to be a critical contributory factor to coronary heart disease (Russek & Zohman, 1958). It is worth noting that the working married woman has a heavy overall workload and is frequently denied the opportunity to recuperate from her remunerative work; this could result in chronic fatigue.

In the contemporary world people at all levels within the organisation have experienced change in the form of downsizing, delayering, outsourcing, and so on, and there is evidence to indicate that this has led to increased workloads and substantially increased job insecurity, lower morale and motivation, and a decline in loyalty to the organisation (Cooper, 2001b). Managers have responsibility for keeping costs and staffing levels in check. In their role of pruning expenditure they will inevitably encounter resistance at the subordinate level, with consequences in terms of damaging relationships of trust and impairing good communications. They also have to contend with pressures from top management who are naturally concerned that policy is implemented in accordance with agreed guidelines. If there are redundancies at shop-floor level and among their colleagues in management, there is a likelihood that their workload will increase. They may also feel that they ought to be seen to be working harder.

With regard to the legal profession, most lawyers in practice charge clients on the basis of billable hours and annual targets can be harsh. It is said that for many lawyers the emphasis on achieving a set number of chargeable hours is the single biggest cause of stress. Of course there are other factors causing stress as well, such as the fear of making costly mistakes, a very competitive environment, and failed job expectations. A spokesperson for LawCare, an organisation set up to help lawyers overcome stress and substance abuse, is reported as saying that when the organisation was founded it was a charity helping lawyers with alcohol-related problems. Now 75% of the calls relate to stress and depression. However, there is still the problem of alcohol, but that arises later in the lawyer's career (SenGupta, 2005).

Certain employees, who have suffered stress due to role overload, have taken legal action. For example, a former junior hospital doctor, backed by the British Medical Association, sued his employers—Bloomsbury Health Authority in London—for stress arising from working excessive hours (nearly 100 hours a week). His claim was that the stress was caused by unreasonable working hours. These conditions left him exhausted and depressed, and endangered the health of his patients (Summers, 1990b). Eventually, he reached the point of total exhaustion and experienced a terrifying incident when he collapsed while driving his car and crashed. He subjected his body to too much pressure and the result was predictable. He received an out of court settlement of £5600 from his former employer. He turned his back on the practice of medicine and subsequently took on modestly remunerated part-time counselling work.

Mr Walker, an Area Social Services Manager in Northumberland, who had previously suffered from a nervous breakdown, left his job due to unbearable pressure, which left him exhausted. He is reported as saying that he felt a "tight band around his head". At work he encountered a five-fold increase in the child abuse caseload and a big increase in demand for services for the elderly and handicapped. A contributory factor to the increased workload was the removal of tiers of management by the employer, leaving those left behind to cope with the workload. In addition, the extra staff promised by the employer were only at the manager's disposal for a very short time. The demands from subordinates were not dealt with adequately and the superiors did not want to know about Mr Walker's difficulties.

The High Court awarded him £175,000 damages because of the employer's failure to provide adequate support. The Court maintained that the County Council was in breach of the care owed to Mr Walker in respect of the second mental breakdown he suffered as a result of the stress and anxiety stemming from his job (Aikin, 1995). The Court also made the point that an employer owes a duty to his employees not to cause them psychiatric damage by the volume or character of work they are required to perform. At the time of the Court award the earnings of the ex-manager, who was then working as a decorator, were a quarter of his previous salary.

Suing for stress has a relatively short history in the UK, but it has been a feature of the US scene for over 30 years. In a report prepared by employment lawyers in the UK, it is suggested that stress cases will follow the path of other injuries at work, and that laws drafted to prevent accidents can easily be directed to include the mental effects of stress. Employers who have taken no steps to identify and reduce stress at work may experience financial sanctions (Kellaway, 1993a). However, one should reflect on the words of a former consultant psychiatrist—Dr Peter Noble, of the Maudsley Hospital, London—who, in a letter to the editor of a daily newspaper, said that the new trend to litigation may compensate some ex-patients, but the main losers apart from employers will be ordinary ex-patients who, having suffered a nervous breakdown, will now face even more disadvantage and discrimination at work.

There is no specific legislation in the UK to control stress at work, but there is legislation that impinges on this area. Under the Health and Safety at Work Act 1974, employers have a duty to ensure so far as reasonably practicable that workplaces are safe and healthy. Under the Management of Health and Safety Regulations 1993, employers are obliged to assess the nature and scale of risk to health in the workplace and base control measures on it. It may be possible under the Disability Discrimination Act 1996 to prosecute employers if they dismiss employees disabled by a stress-related illness stemming from work.

There is an interesting pattern emerging with respect to the destination of incapacity benefits in the UK. The recipients of incapacity benefits on grounds of a mental or behavioural disorder are on the increase, but the recipients of benefits for muscular skeletal disorders are on the decrease in a significant way. The latter has fallen from 194,000 in 1997 to 108,000 in 2003 (Turner, 2004b). This is probably due to the growing awareness of health and safety issues and the continuing decline in manufacturing jobs.

There should be sober reflection on the nature and consequences of overload. Although some people put great pressures on themselves and others, the overload situation may be brought about by poor delegation and poor management of time.

Role underload. The opposite of overload is underload. It could be tantamount to not being sufficiently challenged by work. Role underload could be a feature of repetitive, routine, boring, and under-stimulating work, which can be associated with ill-health (Arnold, 2005). However, certain types of skilled jobs could be associated with underload. For example, airline pilots and workers observing the operation of advanced technological systems in manufacturing have to cope with long spells of time in which they have little to do, but they always have to face the possibility of responding promptly and decisively should an emergency arise. But there are other workers operating in an advanced technological work environment who could be classified as unskilled machine minders, who are also expected to respond promptly if the system malfunctions or fails (Chase & Karowski, 2003).

Role ambiguity

Role ambiguity was introduced and explained in Chapter 10. Sometimes we overlook the importance of clearly specifying what the job requires of the individual. There are a number of circumstances in an organisation when the requirements of a job are unclear as to the objectives laid down and the scope of responsibilities; as a result, colleagues are not altogether clear about what the job entails. In such circumstances a number of undesirable consequences are likely to ensue (Kahn, Wolfe, Quinn, Snoek, & Rosenthal, 1964).

PANEL 19.2: Consequences of stress at work

In a court case in the UK it appears that elements of role overload, role complexity, and role ambiguity were considered prior to the judge awarding £67,000 to a local authority housing officer. This was an important legal case where the employer admitted liability for the illness that led the 44-year-old employee to retire on medical grounds. The amount awarded covered loss of wages, loss of future earnings, and the cost of prescription charges.

The employee in question had spent 26 years with the council, and was promoted to the post of Housing Officer in Birmingham in 1993 where she had to deal with rude and demanding tenants. In addition, she said that she was literally buried in paperwork, and was expected to be a jack-of-all-trades without sufficient briefing from the employer. At times her mind would just go blank. Eventually, she began to suffer panic attacks, anxiety, and depression. It should be noted that the council has since revised its personnel procedures.

(Johnstone, 1999)

These consequences consist of a lowering of job satisfaction, self-confidence, and self-esteem, a general dissatisfaction with life and a feeling that the whole thing is futile, leading to a depressed mood, low motivation to work, an intention to quit the job, and increased blood pressure and pulse rate (French & Caplan, 1970; Margolis et al., 1974). According to Cartwright and Cooper (1997), role ambiguity could also lead to mistrust of colleagues.

In Panel 19.2 there is a description of a case that raises issues connected with different types of role pressure.

Role conflict

Role conflict was introduced and explained in Chapter 10. If a job is arranged in such a way that the individual performing the tasks connected with the job is confused by conflicting demands— e.g., the person is sandwiched between two groups of people who expect a different kind of service, or expect a service different from the one that is presently rendered—or if the person is doing things he or she does not want to do or does not think are part of his or her job description, then the seeds of conflict are sown. As conflict develops, a lowering of job satisfaction is experienced —more so if the conflicting demands originate from the desks of powerful figures in the organisation. In addition, an increase in heart rate and feelings of tension about the job are likely to materialise (French & Caplan, 1970; Kahn et al., 1964). A significant relationship was found between role conflict and coronary heart disease

among managerial employees in the kibbutz system in Israel. However, occupations requiring excessive physical activity (e.g., agricultural work) were associated with a lower incidence of coronary heart disease (Shirom, Eden, Silberwasser, & Kellerman, 1973).

More recent research evidence indicates that role conflict is associated with decreased job satisfaction and higher anxiety levels (Arnold, 2005). Arnold pays particular attention to conflict between the organisational role and the home role, maintaining that it is the subject of increasing comment. The conflict could be reflected in two ways: one where the work role interferes with the family role, and two where the family role interferes with the work role (i.e., the role within the family puts a lot of pressure on the role within the organisation). What seems to be happening is that the quantity of mental processing and energy demanded by one role does not leave behind sufficient personal resources or energy to deal adequately with the demands of other roles. Different types of behaviour required in the two roles could aggravate this; for example, the work role requires a particular type of behaviour (e.g., dominance), while the home role requires more cooperative behaviour. Conflict between work roles and home roles can produce different types of stress. Not being able to devote enough time to a particular role could lead to guilt or anxiety about failure to fulfil one's role properly, with the possibility of low job satisfaction.

An important consideration is role conflict due to lack of energy. This could produce exhaustion or irritability. Conflict based on a clash of values between the organisational role and the family role can lead to a sense of alienation or loss of self-identity (Kossek & Ozeki, 1998). There are further observations on the interaction between work and home life later in this chapter. In certain cases it would be wise to take nonwork roles (incorporating both family and leisure roles) and work roles into account when focusing on stress.

Responsibility for people

Responsibility for people can be stressful. Coronary heart disease, in the form of diastolic blood pressure and serum cholesterol levels, was found to be associated with bearing more responsibility for people than for things (Wardwell, Hyman, & Bahnson, 1964). Having responsibility for people involves spending more time interacting with others, attending more meetings, and keeping to deadlines often working alone. This appears to be the predicament of the older executive who has assumed greater responsibility (Pincherle, 1972). But taking on increasing responsibility is not just the preserve of the older person; increasingly younger people nowadays are assuming significant levels of responsibility.

Just as we identify greater responsibility as a source of stress, the same could be said of too little responsibility.

Machine-paced and repetitive work

The nature of repetitive work varies from company to company, as does the individual's susceptibility to stressful experiences. Nevertheless, repetitive work is said to be potentially stressful, and for certain individuals can threaten the quality of their life and health. Repetition could be compounded by other factors such as the worker's posture, and also shift work. With regard to the latter, night work is critical. The most obvious manifestation of night work is sleep disturbance. According to Cox (1985), repetitive work amounts to a discrete set of activities, repeated over and over again in the same order without planned interruptions by other activities or tasks. The discrete set of activities is simple and unskilled, with perhaps a short time cycle. Features

of reaction to repetitive work are "switching off" and "letting your mind go blank"; these are strategies used by car assembly workers to cope with repetitive and monotonous tasks.

A source of dissatisfaction could be lack of control over the task, whereby workers enjoy little autonomy and experience little responsibility. Under-utilisation of skill is frequently associated with repetitive work, as are relatively high levels of machine pacing (often in a relatively isolated workstation with reduced social contacts) and a conspicuous lack of job complexity and participation.

There is a view that workers engaged in repetitive work practices suffer poorer health than most other occupational groups, and this would be particularly so for those engaged in shift work that involves night working (Cox, 1985). From a starting point that there is no clear evidence to support the suggestion that repetition, pacing, and short cycle time (the so-called "evils" of assembly line work) harm workers' health, a group of researchers undertook a government-backed research study at a large car factory (Broadbent & Gath, 1981). The index of health used in the study consisted of:

- anxiety (feelings of tension and worry);
- depression (lethargy and inability to make an effort);
- somatic symptoms (stomach upsets, giddiness, and similar sensations when mental health is poor); and
- obsessional problems, manifest as obsessional personality (reflected in, for example, perfectionism) and an obsessional stance (reflected in recent failures in the exercise of control due to, for example, unwanted thoughts).

The results to emerge from the study were:

(1) Workers doing repetitive work disliked the job, but were not necessarily unhealthy.
(2) Workers who were machine paced to a marked extent in their work showed a higher level of anxiety.
(3) Workers with a pronounced obsessional personality (i.e., meticulous, conscientious,

and precise) were no less satisfied than other people, but they suffered more anxiety when they worked in machine-paced jobs. Therefore, a particular personality type—the obsessional personality—is unsuited to jobs that are machine paced. It certainly seems reasonable to assume that workers are likely to become anxious if they have no control over the speed of their operations.

(4) Short work cycle (under 1 minute) was not connected with either job dissatisfaction or ill-health, when compared with work cycles of up to half an hour in repetitive jobs.

(5) A slightly higher proportion of workers in machine-paced jobs may need psychiatric help than other people.

From the research evidence it is clear that machine pacing, rather than short cycle times, is a hazard, and that people can become stressed without being dissatisfied with the job. The message for practitioners is that they should be cautious in applying the results of the study, and be aware of the hazardous nature of machine pacing.

Decision latitude and job control

Decision latitude relates to the opportunity for the significant use of judgement and discretion in the job. When this factor was high and combined with a demanding job, people experienced job satisfaction and reduced depression. The opposite appeared to be the case, particularly with respect to satisfaction, when jobs were rated low in terms of decision latitude and demands posed by the task (Karasek, 1979). To relieve job strain it is suggested that the employee should be given greater scope for decision making and use of discretion at work but, at the same time, that this should not be overdone in the quest to obtain more substantial job responsibilities.

In a later study, the positive health implications (i.e., a reduction in illness among full-time workers, including heart disease among males) of greater control in one's job, together with greater opportunities for democratic participation at work, are endorsed (Karasek, 1990). The researcher points out that one of the most disturbing conclusions of his study is that current changes to white-collar jobs often involved less opportunity to exercise control at work, especially for older workers and women. Added to this is the stressful experience of lack of employee involvement in processes leading up to job reorganisation and change. It should be noted that change is potentially stressful because people move from predictable environments where they feel secure. They may take one or two changes in their stride, but if too many things are changed at the same time they may become stressed and defensive.

On the question of job control, Fisher (1985) maintains that when blue-collar workers are compared with white-collar workers, the former fare worse in the sense that they experience less control. The alleged disadvantages accruing to blue-collar workers, which could result in more distress at work, are as follows:

• Blue-collar workers, who operate directly on the line handling a product or process, are more likely to feel helpless in that they are less able to avoid unpleasant conditions, and have less control over how their time is spent at work. By contrast, those in certain managerial posts may have the opportunity to avoid circumstances they do not like, but they have to be careful in case they are penalised for such behaviour.

• Blue-collar workers have less scope to modify the task, because their work is a well-defined process and integrated in an overall production process in a systematic way. Should there be unpleasant conditions in the job—often expressed as a greater range of industrial hazards and uncomfortable working conditions than those experienced by white-collar workers—they are generally lumbered with them, and the only option open to them is to put up with the conditions or leave the job.

• In the sense of marketability, it is not easy for blue-collar workers to change jobs, because of lower income (with consequent lower savings) and reduced options.

• Opportunities for social activity at work are greater if the worker enjoys greater discretion. In this sense the blue-collar worker is at a disadvantage. It is said that the blue-collar worker cannot easily counteract the unfavourable conditions at work by exercising control outside mainstream work activity.

Nowadays there is a tendency to accept the mediating influence of self-efficacy (discussed in Chapters 2 and 4) when examining the relationship between job control and stress. Schaubroeck and Merritt (1997) believe that self-efficacy plays an important role in the way it interacts with job control in reducing the harmful effects of stress. Employees who experience a pronounced level of mastery in their jobs could experience a decrease in stress levels if they are given increasing control over their work. However, for employees with low efficacy, increasing control over their work could lead to much more pressure than before. The message coming across is that it is important for organisations to increase employees' feelings of self-efficacy and mastery than it is, for example, to go down the road of job redesign in order to foster greater self-control.

Shift work

Many workers do jobs requiring them to work in shifts—often rotating shifts. A number of studies have found shift work to be a stress factor at work. It can affect neurophysical rhythms—such as blood temperature, metabolic rate, blood sugar levels, mental efficiency, and work motivation —which may ultimately result in stress-related disease (Monk & Tepas, 1985). In addition, it has a negative impact on sleep patterns and family and social life.

In a study of offshore oil workers it was concluded that the longer the shift the greater the stress, and shift work was listed among the three most important sources of stress (Sutherland & Cooper, 1987). In another study, Demir, Ulusoy, and Ulusoy (2003) found that working night shifts led to greater exhaustion, loss of energy, and sense of depersonalisation than working day shifts.

Doyle (2003), having examined some of the evidence, concludes that night shift work can create stomach upsets, disruption of family and social life, and a greater risk of heart disease. But it should be recognised that it is shift work that has the direct effect of disrupting sleep patterns that causes the most problems. There is evidence to indicate that a substantial proportion (60%) of shift workers either liked shift work or tolerated it. There are further observations on shift work in Panel 19.3.

New technology: VDU work

A feature of recent years has been the development of computer technology and its application

---

PANEL 19.3: Consequences associated with shift work

Drawing on empirical studies, a researcher addressed the issue of shift work, and concluded that the following consequences are associated with it:

* It leaves people's body clocks in a perpetual state of disarray.
* Workers on night shift are more irritable than day workers; they are also less alert, are quicker to make mistakes at work, and are also more lethargic at home. In a North American study, it was found that working night shifts had a modestly negative effect on the quality of a marriage, with issues of jealousy and concerns about infidelity featuring prominently.
* Rotating night shifts can be even worse. Having one's working hours changed every few days or weeks causes not only sleep deprivation, but also has an effect described as having permanent jet lag. This is a fate that affects workers in a range of jobs, including the investment and electronic media, as well as factory production. In one study "over 80% of rotating shift workers experienced serious sleep disruption, including insomnia at home and drowsiness at work, which lowered their productivity as well as the quality of their lives. There was also a higher risk of cardiovascular and digestive tract disorders."
* Shift work can create a sense of isolation by making it much more difficult to see friends, or even to ring someone up for a chat.

(Sigman, 1993)

in a wide variety of industrial and commercial processes. Part of this development is the growth in the use of visual display units (VDUs) and in the use of business machines and equipment, such as word-processors and the growing use of e-mail and the internet.

Concern has been expressed over the direct health effects of VDU operation, particularly the effects of exposure to radiation. Apparently there is no need to fear any threat from radiation emitted by VDUs. Significant improvements in the design of the cathode ray tube (CRT) and associated equipment in recent years have resulted in ionising radiation emission from VDU terminals becoming almost negligible (only fractionally above the level of natural background radiation). A report prepared by the National Radiological Protection Board concluded that radiation from VDUs cannot cause physical injury to either the skin or the eyes of people working with them (Anderson, 1980). A similar conclusion was arrived at in a Health and Safety Executive report (Mackay, 1980).

The majority of problems connected with VDU operation stem from indirect factors of a visual and postural nature, and possibly anxiety related to fatigue (Mackay & Cox, 1984). In recent years there has been much comment on physical disorders—referred to as repetitive strain injury or RSI. This arises when the operator maintains the same posture at a keyboard over time, placing the muscles in the arms and back under constant strain (i.e., static loading), which results in pain.

RSI became an issue in the UK newspaper industry when nine journalists suffering from RSI, as a result of working on computer keyboards,

were informed by their employer—the *Financial Times*—that they should take early retirement on health grounds. The company was served with six writs from RSI sufferers (*Independent*, 1991). An ex-*Financial Times* subeditor failed in a High Court attempt to win damages for injury caused by the alleged negligence of the newspaper in introducing computer technology, the poor ergonomic conditions in the workplace, the repetitive nature of the work, and the lack of proper keyboard training. The subeditor claimed that he had contracted a psychologically based upper limb disorder, which became chronic and rendered him unable to work. The *Financial Times* claimed that he suffered from occupational neurosis caused by tension and nonwork related stress among other factors (Dalby & Wood, 1995). Also, in a court ruling in October 1993, a British judge rejected a claim for damages by an RSI sufferer—a journalist employed by Reuters—and said that the term RSI had no place in the medical books. However, a former typist, now an RSI sufferer, received an out of court settlement (see Panel 19.4).

Williams (1985) feels that RSI emanates from a combination of new technology and the relentless repetition of many traditional office jobs. The design of equipment and furniture has obviously a part to play in solving this problem. However, Williams maintains that job enlargement, rest pauses, and exercise programmes have a greater part to play to counteract the monotony of the keyboard.

The frequency with which a computer terminal is used can have a material influence on the outcome. Johansson and Aronsson (1984) found that those who occasionally used a computer

---

PANEL 19.4: Compensation award for RSI sufferer

A former Inland Revenue typist in the UK was awarded a record £79,000 compensation for the loss of her job because of RSI in an out of court settlement. The typist was forced to leave her job after suffering for 2 years from tennis elbow, which she claimed was caused by using an electronic typewriter. Her condition was related to posture, lack of breaks from typing between 13,000 and 16,000 strokes an hour, the general inadequacy of the office furniture she used, and a putative management environment that emphasised greater effort to achieve higher output.

The former typist is registered as disabled, cannot pick up a 1 lb bag of sugar, and is unable to do housework such as ironing, vacuuming, and cleaning. It is reported that management in the Inland Revenue is planning to pay greater attention to ergonomic aspects of work in the future.

(Donkin, 1994a)

terminal felt that the experience helped them to do their job quicker and better. However, frequent users of the computer suffered stress, eyestrain, headaches, and pains in the arms and shoulders. A primary source of stress resulted from the breakdown of the computer and from phone calls interrupting work. A particular irritation was not knowing how long the interruptions would last and seeing the work pile up. This seemed to influence people's work behaviour because there was a tendency to work harder in the morning in anticipation of a computer breakdown. This resulted in frequently spending more time on the computer than prescribed by the company regulations. A suggested way forward is that work should be planned to allow for computer breakdowns, with the attendant prescription that rest pauses should be scheduled.

Mackay and Cox (1984), based on the outcome of their research, have summarised the impact of VDUs on work under three headings: underload, de-skilling, and control.

- *Underload*. This amounts to being understretched and it is a principal characteristic of many repetitive work practices, particularly machine-paced assembly lines. It is now associated with VDU operation where simple clerical tasks are computerised. Following computerisation, these tasks retain their monotonous and repetitive features, such as short cycle and repetition. In the earlier subsection on machine-paced and repetitive work, the dissatisfying features of repetitive work were described.
- *De-skilling*. When a job is changed to accommodate new technology, an element of de-skilling can occur. Should this happen, it amounts to the loss of some of the past investment in skills development. Therefore, the existing patterns of skills are not fully utilised, with the likely absence of challenge and job interest.
- *Control*. An important factor determining stress-related symptoms among VDU operators is the lack of control. It can increase substantially the number of considerations the operator has to confront, and inevitably leads to fatigue. In some computerised systems the

machine is able to monitor the performance of the operator in keying-in data. The resultant control information could, in many instances, be used to determine levels of remuneration through piece-rate payment systems. Understandably, this type of machine control is often resented and regarded with suspicion by computer operators. Consequently it is associated with feelings of fatigue and stress.

The response of the computer itself following the keying-in of information is also a factor to consider. Where response times are very long, or variable in length, uncertainty and frustration can be created. These problems can be exacerbated by technical disturbances and breakdowns, if they occur frequently. Some ideas about how to tackle the factors identified here as negative outcomes arising from VDU operations are set out in Panel 19.5. (Other aspects of VDU operation are discussed in Chapters 4 and 14.)

Stress from within the individual, plus outside influences

As shown in Table 19.1, this topic will be discussed with reference to personality, work relationships, career development, redundancy and unemployment, early retirement, and family considerations.

Personality

A number of perspectives on personality were discussed in Chapter 2. When considering the effects of stress on executives, it is wise to take into account the individual's personality, and their ability to withstand stressful conditions. As the following studies show, personality appears to be a key factor in this respect. Patients in one study with coronary heart disease or related diseases were considered to be emotionally unstable and introverted (Lebovits, Shekelle, & Ostfeld, 1967). Employees with rigid personalities were more prone to rushing jobs assigned to them from above and to be dependent on other people, whereas those with flexible personalities were more likely to be influenced by others and to suffer from work

---

PANEL 19.5: Counteracting VDU problems

Minimise repetition
The repetitive elements in the operator's task should be minimised by introducing a variable workload during the day, instead of long periods of concentrated work. It is also helpful for operators to know what is in store for them.

Discretion on work allocation
With regard to the allocation of tasks over a set period of time, allow the individual some discretion on how work is allocated. This offers some potential for the use of individual skills.

Introduce challenge
Endeavour to avoid treating the VDU operator as essentially a machine-minder. Where possible, jobs should be designed to be mentally challenging, but at the same time to be within the realm of the operator's abilities.

Screen quality
If the VDU equipment is used intensely and continuously, then there is a need for optimum screen features and good workplace conditions. But if the VDU operator's task consists of a variety of work activities, some of which may include VDU operation, then less than satisfactory screen features could be tolerated.

Design procedures
Improvements in ergonomic aspects of the VDU equipment will have little overall effect if staff are demotivated and suffer from low morale. Any process leading to enrichment of the jobs of VDU operators should involve both the designers and users of the system during the various phases of design and implementation.

Rest breaks
In many jobs we take natural breaks or pauses. For VDU operators this would mean time spent not viewing the VDU screen because they are doing other things, and this distraction would help to prevent the onset of fatigue, which in turn affects performance. But informal breaks are less frequent in certain types of VDU work—for example, data-entry tasks requiring continuous and sustained attention, concentration, and high rates of data entry. In work of this nature the introduction of formal rest pauses should help the maintenance of attention and concentration. Issuing guidance about the duration of rest pauses can prove difficult. Some people complain that they are too short to prevent fatigue occurring, whereas others view them as unnecessarily prolonged and frustrating. In the final analysis the length of a rest pause can only be determined by a consideration of the individual operator's job. However, some general statements can be made (Mackay & Cooper, 1987):

- As adverse symptoms often arise when people try to maintain their performance in the face of accumulated fatigue, rest pauses should be arranged prior to the onset of fatigue, and should not be provided as a means to recuperate from it. The rest pause should be introduced when performance is at a maximum, just before a decrease in productivity sets in.
- Short, frequently occurring rest pauses appear to be more satisfactory than longer pauses taken occasionally.
- Ideally, the break from work should be taken away from the location of the VDU.
- The nature of the work should be considered. Rest pauses are more effective for work that requires concentration than for work that is more or less automatic. The latter leaves the employee free to daydream, converse with others, or to follow similar monotony-reducing strategies.
- Rest pauses are likely to be more useful for relatively ineffective workers.

---

overload. Introverts are said to withdraw from interpersonal relationships that produce stress and, in doing so, complicate matters by preventing communication and making interaction and problem solving more difficult (Kahn et al., 1964).

SenGupta (2005) reports observations of professionals in the legal profession. A spokesperson for White Water Strategies, a London-based executive coaching consultancy, makes reference to the "legal personality" as an accepted term in legal circles. It refers to a highly driven, detail-conscious perfectionist, with a tendency to be pessimistic and blaming themselves for any predicament. The chief executive of LawCare, a UK charity offering support to lawyers, tends to echo this view when she says that lawyers display facets of the obsessive personality: "They have to do a perfect job and if that means giving 110% they do so whatever the price." The result is that lawyers are the professionals most likely to suffer from depression, stress, and alcohol abuse (SenGupta, 2005).

Friedman and Rosenman's research identifies a relationship between certain behavioural traits and a proneness to heart disease (Rosenman, Friedman, & Strauss, 1964). The individuals in their studies were rated on personality factors prior to the actual medical diagnosis, and this was conducted without awareness of the behavioural traits. Those classified as Type A in behaviour were people who exhibited coronary-prone behaviour, which can be expressed as follows:

- extreme competitiveness;
- striving for achievement;
- aggressiveness;
- haste;
- impatience;
- restlessness;
- hyperalertness;
- explosive speech;
- tenseness of facial muscles;
- feelings of being under pressure of time; and
- keenness to assume the challenge of responsibility.

Type A people tend to set deadlines or quotas for themselves at work or at home at least once per week, whereas the opposite—Type B—will do so only occasionally. Type A people tend to bring work home frequently, whereas Type B will rarely do so. Also, Type A people are in general substantially involved and committed to their work, and other aspects of their lives are relatively neglected. They tend to possess the following risk factors: high serum cholesterol levels, elevated beta lipoproteins, decreased blood clotting and elevated daytime excretion of norepinephrine, more incidence of acute myocardial infarction and angina pectoris. In addition, they are less likely to give up smoking. It is also suggested that individuals susceptible to Type A behaviour tend to be professional or managerial staff between the ages of 36 and 55 years, living in urban environments. They show a tendency to suppress stress symptoms and fatigue because they believe that illness might interfere with the completion of various important tasks.

The relationship between Type A behaviour and symptoms of stress is supported in a study of 236 managers in 12 different companies (Howard, Cunningham, & Rechnitzer, 1976). This showed that Type A behaviour was associated in a significant way with high blood pressure and higher cholesterol and triglyceride levels. A high percentage of the managers in each of the age groups studied were cigarette smokers, and Type A managers were less interested in exercise.

In a study of 384 male salaried employees in the USA (based on questionnaires, interviews, and physical examinations), it was found that there was no direct association between Type A behavioural patterns and risk factors connected with coronary heart disease (Chesney et al., 1981), a view that was challenged by Friedman and Booth-Kewley (1987). Other evidence from the USA, where most of the research on this subject originates, shows an absence of data on the association between Type A behaviour and coronary heart disease in women, blacks, Hispanics, and young adults. Also, sufficient data have not been accumulated to show conclusively what aspects of Type A behaviour are coronary-prone, and what aspects are not (Matthews & Haynes, 1986). It is difficult to identify research evidence tracing subjects from the point of selection for a job through their careers in order to discover how changes and influences over time affect their behaviour.

Finally, Baron (2002), having reflected on and recognised Type A behaviour patterns, concludes that this is an aspect of personality with important implications for individuals' health and well-being. He then goes on to say that having the characteristics of a Type A person is not necessarily a death sentence because individuals can learn to reduce their tendency towards Type A behaviour.

Locus of control. The concept of locus of control has been discussed already as a dimension of personality in Chapter 2. A prevailing view of the relationship between locus of control and life stress holds that people who define events in their lives as being outside their control (i.e., external locus of control) will be less able to cope effectively with stress, and are therefore more likely to experience physical and psychological distress than people with internal locus of control beliefs.

Externals see themselves as powerless to influence day-to-day events.

On the other hand, if people define stressful situations as amenable to their own control (i.e., internal locus of control) it is possible that they have sufficient confidence in themselves to deal with stressful situations in a way that minimises the negative impact (Cooper, Dewe, and O'Driscoll, 2001; Krause & Stryker, 1984). This was shown in a study of female student nurses. The internals were more adaptive at modifying their coping strategies after having appraised the particular stressful situation. This flexibility was not evident in the case of the externals, who appeared hardly to alter their mode of coping (Parkes, 1984). But we have to recognise that situations might arise where the person with an internal locus of control outlook may not be able to influence events in the manner indicated and therefore could end up as a frustrated individual (Arnold, 2005).

Apparently, internal locus of control dispositions in a group of undergraduates can be traced back to health habits as a child. Health habits included regular visits by children to medical practitioners for check-ups and vaccinations. Apart from the promotion of good health, these habits—more likely to be found in the higher socio-economic groups—are important in that they contribute to the development of beliefs that underpin sound preventative health behaviour (Lau, 1982). Paradoxically, early experience of illness was not positively related to internal locus of control beliefs in this study. Specific behaviour, where locus of control is related to health, includes seeking information on health hazards and remedies, taking medication, keeping appointments with physicians, maintaining a diet, and giving up smoking. With regard to these types of behaviour, internals fared well, though in some cases externals showed positive interest and action (Wallston & Wallston, 1978).

It is suggested that one should look to the extreme positions on a continuum ranging from "internal" to "external". According to Phares (1976), both the extremely internal and extremely external person may be especially vulnerable to the effects of life stress. In particular, the extremely

internal types who confront stressful conditions may be so overcome with a sense of personal responsibility for the occurrence of the stressful event that they may suffer from anxiety and depressive reactions.

The plight of the extreme internal is substantial at both the theoretical and empirical levels. At the theoretical level it is suggested that extreme internals possess a hysterical rigidity that produces an incapacity to live with uncontrollable events in life, and prevents them from taking effective coping action (Antonovsky, 1979). In an empirical study (Krause & Stryker, 1984) of men aged 45–54, extreme internals (who were gripped by guilt feelings on account of feeling personally responsible for the initial event) were coupled with moderate externals as people who are less likely to initiate constructive efforts to deal with stressful events, because they feel their best attempts cannot influence life events. (The stressful events included financial loss, unemployment, increased job pressure, and retirement.) But the results showed that moderate externals were the most vulnerable to the effects of job and economic stress, whereas the group that came out best in ability to cope effectively with stressful events was the moderate internals.

Work relationships

A number of desirable and undesirable consequences stem from the relationship between superiors, subordinates, and colleagues (Sosik & Godshalk, 2000). When the relationship is good it leads to an improvement in individual and organisational health. When the relationship is deficient or bad, as one finds in circumstances where distrust among staff is rampant, it can give rise to poor or inadequate interpersonal communication, leading to reduced job satisfaction and a feeling of being threatened by one's colleagues and superiors (French & Caplan, 1970; Kahn et al., 1964).

Jealousy, humiliation, arguments, and reprimands all contribute to feelings of stress, and may lead to negative emotions that can be exhausting and debilitating. John Hunter, the 18th century physician, who was prone to angina pectoris, once remarked that his life was in the hands of any rascal who chose to annoy or tease him. He got into an argument with a colleague who contradicted him and became very involved in a verbal encounter; he then stopped talking, left the room, and immediately dropped dead (Barnard, 1981). Where rivalry and office politics occur in relationships between colleagues, support from one's peers in difficult situations may be lacking, with obvious repercussions (Lazarus, 1966).

If a highly competitive atmosphere exists, sharing of problems may cease as an activity because people fear that they may not be able to stand their ground and perform adequately. In today's conditions of constant cuts in expenditure and programmes of rationalisation, quite understandably people feel anxious in the face of uncertainty as to what is going to happen next. In such conditions there is a real danger of losing a sense of belonging and identification with the organisation or part of it, with clear repercussions in terms of anxiety and stress.

The dampening influence emanating from an incompetent superior cannot be overstated. This may be reflected in a number of ways. The superior may be bankrupt technically in conditions where a deficiency in this respect is serious. He or she may be unable to focus seriously on key issues, be prone to digress frequently and listen inattentively, fail to act on sensible ideas or suggestions put forward for serious consideration, and may lack the confidence to take initiatives backed up by a reasonable amount of preparation. In addition, a failure to empathise with others and the lack of a modicum of charisma are limiting factors. The subordinate who expects a better calibre superior, but is encumbered with the type of manager just described, may suffer from some of the classical symptoms of stress.

For a long time the desirability of encouraging managers to adopt a participative leadership style has been advocated. It is believed that the superior who extends the hand of friendship to subordinates, who develops mutual trust, respect, and warmth with subordinates, and who is constructive in his or her criticisms, without playing favourites or taking advantage of subordinates, is likely to go a long way in neutralising pressure that originates from the job (Buck, 1972; Sosik

& Godshalk, 2000). It is claimed that more involvement in the decision-making process by subordinates, where they get feedback on their performance and are duly recognised for their contribution, leads to higher productivity, better relationships between superiors and subordinates, more individual control and autonomy, and less staff turnover, all of which are conducive to good mental health (Coch & French, 1948). Sauter, Hurrel, and Cooper (1989) associate the individual's feeling of control, and the consequent feeling of well-being, with participation in the decision-making process, which fosters identification with the organisation and a sense of belongingness. A similar view is taken by Spector (2000).

On the other hand, lack of participation in decision making is said to promote strain and stress at work because the freedom of thought and movement enjoyed by subordinates is restricted as a result of close supervision and low autonomy (Buck, 1972). One group of researchers claims that failure to allow participation to take root was related in a significant way to a number of risks to personal health. These are poor overall physical health, escapist drinking, depressed mood, low self-esteem, low job satisfaction and satisfaction with life, low levels of motivation to work, an intention to quit, and absenteeism (Margolis et al., 1974).

A word of caution is called for before unequivocally endorsing the participative approach as a panacea for problems connected with management style. To use this approach successfully in managing subordinates, managers must be adept at delegating responsibilities and be able to manage effectively through an open process (Donaldson & Gowler, 1975). Otherwise, a certain level of anxiety, stress, and resentment may arise because managers recognise that their actual power falls short of their formal power and, as a consequence, their formal role and status are eroded. It is also conceivable that the participative approach is seen as "soft" and a waste of time, partly because of the view that subordinates do not wish to get involved or participate in decision making. This eventually places a barrier in the way of doing a good job and achieving a high level of productivity. A full discussion of the participative leadership style, including situations where it may not easily take root, appeared in Chapter 12.

Bullying. Hoel, Rayner, and Cooper (1999) maintain that bullying is quite common in the workplace. It can be reflected in actions designed to deliberately humiliate, ridicule, and socially isolate the person and is a form of behaviour that can be exercised in subtle and devious ways, such as giving the victim an exceedingly difficult work target to achieve or denying the victim crucial information that is necessary to execute a task properly, thereby allowing the perpetrator to criticise the quality of the work performance of the victim. Bullying can take place in the context of normal social interaction when, for example, colleagues make insulting remarks or play practical jokes at another person's expense (Leymann, 1996).

People who are bullied, whether it is at school or in employment, can be traumatised by the experience. Doyle (2003) advises those who feel they are being bullied to keep a diary of incidents because any one incident alone may appear trivial, whereas an aggregation of incidents can create misery and humiliation for those at the receiving end of them, eventually leading to a demoralising experience with a real fear of facing the work day, or perhaps worse.

The following is an example of where bullying at work resulted in a victory for the person bullied. A computer analyst with 9 years' service resigned from a company in the financial services field—Crédit Lyonnais Rouse, London—after being at the receiving end of public abuse from the financial director. Apparently the financial director swore at him in an open-plan office for allowing an old printer to remain on a filing cabinet in contravention of company rules. The case was brought to an industrial tribunal, which heard evidence from the financial director that he was unrepentant, claiming that he gave the analyst "a severe, well-merited and public reprimand". From this statement one can conclude that the financial director's behaviour was not an unexpected aberration but part of his management style. The chairman of the industrial tribunal rebuked the financial

director, saying that he neither apologised nor sought to make amends for his discourteous behaviour. The computer analyst was awarded £11,000 for "constructive dismissal" (Fursland, 1995).

In a more recent case the damages awarded to a senior "bullied" employee were more substantial. Mr Horkulak was a senior director in the UK of Cantor Fitzgerald, the US-based broker, the firm that lost substantial numbers of employees in the 9/11 terrorist attack on the twin-towers in New York. This case was widely reported and raised questions about the extent to which foul language and bullying were part of the dealing room culture. It also raised legal issues about the extent to which top managers were entitled to behave aggressively towards those reporting to them. During the court case Mr Horkulak claimed that Lee Amaitis, the firm's president, regularly screamed obscenities at him and once threatened to break him in two. The firm claimed that Mr Horkulak, who admitted to using cocaine and heavy drinking while working for Cantor Fitzgerald, had a long history of stress and anxiety at work and was said to walk away from difficult situations. The end result was that Mr Horkulak was awarded damages of approximately £900,000 in 2004 because of the bullying, cut by around £116,000 after the case went to the Court of Appeal in London in 2005 (Tait, 2005).

The following is an example of an initiative taken by an organisation committed to confronting bullying and other undesirable practices in the workplace. The director of human resources at Chelsea and Westminster Healthcare NHS Trust is quoted as saying that the Trust is committed to the physical and psychological health, safety, and welfare of its employees (Trust News, 2001):

The trust believes that all individuals have the right to be treated with dignity and respect at work and affirms that harassment, discrimination, or bullying at work, in any form, is unacceptable . . . We are firmly committed to promoting a working environment free from all forms of hostility, so that staff are enabled to achieve their full potential, contribute more effectively to organizational success, and achieve higher levels of job satisfaction.

The Trust introduced a "Dignity at Work Policy", which specified the different forms harassment can take. In this document there is advice on both formal and informal ways in which staff can tackle the problem. In particular it is said that any employee who believes that he or she is being bullied or harassed should avail themselves of the opportunity to discuss the situation confidentially with someone who is impartial, empathetic, and trained in issues of equality. The Trust set about recruiting a team of Harassment Advisers: "The Harassment Adviser will be part of a team. The aim is to provide a professional, yet informal and friendly service, which staff can use with confidence, and which is independent of line management systems." Staff who are interested in this role are asked to come forward, and they will receive special training on a course lasting three and a half days. When trained they will offer confidential advice, guidance, and support to any member of staff who feels they are being harassed.

Career development

Progression in a career (a topic discussed in Chapter 18) is of prime importance to many executives and managers. But with fairly rapid technological, economic, and social change and development in society, uncertainty arises because of the real possibility of having to change career during one's working life. As a consequence, career development stress is likely to occur much more frequently later in life, unless executives and managers adapt their expectations to coincide with these developments. Middle age is a particularly vulnerable stage because it is then that career opportunities can decrease significantly and career progress can grind to a near halt.

In the case of men, various manifestations of the "male menopause"—considered by some to be a myth—are likely to occur (Constandse, 1972). These include:

- a proneness to dwell on fears and disappointments;
- a feeling of being isolated;
- doubting one's ability to get on top of a new assignment or job;
- a belief that the old knowledge and skills are no longer as relevant as they once were;
- a realisation that energy is becoming more scarce or is being channelled into family activities; and
- coping with competition from younger colleagues.

In the case of women, apparently, blockages to career development are pronounced among female managers (Davidson & Cooper, 1983). The most damaging health and job satisfaction factors were associated with career development and related issues—e.g., sex discrimination in promotion, inadequate training, insufficient delegation of assignments to women, and male colleagues being treated more favourably.

At the present time, pruning of expenditure and cutting back on staffing levels are tending to lead to a situation of more competition for the limited number of promotions within organisations. Also, with restricted career opportunities outside the organisation, a number of managers are likely to feel trapped because a barrier is placed in the path to the realisation of their ambition and potential. In circumstances such as these, frustrations develop and can be directed negatively against the organisation, or the system of authority within it, or, where that is not possible, against colleagues and the family (Culbert, 1974). The situation can be even worse if the manager is passed over in the promotion stakes: psychosomatic illness has been attributed to such an event (Morris, 1956). Equally sensitive might be a situation in which a previous subordinate now becomes a person's boss.

In one sense, occupational mobility has a positive aspect to it, but in another sense it may produce negative consequences. Those who were occupationally mobile (four or more job changes) and geographically mobile (two or more cross-border moves) were said to be more vulnerable to heart disease than those who belonged to stable occupational groups (Syme, Hyman, & Enterline, 1964). Some people may feel uneasy about being over-promoted, just as others would feel uneasy about being under-promoted or having reached the end of their career path. The over-promoted manager may be grossly overworked in order to hold down the job and, at the same time, may engage in behaviour designed to mask inner insecurities (McMurray, 1973). People who were fully stretched, having been given responsibility exceeding their ability, were found to progress from minor psychological symptoms to marked psychosomatic complaints and, finally, to mental illness (Brook, 1973). Apparently, under-promoted people, given responsibility below the corresponding level of their ability, suffered similar complaints.

Performance management is a valid concept in the context of career development. Performance appraisal techniques, discussed in Chapter 17, could be used to determine progression within the organisation. However, being evaluated or appraised can be a stressful experience for many employees (Fletcher, 2001). Whether it is the evaluative appraisal or the development appraisal, the experience can be anxiety-arousing for both the appraiser and appraisee. This could stem from the way interpersonal issues are handled in the appraisal process, and also where some appraisers may feel acutely uncomfortable about making decisions that can affect another person's career.

Redundancy and unemployment

Before examining the adverse effects of being without a job, it seems appropriate to dwell for a moment on the significance of work (see Panel 19.6).

Feelings of insecurity arise because of the fear of redundancy or demotion, the fear that one's skills are becoming obsolete, or when there is

---

PANEL 19.6: The nature of work

A job offers us a recognised place in a community, confers self-respect and status, and provides a standard by which others judge us. In social introductions, questions are often asked such as "What do you do?" However, job titles can be misleading because some groups use grandiose titles. Also, where a job title is not considered to be particularly significant, some workers may mention the organisation for which they work. A good fit between the employee's characteristics and the requirements of the job could lead to a satisfied outlook and a balanced disposition. A poor fit, on the other hand, may produce the opposite effect.

Work is generally a highly organised activity and as such provides many people with a number of benefits apart from income. It offers the opportunity to structure a significant part of our waking hours, and forces us to engage in purposeful activities; it provides us with the opportunity to associate with people outside our immediate circle of family and friends; it allows us to test and clarify our own personal impressions about our status and identity; and it can permit the attainment of personal goals while contributing to the achievement of organisational goals.

The work ethic is deeply ingrained in Western industrialised society, and in the UK in the past we tolerated waste and over-manning in order to preserve employment, presumably to ensure that people felt socially useful. Political ideologies focus narrowly on work as the creator of wealth. Though one can draw a distinction between work and leisure, there are certain types of leisure activity that have a number of attributes in common with work. For some people, however, enforced leisure is not a welcome experience because it is an inadequate substitute for work. It is interesting to note that being a lady or gentleman of leisure used to be held in high social esteem, and this was at a time when work was morally justified. The work ethic is unlikely to be dislodged by unacceptably high levels of unemployment, but it could be subjected to a significant overhaul in these circumstances (Shimmin, 1966).

But in contemporary society the nature of work is changing. The redesign of work processes within organisations leads to higher output with fewer workers. The march of automation has removed low-skill jobs, and the computer illiterate with poor interpersonal skills are at a great disadvantage. Generally, developments within organisations are changing job demands and the skills required. Middle managers, who previously acted as filters through which information flowed while performing their coordinating role, are being axed. Those left behind are required to acquire new skills, such as coaching, negotiating, and teambuilding. Computing software is changing the nature of the jobs of professionals, such as lawyers and accountants. Software programs make it possible for the lay person to use specialised knowledge to solve routine problems. In other situations professionals are placing reliance on software to improve their judgement—e.g., software assisting medical doctors to make diagnosis of patients' problems.

In recent years commentators refer to a number of developments likely to affect work in the future, such as greater demand for "knowledge" workers, with less demand for workers with lower-level skills. In addition, it is suggested that security of tenure as existed in the past will become rarer and the growth of the contractual fringe (e.g., self-employed contract workers) will be more pronounced. But there are academics, such as Nolan and Wood (2003), who would challenge these assertions and point out that there has been a reversal in some of the radical practices introduced over the last decade or so.

talk of early retirement. Redundancies among all staff, and executives in particular, have been increasingly common in recent years (Cooper, 1979). Prior to the announcement of any redundancies, rumours circulate and anxiety springs from job insecurity. If redundancy is to be selective, trust and openness suffer, leading to suspicion and perhaps severe competition. Uncertainty about the future develops and, ironically, the actual announcement of the redundancy programme may initially be considered a relief because people know where they stand. But this will soon wear off and the process of instituting the redundancy programme may be equated with an exercise in removing "dead wood". Feelings of guilt and shame arise as a consequence, even though the redundant person obtains the sympathy of colleagues. Events may not take the course outlined in the case of mass redundancies or voluntary redundancies, but it seems plausible that the process in such an eventuality would contain certain similarities.

Having been made redundant, individuals suffer the loss of status that accompanied the job and, for some people, there is the danger of withdrawal due to a sense of failure. Loneliness and a feeling of isolation are not uncommon at this stage, but redundant employees may regard their loss as only temporary and tend to look at the new situation as if it were a long-deserved holiday. They are cushioned by a redundancy settlement and can get on with jobs needed to be done about the house (Fagin, 1979). In the search for another job, extreme competition is encountered and perhaps there is a feeling that a prospective employer may be unfavourably disposed to somebody who has been made redundant. With continual lack of success in securing another job comes an increasingly long period of unemployment. Even for the most optimistic of people, this is something that erodes self-confidence and contributes to depression.

If the main wage earner in a family—traditionally the man—suffers prolonged bouts of unemployment, these create problems of structuring time and organising daily life, and contribute to pessimism, distress, fatalism, and apathy. A spillover to family life is likely as the individual's influence becomes less in the home (Jahoda, 1979). This is due to his own negative view of himself (Archer & Rhodes, 1993), as well as a negative evaluation by the family and, quite naturally, this becomes a source of domestic anxiety. At a time when the wife is suffering strain from the burden of financial worries, and perhaps planning a change in lifestyle, she has also to contend with her husband's need for encouragement and emotional support. This places added strain on her. Eventually the roles may have to be reversed when the wife goes out to work and the former breadwinner stays at home, much to the relief of the wife. The children may suffer a loss of prestige among their friends, and homework may suffer. The waning of the father's authority may encourage disobedience, emotional upset, and antisocial behaviour.

From preliminary studies of redundancies it was shown that, when employees expected plant closures, blood pressure rose, and for those who became unemployed it continued to do so. Feelings of depression, irritation, and low self-esteem were associated with the high blood pressure. Those who found employment experienced rapid reduction in blood pressure levels towards normal. Levels of serum uric acid behaved in a similar fashion to blood pressure as a consequence of unemployment (Kasl & Cobb, 1970). Emotional instability was associated with increasing unemployment among unemployed engineers (Shanthamani, 1973).

Eventually, the job aspirations of the unemployed could be lowered, and a lower-status job with a lower salary accepted. Where the unemployed person cannot secure another job, the individual settles for new standards and a different way of life. Social activities of all sorts are curtailed for emotional and financial reasons, and roles within the family could suffer a dramatic change (Fagin, 1979). In a survey of a small group of unemployed male managerial staff in the UK, it was concluded that, though the men passed through the shock phase on losing their jobs, none had reached the pessimism or acceptance of unemployment stage, whether they had been unemployed for 6 months or over a year (Swinburne, 1981). Though aware of the negative and pessimistic feelings associated with unemployment, they used conscious strategies to delay these feelings—for example, it is to be expected that it will take longer to secure a managerial or professional job; the contemporary unemployment scene makes one realise that the job situation is highly competitive, and failure to land a job is not a personal deficiency. Savings and redundancy payments act as a buffer against the financial hardships of unemployment, and the reduction in the stigma attached to it helps. But "bitchy" neighbours can rub salt in the wound. There is still a reluctance to discuss unemployment.

Fryer and Payne (1986), having examined a number of studies, concluded that "the unemployed as a group have higher mean levels of experienced strain and negative feelings, lower mean levels of happiness and present life satisfaction, with lower mean levels of experience of pleasure and positive feeling than comparable employed people". Similar views have been expressed by Wanberg, Kammeyer-Mueller and Shi (2001). In addition, it was asserted by Fryer and Payne (1986) that there tends to be a view among physicians that the physical health consequences of unemployment were real and possessed serious implications for the health of the community. Three areas of health concern have been identified as worthy of note:

(1) Studies of depression have consistently shown the unemployed to be more affected by depression than the employed (Fryer & Payne, 1986; Murphy & Athanasou, 1999; Whelan, 1992).

(2) The bulk of studies of suicides report higher rates of suicides for the unemployed than for the employed (Fryer & Payne, 1986). But, it is pertinent to ask, were the unemployed group more vulnerable to suicide independent of their state of being without work?

(3) Certain cognitive difficulties could arise. For example, in a study of 954 working-class men, stratified by age and length of unemployment, it was found that 31% of the sample reported taking longer over doing things, had difficulties in concentrating, and got rusty. However, only about 10% reported an increase in making mistakes in shopping or understanding written material (Fryer & Warr, 1984).

The following intervening variables have to be considered when examining the relationship between the person and the unemployed state:

• *Length of unemployment*. It is suggested that the negative mental health consequences of being unemployed occur within the first 3 months after the loss of the job, and remain fairly stable thereafter (Warr & Jackson, 1984). However, one should maintain a flexible position when interpreting the significance of the length of unemployment as an intervening variable in the relationship between ill-health and unemployment.

• *Social class*. It is said that there is not much difference between professional/white-collar workers and semi-skilled/blue-collar workers in terms of reactions to unemployment, except that the working-class group reported greater anxiety over financial difficulties, and greater problems in occupying their time (Fryer & Payne, 1986).

• *Role of the family*. It is suggested that unemployment is associated with increased family stress, particularly among the long-term unemployed and those in the lower occupational groups (Fagan & Little, 1984). However, other evidence emphasises the resilience of the family. For example, it is said that unemployment actually reactivates dormant family ties, and, for a majority of families, including white- and blue-collar workers, a family crisis does not accompany the husband's unemployment (Fryer & Payne, 1986). It is understandable to underline the supportive role of the family in conditions of unemployment, but equally one must acknowledge the potential for power struggles and highly charged emotional exchanges brought about by stringent financial circumstances and changed status.

• *Social support and structuring of time*. High levels of social support and an ability to structure one's time tend to reduce the impact of unemployment on well-being (Arnold, 2005).

Inevitably, there is going to be a reduction in activities where expenditure is involved and this could create certain strains. The plight of the children and family has to be considered (Whelan, 1992). The continuation of unemployment for some months led to economic deprivation, which increased pressure on the social relationships of children, leading to poorer performance at school and a deterioration in emotional and physical health. In some cases matters deteriorated to a point where children were physically abused (Madge, 1983).

Turning unemployment to advantage. Though the negative aspects of unemployment have been highlighted at length, unemployment may be construed as an opportunity (where possible) for somebody to change direction. However, in the chronic unemployment conditions of the early 1990s, such an opportunity could be rather elusive. Nevertheless, unemployed people have the option of being active, relying on their talents, interests, and so on, in order to counteract the malaise of unemployment (Fryer & Payne, 1986).

This could entail engaging in meaningful activities, such as pursuing hobbies, seeing friends, attending to an allotment, do-it-yourself work in the home, etc., as a way of instilling a vestige of nonmaterial meaning in their lives. This could be a welcome change in some respects for the unskilled factory worker, now unemployed, who is no longer subjected to the dehumanising effects of the assembly line. However, a fundamental constraint on the unemployed person's freedom to act, particularly where expense is involved, has to be considered. Due to lack of resources, the unemployed person may not be able to engage in certain types of activities, such as decorating the house or repairing furniture. Where it is possible to purchase inferior materials or tools to do the job, the quality of the outcome may be less than satisfactory. This could engender a sense of failure and lowered self-esteem. Some unemployed people, who take an active stand to cope with their predicament, may break the social security laws in order to maintain their standard of living.

Early retirement

For some managers nearing retirement the call of a job with lighter responsibilities and more flexible hours is attractive, and they decide to move on (Sleeper, 1975). Those who are compelled to retire early and those who are ill-prepared for retirement may feel dissatisfied, as would perhaps those who retire for health reasons, at least initially. There are those who retire early and find it difficult to adjust emotionally to the life of a retired person, and they can feel bored, depressed, and lonely (Cooper, 1979). There are others who miss the social contacts at work, and will be ill-equipped to cope with a situation in which a lot of time is spent with the spouse. However, one must not lose sight of a number of advantages attached to early retirement. These include more personal freedom, more leisure time, more time with the family and friends, and opportunities to pursue hobbies, to travel, and to engage in educational pursuits. These advantages would be even more attractive if the person is provided with an adequate pension and feels financially secure.

Family considerations

There are a number of circumstances that originate outside the organisation that can create stress. These include family problems, life crises, financial difficulties, conflict of personal beliefs with those of the organisation, and family commitments competing with commitments to the organisation.

In the past a topic that has attracted a fair amount of analysis and comment was the relationship between the male manager and his wife and family (Handy, 1975; Pahl & Pahl, 1971). The work and home situation are interrelated because the manager has to rely on support from the home to alleviate stress originating at work, and to keep him in touch with certain realities. In this way the wife's role may be seen as supportive and caring while the "thruster" husband pursues a demanding job in the knowledge that, provided the marital relationship is not in jeopardy, the home environment is a refuge.

The husband may run the risk of strain and ineffectiveness if he tries to execute both the work and home roles to an adequate level. The young executive may find himself in the situation where he has to maintain a distance between his wife and the organisation as he is building up his career and putting a lot of effort into the job, just at the very time his young housebound wife is also making demands on his time. By maintaining the distance between the wife and the organisation he is not forced to choose between the two, at a time when he ought to involve his wife because of the need for her sympathy and understanding (Beattie, Darlington, & Cripps, 1974).

It would be an oversimplification to view the relationship between the husband and his family as being strictly of the nature described here. Some wives, though, acting in a supportive role, are bored and lonely at home and may be jealous of the husband because of his career. Others are very adept at acting as a buffer between problems arising in the home and their husband. In other situations a wife may take an outside interest and step up entertaining on behalf of her husband when the children are grown up, and may find this life absorbing and satisfying. Or, instead of acting in a supportive capacity, a wife may be envious of the fact that the husband has insufficient time to consider her problems or achievements, and as a retaliatory measure object to him bringing work home or moving house because of the job. This could create a situation of overload during office hours, and frustrated ambitions for the husband that he is likely to resent.

There are of course relationships where the wife pursues a career, because to do so is satisfying or financially rewarding, and both husband and wife share the housework. It is when the husband expects his home comforts and does not receive them that problems are likely to arise. Many husbands do not fully appreciate the implications for the wife of moving house as a result of changing jobs. This is even more important when the move is to a foreign country. It is almost inevitable that the mobile family is prone to developing temporary relationships, with a

capacity to live for the present and to turn on instant sociability, as well as an ability to display indifference to the local community (Packard, 1975). From the husband's viewpoint, this may be due to a shortage of time and the realisation that they are short-stay inhabitants. The wife may bear the brunt of the move; she has to attend to a number of matters connected with the house move; she has to create a new life in the new neighbourhood and does not have the advantage of her husband whose job status is transferred; and she is expected to provide a stable environment for the children and her husband and to be in a state of readiness for the next move. In the process she may have had to sever contact with a close circle of friends or family, and this loss is very prevalent soon after the move (Marshall & Cooper, 1976).

Increasing divorce rates in the United States were said to be a consequence of the continuous success of the aspiring senior manager who leaves his socially unskilled wife at home (Immundo, 1974). Alcoholism may be a problem for some corporate wives (Seidenberg, 1973). Perhaps this may be due to frustration and loneliness. Generally the plight of the wife may not be as bad as it seems because she may not encounter too many difficulties getting involved in the community, even if the involvement is transient, and this could act as compensation for being somewhat isolated because of her husband's ambitions and career involvement. It is in the husband's interest to see that his wife has made a successful adjustment following the move.

The position of the working wife of executive rank is considered by some companies (e.g., Sainsbury and ICI in the UK) when a career move is contemplated for her spouse. According to Professor Peter Herriott, the organisations likely to survive in the future will have to accept "couple careers" as well as individual careers (Thomas, 1993). This could be prompted by the growth in the number of female managers. It may be unrealistic to expect wives with established jobs to uproot in order to relocate with career-minded spouses. Career planning is discussed in Chapter 18.

SUGGESTED REMEDIES FOR STRESS

Stress does not have to be viewed as a bad thing, for there is only one kind of person without conflicts—a dead one. However, too much stress is harmful and measures should be taken to tackle it with the hope of eventually reducing it. To cope with tension or stress, drugs or tranquillisers can be used, but this remedy helps the person to deal with the immediate condition or symptoms without equipping him or her to confront future stressful situations. It is suggested that allowing greater individual autonomy and participation by employees in matters that concern them is a useful approach (Elkin & Rosch, 1990). Where there is evidence of deficiencies in personal and interpersonal skills, techniques are available, such as sensitivity training and teambuilding, which are designed to analyse and perfect behavioural skills, but it is by no means conclusive that results following the adoption of these techniques (discussed in Chapter 16) match the expectations of those committed to their use.

One could also create an organisational environment in which people feel free and confident to say they cannot cope, where they can air their basic fears, and invite help if necessary. This would require a significant shift in attitudes because, to many people, an admission of being a victim of stress is tantamount to acknowledging that one is unstable and incompetent. Understandably, people prefer to brush it under the carpet and remain secretive about it.

There are a number of person-centred techniques that are useful in the management of stress. It is important to choose the techniques that suit the individual and with which he or she feels comfortable. The time of the day when best to use a technique may also be considered—(e.g., after work to signify the end of one phase and the beginning of another, or during the work day when cues are identified that signal tension. Suinn (1976), a clinical psychologist, has indicated a number of techniques that the Type A person might use to change his or her habits (see Panel 19.7).

Apart from remedies based on psychotherapy and meditation, regularity of meals and their nutritional balance are of major importance in keeping fit and in raising resistance to stress. Adequate sleep and moderation in the consumption of food, drink, and drugs are also worth pursuing. Regular exercise, which can be pleasurable, at the end of the day, in the lunch break, and at the weekends, can help to get rid of anger, irritation, and frustration. See the funny side of life; enthuse about things generally; put aside time for little things; encourage, pay compliments to, and praise other people when it is appropriate and proper to do so. Nurture friendships, and build a mutual support system so as to be able to discuss stresses with a trusted friend, a relative, or professional helpers. Talking through problems and putting stresses in perspective can be productive and may point in the direction of a solution. Take on hobbies that can be a source of relaxation (Murray-Bruce, 1983, 1990), and strive for a healthy interaction between work and the home.

Cognitive strategies

When we use cognitive strategies to cope with and control or manage stress, our thinking process takes over. However, there are times when people do not confront stressors, instead they withdraw from the stressful situation, though this is not to be recommended in the long term. Similarly, individuals can experience "denial" (a defence mechanism) in response to acute stress —e.g., denial on receiving news of the death of a loved one. This serves to protect the person in the short term so that longer-term strategies can be put in place.

In a cognitive appraisal of a stressful situation we can refer to two approaches—one is problem-focused (i.e., dealing directly with a problem) and the other is emotion-focused (i.e., dealing with how we feel about the problem). An example of the problem-focused approach is the action of a person who is grossly overweight or is a heavy smoker. Having analysed the problem, the person exercises control and adopts a new pattern of behaviour (e.g., goes on a diet or cuts down on cigarettes). An example of an emotion-focused

(1) (a) Select a quiet place in your home; then sit down or lie comfortably and close your eyes. Listen to soothing instrumental music and let yourself float along with the melody. Imagine yourself in a soothing environment and allow the music to relax your muscles.

(b) In an alternate fashion, tighten and relax the muscles of your hands, biceps, face, shoulders, chest, stomach, legs, and feet. Concentrate on the feeling of relaxation that follows the tightening of the muscles.

(c) As you breathe out, repeat the word "one" and maintain this pattern of breathing for 10 minutes. Feel the release of tension with each breath. If you find that you are able to relax by any one of these methods, then use it at times when you feel stress. Take a break from the activity causing the stress and make your way to a private place and relax. Allow your mind to float away from the pressures of daily activities and remember how you felt when you relaxed at home; relive those feelings.

(2) If you have mastered the technique of relaxing quickly, use imagery to neutralise the emotional reactions that arise as a consequence of the pressures you frequently encounter. First relax, and then imagine yourself facing a situation that normally makes you tense—e.g., the pressure that comes about when you face a deadline. You continue to imagine this situation but at the same time you retain an awareness of relaxation. Repeat this several times, and each time imagine that you are handling the situation calmly. Should the visualisation of the stress scene make you feel more tense than relaxed, terminate the exercise temporarily; then repeat it until you work your way through the entire scene without feeling any tension.

(3) Take active steps to control and manage your environment. For example, arrange your appointments realistically and allow enough time in between meetings so that you are not always rushing from one meeting to another. Set your priorities, if you can, in the morning of each day, and adhere to that order. Only undertake a new task when you are finished with the priority items. Learn how to cope with what others expect of you. Be frank and let them know how much effort and time you are prepared to give them, and be honest and direct when you feel you cannot accept their requests. If somebody wants you to take on another task, and you feel your present workload is more than sufficient, get that person to assist you in evaluating the urgency of his or her request and then decide whether it fits among your priority items.

Try to avoid acting in a rushed manner, otherwise you will feel pressure. Take it easy and practise eating with slower movements, putting down your knife and fork between bites. Slow down your steps when you walk and slow down your speech when you talk. Repeat briefly what you hear others say as you are listening to them. This will help you to understand them better and will contribute towards minimising your impatience.

(Suinn, 1976)

approach is the action of a person who changes the way he or she feels about a stressful event after a change in perceptions or attitudes.

A particular cognitive-based technique for dealing with stress is **rational emotive therapy—RET** (Ellis, 1974). In RET the major approach is to confront irrational beliefs and faulty thinking, which lead to unpleasant or harmful consequences (i.e., a stressed state). Examples of irrational beliefs that influence the way we perceive the stressors that confront us, and as a consequence distort reality, are as follows:

- I must receive approval at all times for what I do.
- I must always be in a euphoric state.
- I am not a whole person unless I am always competent with very high levels of achievement.

- I must be in control, and the perfect solution to a problem is there to be grasped.
- Bad behaviour always deserves the allocation of blame, reprimand, and punishment.
- The world should be a just and fair place, and I feel sad when it does not live up to my expectations of it.

RET emphasises the rebuilding of one's thinking process about particular issues, and is designed to help people who over-react to stressful situations by giving them almost complete responsibility to examine their own faulty reactions. The assumption is that they will be able to change their emotional reactions if they modify their ideas, philosophies, and attitudes about various kinds of stressors that impinge on their lives. The technique consists of a multi-pronged attack, at the emotional and intellectual levels, on dysfunctional ways of thinking and behaving. It tries to teach people how to treat themselves—that is, how to cope with present and future stressful conditions by recognising that because these conditions exist they should attempt to cope with them as sensibly as possible, frequently trying to change them for the better by continually confronting them.

Another manifestation of cognitive processes aimed at formulating a response to an event is a dialogue with oneself in order to handle the situation. For example, two courses of action could be open to a motorist when he or she perceives the behaviour of a fellow road user as likely to endanger his or her safety. One option is to view the incident as reckless driving and decide to take retaliatory action ("road rage"). Another option is to converse with the self and eventually decide to stay cool and not over-react, and turn a blind eye to the unsafe incident. If a particular driver were to habitually take the first action (be furious with the offending motorist), we might call it a negative and irrational response based on an unhelpful personal dialogue. However, it is open to the motorist to engage in an alternative personal dialogue where the thought processes lead to a positive and rational response (stay calm and ignore what is seen as an isolated bout of reckless driving).

Notice the emphasis on self-control in the cognitive strategies described above. There is a conscious decision to take charge of our own behaviour, particularly when new challenges arise, and as such it is considered beneficial. However, there are situations when it is not functional to be in control in a cognitive sense, for example, when undergoing hypnosis for the management of stress. It would appear sensible to recognise personality differences between people (and people's medical condition) when specifying the most appropriate stress-relieving techniques to use. For example, meditation may be effective for hypertension, but inappropriate for dealing with a peptic ulcer. In another situation, psychotherapy may be suitable for treating one Type A personality, whereas regular exercise and vacations would suit another.

A related technique is **cognitive behavioural therapy** (CBT) devised by Beck (Beck, Emery and Greenberg, 1985). It focuses on changing illogical patterns of thought that underlie depression. Just like Ellis above, Beck assumes that depressed individuals pursue illogical thinking and this lies at the root of their problem. The techniques of CBT are based on the assumption that cognitive structures shape the way people react and adapt to a variety of situations encountered in their lives. The most widespread use of CBT is for the treatment of depression, but it can also be used to treat anxiety. Beck described the three major cognitive patterns in depression as the cognitive triad: (i) a negative view of oneself; (ii) a negative interpretation of experience; and (iii) a negative view of the future. People with these cognitive patterns are prone to react to situations by interpreting them in the light of the cognitive triad (Andreasen & Black, 2001).

For example, an unsuccessful applicant who applied for a job that attracted many able candidates has his or her perception shaped by the stated cognitive triad, and reasons as follows:

- I did not get the job because I am not really bright, despite my good college record, and the employer was able to figure that out (*negative view of self*).
- Trying to find a decent job is so hopeless that I might as well give up trying (*negative view of experience*).
- I am always going to be a failure; I will never succeed at anything (*negative view of the future*).

The techniques of CBT focus on teaching clients or patients new ways to change their negative beliefs and assumptions about themselves, the world, and the future. As a treatment it tends to be relatively short term and highly structured. The major goal is to help people restructure their negative cognitions so that they view reality in a less distorted way and learn to react accordingly.

In contrast to RET, CBT does not attempt to disprove the ideas harboured by the depressed person. However, even though the specific techniques are different, the major goals of CBT and

RET are similar—helping people to recognise and reject false assumptions that are key ingredients of their problems (Baron, 2002). The therapist and client work together to identify the individual's assumptions, beliefs, and expectations and to formulate ways of testing them. For example, the unsuccessful job applicant referred to above states that he or she is a total failure. The therapist may then ask for a definition of failure, probing the extent of the perceived failure, and later explore areas of the client's life where success has been achieved. There is evidence to indicate that individuals learn to reinterpret negative events with outcomes that are encouraging (Bruder et al., 1997).

Social support

The support of people (**social support**) has been referred to briefly earlier. The study of social support with its group emphasis emerged from almost nowhere in the 1970s, but "support" as a concept has occupied a central position in the social sciences for quite a while. In distant studies of participative management, the principle of supportive relations was recognised as a core element in effective supervision, when supervisors related to subordinates in such a way that the individual's sense of personal worth and importance was enhanced. Supportive behaviour assumes a central position in certain branches of psychotherapy and **counselling** (House & Kahn, 1985).

Although there is not complete agreement as to what constitutes social support, it refers generally to the existence or quality of social relationships, and in a specific sense could refer to a marriage, friendship, or membership of an organisation. It is highlighted in the give and take in interpersonal relationships—i.e., giving and receiving at the emotional level—and also giving and receiving when help and assistance are at stake, but with emotional concern as the central plank. It is suggested that the popularity of social support has been promoted by the recognition of the part it can play in reducing the prevalence and impact of one of the major health hazards of the modern industrial world—i.e., stress inside

and outside work. This is a view shared by Bernin and Theorell (2001), who maintain that adequate social support can be critical to the health and well-being of an individual and to the atmosphere and success of an organisation.

The manner in which supportive social relationships alleviate the problem of stress at work can be viewed as follows (Williams & House, 1985):

(1) Support can enhance health directly by creating the setting in which needs for affection, approval, social interaction, and security are met.

(2) Support can reduce levels of stress directly, and improve health indirectly, by reducing interpersonal tensions as well as having a positive effect generally in the work environment.

(3) Support acts as a buffer between the person and health hazards. As the level of social support increases, health risks decline for individuals exposed to stressful conditions. Conversely, with the decline in social support, the adverse impact of stress on health becomes increasingly apparent.

We must be careful not to be overwhelmed by the alleged beneficial effects of social support, because there are occasions when, for example, social interaction can have a detrimental effect on a person's health. This could arise where conflict and strife are inherent in social relationships. The process of social support is said to vary from one group to another. It was concluded in one study that female managers were more likely to use social support to deal with job-related problems than their male counterparts (Burke & Belcourt, 1974). Apparently, women are more likely to be the providers of support (Belle, 1982), and can become more emotionally affected by the problems of others and, as a consequence, incur higher psychological costs.

Enhancers of social support

Three important measures to enhance social support and improve the flow of supportive behaviour among blue-collar workers have been identified as:

(1)   structural arrangements;
(2)   other organisational change processes; and
(3)   facilitation of supportive supervisory behaviour.

However, it should be stated that these measures have relevance to other occupational groups as well (Williams & House, 1985).

Structural arrangements.   Work is organised in such a way as to facilitate stable interaction between employees in the performance of various tasks, as well as maintaining social ties. Here the importance of social interaction is emphasised as a means to reduce stress in the working environment (Alcalay & Pasick, 1983). It is suggested that people who had a constant set of co-workers (colleagues) had lower cholesterol levels than those whose co-workers changed frequently (Cassel, 1963). This finding is interesting in the light of evidence from the functioning of traditional Japanese organisational systems, where a high level of job security results in membership of a group throughout a person's entire career. The cohort of workers who enter the organisation together develop strong feelings of group solidarity over time. As a consequence, individual interests are said to be absorbed into the work group interests, and the work group offers satisfying emotional support and social ties in a friendly atmosphere (Matsumoto, 1970).

The importance of emotional support is recognised elsewhere. Emotional support among a sample of social workers—in this case the provision of empathy, caring, trust, and concern by co-workers and supervisors—was beneficial in helping them to cope better with stress and strain in the workplace. However, it was not viewed as a total stress-reduction process (Jayaratne & Chess, 1984).

Other organisational change processes.   Other processes, which have been discussed in Chapters 11 and 12 respectively, are quality circles and participative management. Participative management schemes, broadly conceived, have potential not only to improve the quantity and quality of production, but also to increase social support,

reduce stress, and, as a consequence, to enhance health and well-being (Cobb, 1976; Elkin & Rosch, 1990). Involvement in the participative management process is said to enhance employees' psychological and social functioning in ways that make them more effective as spouses, parents, and members of the community. This experience teaches employees new skills and attitudes that are capable of improving the giving and receiving of social support (Crouter, 1984).

Central features of the quality circle of old are the emphasis given to the group process and effective teamwork, with scope for the provision of social support. Some commentators believe that quality circles represent an advanced form of employee participation that is associated with favourable employee attitudes and productivity (Dale, Cooper, & Wilkinson, 1998). It is suggested that social needs are met in quality circles where an outlet is provided for grievances and irritations, and immediate recognition is provided for members' abilities and achievements. It is, therefore, not surprising that quality circles provide workers with a new sense of dignity and a higher level of morale. In addition, the group cohesiveness developed at work spreads to nonwork activities as circle members engage in social activities outside the workplace.

A word of caution about participative management is echoed, because it can have unanticipated negative effects. We are told that employees may feel more responsible for problems on the job, and they worry about these problems. Then they take this new stress into their nonwork life. There is also evidence to suggest that marriage relationships can suffer when employees who are wives transfer the new independence and competence learned at work to the home environment (Crouter, 1984).

Another avenue for delivering social support is through health promotion programmes (discussed later). They could be concerned with the management of stress, and are often group-based rather than person-based. Therefore, they could act as social support interventions and serve as powerful stress-reducing strategies.

The following is an example of a formal social support scheme developed by a large chemical company in the UK. An employee counselling service, with a full-time counsellor having a psychiatric social work background, was set up. The objectives of this service were to provide a confidential counselling service to all employees and their families; to work with outside care agencies for the welfare of employees; and to provide other activities likely to improve the quality of working life. About half the employees who availed themselves of the service came for advice on education, family matters, work-related housing problems, separation, divorce, children, ageing parents, and consumer issues. The other half received longer-term counselling on fundamental personal and interpersonal problems. Over a 4-year period roughly 10% of total employees per annum took advantage of the service. This is the type of programme some would argue should be encouraged to deal with the pressures of modern industrial society (Cooper, 1981).

In the absence of a formal social support system, an informal approach for individuals suffering from stress is suggested as follows (Cooper, 1981):

- Pick somebody at work that you feel you can talk to—someone you don't feel threatened by and to whom you can trustfully reveal your feelings. Don't pick someone who, on reflection, you may be using on an unconscious level as a pawn in a game of organisational politics!
- Approach the person you can trust and explain to him or her that you have a particular problem at or outside work that you would like to discuss. Admit that you need help and that you are consulting the person because you trust their opinion, like them as a person, feel that they can usefully identify with your circumstances, and so forth.
- Try to maintain and build on this relationship, even at times of no crisis or problems.
- Review, from time to time, the nature of the relationship, to see if it is still providing you with the emotional support you need to cope with the difficulties that arise. If the relationship is no longer constructive or the nature of your problems has changed (requiring a different peer counsellor), then seek another person for support.

Facilitation of supportive supervisory behaviour. Supportive behaviour is generally endorsed by a number of empirical studies. Proponents would argue it should be encouraged and expanded, and be adopted at the different layers of the organisation, and that managers and supervisors who use it should receive appropriate recognition and rewards for doing so. Those supervisors and managers who are rewarded solely on the basis of nonsocial criteria, such as a single-minded approach to productivity, are likely to have little motivation to be supportive to subordinates.

Workplace counselling

In general terms, counselling is a process aimed at helping people to explore a problem or issue, and alternative ways of dealing with it, so that something can be done about it. The over-riding goal is to help the clients of the counsellor to help themselves and take responsibility for their own lives. It is based on the belief that within individuals there is a capacity to grow in maturity and take on responsibility if the conditions are right. You would expect the counsellor to be sympathetic, genuine, nonjudgemental, and able to create an atmosphere of trust and acceptance in the quest to understand (in an empathetic way) the client's behaviour and the reasons for it. Other skills used by the counsellor are active listening, clarifying issues, reflecting on what comes across in the disclosures, summarising the position put forward by the client, and offering guidance.

Workplace counselling is somewhat different from counselling in private practice. In the workplace organisational and management constraints associated with legal matters, culture, and practice could pose a challenge to counselling models developed for individual clients (Pickard & Towler, 2003). The fundamental counselling relationship and processes are the same in both workplace counselling and counselling in private practice, but in the workplace the counsellor has to establish a relationship with management as well as pursuing the special relationship with the individual client. This three-cornered contract has to be handled with delicacy in order to ensure the smooth operation of the event. On this general theme, Walton (1997) makes the following observation:

> in workplace counselling counsellors who choose to operate as if they were operating within their private practice are unlikely to appreciate the full range of pressures and vulnerabilities affecting the client, and they run the risk of not being perceived as practical, credible professionals both by their clients and by others with whom they interact within the client organization. It is in the interests of the counsellor and client alike, therefore, that the counsellors in the workplace can draw to mind and use different ways of thinking about organisations, which can be adapted and used by workplace counsellors.

Doyle (2003), an occupational psychologist, seems to be favourably disposed to Egan's (1998) skilled helper model of counselling, as she considers it suitable for application in an organisational setting. Egan's model can be positioned somewhere between the counsellor or therapist that prescribes a course of action and one that acts strictly as a sounding board (i.e., repeats what the client has to say, and then leaves the client to come up with his or her own answer). Egan's model comprises the following:

- Pay close attention to what the client has to say, and the counsellor should make sure that he or she empathises with the client (put oneself in the client's shoes).
- Ask probing questions, forcing the client to work through the problem. This may entail challenging the client, particularly in areas where it is felt that barriers are placed in the path to moving forward (challenging assumptions, etc.).
- Implement the chosen courses of action, and assist the client in this process.

The problems highlighted in Panel 19.8 could lend themselves to analysis and solution using the Egan model.

A question is sometimes asked, as follows: Are line managers and human resource specialists equipped to use counselling skills in the workplace? According to Carroll (1996), it may not be a good idea to expect this category of employee to act formally in a counselling role. The main reason given is role conflict. For example, a line manager or HR specialist is involved in the evaluative appraisal (described in Chapter 17) where evaluation with reference to the determination of rewards takes place. In such a setting it would not be realistic to expect the

---

PANEL 19.8: Problems addressed by workplace counsellors

What type of problems are faced by the workplace counsellor? The answer could be illustrated with the use of examples. First, consider a significant reaction to an organisational stressor when an employee is told that he or she is about to be made redundant. This incident could arouse a range of negative emotions—shock, anger, fear for the future, grief, loss, etc. An approach to dealing with this type of situation is to accept that these feelings are legitimate. In fact they should be allowed to surface and express themselves and the person should be helped to confront them and try to make sense out of them so that he or she can face the future in a constructive way. The end result of this analysis might be that a change of job or career might be worth considering (Doyle, 2003).

Another example is where an employee has an exceptionally heavy workload, and this could be caused by a variety of factors. For example, a rationalisation programme within the company has led to a significant cut back in staffing levels resulting in greater workloads for the survivors. Imagine a survivor who finds it difficult to delegate, has a problem with prioritising work, is too much of a perfectionist, or is deficient in processing the workload quickly. In such a case the workplace counsellor assists with the identification of the problem and getting the client to accept it, and this constitutes the first step in establishing the nature of the problem. Later, various options as to the best way to proceed would be explored (Doyle, 2003).

Other areas requiring the intervention of a workplace counsellor are role ambiguity suffered by the client, continuous conflict between the superior and subordinate (client), bullying of the subordinate (client) by his or her line manager, and the client being stressed because of the nature of the tasks performed.

appraisee to divulge information of a personal nature that is having a negative impact on work performance. The issue of confidentiality (sacred to counsellors) also arises, particularly where the appraiser is already aware of the impact of the personal problem, but there might be an inclination to disclose this information to others within the company because of the effect the personal problem is having on the efficiency of the section or department. Finally, although one may propose that line managers and HR specialists ought not to act formally as workplace counsellors, nevertheless it would be useful if such employees developed counselling skills.

In Chapter 18 when discussing on-the-job training there was an analysis of mentoring. Here we will briefly draw a distinction between counselling and mentoring using a perspective provided by Pickard (1997), a pioneer in workplace counselling (training):

> There are overlaps between counselling and mentoring. Both are concerned with the potential of the individual and draw on counselling skills. But counselling and mentoring remain separate and distinct interventions in the life of people; they set out to achieve different things. The purpose of mentoring is to transmit organizational values and practices and there are usually status differences between the mentor and mentoree, whereas in counselling there is likely to be more equality in the relationship. Mentoring focuses upon the individual in relation to the organization and upon the realization of the individual's personal potential or the resolution of personal issues in relation to organizational needs. Mentoring requires learning, adjustment, and even imitation on the part of the individual (mentoree). Though organizational counselling is concerned with organizational issues, it places more emphasis on the realization of personal potential and the resolution of personal issues for the sake of the individual than does mentoring. However, there will be times when the balance will shift and the two processes may appear indistinguishable.

Finally, how effective is workplace counselling? Doyle (2003), having "reviewed the meagre evidence (at least in the UK)", concluded that at least two factors contributed to the success of counselling interventions: the quality of the counselling, and the perceptions of the workforce that employers care about their well-being.

Health promotion programmes

Health promotion programmes are broader in scope than the preventative strategies outlined earlier. They range from purely educational schemes to promote health, to learning to take one's own blood pressure, using stress management techniques, or altering one's lifestyle.

There has been a steady growth in employee health programmes in recent years. Employers take greater responsibility for paying the health insurance costs of workers in the United States, principally because of the absence of a national health service. However, it is the larger companies that offer the more comprehensive programmes. Perhaps paternalism and philanthropy may have a part to play in this development in some large and long-established companies. However, an increasing number of employees adopt the position that investing in the health of employees produces dividends. The dividends could include increased productivity, lower medical and disability costs, reduced absenteeism and turnover of staff, and improved satisfaction and morale among employees (Murphy, 1984).

It is the substantial increase in medical care expenditure in the United States that has generated interest in health preventative programmes. Also, US employers are most vulnerable to legal action in connection with occupational stress when they have not taken preventative measures. Hence, they are motivated to take such measures. A particular development in the past was the "wellness" movement, which was proactive rather than reactive in the field of preventative health management.

The promotion of wellness can be viewed as a four-step process (Reed, 1984):

(1) Employees are educated about health risk factors such as poor nutrition, lack of

exercise, smoking, drinking and drug abuse, and being overweight.

(2) Employees receive information about their health-risk factors through lifestyle assessments and physical examinations.

(3) Plans are developed for employees to reduce risks through healthier lifestyles.

(4) Employees receive assistance from the organisation to continue with the changes in their lifestyle. This necessitates a process of monitoring and evaluation.

Wellness programmes vary in their degree of comprehensiveness. Some companies merely distribute educational material on desirable lifestyles, whereas others can go as far as providing an indoor track, weightlifting equipment, bicycles,

and workout clothes to their employees, and claim consequential benefits such as reductions in absenteeism, smoking, and excess weight. An example of a wellness programme is the "Staywell" programme introduced in 1979 by Control Data Corporation of the USA (see Panel 19.9).

Beneficial outcomes of wellness programmes include 50% reductions in sickness rates and absenteeism, increases in job performance, improved attitudes towards work, improved stamina, sounder sleep, and loss of weight (Hall & Goodale, 1986). At Control Data, significant reductions in healthcare costs were associated with a decline in cigarette smoking, a lack of hypertension, and an increase in regular exercise. A decrease in absenteeism and lost time due to illness went hand-in-hand with an increase in the number of good

---

PANEL 19.9: The Staywell programme

The programme consisted of creating profiles of health risk, medical screening, health education, and activities to change lifestyles. It was offered to the company's employees in San Diego and New York, and, subsequently, other sites were included (McCann, 1981). The programme was offered without charge to all the company's employees and their spouses. Participation was on a voluntary basis and all activities were provided at the place of work. Employees were allowed time off to attend an orientation session and to participate in other activities such as the health-risk profile and a group interpretation meeting.

Those who signed on for the Staywell programme were weighed and measured, had their blood pressure taken, and gave a blood sample. Also, they completed a questionnaire on their medical outlook. The results of the physical examination and the questionnaire responses were used to provide a computerised health-risk profile on each person. The profile compared the individual's chronological age with his or her "risk age", and it showed how the risk could be improved if the individual changed certain behaviour.

Next, those who participated in the programme were encouraged to select courses from a group of 1-hour health awareness courses. These ranged from how to utilise the healthcare system through to breast self-examination and substance abuse. However, the multi-session behaviour and lifestyle change programmes were the most popular. These covered specific high-risk areas such as smoking, fitness, nutrition and weight control, hypertension, and stress. Specific activities to change lifestyle and improve health were planned for each individual.

An important feature of Staywell was the introduction of a follow-up programme and the use of support systems. One characteristic of the follow-up programme was the formation of employee groups consisting of individuals interested in or troubled by similar problems. Changing the culture at work and people's attitudes would be necessary for the success of the programme.

The group sessions took place at the end of each of the education and lifestyle change courses, and for a certain period had an instructor at their disposal. Eventually, group members learned to help one another to sustain the change in their behaviour, and they practised various techniques and strategies to avoid failure. Support from one's peers in the group, whether it was an exercise in reducing weight or stopping smoking, helped to persuade people to persevere with the modified behaviour. In the mid-1980s it was said that approximately 22,000 people, either employees of Control Data or their spouses, participated in the Staywell programme in 14 US cities.

The Staywell programme at Control Data was based on the following premises (Hall & Goodale, 1986):

• Lifestyle has a major effect on illness and life spans.

• People can change their habits, with appropriate help.

• The workplace is the most effective place to help people change their behaviour, because people spend so much of their time there.

• Companies have a major stake in promoting a healthier lifestyle for their employees because of the potential benefits in terms of reduced insurance costs, decreased absenteeism, improved productivity, and better morale.

health habits developed in the Staywell programme. It is difficult to establish whether or not "wellness" programmes are successful generally, because only a limited amount of evaluation of these programmes has so far taken place. However, there are signs of some promising results for the future.

In the UK it is not surprising that health promotion programmes at the workplace are viewed by many employers as one of the most promising strategies to cope with rapidly increasing health-care costs. For many employers this could be the primary justification for embracing preventative measures (Ashton, 1990). It is interesting to note that in recent years the two major insurance companies in the UK specialising in healthcare (BUPA and PPP) have promoted preventative measures —medical screening, stress management programmes, and occupational health advice—no doubt believing that a healthier workforce will mean fewer claims. This could also mean lower premiums in the future. However, the predicted fall in premiums may not happen, particularly in the short term, because the introduction of medical screening could lead to the diagnosis of illness or disease requiring medical attention. Obviously, this would lead to an acceleration in claims.

What were British companies doing in connection with preventative health measures in the 1990s? There were some interesting developments (Summers, 1990a). For example, in the late 1980s at the headquarters of the Marks & Spencer organisation in London, facilities such as a gym, dentists, doctors, nurses, osteopaths, physiotherapists, and health administrators were provided. According to the company's deputy head of health services at that time there is no doubt that the service reduced absenteeism, increased the efficiency of the workforce, and provided an example of the commitment of the organisation to its staff.

The Post Office took its mobile clinics and health education roadshows to its widely dispersed workforce numbering 200,000. Also, in the early 1990s Professor Cary Cooper spearheaded a stress audit among the 24,000 blue-collar workers of the Scottish & Newcastle Breweries company.

According to the chief medical officer of the company, the results might indicate the need for a number of improvements in organisational practices ranging from encouraging managers to improve the way they work with people to the overhaul of production methods (Summers, 1990b). These are examples of what some large and successful companies were doing in this area.

Du Pont, a US corporation with operations in the UK, has a scheme called "Health Horizons". There is a belief that employees can learn to extend their life expectancy by adopting improved lifestyles. Employees complete a lifestyle questionnaire, which is analysed by computer. The analysis aims to show employees where to concentrate their efforts to improve their health. Also, self-help kits are available, and incentives (e.g., free tracksuits) are provided to encourage appropriate behaviour.

According to Donkin (1995a), Unipart in the UK runs a programme consisting of a health and fitness centre for its employees, which includes a sports hall, squash courts, and aerobics studio, and, for the less athletically inclined, various therapies are offered for which there is a charge. For example, there are beauty treatments, massage, reflexology, aromatherapy, some counselling, and various tips on self-help in rooms not only bearing the names of fruits but also with appropriate scents, colour, and relaxing music. A major motive behind the company's action was to put employees in better shape to handle stress-inducing events, such as learning new skills and coping with change. The company also created a college or training centre (called Unipart University) to develop employees' knowledge and skills.

Little scientifically valid assessment of health promotion programmes in the UK has been undertaken, but in the US the Staywell programme, discussed earlier, appears to be well researched (Cooper, 1986). Generally, companies hold favourable views of these programmes (Gebhart & Crump, 1990), but there is some evidence to suggest that quite a large percentage of employees who took part in wellness programmes stopped doing the exercises and showed an inclination to return to their old lifestyles (Ivancevich & Matteson, 1988).

Employee assistance programmes

The increasing costs of ill-health due to stress, health and safety legislation being broadly interpreted to cover psychological issues, and fear of litigation are influencing a number of organisations to take steps to set up **employee assistance programmes** (EAPs). These programmes—in which employees are counselled on problems ranging from alcohol and drug abuse to financial, marital, and legal difficulties—have a short history in the UK, but have been in existence for quite a while in the USA. The main purpose of EAPs is to enhance the quality of the employee's personal life (Berridge & Cooper, 1993), but offering these programmes could be viewed by some companies as a way of projecting a caring image. A main reason why this service is used by employees is that it gives them the opportunity to address issues connected with relationships, family problems, and financial worries. This may not be a surprising development because in many cases traditional support services (e.g., family, church, and GP) are not readily available.

Although it is changes in the workplace—e.g., widespread downsizing and restructuring often resulting in greater pressure and more work for those left behind—that often persuade companies to introduce EAPs, many of the problems dealt with by the programmes are frequently unrelated to work (Hall, 1995). Normally the types of problem presented vary according to whether they are discussed face to face or over the telephone. According to Michael Reddy of ICAS (an EAP provider), about half the people calling telephone help-lines seek financial or legal help, with less than a third of calls related to work. People may want to talk about drink driving, or social security benefits, or eviction threats by a landlord, or separation, or behavioural problems in children experienced by single mothers, or one partner reluctant to move following the relocation of a job.

SmithKline Beecham (now GSK), the pharmaceutical company, introduced an EAP programme and found that many of the problems presented were not work-related (e.g., Child Support Agency assessments, or meeting the needs of an elderly parent living far away). The company found that those who participated in the programme were subsequently happier, more punctual, and more productive. At the Post Office stress counselling was said to be beneficial in terms of a decline in anxiety levels and depression, improved self-esteem, and a reduction in absenteeism.

The question sometimes asked is whether the provider of the service should be from within the organisation or from an external source. Some organisations, such as BT and the Inland Revenue, prefer an in-house service. However, the use of an outside provider can help reassure staff that their problems remain confidential (Hall, 1995).

In the UK there has been little research undertaken to evaluate the effectiveness of EAPs. Highley and Cooper (1995) evaluated the effectiveness of the Royal Mail EAP and concluded that absenteeism decreased markedly, there was greater awareness of stress and what causes it, and behaviour aimed at coping with stress increased. However, relationships with the employer and job satisfaction showed little improvement. This could be due to the negative impact of the reorganisation of the service and the application of new technology, with a natural fear about job security.

CHAPTER SUMMARY

- Following a definition of stress and its physiological manifestations, which included burnout and PTSD, reference was made to court cases where the victims of stress were compensated.
- Certain stresses and strains were associated with different facets of organisational life. These include role overload, role complexity, role ambiguity, responsibility for people, machine-paced and repetitive work, decision latitude and job control, shift work, new technology in the form of VDU work, work relationships (including bullying), career development, redundancy and unemployment, early retirement, and personality factors including locus of control.
- A number of remedies to counteract a stressful state were suggested. These ranged from psychotherapy and meditation to nutritional balance in intake of food, regular exercise, a balanced personal and social existence, cognitive strategies, RET, CBT, social support, and workplace counselling.
- Finally, the importance of preventative health management was emphasised, and health promotion programmes, including workplace wellness programmes and employee assistance programmes, were mentioned.

QUESTIONS

(1) Distinguish between pressure and stress in an organisational context.

(2) Define PTSD and burnout.

(3) Identify the costs associated with stress at work.

(4) What is the difference between role complexity and role ambiguity?

(5) Consider the nature of bullying and its impact on the victim in contemporary organisations.

(6) Discuss the relevance of the following factors in the context of stress originating from within the organisation: (a) machine-paced/repetitive work; (b) decision latitude/job control; (c) impact of new technology; and (d) self-efficacy as a mediating variable in the relationship between job control and stress.

(7) How important is personality in the relationship between stressful conditions and the individual's response to them?

(8) Comment on the nature of conflict between the organisational role and the family role.

(9) Examine the human costs of unemployment, and the coping strategies used by the unemployed.

(10) Discuss the significance of social support as a technique to cope with stress.

(11) In the control or management of stress explain the following cognitive strategies: (a) problem-focused; (b) emotion-focused; and (c) dialogue with oneself.

(12) Examine the similarities and dissimilarities between CBT and RET.

(13) What are the likely benefits to the organisation and to individuals from health promotion programmes, including "wellness" schemes?

(14) Assess the usefulness of EAPs.

(15) Discuss the significance of workplace counselling as a technique for coping with stress.

SPOTLIGHT ON RELEVANT READING

Carroll, M. (1996). *Workplace counselling*. London: Sage Publications.

Cooper, C.L., Dewe, P., & O'Driscoll, M. (2001). *Organisational stress: A review and critique of theory, research, and application*. London: Sage Publications.

Earnshaw J., & Cooper, C.L. (2001). Stress and employer liability. London: CIPD Books.

Greenberg, J. (2004). Stress fairness to fare no stress. Managing workplace stress by promoting organisational justice. *Organisational Dynamics*, *33*, 352–365.

Wanberg, C.R., Kammeyer-Mueller, J., & Shi, K. (2001). Job loss and the experience of unemployment: International research and perspectives. In N. Anderson, D.S. Ones, H.K. Sinangil, & C. Viswesvaran (Eds.), *Handbook of work, industrial and organisational psychology, Vol. 2*. London: Sage Publications.

Glossary

absolute threshold: each sense receptor requires some minimum level of energy to excite it before perception is organised; the minimum level is called the absolute threshold—a point below which we do not perceive energy.

achievement motivation: a person with a motive to achieve tends to define his or her goals in accordance with some standard of excellence; six suggested components of achievement motivation are a work ethic, the pursuit of excellence, status aspirations, mastery, competitiveness, and acquisitiveness.

action learning: an approach to training whereby students are asked to consider problems for which there are no obvious solutions, but which can be tackled by reinterpreting experience.

action research: action research is the application of the scientific method of fact-finding and experimentation to practical problems awaiting solutions, including action to solve the problems.

adult: a person in a communication network is in the adult state when he or she is a seeker and processor of information.

affinity groups: these teams are composed of professional or knowledge workers who meet regularly to share information, capitalise on opportunities, and solve problems relating to the work team and the wider organisation.

ambiguous figure: an image that can be perceived in more than one way; in experimental psychology it typically consists of a contrived image containing two perceivable figures or interpretations; usually only one of these figures can be perceived at any one moment.

anal stage of psychosexual development: the second stage of personality development in the psychoanalytic approach; the anus is the focal point of the infant's libido.

assessment centres: assessment centres make use of many different methods in personnel selection, including interviews, psychological tests, in-tray exercises, written tasks, and group discussions, and can be considered a systematic, effective, and reliable approach.

assumed similarity: this is the tendency to see others as having characteristics more like our own than is really the case.

attitudes: attitudes are enduring systems of positive or negative evaluations, emotional feelings, and action tendencies with respect to an individual's social world.

attribution theory: attribution theory has been proposed to develop explanations of how we judge people differently depending on the meaning we attribute to given behaviour; the theory suggests that as we observe a person's behaviour, we try to establish whether it was caused by internal or external forces.

authoritarian personality: a personality type hypothesised to be basically insecure and tending to repress or deny their own personal conflicts; they are conventional in their approach to life with explicit values and rules to guide behaviour; they adhere to socially acceptable behaviour that promotes their interests, and tend to be aggressive towards groups not sharing their views (and hence highly prone to prejudice).

behaviour modification: techniques used to control and change behaviour by reinforcing in a systematic way those actions that are considered important or desirable.

behaviourist approach/behaviourism: prominent until the 1950s, this approach focuses on only that which is objective, observable, and measurable; it advocated a scientific means of studying animal and human behaviour in carefully controlled conditions.

bet your company: a type of corporate culture where the heroes are technically competent with respect for authority; they show a tendency to double-check their decisions, are extremely slow, have a tolerance for ambiguity, and a capacity to make breakthroughs in a scientific sense.

"Big Five" factor theory: a way of measuring personality based on the assumption that there are five major dimensions, or traits, to personality.

bonus and profit sharing: a reward system where a bonus could be based on the performance of a unit or organisation, and profit sharing could amount to a distribution of a proportion of profits at a predetermined rate to all employees.

boundaryless organisation: the basic ideology behind the boundaryless organisation is that of trying to eliminate the chain of command, having limitless spans of control, and replacing departments with empowered teams, with a heavy reliance on information technology.

bounded rationality model: a reality-orientated model of decision making in which individuals and organisations seek the best solutions when faced with a choice among alternatives, but they usually settle for considerably less than they would like to have.

brainstorming: in a brainstorming session a group of people are encouraged to exchange ideas freely in an atmosphere characterised by little censorship or criticism.

burnout: the development of negativity in a person's response to others, a lowering of one's estimation of personal achievements, and total exhaustion on all fronts.

business ethics: the principle of business ethics is that companies and their employees need a framework to deal with issues, both internal and external to the organisation, that have a moral dimension.

business process re-engineering: the critical examination of everything the organisation does in order to improve processes.

case study: case studies probe in some detail the activities or behaviour of individuals or groups within an organisation.

Cattell's 16 PF Test: this test measures 16 dimensions of personality; the dimensions have been identified by using a statistical method called factor analysis.

charisma: charismatic leaders, through the force of their personalities and interpersonal skills, are capable of articulating an appealing vision linking the present with the future and are said to have an extraordinary effect on followers or subordinates, without resorting to any formal authority.

child: a person in a communication network is in the child state when he or she is not logical in his or her position or approach, is intent on immediate gratification of impulses, and displays temper tantrums and attention-seeking behaviour.

classical bureaucracy: a theory, based on Weber, that the ideal organisation is hierarchical, with each position in the hierarchy assigned a specific role, where there are clear rules, and where everything done is documented; here the concern is with how to organise effectively large numbers of employees into an overall structure.

classical conditioning: classical conditioning is the learning of an association of one event with another that results in a new pattern of behaviour.

co-acting group: a feature of a co-acting group is the level of independence experienced by group members; they may undertake either similar or dissimilar tasks within the group, but they do so independently of each other.

coercive power: in this type of power the leader is able and willing to use penalties that subordinates dislike—e.g., withdrawal of privileges, allocation of unattractive assignments, denial of promotion opportunities and pay increases, verbal abuse, withdrawal of friendship and emotional support.

cognitive approach: the cognitive perspective, which focuses on the internal mental states and processes of the individual, has been dominant in psychology since the 1970s and is recognised as a major school of thought.

cognitive behavioural therapy: cognitive behavioural therapy focuses on changing illogical patterns of thought that underlie depression; it is assumed that depressed individuals pursue illogical thinking and that this is the root of their problem.

cognitive dissonance theory: cognitive dissonance arises when individuals act in a manner inconsistent with what they feel; if an attitude is important to the individual, then the behaviour that is inconsistent with it creates dissonance or psychological discomfort; the easiest way to get rid of this dissonance is to change the attitude so that it now corresponds more closely with the behaviour.

cognitive learning: a theoretical perspective on learning that contrasts with social learning theory; in cognitive learning it is assumed that there is a change in what the learner knows rather than what he or she does.

cohesiveness: cohesiveness within a group is likely to exist when there is a high level of agreement among group members with respect to values, beliefs, and objectives.

collective unconscious: in Jungian psychology, this contains experiences shared by all human beings and is part of our biological inheritance; in effect the contents of the collective unconscious basically reflect the experiences of our species since it originated on our planet.

collectivism: in a collectivist culture—such as Singapore, the Philippines, and Mexico—the individual receives help and support from the extended family and tribal group, and is expected to reciprocate with loyalty; the emphasis could be on belonging, having a sense of duty, and a strong belief in the power of group decision making.

colour adaptation: the process of adapting to sudden changes in illuminated colour.

common goals: a goal can be defined as something the organisation is striving to achieve. In its broadest sense it refers to the overall purpose of the organisation.

communication networks: networks of communication are systems of information exchange within an organisation.

compliance: in attitude research, compliance is a form of attitude change whereby an attitude is adopted for ulterior motives, such as the desire to make a favourable impression on the individual's boss or client.

conflict: conflict is defined as a process that materialises when an individual or group perceives that another individual or group is frustrating, or about to frustrate, the attempts of the former to attain a goal.

consideration: a dimension of leadership that indicates friendship, mutual trust, respect, and warmth; a leader with a high score on this dimension is likely to be friendly and approachable, with a good rapport and two-way communication with subordinates, and is willing to help with personal problems, and thereby adopts an employee-oriented (i.e., participative and empowered) approach to leadership.

consistency theories: consistency theories of attitude formation hold that people try to establish internal harmony, consistency, or congruity among their opinions, attitudes, knowledge, and values.

constancy: constancy refers to situations where we see objects as stable despite great changes in the stimuli reaching the sensory organs (such as changes in size, orientation, and colour).

contingency approach: this approach challenges the view that there are universal answers to organisational questions; instead, the structure of an organisation is dependent upon its situation.

continuous change process model: a model of organisational change that examines change from the perspective of top management and recognises that change is continuous.

continuous reinforcement: a schedule of reinforcement that involves always giving a reward when the desired behaviour occurs; there is some debate about which is more effective, continuous reinforcement or partial reinforcement (when the desired response is rewarded only some of the time).

control theory of motivation: a general theory of motivation that integrates a number of different cognitive theories of motivation.

core competencies: skills that are crucial for the efficient execution of organisational tasks.

corporate culture: a consideration of organisational values and norms, with the focus on assumptions and beliefs.

cosmopolite: a person in a communication network who acts as a link between the organisation and its external environment, and has a lot of contact with sources outside the organisation.

counselling: a process aimed at helping the clients of the counsellor to explore a problem or issue so that they can help themselves and take responsibility for their own lives.

counteracting groups: these groups have opposing aims and compete for scarce resources; in the process they may engage in a struggle for power and advantage.

critical incidents: a technique for measuring job satisfaction that involves the employee focusing attention on some situation or incident that is related to job satisfaction.

cross-functional teams: these teams are drawn from roughly the same hierarchical level, but from different functional areas within an organisation, or even between organisations, and they come together to perform a particular task.

customer grouping: a way of structuring an organisation where the structures are created to satisfy the needs of particular types of customers under a customer grouping arrangement (e.g., a department store).

decision cycle: a descriptive method for analysing the steps involved in making a choice from among various courses of action open to the decision maker.

decision-support system: a system that provides information to supplement rather than replace managerial decision making.

defence mechanism: in psychoanalytic psychology, defence mechanisms are coping strategies designed to protect the ego from the excessive demands of the id and the super-ego, and to cope with external reality; examples include suppression, repression, and projection.

Delphi group: a type of decision-making group similar to the nominal group, but where members do not meet face-to-face.

dependent variable: in an experiment, the factor that changes as a result of the independent variable, and one that can be measured, such as counting the number of units of production.

descriptive statistics: a method of describing phenomena in statistical terms—e.g., a key characteristic of a sample of managers, such as the average weekly hours spent at work.

differential threshold: the differential threshold is the smallest amount by which two similar stimuli must be different in order to be perceived as different; an example of the differential threshold can be seen in the case of the professional wine taster, who frequently perceives a difference between two bottles of wine that the amateur finds identical.

discrimination: in classical conditioning, discrimination refers to the capacity to distinguish between two stimuli so that the appropriate response to the correct stimulus is made.

dysfunctional or destructive conflict: dysfunctional conflict produces uncontrolled opposition and discontent, hampers communication, undermines cohesiveness, elevates in-fighting between members to a position higher than the achievement of group goals, and eventually has an adverse effect on group effectiveness.

econological model: this model describes a logical and orderly way of processing information and arriving at a decision.

ego: in psychoanalytic psychology, the ego is the main mental force controlling behaviour that realistically pursues pleasure and seeks to avoid unpleasant or anxious situations.

e-learning: this refers to information and knowledge delivered through the medium of information and communication technology, and is typically associated with the internet.

emergent conflict: this is seen when two social forces collide, for example when subordinates are convinced that their level of expertise surpasses that of their superiors.

emotional intelligence: emotional intelligence is concerned with an individual's emotional and social skills, such as emotional self-awareness, emotional management, self-motivation, and self-management skills.

employee assistance programmes: EAPs are programmes through which employees are counselled on problems ranging from alcohol and drug abuse to financial, marital, and legal difficulties; the main purpose is to enhance the quality of the employee's personal life.

empowerment: an approach to job design that implies the creation of conditions by management so that people can experience enhanced motivation to achieve desired levels of performance.

entrepreneur: someone who creates and manages a business in an innovative way, and who has the creative talent to identify a new product or service.

equity theory: a social comparison theory based on the importance of the underlying cognitive processes governing an individual's decision whether or not to put effort into an activity; the main thrust of the theory is that people are motivated to secure what they perceive to be a fair return for their efforts.

ERG theory: Alderfer (1972) proposed a hierarchical theory consisting of three need categories —existence (E), relatedness (R), and growth (G).

escalation of commitment: a decision-making style that arises when there is a tendency to persist in an ineffective course of action, even when evidence suggests that a problem exists and that a particular project is doomed to failure.

ethical issues: issues relating to the way participants are treated in research, and in other areas such as decision making, politics, and employee selection.

expectancy theory: this theory expounds the view that we choose among alternative behaviours— i.e., we anticipate the possible outcome of various actions; we place a weighting or value on each possible outcome, assessing the probability that each outcome will be the result of an alternative action; and, finally, the course of action that maximises our expected value will be chosen.

expert power: this type of power emerges when the leader is seen by subordinates as having superior knowledge and expertise that is relevant to the tasks or activities under consideration.

external validity: external validity is concerned with the extent to which the findings of a piece of research can be generalised beyond the specific confines of the setting in which the study took place.

extinction: in classical conditioning, extinction occurs if the conditioned stimulus is introduced repeatedly without being followed by the unconditioned stimulus, when there will be a gradual weakening of the strength of the conditioned response.

extraneous variable: in an experiment, any variable other than the independent and dependent variables that can influence the outcome of the experiment.

extravert: according to Eysenck, an extravert is a personality type that is sociable, likes parties, has many friends, needs people to converse with, but does not like reading or studying alone.

FIDO principle: the FIDO principle states that learning through communication is enhanced by frequency, intensity, duration, and over again (repetition).

Fiedler's model: a theory of situational leadership that attempts to predict how style of leadership, leader–member relations, the power vested in the position of leader, and the structure of the job or task harmonise to determine the leader's ability to achieve productive output.

field experiment: a field experiment is designed with a view to applying the laboratory method to a real-life situation.

field study: the field study is conducted in a real-life setting and is principally concerned with survey research methods based on questionnaires, interviews, observation, and the analysis of documents.

formal group: in a formal group, important objectives and roles performed by members are predetermined.

functional grouping: a way of structuring an organisation by allowing employees to have most contact with those working in the same function.

functional or constructive conflict: low to moderate levels of subtle and controlled opposition; this conflict is likely to lead to an arousal of motivation and could lend itself to activities such as creative or nonprogrammed decision making.

g factor: the theory of intelligence provided by Spearman proposes that individuals possess a general factor of intelligence in different quantities.

gain sharing: this reward scheme can amount to passing on to employees income or benefits as a result of reductions in costs, or arising from ideas related to improvements.

gatekeeper: a person in a communication network who occupies a strategic position in the network enabling him or her to control information moving in either direction through a particular communication line.

generalisation: in classical conditioning, the phenomenon of generalisation occurs when we attribute to a similar stimulus the characteristics of the conditioned stimulus.

Gestalt laws of organisation: a number of rules or laws governing the organisation of perception are sometimes referred to as the Gestalt laws of organisation—namely, area, proximity, similarity, continuation, common fate, and closure; named after the Gestalt psychologists who first defined them.

goal-setting theory: a cognitive theory of motivation based on the assumption that motivation can be broken down into a series of personal behavioural goals or objectives.

grapevine: a network of relationships between people that arises in a spontaneous way, and one that can be used to supplement formal communication channels.

group demography: the degree to which members of a group share a common demographic attribute such as age, sex, race, educational level, or time spent in the organisation.

group polarisation: this occurs when the group decision is more extreme than the original attitudes and preferences of members of the group.

groupthink: this is the outcome of group pressure, impeding the efficient execution of members' mental faculties and interfering with members' ability to test reality and preserve their judgement; groupthink amounts to an unintentional erosion of one's critical faculties as a result of adopting group norms.

growth curve model of change: a model of organisational change in which the organisation passes through three phases in sequence: formative, normative, and integrative phases.

halo effect: this materialises when we perceive people in terms of the concepts of good and bad; good people possess all the good qualities, whereas bad people possess all the bad qualities.

Harrison's four types: according to Harrison, four types of culture are found in organisations—power culture, role culture, support culture, and achievement culture.

Hersey–Blanchard situational theory: this model adopts consideration (relationship behaviour) and initiating structure (task behaviour) and extends these two dimensions of leadership to form four styles (tell, sell, participation, and delegation); the model places particular emphasis on matching a style of leadership to the maturity of subordinates, and this relationship is said to be crucial in the determination of leadership effectiveness.

heterogeneous group: in the heterogeneous group, the profile of members (e.g., age, experience, education, specialism, and cultural origins) is dissimilar in one or more ways that are relevant to the functioning of the group.

heuristics: in solving problems or making decisions, heuristics are rules that guide the search for alternatives into areas where there is a good chance of finding satisfactory solutions; they reduce to manageable proportions the number of possible solutions through which the decision maker must sift.

hierarchy of needs: Maslow (1954) proposed the theory that individual needs form a hierarchy, with basic needs at the bottom and self-actualisation needs at the top.

high-performance systems: HPS are organisational systems based on the principles of customer-focused operating units, devolved decision making, streamlined management control, including tighter financial control, re-engineering of business processes, and benchmarking of decisions against their contribution to shareholder value.

homogeneous group: a homogeneous group is said to exist when the profile of members (e.g., age, experience, education, specialism, and cultural origins) is similar in one or more ways that are relevant to the functioning of the group.

human relations movement: initiated by Elton Mayo, a social scientist from Harvard University, this is the view that an organisation should be committed to justice and humanity in its dealings with workers.

human resource management: a strategic approach to acquire, develop, manage, and motivate people.

hypothesis: a precise statement about the expected outcome of an experiment, often based on a theoretical prediction or even just a hunch.

id: in psychoanalytic psychology, the id consists of the inherited characteristics of the individual and can be viewed as a collection of instinctive desires, urges, or needs, all demanding immediate gratification.

identification: in attitude research, identification is a form of attitude change that arises when the individual adopts an attitude in order to establish or maintain a satisfying relationship with others.

idiographic approach: when studying personality, the researcher adopting this approach takes the view that the individual is not just a collection of separate traits, but is a well-integrated organism.

illusions: under certain conditions constancy does not hold good, and what we see appears to be quite different from what we know to be true; these manifestations are called illusions.

implicit favourite model: this model postulates the view that individuals solve complex problems by simplifying the decision process; in fact early in the decision process, before seriously exploring all possibilities, a preferred alternative is selected and for the remainder of the time the decision maker places emphasis on confirming that the implicit favourite has been the right choice.

implicit personality: implicit personality theory is part of our cognitive set—in essence, it is a set of concepts and assumptions used to describe, compare, and understand people.

impression management: this refers to the process by which individuals attempt to control the impression others form of them.

incubation: a hypothesised stage of the creative process where reflection and consideration often occur at an unconscious level.

independent variable: in an experiment, the factor that is varied and controlled by the researcher—e.g., the level of illumination during a particular task.

individual conflict: individuals experience frustration when their pathway to achieving personal goals is blocked.

individualism: the individualistic orientation, prevalent in the UK, Canada, and the USA, puts the spotlight on such characteristics as achievement and the use of personal initiative, with more inward concerns based on the self and the family.

indoor/outdoor exercises: an approach to training in which real-life situations are simulated because they are thought to involve an element of stress, the need to inspire teamwork, problem solving, resolution of conflict, the exercise of interpersonal skills, and the maintenance of morale.

industrial psychology: the application of psychology and science to industry to better understand workplace practice.

inferential statistics: a statistical method for drawing inferences from the analysis of data.

influence–power continuum: a leadership continuum used to evaluate the various degrees of sharing influence and power between superiors and subordinates.

informal group: the informal group develops in a spontaneous fashion, and the objectives and roles found in this type of group arise from the current interactions of members.

information-processing: a cognitive view of humans as processors of information where information from a person's environment is processed through pre-existing systems of knowledge abstracted from various memory schemata and experiences.

initiating structure: a dimension of leadership that indicates a concern with defining and organising roles or relationships in an organisation, establishing well-defined forms of organisation, channels of communication and ways of getting jobs done, and trying out new ideas and practices; a high score on this dimension characterises individuals who play an active role in directing group activities through planning, communicating information, scheduling, including assigning group members to particular tasks, and expecting employees to meet particular standards of performance and meet deadlines.

insight: a hypothesised stage of the creative process where, as a result of the previous stages, there is a desired outcome reflected as something new.

institutionalised conflict: this is evident when two or more groups within an organisation vie for advantage over such things as resource allocation; in such circumstances, particular groups are preoccupied with their own vested interests and, given that resources are normally scarce, a gain for one group could be a loss for another.

intensity of motives: perception is selectively affected by personal motives because we pay most attention to stimuli that appeal to fairly intense motives.

interacting group: a type of decision-making group that involves members interacting in the process of generating ideas about ways of tackling a problem, leading eventually to a group decision using majority voting if necessary.

interference: the most common form of forgetting is through interference, which can be when new information corrupts old information (retroactive interference), when old information interferes with the learning of new information (proactive interference), when subconscious forces promote the avoidance of painful memories (repression), and when emotion, such as anxiety, interferes with the retrieval of memories (emotional interference).

internal–external locus of control: in Rotter's theory of personality, people differ in their attitude to control; certain people (externals) feel that the outcome of their efforts is controlled by forces and events external to themselves, such as chance, fate, and powerful figures in authority, whereas others (internals) are convinced that control is an internal matter related to their own efforts and talents.

internal validity: the extent to which the independent variable (e.g., participation in decision making) really does affect the dependent variable (e.g., productivity).

internalisation: in attitude research, internalisation is a more permanent form of attitude change (when contrasted with compliance and identification) that arises when the new attitude is embraced as part of a cluster of attitudes, because the individual feels comfortable subscribing to that attitude.

intrapreneur: a company employee who works independently inside the company to develop a new product or service, and adopts an entrepreneurial perspective with the objectives of the organisation firmly in mind.

introvert: according to Eysenck, an introvert is a personality type that is quiet, retiring, introspective, and fond of books rather than people.

isolate: a person in a communication network who tends to work alone, and communicates little with others.

isolated dyad: a small group of people in a communication network who tend to interact with each other, but communicate little with others.

job analysis: job analysis procedures are designed to produce systematic information about jobs, including the nature of the work performed, the equipment used, the working conditions, and the position of the job within the organisation.

job characteristics model: a numerical method for matching personal needs to a specific job.

job enlargement: an approach to job design that entails an expansion of the worker's job to include tasks previously performed by other workers.

job enrichment: an approach to job design in which positive job-related experiences are promoted, such as a sense of achievement, responsibility, and recognition. It also involves granting the worker more control over the job.

job rotation: a view of job design in which workers are moved in a systematic way from one job to another in order to provide more interest and satisfaction at work.

job satisfaction: job satisfaction is associated with how well our personal expectations at work are in line with outcomes.

job specialisation: a view of job design in which a job is one specialised aspect of a business.

Jung's typology: Jung's theory of personality consists of four types and is based on four functions —sensing, thinking, feeling, and intuition.

just-in-time: a manufacturing and stock system geared to improving productivity, and a feature of it is that component parts arrive just in time to be used in the manufacturing process; this has the effect of reducing the costs of keeping stocks in a warehouse until they are required.

leader–member exchange (LMX) theory: also known as vertical dyad linkage theory, this theory places emphasis on subordinate participation and influence in the decision-making process; it attempts to explain how the nature of the relationship (or linkage) between leader and follower can affect the leadership process.

leadership grid: a model of leadership style, which is not shown as a point on a leadership continuum but rather as a point on a two-dimensional grid, with concern for people and production as the two separate dimensions.

lean production systems: lean production systems revolve round five main principles—teamwork, quality control, customer focus, minimal inventory buffers, and continuous improvement.

legitimate power: this type of power arises if subordinates believe that the leader is endowed with the right to issue orders that they are obliged to accept.

liaison: a person in a communication network who acts as a bridge between groups by promoting closer relationships between them and ensuring that the necessary level of information to integrate group activities is available.

Likert scale: a way of measuring attitudes by using a rating scale with a fixed number of alternatives; the individual is asked not only to indicate agreement or disagreement, but also to signify how strongly he or she agrees or disagrees with a number of statements relevant to the attitude being measured.

Likert's four styles of leadership: under Likert's theory there are four management styles— exploitive authoritative, benevolent authoritative, consultative, and participative.

linear programming: linear programming, which involves presenting very small pieces of information (a frame) at an acceptable level of difficulty to the learner, sometimes using machines, is linked to Skinner's concept of operant conditioning.

long-term memory: when material can be recalled reliably after a day or a week, it is assumed that the information is recalled from long-term memory; the capacity of long-term memory is substantial and forgetting is slow.

management competencies: the successful application of skills, knowledge, and ability to the standards required in employment.

management teams: these teams coordinate the activity of work teams drawn from a number of areas, as well as offering advice and support.

managerial talent: the view that successful management is based on talent (a mixture of personality traits, motives, and skills) rather than on a set of personality traits alone.

matrix organisation: the matrix structure of an organisation integrates two different groupings —for example, a project department is superimposed on a functional grouping.

modelling: an applied learning procedure in which the desired behaviour is firmly kept in mind before selecting the appropriate model capable of exemplifying the way to proceed; this could, for example, be an ideal style of supervision.

Myers-Briggs type indicator: this indicator, or measure, is used to identify managerial decision styles based on Jung's personality typology.

N.Ach: the need to achieve.

N.Pow: the need for power.

needs assessment: a systematic assessment of training needs before training commences.

neo-human relations: this is the view that employees have great potential to perform, and they should not be treated as submissive, compliant creatures; and also the view that there should be greater scientific analysis of organisational functioning.

neurotic: according to Eysenck, a neurotic is a personality type that is prone to worries and anxieties, and is easily upset.

nominal group: a type of decision-making group that involves members physically present at the meeting stating their opinions independently with respect to the problem before the discussion takes place, and remaining silent in relation to such opinions during the discussion.

nomothetic approach: principally concerned with the collection and analysis of data about groups; the main objective of the nomothetic approach is the isolation of one or more of the variables of personality.

nonverbal communication: this concerns all aspects of communication that are not expressed orally or in writing; it includes body movements, the emphasis and intonations we put on words, facial expressions, and the physical distance between the sender and receiver of a message.

observational method: a method of research that involves observing more naturally occurring behaviour than can be found in a laboratory experiment; it is assumed that memories, thoughts, and feelings (nonobservable data) can be inferred from observing behaviour, though sometimes it may be difficult to infer what causes particular behaviour.

operant conditioning: a basic form of learning in which learning occurs after behaviour is rewarded or reinforced.

opportunity power: this category of power is said to exist when someone can exert power by reason of being in the right place at the right time.

oral stage of psychosexual development: the first stage of personality development in the psychoanalytic approach; the mouth is the focal point of the infant's libido.

organisation: an organisation could be described as a collection of individuals who are organised into groups and subgroups and interact with each other in an interdependent relationship.

organisational behaviour: the study of human behaviour in organisations; it is concerned with the relationship between the individual and the group, and how both interact with the organisation.

organisational commitment: the relative strength of an individual's identification with and involvement in an organisation.

organisational development: "The process of planned change and improvement of organisations through the application of knowledge of the behavioural sciences" (Moorhead & Griffin, 2004).

orientation: the particular orientation—the attitude adopted by the perceiver towards a set of physical stimuli, based on interests, background, etc.—is critical to the way something is perceived.

Osgood's semantic differential: a technique for measuring attitudes in which the respondent is asked to give an immediate reaction to pairs of words and to describe the person he or she prefers the least by placing a cross in one of the seven spaces between each pair of words; the individual's score is his or her total score on all scales of the measure used, and the higher the score the more favourable is the respondent's impression of the person assessed.

parapsychology: the scientific study of extrasensory perception and other paranormal events, such as precognition, clairvoyance, telepathy, and psychokinesis; most psychologists are sceptical about the existence of extra-sensory perception.

parent: a person in a communication network is in the parent state when he or she is influenced heavily by childhood perceptions of the behaviour of parents or other important role models.

participant observation: an observational method whereby the observer becomes a member of the group he or she is observing; the group may know they are being observed or the observation may be carried out in secret.

participative leadership: a style of leadership characterised by a high frequency of contact between superior and subordinates, where decision making tends to be pushed down the hierarchy, where superiors are helpful in a constructive way, and generally where good relationships between superiors and subordinates are evident.

path–goal model: the path–goal theory of leadership supposes that the main functions of the leader are to assist the subordinate to attain his or her goals and to ensure that the subordinate finds the experience satisfying; the theory is concerned with explaining the relationship between the behaviour of the leader and the attitudes and expectations of the subordinate.

payment by results: this system links pay to the quantity of the individual's output; a forerunner of PBR is the piece-work system where pay is linked to the number of units of work produced, and this was common in manufacturing industry.

perceptual interpretation: perceptual interpretation occurs when we relate a stimulus (e.g., a physical object or a person) to the individual's cognitive context.

performance appraisal: a process where the performance of subordinates is evaluated by superiors and others as a means of developing human resources, with productivity in mind; the normal practice is for the results of the appraisal process to be shared with the subordinate in a positive way so that the individual concerned is given the support to put right deficiencies or maintain good practice.

performance-related pay: a reward system with a broad interpretation of financial rewards, ranging from pay incentives and bonuses to profit sharing and equity share schemes, with the emphasis on relating rewards to performance.

personal construct theory: the theory of Kelly, under which humans are seen as scientists who are trying to make sense of their world; they are continually testing assumptions about various things with reference to experience and evidence; there is no absolute truth or objective reality, but humans can use constructs to interpret situations in order to improve their understanding and ability to predict future events.

personal power: personal power is attached to the person and it subsumes referent and some traces of expert, coercive, and reward power.

personal space: the distance or physical proximity of others; in interactions with others,

we allow people we know well to enter our personal space; a stranger entering into this territory could be perceived as a threat.

personality: personality consists of the physical, mental, moral, and social qualities of the individual; these qualities are dynamic and integrated.

personality type: a view of personality based on the idea that when a person shares a pattern of traits with a large group of people, he or she is said to belong to a personality type.

phallic stage of psychosexual development: the third stage of personality development in the psychoanalytic approach; the genitals are the focus of the infant's libido.

phenomenological approach/phenomenology: in this approach the emphasis is essentially on people's individual experience rather than their behaviour; our unique perceptions, and action strategies based on them, tend to determine what we are and how we react.

politics: politics in organisations has been defined as those activities carried out by people to acquire, enhance, and use power and other resources to obtain preferred outcomes in situations where there are uncertainties or disagreements.

position power: this category of power is attached to a post, irrespective of who is performing the job, and is limited to the activities within the boundaries of that power.

post-traumatic stress disorder: this occurs in people who have encountered a trauma in which they experienced, witnessed, or were confronted with an event involving actual or threatened death, serious physical injury, or a threat to their physical integrity.

power: this refers to a force at the disposal of one person that can influence the behaviour of another. Therefore, X has the capacity to influence the behaviour of Y in such a way that Y performs tasks he or she would not otherwise do.

prejudice: this is an attitude that predisposes a person to act in an unfavourable or favourable way to another person or group of people.

preparatory set: the preparatory set basically refers to the range of things that, because of our internal state, we are almost programmed to see and register.

primary group: a primary group is small in size, face-to-face contact is generally frequent, and relationships tend to be close and often intimate; a family, a playgroup, a sports team, or a tightly knit group of accountants in an organisation could constitute a primary group.

primary reinforcers: reinforcers used in most animal-learning experiments are examples of primary reinforcers; food, drink, and sex fit into this category.

principles of organisation: a theory expounded by practitioners, such as Fayol (1949) and Urwick (1947), that emphasises the organisation's objective, its division of labour and specialisation, authority and the responsibility that comes with it, modes of effective communication, the need for a chain of command, and continuity and balance between different parts of the organisation.

process culture: a type of corporate culture where the heroes are rather cautious and protective of their position, which requires the display of an eye for detail, order, and punctuality within the context of well-defined procedures.

process grouping: a way of structuring an organisation by allowing employees to have most contact with those working in the same process; the grouping of specific jobs is influenced by a particular work activity.

process model of change: a three-step change process involving unfreezing, changing, and refreezing.

process re-engineering: this is described as a fundamental rethink and redesign of critical organisational processes, getting rid of processes that are unnecessary or redundant, and placing greater reliance on cross-functional teams.

product grouping: grouping members of an organisation by product or service materialises when employees who work on a particular product or service belong to the same unit or department, irrespective of their specialism.

project teams: project teams, drawing their membership from within the organisation, are essentially multifunctional groups that may only

have a temporary existence; they could be formed to solve particular problems and are likely to draw on representatives from different departments, with different backgrounds, values, skills, and affiliations.

protocol analysis: a method of gathering and analysing data based on verbal descriptions of participants' own decisions and behaviour.

psychoanalytical approach/psychoanalysis: initiated by Freud, the prime preoccupation with this approach is providing help for neurotic patients; the central thrust is that people's behaviour can be investigated in a nonexperimental way, that behaviour is determined by some unconscious force, and that behavioural difficulties or abnormalities in adult life spring from childhood.

psychometric testing: the term psychometrics is used to refer to a broad range of different types of assessments and measurements of intelligence, achievement/aptitude, and personality.

punctuated equilibrium model: a model of teambuilding that supposes that there is an initial flurry of activity at the commencement of deliberations—i.e., changing old practices and introducing new ones—followed by a substantial period of inertia as the group puts into action the plans made at the earlier stage; the last meeting of the group is full of activity aimed at finishing the job.

quality circles: a quality circle is a small group of employees (4 to 15) who do similar work and report to the same supervisor; the group meets regularly on a voluntary basis to identify and analyse work problems and provide solutions

rational emotive therapy: RET is a particular cognitive-based technique for dealing with stress, in which irrational beliefs and faulty thinking are confronted.

reference group: reference groups may possess a certain attraction and, as a result, individuals may wish to join them, or merely to identify with them in some way.

referent power: this type of power, similar in concept to charisma, is visible when subordinates think the leader has desirable characteristics that they should imitate.

rehearsal: this is an activity that recycles the same items of information in short-term memory in order to retain the information.

reliability: a reliable measure is one that will provide the same reading if that which is measured remains constant.

reward power: in this type of power the leader is able to control rewards—e.g., pay and promotion—which subordinates consider to be worth striving for.

reward systems: reward systems in organisations are those that are used in order to attract, retain, and motivate people in the desired direction.

risky shift: a phenomenon that often occurs as the consequence of a group decision rather than an individual decision, which is that the group is often prepared to take greater risks than is an individual.

role (of a group member): a role could be defined as a set of expected patterns of behaviour attributable to a person occupying a particular position.

role ambiguity: this arises when people are uncertain about their duties, responsibilities, or authority, or all three.

role conflict: this arises when a person performs more than one role, and performance in one role makes performance in the other more difficult.

role construct repertory test: this is a method, based on the personal construct theory of Kelly, used to arrive at the basic constructs that a person uses, and the interrelationship between them.

Rorschach Test: a projective test consisting of a series of 10 ink-blots or formless shapes in which one half is the mirror image of the other; the subject is asked to say what the blot resembles.

schedules of reinforcement: the various ways in which a response is rewarded in terms of the frequency of the response, the interval between responses, and the frequency of the reinforcer.

schemata: a schemata is an internal structure, developed through experience, that organises incoming information in relation to previous experience.

scientific management: a theory (spearheaded by Taylor, Gilbreth, and Gantt) that emphasises efficiency and productivity in organisations, with the spotlight on the interaction between the person and the job.

script: a script is a sub-component of a schemata that describes a scenario of behaviour applicable to a particular setting, such as a restaurant script—the sequence includes being seated, looking at the menu, ordering food, paying the bill, and leaving.

secondary group: a secondary group assumes more of an impersonal nature and may be geographically distant; a company, a hospital, or a school could fall into this category.

secondary reinforcer: a secondary reinforcer is one that has derived and developed its reinforcement qualities from being associated with one or more primary reinforcers; money would fall into this category.

selective perception: selective perception amounts to attending to those stimuli that are most likely to be important and ignoring the others.

self-actualisation: the view of Maslow that the most difficult personal need to obtain is that of self-actualisation, implying self-fulfilment derived from achievement following the successful accomplishment of, for example, a demanding and challenging assignment at work.

self-concept: according to Carl Rogers' theory, the self comprises the pattern of perception, feelings, attitudes, and values that individuals consider to be unique to themselves.

self-efficacy: a cognitive theory of motivation resting on the assumption that motivation is based on a cognitive judgement by the individual and amounts to a belief in one's capability to execute required actions and produce outcomes for a defined task.

self-managed teams: these teams or groups, with around 10–15 employees, take on the responsibilities of their former supervisors; the work of the team consists of planning and scheduling work, collective control over the pace of work, making operating decisions and solving problems.

self-monitoring: this refers to the tendency of individuals to regulate their behaviour on the basis of internal factors (e.g., own attitudes, values, beliefs), or alternatively external factors (e.g., reactions to other people or requirements of a given situation).

sensation-seeking: sensation-seeking is the desire to explore novel and intense experiences.

sensory adaptation: absolute and differential thresholds are known to fluctuate, and this fluctuation is referred to as sensory adaptation.

shaping: a form of learning or teaching in which an appropriate reinforcer is selected to suit the occasion, and all positive reinforcements are contingent on the organism moving closer to adopting the desired behaviour.

short-term memory: STM is said to have limited storage capacity (about seven—plus or minus two—units of information) and is capable of holding a small amount of information for a short time.

simplification: a decision-making strategy where a simplified model of reality is adopted by the decision maker; familiar situations invite similar responses and a different approach is adopted only if the previous approach did not work out well.

skill-based pay: skill-based or competency-based pay is determined by the range of expertise of the employee (e.g., the number of skills acquired); it allows employees to improve their earnings without having had a promotion.

social identity theory: a theoretical perspective based on personality applied to motivation that supposes that group-based influences play an important motivational role and an individual's social identity is crucial.

social learning theory: a theoretical perspective and practical training method based on the assumption that learning involves associations between behaviour and its consequences, as well as between stimuli and their consequences; most learning in this perspective is assumed to be governed by rewards.

social loafing: this is the term applied to the behaviour of a member of a group who is not conscientious and withholds effort.

social norms: social norms regulate the relationships between individuals in groups; in fact they are guides to behaviour on a number of issues, such as how tasks are performed, the level of output, and the speed of action.

social support: the giving and receiving of help (especially emotional support) from social relationships, such as one's partner, a friend, or through membership of an organisation.

sociometry: using a natural group, every member of the group is asked to name their preferred partner for a specified activity, and they then rank the remainder of the group in order of preference; this method is useful in establishing the popularity of group members.

spirituality: spirituality in the workplace refers to the fact that people have a spiritual side to their make-up, are eager to seek meaning, purpose, and fulfilment in the work they do, and strive for satisfaction from connecting with other people and feeling they are part of a community.

statistical significance: a probability measurement of the likelihood that the differences between the data from at least two groups in an experiment are due to chance.

status: this is the social ranking given to an individual because of the position he or she occupies in a group; various factors may contribute to status, such as seniority, title, salary, and power, and any one of these factors could be critical in bestowing status.

stereotyping: this is a generalised belief about the characteristics, attributes, and behaviour that typically belong to a certain group.

stock ownership plans: a reward system where the employee owns some stock in the company.

stress: any situation that is seen as burdensome, threatening, ambiguous, or boring is likely to induce stress.

structured observation: in structured observation, the observer knows in advance what behaviour is relevant to the research objectives.

subjective rationality: a decision-making strategy where the decision maker becomes more conservative as the complexity of the decision situation grows; at the same time, there is the tendency to cease seeking more information, even though such information could be useful and inexpensive to acquire, and heavy reliance is placed on personal judgement.

super-ego: in psychoanalytic psychology the ego represents the standards and ethical values acquired from parents and society in general.

systems approach: this is the notion that an organisation is an open system (one that is continually adapting to and influencing its external environment) comprised of technical and social elements.

team: a team could be described as a small number of people with complementary skills who are committed to a common purpose, common performance goals, and a common approach for which they hold themselves mutually accountable; a team differs from a group in its job category, authority, and reward systems.

team briefing: the team briefing is a two-way communication process whereby the manager or leader of the group provides up-to-date information to group members, and the latter are given the opportunity to ask questions.

Team Climate Inventory: a survey instrument used to measure team climate and the extent to which the team is effective and supported by management.

territorial grouping: when an organisation is geographically dispersed, groupings are created by region within a country or, where appropriate, by world regions; frequently sales or marketing groups are divided by geographic region.

Thematic Apperception Test: a projective test that consists of 20 pictures of varying degrees of clarity; the subject examines each picture and then tells a story about the scene portrayed.

theory of planned behaviour: an attitude is expressed as a belief about the consequences of behaviour; it is not concerned about general beliefs or feelings related to the object or subject matter of the attitude. As a result, it is said that beliefs are good predictors of behaviour.

theory of reasoned action: in the theory of reasoned action there is the assumption that people's actions are best predicted by their intentions; in turn, intentions are determined by people's attitudes as well as by what they see as expectations of them held by others.

Thurstone Scale: one of the first systematic approaches to attitude measurement was developed by Thurstone and Chave (1929).

time rates: a payment system based on time rates relates to the number of hours worked, and is common in collective bargaining; time rates can be classified as an hourly rate, a weekly wage, or a monthly salary.

top management teams: a relatively small group of the most influential executives at the top of the organisation; its existence is a recognition that the management of an enterprise is typically a shared activity that extends well beyond the chief executive.

total quality management: an organisational technique of satisfying consumer needs and promoting worker satisfaction through the continuous improvement of all organisational processes.

tough-guy macho: a type of corporate culture where the heroes are tough, individualistic, superstitious, and risk-takers, and they keep up with fashion, and embrace trendy lifestyles; they prefer sport that lends itself to solo performance (e.g., squash) and enjoy competitive verbal interactions.

trained incapacity: a situation sometimes develops where the training provided by the organisation actually interferes with the individual's approach to decision making and problem solving.

training objective: a statement of what the employee will be able to do at the end of the training session, often referred to as the behavioural objective.

trait: a trait is an individual characteristic in thought, feeling, and action, either inherited or acquired, and refers to tendencies to act or react in certain ways (e.g., kindness).

transactional leadership: the leader enters into various transactions with subordinates, explaining what is required of them in terms of their contributions, and specifies the compensation or rewards they will receive if they fulfil these requirements; it is a style of leadership appropriate to stable conditions in the environment.

transfer of learning: the transfer of learning (or training) is the process by which the effects of training in one form of an activity are transferred to another form; a claim often made is that the learning of mathematics, or at least the training involved, improves the learner's ability to solve problems requiring logic, whether these are of a mathematical nature or not.

transformational leadership: in transformational leadership the emphasis is on people of vision who are creative, innovative, and capable of getting others to share their dreams while playing down self-interest; and who are able to cooperate with others in reshaping the strategies and tactics of the organisation (e.g., orchestrating a merger, creating a team, or shaping the culture of the organisation) in response to a fast-changing world.

triarchic theory of intelligence: a theory that attempts to identify the mental processes that underlie intelligent behaviour, such as analytical thinking, creative thinking, and real-world intelligence.

Tuckman model: a model of teambuilding that implies that the group must go through five stages (forming, storming, norming, performing, and adjournment) before it can be effective in terms of performance.

typology of organisations: a way of categorising organisations on some basis, such as the primary system of reward used to secure the compliance of members.

unconscious motivation: the Freudian or psychoanalytic notion that the individual can be motivated by forces in the unconscious mind of which he or she is unaware.

unstructured observation: unstructured observation often takes the form of participant observation and is often used in exploratory investigations.

validity: a valid measure is one that measures what it claims to measure, though this is sometimes difficult in the social sciences because we normally try to measure something that cannot be observed from the outside.

values: a value is an ideal to which the individual subscribes, it represents basic convictions that a specific mode of conduct is preferable (in a personal or social sense) to any other, and it is relatively stable and enduring.

venture teams: these teams try to tap the resources of creative departments within the organisation. They are often located out on a limb and are not subjected to the normal rules and regulations of the company.

virtual organisation: the virtual organisation has been defined as a network organisation with a small core of employees that outsources major business functions.

virtual teams: a virtual team has been defined as a physically dispersed task group that conducts its business through modern information technology; members never meet in a room as a group but they relate to each other, audibly and visually, using computers and telecommunications.

visual adaptation: the process of adapting to sudden changes in illumination; temporary blindness can occur with rapid changes in illumination.

Weber's ideal bureaucracy: Weber viewed bureaucratic organisation as technically superior to any other form of organisation and admirably equipped to maintain effective and impartial control; its aim is to accomplish organisational objectives.

Woodcock model: a model of teambuilding based on the notion that the team must go through four stages of development before it becomes effective.

work ethic: a person with a firm attachment to the Protestant work ethic sees work as intrinsically good, from which is acquired a certain dignity; he or she is hard working, keen to accomplish things, rational, economical, thrifty, and can expect to receive adequate extrinsic rewards.

workforce diversity: recognising that differences between people do not only apply to people in a global setting, but also to people within the same country.

work hard, play hard: a type of corporate culture where the heroes are super salespeople, friendly, not superstitious, fairly conventional in dress, prefer team sport, and socialise in the company of others, and they have a high work rate with quick solutions to problems.

work teams: these are relatively permanent teams that are engaged in daily work.

working memory: a type of short-term memory system where information can be manip-ulated, interpreted, and recombined to develop new knowledge, assist learning, facilitate inter-action with the outside environment, and form goals.

References

Ackerman, L.S. (1982). Transition management: An in-depth look at managing complex change. *Organizational Dynamics*, Summer, 46–66.

Adair, J. (1990). *Great leaders*. Brookwood, UK: Talbot Adair Press.

Adams, J.S. (1963). Towards an understanding of inequity. *Journal of Abnormal and Social Psychology*, *67*, 422–436.

Adams, J.S. (1965). Inequity in social exchange. In L. Berkowitz (Ed.), *Advances in experimental social psychology, Vol. 2*. New York: Academic Press.

Adler, N. (2002). *International dimensions of organizational behaviour* (4th ed.). Cincinnati, OH: South Western College Publishing.

Adorno, J.W., Frenkel-Brunswick, E., Levinson, D.J., & Sanford, R.N. (1953). *The authoritarian personality*. New York: Harper & Row.

Ageism in the workplace. (1993, October 7). *Financial Times*, Editorial Comment, p. 23.

Agor, W.H. (1986). The logic of intuition: How top executives make important decisions. *Organizational Dynamics*, Winter, 9.

Aikin, O. (1995, June 29). Be aware of the risks. *People Management*, 25–28.

Ajzen, I. (1991). The theory of planned behaviour. *Organizational Behaviour and Human Decision Processes*, *50*, 179–211.

Ajzen, I. (2001). Nature and operation of attitudes. *Annual Review of Psychology*, *24*, 1251–1263.

Ajzen, I., & Fishbein, M. (1980). *Understanding attitudes and predicting social behaviour*. New York: Prentice Hall.

Ajzen, I., & Madden, J.T. (1986). Prediction of goal-directed behaviour: Attitudes, intentions, and perceived behavioural control. *Journal of Experimental Social Psychology*, *22*, 453–474.

Alcalay, R., & Pasick, R.J. (1983). Psychosocial factors and the technologies of work. *Social Science and Medicine*, *17*, 1075–1084.

Aldag, R.J., & Fuller, S.R. (1993). Beyond fiasco: A reappraisal of the groupthink phenomenon and a new model of group decision making processes. *Psychological Bulletin*, *113*, 533–552.

Alderfer, C.P. (1972). *Existence, relatedness and growth: Human needs in organisational settings*. New York: Free Press.

Alderfer, C.P., & Ferriss, R. (1972). Understanding the impact of survey feedback. In W.W. Burke & H.A. Hornstein (Eds.), *The social technology of organisational development* (pp. 234–243). Fairfax, VA: NTL Learning Resource Corporation.

Aldrich, H.E. (1992). Understanding, not integration: Vital signs from three perspectives on organizations. In M. Reed & M.D. Hughes (Eds.), *Rethinking organizations: New directions in organizational theory and analysis*. London: Sage.

Allen, C.T., & Madden, T.H. (1985). A closer look at classical conditioning. *Journal of Consumer Research*, *12*, 301–313.

Allen, N.J., & Meyer, M.P. (1990). The measurement and antecedents of affective continuance and normative commitment to the organisation. *Journal of Occupational Psychology*, *63*, 1–8.

Allen, R.S., & Montgomery, K.A. (2001). Applying an organizational approach to creating diversity. *Organizational Dynamics*, *30*, 149–161.

Alliger, G.M., Tannenbaum, S.I., Bennett, W. (Jr), Traver, H., & Shotland, A. (1997). A meta-analysis of the relations between training criteria. *Personnel Psychology*, *50*, 341–358.

Allison, R.I., & Uhl, K.P. (1964). Influence of beer brand identification on taste perception. *Journal of Marketing Research*, *1*(August), 80–85.

Allport, G.W. (1935). Attitudes. In C. Murchison (Ed.), *Handbook of social psychology*. Worcester, MA: Clark University Press.

Allport, G.W. (1961). *Pattern and growth in personality*. New York: Holt, Rinehart & Winston.

Allport, G.W. (1965). *Letters from Jenny*. New York: Harcourt Brace & World.

Allport, G.W., Vernon, P.E., & Lindzey, G. (1960). *A study of values: A scale for measuring the dominant interests in personality*. Boston: Houghton Mifflin.

Alvesson, M. (1988). *Management, corporate culture, and labour process in a professional service company*. Unpublished paper presented at the Conference on the Labour Process, Aston/UMIST, UK.

Amason, A.C. (1996). Distinguishing the effects of functional and dysfunctional conflict on strategic decision making: Resolving a paradox for top management teams. *Academy of Management Journal*, February, 123–148.

Amason, A.C., Hockwarter, W.A., Thompson, K.R., & Harrison, A.W. (1995). Conflict: An important dimension in successful management teams. *Organizational Dynamics*, Autumn, 20–33.

Ambrose, M.L., & Kulik, C.T. (1999). Old friends, new faces. Motivation research in the 1990s. *Journal of Management*, *25*, 231–292.

Anastasi, A. (1979). *Fields of applied psychology* (2nd ed.). New York: McGraw-Hill.

Anastasi, A. (1997). *Psychological testing*. New York: Prentice-Hall.

Anderson, D. (1980). VDUs: Eyestrain or eyewash? *Health and Safety at Work*, August, 36–39.

Anderson, J.R. (1983). *The architecture of cognition*. Cambridge, MA: Harvard University Press.

Anderson, J.R. (1987). Skill acquisition: Compilation of weak method problem solutions. *Psychological Review*, *94*, 192–210.

Anderson, L.R. (1990). Toward a two-track model of leadership training: Suggestions from self-monitoring theory. *Small Group Research*, May, 147–167.

Anderson, N., & Prutton, K. (1993). Occupational psychology in business: Strategic resource or purveyor of tests! *The Occupational Psychologist*, *20*, 3–10.

Anderson, N.R., & West, M.A. (1994). *The team climate inventory: Manual and user's guide*. Windsor, UK: NFER-Nelson.

Anderson, N.R., & West, M.A. (1996). The team climate inventory: Development of the team climate inventory and its application in teambuilding for innovativeness. *European Journal of Work and Organizational Psychology*, *5*, 53–66.

Andreasen, N.C., & Black D.W. (2001). *Introductory textbook of psychiatry* (3rd ed.). Washington, DC: American Psychiatric Publishing.

Andrews, B., & Brewin, C.R. (2000). What did Freud get right? *The Psychologist*, *13*, 605–607.

Antonioni, D. (1996). Designing an effective 360 degree appraisal feedback process. *Organizational Dynamics*, Autumn, 24–38.

Antonovsky, A. (1979). *Health, stress and coping*. San Francisco: Jossey-Bass.

Archer, E. (1980). How to make a business decision: An analysis of theory and practice. *Management Review*, February.

Archer, J., & Rhodes, V. (1993). The grief process and job loss: A cross-sectional study. *British Journal of Psychology*, *84*, 395–410.

Argyle, M. (1968). *The psychology of interpersonal behaviour*. Harmondsworth, UK: Penguin.

Argyris, C. (1953). Human problems with budgets. *Harvard Business Review*, *31*(January–February), 97–110.

Argyris, C. (1964). *Integrating the individual and the organization*. New York: Wiley.

Argyris, C. (1973). Personality and organisation theory revisited. *Administrative Science Quarterly*, *18*, 141–167.

Argyris, C. (1991). Teaching smart people how to learn. *Harvard Business Review*, May–June, 99–109.

Arkin, A., & Downard, B. (2005). Reward—eyes on the prize: The process of developing the best packages to attract and retain staff is becoming more complex. *People Management*, 10 February, 29–35.

Armitage, C.J., & Conner M. (2001). Efficacy of the theory of planned behaviour: A meta-analytical review. *British Journal of Social Psychology*, *40*, 471–499.

Armstrong, M. (1992). *Human resource management: Strategy and action*. London: Kogan Page.

Armstrong, M. (2002). *Employee reward*. London: CIPD.

Armstrong, M. (2003). *A handbook of human resource management practice* (9th Ed.). London: Kogan Page.

Arndt, S., Feltes, J., & Hanak, J. (1983). Secretarial attitudes towards word-processors as a function of familiarity and locus of control. *Behaviour and Information Technology*, *2*, 17–22.

Arnold, J. (2005). *Work psychology: Understanding human behaviour in the workplace* (4th ed.). Harlow, Essex: Pearson Education.

Arnold, J., Cooper, C.L., & Robertson, I.T. (1998). *Work psychology: Understanding human behaviour in the workplace* (3rd ed.). London: Financial Times/ Pitman Publishing.

Arroba, T.Y. (1978). Decision-making style as a function of occupational group, decision content, and perceived importance. *Journal of Occupational Psychology*, *51*, 219–226.

Arvey, R.D., & Campion, J.E. (1982). The employment interviews: A summary and review of recent research. *Personnel Psychology*, *35*, 281–322.

Arvey, R.D., McCall, B.P., Bouchard, T.J., & Taubman, P. (1994). Genetic influences on job satisfaction and work values. *Personality and Individual Differences*, July, 21–33.

Asch, S.E. (1952). Effects of group pressure upon the modification and distortion of judgements. In C.E. Swanson, T.M. Newcombe, & E.L. Hartley (Eds.), *Readings in social psychology*. New York: Holt, Rinehart, & Winston.

Ash, A. (1994). Participants' reactions to appraisal of managers: Results of a pilot. *Public Personnel Management, 23,* 237–256.

Asher, J.J. (1972). The biographical item: Can it be improved? *Personnel Psychology, 25,* 251–269.

Ashforth, B.E., & Mael, F. (1989). Social identity theory and the organisation. *Academy of Management Review, 14*(January), 20–39.

Ashmos, D.P., & Duchon, D. (2000). Spirituality at work: A conceptualization and measure. *Journal of Management Inquiry,* June, 139.

Ashton, D. (1990). *The corporate health care revolution.* London: Kogan Page/Institute of Personnel Management.

Ashworth, J. (1999, February 5). Management training is changing: Dramatic change to the art of team building. *The Times,* p. 26.

Assael, H. (1997). *Consumer behaviour and marketing action.* Cincinnati, OH: South Western Publishing Co.

Atkins, R. (2004, June 21). Volkswagen goes down road to flexible working. *Financial Times,* p. 3.

Atkins, R., & Milne, R. (2004, November 22). How a Rhineland behemoth changed course. *Financial Times,* p. 8.

Atkinson, J.W. (1964). *An introduction to motivation.* New York: Van Nostrand.

Atkinson, K. (1986). Intrapreneurs: Fostering innovation inside the corporation. *Personnel Administrator,* January, 43.

Atkinson, R.L., Atkinson, R.C., Smith, E.E., & Hilgard, E.R. (1987). *Introduction to psychology* (9th ed.). Orlando, FL: Harcourt Brace Jovanovich.

Atkinson, R.L., Atkinson, R.C., Smith, E.E., & Hilgard, E.R. (1996). *Introduction to psychology* (12th ed.). Orlando, FL: Harcourt Brace Jovanovich College Publishers.

Austin, J.T., & Bobko, P. (1985). Goal-setting theory: Unexplored areas and future research needs. *Journal of Occupational Psychology, 58,* 289–308.

Ayres, C. (1998, October 26). Angry staff able to wipe out systems. *The Times,* p. 52.

Bachman, J.G., Bowers, D., & Marcus, P.M. (1968). Bases of supervisory power: A comparative study in five organisational settings. In A.S. Tannenbaum (Ed.), *Control in organisations.* New York: McGraw-Hill.

Bachrach, P., & Baritz, M.S. (1962). Two faces of power. *American Political Science Review, 56,* 947–952.

Baddeley, A.D. (1997). *Human memory* (Rev. ed.). Hove, UK: Psychology Press.

Baddeley, A.D. (1999). *Essentials of human memory.* Hove, UK: Psychology Press.

Baddeley, A.D., & Hitch, G.J. (1974). Working memory. In G.A. Bower (Ed.), *The Psychology of Learning and Motivation* (pp. 47–89). New York: Academic Press.

Baddeley, S., & James, K. (1987). Owl, fox, donkey or sheep: Political skills for managers. *Management Education and Development, 18,* 3–19.

Baker, G. (1996, August 13). Japan's dismal banks: The flip side of success. *Financial Times,* p. 12.

Baldry, C., & Fletcher, C. (1997). The integrity of integrity testing. *Selection and Development Review, 13,* 3–6.

Bales, R.F. (1950). A set of categories for the analysis of small group interaction. *American Sociological Review, 15,* 257–263.

Balzer, W.K., & Sulsky, L.M. (1992). Halo and performance appraisal research: A critical evaluation. *Journal of Applied Psychology,* December, 975–985.

Bandura, A. (1969). *Principles of behaviour modification.* London: Holt, Rinehart & Winston.

Bandura, A. (1977). *Social learning theory.* New York: Prentice Hall.

Bandura, A. (1986). *Social foundations of thought and action: A social cognitive theory.* New York: Prentice Hall.

Bandura, A. (1997). The exercise of control. New York: W.H. Freeman.

Bannister, D. (1970). *Perspectives in personal construct theory.* New York: Academic Press.

Barber, A.E., Dunham, R.B., & Formisano, R.A. (1992). The impact of flexible benefits on employee satisfaction: A field study. *Personnel Psychology,* Spring, 55–75.

Barberis, N. (2001, June 18). Investors seek lessons in thinking. *FT, Mastering Investment, Part 6,* 2–4.

Barclay, J. (1999). Employee selection: A question of structure. *Personnel Review, 28,* 134–151.

Barling, J., Wade, B., & Fullagar, C. (1990). Predicting employee commitment to company and union: Divergent models. *Journal of Occupational Psychology, 63,* 49–61.

Barnard, J.M. (1981, July 7). Stress: Its effects on people at work. *Occupational Health,* 353–361.

Barney, J.B. (1986). Organisational culture: Can it be a source of sustained competitive advantage? *Academy of Management Review,* July, 656–665.

Baron, R.A. (1999). *Essentials of psychology* (2nd ed.). Needham Heights, MA: Allyn & Bacon.

Baron, R.A. (2002). *Essentials of psychology* (3rd ed.). Needham Heights, MA: Allyn & Bacon.

Baron, R.A., & Bronfen, M.I. (1994). A whiff of reality. Empirical evidence concerning the effects of pleasant fragrance on work-related behaviour. *Journal of Applied Psychology, 13,* 1179–1203.

Baron, R.A., & Kalsher, M.J. (1996). The sweet smell of safety. *Proceedings of the Human Factors and Ergonomics Society, 40,* 1282.

Barrett, B., & James, P. (1981). How real is employee participation in health and safety. *Employee Relations*, *3*, 4–7.

Barrett, P. (1998). Science, fundamental measurement and psychometric testing. *Selection and Development Review*, *1*(14), 3–10.

Barrett, P., Kline, P., Paltiel, L., & Eysenck, H.J. (1996). An evaluation of the psychometric properties of the concept 5.2. Occupational Personality Questionnaire. *Journal of Occupational and Organisational Psychology*, *69*, 1–19.

Barrick, M.R., & Mount, M.K. (1991). The "Big Five" personality dimensions and job performance: A meta analysis. *Personnel Psychology*, *44*(1), 1–26.

Barrick, M.R., & Mount, M.K. (1993). Autonomy as a moderator of the relationship between the "Big Five" personality dimensions and job performance. *Journal of Applied Psychology*, *78*(1), 111–118.

Barry, B. (1995, November). *Insight into the composition of the management team: A source of competitive advantage!* Paper presented at Monash University (Faculty of Business and Economics), Australia.

Barry, B., & Dowling, P. (1984). *Towards an Australian management style: A study of the personality characteristics and management style of Australian managers*. Victoria, Australia: Australian Institute of Management.

Bartlett, F.C. (1932). *Remembering: An experimental and social study*. London: Cambridge University Press.

Bartram, D. (1995). The predictive validity of the EPI and the 16 PF for military flying training outcomes. *Journal of Occupational and Organisational Psychology*, *68*, 219–236.

Bass, B.M. (1990). From transactional to transformational leadership. *Organizational Dynamics*, *18*, 19–31.

Bass, B.M. (1999). Two decades of research and development in transformational leadership. *European Journal of Work and Organizational Psychology*, *6*, 9–25.

Bass, B.M., & Avolio, B.J. (1990). Developing transformational leadership: 1992 and beyond. *Journal of European Training*, *14*, 21–27.

Bass, B.M., & Leavitt, H. (1963). Some experiments in planning and operating. *Management Science*, *4*, 574–585.

Bass, B.M., & Vaughan, J.A. (1966). *Training in industry: The management of learning*. Belmont, CA: Wadsworth.

Bateman, T., & Strasser, S. (1984). A longitudinal analysis of the antecedents of organisational commitment. *Academy of Management Journal*, *27*, 95–112.

Baum, J.A.C. (1996). Organizational ecology. In C.R. Clegg, C. Hardy, & R. Nord (Eds.), *Handbook of organization studies*. Thousand Oaks, CA: Sage.

Baumeister, R.F., & Leary, M.R. (1995). The need to belong: Desire for interpersonal attachments as a fundamental human motivation. *Psychological Bulletin*, *117*, 497–529.

Bavelas, A. (1960). Leadership: Man and function. *Administrative Science Quarterly*, *4*, 344–360.

Bavelas, A., & Strauss, G. (1970). Group dynamics and inter-group relations. In W.G. Bennis, D. Benne, & R. Chin (Eds.), *The planning of change* (2nd ed.). New York: Holt.

Baxter, A. (1993, August 11). Reorganisation into product divisions at JCB. *Financial Times*, p. 8.

Bayley, N. (1970). Development of mental abilities. In P. Mussen (Ed.), *Carmichael's manual of child psychology, Vol. 1*. New York: Wiley.

Bayne, R. (1994). The "Big Five" versus the Myers-Briggs. *The Psychologist*, January, 14–16.

Beard, D. (1993). Learning to change organisations. *Personnel Management*, January, 32–35.

Beardwell, I., Holden, L., & Claydon, T. (2004). *Human resource management: A contemporary approach* (4th ed.). Harlow, Essex: Pearson Education.

Beattie, A. (2004, October 25). New accounting rules push share option deals further out of favour. *Financial Times*, p. 3.

Beattie, R.T., Darlington, T.G., & Cripps, D.M. (1974). *The management threshold* (BIM Paper OPN II). London: British Institute of Management.

Beck, A.T., Emery G., & Greenberg, B.L. (1985). *Anxiety, disorders, and phobias: A cognitive perspective*. New York: Basic Books.

Becker, T.E., & Billings, R.S. (1993). Profiles of commitment: An empirical test. *Journal of Organizational Behaviour*, *14*, 177–190.

Bedeian, A.G., & Zammuto, R.F. (1991). *Organizations: Theory and design*. Orlando, FL: Dryden Press.

Beech, N., & Cairns, G. (2001). Coping with change: The contribution of post-dichotomous ontologies. *Human Relations*, *54*, 1303–1324.

Beer, M. (1980). *Organisational change and development: A systems view*. Santa Monica, CA: Goodyear.

Beer, M., Eisenstat, R.A., & Spector, B. (1990). Why change programs don't produce change. *Harvard Business Review*, November–December, 158–166.

Beer, M., & Walton, A.E. (1987). Organisational change and development. In M.R. Rosenzweig & L.W. Porter (Eds.), *Annual review of psychology*. Palo Alto, CA: Annual Reviews.

Behling, O., & Eckel, N.L. (1991). Making sense out of intuition. *Academy of Management Executive*, February, 46–47.

Behling, O., & Schriesheim, C. (1976). *Organisational behaviour: Theory, research, and application*. Glenview, IL: Richard D. Irwin.

Belasco, J.A., & Stayer, R.C. (1994). Why empowerment doesn't empower: The bankruptcy of current paradigms. *Business Horizons*, March/April, 29–40.

Belbin, E. (1964). *Problems of progress in industry: No. 15. Training the adult worker*. London: HMSO.

Belbin, R.M. (1981). *Management teams*. London: Heinemann Educational Books.

Belbin, R.M. (1993). *Team roles at work*. Oxford, UK: Butterworth Heinemann.

Bell, C. (1998). *Managers as mentors*. Maidenhead, UK: McGraw-Hill.

Belle, D. (1982). The stress of caring: Women as providers of social support. In L. Golberger & S. Breznitz (Eds.), *Handbook of stress*. New York: Free Press.

Bem, D.J. (1967). Self-perception: An alternative interpretation of cognitive dissonance phenomena. *Psychological Review*, *74*(3), 183–200.

Bem, D.J., & Honorton, C. (1994). Does psi exist? Replicable evidence for an anomalous process of information transfer. *Psychological Bulletin*, *115*, 14–18.

Benders, J., Huijgen, F., & Ulricj, P. (2001). Measuring group work: Findings and lessons from a European survey. *New Technology, Work and Employment*, *16*, 204–217.

Benne, K.D., & Sheats, P. (1948). Functional role of group members. *Journal of Social Issues*, *4*, 41–49.

Bennis, W. (1966). *Changing organisations*. New York: McGraw-Hill.

Bennis, W.G. (2004). The seven ages of the leader. *Harvard Business Review*, January, 46–53.

Bentall, R.P. (1993). Personality traits may be alive, they may even be well, but are they really useful? *The Psychologist*, July, 307.

Berkman, H.W., & Gilson, C.C. (1998). *Consumer behaviour*. Lincolnwood, IL: NTC Publishing Group.

Berkowitz, L., Fraser, C., Treasure, F.P., & Cochran, S. (1987). Pay, equity, job gratifications and comparisons in pay satisfaction. *Journal of Applied Psychology*, November, 544–551.

Bernardin, H.J. (1978). The effects of rater training on leniency and halo errors in student ratings of instructors. *Journal of Applied Psychology*, June, 301–308.

Bernardin, H.J., & Alvares, K. (1976). The managerial grid as a predictor of conflict resolution method and managerial effectiveness. *Administrative Science Quarterly*, *21*(March), 84.

Bernardin, H.J., & Russell, J. (1993). *Human resource management: An experiential approach*. New York: McGraw-Hill.

Berne, E. (1964). *Games people play*. New York: Grove Press.

Bernin, P., & Theorell, T. (2001). Demand-control-support among female managers in eight Swedish companies. *Stress and Health*, *17*, 89–102.

Berridge, J., & Cooper, C.L. (1993). Stress and coping in US organizations: The role of the Employee Assistance Programme. *Work and Stress*, *7*, 89–102.

Berry, A. (1991). Management development. *Manchester Business School Research Newsletter*, *13*, 5.

Berryman-Fink, C. (1985). Male and female managers: Views of the communication skills and training needs of women in management. *Public Personnel Management*, *14*, 307–313.

Bettencourt, L.A., Gwinner, K.P., & Meuter, M.L. (2001). A comparison of attitude, personality, and knowledge predictions of service oriented organizational citizenship behaviours. *Journal of Applied Psychology*, February, 29–41.

Bettman, J.R. (1984). Memory factors in consumer choice—a review. In I. Fenwick & J.A. Quelch (Eds.), *Consumer behaviour for marketing managers*. Newton, MA: Allyn & Bacon.

Bhagat, R.S., Kedia, S.E., Crawford, S.E., & Kaplan, M.R. (1990). Cross-cultural issues in organizational psychology: Emergent trends and directions for research in the 1990s. In C.L. Cooper & I.T. Robertson (Eds.), *International review of industrial and organizational psychology* (Vol. 5, pp. 79–89). Chichester, UK: J. Wiley.

Biberman, G. (1985). Personality and characteristic work attitudes of persons with high, moderate, and low political tendencies. *Psychological Reports*, October, 1303–1310.

Big blue wants to loosen its collar. (1988, February 29). *Fortune Magazine*, p. 8.

Bilmes, L., & Wetzker, K. (1996, June 3). Wise tending in the jobs garden. *Financial Times*, p. 12.

Bion, W.R. (1961). *Experience in groups*. London: Tavistock.

Birkinshaw, J. (2000, December 4). The structures behind global companies. *FT Mastering Management, Part 10*, 2–4.

Birkinshaw, J., & Crainer, S. (2002). *Leadership, the Sven-Goran Eriksson Way*. Albany, OR: Capstone Publishing.

Bjorn-Anderson, N., & Pedersen, P.H. (1977). *Computer systems as a vehicle for changes in the management structure* (ISRG Working Paper No. 77-3). Copenhagen.

Blackler, F., & Shimmin, S. (1984). *Applying psychology in organisations*. London: Methuen.

Blake, R.R., & Mouton, J.S. (1964). *The managerial grid*. Houston, TX: Gulf Publishing.

Blake, R.R., & Mouton, J.S. (1969). *Building a dynamic corporation through grid organisation development*. Reading, MA: Addison-Wesley.

Blake, R.R., & Mouton, J.S. (1985). *The managerial grid III* (Rev. ed.). Houston, TX: Gulf Publishing Co.

Blau, G. (1995). Influence of group lateness on individual lateness: A cross-level examination. *Academy of Management Journal*, October, 1483–1496.

Blau, P.M., Falbe, C.M., McKinley, W., & Tracey, P.K. (1976). Technology and organisation in manufacturing. *Administrative Science Quarterly*, *21*, 20–40.

Blau, P.M., & Schoenherr, R.A. (1971). *The structure of organisations*. New York: Basic Books.

Blau, P.M., & Scott, W.R. (1966). *Formal organizations*. London: Routledge & Kegan Paul.

Blauner, R. (1964). *Alienation and freedom*. Chicago: University of Chicago Press.

Blinkhorn, S., & Johnson, C. (1990). The insignificance of personality testing. *Nature*, *348*, 671–672.

Blinkhorn, S.F. (1997). Past imperfect, future conditional: Fifty years of test theory. *British Journal of Mathematical and Statistical Psychology*, *50*, 175–185.

Boal, K.B., & Cummings, L.L. (1981). Cognitive evaluation theory: An experimental test of processes and outcomes. *Organizational Behaviour and Human Performance*, December, 289–310.

Bobbitt, H.R., & Ford, J.D. (1980). Decision-maker choice as a determinant of organisational structure. *Academy of Management Review*, January, 13–23.

Bobbitt, H.R., Breinholt, R.H., Doktor, R.H., & McNaul, J.P. (1978). *Organisational behaviour: Understanding and prediction*. New York: Prentice Hall.

Bobocei, D.R., & Meyer, J.P. (1994). Escalating commitment to a failing course of action: Separating the roles of choice and justification. *Journal of Applied Psychology*, June, 360–363.

Bodenhausen, G.V. (1988). Stereotypic biases in social decision making and memory: Testing process models of stereotype use. *Journal of Personality and Social Psychology*, *55*, 726–737.

Bohner, G., & Wanke, M. (2002). Attitudes and attitude change. Hove, UK: Psychology Press.

Bolger, A. (1996, November 22). Investors in People: Both sides reap the benefits. *Financial Times*, p. 13.

Bolman, L.G., & Deal, T.E. (2003). *Reframing organizations: Artistry, choice, and leadership* (3rd ed.). San Francisco, CA: Jossey-Bass.

Bond, R., & Smith, P.B. (1996). Culture and conformity. A meta analysis of studies using Asch's (1952, 1956) line judgement task. *Psychological Bulletin*, January, 111–137.

Borgida, E., & Nisbett, R.E. (1977). The differential impact of abstract vs. concrete information on decisions. *Journal of Applied Social Psychology*, July–September, 258–271.

Borman, W.C. (1974). The ratings of individuals in organizations: An alternative approach. *Organizational Behaviour and Human Performance*, August, 105–124.

Botwinick, J. (1984). *Ageing and human behaviour: A comprehensive integration of research findings* (3rd ed.). New York: Springer.

Bouwman, M.J. (1984). Expert vs. novice decision making in accounting: A summary. *Accounting, Organisations and Society*, *9*, 325–327.

Bowen, D.D., & Hisrich, R.D. (1986). The female entrepreneur: A career development perspective. *Academy of Management Review*, April, 393–407.

Bowen, D.D., & Rath, R. (1978). Transactional analysis is OK: Applications within the NTL model. *Academy of Management Review*, *3*, 79–89.

Bower, G.H., Clark, M., Lesgold, A., & Winzenz, D. (1969). Hierarchical retrieval schemes in recall of categorised word lists. *Journal of Verbal Learning and Verbal Behavior*, *8*, 323–343.

Bowman, C. (1990). *The essence of strategic management*. Hemel Hempstead, UK: Prentice Hall.

Boyd, B., & Salamin, A. (2001). Strategic reward systems. A contingency model of pay system design. *Strategic Management Journal*, *22*, 777–792.

Boye, D.M. (1991). The storytelling organization: A study of story performance in an office-supply firm. *Administrative Science Quarterly*, March, 106–126.

Boyle, S. (1997). Researching the selection interview. *Selection and Development Review*, *13*(August), 15–17.

Bradford, D.L., & Burke, W.W. (2004). Is OD in crisis? *Journal of Applied Behavioural Science*, *40*, 369–373.

Brading, L., & Wright, V. (1990). Performance-related pay. *Personnel Management*, Factsheet 30.

Bradley, D. (2004, September 25). References: No comment, no legal action. *Financial Times*.

Bradshaw, D. (1993, October 29). Rewards for the scientists. *Financial Times*.

Bragg, A., & Bragg, M. (2005). *Developing new business ideas*. Harlow, UK: Pearson.

Bragg, M. (1996). *Reinventing influence*. London: Pitman Publishing.

Brand, R.E. (1986). *Contrary investing*. New York: McGraw-Hill.

Brass, D.J. (1984). Being in the right place: A structural analysis of individual influence in an organisation. *Administrative Science Quarterly*, December, 518–539.

Bratkovich, J.R. (1989). Pay for performance boosts productivity. *Personnel Journal*, January, 78–86.

Bray, D.W., & Campbell, R.J. (1974). *Formative years in business: A long-term AT&T study of managerial lives*. New York: Wiley.

Bream, R. (2003, March 27). Tackling the skills shortage. *Financial Times*, p. 16.

Breckler, S.J. (1984). Empirical validation of affect, behaviour, and cognition as distinct components of attitude. *Journal of Personality and Social Psychology*, *47*, 1191–1205.

Brehm, W.J. (1966). *A theory of psychological reactance*. New York: Academic Press.

Brenner, S.N., & Molander, E.A. (1977). Are the ethics of business changing? *Harvard Business Review*, January–February, 57–71.

Brett, J.F., & Atwater, L.E. (2001). 360-degree feedback: Accuracy, reactions, and perceptions of usefulness. *Journal of Applied Psychology*, October, 930–942.

Bretz Jr, R.D., Milkovich, G.T., & Read, W. (1992). The current state of performance appraisal research and practice: Concerns, directions and implications. *Journal of Management*, June, 323–333.

Brindle, D. (1998, May 26). Study shows disabled prejudice. *Guardian*, p. 7.

Briner, R. (1999a). Emotion at work: Feeling and smiling. *The Psychologist*, January, 16–19.

Briner, R. (1999b). The neglect and importance of emotion at work. *European Journal of Work and Organizational Psychology*, 8, 323–346.

Briner, R., & Reynolds, S. (1993). Bad theory and bad practice in occupational stress. *Occupational Psychologist*, 19, 8–13.

Brisco, S. (2004, October 30). Missing data mean causes of lower wages are hard to establish. *Financial Times*, p. 11.

British Psychological Society (1993). *Graphology in personnel assessment*. Leicester, UK: BPS.

British Psychological Society (2000). *Code of conduct, ethical principles, and guidelines*. Leicester, UK: BPS.

British Psychological Society (2004a). *Requirements for continuing professional development*. Leicester, UK: BPS.

British Psychological Society (2004b). *Final report of a working party: A review of the current scientific status and fields of application of the Polygraphic Deception Detection*. Leicester, UK: BPS.

Broadbent, D., & Gath, D. (1981). Ill-health on the line: Sorting out myth from fact. *Employment Gazette*, March, 157–160.

Broadbent, K., & Cooper, P. (1987). Research is good for you. *Marketing Intelligence and Planning*, 5, 3–9.

Brock, T.C., & Becker, L.A. (1965). Ineffectiveness of overheard counter-propaganda. *Journal of Personality and Social Psychology*, 2, 654–660.

Brockner, J. (1992). Managing the effects of layoffs on survivors. *California Management Review*, Winter, 9–28.

Brockner, J., Houser, R., Birnbaum, G., Lloyd, K., Deitcher, J., Nathanson, S., & Rubin, J.Z. (1986). Escalation of commitment to an ineffective course of action: The effect of feedback having negative implications for self-identity. *Administrative Science Quarterly*, March, 109–126.

Bromnell, P. (1981). Participation in budgeting, locus of control, and organisational effectiveness. *The Accounting Review*, October, 844–860.

Brook, A. (1973). Mental stress at work. *The Practitioner*, *210*, 500–506.

Brookes, M.J., & Kaplan, A. (1972). The office environment: Space planning and effective behaviour. *Human Factors*, *14*, 373–391.

Brotherton, C. (1980). Paradigms of selection validation: Some comments in the light of British equal opportunities legislation. *Journal of Occupational Psychology*, *53*, 73–79.

Brotherton, C. (1999). *Social psychology and management*. Milton Keynes, UK: Open University Press.

Brown, B.K., & Campion, M.A. (1994). Bio-data phenomenology: Recruiter's perception and use of biographical information in resume screening. *Journal of Applied Psychology*, *79*, 897–908.

Brown, D. (1992). Outsourcing: How corporations take their business elsewhere. *Management Review*, February, 16–19.

Brown, E., & Gay, P. (1985). *Racial discrimination 17 years after the Act* (Report No. 646). London: Policy Studies Institute.

Brown, G.F., & Read, A.R. (1984). Personnel and training policies: Some lessons for Western companies. *Long Range Planning*, *17*, 48–57.

Brown, J.A.C. (1954). *The social psychology of industry*. Harmondsworth, UK: Penguin.

Brown, J.A.C. (1961). *Freud and the post-Freudians*. Harmondsworth, UK: Penguin.

Brown, R. (1965). *Social psychology*. New York: Free Press.

Brown, R. (2000). *Group processes*. Oxford: Blackwell.

Brown, T. (1990, October). Match up with a mentor. *Industry Week*, *239*.

Brownell, P. (1982). The effects of personality—situation congruence in a managerial context: Locus of control and budgetary participation. *Journal of Personality and Social Psychology*, *42*, 753–763.

Bruder, G.E., Stewart, M.W., Mercier, C., Agosti, M.A., Leite, P., Donovan, S., & Quitkin F.M. (1997). Outcome of cognitive behavioural therapy for depression: Relation to hemispheric dominance for verbal processing. *Journal of Abnormal Psychology*, *106*, 138–144.

Bruner, J.S., & Goodman, C.C. (1947). Value and need as organising factors in perception. *Journal of Abnormal and Social Psychology*, *42*, 33–44.

Brunswick, E. (1955). Representative design and probabilistic theory in a functional psychology. *Psychological Review*, May, 193–217.

Bryan, W.L., & Harter, N. (1899). Studies on the telegraphic language: The acquisition of a hierarchy of habits. *Psychological Review*, *6*, 345–375.

Buchanan, D., & Badham, R. (1999). Politics and organizational change: The lived experience. *Human Relations*, *52*, 609–630.

Buchanan, D., & Huczynski, A. (1997). *Organisational behaviour: An introductory text* (3rd ed.). Hemel Hempstead, UK: Prentice Hall International (UK).

Buchanan, D., & Huczynski, A. (2004). *Organisational behaviour: An introductory text* (5th ed.). Harlow, UK: Pearson Education.

Buchko, A.A. (1993). The effects of employee ownership on employee attitudes: An integrated causal model and path analysis. *Journal of Management Studies*, July, 633–656.

Buck, T. (2002, October 30). Tarnished Browne loses the pixie dust. *Financial Times*.

Buck, T., & Buchan, D. (2002, July 31 & August 1). Lord Browne: The inside story. *Financial Times*, pp. 22–23, p. 21.

Buck, T., Buchan, D., Guha, K., & McNulty, S. (2002, August 2). Oiling the political engine. *Financial Times*, p. 23.

Buck, V. (1972). *Working under pressure*. London: Staples Press.

Buckley, C. (1996, August 14). Teamworking points up the strains in a mail preserve. *The Times*, p. 27.

Bull, P. (2001). State of the art: Non-verbal communication. *The Psychologist*, December, 644–647.

Buller, P.F., & Bell, C.H. (1986). Effects of teambuilding and goal setting on productivity: A field experiment. *Academy of Management Journal*, June, 305–328.

Burgoyne, J., & Germain, C. (1984). Self-development and career planning: An exercise in mutual benefit. *Personnel Management*, April, 21–23.

Burke, R.J., & Belcourt, M.L. (1974). Managerial role stress and coping responses. *Journal of Business Administration*, *5*, 55–68.

Burke, R.J., Weitzel, W., & Weir, T. (1978). Characteristics of effective employee performance at review and development interviews: Replication and extension. *Personnel Psychology*, *31*, 903–919.

Burke, W.W. (1982). *Organisational development: Principles and practice*. Boston, MA: Little, Brown.

Burke, W.W. (2000). The new agenda for organizational development. In W.L. French, C.H. Bell Jr, & R.A. Zawacki (Eds.), *Organizational development and transformation: Managing effective change* (pp. 523–535). Burr Ridge, IL: Irwin McGraw-Hill.

Burnes, B. (1996). No such thing as one best way to manage organizational change. *Management Decision*, *34*, 11–18.

Burnes, B. (2004). Kurt Lewin and the planned approach to change. A reappraisal. *Journal of Management Studies*, *41*, 977–1002.

Burns, R.B., & Dobson, C.B.L. (1984). *Introductory psychology*. Lancaster, UK: MTB Press.

Burns, T., & Stalker, G.M. (1961). *The management of innovation*. London: Tavistock Publications.

Burpeau-Di Gregorio, M.Y., & Dickson, J.W. (1983). Experiences with quality circles in the south-west United States. *Employee Relations*, *5*, 12–16.

Burt, T. (1999, August 31). Daimler Chrysler: Two tribes on the same trail. *Financial Times*.

Buss, A.H. (1989). Personality as traits. *American Psychologist*, November, 1378–1388.

Butcher, D., & Clarke, M. (2002). Organizational politics: The cornerstone for organizational democracy. *Organizational Dynamics*, *31*, 35–46.

Butler, R.J., & Wilson, D.C. (1989). *Managing voluntary and non-profit organisations: Strategy and structure*. London: Routledge & Kegan Paul.

Cabrera, A. (2000, October 2). Making sharing good for all. *FT Mastering Management Series, Part 1*, pp. 12–15.

Cacioppo, J.T., & Petty, R.E. (1989). Effects of message repetition on argument processing, recall, and persuasion. *Basic Applied Social Psychology*, *10*, 3–12.

Caie, B. (1988). Learning in style: Reflections on an action learning MBA programme. *Business Education*, *9*, 109–117.

Campbell, J.P., & Dunnette, M.D. (1968). Effectiveness of T-groups: Experience in managerial training and development. *Psychological Bulletin*, *70*(August), 73–104.

Campion, M.A., & McClelland, C.L. (1993). Follow-up and extension of the interdisciplinary costs and benefits of enlarged jobs. *Journal of Applied Psychology*, June, 339–351.

Campion, M.A., Medsker, G.J., & Higgs, A.C. (1993). Relations between work group characteristics and effectiveness: Implications for designing work groups. *Personnel Psychology*, Winter, 823–850.

Campion, M.A., Palmer, D.K., & Campion, J.E. (1997). A review of structure in the selection interview. *Personnel Psychology*, Autumn, 655–702.

Cannel, M., & Long, P. (1991). What has changed about incentive pay? *Personnel Management*, October, 58–63.

Capaldi, E., Birmingham, K.M., & Alptekin, S. (1995). Memories of reward events and expectancies of reward events may work in tandem. *Animal Learning and Behavior*, *23*, 40–48.

Cappelli, P., & Rogovsky, N. (1997). What do new systems demand of employees? In *Mastering management: Module 6. Organizational behavior* (pp. 224–228). London: FT/Pitman.

Carlson, R.E. (1969). Degree of job fit as a moderator of the relationship between job performance and job satisfaction. *Personnel Psychology*, *22*, 159–170.

Carnal, C. (1990). *Managing change in organizations*. Hemel Hempstead, UK: Prentice Hall.

Carroll, M. (1996). *Workplace counselling*. London: Sage Publications.

Carroll, S.J., & Tosi, H.L. (1970). Goal characteristics and personality factors in a management by objectives programme. *Administrative Science Quarterly*, *15*(September), 295–305.

Carson, J., & Richards, T. (1979). *Industrial new product development*. Farnborough, UK: Gower.

Carson, K.P., & Gillard, D.J. (1993). Construct validity of the Miner Sentence Completion Scale. *Journal of Occupational and Organizational Psychology, 66,* 171–175.

Carsten, J.M., & Spector, P.E. (1987). Unemployment, job satisfaction, and employee turnover: A meta-analytical test of the "Muchinsky Model". *Journal of Applied Psychology*, August, 374–381.

Carter, M. (2002, October, 10). A question of commitment. *Financial Times.*

Cartwright, S., & Cooper, C.L. (1993). The role of cultural compatibility in successful organizational marriages. *Academy of Management Executive*, May, 57–70.

Cartwright, S., & Cooper, C.L. (1997). *Managing workplace stress*. London: Sage.

Cascio, W.F. (1991). *Applied psychology in personnel management* (4th ed.). Englewood Cliffs, NJ: Prentice Hall.

Cascio, W.F. (2000). Managing a virtual workplace. *Academy of Management Executive*, August, 81–90.

Case, P. (1999). Remember re-engineering? The rhetorical appeal of a managerial salvation device. *Journal of Management Studies, 36,* 420–441.

Caspi, A., Harrington, H., Milne, B., Amell, J.W., Theodore, R.F., & Moffitt, T.E. (2003). Children's behavioral styles at age 3 are linked to their adult personality traits at age 26. *Journal of Personality, 71,* August, 495–514.

Cassel, C. (Ed.) (1999). Exploring feelings at work: Emotion at work [Special issue]. *The Psychologist*, January, 15.

Cassel, J. (1963). The use of medical records: Opportunity for epidemiological studies. *Journal of Occupational Medicine, 5,* 185–190.

Cassell, C., & Walsh, S. (1993). Being seen but not heard: Barriers to women's equality in the workplace. *The Psychologist*, March, 110–113.

Cassidy, T., & Lynn, R. (1989). A multifactorial approach to achievement motivation: The development of a comprehensive measure. *Journal of Occupational Psychology, 62,* 301–312.

Catan, T., & Chaffin, J. (2003, May 8). Bribery has been used to land international contracts. New laws will make that tougher. *Financial Times*, p. 19.

Cattell, R.B. (1965). *The scientific analysis of personality*. Harmondsworth, UK: Penguin.

Cattell, R.B. (1974). How good is the modern questionnaire? General principles for evaluation. *Journal of Personality Assessment, 38,* 115–129.

Cattell, R.B. (1995). The fallacy of five factors in the personality sphere. *The Psychologist*, May, 207–208.

Cavanagh, G.F., Moberg, D.J., & Velasquez, M. (1981). The ethics of organisational politics. *Academy of Management Review*, July, 363–374.

CBI (2001). *Understanding absence*. London: CBI.

Chao, G.T., O'Leary-Kelly, A.M., Wolf, S., Klein, H.J., & Gardner, P.D. (1994). Organizational socialization: Its content and consequences. *Journal of Applied Psychology*, October, 730–743.

Chapman, J. (1982). After the inspector's visit: When group loyalty made a mockery of accident prevention. *The Safety Representative*, March, 5.

Chase, B., & Karowski, W. (2003). Advanced manufacturing technology. In D. Holman, T.D. Wall, C.W. Clegg, P. Sparrow, & A. Howard (Eds.), *The new workplace*. Chichester, UK: John Wiley.

Chatman, J.A. (1992). Matching people and organisations: Selection and socialization in public accounting firms. *Human Relations*, April, 459–484.

Chatman, J.A., & Cha, S.E. (2002, November 22). Culture of growth. *FT Mastering Leadership Series, Part 4,* 2–3.

Chatman, J.A., & Jehn, K.A. (1994). Assessing the relationship between industry characteristics and organizational culture: How different can you be? *Academy of Management Journal*, June, 522–553.

Chattopadhyay, A., & Alba, J.W. (1988). The situational importance of recall and inference in consumer decision making. *Journal of Consumer Research, 15,* 1–12.

Chell, E. (1993). *The psychology of behaviour in organizations* (2nd ed.). London: Macmillan.

Chell, E. (1999), The entrepreneurial personality—past, present and future. *Occupational Psychologist, 38,* 5–12.

Chen, C., Gustafson, D.H., & Lee, Y. (2002). The effect of a quantitative decision aid—analytic hierarchic process—on group polarization. *Group Decision and Negotiation, 11,* 329–344.

Chesbrough, H. (2003, August 7). How to generate more innovation for less. *Financial Times*, FT Summer School, p. 11.

Chesney, M.A., Sevelius, G., Black, G.W., Ward, M.M., Swan, G.E., & Rosenman, R.H. (1981). Work environment, Type A behaviour, and coronary heart disease risk factors. *Journal of Occupational Medicine, 23,* 531–555.

Child, I.L., & Whiting, J.W.M. (1954). Determinants of level of aspiration: Evidence from everyday life. In H. Brand (Ed.), *The study of personality*. New York: Wiley.

Child, J. (1972). Organisational structure, environment and performance: The role of strategic choice. *Sociology, 6,* 1–22.

Child, J. (1973). Predicting and understanding organisation structure. *Administrative Science Quarterly, 18*(2), June, 168–185.

Child, J. (1982). Professionals in a corporate world. In D. Dunkerley & G. Salaman (Eds.), *The international yearbook of organisation studies*. London: Routledge & Kegan Paul.

Child, J. (1984a). New technology and developments in management organisation. *Omega*, *12*, 211–223.

Child, J. (1984b). *Organisation: A guide to problems and practice* (2nd ed.). London: Harper & Row.

Child, J. (1987). New technologies in the service class. In K. Purcell, S. Wood, A. Watson, & S. Allen (Eds.), *The changing experience of employment*. London: Macmillan.

Child, J. (1997). Strategic choice in the analysis of action, structure, organizations, and environment: Retrospect and prospect. *Organization Studies*, *18*, 43–76.

Child, J. (2005). *Organizations: Contemporary principles and practice*. Oxford: Blackwell.

Child, J., & Loveridge, R. (1990). *Information technology in European services*. Oxford: Basil Blackwell.

Child, J., & McGrath, R.G. (2001). Organizations unfettered: Organizational form in an information intensive economy. *Academy of Management Journal*, December, 1135–1148.

Child, J., & Rodrigues, S.B. (2003). Corporate goverance and new organizational forms: Issues of double and multiple agencies. *Journal of Management and Goverance*, *7*, 337–360.

Chisseli, E.E., & Brown, C.W. (1955). *Personnel and industrial psychology* (2nd ed.). New York: McGraw-Hill.

Choi, J.N., & Kim, M.U. (1999). The organizational application of groupthink and its limits in organizations. *Journal of Applied Psychology*, April, 297–306.

Ciarrochi, T., Forgas, J.P., & Mayer, J.D. (2001). *Emotional intelligence in everyday life: A scientific inquiry*. Hove, UK: Psychogy Press.

Ciulla, J.B. (1995). Leadership ethics: Mapping the territory. *Business Ethics Quarterly*, January, 5–28.

Clapperton, G. (2003, December 29). Telecommuting: Home work isn't where the heart is. *Financial Times*, p. 8.

Clarke, A., Oswald, A., & Warr, P. (1996). Is job satisfaction U-shaped in age? *Journal of Occupational and Organizational Psychology*, *69*, 57–81.

Clarke, A.E. (1996). Job satisfaction in Britain. *British Journal of Industrial Relations*, *34*, 189–219.

Clarke, L. (1994). *The essence of change*. Hemel Hempstead, UK: Prentice Hall.

Clarkson, G.P.E. (1963). A model of trust investment behaviour. In R.M. Cyert & J.G. Marsh (Eds.), *A behavioural theory of the firm*. New York: Prentice Hall.

Clegg, C.W. (1983). Psychology of employee lateness, absence and turnover: A methodological critique and an empirical study. *Journal of Applied Psychology*, February, 88–101.

Clegg, S. (1977). Power, organisation theory, Marx, and critique. In S. Clegg & D. Dunkerley (Eds.), *Critical issues in organisations*. London: Routledge & Kegan Paul.

Clegg, S. (1990a). *Modern organizations: Organizations in the postmodern world*. London: Sage.

Clegg, S. (1990b). *Frameworks of power*. London: Sage.

Clifford, L., & Bennett, H. (1997). Best practice in 360 degree feedback. *Selection and Development Review*, *13*, 6–9.

Clutterbuck, D. (1986). Mentoring. *Industrial and Commercial Training*, *18*, November.

Clutterbuck, D. (2001a, January 8). Mentoring and coaching at the top. *FT Mastering Management Series, Part 13*, pp. 14–15.

Clutterbuck, D. (2001b). *Everybody needs a mentor* (3rd ed.). London: Chartered Institute of Personnel and Development.

Cobb, S. (1976). Social support as a moderator of life stress. *Psychosomatic Medicine*, *38*, 300–314.

Coch, L., & French, J.R.P. (1948). Overcoming resistance to change. *Human Relations*, *1*, 512–532.

Coggan, P. (2002, November 25). In an uncertain world, rational isn't everything. *Financial Times*.

Cohen, D. (1981). *Consumer behaviour*. New York: Random House.

Cohen, S.G., Ledford Jr, G.E., & Spreitzer, G.M. (1996). A predictive model of self-managing work team effectiveness. *Human Relations*, May, 643–676.

Coles, M. (1999a, July 4). Managers warm to flexible working. *The Sunday Times*, Section 7, p. 18.

Coles, M. (1999b, February 14). Reappraise the way you develop staff. *The Sunday Times*, pp. 7–22.

Collard, R. (1981). The quality circle in context. *Personnel Management*, September, 26–30, 51.

Collins, A.M., & Quillian, M. (1969). Retrieval time from semantic memory. *Journal of Verbal Learning and Verbal Behavior*, *8*, 240–247.

Collins, R., Schmenner, R., & Cordon, C. (1997). Rigid flexibility and factory focus. In *Mastering management: Module 9. Production and operations management* (pp. 311–315). FT/Pitman Publishing.

Comer, D.R. (1995). A model of social loafing in real workgroups. *Human Relations*, June, 647–667.

Conger, J.A., & Kanungo, R.N. (1988a). Behavioural dimensions of charismatic leadership. In J.A. Conger, R.N. Kanungo, and Associates (Eds.), *Charismatic leadership*. San Francisco: Jossey-Bass.

Conger, J.A., & Kanungo, R.N. (1988b). The empowerment process: Integrating theory and practice. *Academy of Management Journal*, *13*(July), 471–482.

Conger, J.A., & Kanungo, R.N. (1994). Charismatic leadership in organizations: Perceived behavioural attributes and their measurement. *Journal of Organizational Behaviour*, *15*, 439–452.

Constandse, W.J. (1972). A neglected personnel problem. *Personnel Journal*, *51*, 129–133.

Control Risks Group. (1998). *A report on corruption and integrity: Best business practice in an imperfect world*. London: Author.

Conway, C. (1994). *Mentoring managers in organizations: A report of a study of mentoring and its application to organizations with case studies*. Berkhamsted, UK: Ashridge Management College.

Conway, J.M. (1996). Analysis and design of multi-trait multi-rater performance studies. *Journal of Management, 22*, 139–162.

Conway, J.M., Jako, R.A., & Goodman, D.F. (1995). A meta analysis of inter-rater and internal consistency reliability of selection interviews. *Journal of Applied Psychology*, October, 565–579.

Conway, M.A. (1992). Developments and debates in the study of human memory. *The Psychologist*, October, 439–440.

Cook, M. (1971). *Interpersonal perception*. Harmondsworth, UK: Penguin.

Cook, M. (1988). Stress management. *Management Services*, November, 18–21.

Cook, M. (1994, January). *Stature, credibility, and true performance*. Paper presented at the Occupational Psychology BPS Conference, Birmingham, UK.

Cook, M. (1998). Personnel selection. *Adding value through people* (3rd ed.). Chichester, UK: Wiley.

Cooke, S., & Slack, N. (1984). *Making management decisions*. Hemel Hempstead, UK: Prentice Hall.

Cooper, C.L. (1979). *The executive gypsy: The quality of managerial life*. London: Macmillan Press.

Cooper, C.L. (1981). Social support at work and stress management. *Small Group Behaviour, 12*, August, 285–297.

Cooper, C.L. (1986). Job distress: Recent research and the emerging role of the clinical psychologist. *Bulletin of the British Psychological Society, 39*, 325–331.

Cooper, C.L. (2001a). Great motivators at work. *The Psychologist, 14*, 95.

Cooper, C.L. (2001b, January 8). *FT Mastering Management*, pp. 12–13.

Cooper, C.L. (2002, July 7). Emails build up to never-ending in-tray. *Sunday Telegraph*, Appointments Section, p. A10.

Cooper, C.L., Dewe, P., & O'Driscoll, M. (2001). Organizational stress. A review and critique of theory, research, and application. London: Sage Publications.

Cooper, C.L., Sadri, G., Alison, T, & Reynolds, P. (1990). Stress counselling in the Post Office. *Counselling Psychology Quarterly, 3*, 3–11.

Cooper, C.L., Sloan, S., & Williams, S. (1987). *Occupational stress indicator*. Walton-on-Thames, UK: NFER-Nelson.

Coopey, J. (1996). *Crucial gaps in the learning organization: Power, politics, and ideology*. London: International Thomson Business Press.

Coopey, J., & Hartley, J. (1991). Reconsidering the case for organizational commitment. *Human Resource Management Journal, 1*, 18–32.

Copperrider, D.L. & Whitney, D. (2000). *Collaborating for change: Appreciative inquiry*. San Francisco, CA: Berrett-Koehler.

Cordery, J.L., & Wall, T.D. (1985). Work design and supervisory practice: A model. *Human Relations, 38*, 425–441.

Cordon, C. (1997). Ways to improve the company. In *Mastering management: Module 9. Production and operations management* (pp. 307–310). London: FT/Pitman Publishing.

Corzine, R. (1998, March 26 & 31). Management inside Royal Dutch/Shell. *Financial Times*.

Cox, T. (1985). Repetitive work: Occupational stress and health. In C.L. Cooper & M.J. Smith (Eds.), *Job stress and blue-collar work*. Chichester, UK: Wiley.

Cox, T. (1994). *Stress research and stress management: Putting theory to work*. Sudbury, UK: Health and Safety Executive.

Cox Jr., T. (1993). *Cultural diversity in organizations: Theory, research, and practice*. San Francisco: Berrett-Koehler.

Craske, S. (1968). A study of the relation between personality and accident history. *British Journal of Medical Psychology, 41*, 399–404.

Crawley, R., & Spurgeon, P. (1979). Computer assistance and the air traffic controller's job satisfaction. In R.G. Sell & P. Shipley (Eds.), *Satisfaction in work design: Ergonomics and other approaches*. London: Taylor & Francis.

Crouter, A.C. (1984). Participative work as an influence on human development. *Journal of Applied Developmental Psychology, 5*, 71–90.

Crozier, M. (1964). *The bureaucratic phenomenon*. London: Tavistock.

Crumley, B. (2004, October 11). Europe: President Sarkozy? *Time Magazine*, 40–43.

Culbert, S. (1974). *The organisation trap*. New York: Basic Books.

Cullen, J.H., & Anderson, K.S. (1986). Blau's theory of structural differentiation revisited: A theory of structural change or scale. *Academy of Management Journal*, June, 203–229.

Cummings, T.G., & Worley, C.G. (2001). *Organization development and change* (7th ed.). Mason: OH: South Western College Publishing.

Currall, S.C., & Epstein, M.J. (2003). The fragility of organisational trust: Lessons from the rise and fall of Enron. *Organizational Dynamics, 32*, 193–206.

Curtis, J.D., & Detert, R.A. (1981). *How to relax: A holistic approach to stress management*. Mountain View, CA: Mayfield Publishing.

Cushman, W.H. (1980). Selection of filters for dark adaptation goggles in the photographic industry. *Applied Ergonomics, 11*, 93–99.

Cyert, R.M., & March, J.G. (Eds.). (1963). *A behavioural theory of the firm*. New York: Prentice Hall.

Daft, R.L. (1998). *Organization theory and design* (6th ed.). Cincinnati, OH: South Western.

Daft, R.L. (2004). *Organization theory and design* (8th ed.). International Student Edition. Mason, OH: South Western.

Dalby, S., & Wood, L. (1995, December 5). Ex-FT subeditor loses injury claim. *Financial Times*.

Dale, B.D., Cooper, C.L., & Wilkinson, A. (1998). *Managing quality and human resources: A guide to continuous improvement*. Oxford, UK: Blackwell.

Dalton, M. (1950). Conflict between staff and line managerial officers. *American Sociological Review*, *15*, 107–120.

Damanpour, F. (1991). Organizational innovation: A meta-analysis of effects of determinants and moderators. *Academy of Management Journal*, September, 555–590.

Dankbaar, B. (1988). New production concepts, management strategies, and the quality of work. *Work, Employment, and Society*, *2*(1), 25–50.

Dansereau, F., Green, G., & Haga, W.J. (1975). A vertical dyad linkage approach to leadership within formal organisations: A longitudinal investigation of the role-making process. *Organisational Behaviour and Human Performance*, *13*, 46–78.

Davey, G.C.L. (1992). Classical conditioning and the acquisition of human fears and phobias. A review and synthesis of the literature. *Advances in Behaviour Research Therapy*, *14*, 29–66.

Davidson, M.J., & Cooper, C.L. (1983). *Stress and the woman manager*. Oxford, UK: Martin Robertson.

Davis, K. (1976). Understanding the organisational grapevine and its benefits. *Business and Public Affairs*, Spring, 5.

Davis, S.M., & Lawrence, P.R. (1977). *Matrix*. Reading, MA: Addison-Wesley.

Davis, T.R.V., & Luthans, F. (1980). A social learning approach to organisational behaviour. *Academy of Management Review*, *5*, 281–290.

Dawkins, W. (1993, December 1). Costly burden of tradition. *Financial Times*, p. 10.

Dawson, P. (2003). *Understanding organizational change: The contemporary experience of people at work*. London: Sage.

Day, D.V., & Silverman, S.B. (1989). Personality and job performance: Evidence of incremental validity. *Personnel Psychology*, *41*, 25–36.

Day, R.H. (1969). *Human perception*. Sydney, Australia: J. Wiley & Son.

Deal, T.E., & Kennedy, A.A. (1982). *Corporate cultures: The rites and rituals of corporate life*. Reading, MA: Addison-Wesley.

Dearborn, D.C., & Simon, H.A. (1958). Selective perception: A note on the departmental identification of executives. *Sociometry*, *21*, 140–144.

Dearlove, D. (1998). *Business: The Richard Branson way*. Oxford: Capstone Publishing.

Dearlove, D. (1999, September 30). Leading with feeling. *The Times*, Section 4, p. 7.

Deary, I.J., & Matthews, G. (1993). Personality traits are alive and well. *The Psychologist*, July, 299–311.

De Bono, E. (1970). *Lateral thinking for management*. New York: McGraw-Hill.

De Chambeau, F.A., & Mackenzie, F. (1986). Intrapreneurship. *Personnel Journal*, July, 40–45.

Deckop, J.R., Mangel, R., & Cirka, C.C. (1999). Getting more than you pay for: Organizational citizenship behaviour and pay-for-performance plans. *Academy of Management Journal*, *42*, 420–428.

Demir, A., Ulusoy, M., & Ulusoy, M.E. (2003). Investigation of factors influencing burnout levels in professional and private lives of nurses. *International Journal of Nursing Studies*, *40*, 807–827.

Den Hartog, D.N., House, R.J., Hanges, P.J., Ruiz-Quintanilla, S., & Dorfman, P.W. (1999). Culture specific and cross-culturally generalizable implicit leadership theories: Are attributes of charismatic/transformational leadership universally endorsed? *Leadership Quarterly*, *10*, 219–256.

De Nisi, A.S., & Mitchell, J.L. (1978). An analysis of peer ratings as predictors and criterion measures and a proposed new application. *Academy of Management Review*, *3*, 369–374.

Denison, D.R. (1996). What is the difference between organizational culture and organizational climate? A native's point of view on a decade of paridigm wars. *Academy of Management Review*, July, 619–654.

Denison, D.R., Hart, S.L., & Kahn, J.A. (1996). From chimneys to cross-functional teams: Developing and validating cross-functional teams. *Academy of Management Journal*, August, 1005–1023.

Dennis, A.R., & Valacich, J.S. (1993). Computer brainstorms: More heads are better than one. *Journal of Applied Psychology*, August, 531–537.

Dermer, J.D. (1973). Cognitive characteristics and the perceived importance of information. *Accounting Review*, July, 511–519.

De Salvo, T. (1999, June). Unleash the creativity in your organization. *HR Magazine*, pp. 154–164.

Deshpande, R., & Parasuraman, A. (1986). Linking corporate culture to strategic planning. *Business Horizons*, *3*, 28–37.

Detert, J.R., Schroeder, R.G., & Mauriel, J.J. (2000). A framework for linking culture and improvement initiatives in organisations. *Academy of Management Review*, *25*, 850–863.

Deutsch, M., & Collins, M.E. (1951). *Inter-racial housing*. Minnesota, MN: University of Minnesota Press.

Devine, P.G. (1989). Stereotypes and prejudice: Their automatic and controlled components. *Personality and Social Psychology*, *56*, 5–18.

Diehl, M., & Stroebe, W. (1987). Productivity loss in brainstorming groups: Towards the solution of a riddle. *Journal of Personality and Social Psychology*, *53*, 497–509.

Diekmann, K.A., Tenbrunsel, A.E., Shah, PP., Schroth, H.A., & Bazerman, M.H. (1996). The descriptive and prescriptive use of previous purchase price in negotiations. *Organizational Behaviour and Human Decision Processes*, *66*, 179–191.

Diener, E., & Seligman, M.P. (2002). Very happy people. *Psychological Science*, *13*, 81–84.

Dillard, J.F. (1984). Cognitive science and decision-making research in accounting. *Accounting, Organisations and Society*, *9*, 343–354.

Dipboye, R.L. (1994). Structured and unstructured selection interviews: Beyond the job-fit model. *Research in Personnel Human Resource Management*, *12*, 79–123.

Di Prete, T.A. (1987). Horizontal and vertical mobility in organisations. *Administrative Science Quarterly*, December, 422–444.

Dirks, K.T. (1999). The effects of interpersonal trust on work group performance. *Journal of Applied Psychology*, June, 445–455.

Dixon, M. (1994, January 12). Bringing in, raising up, throwing out. *Financial Times*, p. 15.

Dobbins, G.H. (1985). Effects of gender on leaders' responses to poor performers: An attributional interpretation. *Academy of Management Journal*, *28*, 587–598.

Dobbins, G.H. (1986). Equity vs equality: Sex differences in leadership. *Sex Roles*, *15*, 513–525.

Dobbins, G.H., & Russell, J.M. (1986). The biasing effects of subordinate likedness on leaders' responses to poor performers: A laboratory and field study. *Personnel Psychology*, *39*, 759–777.

Dobson, P. (1989). Reference reports. In P. Herriot (Ed.), *Assessment and selection in organisations*. Chichester, UK: Wiley.

Dollinger, M.J., & Danis, W. (1998). Preferred decision making styles: A cross-cultural comparison. *Psychological Reports*, *82*, 755–761.

Donaldson, J., & Gowler, D. (1975). Prerogatives, participation, and managerial stress. In D. Gowler & K. Legge (Eds.), *Managerial stress*. Epping, UK: Gower Press.

Donaldson, L. (1987). Strategy and structural adjustment to regain fit and performance: In defence of contingency theory. *Journal of Management Studies*, January, 1–24.

Donaldson, L. (1997). A positive alternative to the structure–action approach. *Organization Studies*, *18*, 77–92.

Donkin, R. (1994a, January 19). Record payout for RSI injury. *Financial Times*, p. 7.

Donkin, R. (1994b, July 27). Redundancy reigns in Metroland. *Financial Times*, p. 8.

Donkin, R. (1994c, May 18). Managing creativity takes talent. *Financial Times*, p. 12.

Donkin, R. (1995a, November). Keeping fit and healthy. *Financial Times*, Health in the workplace (Health and Safety Executive sponsored guide), p. 10.

Donkin, R. (1995b, December 6). Men in empty suits. *Financial Times*, p. 32.

Donkin, R. (1997, November 26). Shoe factory provides an offshore spur. *Financial Times*, p. 19.

Donkin, R. (1998a, October 14). A question of ethics. *Financial Times*, p. 15.

Donkin, R. (1998b, February 18). A stake in the company's future. *Financial Times* (Recruitment section), p. 15.

Donkin, R. (1998c, October 28). Knowledge management (disciplines compete for a newcomer). *Financial Times*, p. 14.

Donkin, R. (2002, October 3). Challenge to human "capital" assumptions. *Financial Times* (Appointments section), p. x.

Donkin, R. (2003a, February 6). F-word missing from a model workplace. *Financial Times* (Appointments section), p. x.

Donkin, R. (2003b, December 4). Home can still be an office with a heart. *Financial Times* (Recruitment section), p. xi.

Donnelly, J. (2003). Blot on the landscape? *The Psychologist*, *16*, 246–249.

Donovan, J.J., & Radosevich, D.J. (1998). The moderating role of goal commitment on the goal difficulty –performance relationship: A meta analytic review and critical reanalysis. *Journal of Applied Psychology*, *83*, 308–315.

Douma, M., Bilderbeek, J., Idenburg, P., & Looise, J.K. (2000). Strategic alliances: Managing the dynamics of fit. *Long Range Planning*, *33*, 579–598.

Downs, S. (1995). Learning to learn. In S. Truelove (Ed.), *The handbook of training and development* (2nd ed.). Oxford: Blackwell.

Doyle, C.E. (2003). *Work and organizational psychology: An introduction with attitude*. Hove, UK: Psychology Press.

Dreher, G., & Ash, R. (1990). A comparative study of mentoring among men and women in managerial, professional and technical positions. *Journal of Applied Psychology*, October, 539–546.

Drever, J. (1964). *A dictionary of psychology*. Harmondsworth, UK: Penguin.

Driver, M.J., & Streufert, S. (1966). *The general incongruity adaptation level (GIAL) hypothesis: An analysis and integration of cognitive approaches to motivation* (Paper No. 114). Krannert School of Industrial Administration, Purdue University, Indiana.

Drucker, P.F. (1988). The coming of the new organisation. *Harvard Business Review*, January–February, 45–53.

Drucker, P.F. (2004). What makes an effective executive? *Harvard Business Review*, June, 58–63.

DuBrin, A.J. (1978). *Winning at office politics*. New York: Ballantine.

DuBrin, A.J. (1990). *Effective business psychology* (3rd ed.). New York: Prentice Hall.

DuBrin, A.J. (2002). *Fundamentals of organizational behavior: An applied approach* (2nd ed.). Mason, OH: South Western/Thomson Learning.

Duchon, D., Green, S.G., & Taber, T.D. (1986). Vertical dyad linkage: A longitudinal assessment of antecedents, measures, and consequences. *Journal of Applied Psychology*, February, 56–60.

Dufty, N.F., & Taylor, P.M. (1970). The implementation of a decision. In L.A. Welsch & R.M. Cyert (Eds.), *Management decision making*. Harmondsworth, UK: Penguin.

Dulewicz, V. (1995). A validation of Belbin's team roles from 16 PF and OQP using bosses' ratings of competence. *Journal of Occupational and Organizational Psychology*, 68, 81–99.

Duncan, D. (1999). The future of psychometric testing: A user's view. *Selection and Development Review*, 15, 16–17.

Duncan, R.B. (1972). Characteristics of organisational environments and perceived uncertainty. *Administrative Science Quarterly*, September, 313–327.

Duncan, W.J. (1981). *Organisational behaviour*. Boston, MA: Houghton Mifflin.

Dunfee, T.W. (1997). Marketing an ethical stance. In *Mastering management: Module 11. Business ethics* (pp. 368–370). London: FT/Pitman Publishing.

Dunham, R., Grube, J.A., & Constaneda, M.B. (1994). Organizational commitment: The utility of an integrative definition. *Journal of Applied Psychology*, 79, 37–80.

Dunphy, D., & Stace, D.A. (1993). The strategic management of corporate change. *Human Relations*, 46, 905–918.

Dupuy, J. (1990). Flexible jobs: Key to manufacturing productivity. *Journal of Business Strategy*, May–June, 28–32.

Dyer, W.G. (1977). *Team-building: Issues and alternatives*. Reading, MA: Addison-Wesley.

Dyer, W.G. (1984). *Strategies for managing change*. Reading, MA: Addison-Wesley.

Eachus, P. (1988). The psychology of the stock market. *The Psychologist*, March, 100–103.

Eaglesham, J. (2005, January 13). Review poses question on bribery curbs. *Financial Times*, p. 2.

Eaglesham, J., Turner, D., & Guthrie, J. (2004, October 30). Mind the gap: Labour puts equal pay for women in its election agenda. *Financial Times*, p. 11.

Eagly, A.H., & Johnson, B.T. (1990). Gender and leadership style: A meta analysis. *Psychological Bulletin*, 108, 233–256.

Eagly, A.H., Karau, S.J., & Makhijani, M.G. (1995). Gender and the effectiveness of leaders: A meta analysis. *Psychological Bulletin*, 117, 125–145.

Earl, M. (2004, August 26). Tantalised by the promise of wisdom. *Financial Times*, FT Summer School, p. 11.

Earley, P.C. (1989). Social loafing and collectivism: A comparison of the United States and the People's Republic of China. *Administrative Science Quarterly*, 34, 565–581.

Earley, P.C. (1993). East meets west meets mideast: Further explorations of collectivist and individualistic work groups. *Academy of Management Journal*, April, 319–348.

Earley, P.C., Connolly, T., & Ekegren G. (1989). Goals, strategy development and task performance: Some limits on the efficacy of goal-setting. *Journal of Applied Psychology*, 74, 24–33.

Earley, P.C., & Lituchy, T.R. (1991). Delineating goal and efficacy effects. A test of three models. *Journal of Applied Psychology*, February, 81–98.

Earley, P.C., Northcraft, G.B., Lee, C., & Lituchy, T.R. (1990). Impact of process and outcome feedback on the relation of goal setting to task performance. *Academy of Management Journal*, March, 87–105.

Earnshaw J., & Cooper, C.L. (2001). *Stress and employer liability*. London: CIPD Books.

Eason, K.D. (1980). Computer information systems and managerial tasks. In N. Bjorn-Anderson (Ed.), *The human side of information processing*. Amsterdam: North-Holland.

Easterby-Smith, M., & Lyles, M. (Eds.) (2003). *The Blackwell handbook of organisational learning and knowledge management*. Oxford: Blackwell Publishing.

Easterby-Smith, M., Thorpe, R., & Lowe, A. (2002). *Management research: An introduction*. London: Sage Publications.

Eaton, M.T. (1969). The mental health of the older executive. *Geriatric*, 24, 126–134.

Ebbinghaus, H. (1885). *Memory: A contribution to experimental psychology*. New York: Columbia University Teachers' College.

Economist, The (1993, January 23). Return of the stop-watch, p. 77.

Economist, The (1994, April 23). Mind over matter, 105–106.

Eden, C., & Huxham, C. (1996). Action research for management research. *British Journal of Management*, 7, 75–86.

Eden, D., & Aviram, A. (1993). Self-efficacy training to speed reemployment. Helping people to help themselves. *Journal of Applied Psychology*, 78, 352–360.

Edenborough, R. (1994). *Using psychometrics: A practical guide to testing and assessment*. London: Kogan Page.

Edwards, M.R. (1983). OJQ offers an alternative to assessment centres. *Public Personnel Management Journal, 12*, 146–155.

Egan, G.E. (1994). *Working the shadow side. A guide to positive behind the scenes management.* San Francisco: Jossey-Bass.

Egan, G.E. (1998). *The skilled helper: A problem-management approach in helping* (6th ed.). Pacific Grove, CA: Brooks Cole.

Eglin, R. (2005, January 23). BT aims to go on the right track. *The Sunday Times* (Appointments section), p. 9.

Egly, D.G. (1982). Cognitive style, categorisation and vocational effects on performance of REL.DATABASE users. *SIGSOC Bulletin, 13*, 91–97.

Ehrlich, D., Guttman, I., Schonbach, P., & Mills, J. (1957). Post decision exposure to relevant information. *Journal of Abnormal and Social Psychology, 54*, 98–102.

Eisenhardt, K.M., & Bourgeois III, L.J. (1988). Politics of strategic decision making in high velocity environments: Towards a mid-range theory. *Academy of Management Journal*, December, 737–770.

Eiser, J.R., & Van der Pligt, J. (1988). *Attitudes and decisions.* London: Routledge.

Ekstrand, B.R. (1972). To sleep perchance to dream: About why we forget. In C.P. Duncan, L. Sechrest, & A.W. Melton (Eds.), *Human memory.* New York: Appleton-Century-Croft.

Elkin, A.J., & Rosch, P.J. (1990). Promoting mental health at the workplace: The prevention side of stress management—state of the art review. *Occupational Medicine, 5*, 739–754.

Ellis, A.A. (1974). *Humanistic psychotherapy: The rational emotive approach.* New York: McGraw-Hill.

Elsmore, T.F., & McBride, S.A. (1994). An eight-alternative concurrent schedule. Foraging in a radial maze. *Journal of Applied Behavior Analysis, 28*, 236.

Emery, F.E., & Trist, E.L. (1965). The causal textures of organisational environments. *Human Relations*, February, 21–32.

Engel, J.F., Blackwell, R.D., & Miniard, P.W. (1995). *Consumer behaviour* (8th ed.). Fort Worth, TX: Dryden Press.

England, G.W. (1991). The meaning of working in the USA: Recent changes. *The European Work and Organizational Psychologist, 1*(2/3), 111–124.

England, G.W., & Lee, R. (1974). The relationship between managerial values and managerial success in the US, Japan, India, and Australia. *Journal of Applied Psychology, 59*, 411–419.

Erez, M. (1977). Feedback: A necessary condition for the goal-setting performance relationship. *Journal of Applied Psychology, 62*, 624–627.

Erez, M., & Somech, A. (1996). Is group productivity loss the rule or the exception? Effects of culture and group-based motivation. *Academy of Management Journal, 39*, 1513–1537.

Esser, J.K. (1998). Groupthink: Alive and well after 25 years—a review of groupthink research. *Organizational Behaviour and Human Decision Processes, 73*, 116–141.

Etzioni, A. (1975). *A comparative analysis of complex organisations.* New York: Free Press.

Evans, M.G. (1996). R.J. House's "A path–goal theory of leadership effectiveness". *Leadership Quarterly*, Fall, 305–309.

Evden, D. (1986). OD and self-fulfilling prophecy: Boosting productivity by raising expectations. *Journal of Applied Behavioural Science, 22*, 1–13.

Eysenck, H.J. (1947). *Dimensions of personality.* London: Routledge & Kegan Paul.

Eysenck, H.J. (1953). *The structure of human personality.* London: Methuen.

Eysenck, H.J. (1954). *The psychology of politics.* London: Routledge & Kegan Paul.

Eysenck, H.J. (1965). *Fact and fiction in psychology.* Harmondsworth, UK: Penguin.

Eysenck, H.J. (1967). *The biological basis of behaviour.* Springfield, IL: C.C. Thomas.

Eysenck, H.J. (1970). *Psychology is about people.* London: Allen Lane.

Eysenck, M.W. (1993). *Principles of cognitive psychology.* Hove, UK: Lawrence Erlbaum Associates Ltd.

Eysenck, M.W., & Keane, M.T. (1995). *Cognitive psychology: A student's handbook* (3rd ed.). Hove, UK: Psychology Press.

Eysenck, M.W., & Keane, M.T. (2000). *Cognitive psychology: A student's handbook* (4th ed.). Hove, UK: Psychology Press.

Fagan, M. (2002, November 3). Is Browne losing his magic? *Sunday Telegraph* (Business section).

Fagan, L., & Little, M. (1984). *The forsaken families.* Harmondsworth, UK: Penguin.

Fagin, L.H. (1979). The experience of unemployment: (1). The impact of unemployment. *New Universities Quarterly*, Winter, 48–64.

Fagley, N.S., & Miller, P.M. (1987). The effects of decision framing on choice of risky vs. certain options. *Organisational Behaviour and Human Decision Processes*, April, 264–277.

Fandt, P.M., & Ferris, G.R. (1990). The management of information and impressions: When employees behaved opportunistically. *Organizational Behavior and Human Decision Processes*, February, 140–158.

Farh, J.L., & Werbel, J.D. (1986). Effects of purpose of the appraisal and expectations on self-appraisal leniency. *Journal of Applied Psychology, 62*, 527–529.

Farmer, E., & Chambers, E.G. (1926). *A psychological study of individual differences in accident rates* (Report No. 38, pp. 1–46). London: Industrial Fatigue Research Board, Medical Research Council.

Farr, J.L., Hoffman, D.A., & Ringenbach, K.L. (1993). Goal orientation and action control theory. In

I.T. Robertson & C.L. Cooper (Eds.), *International review of industrial and organizational psychology, Vol. 8.* Chichester, UK: John Wiley.

Farrar, S. (1998, June 28). Scientists lead out robot guide dog for the blind. *Sunday Times* (News Review), p. 14.

Farrell, D., & Petersen, J.C. (1982). Patterns of political behaviour in organisations. *Academy of Management Review*, July, 403–412.

Farren, C. et al. (1984). Mentoring: A boon to career development. *Personnel*, November/December.

Fayol, H. (1949). *General and industrial management.* London: Pitman.

Fazio, R.H. (1986). How do attitudes guide behaviour? In R.M. Sorrentino & E.T. Higgins (Eds.), *Handbook of motivation and cognition: Foundations of social behaviour.* New York: Guilford Press.

Fazio, R.H. (2000). Acessible attitudes as tools for object appraisal: Their costs and benefits. In G.R. Maio & J.M. Olson (Eds.), *Why we evaluate: Functions of attitudes* (pp. 1–36). Mahwah, NJ: Lawrence Erlbaum Associates Inc.

Fedor, D.B., & Buckley, M.R. (1988). Issues surrounding the need for more frequent monitoring of individual performance in organisations. *Public Personnel Management*, Winter, 435–442.

Feldman, D.C. (1984). The development and enforcement of group norms. *Academy of Management Review*, January, 47–53.

Feldman, D.C., & Arnold, H.J. (1985). Personality types and career patterns: Some empirical evidence on Holland's model. *Canadian Journal of Administrative Science*, June, 192–210.

Feldman, D.C., Doerpinghaus, H.I., & Turnley, W.H. (1994). Managing temporary workers: A permanent HRM challenge. *Organizational Dynamics*, Autumn, 49–63.

Feldman, M.P. (1971). *Psychology in the industrial environment.* Sevenoaks, UK: Butterworth.

Feltham, R., Lewis, C., Anderson, P., & Hughes, D. (1998). Psychometrics: Cultural impediments to global recruitment and people development. *Selection and Development Review*, August, 16–21.

Fenlon, M. (2002, November 22). The public spirit. *FT Mastering Leadership, Part 4*, pp. 4–5.

Ferris, G.R., & Kacmar, K.M. (1992). Perceptions of organizational politics. *Journal of Management*, March, 93–116.

Feshback, S., & Singer, D. (1957). The effects of a vicarious aggressive activity. *Journal of Abnormal and Social Psychology*, *63*, 381–385.

Festinger, L., & Carlsmith, J. (1959). Cognitive consequences of forced compliancies. *Journal of Abnormal and Social Psychology*, *58*, 203–210.

Festinger, L., Schachter, S., & Back, K. (1950). *Social pressure in informal groups: A study of human factors in housing.* New York: Harper & Row.

Festinger, L.A. (1957). *Theory of cognitive dissonance.* Evanston, IL: Row, Peterson.

Fiedler, F.E. (1967). *Theory of leadership effectiveness.* New York: McGraw-Hill.

Fiedler, F.E. (1972). The effects of leadership training and experience: A contingency model interpretation. *Administrative Science Quarterly*, December, 453–470.

Fiedler, F.E. (1995). Cognitive resources and leadership performance. *Applied Psychology: An International Review*, *44*, 5–28.

Fiedler, F.E., & Garcia, J.E. (1987). *New approaches to effective leadership: Cognitive resources and organisational performance.* New York: John Wiley.

Fiegenbaum, A., & Thomas, H. (1988). Attitudes toward risk and the risk return paradox: Prospect theory explanations. *Academy of Management Journal*, *31*, 86–106.

Field, R. (1979). A critique of the Vroom-Yetton model of leadership behaviour. *Academy of Management Review*, *4*, 249–257.

Field, R.H.G., & House, R.J. (1990). A test of the Vroom-Yetton model using manager and subordinate reports. *Journal of Applied Psychology*, *75*, 362–366.

Financial Times (1993, August 13). Editorial comment, p. 13.

Financial Times (1999, August 21). Editorial comment.

Financial Times (2003, September 20). Editorial comment, p. 12.

Financial Times (2004a, July 15). Editorial comment, p. 18.

Financial Times (2004b, November 1). Editorial comment, p. 18.

Financial Times (2004c, January 23). Science update: Determination of sexual identity, p. 17.

Financial Times (2005, February 18). Editorial comment, p. 16.

Finn, A. (1988). Print advertisement recognition readership scores: An information processing perspective. *Journal of Marketing Research*, *25*, 168–177.

Firn, D., & Tait, N. (2003, November 6). Former executives face fraud allegations. *Financial Times*, p. 4.

Fisch, G.G. (1961). Line-staff is obsolete. *Harvard Business Review*, *39*, 67–79.

Fishbein, M., & Ajzen, I. (1975). *Beliefs, attitudes, intention and behaviour: An introduction to theory and research.* Reading, MA: Addison-Wesley.

Fisher, C. (1979). Transmission of positive and negative feedback to subordinates: A laboratory investigation. *Journal of Applied Psychology*, October, 533–540.

Fisher, G.H. (1967). Preparation of ambiguous stimulus materials. *Perception and Psychophysics*, *2*, 421–422.

Fisher, S. (1985). Control and blue-collar work. In C.L. Cooper & M.J. Smith (Eds.), *Job stress and blue-collar work.* Chichester, UK: Wiley.

Fitts, P.M. (1962). Factors in complex skills training. In R. Glaser (Ed.), *Training, research and education*. New York: J. Wiley.

Fitzgerald, N. (1997, May 25). Incentive plans under fire. *The Sunday Times* (Business section), p. 31.

Flanagan, J.C. (1954). The critical incident technique. *Psychological Bulletin*, *51*, 327–358.

Fleishman, E.A., & Harris, E.F. (1962). Patterns of leadership behaviour related to employee grievance and turnover. *Personnel Psychology*, *15*, 43–56.

Fletcher, C. (1984). What's new in performance appraisal? *Personnel Management*, February, 20–22.

Fletcher, C. (1993). *Appraisal: Routes to improved performance*. London: IPM.

Fletcher, C. (1994). Validity, test use and professional responsibility. *The Psychologist*, January, 30–31.

Fletcher, C. (1995). What it means to assess integrity. *People Management*, August, 30–31.

Fletcher, C. (1997). The future of psychometric assessment: Fostering positive candidate attitude and reactions. *Selection and Development Review*, *13*(August), 8–11.

Fletcher, C. (1998). *Assessing the effectiveness of some 360 degree appraisal systems*. Paper presented at the BPS Occupational Psychology Conference, Birmingham, UK.

Fletcher, C. (2000). Performance appraisal. Assessing and developing performance and potential. In N. Chiemel (Ed.), *Introduction to work and organizational psychology: A European perspective*. Oxford: Blackwell.

Fletcher, C. (2001). Performance appraisal and management: The developing research agenda. *Journal of Occupational and Organizational Psychology*, *74*, 473–487.

Fletcher, C., & Williams, R. (1992). The route to performance management. *Personnel Management*, October, 42–47.

Folger, R., & Konovsky, M. (1989). Effects of procedural and distributive justice on reactions to pay raise decisions. *Academy of Management Journal*, *32*, 115–130.

Foran, M.F., & De Coster, D.R. (1974). An experimental study of the effects of participation, authoritarianism, and feedback on cognitive dissonance in a standard setting situation. *Accounting Review*, October, 751–763.

Ford, J.K., & Kraiger, K. (1995). The application of cognitive constructs and principles to the instructional systems model of training: Implications for needs assessment, design and transfer. *International Review of Industrial and Organizational Psychology*, *10*, 1–48.

Ford, R.C., & Randolph, W.A. (1992). Cross-functional structures: A review and integration of matrix organization and project management. *Journal of Management*, *18*, 267–294.

Forester, J. (1984). Bounded rationality and the science of muddling through. *Public Administration Quarterly*, January–February, 23–31.

Forrester, R., & Drexler, A.B. (1999). A model of team-based organization performance. *Academy of Management Executive*, August, 36–49.

Fowler, A. (1988). New directions in performance-related pay. *Personnel Management*, November, 30–34.

Fox, A. (1974). *Beyond contract, power and trust relations*. London: Faber.

Fox, G., & Dinur, Y. (1988). Validity of self-assessment: A field evaluation. *Personnel Psychology*, *41*, 581–592.

Francis, R.D. (1999). *Ethics for psychologists: A handbook*. Leicester, UK: BPS Books.

Franklin, J.L. (1978). Improving the effectiveness of survey feedback. *Personnel*, May–June, 11–17.

Fredrickson, J.W. (1986). The strategic decision process and organisation structure. *Academy of Management Review*, April, 280–297.

Fredrickson, J.W., & Iaquinto, A.L. (1989). Inertia and creeping rationality in strategic decision processes. *Academy of Management Journal*, *32*, 516–542.

Freeman, C. (2004). Viewpoint—Women play salary catch-up: Despite equal opportunities legislation, male workers are still being paid a lot more than their female counterparts. *People Management*, 25 March, 27.

French, J., & Raven, B. (1958). The bases of social power. In D. Cartwright (Ed.), *Studies in social power*. Ann Arbor, MI: Institute for Social Research.

French, J.R.P., & Caplan, R.D. (1970). Psychosocial factors in coronary heart disease. *Industrial Medicine*, *39*, 383–397.

French, W.L., & Bell, C.H. (1978). *Organisational development* (2nd ed.). New York: Prentice Hall.

Frenkel-Brunswick, E., & Sanford, R.N. (1945). Some personality factors in anti-Semitism. *Journal of Psychology*, *20*, 271–291.

Freud, S. (1938). *The basic writings of Sigmund Freud*. New York: Modem Library.

Freud, S. (1955). Group psychology and the analysis of the ego. In J. Strachey (Ed.), *The complete psychological works of Sigmund Freud, Vol. XVIII*. London: Hogarth Press.

Friedlander, F., & Brown, L.D. (1974). Organisational development. In M.R. Rosensweig & L.W. Porter (Eds.), *Annual review of psychology*. Palo Alto, CA: Annual Reviews.

Friedman, H.S., & Booth-Kewley, S. (1987). The disease-prone personality: A meta-analytic view of the construct. *American Psychologist*, June, 539–555.

Fromm, E. (1941). *Escape from freedom*. New York: Rinehart.

Frost, B. (1990, December 19). Firemen awarded £34,000 for trauma after King's Cross. *The Times*, p. 3.

Fryer, D., & Payne, R. (1986). Being unemployed: A review of the literature on the psychological experience of unemployment. In C.L. Cooper & I.T. Robertson (Eds.), *International review of industrial and organisational psychology*. Chichester, UK: Wiley.

Fryer, D.M., & Warr, P. (1984). Unemployment and cognitive difficulties. *British Journal of Clinical Psychology, 23,* 67–68.

Fulmer, R.M. (2004). The challenge of ethical leadership. *Organizational Dynamics, 33,* 307–317.

Furnham, A. (1990). Faking personality questionnaires: Fabricating different profiles for different purposes. *Current Psychology: Research and Reviews*, Spring, 45–55.

Furnham, A. (1992). Personality and learning style: A study of three instruments. *Individual Differences, 13,* 429–438.

Furnham, A. (1993a, January 13). Short cut to the top. *Financial Times*.

Furnham, A. (1993b, March 1). When employees rate their supervisors. *Financial Times*.

Furnham, A. (1997). *The psychology of behaviour at work*. Hove, UK: Psychology Press.

Furnham, A. (1999). *Body language at work*. London: Institute of Personnel and Development.

Furnham, A. (2000). Thinking about intelligence. *The Psychologist, 13,* 510–515.

Furnham, A. (2001a). Keys to unlock path of career fulfillment. *Sunday Telegraph* (Appointments section), p. A1.

Furnham, A. (2001b). Vocational preference and P–O fit: Reflections on Holland's theory of vocational choice. *Applied Psychology: An International Review, 50,* 5–29.

Furnham, A. (2002a, July 5). Freud and the office hoarder. *Financial Times*, p. 12.

Furnham, A. (2002b, May 14). Remember to manage upwards: Five traits are important when assessing the personality of the boss and maintaining a good working relationship. *Financial Times*, p. 17.

Furnham, A. (2005a). *The psychology of behaviour at work* (2nd ed.). Hove, UK: Psychology Press.

Furnham, A. (2005b, February 6). Keeping crooks out of your business. *The Sunday Times* (Appointments section), p. 7.

Furnham, A., & Gunter, B. (1993). Corporate culture: Diagnosis and change. In C.L. Cooper & I.T. Robertson (Eds.), *International review of industrial and organisational psychology*. Chichester, UK: Wiley.

Furnham, A., Steele, H., & Pendleton, D. (1993). A psycho-metric assessment of the Belbin team-role self-perception inventory. *Journal of Occupational and Organizational Psychology, 66,* 245–257.

Fursland, E. (1995, January 2). No place for the bully. *The Times* (Section 3), p. 20.

Gaertner, S.L., Rust, M., Dovidio, J.F., Backman, B.A., & Anastasio, P.A. (1993). The contact hypothesis: The role of common in-group identity on reducing inter-group bias. *Small Groups Research, 25,* 244–249.

Gagne, R.M. (1977). *The conditions of learning* (3rd ed.). New York: Rinehart & Winston.

Galbraith, J.R. (1977). *Organization design*. Reading, MA: Addison-Wesley.

Galunic, D.C., & Eisenhardt, K.M. (1994). Reviewing the strategy-structure performance paradigm. In B.M. Staw & L.L. Cummings (Eds.), *Research in organizational behaviour* (Vol. 16, pp. 215–255). Greenwich, CT: JAI Press.

Gandz, J., & Murray, V.V. (1980). The experience of workplace politics. *Academy of Management Journal*, June, 237–251.

Gardner, H. (1999). *Intelligence reframed*. New York: Basic Books.

Gardner, W.L. (1992). Lessons in organizational dramaturgy: The art of impression management. *Organizational Dynamics*, Summer, 51–63.

Gardner, W.L., & Martinko, M.J. (1988). Impression management: An observational study linking audience characteristics with verbal self-presentations. *Academy of Management Journal, 31,* 42–65.

Garland, H., & Price, K.N. (1977). Attitudes towards women in management and attributions of their success and failure in managerial positions. *Journal of Applied Psychology, 62,* 29–33.

Garvey, C. (2002). Steering teams with the right pay. *HR Magazine*, May, 70–80.

Garvin, D.A. (1993). Building a learning organization. *Harvard Business Review*, July–August, 78–91.

Garvin, D., & Roberto, M. (2001). What you don't know about making decisions. *Harvard Business Review*, September, 108–115.

Gastil, J. (1994). A definition and illustration of democratic leadership. *Human Relations, 47,* 953–975.

Gavin, J.H. (2004). The virtuous organization: The value of happiness in the workplace. *Organizational Dynamics, 33,* 379–392.

Geary, J.F. (1992). Employment flexibility and human resource management: The case of three electronics plants. *Work, Employment and Society, 4,* 157–188.

Gebhart, G.L., & Crump, C.E. (1990). Employee fitness and wellness programmes in the workplace. *American Psychologist, 45,* 262–272.

Gemmil, G.R., & Heisler, W.J. (1972). Machiavellianism as a factor in managerial job strain, job satisfaction, and upward mobility. *Academy of Management Journal, 15,* 53–67.

George, J.M. (1995). Asymmetrical effects of rewards and punishments: The case of social loafing. *Journal of Occupational and Organizational Psychology, 68,* 327–338.

George, J.M., & Jones, G.R. (1996). The experience of mood and turnover decisions: Interactive effects of value attainment, job satisfaction and positive mood. *Journal of Applied Psychology, 81,* 318–325.

George, J.M., & Jones, G.R. (1997). Experiencing work: Values, attitudes and moods. *Human Relations, 50,* 393–416.

Gerth, H.H., & Mills, C.W. (1948). *From Max Weber.* London: Routledge & Kegan Paul.

Gervais, S., & Odean, T. (2001, June 18). The perils for investors of human nature. *FT Mastering Investment,* 6–7.

Geyer, A.L.J., & Speyrer, J.M. (1997). Transformational leadership and objective performance in banks. *Applied Psychology: An International Review, 46.*

Gherardi, S. (1997). Organizational learning. In A. Sorge & M. Warner (Eds.), *The handbook of organizational behaviour* (pp. 542–551). London: International Thomson Business Press.

Ghiselli, E.E. (1971). *Exploration in managerial talent.* Santa Monica, CA: Goodyear.

Ghiselli, E.E. (1973). The validity of aptitude tests in personnel selection. *Personnel Psychology, 26,* 461–477.

Gibbs, N. (1995, October 15). The EQ factor. *Time,* pp. 62–68.

Gibson, C.B., & Zellmer-Bruhn, M.E. (2002). Minding your metaphors: Applying the concept of teamwork metaphors to the management of teams in multicultural contexts. *Organizational Dynamics, 31,* 101–116.

Gibson, E.J. (1969). *Principles of perceptual learning and development.* New York: Appleton-Century-Crofts.

Gilovich, T., & Griffin, D. (Eds.) (2002). *Heuristics and biases: The psychology of intuitive judgement.* New York: Cambridge University Press.

Ginnet, R.C. (1990). The airline cockpit crew. In J.R. Hackman (Ed.), *Groups that work (and those that don't).* San Francisco: Jossey-Bass.

Ginsberg, A., & Ventrakaman, N. (1985). Contingency perspectives of organizational strategy—a critical review of the empirical research. *Academy of Management Review,* July, 412–434.

Gist, M.E. (1987). Self-efficacy: Implications for organizational behaviour and human resource management. *Academy of Management Review,* July, 472–485.

Gist, M.E., & Mitchell, T.R. (1992). Self-efficacy: A theoretical analysis of its determinants and malleability. *Academy of Management Review,* April, 183–211.

Glanzer, M., & Cunitz, A.R. (1966). Two storage mechanisms in free recall. *Journal of Verbal Learning and Verbal Behavior, 5,* 351–360.

Gleitman, H. (1995). *Psychology* (4th ed.). New York: W.W. Norton & Co.

Glendon, A.I., & McKenna, E.F. (1995). *Human safety and risk management: A psychological perspective.* London: Chapman & Hall.

Glisson, C., & Durick, M. (1988). Predictors of job satisfaction and organisational commitment in human service organisations. *Administrative Science Quarterly,* March, 61–81.

Godfrey, R.R. (1986). Tapping employees' creativity. *Supervisory Management,* February, 17–18.

Goffee, R. (1997). Cultural diversity. In *Mastering management: Module 6. Organizational behaviour* (pp. 240–246). FT/Pitman Publishing.

Goffee, R., & Jones, G. (2000). Why should anyone be led by you? *Harvard Business Review,* September–October, 62–70.

Goffee, R., & Jones, G. (2002, November 1). Mantle of authority. *FT Mastering Leadership, Part 1,* 4–5.

Goffman, E. (1961). *Asylums: Essays on the social situation of mental patients and other inmates.* New York: Doubleday.

Goldberg, L.R., & Rosolack, T.K. (1994). The Big Five factor structure as an integrative framework: An empirical comparison with Eysenck's P-E-N model. In C.F. Halverson, G.A. Kohnstamm, & R.P. Martin (Eds.), *The developing structure of temperament and personality from infancy to adulthood.* Hillsdale, NJ: Lawrence Erlbaum Associates Inc.

Goldstein, A.P., & Sorcher, M. (1974). *Changing supervisor behavior.* New York: Pergamon.

Goldstein, I.L. (1978). The pursuit of validity in the evaluation of training programmes. *Human Factors, 20,* 131–144.

Goldstein, I.L. (1980). Training in work organisations. *Annual Review of Psychology, 31,* 229–272.

Goldstein, I.L. (1986). *Training in organisations: Needs, assessment, development, and evaluation* (2nd ed.). Monterey, CA: Brooks/Cole.

Goldthorpe, J.H., Lockwood, D., Bechhofer, F., & Platt, J. (1970). *The affluent worker: Industrial attitudes and behaviour.* Cambridge, UK: Cambridge University Press.

Goleman, D. (1998). *Working with emotional intelligence.* London: Bloomsbury Publishers.

Goleman, D. (2004). What makes a leader? *Harvard Business Review,* January, 82–91.

Golembiewski, R.T., Proehl Jr, C.W., & Sink, D. (1982). Estimating the success of OD applications. *Training and Development Journal,* April, 90–93.

Golzen, G. (1993, February 21). Team up for business success. *The Sunday Times,* p. 4.2.

Goman, C.G. (1989). *Creative thinking in business.* London: Kogan Page.

Gomez-Mejia, L.R., Welbourne, T.M., & Wiseman, R.M. (2000). The role of risk sharing and risk taking under gain sharing. *Academy of Management Review,* July, 492–507.

Goodge, P. (1997). Assessment and development centres: Practical design principles. *Selection and Development Review, 13,* 11–14.

Goodge, P. (2005). How to link 360-degree feedback and appraisal. *People Management*, 27 January, 46–47.

Goodhart, D. (1993, November 3). Rewards for the top performers (curious appeal of UK performance-related pay schemes). *Financial Times*, p. 16.

Goodhart, D. (1994, January 8). Equal pay victory for 1500 women. *Financial Times*, p. 7.

Goodman, A.M. (1990). A model for police officer burnout. *Journal of Business and Psychology*, 5, 85–99.

Goodman, P.S., & Leyden, D.P. (1991). Familiarity and group productivity. *Journal of Applied Psychology*, August, 578–586.

Goodman, P.S., Ravlin, E., & Schminke, M. (1987). Understanding groups in organisations. In L.L. Cummings & B.M. Staw (Eds.), *Research in organisational behaviour, Vol. 9*. Greenwich, CT: JAI Press.

Goodwin, V., Wofford, J.C., & Whittington, J.L. (2001). A theoretical and empirical extension to the transformational leadership construct. *Journal of Organizational Behaviour*, 22, 759–774.

Gordon, G.G., & Di Tomaso, N. (1992). Predicting corporate performance from organizational culture. *Journal of Management Studies*, November, 793–798.

Gordon, R.A. (1993). The effect of strong versus weak evidence on the assessment of race stereotyping and non-stereotypical crimes. *Journal of Applied Social Psychology*, 23, 734–749.

Gover, J.A., Ronning, R.R., & Reynolds, C.R. (1989). *Handbook of creativity*. New York: Plenum Press.

Graen, G., Orris, J.B., & Alvares, K.M. (1971). Contingency model of leadership effectiveness: Some experimental results. *Journal of Applied Psychology*, 55, 196–201.

Graen, G., & Uhl-Bien, M. (1995). Relationship based approach to leadership development of leader–member exchange (LMX) theory of leadership over 25 years: Applying a multi-level multi-domain perspective. *Leadership Quarterly*, Summer, 219–247.

Granrose, C.S., & Portwood, J.D. (1987). Matching individual career plans and organisational careers management. *Academy of Management Journal*, December, 699–720.

Gray, D. (2003). Wanted: Chief Ignorance Officer. *Harvard Business Review*, November, 22–24.

Gray, J.L., & Starke, F.A. (1984). *Organisational behaviour: Concepts and applications* (3rd ed.). Columbus, OH: Charles E. Merrill.

Green, D. (1995, December 15). Woolworth sniffs a seasonal opportunity to increase sales. *Financial Times*, p. 1.

Green, S.G., & Mitchell, T.R. (1979). Attributional processes of leaders in leader–member interactions. *Organisational Behaviour and Human Performance*, 23, 429–458.

Greenberg, J. (1986). Determinants of perceived fairness of performance evaluations. *Journal of Applied Psychology*, May, 340–342.

Greenberg, J. (2004). Stress fairness to fare no stress. Managing workplace stress by promoting organisational justice. *Organizational Dynamics*, 33, 352–365.

Greene, J., & Lewis, D. (1988). *The hidden language of your handwriting*. London: Macdonald & Co.

Greenhalgh, L. (2002, November 29). *FT Mastering Leadership, Part 5*, pp. 2–3.

Greenhaus, J.H., Parasuraman, S., & Wormley, W.M. (1990). Effects of race on organisational experiences, job performance evaluation, and career outcomes. *Academy of Management Journal*, March, 64–86.

Gregory, R.L. (1966). *Eye and brain*. London: Weidenfeld & Nicolson.

Grey, C., & Mitev, N. (1995). Re-engineering organizations: A critical appraisal. *Personnel Review*, 24, 6–18.

Griffeth, R.W., Vecchio, R.P., & Logan, J.W. (1989). Equity theory and interpersonal attraction. *Journal of Applied Psychology*, June, 394–401.

Griffin, M.A., Patterson, M.G., & West, M.A. (2001). Job satisfaction and teamwork: The role of supervisor support. *Journal of Organizational Behaviour*, 22, 537–550.

Griffin, R.W. (1979). Task design determinants of effective leader behaviour. *Academy of Management Review*, 4, 215–224.

Griffin, R.W. (1982). *Task design: An integrative approach*. Glenview, IL: Scott, Foresman.

Griffin, R.W. (1988). A longitudinal assessment of the consequences of quality circles in an industrial setting. *Academy of Management Journal*, June, 338–358.

Griffith, V. (1995, March 3). Hero one day, villain the next. *Financial Times*, p. 13.

Griffith, V. (1998, April 28). Women in the workplace: And the bad news is. . . . *Financial Times*.

Griffiths, P., & Bell, E. (1985). Using assessment centres. *Training Officer*, October, 300–302.

Grubb, E.L., & Hupp, G. (1968). Perception of self, generalised stereotypes and brand selection. *Journal of Marketing Research*, 5, 58–63.

Guardian (1986, October 24). An account of the Colwich Junction train accident.

Guest, D. (1994). Organizational psychology and human resource management: Towards a European approach. *The European Work and Organizational Psychologist*, 4, 251–270.

Guest, D. (2001). Human resource management: When research confronts theory. *International Journal of Human Resource Management*, 12, 1092–1106.

Guest, D., & Conway, N. (2002). *Pressure at work and the psychological contract*. London: Chartered Institute of Personnel and Development.

Guest, D., & King, Z. (2004). Power, innovation, and problem solving: The personnel manager's three steps to heaven. *Journal of Management Studies*, *41*, 401–423.

Guilford, J.P. (1967). *The nature of human intelligence*. New York: McGraw-Hill.

Guirdham, M. (1972). *Marketing: The management of distribution channels*. Oxford: Pergamon.

Guirdham, M. (2002). *Interactive behaviour at work*. Harlow, UK: Pearson.

Gumbel, P. (2004, October 1). Au revoir, les jobs. *Time*, 44–45.

Guthrie, J. (2003a, November 12). Founders of the future. *FT Understanding Entrepreneurship*, pp. 2–3.

Guthrie, J. (2003b, October 21). The millionaire mentality and bumps on the head. *Financial Times*, p. 17.

Guzzo, R.A., & Dickson, M.W. (1996). Teams in organizations: Recent research on performance and effectiveness. *Annual Review of Psychology*, *47*, 307–338.

Hackman, J.R. (1977). Work design. In J.R. Hackman & J.L. Suttle (Eds.), *Improving life at work*. Santa Monica, CA: Scott, Foresman.

Hackman, J.R. (1994). Trip wires in designing and leading workgroups. *Occupational Psychologist*, *23*, 3–8.

Hackman, J.R., & Oldham, G.R. (1975). Development of the job agnostic survey. *Journal of Applied Psychology*, *60*(2), 159–170.

Hackman, J.R., Oldham, G.R., Janson, R., & Purdy, K. (1975). A new stage for job enrichment. *California Management Review*, *17*, 57–71.

Haddon, W., Suchman, E., & Klein, D. (1964). *Accident research: Its methods and approaches*. New York: Harper & Row.

Hagerty, M.R. (1999). Testing Maslow's hierarchy of needs. National quality of life across time. *Social Indicators Research*, *46*, 249–271.

Haire, M. (1950). Projective techniques in market research. *Journal of Marketing*, *14*, 649–656.

Halcrow, A. (1986). Incentive! How three companies cut costs. *Personnel Journal*, February, 12.

Hall, D.T., & Goodale, J.G. (1986). *Human resource management: Strategy, design, and implementation*. Glenview, IL: Scott, Foresman.

Hall, D.T., & Nougaim, K.E. (1968). An examination of Maslow's need hierarchy in an organisational setting. *Organisational Behaviour and Human Performance*, *3*, 12–35.

Hall, J.F. (1976). *Classical conditioning and instrumental learning*. Philadelphia: Lippincott.

Hall, L. (1995, November). More and more companies are using workplace counselling. *Financial Times*, Health in the workplace (Health and Safety Executive sponsored guide), pp. 8–11.

Hall, R.H. (1962). Intra-organisational structural variation: Application of the bureaucratic model. *Administrative Science Quarterly*, December, 295–308.

Halligan, L. (1997, June 10). Performance-related pay attacked. *Financial Times*, p. 8.

Halperin, K., Snyder, C.R., Shenkel, R.J., & Houston, B.K. (1976). Effect of source status and message favourability on acceptance of personality feedback. *Journal of Applied Psychology*, February, 85–88.

Hamblin, A.C. (1974). *Evaluation and control of training*. Maidenhead, UK: McGraw-Hill.

Hambrick, D. (2000, October 9). Putting the team into top management: Skills of management. *FT Mastering Management, Part 2*, pp. 6–7.

Hammer, M., & Champy, J. (1993). *Reengineering the corporation: A manifesto for business revolution*. New York: Harper Business.

Hammond, J.H., Keeney, R.L., & Raiffa, H. (1998). The hidden traps in decision making. *Harvard Business Review*, September–October, 47–58.

Hamner, W.C. (1977). Worker motivation programmes: The importance of climate, structure, and performance consequences. In W.C. Hamner & F.L. Schmidt (Eds.), *Contemporary problems in personnel*. Chicago: St Clair.

Hamner, W.C. (1983). Reinforcement theory and contingency management in organisational settings. In R. Steers & L.W. Porter (Eds.), *Motivation and work behaviour*. New York: McGraw-Hill.

Hamner, W.C., & Hamner, E.P. (1976). Behaviour modification on the bottom line. *Organizational Dynamics*, *4*, 3–21.

Hampden-Turner, C. (1983). Is there a new paradigm? A tale of two concepts. *Personnel Management Review*, *56*.

Hampden-Turner, C. (1990). *Corporate cultures: From vicious to virtuous circles*. London: Random Century.

Hampson, S. (1998, November 10). Directors should be above board. *Financial Times*, p. 16.

Hampson, S. (1999). State of the art: Personality. *The Psychologist*, June, 284–288.

Handy, C. (1975, September 22). Difficulties of combining family and career. *The Times*, p. 16.

Handy, C. (1989). *The age of unreason*. London: Business Books.

Handy, C.B. (1985). *Understanding organisations* (3rd ed.). London: Penguin.

Hanisch, K.A. (1995). Behavioral families and multiple causes: Matching the complexity of responses to the complexity of antecedents. *Current Directions in Psychological Science*, *4*, 156–161.

Hannan, M.T., & Freeman, J.H. (1977). The population ecology of organisations. *American Journal of Sociology*, *2*, 929–964.

Hansen, M. (2002, August 8). Turning the lone star into a real team player. FT Summer School Day 4: Knowledge Management. *Financial Times*, p. 14.

Hantula, D.A., & Bragger, J.L.D. (1999). The effects of feedback equivocality on escalation of commitment.

An empirical investigation of decision dilemma theory. *Journal of Applied Social Psychology*, February, 424–444.

Hardman, D., & Harries, C. (2002). How rational are we? *The Psychologist*, *15*, 76–79.

Hardy, C., & Leiba-O'Sullivan, S. (1998). The power behind empowerment: Implications for research and practice. *Human Relations*, *51*, 451–483.

Hargie, O., Saunders, C., & Dixon, D. (1994). *Social skills in interpersonal communication*. London: Routledge.

Harley, B. (2001). Team membership and the experience of work in Britain: An analysis of the Workplace Employee Relations Survey 1998 data. *Work, Employment and Society*, *15*, 721–742.

Harlow, H.F. (1953). Mice, monkeys, men and motives. *Psychological Review*, *60*, 23–32.

Harnischfeger, U. (1999, March 29). Germany: Second wave causes a ripple. *Financial Times* (Business education supplement), p. 8.

Harris, M.M. (1989). Reconsidering the employment interview: A review of recent literature and suggestions for future research. *Personnel Psychology*, Winter, 691–726.

Harris, M.M., Smith, D.E., & Champagne, D. (1995). A field study of performance appraisal purpose: Research vs administrative-based ratings. *Personnel Psychology*, Spring, 151–160.

Harris, T.A. (1969). *I'm OK—you're OK*. New York: Harper & Row.

Harrison, E.F. (1995). *The managerial decision making process* (4th ed.). Boston: Houghton Mifflin.

Harrison, J.R., & Carroll, G.R. (1991). Keeping the faith: A model of cultural transmission in formal organizations. *Administrative Science Quarterly*, December, 552–582.

Harrison, R. (1972). Understanding your organisation's character. *Harvard Business Review*, May–June, 119–128.

Harrison, R. (2000). *Employee development* (2nd ed.). London: Institute of Personnel and Development.

Hart, E. (1996). Top teams. *Management Review*, February, 43–47.

Hartley, J. (1984). Industrial relations psychology. In M. Gruneberg & T. Wall (Eds.), *Social psychology and organisational behaviour*. Chichester, UK: J. Wiley & Sons.

Hartston, W.R., & Mottram, R.D. (1976). *Personality profiles of managers: A study of occupational differences*. Cambridge, UK: Industrial Training Research Unit.

Harvey, F. (2004, September 27). The office is future-proof. *Financial Times* (FT Special Report on the Future of Work), p. 2.

Harvey, P. (1988). *Health psychology*. Harlow, UK: Longman.

Haslam, S.A., Powell, C., & Turner, J.C. (2000). Social identity, self-categorization and work motivation: Rethinking the contribution to positive and sustainable organizational outcomes. *Applied Psychology: An International Review*, *49*, 319–339.

Hatch, M.J. (1993). The dynamics of organisational culture. *Academy of Management Review*, *18*, 657–693.

Haugtvedt, C., Petty, R.E., Cacioppo, J.T., & Steidley, T. (1988). *Advances in consumer research: Vol. 16. Personality and ad effectiveness: Exploring the utility of need for cognition*. Prova, UT: Association for Consumer Research.

Hawkins, F.H. (1987). *Human factors in flight*. Aldershot, UK: Gower Press.

Hayes, J. (2002). The theory and practice of change management. Basingstoke, UK: Palgrave.

Hayes, J.R. (1968). Strategies in judgemental research. In B. Kleinmuntz (Ed.), *Formal representation of human judgement*. New York: Wiley.

Hayes, N. (1992). *Social identity and organisational consultancy*. Paper presented at the XXVth International Congress of Psychology, Brussels.

Hayes, N. (1993). *Principles of social psychology*. Hove, UK: Lawrence Erlbaum Associates Ltd.

Hayes, N. (1996). *Psychological dimensions of organisational culture*. Paper presented at the BPS Occupational Psychology Conference, Eastbourne, UK.

Hayes, N. (1997). *Successful team management*. London: International Thomson Business Press.

Hayne, C. (1981). Light and colour. *Occupational Health*, April, 198–204.

Heider, F. (1946). Attitudes and cognitive organisations. *Journal of Psychology*, *21*, 107–112.

Held, R., & Hein, A. (1963). Movement-produced stimulation in the development of visually guided behaviour. *Journal of Comparative and Physiological Psychology*, *5*(56), 872–876.

Heller, F. (1983, January 31). The danger of groupthink. *Guardian*, p. 9.

Heller, F.A. (1971). *Managerial decision making: A study of leadership styles and power-sharing among senior managers*. London: Tavistock.

Heller, F.A., & Wilpert, B. (1981). *Competence and power in managerial decision making*. Chichester, UK: John Wiley.

Henchy, T., & Glass, D.C. (1968). Evaluation of apprehension and the social facilitation of dominant and subordinate responses. *Journal of Personality and Social Psychology*, *10*, 445–454.

Henderson, J.C., & Nutt, P.C. (1980). The influence of decision style on decision-making behaviour. *Management Science*, *26*(April), 371–386.

Henderson, M. (2003, August 25). Blind man who regained sight is still in the dark. *The Times*, p. 7.

Hendry, C. (1996). Understanding and creating whole organizational change through learning theory. *Human Relations*, *48*, 621–641.

Hendry, C., Pettigrew, A., & Sparrow, P. (1988). Changing patterns of human resource management. *Personnel Management*, November, 37–41.

Heneman II, H.G. (1974). Comparisons of self and superior ratings of managerial performance. *Journal of Applied Psychology, 59*, 638–642.

Heneman, R.L., Greenberger, D.B., & Strasser, S. (1988). The relationship between pay-for-performance, perceptions and pay satisfaction. *Personnel Psychology*, Winter, 745–759.

Heneman, R.L., & Wexley, K.N. (1983). The effects of time delay in rating and amount observed on performance rating accuracy. *Academy of Management Journal*, December, 677–686.

Herrenkohl, R.C., Judson, G.T., & Heffner, J.A. (1999). Defining and measuring employee empowerment. *The Journal of Applied Behavioural Science, 35*, 373–389.

Herriot, P. (1992). *The career management challenge: Balancing individual and organisational needs*. London: Sage.

Herriot, P., & Pemberton, C. (1995). *New deals: The revolution in managerial careers*. Chichester, UK: Wiley.

Herriot, P., & Pemberton, C. (1996). Contracting careers. *Human Relations, 49*, 757–790.

Hersey, P. (1984). *The situational leader*. New York: Warner Books.

Hersey, P., & Blanchard, K. (1982). *Management of organisational behaviour*. New York: Prentice Hall.

Herzberg, F. (1966). *Work and the nature of man*. London: Staples Press.

Herzberg, F. (1968). How do you motivate employees? *Harvard Business Review*, January–February, 53–62.

Herzberg, F. (1974). The wise old Turk. *Harvard Business Review*, September–October, 70–80.

Hetherington, E.M., & Wray, N.P. (1964). Aggression, need for social approval and humour preferences. *Journal of Abnormal and Social Psychology, 68*, 685–689.

Hewstone, M, Ruibin, M., & Willis, H. (2002). Inter-group bias. *Annual Review of Psychology, 53*, 575–604.

Hickson, D.J., Butler, R.J., Gray, D., Mallory, G.R., & Wilson, D.C. (1986). *Top decisions: Strategic decision makers in organisations*. Oxford, UK: Blackwell.

Hickson, D.J., Hinings, C.R., Lee, C.A., Schneck, R.E., & Pennings, J.M. (1971). A strategic contingencies theory of inter-organisational power. *Administrative Science Quarterly*, June, 216–229.

Highley, J.C., & Cooper, C.L. (1995). *An assessment of UK EAPs and workplace counselling programmes*. London: Health and Safety Executive.

Hilton, J.L., & Von Hippel, W. (1996). Stereotypes. *Annual Review of Psychology, 47*, 237–271.

Hilton, P. (1992). Shepherd defends training policy. *Personnel Management*, December, 11.

Himmelfarb, S. (1974). Resistance to persuasion induced by information integration. In S. Himmelfarb & A. Eagley (Eds.), *Readings in attitude change*. New York: John Wiley & Sons.

Hinkle, C.L., & Kuehn, A.A. (1967). Heuristic models: Mapping to maze for management. *California Management Review, 10*, 59–68.

Hirschfield, A., & Behan, R. (1963). The accident process: Etiological considerations of industrial injuries. *Journal of the American Medical Association*, 19 October, 193.

Hirst, M.K., & Yetton, P.W. (1999). The effects of budget goals and task interdependence on the level of and variance in performance: A research note. *Accounting, Organizations and Society, 24*, 205–216.

Hodgetts, R.M. (1990). *Modern human relations at work* (4th ed.). Orlando, FL: Dryden Press.

Hodgetts, R.M. (1991). *Organizational behavior: Theory and practice*. New York: Macmillan.

Hodgetts, R.M., & Luthans, F. (1991). *International management*. New York: McGraw-Hill.

Hoel, H., Rayner, C., & Cooper, C.L. (1999). Workplace bullying. In C.L. Cooper and I.T. Robertson (Eds.), *International review of industrial and organizational psychology, 14*. Chichester, UK: J. Wiley.

Hoffman, R. (1995). Ten reasons you should be using 360 degree feedback. *HR Magazine*, April, 82–90.

Hofstede, G. (1968). *The game of budget control*. London: Tavistock.

Hofstede, G. (1980a). *Culture's consequences*. Beverley Hills, CA: Sage Publications.

Hofstede, G. (1980b). Motivation, leadership and organization: Do American theories apply abroad? *Organizational Dynamics, 9*, 42–63.

Hofstede, G. (1983). National cultures in four dimensions. *International Studies of Management and Organization*, Spring–Summer, 61.

Hofstede, G. (1991). *Cultures and organizations: Software of the mind*. Maidenhead, UK: McGraw-Hill.

Hofstede, G. (1993). Cultural constraints in management theories. *Academy of Management Executive*, February, 91.

Hogg, C., & McInerney, D. (1990). Team-building. *Personnel Management*, October, Factsheet 34.

Holden, L. (1994). Employee involvement. In I. Beardwell & L. Holden (Eds.), *Human resource management: A contemporary perspective*. London: Pitman.

Holland, J.L. (1997). *Making vocational choices: A theory of vocational personalities and work environment* (3rd ed.). Odessa, FL: Psychological Assessment Resource Inc.

Hollenbeck, J.R., & Klein, H.J. (1987). Goal commitment and the goal-setting process: Problems, prospects, and proposals for future research. *Journal of Applied Psychology, 72*, 212–220.

Hollenbeck, J.R., Williams, C.R., & Klein, H.J. (1989). An empirical examination of the antecedents of commitment to difficult goals. *Journal of Applied Psychology, 74*, 18–23.

Hollingshead, A.B., & McGrath, J.E. (1995). Computer assisted groups: A critical review of the empirical research. In R.A. Guzzo & E. Salas (Eds.), *Team effectiveness and decision making in organisations.* San Francisco, CA: Jossey-Bass.

Hollway, W. (1991). *Work psychology and organizational behaviour.* London: Sage Publications.

Holmes, D.S. (1974). The conscious control of thematic projection. *Journal of Consulting and Clinical Psychology, 42*, 323–329.

Hopper, T. (1978). *Role conflicts of management accountants in the context of their structural relationship to production.* Unpublished MPhil thesis, University of Aston, Birmingham, UK.

Hopwood, A. (1974). *Accounting and human behaviour.* London: Haymarket.

Horner, M.S. (1970). Femininity and successful achievement: A basic inconsistency. In Y. Bardwich et al. (Eds.), *Feminine, personality and conflict.* Belmont, CA: Brooks & Cole.

Horney, K.B. (1945). *Our inner conflicts.* New York: W.W. Norton.

Horton, D.L., & Mills, C.B. (1984). Human learning and memory. *Annual Review of Psychology, 35*, 361–394.

Hosking, D.M., & Morley, I. (1988). The skills of leadership. In J.G. Hunt, B.R. Baliga, H.P. Dachler, & C.A. Schriesheim (Eds.), *Emerging leadership vistas.* Boston, MA: Lexington.

Hosmer, L.T. (1995). Trust: The continuing link between organizational theory and philosophical ethics. *Academy of Management Review*, April, 397–403.

Hough, L. (1992). The "Big Five" personality variables—construct confusion: Description versus prediction. *Human Performance, 5*, 139–155.

Houlder, V. (1995, October 2). Strategic alliances are becoming increasingly popular, but the drawbacks are many. *Financial Times*, p. 14.

Houlder, V. (1996, June 22). Innovation under the spotlight. *Financial Times*, p. 8.

House, J.S., & Kahn, R.L. (1985). Measures and concepts of social support. In S. Cohen & L. Syme (Eds.), *Social support and health.* Orlando, FL: Academic Press.

House, R.J. (1971). A path–goal theory of leader effectiveness. *Administrative Science Quarterly, 16*, 321–338.

House, R.J. (1977). A 1976 theory of charismatic leadership. In J.G. Hunt & L.L. Larson (Eds.), *Leadership: The cutting edge.* Carbondale, IL: Southern Illinois University Press.

House, R.J. (1995) Leadership in the 21st century: A speculative inquiry'. In A. Howard (Ed.), *The changing nature of work*, San Francisco, CA: Jossey-Bass.

House, R.J. (1996). Path goal theory of leadership: Lessons, legacy, and a reformulated theory. *Leadership Quarterly, 7*, 333–352.

House, R.J., & Mitchell, T.R. (1974). Path–goal theory of leadership. *Journal of Contemporary Business, 3*, 81–97.

House, R.J., & Wigdor, L.A. (1967). Herzberg's dual-factor theory of job satisfaction and motivation: A review of the evidence and a criticism. *Personnel Psychology, 20*(4), 369–389.

Hovland, C.I. (1938). Experimental studies in rote learning theory: 111. Distribution of practice with varying speeds of syllable presentation. *Journal of Experimental Psychology, 23*, 172–190.

Hovland, C.I., Harvey, O.J., & Sherif, M. (1957). Assimilation and contrast effects in reactions to communication and attitude change. *Journal of Abnormal and Social Psychology, 55*, 244–252.

Hovland, C.I., Lumsdaine, A.A., & Sheffield, F.D. (1949). *Experiments in mass communication.* Princeton, NJ: Princeton University Press.

Hovland, C.I., & Weiss, W. (1951). The influence of source credibility on communication effectiveness. *Public Opinion Quarterly, 15*, 635–650.

Howard, J.H., Cunningham, D.A., & Rechnitzer, P.A. (1976). Health patterns associated with Type A behaviour: A managerial population. *Journal of Human Stress*, March, 24–31.

Howarth, E., & Browne, A. (1971). An item factor analysis of the 16 PF. *Personality, 2*, 117–139.

Howe, M.J.A. (1998). Can IQ change? *The Psychologist*, February, 69–72.

Howell, J.M., & Avolio, B.J. (1992). The ethics of charismatic leadership: Submission or liberation. *Academy of Management Executive*, May, 43–55.

Howell, J.M., & Avolio, B.J. (1993). Transformational leadership, transactional leadership, locus of control, and support for innovation: Key predictors of consolidated-business unit performance. *Journal of Applied Psychology, 78*, 891–902.

Howitt, D., & Cramer, D. (2000). *First steps in research and statistics.* London: Routledge.

Huber, G.P. (1990). A theory of the effects of advanced information technologies on organisation design, intelligence, and decision making. *Academy of Management Review, 15*, 47–71.

Hudson, L. (1966). *Contrary imaginations.* London: Methuen.

Huffcutt, A.I., & Arthur, W.A. (1994). Hunter and Hunter (1984) revisited: Interview validity for entry level jobs. *Journal of Applied Psychology, 79*, 184–190.

Huffcutt, A.I., Conway, J.M., Roth, P.L., & Stone, N.J. (2001). Identification and meta-analytic assessment of psychological constructs measured in employment interviews. *Journal of Applied Psychology*, October, 910.

Hulin, C.L., & Blood, M.R. (1968). Job enlargement, individual differences, and workers' responses. *Psychological Bulletin*, 69(1), 41–55.

Hulin, C.L., Reznowski, M., & Hachiya, D. (1985). Alternative opportunities and withdrawal decisions: Empirical and theoretical discrepancies and an integration. *Psychological Bulletin*, July, 233–250.

Hulin, C.L., & Smith, P. (1967). An empirical investigation of two implications of the two-factor theory of job satisfaction. *Journal of Applied Psychology*, October, 396–402.

Hull, C.L. (1943). *Principles of behaviour*. New York: Appleton-Century-Crofts.

Hunt, D.M., & Michael, C. (1983). Mentoring: A career training and development tool. *Academy of Management Review*, 8.

Hunt, E. (1985). Verbal ability. In R.J. Sternberg (Ed.), *Human abilities: An information-processing approach*. New York: Freeman.

Hunt, J.W. (2001, August 31). Mentoring: Wise friends in high places. *Financial Times*, p. 10.

Hunt, N. (1997). Trauma of war. *The Psychologist*, August, 357–360.

Hunt, R.G., Krystofiak, F.J., Meindl, J.R., & Yousry, A.M. (1989). Cognitive style and decision making. *Organisational Behaviour and Human Decision Processes*, 44, 436–453.

Huseman, R.C., Hatfield, J.D., & Miles, E.W. (1987). A new perspective on equity theory: The equity sensitivity construct. *Academy of Management Review*, 12, 222–234.

Hussey, D.E. (1985). Implementing corporate strategy: Using management education and training. *Long Range Planning*, 18, 28–37.

Hwang, K.K. (2005). The third wave of cultural psychology. The indigenous movement. *The Psychologist*, February, 80–83.

Hyman, R. (1994). Anomaly or artifact? Comments on Bem and Honorton. *Psychological Bulletin*, 115, 19–24.

Iaffaldano, M.T., & Muchinsky, P.M. (1985). Job satisfaction and job performance: A meta-analysis. *Psychological Bulletin*, 97, 251–273.

Idzikowski, C. (1984). Sleep and memory. *British Journal of Psychology*, 75, 439–449.

Ilgen, D.R. (1999). Teams embedded in organizations: Some implications. *American Psychologist*, 54, 129–139.

Ilgen, D.R., Fisher, C.D., & Taylor, M.S. (1979). Consequences of individual feedback on behaviour in organisations. *Journal of Applied Psychology*, 64, 349–371.

Immundo, L.V. (1974). Problems associated with managerial mobility. *Personnel Journal*, 53, 910.

Income Data Services (1992). *Performance management* (Study No. 518, November). London: Author.

Independent (1991, December 11). Staff at FT angry over retirements.

Industrial Society (1999). *Coaching* (Report). London: Author.

Insko, C., & Wilson, M. (1977). Interpersonal attraction as a function of social interaction. *Journal of Personality and Social Psychology*, December, 903–911.

Institute of Management (1999). *A workstyle revolution* (report). Milton Keynes, UK: Author.

IRS (1991, September). *Employment trends: No. 495. BT managers hostile to PRP*. London: Author.

Isenberg, D.J. (1986). Group polarisation: A critical review and meta-analysis. *Journal of Personality and Social Psychology*, 50, 1141–1151.

Ivancevich, J.M., & Matteson, M.T. (1988). Promoting the individual's health and well being. In C.L. Cooper & R. Payne. (Eds.), *Causes, coping, and consequences of stress at work*. Chichester, UK: J. Wiley.

Ivancevich, J.M., & McMahon, J.T. (1982). The effects of goal setting, external feedback, and self-generated feedback on outcome variables: A field experiment. *Academy of Management Journal*, June, 359–372.

Jack, A., & Dixon, H. (1993, September 17). What price a corporate halo? *Financial Times*, p. 16.

Jackson, D., & Rothstein, M. (1993). Evaluating personality testing in personnel selection. *The Psychologist*, 6(January), 8–11.

Jackson, E., & Schuler, R.S. (1985). A meta-analysis and conceptual critique of research on role ambiguity and role conflict in work settings. *Organisational Behaviour and Human Decision Processes*, August, 16–78.

Jackson, S.E., Stone, V.K., & Alvarez, E.B. (1993). Socialization and its diversity: The impact of demographics on work team old-timers and newcomers. In L.L. Cummings & B.M. Staw (Eds.), *Research in organizational behaviour* (Vol. 15, p. 64). Greenwich, CT: JAI Press.

Jaeger, A.M. (1986). Organisation development and national culture: Where's the fit? *Academy of Management Review*, January, 178–190.

Jahoda, M. (1979). The impact of unemployment in the 1930s and the 1970s. *Bulletin of the British Psychological Society*, 32, 309–314.

James, C.R. (2003). Designing learning organisations. *Organizational Dynamics*, 32, 46–61.

Janis, I.L. (1972). *Victims of groupthink: A psychological study of foreign policy decisions and fiascos*. Boston, MA: Houghton Mifflin.

Janis, I.L., & Feshbach, S. (1963). Effects of feararousing communication. *Journal of Abnormal and Social Psychology*, 48, 78–92.

Janis, I.L., & Mann, L. (1982). A theoretical framework for decision counselling. In I.L. Janis (Ed.),

Counselling on personal decisions. New Haven, CT: Yale University Press.

Jansen, P.G.W., & Stoop, B.A.M. (2001). The dynamics of assessment center validity: Results of a 7-year study. *Journal of Applied Psychology*, August, 741–753.

Jaques, E. (1990). In praise of hierarchy. *Harvard Business Review*, January–February, 127–133.

Jarrett, C. (2005). Out on a limb. *The Psychologist*, March, p. 126.

Jayaratne, S., & Chess, W.A. (1984). The effects of emotional support on perceived job stress and strain. *Journal of Applied Behavioural Science*, 20, 141–153.

Jehn, K. (1995). A multi-method examination of the benefits and detriments of intragroup conflicts. *Administrative Science Quarterly*, June, 256–282.

Jenkins Jr, G.D., Gupta, N., Mitra, A., & Shaw, J.D. (1998). Are financial incentives related to performance? A meta-analytic review of empirical research. *Journal of Applied Psychology*, October, 777–787.

Jenkins, J. (1974). Remember that old theory of memory? Well, forget it! *American Psychologist*, 29, 785–795.

Jenkins, J.G., & Dallenbach, K.M. (1924). Oblivescence during sleep and waking. *American Journal of Psychology*, 35, 605–612.

Jennings, D.F., & Lumpkin, J.R. (1989). Functioning modeling corporate entrepreneurship: An empirical integrative analysis. *Journal of Management*, 15, 485–502.

Jennings, R., Cox, C., & Cooper, C.L. (1994). *Business elites: The psychology of entrepreneurs and intrapreneurs*. London: Routledge.

Jensen, A.R. (1977). Cumulative deficit in IQ of blacks in the rural South. *Development Psychology*, 13, 184–191.

Johansson, G., & Aronsson, G. (1984). Stress reactions in computerised administrative work. *Journal of Occupational Behaviour*, 5, 159–181.

Johns, G. (1993). Constraints on the adoption of psychology-based personnel practices: Lessons from organizational innovation. *Personnel Psychology*, 46, 596–602.

Johnson, H.H., & Scileppi, I.D. (1969). Effects of ego involvement conditions on attitude change to high and low credibility communications. *Journal of Personality and Social Psychology*, 13, 31–36.

Johnson, R. (2004). Diversity—What women want: The glass ceiling is still a firm fixture in most companies, with women finding it difficult to reach board level. *People Management*, 15 January, 26–30.

Johnson, S.T. (1998). Making a difference. Developing management incentives that drive results. *Compensation and Benefits Review*, July/August, 41–48.

Johnstone, H. (1999, July 6). Woman is awarded £67,000 for stress. *The Times*, p. 7.

Jones, M. (2002, October 30). BP slips on oil production growth target. *Financial Times*.

Jones, M., & Buck, T. (2002, October 30). BP hit by third cut to targets. *Financial Times*.

Jones, E.E., & Davis, K.E. (1965). From acts to dispositions: The attribution process in person perception. In L. Berkowitz (Ed.), *Advances in experimental social psychology, Vol. 12*. New York: Academic Press.

Jordan, P.C. (1986). Effects of an extrinsic reward on intrinsic motivation. *Academy of Management Journal*, June, 405–412.

Joseph, M. (1989). *Sociology for business*. Cambridge, UK: Polity Press.

Judge, T.A. (1993). Does affective disposition moderate the relationship between job satisfaction and voluntary turnover. *Journal of Applied Psychology*, June, 395–401.

Judge, T.A., & Bretz, R.D. (1994). Political influence behaviour and career success. *Journal of Management*, 20, 43–65.

Judge, T.A., & Ferris, G.R. (1993). Social context of performance evaluation decisions. *Academy of Management Journal*, February, 80–105.

Judge, T.A., & Hulin, C.L. (1993). Job satisfaction as a reflection of disposition: A multiple source causal analysis. *Organizational Behaviour and Human Decision Processes*, 56, 388–421.

Judge, T.A., Thoreson, C.J., Bono, J.E., & Patton, G.K. (2001). The job satisfaction–job performance relationship. A qualitative and quantitative review. *Psychological Bulletin*, 127, 376–407.

Jung, C.G. (1923). *Psychological types*. London: Routledge & Kegan Paul.

Jung, C.G. (1965). Analytical psychology. In W. Sahakian (Ed.), *Psychology of personality: Readings in theory*. Chicago: Rand McNally.

Kahn, R.L., Wolfe, D.M., Quinn, R.P., Snoek, J.D., & Rosenthal, R.A. (1964). *Organisational stress*. New York: Wiley.

Kahneman, D., & Tversky, A. (1979). Prospect theory: An analysis of decision under risk. *Econometrica*, 47, 263–291.

Kahneman, D., & Tversky, A. (1984). Choices, values and frames. *American Psychologist*, 39, 341–350.

Kakabadse, A. (1991). *The wealth creators*. London: Kogan Page.

Kakabadse, A. (2002, November 1). Groomed for the top. *FT Mastering Leadership, Part 1*, pp. 10–11.

Kalagnanam, S.S., & Lindsay, R.M. (1998). The use of organic models of control in JIT firms: Generalising Woodward's findings to modern manufacturing practices. *Accounting, Organizations, and Society*, 24, 1–30.

Kamin, L.J. (1976). Heredity, intelligence, politics, and psychology. In N.J. Block & G. Dworkin (Eds.), *The IQ controversy*. New York: Pantheon.

Kandola, R. (1995). Managing diversity: New broom or old hat? In C.L. Cooper & I.T. Robertson (Eds.), *International review of industrial and organizational psychology, Vol. 10*. Chichester, UK: J. Wiley.

Kanfer, R., Ackerman, P.L., Murtha, T.C., & Dugdale, B. (1994). Goal setting, conditions of practice and task performance: A resource allocation perspective. *Journal of Applied Psychology*, 79, 826–835.

Kanji, G.K. (1990). Total quality management: The second industrial revolution. *Total Quality Management*, 1, 3–12.

Kanter, R.M. (1984). *The change masters*. London: Unwin.

Kanter, R.M. (1989). *When giants learn to dance: Mastering the challenges of strategy, management, and careers in the 1990s*. London: Unwin.

Kanter, R.M. (1992). *Address to the Institute of Personnel Management National Conference*. Unpublished. London: Institute of Personnel Management.

Kanter, R.M. (1999). Change is everyone's job: Managing the extended enterprise in a globally connected world. *Organizational Dynamics*, Summer, 7–23.

Kanter, R.M., Stein, B.A., & Jick, T.D. (1992). *The challenge of organizational change*. New York: Free Press.

Kanugo, R.N., & Pang, S. (1973). Effect of human models on perceived product quality. *Journal of Applied Psychology*, 57, 172–178.

Kaplan, R., & Norton, D. (1996). *The balanced scorecard: Translating strategy into action*. Boston, MA: Harvard Business School Press.

Kapstein, J. (1989, August 28). Volvo's radical new plant: The death of the assembly line. *Business Week*, pp. 92–93.

Karasek, R.A. (1979). Job demands, job decision latitude, and mental strain: Implications for job design. *Administrative Science Quarterly*, 24(June), 285–309.

Karasek, R.A. (1990). Lower health risk with increased job control among white-collar workers. *Journal of Organisational Behaviour*, 11, 171–185.

Karlins, M., & Abelson, H. (1970). *Persuasion*. London: Crosby Lockwood.

Kasl, S.V., & Cobb, S. (1970). Blood pressure in men undergoing job loss. *Psychosomatic Medicine*, 32, 19–38.

Katz, D. (1960). The functional approach to the study of attitudes. *Public Opinion Quarterly*, 24, 163–204.

Katz, D., & Kahn, R.L. (1978). *The social psychology of organisations* (2nd ed.). New York: John Wiley.

Katz, E., & Lazarsfield, P.F. (1955). *Personal influence*. New York: Free Press.

Katzell, R.A., Thompson, D.E., & Guzzo, R.A. (1992). How job satisfaction and job performance are or are not linked. In C.J. Cranny, P.C. Smith, & E.F. Stone (Eds.), *Job satisfaction* (pp. 195–217). New York: Lexington Books.

Katzenbach, J.R., & Smith, D.K. (1993). *The wisdom of teams*. Boston, MA: Harvard Business School Press.

Kaufman, B.E. (1990). A new theory of satisficing. *Journal of Behavioural Economics*, Spring, 35–51.

Kay, E. (1974). Middle management. In J. O'Toole (Ed.), *Work and the quality of life*. Cambridge, MA: MIT Press.

Kay, J. (2001, March 7). Peak performance. *Financial Times*.

Kazmin, A. (2005, January 7). Aid comes swiftly but hurt minds will take longer to mend. *Financial Times*, p. 6.

Kearns, J.L. (1973). *Stress in industry*. London: Priory Press.

Kehoe, L. (2001, January 17). Hewlett's rich legacy. *Financial Times*.

Kellar, K.L. (1987). Memory factors in advertising. *Journal of Consumer Research*, 14, 316–333.

Kellaway, L. (1993a, August 20). Legal dangers of stress. *Financial Times*, p. 8.

Kellaway, L. (2000, October 16). Everyone loves a character flaw. *Financial Times*, p. 18.

Kellaway, L. (2003a, December 1). In case you don't know, ignorance is the new knowledge. *Financial Times*, p. 11.

Kellaway, L. (2003b, January 27). Doggone smart. *Financial Times*, p. 12.

Keller, F.S. (1959). The phantom plateaux. *Journal of the Experimental Analysis of Behaviour*, 1, 1–13.

Keller, L.M., Bouchard Jr, T.J., Arvey, R.D., Segal, N.L., & Davis, R.V. (1992). Work values, genetic and environmental influences. *Journal of Applied Psychology*, February, 79–88.

Keller, R.T. (1989). A test of the path–goal theory of leadership, with the need for clarity as a moderator in research and development organisations. *Journal of Applied Psychology*, April, 208–212.

Keller, T., & Dansereau, F. (1995). Leadership empowerment: A social exchange perspective. *Human Relations*, 48, 127–146.

Kellett, D., Fletcher, S., Callen, A., & Geary, B. (1994). Fair testing: The case of British Rail. *The Psychologist*, January, 26–29.

Kelley, H.H. (1950). The warm–cold variable in the first impressions of person. *Journal of Personality*, 18, 431–439.

Kelley, H.H. (1967). *Attribution theory in social psychology*. Nebraska Symposium on Motivation. Lincoln, NE: University of Nebraska Press.

Kelley, H.H. (1971). *Attribution in social interaction*. Morristown, NJ: General Learning Press.

Kelley, R.E. (1988). In praise of followers. *Harvard Business Review*, November–December, 142–148.

Kelly, G.A. (1955). *The psychology of personal constructs*. New York: W.W. Norton.

Kelly, J. (1992). Does job design theory explain job redesign outcomes. *Human Relations*, I, 753–774.

Kelly, J. (2000, December 11). Skills Council targets adult illiteracy. *Financial Times*, p. 6.

Kelman, H.C. (1958). Compliance, identification, and internalization: Three processes of attitude change. *Journal of Conflict Resolution*, *2*, 51–60.

Kelman, H.C. (1969). Patterns of personal involvement in the national system: A social psychological analysis of political legitimacy. In J.N. Rosenau (Ed.), *International politics and foreign policy*. New York: Free Press.

Kenis, I. (1977). Effects of budgetary goal characteristics on managerial attitudes and performance. *The Accounting Review*, October, 707–721.

Kenis, I. (1979). Effects of budgetary goal characteristics on managerial attitudes and performance. *Accounting Review*, October, 707–721.

Kenny, D.A., & DePaulo, B.M. (1993). Do people know how others view them: An empirical and theoretical account. *Psychological Bulletin*, *114*, 145–161.

Kerr, S., & Jermier, J.M. (1978). Substitutes for leadership: Their meaning and measurement. *Organisational Behaviour and Human Performance*, *22*, 375–403.

Kerr, S., Klimoski, R.J., Tolliver, J., & Van Glinow, M.A. (1975). Human information processing. In J. Leslie Livingstone (Ed.), *Managerial accounting: The behavioural foundations*. Columbus, OH: Grid Publishing.

Kets de Vries, M., & Balazs, K. (1996). The human side of downsizing. *European Management Journal*, *14*, 111–120.

Kets de Vries, M.F.R., & Miller, D. (1984). *The neurotic organization*. London: Jossey-Bass.

Keys, B., & Case, T. (1990). How to become an influential manager. *Academy of Management Executive*, *4*, 38–51.

Killgren, L. (2000, August 5/6). Unilever splits operations but denies plans for divorce. *Financial Times*, p. 1.

Kipnis, D., Schmidt, S.M., Swaffin-Smith, C., & Wilkinson, I. (1984). Patterns of managerial influence: Shotgun managers, tacticians, and bystanders. *Organizational Dynamics*, Winter, 58–67.

Kirby, S.L., & Davis, M.A. (1998). A study of escalating commitment in principal–agent relationships: Effects of monitoring and personal responsibility. *Journal of Applied Psychology*, April, 206–217.

Kirkpatrick, D.L. (1967). Evaluation of training. In R.L. Craig & L.R. Bittel (Eds.), *Training and development handbook*. New York: McGraw-Hill.

Kirkpatrick, S.A., & Locke, E.A. (1991). Leadership: Do traits matter? *Academy of Management Executive*, May, 48–60.

Kirkpatrick, S.A., & Locke, E.A. (1996). Direct and indirect effects of three core charismatic leadership components on performance and attitudes. *Journal of Applied Psychology*, February, 36–51.

Kirton, M.J. (1984). Adaptors and innovators: Why new initiatives get blocked. *Long Range Planning*, *17*, 137–143.

Kivimaki, M., & Elovainio, M. (1999). A short version of the team climate inventory: Development and psychometric properties. *Journal of Occupational and Organizational Psychology*, *72*, 241–246.

Klein, H.J. (1989). An integrated theory model of work motivation. *Academy of Management Review*, *14*, 150–172.

Klimoski, R.J., & Rafael, A. (1983). Inferring personal qualities through handwriting analysis. *Journal of Occupational Psychology*, *56*, 191–202.

Kline, P. (1987). Factor analysis and personality theory. *European Journal of Personality*, *1*, 21–36.

Kling, R., & Scacchi, W. (1980). Computing as social action: The social dynamics of computing in complex organisations. *Advances in Computers*, *19*, 249–327.

Kluckhohn, F., & Strodtbeck, F.L. (1961). *Variations in value orientations*. Connecticut: Greenwood Press.

Koeske, G., & Crano, W. (1968). The effect of congruous and incongruous source statement combinations upon the judged credibility of a communication. *Journal of Experimental Social Psychology*, *4*, 384–399.

Koestner, R., Bernieri, F., & Zuckerman, M. (1992). Self-regulation and consistency between attitudes, traits, and behaviors. *Personality and Social Psychology Bulletin*, *18*, 52–59.

Kogan, N., & Wallach, M.A. (1967). Risk taking as a function of the situation, person, and the group. In T.M. Newcombe (Ed.), *New directions in psychology, Vol III*. New York: Holt, Rinehart, & Winston.

Kohler, I. (1962, May). Experiments with goggles. *Scientific American*, 62–72.

Kohler, W. (1927). *The mentality of apes*. London: Routledge.

Kohn, A. (1993). Why incentive plans cannot work. *Harvard Business Review*, September/October, 54–63.

Kohn, A. (1998). Challenging behaviourist dogma. Myths about money and motivation. *Compensation and Benefits Review*, March/April, 27, 33–37.

Kolb, D.A. (1974). On management and the learning process. In D.A. Kolb, I.M. Rubin, & J.M. McIntyre (Eds.), *Organisational psychology* (2nd ed.). New York: Prentice Hall.

Komaki, J., Waddell, W.M., & Pearce, M.G. (1977). The applied behavioural analysis approach and individual employees: Improving performance in two small businesses. *Organisational Behaviour and Human Performance*, *19*, 337–352.

Kondrasuk, J.N. (1981). Studies in MBO effectiveness. *Academy of Management Review*, *6*, 419–430.

Konrad, E. (2000). Changes in work motivation during transition. A case from Slovenia. *Applied Psychology: An International Review*, *49*, 619–635.

Koopman, P.L., Den Hartog, D.N., Konrad, E. et al. (1999). National culture and leadership profiles in Europe: Some results from the GLOBE study. *European Journal of Work and Organizational Psychology*, *8*, 503–520.

Korman, A.K. (1968). The prediction of managerial performance: A review. *Personnel Psychology*, *21*, 295–322.

Kossek, E.E., & Ozeki, C. (1998). Work–family conflict policies, and the job–life satisfaction relationship: A review and directions for organizational behaviour—human resources research. *Journal of Applied Psychology*, *83*, 139–149.

Kothandapani, V. (1971). Validation of feeling, belief, and intention to act as three components of attitude and their contribution to prediction of contraceptive behaviour. *Journal of Personality and Social Psychology*, *19*, 321–333.

Kotter, J.P. (1990). What do leaders really do? *Harvard Business Review*, *68*, 103–111.

Kotter, J.P., & Cohen, D.S. (2002). *The heart of change. Real life stories of how people change their organizations*. Boston, MA: Harvard Business School Press.

Kotter, J.P., & Heskett, J.L. (1992). *Corporate culture and performance*. New York: Free Press/Macmillan.

Kotter, J.P., & Schlesinger, L.A. (1979). Choosing strategies for change. *Harvard Business Review*, March–April, 106–114.

Kozan, M.K. (1989). Cultural influences on styles of handling interpersonal conflicts: Comparisons among Jordanian, Turkish, and US managers. *Human Relations*, *42*, 789–799.

Krause, N., & Stryker, S. (1984). Stress and wellbeing: The buffering role of locus of control beliefs. *Social Science and Medicine*, *18*, 783–790.

Krech, D., Crutchfield, R.S., & Ballachey, E. (1962). *Individual in society*. New York: McGraw-Hill.

Kreitner, R., Kinicki, A., & Buelens, M. (2002). *Organizational behaviour* (2nd European ed.). Maidenhead, UK: McGraw-Hill.

Kristof, A.L. (1996). Person–organization fit: An integrated review of its conceptualisations, measurement, and implications. *Personnel Psychology*, Spring, 1–49.

Krueger, J. (1991). Accentuation effects and illusory change in exemplar based category learning. *European Journal of Social Psychology*, *21*, 37–48.

Kruglanski, A.W., & Thompson, E.P. (1999). Persuasion by a single route. A view from the unimodel. *Psychological Inquiry*, *10*, 83–109.

Kumar, N. (2002, December 2). The path to change. *FT Mastering Leadership, Part 6*, pp. 10–11.

Kuratho, D.F., & Hodgetts, R.M. (1989). *Entrepreneurship: A contemporary approach*. Fort Worth, TX: Dryden Press.

Laiken, M.E. (1994). The myth of the self-managing team. *Organization Development Journal*, *12*, 29–34.

Lambert, R. (1986, March 15). Investment-contrary behaviour. *Financial Times*.

Lamm, H., & Trommsdorff, G. (1973). Group vs. individual performance on tasks requiring ideational proficiency (brainstorming). *European Journal of Social Psychology*, *3*, 361–387.

Landon, E.L. (1972). A sex-role explanation of purchase intention differences of consumers who are high and low in need for achievement. In M. Venkatesan (Ed.), *Proceedings of third annual conference* (pp. 1–8). Association for Consumer Research.

Landon, E.L. (1974). Self-concept, ideal self-concept and consumer purchase intentions. *Journal of Consumer Research*, *1*, 44–51.

Landy, F.J., & Becker, W.S. (1987). Motivation theory reconsidered. *Research in Organisational Behaviour*, *9*, 1–38.

Lane, G.S., & Watson, G.L. (1975). A Canadian replication of Mason Haire's shopping list study. *Journal of the Academy of Marketing Science*, *13*(Spring), 48.

Langly, A. (1989). In search of rationality: The purposes behind the use of formal analysis in organizations. *Administrative Science Quarterly*, December, 598–631.

LaPiere, R.T. (1934). Attitudes vs. actions. *Social Forces*, *13*, 230–237.

Larson, C.E., & La Fasto, F.M.J. (1989). *Team-work*. London: Sage.

Larson, E.W., & Gobeli, D.H. (1987). Matrix management: Contradictions and insights. *California Management Review*, Summer, 126–138.

Latane, B., & Darley, J. (1968). Group inhibition of bystander intervention in emergencies. *Journal of Personality and Social Psychology*, *10*, 215–221.

Latane, B., Williams, K., & Harkins, S. (1979). Many hands make light the work: The causes and consequences of "social loafing". *Journal of Personality and Social Psychology*, *37*, 822–832.

Lately, P. (1982). Computing can damage your health. *Practical Computing*, July, 126–127.

Latham, G.P. (1988). Human resource training and development. *Annual Review of Psychology*, *39*, 545–582.

Latham, G.P., Almost J., Mann, S., & Moore, C. (2005). New developments in performance management. *Organizational Dynamics*, *34*, 77–87.

Latham, G.P., & Dossett, D.L. (1978). Designing incentive plans for unionised employees: A comparison of continuous and variable ratio reinforcement schedules. *Personnel Psychology*, *31*, 47–61.

Latham, G.P., & Locke, E. (1979). Goal-setting: A motivational technique that works. *Organizational Dynamics*, Autumn, 68–80.

Latham, G.P., & Saari, L.M. (1984). Do people do what they say? Further studies on the situational interview. *Journal of Applied Psychology*, *69*, 309–314.

Latham, G.P., Skarlicki, D., & Siegel, J.P. (1993). The increasing importance of performance appraisals to employee effectiveness in organizational settings in North America. In C.L. Cooper & I.T. Robertson (Eds.), *International review of industrial and organizational psychology* (Vol. 8). Chichester, UK: J. Wiley.

Latham, G.P., & Steele, T.P. (1983). The motivational effects of participation versus goal-setting on performance. *Academy of Management Journal*, September, 406–417.

Latham, G.P., & Wexley, K.N. (1981). *Increasing productivity through performance appraisal*. Reading, MA: Addison-Wesley.

Lau, R.R. (1982). Origins of health locus of control beliefs. *Journal of Personality and Social Psychology*, *42*, 322–334.

Lawler, E.E. (1977). Reward systems. In J.R. Hackman & J.L. Suttle (Eds.), *Improving life at work*. Glenview, IL: Scott, Foresman.

Lawler, E.E. (1981). *Pay and organisation development*. Reading, MA: Addison-Wesley.

Lawler, E.E. (1984). Whatever happened to incentive pay? *New Management*, *1*, 37–41.

Lawler, E.E., Ledford, G.E., & Chang, L. (1993). Who uses skill-based pay and why? *Compensation and Benefits Review*, March/April, 22.

Lawler, E.E., Mohrman, A.M., & Resnick, S.M. (1984). Performance appraisal revisited. *Organizational Dynamics*, *13*(Summer), 20–35.

Lawrence, P.R., & Lorsch, J.W. (1969). *Organisations and environment: Managing differentiation and integration*. Homewood, IL: Irwin.

Lazarus, R.S. (1966). *Psychological stress and the coping process*. New York: McGraw-Hill.

Lazarus, R.S. (1971). *Personality*. New York: Prentice Hall.

Lazarus, R., & Lazarus, B. (1994). *Passion and reason*. New York: Oxford University Press.

Leavitt, H.J. (1951). Some effects of certain communication patterns on group performance. *Journal of Abnormal and Social Psychology*, *46*, 38–50.

Leavitt, H.J. (2003). Why hierarchies thrive. *Harvard Business Review*, March, 96–1022.

Leavitt, H.J., & Whisler, T.L. (1958). Management in the 1980s. *Harvard Business Review*, *36*, 41–48.

Lebaron, D., & Vaitilingam, R. (1999). *The ultimate investor*. Oxford, UK: Capstone Publishing.

Lebovits, B.Z., Shekelle, R.B., & Ostfeld, A.M. (1967). Prospective and retrospective studies of CHD. *Psychosomatic Medicine*, *29*, 265–272.

Ledger, W. (2002, September 16). Universal answer to a global question. *London Evening Standard*, p. 38.

Lee, R., & Lawrence, P. (1985). *Organisational behaviour: Psychology and work*. London: Hutchinson.

Lee, R.T., & Ashforth, B.E. (1990). On the meaning of Maslach's three dimensions of burnout. *Journal of Applied Psychology*, December, 743–747.

Lee, T. (1993, November 3). Managing your career. *Wall Street Journal*, B3.

Lee, T.W., & Mowday, R.T. (1987). Voluntarily leaving an organisation: An empirical investigation of Steers and Mowday's model of turnover. *Academy of Management Journal*, December, 721–743.

Lefkowitz, J. (1994). Sex-related differences in job attitudes and dispositional variables: Now you see them. *Academy of Management Journal*, *37*, 323–349.

Leibowitz, Z.B., & Schlossberg, N.K. (1981). Training managers for their role in a career development system. *Training and Development Journal*, July, 72–79.

Lengnick-Hall, C.A. (1986). Technology advances in batch production and improved competitive position. *Journal of Management*, Spring, 75–90.

Lengnick-Hall, M.L. (1995). Sexual harassment research: A methodological critique. *Personnel Psychology*, Winter, 841–864.

Leonard, P. (1984). *Personality and ideology: Toward a materialist understanding of the individual*. London: Macmillan.

Leventhal, H., Watts, J.C., & Pagano, F. (1967). Effects of fear and instructions on how to cope with danger. *Journal of Personality and Social Psychology*, *6*, 313–321.

Leventhal, H.R., Singer, P., & Jones, S. (1965). Effects of fear and specificity of recommendation upon attitudes and behaviour. *Journal of Personality and Social Psychology*, *2*, 20–29.

Levy, J. (1985). Right brain, left brain: Facts and fiction. *Psychology Today*, May, 44.

Lewin, K. (1951). *Field theory in social science*. New York: Harper & Row.

Lewin, K. (1958). Group decision and social change. In E.E. Maccoby, T.M. Newcombe, & R.L. Hartley (Eds.), *Readings in social psychology* (3rd ed.). New York: Holt.

Lewin, K. (1964). The psychology of a successful figure. In H.S. Leavitt & L.R. Pondy (Eds.), *Readings in managerial psychology*. Chicago: University of Chicago Press.

Lewis, C. (1984). What's new in selection. *Personnel Management*, January, 14–16.

Lewis, D.J., & Duncan, C.P. (1956). Effect of different percentages of money reward on extinction of a lever pulling response. *Journal of Experimental Psychology*, *52*, 23–27.

Leymann, H. (1996). The content and development of bullying at work. *European Journal of Work and Organizational Psychology*, *5*, 65–184.

Libby, R., & Lewis, B.L. (1982). Human information processing research in accounting: The state of the art in 1982. *Accounting, Organisations and Society*, *7*, 231–285.

Liberman, S. (1956). The effects of changes in roles on the attitudes of role occupants. *Human Relations*, *9*, 385–402.

Liden, R.C., Wayne, S.J., & Stilwell, D. (1993). A longitudinal study of the early development of leader–member exchanges. *Journal of Applied Psychology*, August, 662–674.

Lieberman, M.A., Yalom, I.D., & Miles, M.B. (1973). Encounter: The leader makes a difference. *Psychology Today*, March, 69–76.

Liebowitz, S.J., & De Meuse, K.P. (1982). The application of team-building. *Human Relations*, January, 1–18.

Likert, R. (1932). A technique for the measurement of attitudes. *Archives of Psychology*, *22*, 1–55.

Likert, R. (1961). *New patterns of management*. New York: McGraw-Hill.

Likert, R. (1967). *The human organisation*. New York: McGraw-Hill.

Linder, J., Jarvenpaa, S., & Davenport, T. (2003). Toward an innovation sourcing strategy. *Sloan Management Review*, *44*(4), 43–94.

Lindsey, F. (1980). Accident-proneness: Does it exist? *Occupational Safety and Health*, *10*(February), 8–9.

Lippit, R., & White, R. (1968). Leader behaviour and member reaction in three social climates. In D. Cartwright & A. Zander (Eds.), *Group dynamics —research and theory*. London: Tavistock.

Litterer, J.A. (1973). *The analysis of organisations* (2nd ed.). New York: Wiley.

Littlefield, D. (1999) "Kerry's heroes", *People Management*, *5* (6 May), 48–50.

Locke, E.A. (1968). Toward a theory of task performance and incentives. *Organisational Behaviour and Human Performance*, *3*, 157–189.

Locke, E.A. (1976). The nature and causes of job satisfaction. In M.D. Dunnette (Ed.), *Handbook of industrial and organisational psychology*. Chicago: Rand McNally.

Locke, E.A. (1977). The myths of behaviour modelling in organisations. *Academy of Management Review*, *4*, 543–553.

Locke, E.A. (1991). The motivation sequence, the motivation hub, and the motivation core. *Organizational Behaviour and Human Decision Processes*, December, 288–299.

Loewenthal, K.M. (2001). *An introduction to psychological tests and scales* (2nd ed.). Hove, UK: Psychology Press.

Loftus, E.F. (1975). Leading questions and the eyewitness report. *Cognitive Psychology*, *7*, 560–572.

Loftus, E.F. (2001). Imagining the past. *The Psychologist*, *14*, 584–587.

Logie, R.H. (1999). State of the art: Working memory. *The Psychologist*, April, 174–179.

London, S. (2002, January 10). A most harmonious collaboration. *Financial Times*, p. 13.

London, S. (2004a, May 17). The art of constructive conflict. *Financial Times*, p. 9.

London, S. (2004b, September 27). Intel's success involves a series of key strokes. Special Report on the Future of Work. *Financial Times*, p. 2.

Long, R.J. (1987). *New office information technology: Human and managerial implications*. London: Croom Helm.

Longenecker, C. (1997). Why managerial performance appraisals are ineffective: Causes and lessons. *Career Development International*, 2.

Lord, R.G., DeVader, C.L., & Alliger, G.M. (1986). A meta analysis of the relation between personality traits and leadership perceptions: An application of validity generalization procedures. *Journal of Applied Psychology*, *71*, 402–410.

Lord, R.G., & Hanges, P.J. (1987). A control system model of organisational motivation: Theoretical development and applied implications. *Behavioural Science*, *32*, 161–178.

Lord, R.G., & Hohenfeld, J.A. (1979). Longitudinal field assessment of equity effects on the performance of major league baseball players. *Journal of Applied Psychology*, February, 19–26.

Lord, R.G., & Kernan, M.C. (1987). Scripts as determinants of purposeful behaviour in organisations. *Academy of Management Review*, *12*, 265–277.

Lorenz, C. (1993a, July 23). TQM: Alive and kicking in the US. *Financial Times*, p. 15.

Lorenz, C. (1993b, November 10). 3M's Europe-wide reorganisation (here, there and everywhere). *Financial Times*, p. 11.

Lorenz, C. (1993c, October 25). Strategic alliances (a meeting of minds). *Financial Times*, p. 15.

Lorenz, C. (1993d, May 24). Process re-engineering is sweeping across the Atlantic. *Financial Times*, p. 11.

Lorenz, C. (1993e, October 4). Corporate creativity: No less than rebirth. *Financial Times*, p. 10.

Lorenz, C. (1994a, December 16). Ford's global matrix gamble. *Financial Times*, p. 13.

Lorenz, C. (1994b, December 5). Pioneers and prophets: Tom Burns. *Financial Times*.

Lorenz, C., & Lorenz, C. (1989, November 13). Business ethics: Will the practice ever emulate the theory? *Financial Times*.

Lowe, E.A., & Shaw, R.W. (1968). An analysis of managerial biasing: Evidence from a company's budgeting process. *Journal of Management Studies*, *5*(October), 304–315.

Lowe, E.A., & Shaw, R.W. (1970). The accuracy of short-term business forecasting: An analysis of a firm's sales budgeting. *Journal of Industrial Economics*, *18*, 275–289.

Lowin, A. (1968). Participative decision making: A model, literature critique, and prescription for research. *Organisational Behaviour and Human Performance*, *3*, 69–106.

Lukes, S. (1974). *Power: A radical review*. London: Macmillan.

Lupton, T. (1963). *On the shop floor*. Oxford, UK: Pergamon.

Luthans, F., & Kreitner, R. (1975). *Organisational behaviour modification*. Glenview, IL: Scott, Foresman.

Lykken, D.T. (1974). Psychology and the lie detection industry. *American Psychologist, 29*, 725–739.

Lynch, D. (1986). Is the brain stuff still the right (or left) stuff. *Training and Development Journal*, February, 23–26.

Mabe, P.A., & West, S.G. (1982). Validity of self-evaluation of ability: A review and meta-analysis. *Journal of Applied Psychology*, June, 280–296.

MacCrone, I.D. (1957). *Race attitudes in South Africa*. London: Oxford University Press.

Mackay, C. (1980). *Human factor aspects of visual display unit operation*. London: HMSO.

Mackay, C., & Cox, T. (1984). Occupational stress associated with visual display unit operation. In B.G. Pearce (Ed.), *Health hazards of VDUs*. Chichester, UK: Wiley.

Mackay, C.J., & Cooper, C.L. (1987). Occupational stress and health: Some current issues. In C.L. Cooper & I.T. Robertson (Eds.), *International review of industrial and organisational psychology*. Chichester, UK: Wiley.

Mackay, K. (1973). *An introduction to psychology*. London: Macmillan.

Macy, B.A., & Igumi, H. (1993). Organizational change, design, and work innovations: A meta-analysis of 131 North American field studies, 1961–1991. In W. Pasmore & R. Woodman (Eds.), *Research in organizational change and development* (Vol. 7, pp. 235–313). Greenwich, CT: JAI Press.

Maddocks, J. (1998). Thinking ahead: The future of psychometrics and other approaches to assessment matters. *The National Journal of Vocational Assessment, 7*, 3–4.

Madge, N. (1983). Unemployment and its effects on children. *Journal of Child Psychology and Psychiatry, 24*, 311–319.

Madison, D.L., Allen, R.W., Porter, L.W., Renwick, P.A., & Mayes, B.T. (1980). Organisational politics: An exploration of managers' perceptions. *Human Relations*, February, 79–100.

Mahoney, J. (1997). Gifts, grease and graft. In *Mastering management: Module 11. Business ethics* (pp. 371–374). London: FT/Pitman Publishing.

Maio, G.R. (2002). Values, truth, and meaning. (Spearman Medal Lecture). *The Psychologist, 15*, 296–299.

Maitland, A. (1998, April 21). Benefits all round, thanks to flexible work options. *Financial Times*, p. 22.

Maitland, A. (1999a, January 26). Corporate ethics: A code to export better practice. *Financial Times*, p. 14.

Maitland, A. (1999b, January 21). From ordeal survivor to ideal adaptor. *Financial Times*, p. 14.

Maitland, A. (2003, 25 July). Read the signals on the fast track to executive failure. *Financial Times*, p. 10.

Maitland, A. (2004a, May 17). Shake-ups that leave us shaken but not stirred. *Financial Times*.

Maitland, A. (2004b, September 9). Virtual teams endeavour to build trust. *Financial Times*, p. 13.

Makin, P., Cooper, C., & Cox, C. (1989). *Managing people at work*. London: Routledge/British Psychological Society.

Makin, P., Cooper, C., & Cox, C. (1996). *Organizations and the psychological contract*. Leicester, UK: BPS Books.

Mander, J.M., & Parker, R.E. (1976). Memory for descriptive and spatial information in complex pictures. *Journal of Experimental Psychology: Human Learning and Memory, 2*, 38–48.

Mandler, G., & Pearlstone, Z. (1966). Free and constrained concept learning and subsequent recall. *Journal of Verbal Learning and Verbal Behavior, 5*, 126–131.

Mann, R.B., & Decker, P.J. (1984). The effect of key behaviour distinctiveness on generalisation and recall in behaviour modelling training. *Academy of Management Journal, 27*, 900–910.

Mann, R.D. (1959). A review of the relationship between personality and performance in small groups. *Psychological Bulletin, 56*, 241–270.

Manz, C.C., & Sims, H.P. (1993). *Business without bosses: How self-managing teams are building high performance companies*. New York: John Wiley.

Manzoni, J.F. (2001, October 15). Managing change: How to avoid the seven deadly sins. *FT Mastering People Management, Part 1*, pp. 6, 8.

March, J.G., & Simon, H.A. (1958). *Organisations*. New York: Wiley.

Marchington, M. (1987). Employee participation. In B. Towers (Ed.), *A handbook of industrial relations practice*. London: Kogan Page.

Margerison, C.J., & McCann, D. (1995). *Team management: Practical new approaches*. Cirencester, UK: Management Books 2000.

Margolis, B.L., Kroes, W.H., & Quinn, R.P. (1974). Job stress: An unlisted occupational hazard. *Journal of Occupational Medicine, 16*, 654–661.

Marsden, R. (1993). The politics of organizational analysis. *Organization Studies, 14*, 93–124.

Marsh, P. (2001, June 8). Industry's weakness blamed on management practices. *Financial Times*, p. 5.

Marsh P. (2004, March 5). Manufacturer switches work from Thailand to Britain to cut costs. *Financial Times*, p. 6.

Marshall, J., & Cooper, C.L. (1976). *The mobile manager and his wife*. Bradford, UK: MCB Publications.

Martin, N. (2002). happiness, happiness. *The Psychologist, 15*, 309.

Marx, E. (1999). *Breaking through culture shock.* London: Nicholas Brealey Publishing.

Masie, E. (1999) "Joined-up thinking", *People Management, 5*, 32–6.

Maslow, A.H. (1954). *Motivation and personality* (3rd ed.). New York: Harper & Row.

Maslow, C., Yoselson, K., & London, M. (1971). Persuasiveness of confidence expressed via language and body language. *British Journal of Social and Clinical Psychology, 10*, 234–240.

Maslyn, J.M., & Uhl-Bien, M. (2001). Leader–member exchanges and its dimensions: Effects of self-effort and other's efforts on relationship quality. *Journal of Applied Psychology*, August, 697–708.

Matlin, M.W., & Foley, H.J. (1992). *Sensation and perception* (3rd ed.). Needham Heights, MA: Allyn & Bacon.

Matsumoto, Y.S. (1970). Social stress and coronary heart disease in Japan: An hypothesis. *Millbank Memorial Fund Quarterly, 48*, 9–36.

Matthews, K.A., & Haynes, S.G. (1986). Type A behaviour pattern and coronary disease risk: Update and critical evaluation. *American Journal of Epidemiology, 123*, 923–959.

Mayer, R.C., Davis, J.H., & Schoorman, F.D. (1995). An integrative model of organizational trust. *Academy of Management Review*, July, 715.

Mayes, B.T., & Allen, R.W. (1977). Toward a definition of organisational politics. *Academy of Management Review*, October, 672–678.

Maylor, E.A. (1996). Older people's memory for the past and the future. *The Psychologist*, October, 456–459.

Mayo, E. (1949). *The social problems of an industrial civilization.* London: Routledge & Kegan Paul.

Mayo, M., Pastor, J.C., & Meindl, J.R. (1996). The effects of group heterogeneity on the self-perceived efficacy of group leaders. *Leadership Quarterly*, Summer, 265–284.

Maznevski, M.L. (1994). Understanding our differences: Performance in decision making groups with diverse members. *Human Relations, 47*, 531–552.

McAdams, D.P. (1992). The five-factor model in personality: A critical appraisal. *Journal of Personality, 60*, 329–361.

McBriarty, M.A. (1988). Performance appraisal: Some unintended consequences. *Public Personnel Management*, Winter, 423.

McCann, J.F. (1981). Control Data's Staywell programme. *Training and Development Journal*, October, 39–43.

McClelland, D.C. (1967). *The achieving society.* New York: Free Press.

McClelland, D.C. (1970). The two faces of power. *Journal of International Affairs, 24*(1), 29–47.

McClelland, D.C. (1975a). Good guys make bum bosses. *Psychology Today*, December, 69–70.

McClelland, D.C. (1975b). *Power: The inner experience.* New York: Irvington.

McClelland, D.C., & Boyatzis, R.E. (1982). Leadership motive pattern and long-term success in management. *Journal of Applied Psychology, 67*, 737–743.

McConnell, J.V., Cutier, R.L., & McNeil, E.B. (1958). Subliminal stimulation: An overview. *American Psychologist, 13*, 229–242.

McCormick, D.W. (1994). Spirituality and management. *Journal of Managerial Psychology, 9*, 5.

McCrae, R.R., & Costa, P.T. (1997). Personality trait structure as a human universal. *American Psychologist, 52*, 509–516.

McCune, J.C. (1996). The intranet: Beyond e-mail. *Management Review*, November, 23–27.

McEvoy, G.M., & Buller, P.F. (1987). User acceptance of peer appraisals in an industrial setting. *Personnel Psychology, 40*, 785–797.

McFarlin, D.B., & Sweeney, P.D. (1992). Distributive and procedural justice as predictors of satisfaction with personal and organizational outcomes. *Academy of Management Journal*, August, 626–637.

McGinnies, E. (1949). Emotionality and perceptual defence. *Psychological Review, 56*, 244–251.

McGookin, S. (1993, November 19). Graphology: A waste of money. *Financial Times*, p. 12.

McGrath, J.E. (1976). Stress and behaviour in organisations. In M.D. Dunnett (Ed.), *Handbook of industrial and organisational psychology*. Chicago: Rand McNally.

McGregor, D. (1960). *The human side of enterprise.* New York: McGraw-Hill.

McGuire, W.J. (1968). Personality and susceptibility to social influence. In E. Borgatta & W.W. Lambert (Eds.), *Handbook of personality theory and research, Vol. 3.* Chicago: Rand McNally.

McKee, V. (1999, February 6). How studying Shakespeare's *Henry V* can teach inspirational leadership. *The Times*, p. 27.

McKenna, E. (1978). *The management style of the chief accountant.* Farnborough, UK: Saxon House.

McKenna, E., & Beech, N. (2002). *Human resource management: A concise analysis.* Harlow, UK: FT/Prentice Hall (Pearson Education).

McLeod, J. (1997). *Narrative and psychotherapy.* London: Sage.

McMurray, R.N. (1973). The executive neurosis. In R.L. Noland (Ed.), *Industrial mental health and employee counselling.* New York: Behavioural Publications.

Mead, M. (1935). *Sex and temperament in three primitive societies.* New York: William Morrow.

Meadows, I.S.G. (1980a). Organic structure and innovation in small work groups. *Human Relations, 33*, 369–382.

Meadows, I.S.G. (1980b). Organic structure, satisfaction and personality. *Human Relations, 33*, 383–392.

Meindl, J.R., & Ehrlich, S.B. (1987). The romance of leadership and the evaluation of organizational performance. *Academy of Management Journal, 30*, 91–109.

Melhuish, A.H. (1977). Causes and prevention of executive stress. *Occupational Health, 29*, 193–197.

Memon, A., & Wright, D.B. (1999). Eyewitness testimony and the Oklahoma bombing. *The Psychologist*, June, 292–295.

Menon, S.J. (2001). Employee empowerment: An integrative psychological approach. *Applied Psychology: An International Review, 50*, 153–180.

Mento, A.J., Lock, E.A., & Klein, H.J. (1992). Relationship of goal level to valence and instrumentality. *Journal of Applied Psychology, 77*, 395–405.

Menzies, R. (1937). Conditioned vasomotor response in human subjects. *Journal of Psychology, 4*, 75–120.

Merchant, K.A. (1981). The design of the corporate budgeting system: Influences on managerial behaviour and performance. *Accounting Review*, October, 813–829.

Merrick, N. (2004). Modern romance: Employers are about to be urged to take another look at modern apprenticeships, but are they less cumbersome and bureaucratic now. *People Management*, 25, March, 16–17.

Merton, R.K. (1957). *Social theory and social structure*. Glencoe, IL: Free Press.

Meyer, G.W. (1994). Social information processing and social networks: A test of social mechanisms. *Human Relations*, September, 1013–1045.

Meyer, H.H. (1991). A solution to the performance appraisal feedback enigma. *Academy of Management Executive*, February, 68–76.

Meyer, J. (2001). Action research. In N. Fulop, P. Allen, A. Clarke, & N. Black (Eds.), *Studying the organization and delivery of health services: Research methods*. London: Routledge.

Meyer, J.J. (2000). The future of flexible benefit plans. *Employee Benefits Journal*, June, 3–7.

Meyer, J.P. (1997). Organizational commitment. In C.L. Cooper & I.T. Robertson (Eds.), *International review of industrial and organizational psychology, Vol. 12*. Chichester, UK: J. Wiley.

Meyer, J.P., & Gellatly, J.R. (1988). Perceived performance norm as a mediator in the effect of assigned goal on personal goal and task performance. *Journal of Applied Psychology, 73*, 410–420.

Michaels, A. (2004, June 4). The downside to staying public. *Financial Times*, p. 10.

Michaelsen, L.K., Watson, W.E., & Black, R.H. (1989). A realistic test of individual versus group consensus decision making. *Journal of Applied Psychology*, October, 834–839.

Midgley, D. (2004). The management style of Roman Abramovich (proprietor of Chelsea FC). *Management Today*, November, 76–83.

Milani, K. (1975). The relationship of participation in budget setting to industrial supervisor performance and attitudes: A field study. *Accounting Review*, April, 274–284.

Miles, R.E. (1965). Human relations or human resources. *Harvard Business Review, 43*, 148–163.

Miles, R.E., & Snow, C.C. (1986). Organisations: New concepts for new forms. *California Management Review, 28*, 62–73.

Miles, R.E., & Snow, C.C. (1995). The new network firm: A spherical structure built on human investment philosophy. *Organizational Dynamics*, Spring, 5–18.

Miles, R.H. (1980). *Macro organisational behaviour*. Glenview, IL: Scott, Foresman.

Milgram, S. (1965). Some conditions of obedience and disobedience to authority. *Human Relations, 18*, 57–76.

Miller, D. (1994). What happens after success?: The perils of excellence. *Journal of Management Studies*, May, 11–38.

Miller, E.J., & Rice, A.K. (1967). *Systems of organisation: The control of task and sentient boundaries*. London: Tavistock.

Miller, G.A. (1956). The magical number seven, plus or minus two: Some limits in our capacity for processing information. *Psychological Review, 63*, 81–97.

Miller, K.I., & Monge, P. (1986). Participation, satisfaction, and productivity: A meta-analytic review. *Academy of Management Journal*, March, 748.

Miller, S.M., & Magnan, C.E. (1983). Interacting effects of information and coping style in adapting to gynaecologic stress: Should the doctor tell all? *Journal of Personality and Social Psychology, 45*, 223–236.

Milton, J., & Wiseman, R. (1999). Does psi exist? Lack of replication of an anomalous process of information transfer. *Psychological Bulletin, 125*, 387–391.

Miner, F.C. (1984). Group versus individual decision making: An investigation of performance measures, decision strategies and process losses/gains. *Organisational Behaviour and Human Performance*, February, 112–124.

Miner, J.B. (1978). Twenty years of research on role motivation theory of managerial effectiveness. *Personnel Psychology, 31*, 739–760.

Miner, J.B. (1980). *Theories of organisational behaviour*. Fort Worth, TX: Dryden Press.

Mintzberg, H. (1979). *The structuring of organisations*. New York: Prentice Hall.

Mintzberg, H. (1980). *The nature of managerial work*. New York: Prentice Hall.

Mintzberg, H. (1981). Organisation design: Fashion or fit. *Harvard Business Review*, January–February, 103–116.

Mintzberg, H. (1983a). *Power in and around organisations*. New York: Prentice Hall.

Mintzberg, H. (1983b). *Structures in fives: Designing effective organizations*. Englewood Cliffs, NJ: Prentice Hall.

Mintzberg, H., Raisinghani, D., & Theoret, A. (1976). The structure of unstructured decision processes. *Administrative Science Quarterly*, *21*, 246–275.

Mischel, W. (1968). *Personality and assessment*. New York: Wiley.

Mischel, W. (1973). Toward a cognitive social learning reconceptualisation of personality. *Psychological Review*, *80*, 252–283.

Mischel, W., & Shoda, Y. (1995). A cognitive-affective system theory of personality: Reconceptualising situations, dispositions, dynamics, and invariance in personality structure. *Psychological Review*, *102*, 246–268.

Mitchell, D. (1989). 1992: The implications for management. *Long-range Planning*, *22*, 32–40.

Mitchell, T.R. (1982). Motivation: New directions for theory, research, and practice. *Academy of Management Review*, January, 80–88.

Mitroff, I. et al. (1974). On managing science in the systems' age: Two schemes for the study of science as a whole systems' phenomenon. *Interfaces*, *4*, 50.

Mitroff, I.I., & Kilmann, R.H. (1976). On organisation stories: An approach to the design and analysis of organisation through myths and stories. In R.H. Kilmann, L.R. Pondy, & D.P. Slevin (Eds.), *The management of organisation design, Vol. 1*. New York: Elsevier/North-Holland.

Mohrman, S.A., Cohen, S.G., & Mohrman Jr., A.M. (1995). *Designing team-based organizations*. San Francisco: Jossey-Bass.

Monk, T., & Tepas, D. (1985). Shift work. In C.L. Cooper & M.J. Smith (Eds.), *Job stress and blue-collar work*. Chichester, UK: Wiley.

Montagnon, P. (1998, October 14). Public turning against the use of bribery. *Financial Times*, p. 7.

Montanari, J.R. (1978). Managerial discretion: An expanded model of organisational choice. *Academy of Management Review*, April, 231–241.

Montanari, J.R., & Moorhead, G. (1989). Development of the groupthink assessment inventory. *Educational and Psychological Measurement*, *49*, 209–219.

Moore, T. (1987, December 21). Goodbye corporate staff. *Fortune*, pp. 65–76.

Moore, T.E. (1982). Subliminal advertising: What you see is what you get. *Journal of Marketing*, *46*, 38–47.

Moorhead, G. (1981). Organisational analysis: An integration of the macro and micro approaches. *Journal of Management Studies*, April, 191–218.

Moorhead, G., Ferrence, R.K., & Neck, C.P. (1991). Group decision fiascos continue: Space shuttle "Challenger" and a revised groupthink framework. *Human Relations*, *44*, 539–550.

Moorhead, G., & Griffin, R.W. (1989). *Organizational behaviour* (2nd ed.). Boston, MA: Houghton Mifflin.

Moorhead, G., & Griffin, R.W. (1998). *Organisational behaviour* (5th ed.). Boston, MA: Houghton Mifflin.

Moorhead, G., & Griffin, R.W. (2004). *Organizational behaviour: Managing people and organisations* (7th ed.). Boston, MA: Houghton Mifflin.

Moreno, J.L. (1953). *Who shall survive?* New York: Beacon.

Morgan, G. (1983). More on metaphor: Why we cannot control tropes in administrative science. *Administrative Science Quarterly*, *28*, 605–622.

Morgan, M.A., Hall, D.T., & Martier, A. (1979). Career development strategies in industry: Where are we and where should we be? *Personnel*, March/April, 13–30.

Morgan, R.E. (2003). Outsourcing: Towards the shamrock organisation. *Journal of General Management*, *29*, 35–52.

Morley, I. (1984). Bargaining and negotiation. In C.L. Cooper & P. Makin (Eds.), *Psychology for managers* (2nd ed.). Basingstoke, UK: British Psychological Society/Macmillan.

Morris, J.N. (1956). Job rotation. *Journal of Business*, October, 268–273.

Morris, M.W., & Peng, K.P. (1994). Culture and cause: American and Chinese attributions for social and physical events. *Journal of Personality and Social Psychology*, *67*, 949–971.

Morse, N.C., & Reimer, E. (1956). The experimental change of a major organisational variable. *Journal of Abnormal and Social Psychology*, *52*, 120–129.

Moscovici, S., & Zavalloni, M. (1969). The group as polarizer of attitudes. *Journal of Personality and Social Psychology*, June, 125–135.

Mottaz, C.J. (1988). Determinants of organisational commitment. *Human Relations*, *41*, 467–482.

Moules, J. (2004a, March 27/28). Social goals go hand in hand with success for top companies. *Financial Times*, p. 3.

Moules, J. (2004b, November 17). CBI urges freezing of minimum wage. *Financial Times*, p. 2.

Moules, J. (2004c, October 11). More opting for outside helping hand. *Financial Times*, Special Report: Professional Development, p. 2.

Mowday, R.T., Porter, L.W., & Steers, R.M. (1982). *Employee–organisation linkages: The psychology of commitment, absenteeism, and turnover*. New York: Academic Press.

Mueller, F., Proctor, S., & Buchanan D. (2003). Teamworking in its context(s): Antecedents, nature and dimensions. *Human Relations*, *53*, 1387–1424.

Muir, H. (2003, January 8). Even the men say women are far better bosses. *London Evening Standard*, p. 17.

Mulder, M., de Jong, R.D., Kippelaar, L., & Verhage, J. (1986). Power, situation, and leaders' effectiveness: An organisational field study. *Journal of Applied Psychology*, November, 566–570.

Mullen, B., & Cooper, C. (1994). The relation between group cohesiveness and performance: An integration. *Psychological Bulletin*, March, 210–227.

Mullins, L.J. (1999). *Management and organisational behaviour* (5th ed.). London: FT/Pitman Publishing.

Mullins, L.J. (2002). *Management and organisational behaviour* (6th ed.). Harlow, UK: Pearson Education.

Mumford, A. (1987). Myths and reality in developing directors. *Personnel Management*, February, 29–33.

Mumford, E., & Banks, O. (1967). *The computer and the clerk*. London: Routledge & Kegan Paul.

Mumford, E., & Hendricks, R. (1996). Business process re-engineering RIP. *People Management*, 2, 22–28.

Munter, M. (1993). Cross cultural communication for managers. *Business Horizons*, May–June, 75–76.

Murlis, H., & Fitt, D. (1991). Job evaluation in a changing world. *Personnel Management*, May, 39–44.

Murphy, G.C., & Athanasou, J.A. (1999). The effect of unemployment on mental health. *Journal of Occupational and Organizational Psychology*, 72, 83–99.

Murphy, L.R. (1984). Occupational stress management: A review and appraisal. *Journal of Occupational Psychology*, 57, 1–15.

Murray, B., & Gerhart, B. (1998). An empirical performance of a skill-based pay programme and plant performance outcomes. *Academy of Management Journal*, February, 68–78.

Murray-Bruce, D.J. (1983). Promoting the healthy banker: Stress. *Journal of the Institute of Bankers*, April, 62–63.

Murray-Bruce, D.J. (1990). *Promoting employee health*. Basingstoke, UK: Macmillan.

Myer, J.P., Paunonen, S.V., Gellatly, I.R., Goffin, R.D., & Jackson, D.N. (1989). Organisational commitment and job performance: It's the nature of the commitment that counts. *Journal of Applied Psychology*, 74, 152–156.

Myers, I.B. (1962). *Myers-Briggs type indicator*. Palo Alto, CA: Consulting Psychologists Press.

Myers, J.H., & Reynolds, W. (1967). *Consumer behaviour and marketing management*. Boston, MA: Houghton, Mifflin.

Nadler, D.A. (1983). Concepts for the management of organisational change. In J.R. Hackman, E.E. Lawler III, & L.W. Porter (Eds.), *Perspectives on behaviour in organisations* (2nd ed.). New York: McGraw-Hill.

Nagy, M.S. (2002). Using a single item approach to measure facet job satisfaction. *Journal of Occupational and Organizational Psychology*, 75, 77–86.

Nakamoto, M. (1993, December 1). When seniority is replaced by merit. *Financial Times*, p. 10.

Nakamoto, M. (1995, April 19). The bitter taste of salarymen's *sake*. *Financial Times*.

Nakamoto, M. (1998, December 22). Performance begins to win a wider audience. *Financial Times*, p. 12.

Nakamoto, M. (2001, March 14). Japanese management, Part 1. *Financial Times*, p. 16.

Nasby, W., & Read, N.W. (1997). The inner and outer voyages of a solo circumnavigator. An integrative case study. *Journal of Personality*, 65, 757–1116.

Natham, R., & Hill, L. (1992). *Career counselling*. London: Sage.

Nathan, B.R., Mohrman, A.M., & Milliman, J. (1991). Interpersonal relations as a context for the effects of appraisal interviews on performance and satisfaction: A longitudinal study. *Academy of Management Journal*, June, 352–369.

Neck, C.P., & Manz, C.C. (1994). From groupthink to teamthink: Toward the creation of constructive thought patterns in self-managing work teams. *Human Relations*, 47, 929–952.

Neck, C.P., & Moorhead, G. (1995). Groupthink remodelled: The importance of leadership, time pressure, and methodical decision making procedures. *Human Relations*, May, 537–558.

Needle, D. (2004). *Business in context: An introduction to business and its environment* (4th ed.). London: Thomson Learning.

Nemecek, J., & Grandjean, E. (1973). Noise in landscaped offices. *Applied Ergonomics*, 4, 19–22.

Nemeth, C.J. (1986). Differential contributions of majority and minority influence. *Psychological Review*, 93, 23–32.

Nevels, P. (1989). Why employees are being asked to rate their supervisors. *Supervisory Management*, December, 5–11.

Newcombe, T.M. (1943). *Personality and social change: Attitude formation in a student community*. New York: Holt, Rinehart & Winston.

Newcombe, T.M. (1967). *Resistance and change: Bennington College and its students after 25 years*. New York: Wiley & Sons.

Ng, K.Y., & Van Dyne, L. (2001). Individualism–collectivism as a boundary condition for effectiveness of minority influence in decision making. *Organizational Behavior and Human Decision Processes*, 84, 198–225.

Nicol-Maveyraud, J. (2003). Mind over money. *The Psychologist*, 16, 240–242.

Nicholson, N. (1990). The transition cycle: Causes, outcomes, processes, and forms. In S. Fisher &

C.L. Cooper (Eds.), *On the move: The psychology of change and transition*. Chichester, UK: J. Wiley.

Nicholson, N. (2001). The new word on gossip. *Psychology Today*, June, 4–45.

Nicholson, N. (2002, November 8). To the manner born. *FT Mastering Leadership, Part 2*, 4–5.

Nicholson, N. (2003). How to motivate your problem people. *Harvard Business Review*, January, 57–65.

Nicholson, N., & Arnold, J. (1989). Graduate early experience in a multinational corporation. *Personnel Review, 18*, 3–14.

Noer, D.M. (1993). *Healing the wounds: Overcoming the traumas of layoffs and revitalizing downsized organizations*. San Francisco: Jossey-Bass.

Nolan, P., & Wood, S. (2003). Mapping the future of work. *British Journal of Industrial Relations, 41*, 165–174.

Nonaka, I., Umemoto, K., & Sasaki, K. (1999). Three tales of knowledge creating companies. In G. von Krogh, J. Roos, & D. Kleine (Eds.), *Knowing in firms: Understanding, managing, and measuring knowledge* (pp. 146–172). London: Sage.

Nord, W.R. (1976). *Concepts and controversy in organisational behaviour* (2nd ed.). Pacific Pallisades, CA: Goodyear.

Nota, B. (1988). The socialisation process of high commitment organisations. *Personnel, 65*, 20–23.

Nugent, P.S. (2002). Managing conflict: Third party interventions for managers. *Academy of Management Executive, 16*, 139–155.

Nusbaum, A. (1999, January 20). Salarymen's fat bonus goes west. *Financial Times*, p. 14.

Nutt, P.C. (1990). Strategic decisions made by top executives and middle managers with data and process-dominant styles. *Journal of Management Studies, 27*, 173–194.

Nutt, P.C. (1993). The formulation process and tactics used in organizational decision making. *Organization Science, 4*, 226–236.

Oborne, D.J. (1994). *Computers at work: A behavioural approach* (3rd ed.). Chichester, UK: Wiley.

Oborne, D.J. (1995). *Ergonomics at work* (3rd ed.). Chichester, UK: John Wiley & Sons.

O'Brien, V. (1998). *Success on our own terms*. New York: J. Wiley.

Ocasio, W. (1994). Political dynamics and circulation of power: CEO succession in US industrial corporations (1960–1990). *Administrative Science Quarterly*, June, 285–312.

Odean, T., & Barber, B. (1999). Do investors trade too much? *American Economic Review, 89*, 1279–1298.

Odean, T., & Barber, B. (2000). Trading is hazardous to your health: The common stock investment performance of individual investors. *Journal of Finance, 5*, 773–806.

Offerrmann, L.R., & Gowing, M.K. (1990). Organizations of the future. *American Psychologist, 45*, 95–108.

Oglonna, E. (1992). Managing organisational culture: Fantasy or reality. *Human Resource Management Journal*, Winter, 42–54.

O'Leary-Kelly, A., Griffin, R.W., & Glew, D.J. (1996). Organization—motivated aggression: A research framework. *Academy of Management Review*, January, 225–253.

O'Leary-Kelly, A.M., Martocchio, J.J., & Frink, D.D. (1994). A review of the influence of group goals on group performance. *Academy of Management Journal*, October, 1285–1301.

Olshavsky, R.W., & Granbois, D.H. (1979). Consumer decision making—fact or fiction. *Journal of Consumer Research, 6*, 93–100.

O'Neill, J. (1986). The disciplinary society: From Weber to Foucault. *British Journal of Sociology, xxxvii*, 42–60.

Ones, D.S., Viswesvaran, C., & Schmidt, F.L. (1993). Comprehensive meta-analysis of integrity test validities: Findings and implications for personnel selection and theories of job performance. *Journal of Applied Psychology*, August, 679–703.

O'Reilly, C.A. (1989). Corporations, culture, and commitment: Motivation and social control in organisations. *California Management Review, 31*(Summer), 19–23.

O'Reilly, C.A., Caldwell, D.F., & Barnett, W.P. (1989). Work group demography, social integration and turnover. *Administrative Science Quarterly, 34*, 21–37.

O'Reilly, C.A., & Chatman, J.A. (1996). Culture as social control: Corporations, cults, and commitment. In B.M. Staw & L.L. Cummings (Eds.), *Research in organizational behaviour* (Vol. 18, pp. 157–200). Greenwich, CT: JAI Press.

O'Reilly, C.A., Chatman, J.A., & Caldwell, D.F. (1991). People and organizational culture: A profile comparison approach to assessing people–organization fit. *Academy of Management Journal*, September, 487–516.

O'Reilly, S. (1998a, March 1). Age of the older worker dawns. *The Sunday Times*, p. 7.20.

O'Reilly, S. (1998b, June 7). Banks lend an ear to ethical lobby. *The Sunday Times*, p. 7.16.

O'Reilly, S. (1998c, June 21). Outdoor training aids leadership. *The Sunday Times*, p. 7.14.

O'Reilly, S. (1998d, July 12). Smart money goes on coaching. *The Sunday Times*, p. 7.14.

Organ, D.W., & Ryan, K. (1995). A meta-analytic review of attitudinal and dispositional predictors of organizational citizenship behavior. *Personnel Psychology, 48*, 775–802.

Orner, R. (1997). What lies ahead as they emerge from obscurity? Falklands war veterans. *The Psychologist*, August, 351–355.

Ornstein, R.E. (1977). *The psychology of consciousness*. New York: Harcourt Brace Jovanovich.

Orth, C.D., Wilkinson, H.E., & Benfari, R.C. (1987). The manager's role as coach and mentor. *Organizational Dynamics*, Spring, 67.

Osborn, A. (1957). *Applied imagination*. New York: Scribners.

Osgood, C.E., Suci, G.J., & Tannenbaum, P.H. (1957). *The measurement of meaning*. Urbana, IL: University of Illinois Press.

Osgood, C.E., & Tannenbaum, P.H. (1955). The principle of congruity in the prediction of attitude change. *Psychological Review*, *62*, 42–55.

Ostroff, C. (1992). The relationship between satisfaction, attitudes and performance: An organizational level analysis. *Journal of Applied Psychology*, December, 963–974.

Otley, D.T. (1977). Behavioural aspects of budgeting. *Accountants' Digest ICAEW (Institute of Chartered Accountants in England and Wales)*, *49*, Summer.

Ouchi, W.G. (1981). *Theory Z: How American business can meet the Japanese challenge*. Reading, MA: Addison-Wesley.

Overell, S. (2000, August 18). Learning to trust that gut feeling. *Financial Times*, p. 12.

Overell, S. (2002a, January 24). A working recipe for quality of life. *Financial Times*, p. 13.

Overell, S. (2002b, December 5). The right personalities in store. *Financial Times*, p. 12.

Overell, S. (2003, March 3). Employee appraisals: Let's have a little chat about work, shall we? *Financial Times*, p. 13.

Owens, J., Bower, G.H., & Black, J.B. (1979). The soap opera effect in story recall. *Memory and Cognition*, *7*, 185–191.

Owens, W.A., & Schoenfeldt, L.F. (1979). Towards a classification of persons. *Journal of Applied Psychology*, *64*, 569–607.

Pace, R.W. (1983). *Organisational communication: Foundations for human resource development*. New York: Prentice Hall.

Packard, V. (1975). *A nation of strangers*. New York: McKay.

Pahl, J.M., & Pahl, R.E. (1971). *Managers and their wives*. London: Allen Lane.

Paivio, A. (1969). Mental imagery in associative learning and memory. *Psychological Review*, *76*, 241–263.

Park, W. (2000). A comprehensive empirical investigation of the relationship among variables of the groupthink model. *Journal of Organizational Behaviour*, *21*, 873–887.

Parker, C.P., Dipboye, R.L., & Jackson, S.L. (1995). Perceptions of organizational politics: An investigation of antecedents and consequences. *Journal of Management*, *21*, 891–912.

Parker, L.D. (1979). Participation in budget planning: The prospects surveyed. *Accounting and Business Research*, Spring, 123–137.

Parker, S.K. (1998). Enhancing role breadth self-efficacy. The roles of job enrichment and other organizational interventions. *Journal of Applied Psychology*, December, 835–852.

Parkes, K.R. (1984). Locus of control, cognitive appraisal, and coping in stressful episodes. *Journal of Personality and Social Psychology*, *46*, 655–668.

Parsons, M.B., Schepis, M.M., Reid, D.H., McCarn, J.E., & Green, C.W. (1987). Expanding the impact of behavioural staff management: A large-scale, long-term application in schools serving severely handicapped children. *Journal of Applied Behaviour Analysis*, *20*, 139–150.

Pasmore, W.A. (1978). The comparative impacts of socio-technical system, job redesign and survey feedback intervention. In W.A. Pasmore & J.J. Sherwood (Eds.), *Socio-technical systems: A sourcebook*. La Jolla, CA: University Associates.

Pasmore, W.A. (1995). Social science transformed: The socio-technical perspective. *Human Relations*, *48*, 1–21.

Pasmore, W.A., & Fagans, M.R. (1992). Participation, individual development and organizational change: A review and synthesis. *Journal of Management*, June, 375–397.

Pastor, J.C., Meindl, J., & Mayo, M. (2002). A network effects model of charisma attributions. *Academy of Management Journal*, *45*, 410–420.

Patrick, J. (1992). *Training: Research and practice*. London: Academic Press.

Paulhus, D.L., Bruce, M.N., & Trapnell, P.D. (1995). Effects of self-presentation on the validity of personality impressions: A longitudinal study. *Personality and Social Psychology Bulletin*, *21*, 100–108.

Paulos, J.A. (2003, July 12). A mathematician plays the market. *The Times*.

Paulus, P.B. (2000). Groups, teams, and creativity: The creative potential of idea-generation groups. *Applied Psychology: An International Review*, *49*, 237–262.

Pavlov, I.P. (1927). *Conditioned reflexes*. New York: Oxford University Press.

Peck, D., & Whitlow, D. (1975). *Approaches to personality theory*. London: Methuen.

Pedlar, M., Boydell, T.H, & Burgoyne, J.G. (1988). *Learning company project*. London: Manpower Services Commission.

Pedlar, M., Boydell, T.H., & Burgoyne, J.G. (1989). Towards a learning company. *Management Education and Development*, *2*, 19–41.

Peiperl, M. (1997). Does empowerment deliver the goods? In *Mastering management: Module 8. Managing people* (pp. 283–287). London: FT/Pitman Publishing.

Penn, R., Lilja, K., & Scattergood, H. (1992). Flexibility and employment patterns in the contemporary paper industry. *Journal of Industrial Relations*, 23.

Pennington, D.C. (1986). *Essential social psychology*. Sevenoaks, UK: Edward Arnold.

Pennington, D.C., Gillen, K., & Hill, P. (1999). *Social psychology*. London: Arnold.

Perlow, L. (2003). *When you say yes but mean no: How silencing conflict wrecks relationships and companies*. New York: Crown Business.

Persaud, R. (2004, August 28). The animal urge, No, not that one, it's trust. *FT Magazine*, pp. 23–25.

Perrin, S., & Spencer, C. (1980). The Asch effect: A child of its time? *Bulletin of the British Psychological Society*, 32, 405–406.

Perrow, C.B. (1970). *Organisational analysis: A sociological view*. London: Tavistock Publications.

Peters, T. (1992). *Liberation management: Necessary disorganisation for the nanosecond nineties*. New York: Alfred Knopf.

Peters, T.J., & Waterman, R.H. (1982). *In search of excellence: Lessons from America's best-run companies*. New York: Harper & Row.

Peterson, M.F. et al. (1995). Role conflict, ambiguity and overload: A 21-nation study—research note. *Academy of Management Journal*, 38, 429–452.

Petrides, K.V., Furnham, A., & Frederickson N. (2004). Emotional intelligence. *The Psychologist*, October, 574–577.

Pettigrew, A. (1973). *The politics of organisational decision making*. London: Tavistock.

Pettigrew, A.M. (1979). On studying organisational culture. *Administrative Science Quarterly*, December, 570–581.

Pettigrew, A.M. (1985). *The awakening giant: Continuity and change in ICI*. Oxford, UK: Blackwell.

Pettigrew, A.M. (1990). Is corporate culture manageable? In D.C. Wilson & R.H. Rosenfeld (Eds.), *Managing organisations: Text, readings, and cases*. Maidenhead, UK: McGraw-Hill.

Petty, M.M., McGee, G.W., & Cavender, J.W. (1984). A meta-analysis of the relationship between individual job satisfaction and individual performance. *Academy of Management Review*, October, 712–721.

Petty, R.E., & Cacioppo, J.T. (1985). The elaboration likelihood model of persuasion. In L. Berkowitz (Ed.), *Advances in experimental social psychology, Vol. 19*. New York: Academic Press.

Petty, R.E., & Wegener, D.J. (1999). The elaboration likelihood model: Current status and controversies. In S. Chaiken & Y. Trope (Eds.), *Dual process theories in social psychology* (pp. 41–72). New York: Guilford.

Pfeffer, J. (1981a). Management as symbolic action: The creation and maintenance of organisational paradigms. In L.L. Cummings & B.M. Staw (Eds.), *Research in organisational behaviour* (Vol. 3). Greenwich, CT: JAI Press.

Pfeffer, J. (1981b). *Power in organisations*. Marshfield, MA: Pitman Publishing.

Pfeffer, J. (1992). *Managing with power: Politics and influence in organizations*. Boston, MA: Harvard Business School Press.

Phares, E. (1976). *Locus of control in personality*. Morristown, NJ: General Learning Press.

Phares, E.J., & Chaplin, W.F. (1998). *Introduction to personality*. New York: Longman Inc.

Phillips, A.P., & Dipboye, R.L. (1989). Correlational tests of predictions from a process model of the interview. *Journal of Applied Psychology*, February, 41–52.

Phillips, A.S., & Bedeian, A.G. (1994). Leader–follower exchange quality: The role of personal and interpersonal attributes. *Academy of Management Journal*, 37, 990–1001.

Pickard, E. (1997). Developing training for organizational counselling. In M. Carroll & M. Walton (Eds.), *Handbook of counselling in organizations* (pp. 325–341). London: Sage Publications.

Pickard, E., & Towler, J. (2003). The invisible client. *Counselling at Work*, Autumn, 2–4.

Pierce, J.L., & Furo, C.A. (1990). Employee ownership: Implications for management. *Organizational Dynamics*, Winter, 32–43.

Pignitore, R., Dugoni, B.L., Tindale, R.S., & Spring, B. (1994). Bias against overweight job applicants in a simulated interview. *Journal of Applied Psychology*, 79, 909–917.

Pike, A. (1996, November 22). Skills for prosperity. *Financial Times*, p. 12.

Pike, A. (1999, October 14). Employers and unions attack new skills plans. *Financial Times*, p. 3.

Pilling, D. (2004, July 5). Japan's job spin out of Tokyo. *Financial Times*, p. 8.

Pincherle, G. (1972). Fitness for work. *Proceedings of the Royal Society of Medicine*, 65, 321–324.

Pinder, C. (1984). *Work motivation*. Glenview, IL: Scott, Foresman.

Pinkley, R.L., & Northcraft, G.B. (1994). Conflict frames of reference: Implications for dispute processes and outcomes. *Academy of Management Journal*, February, 193.

Piper, W.E., Marrache, M., Lacroix, R., Richardson, A.M., & Jones, B.D. (1983). Cohesion as a basic bond in groups. *Human Relations*, February, 93–108.

Pizam, A. (1975). Social differentiation: A new psychological barrier to performance appraisal. *Public Personnel Management*, July/August, 244–247.

Plimmer, G. (2004, October 11). Emphasis should be on more skills investment. Professional Development (Special Report), *Financial Times*, p. I-2.

Plowin, R. (2001). Genetics and behaviour. *The Psychologist*, 14, 134–139.

Pocock, P. (1989). Is business ethics a contradiction in terms? *Personnel Management*, November, 60–63.

Podsakoff, P.M., MacKenzie, S.B., Aherne, M., & Bommer, W.H. (1995). Searching for a needle in a haystack: Trying to identify the illusive moderators of leadership behavior. *Journal of Management, 1*, 422–470.

Podsakoff, P.M., MacKenzie, S.B., & Bommer, W.H. (1996). Meta analysis of the relationships between Kerr & Jermier's substitutes for leadership and employee attitudes, role perceptions, and performance. *Journal of Applied Psychology*, August, 380–399.

Podsakoff, P.M., & Schriesheim, C.A. (1985). Field studies of French and Raven's bases of power: Critique, re-analysis, and suggestions for future research. *Psychological Bulletin, 97*(3), 387–411.

Politi, J. & Foster, L. (2004, November 18). Corporate cultures will have to be merged. *Financial Times*, p. 32.

Pollack, A. (1993, May 22/23). New skill in Japan: Learning to cope when lifetime contract is broken. *International Herald Tribune*, p. 5.

Pollert, A. (1988). The flexible firm: Fixation or fact. *Work, Employment, and Society, 2*, 281–316.

Poppleton, S.E. (1975). *Biographical and personality characteristics associated with success in life assurance salesmen.* Unpublished MPhil thesis, Birkbeck College, University of London.

Porteous, M. (1997). *Occupational psychology.* Hemel Hempstead, UK: Prentice Hall.

Porter, L.W., & Lawler, E.E. (1968). *Managerial attitudes and performance.* Homewood, IL: R.D. Irwin.

Porter, L.W., & Lawler, E.E. (1975). *Behaviour in organisations.* New York: McGraw-Hill.

Posthuma, R.A., Moregeson, F.P., & Campion, M.A. (2002). Beyond employment interview validity: A comprehensive narrative of recent research and trend over time. *Personnel Psychology, 55*, 1–82.

Power, D.J., & Aldag, R.L. (1985). Soelberg's job search and choice model: A clarification, review, and critique. *Academy of Management Review*, January, 48–58.

Pratkanis, A.R., & Turner, M.E. (1994). Of what value is a job attitude? A socio-cognitive analysis. *Human Relations, 47*, 1545–1576.

Price, A. (1997). *Human resource management in a business context.* London: International Thomson Business Press.

Price, D.L., & Lueder, R.K. (1980). Virginia union and industry management attitudes toward safety and the Occupational Safety and Health Act. *Journal of Safety Research, 12*(Fall), 99–106.

Priem, R.J., Harrison, D.A., & Muir, N.K. (1995). Structured conflict and consensus outcomes in group decision making. *Journal of Management, 21*, 691–710.

Pritchard, R.D., Jones, S.D., Roth, P.L., Stuebing, K.K., & Ekeberg, S.E. (1988). Effects of group feedback, goal setting and incentives on organizational productivity. *Journal of Applied Psychology, 73*, 337–358.

Proctor, R.A. (1991). The importance of creativity in the management field. *British Journal of Management, 2*, 223–230.

Proctor, S. & Currie, G. (2002). How teamworking works in the Inland Revenue: Meaning, operation and impact. *Personnel Review, 31*, 304–319.

Prowse, M. (2003, September 1). Nurture versus nature is a childish debate. *Financial Times*, p. 17.

Pugh, D.S., Hickson, D.T., Hinings, C.R., & Turner, C. (1968). Dimensions of organisation structure. *Administrative Science Quarterly, 13*, 65–105.

Pugh, D.S., Hickson, D.T., Hinings, C.R., & Turner, C. (1969). The context of organisation structures. *Administrative Science Quarterly, 14*, 91–114.

Pulakos, E.D., Schmitt, N., Whitney, D., & Smith, M. (1996). Individual differences in interviewer ratings: The impact of standardization, consensus, and sampling error on the validity of a structured interview. *Personnel Psychology, 49*, 85–102.

Putman, R. (2000). *Bowling alone: The collapse and revival of the American community.* New York: Simon & Schuster.

Quick, J.C. (1992). Crafting an organization culture: Herb's hand at Southwest Airlines. *Organizational Dynamics*, Autumn, 50–53.

Radke, M., & Klisurich, D. (1958). Experiments in changing food habits. In E.E. Maccoby, T.M. Newcombe & R.L. Hartley (Eds.), *Readings in social psychology* (3rd ed.). New York: Holt.

Rafaeli, A. (1989). When cashiers meet customers: An analysis of the role of supermarket cashiers. *Academy of Management Review, 32*, 245–273.

Rajan, A., Lank, E., & Chapple, K. (1998). *Good practices in knowledge creation and exchange.* London: Centre for Research in Employment and Technology in Europe (CREATE), Focus.

Randall, F.D. (1955). Stimulate your executives to think creatively. *Harvard Business Review*, July–August, 121–128.

Randolf, W.A. (1995). Navigating the journey to empowerment. *Organizational Dynamics*, Spring, 19–31.

Randsepp, E. (1978). Are you a creative manager? *Management Review, 58*, 15–16.

Rao, R. (2004, August 25). How to tap the opportunities for outsourcing. FT Summer School, *Financial Times*, p. 11.

Reason, J. (1987). The Chernobyl errors. *Bulletin of the British Psychological Society, 40*, 201–206.

Ree, M.J., Earles, J.A., & Teachout, M.S. (1994). Predicting job performance: Not much more than "g". *Journal of Applied Psychology, 79*, 518–524.

Reed, M. (1989). *The sociology of management*. Hemel Hempstead, UK: Harvester Wheatsheaf.

Reed, M. (1992). Introduction. In M. Reed & M. Hughes (Eds.), *Rethinking organisation: New directions in organisation theory and analysis*. London: Sage Publications.

Reed, R.W. (1984). Is education the key to lower health care costs? *Personnel Journal*, *63*, 40–46.

Rees, R. (1993, October 17). Transformation scenes—re-engineering: Back to the black. *The Sunday Times*, p. 90.

Reich, B., & Adcock, C. (1976). *Values, attitudes and behaviour change*. London: Methuen.

Reichers, A.E. (1985). A review and re-conceptualisation of organisational commitments. *Academy of Management Review*, *10*, 465–476.

Reid, J.M.V. (1997). Standardised ability testing for vocational rehabilitation in visually impaired adults: A literature review. *Journal of Visual Impairment and Blindness*, *91*, 546–554.

Revans, R.W. (1971). *Developing effective managers*. London: Praeger.

Reynolds, J. (2002). Method and madness: The real value of e-learning. *People Management*, 4 April, 42–43.

Reynolds, J., & Slowman, M. (2004). In the driving seat: Traditional training has its place, but is teaching people what the organisation wants them to know the best way to unlock their potential. *People Management*, 12 February, 40–42.

Rhodes, T. (1998, March 19). Asia culture links in jet crash. *The Times*, p. 19.

Ribot, T. (1882). *Diseases of memory*. New York: Appleton.

Rice, G.H., & Lindecamp, D.P. (1989). Personality types and business success of small retailers. *Journal of Occupational Psychology*, *62*, 177–182.

Richards, M.D., & Greenlaw, P.S. (1972). *Management: Decisions and behaviour*. Glenview, IL: Richard D. Irwin.

Richards, T. (1990). *Creativity and problem solving at work*. Farnborough, UK: Gower.

Rick, J., & Briner, R.B. (2000). Trauma management vs stress debriefing: What should responsible organizations do? *BPS Occupational Psychology Book of Proceedings* (pp. 126–130). Leicester, UK: British Psychological Society.

Ridley, M. (2003). *Experience and what makes us human*. London: Fourth Estate.

Ridgeway, C. (1998). The strategic occupational psychologist. *The Occupational Psychologist*, December, 18–20.

Roadman, H.E. (1964). An industrial use of peer ratings. *Journal of Applied Psychology*, *48*, 211–214.

Robbins, S.P. (1974). *Managing organisational conflict*. New York: Prentice Hall.

Robbins, S.P. (1991). *Organisational behaviour: Concepts, controversies, and applications* (5th ed.). New York: Prentice Hall.

Robbins, S.P. (1998). *Organizational behaviour: Concepts, controversies, applications* (8th ed.). Upper Saddle River, NJ: Prentice Hall.

Robbins, S.P. (2003). *Organisational behaviour* (10th ed.). Upper Saddle River, NJ: Prentice Hall/Pearson Education International.

Robbins, S.P., & Hunsaker, P.L. (1996). *Training in interpersonal skills: Tips for managing people at work* (2nd ed.). Upper Saddle River, NJ: Prentice Hall.

Robbins, S.P., Millett, B., Cacioppe, R., & Waters-Marsh, T. (2001). *Organizational behaviour: Leading and managing in Australia and New Zealand* (3rd ed.). French's Forest, NSW: Pearson Education Australia.

Robbins, T.L. (1995). Social loafing on cognitive tasks: An examination of the sucker effect. *Journal of Business and Psychology*, Spring, 337.

Roberts, D. (2004, June 1). The boardroom burden: Calls for reform are replaced by concern that corporate shake-up has gone too far. *Financial Times*, p. 15.

Roberts, G.E. (1994). Maximising performance appraisal systems effectiveness: Perspectives from municipal government personnel administrators. *Public Personnel Management*, *23*, 525–549.

Robertson, I.T. (1985). Human information processing strategies and style. *Behaviour and Information Technology*, *4*, 19–29.

Robertson, I.T. (1994). Personnel selection research: Where are we now? *The Psychologist*, January, 17–21.

Robertson, I.T. (1998). Personality and organizational behaviour. *Selection and Development Review*, *14*(4), August, 11–15.

Robertson, I.T., & Cooper, C.L. (1983). *Human behaviour in organisations*. Plymouth, UK: Macdonald and Evans.

Robertson, I.T., & Downs, S. (1989). Work-sample tests of trainability: A meta-analysis. *Journal of Applied Psychology*, *74*, 402–410.

Robertson, I.T., Gratton, L., & Rout, U. (1990). The validity of situational interviews for administrative jobs. *Journal of Organisational Behaviour*, *11*, 69–76.

Robertson, I.T., & Kandola, R.S. (1982). Work-sample tests: Validity, adverse impact, and applicant reaction. *Journal of Occupational Psychology*, *55*, 171–183.

Robertson, I.T., & Kinder, A. (1993). Personality and job competences: The criterion-related validity of some personality variables. *Journal of Occupational and Organisational Psychology*, *66*, 225–244.

Robertson, I.T., & Makin, P.J. (1986). Management selection in Britain: A survey and critique. *Journal of Occupational Psychology*, *59*, 45–58.

Robertson, I.T., & Smith, M. (1989). Personnel selection methods. In M. Smith & I.T. Robertson (Eds.), *Advances in selection and assessment*. Chichester, UK: Wiley.

Robertson, I.T., & Smith, M. (2001). Personnel selection. *Journal of Occupational and Organizational Psychology*, *74*, 441–472.

Robertson, P.J., Roberts, D.R., & Porras, J.I. (1993). Dynamics of planned organizational change: Assessing support for a theoretical model. *Academy of Management Journal*, June, 619–634.

Robey, D. (1977). Computers and management structures: Some empirical findings re-examined. *Human Relations*, *30*, 963–976.

Robins, R.W., Gosling, S.D., & Craik, K.H. (1999). An empirical analysis of trends in psychology. *American Psychologist*, February, 117–128.

Robinson, S.L., Kraatz, M.S., & Rousseau, D.M. (1994). Changing obligations and the psychological contract: A longitudinal study. *Academy of Management Journal*, February, 137–152.

Rodger, A. (1952). *The seven-point plan*. London: National Institute of Industrial Psychology.

Rodgers, R., & Hunter, J.E. (1991). Impact of management by objectives on organizational productivity. *Journal of Applied Psychology*, April, 151–155.

Rodgers, R., Hunter, J.E., & Rogers, D.L. (1993). Influence of top management commitment on management programme success. *Journal of Applied Psychology*, February, 151–155.

Roe, R.A., & Van den Berg, P.T. (2003). Selection in Europe: Context, developments, and research agenda. *European Journal of Work and Organisational Psychology*, *12*, 257–287.

Roe, R.A., Zinovieva, I.L., Dienes, E., & Tenttorn, L.A. (2000). A comparison of work motivation in Bulgaria, Hungary, and the Netherlands: Test of a model. *Applied Psychology: An International Review*, *49*, 658–687.

Roethlisberger, F.J., & Dickson, W.J. (1939). *Management and the worker*. Cambridge, MA: Harvard University Press.

Roffey Park Newsletter (2004). *Opening up OD for managers and developers*. Autumn, p. 6.

Roffey Park Newsletter (2005). *Introducing a dramatic change in leadership*. Spring, p. 1.

Rogers, A. (1998, August 9). Psychometric tests go on trial. *The Sunday Times*, p. 7.7.

Rogers, C.A. (1974). Feedback precision and post-feedback interval duration. *Journal of Experimental Psychology*, *102*.

Rogers, C.R. (1951). *Client-centred therapy*. Boston: Houghton Mifflin.

Rogers, C.R. (1959). A theory of therapy, personality and interpersonal relationships as developed in the client-centred framework. In S. Koch (Ed.), *Psychology: A study of a science* (Vol. 3). New York: McGraw-Hill.

Rogers, L. (1993, September 5). Absorbing the shock waves. *The Sunday Times* (Style and travel section), p. 23.

Rogers, R.W., & Mewborn, C.R. (1976). Fear appeals and attitude change: Effects of a threat's noxiousness, probability of occurrence, and the efficacy of coping responses. *Journal of Personality and Social Psychology*, *34*, 54–61.

Rokeach, M. (1968). *Beliefs, attitudes, and values*. San Francisco: Jossey-Bass.

Rokeach, M. (1973). *The nature of human values*. New York: Free Press.

Rokeach, M., & Ball-Rokeach, S.J. (1989). Stability and change in American value priorities, 1968–1981. *American Psychologist*, May, 775–784.

Romanelli, E., & Tushman, M.L. (1994). Organizational transformation as punctuated equilibrium: An empirical test. *Academy of Management Journal*, October, 1141–1166.

Romzek, B.S. (1989). Personal consequences of employee commitment. *Academy of Management Journal*, September, 649–661.

Ronen, S., & Shenkar, O. (1985). Clustering countries on attitudinal dimensions: A review and synthesis. *Academy of Management Journal*, September, 435–454.

Rosenfeld, P., Giacalone, R.A., & Riordan, C.A. (1995). *Impression management in organizations: Theory, measurement and practice*. London: Routledge.

Rosenman, R.H., Friedman, M., & Strauss, R. (1964). A predictive study of CHD. *Journal of the American Medical Association*, *189*, 15–22.

Ross, I.C. (1957). *Role specialisation in supervision*. Unpublished PhD thesis, Columbia University.

Rosse, J.G., Miller, J.L., & Ringer, R.C. (1996). The deterrent value of drug and integrity testing. *Journal of Business and Psychology*, *10*, 477–485.

Rothman, A.J., & Salovey, P. (1997). Shaping perceptions to motivate healthy behaviour. The role of message framing. *Psychological Bulletin*, *121*, 3–19.

Rothstein, M., & Jackson, D.N. (1984). Implicit personality theory and the employment interview. In M. Cook (Ed.), *Issues in person perception*. London: Methuen.

Rotter, J.B. (1954). *Social learning and clinical psychology*. New York: Prentice Hall.

Rotter, J.B. (1966). Generalised expectancies for internal versus external control of reinforcement. *Psychological Monographs*, *8*(1, Whole No. 609).

Rotter, J.B. (1975). Some problems and misconceptions related to the construct of internal versus external locus of control of reinforcement. *Journal of Consulting and Clinical Psychology*, *43*, 56–67.

Rowe, A.J., & Boulgarides, J.D. (1992). *Managerial decision making*. Upper Saddle River, NJ: Prentice Hall.

Roy, D.F. (1960). Banana time: Job satisfaction and informal interaction. *Human Organisation*, *18*, 156–168.

Royal Society (1985). *The public understanding of science* (Report). London: Author.

Russek, H.I., & Zohman, B.L. (1958). Relative significance of hereditary and occupational stress in CHD of young adults. *American Journal of Medical Science*, *235*, 266–275.

Russell, J.A. (1994). Is there universal recognition of emotion from facial expression? A review of the cross-cultural studies. *Psychological Bulletin*, *115*, 102–141.

Rynes, S., & Rosen, B. (1994). What makes diversity programmes work. *HR Magazine*, October, 67–73.

Saal, F.E., & Knight, P.A. (1995). *Industrial organisational psychology* (2nd ed.). Pacific Grove, CA: Brooks Cole Publishing.

Sackmann, S.A. (1992). Culture and sub-cultures: An analysis of organizational knowledge. *Administrative Science Quarterly*, March, 140–161.

Sacks, O. (1993, May 10). To see and not to see: A neurologist's notebook. *The New Yorker*, pp. 59–73.

Sadler, P. (1988). *Managerial leadership in the post-industrial society*. Aldershot, UK: Gower Publishing.

Sadler, P.J. (1993). *Managing talent: Making the best of the best*. London: Century Books.

Sadler-Smith, E., & Shefy, E. (2004). The intuitive executive (understanding and applying "gut feel" in decision making). *Academy of Management Executive*, *18*, 76–91.

Sagie, A., Elizur, D., & Yamauchi, A. (1996). The structure and strength of achievement motivation: A cross-cultural comparison. *Journal of Organizational Behavior*, *17*, 431–444.

Salancik, G., & Pfeffer, J. (1978). A social information processing approach to job attitudes and task design. *Administrative Science Quarterly*, *23*, 224–253.

Salgado, J.F., Viswesvaran, C., & Ones, D. (2001). Predictors used for personnel selection: An overview of constructs, and techniques. In N. Anderson, D. Ones, H.K. Sinangil, & C. Viswesvaran (Eds.), *Handbook of industrial, work, and organizational psychology* (pp. 165–200). London: Sage.

Sankowsky, D. (1995). The charismatic leader as narcissist: Understanding the abuse of power. *Organizational Dynamics*, Summer, 56–67.

Saul, F.E., & Moore, S.C. (1993). Perceptions of promotion fairness and promotion candidates' qualifications. *Journal of Applied Psychology*, *78*, 105–110.

Sauter, S., Hurrel, J.T., & Cooper, C.L. (1989). *Job control and worker health*. Chichester, UK: J. Wiley.

Saville & Holdsworth Ltd. (1984). *The Occupational Personality Questionnaires*. Thames Ditton, UK: Author.

Scarborough, H., & Corbett, J.M. (1992). *Technology and organization: Power, meaning and design*. London: Routledge.

Scarpello, V., & Campbell, J.P. (1983). Job satisfaction: Are all the parts there? *Personnel Psychology*, Autumn, 577–600.

Schachter, S. (1959). *The psychology of affiliation*. Palo Alto, CA: Stanford University Press.

Schachter, S., Ellertson, N., McBride, D., & Gregory, D. (1951). An experimental study of cohesiveness and productivity. *Human Relations*, August, 229–239.

Schaubroeck, J., & Merritt, D.E. (1997). Divergent effects of job control on coping with work stressors: The key role of self-efficacy. *Academy of Management Journal*, *40*, 738–754.

Schein, E.H. (1956). The Chinese indoctrination programme for prisoners of war. *Psychiatry*, *19*, 149–172.

Schein, E.H. (1969). *Process consultation: Its role in organisational development*. Reading, MA: Addison-Wesley.

Schein, E.H. (1985). *Organizational culture and leadership*. San Francisco: Jossey-Bass.

Schein, E.H. (1987). *Process consultation: Vol. II. Lessons for managers and consultants*. Reading, MA: Addison-Wesley.

Schein, E.H. (1988). *Organizational psychology* (3rd ed.). Englewood Cliffs, NJ: Prentice Hall International.

Schein, E.H. (1990). Organisational culture. *American Psychologist*, *45*, 109–119.

Schein, E.H. (1996). Career anchors revisited: Implications for career development in the 21st century. *Academy of Management Review*, *10*, 80–88.

Schein, E.H. (2001, January 8). The anchors that dictate our careers. *FT Mastering Management Series, Part 13*, pp. 2–4.

Schiff, M., & Lewin, A.J. (1970). The impact of people on budgets. *Accounting Review*, April, 259–268.

Schindler, P.L., & Thomas, C.C. (1993). The structure of interpersonal trust in the workplace. *Psychology Reports*, October, 563–573.

Schlenker, B. (1980). *Impression management*. Monterey, CA: Brookes Cole.

Schmidt, F.L., & Hunter, J.E. (1998). The validity and utility of selection methods in personnel psychology: Practical and theoretical implications of 85 years of research findings. *Psychological Bulletin*, September, 262–274.

Schneider, R.J., & Hough, L.M. (1995). Personality and industrial/organizational psychology. In C.L. Cooper & I.T. Robertson (Eds.), *International review of industrial and organizational psychology* (Vol. 10, pp. 75–130). Chichester, UK: J. Wiley.

Schneier, C.E. (1977). Operational utility of BES: A cognitive re-interpretation. *Journal of Applied Psychology*, *62*, 541–548.

Schoonmaker, A.N. (1969). *Anxiety and the executive.* New York: American Management Association.

Schottenfeld, R.S., & Cullen, M.R. (1986). Recognition of occupation induced post-traumatic stress disorders. *Journal of Occupational Medicine, 28,* 365–369.

Schriesheim, C.A., Castro, S.L. , Zhou, X., & Yamarino, F.J. (2001). The folly of theorizing "A" but testing "B": A selective level-of-analysis view of the field and a detailed leader–member exchange illustration. *Leadership Quarterly,* Winter, 515–551.

Schriesheim, C.A., Cogliser, C.C., & Neider, L.L. (1995). Is it trustworthy? A multiple levels of analysis reexamination of an Ohio State leadership. *Leadership Quarterly,* Summer, 111–145.

Schriesheim, C.A., & Neider, L.L. (1996). Path–goal leadership theory: The long and winding road. *Leadership Quarterly,* Fall, 317–321.

Schriesheim, C.A., Tepper, B.J., & Tetrault, L.A. (1994). Least preferred co-worker score, situational control and leadership effectiveness: A meta analysis of contingency model performance predictions. *Journal of Applied Psychology,* August, 561–573.

Schroder, H.M., Driver, M.J., & Streufert, S. (1967). *Human information processing.* New York: Holt, Rinehart & Winston.

Schroeder, D.M., Congden, S.W., & Gopinath, C. (1995). Linking competitive strategy, structure, and technology. *Journal of Management Studies, 32,* 163–189.

Schultz-Hardt, S., Jochims, M., & Frey, D. (2002). Productive conflict in group decision making: Genuine and contrived dissent as strategies to counteract biased information seeking. *Organizational Behaviour and Human Decision Processes, 88,* 563–586.

Schurr, P.H. (1987). The effects of gain and loss decision frames on risky purchase negotiations. *Journal of Applied Psychology,* August, 351–359.

Schwartz, S. (1992). Universals in the context and structure of values: Theoretical advances and empirical tests in twenty countries. In M. Zanna (Ed.), *Advances in experimental social psychology* (pp. 1–65). New York: Academic Press.

Schwenk, C.R. (1985). The use of participant recollection in the modelling of organisational decision processes. *Academy of Management Review,* July, 496–503.

Scott, E.D., & Taylor, G.S. (1985). An examination of conflicting findings on the relationship between job satisfaction and absenteeism: A meta-analysis. *Academy of Management Journal,* September, 599–612.

Secord, P.F., & Beckman, C.W. (1974). *Social psychology.* New York: McGraw-Hill.

Secord, P.F., Bevan, N., & Katz, B. (1956). Perceptual accentuation and the Negro stereotype. *Journal of Abnormal and Social Psychology, 59,* 309–315.

Sederburg, M.E., & Rogelberg, S.G. (1999). Implementing 360 degree feedback: Methodological advice from multiple sources. *Selection and Development Review, 15,* 9–15.

Seidenberg, R. (1973). *Corporate wives—corporate casualties.* New York: American Management Association.

Seifter, H. (2002). *Leadership Ensemble: Lessons in collaboration management from the world's only conductorless orchestra.* New York: Times Books.

Sekuler, R., & Blake R. (2002). *Perception* (4th ed.). New York: McGraw-Hill.

Selznick, P. (1984). *Leadership in administration.* Berkeley, CA: University of California Press.

Senge, P. (1990). *The fifth discipline: The art and practice of the learning organisation.* New York: Random House.

Senge, P., Kleiner, A., Roberts, C., Ross, R., Roth, G., & Smith, B. (1999). *The dance of change: The challenges of sustaining momentum in learning organizations.* London: N. Brealey Publishing.

SenGupta, R. (2005, January 13). Stress at work. Lawyers laid low by time sheets. *Financial Times,* p. 12.

Settoon, R.P., Bennett, N., & Liden, R.C. (1996). Social exchange in organizations: Perceived organizational support, leader–member exchange, and employee reciprocity. *Journal of Applied Psychology,* June, 219–227.

Shackleton, V. (1995). *Business leadership.* London: Routledge.

Shackleton, V., & Newell, S. (1991). Management selection: A comparative survey of methods used in top British and French companies. *Journal of Occupational Psychology, 64,* 23–36.

Shackleton, V., & Newell, S. (1994). European management selection methods: A comparison of five countries. *International Journal of Selection and Assessment, 2,* 91–102.

Shalley, C.E. (1991). Effects of productivity goals, creativity goals, and personal discretion on individual creativity. *Journal of Applied Psychology,* April, 179–180.

Shamir, B. (1992). Attribution of influence and charisma to the leader: The romance of leadership revisited. *Journal of Applied Social Psychology,* March, 386–407.

Shamir, B., House, R.J., & Arthur, M.B. (1993). The motivational effects of charismatic leadership: A self-concept theory. *Organization Science,* November, 577–594.

Shamoon, S. (1999, November 27). Investment Psychology. Think your way to wealth. *Financial Times* (Money section), p. 4.

Shani, A.B., & Pasmore, W.A. (1985). Organization inquiry: Towards a new model of the action research process. In D.D. Warwick (Ed.), *Contemporary organization development: Current thinking and applications* (pp. 438–448). Glenview, IL: Scott, Foresman.

Shanthamani, V.S. (1973). Unemployment and neuroticism. *Indian Journal of Social Work, 34,* 83–102.

Shaw, M.E. (1964). Communication networks. In L. Berkowitz (Ed.), *Advances in experimental social psychology, Vol. 1.* New York: Academic Press.

Shaw, M.E. (1981). *Group dynamics: The psychology of small group behaviour* (3rd ed.). New York: McGraw-Hill.

Shein, V.E. (1985). Organisational realities: The politics of change. *Training and Development Journal,* February, 37–41.

Sheldon, W.H. (1954). *A guide for somatotyping the adult male at all ages.* New York: Harper.

Sheppard, B.H., Hartwick, T., & Warshaw, P.R. (1988). The theory of reasoned action. A meta-analysis of past research with recommendations for modifications and future research. *Journal of Consumer Research, 15,* 325–343.

Sheridan, J.E. (1992). Organizational culture and employee retention. *Academy of Management Journal,* December, 1036–1056.

Sherif, M. (1936). *The psychology of social norms.* New York: Harper & Row.

Sherif, M. (1967). *Group conflict and co-operation: Their social psychology.* London: Routledge & Kegan Paul.

Sherif, M., & Sherif, C.W. (1967). Attitude as the individual's own categories: The social judgement involvement approach to attitudes and attitude change. In C.W. Sherif & M. Sherif (Eds.), *Attitude, ego-involvement, and change.* New York: John Wiley & Sons.

Sherwood, B. (2004, November 5). BAE "gifts" claim highlight rules for companies operating overseas. *Financial Times,* p. 3.

Shevels, T. (1998). Competencies, competences, and confusion. *Selection and Development Review, 14,* 17–18.

Shields, J.F., & Shields, M.D. (1998). Antecedents of participative budgeting. *Accounting, Organizations and Society, 23,* 49–76.

Shiffrin, R.M., & Atkinson, R.C. (1969). Storage and retrieval processes in long-term memory. *Psychological Review, 76,* 179–193.

Shiller, R. (1990). *Market volatility.* Boston: MIT Press.

Shimmin, S. (1966). Concepts of work. *Occupational Psychology, 40,* 195–201.

Shimmin, S., & Wallis, D. (1994). *Fifty years of occupational psychology in Britain.* Leicester, UK: The British Psychological Society.

Shipper, F., & Manz, C.C. (1992). Employee self-management without formally designated teams: An alternative road to empowerment. *Organizational Dynamics,* Winter, 48–61.

Shirom, A., Eden, D., Silberwasser, S., & Kellerman, J.J. (1973). Job stress and the risk factors in coronary heart disease among occupational categories in Kibbutzim. *Social Science and Medicine, 7,* 875–892.

Sigman, A. (1993). Working shifts on the "red eye". *Personnel Management Plus,* October, 19.

Siklos, R. (2002, December 22). Vodafone's Indian worker. *Sunday Telegraph* (Business section), p. 3.

Silver, J. (1987). The ideology of excellence: Management and neo-conservatism. *Studies in Political Economy, 24*(1), 5–29.

Silvester, J., & Chapman A.J. (1996). Unfair discrimination in the selection interview: An attributional account. *International Journal of Selection and Assessment, 4,* 63–70.

Silvester, J., Patterson, E., & Ferguson, E. (2003). Comparing two attributional models of performance in retail sales. *Journal of Occupational and Organizational Psychology, 76,* 115–132.

Simon, H.A. (1957a). *Administrative behaviour.* New York: Free Press.

Simon, H.A. (1957b). *Models of man.* New York: Wiley.

Simon, H.A. (1960). *The science of management decisions.* New York: Harper & Row.

Simon, H.A. (1964). On the concept of organizational goals. *Administrative Science Quarterly, 10,* 21.

Simon, H.A., & Newell, A. (1971). Human problem solving: The state of the theory in 1970. *American Psychologist, 26,* 145–159.

Simon, S. (2005, March 21). Corporate turnround: Chrysler's magic formula. *Financial Times,* p. 11.

Simonson, I., & Staw, B.M. (1992). De-escalation strategies: A comparison of techniques for reducing commitment to losing courses of action. *Journal of Applied Psychology, 77,* 419–426.

Singer, J.A., & Salovey, P. (1994). *Remembered self: Emotion and memory in personality.* New York: Free Press.

Sisson, K., & Storey, J. (1988). Developing effective managers: A review of the issues and an agenda for research. *Personnel Review, 17,* 3–8.

Skapinker, M. (2000, October 20). An open relationship. *Financial Times,* p. 17.

Skinner, B.F. (1951). How to teach animals. *Scientific American, 185,* 26–29.

Skinner, B.F. (1961). *Analysis of behaviour.* New York: McGraw-Hill.

Skinner, B.F. (1974). *About behaviourisim.* London: Jonathan Cape.

Sleeper, R.D. (1975). Labour mobility over the life cycle. *British Journal of Industrial Relations, XIII*(2).

Sloman, M. (1994). Coming in from the cold: A new role for trainers. *Personnel Management,* January.

Small is beautiful now, in manufacturing. (1984, October 22). *Business Week,* pp. 65–76.

Smith, D.B., Grojean, M.W., & Ehrhart, M. (2001). An organizational climate regarding ethics: The outcome of leader values and practices that reflect them. *Leadership Quarterly*, Summer, 197–217.

Smith, D.E. (1986). Training programs for performance appraisal: A review. *Academy of Management Review*, *11*, 22–40.

Smith, E.R., & Henry, S. (1996). An in-group becomes part of the self: Response time evidence. *Personality and Social Psychology Bulletin*, *22*, 635–642.

Smith, G.P. (1967). *The motivation of sales executives* (Ashridge Papers in Management Studies, No. 2, Autumn). Berkhamsted, UK: Ashridge Management College.

Smith, M. (1978). Using repertory grids to evaluate training. *Personnel Management*, February, 36–37.

Smith, P.B. (2004). Nations, cultures, and individuals. *Journal of Cross Cultural Psychology*, *35*, 6–12.

Smith, P.B., & Bond, M. (1993). *Social psychology across cultures: Analysis and perspective*. London: Harvester-Wheatsheaf.

Smith, P.B., Misumi, J., Tayeb, M., Peterson, M., & Bond, M. (1989). On the generality of leadership style measures across cultures. *Journal of Occupational Psychology*, *62*, 97–109.

Smith, P.B., & Peterson, M.F. (1988). *Leadership, organisations and culture*. London: Sage.

Smith, P.C., & Kendall, L.M. (1963). Retranslations of expectations: An approach to the construction of unambiguous anchors for rating scales. *Journal of Applied Psychology*, *48*, 149–155.

Smith, R.A., & Houston, M.J. (1985). A psychometric assessment of measures of scripts in consumer memory. *Journal of Consumer Research*, *12*, 214–224.

Snell, R.S. (1996). Complementing Kohlberg: Mapping the ethical reasoning used by managers for their own dilemma cases. *Human Relations*, January, 23–50.

Snow, C.C., Miles, R.E., & Coleman, H.J. (1992). Managing 21st century network organisations. *Organizational Dynamics*, Winter, 5–20.

Snowball, D. (1980). On the integration of accounting research in human information processing. *Accounting and Business Research*, *10*, 307–318.

Snyder, C., & Luthans, F. (1982). The application of OB modification to increase the productivity of hospital personnel. *HR Magazine* (formerly *Personnel Administrator*), August, 72.

Snyder, M., & Gangestad, S. (1987). On the nature of self-monitoring: Matters of assessment, matters of validity. *Journal of Personality and Social Psychology*, *51*, 125–139.

Snyder, N.H., & Graves, M. (1994). Leadership and vision. *Business Horizons*, January–February, 1–2.

Soelberg, P.O. (1967). Unprogrammed decision making. *Industrial Management Review*, *8*, 19–29.

Sofer, V. (1970). *Men in mid-career*. Cambridge, UK: Cambridge University Press.

Solomon, M.R. (1983). The role of products as social stimuli: A symbolic interactionism perspective. *Journal of Consumer Research*, *10*, 319–329.

Sommer, R. (1967). Small group ecology. *Psychological Bulletin*, *67*, 145–152.

Sorcher, M., & Spence, R. (1982). The interface project: Behaviour modelling as social technology in South Africa. *Personnel Psychology*, *35*, 557–581.

Sosik, I.J., & Godshalk, V.W. (2000). Leadership styles, mentoring functions received and job-related stress. A conceptual model and preliminary study. *Journal of Organizational Behaviour*, *21*, 365–390.

Spearman, C. (1904). "General intelligence" objectively determined and measured. *Journal of Psychology*, *15*, 201–293.

Spector, P.E. (2000). A control theory of the job stress process. In C.L. Cooper (Ed)., *Theories of organizational stress*. Oxford: Oxford University Press.

Spector, P.E., Brannick, M.T., & Coovert, M.D. (1989). Job analysis. In C.L. Cooper & I.T. Robertson (Eds.), *International review of industrial and organisational psychology*. Chichester, UK: J. Wiley.

Spence, K.W., Farber, I.E., & McFann, H.H. (1956). The relation of anxiety (drive) level to performance in competitionial and non-competitional paired-associated learning. *Journal of Experimental Psychology*, *52*, 296–305.

Spencer, D.G., & Steers, R.M. (1981). Performance as a moderator of the job satisfaction–turnover relationship. *Journal of Applied Psychology*, August, 511–514.

Stace, D., & Dunphy, D. (2001). *Beyond the boundaries: Leading and creating the successful enterprise*. Sydney: McGraw-Hill.

Stace, D.A. (1996). Transitions and transformations: Four case studies in business-focused change. In J. Storey (Ed.), *Cases in human resource and change management* (pp. 43–72). Oxford, UK: Blackwell Business.

Stahl, M.J., & Harrell, A.M. (1982). Evolution and validation of a behavioural decision theory measurement approach to achievement, power, and affiliation. *Journal of Applied Psychology*, December, 744–751.

Stangor, C., & McMillan, D. (1992). Memory for expectancy-congruent and expectancy-incongruent information: A review of the social and social development literatures. *Psychological Bulletin*, *111*, 42–61.

Starbuck, W.H., & Mezias, J.M. (1996). Opening Pandora's Box: Studying the accuracy of managers' perceptions. *Journal of Organizational Behaviour*, *17*, 99–117.

Starch, D. (1961). Do inside positions differ in readership? Consultancy report cited in A. Anastasi (1979). *Fields of applied psychology* (2nd ed.). New York: McGraw-Hill.

Staw, B.M. (1981). Escalation of commitment to a course of action. *Academy of Management Review*, October, 577–587.

Staw, B.M., & Ross, J. (1988). Good money after bad. *Psychology Today*, February, 30–33.

Steckler, N., & Fondas, N. (1995). Building team leadership effectiveness: A diagnostic tool. *Organizational Dynamics*, Winter, 20.

Stedry, A.C. (1960). *Budget control and cost behaviour*. New York: Prentice Hall.

Stedry, A.C., & Kay, E. (1964). *The effects of goal difficulty on performance: A field experiment*. MIT: Sloan School of Management.

Steedman, H. (1998, August 26). Basics are essential: Vocational training must include literacy and numeracy. *Financial Times*, p. 9.

Steel, R.P., & Rentsch, J.R. (1995). Influence of cumulation strategies on the long range prediction of absenteeism. *Academy of Management Journal*, December, 1616–1634.

Steers, R.M. (1977). Antecedents and outcomes of organisational commitment. *Administrative Science Quarterly*, *22*, 46–56.

Steiner, S. (1999, June 15). Ageism code condemned as toothless. *The Times*, p. 10.

Sternberg, R.J. (1985). *Beyond IQ: A triarchic theory of human intelligence*. New York: Cambridge University Press.

Sternberg, R.J. (2000). In search of the zipperump-a-zoo (Broadbent Lecture on Intelligence). *The Psychologist*, *13*, 250–255.

Sternberg, R.J., Grigorenko, E.L., Ferrar, M., & Clinken-Beard, P. (1999). A triarchic analysis of an aptitude-treatment interaction. *European Journal of Psychological Assessment*, *15*, 1–11.

Sternberg, R.J., & Soriano, E.J. (1984). Styles of conflict resolution. *Journal of Personality and Social Psychology*, July, 115–126.

Stevens, C.K., & Gist, M. (1997). Effects of self-efficacy and goal orientation training in negotiation skill maintenance. What are the mechanisms? *Personnel Psychology*, *50*, 955–978.

Stevens, C.K., & Kristof, A.L. (1995). Making the right impression: A field study of applicant impression management during job interviews. *Journal of Applied Psychology*, October, 587–606.

Stevens, M.J., & Campion, M.A. (1994). The knowledge, skill, and ability requirements for teamwork: Implications for human resource management. *Journal of Management*, Summer, 503–530.

Stewart, J., & Tansley, C. (2002). Training in the knowledge economy. London: CIPD.

Stewart, R. (1982). A model for understanding managerial jobs and behaviour. *Academy of Management Review*, *7*, 7–13.

Stewart, T.A. (1999, January 11). The contest for Welch's throne begins: Who will run GE? *Fortune*, p. 27.

Stogdill, R.M. (1948). Personal factors associated with leadership: A review of the literature. *Journal of Psychology*, *25*, 35–71.

Stogdill, R.M. (1974). *Handbook of leadership*. New York: Free Press.

Stokes, G.S., & Reddy, S. (1992). Use of background data in organizational decisions. In C.L. Cooper & I.T. Robertson (Eds.), *International review of industrial and organizational psychology*. Chichester, UK: J. Wiley.

Stoner, J.A.F. (1961). *A comparison of individual and group decisions involving risk*. Unpublished thesis, School of Industrial Management, MIT, New York.

Stouffer, S.A., Suchman, E.A., Devinney, L.C., Star, S.A., & Williams, R.N. (1949). *The American soldier: Vol. 1. Adjustment during army life*. Princeton, NJ: Princeton University Press.

Strassman, P.A. (1982). Overview of strategic aspects of information management. *Office: Technology and People*, *1*, 71–89.

Strauss, G. (1968). Human relations—1968 style. *Industrial Relations*, *7*, 262–276.

Strauss, G., & Sayles, L.R. (1960). *Personnel: The human problems of management*. New York: Prentice Hall.

Stuttaford, T. (1999, 14 October). Addicted to risk? It's your novelty gene. *The Times*, p. 38.

Suinn, R.M. (1976). How to break the vicious cycle of stress. *Psychology Today*, December, 59–60.

Sulin, R.A., & Dooling, D.J. (1974). Intrusion of a thematic idea in retention of prose. *Journal of Experimental Psychology*, *103*, 244–262.

Summers, D. (1990a, November 23). An act of faith that can reap rewards. *Financial Times*.

Summers, D. (1990b, December 7). Testing for stress in the workplace. *Financial Times*.

Sunday Times (1986, September 21). An account of the Colwich Junction train accident.

Sundstrom, E., De Meuse, K.P., & Futrell, D. (1990). Work teams: Applications and effectiveness. *American Psychologist*, February, 120–133.

Sutherland, V., & Cooper, C.L. (1987). *Man and accidents offshore*. London: Lloyds.

Sutton, S.R. (1982). Fear-arousing communications: A critical examination of theory and research. In J.R. Eiser (Ed.), *Social psychology and behavioural medicine*. Chichester, UK: Wiley.

Swann, W.B., & Ely, R.J. (1984). A battle of wills: Self-verification versus behavioural confirmation. *Journal of Personality and Social Psychology*, *46*, 1287–1302.

Swinburne, P. (1981). The psychological impact of unemployment on managers and professional staff. *Journal of Occupational Psychology*, *54*, 47–64.

Syme, S.L., Hyman, M.M., & Enterline, P.E. (1964). Cultural mobility and the occurrence of coronary heart disease. *Journal of Health and Human Behaviour*, 6, 178–189.

Szilagi, A.D., & Wallace, M.J. (1983). *Organisational behaviour and performance* (3rd ed.). Glenview, IL: Scott, Foresman.

Taggart, W., & Robey, D. (1981). Minds and managers: On the dual nature of human information processing and management. *Academy of Management Review*, April, 190.

Tailby, S., & Turnbull, P. (1987). Learning to manage just-in-time. *Personnel Management*, January.

Tait, N. (1999, August 31). Daimler Chrysler: Corporate TV counts. *Financial Times*.

Tait, N. (2005, March 22). Cantor close to settlement with bullied trader. *Financial Times*, p. 2.

Tajfel, H. (1970). Experiments in inter-group discrimination. *Scientific American*, 223, 96–102.

Tajfel, H., & Turner, J.C. (1985). The social identity theory of inter-group behaviour. In S. Worchel & W.G. Austin (Eds.), *Psychology of inter-group relations* (2nd ed.). Chicago: Nelson-Hall.

Tang, S.F.Y., & Kirkbridge, P.S. (1986). Developing conflict management in Hong Kong: An analysis of some cross-cultural implications. *Management Education and Development*, 17, 287–301.

Tannenbaum, A.S. (1962). Control in organisations: Individual adjustment and organisational performance. *Administrative Science Quarterly*, 7, 236–257.

Tannenbaum, R., & Schmidt, W.H. (1973). How to choose a leadership pattern. *Harvard Business Review*, May–June, 162–180.

Tannenbaum, S.I., & Yukl, G.A. (1992). Training and development in work organizations. *Annual Review of Psychology*, 43, 399–441.

Tapsell, J., & Cox, J. (1997). The writing on the wall: Graphology and its validity in personnel assessment. *Selection and Development Review*, 13, 3–6.

Taylor, A. (2005, February 23). Teenage talent wasted by ageism at work. *Financial Times*, p. 6.

Taylor, D. (1996). The healing power of stories. *The Therapist*, 14, 8–13.

Taylor, F.W. (1947). *Scientific management*. New York: Harper & Row.

Taylor, M.S., Tracy, K.B., Renard, M.K., Harrison, J.K., & Carrol, S.J. (1995). Due process in performance appraisal: A quasi-experiment in procedural justice. *Administrative Science Quarterly*, September, 495–523.

Taylor, R. (1993, September 1). Not a penny more, not a penny less. *Financial Times*.

Tedeschi, J., Schlenker, B., & Bonoma, T. (1973). Cognitive dissonance: Private rationalisation or public spectacle. In W. Scott & L. Cummings (Eds.), *Readings in organisational behaviour and human performance*. Homewood, IL: Richard Irwin.

Teel, K.S. (1978). Self-appraisal revisited. *Personnel Journal*, 57, 364–367.

Terman, L.W. (1904). A preliminary study of the psychology and pedagogy of leadership. *Journal of Genetic Psychology*, 11, 413–451.

Terpstra, D.E. (1981). Relationship between methodological rigour and reported outcomes in organisation development evaluation research. *Journal of Applied Psychology*, 66, 541–543.

Terry, D.J., Hogg, M.A., & White, K.M. (1999). The theory of planned behaviour: Self-identity, social identity and group norms. *British Journal of Social Psychology*, 38, 225–244.

Terry, G.R. (1968). *Principles of management*. Homewood, IL: Richard D. Irwin.

Tesser, A., & Shaffer, D. (1990). Attitudes and attitude change. In M.R. Rosenzweig & L.W. Porter (Eds.), *Annual review of psychology, Vol. 41*. Palo Alto, CA: Annual Reviews Inc.

Thach, L., & Woodman, R.W. (1994). Organizational change and information technology: Managing on the edge of cyberspace. *Organizational Dynamics*, Summer, 30.

Thaler, R.H., & Johnson, E.J. (1990). Gambling with house money and trying to break even. The effects of prior outcomes on risky choice. Management Science, 36, 643–660.

Thatcher, M. (1997, May 15). A test of character. *People Management*.

Thayer, P.W. (1997). A rapidly changing world: Some implications for training systems in the year 2001 and beyond. In M.A. Quinones & A. Ehrenstein (Eds.), *Training for a rapidly changing workplace: Applications of psychological research*. Washington, DC: American Psychological Association.

Thierren, L. (1989, November 13). The rival Japan respects. *Business Week*, pp. 108–120.

Thomas, J., & Griffin, R.W. (1983). The social information processing model of task design: A review of the literature. *Academy of Management Review*, October, 672–682.

Thomas, K.W. (1977). Toward multi-dimensional values in teaching: The example of conflict behaviours. *Academy of Management Review*, 2(July), 484–490.

Thomas, K.W. (1992). Conflict and negotiation processes in organizations. In M.D. Dunnette & L.M. Hough (Eds.), *Handbook of industrial and organisational psychology* (2nd ed., Vol. 3). Palo Alto, CA: Consulting Psychologists Press.

Thomas, T. (1993, February 14). Move me, move my spouse. *Sunday Times*, p. 4.2.

Thompson, J.D. (1967). *Organisations in action*. New York: McGraw-Hill.

Thompson, P., & McHugh, D. (1995). *Work organisation: A critical introduction* (2nd ed.). London: Macmillan Education.

Thompson, P., & McHugh, D. (2002). *Work organizations* (3rd ed.). Basingstoke, UK: Palgrave.

Thompson, S.B.N. (1997). War experiences and post-traumatic stress disorder. *The Psychologist*, August, 349–350.

Thomsett, R. (1980). *People and project management*. New York: Yourdon Press.

Thorndike, E.L. (1911). *Animal intelligence*. New York: Macmillan.

Thorndike, E.L., Hagen, E.P., & Satlet, J.M. (1986). *Stanford-Binet intelligence scale: Guide for administering and scoring the fourth edition*. Chicago: Riverside Publishing.

Thornhill, J. (2000, August 5/6). Unilever's rejig takes inspiration from its origin. *Financial Times*, p. 12.

Thornton, G.C. (1992). *Assessment centers in human resource management*. Reading, MA: Addison Wesley.

Thottam, J. (2003, August 18). Where the good jobs are going. *Time*, pp. 34–36.

Thurstone, L.L. (1938). *Primary mental abilities* (Psychometric Monographs, No. 1). Chicago: University of Chicago Press.

Thurstone, L.L., & Chave, E.J. (1929). *The measurement of attitudes*. Chicago: University of Chicago Press.

Thurstone, L.L., & Thurstone, T.G. (1942). Factorial studies of intelligence. *Psychometric Monographs*, No. 2.

Thurstone, L.L., & Thurstone, T.G. (1963). *SRA primary abilities*. Chicago: Science Research Associates.

Tichy, N.M., & Devanna, M.A. (1986). *The transformational leader*. New York: John Wiley.

Tichy, N.M., & Ulrich, D.O. (1984). The leadership challenge: A call for the transformational leader. *Sloan Management Review*, Fall, 59–68.

Tiffin, J., & McCormick, E.J. (1969). *Industrial psychology* (3rd ed.). London: George Allen & Unwin.

Time (2002, July 8). How to hide US$3,852,000,000: p. 28.

Timmins, N. (2002, May 1). Work myths study shows rise in staff discontent. *Financial Times*, p. 5.

Tjosvold, D., & Deemer, D.K. (1980). Effects of controversy within a co-operative or competitive context on organisational decision making. *Journal of Applied Psychology*, 65, 590–595.

Tjosvold, D., Wedley, W.C., & Field, R.H.G. (1986). Constructive controversy, the Vroom-Yetton model, and managerial decision making. *Journal of Occupational Behaviour*, 7, 125–138.

Tolman, E.C. (1948). Cognitive maps in rats and men. *Psychological Review*, 55, 189.

Toplis, J., Dulewicz, V., & Fletcher, C. (1987). *Psychological testing: A practical guide for employers*. London: Institute of Personnel Management.

Torrington, D., Hall, L., & Taylor, S. (2002). *Human resource management* (5th ed.). Harlow, UK: FT Prentice Hall.

Torrington, D., Hall, L., & Taylor, S. (2005). *Human resource management* (6th ed.). Harlow, UK: Pearson Education.

Tourish, D. & Pinnington, A. (2002). Transformational leadership, corporate cultism, and the spirituality paradigm: An unholy trinity in the workplace. *Human Relations*, 55, 147–172.

Townsend, A.M., DeMarie, S.M., & Hendrickson, A.R. (1998). Virtual teams: Technology and the workplace of the future. *Academy of Management Executive*, August, 17–29.

Traini, R. (1983, January 16). Computer detection. *The Sunday Times*.

Trevino, L.K., & Nelson, K.A. (1995). *Managing business ethics: Straight talking about how to do it right*. New York: Wiley.

Trice, H.M., & Beyer, J.M. (1984). Studying organisational cultures through rites and rituals. *Academy of Management Review*, 9, 653–669.

Trice, H.M., & Beyer, J.M. (1991). Cultural leadership in organizations. *Organization Science*, May, 149–169.

Trist, E.L., & Bamforth, K.W. (1951). Some social and psychological consequences of the longwall method of coal-getting. *Human Relations*, 4, 3–38.

Trompenaars, A. (1993). *Riding the wave of culture: Understanding cultural diversity in business*. London: Nicholas Brealey.

Tubbs, M.E. (1993). Commitment as a moderator of the goal–performance relation: A case for clearer construct definition. *Journal of Applied Psychology*, February, 86–97.

Tucker, S. (2004, August 2). Executive bonuses poorly linked to success. *Financial Times*, p. 1.

Tuckman, B.W. (1965). Development sequence in small groups. *Psychological Bulletin*, 63, 384–399.

Tulving, E. (1968). Theoretical issues in free recall. In T. Dixon & D. Horton (Eds.), *Verbal behaviour and general behaviour theory*. New York: Prentice Hall.

Tulving, E. (1985). How many memory systems are there? *American Psychologist*, 40, 385–398.

Turban, D.B., & Dougherty, T.M. (1994). Role of protégé personality in receipt of mentoring and career success. *Academy of Management Journal*, 37, 688–702.

Turner, A.N., & Lawrence, P.R. (1965). *Industrial jobs and the worker*. Cambridge, MA: Harvard University Press.

Turner, D. (2004a, October 6). Pay rates reflect action on national minimum wage. *Financial Times*, p. 4.

Turner, D. (2004b, March 1). Work offers cures as stress tops the sick list. *Financial Times*, p. 4.

Turner, J.C. (1981). The experimental social psychology of inter-group behaviour. In J.C. Turner & H. Giles (Eds.), *Inter-group behaviour*. Oxford, UK: Blackwell.

Tushman, M., & O'Reilly, C.A. (1996). *Staying on top. Managing strategic innovation and change for long term success*. Boston: Harvard Business Press.

Tversky, A., & Kahneman, D. (1974). Judgement under uncertainty: Heuristics and biases. *Science, 185,* 1124–1131.

Tversky, A., & Kahneman, D. (1981). The framing of decisions and the psychology of choice. *Science, 211,* 453–458.

Tyson, S., & Jackson, T. (1992). *The essence of organisational behaviour.* Hemel Hempstead, UK: Prentice Hall.

Underwood, B.J. (1964). The representativeness of rote verbal learning. In A.W. Melton (Ed.), *Categories of human learning.* New York: Academic Press.

Urwick, L. (1947). *The elements of administration.* London: Pitman.

Urwick, L. (1952). *Notes on the theory of organization.* New York: American Management Association.

Useem, M. (1997). The true worth of building high-performance systems. In *Mastering management: Module 8. Managing people in organizations* (pp. 288–292). London: FT/Pitman Publishing.

Useem, M. (2000, November 20). Skills of management. How to groom the leaders of the future. *FT Mastering Management, Part 8,* pp. 8–10.

Useem, M. (2001, October 29). The ups and downs of leading people. *FT Mastering People Management,* pp. 6, 8.

Van Aken, E.M., Monetta, D.J., & Scott Sink, D. (1994). Affinity groups: The missing link in employee involvement. *Organizational Dynamics,* Spring, 38–54.

Van der Zee, K.I., Atsma, N., & Brodbeck, P. (2004). The influence of social identity and personality outcomes of cultural identity in teams. *Journal of Cross Cultural Psychology, 35,* 283–303.

Van der Zee, K.I., Bakker, A.B., & Bakker, P. (2002). Why are structured interviews so rarely used in personnel selection? *Journal of Applied Psychology,* February, 176–184.

Van de Ven, A.H., & Delbecq, A.L. (1974). The effectiveness of nominal, delphi, and interacting group decision-making processes. *Academy of Management Review,* December, 606–615.

Van de Vliert, E. (1985). Escalative intervention in small groups. *Journal of Applied Behavioural Science, 21,* 19–36.

Van de Vliert, E., & De Dreu, C.K.W. (1994). Optimising performance by conflict stimulation. *International Journal of Conflict Management,* July, 211–222.

Van de Vliert, E., & Kabanoff, B. (1990). Toward theory-based measures of conflict management. *Academy of Management Journal, 33,* 199–209.

Van Eerde, W., & Thierry, H. (1996). Vroom's expectancy models and work-related criteria: A meta-analysis. *Journal of Applied Psychology,* October, 575–586.

Van Fleet, D. (1983). Span of management research and issues. *Academy of Management Journal,* September, 546–552.

Van Fleet, D.D., & Yukl, G.A. (1989). A century of leadership research. In W.E. Robsenbach & R.L. Taylor (Eds.), *Contemporary issues in leadership* (2nd ed.). London: Westview Press.

Van Hiel, A., & Mervielde, I. (2001). Preferences for behavioral style of minority and majority members who anticipate group interaction. *Social Behavior and Personality, 29,* 701–710.

Van Knippenberg, A. (1984). Intergroup differences in group perceptions. In H. Tajfel (Ed.), *The social dimension: European developments in social psychology, Vol. 2.* Cambridge, UK: Cambridge University Press.

Van Knippenberg, D. (2000). Work motivation and performance: A social identity perspective. *Applied Psychology: An International Review, 49,* 357–371.

Van Maanen, J., & Schein, E.H. (1977). Career development. In J.R. Hackman & J.L. Suttle (Eds.), *Improving life at work.* Santa Monica, CA: Goodyear.

Vaughn, L.A. (1999). Effects of uncertainty on use of the availability heuristic for self-efficacy judgements. *European Journal of Social Psychology,* March–May, 407–410.

Vecchio, R.P. (1987). Situational leadership theory: An examination of a prescriptive theory. *Journal of Applied Psychology, 72,* 444–451.

Vecchio, R.P. (1990). Theoretical and empirical examination of cognitive resource theory. *Journal of Applied Psychology,* April, 141–147.

Vecchio, R.P. (1995). *Organizational behavior* (3rd ed.). Orlando, FL: Dryden Press.

Vecchio, R.P. (2003). *Organizational behavior: Core concepts* (5th ed.). Mason, OH: Thomson South Western.

Vecchio, R.P., & Gobdel, B.C. (1984). The vertical dyad linkage model of leadership: Problems and prospects. *Organisational Behaviour and Human Performance, 34,* 5–20.

Vecchio, R.P., & Keon, T.L. (1981). Predicting employee satisfaction from congruency among individual need, job design, and system structure. *Journal of Occupational Behaviour, 2,* 283–292.

Vega, G. (2003). *Managing teleworkers and telecommunicating strategies.* London: Praeger.

Venkatesan, M. (1966). Experimental study of consumer behaviour: Conformity and independence. *Journal of Marketing Research, 3,* November, 384–387.

Vernon, P.E. (1956). *The measurement of abilities.* London: University of London Press.

Veroff, J. (1953). Development and validation of a projective measure of power motivation. *Journal of Abnormal and Social Psychology, 55,* 1–8.

Voke, J. (1982). Colour vision problems at work. *Health and Safety at Work,* January, 27–28.

Volkema, R.J., & Bergmann, T.J. (1995). Conflict styles as indicators of behavioural patterns in interpersonal conflicts. *Journal of Social Psychology*, February, 5–15.

Von Neumann, J., & Morgenstern, O. (1953). *Theory of games and economic behaviour*. Princeton, NJ: Princeton University Press.

Voyle, S. (2003, June 13). Why Sainsbury put its money on a wholesale system change. *Financial Times*.

Vroom, V.H. (1964). *Work and motivation*. New York: Wiley.

Vroom, V.H. (2000). Leadership and the decision making process. *Organizational Dynamics*, Spring, 82–93.

Vroom, V.H., & Jago, A.G. (1988). *The new leadership: Managing participation in organisations*. New York: Prentice Hall.

Vroom, V.H., & Jago, A.G. (1995). Situational effects and levels of analysis in the study of leader participation. *Leadership Quarterly*, Summer, 169–181.

Vroom, V.H., & Yetton, P.W. (1973). *Leadership and decision making*. Pittsburgh, PA: University of Pittsburgh Press.

Wagner, J.A. (1994). Participation's effects on performance and satisfaction: A reconsideration of the research evidence. *Academy of Management Review*, *19*, 312–330.

Wagstyl, S. (1996, July 29). Lifeblood from transplants: A revolution in British manufacturing has been heavily influenced by Japanese groups such as Nissan. *Financial Times*, p. 15.

Waister, E., & Festinger, L. (1962). The effectiveness of overheard persuasive communications. *Journal of Abnormal and Social Psychology*, *65*, 3–402.

Walker, C.R., & Guest, R. (1952). *The man on the assembly line*. Cambridge, MA: Harvard University Press.

Walker, M.J., Huber, G.P., & Glick, W.H. (1995). Functional background as a determinant of executive's selective perception. *Academy of Management Journal*, August, 943–974.

Wall Jr, J.A., & Callister, R.R. (1995). Conflict and its management. *Journal of Management*, *21*, 515–558.

Wall, T.D., Corbett, J.M., Jackson, C.W., & Martin, R. (1990). Advanced manufacturing technology and work design: Towards a theoretical framework. *Journal of Organisational Behaviour*, *11*, 201–219.

Wall, T.D., Cordery, J.L., & Clegg, C.W. (2002). Empowerment, performance and operational uncertainty: A theoretical integration. *Applied Psychology: An International Review*, *51*, 146–169.

Wall, T.D., Kemp, N.J., Jackson, P.R., & Clegg, C.W. (1986). Outcomes of autonomous work groups: A long-term field experiment. *Academy of Management Journal*, June, 280–304.

Wallace, L.M. (1986). Communication variables in the design of pre-surgical preparatory information. *British Journal of Clinical Psychology*, *25*, 111–118.

Wallach, M.A., & Kogan, N. (1965). The roles of information, discussion, and consensus in group risk taking. *Journal of Experimental Social Psychology*, *1*, 1–19.

Wallis, C. (2005, February 7). The new science of happiness. *Time*, pp. 45–50.

Wallston, B.S., & Wallston, K.A. (1978). Locus of control and health. *Health Education Monographs*, Spring, 107–115.

Walton, M. (1997) Organization culture and its impact on counselling. In M. Carroll and M. Walton (Eds.), *Handbook of counselling in organizations* (pp. 92–109). London: Sage Publications.

Walton, R.E. (1969). *Interpersonal peacemaking: Confrontations and third party consultation*. Reading, MA: Addison-Wesley.

Wanberg, C.R., Kammeyer-Mueller, J., & Shi, K. (2001). Job loss and the experience of unemployment: International research and perspectives. In N. Anderson, D.S. Ones, H.K. Sinangil, & C. Viswesvaran (Eds.), *Handbook of work, industrial and organizational psychology, Vol. 2*. London: Sage Publications.

Wardwell, W.I., Hyman, M., & Bahnson, C.B. (1964). Stress and coronary disease in three field studies. *Journal of Chronic Diseases*, *17*, 73–84.

Warner, M., & Witzel, M. (2004). *Managing in virtual organizations*. London: Thomson.

Warr, P., & Ainsworth, E. (1999). 360-degree feedback: Some recent research. *Selection and Development Review*, *15*, 3–6.

Warr, P., Cook, J., & Wall, T. (1979). Scales for the measurement of some work attitudes and aspects of psychological well-being. *Journal of Occupational Psychology*, *52*, 129–148.

Warr, P.B., & Jackson, P.R. (1984). Men without jobs: Some correlates of age and length of unemployment. *Journal of Occupational Psychology*, *57*, 77–85.

Warr, P.B., & Knapper, G. (1968). *The perception of people and events*. Chichester, UK: J. Wiley & Son.

Warrington, E.K., & Sanders, H. (1972). The fate of old memories. *Quarterly Journal of Experimental Psychology*, *23*, 432–442.

Warwick, K. (2004, April 8). Wired learning: Mind blending. *People Management*, pp. 32–33.

Wastell, D.G., White, P., & Kawalek, P. (1994). A methodology for business process redesign: Experience and issues. *Journal of Strategic Information Systems*, *3*, 23–40.

Waters, R. (1998, September 15). Aiming for moving goalposts. *Financial Times*, p. 19.

Watkin, C. (1999). Emotional Competency Inventory (ECI). *Selection and Development Review*, October, 13–16.

Watson, J.B., & Rayner, R. (1920). Conditioned emotional reactions. *Journal of Experimental Psychology*, *3*, 1–14.

Watson, T. (1994). *In search of management: Culture, chaos, and control in managerial work.* London: Routledge.

Watson, T.J. (2004). HRM and critical social science analysis. *Journal of Management Studies, 41,* 447–467.

Watson, W.E., Kumar, K., & Michaelsen, L.K. (1993). Cultural diversity's impact on interaction process and performance: Comparing homogeneous and diverse task groups. *Academy of Management Journal,* June, 590–602.

Waugh, N.C., & Norman, D.A. (1965). Primary memory. *Psychological Review, 72,* 89–104.

Wayne, S.J., & Kacmar, K.M. (1991). The effects of impression management on the performance appraisal process. *Organizational Behaviour and Human Decision Processes,* February, 70–88.

Weaving, K. (1995, March 3). Sweeping fear from the floor. *Financial Times,* p. 13.

Weber, M. (1947). *The theory of social and economic organization* (Trans.). Oxford, UK: Oxford University Press.

Weber, M. (1958). *The protestant ethic and the spirit of capitalism* (Trans.). New York: Scribner.

Webster, F.E., & Von Pechmann, F. (1970). A replication of the shopping list study. *Journal of Marketing, 34,* 61–77.

Wechsler, D. (1981). *Manual for Wechsler adult intelligence scale* (Rev. ed.). San Antonio, TX: The Psychological Corporation.

Wegge, J. (2000). Participation in group goal setting: Some novel findings and a comprehensive model as a new ending to an old story. *Applied Psychology: An International Review, 49,* 498–516.

Wehner, R., & Menzel, R. (1990). Do insects have cognitive maps? *Annual Review of Neuroscience, 13,* 403–414.

Weiner, B., Frieze, I., Kukla, A., Reid, L., Rest, S., & Rosenbaum, R.M. (1972). Perceiving the causes of success and failure. In E.E. Jones, D.E. Knouse, H.H. Kelley, R.E. Nisbett, S. Valins, & B. Weiner (Eds.), *Attribution: Perceiving the causes of behavior.* Morristown, NJ: General Learning Press.

Weiner, I.B. (2001). Advancing the science of psychological assessment: The Rorschach inkblot method as exemplar. *Psychological Assessment, 13,* 423–432.

Weiss, H.M., & Cropanzano, R.R. (1996). Affective events theory: A theoretical discussion of the structure, causes and consequences of affective experiences at work. In B.M. Staw & L.L. Cummings (Eds.), *Research in organizational behaviour* (Vol. 18, pp. 1–3). Greenwich, CT: JAI Press.

Weissenberg, P., & Kavanagh, M.J. (1972). The independence of initiating structure and consideration: A review of the evidence. *Personnel Psychology, 25,* 119–130.

Weist, J.D. (1966). Heuristic programs for decision making. *Harvard Business Review,* September–October, 129–143.

Wellins, R.S., Byham, W.C., & Dixon, G.R. (1994). *Inside teams.* San Francisco: Jossey-Bass.

Wells, W.D., & Tigert, D.J. (1971). Activities, interests and opinions. *Journal of Advertising Research, 11,* 27–35.

Wernimont, P. (1966). Intrinsic and extrinsic factors in job satisfaction. *Journal of Applied Psychology, 50*(1), 41–50.

West, M. (1998, November). *Job satisfaction.* Paper presented at the Institute of Personnel and Development Conference, Harrogate, UK.

West, M. (2000). Creativity and innovation at work. *The Psychologist, 13,* 460–463.

West M. (2002). Sparkling fountains or stagnant ponds. An integrative model of creativity and innovation implementation in work groups. *Applied Psychology: An International Review, 51,* 355–387.

Westley, F., & Mintzberg, H. (1989). Visionary leadership and strategic management. *Strategic Management Journal, 10,* 17–32.

Westwood, R. (1992). *Organisational behaviour: Southeast Asia perspectives.* Hong Kong: Longman (Far East).

Wexley, K.N. (1984). Personnel training. *Annual Review of Psychology, 35,* 519–551.

Whelan, C.T. (1992). The role of income, life-style deprivation and financial strain in mediating the impact of unemployment on psychological distress: Evidence from the Republic of Ireland. *Journal of Occupational Psychology, 65,* 331–344.

Where are the leaders? (1993, July 12). *Time,* pp. 12–17.

Whisler, T.L. (1970). *The impact of computers on organisations.* New York: Praeger.

White, D. (2002, April 1). Away-days. How to build boats and boost morale. *Financial Times,* p. 8.

White, R.W. (1960). Competence and psychosexual stages of development. In M.R. Jones (Ed.), *Nebraska symposium on motivation* (pp. 97–141). Lincoln, NE: University of Nebraska Press.

Whitelaw, W. (1989). *The Whitelaw memoirs.* London: Aurum Press.

Whyte, G. (1989). Groupthink reconsidered. *Academy of Management Review, 14,* 40–56.

Wickens, P. (1987). *The road to Nissan: Flexibility, quality, teamwork.* Basingstoke, UK: Macmillan.

Wickham, T. (1993, October 17). Time is of the essence: Back to the black. *Sunday Times,* p. 7.

Wicks, R.P. (1984). Interviewing: Practical aspects. In C.L. Cooper & P. Makin (Eds.), *Psychology for managers.* Basingstoke, UK: BPS/Macmillan Publishers.

Wighton, D. (2005, March 2). Citigroup in global drive to boost standards. *Financial Times,* p. 29.

Williams, D.E., & Page, M.M. (1989). A multi-dimensional measure of Maslow's hierarchy of needs. *Journal of Research in Personality, 23,* 192–213.

Williams, D.R., & House, J.S. (1985). Social support and stress reduction. In C.L. Cooper & M.J. Smith (Eds.), *Job stress and blue-collar work.* Chichester, UK: Wiley.

Williams, M. (2001). In whom we trust. Group membership as an affective context for trust development. *Academy of Management Review,* July, 377–396.

Williams, M.L., Podsakoff, P.W., Lodor, W.S., Huber, V.L., Howell, J.P., & Dorfman, P.W. (1988). A premliminary analysis of the construct validity of Kerr and Jermier's substitutes for leadership scales. *Journal of Occupational Psychology, 61,* 307–333.

Williams, R. (1984). What's new in career development. *Personnel Management,* March, 31–33.

Williams, R. (1998). *Performance management.* London: Thompson Business Press.

Williams, T. (1985). Visual display technology, worker disablement, and work organisation. *Human Relations, 38,* 1065–1084.

Willman, J. (2000, August 8). Investment, but not as we know it. *Financial Times,* p. 17.

Wills, J. (1999). European Works Councils in British firms. *Human Resource Management Journal, 9,* 19–38.

Wilson, D.C. (1992). *A strategy of change.* London: Routledge.

Winnett, R. (2005, January 30). Lie detector machines planned to tackle benefit fraud. *The Sunday Times* (News section), p. 3.

Withey, M.J., & Cooper, W.H. (1989). Predicting exit, voice, loyalty, and neglect. *Administrative Science Quarterly,* December, 521–539.

Witkin, H.A. (1965). Psychological differentiation and forms of pathology. *Journal of Abnormal and Social Psychology, 70,* 317–336.

Witt, L.A., & Nye, L.G. (1992). Gender and the relationship between perceived fairness of pay or promotion and job satisfaction. *Journal of Applied Psychology,* December, 910–917.

Witzel, M. (2004, December 12). Memo to the CEO (Part 4): Why businesses must stay in training. *Financial Times,* p. 7.

Woehr, D.J., & Feldman, J. (1993). Processing objective and question order effects on the causal relation between memory and judgement in performance appraisal: The tip of the iceberg. *Journal of Applied Psychology,* April, 232–241.

Wofford, J.C., & Liska, L.Z. (1993). Path–goal theories of leadership: A meta-analysis. *Journal of Management,* Winter, 857–876.

Wolfe, J.B. (1936). Effectiveness of token rewards for chimpanzees. *Comparative Psychology Monographs, 12*(Whole No. 60).

Womack, J.P., Jones, D.T., & Roos, D. (1990). *The machine that changed the world.* New York: Macmillan.

Wood, J.D. (1997). Culture is not enough. In *Mastering management: Module 13. Managing across cultures* (pp. 414–418). FT/Pitman Publishing.

Wood, J.D., & Colosi, T.R. (1997). The subtle art of negotiation. In *Mastering management: Module 13. Managing across cultures* (pp. 419–425). London: FT/Pitman Publishing.

Wood, J.M., & Lilienfeld, S.O. (1999). The Rorschach Inkblot Test: A case of overstatement. *Assessment, 6,* 341–351.

Wood, L. (1993, November 17). Take care when rewarding high flyers. *Financial Times,* p. 22.

Wood, L. (1998, October 5). Negotiating skills: Dealing across the cultures. *Financial Times* (Business Education), p. 4.

Wood, L., & Goodhart, D. (1993, September 20). Workers give job security lower priority. *Financial Times,* p. 80.

Wood, R.E., & Atkins, P. (2000). Self-efficacy and strategy on complex tasks. *Applied Psychology: An International Review, 49,* 430–446.

Wood, W. (2000). Attitude change: Persuasion and social influence. *Annual Review of Psychology, 51,* 539–570.

Wood, W., & Kallgren, C.A. (1988). Communicator attributes and persuasion: Recipients' access to attitude-relevant information in memory. *Personality and Social Psychology Bulletin, 14,* 172–182.

Wood, W., Lundgren, S., Ouellette, J.A., Buscene, S., & Blackstone, T. (1994). Minority influence: A meta analytic review of social influence processes. *Psychological Bulletin, 115,* 323–345.

Woodcock, M. (1979). *Team development manual.* Farnborough, UK: Gower Publishing.

Woodhead, M. (1998, September 20). Daimler's culture collide. *The Sunday Times* (Business section), pp. 3–10.

Woodruffe, C. (1993). What is meant by competency? *Leadership and Organization Journal, 4,* 27–36.

Woodruffe, C. (2000a). Emotional intelligence. Time for a time out. *Selection and Development Review, 16,* 3–9.

Woodruffe, C. (2000b). *Development and assessment centers. Identifying and assessing competence.* London: Chartered Institute of Personnel and Development.

Woodward, H., & Bucholtz, S. (1987). *Aftershock: Helping people through corporate change.* New York: Wiley.

Woodward, J. (1965). *Industrial organisations: Theory and practice.* London: Oxford University Press.

Woodward, J. (1970). *Industrial organisations: Behaviour and control.* London: Oxford University Press.

Work Research Unit, Department of Employment. (1983). *Small group activities: Quality circles.* Review of a conference organised by the Work Research Unit and sponsored by the National Economic Development Office, March. London: Author.

Worren, N.A.M., Ruddle, K., & Moore, K. (1999). From organizational development to change management: The emergence of a new profession. *Journal of Applied Behavioural Science, 35,* 273–286.

Worthy, J.C. (1950). Organisational structure and employee morale. *American Sociological Review, 15,* 169–179.

Wright, D.S., Taylor, A., Davies, D.R., Sluckin, W., Lee, S.G.M., & Reason, J.T. (1970). *Introducing psychology: An experimental approach.* London: Penguin.

Wright, G., van der Heijden, K., Bradfield, R., & Cairns, G. (2004). The psychology of why organisations can be slow to adapt and change. *Journal of General Management, 29,* 21–36.

Wright, P.L., & Taylor, D.S. (1984). *Improving leadership performance.* New York: Prentice Hall.

Wright, P.M., O'Leary-Kelly, A.M., Cortina, J.M., Klein, H.J., & Hollenbeck, J.R. (1994). On the meaning and measurement of goal commitment. *Journal of Applied Psychology, 79,* 795–803.

Wrightsman, L. (1960). Effects of waiting for others on changes in level of felt anxiety. *Journal of Abnormal and Social Psychology, 61,* 216–222.

Xenikou, A., & Furnham, A. (1996). A correlational and factor analytic study of different measures of corporate culture. *Human Relations, 49,* 349–371.

Xin, K.R., & Tsui, A.S. (1996). Different strokes for different folks? Influence tactics by Asian-American and Caucasian-American managers. *Leadership Quarterly,* Spring, 109–132.

Yablonsky, L. (1967). *The violent gang.* Harmondsworth, UK: Penguin.

Yammarino, F.J., & Dublinsky, A.J. (1994). Transformational leadership theory: Using levels of analysis to determine boundary conditions. *Personnel Psychology, 47,* 787–800.

Yearta, S.K., Maithis, S., & Briner, R.B. (1995). An exploratory study of goal setting in theory and practice: A motivational technique that works. *Journal of Occupational and Organizational Psychology, 68,* 237–252.

Young, M., & Post, J.E. (1993). Managing to communicate, communicating to manage: How leading companies communicate with employees. *Organizational Dynamics,* Summer, 31–43.

Yuchtman, E., & Seashore, S. (1967). A system resource approach to organisational effectiveness. *American Sociological Review,* December, 891–903.

Yukl, G.A. (1994). *Leadership in organizations* (3rd ed.). Englewood Cliffs, NJ: Prentice Hall.

Yukl, G.A., & Falbe, C.M. (1990). Influence tactics in upward, downward, and lateral influence attempts. *Journal of Applied Psychology, 75,* 132–140.

Yukl, G.A., Kim, H., & Falbe, C. (1996). Antecedents of influence outcomes. *Journal of Applied Psychology,* June, 309–317.

Yukl, G.A., Latham, G.P., & Elliott, D.P. (1976). The effectiveness of performance incentives under continuous and variable ratio schedules of reinforcement. *Personnel Psychology, 29,* 221–231.

Yukl, G.A., & Tracey, J.B. (1992). Consequences of influence tactics used with subordinates, peers, and the boss. *Journal of Applied Psychology, 77,* 522–535.

Zairi, M., Letza, S., & Oakland, J. (1994). Does TQM impact on bottom line results. *TQM Magazine, 6,* 38–43.

Zajonc, R.B., & Markus, H. (1982). Affective and cognitive factors in preferences. *Journal of Consumer Research, 9.*

Zajonc, R.B., & Sales, S.M. (1966). Social facilitation of dominant and subordinate responses. *Journal of Experimental Social Psychology, 2,* 160–168.

Zaleznik, A. (1986). Managers and leaders: Are they different? *Harvard Business Review,* May–June, 54.

Zaltman, G., & Duncan, R. (1977). *Strategies for planned change.* New York: John Wiley.

Zaltman, G., & Wallandorf, M. (1979). *Consumer behaviour: Basic findings and managerial implications.* New York: John Wiley & Sons.

Zander, A. (1982). *Making groups effective.* San Francisco: Jossey-Bass.

Zaremba, A. (1988). Working with the organisational grapevine. *Personnel Journal,* July, 38–42.

Zeelenberg, M., Beattie, J., Van Der Plight, J., & DeVries, N.K. (1996). Consequences of regret aversion: Effects of expected feedback on risky decision making. *Organizational Behavior and Human Decision Processes, 65,* 148–158.

Zhou, J., & George, J.M. (2001). When job satisfaction leads to creativity: Encouraging the expression of voice. *Academy of Management Journal, 44,* 682–696.

Zohar, D. (1980). Prompting the use of personal protective equipment by behaviour modification techniques. *Journal of Safety Research, 12*(Summer), 78–85.

Zuckerman, M. (1990). The psychophysiology of sensation seeking. *Journal of Personality, 58,* 313–345.

Zuckerman, M. (1995). Good and bad humours: Biochemical basis of personality and its disorders. *Psychological Science, 6,* 325–332.

Author index

Subject index